Deep South

Kap Stann

Diane Marshall

John T Edge

Deep South

1st edition

Published by
  Lonely Planet Publications
  Head Office: PO Box 617, Hawthorn, Vic 3122, Australia
  Branches: 155 Filbert St, Suite 251, Oakland, CA 94607, USA
                  10A Spring Place, London NW5 3BH, UK
                  71 bis rue du Cardinal Lemoine, 75005 Paris, France

Printed by
  SNP Printing Pte Ltd, Singapore

Photographs by
  Front cover: Bob Krist

  Jan Butchofsky-Houser   Louisiana Office of Tourism
  John T Edge   Diane Marshall
  Greg Elms   Memphis Convention & Visitors Bureau
  James Fraher   Nashville Convention & Visitors Bureau
  Rick Gerharter   Kap Stann
  Dave G Houser   University of Mississippi Special Collections
  Dorothea Lange   Marion Post Walcott

Published
  April 1998

Although the author and publisher have tried to make the information as accurate as possible, they accept no responsibility for any loss, injury or inconvenience sustained by any person using this book.

National Library of Australia Cataloguing in Publication Data

  Stann, Kap.
  Deep South.

  Includes index.
  ISBN 0 86442 486 8.

  1. Southern States - Guidebooks. 2. United States - Guidebooks.
  I. Marshall, Diane. II. Edge, John T. III. Title.

917.504

text & maps © Lonely Planet 1998
photos © photographers as indicated 1998

All rights reserved. No part of this publication may be reproduced, stored in a retrieval system or transmitted in any form by any means, electronic, mechanical, photocopying, recording or otherwise, except brief extracts for the purpose of review, without the written permission of the publisher and copyright owner.

Kap Stann

A native New Yorker who now lives in California, Kap first traveled to the American South 10 years ago and has been writing about it ever since. Kap contributed to Lonely Planet's *Washington, DC & the Capital Region* and has written guides to Georgia and South Carolina. Kap and her daughter, Cory, live in Berkeley.

Diane Marshall

Born in Texas into a military family, Diane has been traveling since she moved to Europe at age six. Since then, she has lived in France, Spain and the Philippines and traveled to more than 30 other countries. Visits to her grandparents and other relatives in Louisiana have brought her back to the South frequently. Before working on this book, she wrote guides to Miami, Orlando, the Everglades and the Florida Keys, where she now lives with her husband and two German shorthaired pointer/Labrador mix dogs, affectionately known as the Pointer Sisters.

John T Edge

A recent refugee from corporate America, John T is a freelance food and travel writer doing postgraduate work at the University of Mississippi's Center for the Study of Southern Culture. When he is not traveling the two-lane blacktops of the South in search of the perfect pulled pork barbecue sandwich, he can often be found on the front porch of his Oxford, Mississippi, home, sipping a little bourbon and listening to the music of Lucinda Williams.

From the Authors

Kap Stann Thanks to all the wonderfully hospitable folks throughout the region who generously aided in my research. In Louisiana, thanks to Bruce Morgan, Beverly Gianna and Kelly Strenge; in Mississippi, thanks to Steve Martin and his associates; and in Tennessee, thanks to Mary Belle Grande, Cindy Ford-Sanders and Kimmie Vaulx.

Thanks particularly to old friends and new who made my trips a whole lot of fun – to Ina and Bob and Camille, my blood sister Carol, and Mary Crichton. Thanks to all the wonderful folks in Oxford – to Jerry at Smitty's for the introductions, to Mr Ferris, JT, the Sincere Ramblers, and Tommy at the Blue Room.

Thanks to Patrick Peterson and Louis Skrmetta for enlightening trips out to the islands, and to all the boys at Anthony's in West Point. Thanks to *Tribe* refugees in New Orleans and to Kendall in Mamou (who still owes me a fish). Thanks to Belle and Doug for their always spirited company and for asking the right questions (Doug's advice: 'Never leave the Quarter'). For encouragement and friendship I thank Sally, for inspiration I thank Cory, and with all-around gratitude I thank my parents, once again reunited.

Diane Marshall Many thanks to all the Alabamians who opened their hearts and minds to 'the woman taking notes' in museums, stores, parks, hotels, historic homes and churches. They showed me the real Alabama. Special thanks to John Hammerstrom, Tom Brosnahan, Caroline Liou, Kate Hoffman, Ami Simpson, Russ Martin, Squee Bailey, George Lair, Melissa Beasley, Heather Rickles, Daneen Buck, Butler Sheldon and Jan Weiler. They made it happen.

John T Edge Thanks to the following people for their help: Raj Betapuldi, Rick Seale, Nelson Ross, Sarah Torian, Allison Finch, Karen Glynn, Mike Luster and the nice folks at Herby K's.

From the Publisher

This 1st edition of *Deep South* was edited in Lonely Planet's Oakland office by Brigitte Barta and Michelle Gagné Ballard with assistance from Michael Walker and Kate Hoffman. Jeff Campbell and Caroline Liou helped with proofing. David Zingarelli and Arun Rasiah checked layout, Sacha Pearson lent a hand with indexing and map proofing, and Jo-Ann Cabello did some fast fact checking. Beca Lafore designed and laid out the book. Alex Guilbert coordinated a mapping team consisting of Beca, Margaret Livingston, Scott Noren and Hayden Foell. Hayden, Rini Keagy, Hugh D'Andrade and Lisa Summers did the illustrations, and Hugh designed the cover. Thanks to both Kate and Alex, who oversaw the project from start to finish.

This Book

Kap Stann wrote the Mississippi and Tennessee sections as well as New Orleans, Cajun Country, Facts about the Deep South, Facts for the Visitor, Getting There & Away, and Getting Around. Diane Marshall covered Alabama and Plantation Country and portions of Around New Orleans. John T Edge contributed the Northern and Central Louisiana chapters, as well as the Literature section. Much of the New Orleans text was drawn from Robert Raburn's material in the *New Orleans* city guide.

Warning & Request

Things change – prices go up, schedules change, good places go bad and bad places go bankrupt. Nothing stays the same. So, if you find things better or worse, recently opened or long since closed, please tell us and help make the next edition even more accurate and useful.

We value all of the feedback we receive from travelers. A small team reads and acknowledges every letter, postcard and email, and ensures that every morsel of information finds its way to the appropriate authors, editors and publishers. Everyone who writes to us will find their name in the next edition of the appropriate guide and will also receive a free subscription to our quarterly newsletter, *Planet Talk*. The very best contributions will be rewarded with a free Lonely Planet guide.

Excerpts from your correspondence may appear in new editions of this guide, in our newsletter, or in the Postcards section of our website. Please let us know if you don't want your letter published or your name acknowledged.

Contents

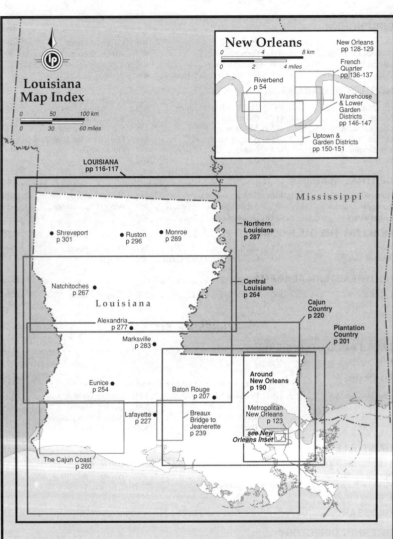

Louisiana Map Index

0   50   100 km
0   30   60 miles

New Orleans

0   4   8 km
0   2   4 miles

New Orleans
pp 128-129

French
Quarter
pp 136-137

Riverbend
p 54

Warehouse
& Lower
Garden
Districts
pp 146-147

Uptown &
Garden Districts
pp 150-151

LOUISIANA
pp 116-117

Mississippi

● Shreveport
p 301

● Ruston
p 296

● Monroe
p 289

**Northern
Louisiana
p 287**

Natchitoches ●
p 267

**Central
Louisiana
p 264**

Louisiana

**Cajun
Country
p 220**

Alexandria ●
p 277

**Plantation
Country
p 201**

Marksville ●
p 283

**Around
New Orleans
p 190**

Eunice ●
p 254

Baton Rouge
p 207 ●

Metropolitan
New Orleans
p 123

Lafayette ●
p 227

Breaux
Bridge to
Jeanerette
p 239

*see New
Orleans inset*

The Cajun Coast
p 260

OTHER MAPS
· Locator map p 13
· Deep South map between pp 16 & 17
· Natchez Trace maps pp 110-111
· Civil War map p 26
· Music Highlights p 53

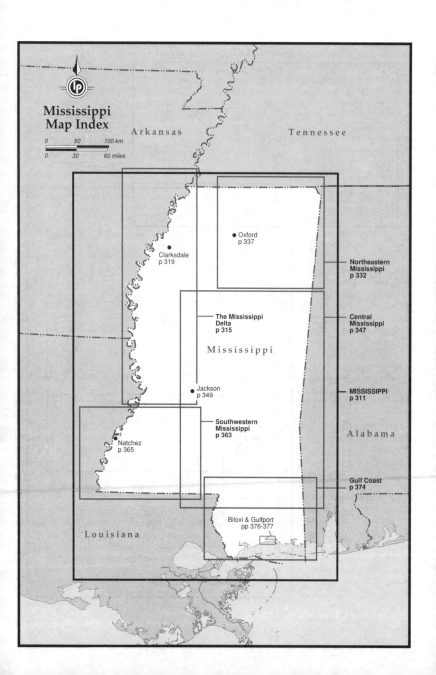

Mississippi
Map Index

0   50   100 km
0   30   60 miles

Arkansas   Tennessee

● Oxford
  p 337

● Clarksdale
  p 319

Northeastern
Mississippi
p 332

The Mississippi
Delta
p 315

Central
Mississippi
p 347

Mississippi

● Jackson
  p 349

MISSISSIPPI
p 311

Southwestern
Mississippi
p 363

Alabama

● Natchez
  p 365

Gulf Coast
p 374

Louisiana

Biloxi & Gulfport
pp 376-377

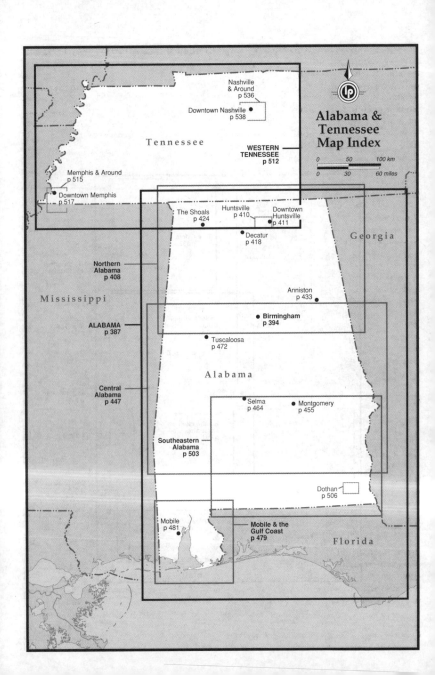

Nashville & Around p 536

Downtown Nashville p 538

Tennessee

WESTERN TENNESSEE p 512

Alabama & Tennessee Map Index

0   50   100 km
0   30   60 miles

Memphis & Around p 515

Downtown Memphis p 517

The Shoals p 424

Huntsville p 410

Downtown Huntsville p 411

Decatur p 418

Georgia

Northern Alabama p 408

Mississippi

Anniston p 433

ALABAMA p 387

Birmingham p 394

Tuscaloosa p 472

Alabama

Central Alabama p 447

Selma p 464

Montgomery p 455

Southeastern Alabama p 503

Dothan p 506

Mobile p 481

Mobile & the Gulf Coast p 479

Florida

Map Legend

BOUNDARIES

—·—·—·—·— International Boundary

—··—··—··— State Boundary

AREA FEATURES

Park

Forest

Reservation

HYDROGRAPHIC FEATURES

Water

Coastline

Beach

River, Waterfall

Swamp, Spring

ROUTES

Freeway

Toll Freeway

Primary Road

Secondary Road

Tertiary Road

Unpaved Road

Trail

Ferry Route

Railway, Train Station

Mass Transit Line & Station

ROUTE SHIELDS

(10) Interstate Freeway

84 US Highway

229 County Road

State Highways

(10) Louisiana, Alabama, Mississippi

(100) Tennessee

SYMBOLS

☼ **NATIONAL CAPITAL**	✈ Airport	❖ Garden
◉ **State Capital**		⬛ Gas Station
● **City**	∴ Archaeological Site, Ruins	⌐ Golf Course
● City, Small	❸ Bank, ATM	♨ Hindu Temple
● Town	Baseball Diamond	✚ Hospital, Clinic
	✕ Battlefield	❶ Information
	⚑ Beach	⚲ Lighthouse
■ Hotel, B&B	✦ Border Crossing	✳ Lookout
▲ Campground	⊥ Buddhist Temple	▲ Monument
⌂ Hostel	⊖ Bus Depot, Bus Stop	⚑ Mosque
▥ RV Park	▱ Cathedral	▲ Mountain
▼ Restaurant	⌢ Cave	⛨ Museum
⛾ Bar (Place to Drink)	† Church	← One-Way Street
☕ Cafe	◗ Embassy	⌂ Observatory
	⋈ Foot Bridge	♠ Park

◻ Parking	
)(Pass	
⋔ Picnic Area	
★ Police Station	
▭ Pool	
✉ Post Office	
↘ Shipwreck	
❖ Shopping Mall	
⛫ Stately Home	
✡ Synagogue	
☎ Telephone	
▣ Tomb, Mausoleum	
⚑ Trailhead	
⚘ Winery	
⛺ Zoo	

Airfield ✚

Note: Not all symbols displayed above appear in this book.

Introduction

The complex history and heritage of the Deep South, combined with its richly diverse landscape, have created a steadfast, distinctly American culture that is often at odds with itself and the country around it.

The lower Mississippi valley was the homeland of the Choctaw, Chickasaw and Creek before the French, Spanish and English arrived in the 16th and 17th centuries to fight over it. The Americans finally took it in the 18th century, and the defining historical event of the Deep South remains the Civil War, fought from 1861 to 1865. In this region all Confederate statues face south, and Robert E Lee's birthday is still a state holiday. And yet, though the Deep South romanticizes antebellum plantation life – built on slavery – it is also the birthplace of the modern civil rights movement. Today there are more African-Americans elected to public office in the South than in any other part of the nation.

Perhaps most characteristic of Southern culture is what writer Eudora Welty called 'a sense of place.' Southerners don't move around to the extent that most Americans do; they often remain rooted to the land, to family and to community. This intimate experience of a compact universe is revealed most eloquently in Southern literature – writer William Faulkner lamented that he'd never live long enough to exhaust the wealth of stories springing from his 'little postage stamp of native soil.' Visitors who slow down long enough to join locals on front porches or over fences while they spin yarns, family histories and tall tales will experience this sense of place first-hand.

The Deep South also possesses a rich and innovative musical heritage. Here African rhythms took a zesty turn to form jazz, a lamenting turn to form the blues and were combined with hillbilly music to create rock 'n' roll. Perhaps there's no better way to understand the life of the Deep South than to take a tour through its musical landscape – soulful blues, brassy jazz, country twang, Cajun accordions, zydeco washboards, riverboat calliopes and Sunday morning gospel choirs.

Festivals and special events are another great way to experience the local culture, from the world-famous Mardi Gras celebration in New Orleans to homey small-town

parades and festivals featuring the crowning of the local Catfish Queen, a mullet toss or a mudbug race. At festivals you can also sample the local cuisine – make sure you try Southern fried chicken and sweet potato pie as well as exotic Cajun and Creole specialties such as crawfish étouffée, andouille and boudin sausage, and gumbo.

Like the people, the landscape varies tremendously – from the damp sugar-cane fields of south Louisiana and the sunny beaches of Mississippi's Gulf Coast to the hardscrabble Appalachian reaches of northern Alabama and the rolling uplands of middle Tennessee. You'll need a boat to fully experience the region's bayous, swamps, rivers and lakes. There are also ample opportunities to hike piney woods and forests of live oak strewn with Spanish moss, and to enjoy city gardens filled with magnolia, crape myrtle, rhododendron and azalea – all flowering varieties common to the South.

Louisiana is perhaps the most distinctive of all Deep South states – ecologically, historically and culturally. Settled by the French and long ruled by the Spanish, the Isle of Orleans was built at a sharp swampy bend of the Mississippi River. This important port town has evolved into a hedonistic, vibrant city that moves to its own atypical rhythm. Southern Louisiana's Cajun Country harbors the largest French-speaking community in the US.

Mississippi also offers a variety of experiences, including pilgrimages to the Mississippi Delta, home of the blues, to wilderness adventures on deserted islands in the Gulf of Mexico. There are also plenty of small Southern towns that still revolve around the town square and local feed-and-seed; many can be seen as detours off the Natchez Trace Parkway.

Alabama offers more diversions, from the birthplace of blues legend WC Handy near the Tennessee River to house tours in the Piedmont. Mobile, the last city to be ceded by the Spanish and the last to surrender during the Civil War, has a history all its own.

The Deep South's musical blessings continue in western Tennessee: Memphis is the birthplace of rock 'n' roll, and Nashville is the country music capital of the world. Despite the hype, Graceland and the Grand Ole Opry are still authentic touchstones of American culture.

Across the Deep South, visitors will undoubtedly discover that the region and its people are diverse and compelling. Take the time to enjoy a little good ol' Southern hospitality, and ease into the evocative mix of rhythms, images and traditions that gives the Deep South its distinctive identity.

Facts about the Deep South

HISTORY

More than any other region in the US, the American South lives intimately with its unusual past. Southerners have a highly personal sense of this history that is closely connected to the land. Where a visitor might see a mound of earth, the Choctaw see remnants of an ancestral civilization. Heirs to the Lost Cause might come across a quiet river bluff and see the setting of a painful siege. Milewide cotton fields in the Mississippi Delta are more than cropland; to African Americans they are the setting of a wrenching oppression lamented in the blues. As William Faulkner explained, 'The past is never dead. It's not even past.'

Original Peoples

As the rising and falling waters of each successive ice age alternately submerged and exposed the stretch of land connecting Asia and Alaska, waves of immigrants from Siberia crossed over to North America. These nomadic people migrated throughout the Americas. How long ago the earliest migration occurred is a matter of scientific debate: conservative estimates place it at around 15,000 years ago, while other estimates speculate at least twice that long ago.

Some of the earliest evidence of human habitation has been found in northern Alabama's cave country. Crude stone tools found alongside projectile points are attributed to the oldest Paleo-Indian period, at least 11,000 years ago. During the following Archaic period (9000-1000 BC), Russell Cave (now a national park in northeastern Alabama) was inhabited. During this period, the first evidence of crop cultivation appears with the earliest settlements.

Adaptation to warmer climates marks the end of the Pleistocene era. Evidence of this transition has been found on the lower Tennessee River in shell-and-earth 'middens' (prehistoric garbage heaps). Refuse indicates reliance on freshwater mussels, fish and game (primarily deer). Ready access to a greater variety of food sources gave early inhabitants the time for other pursuits – pottery and such personal adornments as beads and pendants first appeared, and burial techniques reveal the beginnings of mortuary practices and traditions that would grow increasingly elaborate in time.

In the Woodland period (1000 BC-AD 900) an increasingly sophisticated civilization established fully realized villages and croplands. Pottery was stylized with stamped patterns. The widespread distribution of shells from the Gulf and ocean, and mica from the Great Lakes reveals an extensive trade network. But most distinctive among the Woodland traditions was the first appearance of laboriously constructed earthen mounds. One of the archaeologically richest sites from this period can be seen today in northeastern Louisiana at Poverty Point, a site so vast its full extent was not recognized until aerial observation became possible. Though mounds had become commonplace across the South by this time, mound construction reached a refined state of development in the subsequent Mississippian period.

Mississippian Civilization

The culture that developed along the lower Mississippi River around 700 AD – dubbed 'Mississippian' – spread throughout the Southeast, reaching its height around 1200 AD. This Mississippian civilization represents the highest state of cultural development in the pre-Columbian southeast, or even, as some anthropologists argue, in all of aboriginal North America.

The Mississippian culture is most noted for refining mound construction and making mounds the centerpiece of village life and religious traditions. Typically, Mississippian mounds had steep-sided walls like a pyramid, but they were rectangular and the top was flattened. These flat tops were used as temple grounds for religious ceremonies and also held the houses of tribal leaders. Once a tribal leader died, his house was destroyed and he was buried under a fresh layer of soil. The new leader then built a house on top and the cycle would repeat itself.

At the Chucalissa site above the Mississippi River in Memphis, Tennessee, a cutaway trench reveals this layering technique. The cropland surrounding this 15th-century village was planted with corn, beans and squash (called the 'three sisters'), which remain staples of Southern cuisine to this day.

The 300-acre Moundville site in Alabama (south of Tuscaloosa) preserves 20 square and oval platform mounds. Decorative artifacts excavated here help to shed light on the belief system of the Mississippian inhabitants (see the Mississippian Mythology sidebar).

Mounds throughout the South are today so integrated with the landscape that they can easily be mistaken for natural features of an uncommonly geometric shape. Many examples have been preserved as historical sites, and some mounds are still considered sacred in the mythology of today's southeastern Indian nations. One such site is Nanih Waiya in eastern Mississippi, the legendary birthplace of the Choctaw Nation.

Amer-Indian Nations

The decline of the Mississippian civilization accelerated after European contact in the mid-15th century (see European Exploration below). Europeans brought diseases that decimated whole tribes. Survivors were dominated by the groups that became known as the Five Civilized Tribes – the Cherokee, Choctaw, Chickasaw, Creek and Seminole – so named by Europeans for their sophisticated agriculture and political organization.

The Cherokee Nation was centered in the Appalachian Mountains, extending to northeastern Alabama's foothills and plateau. The antagonistic but culturally similar Choctaw and Chickasaw occupied the Mississippi region up into Tennessee. The Creek Confederacy stretched from around the Tombigbee River in western Alabama to the Atlantic Coast. The Seminoles broke

Mississippian Mythology

The Amer-Indian Mississippian culture, which reached its height in the southeast around 1200 AD, had a complex belief system that centered around three worlds: the earth, the upper world and the underworld. According to these beliefs, the earth upon which they lived was a large island floating on the sea. Above this land was the 'Sky Vault,' the upper world, which represented perfection. There lived the same creatures as on earth but in gigantic proportions. Below the earth was the Underworld, which represented chaos and disorder. The features of the Underworld were inverted from the earth world – for example, when it was summer on earth, it was winter below. Bubbling springs that felt cold in summer and warm in winter were considered proof of this belief.

Many Mississippian traditions reveal Mesoamerican influences, presumed to be introduced by Aztec traders (yet no evidence of direct contact currently exists). Mississippian mounds can be seen as earthen versions of stone Aztec temples, and artifacts unearthed in Moundville, Alabama, in particular bear a striking resemblance to Mesoamerican styles and designs. The dominant crop for both cultures was corn, and the similarities extend to mythological beliefs as well. The Natchez of the lower Mississippi, for example, worshipped the sun and moon as male and female deities, and considered the stars the children of the sun and moon – beliefs identical to those of the Andean people of South America. Many indigenous cultures of the pre-Columbian Americas also shared a common prophecy that 'strangers from across the sea' would come and destroy their people. ■

JOHN T EDGE

JOHN T EDGE

DAVE G HOUSER

JAN BUTCHOFSKY-HOUSER

Top: Inside Fertitta's, Shreveport, LA
Middle Left: Marksville, LA
Bottom Left: The Crawfish Palace Café, Eunice, LA

Bottom Right: Paddle wheel on Delta Queen, Mississippi River

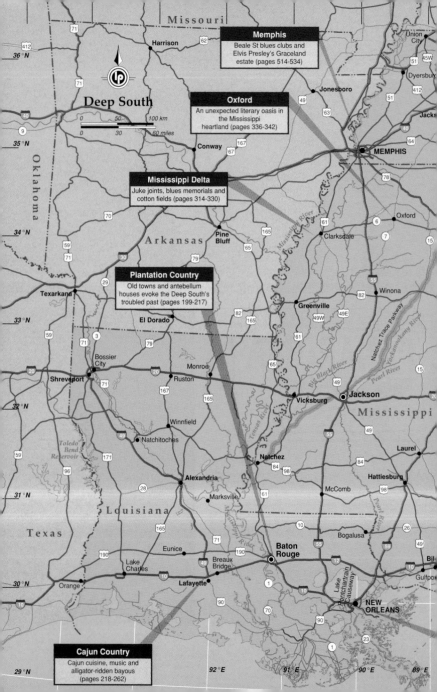

Missouri

Deep South

0   50   100 km
0   30   60 miles

Memphis
Beale St blues clubs and
Elvis Presley's Graceland
estate (pages 514-534)

Oxford
An unexpected literary oasis in
the Mississippi
heartland (pages 336-342)

Mississippi Delta
Juke joints, blues memorials and
cotton fields (pages 314-330)

Plantation Country
Old towns and antebellum
houses evoke the Deep South's
troubled past (pages 199-217)

Cajun Country
Cajun cuisine, music and
alligator-ridden bayous
(pages 218-262)

Oklahoma

Arkansas

Mississippi

Louisiana

Texas

MEMPHIS

Harrison
Jonesboro
Union City
Dyersburg
Jacks
Conway
Oxford
Clarksdale
Pine Bluff
Winona
Greenville
El Dorado
Texarkana
Bossier City
Shreveport
Monroe
Ruston
Vicksburg
Jackson
Winnfield
Natchitoches
Laurel
Alexandria
Natchez
Hattiesburg
Marksville
McComb
Eunice
Lake Charles
Breaux Bridge
Baton Rouge
Bogalusa
Orange
Lafayette
Gulfpor
NEW ORLEANS
Bil

Mississippi River
Natchez Trace Parkway
Yockanookany River
Big Black River
Pearl River
Toledo Bend Reservoir
Lake Pontchartrain Causeway

36° N
35° N
34° N
33° N
32° N
31° N
30° N
29° N

92° E
91° E
90° E
89° E

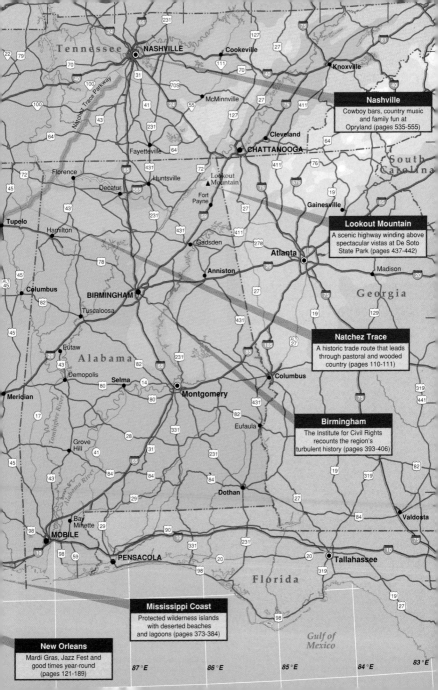

Nashville
Cowboy bars, country music and family fun at Opryland (pages 535-555)

Lookout Mountain
A scenic highway winding above spectacular vistas at De Soto State Park (pages 437-442)

Natchez Trace
A historic trade route that leads through pastoral and wooded country (pages 110-111)

Birmingham
The Institute for Civil Rights recounts the region's turbulent history (pages 393-406)

Mississippi Coast
Protected wilderness islands with deserted beaches and lagoons (pages 373-384)

New Orleans
Mardi Gras, Jazz Fest and good times year-round (pages 121-189)

Tennessee

NASHVILLE
Cookeville
Knoxville
McMinnville
Cleveland
CHATTANOOGA
South Carolina
Fayetteville
Florence
Huntsville
Lookout Mountain
Decatur
Fort Payne
Gainesville
Tupelo
Hamilton
Gadsden
Atlanta
Anniston
Madison
Columbus
BIRMINGHAM
Tuscaloosa
Georgia
Eutaw
Alabama
Columbus
Demopolis
Selma
Meridian
Montgomery
Grove Hill
Eufaula
Bay Minette
Dothan
Valdosta
MOBILE
PENSACOLA
Tallahassee
Florida
Gulf of Mexico

Natchez Trace Parkway

87 °E   86 °E   85 °E   84 °E   83 °E

KAP STANN

JAN BUTCHOFSKY-HOUSER

JAN BUTCHOFSKY-HOUSER

RICK GERHARTER

Top Left: Louisiana swamp boat
Bottom: Bayou near Houma, LA

Top Right: Atchafalaya Swamp, LA
Middle Right: Atchafalaya Swamp resident

Mississippi Choctaw group, 1908

away from the Creek ('seminole' is Creek for 'runaway' or 'separatist') and settled in southern Alabama and Georgia along the Chattahoochee River before they were pushed farther south into Florida.

In Louisiana, the Caddo Nation predominated. Smaller groups along the Gulf of Mexico, such as the Biloxi, had coastal cultures that were distinct from inland cultures.

Over the three hundred years following European contact, the southeastern nations were conquered by Europeans with an insatiable desire for new land on which many hoped to grow cotton. The means by which Europeans acquired this land varied. Some groups were conquered by military might, among them the Natchez of the lower Mississippi, who were vanquished after a thorough assault by the French in 1729. But most were defrauded by economic pressure.

The US government's strategy (originally devised by Thomas Jefferson) was to establish trading posts among the Indians, to encourage a dependence on European goods, to allow the Indians to fall into debt and then to force them to cede lands as repayment. Treaties sealed the deal.

The Choctaw experience was typical. In 1805 the Choctaw surrendered more than four million acres in south Mississippi to forgive a $48,000 trading debt. More treaties in 1820 and 1826 further eroded Choctaw territory until in 1830 the Treaty of Dancing Creek surrendered most all remaining Choctaw land. Greenwood Le-Flore was among the handful of Indian leaders bribed by President Andrew Jackson into signing. In exchange for signing away the homeland of his kin, LeFlore was enriched with a large estate. Hundreds of such forced or fraudulent treaties appropriated Indian land throughout the southeast.

But even that was not enough for the Southern planters and land speculators eyeing remaining Indian enclaves and eager to rid the region of a people they regarded as a nuisance. The final assault came in the 1830s. Jackson issued an ultimatum to move voluntarily to Indian Territory out west or be 'removed' by force.

Of all the southeastern Indians, the Cherokee fought the most determined legal battle against removal. In 1827, they formalized their own sovereignty as the Cherokee Nation by adopting a constitution based on the US model. In 1829, the state of Georgia passed legislation annexing a large portion of Cherokee territory and declaring Cherokee law null and void. The Cherokee appealed all the way to the Supreme Court. In *Worcester* v *the State of Georgia*, Chief Justice John Marshall found these Georgia laws unconstitutional. Nonetheless, in contempt of the authority of the Supreme Court, President Jackson is reported to have said: 'John Marshall has rendered his decision, now let him enforce it.' In 1838, the US Army along with local militias forced 18,000 Cherokee off their land and sent them west with little more than the clothes on their backs; 4000 Cherokee died en route.

Besides the Choctaw and Cherokee, other southeastern nations were similarly banished and forced along a route that has come to be remembered as the Trail of Tears. Survivors established communities in what is now Oklahoma, and their descendants remain there still.

Isolated Amer-Indian communities managed to remain in the southeast and some were eventually granted trust land. Today, the 6000-member Mississippi Band of the Choctaw Indians in central Mississippi and the Chitimacha of south Louisiana's Bayou Teche have built thriving reservations on portions of their ancestral lands (thanks largely to casino dollars). Other Amer-Indian communities remain sprinkled throughout the region without trust land.

Native American traditions and powwows are celebrated on reservations and at historic sites throughout the region.

Ironically, though the US government stopped only one step short of outright genocide in its attempt to rid the southeast of Native Americans, it readily adopted Indian names for the territories it claimed, among them Mississippi and Alabama.

European Exploration

In 1540, the Spanish explorer Hernando de Soto led an army of 900 soldiers and hundreds of horses through the southeast in search of gold to rival the looting of Peru's Inca empire. His route led from the Atlantic Coast through Alabama, across the northern part of Mississippi, through Louisiana, down the Mississippi River and across the Gulf of Mexico back to Florida. Though he charged through the southeast on the attack, the greatest damage he wrought was effected not by brutal encounters but by exposing the Amer-Indian populations to devastating diseases.

A major battle fought in southern Alabama signaled a turning point in the expedition. Although the Indian foot soldiers were superior warriors, they were no match for the Spanish Cavalry, and after great numbers of Indian casualties, the Spanish were victorious. Yet the Spanish were convinced that these inhabitants were unlike the native peoples de Soto had encountered in Mexico and Peru.

According to de Soto historian Edward G Bourne, the Spanish became convinced that it was 'impossible to dominate such bellicose people or to subjugate men who were so free, and that because of what they had seen up until that time, they felt they could never make the Indians come under their yoke either by force or trickery, for rather than do so these people would all permit themselves to be slain.'

As de Soto stepped up his attacks, the Choctaw and Chickasaw in Mississippi were becoming more effective opponents and continued harassing raids against the Spanish. After burning several towns in a densely populated area of eastern Louisiana, de Soto fell ill and died in May 1542. His body was laid afloat down the Mississippi River. His successor led about 300 survivors down the river to the Gulf and back to Spanish Florida.

La Louisiane

It was more than a century before Europeans returned to the Mississippi River, and this time it was the French. In 1673, the team of Father Marquette and trader Joliet sailed downriver from French outposts at the Great Lakes to the lower Mississippi before heeding warnings about hostile tribes and turning back. Nine years later, René Robert Cavelier, Sieur de la Salle headed an expedition of 23 French and 18 Native Americans that pushed through to the Gulf of Mexico. Upon reaching the Gulf, La Salle staged a ceremony to claim the Mississippi River and all its tributaries for France, naming it *La Louisiane* in honor of reigning King Louis XIV.

La Salle was not the only European to lay claim to the region. The lower portion of the land La Salle declared Louisiana was considered by the British to be part of a vaguely mapped 1629 Carolina Grant that essentially claimed everything west of Charleston as British territory. Furthermore, Spanish outposts scattered from Florida to Texas established an equally broad Spanish claim to dominion over the Gulf Coast. The three powers would continue to exercise power within the region for nearly two centuries (and the newly formed US would enter the fray after 1776).

France knew it needed to occupy its new colony to strengthen its claim. In 1699, two Quebecois brothers – Pierre Le Moyne, Sieur d'Iberville and Jean Baptiste Le Moyne, Sieur de Bienville - were sent to found France's first permanent settlement in the South. They established Fort de Maurepas at what is now Ocean Springs, Mississippi. The brothers set up trading operations with the Biloxi Indians, and peopled the settlement with 200 colonists,

mostly male. The fort became the seat of government for the new colony. (Ocean Springs remains the second-oldest European settlement to endure in the US after St Augustine, Florida.)

In 1702, England declared war on France, leading the French king to order the new colony moved to the Mobile River to be closer to allies at Fort Pensacola in Spanish Florida. Though the Fort de Maurepas settlement was not completely abandoned, the seat of Louisiana government moved to this new fort, named Louis de la Mobile.

In 1704, the French government sponsored the transport of 20 young women as prospective brides for the colonists. Dubbed 'cassette girls,' these orphans and peasants were 'stationed' on Ship Island (off the Mississippi coast) with their suitcases *(cassettes)* bearing their state-issued trousseaux. This was the first of several such boatloads of French women.

The Le Moyne brothers continued westward to explore the Mississippi River Delta, which had previously eluded European explorers on the Gulf. With a Native American guide, the brothers sailed up the Mississippi, taking note of the spit of land between the river and a huge lake, linked by a narrow portage route – the future site of New Orleans. Upriver, they established Fort Rosalie in 1716 at the future site of Natchez, Mississippi.

In 1718, Bienville laid out the city of New Orleans. The first colonists included 30 convicts, six carpenters and four Canadians, who struggled against the floods and yellow-fever epidemics endemic to the region. But promoters omitted these harsher details of colonial life, and French, Canadian and a few German immigrants were drawn to the new colony. The capital of La Louisiane was moved from Mobile to New Orleans in 1722. At this time, New Orleans had a population of 370 – 147 male and 65 female colonists, 38 children, 73 slaves and 21 Indians. Over the next 20 years, New Orleans grew to a population of around 5000, more than half of whom were enslaved Africans. Offspring of free foreign immigrants born in the colony were called Creoles.

Not all blacks were slaves. Once manumitted (released from slavery), blacks joined free black communities the French called *les gens de couleur libre*, the free people of color. Louisiana's Code Noir (Black Code), adopted in 1724, regulated the treatment and rights of slaves and 'freemen of color' (see Freemen of Color sidebar below). Free black men and women still had to carry passes to identify their status and were restricted from voting, holding public office or marrying outside their race.

Money Talks

Spanish coinage can help define the word that appears on the masthead of the New Orleans daily newspaper, the *Picayune*. The Spanish peseta, otherwise known as a 'piece of eight,' is the forerunner of our own silver dollar and its fractional divisions. Often the coin was inscribed so that the user could break it into quarters representing two *reales* or two bits with each bit worth 12-1\2¢. Further subdivision of a bit to its smallest possible fraction resulted in the picayune. The cost for a *Times-Picayune* was once a little more than a nickel, or 6-1\4¢. Hence a 'picayune' is something exceedingly small.

Prior to the Civil War, the Citizen's Bank of New Orleans minted $10 bank notes. On the back of these bills appeared the French word *dix* (10). Southerners handling these bills came to refer to them as 'Dixies.' Eventually, Dixie stuck as a nickname for the American South.

New Orleans also played a role in the origin of the US dollar sign. During the Spanish colonial period of the late 1700s, Oliver Pollack, a wealthy Irish merchant engaged in Mississippi River trade, made notations in his ledger for the peso that by 1778 had evolved from a separate 'P' and 'S' to an overlapping symbol. Further shorthand reduced the 'P' to a single slash. ■

Louisiana became a drain on the French treasury, which was already strapped with the expenses of waging war against England, so French officials negotiated a secret pact with Spanish King Charles III – the 1762 Treaty of Fountainbleu. In return for ceding to Spain the remote and unprofitable Louisiana territory west of the Mississippi along with the 'Isle of Orleans,' France gained an ally in its war against England. Louisiana provided a buffer between Spain's possessions in New Spain and English colonies along the Atlantic Coast.

In 1763 under the Peace of Paris, Britain acquired France's Louisiana territory east of the Mississippi and north of New Orleans. Spain ceded to Britain its territories of East and West Florida. In 1779, war broke out between Spain and Britain; the Spanish captured the British outpost in Baton Rouge, Louisiana. As a result of this victory, portions of West Florida were returned to Spain.

Two important events in the Americas brought tremendous changes to Louisiana's population. Around the onset of Spanish control, French refugees from L'Acadie (now Nova Scotia) began arriving after the British seizure of French Canada. The British banished thousands of Acadians in 1755. In 1765, France began transporting the forlorn Acadians to New Orleans, hoping to advance French interests in Louisiana. The Acadians (or 'Cajuns' as they came to be called) settled in south Louisiana west of the Mississippi River (the region that remains 'Cajun Country' today). Then in 1791, the slave revolt in St Domingue (Haiti) and ensuing turmoil led thousands of former black slaves to seek refuge in Louisiana as freemen.

Louisiana Purchase

By the late 18th century, Louisiana was proving as troublesome and costly to the Spanish as it had been to the French. Spain also feared that it would have to fight the upstart Americans to retain control. So when Napoleon Bonaparte offered to retake control in 1800, Spain jumped at the

Floating Palaces & Crop Couriers

I'm waiting on the levee for the steamboat to come round,
I think she's loaded heavy, I think she's loaded down.
I hear that steamboat whistle, blowing clear and free,
I think she is the Natchez or the Robert E Lee.
                                    – traditional song

Rafts, flatboats and keelboats floated downstream from early colonial days onward, carrying goods to market. Most traffic remained downstream until 1811, when the steamboat *New Orleans* departed her namesake city by way of the Mississippi River for points north. With her maiden voyage, river transportation was changed forever.

The Mississippi River remained the primary waterway throughout the late 1800s. However, the South abounded with navigable rivers plied by steamboats both large and small during the golden age of riverboat transportation.

Whether serving as floating palaces bedecked with chandeliers and skylights or as de facto barges loaded down with cotton en route to market, the steamboat's familiar bells, whistles and billowing smoke symbolized modernity for the farmers and townspeople who gathered at river whenever the boats arrived. Though as many boats provided crop transport as luxury passenger service, the most fondly remembered of these great vessels were the luxury passenger service, the most fondly remembered of these great vessels were the luxury passenger service. Foremost among these was the *Robert E Lee*.

Built in 1866 for the then astronomical sum of $200,000, the *Lee* boasted an opulent main cabin outfitted with crystal chandeliers, stained-glass skylights, rosewood furniture and Egyptian marble sills. Its opulent appointments were emblematic of an elegance that historian Louis C Hunter dubbed 'steamboat gothic.'

For its time, the *Lee* was an exceedingly fast craft, able to reach neck-wrenching speeds of close to 20 miles per hour. Its closest competitor in opulence and power was the *Natchez*. In 1870, the two steamboats raced from New Orleans to St Louis for bragging rights to the title of the best boat on the river. On June 30, the *Lee* steamed into St Louis after traveling 1218 miles in 80 hours and 30 minutes. It was six hours ahead of the *Natchez*.

Despite the popularity of steamboat travel, by the late 1800s another form of steam transportation began overshadowing it. As railroads became the more economical and practical means of moving people and goods, the once grand steamboats were either taken out of service or relegated to lesser routes.

Today, steamboats are enjoying something of a renaissance. Refurbished treasures like the *Delta Queen* offer luxury cruises and have achieved the status of national landmarks, but most of today's steamboats are nothing more than gutted floating facades, outfitted with slot machines and the like to take advantage of newly enacted laws that allow water-based gambling. ∎

– John T Edge

Steamer American at Landing, Vicksburg, Miss.

chance and ceded territory in another secret pact. (France did not actually resume control until November 1803.)

Meanwhile, President Thomas Jefferson recognized that seizing the river capital New Orleans would promote US western expansion. Bonaparte needed to raise funds, feared losing New Orleans to the British and preferred to see the territory in American hands, so he offered the Louisiana territory to the US for a price of $15 million, a purchase that would double the country's national domain. On the final day of November 1803 in the Place d'Armes in New Orleans, the Spanish flag was quietly replaced by the French flag, which in turn was replaced by the American flag on December 20.

In 1812, Louisiana joined the Union as the 18th state. In the same year, the US declared war against England. With the British navy approaching from the Gulf of Mexico, General Andrew Jackson assembled a ragtag band of pirates, Indians and volunteer militia. These troops fought the British at the Battle of New Orleans in 1815 and won (the war had actually been declared over before the battle, but neither side had been alerted).

Though Spain had relinquished its lands west of the Mississippi, it held onto West Florida, its lands east of the river. The US contested this assertion, claiming it was all US territory as a result of the French concession. Americans within this region began to rebel against Spanish rule; residents of the eastern Louisiana region still known today as 'the Florida Parishes' briefly declared themselves an independent republic in 1810. With the US Army in active duty during the War of 1812, the US took the opportunity to seize control of the disputed territory. Mobile, an isolated European outpost, finally came under American control in 1812.

With US dominion firmly in place, the government began to plot state lines. Boundaries were contested by various factions for years, but the new states of Mississippi and Alabama joined the Union in

1817 and 1819, respectively, with borders close to those in effect today. Indian removal in the 1830s opened up free and easily cultivated land. Speculators and settlers from the Piedmont region of the Southern Atlantic seaboard populated the region and expanded cotton cultivation. In southern Louisiana, sugar cane dominated the economy, and rice and indigo flourished on Alabama's Gulf Coast.

The Mississippi River served as a primary transportation corridor. Goods from as far away as Pittsburgh and St Louis passed through New Orleans on their way abroad. Steamboats plied the navigable waters of the river's entire Mississippi drainage basin. At first riverboats were welcomed in river towns with calliope steam-organ music announcing their arrival, but soon they transported as many shady characters as freight and became an unwelcome nuisance (see Floating Palaces & Crop Couriers sidebar). Many trading boatsmen found it easier to sell the boat lumber than to fight their way back upstream; they returned north on foot via the Natchez Trace. (As early as 1801 the US government had secured a right-of-way treaty along this ancient buffalo trail through Chickasaw territory.)

'King Cotton'

The economy of the Deep South was overwhelmingly dependent upon a single crop: cotton. Not only was the soil and climate ideally suited for cotton production, but it seemed as if the European market in the 18th and 19th centuries could not get enough of the commodity. Production started to lag in the latter half of the 18th century, but the 1793 invention of the cotton gin – which mechanized the laborious task of separating seeds and hulls from cotton fibers – was a tremendous boon to the industry and to the South.

While small owner-operated farms grew cotton across the South, certain specific areas supported the large-scale 'plantations' so commonly associated with the region. These were concentrated across the 'Black Belt' (so named for its fertile dark soil) of central Alabama and in the alluvial plain of the Mississippi Delta along the lower Mississippi River.

Historian Ulrich B Phillips described the plantation economy as a 'kind of agribusiness whose machines were human beings.' These laborers were slaves.

The Slave Economy

The gruesome slave trade brought to South America, the Caribbean and North America at least 10 million Africans – some estimates are upwards of 20 million. This commerce in humans reached its height in the 18th century.

From the 1400s to the 1800s, the slave trade operated from Africa's west coast in the region stretching from Senegal to Angola, principally the central 'Gold Coast' region (now Ghana, Togo, Benin and Nigeria). At first, captives were largely prisoners of local wars sold by the chieftains of victorious tribes. Later, as demand soared, raiders throughout West Africa kidnapped men, women and children, and drove them to the coast, where they were held in stockades before being loaded onto ships bound for the Americas. An overwhelming number – 95% – were brought to the Caribbean and Central and South America; the remaining 5% arrived in North America.

During the 'Middle Passage' across the Atlantic, captives were packed shoulder-to-shoulder in inhumane and unsanitary conditions for six to 12 weeks before reaching shore. One-third of the captives did not survive the ordeal (sharks commonly followed slave ships in anticipation of the bodies thrown overboard). The ones who did endure were fattened as they reached port and oiled upon arrival to appear healthy for auction.

In 17th-century America, planters considered Africans an ideal source of labor. The first Africans in the colonies were indentured servants, but ruthless planters soon saw that they could exploit these servants beyond the years of their contracts. As servants, the Africans' distinctive appearance and unfamiliarity with local languages and terrain made it harder for them to escape or blend in. This unfamiliarity also made it easy for the planters to codify permanently their secondary status. The transition to outright slavery was swift; the first laws addressing slave labor appeared in 1662. As settlement and cotton cultivation spread west throughout the South, so did slavery.

In addition to having their labor exploited, slaves were denied most basic human liberties. In the American South, clans and families were separated, slave marriages were not recognized, and women were routinely exploited sexually. African culture was likewise suppressed: any expression of African languages, religious worship and cultural rituals was strictly prohibited. It was a crime to teach a slave to read. Though some slaves rose in stature by learning trades or becoming house servants, the great majority were field workers whose legal status was roughly equivalent to that of domestic animals.

Skilled slaves were expensive, so slave-owning was beyond the reach of the great majority of Southern farmers. The overwhelming number of farms – over

Freemen

Most blacks in the antebellum South were slaves, though a small but significant number were not. These 'free men of color' gained their freedom in a wide variety of ways. Some were released from slavery (manumitted) and some escaped their masters. Any free person could join isolated, self-regulated free black communities.

Many slaves were able to escape to freedom in the north via the figurative 'Underground Railroad' – 'conductors' such as the famous escaped slave Harriet Tubman escorted fleeing slaves in concert with local sympathizers who provided waystations and transportation. ■

two-thirds – held no slaves. Of those that did, the greatest proportion held only one slave. The popular image of huge plantations with hundreds of slaves (such as in the novel *Gone With the Wind*) actually accounted for only a small number of Southern farms. Yet enriched by slave labor, the elite ruling class that owned these large plantations dominated the economy, society and plantation life of the South far out of proportion to its size.

Plantation Life

On large plantations, planters lived in the 'Big House' so commonly associated with plantation mythology, supported by the labor of the slaves who lived in shacks out back. The planter's wife was generally responsible for doctoring the ailments of the residents. Although it would have been within a planter's best economic interest to ensure adequate food and health care for slaves, brutality and generally dehumanizing conditions served to underscore the authority of the 'master' and to repress the potential for rebellion.

There was a wide gulf between the status and treatment of household servants and field hands. Black house servants attended to the domestic needs of the white household, including cooking, craftwork, child-raising and even wet-nursing. Female slaves were subject to sexual exploitation. The mulatto children of these unions (or rare elective white-black liaisons) often fared better than their black siblings, encouraging a color-stratified class society within the black culture.

The close proximity between races and classes spurred the creation of strict social boundaries. For instance, blacks could enter by the back door but not the front or sit in the church balcony but not the pews. These social rules of conduct seemed peculiarly arbitrary in the eyes of Northerners.

The Abolitionist Debate

While the South was never monolithic in its support of slavery, few abolitionists there were able to openly criticize the prevailing pro-slavery forces without fear of

reprisals. In the North the economy was based on industry and the culture was never dependent upon slavery. The abolitionist movement in the North gained strength throughout the early 19th century, and by 1846 all Northern states had outlawed slavery. Meanwhile, New Orleans had become the South's largest slave-trading center, with some 25 slave markets.

In 1852, publication of Harriet Beecher Stowe's landmark book *Uncle Tom's Cabin*, which described the hardships of slavery on a fictional Red River estate in Louisiana, hardened opposition to slavery in the North.

The fragile 30-year truce of the *Missouri Compromise*, which established a boundary between 'slave states' and 'free states' at the 36°30'N parallel, was threatened by the increasingly emotional debate. In 1854, US Senator Steven Douglas of Illinois introduced a bill that would allow settlers in new western territories (at the time, Kansas and Nebraska) to decide for themselves whether to be a slave or free state. As a result, Kansas settlers from the South and North on opposing sides of the debate were soon at each other's throats. 'Bleeding Kansas' intensified the polarized divisions between pro-slavery and anti-slavery lobbies. In 1857, the Supreme Court ruled in its *Dred Scott* decision that Congress would not interfere with a state's choice to allow or prohibit slavery – in effect, sanctioning slavery as national policy.

Abraham Lincoln of Illinois gained a name for himself debating the issue against his opponent Douglas in the 1858 campaign for the US Senate. During one of these debates Lincoln declared, 'A house divided against itself cannot stand – I believe this government cannot endure permanently half slave and half free.' Though Douglas won the Senate seat, Lincoln's position on the national political stage was set, and the following year Lincoln was selected as the Republican candidate for the US presidential race. In November 1860, Lincoln was elected president with a plurality of the popular vote (around 40%) and over half the electoral college votes.

Civil War in the Western Theater

Sparked by the slavery debates, chronic sectionalism and Lincoln's election, South Carolina and then Mississippi seceded from the Union, asserting their 'states' rights' against centralized control. Nine more states soon joined them. On February 4, 1861, at a convention in Montgomery, Alabama, delegates from Alabama, Mississippi, Louisiana, Georgia, South Carolina, Florida and Texas created the provisional government of the Confederate States of America. Mississippian Jefferson Davis, former US Secretary of War, was named the Confederate President. Virginia, Tennessee, Arkansas and North Carolina later joined the Confederate effort. Montgomery remained the seat of the Confederate government until May 1861, when it was moved to Richmond, Virginia (the original Confederate White House in Montgomery can be toured today).

In response to Lincoln's decision to resupply troops at Fort Sumter in South Carolina, Jefferson Davis sent orders to fire the first shot of what would prove to be the bloodiest war in US history. That shot rang out on April 12, 1861. Many of the Civil War's early battles were likewise fights for control of coastal forts along the Atlantic Ocean and Gulf of Mexico. Among these battles was one at Fort Massachusetts on Ship Island off the Mississippi coast, which was occupied by Union troops on December 3, 1861.

A key Union objective from the outset was to control the Mississippi, which would cut an important lifeline for Southern states and divide the Confederacy in two. The Union blockade at the mouth of the Mississippi began in 1861. Later that year, major campaigns were launched simultaneously upriver from the Gulf and downriver along the Mississippi and its tributaries from the Union position in Kentucky.

In the spring of 1862, Union troops took Nashville – a Cumberland River port, railroad hub and Confederate supply depot and arsenal – opening a pathway for a Union invasion of the Deep South. Continuing their advance, Union troops met the Confederate army in Shiloh, Tennessee, on April 6, 1862. Two days of battle resulted in a Union victory at a cost of 23,746 lives on both sides, making it one of the bloodiest battles of the war. Crossing into Mississippi, the Federals besieged Corinth from April 29 to May 30 until the Confederates evacuated. To the west, Union forces seized Memphis on June 6.

Meanwhile, US Admiral David Farragut and the US Navy secured the surrender of New Orleans, Baton Rouge and Natchez by the middle of 1862. They tried to take Vicksburg but failed and withdrew in July. As the strongest Confederate holdout between Union-occupied Memphis and Natchez, Vicksburg became the primary target of the Union's Western Theater operations. 'Vicksburg is the key,' said Lincoln. 'The war can never be brought to a close until that key is in our pocket.'

Union General Ulysses S Grant launched his first campaign towards Vicksburg in October 1862, but a series of daring Confederate raids against his supply lines led Grant to abandon it. These raids included one by Nathan Bedford Forrest in West Tennessee (December 11-January 1) and another by Earl Van Dorn in Holly Springs (December 17-28).

Grant began a second offensive the following spring. His 45,000 troops failed to take Vicksburg by storm, so instead they encircled it and imposed a siege that lasted 48 days before the city surrendered 31,000 Confederate troops on July 4, 1863. When Port Hudson, the last Confederate stronghold on the Mississippi, fell five days later, Lincoln declared 'The Father of Waters again goes unvexed to the sea.'

Union General Tecumseh Sherman moved east to Meridian, Mississippi, testing his 'total war' technique (remembered as an unprecedented assault on nonmilitary targets). Later in the year, he perfected the technique in his Atlanta campaign (also known as the 'March to the Sea').

In Louisiana, a Union offensive headed up the Red River, but despite reinforcements

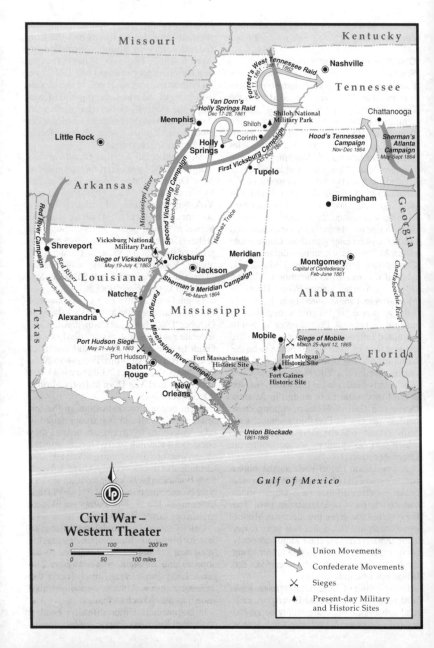

Civil War –
Western Theater

Union Movements

Confederate Movements

× Sieges

▲ Present-day Military
and Historic Sites

on the way from the north, the Federals were forced to withdraw. In the summer of 1864, the fall of forts guarding Mobile Bay enabled Union forces to threaten the city of Mobile.

Confederate General John B Hood, licking his wounds after his defeat to Sherman in Atlanta in September 1864, regrouped and launched a major offensive through Alabama to Tennessee in the hopes of retaking Nashville, but after several engagements his army was largely destroyed.

After Sherman captured the Confederate capital of Richmond, Virginia, on April 3, 1865, the war was all but over. Confederate General Robert E Lee surrendered to General Grant in Appomattox, Virginia, on April 7, 1865. Five days later Mobile surrendered to the Union siege. Two days after that, President Lincoln was assassinated in Washington, DC, by John Wilkes Booth, an avowed white supremacist.

The prolonged war destroyed the economy of the South and spent an entire generation of Southern white men. (By war's end, the state of Mississippi had sent 80,000 enlistees into battle – a figure greater than the state's total number of white males between the ages of 18 and 45 cited in the 1860 census.)

The Confederate cause is remembered with monuments and memorials, and is relived in battle reenactments throughout the South. Its heroes are revered in state holidays – even today, state offices may be closed on Robert E Lee Day, Jefferson Davis' birthday and Confederate Memorial Day.

Reconstruction & 'Redemption'

After Lincoln's assassination Vice President Andrew Johnson was sworn in and oversaw the ratification of the 13th, 14th and 15th Amendments, which outlawed slavery and granted equal protection for blacks under the Constitution.

In 1864, General Sherman had issued Field Order 15, allotting '40 acres and a mule' for former slaves, but federal legislation during Reconstruction rescinded

Emancipation

Though at the start of the Civil War Lincoln had vowed not to touch slavery, after two years of fighting he recognized the issue as his trump card. In June 1862, slavery was outlawed in the territories (reversing the 1857 *Dred Scott* decision). On September 27, Lincoln issued his *Emancipation Proclamation*, which emancipated the four million slaves in rebel states effective January 1, 1863. The proclamation paved the way for blacks to formally enlist in the Union forces, significantly strengthening the Union effort. Though blacks accounted for less than 1% of the population in the North, by the war's end they constituted 10% of the Union Army. A small number of blacks fought on the side of the Confederacy, largely Creole landowners from Louisiana. ∎

Sherman's generosity. Liberated slaves were left with 'nothing but freedom' – landless, powerless and impoverished.

Great economic, political and social instability prevailed throughout the South. Farms lay fallow, and an agrarian depression loomed. Many families were financially ruined, and many had lost members to the war and were overcome with grief. Federal troops descended on the chaos to impose a mandatory 'reconstructed' system of society, labor and government. Former members of the Confederate government were disqualified from holding office, and in their places the Federals installed blacks and Union-sympathizing whites.

To black Southerners, Reconstruction represented the first taste of liberty since their ancestors were captured in Africa generations ago. It transformed slaves into citizens; all former slaves were guaranteed the right to an education and could engage in an unprecedented interracial democracy. Black men could vote. The blacks elected or appointed to positions of power were largely drawn from the small but highly significant free black community, which had been quietly building a black middle class of doctors, dentists, lawyers and other educated professionals throughout slavery days. After the war, many Northern religious communities sent teachers to the South to start schools for former slaves.

Reconstruction drew many opportunists bent on exploiting the defeated South, and some of these brought corruption to Reconstruction governments. Opportunists from the North who arrived with tapestry duffels in hand were derided by many white Southerners as 'carpetbaggers' and their local collaborators (often drawn from the white lower class) as 'scalawags.'

After six years of frustrated intervention in the region's internecine struggles, the federal government withdrew, leaving the door wide open for the return of white supremacy. Former Confederates returned to power. In 1890, Mississippi – a state with over half of its population black – led the way in formal disenfranchisement of blacks by adopting a state constitution that imposed literacy tests, a $2 poll tax and other restrictions on voting. An estimated 123,000 blacks lost their right to vote

almost overnight. Within a few years, almost every Southern state had copied Mississippi's example – 'redeeming' their state from the 'sins' of Reconstruction. Reconstruction's ambitious libertarian goals didn't meaningfully resurface until the modern civil rights movement.

The Jim Crow South

'Jim Crow' was originally a derogatory term for blacks. In 1832, white performer Thomas 'Daddy' Rice won raves for his caricature of a fictitious black minstrel, Jim Crow, further popularizing the term. By the early 1900s, 'Jim Crow' described the official system of apartheid in the American South. This system came to include segregation by race of transportation modes, waiting rooms, hotels and restaurants, parks and theaters. Separate public institutions, usually of inferior quality, were created, including schools and hospitals.

The strict social boundaries between blacks and whites were unofficially enforced by the white supremacist Ku Klux Klan, which employed violent tactics such as brutal beatings, cross burnings, church

DOROTHEA LANGE

Women hoeing (Mississippi Delta, late 1930s)

firebombings, lynchings and other intimidation techniques to keep blacks from realizing their constitutional rights.

In 1896 a Supreme Court decision solidified institutionalized racism. Earlier that year, Homer Plessy, a quadroon from Louisiana, bought a train ticket from New Orleans to Covington. He took a seat in the whites-only car and refused to move to the 'colored' car when directed by the conductor. He was arrested for violating segregation laws. Plessy sued the railroad, arguing that segregation was illegal under the 14th Amendment. The *Plessy* v *Ferguson* case came before the US Supreme Court, which decided that separation of the races was within the bounds of the Constitution as long as equal accommodations were made for blacks, underpinning the 'separate-but-equal' doctrine for decades.

The Sharecropper Economy

Industry came slowly to the South – first the railroads, then logging – but the region continued to be dependent upon agriculture, primarily cotton. 'Sharecropping' replaced the institution of slavery and became the predominant labor system for poor whites and blacks throughout the South. Under this system, tenant farmers worked a certain portion of the property owner's land in exchange for a portion of the cash crop they produced. In practice, the system cyclically exploited tenant farmers, driving them into permanent debt. Early on in the growing season, share-croppers borrowed against the crop for their seeds, tools and subsistence; at each harvest they delivered their bales and realized they were still in debt to the landowner, who would set the terms of the exchange to his own advantage.

In 1914, the boll-weevil infestation ravaged cotton crops across the South and revealed the folly of dependence on a single crop. Blacks were hit the hardest and left the South by the thousands (a time remembered as the 'Great Migration') to look for work in factories booming in such northern cities as Detroit and Chicago. When the Great Depression struck in 1929,

> ### Hail, the Boll Weevil!
> King cotton dominated the economy of the Deep South throughout the 19th and early 20th century. Then the boll weevil descended on crops in Louisiana, Mississippi and Texas. In 1915 it arrived in Alabama and dethroned the king by devouring two-thirds of the state's cotton crop. Coffee County, the area around Enterprise, was one of the hardest hit. Ironically, the weevil forced farmers to diversify and the area eventually prospered. In thanks, Enterprise erected a statue of a woman holding a boll weevil above her head in the middle of the intersection of Main and Glover Sts. The inscription reads 'In profound appreciation of the boll weevil and what it has done.' ■
>
> – Diane Marshall

the crippled Southern economy sunk even further.

From all this pain and poverty arose some of the greatest contributions the South has made to American culture. The early 20th century saw the birth of jazz and the blues ('takes a man what knows the blues to sing the blues'). Likewise, the literary arts flourished; Mississippians Faulkner and Williams, and Tennessee's Agrarian Poets gave rise to a Southern literature drawn from the everyday struggles and dramas of rural society (see the Music and Literature sections).

New Deal Society

In the 1940s the New Deal programs introduced by President Franklin Delano Roosevelt brought some respite to the region, addressing environmental destruction caused by soil erosion and clear-cut forestry. The parks and recreation areas constructed by skilled WPA laborers and craftsworkers remain in constant use today.

During the two world wars, Southerners joined the military. While enlisted, black soldiers experienced less-racist societies in the North and in Europe. The US military was at the time uncommonly progressive, at least in terms of pay scales: the rate of pay for black and white soldiers had been equal since the Civil War due to protests by the 34th Massachusetts, a famous black unit. When black soldiers returned to the South, they were rendered second-class citizens once more.

In 1934, the National Association for the Advancement of Colored People (NAACP) was founded to advocate for civil rights. By the early 1950s, literacy programs were established across the South to increase black participation in the political process, but gains were small and slow.

The Civil Rights Movement

For most Americans, the civil rights movement began on May 17, 1954, when the Supreme Court handed down its decision in the *Brown* v *Board of Education* case outlawing segregation in public schools. Since the rise of Jim Crow segregation, schooling in the South was separate but not equal; it was common for Southern states to spend five times more educating white children than black children.

From this decision until the passage of the Voting Rights Act in 1965, the US experienced more social change, court decisions and legislation in the name of civil rights than in any other decade of US history, and many of these pivotal events occurred in the Deep South. Though the period is remembered for its violent clashes, many advocates for change were committed to nonviolence (inspired by Mahatma Gandhi). This strategy enabled such dramatic social change to occur without the massive bloodshed that typically accompanies revolution.

School Desegregation The *Brown* decision did not automatically lead to school desegregation. In the decade that followed, some schools defied the court order, necessitating the arrival of federal troops to guarantee that black students could register. In 1954, Mississippi state voters approved a constitutional amendment allowing the legislature to abolish public schools rather than integrate them. It took President Eisenhower dispatching

the 101st Airborne Division for the 'Little Rock Nine' to integrate Central High School in Little Rock, Arkansas.

In Alabama, Governor George Wallace personally stood in the doorway at the University of Alabama to block the entrance of James Hood and Vivian Malone. (In 1996, George Wallace would attend a 'reconciliation' ceremony with the former Miss Malone.) At the bastion of the Old South, the 'Ole Miss' campus of the University of Mississippi in Oxford, it took thousands of state and federal guardsmen to quell the riots that broke out when James Meredith attempted to register in 1962; the price of opposition to Meredith's admission was 160 injured marshals and two deaths.

Montgomery Bus Boycott Throughout the South, laws mandated that blacks had to board buses up front to pay their fare and then reboard through the rear door to take seats in the back; laws also specified that black riders had to yield their seats to whites. In 1953, bus riders in Baton Rouge, Louisiana, petitioned for first-come, first-served seating, and by leading a boycott of the buses, they were able to reach a compromise.

On December 1, 1955, in Montgomery, Alabama, 42-year-old seamstress Rosa Parks refused to surrender her seat to a white passenger and was arrested for violating the segregation laws. The black community mobilized a citywide boycott galvanized by the leadership of Reverend Martin Luther King Jr. The boycott that few expected to last a week continued 13 months before the Supreme Court affirmed a lower court's ruling outlawing segregation. (In 1996, Parks would receive the Presidential Medal of Freedom – the nation's highest civilian honor.)

Despite a violent backlash that included the bombing of King's home, the Montgomery boycott inspired blacks in neighboring Birmingham and Mobile to boycott for change in their cities. Birmingham was later the scene of mass demonstrations calling for wider desegregation. In 1963, Martin Luther King Jr was among nearly

15,000 protesters arrested in Birmingham; as a prisoner he wrote the inspirational civil-rights manifesto remembered as 'Letter from Birmingham Jail.'

Nashville Sit-Ins Department stores in the South sold goods to blacks, but they reserved their lunch counters for whites only. In 1960 when a group of black college students refused to leave a Woolworth's lunch counter in Greensboro, North Carolina, Woolworth's closed the lunch counter rather than serve them. The students returned day after day. The news of the sit-ins spread and students throughout the region – who had grown up in the post-*Brown* era – organized other sit-ins.

Despite harassment and mob violence, over 50,000 people participated in a non-violent campaign, which culminated in a silent march to city hall. Fearful of violence and the economic damage such sit-ins wrought, the mayor agreed to desegregate the city's lunch counters.

Such student demonstrations across the South shifted the battle from the courts to the marketplace. The movement gained momentum with the 1960 presidential election of John F Kennedy (he won 68% of the black vote), and it drew inspiration as 11 African nations won independence in a single year (June 1960 to June 1961).

Freedom Riders Though the federal government outlawed segregation in interstate travel in 1955, Southern states routinely ignored federal policy and continued to separate white and colored waiting rooms, bathrooms and water fountains. In 1961 civil-rights activists organized a 'Freedom Ride,' intending to ride buses from Washington, DC, to New Orleans. Riders were beaten in south Carolina. When they crossed into Alabama, the bus was firebombed; they were again stopped by a violent attack in Birmingham. More Freedom Riders volunteered to continue the route, and flank upon flank the volunteers were met by mob violence. When they reached Jackson, Mississippi, the riders were followed by police through the whites-only waiting room and then jailed for violating state segregation laws.

More than 300 Freedom Riders traveled through the Deep South to challenge local segregation practices, but the ensuing violence led the movement to shift the strategy to voter registration, which was thought to be a less-confrontative avenue for activism.

Mississippi Burning In the 1950s, the population of Mississippi was 45% black, the highest of any state in the nation, yet only 5% of voting-age blacks were registered, the lowest of any state. With majorities in many counties, blacks might well have controlled local politics through the ballot box, a fact not lost on local segregationists, who did whatever it took to suppress black voter registration. Blacks attempting to register to vote were subjected to economic or violent retribution against them or their families. Churches, the mainstay of the black community, were often targets of firebombings designed to suppress the pursuit of civil rights.

Already well known nationally for its routine repression of blacks, Mississippi increased its notoriety through the ignominious activities of its white Citizens Council (founded in 1954), a white-collar equivalent of the Ku Klux Klan that was supported by the state government and dedicated to maintaining segregation at any cost. (In 1996, federal courts would finally order the state to unseal its Citizens Council records; the files are now under review by the American Civil Liberties Union.)

On June 12, 1963, Medgar Evers, field secretary of the NAACP, was shot to death in the driveway of his home outside Jackson. It took 30 years and two trials for his murderer, Brian de la Bequith, to be brought to justice (see the sidebar entitled 'The Content of Their Character' in the Central Mississippi chapter).

On June 21, 1964, the disappearance of three civil rights workers on a voter registration drive through Mississippi prompted an FBI investigation. Kennedy had been assassinated the previous November, and

Vice President Lyndon Johnson had assumed the job of bringing civil rights to the South. Johnson sent in sailors to aid the search. On August 4, the bodies of the three were pulled from an earthen dam outside Meridian. Though murder charges were dropped in state court, six of the accused white men were found guilty of violating federal civil rights laws and were sentenced to jail.

The March from Selma to Montgomery Though the Civil Rights Act of 1964 was intended to protect equal voting rights, Southern states continued to put up barriers specifically designed to restrict the black vote. To protest such practices and gain full enfranchisement, grassroots organizers planned a march from Selma, Alabama, to the state capitol in Montgomery, 58 miles east. On March 7, 1965, 500 marchers – mostly black, but many white as well – started out from the Brown Chapel AME Church. They got no further than six blocks. At the Edmund Pettus Bridge over the Alabama River, state troopers standing three-deep and on horseback blocked Highway 80. They descended on the marchers with nightsticks, bullwhips and tear gas. Three marchers died (including a white man, which drew increased media attention) and 87 were injured. The sight of the battered band bleeding and limping in retreat immemorialized the event as 'Bloody Sunday.'

As the scene was broadcast around a shocked nation, President Johnson, in one of the most stirring speeches of his presidency, was moved to proclaim: 'At times, history and fate meet in a single place to shape a turning point in man's unending search for freedom. So it was at Lexington and Concord. So it was a century ago at Appomattox. So it was last week in Selma, Alabama.'

Two weeks after Bloody Sunday, Dr Martin Luther King Jr returned from Norway after accepting the Nobel Peace Prize and in Selma joined 4000 black and white demonstrators to renew the march – their

numbers swelled to 25,000 as they proceeded up the Jefferson Davis Hwy to Montgomery. They climbed the steps of the State Capitol, with its Confederate battle flag waving outside, but their request to see Governor Wallace was refused.

The Voting Rights Act of 1965 Four months after Bloody Sunday, LBJ signed into law the Voting Rights Act of 1965, which banned literacy tests as a prerequisite to voting and other obstacles designed to block the black franchise. Significantly, the act shifted 'the burden of proof' to state governments, meaning it was now up to the states to prove they hadn't intended to discriminate. The act required all or part of seven states – Alabama, Georgia, Louisiana, Mississippi, Virginia and the Carolinas – to have every change in local or state election laws approved by the US Justice Department or federal courts in Washington, DC.

Enforcement of the act led to sweeping changes in the nature of the American political process. In Louisiana, black registered voters rose from 32% of those eligible in 1964 to 47 % in 1966. In Alabama during that same period, the gain was from 23% to 51% of eligible blacks. In Mississippi, the percentage of registered eligible black voters skyrocketed from 7% in 1964 to 33% just two years later. By 1984 it would rise to 86% of the state's black voting-age population, a higher proportion of registration among eligible blacks than eligible whites.

When Johnson declared the new act 'one of the most monumental laws in the entire history of American freedom,' there were only 300 black elected officials in the nation. Twenty years later, there were more than 2300 in the seven states first covered by the Voting Rights Act alone. Sixty percent of the increase in black officials nationwide had occurred in the South. These officials included mayors in New Orleans, Birmingham, Atlanta and many smaller cities and towns throughout the Deep South.

However, the act was no panacea. Stalwart segregationists derided its enforcement as a 'second Reconstruction' and found ingenious ways to continue to impede the black vote. In 1985, a Justice Department official reflecting on the number of federal observers still dispatched to enforce the act said, 'We're far from going out of business.' Intimidation also continued, and a segregationist backlash intensified in the decade following the 1965 legislation; Ku Klux Klan activities reached their height in the 1970s. Economically, gaining the vote could only begin to reverse centuries of oppression – blacks in the region (as well as in the nation) continued to trail far behind whites in every economic measure.

Nonetheless, much change was swift and visible. When the Selma-to-Montgomery march was reenacted in 1985, the Alabama state troopers – including black officers formerly barred from the force – served as guardians to protect the marchers. At the Capitol, the group was welcomed by Governor Wallace, whose reelection now depended on black voters.

King's Assassination On April 4, 1968, Dr Martin Luther King Jr was assassinated on the second-story balcony of the Lorraine Motel in downtown Memphis, Tennessee. King's assassination delivered a tremendous blow to the movement and the cause of civil rights in general. His absence from the national stage left a vacuum that remains unfilled even 30 years later.

Aftermath To go through the South now is to witness the dismantlement of apartheid. To view the battlegrounds of the civil rights movement – Jackson, Meridian, Selma, Montgomery, Birmingham, Nashville and Memphis – is to witness a transformation in American society no less sweeping than the Civil War.

Today the struggle is memorialized in monuments and exhibits across the South. The Lorraine Motel is now preserved as the National Civil Rights Museum, as a tribute to Dr King, to those who died in the civil-rights struggle and to the cause of nonviolent social change. Birmingham also maintains a museum dedicated to civil rights, and there's a Voting Rights Museum in Selma. In Montgomery, a civil-rights fountain designed by Vietnam Veterans Memorial architect Maya Lin stands outside the Southern Poverty Law Center. The memory of Martin Luther King Jr is now marked by a national holiday on his birthday in January.

In major cities across the region blacks and whites mingle together in many restaurants, shopping centers, schools and churches. In many others, and in smaller cities and towns, there remains an invisible but stark line dividing white and black.

For recent history, see state chapters.

GEOGRAPHY

From the Appalachian heights in northeast Alabama to Louisiana's low-lying coastal wetlands (much of New Orleans is actually below sea level), the Deep South slopes slowly downhill in a fan shape. (Definitions of 'Deep South' often include the states of Georgia and South Carolina; for the purposes of this guide, we include only Alabama, Louisiana, Mississippi and western Tennessee.) The primary geographical feature of the Deep South is the great Mississippi River, which meanders along the state borders of Mississippi, Louisiana and western Tennessee.

In Alabama, the geographical features of the Atlantic Seaboard meet those of the Gulf states. Three provinces related to the Appalachian mountain range extend into eastern Alabama: the Cumberland Plateau (reaching a maximum height of 2407 feet), the Ridge-and-Valley region in the north and the central Piedmont Plateau. In southern Alabama, the wide Atlantic Coastal Plain meets the Gulf Coastal Plain, which stretches west through lower Mississippi and Louisiana. In upper Mississippi, the Central Plateau rises to a maximum elevation of 780 feet in the northeast corner and drops to 535 feet in northern Louisiana.

The Mississippi River has a unique geography and ecology that dominates the central US. Left to its own devices, the Mississippi could change course and flood periodically, replenishing the fields of the alluvial basin; if not for human intervention, it would today be emptying into the Atchafalaya River. For centuries humans have worked to control the river's flow to maintain a single shipping channel and to protect cities, industries and farmland along the riverbanks. An impressive arsenal of artificial levees, reservoirs, pumping stations and dredging fleets has – so far – proven successful. This technology has altered the topography of the region, diverting waters that would naturally flow elsewhere and carrying silt deposits down a stream-lined shipping channel to build up at the river's mouth in the Gulf of Mexico (an estimated two million tons of sediment per day).

Most of the other major rivers in the region – the Tennessee River in Tennessee and Alabama, the Yazoo River in Mississippi and Louisiana's Red River and Ouachita Rivers – are part of the Mississippi River navigation system. The Mobile drainage basin consists of the Black Warrior and Alabama Rivers in Alabama and the Tombigbee River in Mississippi; these rivers meet the Gulf in Mobile Bay. (A note on the regional lexicon: Though the Mississippi River disperses through a fringed delta at Louisiana's Gulf shore, the leaf-shaped alluvial basin from Memphis to Vicksburg is known locally as the 'Mississippi Delta,' or just 'the Delta.')

Barrier islands in the Gulf of Mexico are also distinctive. Sandbars that evolved to support maritime forests, the Gulf Islands (now preserved as the Gulf Islands National Seashore) off the southern coast are forever shifting. Petit Bois Island, for example, was partially in Alabama as late as 1950; now it's entirely in Mississippi. Hurricanes, common to the coast, can also influence geography – Ship Island was split in two by Hurricane Camille in 1965; now it's known as West and East Ship.

The wetlands of southwestern Louisiana represent another unique environment comprising swamps, marshes and bayous. The region's only natural areas of solid ground are the indigenous river levees. Swamps are permanently waterlogged areas that often exhibit tree growth. Marshes tend to be poorly drained areas that may be only periodically inundated. Bayous are the sluggish freshwater tributaries of the main river channel, often becoming cut-off and abandoned bodies of water. The combination of elevated land (however slight), a rich freshwater environment and removal from the threat of over-bank river flooding makes bayous relatively attractive settlement areas – at least when compared with other wetland environments.

GEOLOGY

Alabama is the most geologically diverse state in the region. In its northeastern Appalachian corner numerous caves are hidden among limestone deposits; some, such as Russell Cave, hold tremendous archaeological significance. Natural bridges, springs and waterfalls make this limestone-and-shale landscape dramatic, particularly so at De Soto State Park. South of the Tennessee River, a mineral belt contains vast deposits of coal, iron, ore and other minerals, and its Piedmont region soils consist of sandy loam and red clay.

Southern Alabama's diverse geology holds much in common with the other states in the region. The 'Black Belt' – so-called for its sticky, black calcareous clay soil – stretches from Georgia to Texas and, along with the rich alluvial soils of the Mississippi River basin, supports the fertile fields that are responsible for the region's cotton industry. A sandy-soiled pine belt, stretching nearly as wide, is the source of the region's lumbering and pulp-and-paper industries.

In Mississippi, loess bluffs shoulder the eastern boundary of the alluvial basin. Many antebellum houses still stand on these 'Bluff Hills' of brown loam, which are underlain by a yellowish calcareous silt layer.

The region's Gulf shore holds oil deposits in submerged salt domes, particularly at the neck of the Mississippi River. While offshore drilling for oil and gas in the region is concentrated off the Louisiana coast, you'll also see rigs offshore in Mississippi and Alabama. This is often the source of local controversy; see Ecology & Environment below.

CLIMATE

The low-lying subtropical coastal plain in the lower half of the region is hot, wet and sticky most of the year – other times it's just wet, receiving around 60 inches of precipitation annually. The climate is cooler and drier at the higher elevations in the upper half of the region. Spring is the most colorful season, with wildflowers and gardens in bloom, and fall is the driest season.

In New Orleans and across the coastal plain, summer is extremely humid, with temperatures reaching 100°F in the shade during the dog days of July and August. The high humidity is broken daily by afternoon thundershowers. City folk head to Gulf Coast beaches to find a breeze, or they head north. Summer nights are languidly hot.

The mountainous region of northeastern Alabama has the coolest temperatures, and the most varied forest colors in fall, though you can find fall colors on trees throughout the upper half of the region. Alabama's mountains get some snow each winter, and the occasional odd storm will also bring frost and even snow to the coastal plain. A freak storm in the winter of 1996 coated coastal palmettos with snow. But generally it rarely drops below 50°F even in midwinter at the lower elevations.

Hurricane season, which brings severe periodic storms that last a day or two, begins in June and usually ends in October, but can continue through November. If you plan to travel the Gulf region during this time pay particular attention to Gulf and Caribbean storm forecasts.

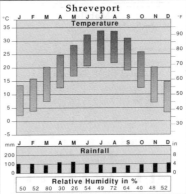

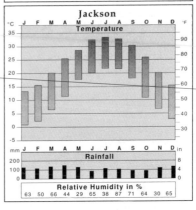

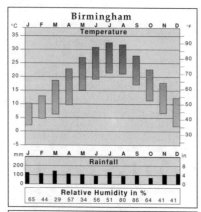

Birmingham

Temperature

Rainfall

Relative Humidity in %
65 44 29 57 34 56 51 80 86 64 41 41

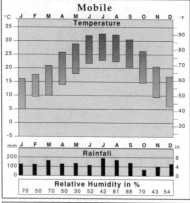

Mobile

Temperature

Rainfall

Relative Humidity in %
70 50 70 50 30 52 42 81 88 70 43 54

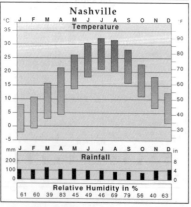

Nashville

Temperature

Rainfall

Relative Humidity in %
61 60 39 83 45 49 46 69 79 56 40 63

ECOLOGY & ENVIRONMENT

The environmental ravaging of the South's many natural riches is legendary. Exploitation of the region has continued almost unabated since colonial times. Even today, vestiges of a near-feudal mentality among politicians and industrialists remain intact, encouraging a system of patronage that allows predominant industries to go about their business with little oversight from local authorities.

By the early part of the 20th century, poor land management of the singly important cotton crop had exhausted the soil, perhaps the costliest environmental degradation in the South. Artificial levees restricting the rejuvenating cycles of river flow were also hurting the soil and sending silt to clog the coastal delta. Vital wetlands were being drained or filled for agricultural development.

During this same period, timber companies swooped in and cleared whole regions of forest, destroying habitats and further eroding the soil in their wake. In the 1930s, the Civilian Conservation Corps – called 'Roosevelt's Tree Army' in these parts – performed restorative work by replanting trees and establishing erosion controls, in addition to building recreation areas.

This did little to stop the destruction. As the 20th century progressed, the Corps of Engineers dammed rivers for reservoirs, giant paper mills replaced varied forests with biologically sterile pine plantations and more wetlands disappeared. In fact, of all wetlands destruction in the nation – saltwater and fresh – the southeast has been hardest hit.

Today, industrial toxins add insult to injury – according to the Institute for Southern Studies Green Index, the region leads the nation in per-capita exposure to industrial toxins in the air and water, yet when it comes to state spending on waste management, the Deep South states are at the bottom of the list. Not surprisingly, the worst dumps and hazards are located near poor communities, especially those with minority residents.

Environmental advocates have now begun to speak out and defend the region's natural resources more vigorously, though state governments continue to accommodate polluting industries. In Alabama, state officials often look the other way when influential, job-providing, land-owning pulp-and-paper companies release dioxin into state waters exceeding EPA standards. In Louisiana, giant polluting corporations are given tax breaks instead of getting slapped with fines.

Though current offshore oil and gas drilling in the Gulf remains a potentially serious threat, companies in the region have so far maintained standards for environmental protection and records free of major accidents. Nevertheless, coastal residents view drilling as visual pollution – in Mississippi, for example, coastal residents are mounting a drive to keep oil drilling out of sight of the nationally protected Horn Island wilderness.

The many container ships that pass the shoreline as they travel the Intracoastal Waterway may represent a greater threat of spills – with their loads of chemicals and who knows what all – but again, so far there have been no major accidents.

Of course, natural disasters such as hurricanes have always wreaked enormous havoc on the coast. The last occurred when hurricane Betsy crashed ashore in early September 1965, taking 74 lives throughout coastal Mississippi and Louisiana. The hurricane cycle is in itself an argument for keeping coastal development of housing and industry to a minimum, but this logic routinely goes unheeded.

There are few silver linings in this cloud, except that environmental organizations are now on guard and have teamed up with local advocates who are vocal in their opposition to any offense to their land. Properties that are now protected, and habitats that have been restored, if only on a small scale, represent major miracles.

FLORA & FAUNA

The South's lush flora and abundant wildlife are what draw many people to visit and live in the region. The incredibly varied woodlands, the moody swamps and bayous, and the sounds of katydids and

Reining in the Mighty Mississippi

Geologists know it's just a matter of time before the Mississippi River shifts its course again, as it has done many times over the last millennia. In *The Control of Nature* (1989), author John McPhee describes such an event:

Southern Louisiana exists in its present form because the Mississippi River has jumped here and there within an arc about two hundred miles wide, like a pianist playing with one hand – frequently and radically changing course, surging over the right or left bank to go off in utterly new directions. Always it is the river's purpose to get to the Gulf by the shortest and steepest gradient.

The likely breech will occur at the Old River Control Auxiliary Structure, 200 miles upriver from New Orleans, where the US Army Corps of Engineers operates a navigation lock that offers a shortcut to the Gulf via the Atchafalaya River and that diverts excess water flow. In 1973 the force of the river at flood stage partially undermined this keystone safety valve. A rebuilt and reinforced structure repelled repeated floods in 1983 and 1993; yet none of these events matched the flow of the '100-Year Flood' of 1927. Most observers agree that the structures will not withstand another cataclysmic flood. All told, human intervention in large-scale hydrologic processes is only temporary in geological time.

The Flood Museum in Greenville is devoted to interpreting the 1927 flood. Mud Island in Memphis also contains exhibits about river ecology. ■

whippoorwills have been memorialized and romanticized in Southern literature for generations.

Flora

At the Davis Bayou on the Mississippi Gulf Coast, the back deck of the ranger station overlooks the water's edge. A short boardwalk leads down to the reedy marshland through a typical Southern forest – chinquapin, pawpaw, sassafras, holly, cypress and several species of pine and oak, for starters. Along this 30-foot path, a naturalist could spend half a day cataloging and enjoying the fascinating variety of trees, understory plants and aquatic vegetation.

This is the richness of the Southern landscape – incredible diversity within a compact area. Residents quickly fall in love with their particular parcel of countryside, from the colorful Southern Appalachian Forest of northern Alabama's Cumberland Plateau to Louisiana's cypress-filled bayous. Locals become attuned to nuances in a forest's mood and subtleties in animal behavior. Whether you immerse yourself in one region or visit several, you'll find that each landscape is unique, intricate and evocative.

The South is well known for many flowering species of trees, shrubs and flowers – 1500 varieties in all. From the blooming of the first white serviceberry in early March until the last yellow witch hazel petal drops in December, Southern blossoms can be seen throughout most of the year. Some of the common flowering species include southern magnolia (Mississippi is the Magnolia State), azalea, rhododendron, mountain laurel, dogwood, redbud, chinaberry, crepe myrtle, wisteria and a variety of wildflowers, such as violets, goldenrod and the Cherokee rose. Southern gardeners make the most of this natural abundance, beauty and fragrance.

Perhaps the most evocative image of the South is of wispy tendrils of Spanish moss draped from the broad limbs of a live oak. However, despite its name, Spanish moss is neither moss nor Spanish. Related to the pineapple, the flowering plant is an epiphyte: it takes all the nutrients its needs from the air. The plant's name was supposedly derived from its resemblance to a Spaniard's beard. It clings to live oaks because the craggy bark gives seeds a secure hold, and long limbs that never lose their leaves provide protection from the wind and sun. Between 1900 and 1940, Spanish moss was 'ginned' in Louisiana and neighboring states, and used to stuff upholstery and repair fishing nets.

Varied Southern habitats harbor distinct plant communities such as cordgrass-lined bayous, cypress swamps, piney woods, canebrakes and maritime forests of palmetto, pine and oak. The Southern Appalachian Forest – vestiges of which can be found in northeastern Alabama – contains more tree types than can be found in all of Europe (130 compared to 85), including towering hardwoods and softwoods and deciduous and evergreen varieties. There's even a 'petrified forest' outside the town of Flora in central Mississippi, said to be the only one of its kind in the eastern US.

Another common sight – and common blight – of Southern landscapes is the unstoppable kudzu vine, which seems to shroud whole forests along interstate byways, choking growth and killing native species. Originally imported from Japan in the early 19th century for erosion control, kudzu exploded without any natural controls in the American South.

Fauna

Mammals White-tailed deer are by far the most significant large mammal inhabiting Southern forests. The primary food source for centuries of Native American inhabitants, deer is still prized game for Southern hunters. But what you'll see most frequently are the smaller mammals, primarily raccoon, opossums (called possums in the South), rabbits, squirrels, bats and strange creatures called armadillos.

The armadillo has an interesting history in these parts. As the story goes, a pair of native South American armadillos escaped from a circus truck in Florida in the early 1900s and spread like wildfire throughout the South. They've proliferated so much, in fact, that they are now called 'weed' wildlife (another nickname is 'possum-on-the-half-shell'). They're slow-moving creatures, and sadly you'll see them most often littered alongside Southern roads (which is inspiration for the local joke: 'Why did the possum cross the road? To show the armadillo it could be done!')

The short-haired Catahoula leopard dog is a breed native to Louisiana. The hound is a cross between a domestic dog raised by Indians of the Catahoula Lake region and a Spanish 'war dog' that came through the area in the early 1500s.

The nutria, a large rodent, thrives in Louisiana bayous and swamps. It goes by the name 'coypu' in its native South America and is sometimes called a 'mouse beaver.' The nutria was imported to the South for its fur. An accident during a storm in 1938 allowed nutrias to escape from cages kept by the McIlhenny family on Avery Island, after which they proliferated in the wild.

In the Gulf, bottle-nosed dolphins can often be seen accompanying boats out to the Gulf Islands.

Fish Mississippi leads the nation in farm-raised catfish, capitalizing on the native species named for the long whiskerlike barbels extending from its lower jaw. (Belzoni, Mississippi, calls itself the 'Catfish Capital of the World' and crowns a Catfish Queen at its annual catfish festival.) On the coast, mullet was such an important food source during the beefless days of WWII that it earned the nickname 'Biloxi Bacon,' and it's commemorated at the annual Mullet Festival. Bass, speckled trout, white perch and the Gulf Coast redfish are also prime Southern catches.

Also lurking in the Mississippi River are ancient species such as the paddlefish, a Paleozoic monster that grows up to six feet long and shares characteristics of both bony fish and cartilaginous sharks. Now protected, their numbers were reduced by commercial fishing for its roe. The alligator gar – which grows up to 9 feet with plate-like scales reputed to turn an ax – inhabits shallow water, where it captures fish in its ferocious-looking jaws. You can see some of these exotic species at the Aquarium of the Americas in New Orleans.

Crustaceans, Marine Invertebrates & Mollusks The best-known regional crustacean is the crawfish (aka crayfish, crawdad), found in swamps and marshes; the Louisiana crawfish is a highly sought-after and much-celebrated delicacy. Freshwater and saltwater shellfish include mussels and clams, and the Gulf of Mexico provides an abundance of local oysters and shrimp.

Jellyfish and Portuguese man-o'-war are common in Gulf waters and should be avoided when swimming (applying meat tenderizer is said to be effective treatment for stings).

Birds The naturalist John James Audubon (1785-1851) painted over 80 of his beautiful folios for the monumental *The Birds of America*, while staying in New Orleans and near St Francisville, Louisiana, during 1821 and 1822.

The Mississippi Flyway is one of the four flyways across the North American continent. Migratory birds travel along it to wetlands up and down the Mississippi River basin. Many of these wetlands are protected as national wildlife refuges for wintering waterfowl, mostly ducks. In April and May, over 70 species of thrushes, warblers, buntings, vireos, grosbeaks and tanagers arrive from South America. Many fly the 800-mile journey over the Gulf of Mexico in a single night.

Year round you'll find all manner of herons, egrets, ibis and anhingas roosting in the region's wetlands. In the woodlands you'll hear many songbird varieties, including warblers, sparrows, mockingbirds and thrashers. Gulf shorebirds include gulls, terns, brown pelicans and several dozen species of sandpiper and plover. Southern gardens attract ruby-throated humming-birds.

The wild turkey is the most popular native game bird, along with the quail and dove.

Amphibians & Reptiles The American alligator (or 'gator') inhabits the bayous, creeks and lowland marshes of the Deep South. Formerly hunted to dwindling numbers for its valuable hide, the alligator has made a remarkable comeback due to the protection provided by the Endangered Species Act. However, Louisiana has reinstated a legal cull, and today visitors will see lacquered alligator heads for sale at the French Market in New Orleans and elsewhere.

A rare, blind, lungless salamander native to the cave region in northeastern Alabama is one of many species of lizards, skinks and newts found in the South. Freshwater turtles are abundant (the soft-shelled variety is considered the most tasty and is marketed commercially), but sea turtles, some of which are endangered, are seen only rarely. Oak toads are one of the distinctly Southern varieties of the many common toads and bullfrogs in the region. (The South's most famous amphibian is Kermit the Frog, mascot of his Leland, Mississippi, birthplace.)

Poisonous snakes are present but are encountered rarely. Water moccasins – called 'cottonmouths' for the white lining they reveal when extending their jaw – live in the coastal plain, but because the common Southern water snake so closely resembles a cottonmouth, alleged sightings far outnumber actual encounters. Copperheads are found at the region's higher elevations.

Insects The South has many varieties of huge and colorful butterflies, which are drawn to the region's abundant flowering plants; indeed, some gardens are specially designed to attract butterflies. Dragonflies inhabit the wetlands, and katydids and crickets chirp through the night.

Mosquitoes – vampires of the marshes – are the most feared wildlife in the region; listen for the soft drone in the still air of early evening that signals their emergence. You'll also make the acquaintance of nuisance gnats that are so small they're called 'no-see-ums.'

Huge, brown, winged cockroaches are another pest; they grow up to three inches long, can fly and live both indoors and out.

Endangered Species
Before European settlement, the continent's southern wilderness was full of bison, bear, wildcat, wolf and cougar; beaver, muskrat, mink and otter were also plentiful. Indiscriminate trappers annihilated these species, though recent efforts have been aimed at saving the remaining species and reintroducing lost species.

In Louisiana, about a hundred black bears remain, and habitat preservation has been dedicated to their survival. The preserved wilderness of several Gulf Islands provides ideal habitats for the reintroduction of diminishing or disappeared species. A pair of red wolves was reintroduced to the Horn Island wilderness, for example. Bald eagles have also returned to the islands as a result of coastal conservation efforts.

A local variety of sandhill crane neither migrates nor interbreeds with other varieties; the crane's survival is dependent on the preservation of their favored water-logged savanna habitat. The Sandhill Crane National Wildlife Refuge near the Mississippi-Alabama border is devoted to this cause.

Native to the Southern woods, the red-cockaded woodpecker – with its distinctive 'Woody the Woodpecker' cry – is now endangered. Many programs throughout the region are dedicated to its preservation.

According to Elizabeth Rooks, executive director of the Mississippi Wildlife Federation, 'the greatest threat to wildlife in Mississippi today is loss of habitat due to changes in land use, plain and simple.'

The same could be said for the rest of the Deep South.

GOVERNMENT & POLITICS

Each US state is a separate governing entity that sends representatives and senators to Congress in Washington, DC. Each state is headed by a governor. In keeping with the nature of complex Southern history, Southern states like to operate as independently as the federal government will allow, while the legacy of a feudal plantation culture favors state control over individual liberties. State identification is a tremendous source of local pride and loyalty.

In its political organization, as in so many other ways, Louisiana is an American anomaly due to its founding as a French colony. While other states are based on the Common Law of England, Louisiana's political foundation is drawn from the Napoleonic Code of France. While other states in the region are subdivided into political units called counties, Louisiana retains the Catholic designation of 'parishes.' While political corruption elsewhere is generally regarded as a sinister and a serious offense, Louisiana has historically been led by a string of colorful characters who have artfully managed to turn corruption into political theater.

The entire South has undergone a radical political shift in the last decade. After the Civil War, Southern whites shunned the Republican party of Abraham Lincoln, even though as the 20th century progressed the Democratic party became more closely aligned with Lincolnian principles. This created a region of 'Dixiecrats' – whites on the Democratic rolls whose conservative voting records departed from the liberalism of the rest of the party. In the last 10 years, even old-line Dixiecrats have changed camps and 'come out' as Republicans, joining the party that, today, is more consistent with their beliefs and values.

African Americans in the South historically aligned with the Republican party of Reconstruction, but the civil rights efforts of Kennedy's Democratic administration caused many to register as Democrats.

The voting rights struggles of the 1960s continue in more subtle campaigns today.

One of the most significant and controversial is redistricting. How district lines are drawn – the degree to which they highlight or diminish minority population areas – can mean the difference in the election of minority or majority candidates.

The South's conservative agenda has historically set the region apart, but recently the entire US has moved to the right, and now the South appears less isolated – a Southern platform that appeared extremely conservative 20 years ago now seems more mainstream. Regional politicians largely support prayer in schools, anti-abortion and capital punishment, but there are exceptions. New Orleans, for example, represents one comparatively liberal pocket in a region dubbed the 'Bible Belt' due to its largely conservative stance. Mississippi Attorney General Michael Moore is another liberal voice; Moore is aggressively pursuing a lawsuit against tobacco companies (a historically Southern industry, yet!) to recover $240 million of state health care costs for smoking-related illnesses.

ECONOMY

Agriculture and other industries based on natural resources continue to dominate the economies of the region. The South's historical reliance on cotton has been diversified and supplemented with soybeans and sugar cane. Lumbering and pulp-and-paper mills continue to be mainstays of many local economies. The coastal seafood industry peaked a few decades back, but it continues to make its contribution. Mississippi raises more catfish on fish farms than any other state.

Louisiana's oil and gas industry was an important economic force until 1982, when the region's oil boom went bust. Production has declined seriously since with little hope for recovery to previous levels. The oil industry is also active in coastal Mississippi (the Chevron refinery there is reportedly the state's single largest employer) and in Alabama. The river and Gulf ports of the region, including those in New

Orleans, Mobile and Memphis, drive local economies, and the shipping business is on the rise.

Of course, tourism has become a major industry in exotic New Orleans and the surrounding area and is also important in Memphis and Nashville. But it's had little impact in the rest of the economically depressed Deep South.

As for manufacturing, Mississippi is the largest manufacturer of upholstered furniture in the country.

The South was formerly the center of textile manufacture (related to its cotton production), but this industry has declined considerably over the last decade. For many years the anti-union South was a haven for manufacturing businesses eager to relocate from the pro-union North. The 1996 passage of the North American Free Trade Agreement (NAFTA) caused many businesses to look to foreign countries as a cheaper alternative to the South. Many of these businesses have begun to leave the US entirely, stranding thousands of textile workers with skills not readily adaptable to other industries.

In 1994, the three states with the lowest per-capita wages in the US were Mississippi, Arkansas and Louisiana. The Deep South states also have the highest poverty rates nationally – 24% of the population in Mississippi, 22% in Louisiana and 19% in Alabama (the national average is 14%).

Lackluster local economies have resulted in the explosive expansion of gaming casinos in the region. While riverboat gambling is a long-romanticized Southern tradition, it bears little resemblance to the huge Vegas-style casinos dropped onto small waterfront communities in rural Mississippi in recent years. Unfortunately, many of these casinos are a drain on the local economy rather than a boon – more locals find employment, but many are tempted to spend their service salaries at gambling tables, which siphons monies from local economies to out-of-state casino operators.

POPULATION & PEOPLE

Deep South state populations are as follows: Louisiana 4,315,000, Mississippi 2,570,000 and Alabama 4,219,000. While

Aquaculture – Crawfish & Catfish Farming

Though generations of Southerners have made crawfish and catfish staples of their diet, until recently, these bottom-dwelling creatures were dismissed by many as 'mudbugs' or 'trash fish.' Thought to be inferior to other crustaceans and fish, they were consumed mainly by poorer Southerners, who were accustomed to eking out a living from the lands and waters of the region.

But with the advent of commercial aquaculture in the 1970s, what was once the province of folks with cane poles and croaker sacks is now big, big business. It turns out that the flat lands of the Mississippi Delta are ideally suited for catfish ponds, while the equally flat Louisiana rice fields are well suited for raising crawfish.

Thanks to aggressive marketing campaigns and concerted efforts to maintain high quality and high prices, crawfish and, to an even greater degree, catfish farmers are enjoying great returns on their watery investments. Today, more than 100,000 acres of Mississippi are devoted to catfish ponds, with more being added yearly. And, though crawfish lags far behind in number of acres under cultivation, the future looks bright, as the nation's curiosity about all things Cajun shows no sign of ending.

But, all is not good news, especially for the catfish industry. Many of the people who work for minimum wage in catfish processing plants scattered about the region will tell you that chopping catfish is not very different from picking cotton like their ancestors did before them. Driven by quotas and afflicted by carpal tunnel syndrome, these workers are seeing none of the profits and feeling much of the pain. But, in a region where unemployment can reach 25%, these jobs are still sought after.

– John T Edge

these populations break down into distinct racial demographic groups, it should be noted that there has also been much cultural and racial intermixing over the past 200 years, and that racial categories and definitions are often not as sharp as they appear. The following descriptions are in order of prevalence in the population.

Caucasians Describing racial intermixing, former Louisiana governor Huey Long said that all the 'pure whites' in Louisiana could be fed 'with a nickel's worth of red beans and a dime's worth of rice.' But white people are still the majority in the Deep South, and there's a big cultural difference between the heritages of whites in inland areas and those in New Orleans and along the coast. The city and coast were settled early in the colonial period by Europeans, largely French and Spanish Catholics. The inland areas were settled almost a century later by Anglo-Saxon Protestants from the Piedmont areas of the Atlantic Coast states (principally Virginia). While these white populations may appear homogeneous compared to other racial groups, they come from historically distinct cultures that can still be distinguished today.

African Americans The majority of blacks in the Deep South today are descended from the African slaves who were brought to the Americas to work on plantations, and the majority of blacks in the United States continue to live in the South. In 1900, 35 years after the Civil War, over 90% of African Americans in the US lived in the states that had made up the Confederacy. During the Depression years of the 1930s and 1940s, millions of African Americans migrated north to escape economic hardship and entrenched racism. And yet today, the Deep South states are still among the five states in the nation with the greatest proportion of blacks: 26% in Alabama, 30% in Louisiana and 36% in Mississippi (the only state in the nation whose population is over one-third African American). Significantly,

African Americans are now relocating back to the South in record numbers. Between 1990 and 1995, a net total of 369,000 people have relocated to 15 Southern states at a rate 92% higher than in the 1980s.

Creoles Perhaps no ethnic definition has caused more confusion than the term Creole. From the Spanish *criollo* (person native to a locality), the term was first coined in the early 18th century to describe children born of French immigrants in the Louisiana colony. The term also applied to the children of the slaves of these immigrants. Members of this early Creole community considered France their motherland, sent their sons to be educated in France and published newspapers in French. After the Civil War, relations between white Creoles and blacks became strained as Creole culture itself was increasingly marginalized by the prevailing American culture. White Creoles continued to maintain French-language newspapers and literary societies into the early 20th century, but the culture largely died out before WWI, surviving only in certain families and constricted social circles. Today the term Creole is most often applied to the descendants of the former slaves of the white Creoles. New Orleans is the seat of Creole culture, and zydeco music is its most tangible legacy.

Cajuns Cajuns are descendants of 17th-century French settlers from Nova Scotia (L'Acadia), many of whom were deported by the British beginning in 1755 after Britain wrested control of Canadian territories from France. After nearly a decade of exile, the majority of the dispersed Acadians (later shortened to Cajuns) migrated to south Louisiana, where they reestablished themselves in the wetlands and prairie regions west of New Orleans. Today, the 22-parish (or county) region is dubbed 'Acadiana.' The Cajun dialect mixes French, Southern and English pronunciations and terms. Cajun cuisine, folkways and music are also distinctive. See the Cajun Country chapter of Louisiana.

Native Americans As is true everywhere in the United States, the Deep South has been home to Native Americans from prehistory to the present, and the indigenous Mississippian culture of 700 to 1200 AD is considered one of the greatest in North America. However, disease, war and forcible removal wiped out many of the local Native American tribes in the 18th and 19th centuries. Several Native American communities live on state and federal reservations in the Deep South, though their current lands and numbers are small compared to others in the United States.

In Mississippi, the thriving Choctaw federal reservation, northwest of Meridian, has 6000 residents, and the smaller Chickasaw reservation is outside Tupelo.

In Alabama, there's a Creek community northeast of Mobile.

In Louisiana, a federal Chitimacha reservation is in the heart of Cajun Country; the state is also home to Choctaw, Tunica, Coushatta and Houma communities without trust land.

As a result of widespread racial intermixing in the Deep South, many individuals of mixed race claim some Indian blood.

Other Minorities The Deep South has a smattering of many different ethnic and racial minorities. For example, Chinese and Lebanese laborers and tradespeople emigrated to the agribusiness zone of the Mississippi Delta earlier this century, and their descendants remain. A US government resettlement program in the 1960s brought Vietnamese families to the Gulf Coast because they were skilled at fishing; today you can find Vietnamese cuisine and Buddhist temples in many areas of the Mississippi outback.

EDUCATION

Southern schools were the battlegrounds of integration during the civil rights era after the Supreme Court outlawed segregation in its *Brown* v *Board of Education* ruling in 1954. Many white politicians fought segregation in the following decade, but none more vocally than George Wallace, who vowed to defy federal law ordering integration of Alabama public schools.

As integration of the schools became a reality in the 1960s, many white families enrolled their children in somewhat hastily established private academies, leading many public schools to become predominantly black, especially in the cities. In the last decade or so, however, the private academies have lost some of their allure, mostly because of rising fees, and more white families are enrolling their children in public schools. Integration can vary dramatically from district to district – for example, a school district with a good academic record and reputation can draw a more equitable racial mix than a neighboring district with lower achievement test scores.

Overall today, education in the Deep South suffers from neglect and apathy. In national educational achievement rankings, Louisiana, Mississippi and Alabama fall among the lowest seven states (and below national averages) for per capita government expenditures for education and for percentages of the population completing high school or earning a bachelors degree. Frequently, those with higher degrees find little economic opportunity in the region, and so they leave, creating a downward spiral for educational spending.

These statistics are not the whole story, of course, and in the extremely stratified Deep South, there's an upper section of highly educated folks and a number of fine institutions, both public and private.

Distinguished universities in Louisiana include Tulane and Loyola, both well-known institutions in New Orleans that attract students from all over the country. The bastion of the Old South, the University of Mississippi (called 'Ole Miss'), is in Oxford. Mississippi's Alcorn State University was the nation's first land-grant university for African Americans in 1875. In Alabama, Tuskegee University was founded by Booker T Washington in 1881. Tuskegee's graduates include Rosa Parks and the 'Tuskegee Airmen'; its professors included agronomist George Washington Carver. In Nashville, Tennessee, Fisk and Vanderbilt Universities are both historic and distinguished.

ARTS

One of the best reasons to visit the South is to experience the distinctive cultural arts the region has produced – arts that are intimately linked with the history, the land and the Southern experience.

Literature

Sahara of the Bozarts In a column for the *New York Evening Mail* published in 1917, cultural critic HL Mencken dubbed and damned the South the 'Sahara of the Bozarts,' charging that the region was 'almost as sterile, artistically, intellectually, culturally as the Sahara Desert.' As was to be expected, Mencken's words irked not a few chauvinistic Southerners. However, by the artistic standards of Mencken's day, the hyperbole was true.

Today, Southern artistic expression is celebrated around the world. The fictional works of Richard Wright, Eudora Welty and William Faulkner are recognized as among the most original and important of the 20th century. Yet there was a time when the Deep South was indeed almost bereft of 'great art.'

While South Carolina and Virginia claim a long and storied literary legacy, the states of Alabama, Louisiana, Mississippi and Tennessee are comparative latecomers to literary enterprise. Settled much later than the Upland South, the Deep South was considered a frontier area through much of the late 1800s. Ironically enough, this frontier mystique gave rise to the area's first literary movement.

19th-Century Humorists

The most influential Southern writers of the antebellum years were not writers at all but doctors, lawyers, salesmen and other professionals whose work required travel and whose comparative wealth and education afforded the perspective and ability to translate the region's rich oral culture into written dispatches from the American hinterlands.

Often first published in Northern newspapers, the tales told were bawdy, vulgar, violent and often hilarious. Among the most accomplished of the southwestern humorists was a Tennessean, George Washington Harris (1814-69). Best remembered for his 1867 publication *Sut Lovingood: Yarns Spun by a 'Nat'ral Born Durn'd Fool,'* Harris created protagonists 'full of fun, foolery and mean whisky' who displayed a rough-hewn, subversive humor.

By reading Harris and other humorists of the old southwest, Missouri-born Samuel Clemens (pseudonym Mark Twain, 1835-1910) learned the writing trade. His first sketches bear the unmistakable imprint of those, like Harris, who went before him. Twain, who worked as a Mississippi River steamboat pilot from 1857 to 1861, immortalized life along the Mississippi in his masterwork *The Adventures of Huckleberry Finn*, a poignant satire of Southern race relations and attitudes that tells of the unlikely friendship between Huck, a white boy, and Jim, a black man.

Local Color While the humorists of the old southwest were writers by circumstance or default, the next breed of writers from the Deep South were more purposeful. Though still concerned with the eccentricity and vagaries of Southern life, this postwar movement sold a romanticized Southern lifestyle to Northern editors intent on depicting the South as a 'land out of time,' where simplicity, honor and insularity prevailed. Two authors from Louisiana, Kate Chopin (1851-1904) and George Washington Cable (1844-1925), were among the foremost practitioners of this 'local-color' style.

Though a native of St Louis, Missouri, Kate Chopin is identified most closely with Louisiana, where much of her work is set and where she once lived. During her lifetime, *Bayou Folk* (1894), a collection of local color sketches, was regarded as her best work, but lately her second novel has risen to the forefront. In *The Awakening* (1899), a tormented woman embraces adultery and later suicide along the path to enlightenment. In its day, the novel was scandalous; today it is revered as a prototype of feminist literature.

George Washington Cable is remembered both for his courageous stand in favor of civil rights in *The Negro Question* (1890) and for his writings about Creole life in New Orleans as depicted in *The Grandissimes* (1880) and *Old Creole Days* (1879). Balancing criticism and understanding of Southern culture, his work is a link to the modernist styles that followed.

Southern Renaissance As the rest of the US grew into 20th-century prosperity, the South lagged far behind in terms of education, race relations and nutrition – not to mention high art and literature. Yet, sometime early in the century, this region came alive with great literature. Its storytellers, steeped in the oral tradition, their skills honed on the front porches of African-American homes, told tales suffused with Native American myths and adapted from European balladeers.

Perhaps the phenomenon was a result of the long period of regional self-analysis brought about by military defeat and Reconstruction. Perhaps it was a result of lingering guilt over the treatment of African Americans. In any case, the generation of Southern writers who emerged in the early and mid-20th century remains among the most well regarded in world literature.

An exhaustive accounting of the Deep South's primary Renaissance writers and accompanying themes would be an encyclopedic undertaking; what follows is only a short overview.

Faulkner It doesn't all start and end with William Faulkner, but it might as well. As Georgia-native Flannery O'Connor (perhaps the greatest short story writer of the 20th century) commented: 'The presence alone of Faulkner in our midst makes a great difference in what the writer can and cannot permit himself to do. Nobody wants his mule and wagon stalled on the same tracks the Dixie Limited is roaring down.'

Faulkner won the Nobel Prize in 1949, and in 1955 he won both the Pulitzer Prize and the National Book Award. Ironically, he received this acclaim after breaking all the rules of literature. In a style inspired by James Joyce, Faulkner wrote stream-of-consciousness accounts of his 'own native postage stamp of soil,' thinly disguised as Yoknapatawpha County with its county seat of Jefferson. In so doing, he grappled with the universality of man's inhumanity to man, and changed the way people of all nations will read and write for generations to come.

Born William Cuthbert Falkner (the 'u' was added in later life) on September 25, 1897, this slight, intensely private man is best remembered for his Yoknapatawpha County novels: *The Sound and the Fury* (1929), a multigenerational account of the Compson family, and *Absalom, Absalom!* (1936). Also of note are the novels *As I Lay Dying* (1930) and *Light in August* (1932).

Faulkner spent stretches of time in Hollywood, Paris and New Orleans, but he always returned to live and write in the hills of northern Mississippi and the town of Oxford, for it was from those hills and from its people that he drew his inspiration.

He was often derided by local townspeople, who thought his work unreadable and his habits uncouth, and Faulkner struggled throughout his life to make ends meet. Despite their critical acclaim, all of his earlier novels were out of print by the mid-1940s. It was not until the 1946 publication of *The Portable Faulkner* that his work began to reach a wider audience.

Faulkner died on July 6, 1962. Today, his home, Rowan Oak, is maintained by the University of Mississippi as a literary landmark and is open to the public (see Oxford in the Northeastern Mississippi chapter).

Faulkner's Contemporaries Among the few influential writers on the cusp of the Renaissance was William Alexander Percy (1885-1942). The offspring of a wealthy Greenville, Mississippi, family, Percy was a poet, novelist, farmer and lawyer. (His nephew, novelist Walker Percy, spent much of his childhood in Uncle Will's care.) His autobiographical novel *Lanterns on the Levee* (1941) is a paean for a way of life on the wane, which, when read today, is seductive in its use of language if not its sentiment.

In 1922, a group of young Vanderbilt professors including John Crowe Ransom and Donald Davidson and their students, including Robert Penn Warren and Allen Tate, began publication of a small literary magazine called *The Fugitive*, which was dedicated to poetic expression. The title referred to the authors as fugitives from Victorian sentimentalism. Though the Nashville-based magazine lasted but three years, the literary group gave birth to one of the South's most enduring (and some would say cantankerous) documents. The group members, along with eight others, published *I'll Take My Stand* (1930), a collection of essays that was an agrarian manifesto, pointing to the virtues of the agrarian South in the face of America's creeping industrialism. The Agrarian movement, which emerged around 1928, died around 1935.

Though all were of great intellect and influence throughout American literature, today only Warren is still widely read. In collaboration with Cleanth Brooks (one of Ransom's students and a prominent Faulkner biographer), Warren developed a new formalist approach to literature called the New Criticism, which eschewed context for text. But Warren (1905-89) will be best remembered for his Pulitzer Prize-winning novel *All the King's Men* (1946). Inspired by the life of Louisiana politician Huey Long, the novel is a meditation on history and self-determination.

Tennessean Peter Taylor (1917-), a master of the short story, was influenced by New Criticism; his collections include *A Long Fourth* (1948). His novel *A Summons to Memphis* was published in 1987, for which he won the Pulitzer Prize.

Like Faulkner, Richard Wright (1908-60) was a native of Mississippi. In both his nonfiction *(Black Boy*, 1945) and fiction *(Native Son*, 1940), Wright wrote of the suffocating despair and poverty that informed black life in America. His works are now appreciated as among the first and most enduring of black protest novels.

Along the Same Path Though her age makes her a contemporary of Wright's, Eudora Welty's (1909-) style and subject matter stand in stark contrast to the works of her fellow Mississippian. Best known for her short stories (like 'Why I Live at the PO' and 'A Worn Path'), Welty, in a style some describe as sentimental, masterfully evokes the Southern attachment to place and family. Both stories can be found in *The Collected Stories of Eudora Welty* (1980).

From the town of Monroeville, Alabama, came two of the South's most original voices: Harper Lee (1926-) and Truman Capote (1924-84).

Lee is the author of but one work of fiction. Yet, her Pulitzer Prize-winning meditation on race and the guilelessness of youth, *To Kill a Mockingbird* (1960), places her in the upper tier of Southern writers. Truman Capote, who grew up with Lee in the same small Alabama town, is perhaps best known for *Breakfast at Tiffany's* (1958), the tale of a lovely but sad Southern girl who comes to New York to escape her past, and the genre-bending *In Cold Blood* (1965), a 'nonfiction novel' about the mass-murder of a Kansas family.

Tennessee Williams (1911-83), a native of Mississippi who lived much of his life in New Orleans, was America's preeminent playwright during his lifetime. His works explore the Southern penchant for romanticizing the past while denying the reality of the present. Among his best

John Kennedy Toole is known for his comedic tour de force *A Confederacy of Dunces* (1980). Toole's portrait of the pompous, flatulent, over-educated Ignatius Reilly is rivaled only by his perfect rendition of the wretched excesses of New Orleans. Unfortunately, the book was not released until long after Toole's suicide in 1969, when his mother sought Walker Percy's help in getting the manuscript published.

Raised in Henning, Tennessee, Alex Haley (1921-92) is best known for his coauthoring of the *Autobiography of Malcom X* (1965) as well as writing *Roots* (1976), a combination of history and fiction. An account of Haley's own journey to find his ancestors, *Roots* quickly rose to the top of the bestseller list. It also won the Pulitzer Prize in 1977, and inspired the TV miniseries that remains one of the most-watched shows in history.

Other influential works included Margaret Walker Alexander's *Jubilee* (1966), a classic work in the African-American tradition. Ernest Gaines' *The Autobiography of Miss Jane Pittman* (1971) is a black history beginning with the Civil War. Will Campbell, a Mississippian by birth, is the author of *Brother to a Dragonfly*, one of the most poignant memoirs of family fidelity ever published. And Nobel Prize-winner Martin Luther King Jr wrote perhaps the most evocative appeal for human understanding ever in his 'Letter from Birmingham Jail' (1963).

A new generation of writers are honing their craft in the Deep South. One of the best working today is Pulitzer Prize-winning novelist Richard Ford, a native of Mississippi now living in Louisiana. His most acclaimed works are *The Sportswriter* (1986) and *Independence Day* (1995), both of which track the inner turmoil of everyman Frank Bascomb. According to some literary critics, he is a perfect example of the postmodern Southern writer, and his New Jersey landscapes are emblematic of a suburban new South.

Tennessee Williams

works are *The Glass Menagerie* (1945) and *Cat on a Hot Tin Roof* (1955). *A Streetcar Named Desire* (1947) introduced two of the most enduring characters in American letters – Stanley Kowalski, the brutish interloper, and Blanche Dubois, the myopic fallen woman.

Walker Percy (1916-90), a native of Alabama, lived much of his life in Mississippi and Louisiana. After contracting tuberculosis, Percy abandoned a medical career to work as a novelist and thinker. His first novel, *The Moviegoer* (1961), as well as subsequent works like *Lancelot* (1977), portray humanity as alienated and adrift. Percy's boyhood friend, Mississippian Shelby Foote (1916-), is best known for his three-volume history *The Civil War: A Narrative*, completed in 1974.

Contemporary Southern Fiction Despite popular perceptions, contemporary Southern literature is more than the sum of John Grisham's predictable plots and Anne Rice's horror-stoked gothic romances.

Larry Brown, also of Mississippi, writes about the Mississippi backwoods as if he owns them outright. Recent novels like *Father and Son* (1996) and short story collections like *Big Bad Love* (1990) have ensured Brown's stature in the world of contemporary Southern letters.

Of the themes most prevalent in today's Southern fiction, most obvious and affecting is the South's struggle to come to terms with its troubled past. For the writers of the Southern Renaissance, that troubled past was a legacy of slavery and racial suppression that was to have culminated with the Civil War, and yet it lived on. For the writers of this newer generation, racism is still a haunting legacy.

Some authors, like Alabama's Mark Childress, deal with the horror in a lighthearted way. His *Crazy in Alabama* (1993) sets a boy's coming of age against the backdrop of the civil rights movement. Vicki Covington, also of Alabama, offers up a female perspective on the same period in her novel *The Last Hotel for Women* (1996), while Mississippi native Lewis Nordan uses magical realism in a fictionalized account of the 1955 murder of young Emmett Till in *Wolf Whistle* (1993).

Architecture

The architecture most commonly associated with the South is the neoclassical antebellum plantation house. The plantation regions along the lower Mississippi River where Mississippi and Louisiana come together, and Alabama's Black Belt region, hold the highest concentrations of these homes. The small city of Natchez boasts an exceptional collection. ('That's because *they* surrendered,' explained one envious Vicksburg neighbor.)

Throughout the Deep South, many antebellum mansions are open to public tours. Houses are carefully restored and decorated, both by local historical societies and by individuals, with elaborate interior furnishings in period style; many display the furnishings of the original residents. On guided tours you'll find that each piece has a story to tell, and the history of the family is at least as important as the house (if not more so). Often, the original architectural craftwork was done by slaves, and a few antebellum houses retain their original slave cabins.

Distinctive architecture is also a major draw for visitors to New Orleans. Homes combine features brought from France, Spain and the Caribbean, including the Creole style of verandas, overhanging balconies (called 'galleries'), colorful palettes, lacy iron railings and ornamenture. Of later origin, many Greek revival mansions remain visible in the city's Garden District. The ultimate in Grecian architecture, however, is found in Nashville, Tennessee, where you'll find a full-size reproduction of the Greek Parthenon, built in 1897, including a 42-foot statue of the goddess Athena.

The humble houses of the working class also make a striking impression. A block and a half from Mississippi's grand capitol, for example, there's a juxtaposing neighborhood of shotgun shacks shaded by palmettos. You see these narrow, often unpainted shacks all over the South. Their rooms are lined up one after another – behind the small porch, there's a living room, then a bedroom, then a kitchen – affording little privacy for whole families. The term shotgun stems from the ability to stand at the front porch and shoot straight through the back door. In an effort to keep out the draft, the single-wall construction is 'insulated' with layers of newspaper, posters and, sometimes, wallpaper.

You'll also notice that many families in poorer communities live out of trailers and keep a 'swept lawn' in the dirt apron out front.

Pioneer architecture, common to the hill regions of Mississippi and Alabama, is exemplified by 'dogtrot' cabins, so-called for the central breezeway constructed between the living quarters and the kitchen. Only isolated examples of early colonial architecture remain, such as the Old Spanish fort in Pascagoula,

Mississippi, constructed from 'tabby' – an adobe-like mixture of ground oyster shells, clay and Spanish moss.

Ideal places to see examples of the South's architecture are recreated towns, such as Montgomery's Old Alabama Town and Huntsville's Constitution Village, where historic buildings – from simple dogtrots to antebellum mansions – have been relocated to give a view of how people lived and worked in the state. In Mississippi, the premier reconstructed village is at the Agriculture and Forestry Museum in Jackson. In Louisiana, the Folklife Center in Baton Rouge contains pioneer restorations, and plantation houses are seen along River Road north of New Orleans.

Perhaps the most distinctive modern architectural skyline is found in Memphis, where the recent addition of a mirrored pyramid, housing a convention center, creates a striking impression.

Elaborate Southern gardens feature exquisite landscaping and are often meticulously designed, accompanied by statuary, sculpture, fountains and monuments. A prime example of a Southern garden is Bellingrath, outside Mobile, Alabama, with its profusion of azaleas, dogwoods and rhododendrons. It was originally a swampside fishing camp, and part of it has been left that way to show just how much work has been done. New Orleans' house and garden tours take visitors to inviting gardens with dramatic secluded courtyards.

Visual Arts

Fine art museums can be found in New Orleans, Nashville, Memphis, Jackson, Birmingham, Montgomery and Tuscaloosa, all of which have excellent permanent collections of classical and/or contemporary works. Many emphasize American paintings, though there's a strong regional appetite for European impressionism.

Locally produced artwork is very distinctive and worthwhile to see in its native context. Folk arts, for example, express the self-taught artistry of Southerners and reflect their connection to the landscape. Many works explore Southern themes and rural scenes in self-styled media – quilts, recycled scrap wood and other found objects. Fascinating environmental works include Earl's Art Gallery in Bovina, Mississippi, where proprietor/artist Earl Simmons has made his house into a colorful living sculpture. In Lucedale, Mississippi, the late Reverend Harvell Jackson was inspired to build a miniature version of the Holy Land he called Palestinian Gardens. In Memphis, the First Church of the Elvis Impersonator exhibits an artful kinetic shrine of Elvisabilia that operates when you drop in a quarter.

The region is also famous for its crafts, especially pottery and woodwork made from native materials; traditions range from the fluid styles of Mississippian George E Ohr ('the Mad Potter of Biloxi') to handmade accordions for sale in Cajun Country.

Performing Arts

Social dancing is a highly valued traditional pastime, especially in Cajun Country, where the Cajun two-step and waltz takes over the dance floor. Jackson, Mississippi, is regarded as a regional center for ballet, and it hosts an international ballet competition every four years.

The Alabama Shakespeare Festival in Montgomery, Alabama, has one of the world's best Shakespeare companies. Also, once a year the festival stages a production of a play by a Southern writer under its Southern Writers Project.

As for film, the South is not known for independent filmmaking, yet many independent and Hollywood filmmakers are drawn to the region to evoke the mystery, drama and landscape of the Deep South. For a list of titles, see Films under Facts for the Visitor.

Music

Jazz New Orleans is the birthplace of jazz, perhaps the primary musical movement of the modern era and one that has evolved into a number of distinct styles. The origins of jazz have been traced back to slaves who gathered to dance and sing to drums in Congo Square on Sunday. Singing was a means of communication among slaves where talking was prohibited. By the 1830s, they were adding violins and banjos. Black gospel singers of the time were noted for improvisation in which a leader was followed by others singing refrain.

White minstrel performers in blackface late in the century contributed to the staging of what became known as folk music. Another influence (as noted at the New Orleans' Old Mint Jazz Exhibit) included a 60-piece Mexican Calvary Band that inspired local brass musicians at the International Cotton Exposition in 1884.

Most agree, however, that Buddy Bolden, a New Orleans Uptown musician, was the innovator who brought jazz into being. His bluesy improvisations and dynamic chords were called 'ratty music' at the time. Unfortunately, no recordings exist of Bolden, who began playing coronet in 1894 and was dubbed 'The King' by 1905.

By the turn of the century, 'ragged' music and spasm bands proliferated, though professional musicians disdained them. Some members of the American Federation of Musicians spoke about 'suppressing such musical trash as ragtime.' This response was as much a reaction to the social origins of jazz as to the music itself, which was complex and required skill and dexterity to play. It was marked by lively syncopated rhythms and emotional improvisations. New Orleans' notorious Storyville district was the heart of the movement until the neighborhood was shut down in 1917. From there, musicians dispersed to Chicago, and then to Kansas City and New York, and coupled with the advent of recording technology, jazz traveled from New Orleans to the rest of the country and into popular culture.

> Jazz I regard as an American folk music; not the only one but a very powerful one which is probably in the blood and feeling of the American people more than any other style.
>
> – George Gershwin

Soon, New Orleans performers like Jelly Roll Morton, Mahalia Jackson and Joseph 'King' Oliver had developed international reputations, and today, Congo Square is dedicated to New Orleans' native son Louis 'Satchmo' Armstrong (1900-71), who established the solo improvisation as central to jazz and was beloved worldwide for his distinctive voice and exuberant trumpet.

In New Orleans, Bourbon St today is a disappointment – you're more likely to hear rock music blaring from the open doors of a club than traditional Dixieland jazz. But this 'old-time' jazz is still alive in the city – in addition to the unsanctioned street scene in which performers play for coins, good jazz is played at select clubs sometimes off the beaten tourist track.

Traditional jazz evolved steadily in the decades following 1920, becoming swing, bop, progressive, hard-bop, mainstream, fusion and free jazz. For some, jazz today is the clean piano of classical jazz artist Ellis Marsalis, who teaches at the University of New Orleans. His sons – Wynton, Branford and Jason – have each garnered acclaim with their own surprising innovations. Gospel and blues music are also important influences in jazz, and the interested visitor to the Deep South will find it nearly impossible to exhaust the opportunities to learn about jazz's history and to experience it live in its many forms.

For a complete immersion in the jazz experience, make sure to attend the annual New Orleans Jazz & Heritage Festival, which brings together national performers like the Neville Brothers and Dr John, along with popular local players in jazz, reggae, zydeco and other major genres.

Cajun & Zydeco Combine the Spanish guitar, African triangle, French fiddle and German accordion and you have the basic components of a Cajun band. A recent renaissance of Cajun music, starting in 1960s, has popularized the style nationally.

The traditional Cajun dance party is called a *fais-do-do*, which translates to 'make sleep'; the term is said to come from a young mother's eagerness for her child to fall asleep at the dance hall so that she could get back out to the dance floor.

Using the same instruments, black Creoles created the fast syncopated dance music called zydeco. In addition, zydeco bands often employ the vest *frottoir*, a metal washboard-like instrument most often played with spoons. Swamp boogie is rock 'n' roll with a Cajun accent.

Beausoleil was one popular group that first brought Cajun music to folk festivals around the country in the 1970s. Queen Ida is a zydeco performer who attracts a national audience. Filmmaker Les Blank looks at the Cajun musical heritage in two interesting, affectionate, modern documentaries: *Les Bon Temps Roulez* and *Marc and Ann*.

Delta Blues From the hardship endured by generations of cotton-pickers in paper-insulated shacks in the Mississippi Delta rose a distinctive style of indigenous American music called the blues. Inspired by the work chants common in slavery, and based on African musical traditions, the blues moved from the Delta north via the rail lines and Hwy 61 to Chicago along with the Great Migration of blacks in the Depression era.

Blues music consists of a three-line 12-bar pattern; each line of the verse corresponds to four measures of the music. Its characteristic 'call-and-response' pattern draws on traditions in the black church. But the music's true soul is more evocatively described by bluesman Arthur Lee Williams:

Blues actually is around you every day. That's just a feeling within a person, you know. You have a hard time and things happen. Downheartedness, that's all it is, hardship. You express it through your song.

Many blues musicians – Robert Johnson, Muddy Waters, 'Sonny Boy' Williamson and BB King, to name a few – got their start in the Mississippi Delta, a land of algae swamps and relentless cotton fields, where still today there can be palpable racial tension and a proliferation of guns. Just driving through the Delta you begin to understand the blues in a way no recording, book or live performance anywhere else can communicate.

Too poor to afford instruments (except for the inexpensive harmonica – the indispensable blues 'harp'), many blues musicians would construct a primitive string instrument using a wire or broom strand nailed to a wall. A bottleneck could be used to vary the sound. These 'one-strands' (found fastened to front porches across the Delta) are also called 'diddley bows.' One Delta musician inverted this term and adopted it for his stage name, becoming the famous Bo Diddley.

Gospel Traditional African-American gospel music can best be heard in churches throughout the Deep South, though gospel radio programs and all-night gospel 'sings' (concerts featuring many performers) also feature this sacred music. Many spirituals originated in slavery, and their Biblical themes of freedom and return to the promised land were significant anthems of emancipation. The spirituals were later resurrected as protest songs during the civil rights movement of the 1960s. White gospel music, though still celebrated in Southern churches, has been popularly eclipsed by 'Christian music.' Even in the smallest markets around the South, there's usually at least one radio station broadcasting a Christian music format.

Country & Bluegrass Nashville is indisputably the country music capital of the

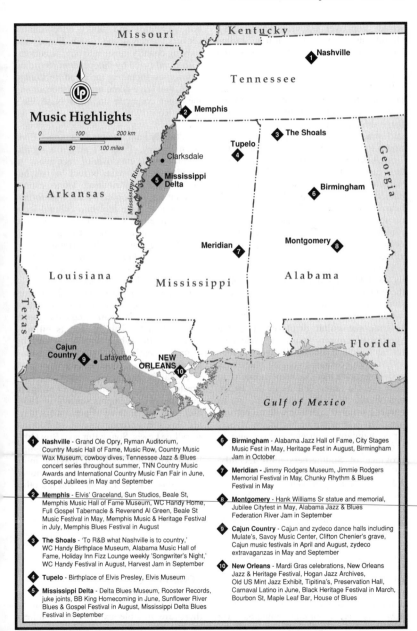

Music Highlights

0   100   200 km
0   50   100 miles

Missouri

Kentucky

Tennessee

Nashville 1

Memphis 2

The Shoals 3

Tupelo
4

Clarksdale •

Mississippi Delta 5

Arkansas

Georgia

Birmingham 6

Meridian
7

Montgomery 8

Louisiana

Mississippi

Alabama

Texas

Florida

Cajun Country 9   Lafayette

NEW ORLEANS 10

Gulf of Mexico

Mississippi River

1 **Nashville** - Grand Ole Opry, Ryman Auditorium, Country Music Hall of Fame, Music Row, Country Music Wax Museum, cowboy dives, Tennessee Jazz & Blues concert series throughout summer, TNN Country Music Awards and International Country Music Fan Fair in June, Gospel Jubilees in May and September

2 **Memphis** - Elvis' Graceland, Sun Studios, Beale St, Memphis Music Hall of Fame Museum, WC Handy Home, Full Gospel Tabernacle & Reverend Al Green, Beale St Music Festival in May, Memphis Music & Heritage Festival in July, Memphis Blues Festival in August

3 **The Shoals** - 'To R&B what Nashville is to country,' WC Handy Birthplace Museum, Alabama Music Hall of Fame, Holiday Inn Fizz Lounge weekly 'Songwriter's Night,' WC Handy Festival in August, Harvest Jam in September

4 **Tupelo** - Birthplace of Elvis Presley, Elvis Museum

5 **Mississippi Delta** - Delta Blues Museum, Rooster Records, juke joints, BB King Homecoming in June, Sunflower River Blues & Gospel Festival in August, Mississippi Delta Blues Festival in September

6 **Birmingham** - Alabama Jazz Hall of Fame, City Stages Music Fest in May, Heritage Fest in August, Birmingham Jam in October

7 **Meridian** - Jimmy Rodgers Museum, Jimmie Rodgers Memorial Festival in May, Chunky Rhythm & Blues Festival in May

8 **Montgomery** - Hank Williams Sr statue and memorial, Jubilee Cityfest in May, Alabama Jazz & Blues Federation River Jam in September

9 **Cajun Country** - Cajun and zydeco dance halls including Mulate's, Savoy Music Center, Clifton Chenier's grave, Cajun music festivals in April and August, zydeco extravaganzas in May and September

10 **New Orleans** - Mardi Gras celebrations, New Orleans Jazz & Heritage Festival, Hogan Jazz Archives, Old US Mint Jazz Exhibit, Tipitina's, Preservation Hall, Carnaval Latino in June, Black Heritage Festival in March, Bourbon St, Maple Leaf Bar, House of Blues

world. For over 60 years, Nashville's Grand Ole Opry and recording studios have popularized what's been called the 'white man's soul music.'

Country music descended from the folk music of Elizabethan England, Scotland and Ireland, yet American pioneers made those traditions their own – in fact, some historic musical traditions were still practiced here in the Appalachian South long after they had died out in the United Kingdom. Elizabethan-type ballads can still be heard in the Deep South (largely in the uplands), sometimes accompanied by the dulcimer. Bluegrass, still heard largely in the hill regions, carries on this tradition with music made from violins (called fiddles), guitars, mandolins, five-string banjo, bass and dobro guitar.

Country first became distinguished for its fast fiddlin', and it was carried through the hinterlands by traveling minstrels and snake-oil salesmen (seriously). Fiddle music swept through the rural southeast. In time the guitar displaced it as the symbol of country music. Classic performers include Jimmie Rodgers (1897-1933), who combined country blues with yodeling (more like mountain 'hollerin' to hear the old-timers tell it) in the 1920s, and he was the first country music star to attract a national audience with his recordings. His hometown of Meridian, Mississippi, maintains a museum in his honor.

Country music has largely been the sole province of Southerners until recently. While individual performers such as Johnny Cash have broken out (or 'crossed over') to become widely popular with increasing frequency, over the last five years or so country music has exploded wildly, attracting a national audience. (It's speculated that baby boomers aging past their attraction to rock music account for the increase.) Country is currently the nation's largest radio format, with 2600 radio stations – 1400 more than the nearest competing radio format. Today, strange new fusions, including bluegrass-jazz

banjo combos and punky retro-country rockers, are gaining an audience and moving country music into new directions. This trend is led by independent recording companies, including the Dead Reckoning label, that have taken up residence among the larger, corporate studios on Nashville's Music Row.

Rockabilly Patron saint of Memphis, Elvis Aron Presley (1935-77) played a significant role in the crossover of 'race music' to the mainstream origins of rock 'n' roll, but his musical contribution alone cannot account for his popularity and transformation from teenage idol into cultural icon. His humble origins (his two-room cottage birthplace can be seen in Tupelo, Mississippi) make him a Southern Horatio Alger who has given hope to a generation of poor whites. His Graceland estate in Memphis is a pilgrimage site for his fans.

Elvis dared to add a then-shocking sexuality to his music. His mixture of rhythm and blues and his native country gospel was termed 'rockabilly' for its hillbilly influences. Rockabilly typically is made by a small ensemble, often a trio, with strong vocalizing over a light but persistent beat. The classic rockabilly sound of Elvis Presley was engineered by Sam Phillips of Sun Studio in Memphis starting in 1954. Sun soon had a stable of performers playing this style, among them Carl Perkins, Jerry Lee Lewis, Sonny Burgess, Roy Orbison and Conway Twitty. The style diminished when Elvis began playing more mainstream rock 'n' roll after he moved from Sun to RCA Records, and the other rockabilly artists evolved in different directions as well.

The style is currently undergoing a revival, particularly in Nashville, popularized by BR5-49 and other alternative country bands.

SOCIETY & CONDUCT

Though you could generalize that the South is overwhelmingly conservative, there are notable exceptions. Southern hospitality is legendary, and most folks are friendly, accessible, hospitable and courteous, though they can be a bit xenophobic regarding outsiders perhaps due in part to the stereotypical and generally negative image of Southerners broadcast by the mainstream media.

African-American culture has developed alongside of but distinct from white Southern culture. One of the most interesting things about traveling in the South is learning about these separate heritages, discovering where they intersect in addition to how they differ.

Locals may get edgy discussing Southern racial dynamics. Be cautious about initiating such a discussion until you've established a good rapport with someone. Simple politeness will keep your curiosity from inadvertently causing offense.

Southerners have a well-earned reputation for storytelling that springs from an extensive oral tradition, so once you get someone started, make yourself comfortable to enjoy a long tale. You'll notice, too, that time moves more slowly in the subtropical South than in other regions of the country. Travelers who can adopt the local pace will avoid frustrations and get the most out of their visit.

Be aware that being clean and tidy is very important in the class-conscious South, and visitors who appear unkempt (wearing cut-offs, flip-flops or anything too revealing) will draw negative attention to themselves.

Dos & Don'ts

Southern rules of courtesy demand that locals use formal rules of address – no sir, yes ma'am – but they don't necessarily expect outsiders to be so polite. However, such small courtesies will certainly be noticed and appreciated; being extraordinarily polite and not coming on too strong will ease social interaction tremendously. Being sincerely curious, nonjudgmental, patient and deferential will also stand you in good stead for a trip through the South.

RELIGION

Religious conviction plays a large role in Southern culture. In the words of Victorian rationalist Sir William Archer:

> The South is by a long way the most simply and sincerely religious country I ever was in. It is not, like Ireland, a priest-ridden country; it is not, like England, a country in which the strength of religion lies in its social prestige; it is not, like Scotland, a country steeped in theology. But it is a very large factor in life, and God is very real and personal.

More recently in the US, the South has been labeled the 'Bible Belt' to describe its commonly conservative, fundamentalist stance, which is dominated by Southern Baptists. In the past, the South has been nearly as divided over religion as it has been over race. Protestants did not tend to associate with Catholics or Jews, and intermarriage between faiths, even among different Protestant branches, was scandalous. The Klan persecuted Catholics and Jews along with blacks. Today it's still common for whites and blacks to attend their own churches.

Any sincere visitor with an open heart will be welcome at churches in the region. Learning about different faiths can be a very powerful experience, and it's a fascinating window into the local culture and community. Some tips: Arrive early, dress well, be generous with your contributions, and be prepared to sit through a long service. Sunday services in Southern churches typically last from 11 am to 1 or 2 pm. Note also that since everyone – at least in the rural areas – is expected to be attending church, most businesses will be closed and few people will be out at this time.

In a typical Sunday service, dress is semiformal and modest. Even in the humblest communities, men wear jackets and ties and women wear dresses, though visitors not meeting this criteria are easily forgiven if they've made some effort to be presentable. Visitors are commonly announced (the preacher may even ask visitors to stand up to be recognized during the service) and greeted by church elders and members of the congregation. Note also that some churches assemble the children up front for a short separate sermon during the service, and visiting children would most likely be expected to join.

Southerners are very up-front about their religious beliefs, and you might be asked about yours. A question like 'Do you accept Jesus Christ into your life?' may be merely a conversation starter and not an evangelical query.

In Catholic churches, only baptized and indoctrinated Catholics are invited to participate in the Communion ritual of bread and wine. Protestant churches are more liberal in sharing their rituals.

Many visitors to Memphis, Tennessee, are attracted to the Full Gospel Tabernacle, which is presided over by Reverend Al Green. Reverend Green was formerly a popular rhythm and blues singer when, at the height of his recording career, he got the calling to leave his secular profession and begin preaching. He preaches now with the accompaniment of bass and lead guitarists, a drummer and a keyboardist, who also back up the soulful gospel choir (see Memphis).

Protestantism Fire-and-brimstone sermons, creekside baptisms, vacation bible school and strict blue laws are all part of a standard Bible Belt experience today. The Southern Baptists that now prevail in the South are a product of a split in the Baptist Church in antebellum times. During the 1840s debates occurred over the interpretation of the religious constitution concerning slavery, resulting in the establishment of the pro-slavery Southern Baptist Convention in 1845. Other mainstream Protestant sects represented in the region include Methodists, Lutherans, Presbyterians and Episcopalians.

African-American Christianity During the slave era, all expressions of African and Haitian religious traditions were prohibited and repressed, and had to be carried out in secrecy. Slaves were allowed (many were obligated) to attend Sunday services at their white slave-owner's church; some early black communities even founded their own churches during slavery. After emancipation, missionaries from Northern churches successfully established congregations in black communities; the African-Methodist Episcopal church helped found many of the AME churches now prolific throughout the South.

Black poet James Weldon Johnson, writing in the early 1900s, found it remarkable that Christianity should have been so earnestly embraced by slaves, in view of 'the vast gulf between the Christianity that was preached and the Christianity that was practiced by those who preached.' Johnson ascribed the sustaining influence to the Old Testament chronicle of the Jews. 'This story at once caught and fired the imagination of the Negro bards, and they sang their hungry listeners into a firm faith that as God saved Daniel in the lion's den, so would He save them; as God delivered Israel out of bondage in Egypt, so would He deliver them.'

The church has always been a powerful unifying force in African-American communities. Early civil rights leaders like Reverend Martin Luther King Jr came from the preacher's ranks. Black churches have been the target of numerous racially motivated attacks, both historically (most well remembered during the civil rights era) and in a rash of arson across the South in 1995 that prompted a federal investigation.

Roman Catholicism Roman Catholics predominate in southern Louisiana, creating an anachronism amid the Protestant 'Bible Belt' that shapes much of the South. French and Spanish heritages, along with a later Irish influx among others, account for the Catholic preeminence. Slaveholders were required by Bienville's 1724 Code Noir to baptize and instruct their slaves in the Catholic faith – an edict not rigidly followed – and black Catholicism abounds today.

New Orleans' signature celebration – Mardi Gras – is rooted in Catholic beliefs. Carnival begins on 'Twelfth Night,' (January 6; the twelfth night following Christmas), and continues until Mardi Gras, or 'Fat Tuesday.' Catholics traditionally feast to celebrate Jesus before Ash Wednesday, the beginning of Lent and a period of penitence that continues through Easter. Celebrations also take place in Lafayette and across Cajun Country, and along the Gulf Coast in Biloxi and Mobile.

Judaism While Judaism is not often associated with the South, a significant Jewish community took up early residence here, particularly in river cities. Scattered temples attest to its presence, as does the Museum of the Southern Jewish Experience in Utica, Mississippi.

Voodoo African slaves transported to Haiti (a New World clearinghouse port for the slave trade) brought an Afro-Haitian amalgamated voodoo (also called hoodoo) tradition to the Mississippi Valley. Much conjecture about voodoo focuses on its mystery and on ceremonies where worshipers enter a trance. As these colonized peoples had Christianity imposed on them, Catholic saints and Christian beliefs began to mingle with the pagan idols of African voodoo traditions. In New Orleans, the Voodoo Spiritual Temple is a local center for followers. The black-dominated Mississippi Delta region in northwestern Mississippi also has many voodoo believers and practitioners – many blues musicians carry talismans of traditional voodoo charms, such as a root called 'High John the Conqueror' held in red flannel 'mojo' bags worn around the neck or tacked to corners of rooms.

LANGUAGE
Southern Dialect Southern variations on standard English are well known and rampant – in fact, you're not likely to hear any standard English except in some cities and along the Gulf. Southern dialects vary widely in pronunciation, pace, delivery and often, lexicon. They vary not only by geography – accents in New Orleans differ from the Mississippi Delta, which differ from Northern Alabama and so on – but also by race and social class.

For general reference, Louisiana is pronounced 'LOOZ-ee-ana,' New Orleans is 'New OR-lins,' and Tupelo is 'TOO-pill-oh.' The distinction between second person singular and second person plural is not made in standard English, but is found in the Southern speech of both whites and blacks as *y'all*.

Black English Most African Americans in the US descend from two linguistic 'families': the Sudanic of the West African coast and the Bantu in East and Central Africa. Although there are many different languages within these two groups, there remains a foundational structural similarity. Today, some of these syntactical features have been retained in Black English – the folk dialect of African Americans. (the term 'ebonics,' a fusion of 'ebony' and 'phonics,' was coined to describe this dialect.)

Black English emerged in Africa in the 17th century as a trade language used in negotiations with English ships, and it was transported to North America via Jamaica. The common colonial policy of dispersing homogeneous groups caused Africans to rely on this *lingua franca* to communicate with each other.

According to Ivan Vansertima's study in *African Linguistic & Mythological Structures in the New World*, the primary characteristics of Black English are the absence of the phoneme *th* and an absence of the connecting link between subject and predicate (for example, 'he is black' in standard English becomes 'he black' in Black English; 'who is he' contracts into 'who he'). There is also no obligatory linguistic marker in Black English for the plural (one cent, two cent) or for the possessive ('teacher's book' collapses to 'teacher-book').

French Dialects Louisiana's Cajun population speaks its own dialect of French, which is widely spoken in Cajun Country, though mostly among old people and schoolchildren, as the language is enjoying a revival after many years of repression. New Orleans and lower Louisiana retains its historically French-speaking roots in its lexicon, but an outside French-speaker will likely have trouble comprehending the local dialect, mostly because of pronunciation.

Facts for the Visitor

PLANNING

At most times, most destinations in the Deep South can be visited without a whole lot of planning beyond looking for bargain airfare. During special events (and you may want to plan your trip to coincide with a festival), planning is more important, particularly during Mardi Gras, when the most desirable hotel rooms may be booked up a year in advance. Reservations are necessary during Mardi Gras and for Jazz Fest in New Orleans. Popular festivals in smaller towns, such as blues festivals in the Mississippi Delta, can exhaust the limited local motel room supply quickly; here, too, reservations would be a good idea. Cities on busy interstate highways – such as Memphis, Nashville and Lafayette – rarely exhaust their abundance of motel rooms.

When to Go

Spring and fall are the most temperate seasons for travel in the Deep South, and many regional festivals are scheduled to coincide with the agreeable climate. These are also the most scenic seasons – spring is beautifully lush with fresh blooms and high rivers, and colorful fall foliage covers upland woodlands in October.

New Orleans celebrates Mardi Gras (see Special Events for dates). Tamer carnival celebrations can be found in Cajun Country and along the Gulf Coast (such as in Biloxi or Mobile).

The summer months of July and August are the least comfortable season in the Deep South. Heat and humidity (see Climate in Facts about the Deep South) can reach insufferable extremes during the day. Anyone unaccustomed to a tropical climate will probably want to seek refuge in air-conditioning until the sun goes down. On the bright side, nocturnal travelers can enjoy sultry Southern nights languidly sipping a Dixie beer and listening to soulful music. And despite the weather,

since most schools are not in session, summers are when most people travel through the region.

In winter you'll find special holiday events and off-peak accommodation discounts. Although temperatures are chilly for the region, they're balmy in comparison to most of the US.

What Kind of Trip?

Rural destinations can most readily be visited (and sometimes can only be visited) by private car. Travelers without a car are limited to large cities if they travel by plane or train, or large and small cities if they travel by bus.

Outdoor adventuring – say, camping, backpacking or bike touring – is good most of the temperate months, though rain is frequent (RV camping is more popular than tent camping). Fall is the most predictably dry for long stretches.

Maps

As for most of the US, you can find good state and city maps for the Deep South. New Orleans and major cities will of course have the greatest map selection and availability for free or purchase. Regional and backroads maps, however, can be difficult to come by. But considering how many places are unmarked or unnamed and known only by local landmarks, maps serve only a limited use in the Deep South anyway. In smaller towns, chambers of commerce usually distribute county and city maps, though these are not designed with tourists in mind. Outdoor stores are a good source for backwoods maps.

The American Automobile Association (AAA) issues the most comprehensive and dependable highway maps, which are free with AAA membership (see Useful Organizations below) and available for a price to nonmembers. These range from national, regional and state maps to very detailed maps of cities, counties and even relatively small towns.

The US Geological Survey (USGS), a federal agency, publishes very detailed topographic maps of the entire country, at different scales up to 1:250,000. Maps at 1:62,500, or approximately 1 inch=1 mile, are ideal for backcountry hiking and backpacking. Some private cartographers are producing updated versions of old USGS maps at 1:62,500. Specialty bookstores and outdoor equipment specialists may carry topographic maps.

What to Bring

Casual clothing is largely fine, though it's good to pack a dress outfit for fancier social, business or church functions. Summer travelers should expect their feet to swell in the heat; pack only shoes with room to expand. Sunscreen, insect repellent and a hat are also good to bring.

For outdoor adventuring, only light hiking boots are ever necessary; an old pair of sneakers will often suit for river floats or exploring muddy bayous. In winter, a light overcoat and gloves are comfortable.

Outside of the major cities there are few bookstores, so bring the paperbacks and periodicals you want to read.

SUGGESTED ITINERARIES

A Deep South travel itinerary would generally always include New Orleans, though as an inexpensive airline hub, Memphis is also a common starting point.

The corridor between the two cities holds many attractions: from New Orleans the route can detour through Plantation Country and run through the town of Natchez and the rugged Mississippi Delta to Memphis. Travelers should plan more than a week for this one-way route, particularly considering that beyond major cities live entertainment is most often heard on weekends only.

Between New Orleans, Cajun Country and Plantation Country, south Louisiana alone makes an exotic destination that could be covered in as short a time as a week (though many who visit New Orleans just make a day trip of the two other regions).

Blues pilgrims make a single trip of touring Memphis and the Mississippi Delta. A yin-and-yang tour of Memphis and Nashville could be accomplished in a few days in each city, though again for the greatest entertainment choices a weekend night in each city is best.

Travelers can easily plan a trip around music (see Music Highlights map in Facts about the Deep South) and weekend festivals are a good excuse for a trip to a single destination.

History buffs and fans of antebellum architecture will find preserved battlefields, monuments, battle reenactments, historic house museums and 'pilgrimage' home tours at every turn.

A Native American heritage tour would include Poverty Point in Louisiana and Moundville in Alabama as among the highlights, with a stop at casinos on the Chitimacha reservation in Louisiana or Choctaw reservation in Mississippi to close the circle.

An African-American heritage tour could examine civil rights history starting at the National Civil Rights Museum in Memphis, and then take in the Civil Rights Institute in Birmingham, the Voting Rights Museum in Selma and memorials in Montgomery and Philadelphia.

Outdoor adventurers will find exotic variety throughout the region – from caving in northern Alabama and rural bike tours of the midlands to a sea-kayak trip out to wilderness Gulf islands and swamp tours in the Cajun wetlands. Beachgoers aim for the Mississippi Coast (better yet, Ship Island); the beaches in Louisiana are undesirable.

TOURIST OFFICES

The following tourist offices distribute statewide guides, maps, events calendars and often specialized guides such as B&B listings, African-American heritage sites or Civil War sites – all free of charge.

Each state also operates welcome centers at its borders, usually at major interstate highways. Some welcome centers can arrange lodging or distribute coupons for discounts at local motels. City welcome centers are often in the heart of tourist districts and are a good source for maps and brochures.

Alabama
> Alabama Bureau of Tourism & Travel, PO Box 4927, Montgomery, AL 36103 (☎ 800-252-2262)

Louisiana
> Louisiana Office of Tourism, PO Box 94291, Baton Rouge, LA 70804 (☎ 504-342-8119, 800-414-8626)

Mississippi
> Mississippi Division of Tourist Development, PO Box 1705, Ocean Springs, MS 39566-1705 (☎ 800-927-6378)

Tennessee
> Tennessee Department of Tourist Development, PO Box 23170, Nashville, TN 37202 (☎ 615-714-2158)

Tourist Offices Abroad

The USA does not have a well-developed overseas tourist-office system. However, some states have information hotlines in the UK (there is no walk-in service). These include Louisiana (☎ 0181-760-0337), Mississippi (☎ 01462-440784) and Tennessee (☎ 01462-440784). Contact your local US diplomatic office for information supplied by the US Travel & Tourism Administration (USTTA).

VISAS & DOCUMENTS

In addition to required documents, visitors should also bring their driver's license and any health insurance or travel insurance cards. You'll need a picture ID to show that you are over 21 to buy alcohol or to gain admission to bars or clubs (make sure your driver's license has a photo on it, or else get some other form of photo ID).

Passport

With the exception of Canadians, who need only proper proof of Canadian citizenship, all foreign visitors to the USA must have a valid passport and most also are required to have a US visa. It's a good idea to keep

photocopies of these documents; in case of theft, they'll be a lot easier to replace.

Visas

Apart from Canadians, and those entering under the Visa Waiver Pilot Program (see below), all foreign visitors need to obtain a visa from a US consulate or embassy. In most countries the process can be done by mail or through a travel agent.

Your passport should be valid for at least six months longer than your intended stay in the USA, and you'll need to submit a recent photo (37 x 37 mm) with the application. Documents of financial stability and/or guarantees from a US resident are sometimes required, particularly for those from Third World countries.

Visa applicants may be required to 'demonstrate binding obligations' that will ensure their return back home. Because of this requirement, those planning to travel through other countries before arriving in the USA are generally better off applying for their US visa while they are still in their home country – rather than while on the road.

The most common visa is a Non-Immigrant Visitors Visa, B1 for business purposes, B2 for tourism or visiting friends and relatives. A visitor's visa is good for one or five years with multiple entries, and it specifically prohibits the visitor from taking paid employment in the USA. The validity period depends on what country you're from. The length of time you'll be allowed to stay in the USA is ultimately determined by US immigration authorities at the port of entry. If you're coming to the USA to work or study, you will probably need a different type of visa, and the company or institution you're connected with should make the arrangements. Allow six months in advance for processing the application.

For further information on work visas, see Work below.

Entering the USA If you have a non-US passport, with a visa, you must complete an

Arrival/Departure Record (form I-94) before you go to the immigration desk. It's usually handed out on the plane, along with the customs declaration. It's a rather badly designed form, and lots of people take more than one attempt to get it right. Some airlines suggest you start at the last question and work upwards. Answers should be written *below* the questions. For question 12, 'Address While in the United States,' give the address of the location where you will spend the first night. Complete the Departure Record, too (the lower part of the form), giving exactly the same answers for questions 14 to 17 as for questions 1 to 4.

The staff of the Immigration & Nationalization Service (INS) can be less than welcoming. Their main concern is to exclude those who are likely to work illegally or overstay, so visitors will be asked about their plans, and perhaps about whether they have sufficient funds for their stay. If the INS thinks you're OK, a six-month entry is usually approved.

It's a good idea to be able to list an itinerary that will account for the period for which you ask to be admitted, and to be able to show you have $300 or $400 for every week of your intended stay. These days, a couple of major credit cards will go a long way toward establishing 'sufficient funds.' Don't make too much of having friends, relatives or business contacts in the USA – the INS official may decide that this will make you more likely to overstay.

Visa Waiver Pilot Program Citizens of certain countries may enter the USA without a US visa, for stays of 90 days or less, under the Visa Waiver Pilot Program. Currently these countries are Andorra, Argentina, Australia, Austria, Belgium, Brunei, Denmark, Finland, France, Germany, Iceland, Ireland, Italy, Japan, Liechtenstein, Luxembourg, Monaco, the Netherlands, New Zealand, Norway, San Marino, Spain, Sweden, Switzerland, and the UK. Under this program you must have a roundtrip ticket that is nonrefundable in the USA, and you will not be allowed to extend your stay beyond 90 days. Check with the US embassy in your home country for any other requirements.

Visa Extensions & Re-Entry If you want, need or hope to stay in the USA longer than the date stamped on your passport, go

---

HIV & Entering the USA

Everyone entering the USA who isn't a US citizen is subject to the authority of the Immigration & Naturalization Service (INS), regardless of whether that person has legal immigration documents. The INS can keep someone from entering or staying in the USA by excluding or deporting them. This is especially relevant to travelers with the HIV virus. Though being HIV-positive is not a ground for deportation, it is a 'ground of exclusion' and the INS can invoke it to refuse admission.

Although the INS doesn't test people for HIV at customs, it may try to exclude anyone who answers yes to this question on the non-immigrant visa application form: 'Have you ever been afflicted with a communicable disease of public health significance?' INS officials may also stop people if they seem sick, are carrying AIDS/HIV medicine or, sadly, if the officer happens to think the person looks gay, though sexual orientation is not legally a ground of exclusion.

It's imperative that visitors know and assert their rights. Immigrants and visitors should avoid contact with the INS until they discuss their rights and options with a trained immigration advocate. For legal immigration information and referrals to immigration advocates, contact the National Immigration Project of the National Lawyers Guild (☎ 617-227-9727), 14 Beacon St, Suite 506, Boston, MA 02108; or Immigrant HIV Assistance Project, Bar Association of San Francisco (☎ 415-267-0795), 685 Market St, Suite 700, San Francisco, CA 94105. ■

to the local INS office (or call ☎ 800-755-0777, or look in the local white pages telephone directory under US Government) *before* the stamped date to apply for an extension. Anytime after that will usually lead to an unamusing conversation with an INS official who will assume you want to work illegally. If you find yourself in that situation, it's a good idea to bring a US citizen with you to vouch for your character. It's also a good idea to have some verification that you have enough money to support yourself.

Alternatively, travel across the border into Mexico, and apply for another period of entry when you come back. US officials don't usually collect the Departure Record cards from your passport when you leave at a land border, so they may not notice if you've overstayed by a couple of days. Returning to the USA, you go through the same procedure as when you entered the USA for the first time, so be ready with your proposed itinerary and evidence of sufficient funds. If you try this border hopping more than once, to get a third six-month period of entry, you may find the INS very strict. Generally it seems that they are reluctant to let you stay more than a year.

International Driving Permit

An International Driving Permit is a useful accessory for foreign visitors in the USA. Local traffic police are more likely to accept it as valid identification than an unfamiliar document from another country. Your national automobile association can provide one for a small fee. They're usually valid for one year.

EMBASSIES & CONSULATES
US Embassies Abroad

US diplomatic offices abroad include the following:

Australia
    21 Moonah Place, Yarralumla ACT 2600
    (☎ 2-6270-5900)
    Level 59 MLC Center 19-29 Martin Place, Sydney NSW 2000 (☎ 2-9373-9200)
    553 St Kilda Rd, Melbourne, Victoria
    (☎ 3-9526-5900)

Austria
    Boltzmanngasse 16, A-1091, Vienna
    (☎ 1-313-39)
Belgium
    Blvd du Regent 27, B-1000, Brussels
    (☎ 2-513-38-30)
Canada
    100 Wellington St, Ottawa, Ontario K1P 5T1
    (☎ 613-238-5335)
    1095 W Pender St, Vancouver, BC V6E 2M6
    (☎ 604-685-1930)
    1155 rue St-Alexandre, Montreal, Quebec
    (☎ 514-398-9695)
Denmark
    Dag Hammarskjolds Allé 24, Copenhagen
    (☎ 31-42-31-44)
Finland
    Itainen Puistotie 14A, Helsinki
    (☎ 0-171-931)
France
    2 rue Saint Florentin, 75001 Paris
    (☎ 01 42 96 12 02)
Germany
    Deichmanns Aue 29, 53179 Bonn
    (☎ 228-33-91)
Ireland
    42 Elgin Rd, Ballsbridge, Dublin
    (☎ 1-687-122)
Israel
    71 Hayarkon St, Tel Aviv
    (☎ 3-517-4338)
Italy
    Via Vittorio Veneto 119a-121, Rome
    (☎ 6-46-741)
Japan
    1-10-5 Akasaka Chome, Minato-ku, Tokyo
    (☎ 3-224-5000)
Mexico
    Paseo de la Reforma 305, Cuauhtmoc, 06500 Mexico City (☎ 5-211-0042)
Netherlands
    Lange Voorhout 102, 2514 EJ The Hague
    (☎ 70-310-9209)
    Museumplein 19, 1071 DJ Amsterdam
    (☎ 20-310-9209)
New Zealand
    29 Fitzherbert Terrace, Thorndon, Wellington (☎ 4-722-068)
Norway
    Drammensvein 18, Oslo (☎ 22-44-85-50)
Russia
    Novinskiy Bulivar 19/23, Moscow
    (☎ 095-252-2451)
South Africa
    877 Pretorius St, Box 9536, Pretoria 0001
    (☎ 12-342-1048)

Spain
    Calle Serrano 75, 28006 Madrid
    (☎ 1-577-4000)
Sweden
    Strandvagen 101, S-115 89 Stockholm
    (☎ 8-783-5300)
Switzerland
    Jubilaumsstrasse 93, 3005 Berne
    (☎ 31-357-70 11)
UK
    5 Upper Grosvenor St, London W1
    (☎ 171-499-9000)
    3 Regent Terrace, Edinburgh EH7 5BW
    (☎ 31-556-8315)
    Queens House, Belfast BT1 6EQ
    (☎ 232-328-239)

Consulates in New Orleans
Many countries do not have diplomatic
representation in the Deep South region
covered in this guide; what consulates
there are are located in New Orleans. Most
countries have representation in Washington, DC; call that city's directory assistance (☎ 202-555-1212) for information.
Canada does not have a consulate in New
Orleans; the nearest is in Miami, Florida.
Consulates in New Orleans include:

Austria
    Consulate of Austria, 755 Magazine St
    (☎ 504-581-5141)
Britain
    Honorary Consulate of Great Brittain, 321 St
    Charles Ave (☎ 504-524-4180)
Denmark
    Consulate of Denmark, 321 St Charles Ave
    (☎ 504-586-8300)
Finland
    Consulate of Finland, 1100 Poydras Ave
    (☎ 504-523-6451)
France
    Consulate-General of France, 300 Poydras
    Ave (☎ 504-523-5772)
Germany
    Honorary Consulate of the Federal Republic
    of Germany, 2 Canal St (☎ 504-558-3777)
Italy
    Consulate of Italy, 630 Camp St
    (☎ 504-524-2271)
Japan
    Consulate-General of Japan, 1 Poydras Plaza
    (☎ 504-529-2101)
Mexico
    Consulate-General of Mexico, 2 Canal St
    (☎ 504-522-3596)

Netherlands
    Consulate of the Netherlands,
    643 Magazine St (☎ 504-596-2838)
Spain
    Consulate-General of Spain, 2 Canal St
    (☎ 504-525-4951)
Sweden
    Consul of Sweden, 2640 Canal St
    (☎ 504-827-8600)

CUSTOMS
US Customs allows each person over the
age of 21 to bring one liter of liquor and
200 cigarettes duty free into the USA. US
citizens are allowed to import, duty free,
$400 worth of gifts from abroad, while
non-US citizens are allowed to bring in
$100 worth. See also the Currency &
Exchange section, below.

MONEY
Costs
Costs for accommodations vary seasonally
in the region, between the cities and the
countryside, and between resorts and everywhere else. Generally rates are higher during
major festivals and in summer at beach
resorts. Winter rates are the lowest. The
cheapest motel rates will usually be in the
$20 to $30 range. Rustic camping is inexpensive, only about $5 or so per night, but
only costlier formal sites have amenities
like hot showers.

Food is very reasonable. The occasional
splurge at a first-rate restaurant will cost
anywhere between $25 and $50 per person
depending on where you are, but good
restaurant meals can be found for $10 – or
even half that for some lunch specials. If
you purchase food at markets, you may get
by even more cheaply.

The USA is quite possibly the most
promotion-oriented society on Earth.
Though the bargaining common in many
other countries is not generally accepted
in the US, you can work angles to cut
costs. For example, at hotels in the off-
season, casually and respectfully mentioning a competitor's rate may prompt a
manager to lower the quoted rate. Discount
coupons are widely available – check cir-
culars in Sunday papers, at supermarkets,

Top Left: Jack Owens and Bud Spires at the Sunflower River Blues & Gospel Festival, Clarksdale, MS
Middle Left: Street musician, New Orleans, LA

Top Right: Young Elvis impersonator, Memphis, TN
Bottom: Frank Frost, Sunflower River Blues & Gospel Festival, Clarksdale, MS

Top Left: Auburn House's most noted feature, Natchez, MS
Bottom Left: Ave Maria Grotto, Roman miniatures, Cullman, AL

Top Right: Interior with Zubar wallpaper, Monmouth Plantation, Natchez, MS
Bottom Right: Windsor ruins, MS

tourist offices, chambers of commerce and welcome centers.

Intracity public transportation is relatively inexpensive; buses or streetcars cost anywhere from 80¢ to $1.50 depending on distance and the system. Owning or renting a car is much less expensive than in other parts of the world. In some areas a car is the only way of getting around; rentals are fairly inexpensive in large cities, and gasoline costs a fraction of what it does in Europe and most of the rest of the world. For more information on purchasing and operating a car, see the Getting Around chapter.

Carrying Money

Carry your money (and only the money you'll need for that day) somewhere inside your clothing (in a money belt, a bra or socks) rather than in a handbag or an outside pocket. Put the money in several places. Most hotels and hostels provide safes, so you can leave your money and other valuables with them. Hide, and avoid wearing, any valuable jewelry. A safety pin or key ring to hold the zipper tags of a daypack together can also help deter theft.

Cash & Traveler's Checks

Though carrying cash is more risky, it's still a good idea to travel with some for the convenience; it's useful to help pay for all those tips, and some smaller, more remote places might not accept credit cards or traveler's checks. Traveler's checks offer greater protection from theft or loss and in many places can be used as cash. American Express and Thomas Cook are widely accepted and have efficient replacement policies.

Keeping a record of the check numbers and the checks you have used is vital when it comes to replacing lost checks. Keep this record separate from the checks themselves.

You'll save yourself trouble and expense if you buy traveler's checks in US dollars. The savings you *might* make on exchange rates by carrying traveler's checks in a foreign currency don't make up for the hassle of exchanging them at banks and other facilities. Restaurants, hotels and most stores accept US-dollar traveler's checks as if they were cash, so if you're carrying traveler's checks in US dollars, the odds are you'll rarely have to use a bank or pay an exchange fee.

Take most of the checks in large denominations. It's only toward the end of a stay that you may want to change a small check to make sure you aren't left with too much local currency.

ATMs

Automated teller machines (ATMs) are a convenient way of obtaining cash from a bank account within the USA or abroad. Most banks charge a $1 to $4 fee for using their ATM with a card not issued by them – it's federal law that you must be warned in advance of how much your account will be charged.

However, their convenience can't be beat: small-town banks in the middle of nowhere have ATMs, they are common in most shopping areas, and they often operate 24 hours a day. There are various ATM networks (Exchange, Accel, Plus and Cirrus are widespread throughout the US) and most banks are affiliated with several.

Using a credit, debit or charge card, you can withdraw money from an ATM with a 2% fee ($2 minimum) plus the non-issuing bank service charge. Check with your credit card company or bank for exact information.

Credit & Debit Cards

Major credit cards are accepted at hotels, restaurants, gas stations, shops and car rental agencies throughout the USA. In fact, you'll find it hard to perform certain transactions without one, such as renting a car or purchasing tickets to performances.

Even if you prefer to rely on traveler's checks and ATMs, it's a good idea to carry a credit card for emergencies. If you're planning to rely primarily upon credit cards, it would be wise to have a Visa or MasterCard in your deck, since other cards aren't as widely accepted.

Places that accept Visa and MasterCard are also likely to accept debit cards. Unlike a credit card, a debit card deducts payment directly from the user's checking account. Instead of an interest rate, users are charged a minimal fee for the transaction. Be sure to check with your bank to confirm that your debit card will be accepted in other states – debit cards from large commercial banks can often be used worldwide.

Carry copies of your credit card numbers separately from the cards. If you lose your credit cards or they get stolen, contact the company immediately. Following are toll-free numbers for the main credit card companies.

Visa	☎ 800-336-8472
MasterCard	☎ 800-826-2181
American Express	☎ 800-528-4800
Discover	☎ 800-347-2683
Diners Club	☎ 800-234-6377

International Transfers
You can instruct your bank back home to send you a draft. Specify the city, bank and branch to which you want your money directed, or ask your home bank to tell you where a suitable one is, and make sure you get the details right. The procedure is easier if you've authorized someone back home to access your account.

Money sent by telegraphic transfer should reach you within a week; by mail allow at least two weeks. When it arrives it will most likely be converted into local currency – you can take it as cash or buy traveler's checks.

You can also transfer money by American Express, Thomas Cook or Western Union, though the latter has fewer international offices.

Currency & Exchange
The US dollar is divided into 100 cents (¢). Coins come in denominations of 1¢ (penny), 5¢ (nickel), 10¢ (dime), 25¢ (quarter), and the seldom seen 50¢ (half-dollar) and $1. Quarters are the most commonly used coins in vending machines and parking meters, so it's handy to have a

stash of them. Notes, commonly called bills, come in $1, $2, $5, $10, $20, $50 and $100 denominations – $2 bills are rare, but perfectly legal. There is also a $1 coin that the government has tried unsuccessfully to bring into mass circulation; you may get them as change from ticket and stamp machines. Be aware that they look similar to quarters.

US law permits you to bring in, or take out, as much as US$10,000 in US or foreign currency, traveler's checks or letters of credit without formality. Larger amounts of any or all of the above – there are no limits – must be declared to customs.

Most banks in major cities, especially those downtown, will exchange cash or traveler's checks in major foreign currencies, though banks in smaller cities and outlying areas don't do so very often, and it may take them some time. It's probably less of a hassle to exchange foreign currency in larger cities. Additionally, Thomas Cook, American Express, and exchange windows in airports offer exchange (although you'll get a better rate at a bank).

At press time, exchange rates were:

Australia	A$1	=	$0.69
Canada	C$1	=	$0.71
France	FF1	=	$0.17
Germany	DM1	=	$0.58
Hong Kong	HK$10	=	$1.29
Japan	¥100	=	$0.79
New Zealand	NZ$1	=	$0.62
United Kingdom	UK£1	=	$1.71

Tipping
Tipping is expected in restaurants and better hotels, and by taxi drivers, hairdressers and baggage carriers. In restaurants, wait staff are paid minimal wages and rely upon tips for their livelihoods. Tip 15% unless the service is terrible (in which case a complaint to the manager is warranted) or up to 20% if the service is great. Never tip in fast-food or take-out restaurants. At Southern cafeterias or buffet-style restaurants with drink waiters, it's customary to leave $1 or $2, depending on the size of your party or your requests.

Taxi drivers expect 10% and hairdressers get 15% if their service is satisfactory. Baggage carriers (skycaps in airports, attendants in hotels) get $1 per bag and 50¢ for each additional bag.

Taxes & Refunds

Almost everything you pay for in the USA is taxed. Occasionally, the tax is included in the advertised price (eg, plane tickets, gas, drinks in a bar and entrance tickets for museums or theaters). Restaurant meals and drinks, accommodations and most other purchases are taxed, and this is added on top of the advertised cost. Unless otherwise stated, the prices given in this book don't reflect local taxes. International visitors should inquire about sales tax refunds, especially in Louisiana. See the 'Facts about' chapters for each state for details on taxes.

When inquiring about hotel or motel rates, be sure to ask about tax amounts.

POST & COMMUNICATIONS
Postal Rates

Postage rates increase every few years; the next increase (10%) is expected in 1998. Currently, rates for 1st-class mail within the USA are 32¢ for letters up to one ounce (23¢ for each additional ounce) and 20¢ for postcards.

International airmail rates (except to Canada and Mexico) are 60¢ for a half-ounce letter, $1 for a one-ounce letter and 40¢ for each additional half-ounce. International postcard rates are 50¢. Letters to Canada are 46¢ for a half-ounce letter, 52¢ for a one-ounce letter and 40¢ for a postcard. Letters to Mexico are 40¢ for a half-ounce letter, 46¢ for a one-ounce letter and 35¢ for a postcard. Aerogrammes are 50¢.

The cost for parcels airmailed anywhere within the USA is $3 for two pounds or less, increasing by $1 per pound up to $6 for five pounds. For heavier items, rates differ according to the distance mailed.

Sending Mail

If you have the correct postage, you can drop your mail into any blue mailbox. However, to send a package 16 ounces (one lb) or larger, you must bring it to a post office. If you need to buy stamps or weigh your mail, go to the nearest post office. The address of each town's main post office is given in the text. In addition, larger towns have branch post offices and post office centers in some supermarkets and drug stores. For the address of the nearest, check the telephone directory.

Usually, post offices are open from 8 am to 5 pm weekdays and 8 am to 3 pm on Saturday, but it all depends on the branch.

Receiving Mail

You can have mail sent to you c/o General Delivery at any post office that has its own zip (postal) code. Mail is usually held for 10 days before it's returned to sender; you might request your correspondents to write 'hold for arrival' on their letters. You can also rent a 'Post Office Box' at US post offices or at businesses like Mail Boxes Etc if you're staying a month or more. Alternatively, have mail sent to the local representative of American Express or Thomas Cook, which provide mail service for their customers.

Telephone

All phone numbers within the USA consist of a three-digit area code followed by a seven-digit local number. If you are calling locally, just dial the seven-digit number. If you are calling long distance, dial 1 + the three-digit area code + the seven-digit number. If you're calling from abroad, the international country code for the USA is 1.

For local directory assistance dial ☎ 411. For directory assistance outside your area code, dial ☎ 1 + the three-digit area code of the place you want to call + 555-1212. For example, to obtain directory assistance for New Orleans, dial ☎ 1-504-555-1212.

A local and national area code map is in the telephone directory. Be aware that metropolitan areas are being divided into multiple new area codes. These changes are not reflected in older phone books. When in doubt, ask the operator.

The 800, 877 and 888 area codes are designated for toll-free numbers within the

USA and sometimes Canada as well. Calling areas can be restricted to outside the local area or within the US. For toll-free directory assistance, call ☎ 800-555-1212.

Local calls usually cost 35¢ at pay phones. Long-distance rates vary depending on the destination and which telephone company you use – call the operator for rate information. Don't ask the operator to put your call through, however, because operator-assisted calls are much more expensive than direct-dial calls. Generally, nights (11 pm to 8 am), all day Saturday and from 8 am to 5 pm Sunday are the cheapest times to call (60% discount from business-hour weekday rates).

In an attempt to make their phone numbers snappy and memorable, many businesses use words, which translate to numbers on the phone keypad. To translate: 1 is unassigned; 2 – ABC, 3 – DEF, 4 – GHI, 5 – JKL, 6 – MNO, 7 – PRS, 8 – TUV, 9 – WXY. Sorry no Qs or Zs.

International Calls To make a direct international call, dial ☎ 011, then the country code, followed by the area code and the phone number. You may need to wait as long as 45 seconds for the ringing to start. International rates vary depending on the time of day and the destination. Call the operator (☎ 0) for rates. The first minute is always more expensive than additional minutes.

Hotel & Pay Phones Many hotels (especially the more expensive ones) add a service charge of 50¢ to $1 for each local call made from a room phone, and they also have hefty surcharges for long-distance calls. Public pay phones, which can be found in most lobbies, are always cheaper. You can pump change into, use a credit or phone card with, or make collect calls from pay phones.

Phone Debit Cards A new long-distance alternative is the phone debit card, which allows purchasers to pay for phone time in advance. Worth varying amounts, these are widely available in airports, at US post

offices, from Western Union, and from some other sources.

When using phone cards, be cautious of people watching you dial – thieves will memorize the numbers and use them to make phone calls to all corners of the Earth.

Fax

Fax machines are easy to find in the USA, at shipping companies like Mail Boxes Etc, photocopy services and hotel business service centers, but be prepared to pay high prices (over $1 a page).

Email

Email is fast becoming a preferred method of communication; however, unless you have a laptop and modem that can be plugged into a telephone socket, it's difficult to get online. Campus or public libraries may provide connections, as well as hotel business service centers. Restaurants and cafes in major cities sometimes offer Internet service.

Setting up a universal email address is getting easier and it's really cheap. It's a service called Freemail, which is subsidized by advertising. Rocketmail (Net) and Hotmail (Net) will set up an absolutely free email address for you that you can access from any Web-connected computer anywhere in the world. Email services are

---

Online Services

Quite a few attractions, hotels and motels, local chambers of commerce and other tourist-friendly places, maintain websites posting hours of operation, rates, current events and email addresses for reservations.

All the Deep South states are somewhat well-represented online. In addition to listing sites that are useful resources for our Internet-savvy readers, we've gathered email and website addresses for some places in the Internet directory. In this guide, 'Net' alongside phone and fax numbers denotes that the organization or business has an Internet address in the directory. ■

complete (attachments, address book, copying multiple recipients). These services require you to submit a personal profile to better categorize you for target marketing. Read the privacy policies on the Web before you register.

BOOKS

Beyond the wealth of evocative Southern literature that you might wish to read before a trip to the Deep South (see Literature in Facts about the Deep South), non-fiction books can also enhance your visit tremendously. Visitors should note, however, that outside of major cities and university towns there are few high-quality bookstores in the region. Bookstores with exceptional collections of works on Southern subjects and themes can be found most easily in New Orleans, Oxford and Memphis. Major chains such as Barnes & Noble and Books-A-Million are found in major cities throughout the region. If you're bypassing major cities, you may have better luck finding books on the South in your hometown than in the South itself. Select titles can be mail-ordered from Square Books (☎ 601-236-2262) in Oxford.

Guidebooks

Lonely Planet's guide to New Orleans by Robert Raburn contains comprehensive information for city visitors.

The Sierra Club's *Trail Guide to the Delta Country*, edited by John P Sevenair, explores the natural world of the lower Mississippi River and around. It describes hikes, backpacking and canoeing trips and bike routes from the Delta region to the Gulf of Mexico. It may be hard to find. *Hiking Mississippi* by Helen McGinnis is a comprehensive guide to state trails. *Only in Mississippi* by Lorraine Redd is a guide to the more offbeat attractions of the Magnolia State.

The *Smithsonian Guide to Historic America: Deep South* emphasizes historic architecture and design in landmark buildings throughout the region.

Members of the American Automobile Association may want to carry AAA's free

TourBook covering Alabama, Louisiana and Mississippi (another edition covers Tennessee along with Kentucky), which contains mostly listings for most chain motels and hotels, and select restaurants.

History & Culture

Charles Hudson's *The Southeastern Indians* is considered the seminal work on the area's archaeological and Native American history. The heritage of northeastern Alabama's Cherokee Indians is explored in adult and children's books in a range of works on history, folklore and spirituality distributed by the Eastern Band of the Cherokee; write for their catalog (Box 256, Cherokee, North Carolina).

The fascinating development of Afro-Creole culture is documented in *Africans in Colonial Louisiana* by Gwendolyn Midlo Hall and *The Free People of Color of New Orleans* by Mary Gehman.

Of the tomes written on the Civil War, one considered a major sourcebook is the three-volume *The Civil War: A Narrative*, written by Mississippi historian Shelby Foote (whose wry and poignant observations appeared throughout the PBS *Civil War* TV series). The *Civil War Almanac*, edited by John S Bowman and introduced by noted historian Henry Steele Commager, is an authoritative single-volume book with a detailed chronology and biographies of key players.

Been in the Storm So Long by Leon Litwak (the book takes its title from a 19th-century black spiritual) explores the aftermath of slavery in the South through moving and revealing personal accounts of ex-slaves and former slaveholders.

Let Us Now Praise Famous Men by James Agee and Walker Evans is a stark portrait of poor white tenant farmers in Alabama in the 1930s. *Coming of Age in Mississippi*, the autobiography of Ann Moody, describes the harsh life of a black sharecropping family in the Mississippi Delta in the 1950s. Stetson Kennedy's 1959 *Jim Crow Guide: The Way It Was* is an eye-opening survey of the Jim Crow South. The civil rights era from 1954 to

1965 is chronicled in Juan William's *Eyes on the Prize* (also a PBS documentary series by the same name). *Free at Last* by Margaret Edds covers the behind-the-scenes struggles for civil rights in several Southern cities.

Folktales are a rich source of cultural entertainment; try *Gumbo Ya Ya* or the Tar Baby stories that describe the exploits of Br'er Rabbit and his pals. Br'er – short for Brother – Rabbit stories are also available in the *Uncle Remus Stories*.

VS Naipaul, an East Indian who grew up on an eastern Caribbean island, shares his observations on the modern South, particularly as it relates to race, in *A Turn in the South*.

Dixie Rising by Yankee observer and *New York Times* reporter Peter Applebome is the most recent contribution to sociopolitical observations on the Southern region. Other scholars and historians who have authored dissections of Southern culture as it relates to politics include C Vann Woodward, John Hope Franklin, George Tindall and Dan Carter.

The gargantuan *Encyclopedia of Southern Culture*, edited by Charles Reagan Wilson and William Ferris, covers everything from agriculture to 'women's life.' The section on Southern politics draws from the authoritative work of Merle and Earl Black.

FILMS

Many films set in the Deep South give a flavor for the region, especially films made from books listed under Literature in Facts about the Deep South. Apart from this, and available on home video, the PBS-produced *Civil War* series sheds a drawn-out light on this Southern history. *Eyes on the Prize* is a good film that details civil rights history.

Some of the music of the region has been documented on film, whether it be to illustrate a storyline or for its own sake. Anything starring Elvis is haute-Hollywood (*Jailhouse Rock* and *King Creole*), but it gives viewers an idea of the man, his music and his appeal. New Orleans' own Louis

Armstrong is immortalized in a number of films, including *New Orleans* (1947) and *Hello Dolly!* (1969), a very popular musical. In the cult favorite *Down by Law*, John Lurie (noted jazzman of the group the Lounge Lizards), Tom Waits (noted cult figure and songwriter) and Roberto Benigni (crowned prince of Italian slapstick) do their best to break out of Orleans Parish prison. It's a 1986 black & white film with songs by Waits and background music by Lurie. The little-known film *Crossroads* is set in the Mississippi Delta and tries to evoke the legend of Robert Johnson. Robert Altman's *Nashville* is more about the people who live there rather than about the place or music.

Louisiana is often in the movies. In 1996, the state's (and America's) death penalty legislation came under scrutiny in the affecting *Dead Man Walking*, a true story about the work of Sister Helen Prejean. Former governor Earl Long is memorialized by Paul Newman in the comedic *Blaze*. The former governor Huey Long (Earl's brother) is fictionalized in *All the King's Men* and *A Lion Is in the Streets*. Academy Award-winning performances enhance Tennessee Williams' play *A Streetcar Named Desire*. This film was so popular and influential it could be credited for establishing modern Southern stereotypes. Louis Malle filmed a cheeky 16-year-old Brooke Shields in *Pretty Baby* at the Columns Hotel in New Orleans. The 1945 semi-documentary film *The Louisiana Story* is about a Cajun boy who scouted the swamps for oil drillers – it's an interesting insight into the region, but it's a somewhat skewed vision as the production was partially funded by Standard Oil.

Films set in Mississippi include *Mississippi Masala*, a biracial romance filmed partially in Biloxi. *Biloxi Blues* is the Neil Simon comedy in which a character from New York remarks on the heat of the Gulf South: 'It's not just hot; it's Africa-hot.' Dramatizations of civil rights struggles include *Mississippi Burning*, an intense account of events in the rural town of Philadelphia. *Ghosts of Mississippi* dramatizes the trial for the murderer of Medgar

Evers. Both of the latter films were somewhat criticized for enlarging the role of whites as 'rescuers.'

Everything from Alabama's racism *(To Kill a Mockingbird)* to its space industry *(Space Camp)* has been fodder for filmmakers. Eccentric or exceptional characters have proved equally worthy of footage: the fictional *Forrest Gump* and the women of *Fried Green Tomatoes*, and the biographical films *The Miracle Worker* (about Helen Keller), *Buffalo Soldiers* and *Your Cheatin' Heart*.

NEWSPAPERS & MAGAZINES
No single paper speaks for the region; dailies in New Orleans, Memphis, Nashville, Jackson and Montgomery cover local news the best, but also attempt to cover the state, region and beyond. The *Atlanta Constitution* purports to speak for the region, but its coverage of neighboring Alabama is more thorough than other Southern states farther afield. Newspapers from outside the region, such as the *New York Times* or the *Wall Street Journal* can be found in major cities only, and often not readily.

The *Oxford American* is a provocative monthly literary magazine produced from the University of Mississippi that also covers regional issues. The bimonthly *Southern Exposure* carries on the muckraking tradition of Stetson Kennedy's 1946 book by the same name.

Several slick monthly magazines cover the upscale beat – *New Orleans*, *Coast* magazine for Gulf Coast coverage from Mississippi to Florida, and *Southern Living*, the home-decoration magazine of choice south of the Mason-Dixon line.

TV & RADIO
Television sets in all but the smallest towns will usually receive the major American TV networks as well as PBS, the Public Broadcasting System. 'Cable' TV guarantees clear reception and will include CNN and TBS – two cable channels originating out of Atlanta.

Local PBS radio stations usually air nationally syndicated news and feature programs, such as 'All Things Considered' and 'Fresh Air.'

You can hear wonderful music programs – especially jazz, blues, country and gospel – on radio stations throughout the region, though a regional format called 'Southern rock' and Top 40 pop tunes are predominant. In some regions, all you may be able to pick up is the local Christian station featuring 'Christian music' and commentary.

PHOTOGRAPHY & VIDEO
Traveling photographers will want to have cameras and bags hand-checked when passing through airport security. Summertime travelers need to be aware that the South's extreme heat can damage film. For purchasing film, only stores in major cities will offer a wide selection of specialty film (black & white, extremely high speed, etc); check expiration dates on film. Inexpensive, quick film processing is widely available; if you care about the quality of your photos, look for a quality photo shop to develop them, which will take more time.

Tips for the best photography and videography: avoid midday, which may create glaring shadows or washed out images. The magic hours around dawn and dusk offer the most dramatic lighting. Always protect camera lenses with a haze or ultraviolet (UV) filter.

Some poorer communities may make riveting subjects for photography, yet locals may be understandably sensitive about being the subject of such a portrait. Be sure to ask before photographing people, and be prepared for a possible refusal.

Overseas visitors considering buying videotapes should note that the USA uses the National Television System Committee (NTSC) color TV standard, which is incompatible with other standards, such as Phas Alternative Line (PAL).

TIME
The region covered in this guide falls under Central Standard Time, six hours behind Greenwich Mean Time. Alabamian communities on the Georgia border, such as

Phenix City, may observe Georgia time (Eastern Standard Time, which is one hour earlier). All Deep South states observe daylight saving time (comparable to Summer Time in Britain).

ELECTRICITY
Electric current is 110-120 volts, 60-cycle. Appliances built to take 220-240 volt, 50-cycle current (as in Europe and Asia) will need a converter (transformer) and a US-style plug adapter with two flat pins.

WEIGHTS & MEASURES
The USA uses a modified version of the traditional English measuring system of feet, yards, miles, ounces, pounds and gallons. Three feet equals one yard (0.914 meters); 1760 yards or 5280 feet are one mile. Dry weights are in ounces (oz), pounds (lbs) and tons (16 oz equal one lb; 2000 lbs equal one ton), but liquid measures differ from dry measures. One pint equals 16 fluid ounces; two pints equal one quart, a common measure for liquids like milk, which is also sold in half gallons (two quarts) and gallons (four quarts). Gasoline is dispensed by the US gallon, which is about 20% less than the Imperial gallon. See the back of this book for conversion charts.

LAUNDRY
Pricier hotels and motels usually provide laundry service, and many budget motels provide coin-operated washers and dryers. You can also find either self-service laundries (called 'washaterias' or 'washerettes') or wash-and-fold service in most towns. Laundries usually have machines to dispense change and to sell single-serving supplies of detergent. A wash costs around $1, a dry another $1. You can find laundry and dry cleaning services under 'Laundries' or 'Cleaners' in the Yellow Pages telephone directory.

TOILETS
You will find relatively clean toilets (most often marked 'restrooms') in airports, attractions, restaurants, hotels, visitor information centers and more upscale bars and clubs. The ones in funkier restaurants and bars, and in bus and train stations, at highway rest areas or fuel stations may or may not be as well maintained, but are generally usable (they commonly run low on toilet tissue, soap and towels). The quality of public facilities in parks and off the street may vary considerably, if available.

Only the most enlightened establishments, most often attractions that cater to upscale families, provide diaper-changing 'decks' in women's restrooms (write if you find one in a men's restroom in the Deep South). Many women's restrooms provide tampon vending machines. In some bars and nightclubs, restroom vending machines dispense condoms.

HEALTH
For most foreign visitors no immunizations are required for entry, though cholera and yellow fever vaccinations may be required of travelers from areas with a history of those diseases. There are no unexpected health dangers, excellent medical attention is readily available, and the only real health concern is that a collision with the medical system can cause severe injuries to your financial state.

Hospitals and medical centers, walk-in clinics and referral services are easily found throughout the region.

In a serious emergency, call ☎ 911 for an ambulance to take you to the nearest hospital's emergency room. But note that charges for this service in the USA are incredibly high.

Predeparture Preparations
Make sure you're healthy before you start traveling. If you are embarking on a long trip, make sure your teeth are in good shape. If you wear glasses, take a spare pair and your prescription. You can get new spectacles made up quickly and competently for well under $100, depending on the prescription and frame you choose. If you require a particular medication, take an adequate supply and bring a prescription in case you lose it.

Health Insurance A travel insurance policy to cover theft, lost tickets and medical problems is a good idea, especially in the USA, where some hospitals will refuse care without evidence of insurance. There are a wide variety of policies and your travel agent will have recommendations. International student travel policies handled by STA Travel and other student travel organizations are usually a good value. Some policies offer lower and higher medical expenses options, and the higher one is chiefly for countries like the USA with extremely high medical costs. Check the fine print.

Some policies specifically exclude 'dangerous activities' like scuba diving, motorcycling and even trekking. If these activities are on your agenda, avoid this sort of policy.

You may prefer a policy that pays doctors or hospitals directly, rather than one where you pay first and claim later. If you have to claim later, keep *all* documentation. Some policies ask you to call back (reverse charges) to a center in your home country for an immediate assessment of your problem.

Check whether the policy covers ambulance fees or an emergency flight home. If you need two seats, somebody has to pay for it!

Travel & Climate-Related Problems

Motion Sickness Eating lightly before and during a trip will reduce the chances of motion sickness. If you are prone to motion sickness, try to find a place that minimizes disturbance, for example, near the wing on aircraft or near the center on buses. Fresh air usually helps. Commercial anti-motion sickness preparations, which can cause drowsiness, have to be taken before the trip commences; once you feel sick, it's too late. Ginger, a natural preventative, is available in capsule form from health food stores.

Jet Lag Jet lag is experienced when a person travels by air across more than three time zones (each time zone represents a one-hour time difference). It occurs because many of the functions of the human body are regulated by internal 24-hour cycles called circadian rhythms. When we travel long distances rapidly, our bodies take time to adjust to the 'new time' of our destination, and we may experience fatigue, disorientation, insomnia, anxiety, impaired concentration and loss of appetite. These effects will usually be gone within three days of arrival, but there are ways of minimizing the impact of jet lag:

- Rest for a couple of days prior to departure; try to avoid late nights and last-minute dashes for traveler's checks or your passport.

- Try to select flight schedules that minimize sleep deprivation; arriving in the early evening means you can go to sleep soon after you arrive. For very long flights, try to organize a stopover.

- Avoid excessive eating (which bloats the stomach) and alcohol (which causes dehydration) during the flight. Instead, drink plenty of noncarbonated, nonalcoholic drinks such as fruit juice or water.

- Make yourself comfortable by wearing loose-fitting clothes and perhaps bring an eye mask and ear plugs to help you sleep.

- Avoid smoking (when permitted on international flights) as this reduces the amount of oxygen in the airplane cabin even further and causes greater fatigue.

Heat Exhaustion Without heeding certain precautions, visitors unacclimated to a subtropical climate may experience discomfort from extreme summertime heat, humidity and overexposure to the sun. Avoid exposure to the midday sun and heat – have a plan to be indoors – and confine strenuous activity to early morning and late afternoon (locals have made a sport of 'mall-walking' to get exercise within an air-conditioned environment). Wear sunscreen and a hat, and even carry an umbrella to shield more sensitive types from the sun. Rent a car with air-conditioning and light-colored interiors. Drinking lots of water is also good.

Note also that many establishments overcompensate for the heat by overchilling their interiors – brace yourself for the bodily shock of alternating between the 100°F (38°C) exterior and 70°F (21°C) interiors. Carry a cover-up.

Fungal Infections Fungal infections, which occur with greater frequency in hot weather, are most likely to occur on the scalp, between the toes or fingers (athlete's foot), in the groin (jock itch or crotch rot) and on the body (ringworm). You get ringworm (which is a fungal infection, not a worm) from infected animals or by walking on damp areas, like shower floors.

To prevent fungal infections, wear loose, comfortable clothes, avoid artificial fibers, wash frequently and dry carefully. If you do get an infection, wash the infected area daily with a disinfectant or medicated soap and water, and rinse and dry well. Apply an antifungal powder and try to expose the infected area to air or sunlight as much as possible. Change underwear and towels frequently and wash them often in hot water.

Infectious Diseases

Diarrhea A change of water, food or climate can all cause the runs; diarrhea caused by contaminated food or water is more serious, but it's unlikely in the USA. Despite all your precautions you may still have a mild bout of traveler's diarrhea from exotic food or drink. Dehydration is the main danger with any diarrhea, particularly for children, where dehydration can occur quite quickly. Fluid replacement remains the mainstay of management. Weak black tea with a little sugar, soda water or soft drinks diluted 50% with water are all good. With severe diarrhea, a rehydrating solution is necessary to replace minerals and salts. Such solutions, like Pedialyte, are available at pharmacies throughout the region.

Hepatitis Hepatitis is a general term for inflammation of the liver. There are many causes of this condition: poor sanitation, contact with infected blood products, drugs, alcohol and contact with an infected person are but a few. The symptoms are fever, chills, headache, fatigue, and feelings of weakness and aches and pains, followed by loss of appetite, nausea, vomiting, abdominal pain, dark urine, light-colored feces and jaundiced skin. The whites of the eyes may also turn yellow. Viral hepatitis is an infection of the liver, which can have several unpleasant symptoms, or no symptoms at all, with the infected person not knowing that they have the disease. The discovery of new strains has led to a virtual alphabet soup, with hepatitis A, B, C, D and E. Hepatitis D and E are fairly rare.

Tetanus Tetanus is difficult to treat but is preventable with immunization. Tetanus occurs when a wound becomes infected by a germ that lives in the feces of animals or people, so clean all cuts, punctures or animal bites.

HIV/AIDS Exposure to blood, blood products or bodily fluids may put an individual at risk for getting HIV/AIDS. Infection can come from unprotected sex or sharing contaminated needles. Apart from abstinence, the most effective preventative is always to practice safe sex using condoms. It is impossible to detect a person's HIV status without a blood test.

HIV/AIDS can also be spread through infected blood transfusions, though the blood supply in the USA is now well screened. It can also be spread if needles are reused for acupuncture, tattooing or body piercing.

A good resource for help and information is the Centers for Disease Control and Prevention (check the local phone book). The US AIDS hotline (☎ 800-342-2437, in Spanish 800-344-7432) offers advice and support.

Cuts, Bites & Stings

Cuts & Scratches Skin punctures can easily become infected in hot climates and heal slowly. Treat any cut with an antiseptic such as Betadine. Where possible avoid bandages and Band-aids, which can keep wounds wet.

Bites & Stings Bee and wasp stings and nonpoisonous spider bites are usually more painful than dangerous. Calamine lotion will give relief, and ice packs will reduce the pain and swelling. More common are mosquito bites. Mosquitoes usually appear at dusk, and can be found around stagnant water. Use insect repellent: *Consumer Reports* rates a product called 'Ultra Muskol' the highest, though locals use Avon's 'Skin So Soft' hand lotion for everyday repelling. You might want to carry an insect bite cream, such as Benadryl. Clothing that covers your limbs is a good deterrent to insects.

Ticks are a parasitic arachnid that may be present in brush, forest and grasslands, where hikers may get them on their legs or in their boots. The adults suck blood from hosts by burying their head into skin, but they are often found unattached and can simply be brushed off. However, if one has attached itself to you, pulling it off and leaving the head in the skin increases the likelihood of infection or disease, such as Lyme disease.

Always check your body for ticks after walking through a high-grass or thickly forested area. If you do find a tick on you, induce it to let go by rubbing on oil, alcohol or petroleum jelly, or press it with a very hot object such as a match or a cigarette. The tick should back out and can then be disposed of. If you feel at all ill in the next couple of weeks, make sure you consult a doctor.

AFRICAN-AMERICAN TRAVELERS
African Americans are as much a part of the South as grits, blues, jazz, plantations and the Mississippi River. Their heritage is a major reason why visitors from around the globe come to the region.

The stereotype of redneck Southern whites lynching blacks is drawn from a bygone era and does not reflect today's Deep South. True, there are occasional racial incidents, but they are more a reflection of individual bigotry than widespread attitudes. In all but a few isolated pockets – and certainly at all tourist attractions – black visitors will feel welcome. In those rare areas where blacks may find themselves uncomfortable, outsiders of any color or culture are generally spurned.

Although most blacks and whites comfortably coexist in the Deep South, centuries of discrimination and segregation have resulted in many communities, churches and institutions – at almost every socioeconomic level – that remain predominantly black or white. Churches may have a sprinkling of other races in their congregations, but, in general, they are attended by one race. While casual attire is acceptable in Northern churches, the dress code in black churches in the South is much more formal. Southern colleges and universities are open to all races, but there are numerous highly regarded learning institutions that are historically black, including Alabama's Tuskegee University and Alabama A&M in Huntsville, Tennessee's Fisk University in Nashville, Louisiana's Xavier University in New Orleans, and Southern University in Baton Rouge, and Mississippi's Alcorn State University in Lorman. These institutions host many African-American related lectures, exhibitions and cultural events that both blacks and whites attend. Some also operate radio stations that broadcast soul, rhythm and blues and jazz programs.

The region's nightlife ranges from dance clubs and bars to theaters and performance centers. Black visitors can enjoy nightlife in traditionally African-American neighborhoods as well as other parts of town. However, outsiders of any color should avoid bars with parking lots full of pickup trucks bearing bumper stickers reading, 'The South Will Rise Again,' 'Keep the Confederate Flag Flying' or related slogans.

At golf courses, tennis courts, stables, parks, pools, beaches and sporting events blacks are welcome. With that said, keep in mind that there are still private clubs with white-only membership policies. It wasn't until 1990 that Birmingham's Shoal Creek Country Club offered admission to blacks and that was only after the club's racist policy drew public outcry as the club prepared to host a Professional Golf Association (PGA) championship.

Resources & Organizations

If you find your rights jeopardized, call the police or one of the following agencies. The National Association for the Advancement of Colored People (NAACP) (☎ 202-638-2269, Net) is the largest civil rights organization in the United States and has branches throughout the country. Its Legal Affairs Department (☎ 410-358-8900, Net) can refer you to a local branch where you can get guidance. The Southern Poverty Law Center (☎ 334-264-0286, Net) handles extreme cases of civil rights violations; its office is in Montgomery, Alabama. If you need an attorney, contact the National Legal Aid & Defender Association (☎ 202-452-0620, Net), which provides low-cost legal assistance and has offices in major cities around the country. Call the main number or check with local directory information under Legal Aid Society or Legal Services for an office near you. You can also contact the American Bar Association's (☎ 312-988-5522) state referral services for a directory of attorneys in Alabama (☎ 334-269-1515), Louisiana (☎ 504-561-8828) and Mississippi (☎ 601-948-5488).

The Greater New Orleans Black Tourism Network (☎ 504-523-5652) in the Superdome at 1520 Sugar Bowl Dr, New Orleans, LA 70112, provides guides to heritage sites and directories to minority-owned businesses. The Heritage Tourism Program (☎ 601-446-6345, 800-647-6724) administered by the Natchez Visitors Bureau, 422 Main St, Natchez, MS 39120, offers a similar service.

In Tennessee, the state (☎ 615-741-2159) produces the *African American Guide to Cultural & Historical Sites*, available from the Tennessee Department of Tourist Development at the Rachel Jackson Bldg, 5th floor, 320 6th Ave N, Nashville, TN 37243.

Alabama's Black Heritage is a 56-page guide to more than 300 African-American historical and cultural sites. It's produced by the Bureau of Tourism & Travel (☎ 334-242-4169, 800-252-2262), PO Box 4927, Montgomery, AL 36103. Special-interest groups can contact the black heritage coordinator (☎ 334-242-4493). Birmingham's convention and visitors bureau (☎ 205-458-8000, 800-458-8085), 2200 Ninth Ave N, maintains a list of tour operators providing individual and group tours. The Historical 4th Ave Visitors & Information Center (☎ 205-328-1850), 319 17th St N, provides information and guided walking tours of Birmingham's historic black business district.

Roots & Wings (☎ 334-262-1700), 1345 Carter Hill Rd, Montgomery, champions African-American culture through fiction, nonfiction, children's books, cards, calendars, magazines, recordings, art exhibitions and readings, lectures and storytelling sessions. Two Birmingham bookstores specialize in African-American fiction and nonfiction: Yamini's Books (☎ 205-322-0037), 1417 4th Ave N, and the Civil Rights Institute Book Shop (☎ 205-328-9696), 520 16th St N. The weekly *Birmingham World* has served the black community since 1930.

WOMEN TRAVELERS

If you are a woman traveler, especially a woman traveling alone, it's not a bad idea to get in the habit of traveling with a little extra awareness of your surroundings. Conducting yourself in a common-sense manner will help you to avoid most problems. For example, you're more vulnerable if you've been drinking or using drugs than if you're sober; you're more vulnerable alone than if you're with company; and you're more vulnerable in a high-crime urban area than in a 'better' district.

In general, exercise more vigilance in large cities than in rural areas. Try to avoid the 'bad' or unsafe neighborhoods or districts; if you must go into or through these areas, it's best to go in a car or taxi. Nighttime is more dangerous, but in the worst areas crime can occur even in the daytime. If you are unsure which areas are considered unsafe, ask at your hotel or telephone the tourist office for advice. Tourist maps can sometimes be deceiving, compressing areas and making distances look shorter than they are.

While there is less to watch out for in rural areas, women may still be subject to unwelcome attention by men unaccustomed to seeing women traveling independently. Try to avoid hiking or camping alone, especially in unfamiliar places. Hikers all over the world use the 'buddy system,' not only for protection from other humans, but also for aid in case of unexpected falls or other injuries.

In an emergency, call the police (☎ 911). In rural areas where ☎ 911 is not active, just dial '0' for the operator and ask for the police. Cities and larger towns have crisis centers and women's shelters that provide help and support; they are listed in the telephone directory, or the police can refer you to them.

Men may interpret a woman drinking alone in a bar as a bid for male company, whether you intend it that way or not. If you don't want the company, most men will respect a firm but polite 'no thank you.'

At night avoid straying from your car to flag down help; turn on your hazard lights, put up the hood and wait for the police to arrive. If you're planning extensive solo driving, consider renting a cellular phone (available from major car rental agencies) as an all-around extra precaution. Be extra careful at night on public transit, and remember to check the times of the last bus or train before you go out.

To deal with potential dangers, many women protect themselves with a whistle, mace, cayenne pepper spray or some karate training. Laws regarding sprays vary, so be informed based on your destination. It is a federal felony to carry pepper spray, due to its combustible design, on board an airplane.

Resources & Organizations

Women's bookstores are good places to find out about gatherings, readings and meetings, and they often have bulletin boards where you can find or place travel and short-term housing notices.

National resources with regional affiliates include:

National Organization for Women (NOW)
   A good resource for related information. The national center can refer you to state and local chapters. 1000 16th St NW, Suite 700, Washington, DC 20036 (☎ 202-331-0066)
Planned Parenthood
   Can refer you to clinics throughout the country and offer advice on medical issues. 810 Seventh Ave, New York, NY 10019 (☎ 212-541-7800)

Several well-established women's resources in Memphis serve as regional resources as well:

Center for Research on Women
   A resource center and clearinghouse for information for and about Southern women and women of color. University of Memphis, TN 38152 (☎ 901-678-2770)
Memphis Center for Reproductive Health
   Women's health clinic that also offers counseling and referrals. 1462 Poplar Ave, Memphis, TN 38104 (☎ 901-274-3550, outside Tennessee 800-843-9895)
Meristem Bookstore
   Books and more for women and their friends. 930 S Cooper, Memphis, TN 38104 (☎ 901-276-0282)

GAY & LESBIAN TRAVELERS

There are gay people everywhere in the USA, but those in the major cities are by far the most visible. In the cities and on both coasts it is easier for gay men and women to live their lives with a certain amount of openness. As you travel into the middle of the country it is much harder to be open. Gay travelers should be careful, *especially* in the rural areas where holding hands might get you bashed.

New Orleans has quite a large gay community which is centered in the lower French Quarter. People around greater New Orleans and the Gulf Coast are generally fairly open-minded about gays and lesbians.

In most of the Bible Belt, however, you might expect a reception ranging narrowly from intolerant to hostile. But it's hard to say; the South is full of contradictions. While the women at Camp Sister Spirit in Mississippi came under attack by locals when starting up, after years of maintaining a local food bank and clothes closet they're a welcome part of the community. Fellow tourists on one recent Natchez tour included a gay couple from California; the two men reported nothing but the most welcoming hospitality. Nashville, a fundamentalist Christian Shangri-la, seems surprisingly tolerant of the local gay population. As is true for all travelers to the South, a respectful attitude and a modest decorum are key, yet there's always the chance you'll run into reactionaries.

See the New Orleans chapter for local periodicals and resources for the gay and lesbian community.

Resources & Organizations

The Women's Traveller, which lists lesbian resources, and *Damron's Address Book* for men are both published by Damron Company (☎ 415-255-0404, 800-462-6654), PO Box 422458, San Francisco, CA 94142-2458. *Ferrari's Places for Women* and *Places for Men* are also useful. Neil Miller's *In Search of Gay America*, a book about gay and lesbian life across America in the 1980s, is a bit dated but gives a good view of life outside major cities.

The Gay Yellow Pages (☎ 212-674-0120), PO Box 533, Village Station, NY 10014-0533, has good national and regional editions.

Useful national resources include: National AIDS/HIV Hotline (☎ 800-342-2437), National Gay/Lesbian Task Force (☎ 202-332-6483 in Washington, DC) and Lambda Legal Defense Fund (☎ 212-995-8585 in New York City, 213-937-2728 in Los Angeles).

Regional resources include Camp Sister Spirit (☎ 601-344-2005), PO Box 12, Ovett, MS 39462, a feminist educational retreat center in southeastern Mississippi (camping and dorm beds available for $15 to $20 a night including communal meals). The South's oldest gay bookstore is the Faubourg Marigny Book Store (☎ 504-942-9875) in New Orleans at 600 Frenchman St. The *Pink Pages of Greater New Orleans*

is a free bimonthly guide to gay and lesbian businesses, entertainment, hotels and guesthouses. The New Orleans AIDS task force hotline is ☎ 504-944-2437, 800-992-4379.

DISABLED TRAVELERS

Travel within the US is becoming easier for people with disabilities. Public buildings are now required by law to be wheelchair accessible and have accommodating restrooms, and transportation must be made accessible to all. Telephone companies are required to provide relay operators for the hearing impaired. The most compliance is found in federal facilities and in modern and newly renovated properties in larger cities. Look to chain motels for the most modern accessible rooms and fully equipped suites. Many banks now provide ATM instructions in Braille. Major car rental agencies in larger cities offer hand-controlled models at no extra charge.

All major airlines, Greyhound buses and Amtrak trains allow service animals to accompany passengers and frequently sell two-for-one packages when attendants of seriously disabled passengers are required. Airlines will also provide assistance for connecting, boarding and deplaning the flight – just ask for assistance when making your reservation. (Note: airlines must accept wheelchairs as checked baggage and have an onboard chair available, though some advance notice may be required on smaller aircraft.)

Of course, the more populous the area, the greater the likelihood of facilities for the disabled. But the South has few big, modern cities, so it's important to call ahead to see what is available. Some of the best attractions in the South are historic buildings including house museums and B&B lodging, and these are not generally handicap accessible, or may have only select accessible rooms.

Resources & Organizations

A number of organizations and tour providers specialize in the needs of disabled travelers (see also the Internet directory):

Access-Able Travel Source
Online information for disabled travelers, with extensive links to other Internet sites (Net).

Mobility International USA
Advises disabled travelers on mobility issues. It primarily runs an educational exchange program. PO Box 10767, Eugene, OR 97440 (☎ 541-343-1284, fax 541-343-6812, Net)

Moss Rehabilitation Hospital's
Travel Information Service
1200 W Tabor Rd, Philadelphia, PA 19141-3099 (☎ 215-456-9600, TTY 456-9602)

SATH
Society for the Advancement of Travel for the Handicapped, 347 Fifth Ave, No 610, New York, NY 10016 (☎ 212-447-7284)

Twin Peaks Press
A quarterly newsletter; also publishes directories and access guides. PO Box 129, Vancouver, WA 98666 (☎ 360-694-2462, 800-637-2256)

Some regional resources and places of special interest: Helen Keller's hometown of Tuscumbia (near Florence, Alabama) opens her home to public tours and sponsors a festival in honor of Annie Sullivan's famous student every June. You can reach the Alabama Institute for the Deaf and Blind at ☎ 205-761-3206.

SENIOR TRAVELERS

Culturally, elders are more venerated in the South than in many other regions of the US, and consequently many seniors particularly enjoy the respectful and welcoming reception they generally receive. The usually mild climate, low prices, golf courses and extensive camping opportunities for RVs also appeal to many seniors. A 1995 tourism study revealed that one-third of the visitors to Mississippi, for example, were over the age of 50.

Senior travelers can find many discounts at hotels, campgrounds, restaurants, parks, museums and other attractions. The age at which senior discounts apply generally starts at 50, though it more commonly applies to those 65 or older. Be sure to inquire about discount rates when you make your reservation.

Visitors to national parks and campgrounds can cut costs greatly by using the 'Golden Age Passport'; see NPS under Useful Organizations below.

Resources & Organizations

National advocacy groups that can help in planning your travels include the following:

American Association of Retired Persons
AARP is an advocacy group for Americans 50 years and older and is a good resource for travel bargains. US residents can get one-year/three-year memberships for $8/20. Citizens of other countries can get the same memberships for $10/24. 601 E St NW, Washington, DC 20049 (☎ 800-424-3410)

Elderhostel
This organization is a nonprofit that encourages travel through scholarship. The programs, which are conducted throughout the Deep South, last one to three weeks and include meals and accommodations; they are open to people 55 years and older and their companions. The cost is extremely reasonable. The organization also has service programs in association with Habitat for Humanity. Write to 75 Federal St, Boston, MA 02110-1941 (☎ 617-426-8056)

Grand Circle Travel
This group offers escorted tours and travel information in a variety of formats. 347 Congress St, Boston, MA 02210 (☎ 617-350-7500, fax 617-350-6206)

National Council of Senior Citizens
Membership in this group (you needn't be a US citizen) gives access to added Medicare insurance, a mail-order prescription service and a variety of discount information and travel-related advice. Fees are $13/30/150 for one year/three years/lifetime. 1331 F St NW, Washington DC, 20004 (☎ 202-347-8800)

TRAVEL WITH CHILDREN

The Deep South is an exceptionally family-friendly destination with many discounts, services, facilities and attractions designed to entertain kids, including such considerate touches as high chairs on wheels at cafeterias. Some casinos feature elaborate child-care rooms. Attitudes toward children and parents are generally welcoming and understanding. Note that Southern children address adults as Sir or Ma'am as a sign of respect; Southerners would be pleased to hear visiting children do the same. Southerners like to offer candy to children; some may pat children on the head.

Though New Orleans is typically considered an adult playground, many city attractions are designed for kids and families, including the zoo and children's museum. Check with B&Bs for age restrictions (see Accommodations below).

For general information, see Lonely Planet's *Travel with Children* by Maureen Wheeler.

USEFUL ORGANIZATIONS
American Automobile Association
For its members, AAA provides great travel information, distributes free road maps and guidebooks and sells American Express traveler's checks without commission. The AAA membership card will often get you discounts for accommodations, car rental and admission charges. If you plan to do a lot of driving – even in a rental car – it is usually worth joining AAA. It costs $56 for the first year and $39 for subsequent years.

Members of other auto clubs, like the Automobile Association in the UK, are entitled to the same services if they bring their membership cards and/or a letter of introduction.

AAA also provides emergency roadside service to members in the event of an accident or breakdown or if you lock your keys in the car. Service is free within a given radius of the nearest service center, and service providers will tow your car to a mechanic if they can't fix it. The nationwide toll-free roadside assistance number is ☎ 800-222-4357 (800-AAA-HELP). All major cities and many smaller towns have a AAA office where you can start membership.

National Park Service & US Forest Service
The federal government controls public lands through at least two groups. The National Park Service (NPS) administrates the use of designated national parks. The US Forestry Service (USFS) administrates the use of designated national forests. National forests are less protected than parks, allowing commercial use (including logging and mining) of some areas.

National park campground and reservations information can be obtained by calling ☎ 800-365-2267 (Net) or writing to National Park Service Public Inquiry, Dept of Interior, PO Box 37127, Washington, DC 20013-7127.

Current information about national forests can be obtained from ranger stations, which are listed in the text. National forest campground and reservation information can be obtained by calling ☎ 800-280-2267.

General information about other publicly owned land is available from each state's Fish & Wildlife Service.

Golden Passports You can apply in person for any of the following Golden Passports at any national park or regional office of the USFS or NPS.

Golden Eagle Passports cost $50 annually and offer one-year entry into national parks to the holder and accompanying guests.

Golden Age Passports are free and allow US residents 62 years and older unlimited entry to all sites in the national park system, with discounts on camping and other fees.

Golden Access Passports offer the same to US residents who are medically blind or permanently disabled.

DANGERS & ANNOYANCES
Personal Security & Theft
Although street crime is a serious issue in large urban areas, most notably New Orleans, visitors need not be obsessed with security.

Always lock cars and put valuables out of sight, whether leaving the car for a few minutes or longer, and whether you are in a town or in the remote backcountry. Make sure you rent a car with a lockable trunk. If your car is bumped from behind in a remote area, it's best to keep going to a well-lit area or service station.

Be aware of your surroundings and who may be watching you. Avoid walking on dimly lit streets at night, particularly when alone. Walk purposefully. Avoid unnecessary displays of money or jewelry. Try to use ATMs in well-trafficked areas.

In hotels, don't leave valuables lying around your room. Use safety-deposit boxes or at least place valuables in a locked bag. Don't open your door to strangers – check the peephole or call the front desk if unexpected guests try to enter.

Visitors to New Orleans should be aware of the city's reputation for high crime. As in cities throughout the world, the majority of crimes occur in the poorest neighborhoods among local residents.

Guns The USA has a widespread reputation, partly true but also propagated and exaggerated by the media, as a dangerous place because of the availability of firearms. Guns do play a significant role in the lives of a hunting and self-protecting rural culture throughout the Deep South. Many people own guns, and some people may carry guns.

When walking in the woods during hunting seasons (generally fall and winter; inquire locally), rangers recommend hikers wear 'blaze' orange vests.

EMERGENCY
Throughout most of the USA, dial ☎ 911 for emergency service of any sort. This is a free call from any phone. Rural phones might not have this service, in which case dial 0 for the operator and ask for emergency assistance – it's still free. Each state also maintains toll-free numbers for traffic information and emergencies.

Lost or Stolen Documents
Carry a photocopy of your passport separately from your passport. Copy the pages with your photo and personal details, passport number and US visa. If it is lost or stolen, this will make replacing it easier. In this event, you should call your embassy.

Similarly, carry copies of your traveler's check numbers and credit card numbers.

LEGAL MATTERS
If you are stopped by the police for any reason, bear in mind that there is no system of paying fines on the spot. For traffic offenses, the police officer will explain your options to you. Attempting to pay the fine to the officer is frowned upon at best and may compound your troubles by resulting in a charge of bribery. Should the officer decide that you should pay up front, the officer can exercise his or her authority and take you directly to the magistrate instead of allowing you the usual 30-day period to pay the fine.

If you are arrested for more serious offenses, you are allowed to remain silent. There is no legal reason to speak to a police officer if you don't wish, but never walk away from an officer until given permission. All persons who are arrested are legally allowed (and given) the right to make one phone call. If you don't have a lawyer or family member to help you, call your embassy. The police will give you the number upon request.

Drinking & Driving Laws
Each state has its own laws, and what is legal in one state may be illegal in others. Some general rules are that you must be at least 16 years of age to drive (older in some states). Seat belts and motorcycle and bicycle helmets must be worn in most states.

Speed limits are 65 mph on interstates and freeways unless otherwise posted. Speed limits on other highways are 55 mph or less. In cities, limits vary from 25 to 45 mph. In small towns, driving over the posted speed by any amount may attract attention. Watch for school zones, which can be as low as 15 mph during school hours – these limits are strictly enforced and result in very costly tickets should you be pulled over for exceeding them.

The drinking age is 21 and you need an ID (identification with your photograph on it) to prove your age. Drinking and driving is a serious offense; you could incur stiff fines, jail time and penalties if caught driving under the influence of alcohol (called 'D-U-I' or 'DWI'). It is illegal to even carry an open container of alcohol in a car. In Tennessee, a driver found to be DUI with a child under 12 in the car could be charged with felony child endangerment. During some holidays and special events, road blocks are sometimes set up to deter drunk drivers.

BUSINESS HOURS & PUBLIC HOLIDAYS

While in New Orleans business hours may be seasonal or casual and a few establishments operate around the clock, in the rest of the region standard US business hours prevail. Public and private office hours are normally 9 am to 5 pm weekdays (Monday through Friday). Most stores are open Monday through Saturday, from 10 am to around 6 pm, or later in big cities or shopping malls. Some convenience stores or fuel stations may be open 24 hours, usually in the larger cities or at interstate freeway exits.

In the South, most businesses are closed Sunday. Even tourist-oriented businesses and attractions are usually closed Sunday morning. Many tourist-oriented restaurants and shops may stay open weekends but then close Monday or Tuesday.

On major holidays expect celebrations, parades or observances, and be prepared for the closure of banks, federal and state offices.

January 1
  New Year's Day
Third Monday in January
  Martin Luther King Jr Day
January 19
  Robert E Lee's Birthday
47 days before Easter
  Mardi Gras (New Orleans and Gulf Coast)
Third Monday in February
  Presidents' Day
First Sunday after a full moon in March or April
  Easter
April 26
  Confederate Memorial Day
Last Monday in May
  Memorial Day
First Monday in June
  Jefferson Davis' Birthday
July 4
  Independence Day
First Monday in September
  Labor Day
Second Monday in October
  Columbus Day
November 11
  Veterans' Day
Fourth Thursday in November
  Thanksgiving
December 25
  Christmas

SPECIAL EVENTS

Beyond holiday celebrations that accompany the dates above, the region also celebrates many events geared around the life of the Deep South. For a taste of the region's folk culture, don't bypass an opportunity to attend a local turkey-calling contest, barbecue cookoff, rattlesnake rodeo, mullet toss, catfish-eating contest or county or state fair.

See the destination chapters for more events and complete information on those mentioned below.

Regional Calendar

Fans of Elvis will note a surge of activity at Elvis shrines in Tupelo and Memphis around the King's January 8 birthday and the anniversary of his death on August 16.

Extended house and garden tours, led by guides in period costume, are known as

---

Future Mardi Gras Dates

Mardi Gras can occur on any Tuesday from February 3 to March 9, depending on the date of Easter. Here are the dates for the next few years:

1999	February 16
2000	March 7
2001	February 27
2002	February 12
2003	March 4
2004	February 24

'pilgrimages.' The gardens are best seen in full bloom in springtime, though fall is also nice.

Jubilee is a rare phenomenon in which crabs, fish, shrimp and other sea life swim to the shallow waters along the eastern shore of Mobile Bay, Alabama. Local residents put out the call for Jubilee! and run to the shore to gather buckets full of fresh seafood. The exact date is not predictable, but it generally occurs two to five times a year between June and September.

January
Elvis' Birthday
This is celebrated in the King's hometown, Tupelo, MS, during a weeklong festival around January 8. In Memphis, Elvis fans will also find weeklong tributes, including all-night candlelight vigils near the grave at Graceland.

February
Mardi Gras
New Orleans is nationally known for this celebration and the carnival season of parades, balls and social events that precedes it. Mardi Gras is also celebrated throughout south Louisiana, most notably in Cajun Country. In Mississippi, it's celebrated along the coast, principally in Biloxi. Mobile, AL, has the country's oldest Mardi Gras celebration with smaller, more manageable and more family-oriented parades than in New Orleans.

Africatown Folk Festival
This is organized by the descendants of the *Clotilde*, the last known slave ship to arrive in the US. The festival honors folk arts and traditions of African Americans in Mobile, Alabama.

Azalea Trail
Colorful azaleas are ablaze from February to March – numerous events celebrate this flower in Mobile, Alabama.

March
Cajun Crawfish Festival
This is held in Biloxi, Mississippi.
pilgrimage tours
Antebellum mansions are open for public tours in Natchez, Vicksburg and Holly Springs, Mississippi, and in Mobile and Selma, Alabama.

Tennessee Williams Literary Festival
This is held the last weekend of the month in New Orleans.

April
Catfish Festival
This occurs the first Saturday of the month in Belzoni, Mississippi.
MLK Memorial March
The anniversary of the assassination of Dr Martin Luther King Jr is remembered with this march on April 4 in Memphis.
French Quarter Festival
New Orleans hosts this event, which features bands on 12 stages during the second weekend of the month.
Festival International de Louisiane
French-speaking cultures celebrate with six days of music and performing arts in Lafayette, Louisiana.
Landing of D'Iberville
This folksy reenactment of the 1699 landing takes place in Biloxi, Mississippi.
Civil War reenactments
Several of these occur in April: the Battle of Mobile Bay assembles the troops at Fort Gaines (Dauphin Island), Alabama; the Battle of Selma brings them to Selma, Alabama.
pilgrimage tours
These include historic homes in the Alabama towns of Eufaula, Marion, Huntsville, Talladega, Tuscaloosa, and Athens.
Tin Pan South
This tribute to songwriters is a major musical event in Nashville.
New Orleans Jazz & Heritage Festival
This is New Orleans' second-largest draw. 'Jazz Fest' is held over two weekends in late April and early May.

May
Memphis in May Festival
This is held mid-month and includes a barbecue cook-off and the Beale St Music Festival.
Crawfish Festival
With Cajun music, crawfish-eating contests and mudbug races, this takes place in Breaux Bridge, Louisiana.
pilgrimage tours
These are sponsored in Prattville and Cullman, Alabama.
Mississippi Crossroads Blues Festival
This is held the last Saturday of the month in Greenwood, Mississippi.
Siege of Vicksburg
This is commemorated with reenactments in late May in Mississippi.
Gospel Jubilee
This is held on Memorial Day weekend at Opryland in Nashville.

June

Hank Williams Fest

Fans get together with country music stars for this tribute to the late singer in Evergreen, Alabama.

TNN Country Awards

These are held at Opryland in Nashville.

International Country Music Fan Fair

This is held mid-month in Nashville.

Chet Atkin's Musician Days

This tribute to session musicians is held in late June in Nashville.

Helen Keller Festival

This takes place during the last weekend of June, opening the two-month seasonal production of *The Miracle Worker* at Ivy Green, Alabama.

July

Memphis Music & Heritage Festival

This major three-day cultural and musical event is held the second weekend of the month in Memphis.

Choctaw Indian Fair

Traditional dances and costumes are a highlight of this festival held late July in Philadelphia, Mississippi.

Faulkner Conference

This is held in late July/early August in Oxford, Mississippi.

August

Louisiana Shrimp & Petroleum Festival

This is held in Morgan City, Louisiana.

Sunflower Blues Festival

This takes place the first weekend in August in Clarksdale, Mississippi.

Elvis Tribute

The anniversary of Elvis' death on August 16 inspires a week-long tribute. Events include all-night candlelight vigils at the grave at Graceland in Memphis.

Civil War reenactment

The encampment and siege at Fort Morgan (Gulf Shores), Alabama, occurs this month.

Creek War reenactment

The Indian attack that signaled the beginning of the Creek Indian War of 1813 is remembered this month at Fort Mims (Bay Minette), Alabama.

WC Handy Music Festival

Celebrating the 'Father of the Blues', this festival highlights jam sessions and concerts in Florence, Alabama.

Bluegrass Festival

This takes place at the Central Alabama Music Park in Jemison, Alabama.

September

Gospel Jubilee

This is held at Opryland over Labor Day weekend in Nashville.

Civil War reenactment

An encampment that re-creates the Union occupation occurs in early September in Nashville.

Southwest Louisiana Zydeco Festival

The premier zydeco event in the world, this features a 13-hour concert in Plaisance, Louisiana.

Festivals Acadiens

The foremost Cajun festival celebrates with music, food and traditional Acadian crafts in Lafayette, Louisiana.

September Skirmish

This Civil War reenactment takes place in Decatur, Alabama.

Mississippi Delta Blues Festival

This is held the third weekend of the month in Greenville, Mississippi.

Louisiana Sugar Cane Festival

This is held at the end of September in New Iberia, Louisiana.

Tennessee State Fair

Held in Nashville, this fair features livestock and midway rides.

October

Moundville Native American Festival

Native American heritage is celebrated with dancing, crafts demonstrations and traditional foods. It's held the first week of the month at the University of Alabama's Moundville Archaeological Park, 20 miles south of Tuscaloosa, Alabama.

Alligator Festival

Franklin, Louisiana hosts this festival.

Louisiana Folklife Festival

The state's finest musicians are showcased the second week of the month in Monroe, Louisiana.

BB King's Homecoming

This is marked in Indianola, Mississippi.

King Biscuit Blues Festival

This takes place the second weekend in Helena, Arkansas (neighbor to Indianola, Mississippi).

Tennessee Williams Festival

This features readings and performances mid-month in Clarksdale, Mississippi.

Rice Festival

This festival is held mid-month in Crowley, Louisiana.

Mullet Festival
  The highlight of this festival held mid-month at the Gulf Coast in Gautier, Mississippi, is a mullet toss.

Fall Muster
  This 'gathering of troops,' is held at the former home of Confederate president Jefferson Davis in Biloxi, Mississippi.

National Shrimp Festival
  Nearly 200,000 visitors flock to Gulf Shores, Alabama, for this festival.

pilgrimage tours
  Antebellum homes are open for inspection in Natchez, Mississippi.

Kentuck Festival
  One of the South's biggest arts and crafts festivals, this has everything from storytelling and jazz to blacksmithing and quilting; it's held the third weekend of the month in Northport/Tuscaloosa, Alabama.

Tale Tellin' Festival
  Storytellers from around the South gather in the 'Tale Tellin' Capital of Alabama,' Selma, Alabama.

Mid-South Fair
  This is held in late September in Memphis.

Halloween
  On October 31, this is grandly celebrated in New Orleans.

November

Celebration of the Giant Omelet
  This involves more than 5000 eggs in Abbeville, Louisiana.

Country Christmas
  Opryland in Nashville hosts events and is specially decorated from November 1 till Christmas.

December

Christmas
  Bonfires along the Mississippi River levees light the way through Louisiana's Plantation Country. There's a Christmas boat parade in Biloxi, Mississippi. Graceland is specially lit for Christmas in Memphis.

pilgrimage tours
  Antebellum homes are open for tours in the second part of the month in Natchez, MS.

ACTIVITIES

The most common mainstream outdoor activities in the Deep South are fishing, hunting and golfing, followed by camping aboard RVs and boating. This leaves less-common pursuits, such as sea kayaking, river-running, mountain biking and backpacking, uncrowded. While recreational equipment and supplies for these activities can be found in the larger cities, rentals elsewhere are scarce.

Beach swimming, sunbathing, boating and saltwater fishing are popular along the Gulf Coast in Mississippi and Alabama. The most pristine and deserted beaches are found on Mississippi's Gulf Islands, which require a 12-mile sea kayak ride through the relatively calm Mississippi Sound to get there. Primitive camping is allowed on the protected islands. There is no scuba or surfing activity to speak of along the coast.

The 440-mile Natchez Trace Parkway is a well-known bicycle-touring corridor between Natchez and Nashville (see Getting Around).

For Louisiana outdoor adventures, Pack & Paddle (☎ 318-232-5854, 800-458-4560), in Lafayette, organizes biking, kayaking, canoeing and hiking trips. They rent equipment, distribute maps and guides, and host classes in kayaking, backpacking and in-line skating.

Off-road biking trails can be found in the region's national forests, but forest service roads themselves are also well suited for mountain or dirt biking. Contact the USFS (see Useful Organizations above) or see national forest listings in state chapters.

Backpacking opportunities are scattered but available. In Louisiana, Chicot State Park maintains a backpacking loop around a lake in Cajun Country, while the Kisatchie National Forest has many areas around the state with forested terrain. In Mississippi, the Black Creek Trail runs along a designated 'wild and scenic' river corridor. In Alabama the 102-mile Pinhoti Trail is the state's longest and most popular trail.

Hiking trails throughout the region offer a variety of terrain, from bayou to beach to woodlands to canyons. National forests, along with state parks, offer some of the most developed trails in each state. National wildlife refuges offer the best chance to see local wildlife (particularly birds along the Mississippi Flyway) in a variety of peaceful settings – from the coastal marshes of the Sabine refuge in southwestern Louisiana or the Sandhill Crane refuge on the Mississippi Gulf Coast to the Noxubee refuge in northeastern Mississippi or the Eufala refuge in southeastern Alabama.

Boating is particularly popular through the wetlands in the southern part of the region. While independent travelers might enjoy wandering around the area's swamps and bayous on their own, everyone should take a guided tour as a window to the local culture. See Cajun Country chapter for more information. The Pearl River, near Bogalusa in Louisiana, offers a chance to canoe through a protected wildlife management area of cypress and tupelo swamp and hardwood forest. In Mississippi, local outfitters run trips down the wild and scenic Black Creek River in the Mississippi Gulf Coast region.

The cave region in TAG country (at the intersection of Tennessee, Alabama, and Georgia) is a nationally known destination for spelunkers. The National Speleological Society (☎ 205-852-1300), 2813 Cave Ave, Huntsville, AL 35810, can provide detailed information. (Also see Fort Payne, Alabama, for local outfitters.)

WORK

The USFS puts volunteers to work as campground hosts and forest hands. Each state has its own USFS headquarters; the regional Southern USFS Information Center is in Atlanta (☎ 404-347-2384), 1720 Peachtree Rd NW, Atlanta, GA 30367.

In New Orleans, many bars and restaurants hire seasonal labor – many get desperate for reliable help during carnival and Jazz Fest. Year-round, you can push a mobile hot dog cart for Lucky Dogs (☎ 504-523-9260), 517 Gravier.

If you're not a US citizen, you'll need to apply for a work visa from the US embassy in your home country before you leave. The type of visa varies depending on how long you're staying and the kind of work you plan to do. Generally, you'll need

either a J-1 visa, which you can obtain by joining a visitor-exchange program, or an H-2B visa, which you get when being sponsored by a US employer. The latter is not easy to obtain (since the employer has to prove that no US citizen or permanent resident can do the job); the former is issued mostly to students for work in summer camps.

ACCOMMODATIONS

Of the many types of overnight accommodations available in the Deep South – from a state park cabin in the woods to a luxurious suite overlooking the French Quarter – perhaps the most distinctive lodging the region has to offer is in historic homes transformed into B&Bs and inns.

Budget travelers can find plenty of roadside chain motels for comfortably predictable accommodations.

It's a general rule of thumb that visiting cities on the weekends and the country during the week helps keep costs down, but many other factors (festivals and seasonal appeal are two) also come into play. During peak seasons or festivals, it's wise to reserve well in advance to get your first choice. This is particularly true of B&Bs and inns. Prices in this guide can only be an approximate guideline at best. Also, be prepared to add room tax. Children often stay free with their parents, but rules for this vary; inquire if traveling with a family.

The prices advertised are called 'rack rates' and are not written in stone. If you simply ask about any specials that might apply, you can often save quite a bit of money. Booking through a travel agent also saves. Members of AARP or AAA can qualify for a discount at several chains.

Reservations

Among the many motel and hotel chains in the USA, the level of quality and style tends to be consistent throughout the chain. For some chains, frequent-guest programs offer discounts and guaranteed reservations.

The cheapest bottom-end hotels and motels may not accept reservations, but at least phone from the road to see what's available; even if they don't take reservations, they'll often hold a room for an hour or two.

Normally, you have to give a credit-card number to make a room reservation. If you don't show and don't call to cancel, you will be charged the first night's rental. Cancellation policies vary, so find out when you book. Make sure to let the place know if you plan on a late arrival – many will give your room away if you haven't arrived or called by 6 pm.

Reservationists at toll-free numbers might not be aware of local special discounts and availability. The reservation numbers of some of the best known chains are:

Best Western	☎ 800-528-1234
Comfort Inn, Sleep Inn	☎ 800-221-2222
Days Inn	☎ 800-329-7466
E-Z 8 Motels	☎ 800-326-6835
Econo Lodge, Rodeway Inn	☎ 800-424-4777
Howard Johnson	☎ 800-446-4656
Motel 6	☎ 800-466-8356
Super 8 Motel	☎ 800-800-8000
Travelodge	☎ 800-578-7878

Hostels
There is only one hostel affiliated with HI-AYH in the region – in New Orleans (see city chapter). An independent hostel operates in Memphis.

Camping
Camping is the cheapest, and can be the most enjoyable, approach to a vacation. Visitors with an RV – or a car and a tent or jungle hammock – can take advantage of hundreds of private and public campgrounds and RV parks at prices of $10 per night or even less.

National wilderness areas offer the most natural and rugged camping adventures in the Deep South. If you can get a boat out (or sea kayak), you can camp out on the Gulf Islands off the Mississippi Coast.

National parks maintain impressive campgrounds often in beautiful areas. The campground in Davis Bayou near Ocean Springs, Mississippi, the mainland component of the Gulf Islands National Seashore, is a particularly nice spot. Wooded campgrounds along the Natchez Trace Parkway are also scenic and well maintained.

National forests in all Deep South states provide primitive campsites – tables, grills, drinking water, vault toilets, some cold showers – for around $6 a night. These are first-come, first-served, and the maximum stay is 14 nights. You may also camp anywhere in the national forest unless posted otherwise; no fee or permit is required.

State park campgrounds are more developed, often with flush toilets and hot showers, some with hookups and disposal stations, in addition to access to the park's other facilities. Most are first-come, first-served. Fees vary slightly depending on location and equipment – higher for hookups, lower for walk-in sites – but are generally around $10 (senior discounts available). Of the Deep South states, Louisiana and Alabama maintain the nicest state park facilities. Mississippi's facilities are shabby by comparison (with office trailers where the other states have fancy visitor centers), but will likely appeal to those who like their natural areas only lightly touched and not overdeveloped or interpreted.

County parks or recreational areas may also offer camping; facilities vary considerably but are not likely plush.

Private campgrounds may run the gamut, but are most often on the 'camping resort' side of things, including developed sites, RV hookups and usually some other amenities, such as a swimming pool, a stocked trout pond or even hayrides. These can climb to rates of around $20. Kampgrounds of America (KOA) is a national network of private campgrounds with sites usually ranging from $12 to $15, depending on hookups. You can get the annual directory of KOA sites by calling or writing: KOA (☎ 406-248-7444), PO Box 30558, Billings, MT 59114-0558.

Low-end camping can be found in funky low-cost fish camps throughout the region, usually on private land near small marinas or boat launches at the shore of the region's lakes.

Many of the lakes are reservoirs that are managed by the Army Corps of Engineers or the local utility company. Facilities tend to be well maintained but often sterile, more suited for RV anglers than back-to-the-land types.

To make reservations at national, state and local parks, you must pay with Visa, MasterCard or Discover. If you know what state park or national forest campground you'd like to stay at, call ☎ 800-280-2267 for reservations. For sites in national parks, call Destinet at ☎ 800-365-2267.

A Note on Camping When camping in an undeveloped area, choose a campsite at least 200 yards (approximately 70 adult steps) from water and wash up at camp, not in the stream, using biodegradable soap. Dig a six-inch-deep hole to use as a latrine and cover and camouflage it well when leaving the site. Burn toilet paper, unless fires are prohibited. Carry out all trash. Use a portable charcoal grill or camping stove; don't build new fires. If there already is a fire ring, use only dead and downed wood or wood you have carried in yourself. Make sure to leave the campsite as you found it.

Even though developed areas usually have toilets and drinking water, it is always a good idea to have a few gallons of water when venturing out to the boonies.

Cabins
Renting a cabin for a week or two is popular for families in the Deep South, but not particularly easy for those who do not live in the region, except at state park cabins. Most state parks offer cabin rentals that can accommodate eight to 12 people; prices are extremely reasonable. These are no shacks – they usually have central heating and air-conditioning, and they supply all the necessary dishware, cookware and linens. Some were built by the Civilian Conservation Corps in the 1930s; these CCC-built stone-and-wood cabins are the most desirable picks today. But because of their popularity

and low rates, cabins may be booked up months in advance.

Local chambers of commerce generally maintain listings of private cabins available for short-term rental. Note that since many cabins are outfitted to accommodate families, some bedrooms are likely to have twin rather than double beds and may not be suitable for several couples traveling together.

Motels
Motels with $20 rates can be found, especially in small towns on major highways and in the motel strips of larger towns. At this price the beds will likely sag, the decor and furnishings will be worn, heat or air-con may be uneven, and the odor of disinfectant or incense may be powerful.

The consistently cheapest national chain is Motel 6. Rooms start in the low $30s for a single in smaller towns, in the $40s in larger towns. They usually charge a flat $6 for each extra person. Super 8, Days Inn or Econo Lodge are a little more expensive. These provide basic clean rooms with TVs, phone and private bath; most have pools.

Stepping up to chains with rates in the $45 to $80 range (depending on location), you'll find nicer rooms; cafes, restaurants or bars may be on the premises; the swimming pool may be indoors with a spa or exercise room also available. Best Western, La Quinta, Comfort Inn and Sleep Inn are in this category.

Some of even the cheapest motels may advertise kitchenettes. These may cost a few dollars more but give you the chance to cook a simple meal for yourself. Kitchenettes vary from a two-ring burner to a spiffy little mini-kitchen and may or may not have utensils. If you plan on doing a lot of kitchenette cooking, carry your own set.

Hotels
Besides New Orleans and casino hotels, most city hotels in the region will be geared to business travelers. Such chains as Marriott and Sheraton provide rooms from $80 a night; in larger cities prices are higher. These may include health clubs

with sauna and hot tub, room service and restaurants and taverns on the premises. Casino hotels along the Mississippi River and at the Gulf Coast provide nicer rooms than non-gaming hotels (they expect to make up the difference in the casino).

Inns & B&Bs

European visitors should be aware that North American B&Bs are much less the casual, inexpensive sort of accommodations found on the continent or in Britain. Many wonderfully preserved historic homes in the Deep South now serve as inns or B&Bs, offering visitors a personal up-close look at the architectural and cultural heritage of the South. These accommodations can vary widely, from a hotel-like inn with many guests and little personal contact to a home-like experience where your hosts live in the property and treat you as their personal guests. Particularly in the South, with its reputation for hospitality, hosts are often eager to lavish attention on their guests, and they will regale them with stories if offered the opportunity.

The nature of the rooms may also vary widely – some inns have all the modern conveniences (private baths, TV, phones, heat and air-conditioning), others maintain a historic authenticity (shared baths, no TV or phone, ceiling fans, quirky plumbing and the like). They may be furnished with period reproductions or antiques. Rates range widely, from $50 for a weeknight stay at a small place to $200 for an all-out historic plantation house.

Be aware that B&B conditions may vary considerably. Some welcome small children, while others have an age minimum, usually around 12 years. Most B&Bs prohibit smoking, if not entirely, at least in rooms. A continental or full Southern breakfast is almost always included, but other meals may be provided as well. Check whether a certain room (view, private bath) can be reserved, or if room choice is on a first-come, first-served basis. Finally, find out whether credit cards, personal or traveler's checks are accepted, or if payment is by cash only.

FOOD

Southern-style American cuisine is found throughout the region, along with traditional American foods. It's inexpensive – fine dining in New Orleans being the exception – and you're served lots of it. Southerners take their time preparing and serving meals, and the local preference seems to be for food served less than piping hot.

Restaurants serve breakfast from around 6 to 11 am; some budget motels put out a simple complimentary breakfast bar (juice, pastries, cold cereals) from around 7 to 9 am, which can be a good way to save time as well as money. Otherwise, standard breakfast choices range from a Danish and coffee for under $2 to a full Southern breakfast of eggs, breakfast meat (bacon, ham or beef), 'grits' (a hot cereal of ground hominy seasoned with butter and salt) and biscuits-and-gravy, all for around $6 with juice and coffee. Several fast-food coffee shop chains, such as the Waffle House, offer breakfast around-the-clock.

Lunch is served from around 11:30 am to 2 or 3 pm; sandwiches, salads, hamburgers and other short orders for around $4 to $5 are common choices. At better restaurants, many lunch entrees are identical to their dinner choices but nearly half the cost (a $12 dinner plate might go for $7 at lunch). Many restaurants also serve all-you-can-eat lunch buffets, which are a good value for larger appetites.

Dinner is the largest meal of the day, starting around 6 pm (later in New Orleans, around 8 pm). Sunday dinner is eaten earlier, as early as noon. Many restaurants close early that day, around 2, 3, or 4 pm; visitors whose timing is off may be stranded. The regional custom is to go out to a restaurant after church, so Sunday dress is the standard attire (though not required). Some city hotels and restaurants offer elaborate Sunday brunch buffets, but many restaurants are closed until midday.

Budget travelers will want to seek out farmers markets for the freshest produce at the lowest prices. Grocery stores and deli counters commonly offer prepared foods for take-out bargains. Restaurants offer discounts on meals for children and seniors, sometimes also for military and clergy in uniform.

Regional chain restaurants offer a healthier and more regionally distinctive alternative to standard American fast food; cafeterias in particular are often just as cheap and quick (and you can see what looks good before ordering). Two that are good and reliable are Morrison's Cafeterias and Piccadilly Cafeterias; you can generally find them near shopping malls off freeway exits. For table service, there's the hick-themed Po' Folks and Cracker Barrel and the more upscale newcomer Black-eyed Pea.

Most restaurants offer the choice of nonsmoking and smoking areas; some prohibit smoking. Many restaurants are air-conditioned to the point of refrigeration; even if it's 100°F out, you might have a sweater handy for lunch.

Traditional Southern Cuisine

Classic Southern country-cookin' means heaps of crispy fried chicken, country-fried steak or hickory-smoked barbecue ribs, all served with several vegetables and your choice of a flaky biscuit or cornbread (called 'hushpuppies' when fried in small balls, or 'corn pone' if it's cylindrical or triangular). A 'meat-and-three' plate means you pick an entree and three vegetables from a list of choices.

If you can forgo the meat, an inexpensive 'vegetable plate' offers you the choice of three or four vegetables. Fried okra, corn-on-the-cob, black-eyed peas, and collard greens are typical selections. Strict vegetarians should ask if the vegetables have been cooked with meat products; many traditionally are.

Southerners have more of a sweet tooth than other Americans, so you will find such wonderful desserts as pecan pie, banana and bread pudding, and peach cobbler. Even meats and vegetables are sometimes laced with sugar, like honey-roasted ham and sweet potato souffle, for example.

Not only is the food unique and the portions larger in the South, but the style of service may differ from other regions. Luncheon and dinner buffets are common in the South (cafeterias are very popular), and many restaurants serve 'family-style,' seating unrelated groups at the same table to pass plates around and serve yourself. Note that many Southern families say a prayer before eating; restaurant patrons would not necessarily be expected to join in (guests *would* be expected to do so at a family's home) but it would be respectful to wait silently until they're done before serving or eating. Server tips are slightly lower at buffet-style and family-style restaurants (around 10%); at cafeterias it's kind to leave a tip for the table-clearer ($1 or $2).

Traditional soul food, the ethnic cuisine of African Americans, includes all the above plus exotic meats that were considered castoffs in slavery days, such as chitterlings (fried tripe, called 'chitlins') and pigs' feet. Okra was brought to the US from Africa by slaves.

A particularly revered Southern cuisine, barbecue can be made with smoked or marinated meat, which is grilled and then smothered in a tangy, spicy sauce. Pork is the he-man meat of choice (offered chopped, sliced, or in ribs), but barbecued chicken and beef are also widely available. 'Cue sauces can be mustard, vinegar or tomato-based (or a combination of all three; recipes are often closely guarded family secrets), and meats are usually served with a slice of white bread and a side of cole slaw or baked beans. The classic venue is a no-frills roadside stand with long picnic tables out front and a hickory-scented smoking chimney out back.

Seafood Specialties

The Gulf Coast is famous for its fleet-fresh fish and shellfish. Oysters, shrimp and mullet are usually served either on a you-crack-'em plate or prepared in a variety of dishes. Mullet was so popular as a substitute for scarce meat during WWII that it earned the name 'Biloxi bacon,' and still today an annual mullet festival honors the local mascot and features a mullet toss competition.

Creole & Cajun Cuisine

Creole and Cajun cuisines, two of the world's most unique, use ingredients and cooking styles that reflect the geography and history of Louisiana. For example, colonial chefs used the Native American technique of ground sassafras leaves (filé powder) as a thickener instead of flour. Africans introduced okra as well as rice and yams as potato substitutes. Spanish colonies throughout the Americas shared spicy peppers and sugar. German immigrants contributed sausage. Everyone, of course, found that the local fisheries provided an abundance for the settlers – they still do.

Many people are unaware of the differences between Creole and Cajun cooking. The two are very similar and share the use of filé powder and 'the holy trinity' of chopped celery, onion and green peppers. Creole cooking developed from French, Spanish and African cuisines and tends to use butter and cream heavily; gumbo is a Creole dish. Cajun cooking is derivative of French and Southern cuisines and tends to use lard (often pork), a roux (a mixture of flour and lard) for thickening, and is highly spiced; jambalaya is Cajun. An easy way to distinguish them is to identify Creole cooking with the city, and therefore more sophisticated, and Cajun cooking with the country, which tends to be more hearty. The confusion enters because both styles are often found on the same New Orleans or Cajun Country menu.

Spiciness, from onions and garlic to fresh hot peppers or bottled pepper sauces like Tabasco, gives either cuisine an unusual appeal. Staple dishes served with (or containing) white rice – gumbo, jambalaya, crawfish étouffée and red beans – are excellent and cheap and can be found in abundance throughout Louisiana.

DRINKS
Nonalcoholic Drinks

Most Americans start the day with a cup of coffee; in New Orleans and other major cities you can find espresso and its varieties (though Americans prefer weaker roasts than Europeans). Popular 'gourmet' coffees are flavored with such things as mint, anise, hazelnut and cinnamon. Brewed decaffeinated coffee is widely available.

Iced tea, sweetened or unsweetened with a slice of lemon, is considered the 'house wine' of the South. This is what they'll bring if you ask for 'tea.' If you want hot tea, you'll have to be specific. Coca-Cola, 7-Up, root beer and the like are also common choices; lemonade is a popular summer drink. Restaurants serve iced tap water (safe to drink) on request at no charge with a meal.

Alcoholic Drinks

Wine is commonly served at dinner but not exclusively so; in many places it isn't uncommon to drink only iced tea with dinner. Microbrewed beer is increasingly popular, and you'll find cozy brewpubs in most cities. Hard liquor is widely available; favorite drinks feature rum, gin, scotch or bourbon. In general, Southerners are not big consumers of alcohol, though the cities, and Louisiana as a whole, tend to be exceptions.

Beverage laws vary from state to state, and liquor sales in stores and restaurants may be restricted on Sunday throughout the region. 'Dry counties,' counties in which the sale of alcohol is illegal, are scattered throughout the region, but proliferate in Alabama. It's illegal to drive with open containers of alcohol in the car; drunk driving is a serious felony offense. Drinking alcohol outdoors is generally prohibited, but it's tolerated at festivals, on Bourbon St in New Orleans and on Beale St in Memphis.

The minimum drinking age throughout the region is 21, and photo identification (driver's license or passport) is often requested at stores and restaurants as proof of age (this ritual is called being 'carded'). Persons under 21 (minors) are not allowed to enter bars and pubs, even to order non-alcoholic beverages. Unfortunately, this means that most dance clubs are also off-limits to minors. Minors are, however, welcome in the dining areas of restaurants where alcohol may be served. That said, New Orleans is extremely lax about carding underage drinkers.

ENTERTAINMENT
Music & Clubs
From the bluesy homespun 'juke joints' of the Mississippi Delta to the barn dance atmosphere at the Grand Ole Opry to the outdoor New Orleans Jazz & Heritage Festival, you will find wonderful live music performed in a variety of inviting venues throughout the region – it's a primary draw for visitors.

Discos and nightclubs without live music often feature disc jockeys spinning records and inciting the crowd to dance. Bars and pubs sometimes feature juke-boxes and often set up pool tables or dart boards. However, take every opportunity to hear live music – it's widely available, diverse, regionally distinctive and usually inexpensive.

Performing Arts
New Orleans is the region's hub for cultural arts (see city chapter) – but it often falls short of international standards. In New Orleans as well as throughout the region, folk arts are the highlight. A few exceptions are worth noting.

Jackson hosts an international ballet competition every four years. This international affair, which brings famous dance companies from as far as Russia and Asia, lends renown to the local Jackson Ballet. In Montgomery, the Alabama Shakespeare Festival is nationally recognized. They perform repertory theater year-round and host an annual festival.

Performing arts troupes are organized in nearly every major city; colleges and universities also host performing arts events open to the public.

Gambling
Casinos can be found in Shreveport, along the Mississippi Gulf Coast and up the Mississippi River (in Natchez, Vicksburg and in Tunica County just south of Memphis). The casinos are open 24 hours a day, and only people age 21 or over are allowed entry. They're heralded by local promoters for bringing in employment, sales taxes and frequently other services as well (expanded transportation options, for example), and for visitors casinos often offer inexpensive lodging, entertainment, food and car rental.

SPECTATOR SPORTS
Sports are a way of life in the South. Folks root for their local team – whether it's major league, minor league, college or high school – with fierce loyalty. One of the best ways to experience local culture is to sit elbow to elbow with cheering fans of all ages at a local sporting event.

Some of favorite local attractions pay homage to sports heroes, notably in the sports halls of fame in Birmingham and Jackson. In Tuscaloosa a museum dedicated to the career of 'Bear' Bryant attests to the popularity of the former University of Alabama (U of A) football coach, who led the school to national notoriety.

Football
The New Orleans Saints play professional NFL football at the Superdome. Nashville will host NFL football in 1999.

Grambling University, a historically black school in Louisiana, remains home to Eddie Robinson, the winningest college football coach in the US. Other college teams in the state include Louisiana State University (LSU), Tulane and Southwestern Louisiana State University. Ole Miss has a competitive team. The U of A also attracts loyal crowds to games. The Sugar Bowl, an NCAA championship game, is played at the Superdome in New Orleans on New Year's Day.

Baseball
The region is not host to a major league team – but this makes attending a game all

the more fun. Minor league and college games are cheap, fun and a good way to experience a community.

The region's minor league baseball teams include the Jackson Generals, the Memphis Chicks, the New Orleans Zephyrs, the Shreveport Captains, the Mobile Bay-Bears, the Birmingham Barons and the Greenville Braves. Inquire at local chambers of commerce for schedules and game details.

As for college teams, the Bulldogs of Mississippi State University at Starkville are well known in the region. LSU, Tulane, Ole Miss and U of A also field respectable teams. In late February, college teams from Mississippi pair off against teams from Louisiana in the Winn-Dixie Showdown, a three-day series of doubleheaders in the Superdome.

Basketball

There are no professional basketball teams in the region.

Highly ranked women's collegiate basketball teams include the University of Tennessee, Ole Miss and Mississippi State University. Tulane, LSU and U of A have good teams also.

In men's college basketball, LSU is consistently highly ranked and notable as the former team of pro player Shaquille O'Neal. Other outstanding NCAA Division I men's teams include Ole Miss, Mississippi State University, Memphis State University and Tulane.

THINGS TO BUY

Traditional Southern crafts are available throughout the region – handmade quilts, pottery and baskets made from native materials, and woodworking from rough to fine.

Historic house museums often have nice little gift shops with a dainty collection of souvenirs, such as cotton boll wreaths or anything with a magnolia on it. Packages of gift-wrapped Southern food specialties available throughout the region make inexpensive souvenirs – it's easy to find fancy stone-ground grits in small canvas sacks, jars of local fruit preserves and syrups daintily topped with calico-print fabric, and colorful pickled relishes made of corn, cucumber and red pepper.

African crafts – masks, wooden figurines, as well as a variety of fine and folk arts – are produced by local African-American artists.

Textile companies in the region retain some outlet stores, but the low quality of goods makes them not worth going out of the way for.

Every city has its shopping mall, where you can find all the necessities – clothing, traveling supplies, recreational and sporting equipment, you name it.

Throughout the region you can sift through antique stores and flea markets for one-of-a-kind souvenirs – from refined crystal and china to dusty old washboards and hand-cranked coffee grinders. Prices may be negotiable for antiques.

Music recordings of bands you've heard are a great souvenir; tapes and CDs can be cheaper if bought at the venue than in stores.

New Orleans has wonderfully weird things to buy: voodoo charms, amulets, beads, feathered Mardi Gras masks, Cajun spices and cookbooks, street art, handmade accordions, alligator skulls – stuff you can't imagine.

Getting There & Away

The two most common ways to reach the Deep South are by air and by car, but you can also get there by train and by bus. Most US travelers from the Midwest, mid-Atlantic states and Great Plains states will simply drive their own cars to visit the Deep South (provided they have air-conditioning); travelers from outside this general radius will likely fly in, then rent a car.

No matter how you're traveling, make sure you take out travel insurance (this is notably important for international travelers). Insurance not only covers you for medical expenses and luggage theft or loss but for cancellation or delays in your travel arrangements (you might fall seriously ill two days before departure, for example), and everyone should be covered for the worst possible case, such as an accident that requires hospital treatment and a flight home. Coverage depends on your insurance and type of ticket, so ask both your insurer and your ticket-issuing agency to explain the finer points. Ticket loss is also covered by travel insurance. Make sure you have a separate record of all your ticket details – or better still, a photocopy of your ticket. Also make a copy of your policy, in case the original is lost.

Buy travel insurance as early as possible. If you buy it the week before you fly, you may find, for instance, that you're not covered for delays to your flight caused by strikes or other industrial action that may have been in force before you took out the insurance.

If you're planning to travel a long time, the insurance may seem very expensive – but if you can't afford it, you certainly won't be able to afford a medical emergency in the USA.

AIR

US domestic airfares vary tremendously depending on the season you travel, the day of the week you fly, the length of your stay and the flexibility the ticket allows for flight changes and refunds. Still, nothing determines fares more than demand, and when things are slow, regardless of the season, airlines will lower their fares to fill empty seats. There's a lot of competition, and at any given time any one of the airlines could have the cheapest fare. (See also the Internet directory for a list of airline websites.)

Airports & Airlines

There are very few direct international flights to Deep South hubs; travelers from abroad usually arrive on connecting flights from traditional ports of entry such as New York, Los Angeles and Miami. Expanded international service to Hartsfield airport (☎ 404-530-6834) in Atlanta, Georgia, may provide additional direct service to the South.

The following list of major airports runs roughly from largest on down. Regional airports are covered in the Getting Around chapter.

Memphis international airport (☎ 901-922-8000) is a major hub for Northwest Airlines, which is closely affiliated with KLM Royal Dutch Airlines. KLM provides direct flights from Amsterdam and has connections from other European countries.

New Orleans international airport (☎ 504-464-3547) is served by major carriers, including Aeromexico and Lacsa.

Nashville international airport (☎ 615-275-1600) is served by major carriers, but is generally more expensive to fly into than Memphis or New Orleans.

Jackson international airport (☎ 601-939-5631) in Mississippi is a minor airport, though it's the state's largest. Traveler's should consider flying into New Orleans.

Birmingham international airport (☎ 205-595-0533) is Alabama's largest, but it's only a minor airport for the region as a whole. Travelers considering flying into Birmingham should first check fares to Atlanta's Hartsfield airport.

Major international airlines serving the US include:

Air Canada	☎ 800-776-3000
Air France	☎ 800-237-2747
Air New Zealand	☎ 800-262-1234
American Airlines	☎ 800-624-6262
British Airways	☎ 800-247-9297
Canadian Airlines	☎ 800-426-7000
Continental Airlines	☎ 800-231-0856
Japan Air Lines	☎ 800-525-3663
KLM	☎ 800-374-7747
Northwest Airlines	☎ 800-447-4747
Qantas Airways	☎ 800-227-4500
TWA	☎ 800-221-2000
United Airlines	☎ 800-631-1500
US Airways	☎ 800-428-4322
Virgin Atlantic	☎ 800-862-8621

Major domestic airlines in the US include:

AirTran Airlines	☎ 800-247-8726
Alaska Airlines	☎ 800-426-0333
America West	☎ 800-235-9292
American Airlines	☎ 800-433-7300
Continental Airlines	☎ 800-525-0280
Delta Airlines	☎ 800-221-1212
Hawaiian Airlines	☎ 800-367-5320
Northwest Airlines	☎ 800-225-2525
Southwest Airlines	☎ 800-435-9792
TWA	☎ 800-892-4141
United Airlines	☎ 800-241-6522
US Airways	☎ 800-428-4322

Buying Tickets

Rather than just walking into the nearest travel agent or airline office, you should do a bit of research and shop around first. If you are buying tickets within the US, the *New York Times*, *Los Angeles Times*, *Chicago Tribune*, *San Francisco Examiner* and other major newspapers all produce weekly travel sections with numerous travel agents' ads. Council Travel (☎ 800-226-8624, Net) and STA (☎ 800-777-0112) have offices in major cities nationwide. The magazine *Travel Unlimited* (PO Box 1058, Allston, MA 02134) publishes details of the cheapest airfares and courier possibilities.

Those coming from outside the US might start by perusing the travel sections of magazines like *Time Out* and *TNT* in the UK, or the Saturday editions of newspapers like the *Sydney Morning Herald* and *The Age* in Australia. Ads in these publications offer cheap fares, but don't be surprised if they happen to be sold out when you contact the agents: they're usually low-season fares on obscure airlines with conditions attached.

The plane ticket will probably be the single most expensive item in your budget, and buying it can be intimidating. It is always worth putting aside a few hours to research the current state of the market. Start shopping for a ticket early – some of the cheapest tickets must be bought months in advance, and some popular flights sell out early. Talk to other recent travelers – they may have other, more specific cost-saving advice. Look at the ads in newspapers and magazines, consult reference books and watch for special offers.

Note that high season for nationwide airline travel rates in the USA is mid-June to mid-September (summer) and the one week before and after Christmas. The best rates for travel to and in the USA are found November 1 to March 31.

Phone travel agents for bargains. Airlines themselves can supply information on routes and timetables, but except at times of fare wars, they do not supply the cheapest tickets. Airlines often have competitive low-season, student and senior citizens' fares. Find out the fare, the route, the duration of the journey and any restrictions on the ticket.

Cheap tickets are available in two distinct categories: official and unofficial. Official ones have a variety of names including advance-purchase fares, budget fares, Apex and super-Apex. Unofficial tickets are simply discounted tickets that the airlines release through selected travel agents (not through airline offices). The cheapest tickets are often nonrefundable and require an extra fee for changing your flight. Many insurance policies will cover this loss if you have to change your flight for emergency reasons. A return (roundtrip) ticket usually works out cheaper than two one-way fares – often *much* cheaper. However the recent emergence of smaller airlines specializing in one-way fares is making it much easier to avoid buying roundtrip fares. America West and Southwest, from the western US, and AirTran Airlines, from the east, sell one-way fares that are half as much as regular roundtrip fares. These airlines also connect major airports with smaller, regional airports.

Use the fares quoted in this book as a guide only. They are approximate and based on the rates advertised by travel agents and airlines at press time. Quoted airfares do not necessarily constitute a recommendation for the carrier.

If traveling from the UK, you will probably find that the cheapest flights are advertised by obscure bucket shops whose names haven't yet reached the telephone directory. Many such firms are honest and solvent, but there are a few rogues who will take your money and disappear, to reopen elsewhere a month or two later under a new name. If you feel suspicious about a firm, don't give them all the money at once – leave a deposit of 20% or so and pay the balance on receiving the ticket. If they insist on cash in advance, go elsewhere. And once you have the ticket, ring the airline to confirm that you are booked on the flight.

You may decide to pay more than the rock-bottom fare by opting for the safety of a better known travel agent. Established firms like STA Travel, which has offices worldwide, Council Travel in the USA or Travel CUTS in Canada are valid alternatives, and they offer good prices to most destinations.

Once you have your ticket, write down its number, together with the flight number and other details, and keep the information separate from the ticket. If the ticket is lost or stolen, this will help you get a replacement.

Remember to buy travel insurance as early as possible (see the introduction to this chapter for details).

Visit USA Passes Almost all domestic carriers offer Visit USA passes to non-US citizens. The passes are actually a book of coupons that you buy – each coupon equals a flight. The following airlines are the most representative, but it's a good idea to ask your travel agent about other airlines that offer the service. These must be booked outside the US, and you must be a non-US resident and have a return ticket to a destination outside the US.

Continental Airlines' Visit USA pass can be purchased in countries on both the Atlantic and Pacific sides. All travel must be completed within 60 days of the first flight into the US or 81 days after arrival in the US. You must have your trip planned out in order to purchase the coupons. If you decide to change destinations once in the US, you will be fined US$50. High-season prices are US$419 for three flight coupons (minimum purchase) and US$729 for eight (maximum purchase). Low season rates are US$369/669.

Northwest offers the same deal, but you can reserve flights beforehand or fly standby.

American Airlines uses the same coupon structure and also sells the passes on the Atlantic and Pacific sides. You must know where you want to go on your first flight and stick to that schedule or be penalized. You must also reserve flights one day in advance, and if a coupon only takes you halfway to your destination, you will have to buy the remaining ticket at full price. A pack of 10 coupons costs US$829.

Delta has two different systems for travelers coming across the Atlantic. Visit USA gives travelers a discount, but you need to have your itinerary mapped out to take advantage of this. Visit USA is based on a point-to-point ticketing system; they will give you the cheapest fare between the two places but not a set ticket price. If there is no cheap fare, then you are stuck. The other option is Discover America, in which a traveler buys coupons good for standby travel anywhere in the continental USA. One flight equals one coupon. Only two transcontinental flights are allowed. Three coupons cost about US$439, 10 cost US$1249. Children's fares are US$399 for three coupons, or about US$40 less. In

Top: French Quarter detail, New Orleans, LA
Bottom Left: Mardi Gras, New Orleans, LA

Middle Right: Babylon, New Orleans, LA
Bottom Right: Lafayette Cemetery, New Orleans, LA

RICK GERHARTER

RICK GERHARTER

RICK GERHARTER

RICK GERHARTER

Top Left: A man on the move, New Orleans, LA
Bottom Left: Mardi Gras, New Orleans, LA

Top Right: Sea fare in New Orleans, LA
Bottom Right: St Louis Cathedral, New Orleans, LA

order to purchase coupons, the transatlantic flight must be paid in advance.

When flying standby, call the airline a day or two before and make a 'standby reservation.' This way you get priority over all the others who just appear and hope to get on the flight the same day.

Round-the-World Tickets Round-the-world (RTW) tickets have become very popular in the last few years. Airline RTW tickets are often real bargains and can work out to be no more expensive or even cheaper than an ordinary return ticket. Prices start at about UK£850 and A$2399 (low season) or A$2699 and US$2500 (high season).

The official airline RTW tickets are usually put together by a combination of two airlines, and permit you to fly anywhere you want on their route systems as long as you do not backtrack. Other restrictions are that you must usually book the first sector in advance and cancellation penalties apply. There may be restrictions on the number of stops permitted, and tickets are usually valid from 90 days up to a year. An alternative type of RTW ticket is one put together by a travel agent using a combination of discounted tickets.

Although most airlines restrict the number of sectors that can be flown within the USA and Canada to four, and some airlines black out a few heavily traveled routes (like Honolulu to Tokyo), stopovers are otherwise generally unlimited. In most cases 14 days advance purchase is required. After the ticket is purchased, the dates can be changed without penalty and tickets can be rewritten to add or delete stops for $50 each.

The majority of RTW tickets restrict you to just three airlines. British Airways, US Airways and Qantas Airways offer a RTW ticket called the Global Explorer that allows you to combine routes on these airlines to a total of 28,000 miles for US$3100 or A$3192 (high season). It allows six flights.

Qantas also flies in conjunction with American, Delta, Northwest, Canadian, Air France and KLM. Qantas RTW tickets, with any of the aforementioned partner airlines, cost US$3300/3100 (high/low) or A$3279/3079 (high/low).

Canadian Airlines offers numerous RTW combinations using a maximum of two other carriers. North Pacific routes with RTW flying one-way west-to-east runs US$2570 or C$3110. Their South Pacific route is US$3247 or C$3615.

Air Canada offers a base fare of US$2458 or C$3287, with two other carriers (additional cost for additional carriers).

Many other airlines also offer RTW tickets. Continental Airlines, for example, links up with either Malaysia Airlines, Singapore Airlines or Thai Airways for a base fare of around US$2570. (Depending on what they can set up with other airlines – Continental takes your itinerary and tries to find the lowest cost flights available.) TWA's lowest priced RTW, linking up with Korean Air, costs from US$2200 to US$3200 and allows stops in Honolulu, Seoul, Tel Aviv, Amsterdam and Paris or London.

Circle Pacific Tickets Circle Pacific tickets use a combination of airlines to circle the Pacific – combining Australia, New Zealand, North America and Asia. Rather than simply flying from point A to point B, these tickets allow you to swing through much of the Pacific Rim and eastern Asia taking in a variety of destinations as long as you keep traveling in the same circular direction. As with RTW tickets, there are advance purchase restrictions and limits on how many stopovers you can take. These fares are likely to be around 15% cheaper than RTW tickets.

Circle Pacific routes essentially have the same fares: A$3500 if purchased in Australia, US$2449 if purchased in the USA, and C$2979 if purchased in Canada. Circle Pacific fares include four stopovers with the option of adding stops at US$50 each. There's a 14-day advance purchase requirement, a 25% cancellation penalty and a maximum stay of six months. There are also higher business class and 1st-class fares. Departure and airport-use taxes, which will vary with the itinerary, are additional.

Qantas Airways offers Circle Pacific routes in partnership with Delta Air Lines, Japan Air Lines, Northwest Airlines or Continental Airlines. In the off-season, the Australian winter, Qantas occasionally offers discounts on tickets that use Qantas as the primary carrier. The standard fare starts at A$2297 (US$1700).

United Airlines flies in conjunction with Cathay Pacific, Qantas, Ansett, Malaysia Airlines or British Airways. Canadian Airlines has Circle Pacific fares from Vancouver that include, in one combination or another, virtually all Pacific Rim destinations. Prices for Canadian Airlines are C$2979 (US$2579). Canadian's partners include Qantas, Air New Zealand, Singapore, Garuda, Cathay Pacific or Malaysia Airlines.

Travelers with Special Needs

If you have special needs of any sort – a broken leg, dietary restrictions, dependence on a wheelchair, responsibility for a baby, fear of flying – you should let the airline know as soon as possible so that they can make arrangements accordingly. You should remind them when you reconfirm your booking (at least 72 hours before departure) and again when you check in at the airport. It may also be worth ringing round the airlines before you make your booking to find out how they can handle your particular needs.

Airports and airlines can be surprisingly helpful, but they do need advance warning. Most international airports can provide escorts, when needed, from check-in desk to plane, and there should be ramps, lifts, accessible toilets and reachable phones. Aircraft toilets, on the other hand, are likely to present a problem; travelers should discuss this with the airline at an early stage and, if necessary, with their doctor.

Guide dogs for the blind often have to travel in a specially pressurized baggage compartment with other animals, away from their owner, though smaller guide dogs may be admitted to the cabin. Guide dogs are not subject to quarantine as long as they have proof of being vaccinated against rabies.

Deaf travelers can ask for airport and in-flight announcements to be written down for them.

Children under two travel for 10% of the standard fare (or free, on some airlines), as long as they don't occupy a seat. (They don't get a baggage allowance either.) 'Skycots' should be provided by the airline if requested in advance; these will take a child weighing up to about 22 lbs. Children between two and 12 can usually occupy a seat for half to two-thirds of the full fare, and do get a baggage allowance. Strollers can often be taken on as hand luggage.

Flight Restrictions

Baggage On most domestic and international flights you are limited to two checked bags, or three if you don't have a carry-on. There could be a charge if you bring more or if the size of the bags exceeds the airline's limits. It's best to check with the individual airline if you are worried about this. On some international flights the luggage allowance is based on weight; again, check with the airline.

If your luggage is delayed upon arrival (which is rare), some airlines will give a cash advance to purchase necessities. If sporting equipment is misplaced, the airline may pay for rentals. Should the luggage be lost, it is important to submit a claim. The airline doesn't have to pay the full amount of the claim, rather they can estimate the value of your lost items. It may take them anywhere from six weeks to three months to process the claim and pay you.

Smoking Smoking is prohibited on all domestic flights within the USA. Many international flights are following suit, so be sure to call and find out. Incidentally, the restriction applies to the passenger cabin and the lavatories but not the cockpit. Many airports in the USA also restrict smoking, but they compensate by having 'smoking rooms.'

Illegal Items Items that are illegal to take on a plane, either checked or as carry-on, include aerosols of polishes, waxes, etc; tear gas and pepper spray; camp stoves with fuel; and divers' tanks that are full. Matches should not be checked.

Getting Bumped

Airlines bump passengers off flights when they overbook them. If you are involuntarily 'bumped,' you'll have to wait around for the next flight. Avoid this by reconfirming your flight and checking in early. If you aren't traveling on a tight schedule, though, try volunteering to be bumped and take advantage of the deals airlines give as compensation. Here's how to get bumped if you're on a full flight: when you check in, ask if they will need volunteers and give your name if they do. Be sure to ask when they can get you on a flight to your destination, and try to confirm that flight so you aren't stuck in the airport for too long. If you have to spend the night, check whether the airline will provide a hotel room and money for meals.

Arriving in the USA

Even if you are continuing immediately to another city, the first airport that you land in is where you must carry out immigration and customs formalities. Even if your luggage is checked from, say, London to Denver, you will still have to take it through customs if you first land in New York.

If you have a non-US passport, with a visa, you must complete an Arrival/Departure Record (form I-94) before going to the immigration desk. See Visas & Documents in Facts for the Visitor for advice on filling out this form and for information on what to expect from immigrations officials.

Departure Taxes

Airport departure taxes are normally included in the cost of tickets bought in the USA, although tickets purchased abroad may not have this included. There's a $24 airport departure tax charged to all passengers bound for a foreign destination. However, this fee, as well as a $6.50 North American Free Trade Agreement (NAFTA) tax charged to passengers entering the USA from a foreign country, are hidden taxes added to the purchase price of your airline ticket.

Within the USA

East Coast The lowest roundtrip non-refundable airfare at press time from New York to Memphis or New Orleans was $178, to Atlanta $158.

From Boston, the roundtrip fare to Memphis was $236, to New Orleans $178, to Atlanta $178. From Washington, DC, to Memphis was $198, to New Orleans $178, to Atlanta $118. From Miami to Memphis was $200, to New Orleans $290, to Atlanta $240.

West Coast The lowest nonrefundable airfare from San Francisco (California) to Memphis or Atlanta at press time was $218 roundtrip, to New Orleans $436, to Nashville $358, to Birmingham $438.

From San Diego, roundtrip fare to Memphis was $218, to Atlanta $338, to New Orleans $198. From Los Angeles to Memphis was $260, to Atlanta $340, to New Orleans $200. From Seattle to Memphis was $510, to Atlanta $350, to New Orleans $440.

Elsewhere in the USA From Chicago, the lowest roundtrip airfare to New Orleans was $340, to Nashville $118, to Memphis $198.

From Phoenix to New Orleans was $250, to Memphis $340, to Atlanta $320. From Denver to New Orleans was $310, to Memphis $350, to Atlanta $200.

Within the South, low-season roundtrip airfare from Memphis to Nashville was $210, to New Orleans $240, to Lafayette $240. From Dallas, roundtrip airfare to New Orleans was $138, to Memphis $118. From Houston to New Orleans was $100, to Memphis $250.

Canada

Travel CUTS has offices in all major cities. The Toronto *Globe & Mail* and *Vancouver Sun* carry travel agents' ads. Low-season roundtrip airfares from Vancouver to Atlanta were C$807, to New Orleans C$687, to Memphis C$1062. Airfares from Toronto to Atlanta were C$609, to New Orleans C$782, to Memphis C$673. And airfares from Montreal to Atlanta were C$581, to New Orleans C$807, to Memphis C$751.

The UK & Ireland

Check the ads in magazines like *Time Out*, plus the *Evening Standard* and *TNT*. Also check the free magazines widely available in London – start by looking outside the main railway stations.

Most British travel agents are registered with the ABTA (Association of British Travel Agents). If you have paid an ABTA-registered agent for your flight, who then goes out of business, ABTA will guarantee a refund or an alternative. Unregistered bucket shops are riskier but sometimes cheaper.

London is arguably the world's headquarters for bucket shops, which are well advertised and can usually beat published airline fares. Three good, reliable agents for cheap tickets in the UK are Trail-finders (☎ 0171-937-5400), 194 Kensington High St, London, W8 7RG; Council Travel (☎ 0171-437-7767), 28a Poland St, London, W1; and STA Travel (☎ 0171-937-9971), 86 Old Brompton Rd, London SW7 3LQ. Trailfinders produces a lav-ishly illustrated brochure including airfare details.

The Globetrotters Club (BCM Roving, London WC1N 3XX) publishes a news-letter called *Globe* that covers obscure destinations and can help you find traveling companions.

American Airlines has a roundtrip fare from London to Denver of £299 via Chicago/New York, which allows a six-month maximum stay and has a seven-day advance purchase requirement. Other low-season airfares are around £290, while other high-season airfares from London to Denver can be around £518.

Virgin Atlantic has a roundtrip high-season fare from London to New York for £452, which allows a one-month maximum stay and requires a three-week advance purchase. Off-peak flights from London to New York range from £240 to £508; to Los Angeles they start at £280.

British Airways has low-season, round-trip, direct flights from London to Atlanta for £281, students £225; to Houston for £339, students £279; and to Dallas £315. They also have flights to Memphis and New Orleans through Chicago; there's an additional £46 tax on all flights.

From Ireland, KLM and Northwest have good prices. Roundtrip, low-season airfares from Belfast to Atlanta were IR£641, to New Orleans IR£830, and Memphis IR£731.

Continental Europe

In Amsterdam, NBBS is a popular travel agent. KLM has low-season, roundtrip, direct flights from Amsterdam to Memphis for f1435 and nondirect flights as low as f941. Other direct flights from Amsterdam include Atlanta for f1477, Houston for f2116 and Dallas for f2116. There's an additional f83 tax on all flights.

In Paris, Council Travel is at 22, rue des Pyramides, 75001 Paris (☎ 01 44 55 55 44). Or try FUAJ (Fédération unie des auberges de jeunesse) at 10, rue Notre-Dame-de-Lorette, 75009 Paris (☎ 01 42 85 55 40), or at 9, rue Brantôme, 75003 Paris (☎ 01 48 04 70 40). For great student fares, contact USIT Voyages at 6, rue de Vau-girard, 75006 Paris (☎ 01 42 34 56 90).

For a Paris/Los Angeles flight, a return ticket runs 3300FF with KLM or 3600FF with Air France. Paris to New York City return tickets run from 1890FF to 2200FF in the low season; special student fares can run as low as 2290FF in the high season and about 3000FF for others. Air France has direct roundtrip service from Paris to Dallas for 4103FF, but all flights from Paris to Memphis, New Orleans, or Atlanta must go through NYC.

Virgin Atlantic roundtrip flights from Paris to New York with seven-day advance purchase range from 3790FF to 4530FF. Virgin does not fly direct from Paris; you would have to change airlines in London.

United, Delta and Continental offer similarly priced service from a number of European cities. United from Paris via Washington to NY is 2650FF.

Australia & New Zealand
In Australia and New Zealand, STA Travel and Flight Centres International are major dealers in cheap air fares; check the travel agents' ads in the Yellow Pages and ring around. Qantas flies to Los Angeles from Sydney, Melbourne (via Sydney or Auckland) and Cairns. United flies to San Francisco from Sydney and Melbourne (via Sydney) and also flies to Los Angeles.

The cheapest tickets have a 21-day advance-purchase requirement, a minimum stay of seven days and a maximum stay of 60 days. Qantas flies from Melbourne or Sydney to Los Angeles for A$1799/2199 one-way/roundtrip in the low season and A$1820 in the high season. Qantas flights from Cairns to Los Angeles cost A$1750/2145 in the low season and A$1919 in the high season.

Flying with Air New Zealand is slightly cheaper, and both Qantas and Air New Zealand offer tickets with longer stays or stopovers, but you pay more. Full-time students can purchase tickets for NZ$1610 or A$1990 on roundtrip fares to the USA.

Roundtrip flights from Auckland to Los Angeles on Qantas cost NZ$1720 in the low season. (This is the quoted student fare.)

Asia
Hong Kong is the discount plane ticket capital of the region, but its bucket shops can be unreliable. Ask the advice of other travelers before buying a ticket. STA Travel, which is dependable, has branches in Hong Kong, Tokyo, Singapore, Bangkok and Kuala Lumpur. Many if not most flights to the USA go via Honolulu, Hawaii.

United Airlines has three flights a day to Honolulu from Tokyo with connections to West Coast cities. Northwest and Japan Air Lines also have daily flights to the West Coast from Tokyo; Japan Air Lines also flies to Honolulu from Osaka, Nagoya, Fukuoka and Sapporo.

Central & South America
Most flights from Central and South America go via Miami, Houston or Los Angeles, though some fly via New York. Most countries' international flag carriers (like Aerolíneas Argentinas and LAN-Chile), as well as US airlines like United and American, serve these destinations, with onward connections. Continental has flights from about 20 cities in Mexico and Central America, including San José, Guatemala City, Cancún and Mérida

BUS
Greyhound (☎ 800-231-2222 for reservations, Net) is the only nationwide bus company. Because buses are so few, schedules are often inconvenient, fares are relatively high and bargain airfares can undercut buses on long-distance routes; in some cases, on shorter routes, it can be cheaper to rent a car than to ride the bus. However, very-long-distance bus trips are often available at bargain prices by purchasing or reserving tickets three days in advance. For more fare details, see Bus in the Getting Around chapter.

AmeriCan Adventures (see Organized Tours below) offers a hop-on/hop-off 'Us Bus' service in which buses offer transportation from city to city around the US. Rates depend on the dates of your travel, but are structured similarly to a EuroRail pass offering unlimited travel in blocks of time from five days to 45 days. Buses run more frequently in the summer than in the off-season.

Green Tortoise (☎ 415-956-7500, 800-867-8647) runs from San Francisco to Boston via New Orleans in April, May and September. Fares for the 11-day journey to New Orleans start at $380 (including meals).

TRAIN
Amtrak (☎ 800-872-7245, Net) provides cross-country passenger service between the West Coast and Chicago; travelers from the East Coast must make connections in Chicago. Schedules are often very tenuous the farther you are from the starting point.

Service through the Deep South is not as comprehensive as in Amtrak's busy north-eastern USA corridor, but certain routes are well-covered – particularly to New Orleans – and worth considering if they coincide with your itinerary.

From Chicago, Amtrak's *City of New Orleans* rides the same rails upon which blues music first traveled to Chicago. The route runs through Memphis, the Mississippi Delta and Jackson before arriving in New Orleans. Altogether it's a 19-hour trip.

From Washington, DC, Amtrak's *Crescent* runs through Atlanta with stops in Birmingham and Meridian before arriving in New Orleans. The trip is 25½ hours from DC; 11½ hours from Atlanta.

From Houston, Amtrak's *Sunset Limited* takes 8½ hours to New Orleans. The same *Sunset Limited* begins in Los Angeles and includes points west. From New Orleans, the route continues east through Mississippi, Alabama and Florida along the Gulf Coast to Jacksonville, Florida, at the Atlantic Coast (a 14½-hour trip from New Orleans to Jacksonville). In Jacksonville, the route intersects with Amtrak's coastal Atlantic route, providing transfers south to Miami and north to Richmond, Virginia.

Certain prices apply to travel within one of Amtrak's defined 'zones.' All Deep South destinations fall within Amtrak's Midwest zone (such northern cities as Chicago and Detroit also fall within this zone). For a fare of $327 peak (May through September and around Christmas) or $279 off-peak (all other times), you can travel within the zone making three stops with no extra charge. (It's about $50 higher to cross a zone.)

The best value overall is the All Aboard America fare. This costs $318 for adults and enables you to travel anywhere you want. There are limitations, however. Travel must be completed in 45 days, and you are allowed up to three stopovers. Additional stopovers can be arranged at extra cost. Your entire trip must be reserved in advance and the seats are limited, so book as far ahead as possible. Travel between mid-June and late August costs

$378. If you want to travel in just one region – the eastern, central or western parts of the country – All Aboard America fares are $228/198 peak/off-peak. For two regions, the prices are $318/258.

For non-US citizens, the USA Rail Pass comes in three types and must be purchased outside the US (check with your travel agent). For a national pass, the 15-day pass costs $355/245; the 30-day pass costs $440/350. Regional passes vary: the 15-day pass costs $175 to $265 (peak) and $155 to $215 (off-peak); the 30-day pass costs $205 to $330 (peak) and $195 to $290 (off-peak).

All fares are for reclining seats; sleeping cars cost extra. Advanced booking is recommended, especially during the peak season. Meals are included only if you travel 1st class in a 'club' or sleeping car; other passengers can buy food on board or bring their own. Smoking is not permitted on most routes; however, on some routes smoking is allowed in private rooms and in the lounge car during specific times.

CAR

Foreign drivers of cars and riders of motorcycles will need their vehicle's registration papers, liability insurance and an international driver's permit, in addition to their domestic driver's license. Canadian and Mexican drivers' licenses are accepted.

See Getting Around for more information on driving in the region.

ORGANIZED TOURS

In getting to and from the Deep South, package tours can be an efficient and relatively inexpensive way to go, especially for those interested in seeing the whole country. However, many tours do not focus on the Deep South and instead give travelers only one or two days in either New Orleans or Memphis and Nashville.

TrekAmerica (☎ 201-983-1144, 800-221-0596, fax 201-983-8551, Net), PO Box 189, Rockaway, NJ 07866, offers roundtrip camping tours to different areas of the country. In England, they are at 4 Water Perry Court, Banbury, Oxon OX16

8QG (☎ 01295-256777, fax 257399), and in Australia contact Adventure World, 75 Walker St, North Sydney, NSW 2060 (☎ 9956-7766, 800-221-931, fax 4956-7707). These tours are designed for small, young international groups. Tour prices vary with season, with July to September being the highest, and don't include airfare. Some side trips and cultural events are included in the price, and participants help with cooking and camp chores. Tours, including food and occasional hotel nights, cost about $1000 for a 10-day tour to $3500 for a nine-week tour of the entire country. Currently, TrekAmerica has two tours that dip into the Deep South: a Dixieland Tour that begins in Miami and spends all of its time in the South, and a longer Atlantic Dream tour that also begins in Florida, goes through the region and ends in New York.

AmeriCan Adventures (☎ 617-984-1556, 800-864-0335, fax 617-984-2045, Net), 1050 Hancock, Quincy, MA 02169, offers seven to 21-day camping trips to different parts of the USA. Prices range from $450 for seven days to $1200 for 21 days. They also have offices in the UK (☎ (01892) 512 700, fax (01892) 522 066, Net), 64 Mount Pleasant Ave, Tunbridge Wells, Kent TN1 1QY. Affiliated with AmeriCan is Road Runner worldwide hosteling treks (☎ 800-873-5872), which organizes one and two-week treks in conjunction with Hostelling International to regions of the USA and across the country. The Confederate Trail tour begins in New York and ends in Florida, but spends a bit of time in the Deep South; costs start from $650.

Green Tortoise (☎ 415-956-7500, 800-867-8647), at 494 Broadway, San Francisco, CA 94133, provides alternative cross-country bus transportation with stops at places like hot springs and national parks. Meals are cooked cooperatively and you sleep on bunks on the bus

or camp. From San Francisco, the company has a 16-day Mardi Gras voyage for $369 plus food. Otherwise, New Orleans is the only Deep South stop on the cross-country routes.

An international company called Suntrek has similar tours. Memphis, Nashville and New Orleans are stops on a few of them, but the Deep South region itself is not a focus.

Specialized Tours
Bicycling, hiking and walking tours around the region are another possibility, with companies like Backroads (☎ 510-527-1555, 800-462-2848), 801 Cedar St, Berkeley, CA 94710. Backroads has two bicycling tours of the region that have multiple starting dates in the spring and a couple in the fall: the Cajun & Plantation Country tour is six days for $1350; the Natchez Trace tour is six days for $1400.

WARNING
The information in this chapter is particularly vulnerable to change: prices for international travel are volatile, routes are introduced and canceled, schedules change, special deals come and go, and rules and visa requirements are amended. Airlines and governments seem to take a perverse pleasure in making price structures and regulations as complicated as possible. You should check directly with the airline or a travel agent to make sure you understand how a fare (and ticket you may buy) works. In addition, the travel industry is highly competitive and there are many lurks and perks.

The upshot of this is that you should get opinions, quotes and advice from as many airlines and travel agents as possible before you part with your hard-earned cash. The details given in the chapter should be regarded as pointers and are not a substitute for your own careful, up-to-date research.

Getting Around

If you want to see the dispersed rural attractions that are so closely associated with a trip to the South, the best way is by car. The highways are good, and public transportation is not as frequent or as widespread as in some other countries. A more focused trip – say a music tour, for instance – could be accomplished by air, train or bus transit between major destinations.

AIR

Flying into small regional airports is frequently the most expensive way to travel, and service to them is primarily designed for business passengers. Though service may be infrequent, the quality of facilities and ground transportation for regional airports is generally very high. If you're intent upon arriving at somewhere like Tupelo and you're coming from abroad or another major US airport, it's usually much cheaper to buy a through-ticket to regional airports as part of your fare rather than separately.

For short trips, trains or buses can land you closer to your destination (though less quickly).

Regional Airports & Airlines

In Louisiana, the Baton Rouge metropolitan airport (☎ 504-355-0333) is served by several major airlines, but it's expensive and so close to New Orleans it's often not useful for tourists. The Lafayette regional airport (☎ 318-266-4400) is served by American Eagle, Atlantic Southeast, Continental and Northwest. It's at the center of Louisiana's Cajun Country, a region in which a car is a necessity and which is only a two-hour drive (or ride) from New Orleans. For a town its size, the Monroe regional airport (☎ 318-329-2461) is exceptionally well served by Delta Airlines. Delta was founded here and continues to use it as a mini-hub. Monroe is in northern Louisiana

and is convenient pretty much for that region alone.

In Mississippi, the Greenville municipal airport (☎ 601-334-3121) is served by Northwest Airlink, and is in the heart of the Mississippi Delta. The Biloxi/Gulfport regional airport (☎ 601-863-5953) is served by Northwest Airlink, Continental Express, Atlantic Southeast and American Eagle; since Biloxi is two hours by highway outside of New Orleans on the Gulf Coast, travelers should consider flying there instead. Tupelo municipal airport (☎ 601-841-6571) is served by American Eagle and Northwest Airlink; Tupelo is an hour by highway outside Memphis. Meridian municipal airport (☎ 601-483-0364), in the east-central part of Mississippi, is served by Atlantic Southeast and Northwest Airlink.

In Alabama, the Huntsville international airport (☎ 205-772-9395), in the northern part of the state, is served by American, Comair, Delta, Northwest, Northwest Airlink, US Airways and US Airways Express. Mobile municipal airport at Bates Field (☎ 334-633-0313) is on the Gulf Coast, and is served by AirTrans, Continental Express, Delta and Northwest Airlines. Montgomery's Dannelly Field airport (☎ 334-281-5040) is served by Atlantic Southeast, Delta, Northwest Airlink and US Airways Express.

Contact these airlines for regional flight information:

AirTran Airlines	☎ 800-247-8726
American Eagle	☎ 800-433-7300
Atlantic Southeast	☎ 800-282-3424
Comair	☎ 800-354-9822
Continental Express	☎ 800-525-0280
Delta Airlines	☎ 800-221-1212
Gulfstream International Airlines	☎ 800-992-8532
Northwest Airlink	☎ 800-225-2525
TWExpress	☎ 800-221-2000
US Airways Express	☎ 800-428-4322

BUS

Bus transit, mainly by Greyhound (☎ 800-231-2222 for reservations), efficiently links the dispersed smaller cities of the Deep South. The quality of the neighborhoods in which bus stations are located, and the facilities offered there, may vary widely, but generally many are modern, well-maintained and staffed stations in okay areas. See destination chapters for specific information.

One well-served route (also, however, well served by interstate freeways and rail) is the Memphis-Jackson-New Orleans corridor. The Memphis-to-Jackson leg takes a little over five hours and costs around $40 one-way; an express bus is available at a slightly higher cost, and there are discounts for roundtrip tickets. The Jackson-to-New Orleans leg takes a little over four hours and costs around $36 one-way.

Other popular corridors are between Birmingham and Atlanta ($26 one-way, seven trips daily) and between Mobile and New Orleans ($21 one-way, eight trips daily).

Buying Tickets

Tickets can be bought over the phone with a credit card (MasterCard, Visa or Discover) and then mailed if purchased 10 days in advance or else picked up at the terminal with proper identification. Greyhound terminals also accept American Express, traveler's checks and cash. Note that all buses are nonsmoking, and reservations are made with ticket purchases only.

Greyhound occasionally introduces a mileage-based discount fare program that can be a bargain, especially for very long distances, but it's a good idea to check the regular fare anyway. As with regular fares, promotional fares are subject to change.

Bus Passes

Ameripass Greyhound's Ameripass is potentially useful, depending on how much you plan to travel, but the relatively high prices may impel you to travel more than you normally would simply to get your money's worth. There are no restrictions on who can buy an Ameripass; it costs $179 for seven days of unlimited travel year round, $289 for 15 days of travel and $399 for 30 days of travel. Children under 11 travel for half-price. You can get on and off at any Greyhound stop or terminal, and the Ameripass is available at every Greyhound terminal.

International Ameripass This can be purchased only by foreign tourists and foreign students and lecturers (with their families) staying less than one year. These prices are $89 for a four-day pass for unlimited travel Monday to Thursday, $149 for a seven-day pass, $209 for a 15-day pass and $289 for a 30-day pass. The International Ameripass is usually bought abroad at a travel agency, or it can be bought in the USA through the Greyhound International depot in New York City (☎ 212-971-0492) at 625 8th Ave at the Port Authority Subway level; it's open Monday to Friday from 9 am to 4:30 pm. New York Greyhound International accepts MasterCard and Visa, traveler's checks and cash, and you can buy tickets over the phone.

To contact Greyhound International to inquire about regular fares and routes, call ☎ 800-246-8572. Those buying an International Ameripass must complete an affidavit and present a passport or visa (or waiver) to the appropriate Greyhound officials.

There are also special passes for travel in Canada that can be bought only through the New York City office or abroad.

SHUTTLE

Coastline Transportation (☎ 601-432-2649, 800-647-3957) runs nine shuttles each way between the New Orleans airport and the Mississippi Gulf Coast. The shuttle will drop you wherever you need to go, whether it be a hotel or car rental office. Reservations are suggested.

TRAIN

Amtrak (☎ 800-872-7255) routes throughout the Deep South are covered in the Getting There & Away chapter. Trains can be an efficient way to travel through popular corridors, such as the Memphis-Jackson-New Orleans route.

As with bus transit, the quality of the neighborhoods in which train stations are located, and the facilities offered there, may vary widely. See destination chapters for more information.

CAR & MOTORCYCLE

Driving a car or motorcycle offers visitors the most flexibility at a reasonable cost. For visitors traveling alone, cars are convenient but isolating and possibly expensive; bus and train fares become more competitive with car rental costs for single travelers. However, since distances are great and buses can be infrequent, car transport is worth considering despite the expense.

Officially, foreign visitors must have an International or Inter-American Driving Permit to supplement their national or state driver's license, but US police are more likely to want to see your national, provincial or state driver's license.

Rental

Major international rental agencies like Hertz, Avis, Budget and A-1 have offices throughout the region, but there are also local agencies. To rent a car, you must have a valid driver's license, be at least 25 years of age and present a major credit card, like MasterCard or Visa, or else a large cash deposit.

Many rental agencies have bargain rates for weekend or week-long rentals, especially outside the peak summer season or in conjunction with airline tickets. Prices vary greatly in relation to region, season and type or size of car you'd like to rent.

If you take a bus or train to a city, or otherwise decide to rent a car but not at an airport, one agency, Enterprise, offers a unique free service in which they deliver you to and from their rental office. The service extends to a 10-mile radius of one of their offices, and saves on taxi fares from a hotel or bus or train station. You need to supply them with a telephone number to determine whether or not they can serve you.

Some agencies tack on a fee for each additional driver in the car. Be aware that some major rental agencies may no longer offer unlimited mileage in less competitive markets – be sure to calculate the cost of your estimated mileage before you rent.

Basic liability insurance, which will cover damage you may cause to another vehicle, is required by law and comes with the price of renting the car. Liability insurance is also called third-party coverage.

Collision insurance, also called the Liability Damage Waiver, is optional; it covers the full value of the vehicle in case of an accident, except when caused by acts of nature or fire. For a mid-size car rented out of Memphis or New Orleans, the cost for this extra coverage is $17 per day. You don't need to buy this waiver to rent the car. Some credit cards, such as the Master-Card Gold Card, will cover collision insurance if you rent for 15 days or less and charge the full cost of rental to your card. If you opt to do that, you'll need to sign the waiver, declining the coverage. If you already have collision insurance on your personal policy, the credit card will cover the large deductible. To find out if your credit card offers such a service, and the extent of the coverage, contact the credit card company.

Here is a list of some of the major car rental agencies:

Alamo	☎ 800-327-9633
Avis	☎ 800-831-2847
Budget	☎ 800-527-0700
Dollar	☎ 800-800-4000
Enterprise	☎ 800-325-8007
Hertz	☎ 800-654-3131
Thrifty	☎ 800-367-2277

Purchase

If you're spending several months in the USA, purchasing a car is worth considering; a car is more flexible than public transport and likely to be cheaper than rentals, but buying one can be very complicated and requires plenty of research.

It's possible to purchase a viable car in the USA for about $1500, but you can't expect to go too far before you'll need some repair work that could cost several hundred dollars or more. It doesn't hurt to spend more to get a quality vehicle. It's also worth spending $50 or so to have a mechanic check it for defects. (Some AAA offices have diagnostic centers where they can do this on the spot for its members and those of foreign affiliates.) You can check out the official valuation of a used car by looking it up in the *Blue Book*, a listing of cars by make, model and year issued and the average resale price. Local public libraries have copies of the *Blue Book*, as well as back issues of *Consumer Reports*, a magazine that annually tallies the repair records of common makes of cars.

If you want to purchase a car, the first thing to do is contact AAA (☎ 800-477-1222) for some general information. Then contact the Department of Motor Vehicles to find out about registration fees and insurance, which can be very confusing and expensive. As an example, say you are a 30-year-old non-US citizen and you want to buy a 1984 Honda. If this is the first time you have registered a car in the USA, you'll have to fork over about $300 first and then about $100 to $200 more for general registration.

Inspect the title carefully before purchasing the car; the owner's name that appears on the title must match the identification of the person selling you the car. If you're a foreigner, you may find it very useful to obtain a notarized document authorizing your use of the car, since the motor vehicle bureau in the state where you buy the car may take several weeks or more to process the change in title.

Insurance While insurance is not obligatory in every state, all states have financial responsibility laws and insurance is highly desirable; otherwise, a serious accident could leave you a pauper. In order for you to get insurance, some states require you to have had a US driver's license for at least 18 months. If you meet this qualification, you may still have to pay anywhere from $300 to $1200 a year for insurance, depending on where the car is registered and the state. Rates are generally lower if you register it at an address in the suburbs or in a rural area, rather than in a central city. Collision coverage has become very expensive, with high deductibles, and is generally not worthwhile unless the car is somewhat valuable. Regulations vary from state to state but are generally becoming stringent throughout the USA.

Obtaining insurance, however, is not as simple as walking into an agency, filling out a form and paying for it. Many agencies refuse to insure drivers who have no car insurance (a classic catch-22!); those who do often charge much higher rates because they presume a higher risk. Male drivers under the age of 25 will pay astronomical rates. The minimum term for a policy is usually six months, but some insurance companies will refund the difference on a prorated basis if the car is sold and the policy voluntarily terminated. It is advisable to shop around.

Drive-aways
A drive-away is a car that belongs to an owner who can't drive it to a specific destination but who is willing to allow someone else to drive it for them. For example, if somebody moves from Boston to Portland, they may elect to fly and leave the car with a drive-away agency. The agency will find a driver and take care of all necessary insurance and permits. If you happen to want to drive from Boston to Portland, have a valid driver's license and a clean driving record, you can apply to drive the car. Normally, you have to pay a small refundable deposit. You pay for the gas (though sometimes a gas allowance is given). You are allowed a set number of days to deliver the car – usually based on driving eight hours a day. You are also allowed a limited number of miles, based on the best route and allowing for reasonable side trips, so you can't just zigzag all over the country. However, this is a cheap way to get around if you like long-distance driving and meet eligibility requirements.

Drive-away companies often advertise in the classified sections of newspapers under 'Travel.' They are also listed in the Yellow Pages telephone directory under 'Automobile Transporters & Drive-away Companies.' You need to be flexible about dates and destinations when you call. If you are going to a popular area, you may be able to leave within two days or less, or you may have to wait over a week before a car becomes available. The routes that are most easily available are coast to coast, although intermediate trips are certainly possible.

Shipping a Vehicle

In general, because good used cars and motorcycles are cheap in the USA, it is usually unnecessary to ship a car, but a surprising number of people take their own transport to the USA and beyond. Jonathon Hewat, who drove a VW Kombi around the world, wrote a book called *Overland and Beyond* (Roger Lascelles, 47 York Rd, Brentford, Middlesex TW8 0QP, UK), which is worthwhile for anyone contemplating such a trip.

Air-cargo planes do have size limits, but a normal car or even a Land Rover can fit. For motorcyclists, air is probably the easiest option; you may be able to get a special rate for air cargo if you are flying with the same airline. Start by asking the cargo departments of the airlines that fly to your destination. Travel agents can sometimes help as well.

Dangers & Annoyances

To avert theft, do not leave items such as cell phones, purses, compact discs, cameras, baggage or even sunglasses visible inside the car. Tuck items under the seat, or even better, put items in the trunk and make sure your car does not have trunk entry through the back seat; if it does, make sure this is locked. Don't leave anything in the car overnight.

Scenic Routes

The **Great River Road** (also called the River Road), as its name implies, is a series of roads running roughly parallel to the Mississippi River on either bank as it travels from its beginnings in Wisconsin and Minnesota to the Midwest and through the Deep South to the Gulf of Mexico.

In Louisiana, the route begins south of New Orleans and rolls through the Cajun wetlands and up through Plantation Country. (While the stretch below New Orleans is interesting for those who have the time, it makes sense to begin a drive following the River Road north from Hwy 90.) In Mississippi's Delta region, the River Road runs through a quiet corner of the state (here you may find Hwy 61 a more engaging alternative; see below).

In the southwestern corner of Louisiana, the **Creole Nature Trail** loops 180 miles past coastal marshlands, including four national wildlife refuges. The wetlands provide sanctuary for migrating birds along the Mississippi and Central Flyways, so naturally the slow, quiet region is a haven for birdwatchers.

Hwy 61, celebrated regionally just as Route 66 is nationally, is the route along which black emigrants from the Mississippi Delta carried blues music north to Chicago and south to New Orleans. Memorialized in blues songs, Hwy 61 through the Delta is the most ideal route in the region for a motorcycle trip – strap a jungle hammock on the back and don't forget to pack your blues harp.

Alabama's most famous motorcycle route is the **Trail of Tears** corridor, which stretches 200 miles from Ross Landing in Chattanooga, Tennessee, to Waterloo, Alabama, tracing the official 'Indian Removal Act of 1830' route Native Americans were forced to walk. There are historic markers and signs along the route, which follows much of what is now Hwy 72. An annual motorcycle ride is held in September honoring the Native Americans who suffered and died en route.

In the northeastern corner of Alabama, **Lookout Mountain Parkway** follows the high plateau along the west rim of Little River Canyon in DeSoto State Park on Hwy 176. There are frequent overlooks.

A famous Alabama route that's more historic than scenic is the **Selma-to-Montgomery March**, following the path blazed by civil rights advocates marching to the state capital in 1965.

The **Natchez Trace** (see the Natchez Trace sidebar and maps, below) and the Selma-to-Montgomery March are two of six highways in the US designated 'All-American Roads' by the Federal Highway Administration. These two and the Creole Nature Trail are three of 14 routes in the US designated National Scenic Byways by the Transportation Secretary. Write or call for a free copy of the brochure mapping all 14 routes from the National Scenic Byways Clearinghouse (☎ 800-429-9297, select Clearinghouse option), 1440 New York Ave NW, Suite 202, Washington, DC 20005.

BICYCLE

Conditions are generally amenable to bike touring in the Deep South, though bicycling is not common among residents, except perhaps in south Louisiana. The topography throughout the region is largely flat, and motorists are generally courteous. Some cities require helmets, others don't, but as a safety precaution helmets should always be worn. Also as a safety measure, cyclists should carry at least two full water bottles and refill them at every opportunity. The availability of spare parts and repair shops vary from plentiful in New Orleans and south Louisiana to adequate along the Natchez Trace, to unheard-of in more remote parts. It's important to be able to do basic mechanical work, like fixing a flat, yourself.

In south Louisiana, Pack & Paddle (☎ 318-264-9707, 800-458-4560), 601 E Pinhook Rd, Lafayette, can get you oriented and outfitted for an extended adventure. See Organized Tours, below, for more bike touring information.

The harsh summer temperatures should be generally avoided, and frequent rains may dampen bicyclists. Fall is the most consistently dry season, and many outfitters schedule group tours during that time.

For independent bicyclists, rentals are extremely limited in the region, so you

may want to bring your bike with you. Bicycles can be transported by air. You can disassemble them and put them in a bike bag or box, but it's much easier simply to wheel your bike to the check-in desk, where it should be treated as a piece of baggage. You may have to remove the pedals and front tire so that it takes up less space in the aircraft's hold; check all this with the airline well in advance, preferably before you pay for your ticket. Be aware that some airlines welcome bicycles, while others treat them as an undesirable nuisance and do everything possible to discourage them.

HITCHHIKING

Hitchhiking is never entirely safe in any country in the world, and we don't recommend it. Travelers who decide to hitch should understand that they are taking a small but potentially life-threatening risk. You may not be able to identify the local rapist, murderer, thief, or even a driver who's just had too much to drink, before you get into the vehicle. People who nevertheless choose to hitch will be safer if they travel in pairs, let someone know where they are planning to go, keep their luggage light and with them at all times, and sit by a door.

WALKING

Pedestrians, as with bicyclists, will find that walking as a leisure activity or for transportation is an uncommon pursuit in the largely rural car-dependent region.

That said, the **Natchez Trace Parkway** (see sidebar and maps, below) permits pedestrians and preserves portions of the original trace as a footpath. As well, the **Bartram Trail** near Tuskegee, Alabama, traces a route explored by 18th-century naturalist William Bartram through what is now the Tuskegee National Forest.

BOAT

Excursions up the Mississippi River are mostly for pleasure, and are organized by tour companies (see Organized Tours, below). Rivers in the region are good for

The Natchez Trace Parkway

This nationally designated parkland corridor maintained by the National Park Service (NPS) is the best-known scenic route in the region. It rolls approximately 200 miles from below Nashville, Tennessee, southwest to Natchez, Mississippi, along a route that was originally an ancient buffalo trail, then an Indian footpath, then a trade route for early European settlers, then an American post road. Today the scenic parkway is a leisurely, bucolic drive (maximum speed 50 mph, commercial traffic prohibited) and a popular bicycle touring route (see Organized Tours, below). The parkway is dotted with historic sites, interpretive trails, very well maintained woodland campgrounds, ranger stations and restrooms. While it sounds ideal, the route can sometimes feel strangely anachronistic and isolated, even a little sanitized; if you're interested in getting beyond this, ample detours offer local color that has less of a museum quality to it. Drivers accustomed to interstate travel will need to slow their pace and not take gas stations for granted. There is only one gas station on the actual parkway itself, and detours for gas and food may be long — fill up when you have the chance, and carry snacks, drinks and other supplies such as picnic gear and film. Detailed information is available in the Southwestern, Central and Northeastern Mississippi chapters as well as the Nashville chapter. ■

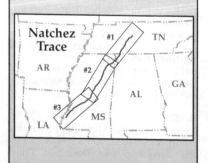

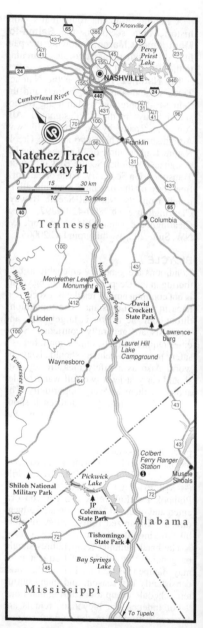

Natchez Trace Parkway #1

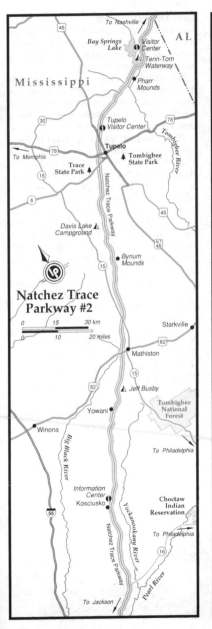

adventure excursions (see Activities in Facts for the Visitor), but are rarely utilized for passenger transportation between cities.

LOCAL TRANSPORT

Cities and metropolitan areas operate local bus transit, but coverage and service is extremely limited compared to cities of comparable size in other parts of the country. Historically, public transit has been largely the domain of poorer and generally underserved residents, and it's not uncommon for municipal transit systems in the Deep South to exist largely to transport domestic workers from poor neighborhoods to places of employment in rich neighborhoods – routes incompatible with the needs of travelers. Often harsh temperatures may also discourage travelers.

In historic towns or resort areas (such as the Gulf Coast), local 'trolleys' (buses resembling trolley cars) may provide localized transportation to major sights, along with a commentary. In casino areas (principally along the Mississippi River and along the Gulf Coast), casinos sponsor shuttles to and from area motels/hotels.

Taxis are common in downtown New Orleans and Memphis and can easily be flagged for a fare there. Outside of this, you generally must phone for taxi service, and since distances are longer, taxis will be more expensive, especially if you're traveling alone. Average fare for taxis is $2 for the first mile, $1 for each additional, with an added 10% tip (possibly more in cities).

ORGANIZED TOURS

For adventure excursions or specialized tours – such as swamp exploring or African American heritage sights – an organized tour might be your best bet.

For outdoor activities, operators provide all equipment and provisions, and guides know the territory best. Most of these are localized (see destination chapters), but a few will traverse the region.

Bicyclists may request a packet of bike-touring information from Natchez Trace Parkway headquarters (☎ 601-842-1572), Rural Route 1, NT-143, Tupelo, MS 38801. In Nashville, Tally Ho (☎ 615-354-1037), 6501 Hardin Rd No B-26, organizes overnight bike tours of the trace. Backroads (☎ 510-527-1555, 800-462-2848), 801 Cedar St, Berkeley, CA 94710, has two bicycling tours in the region that have multiple starting dates in the spring and a couple in the fall: the Cajun & Plantation Country tour is six days for $1350; the Natchez Trace tour is six days for $1400. Backroads may also do walking tours in the future.

Paddleboat cruises up the Mississippi River are organized by the Delta Queen Steamboat Co (☎ 800-543-1949), based in New Orleans. Excursions from two to 14 nights typically include stops in Natchez, Vicksburg and Memphis. The company also runs theme tours, such as a Civil War tour.

New Orleans is the home port for many passenger liners that cruise the Gulf of Mexico and the Caribbean, such as Carnival Cruises (☎ 800-327-7276).

Louisiana

Facts about Louisiana

Louisiana's distinct heritage as a French colony makes it unique among American states. Structurally, for example, the state's geopolitical units are drawn into parishes instead of counties, and while the rest of the US legal system has its foundation in British law, Louisiana's legal system retains vestiges of the Napoleonic Code. The sporting political style for which the state is well known (see Government & Politics, below) is another remnant of its colonial history. Louisiana is also home to the greatest concentration of French-speaking citizens in the US, despite years of official language suppression.

But for most visitors, Louisiana (locally pronounced LOOZ-ee-ana) is distinguished for its exotic landscapes, cuisine and music, and for a joie de vivre such as you'll find nowhere else in the country. Take Mardi Gras, for instance, when Louisiana celebrates the traditional pre-Lenten blow-out with costumes of sparkling sequins and feathers, showers of golden confetti and noisy processions of brass bands leading a gyrating parade of 'second line' celebrants flinging colorful strings of beads and baubles.

The city of New Orleans lends Louisiana its reputation for the high life, and deservedly so. Music, food and drink flow around the clock in the beautiful historic city, and not only along famed Bourbon St but throughout the preserved French Quarter and bohemian neighborhoods. The steamy subtropical city offers an intoxicating mix of indulgences, from sugar-dusted beignets to Hurricanes – potent concoctions of pineapple juice and grenadine laced with 151-proof rum. Not only does the city celebrate the carnival season, which culminates with Mardi Gras, but two months later the New Orleans Jazz & Heritage Festival is another major event.

From New Orleans, traveling upriver on the Mississippi will bring you to the state capital at Baton Rouge and on through Plantation Country, where antebellum mansions stand as reminders of the legacy of King Cotton. Inviting small towns along the route, including St Francisville, retain their historic heritage through architectural preservation and festivals. At Christmas, bonfires along the river's levee blaze the way for Papa Noel, as they have for more than a century.

The unofficial state motto, *laissez les bons temps rouler* (let the good times roll), aptly befits Cajun Country, the region around Lafayette in south Louisiana. Cajun Country harbors one of the USA's largest and most distinct cultural enclaves in one of its most exotic locales. The area's bayous and swamps are havens for birds, alligators and other wildlife, as well as being the home of Cajun music, zydeco and swamp pop. You can easily pick up the two-step at dance halls, block parties and festivals throughout the year, but try to visit in spring during crawfish season and join in the tasty head-sucking and tail-squeezing rituals.

In the narrow waist of Central Louisiana, the landscape of swamps and prairies gives way to forested midlands, a quiet neutral ground between the historically French Catholic communities to the south and the Anglo-Protestants to the north. The various regions of the Kisatchie National Forest are favorites for hiking and canoeing, and other area attractions include the Native American ruins at Marksville and a visit to the home of the South's best-known demagogue, Huey Long.

North Louisiana is most often seen off the shoulder of the I-20 thoroughfare, but even through-travelers will find local diversions – including Poverty Point, one of the most significant Native American sites in North America. In mid-September, the region's highlight is the Louisiana Folklife Festival, held each year in Monroe.

History

The European history of Louisiana's Mississippi River region starts with the expedition of de Soto in 1541. The following century, in 1682, La Salle came down the river and liberally claimed the entire Mississippi basin for France. The town of Natchitoches was settled in 1714, and New Orleans was founded four years later.

Considering Louisiana a drain on the French treasury (there was the French & Indian war to fight, and oversees investments never lived up to expected returns), French officials quietly negotiated to pass off the territory west of the Mississippi to Spain in 1762; territory east of the Mississippi (except New Orleans) was ceded to England in 1763. Interestingly, these changes weren't announced until 1764.

During the American Revolutionary War, Spain aided the revolutionaries, using New Orleans and the Mississippi River as an important supply and trade route to the interior of the new nation. By 1779, Spain itself was in a costly war with Britain (through regained territories east of the Mississippi), and Napoleon was advancing French interests in the New World. In a secret treaty with Napoleon in 1800, the King of Spain ceded the Louisiana Territory back to France – with the caveat that it never be ceded to another country. However, Napoleon also was slowly losing a war with the British and needed funds.

It had become apparent to US president Thomas Jefferson that whoever controlled the port at New Orleans would also control the Mississippi River and US western expansion and midwestern trade. After the disclosure of Napoleon's secret acquisition, James Monroe and French foreign minister Robert Livingston were authorized to offer $10 million for New Orleans. Seeking funds, Napoleon shamelessly jumped at the chance to sell off not only New Orleans but all of the western territory ceded to him from the King of Spain. This became the Louisiana Purchase of 1803, and it doubled the national domain of the US.

Louisiana became a state in 1812, just in time for Andrew Jackson to fight the Battle of New Orleans at the close of the War of 1812 between the US and Britain. Louisiana was for a brief time an independent republic before it joined the Confederate States of America in 1861, and at the end of the Civil War, Louisiana rejoined the Union after enduring a long Yankee occupation.

In 1901, the state's first oil well was struck, ushering in Louisiana's modern economy. Mineral resources have come to be an important factor in the state's political history.

The recent popularity of Cajun folklife, cuisine and music has been one of Louisiana's most significant contributions to modern American culture (see Cajun Country chapter).

Geography

The boot-shaped state of Louisiana is bounded on the north by Arkansas, on the east by Mississippi, on the west by Texas and on the south by the Gulf of Mexico. Slightly larger than New York state, Louisiana encompasses 48,114 sq miles, of which nearly 4000 sq miles are water. The state's elevation slopes downward from the 400-foot uplands of north Louisiana to two feet below sea level in New Orleans.

The Mississippi River, along with its primary tributary the Atchafalaya River, dominates the geography (and history, and culture, and economy…) of southern Louisiana. Second only to these natural wetlands are the levees, basins, dams, and channels built to control and constrain the river system. Both the historic capital, New Orleans, and the modern capital, Baton Rouge, are set on the Mississippi's banks. Other significant waterways include the Sabine River at the Texas border, the Pearl River at the southeasternmost border with the state of Mississippi and the Red River, which flows diagonally through the center of the state.

The forested midlands and uplands of central and north Louisiana provide a sharp contrast to the lowland swamps and prairies – a contrast also manifested in the divergent cultures of north and south Louisiana.

LOUISIANA

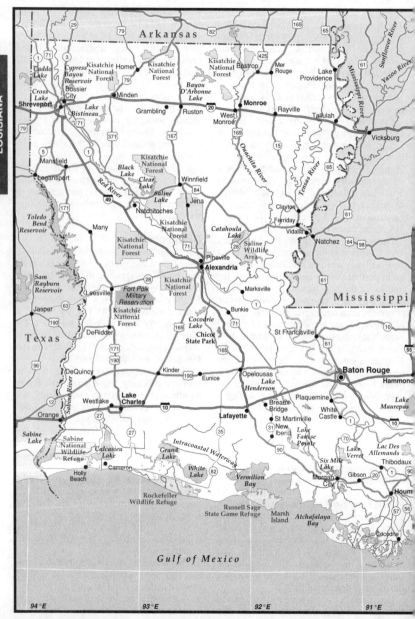

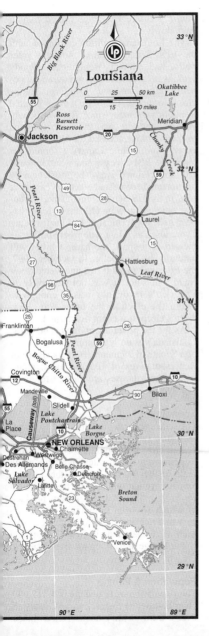

LOUISIANA

Government & Politics

Ever since 1682 when La Salle extravagantly laid claim to the bulk of the continent with a wave of his hand, Louisiana's promoters have been well known for theatrical excess.

The most legendary modern actor in Louisiana political theater was the irrepressible Huey Long (1893-1935). By the time of his assassination, Long had risen to mythical stature as a Louisiana-style Robin Hood. The charismatic Long was first elected governor in 1928, and over the course of his growing regime he dominated state politics with a nearly despotic ruthlessness, which he threatened to carry onto the national political scene.

As a populist demagogue, Long ushered in an era of public works, building a modern infrastructure that brought Louisiana out of post-Reconstruction antiquity. In exchange for such good works Long presumed the authority to sidestep the democratic process to achieve his goals. Graft, corruption, intimidation and bribery characterized his administration, and he'd positioned himself to make a run for the US presidency when he was struck down in the state capitol by an assassin.

The winking good-ole-boy style of state politics was given a brief respite in 1943 with the gubernatorial election of country music singer Jimmie Davis, a Baptist from northern Louisiana. He is still the only governor elected to the Country Music Hall of Fame, the Nashville Songwriters Hall of Fame and the Gospel Music Hall of Fame, and his hit song 'You Are My Sunshine' has since been adopted as the state anthem. Despite an optimistic start, Davis' reputation was in time corrupted by handlers who sought to maintain the governor's power through racist appeals.

Then, in 1959, the Longs returned to center stage when Huey's brother Earl was elected governor. The 'Earl of Louisiana' never quite lived up (or down) to Huey's nefarious reputation, but he steadfastly maintained the low standards expected of Louisiana's politicians with a series of embarrassing personal scandals. (For more on the Longs, see the Central Louisiana chapter.)

More disturbing political weirdness took place in 1988, when voters from the New Orleans suburb of Metairie sent David Duke – an acknowledged former Grand Wizard of the Ku Klux Klan – to the state capital as their representative. Three years later, Duke's race for governor gave voters the unenviable choice of either him or opponent Edwin Edwards, who had a reputation for being a crook. During the campaign Edwards quipped: 'The only way I won't get re-elected is if I get caught in bed with a live boy or a dead woman.' National attention created curious allies for Edwards, whose supporters displayed bumper stickers declaring, 'Vote for the Crook – It's Important.' Edwards narrowly won with 34% of the vote (compared to Duke's 32%) and went on to serve an unprecedented fourth term as governor, which ended in 1996. Duke, meanwhile, set his sights on the US Senate in 1990 and 1996, but was unsuccessful both times.

Current Republican governor Mike Foster seems to have no trouble living up to Louisiana's notorious legacy. Foster may not be up to Long's reputation for drinking, nor Edwin Edwards' glib quips, but so far he has not disappointed political observers. Foster's lament on election day, for example, was that it inconveniently coincided with the opening of duck-hunting season. While Foster missed the hunt, he did send mailers to duck-stamp holders encouraging them to vote absentee. Another Foster comment exclaimed his inclination, like 'any good Christian person,' to support David Duke for US Senate if the race was to come down to a runoff against a Democrat.

Foster hails from a political dynasty that includes his great-grandfather, Governor Murphy J Foster, who enacted the poll tax after his election in 1892 and required property ownership to vote. Following his great-grandfather's lead and the Republican national agenda, Governor Foster recently issued an executive order banning state affirmative action programs;

public pressure has since forced him to back down.

The Louisiana tradition continued with the 1996 Senate election. Advance voter polls had shown Republican Woody Jenkins favored over his Democratic opponent Mary Landrieu, bringing Jenkins close to being the state's first elected Republican senator since Reconstruction. When Landrieu was narrowly elected instead, Jenkins accused the Democrats of voter fraud. While Landrieu served her term, the FBI investigated what Jenkins' attorney claimed was 'the most heavily documented (contested election) case ever filed in the US Senate.' Interestingly, popular opinion (in New Orleans at least) has been generally critical of Jenkins for being a sore loser, as if in a state where politics is viewed as a sport, the hardest hitter will naturally be the victor. In October 1997, the FBI announced it had uncovered voter fraud, but since it was not decisively in Landrieu's favor, nor was it enough to swing the election the other way, Landrieu's election was not overturned.

As for the governmental nuts and bolts, Louisiana's state legislature is composed of a Senate of 39 members and a House of Representatives of 105 members; members of both houses are elected for four-year terms.

Economy
The state's economy is dominated by manufacturing (accounting for $4.3 billion a year of gross state product), which includes its petroleum and chemical industries along with smaller outfits such as the Tabasco empire. Agricultural production accounts for $1.92 billion of the gross state product, of which soybean production constitutes 13% and rice and sugarcane represent 11% each. Port operations in New Orleans and Baton Rouge are among the five busiest in the US.

Population & People
The population of Louisiana is 4,315,100. Over half define themselves as Caucasian, over a third identify themselves as black.

Slightly less than a quarter are Hispanic, and only a small fraction are Asian. The Caucasian population is divided evenly between urban areas and rural areas; the remaining ethnic groups are predominantly found in urban areas.

There is a wide difference between those folks who settled in the south and those in the north, and the cultural differences continue today. While the southern portion of the state was settled by French Catholics, north Louisiana was settled by Appalachian immigrants of largely Scottish and Irish descent who adopted the Southern Baptist faith. These very different groups often hold widely divergent opinions on matters of state.

Other significant ethnic groups are the Cajuns and Creoles, terms that can be confusing to outsiders. Cajun describes residents of Acadian heritage, and it applies largely to white people. Creole, while first used to describe Louisiana-born offspring of free immigrants – white or black – now is largely used to describe a predominantly black population whose heritage may include European, Native American and/or Caribbean roots.

Louisiana's multicultural diversity can best be experienced in New Orleans, where descendants of immigrants from many European, Asian and African nations maintain distinct ethnic traditions.

Information

Tourist Offices The Louisiana Department of Culture, Recreation & Tourism (☎ 504-342-8119, 800-633-6970, Net), PO Box 94291, Baton Rouge, LA 70804-9291, oversees historic preservation and the tourist bureaus, state museums and state parks (for more information on parks, see below). In the UK, you can contact the New Orleans & Louisiana tourist office at ☎ 0181-760-0377; there are no walk-in facilities.

Louisiana maintains 10 state welcome centers located at state borders on major freeways, in Baton Rouge and in New Orleans. All centers are open daily (excluding major holidays), and are good

resources for maps, events calendars and sightseeing information. They are also convenient pit stops.

Taxes In Louisiana, sales tax is 4% statewide and there are additional local levies. New Orleans sales tax totals 9%, and the city also levies an additional 5% on food and beverage sales, a 5% tax on amusements and a total accommodations tax of 11% plus $1 per person. At New Orleans international airport, taxes total 12% on all retail purchases – try to avoid buying anything there.

Driving Laws The minimum driving age is 16. Motorcycle helmets are required throughout the state.

Liquor Laws The minimum drinking age is 21 years (but this is not strictly enforced

---

Tax-Free Shopping

International visitors to Louisiana can receive refunds of up to 10% on sales taxes from over a thousand Louisiana Tax Free Shopping (LTFS) stores. Look for the 'Tax Free' sign in store windows. Foreign visitors must show participating LTFS merchants a valid passport (Canadians may substitute a birth certificate or driver's license) to receive a tax-refund voucher. At the LTFS refund center at New Orleans international airport you must present the following: voucher(s) with associated sales receipts, passport and roundtrip international ticket for under 90 days' stay. Refunds under $500 are made in cash; otherwise a check will be mailed to the visitor's home address.

A complete listing of LTFS merchants is included in the *New Orleans Visitor Guide* available free from the tourist and convention bureau (☎ 504-566-5003). The guide includes instructions printed in French, German, Italian, Japanese, Portuguese and Spanish. Also included is a useful description of each store plus its address, hours, telephone number, credit cards accepted and languages spoken. ■

LOUISIANA

Daiquiri Shops
When travelers in the other 49 states pull up to a fast-food chain's lighted sign and the voice over the speaker asks, 'Can I take your order, please,' they drive away with Happy Meals and tacos. In Louisiana, daiquiri chains are as ubiquitous as fast-food chains. Here you can order your favorite flavor of the frozen libation (with alcohol), then drive away.

True, it's illegal to drink and drive or to drive with an open container of alcohol in Louisiana. However, daiquiri dealers get around this by filling the paper or plastic cup and putting a plastic lid on it, albeit with a convenient hole in the middle for your straw.

– Diane Marshall

in New Orleans). In New Orleans, liquor sales are permitted around the clock.

Gambling The minimum age for gambling is 21 years.

State Parks For information on Louisiana's parks, call either ☎ 504-342-8111 or ☎ 888-677-1400.

The Louisiana Department of Wildlife & Fisheries in Baton Rouge (☎ 504-765-2800) issues fishing licenses and information. To use a Louisiana Wildlife Management Area, visitors between 16 and 59 years old must possess one of the following Louisiana licenses: a valid wildlife stamp, a fishing license or a hunting license. You can purchase them at sheriff's departments, the Department of Wildlife and Fisheries, fishing outfitters and some stores around the state.

A multitude of other national, state and local authorities oversees other natural areas in Louisiana; see destination chapters for detailed information.

New Orleans

There is perhaps no city in the US more sensuous than New Orleans. Naturally languid from the subtropical heat and humidity, nothing ever goes too fast or grows too worrisome. The food is rich, music is everywhere, the historic district is beautiful and lived-in, Mardi Gras is an incomparable visual spectacle, and you'd have to work awfully hard to not have a good time.

Hot brass bands, jazz performers, and Cajun and zydeco groups play music such as you've likely never heard before. Whether at a local dive, Jazz Fest or a concert hall hosting top performers from around the country, the music of New Orleans inspires audiences to *laissez les bons temps rouler*.

New Orleans also offers some of the best food in the US. African, Spanish, French, Italian and Caribbean culinary influences reflect the city's cultural diversity. From world-renowned restaurants and romantic bistros to corner cafes and oyster shacks, celebrity and everyday chefs make their mark. Start out with café au lait and beignets for breakfast, and graze through the day sampling jambalaya, crawfish étouffée or andouille sausage, along with down-home fried green tomatoes, red beans and rice, and banana pudding.

Though all city festivals offer good times – and Bourbon St hosts a nearly continuous block party year-round – New Orleans is most notorious for its raucous Mardi Gras celebration, preceded by a month-long season of carnival balls and festivities. A good way to get into the spirit is to costume up and join the parade. The more feathers, beads and sequins, the better (though lots of flesh will also do) – and feel free to borrow liberally from grotesque mythology, voodoo or aberrant fantasies. Strands of gold, purple and green beads continue to decorate trees and wrought-iron balconies along the parade route from past pagan processions.

HIGHLIGHTS

- Getting in costume for wild antics during Mardi Gras
- Live jazz, zydeco, bluegrass and R&B at the Jazz & Heritage Festival
- A walking tour around the historic French Quarter
- Bar-hopping on Bourbon St
- Sampling Creole and Cajun specialties such as gumbo, jambalaya and crawfish étouffée

In the French Quarter, compact blocks of colorful Spanish architecture surround Jackson Square in the 18th-century historic district first settled in 1718. After the Louisiana Purchase in 1803, the Americans moved in, building grand homes upriver along the St Charles Ave streetcar line that was established in 1835. 'Uptown' today encompasses the Garden District, a few university campuses and the Riverbend area. Older, crowded faubourgs ('false towns' or suburbs) border the French Quarter: Faubourg Marigny appeals to a Bohemian mix of gays and straights, while the rugged Tremé district still thrives on music as it has since jazz first emanated from its historic square. Watch for the emergent avant-garde in Bywater and the Lower Garden District.

The Crescent City, so-called for its position at a bend in the Mississippi River, goes by quite a few nicknames. The Big Easy best characterizes its easygoing nature. But you'll find that residents aren't forgiving if you mispronounce the city's official name: it should be N'AW-lins, New OR-lins, or even New OR-le-uns, but *never* New Or-LEENS.

History

Founded by the French in 1718, New Orleans was ruled by the Spanish from 1764 until the French resumed control in 1803. Within days, Napoleon gave the city and its unhappy Creole residents to the US as part of the vast Louisiana Purchase. Soon the French Creoles and African slaves were joined by Anglo-Americans who built the region's powerful plantation economy on the backs of slaves.

By 1840, New Orleans was the nation's fourth city to exceed 100,000 inhabitants, joining New York, Philadelphia and Baltimore. It survived the Civil War as the South's largest city, remaining so until in the 1960s when a booming Atlanta, Georgia, eclipsed New Orleans in population. Despite the onslaught of hurricanes, floods and epidemics through the city's history, it miraculously perseveres, celebrating its unique heritage with an extraordinary joie de vivre.

French Settlement When French explorers Pierre Le Moyne, Sieur d'Iberville, and his brother Jean-Baptiste Le Moyne, Sieur de Bienville, sailed up the Mississippi River in 1699, they noticed a small portage that led across a narrow spit of land from the great river to a large lake. The portage was later named Bayou St John; the lake, Lake Pontchartrain; and the spit of land, Nouvelle Orléans.

In 1718, Bienville laid out the city of New Orleans. With a child king on the French throne and the regent's hands full, responsibility for promotion of the new settlement fell to John Law, head of the Company of the Indies, which controlled France's world trade. As Bienville's original group of 30 convicts, six carpenters and four Canadians struggled against yellow-fever epidemics and floods in the subtropical mire, Law liberally portrayed Louisiana as heaven on Earth to prospective European settlers. One painting depicted New Orleans bustling against a backdrop of snow-capped mountains!

Early immigrants arrived from France, Canada and Germany. The French also imported thousands of African slaves. By 1746, African slaves in New Orleans numbered over 3000, exceeding the French settlers by a factor of two. Yet not all blacks were slaves. Once freed from slavery, Africans joined the community known as *les gens de couleur libre* (free people of color). These ex-slaves were subject to the Code Noir (Black Code), which restricted their ability to vote, hold public office, and marry outside their race. Any offspring born in the colony to free foreign immigrants, be they European or African, were called Creoles.

Colonial mercantilism was an economic failure and the harsh realities of life in New Orleans inhibited civilian immigration – especially by women. The colonists created an exchange economy based on smuggling and local trade, and the city developed a reputation for its extralegal enterprise and swarthy character. When the Ursuline nuns arrived in 1728, Sister Hachard observed: 'the devil here has a very large empire.'

Spanish Domination The essential French character of New Orleans was little affected by the change from French to Spanish rule in 1764, though growing resentments over Spanish control later prompted a small local rebellion against the Spanish regime.

During this time, Acadian refugees from Canada arrived in New Orleans and were shunted off to westward swamplands (see the Cajun Country chapter). After the 1791 slave revolt in the French colony of St Domingue (now Haiti), thousands of former slaves emigrated to New Orleans (and to neighboring Acadiana) as free people of color.

Louisiana Purchase & Antebellum New Orleans The Louisiana Purchase of 1803 saw New Orleans pass into American

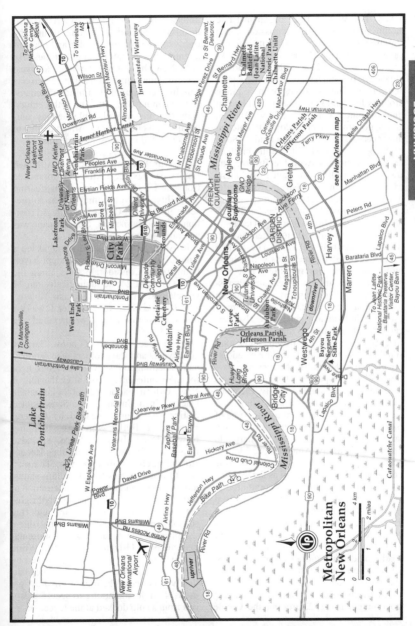

Metropolitan New Orleans

LOUISIANA

hands. The War of 1812 began just one month after Louisiana's admission to the Union as the 18th state. As British forces gathered in Jamaica, General Andrew Jackson assembled in New Orleans a motley alliance of free blacks, Acadians, Choctaws and pirates. The escapades of the pirating brothers Jean and Pierre Lafitte had by that time become legendary in New Orleans, and a government crackdown threatened their successful smuggling operation. So in exchange for amnesty, the Lafitte brothers decided not to side with the British. The Battle of New Orleans engaged the Americans against the British in Chalmette, downriver from the city. The American victory (291 British lives lost versus 13 US losses) made a national hero of Jackson.

In town, the adjustment to American control was less than welcome. The French Creoles associated Americans with a boisterous and domineering culture that they considered vulgar. The Americans' Protestant beliefs and support for English common law, emphasizing corporate interests over individual rights, were also perceived as threatening to the Creole way of life. In 1808 the territorial legislature sought to preserve Creole culture by adopting elements of Spanish and French laws – especially the Napoleonic Code as it relates to equity, succession and family. Elements of the code persist in Louisiana today.

In the 1830s, a merchant by the name of Samuel Jarvis Peters purchased plantation land upriver from the French Quarter to create a distinctly American residential section separate from the Quarter's Creole community. Canal St served as the dividing line between the antagonistic communities, and its median was considered 'neutral ground.' Developers further transformed 15 riverbank plantations into ostentatious residences for the new Americans. By 1835 the New Orleans & Carrollton Railroad provided horse-drawn transit along St Charles Ave, where the present streetcar line remains today.

Americans took control of the municipal government in 1852, eroding the Creole influence in New Orleans. Americans also dismissed the Code Noir, diminishing the rights of free people of color and marginalizing their economic opportunities. By 1850 New Orleans was the South's largest slave-trading center with some 25 markets handling an internal US traffic in humans.

Throughout the 18th and 19th century, New Orleans was also plagued by outbreaks of yellow fever. An epidemic in 1853 resulted in almost 8000 deaths.

Civil War & Reconstruction Although Louisiana was the sixth state to secede from the US, New Orleans itself, fearing instability, had voted three-to-one to preserve the Union. Given its strategic position on the Mississippi, New Orleans was naturally a prime Union target.

In April, Admiral David Farragut led a Union squadron up the Mississippi River, bombarding Confederate forts along the way. On April 24, he dramatically ran 17 vessels past a river blockade and captured New Orleans only two days later. It was the first Confederate city to be captured and occupied.

Some free people of color, largely landowners and slaveholders who felt they had something to lose, volunteered to fight for the Confederacy. But after the fall of New Orleans about 24,000 Louisiana blacks joined Union forces. Some joined Native Guard units headed by General Benjamin F Butler who was occupying New Orleans. Butler's force was also responsible for initiating Lincoln's Reconstruction policies after the war. The plan was to restore states to antebellum status, minus slavery and without compensation to former slaveholders. Voting and civil rights were extended to black males and free schools were established in each parish.

Opposing these gains, white supremacists in New Orleans formed the White League to oust the government elected by newly enfranchised black voters. They battled with police at the foot of Poydras Ave in 1874 while attempting to secure weapons from a ship docked at the levee.

After occupying troops left in 1877, many civil rights gains were lost as Jim Crow segregation became commonplace. One of the most significant challenges to segregation – the court case of *Plessy* v *Ferguson* – was instigated in 1896 by a New Orleans quadroon named Homer Plessy. The 'separate but equal' policy that sprung from this case established official racial segregation in the South for 58 years.

The Jazz Age By the early 20th century all the cultural elements were ripe for the musical revolution that gave birth to jazz. Ever since arriving in America as slaves, Africans had been congregating in Congo Square every Sunday to dance and sing to an African drumbeat – the only place in the South where this was permitted – adding violins and banjos by the 1830s.

Eventually, the indigenous musical genre called jazz took shape with performers such as Jelly Roll Morton and band leader Buddy Bolden. Many early jazz musicians performed in the red-light district of Storyville (ignominiously named after alderman Albert Story, who fought to restrict vice to this small quadrant).

With the advent of recording technology, the unstoppable export of jazz from New Orleans began in 1917 when the Original Dixieland Jazz Band (a white band) recorded *At the Darktown Strutters' Ball*. Today Congo Square has been renamed Louis Armstrong Park, in honor of the city's famous native son.

Modern Economic Development In the 1960s, the city's historic trade connection with Latin America – responsible for bringing the scent of roasting coffee and imported tropical fruits to the city – lost ground to Miami.

From 1972 to 1981 New Orleans enjoyed a booming economy propelled by the manufacture and financing of offshore oil rigs. The economic turmoil of the 1981 oil surplus and ensuing price crash reverberated

Louis Armstrong

throughout the state in the following years. Energy produced 41% of the state's revenues in 1982, but had plummeted to 13% in 1992.

The steady growth of tourism (despite reports of the city's high crime rate) provides many service jobs in hotels, restaurants and museums, making up an increasing share of the employment opportunities in New Orleans.

Population & People
Metropolitan New Orleans has a population of over 1.2 million. African Americans constitute the majority at 62% of the population; Anglo-Americans comprise 35%. The total Hispanic population is 3%, including the well-established Cuban community and more recent immigrants from Central America. Though statistically less significant, a community of upwards of 12,000 Vietnamese and other Asians have settled at the far eastern edge of the city around Versailles.

The gulf between the wealthy upper crust and poor lower classes is very wide here. One person in four lives below the poverty line in New Orleans.

Orientation

New Orleans is bounded by the Mississippi River to the south and Lake Pontchartrain to the north. Local orientation is relative to these two bodies of water: things are either lakeside or riverside, upriver or downriver. It's a simple system if you know where the river is, but at times it can be confusing. For example, though the convention center is southwest of the French Quarter, locals will send you 'upriver.' On maps, the Lower Garden District is situated above the central Garden District to the south, but because it's downriver, it's considered 'lower.'

In New Orleans, avenues are generally four-lane major thoroughfares, and streets usually have two-lanes. Street numbering between the river and lake typically starts at the river. For routes that run parallel to

the river, street numbers begin at Canal St. Due to the vagaries of the river, Uptown streets are labeled 'south' and streets east of Canal St are 'north' whether or not a compass would prove that true.

The city's historic French Quarter (Vieux Carré) is made up of 80 blocks around Jackson Square. The 'upper' Quarter (upriver), bounded by Canal St, is where most large convention-style hotels are situated. The 'lower' Quarter, downriver from the square, is quieter and largely residential. Stretching upriver from the Canal St ferry landing to the riverfront streetcar terminus on Esplanade Ave is the tourist zone where you'll find attractions such as the aquarium, Jackson Brewery and the French Market.

The Faubourg Marigny, a lively and predominantly gay district centered on Frenchmen St, is downriver from Esplanade Ave. Beyond the Marigny is the rugged Bywater district, where a few hipster hangouts are dispersed. Up Esplanade Ave from the Marigny towards the lake you'll find City Park and the Fair Grounds Race Track.

The Tremé district, one of the original faubourgs designed by colonial developers, is centered around Louis Armstrong Park, which is on the lakeside boundary of the French Quarter along N Rampart St (named after the fortification that once surrounded the city). This is a predominantly African-American residential district.

The Central Business District (CBD) stretches upriver from the historic Canal St boundary to around Lee Circle at the freeway overpass. The CBD offers little for visitors, but recent development along the riverfront is helping to transform the old Warehouse District at the riverside fringe of the CBD into an appealing arts center.

Uptown, historically considered anything upriver from Canal St, is now used to refer to the largely residential communities southwest of the CBD, across the freeway. The central thoroughfares of St Charles Ave, with its historic streetcar, and Magazine St (a bus route) transport people to Uptown's many distinct neighborhoods.

Isle of Orleans

Were it not for human intervention, much of present-day New Orleans would be under water – the city's elevation averages two feet *below* sea level. Elevated land, formed naturally when silt was moved by floods, exists near the river levees that generally serve as the city's crescent-shaped southern boundary.

Local drainage flows northward toward Lake Pontchartrain, a shallow body of saltwater that washes against the northern edge of New Orleans. By reclaiming low-lying swamps along the lake, engineers have created neighborhoods that are dependent on massive pumps which keep rising waters at bay.

New Orleans is surrounded by 130 miles of levees. We can assume that Fats Domino's hit song 'Walkin' to New Orleans,' refers to travel along the river levees. No other land connections exist. Motorists heading toward New Orleans on I-10 from either the east or west travel over waterways on elevated freeways. ■

Directly across the freeway from the CBD, the Lower Garden District is the low-rent cousin of its chichi neighbor upriver. This largely ramshackle neighborhood offers budget guesthouses and a bohemian enclave at the elbow where Magazine St meets Camp St at Sophie Wright Place.

The lovely adjacent Garden District, which is well known for its walking tours past historic homes, is bounded lakeside by St Charles Ave, riverside by Magazine St, with Louisiana and Jackson Aves forming the respective upper and lower boundaries.

The Riverbend area along S Carrollton Ave at the corner of St Charles Ave is populated by many university students. Both City Park and the Fair Grounds are accessible from the Riverbend via S Carrollton Ave, which becomes Wisner Blvd as it heads toward the lake.

The geographic center of the city, between the established riverfront and lakefront corridors, is called Mid-City. It holds the least appeal for visitors, and is most often traversed only on the elevated interstate that shadows its neighborhoods.

Maps Good-quality maps of New Orleans are available from most bookstores, and less comprehensive free maps are also widely available. Rental-car firms have heaps of maps but the best is the excellent *New Orleans Street Map & Visitor Guide* available free from tourist offices. It depicts Regional Transit Authority (RTA) bus routes and also includes a street index.

Rand McNally's *New Orleans City Map* has a street index and an up-to-date depiction of all streets in the city. AAA's *New Orleans & Vicinity Map* is a compact guide that details the CBD and French Quarter but simplifies the rest of town; members can ask for a comprehensive city map as well.

Information
Tourist Offices Looking out over Jackson Square from the historic Lower Pontalba Building in the heart of the French Quarter, the welcome center (☎ 504-566-5031), at

529 St Ann St, offers brochures, listings of upcoming events, and discount RTA passes. It also offers free copies of the *African American Heritage Map*, which highlights historic landmarks. Helpful staff-members can answer questions and offer advice about New Orleans; however, few resources are available for the non-English speaker. It's open daily from 9 am to 5 pm. Small, staffed information kiosks scattered throughout the main tourist areas stock many of the same materials offered at the welcome center.

Travelers' Aid (☎ 504-528-9026) has an information booth at the airport; it operates daily from 9 am to 9 pm.

For information on Louisiana write to the Louisiana Office of Tourism (☎ 504-342-8119, 800-414-8626), PO Box 94291, Baton Rouge, LA 70804. In the UK, you can contact the New Orleans & Louisiana tourist office at ☎ 0181 760 0377; there are no walk-in facilities. French visitors should contact Claude Teboul at France Louisiane de la Nouvelle Orléans (☎ 01 45 77 09 68), 28 boulevard de Strasbourg, 75010 Paris.

The easiest way to have local information sent by mail is to call the welcome center (☎ 504-566-5031) day or night. Both the New Orleans Metropolitan Convention and Visitors Bureau (☎ 504-566-5003, 800-672-6124, Net) and the Greater New Orleans Black Tourism Network (☎ 504-523-5652) are only open on weekdays and share an address in the Superdome at 1520 Sugar Bowl Dr, New Orleans, LA 70112.

On the Internet, the Greater New Orleans Free-Net and the New Orleans Connection are two sites with a wide range of tourist information (see Internet directory).

Consulates See Embassies & Consulates in Facts for the Visitor for a list of foreign consulates in New Orleans.

Money There are many ATMs around New Orleans offering the usual services.

First NBC bank contributed to producing the free *New Orleans Street Map*; naturally

LOUISIANA

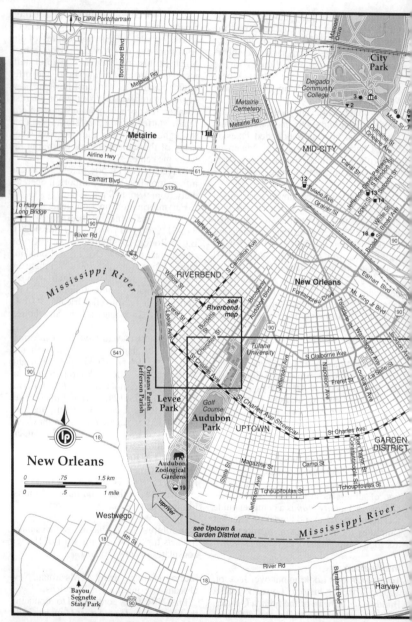

New Orleans

0   .75   1.5 km
0   .5   1 mile

To Lake Pontchartrain

City Park

Metairie

MID-CITY

New Orleans

RIVERBEND

see Riverbend map

Tulane University

Levee Park

Golf Course

Audubon Park

UPTOWN

GARDEN DISTRICT

Audubon Zoological Gardens

Mississippi River

see Uptown & Garden District map

Mississippi River

Westwego

Harvey

River Rd

Bayou Segnette State Park

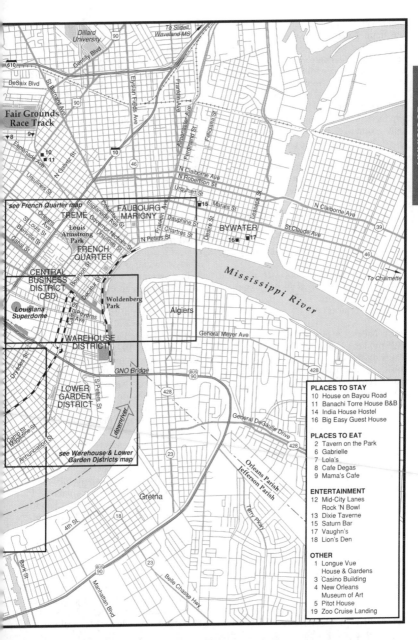

LOUISIANA

PLACES TO STAY
10 House on Bayou Road
11 Banachi Torre House B&B
14 India House Hostel
16 Big Easy Guest House

PLACES TO EAT
2 Tavern on the Park
6 Gabrielle
7 Lola's
8 Cafe Degas
9 Mama's Cafe

ENTERTAINMENT
12 Mid-City Lanes
   Rock 'N Bowl
13 Dixie Taverne
15 Saturn Bar
17 Vaughn's
18 Lion's Den

OTHER
1 Longue Vue
   House & Gardens
3 Casino Building
4 New Orleans
   Museum of Art
5 Pitot House
19 Zoo Cruise Landing

it marks all their branch offices and ATMs. The main American Express Travel Services office (☎ 504-586-8201) at 158 Baronne St offers currency exchange along with cash advances for members. It's open Monday to Friday from 9 am to 5 pm.

The *Times-Picayune*'s Sunday travel section publishes current exchange rates as provided by American Express. Independent exchange bureaus can be easily found. In the airport terminal (near Delta) you can change money at Travelex (☎ 504-465-9647), open daily from 6 am to 7 pm, and at Whitney Bank (☎ 504-838-6492). Since the exchanges are so close, get quotes from both.

Downtown outlets generally offer the best rates of exchange. Besides American Express, try the main offices of banks such as First NBC (☎ 504-561-1371), 210 Baronne St.

The AAA office (☎ 800-926-4222) at 3445 N Causeway Blvd in the suburb of Metairie also offers foreign currency exchange services.

Post The main post office (☎ 504-589-1135) is near Union passenger terminal at 701 Loyola Ave. General delivery mail (poste restante) can be sent to you here marked c/o General Delivery, New Orleans, LA 70112. General delivery mail is only held for 30 days and it's not advisable to get general delivery mail sent to other post offices in New Orleans. There are other post offices at the airport mail center (☎ 504-589-1296) in the passenger terminal; the World Trade Center (☎ 504-524-0033), 2 Canal St; in the French Quarter (☎ 504-524-0072), 1022 Iberville St; and in the CBD on Lafayette Square (☎ 504-524-0491), 610 S Maestri Place.

Fax Fax machines are easy to find at storefront shipping outlets such as Mail Boxes Etc, at photocopy shops and at hotel business service centers, but be prepared to pay over $1 a page. Most hotels provide a limited fax service free for guests. Commercial fax services are available at the French Quarter Postal Emporium

(☎ 504-525-6651, fax 504-525-6652), 940 Royal St at St Philip St.

Kinko's Copy Centers, where you can send and receive faxes, are open 24 hours at two locations: in the CBD at 762 St Charles Ave (☎ 504-581-2541, fax 504-525-6272), and Uptown at the Riverbend near the universities, 1140 S Carrollton Ave (☎ 504-861-8016, fax 504-866-0502).

Email Terminals in the main library are equipped to allow Web browsing and access to chat groups, though not to send or receive email. You should carry your own laptop to log on or send email; when making hotel reservations inquire if your room is equipped with a modem line.

Newspapers & Periodicals The daily *Times-Picayune* has the largest circulation of any newspaper in Louisiana. It offers a daily entertainment calendar, and Friday's edition features an expanded 'Lagniappe' entertainment guide. See the Internet directory at the back of this book for details of the paper's Website.

The *Louisiana Weekly*, published in New Orleans since 1925, offers an African-American perspective on local and regional politics and events. Billing itself as 'the people's paper,' *New Orleans Data News Weekly* focuses on local news. Hispanic readers should pick up *La Prensa*, a monthly newspaper that features bilingual articles.

For alternative news and entertainment listings, pick up a copy of the free weekly newspaper *Gambit*. The free monthly *Offbeat* has a comprehensive club calendar and reviews of local performances. Find these indispensable resources in hotel lobbies, at coffee shops, record stores or the Riverwalk Mall.

The glossy monthly *New Orleans Magazine* offers higher-quality writing on the city.

Radio A community radio station, WWOZ-FM at 90.7, offers the most jazz, as well as a mix of blues and R&B. WWNO-FM at 89.9 mainly broadcasts classical music but plays jazz from 10:30 pm to 1 am – it's the city's only National Public Radio (NPR) affiliate and offers morning and evening news programs. KLGZ-FM at 106.7 plays 'smooth jazz.' There's a zydeco program on Sunday from 4 to 6 pm on WSLA-AM at 1560. News and lengthy literary programming is broadcast by WRVH-FM at 88.3. They read the entire local paper – including Ann Landers' advice column – on air for the blind 'and print handicapped.' A lewd counterpoint is the nightly 'passion show' or 'love phones' program on WEZB-FM at 97.1 with sexual decadence befitting the city.

Photography & Video Liberty Camera Center (☎ 504-523-6252) at 337 Carondelet St, provides professional photo processing and services downtown (expect about four days wait for Kodachrome processing). Downtown Fast Foto (☎ 504-525-2598), 327 St Charles Ave, offers quick color print and E-6 slide processing. They also have color copy machines. French Quarter Camera (☎ 504-529-2974) is across from Café du Monde at 809 Decatur St. For camera repairs and used gear there's Alfredo's Cameras (☎ 504-523-2421), 916 Gravier St.

Travel Agencies The *Times-Picayune* Sunday travel section is a good place to search for discount travel deals. Local agencies that advertise discounted airline tickets include Omega World Travel (☎ 504-525-8900), 201 St Charles Ave, and Deviney's Associated Travel (☎ 504-837-9907), 2305 Veterans Memorial Parkway, Metairie. A few full-service travel agencies offer more than just cheap airline seats: student and budget travelers can pick-up Eurail passes and other tickets from Council Travel (☎ 504-866-1767), 6363 St Charles Ave at the Loyola University Student Center.

AAA Travel Agency (☎ 504-838-7500, 800-452-7198), 3445 N Causeway Blvd, Metairie, offers complete travel planning for nonmembers and free maps and assistance for its members. American Express

(☎ 504-586-8201) operates a travel office and currency exchange at 158 Baronne St.

Bookstores Book-lovers will find plenty of good independent bookstores in New Orleans. Most second-hand bookstores carry some new titles, including city guides and books by local authors, in addition to used books. Look for the map of New Orleans' second-hand bookstores compiled by Russell Desmond, owner of Arcadian Books & Art Prints (☎ 504-523-4138), 714 Orleans St. Desmond speaks French fluently and is a wonderful (yet cynical) ambassador for New Orleans.

General Bookstores Bookstar (☎ 504-523-6411) at 414 N Peters St near the Hard Rock Cafe in the French Quarter is a large chain outlet that carries a wide variety of new books and periodicals. In the same building, Tower Records (☎ 504-529-4411) offers magazines, underground comics and obscure publications.

In the CBD, DeVille Books (☎ 504-525-1486), 344 Carondelet St, mixes a few fine used volumes with new offerings, including LP travel guides and maps.

The Garden District Bookshop (☎ 504-895-2266), 2727 Prytania St in The Rink shopping center at Washington Ave, offers a select collection of first editions and collector books on the region. Also Uptown, Beaucoup Books (☎ 504-895-2663), 5414 Magazine St, offers a good New Orleans selection, plus large stocks of foreign-language books, travel and fiction. In the Riverbend district, you'll find the Maple Street Bookstore (☎ 504-866-4916) at 7523 Maple St.

Specialty & Used Bookstores A French Quarter landmark, Faulkner House Bookshop (☎ 504-524-2940), 624 Pirates Alley, offers a good selection of literature and rare books along with new paperbacks by local and Southern authors.

On Royal St, you'll find a small collection of new and used books on regional history and politics at the Historic New Orleans Collection (☎ 504-523-4662) at No 533;

voodoo and occult works are available from Starling Books (☎ 504-595-6777), No 1022; books on Native Americans at Vision Quest (☎ 504-523-0920), No 1034; and quality used children's books at Old Children's Books (☎ 504-525-3655), No 734.

Among the French Quarter's second-hand stores you will find two floors of used books at Beckham's Book Store (☎ 504-522-9875), 228 Decatur St. Nearby, Crescent City Books (☎ 504-524-4997), 204 Chartres St, offers a variety of used works at reasonable prices, plus a few new titles. In the far reaches of the lower Quarter, Kaboom Books (☎ 504-529-5780), 901 Barracks St, is a worthwhile store to visit for its large and varied collection.

Larger collections are shelved at the Uptown shops of George Herget (☎ 504-891-5595), 3109 Magazine St, and the Great Acquisitions Book Service (☎ 504-861-8707), 8200 Hampson St near the Riverbend and Maple St shops.

For books written by or for African Americans, head to Vera Walker's Community Book Center (☎ 504-822-2665), 217 N Broad St, near the Fair Grounds. At the Uptown Square Book Store (☎ 504-865-8310), 200 Broadway in the mall, Mark Zumpke specializes in African-American literary fiction.

Libraries The Louisiana Room (☎ 504-596-2610), on the 3rd floor of the public library (☎ 504-529-7323, Net), 219 Loyola Ave in the CBD, is an excellent resource for books, newspapers and maps. You can search the library's online catalog via NOPLine (☎ 504-595-8930).

Campuses New Orleans' foremost private universities are Tulane and Loyola, with spacious campuses Uptown off St Charles Ave across from Audubon Park.

Tulane University (☎ 504-865-5000), 6823 St Charles Ave, was founded by seven physicians in 1834 in response to cholera and yellow-fever epidemics. It now enrolls 12,000 students in 11 colleges and schools, including a law school and school of medicine. Among Tulane's most noted

graduates are the president of France, Jacques Chirac (who wrote his thesis on the port of New Orleans), and US Speaker of the House of Representatives, Newt Gingrich, who opposed university censorship of the student newspaper in 1968. The Amistad Research Center – the world's largest African-American archive – and the WR Hogan Jazz Archives are two of Tulane's attractions.

Loyola University (☎ 504-865-2011), 6363 St Charles Ave, was founded by the Jesuits in 1917. The Roman Catholic university is best known for its College of Music, School of Business and Department of Communications.

Dillard and Xavier Universities are the city's historic African-American schools. Founded in 1869, Dillard University (☎ 504-283-8822), 2601 Gentilly Blvd, was an important meeting site for civil rights leaders. The oldest building on campus is the 1934 library building, but the stately Avenue of the Oaks is the campus's most attractive feature. Established in 1915, Xavier University (☎ 504-486-7411), 7325 Palmetto St, is the only historically black Roman Catholic university in the US. Xavier boasts an exceptional College of Pharmacy.

The largest public campus in town, the University of New Orleans (UNO; ☎ 504-280-6000) on the lakefront enrolls 16,000 students. Its Kiefer Arena hosts large concerts and events.

Cultural Centers Operated by the National Park Service, the Jean Lafitte National Historic Park does a great job of detailing the wide variety of cultural communities in New Orleans at its headquarters in the French Market on N Peters St. The cultural organizations that hold regular gatherings include:

Cuban American Association	☎ 504-523-2600
Chinese Association	☎ 504-887-8328
Deutsches Haus	☎ 504-522-8014
Filippino American Goodwill Society	☎ 504-945-3536
Korean Association of Greater New Orleans	☎ 504-456-1606

Asociación de Guatemala en Louisiana	☎ 504-733-5070
Honduran Association of Louisiana	☎ 504-456-0900
Irish Cultural Society	☎ 504-861-3746
American Italian Museum	☎ 504-891-1904
Japan Society	☎ 504-283-4890
Japan Club	☎ 504-589-6893
Jewish Community Center	☎ 504-897-0143
Club Social Nicaraguense	☎ 504-524-1329

International visitors might also contact the University of New Orleans' Council for International Visitors (☎ 504-286-7266) or Alliance Française (☎ 504-568-0770), 1519 Jackson Ave.

Laundry A few bars in New Orleans offer self-service laundry facilities. If one is not nearby, Hula Mae's laundry (☎ 504-522-1336) at 832 N Rampart St will pick you up.

Medical Services The Charity Hospital (☎ 504-568-2311), 1532 Tulane Ave, offers free services to those who qualify and pro-rates fees on a sliding scale for others.

Walgreens offers two 24-hour locations within a short drive from the French Quarter at 3311 Canal St at Jefferson Davis Parkway (☎ 504-822-8073) and 1100 Elysian Fields Ave near St Claude Ave (☎ 504-943-9788). Many outlying K&B Drug Stores are open 24 hours; the closest to the French Quarter is at 3401 St Charles Ave (☎ 504-895-0344) at Louisiana Ave in the Garden District. Condoms are commonly available from vending machines in public restrooms at bars and some restaurants.

Dangers & Annoyances New Orleans has a seriously high violent-crime rate (in 1995 there was an average of one homicide per day), and tourists are not immune. Wide income disparities, drug use and police corruption all contribute to the problem. Though a new police chief hired with national fanfare in 1996 promises to reduce crime, visitors must take every precaution to avoid becoming a target. Use common sense: travel in pairs or groups; leave flashy jewelry or valuables

at home; stick to routes that are well traveled and well peopled, particularly at night; and budget for a taxi fare to avoid dark walks to nightspots or hotels. Use money belts and hotel safes to store valuables, and carry a small, easily accessible stash of cash to throw down if ever accosted.

Though crime may occur throughout the city, visitors would be wise to avoid certain areas where crime occurs most frequently. Since most crime is perpetrated on the impoverished residents of poor neighborhoods, staying out of such areas makes sense. Note that neighborhoods may shift abruptly from relatively safe to dangerously unsafe. Desolate areas with only short sight lines, including St Louis Cemetery No 1 and Louis Armstrong Park, have a particularly bad reputation. These worthwhile sights can be more safely visited in groups or on a tour (independent travelers may want to wait and slide up as a tour group enters).

That said, it would be a shame to spend your vacation preoccupied with safety. Most visitors to New Orleans are able to thoroughly enjoy the city's many attractions and friendly people, discovering exciting nightspots, drinking, dancing and staying out late, without encountering anything seedier than a request for spare change. A wrong turn onto a rundown street is not a death sentence; you'll likely find a helpful resident to set you back on course. But it is not a city to be careless in. It's especially easy to become disoriented and vulnerable after drinking.

As for pedestrian safety, be mindful of traffic. Pedestrians do not have the right of way and motorists (unless they are from out of state) do not yield.

Be wary too of street hustlers who come up with creative scams to separate tourists from their money. This one's a classic: the hustler approaches a tourist and challenges 'I bet I can tell you where you got them shoes.' After they wager and shake on it, the hustler announces triumphantly 'You got them on your feet on Bourbon St in New Orleans!'

LOUISIANA

FRENCH QUARTER

Nowhere else in the US can you see such an extensive array of architecture as in New Orleans' French Quarter. At its heart is the French and Spanish colonial heritage of Jackson Square, offering pristine architectural symmetry and modern cultural chaos – because this historic district remains so well-used and lively, it has a European feel.

The NPS oversees architectural preservation efforts in the Quarter, and rangers offer free walking tours of the area. By strolling through the residential lower Quarter in particular you can absorb a sense of the place – its lacy ironwork balconies,

---

Architecture

On the eve of Spanish control, New Orleans was a symmetrical grid of 44 blocks formally centered about the Place d'Armes (now Jackson Square) – a muddy parade ground facing the river and surrounded on three sides by religious and government buildings. As yet, a quarter of the blocks were unoccupied, and a few residents were in the process of replacing earlier wooden structures with Spanish-style brick houses with red-tile roofs. Better suited to the tropical climate than French architecture, Spanish architecture features cross ventilation and shaded interior courts. Among the most readily identified Spanish elements are broad window openings crowned by graceful arches. There are handsome fan-shaped transoms above many entrances.

Fires in 1788 and again in 1794 wiped out most remaining French architecture. The Cabildo (Spanish council chamber) mandated post-fire building codes that specified brick construction and tile or slate roofs. Houses facing the levee were to be two stories with a gallery in front and residence on the upper floor.

The first efforts to preserve the quaint and distinctive elements of the Quarter began in 1937, when the French Quarter acquired historic-district status, and the federal government enlisted the unemployed to restore the French Market and Pontalba Buildings. Today, the Quarter's overwhelming assortment of Creole townhouses and simple cottages with overhanging balconies decorated with lacy iron railings are among the most emblematic features of the city. Jackson Square itself qualifies as one of the finest architectural spaces in the country. Built in 1745, the old Ursuline Convent is the oldest building in New Orleans and remains impressively preserved.

However, historic preservation of the French Quarter has led some critics to regard it as a Creole Disneyland. Since 1937, the Quarter's population has plummeted from 12,000 to about 5000 today. The Quarter's working-class population, unable to afford the high rents in the gentrified neighborhood, has now gone. Most notable is the decline in the number of blacks and families.

Many visitors may question the inauthentic character of the Quarter's riverfront buildings on Decatur and N Peters Sts – Jackson Brewery (once fully operational producing Jax beer, now a mall), Planet Hollywood, Tower Records, and the like. These have not displaced historic structures: since the city was founded the river has altered its course, exposing the land on which they stand.

The most renowned of New Orleans' architects is Benjamin Henry Latrobe. Latrobe was the noted architect of the Capitol in Washington, DC, and the Baltimore Cathedral. After arriving in New Orleans in 1819, his early commissions included the St Louis Cathedral tower, and construction of the waterworks with their innovative pumping stations. Before he succumbed to yellow fever, Latrobe designed the Louisiana State Bank building at 403 Royal St.

Also well known are James Gallier Sr, father of distinguished architect James Gallier Jr. Gallier Sr is best known for Greek revival Gallier Hall, 545 St Charles Ave, where Farragut's forces took control of the city in 1862. He also took part in designing the Pontalba Buildings fronting Place d'Armes. Appreciation of Gallier Jr's contributions to the city best begins at the house he built for his family at 1132 Royal St; it's now the Gallier House Museum and is open to public tours. ∎

rows of shops in hues from royal blue to vivid orange, and fragrances wafting from flowerpots and lush pocket gardens.

Within the upper Quarter are the tourist areas which are equated with New Orleans throughout the world. The bright lights and noisy bars along Bourbon St are in stark contrast to Royal St, with its tony antique shops and galleries. Both streets offer some of the finest old-line Creole restaurants in the city. On any given night on Bourbon St you can sample rock, jazz and Cajun music only footsteps apart. If the shops along Royal St are too regal for your tastes, try the French Market, which houses the Farmers Market and Flea Market, offering inexpensive goods from Louisiana and around the world.

Royal St Walking Tour
As the main street of the French Quarter, Royal St has long been the most prestigious address in town. Today the stretch of Royal St near Jackson Square holds the city's finest shops and galleries. Downriver toward Esplanade Ave is a residential section with the Gallier House Museum among its distinguished houses.

Start the walking tour around St Philip St at the Cornstalk Fence Hotel at 914 Royal St (see Places to Stay). The fence out front is made of cast iron and dates from 1859.

Turn left for a short side trip to the French colonial house built in 1788 at 632 Dumaine St before returning to Royal St. This was the setting for the popular story 'Tite Poullette' by New Orleans writer George Washington Cable. The house has several distinctive features: its raised brick basement offered protection from floods, and the roof follows an African design.

Back on Royal St, the house at No 823 belonged to Daniel Clark, an Irish-born merchant who aided Thomas Jefferson in negotiating the Louisiana Purchase. His lasting notoriety came from wounding Governor Claiborne in a duel brought about by charges that he was involved in the Aaron Burr conspiracy.

As you pass behind St Louis Cathedral, off Jackson Square, you'll see the lush tropical plants that fill St Anthony's Garden. On either side are narrow pedestrian alleyways sheltering hidden bookstores, shops and cafes. In 1925, when William Faulkner lived at 624 Pirates Alley, it was officially named Orleans Alley. There is no evidence of pirate activity here; in fact, the pirates associated with the infamous Jean Lafitte were already history when the passageway opened in 1831.

You'll hear camera shutters clicking at St Peter St where visitors are drawn to photograph the lacy cast-iron galleries on the Labranche buildings. The 11 three-story brick houses at 708 Royal St, 621 to 639 St Peter St, and 622 to 624 Pirates Alley were built by sugar-planter Jean-Baptiste Labranche between 1835 and 1840 in the Greek revival style.

One block toward the river at 616 St Peter St stands Le Petit Théâtre du Vieux Carré, a playhouse built in 1922 in traditional colonial style with a handsome courtyard. Up to this time, construction in the Quarter had followed contemporary designs; the playhouse was an important instigator of the modern preservation movement. See Entertainment for information on the company.

From the solid line of façades built to the *banquette* (sidewalk), it's difficult to imagine that the block between St Peter and Toulouse Sts offers significant open space to merchants and residents, but large interior courtyards are hidden behind many entryways. Patti's Court, behind the entry to Old Town Praline Shop at 627 Royal St, is open to the public. Next to the small courtyard leading to Royal Blend at 623 Royal St, the Court of the Two Sisters, 613 Royal St, is now an expensive buffet restaurant. Across the street a tunnel-like arching corridor leads to the Spanish Courtyard, which is guarded by handsome wrought-iron gates that once graced the Masonic Temple.

From Toulouse to St Louis Sts are many fine homes and courtyards, including the Court of Two Lions at 541 Royal St, built by Jean François Merieult in 1798. The Toulouse side of the court has marble lions

LOUISIANA

LOUISIANA

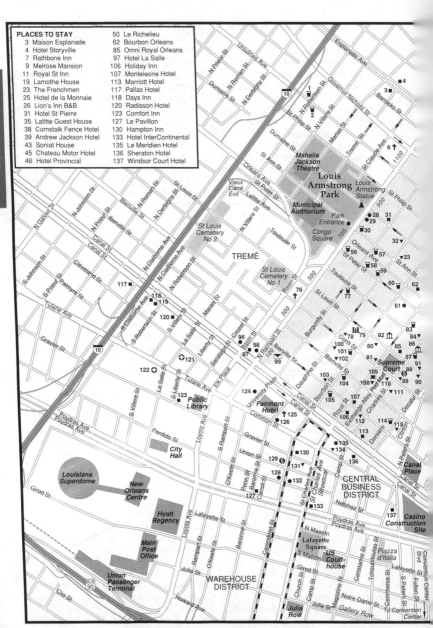

PLACES TO STAY

3 Maison Esplanade	50 Le Richelieu
4 Hotel Storyville	62 Bourbon Orleans
7 Rathbone Inn	85 Omni Royal Orleans
9 Melrose Mansion	97 Hotel La Salle
11 Royal St Inn	106 Holiday Inn
19 Lamothe House	107 Monteleone Hotel
23 The Frenchmen	113 Marriott Hotel
25 Hotel de la Monnaie	117 Pallas Hotel
26 Lion's Inn B&B	118 Days Inn
31 Hotel St Pierre	120 Radisson Hotel
35 Lafitte Guest House	123 Comfort Inn
38 Cornstalk Fence Hotel	127 Le Pavillon
39 Andrew Jackson Hotel	130 Hampton Inn
43 Soniat House	133 Hotel InterContinental
45 Chateau Motor Hotel	135 Le Meridien Hotel
46 Hotel Provincial	136 Sheraton Hotel
	137 Windsor Court Hotel

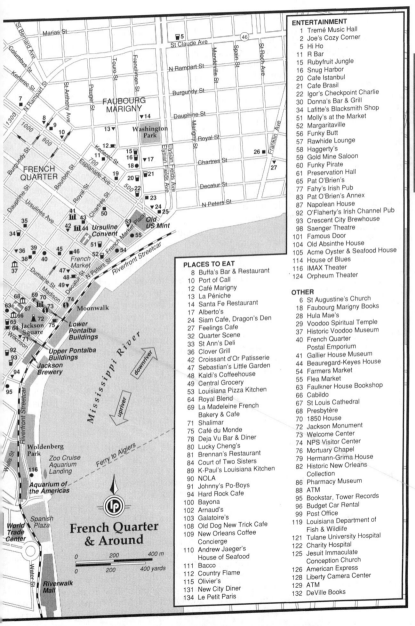

LOUISIANA

ENTERTAINMENT
1 Tremé Music Hall
2 Joe's Cozy Corner
5 Hi Ho
11 R Bar
15 Rubyfruit Jungle
16 Snug Harbor
20 Cafe Istanbul
21 Cafe Brasil
22 Igor's Checkpoint Charlie
30 Donna's Bar & Grill
34 Lafitte's Blacksmith Shop
51 Molly's at the Market
52 Margaritaville
56 Funky Butt
57 Rawhide Lounge
58 Haggerty's
59 Gold Mine Saloon
60 Funky Pirate
61 Preservation Hall
65 Pat O'Brien's
77 Fahy's Irish Pub
83 Pat O'Brien's Annex
87 Napolean House
92 O'Flaherty's Irish Channel Pub
93 Crescent City Brewhouse
98 Saenger Theatre
101 Famous Door
104 Old Absinthe House
105 Acme Oyster & Seafood House
114 House of Blues
116 IMAX Theater
124 Orpheum Theater

OTHER
6 St Augustine's Church
18 Faubourg Marigny Books
28 Hula Mae's
29 Voodoo Spiritual Temple
37 Historic Voodoo Museum
40 French Quarter
   Postal Emporium
41 Gallier House Museum
44 Beauregard-Keyes House
54 Farmers Market
55 Flea Market
63 Faulkner House Bookshop
66 Cabildo
67 St Louis Cathedral
68 Presbytère
70 1850 House
72 Jackson Monument
73 Welcome Center
74 NPS Visitor Center
76 Mortuary Chapel
79 Hermann-Grima House
82 Historic New Orleans
   Collection
86 Pharmacy Museum
88 ATM
95 Bookstar, Tower Records
96 Budget Car Rental
99 Post Office
119 Louisiana Department of
   Fish & Wildlife
121 Tulane University Hospital
122 Charity Hospital
125 Jesuit Immaculate
   Conception Church
126 American Express
128 Liberty Camera Center
129 ATM
132 DeVille Books

PLACES TO EAT
8 Buffa's Bar & Restaurant
10 Port of Call
12 Café Marigny
13 La Péniche
14 Santa Fe Restaurant
17 Alberto's
24 Siam Cafe, Dragon's Den
27 Feelings Cafe
32 Quarter Scene
33 St Ann's Deli
36 Clover Grill
42 Croissant d'Or Patisserie
47 Sebastian's Little Garden
48 Kaldi's Coffeehouse
49 Central Grocery
53 Louisiana Pizza Kitchen
64 Royal Blend
69 La Madeleine French
   Bakery & Cafe
71 Shalimar
75 Café du Monde
78 Deja Vu Bar & Diner
80 Lucky Cheng's
81 Brennan's Restaurant
84 Court of Two Sisters
89 K-Paul's Louisiana Kitchen
90 NOLA
91 Johnny's Po-Boys
94 Hard Rock Cafe
100 Bayona
102 Arnaud's
103 Galatoire's
108 Old Dog New Trick Cafe
109 New Orleans Coffee
   Concierge
110 Andrew Jaeger's
   House of Seafood
111 Bacco
112 Country Flame
115 Olivier's
131 New City Diner
134 Le Petit Paris

**French Quarter
& Around**

0   200   400 m
0   200   400 yards

atop the entry posts. Merieult built the neighboring house at 527 to 533 Royal St in 1792; a rare survivor of the 1794 fire, it's now home to the Historic New Orleans Collection. Following service in the Battle of New Orleans, Bordeaux native François Seignouret built the Brulatour Courtyard at 520 Royal St to house his wine-importing business. You can enter the distinctive courtyard, which now houses WDSU-TV studios. The opening of the prestigious Royal Orleans Hotel (now the Omni Royal Orleans) in 1960 initiated a hotel construction boom in the Quarter.

The massive Supreme Court building dominates the block between St Louis and Conti Sts. The white-marble courthouse opened in 1909 and after years of extensive refurbishment and asbestos removal is due to reopen in 1998. Scenes from the movie *JFK* were filmed here several years back. Since 1955, Brennan's restaurant across the street has occupied the former Banque de la Louisiane, the first bank established after the Louisiana Purchase. Vincent Rillieux, the great-grandfather of artist Edgar Degas, built the structure after the devastating 1794 fire. At Royal and Conti Sts, nationally acclaimed architect Benjamin Henry Latrobe designed the Louisiana State Bank (1820), shortly before his death from yellow fever.

At the corner of Conti St, the 1826 Greek revival Bank of Louisiana has housed a variety of tenants since being liquidated in 1867, including the state capitol. Next door, the New Orleans Coffee Concierge maintains a binder filled with menus from local restaurants. On the other corner at 343 Royal St, the Planters Bank is another former bank and was built by Rillieux between 1795 and 1800. Its wrought-iron balconies and knee braces are notable examples of Spanish colonial design.

The first large hotel to open in the French Quarter, the Monteleone, dominates the entire block between Bienville and Iberville Sts. In the block preceding Canal St (with the Holiday Inn) you leave the historic district and step abruptly into a modern urban milieu.

Jackson Square

In 1721, Audrien de Pauger laid out the city about Place d'Armes, and today Jackson Square remains the central and most important starting point for visitors to the French Quarter. Its cultural scene offers a constantly changing assortment of street musicians, artists, tarot-card readers and mimes competing for attention on the sidewalk. Overlooking the square from the top of the levee is so-called 'hippie hill,' a congregating point for youths, panhandlers and scam artists. From the river levee you can sit and watch ships turning the bend of the Mississippi. There's a visitor center on the square, and horse-drawn carriage tours leave from the riverside on Decatur St.

The centerpiece of the square itself is a monument to General Andrew Jackson, after whom the plaza was renamed. The statue's inscription proclaims 'The Union Must and Shall be Preserved' – an unwelcome sentiment added by the Yankee commander of occupying forces in 1862, General Benjamin Butler.

Towering over the formal square is the grand St Louis Cathedral, which is flanked by the matching Cabildo and Presbytère buildings. These contain the major collections of the Louisiana State Museum. Alongside Jackson Square are the 1850 Pontalba Buildings. In the Lower (downriver) Pontalba Building, the Louisiana State Museum offers tours of a restored 1850 household.

St Louis Cathedral In 1722 a hurricane destroyed the first of three sanctuaries built here by the St Louis Parish. Architect Gilberto Guillemard dedicated the existing cathedral on Christmas Eve in 1794, only weeks after it survived that year's devastating fire. In 1850 the cathedral was designated as the metropolitan church of the Archdiocese of New Orleans. Pope Paul VI awarded it the rank of minor basilica in 1964. For a schedule of Masses (on Christmas Eve, the cathedral's midnight Mass is the most popular draw in the city) contact the Oblates of Mary Immaculate (☎ 504-525-9585), 615 Pere Antoine Alley. The

Prytania St
New Orleans

cathedral is open for tours Monday to Saturday from 9 am to 5 pm, and Sunday from 1 to 5 pm. Donations are accepted.

Cabildo The first Cabildo was a single-story structure destroyed by the Good Friday fire of 1788. Reconstruction was delayed by the city's more pressing needs for a prison, a cathedral, and police and fire structures. It's a good thing that architect Don Gilberto Guillemard, who was busy with the St Louis Cathedral, did not hurry the reconstruction: the December 1794 fire would likely have destroyed it. Tenants in the rebuilt Cabildo, dedicated in 1799, have included the Spanish council for which the building is named, the City Hall government (1803 to 1853), the Louisiana Supreme Court (1853 to 1910), and the Louisiana State Museum (1911 onwards).

Three floors of exhibits emphasize the significance of New Orleans in a regional, national and international context. It is a challenge to see it all in part of a day. You might try to quickly survey the lower floor, paying attention to the pre-Columbian Indian artifacts and the colonial exhibits that most interest you. The Sala Capitular (council room) on the 2nd floor overlooking Jackson Square is where the historic Louisiana Purchase documents were signed. Other displays depict the Battle of New Orleans, including the role played by free blacks and members of the Choctaw tribe. The most interesting 3rd-floor exhibits are the shocking depictions of slavery juxtaposed with stories of black Confederate troops.

The Cabildo (☎ 504-568-6968) at 701 Chartres St is open Tuesday through Sunday from 9 am to 5 pm.

Presbytère Although architect Gilberto Guillemard originally designed the Presbytère to be a rectory for the St Louis Cathedral, after it was completed in 1813 the building was never used by the church. Instead, the cathedral administrators rented the building to the city for use as a courthouse before selling it to them in 1853. Ownership was transferred to the Louisiana State Museum in 1911.

In contrast to the Cabildo's collection signifying the external impact of New Orleans, the Presbytère primarily showcases the local history of the city and its citizens. In addition, the museum includes art and furniture treasures. One display features local Newcomb pottery, with decorations based on Southern flora and fauna, which was part of the influential

Arts & Crafts movement of the early 20th century. Photographs and maps of the great flood of 1927 follow exhibits on riverboat commerce. Somewhat out of place and dis-organized is the exhibit on Louisiana native son Zachary Taylor, a slave owner from Baton Rouge elected from the Whig party as the 12th president of the US in 1848.

The Presbytère (☎ 504-568-6968), 751 Chartres St, is open Tuesday through Sunday from 9 am to 5 pm.

1850 House The 1850 House is one of the apartments in the Lower Pontalba Build-ing. Madame Micaëla Pontalba, daughter of Don Almonaster y Roxas, continued her father's improvements around Jackson Square by building the long rows of red-brick apartments flanking the upper and lower portions of the square. She was also responsible for renaming the once barren parade grounds, the Place d'Armes, after her friend Andrew Jackson. Initial plans for the apartments were drawn by the noted architect James Gallier Sr. In 1927, the Lower Pontalba Building was bequeathed to the Louisiana State Museum; in 1930 the city acquired the Upper Pontalba Build-ing where Micaëla once lived.

Volunteers offer guided tours of the apartment that includes a central court and servants' quarters with period furnishings. Repeated along the railings are the initials AP, signifying the union of Almonaster and Pontalba wealth.

The 1850 House (☎ 504-568-6968), 523 St Ann St, is open for self-guided tours Tuesday through Sunday from 9 am to 5 pm. Volunteer guides are available Tuesday through Friday from 11 am to noon and 1 to 2 pm, and Saturday from 11 am to noon.

Old US Mint
Even if you wouldn't give a nickel to see where coins were once minted, the exhibits on New Orleans jazz and the history of Mardi Gras at the Old US Mint (☎ 504-568-6968), 400 Esplanade Ave, should get your attention.

Madame Pontalba

Madame Micaëla Pontalba, mistress of the landmark Pontalba Buildings flank-ing Jackson Square, is often mistakenly referred to as a baroness (she divorced her husband before he inherited the title of baron). Yet her wealth and power cause many to presume nobility – the present American embassy in Paris was originally built as her private home. She was able to fuse the wealth of the two richest families in Louisiana – Almonaster and Pontalba – through her own shrewd dealings after an ill-fated attempt on her life by her father-in-law.

Micaëla was born in 1795 when her father, Don Almonaster y Roxas was 71. He had arrived in Louisiana as a penni-less Spanish notary in 1769 and some-how amassed a fortune through land transfers and rental income. At 16, Micaëla married her cousin, Joseph Xavier Célestin Delfau de Pontalba. She was unhappy and gained a separation in 1834. Micaëla, however, was unwilling to give up her share of the Pontalba riches. Angered by her demands, her husband's father, Baron Joseph Xavier de Pontalba, shot her while she was visiting in France. Thinking that she was dead, the baron turned the gun on him-self and committed suicide. Though seriously injured, she survived and left Paris with two of her three sons for her native New Orleans in 1848, sans title but with her wealth intact. ■

On this site from 1838 to 1861 and again from 1879 to 1910, the mint struck US coinage bearing the 'O' mint mark. The Confederate States of America briefly pro-duced coins here, after seizing the mint in 1861. The minting exhibits are the most meager of the three exhibits housed here, but the site itself is evocative and the gift shop offers great souvenirs for the numis-matically inclined.

The wonderful **jazz exhibit** here tells the story of the evolution of the genre while music fills the air. Three huge murals depict Storyville, the historic red-light dis-trict (redeveloped into the civic center area around city hall) where many jazz musicians, including Louis Armstrong, began their careers. Visitors can spend hours in the comfortable air-conditioned exhibit discovering how jazz evolved from its African roots in Congo Square. A gift shop offers a good selection of historic and current jazz recordings and other select jazz souvenirs.

The **carnival exhibit** explains the origins of the city's most notorious celebration, and displays spectacular Mardi Gras costumes and paraphernalia – including historic 'throws' (souvenir trinkets and baubles tossed to the crowd) and examples of Cajun traditions.

Admission to the mint, one of four units of the Louisiana State Museum, is $4 ($3 for students and seniors). A combination ticket admits ticket-holders to all four units for $10 ($7.50 for students and seniors). The mint is open Tuesday through Sunday from 9 am to 5 pm.

Historic New Orleans Collection

The Historic New Orleans Collection (☎ 504-523-4662), 533 Royal St, is a complex of historic buildings anchored by **Merieult House**. A survivor of the 1794 fire, the historic house displays the original transfer documents of the Louisiana Purchase of 1803, early maps showing the city's evolution, and artifacts such as an 1849 broadside advertising '24 Head of Slaves,' ($500 for individual children or $2400 for entire families). Unlike the undocumented anecdotes fed to tourists by carriage guides, the history explained here is meticulously researched – you could find no better condensed introduction to New Orleans' past.

The house itself is an almost overlooked part of the tour. Extensive remodeling in 1832 reflects the American influence of the period. In one room, a removed section of plaster reveals the briquette-entre-poteaux construction; in another the walls are sheathed with barge boards from riverboats dismantled at the end of a downriver trip. House tours cost $4, and run Tuesday through Saturday at 10 and 11 am, and 2 and 3 pm.

The **Williams Gallery** has rotating exhibits on local history. It's open Tuesday through Saturday from 10 am to 4:45 pm, and admission is free.

History scholars are drawn to the research facilities at the **Williams Research Center** (☎ 504-523-4662), 410 Chartres St, which is housed in a beautifully refurbished police station.

Pharmacy Museum

The Pharmacy Museum (☎ 504-565-8027), 514 Chartres St, occupies a shop established in 1823 by the nation's first licensed pharmacist, Louis J Dufilho Jr.

Dufilho dispensed gold-coated pills to the rich, along with opium, alcohol and cannabis to those who really needed to feel better. If the globe in the window was filled with red liquid, a yellow fever or cholera epidemic was at large. Admission costs $2. It's open Tuesday through Sunday from 10 am to 5 pm.

St Louis Cemetery No 1

Death was a central fixture of old New Orleans – during frequent epidemics deaths greatly exceeded births. St Louis Cemetery No 1, in the Tremé district, received the remains of most early Creoles, as well as Americans before the Protestant Uptown cemeteries and Metairie Cemetery came into fashion. At one time, the small Protestant section was fenced off from Catholic tombs. The present entrance on Basin St is near the middle of the original cemetery which extended to Rampart St – construction of Basin St cut a swath through the old grounds.

Above-ground burials, necessitated by shallow water tables, took place in family tombs or the long rows of 'oven' vaults that often line the walls. Large mausoleums, such as the impressive tomb of the Italian Mutual Benefit Society, contain the remains of groups with shared histories. The density of the dead within the lifeless compound is incredible, particularly in comparison with standard burial plots. As the multiple inscriptions imply, each tomb held many remains. The heat and humidity united to reduce the flesh within a year after interment. After this period, the tomb was opened and the bones deposited in a crypt, while the casket was burned. In the same manner, the ovens were traditionally rented for a year and a day, after which the remains would be pushed to the rear or scattered and the coffin destroyed.

Within a few steps from the entrance gate and to the left is the purported resting site of voodoo queen Marie Laveau, the most visited tomb in all of New Orleans. It's easily recognized as the unkempt tomb covered with chalked X's. A bizarre mixture of offerings typically litter the ground. The tomb next to her belongs to Ernest 'Dutch' Morial, mayor from 1978 to 1986 and father of present mayor Marc Morial.

It is strongly recommended that visitors do not enter this cemetery alone – even tour operators print disclaimers that they are not responsible for any mishaps on their tours, and they are not referring to the occult. During a police strike a few years ago, one group witnessed a murder.

Mortuary Chapel

An unfounded fear of yellow-fever contagion led the city to forbid funerals for fever victims at the St Louis Cathedral. Built near the St Louis Cemetery No 1 in 1826, the Mortuary Chapel, 401 N Rampart St, its bell tolling constantly during epidemics, offered hasty services for victims. In 1931 it was renamed Our Lady of Guadeloupe Church.

Jazz Funerals

A uniquely New Orleans phenomenon is the jazz funeral. A parading band of musicians heralding the dead with brassy jazz head up a 'second line' of mourners (and funeral crashers) in a celebratory street dance. As part of the second line, folks play tambourines, toss traditional Mardi Gras 'throws' such as gold coins and trinkets, and carry brightly ornamented decorative umbrellas. Jazz parades also accompany weddings and other festive occasions. ■

Voodoo Spiritual Temple

At the Voodoo Spiritual Temple (☎ 504-522-9627), 828 N Rampart St, the priestess Miriam Chamani practices spiritual healing rituals, based on Afro-centric American Voodooism. Her temple features neither white nor black magic, but instead focuses on 'true spiritual power for friendly people.' She continues a tradition established by her New Orleans ancestors: Dr John, Marie Laveau and Leafy Anderson.

Drop by the small storefront temple to chat, pick up books on the occult and check out the small collection of artifacts from around the world. Donations are accepted.

Historic Voodoo Museum

Two jam-packed rooms of voodoo charms, potions, powders and mojos (voodoo talismans) are tucked behind a storefront at 724 Dumaine St (☎ 504-523-7685). The $6.30 admission is steep for exhibits which are visually intriguing but not explained; it's a better deal if the store is not crowded and someone's willing to show you around. The store sells some of the same substances displayed in the museum.

Ursuline Convent

After a five-month voyage from Rouen, France in 1827, 12 Ursuline nuns arrived in New Orleans to care for the French garrison's 'miserable little hospital' and educate the young girls of the colony. The French colonial army built the existing Ursuline convent and girls' school between 1745 and 1752; today, it is the oldest structure in the French Quarter. It is also one of the few surviving examples of French colonial architecture. Tours of the fully restored convent include a visit next door to the Chapel of Archbishops, built in 1845, where stained-glass windows pay tribute to the Battle of New Orleans (Andrew Jackson credited his victory to the Ursulines' prayers for divine intervention) and the Sisters of the Holy Family, the order of black Creole nuns established in 1842 by Archbishop Antoine Blanc.

The Ursuline Convent (☎ 504-529-3040) is at 1100 Chartres St. Guided tours are offered Tuesday through Friday at 10 and 11 am, and 1, 2 and 3 pm; and on weekends at 11:15 am, and 1 and 2 pm. Admission costs $4 ($2 for children).

Beauregard-Keyes House

Greek revival structures, like this house built in 1826 with slave quarters and rear courtyard, are uncommon in the French Quarter. After the war it was home to Confederate general PGT Beauregard, best known for ordering Confederate forces to fire upon Fort Sumpter in Charleston, South Carolina, thereby initiating the Civil War in 1861. Its other illustrious resident (from 1944 until her death in 1970) was the author Francis Parkinson Keyes, who had 51 novels published. Unfortunately, tours of the house (☎ 504-523-7257) at 1113 Chartres St are less interesting than its former residents. The gift shop sells most of Keyes' books. Guided tours are $4. The house is open Monday through Saturday from 10 am to 3 pm; tours are on the hour.

Gallier House Museum

James Gallier Sr and his son James Gallier Jr were both architects credited with popularizing the Greek revival style in New Orleans through landmarks such as St Patrick's Church and the Gallier Hall municipal building. In 1857 the son began work on this impressive French Quarter townhouse, incorporating numerous innovations – such as interior plumbing, skylights and ceiling vents – into the design. A view of Royal St from the gallery is a highlight of the worthwhile tour. The Gallier House Museum (☎ 504-525-5661), 1118 Royal St, is open Monday through Saturday from 10 am; the last tour is at 3:30 pm. Guided tours are $5 ($4 for children).

Hermann-Grima House

Samuel Hermann, a Jewish merchant who married a Catholic, introduced the unique American-style Federal design to the French Quarter in 1831. Hermann sold the house in 1844 to Judge Grima, a slaveholder, after he reportedly lost $2 million during the financial panic of 1837. Cooking demonstrations

Historic House Tours

New Orleans offers a tremendous array of houses that are open for tours. You can observe the evolution of style by following a chronological sequence when visiting the houses.

A few aspects of house design and layout are worth noting. The simplicity of French colonial designs and furnishings contrasts with the elaborate Spanish and American period homes. Slave quarters were common components of antebellum homes. Fire hazards and heat caused most early kitchens to be located outside the main house.

The following list includes a few of the more significant city homes open for tours and their dates of construction. The two earliest homes on the list are French colonial city and plantation houses.

Merieult House, French Quarter	1792/1832
Pitot House, Fair Grounds	1799
Beauregard-Keyes House, French Quarter	1826
Hermann-Grima House, French Quarter	1831
1850 House, French Quarter	1850
Gallier House, French Quarter	1857

in the authentic open-hearth kitchen are a special treat on Thursdays from October through May. Tours of Hermann-Grima House (☎ 504-522-5661), 818 St Louis St, are offered Monday through Saturday from 10 am to 3:30 pm. Admission costs $5 ($3 for children).

Faulkner House

Considered one of the greatest American novelists, William Faulkner (1897-1962) moved to New Orleans from Mississippi in 1935. He worked as a journalist at the *Times-Picayune*, and met Sherwood Anderson who helped him publish his first novel, *Soldier's Pay* (1926). He also contributed to the *Double Dealer*, a literary magazine published in the city. The site of his New Orleans stay is now a bookstore and the home of the nonprofit Pirates Alley Faulkner Society. The literary society holds monthly meetings and sponsors writing contests. Faulkner House Books (☎ 504-524-2940), 624 Pirates Alley, is open daily from 10 am to 6 pm.

French Market

This area really consists of three types of market: a bevy of air-conditioned stores; an open-air farmers market; and an open-air flea market where wares from Louisiana and around the world are sold. While trading here dates back to Indian times, most of the current structures date from 1975. Cafes have occupied the Butcher's Market building since 1860; Café du Monde, the market's oldest tenant, is open 24 hours. There is a public restroom in Building II near the NPS visitor center on N Peters St.

The **Farmers Market**, on Ursulines St between St Peters St and French Market Place, was built in 1937 by the WPA to serve as the main wholesale produce terminal for the 18 municipal markets throughout the city. Merchants offer fresh fruits and vegetables, kitchen supplies, spices (a large selection of hot sauces), garlic and chili strings, and cookbooks for the tourist trade. The Farmers Market is open 24 hours a day.

At the **Flea Market**, shoppers can pick up some unique southern Louisiana products as well as African art, well-priced hand-crafted sterling-silver jewelry, inexpensive Chinese-made Mardi Gras masks and dolls, musical tapes and CDs of dubious origin, and preserved alligator heads.

St Augustine's Church

Lakeside of the French Quarter's early walls (now N Rampart St) grew New Orleans first suburb, the Tremé district, an area traditionally populated by black Creoles. The celebrated architect who virtually rebuilt the St Louis Cathedral in 1849-51, JNB DePouilly, designed St Augustine's

Church (☎ 504-525-5934), 1210 Governor Nichols St. It opened in 1842 and is the second-oldest African-American Catholic church in the country. One of its stained-glass panels depicts the Sisters of the Holy Family, the order of black Creole nuns founded in 1842 by Henriette Delille. Today the small congregation works to provide food for the needy and maintains the Tomb of the Unknown Slave.

CENTRAL BUSINESS DISTRICT (CBD)

Algiers Ferry

The short ferry ride from the foot of Canal St gets you out on the water and provides a view of the city from the traditional river approach. Ride on the lower deck next to the water and you're likely to see the state bird, the brown pelican. The free state-run ferry runs between 6 am and midnight, leaving Canal St on the hour and half-hour, returning from Algiers on the quarter-hour.

Woldenberg Park

Woldenberg Park offers a promenade along the riverfront, and a grassy strip where civic events and concerts are frequently staged. It's a comfortable place to eat your po-boy while watching river traffic. The park ends at the aquarium and Spanish Plaza.

Aquarium of the Americas

At this aquarium you can go eye to eye with giant tropical creatures like the arapaima that inhabit the Amazon basin, see Caribbean reef inhabitants like spotted moray eels and hawksbill in a walk-through acrylic tunnel, or watch incredible specimens of Gulf of Mexico species through 14-foot-high windows. Mr Bill the 40-year-old sawfish shares the giant Gulf tank with an oil platform. Of course there are displays on the Mississippi River and Delta wetlands, and Arctic environments are included too.

Operated by the Audubon Institute, the air-conditioned aquarium (☎ 504-861-2537) at the foot of Canal St is adjacent to Woldenberg Park and next to the Algiers ferry. Use the Riverfront streetcar if you don't want to walk from the French Quarter. Be sure to pick up a program listing times for special presentations like the penguin feed. The gift shop is a good place to pick up books on Louisiana's natural history. The aquarium is open daily at 9:30 am; closing hours vary from 5 to 7 pm. Admission costs $10.50 for adults, $8 for seniors and $5 for children.

Discounts on admission are continually offered in tourist magazines such as *Where*. In addition, the *Audubon* zoo cruise docks here, and you can get a variety of combination tickets to both the Audubon Zoo and the aquarium that include the price of the cruise (see Audubon Zoological Gardens, below). Double-check the coupon offers against combination tickets for the best price. Other combination tickets with the aquarium and adjacent **IMAX theater** (see Entertainment) offer savings of about 15%.

World Trade Center
The 33-story World Trade Center, 2 Canal St, completed in 1968, is a member of the 'revolving observation deck' club that consists of some 87 buildings in North America. The slowly revolving *Top of the Mart Lounge* (☎ 504-522-9795) offers spectacular views for the price of a mixed drink. Also check out the stained-glass murals by Milton Pounds that depict local history. Another option for a more limited high-rise view of the city is to ride the glass elevator for $2 ($1 for kids); it's open 9 am to 5 pm.

WAREHOUSE DISTRICT
On the upriver side of Canal St a nexus of factories and warehouses evolved near the river piers with financial offices quartered nearby, mostly along St Charles Ave and Carondelet St. Lee Circle and Howard Ave are generally considered the boundary between this area and the residences of the Lower Garden District.

Former warehouses serve as lofts and exhibit spaces for artists who moved into the Warehouse District following the 1984 Louisiana World Exposition. Julia St, between Commerce and Baronne Sts, is a corridor lined with about a dozen galleries. Bistros and cafes in the area are good places to take a break. Also nearby is Charles Moore's postmodern Piazza d'Italia (1979), at Tchoupitoulas and Lafayette Sts, where the cascading pools offer cheap baths for winos.

You can pick up a pamphlet, *The Arts District*, which has a map and listing of current galleries, at True Brew Theatre (also a cafe; ☎ 504-522-2907), 200 Julia St, or from almost any of the galleries along the way. The first Saturday of each month marks the opening of new exhibits.

Riverwalk
For nearly half a mile upriver from the Algiers ferry, the Riverwalk Mall borders the Mississippi River. When Bienville founded New Orleans in 1718, this site was in the middle of the river – an 1800-foot shift has since occurred. The mall is air-conditioned and full of stores that mainly attract tourists. An uncrowded walkway along the river is a worthwhile ramble and features a number of informative plaques along with views of the river bend; there are also binoculars with which you can spy on ships and riverboats.

Contemporary Arts Center
This exhibition and performance space occupies a renovated warehouse. Dozens of exhibits appear each year in the gallery spaces, and its two stages host plays, performance art, dance and musical concerts. Call the box office (☎ 504-528-3800) for information about performances. Admission to the Contemporary Arts Center (☎ 504-523-1216), 900 Camp St, costs $3 ($2 for kids), except on certain Thursdays when it's free. It's open Monday through Saturday from 10 am to 5 pm, and Sunday from 11 am to 5 pm.

Louisiana Children's Museum
Generous corporate sponsors have helped create hands-on exhibits like a supermarket, complete with stocked shelves and check-out registers, and a TV news studio where young anchors can see themselves

LOUISIANA

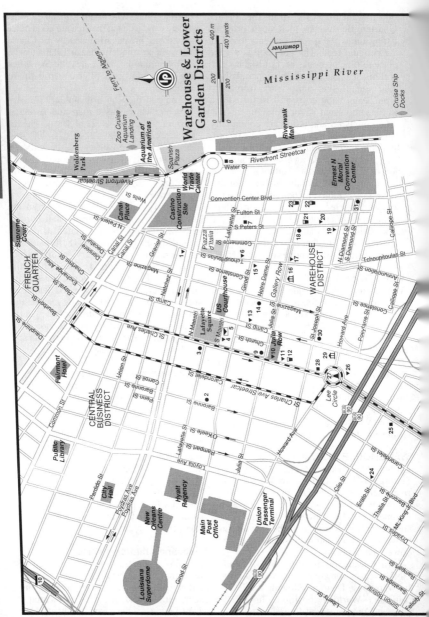

Warehouse & Lower Garden Districts

Mississippi River

downriver

Cruise Ship Docks

Riverwalk Mall

Ernest N Morial Convention Center

WAREHOUSE DISTRICT

Riverfront Streetcar

Water St

World Trade Center

Casino Construction Site

Convention Center Blvd

Spanish Plaza

Aquarium of the Americas

Zoo Cruise Aquarium Landing

Woldenberg Park

Ferry to Algiers

Riverfront Streetcar

Canal Place

Supreme Court

FRENCH QUARTER

CENTRAL BUSINESS DISTRICT

Lafayette Square

US Courthouse

Gallery Row

Julia Row

Lee Circle

St Charles Ave Streetcar

Fairmont Hotel

Public Library

City Hall

New Orleans Centre

Hyatt Regency

Main Post Office

Union Passenger Terminal

Louisiana Superdome

LOUISIANA

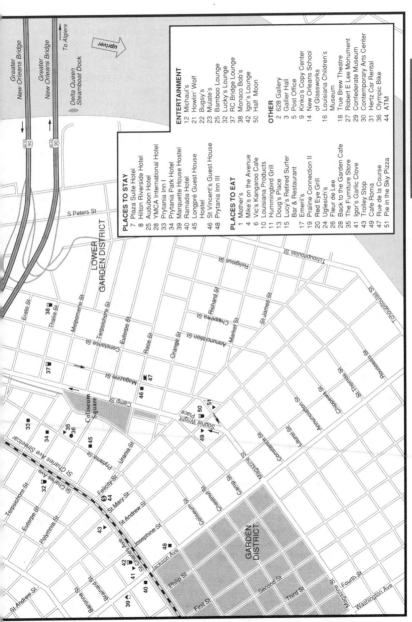

PLACES TO STAY
7   Plaza Suite Hotel
8   Hilton Riverside Hotel
25 Audubon Hotel
28 YMCA International Hotel
33 Prytania Inn I
34 Prytania Park Hotel
39 Marquette House Hostel
40 Ramada Hotel
45 Longpré Guest House
46 St Vincent's Guest House
    Hostel
48 Prytania Inn III

PLACES TO EAT
1   Mother's
4   Mike's on the Avenue
6   Vic's Kangaroo Cafe
10 Louisiana Products
11 Hummingbird Grill
13 Doug's Place
15 Lucy's Retired Surfer
    Bar & Restaurant
17 Emeril's
19 Praline Connection II
20 Red Eye Grill
24 Uglesich's
26 Fleur de Lee
28 Back to the Garden Cafe
35 The Furniture Store
41 Igor's Garlic Clove
43 Trolley Stop
49 Cafe Roma
47 Rue de la Course
51 Pie in the Sky Pizza

ENTERTAINMENT
12 Michaul's
21 Howlin' Wolf
22 Bugsy's
23 Mulate's
25 Bamboo Lounge
32 Lucky's Lounge
37 RC Bridge Lounge
38 Monaco Bob's
42 Igor's Lounge
50 Half Moon

OTHER
2   628 Gallery
3   Gallier Hall
5   Post Office
9   Kinko's Copy Center
14 New Orleans School
    of Glassworks
16 Louisiana Children's
    Museum
18 True Brew Theatre
27 Robert E Lee Monument
29 Confederate Museum
30 Contemporary Arts Center
31 Hertz Car Rental
36 Olympic Bike
44 ATM

on monitors as they forecast a July snow-storm in New Orleans. In the rush to build newer, bigger and better exhibits, the museum has failed to maintain some of the existing displays – mayday calls on the tugboat radio go unheard and most kids abandon ship. Overall, however, the non-profit museum and volunteers have done a good job in providing attractions for everyone from toddlers to 12-year-olds.

The Louisiana Children's Museum (☎ 504-523-1357), 420 Julia St, is open Tuesday through Saturday, 9:30 am to 5:30 pm; Sunday from noon to 5:30 pm; and on Monday during the summer months. Chil-dren under 16 must be accompanied by an adult. Admission for anyone over a year old costs $5.

New Orleans School of Glassworks

At this large indoor glass studio you can watch students craft molten glass and pot-tery. All the work is for sale and is so accomplished that one Saks Fifth Avenue department store merchandiser mistook the children's artwork for graduate-level work, so the story goes. The school (☎ 504-529-7277), 727 Magazine St, is open daily except Sunday, but few folks are firing kilns in the hot summer months. Admis-sion is free.

Julia Row

Julia Row, 13 identical red-brick houses at 600 to 648 Julia St, was built in 1832. Architect Henry Hobson Richardson lived here as a child, and his 'Richardson-Romanesque' Field's Wholesale House in Chicago (1885) shares many elements with his early home. Field's was one of the most copied and admired buildings in the US.

In 1976 the Preservation Resource Center (☎ 504-581-7032, Net) instigated restoration of the block after they refur-bished the building at 604 Julia St. Pick up a copy of their publication *Preservation in Print*. In 1988 the PRC initiated a program called Operation Comeback (☎ 504-523-4064) to help renovate vacant and aban-doned properties worthy of restoration.

Confederate Museum

Don't expect apologies from the stars and bars crowd that operate the two large rooms of exhibits in Louisiana's oldest museum, opened in 1891. The museum (☎ 504-523-4522), 929 Camp St, is housed in Memorial Hall, a red-brick Romanesque-style building designed by Thomas Sully to harmonize with the adjoining Howard Memorial Library which was designed by Henry Hobson Richardson. Admission costs $4. It's open Monday through Saturday from 10 am to 4 pm.

UPTOWN & GARDEN DISTRICT

Following the Louisiana Purchase in 1803, the area upriver from the CBD and Ware-house District became the preferred area for American settlement while the Creoles remained in the French Quarter. The sub-division of former plantation lands for indi-vidual homes began in the area now known as the Lower Garden District. Building extended Uptown following the steam railway on St Charles Ave (now the St Charles Ave Streetcar) – many elegant mansions line the route. Unlike the town-houses built in the business district near Lafayette Square in the 1830s, the Uptown area developed a more open character, with residences surrounded by greenery: trees (live oaks and palms), grass yards, lush, fragrant floral gardens. The city's evolu-tion of American design is seen beginning in the Lower Garden District followed by the Garden District proper.

During the 1850s and 1860s, wealthy Americans built massive Greek revival mansions as a symbol of staunch classical tastes in the Garden District. Like the French Quarter, the Garden District is a National Historic District, where architec-tural preservation ordinances attempt to maintain the character of the area. Its boundaries are St Charles Ave to Magazine St, from Jackson Ave upriver to Louisiana Ave. The NPS offers free interpretive ranger-led tours of the well-maintained Garden District. It's also a great area to bike around.

Between 1884 and 1885, Audubon Park was the site of the World's Industrial & Cotton Centennial Exposition, which celebrated the centenary of a shipment of six bales of cotton from Charleston to Liverpool in 1784. The adjacent Tulane and Loyola campuses also attracted development to the then sparsely settled area. Today this residential area offers architectural diversity: there are modest shotgun shacks next to multi-story Arts & Crafts bungalows, Gothic stone campus buildings, and immense Greek revival mansions surrounded by innumerable towering white columns.

Lafayette Cemetery No 1

Established in 1833 by the former City of Lafayette, this cemetery features German and Irish names on its above-ground tombs. Not far from the entrance, on the right, is a low tomb containing the remains of an entire family who died of yellow fever. Another fever victim's memorial was inscribed by his employer. Fraternal organizations and groups like the Jefferson Fire Company No 22 buried members and their families in large shared crypts. The 'ovens' that line the walls provided space for indigents, which explains why few are inscribed. Tombs of the wealthier families were built of marble, with elaboration that mimicked the finest architecture in the district. Most tombs, however, were built of inexpensive whitewashed brick and the cemetery filled within decades of opening, before many of the opulent residences were built nearby. By 1872 the prestigious Metairie Cemetery appealed to those with extravagant tastes. (Anne Rice fans will recognize this cemetery as the place where vampire LeStat took his long sleep.)

Volunteers from the nonprofit group Save our Cemeteries (☎ 504-588-9357) offer tours on Monday, Wednesday and Friday at 10:30 am. Tours cost $5, payable at the Washington Ave gate. Proceeds go to restoration efforts. The gates are closed at 2:30 pm; don't get locked in!

Uptown Literary Retreats

As all of the following literary sites are private homes, passers-by are urged to respect the privacy of residents.

Anne Rice fans know that the Garden District is the setting for the witchcraft and vampire bloodletting in many of her best-selling novels. After a 25-year hiatus in Texas and California, Rice returned to the large raised Greek revival cottage at 2524 St Charles Ave. She also owns another mansion at 1329 Third St, at the corner of Chestnut St.

Romanian-born Andrei Codrescu, another contemporary author, lives in the Garden District.

Mark Twain was often a guest of George Washington Cable's house built in 1874; it's at 1313 Eighth St, between Coliseum and Chestnut Sts. At a time when black politicians were faring badly against white resistance to Reconstruction, Cable's works advocated African-American civil rights.

The enlightened feminist author Kate Chopin lived at 1413 Louisiana Ave, between Prytania and Coliseum Sts, from 1876 to 1879. For more on Chopin see the Central Louisiana chapter.

While working on *This Side of Paradise* in 1920, F Scott Fitzgerald rented the small white house at 2900 Prytania St overlooking Lafayette Cemetery No 1. Continue toward downtown to the Lower Garden District boarding house at 1718 Prytania St where Lillian Hellman, who was born in New Orleans, wrote *The Children's Hour* in 1934. ∎

Audubon Zoological Gardens

Among the country's best zoos, this is also the headquarters of the Audubon Institute, which maintains Woldenberg Park and the Aquarium of the Americas.

The **Louisiana Swamp** exhibit displays flora and fauna amid a Cajun cultural setting that includes details such as the Spanish moss harvested for use as furniture stuffing, and a fishing camp complete with shrimp trawls, crawfish traps and an oyster dredge. Of course there are alligators milling about the muddy bank of

LOUISIANA

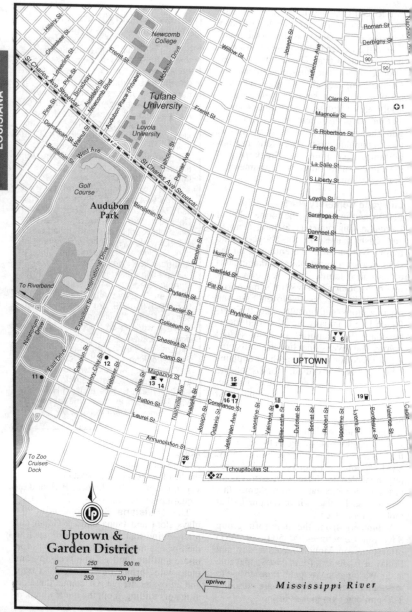

Newcomb College

Tulane University

Loyola University

Golf Course

Audubon Park

To Riverbend

To Zoo Cruises Dock

UPTOWN

Mississippi River

upriver

Uptown & Garden District

0   250   500 m
0   250   500 yards

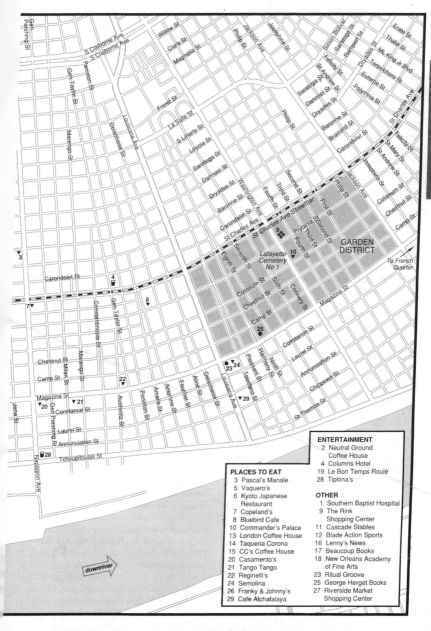

LOUISIANA

GARDEN DISTRICT

Lafayette Cemetery No 1

To French Quarter

downriver

PLACES TO EAT
3 Pascal's Manale
5 Vaquero's
6 Kyoto Japanese Restaurant
7 Copeland's
8 Bluebird Cafe
10 Commander's Palace
13 London Coffee House
14 Taqueria Corona
15 CC's Coffee House
20 Casamento's
21 Tango Tango
22 Reginelli's
24 Semolina
26 Franky & Johnny's
29 Cafe Atchafalaya

ENTERTAINMENT
2 Neutral Ground Coffee House
4 Columns Hotel
19 Le Bon Temps Roulé
28 Tipitina's

OTHER
1 Southern Baptist Hospital
9 The Rink Shopping Center
11 Cascade Stables
12 Blade Action Sports
16 Lenny's News
17 Beaucoup Books
18 New Orleans Academy of Fine Arts
23 Ritual Groove
25 George Herget Books
27 Riverside Market Shopping Center

the bayou when they're not hibernating during the winter. But year-round in the exhibit you'll see bobcats, red foxes, endangered Louisiana black bears and alligator snapping turtles.

The **Audubon Flight Exhibit** is best on quiet days, when visitors can enter the giant cage to sit and observe the bird species that John James Audubon portrayed in his book *Birds of America*. Of course there are ducks galore, but you will be mesmerized by the brilliant plumage of species like the scarlet ibis and glossy ibis, among others.

Most visitors are awed by the 'magnificent seven' in the **Reptile Encounter** display which houses representatives of some of the largest snake species in the world, from the king cobra that grows to over 18 feet in length to the green anaconda that reaches 38 feet. Many local snake species are also on display.

The **Butterflies in Flight** exhibit features a video about metamorphosis and migration, shown before you enter the greenhouse filled with thousands of fluttering exotic butterflies, including tropical swallowtails and the iridescent morphos. Tropical birds and plants are also on display. It's worth the additional $2 admission cost. (Shed unnecessary layers before entering.)

The zoo (☎ 504-861-2537), on the river side of Magazine St and Audubon Park, is accessible from the French Quarter via the No 11 Magazine bus or the St Charles Ave streetcar (with a 1½-mile walk through Audubon Park).

The *Audubon* zoo cruise offers a glamorous way to reach the zoo and the Levee Park area from Woldenberg Park downtown. Tickets for the riverboat cruise, zoo and aquarium can be bought either independently or in combination (adults $26 for all three, children $13.25). The zoo cruise departs the aquarium at 10 am, noon, 2 and 4 pm. The cruise leaves the zoo at 11 am, 1, 3 and 5 pm. (Call ☎ 504-581-4629 to confirm current schedule before setting out.)

The zoo is open daily from 9:30 am to 5 pm. Admission costs $8 ($4 for seniors and children). Look for discount coupons in tourist magazines such as *Where*.

Tulane University

Tulane University (☎ 504-865-4000) was founded in 1834 as the Medical College of Louisiana in an attempt to control repeated cholera and yellow-fever epidemics. In 1847 the University of Louisiana merged with the school. Paul Tulane's $1 million donation in 1883 initiated significant expansion – and immortalized his name.

The University Center, near Freret St on McAlister Dr, features a bookstore, ATM, apartment-rental and sublet and ride-share bulletin board (downstairs) and sporting and special events ticket office (☎ 504-861-9283). The *Hullabaloo*, the campus newspaper published during the school year, lists campus events (free Friday open-air concerts) and job openings.

The **Amistad Research Center** (☎ 504-865-5535) is one of the nation's largest repositories of African-American history. The archive is in Tilton Hall, 6823 St Charles Ave (open weekdays only).

To hear the earliest jazz recording made by the Original Dixieland & Jazz Band in 1917 and to have any questions on jazz history answered, the **Hogan Jazz Archive** offers a cozy space to pursue your research. Their twice-yearly publication *The Jazz Archivist* contains historical accounts on musicians, their music and the venues. The archive (☎ 504-865-5688) is on Freret St in Howard Tilton Memorial Library, 4th floor (open weekdays only).

Tulane's H Sophie Newcomb College, founded in 1886, was the first degree-granting women's college in the US established as a coordinate division of a men's university. It maintains an adjacent campus facing Broadway. **Newcomb Art Gallery** (☎ 504-865-5327) exhibits the college's collection, including Arts & Crafts-style Newcomb pottery (see the sidebar in Arts in the Facts about the Deep South chapter). Admission is free (open weekdays only).

La Amistad

In 1839, the slave ship *La Amistad* sailed from Havana with 53 captives abducted from West Africa. Three days from port the Africans revolted and demanded the Cubans sail into the rising sun toward Africa, but the Cubans reversed direction each night. After two months of aimless oscillations, *La Amistad* arrived at Long Island, New York. The Africans were jailed and charged with piracy and murder.

Their legal defense, the Amistad Committee, was aided by Lewis Tappan and former US President John Quincy Adams. The case went to the US Supreme Court which ruled that the Africans were free. The Amistad Committee evolved into the American Missionary Association which founded a race relations department at Fisk University in Nashville, Tennessee. Tulane University's Amistad Research Center developed from this enterprise and moved to New Orleans in 1969.

This heroic American story is told in the film *Amistad*, directed by Steven Spielberg. ■

CITY PARK & FAIR GROUNDS

The 'Esplanade Ridge' neighborhood and fellow residents near Bayou St John are making a brave attempt to restore their district to its former grandeur. The shopping focus for the area is near the corner of Esplanade Ave and Ponce de Leon St. Visitors are attracted to the great live oaks at City Park, site of the New Orleans Museum of Art.

Of course, in addition to hosting a regular horseracing season, the Fair Grounds are also the site of the huge springtime New Orleans Jazz & Heritage Festival (see Special Events).

The natural raised levee along Bayou St John, which once served as the Old Portage linking Lake Pontchartrain with the Mississippi River, today offers a pleasant stroll past the Pitot House museum and private historic homes.

City Park

The 1500-acre City Park (☎ 504-482-4888), the nation's fifth-largest urban park, is home to the New Orleans Museum of Art (see below), botanical gardens and sport centers. Acquired in 1850, the park is deservedly famous for its huge moss-draped live oaks and scenic bayou lagoons, especially along the narrow strip fronting City Park Ave. Unfortunately, I-610 slices through the park, interrupting the peace and quiet. The larger lakeside portion contains four golf courses, and a riding stable (see Activities, below, for details). Most visitors explore the third of the park on the river side of I-610.

The seven-acre **botanical gardens** built by the WPA feature a showpiece art deco pool and fountain. Both native and exotic plant specimens from tropical and semi-tropical environments stimulate the senses. Admission to the botanical gardens (☎ 504-483-9386) costs $3 (children $1). It's open Tuesday through Sunday from 10 am to 4:30 pm.

The centerpiece of **Storyland** is a vintage carousel, recently restored to pristine condition. The children's amusement area also includes a variety of other rides and appealing attractions. Storyland (☎ 504-483-9382) is open Wednesday through Sunday, 10 am to 4:30 pm. Admission costs $1.50/3 day/night.

Canoes ($6) and pedal boats ($8) are available at the casino building (☎ 504-483-9371). Here you can also find a surprisingly impressive selection of food, and buy cane fishing poles (daily fishing permits cost $2/1 adults/children); the season opens in March. The casino is open Wednesday through Friday from 8:30 am to 5 pm, and weekends from 7 am to 7 pm.

One of two **Dueling Oaks** still stands near the park's art museum. Here in the 19th century, challenges to Creole honor were often cause to meet under the great oaks. The famous duel between a Baton Rouge newspaper editor who offended Alcée La Branche refutes the notion that the pen is mightier than the sword. After

LOUISIANA

three attempts where the combatants missed each other from 40 yards, the fourth duel felled the editor.

From the French Quarter, City Park is easily reached aboard the No 48 Esplanade bus. Esplanade Ave ends at the park entrance.

New Orleans Museum of Art

Founded in 1910 by philanthropist Isaac Delgado, this museum continues to grow. The collection of fine art is now valued at over $200 million and covers three large floors. On the 1st floor are major traveling exhibits that typically feature associated lectures, films and workshops.

If you're not here for a special exhibit, you might want to start with the 3rd-floor permanent exhibits, which feature pre-Colombian and African art.

The New Orleans Museum of Art (☎ 504-488-2631) can be reached from the French Quarter on the No 48 Esplanade bus. You can also get there from the Riverbend area aboard the No 90 Carrollton bus. Admission is $6 (seniors $5 and children $3). The museum is open Tuesday through Sunday from 10 am to 5 pm. The *Courtyard Café* offers lunch and snacks from 10:30 am to 4:30 pm.

Pitot House

On the banks of Bayou St John sits Pitot House, a French colonial plantation-style house built in 1799. James Pitot, the first mayor of the incorporated city of New Orleans, acquired it in 1810. In 1904 it was purchased by the Missionary Sisters of the Sacred Heart who used it as a day-care center and girls' orphanage. The sisters were guided by Mother Frances Xavier Cabrini, who in 1946 became the first US citizen canonized as a saint. In 1964 the sisters performed yet another act of charity by donating the house to the Louisiana Landmarks Society, which moved it a short distance to its present site and restored it from floor to ceiling.

Built without corridors, the adjoining interior rooms allow air to circulate through the louvered shutters on the windows and

upstairs back porch. It features a double-pitched roof and briquette-entre-poteaux construction. Guided tours cost $4. The house (☎ 504-482-0312), 1440 Moss St, is open Wednesday through Saturday from 10 am to 3 pm.

Lakeshore Park

This park, stretching nearly 10 miles along a narrow shoreline strip fronting Lake Pontchartrain, is where locals cool off and bike, skate or just check each other out. The park extends from the Southern Yacht Club, marked by the lighthouse, to the Inner Harbor Navigation Canal. It's still a long way from Santa Monica, and you shouldn't enter the polluted water, but it beats driving across the mind-numbing Pontchartrain Causeway to see the lake (see Around New Orleans, below). Near the yacht club are numerous restaurants suitable for lunch, but don't make a special trip for dinner.

ACTIVITIES

Besides being a great town for **bicycling** (see Getting Around for more information), New Orleans offers plenty of other outdoor activities, many of which take place in City Park and Audubon Park.

If you want to play **golf** head to City Park's North, South, East and West Bayou Oaks courses. The Bayou Oaks Clubhouse & Restaurant (☎ 504-483-9396), 1040 Filmore Ave, serves the East, West and North courses. The Bayou Oaks South course straddles the freeway and its clubhouse (☎ 504-483-9396) is on Zachary Taylor Dr, lakeside of the freeway. Greens fees range from $7 ($5 after 2 pm) at the South course to $17 at the East and West championship courses. Audubon Park also offers an 18-hole course, easily accessible from the St Charles Ave streetcar line.

Casual anglers can try for the catfish and *sacalait* in Bayou Metairie at City Park. The fishing season begins in March. There's no equipment rental but cane poles are sold for $4 at the boat rental place near the casino building (see City Park, above).

For **horseback riding**, City Park Riding Stables (☎ 504-483-9398), 1001 Filmore

St, offers English-style rides accompanied by an instructor. The rides cost $20 per hour with a group, or $25 per half-hour for private lessons (no unaccompanied riders). They're open weekdays from 9 am to 7 pm, and close at 5 pm on weekends. Within Audubon Park, Cascade Stables (☎ 504-891-2246) offers pony rides.

Audubon Park is an excellent **in-line skating** area. You can circle the park or concentrate on speed near the river in adjacent (across Magazine St) Levee Park where you are unlikely to crash into other park users. Blade Action Sports (☎ 504-891-7055), 6108 Magazine St, rents skates near the park. Lakeshore Park is also a great place to blade on long, paved trails.

For **gym** facilities, the Lee Circle YMCA (☎ 504-568-9622), 920 St Charles Ave, has complete and reasonably priced facilities, including a swimming pool appropriate for laps. Entry is $8; $5 if you are staying at a local hotel (show a key).

The City Park Tennis Center (☎ 504-483-9382) offers 36 lighted **tennis** courts. Both hard and soft courts are available along with locker rooms, racquet rental, a pro shop and lessons from USPTA pros. It's open Monday through Thursday from 7 am to 10 pm, and Friday through Sunday from 7 am to 7 pm.

The best uninterrupted **jogging** paths are along the west bank levee and the levee above Audubon Park. Joggers have also worn pathways between the St Charles Ave streetcar tracks. (Be sure to run facing the approaching streetcar so you can see it coming.) Many joggers also circle the Superdome on the plaza level – each lap is a quarter-mile.

ORGANIZED TOURS

Few cities offer the variety of worthwhile organized tours that visitors to New Orleans may select from. Even independent travelers who generally resist group tours will get a lot out of a select New Orleans tour, especially one which covers sights in dodgy areas you might not want to visit alone.

It is always wise to call to confirm current schedules, departure locations and prices before setting out. Note that some operators require reservations.

For a tour of the city that begins from the North Shore of Lake Pontchartrain, see that section in Around New Orleans.

Walking Tours
NPS Ranger-Led Tours Your first stop should be the National Park Service (NPS) visitor center, 916 N Peters St, where you sign up for the free guided walking tours of the French Quarter and the Garden District. NPS rangers present a thorough introduction to the city's history and to the architecture of these two historic preservation districts. The History of New Orleans tour in the French Quarter starts daily (except Christmas and Mardi Gras) at 10:30 am and the Faubourg Promenade through the Garden District starts at 2:30 pm.

Participants are given directions for taking the streetcar to the Garden District assembly spot (French Quarter tours depart from the visitors center). In addition, rangers occasionally lead tours that begin at 11:30 am and cover special topics in the French Quarter. Call the visitor center (☎ 504-586-2636) for information about the special tours, but phone reservations are not accepted.

Friends of the Cabildo This nonprofit historical society (☎ 504-523-3939) offers volunteer-led walking tours of the French Quarter daily. Tours last two hours and emphasize history, folklore and architecture. The cost is $10 for adults and $8 for students and seniors (no charge for children under 12). As a worthwhile bonus, the price includes admission to any two of the four Louisiana state museums ($4 admission otherwise): the Cabildo, the Presbytère, the Old US Mint or the 1850 House. Tours starting at the 1850 House museum store, 523 St Ann St, leave at 10 am and 1:30 pm Tuesday through Sunday, and at 1:30 pm on Monday.

Voodoo & Cemetery Tours Of the many voodoo tours available, voodoo proponents most highly regard the no-hype cemetery and voodoo history tour sponsored by Historic New Orleans Walking Tours (☎ 504-947-2120). Two-hour tours cover St Louis Cemetery No 1, Marie Laveau's house and grave, Congo Square and the Voodoo Spiritual Temple. Tours are offered Monday through Saturday at 10 am and 1 pm, and on Sunday at 10 am. The cost is $12 per person. Tours leave from Café Beignet at 334B Royal St; reservations are not required.

Also recommended are Magic Walking Tours (☎ 504-588-9693). Tours depart daily from the Pirates Alley Cafe, 622 Pirates Alley, at 10:30 am and 1:15 pm. The 1½-hour tours cost $13 ($10 for students and seniors).

Save Our Cemeteries (☎ 504-588-9357, 888-721-7493), a nonprofit preservation society, sponsors cemetery tours that emphasize historical accuracy over theatrics. Proceeds help maintain above-ground crypts and ovens. Volunteer guides offer one-hour tours of St Louis Cemetery No 1 on Sunday at 10 am for $12 ($10 for seniors and students, free for children under 12). Tours leave from the courtyard at 623 Royal St. Their unreserved tours of the Uptown Lafayette Cemetery No 1 cost $6 ($5 for seniors and students) and meet at the Washington Ave gate between Prytania and Coliseum Sts on Monday, Wednesday and Friday at 10:30 am.

Bicycle Tours

Olympic Bicycle's city-wide bike tour explores the Garden District, Tulane campus area and City Park on a 25-mile ride. It costs $45, including bike and helmet rental. Their Bike the Bayou tour is a 15-mile excursion (one-way) across the Mississippi River to Jean Lafitte National Park's Barataria Preserve (see Around New Orleans for a description of the preserve); it costs $55 and includes canoe rental and lunch.

Carriage Rides

Mule-drawn carriage rides are a great way to see the French Quarter. The slow pace suits the narrow streets of the historic district, and drivers aim to be entertaining (often at the expense of historical accuracy). Carriages depart day and night, until midnight, from Jackson Square. Half-hour tours for up to four people cost around $40, plus tip.

Riverboat Cruises

Take a paddlewheel riverboat cruise on the Mississippi aboard the *Creole Queen* to visit the 1815 Battle of New Orleans site at Chalmette, a unit of the Jean Lafitte National Historic Park (☎ 504-589-4430). A brief walking tour of the battle grounds and Beauregard-Keyes House are included in the 2½-hour excursion. Cruises leave daily at 10:30 am and 2 pm from Spanish Plaza at the foot of Canal St. Tours cost $14/7 for adults/children aged three to 12. On the *Creole Queen* you can also dine and dance or just dance to live jazz as it cruises the Mississippi River. Board at the Canal St wharf at 7 pm to depart at 8 pm. Tickets are around $40 per person for the dinner dance.

A more mundane boat, the *Cajun Queen*, offers 90-minute sightseeing cruises that depart from the Canal St wharf daily at 11 am, 1:15 and 3:30 pm. Tickets cost $12/6.

Reservations and information about either cruise option are available from New Orleans Tours (☎ 504-592-0560, 504-524-0814). Tickets may be purchased at the aquarium dock, the Spanish Plaza dock and at selected hotels.

Calliope music announces the boarding of the *Natchez*, a steam-powered paddlewheeler that departs on two-hour harbor cruises from behind the Jackson Brewery daily at 11:30 am and 2:30 pm. Tickets cost $14.75/7.25 for children six to 12, and are sold at the dock by the New Orleans Steamboat Company (☎ 504-586-8777).

A river cruise on the *Audubon* will take you from the zoo to the aquarium or vice versa; find details in the text on Aquarium of the Americas.

SPECIAL EVENTS

Just after New Year's Eve (which is no slouch celebration here), when other cities succumb to the doldrums of post-holiday despair, New Orleans residents break out

the king cakes and spirits to begin cele-
brating carnival. And the party doesn't end
with Mardi Gras – costumes abound during
St Patrick's Day as well as Halloween.
Other excuses to celebrate include Jazz
Fest in late April and early May.

January
NCAA Sugar Bowl
  This game between two of the nation's top-
  ranked college football teams takes place on
  or around New Year's Day. It originated in
  1935 and fills the Superdome to capacity;
  call ☎ 504-525-8573 for information.
Twelfth Night
  The feast of the Epiphany on January 6 (12
  nights after Christmas) marks the official
  start of carnival. The Phunny Phorty Phel-
  lows dust off their costumes and assemble at
  the Willow St car barn prior to an evening
  ride on the St Charles Ave streetcars.
Battle of New Orleans Celebration
  On the weekend closest to January 8, this
  event re-creates the decisive victory over the
  British at the original battleground in Chalmette National Historical Park (☎ 504-589-
  4430). A midday commemoration in Jackson
  Square on Sunday features a military guard
  in period dress.
Mardi Gras
  Early parades in January or February tend to
  be the most outlandish. In 1996 the Krewe
  du Vieux celebrated their 'decade-ence' followed by their 10th annual ball. The Krewe
  of Funky Butts, named after an early jazz
  hall, presents a jazz and art parade through
  the Warehouse District staged by the Contemporary Arts Center (☎ 504-528-3800).

February
Mardi Gras
  The parades heat up during the three weeks
  before Mardi Gras. Routes vary but the
  largest krewes stage massive parades with
  elaborate floats and marching bands that run
  along portions of St Charles Ave and Canal
  St. On Mardi Gras itself, in late February or
  early March, the outrageous activity reaches
  a crescendo and the French Quarter nearly
  bursts with costumed celebrants. It all ends
  at midnight with the beginning of Lenten
  penitence. See the sidebar for details.

March
Black Heritage Festival
  Held on the second weekend in March at the
  Audubon Zoo (☎ 504-861-2537), this festival
celebrates African-American contributions to
food, music and the arts.
St Patrick's Day (March 17)
  Just when you thought things would calm
  down, a major Irish pub crawl through the
  French Quarter follows a parade through the
  Irish Channel starting at Race and Annunciation Sts in the Lower Garden District. The
  prior weekend also features a motley parade,
  beginning at Molly's at the Market (☎ 504-
  525-5169), where a boisterous group tosses
  cabbage to the lasses in exchange for kisses.
Tennessee Williams Literary Festival
  Three days of plays, readings and lectures
  honoring one of the most decadent individuals ever venerated take place on the last
  weekend in March; the festival is coordinated by the University of New Orleans
  (☎ 504-286-6680).

April
Spring Fiesta
  Since 1935 locals have donned antebellum
  outfits when showing visitors through his-
  toric homes normally closed to the public.
  Tours are given over a five-day period in
  April or May beginning on the first Friday
  after Easter. Fees vary, but you can receive
  details by contacting the Spring Festival
  Association (☎ 504-581-1367), 826 St Ann
  St, New Orleans, LA 70116.
Crescent City Classic
  Runners from all over the globe come to
  compete in this 10-km race from the Jackson
  Brewery to Audubon Park on the first Sat-
  urday of the month. Contact the *Times-
  Picayune* (☎ 504-861-8686) for details.
French Quarter Festival
  Held on the second weekend in April, this
  music festival features local bands per-
  forming on 12 stages throughout the Quarter.
Jazz Fest
  Held at the Fair Grounds Race Track (and at
  night all over town), Jazz Fest reverberates
  with good sounds, plus food and crafts, over
  two weekends in late April and early May.
  See sidebar for admission and other details.

May
Greek Festival
  On Memorial Day weekend, the Greek community offers food and the entertaining Hel-
  lenic Dancers. The festival is held on the
  grounds of the Greek Orthodox Cathedral
  of the Holy Trinity Church (☎ 504-282-
  0259), near Bayou St John at 1200 Robert E
  Lee Blvd.

LOUISIANA

LOUISIANA

Mardi Gras

Mardi Gras, French for 'Fat Tuesday,' began as a pagan rite of spring and evolved into a bacchanalia before being subsumed as a Roman Catholic celebration to usher in the 40-day Lenten season that precedes Easter. Mardi Gras falls the day before Ash Wednesday, and as Lent demands fasting, Mardi Gras has always represented the last chance to indulge. Mardi Gras itself is the culmination of the celebratory season of carnival starting on Twelfth Night (January 6), also known as the Feast of Epiphany, which falls 12 days after Christmas.

Today around the Gulf South, carnival and Mardi Gras have come to take on a meaning far removed from their religious underpinnings, though some rituals and the spirit of pagan indulgence continue. For example, in parts of France a roast *boeuf gras* leads the procession to remind celebrants that Mardi Gras is the last meat before Lent. In New Orleans, a papier-mâché beouf gras on a float is nearly lost amid the calamity of beer and beads.

Historically, in Europe, Mardi Gras was an opportunity to mock the aristocracy with ridiculously regal antics, and the Creoles in New Orleans maintained that tradition. When the Creoles sniffed at the presence of Americans in the early 1800s, the Americans exploited the tradition to make Creoles the target of Mardi Gras spoofs. The parody of Creole society came to permeate every aspect of the local carnival. Yet, as carnival became institutionalized in the late 19th century, with 'krewes' (men-only social clubs) reflecting white, Protestant Uptown society, the regal trappings surrounding the many parades and masquerade balls began to lose their jestful luster. Kings were anointed in elaborate ceremonies at grand Mardi Gras balls, and their krewes pompously arrived at the riverfront docks by steamboat.

But no elite remains safe from knee-buckling Mardi Gras traditions for long. In 1906, Mr Big Shot led the Zulu Social Aid & Pleasure Club (formerly the Black Tramps) by rowboat across the fetid Basin Canal. With a porkpie hat and oversize cigar, Mr Big Shot and his spear-and-coconut-wielding group in grass skirts revived the outrageous silliness of the event. The all-women Isis krewe also defied the Uptown male establishment when they organized in 1917. In the 1950s, drag queens and gay masquerade balls became a popular mode of parody, and they are still a vital component of Mardi Gras. Today, blacks elaborately costumed as 'Mardi Gras Indians' continue to upstage the major krewes.

Rex and Zulu krewe parades remain the highlight of Fat Tuesday. A wide range of other krewes also host parties and parades in the weeks leading up to Mardi Gras. Most parades are held Uptown, along St Charles Ave to Canal St. The only krewe to parade through the French Quarter is the Krewe du Vieux, whose procession three weeks before Mardi Gras has brass-band accompaniment and some 15 subkrewes, including the Krewe of the Mystic Inane and Krewe of CRUDE (Committee for the Revival of Urban Decadent Entertainment). Their annual ball – the Krewe du Vieux Doo – follows the parade and is open to the most perverse members of the public. (Look for their newsletter *Le Monde de Merde* in laundries and toilet stalls.)

Information You can find a complete description of the krewes and parade route maps in the *Times-Picayune Mardi Gras Supplement* (☎ 504-822-6660), published on a Wednesday two weeks prior to Mardi Gras. A glossy magazine, *Arthur Hardy's Mardi Gras Guide*, published by Arthur Hardy (☎ 504-838-6111), appears in bookstores about a month before Mardi Gras. It's a worthwhile purchase and contains a good history along with detailed descriptions and maps of all parades.

Costumes If you arrive at Mardi Gras with only a T-shirt, you should be able to catch enough beads for a decent costume. (Women who lift their shirts get showered with beads.) But at least add a goofy hat to your ensemble – a good one will be handy if it rains. Even a simple mask can transform you into a worthy party peer. More elaborate costumes will require rummaging at thrift stores, hardware stores and hobby shops. Thrift

City (☎ 504-482-0736), 4125 S Carrollton Ave, next to Mid-City Lanes Rock 'N Bowl, is a good place to look for a cape or drag costume. It's really worth the effort as the fun seems to increase in proportion to the number of people in costume.

Add a good pair of walking shoes; plenty of revelers make the trek from the Uptown parade routes to the downtown party.

Balls & Parades With few exceptions, most krewe balls held during carnival season are exclusive events open only to members and guests. Without wrangling an invitation, most folks get in the spirit by attending the many parades, related events and continuous nightlife that starts to really heat up around two weeks before Mardi Gras. Nonstop frivolity starts the Thursday before.

Krewe parades usually feature a dozen or more tractor-drawn floats and marching bands. With a full line of tubas blasting away, bands like the St Augustine Purple Knights represent the progeny of the local music scene and attract out-of-town competition. At dramatic nighttime parades, *flambeaux* carriers wield fiery torches.

Onlookers' screams of 'Hey, mister! Throw me something!' merit a handful of goodies tossed their way, and the crowd scrambles for the souvenir 'throws' – often beads, doubloons (golden coins), condoms or candy. Locals set up banks of ladders for the best views and the most trinkets. The krewe of Zulu is no longer permitted to throw their prized coconuts – too many visitors and police were clobbered by the golden nuggets – but a few are handed out along the route.

Following the Orpheus parade on Lundi Gras (Fat Monday) head for Woldenberg Park with your mask to the city-sponsored bash which features fireworks.

A little planning will help you negotiate the gridlock that accompanies the parades and nightlife. From the last weekend before Mardi Gras onward, the Quarter – including the wide Canal St sidewalks – is jammed, making pedestrian movement difficult and especially frightening for youngsters.

The logistics of seeing the two big parades on Mardi Gras (Fat Tuesday) – Zulu and Rex – and getting to the costume party in the French Quarter may be too much for many people. Forget about relying on cabs, buses or streetcars. If your car is already in a secure spot, don't move it! Bicyclists must also negotiate shoulder-to-shoulder crowds and many barricaded streets.

Before sunrise the entire parade corridor along St Charles Ave is lined with people staking out prime spots with chairs, ladders and coolers. The neutral ground along Napoleon Ave serves as a campground for many of the early risers and those who never went to bed.

Zulu's parade route in particular provides a great opportunity to visit neighborhoods such as the Tremé which are typically avoided by most tourists. Zulu moves out at dawn to its starting point at the statue of Martin Luther King Jr at the corner of S Claiborne Ave and Martin Luther King Jr Blvd. At 8:30 am over 30 floats and 30 marching bands begin rolling down Jackson Ave toward St Charles Ave before continuing past Lee Circle to Canal St and through the Tremé district along N Galvez St and Orleans Ave.

After Zulu, the Rex krewe begins their elaborate procession at about 10 am farther up S Claiborne Ave at Napoleon Ave. Then Rex travels along St Charles Ave from Jackson Ave to Canal St. So-called truck parades pulling decorated floats follow Rex and continue to shower the crowds with throws. By mid-afternoon, it's beer and beads on Bourbon St. By the evening, a besotted mass of humanity is tightly wedged on the street as the galleries above sag beneath the weight of bead-flinging throngs. Usually only the rich can afford to snag the coveted overlooks at hotels, bars and private homes (often reserved over a year in advance).

People with spectacular costumes seem to avoid the elbow-to-elbow Bourbon St crowd. Celebrations in the lower Quarter vary from block to block – check out the ribald costume contest in front of the Rawhide Lounge at 740 Burgundy St and the festivities across from the Quarter on Esplanade Ave at Dauphine St or at Chartres and Frenchmen Sts. ∎

LOUISIANA

June

French Market Tomato Festival
On the first weekend of June, celebrate with food and entertainment in the French Market (☎ 504-522-2621).

Grand Prix du New Orleans
Over the second weekend in June the city becomes a racetrack.

Carnaval Latino
On the last weekend in June, the riverfront comes alive with the sounds and flavors of Latin America. For information contact the New Orleans Hispanic Heritage Foundation (☎ 504-522-9927).

Wine & Food Experience
Find out what wine to drink with catfish during this four-day gourmet event usually held in late June.

July

Independence Day (July 4)
Food and entertainment are followed by fireworks at the downtown riverfront. On Independence Day weekend, *Essence Magazine* sponsors star-studded musical performances at the Superdome. Call ☎ 504-941-5100 for details.

August

Blessing of the Shrimp Fleet
Traditional Isleño festivities alternate annually between the fishing villages at Delacroix and Yscloskey in St Bernard Parish east of New Orleans. Contact the Museo de los Isleños (☎ 504-682-0862) for information (see also Around New Orleans).

October

New Orleans Film & Video Festival
Arthouse films and independent features are shown mid-month.

Swamp Festival
For four days in early October, the Audubon Institute (☎ 504-861-2537) releases swamp critters into the hands of visitors at both the Audubon Zoo and Woldenberg Park. Both locations feature Cajun food, music and crafts.

Halloween (October 31)
Most of the fun takes place at the giant costume party in the French Quarter. In addition, the visitors bureau (☎ 504-566-5055) coordinates a parade, and Anne Rice hosts a Vampire LeStat Extravaganza at the convention center.

November

All Saints' Day (November 1)
Many residents honor the dead by sprucing up local cemeteries.

Celebration in the Oaks
A drive-through exhibit of holiday lights and decorations is held from the last week of the month through the first week of January in City Park (☎ 504-482-4888). Unfortunately, bicyclists and pedestrians are not allowed. Admission is around $5 per car.

Bayou Classic
Southern University (see Plantation Country chapter) and Grambling University (see Northern Louisiana chapter) play their traditional end-of-the-season football game at the Superdome (☎ 504-523-5652); it's held on the last weekend in November.

December

Christmas
Historic homes are dressed up in old holiday decorations, carolers sing in Jackson Square, and the choir performs at the St Louis Cathedral – especially notable is the tremendous turnout for midnight Mass on Christmas Eve. Many restaurants offer *réveillon* on Christmas Eve, a traditional New Orleans feast. Not to be missed is a stroll through the 180-foot canopied lobby of the Fairmont Hotel. Contact French Quarter Festivals (☎ 504-522-5730), 100 Conti St, New Orleans, LA 70130, for a complete schedule of events, open homes and list of réveillon menus.

New Year's Eve
Revelers pack the French Quarter before heading to the riverbank to watch a spectacular fireworks display and listen to performers at the Jackson Brewery.

PLACES TO STAY

Most visitors to New Orleans stay within easy reach of the French Quarter or in the Quarter itself. Though accommodations here are more expensive than a similar room elsewhere, the ambiance and convenience are well worth it if you have the money to spend. Budget travelers often aim for backpacker hostels and guesthouses in the Lower Garden District, relying on buses, bikes or the St Charles Ave streetcar to reach the Quarter. The city's central hotel district, with the Monteleone and Royal Orleans as well as

New Orleans Jazz & Heritage Festival

The first Jazz Fest (1968), celebrating the city's 250th anniversary, featured the likes of Louis Armstrong, Dave Brubeck, Duke Ellington, Woody Herman, Ramsey Lewis and Pete Fountain. In 1972 the festival expanded to two weekends in late April and early May, moved to the Fair Grounds, and began showcasing a variety of musical styles in addition to jazz.

Today, Jazz Fest features thousands of performers on more than 10 stages. Styles range from bluegrass to zydeco, with ample portions of R&B, gospel, rock, reggae and, of course, many variations of jazz. The 'heritage' part of the title refers to Louisiana's local arts, crafts and food. This continues downtown at Armstrong Park's Congo Square, where African food and crafts are emphasized.

Arrive at the Fair Grounds hungry – the plethora of eating options is staggering, and prices are reasonable for delicacies such as boiled crawfish (in peak season!), shrimp étouffée, catfish or oyster po-boys, soft-shell crab (in-season!), crawfish pie, gumbo, barbecue, and world cuisine from gyros to fried plantains. In addition, plan for heat, sun and long periods on your feet. Only a few tents are ventilated and most stages are open-air. Bring sunscreen and a brimmed hat, carry water, and wear light-colored clothing and sturdy sandals or walking shoes. A blanket or ground cover would enable you to rest comfortably between concerts, and a rain poncho is an added precaution.

Performance schedules become available in January. Early reservations assure you your first choice of dates. Daily passes cost $13 in advance or $16 at the gate. During Jazz Fest, the Fair Grounds are open daily from 11 am to 7 pm, plus there are many nightly performances at other sites throughout New Orleans. For information call or write to New Orleans Jazz & Heritage Festival (☎ 504-522-4786), 2200 Royal St, New Orleans, LA 70117. Tickets are available through TicketMaster (☎ 504-522-5555). Parking is an additional $10 and availability is limited; most people take a bus. The RTA (☎ 504-569-2700) operates a regularly scheduled No 82 Esplanade bus to/from the French Quarter. Air-conditioned shuttle buses run back and forth from major hotels on Canal St. Combination tickets include Jazz Fest admission and shuttle transit for around $18. If you can find a taxi, the special event price from the Quarter is around $5 per person. ■

---

numerous convention-oriented hotels, is concentrated on and around Canal St at the boundary between the CBD and the upper Quarter.

Room rates vary, depending on the time of year, peaking during Mardi Gras and Jazz Fest. During the hot, sticky summer months (June through August) rates fall, possibly by as much as 50%. Note that many hotels require minimum stays, deposits and up to two month's cancellation notice for rooms during carnival or Jazz Fest. Early reservations, at least two months in advance for Mardi Gras, are a must.

At any time of year, even walk-in visitors can negotiate down from the official 'rack rate.' Discounts of 10% or more are commonly granted to members of the American Automobile Association (AAA), as well as to senior citizens, students and some corporate affiliations. Ask your shuttle or taxi driver how business is in town; you'll have less luck bargaining if you're competing with a convention. Note also that toll-free numbers for chain hotels are not always as reliable as the properties themselves for quoting occupancy or the lowest available rate. Additional charges include room tax at 11% plus $1 per person occupancy tax. Parking adds about $15 a day in the French Quarter or CBD.

Guesthouses in New Orleans provide inexpensive lodging. Rooms start below $40 in the larger guesthouses and generally include a continental breakfast. More upscale B&Bs typically cater to a small number of guests and offer antique furnishings and full breakfasts; expect to pay $80 and up. Bed & Breakfast, Inc (☎ 504-488-4639, 800-729-4640), PO Box 52257, New Orleans, LA 70152-2257, makes free reservations at selected B&Bs to suit a wide variety of preferences and budgets. They promptly send or fax illustrated descriptions. The Louisiana B&B Association (☎ 504-346-1857), PO Box 4003, Baton Rouge, LA 70821-4003, offers a free illustrated guide to member B&Bs throughout the state.

For house rental (ideal for larger groups), check with the B&B associations or the classified ads in the Sunday *Times-Picayune* a few months before the event. Be sure to pinpoint the nearest cross street on a map; homes advertised 'near the French Quarter' could be either a long taxi ride away or in a dodgy neighborhood.

Camping

There are four state parks within a half-hour drive of New Orleans and all offer well-maintained camping facilities, with toilets, hot and cold running water, showers, electrical hookups and shaded sites.

The most convenient is about 13 miles south of New Orleans at *St Bernard Parish State Park* (☎ 504-682-2101). It's near the Mississippi River and features wooded lagoons, short nature trails and a swimming pool. Take Hwy 46 along the east bank to Bayou Rd and turn right on Hwy 39. The park entrance is within a mile on your left. Campsites run on a first-come, first-served basis and include water and electricity in the $12 fee.

On the west bank at *Bayou Segnette State Park* (☎ 504-736-7140) are 100 campsites, with water and electricity, for $12 per night. Cabins that can accommodate eight are $65, including linens and cookware. The park is built at the confluence of several canals and offers good boat access to swamps and bayous all the way to the Gulf; its popular boat launch is open 24 hours. To get there from New Orleans, cross the Greater New Orleans Bridge and follow Business Hwy 90 (Westbank Expressway) upriver about 10 miles to the bayou entrance on your left at Drake Ave.

On the North Shore of Lake Pontchartrain (see Around New Orleans, below), *Fontainebleau State Park* (☎ 504-624-4443) offers hundreds of improved ($12)

and unimproved sites ($10). Pine and hardwood forests shade most campsites, and there is a swimming beach, pool and nature trail. It's across the Lake Pontchartrain Causeway and about four miles east on Hwy 190.

The closest privately operated RV parks and campgrounds are along the Chef Menteur Hwy (Hwy 90) in eastern New Orleans (east of the Inner Harbor Canal). The *Jude Travel & Trailer Park* (☎ 504-241-0632), 7400 Chef Menteur Hwy, offers a pool, hot tub, showers and laundry along with full hookups starting at $19 (tent sites a bit less). The No 66 Chef Menteur Express bus stops nearby. Or try the *Mardi Gras Campground* (☎ 504-243-0085), 6050 Chef Menteur Hwy, near I-10 exit 240A, which charges $15 for a hookup site or separate tent site. There is a pool.

Not far from the New Orleans international airport, the *New Orleans West KOA* (☎ 504-467-1792, 800-562-5110), 11129 Jefferson Hwy, offers tent sites for $21 and RV sites for $27.

Hostels

There are three backpacker hostels within reach of the French Quarter on public transit: two in the Lower Garden District, and one with a pool in Mid-City near Canal St. All are well known to airport shuttle drivers. The hostels all offer kitchens, baggage storage, heat or air-conditioning and communal areas where it's easy to make friends; there are no curfews. Laundry facilities are either located within or nearby.

Hostelling International operates the 162-bed *Marquette House Hostel* (☎ 504-523-3014) at 2253 Carondelet St on the margins of the Lower Garden District. A night's stay in a dormitory costs $14 for members or $17 for nonmembers, including tax. Discounted weekly rates for members run about $80. Sheet rental is an additional $2.25; bring your own towel. A few private rooms with linens and kitchen are also available; a double that sleeps four costs $40, and a large two-bedroom unit runs about $70. To get there from the Union passenger terminal: walk five blocks toward the river on Howard Ave to St Charles Ave and take the uptown streetcar to Jackson Ave. You'll be facing in the right direction when you get off – walk one block to Carondelet St.

The *Longpré Guest House Hostel* (☎ 504-581-4540), 1726 Prytania St, has 24 dorm beds in an 1850s Italianate-style home in the Lower Garden District. Bunks come with linens for $12 including tax if you carry a student card or foreign passport, or $16 without. Private rooms with shared shower are $35 a single. Bike rentals are available nearby. To get there from downtown take the St Charles Ave streetcar and get off at Euterpe St; walk one block toward the river to Prytania St.

The *India House Hostel* (☎ 504-821-1904), in Mid-City off Canal St at 124 S Lopez St, has a swimming pool behind the two homes that serve as dorms. Bunks cost $12 including linens and tax; simple private cabins are available for $30. You must have either a student ID or a foreign passport to stay here. To get there from the Union passenger terminal, cross Loyola Ave in front of the depot and board a bus ($1.10 fare with transfer) to Claiborne Ave; only go as far as Canal St and transfer to any Canal St bus heading toward the lake. Cross Canal St after you get off at Lopez St. Taxis cost $6. (Check out the *Dixie Taverne* (☎ 504-822-8268) nearby at 3340 Canal St, where pitchers of beer cost $3 and women drink for free each Thursday.)

During summer (roughly mid-May to mid-August), *Loyola University* (☎ 504-865-3622) rents out dormitory rooms on its Uptown campus for $35 a night. Be patient; room rental is not their primary mission.

Hotels, Motels & B&Bs
French Quarter At the bottom end, *Hotel La Salle* (☎ 504-523-5831, 800-521-9450), on the edge of the Quarter at 1113 Canal St, offers decent singles/doubles with shared bath for $30/34 or $55/65 with private bath. All rooms include TV and phone.

There are many wonderful mid-range hotels to choose from. *Chateau Motor Hotel* (☎ 504-524-9636), 1001 Chartres St in a quiet part of the Quarter, offers singles from $79, including continental breakfast and parking. For a little more you can jump up considerably in quality to the effortlessly elegant *Le Richelieu* (☎ 504-529-2492, 800-535-9653), 1234 Chartres St, with its own bar and pool. Single/double rooms start at $85/100. (Drivers note: free parking, no valets, easy in and out!)

The *Cornstalk Fence Hotel* (☎ 504-523-1515), 915 Royal St, occupies a historic house. Rooms with high ceilings, antique furnishings and private bath cost $125/155 a single/double, but can drop to $75 in the low season.

Hotel St Pierre (☎ 504-524-4401, 800-225-4040), 911 Burgundy St, is a group of historic Creole cottages (note the brick construction and courtyard interiors) with modern furnishings, a pool and rates that start at $110/130. The same owners operate the *Andrew Jackson Hotel* (☎ 504-561-5881, 800-654-0224), 919 Royal St; rates start at $109 including continental breakfast; there's no pool.

The commotion rarely extends down Bourbon St to the *Lafitte Guest House* (☎ 504-581-2678), 1003 Bourbon St, an elegant three-story French manor house that offers 14 rooms at prices from $99 to $165 during peak season, or $59 in the off-season.

Climbing up in price, the finely restored buildings of the *Hotel Provincial* (☎ 504-581-4995, 800-535-7922), 1024 Chartres St, offer about 100 high-ceiling rooms, suites that open onto interior courtyards, two pools and a cafe and bar. Doubles start at $145, but off-peak discounts drop to $79. Parking adds $8 a night.

The venerable Monteleone and Omni Royal Orleans head the list of prominent large hotels. Opened in 1907, the *Monteleone* (☎ 504-523-3341, 800-535-9595), 214 Royal St, offers glamorous singles/doubles for $130/150, except during the summer months and Christmas when all rooms cost $90. It has a rooftop pool and some rooms have river views. Parking costs $11 a night. The *Omni Royal Orleans* (☎ 504-529-5333, 800-843-6664), 621 St Louis St, offers the best furnishings and in-room amenities (rooftop pool, fitness center) of any large hotel in town. Rooms start at $244 and parking adds $14.

Among small hotels, the 33-room *Soniat House* (☎ 504-522-0570, 800-544-8808), 1133 Chartres St, is the place where local innkeepers send their friends for Creole-style elegance. This meticulously restored 1830 townhouse in the lower Quarter features fine antique furnishings in rooms that start at $160 (note there is at least three-night minimum for most of the year). Parking costs $14 a night.

Faubourg Marigny Lodgings on Esplanade Ave across from the Quarter provide easy access to sights. Nearby, around Frenchmen St, is the heart of the city's gay and bohemian district.

The *Rathbone Inn* (☎ 504-947-2100, 800-947-2101), 1227 Esplanade Ave, offers rooms in an 1850s mansion. The rooms, starting at $90, have private bath and kitchenette, and the rate includes continental breakfast. Nearby, the small *Lamothe House* (☎ 504-947-1161, 800-367-5858), 621 Esplanade Ave, offers nine antique-furnished rooms that start at $175 in peak season; a two-night minimum stay is required on weekends.

Up Esplanade Ave across Rampart St, *Maison Esplanade* (☎ 504-523-8080, 800-892-5524), 1244 Esplanade Ave, offers 10 rooms in a historic home furnished with antiques; rates start at $139. Across the street, the *Hotel Storyville* (☎ 504-948-4800), 1261 Esplanade Ave, is a thoroughly modern lodging that was built to look old on the outside. Spotless suites sleep four and cost between $109 and $125 ($199 to $250 with kitchenettes).

On the riverfront, across from the Old Mint and near the streetcar terminus, *Hotel de la Monnaie* (☎ 504-947-0009), 405 Esplanade Ave, offers time-share condominiums in a building designed to pass for historic. The best value here are two-bedroom suites with kitchenette; these sleep six for $190 a night ($270 during special events). One-bedroom suites sleep four for $140.

At the top end in this area, *Melrose Mansion* (☎ 504-944-2255), 937 Esplanade Ave, pampers guests with elegant accommodations in an 1884 Victorian mansion with fine antiques. To get there, just hop in the stretch limo at the airport after making a reservation; rooms start at $225.

Several smaller places in the heart of the Marigny offer less-expensive lodgings with more of a taste of the neighborhood. The *Royal St Inn* (☎ 504-948-7499) operates a 'bed and beverage' out of the hipster R Bar at the corner of Royal and Kerlerec Sts. Comfortable small rooms that open onto the street are $75, while bigger rooms that sleep four are $100; the attic room has a kitchenette. *The Frenchmen* (☎ 504-948-2166, 800-831-1781), 417 Frenchmen St, is a small refurbished 1850s Creole townhouse with an inviting interior court and pool; rates start at $84.

Across Elysian Fields Ave, the *Lion's Inn B&B* (☎ 504-945-2339), 2517 Chartres St, 'welcomes all sexual persuasions;' it has four nice rooms in a renovated house, and rates range from $65 to $90.

Farther out in the raw Bywater district downriver from the Marigny, bargain-hunters will find the *Big Easy Guesthouse* (☎ 504-943-3717, 800-679-0640) at 2633 Dauphine St (near a popular nightclub called Vaughn's). Here a small cottage built of barge boards in 1836 has rooms with shared/private bath for $50/75.

CBD Singles/doubles at the *Pallas Hotel* (☎ 504-558-0201), 1732 Canal St, start at $89/99; discounts are available to AAA members or almost anybody who complains about the long walk along a threatening vacant stretch to the French Quarter.

This area contains the bulk of chain hotels (also see the list of convention hotels, below). Next to the noisy freeway, the *Days Inn* (☎ 504-586-0110, 800-232-3297) at

1630 Canal St offers rooms that start at $50 on weekdays and $60 on weekends. The high-rise *Comfort Inn* (☎ 504-586-0100, 800-228-5150), near City Hall at 1315 Gravier St, has well-worn rooms; rates start at $65/90 weekday/weekend. A step up and only two blocks from Bourbon St is the *Hampton Inn* (☎ 504-529-9990, 800-426-7866), 226 Carondelet St, a new hotel offering free local calls and continental breakfast in modern rooms starting at $119 on weekends.

Large high-rise chain hotels clustered near Canal St offer predictable standards at competitive rates. (The Hyatt Regency is adjacent to the Superdome.) Typical room rates start at about $100 and range to $200 and up at the Hotel InterContinental, Hilton Riverside Hotel and Le Meridien Hotel.

New Orleans' convention hotels include:

Hyatt Regency, 500 Poydras St
  (☎ 504-561-1234, 800-233-1234)
InterContinental, 444 St Charles Ave
  (☎ 504-525-5566, 800-332-4246)
Le Meridien Hotel, 614 Canal St
  (☎ 504-525-6500, 800-543-4300)
Marriott, 555 Canal St
  (☎ 504-581-1000, 800-228-9290)
Radisson, 1500 Canal St
  (☎ 504-522-4500, 800-333-3333)
Sheraton Hotel, 500 Canal St
  (☎ 504-525-2500, 800-325-3535)
Westin Canal Place, 100 Iberville St
  (☎ 504-566-7006, 800-228-3000)

Among the area's other major lodgings, a few rise above the standard overpriced convention-goers' quarters. *Le Pavillon* (☎ 504-581-3111, 800-535-9095), 833 Poydras Ave, a large full-service hotel since 1907, offers a lovely marble lobby and plush updated rooms for around $149, or $230 in peak season.

At the top end, the *Fairmont Hotel* (☎ 504-529-7111, 800-527-4727) at 123 Baronne St has been among the city's best hotels since it was opened in the 1920s as the Roosevelt Hotel. Its location opposite the richly ornamented Orpheum Theater is adjacent to the French Quarter and close to public transit. Rooms have recently been renovated and cost $229, dipping slightly in summer.

Offering a high tea, fine English paintings and antique European furnishings, the *Windsor Court Hotel* (☎ 504-523-1236, 800-237-1236), 300 Gravier St, represents the greatest English invasion of New Orleans since General Pakenham's army. It was founded in 1984 by the British honorary consul, who felt that New Orleans needed luxurious accommodations with traditional grand service. Rooms start at $230.

Warehouse & Lower Garden Districts

The greatest concentration of decent low-priced lodgings in the city is in this area. At the bottom end, the *YMCA International Hotel* (☎ 504-568-9622) on Lee Circle at 920 St Charles Ave, offers spartan rooms with shared bath for only $29/35 a single/double, plus a $5 key deposit. Guests have access to the gym facilities, swimming pool and restaurant.

The newest offering is the *Audubon Hotel* (☎ 504-568-1319), 1225 St Charles Ave, with rooms above the arty Audubon Lounge. Renovations are still in progress and, for the time being, spartan singles and doubles rent for $25/35 with shared/private bath. Those with kitchens attract local hipsters and cost $110 a week. It's right on the streetcar line.

Among the city's best-value guesthouses are the *Prytania Inns I, II & III* (☎ 504-566-1515). The office for all three separate properties is within Prytania I at 1415 Prytania St. Spare, clean, comfortable singles/doubles with private bath start at $35/45 without breakfast; add $5 for a full breakfast. One of the managers speaks Japanese, German, French, Spanish, Chinese and Thai (as well as English). Prytania III is costlier and more upscale than the other two and occupies a historic house that has been the setting for Halloween parties hosted by Anne Rice.

St Vincent's Guest House (☎ 504-523-3411), 1507 Magazine St, is yet another inn operated by the Prytania folk. Situated in a former orphanage furnished with plenty of wicker, immaculate singles/doubles with private bath are $59/69 including full breakfast. A high tea is served from noon to 4 pm.

The *Prytania Park Hotel* (☎ 504-524-0427, 800-862-1984), 1525 Prytania St, offers a modern motel with 49 small but nicely appointed rooms, and a restored 1850s guesthouse with 13 rooms. Single/double rates are $129/149 with continental breakfast, but discounts are easily obtained when few cars appear in the free parking lot.

In the Warehouse District, the small *Plaza Suite Hotel* (☎ 504-524-9500, 800-770-6721), 620 S Peters St, occupies a former fire house built near the river in 1870. Each suite sleeps four with a fold-out couch in the living room, and go for around $135.

City Park & Fair Grounds While accommodations here are convenient for Jazz Fest, most people prefer to stay closer to downtown and bus up. Nevertheless, there are some distinctive options for lodging in the area. The *Benachi Torre House B&B* (☎ 504-525-7040, 800-308-7040), 2257 Bayou Rd at Rocheblave St (near Esplanade Ave), occupies a mansion built in 1859 for the Greek consul. It sits within a large iron-fenced lot, complete with carriage house and original cistern. Handsome restored rooms cost $95/105 with shared/private bath. The owners also operate an all-suite property nearby with prices starting at $125.

Neighbors operate the *House on Bayou Road* (☎ 504-945-0992, 800-882-2968) at 2275 Bayou Rd, a top-end B&B in a Creole plantation home surrounded by two acres of former plantation land. Rooms in the main house start around $115 a double. A private cottage is also offered and guests may take a cooking course as part of a two or five-night package.

Airport Plenty of chain hotels and motels are located near the airport. The cheapest rooms are available at *Days Inn* (☎ 504-

469-2531), 1300 Veterans Blvd, and *Comfort Inn* (☎ 504-467-1300), 1700 I-10 Service Rd. *La Quinta New Orleans Airport* (☎ 504-466-1401), 2610 Williams Blvd, has renovated rooms with king-size beds for $77 a double ($65 with AAA membership). The *New Orleans Airport Hilton* (☎ 504-469-5000), 901 Airline Hwy, and *Best Western New Orleans Inn at the Airport* (☎ 504-464-1644) are literally across the street from the airport. The Hilton is pricey and considered a fine, standout hotel, but the Best Western can offer rooms for as low as $50 a double. Ask at any of the above hotels for discount shuttles to town. These are good options for your last night in the city if you have an early flight to catch.

PLACES TO EAT

One of the most entertaining things to do in New Orleans is eat.

Creole and Cajun cuisines are among the world's most unique culinary traditions and are the result of the region's diverse heritage. See Food in the Facts for the Visitor chapter for a comparison of Creole and Cajun cooking.

Not only is the food delicious, but dining rises to a high art in New Orleans. Meals are accompanied by a wonderful ambiance whether you're enjoying an elegantly presented plate of blackened redfish at a romantic French Quarter bistro or you're at a dockworker dive where the waiter has just slapped a tin tray of steaming crawfish on your newsprint-covered table.

French Quarter

Eating in the crowded tourist areas along the river and in the lower Quarter offers everything from Lucky Dogs sold by street vendors to splurging on the splendor and service offered at the many restaurants. The middle range is better represented in the lower Quarter, where it's also possible to avoid the crowds.

Budget The Quarter's many cafes offer respite from the crowds, and inexpensive eats. The classic choice, *Café du Monde* (☎ 504-581-2914), 800 Decatur at the

French Market, is a New Orleans institution that has not exploited its fame and convenient riverside location opposite Jackson Square by charging astronomical prices or adding new menu selections. Many visitors and locals have weathered sudden showers or drunken escapades under their patio awning while a server delivers café au lait and an order of beignets dusted with powdered sugar ($2). It's open 24 hours a day.

A spacious, local alternative is *Kaldi's Coffeehouse* (☎ 504-586-8989), 941 Decatur St, where you can usually find copies of *Offbeat* along with old copies of the *New York Times* and other cafe standards. The former bank building also contains a fledgling collection of old coffee grinders and roasters.

The 'concierge' at *New Orleans Coffee Concierge* (☎ 504-524-5530), 334B Royal St, is an invaluable binder filled with menus and brochures from local restaurants. They serve quiche, omelets and waffles for under $6 along with light lunches and suppers. *Royal Blend* (☎ 504-523-2716), 621 Royal St, makes another easy coffeehouse stop, with a pleasant garden courtyard popular with tourists.

La Madeleine (☎ 504-568-9950) overlooks the Jackson Square scene at 547 St Ann St. This French bakery and cafe offers the flakiest quiche crusts on the planet – crawfish and spinach quiche with juice and coffee costs under $8. Not all of their pastries are French – try their delicious bran muffins.

Tucked in the lower Quarter, *Croissant d'Or Patisserie* (☎ 504-524-4663) at 617 Ursulines Ave (between Chartres and Royal Sts) offers fluffy individual quiches, filled croissants, birthday cakes and a small restful courtyard.

A good no-frills breakfast is available for under $4 at *St Ann's Deli* (☎ 504-529-4421), 800 Dauphine St at St Ann St. It also offers sandwiches, salads, soups and spinach pie. It's open late and offers bicycle delivery within the Quarter.

The best late-night menu can be found at the *Quarter Scene* (☎ 504-522-6533),

Cooking Classes

New Orleans attracts chefs from around the world who come to learn from the locals. Visitors can pick up some of the culinary mystique by enrolling in the cooking classes offered in town. You may not learn how to make complex French sauces in an afternoon class, but you will be able to add to your repertoire a few of the delicious one-dish Cajun and Creole specialties that are relatively easy to prepare. The first two courses below offer entertaining lectures followed by a lunch from the dishes you have watched the chefs prepare. If you're in town for a couple of days, you might take both courses; they're not much more expensive than lunch alone.

New Orleans School of Cooking The three-hour demonstration features everyday Creole cooking. An introduction to the area's geography and history is woven into the course. The menu consists of gumbo, jambalaya, bread pudding and pralines served with a Dixie beer. The New Orleans School of Cooking (☎ 504-525-2665) is in the Jackson Brewery, 620 Decatur St, in the Louisiana General Store. The class begins daily at 10 am and costs $20.

Cookin' Cajun The two-hour demonstration is a bit more rushed than the above course, leaving out the geography and history lesson, and the menu typically features either gumbo or jambalaya. Cookin' Cajun (☎ 504-733-4406) is in the Riverwalk Mall, in the Creole Delicacies Gourmet Shop. Classes start daily at 10 am and 1 pm, and cost $15.

Cuisine Eclairée Cooking School If you're interested in a more in-depth cooking class consider the Cuisine Eclairée Cooking School (☎ 504-945-0992, 800-882-2968), 2275 Bayou Rd. Classes are taught by acclaimed chef Gerard Maras. They're offered as part of a two or five-night package at the House on the Bayou, a top-end B&B (see Places to Stay). ∎

LOUISIANA

900 Dumaine St at Dauphine St, offering a spicy grilled vegetable plate with rice or pasta that comes with salad for $7 (add $2 to include grilled chicken or shrimp). It's a linen-napkin sort of place open until midnight on weekdays and around-the-clock on weekends.

For a sausage omelet or burger, check out the buns at the counter of the 24-hour *Clover Grill* (☎ 504-523-0904), 900 Bourbon St, where everyone enjoys a good sense of humor.

Deja Vu Bar & Diner (☎ 504-568-1771), on Conti St between Dauphine and Bourbon Sts, offers around-the-clock budget food. Breakfast starts at $2; garden burgers and seafood gumbo are under $6.

At *Johnny's Po-Boys* (☎ 504-524-8129), 511 St Louis St, ask for your sandwich 'dressed' if you want lettuce, tomato and mayonnaise (extra charge). It also offers budget hot plates for breakfast and lunch, and the potato salad is a delicious vegetarian option. You can call for delivery.

Cheap yet substantial Cuban and Mexican dishes keep the picnic tables filled at the *Country Flame* (☎ 504-522-1138), 620 Iberville St. Stick with the vegetarian fajita, served with yucca, guacamole, beans, rice and tortillas for $5 – the meat dishes and bargain empanadas tend to be overly greasy.

Opposite the Old US Mint at 95 French Market Place, the *Louisiana Pizza Kitchen* (☎ 504-522-9500) is a popular local chain offering wood-fired individual pizzas topped with treats such as artichokes, feta and roasted garlic (from $6).

An 18-seat vegetarian cafe, *Old Dog New Trick Cafe* (☎ 504-522-4569), 307 Exchange Alley, offers dinner entrées like polenta stuffed with black beans and feta, and grilled tofu with peanut ginger sauce, both served with grilled vegetables, for $8. Their tasty soups make inexpensive meals and their fresh-baked cakes are always winners.

Moderate & Top End The splendid menu at chef Emeril Lagasse's *NOLA* (☎ 504-522-6652), 534 St Louis St, is a welcome

alternative to the standard Cajun fare. Vegetarian, meat and seafood entrées go for under $20. Part of the fun is watching the kitchen staff while waiting at the bar for a seat.

Chef Armand Olivier combines modern innovations with his African Creole family traditions at *Olivier's* (☎ 504-525-7734), 204 Decatur St across from the House of Blues. Start with the pecan-breaded oysters with pickled okra and baby corn for $6, then choose from seafood and meat entrées that come with salad (the honey mustard horseradish dressing is hot!) and side dishes for $12 to $18.

Spicy Creole sauces on pasta and seafood dishes are specialties at *Sebastian's Little Garden* (☎ 504-524-2041), 538 St Philip St, but close attention is also paid to side dishes like stir-fried vegetables, meatless red beans and rice, plus the soup and salad that come with dinners for under $15. Finish with one of their excellent freshly made desserts.

Pasta and seafood-lovers appreciate the offerings at *Andrew Jaeger's House of Seafood* (☎ 504-522-4964), 621 Conti St. Vegetarians can order the spicy pasta dishes sans seafood. Dinners in the three-story restaurant with piano entertainment cost between $10 and $20.

At *Lucky Cheng's* (☎ 504-529-2045), 720 St Louis St, Asian drag-queen waitresses serve spicy 'Asian Creole' dishes. It's a fun place to take unsuspecting friends. Dinners cost $17 to $31; lunch is $8. Their brunch features bottomless mimosa cocktails.

For Indian cuisine amid splendid furnishings try *Shalimar* (☎ 504-523-0099), 535 Wilkinson Row, where dinners cost $13 to $20 for most traditional tandoori and a few of the more exotic dishes from South India.

Paul Prudhomme, the mentor for an entire new generation of New Orleans chefs since his days at Commander's Palace in the early 1970s, runs *K-Paul's Louisiana Kitchen* (☎ 504-596-2530), 416 Chartres St. Communal seating and prices in the $30 to $40 range help keep away the locals, but it's fun to meet people while

The Muffuletta – Louisiana's Signature Sandwich

Created in 1906 by Sicilian immigrant Salvatore Lupo, the muffuletta gets its name from a round, seeded loaf of bread, indigenous to Sicily. According to Lupo family lore, Salvatore Lupo, the proprietor of New Orleans' Central Grocery, first made the sandwich for the local workers who stopped in his shop each afternoon to get the ingredients for a four-course meal: meats, cheese, olive relish and bread.

Lupo merely combined their four-course meal into sandwich form. Today, the sandwich is made by layering ham, salami and provolone onto the same round, seeded muffuletta loaf that Lupo used. The sandwich is then crowned with a heaping helping of oily olive relish, quartered and served wrapped in butcher's paper to the throngs of locals and tourists who descend upon the Central Grocery each day.

Though the sandwich owes its name to the distinctive bread on which it is served, its fame is surely attributable to the olive relish. With each bite of a muffuletta, capers, green and black olives, carrots, garlic, celery, pimentos and bits of cauliflower ooze out of the sandwich (and onto your shirt front).

From its point of origin in the French Quarter, the muffuletta has spread statewide, even nationwide. One of the more compelling derivations is found at Fertitta's in Shreveport, Louisiana (see Northern Louisiana chapter), where they serve a 'muffy,' so-named because the owners opted to shorten the sandwich name rather than pay for the extra five letters on the neon sign that still blinks above the entrance. Fertitta's adds mustard, turkey, bologna and finely chopped olive relish to the mix, and then warms the sandwich in the oven – changes that the owners attribute to their close proximity to Texas. (We don't quite understand this either.)

Though there are now as many variations as there are sandwiches, for a taste of the real thing you are advised to start where it all began. The motherchurch of muffulettas, *Central Grocery* (☎ 504-523-1620), is at 923 Decatur St between Dumaine and St Phillip Sts. Half a muffuletta will satisfy most appetites. Order it to go and eat it in the plaza across the way or fight for counterspace in the back of the air-conditioned market. The *Progress Grocery* next door makes an equally good muffuletta. *Napolean House* (☎ 504-524-9752), 500 Chartres St, serves the best sit-down muffuletta in the Quarter – in a cool, dark bar built in 1797.

– John T Edge

sharing outrageously rich and flavorful Cajun and Creole food.

Chef Susan Spicer's innovative cooking at *Bayona* (☎ 504-525-4455), 430 Dauphine St, draws rave reviews and keeps her reservations-only restaurant filled. Her polenta appetizer is a hit, as are the choice of entrées that hover around the $14 to $20 range. A roasted vegetarian tamale with black beans costs $14.

Men will need a jacket at *Arnaud's* (☎ 504-523-5433), 813 Bienville St, a New Orleans institution serving rich Creole cuisine. They offer a few dishes made with Gulf pompano (a fish Mark Twain said was as 'delicious as the less criminal forms of sin'), such as the pompano en croûte. Without wine, à la carte items easily exceed $30. The main dining room

is preferable to the back room fronting noisy Bourbon St. Upstairs, check out the Mardi Gras collection of vintage costumes, photos and other memorabilia.

Families in Sunday clothes walk past strip joints to enter the elegant turn-of-the-century dining room at *Galatoire's* (☎ 504-525-2021), 209 Bourbon St. A no-reservation policy assures that everyone is treated alike – from the royal heads of carnival to visitors from the rural backwaters. Lunch can last for hours and the bar tab may be a shock. Plan on spending about $30 per person – more if your party gets into the 'eat drink and be merry' mood.

For generations, tourists have breakfasted at *Brennan's Restaurant* (☎ 504-525-9711), 417 Royal St, where a traditional

Creole meal in one of the 12 elegant dining rooms surrounding the courtyard costs about $35. That's a bit steep for eggs, even if they are eggs Sardou (poached on artichoke bottoms in a bed of creamed spinach).

The Brennan dynasty also offers modern northern Italian cuisine at *Bacco* (☎ 504-522-8792), 310 Chartres St, where you can come as you are to enjoy chef Haley Gabel's creative work – she is the first female head chef in any of the Brennan family restaurants. Try the oyster and eggplant ravioli appetizer; risotto or cannelloni entrées cost under $20. An elegant egg breakfast with juice is under $8.

Faubourg Marigny

Get started at *PJ's Coffee & Tea* (☎ 504-949-2292), 634 Frenchmen St, one branch of a local chain of cafes known for good coffee and pastries. *Café Marigny* (☎ 504-945-4472), 1913 Royal St, is another option, and it exhibits local art. There is a $1 cappuccino happy hour from 4 to 6 pm on weekdays.

For lunch, there are a couple of classic dives on Esplanade Ave left over from before the neighborhood turned hip. *Port of Call* (☎ 504-523-0120), 838 Esplanade Ave, serves some of the best burgers in the city ($7 with a baked potato). *Buffa's Bar & Restaurant* (☎ 504-945-9397), 1001 Esplanade Ave, serves old-fashioned meat and potato plates for under $7.

Despite the unappealing name, *Feelings Cafe* (☎ 504-945-2222), 2600 Chartres St (near Franklin Ave), has a wonderfully romantic setting (couples should reserve a gallery table; groups, the patio) for seafood and nice wines overlooking the fountain. Entrées are around $12.

The neighborhood also offers a couple of exotic choices. *Santa Fe* (☎ 504-944-6854), 801 Frenchmen St, serves a chili relleno dinner for $10. The *Siam Cafe* (☎ 504-949-1750), 435 Esplanade Ave, offers spicy vegetarian curries and seafood noodle dishes ($7 to $13). You can sit on traditional mats or on standard Western chairs. A popular nightclub is upstairs.

Open 24 hours, *La Péniche* (☎ 504-943-1460), 1940 Dauphine St at Touro St, is largely a late-night spot. Surly waiters serve a range of foods from red beans and rice for under $4 to shrimp and oyster dinners for $13.

CBD

On weekdays, the small *Le Petit Paris* (☎ 504-524-7660), 731 Common St, offers French pastries, omelets and delicious individual quiches. Try the 'croissant la Seine,' which is filled with crawfish and béchamel sauce. All items are under $4, and they speak French. It's closed on weekends.

In the heart of the CBD you can't miss the cafeteria-style *New City Diner* (☎ 504-522-8198), 828 Gravier St, where full breakfasts are $3 and hot-plate lunch specials cost $6.

At the Windsor Court's world-class *Grill Room* (☎ 504-522-1992), inside the hotel at 300 Gravier St, elegant dinners with accommodating service are priced in the $40 to $60 range. Their Christmas Eve réveillon dinner re-creates the traditional New Orleans feast. You can sample the upper-crust atmosphere for only $17 at high tea.

Warehouse District

Budget On Lee Circle within the YMCA, *Back to the Garden* (☎ 504-522-8792), 920 St Charles Ave, offers healthy breakfasts and lunch plates for under $6, plus they make inexpensive smoothies.

You might hesitate entering the dingy 24-hour *Hummingbird Grill* (☎ 504-561-9229), 804 St Charles Ave. Don't worry, you will not be the only patron without a bottle of cheap wine in a paper bag. The French toast is good and the service is friendly.

Neighbors rely on Martha's daily lunch special and bargain prices at *Louisiana Products* (☎ 504-529-1666), 618 Julia St, a small store with limited seating offering chicory coffee for 50¢, an egg on a French roll for $1 and soup.

Granola with yogurt and bran muffins are a rarity in New Orleans, as are appetizing Mexican dishes served by 'retired surfers'. All of these are on offer at *Lucy's Retired Surfer Bar & Restaurant* (☎ 504-523-8995), 701 Tchoupitoulas St. Be aware that surfers sleep in late.

Across the street is yet another oddity, *Vic's Kangaroo Cafe* (☎ 504-524-4329), 636 Tchoupitoulas St – an Australian pub that provides a taste of down under by serving pies for under $5 until 2 am. Try the chook pie or feta with spinach and tomato, and wash it down with a draft Fosters. Ahh.

The *Red Eye Grill* (☎ 504-593-9393), 852 S Peters St, is strictly a late-night place to get a greasy burger and fries.

At *Mother's* (☎ 504-523-2078), 401 Poydras at Tchoupitoulas St, they serves up their classic 'pile of debris' (shredded beef with pan drippings, $7) even on Mardi Gras morning. This is a good place to try an inexpensive plate of red beans and rice with andouille sausage done right; you might drop back in later for a quick slice of fresh pie.

Moderate At *Doug's Place* (☎ 504-527-5433), 748 Camp St across from the lighthouse building, lunch offerings range from fettuccine ($7) to prime-cut T-bone steak ($22). The real attraction in this former recording studio is the Music Hall of Fame which includes 45 rpm singles recorded by local musicians, including Fats Domino's 'Walking to New Orleans.' The music that's played in the restaurant was recorded there.

For reasonably priced but uncommonly small portions of Creole soul food with blues and gospel entertainment on the weekend (including during Sunday brunch), check out the *Praline Connection II* (☎ 504-523-3973), 907 S Peters St at the corner of St Joseph St in the Warehouse District. Vegetarian lunches start at $4, and dinner entrées cost between $8 and $14. The gumbo Zaire is especially worthwhile.

Two Cajun family restaurants close to the convention center – *Michaul's* and *Mulate's* – offer dining and dancing. Their food is good and authentic, but overpriced to cover the entertainment. See the Entertainment section.

Top End On Gallery Row at 800 Tchoupitoulas St, *Emeril's* (☎ 504-528-9393) is Emeril Lagasse's showcase for updated south Louisiana culinary traditions. Dinner prices range from $25 to $45, while lunches are between $12 and $17.

On Lafayette Square, chef Michael Fennelly is responsible for the artwork as well as the eclectic menu at *Mike's on the Avenue* (☎ 504-523-1709), 628 St Charles Ave. The menu reflects his work as a chef in Santa Fe but there are also Asian influences.

Lower Garden District

For breakfast, lunch or a late-night meal, the restaurants here are conveniently close to the many guesthouses in the area. The place to get started is at the *St Vincent's Guest House* (☎ 504-523-2318), 1507 Magazine St, where $5 buys a complete home-style breakfast with coffee and juice in a grand dining room with real Southern hospitality. They also offer a daily set tea from noon to 4 pm for $6. Across the street, *Rue de la Course* (☎ 504-529-1455), 1500 Magazine St, is a comfortable coffee shop hangout.

Down-home Louisiana-style cooking at *The Furniture Store* (☎ 504-566-1707), 1600 Prytania St, attracts a business crowd and serves lunches that cost around $5. It's not advertised out front; patrons must pass through the retail furniture store and go upstairs.

Vegetarian pizza pies with a whole-wheat crust make *Pie in the Sky* (☎ 504-522-6201), 1818 Magazine St, a hit in a hip atmosphere amid art galleries. Slices cost under $2.50. You can also get whole pizzas (about $15) and pasta nearby at the upscale at *Cafe Roma* (☎ 504-524-2419), 1901 Sophie Wright Place. It's cheap chic with linen-covered tables next to tall arched doorways open to the street.

At 1 am in the 24-hour *Trolley Stop* (☎ 504-523-0090), 1923 St Charles Ave, you're likely to find patrons wearing camouflage next to others wearing cummerbunds. The funky former gas station offers ham and eggs for $4, and even cheaper baked potatoes.

Uglesich's (☎ 504-523-8571) at 1238 Baronne St, a funky low-rent institution since 1927, serves the best oysters in the city. You're likely to see the local elite in the crowded and noisy lunch spot where a bowl of crawfish bisque costs $7 and a cat-fish plate goes for $9. A half-dozen oysters costs $6. It's only open weekdays from 9 am to 4:30 pm.

For even finer dining, *Fleur de Lee* (☎ 504-588-2616), on Lee Circle, offers avant-garde food to the swing set.

Uptown & Garden District

The corridor that extends along St Charles Ave and Magazine St from the Lower Garden District to Audubon Park encompasses some of the wealthiest residential areas in the city. Many restaurants cater to discriminating (also homogeneous and fairly suburban) residents along with students from Tulane and Loyola by offering good value on an everyday basis. Closer to the river one finds a few older working-class places.

Budget Across from Lafayette Cemetery No 1, The Rink shopping center at 2727 Prytania St, houses a *PJ's Coffee & Tea*. Check out the historical photo exhibit in the former skating rink. Or, hang at *CC's Coffee House*, 900 Jefferson Ave at Magazine St. Located closer to Audubon Park on Magazine St, the *London Coffee House* (☎ 504-897-4000), 721 State St, offers soups, salads and sandwiches.

Medical students from nearby hospitals pack the *Bluebird Cafe* (☎ 504-895-7166), 3625 Prytania St at the corner of Antonine St, to enjoy innovative and healthy breakfast and lunch dishes for about $5. Try the huevos rancheros or just grab a seat at the counter for a quick slice of pecan pie. When all the seats are taken (often) you must wait outside.

Order a platter of boiled crawfish and beers for your party before choosing from appetizers like alligator pie and turtle soup, or fried fish entrées at *Franky & Johnny's* (☎ 504-899-9146), a riverfront shanty at 321 Arabella St and Tchoupitoulas St. Five

wild-and-crazy guests can eat and drink for under $100, including a 20% tip for a crawfish-eating lesson.

You step back in time when you enter the impeccably clean, tiled dining room at *Casamento's* (☎ 504-895-9761), 4330 Magazine St near Napoleon Ave. The family remodeled the place in 1949 but kept the same menu featuring a light roux-based gumbo and the oyster loaf (a sandwich of breaded and fried oysters on buttered white bread). They also upheld one other tradition – they close during the summer.

A muy popular place with students is *Taqueria Corona* (☎ 504-897-3974), 5932 Magazine St, offering fresh ingredients and an excellent pico de gallo but surprisingly small portions and a limited beer selection. Burritos start at $3.

Moderate A neighborhood favorite a bit out of the way is *Cafe Atchafalaya* (☎ 504-891-5271), 901 Louisiana Ave between Laurel and Annunciation Sts. Besides meat and seafood entrées, you can make a meal of appetizers and side dishes, from classic fried green tomatoes and crab cakes to a more inventive roasted onion concoction. A light dinner of three vegetables and salad costs just $6.

Locals love the international variety of pasta dishes at *Semolina* (☎ 504-895-4260), 3242 Magazine St, where you can feast on large portions of pasta jambalaya with andouille sausage and bell pepper or pad Thai with shrimp, shitake mushrooms and peanuts for about $10. If it's too busy, go next door to *Cafe Italiano* (☎ 504-891-4040), 3244 Magazine St, for untrendy fettuccine Alfredo or veal scaloppini in the $7 to $11 price range.

A great place for lunch while you're checking out nearby art galleries and antique shops is *Reginelli's* (☎ 504-895-9229) at 3923 Magazine St. The Italian dishes are first rate, but a bit on the expensive side.

In the same area you can eat tapas and Latin Creole dishes for $8 to $19 at *Tango Tango* (☎ 504-895-6632), 4100 Magazine St. They offer live flamenco entertainment on Saturday nights and a Sunday Latin Jazz brunch.

Upscale Uptowners pack the popular *Vaquero's* (☎ 504-891-6441), 4938 Prytania St near Robert St, to sample Native American and Southwestern cuisine, including outstanding grilled veggie appetizers.

Nearby, the *Kyoto Japanese Restaurant* (☎ 504-891-3644), 4920 Prytania St, is a sushi bar that is an undiscovered gem. Dinners cost between $12 and $25.

Pascal's Manale (☎ 504-895-4877) at 1838 Napoleon Ave serves Italian dishes and seafood, notably barbecued shrimp, that locals seem to adore, despite the windowless dining hall and stiff service. Entrées cost from $8 to $16.

Top End One of the top restaurants in the nation, *Commander's Palace* (☎ 504-899-8221), at 1403 Washington Ave across from Lafayette Cemetery No 1, features the most attentive service imaginable and outstanding dishes guided by chef Jamie Shannon. The menu emphasizes fresh, local produce; lunches cost about $20, while four-course dinners start at $42. Reservations and a tie are required.

Riverbend
A cluster of restaurants, bars and shops appear where the St Charles streetcar turns onto S Carrollton Ave. Most restaurants are oriented to the day visitor, but a few special dinner spots are hidden from the typical tourist excursion.

The immensely popular counter in the *Camellia Grill* (☎ 504-866-9573) at 626 S Carrollton Ave offers creamy milkshakes and standard short-order items like burgers and fries. It's the interaction with your neighbor or server that make it special, but the pecan waffle will definitely satisfy your sweet tooth. They're open until 3 am on Friday and Saturday nights. Another late-night munchie spot is *Rick's Pancake Cottage* (☎ 504-822-2630), 1438 S Carrollton Ave, where you can get a blintz with blueberries and cream cheese.

For a po-boy on fresh French bread stop by *Streetcar Sandwiches* (☎ 504-866-1146),

1434 S Carrollton Ave, and watch the streetcars from a sidewalk table. The large rack of hot sauces gives visitors an opportunity to sample everything from mild chilis to the sizzling hot habañero pepper sauces.

Maple St is a popular neighborhood shopping district and hangout for Tulane students. Here you will find a *PJ's Coffee & Tea* at 7624 Maple St. Head to *Figaro's Pizzerie* (☎ 504-866-0100), 7900 Maple St, for pizza or pasta with a pitcher of Abita bock while watching the street activity. Try their eggplant and tomato pasta. A spicy choice for vegetarians or meat-eaters is *Bangkok Thai* (☎ 504-861-3932), at 513 S Carrollton Ave and St Charles Ave.

A cookbook from turn-of-the-century New Orleans noted that it was a poor Creole family that did not have cheese at every meal. The *Chicory Farm Cafe* (☎ 504-866-2325), 723 Hillary St, follows on the success of their nationally renowned cheese-making and organic produce farm at Mt Hermon, Louisiana. A four-course Creole-style vegetarian lunch or dinner for two costs $25 to $30.

Frank Brigtsen apprenticed under Paul Prudhomme; now his popular top-end *Brigtsen's Restaurant* (☎ 504-861-7610), 723 Dante St near River Rd, is Cajun influenced but modern and innovative. He changes the menu daily and most entrées cost between $15 to $20 – but wine and dessert will significantly escalate the bill. You must make reservations for seating in the crowded cottage.

City Park & Fair Grounds Area
Neighborhood markets, such as the Whole Foods Market (☎ 504-943-1626), 3135 Esplanade Ave, have fresh-baked bread, salads, deli items and fresh produce.

Mama's Cafe (☎ 504-947-3141), 1605 Gentilly Blvd, a minuscule joint with barely enough room for a counter, serves tasty cooked-to-order dishes like red beans and rice with fried chicken, salad and bread for around $4.

Chef Angel Miranda offers Spanish-style cuisine in the small cafe at *Lola's*

LOUISIANA

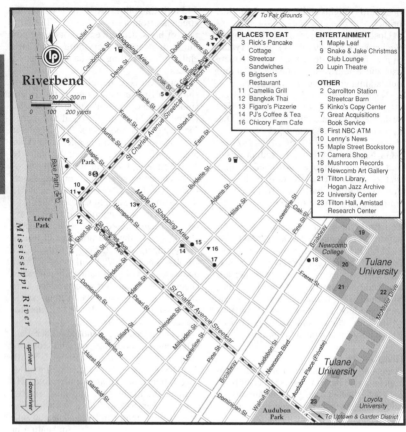

Riverbend

0   100   200 m
0   100   200 yards

Mississippi River

Levee
Park

Bike Path

upriver

downriver

To Fair Grounds

PLACES TO EAT
3 Rick's Pancake
   Cottage
4 Streetcar
   Sandwiches
6 Brigtsen's
   Restaurant
11 Camellia Grill
12 Bangkok Thai
13 Figaro's Pizzerie
14 PJ's Coffee & Tea
16 Chicory Farm Cafe

ENTERTAINMENT
1 Maple Leaf
9 Snake & Jake Christmas
   Club Lounge
20 Lupin Theatre

OTHER
2 Carrollton Station
   Streetcar Barn
5 Kinko's Copy Center
7 Great Acquisitions
   Book Service
8 First NBC ATM
10 Lenny's News
15 Maple Street Bookstore
17 Camera Shop
18 Mushroom Records
19 Newcomb Art Gallery
21 Tilton Library,
   Hogan Jazz Archive
22 University Center
23 Tilton Hall, Amistad
   Research Center

Newcomb
College

Tulane
University

Tulane
University

Loyola
University

Audubon
Park

To Uptown & Garden District

(☎ 504-488-6946), 3312 Esplanade Ave. His pasta or rice-based plates are laced with garlic and olive oil and feature either chicken, seafood or vegetables starting from under $10.

Greg Sonnier captures the attention of both locals and a national audience with his innovative mixture of Creole and Cajun dishes served in modest surroundings at *Gabrielle* (☎ 504-948-6233), 3201 Esplanade Ave. Dinner entrées cost between $15 and $25. Save room for dessert as Greg's wife, Mary, creates outstanding pastries.

Tavern on the Park (☎ 504-486-3333), 900 City Park Ave, housed in the 1860 Jean Marie Saux Building opposite the former main gate to City Park, is now a seafood and steak restaurant. The wood-paneled dining room, which is otherwise romantic, features the owner's collection of military weapons.

Fine French cuisine at a moderate price is offered at *Café Degas* (☎ 504-945-5635), 3127 Esplanade Ave. The à la carte dinner menu ranges from under $10 for sautéed vegetables with wild rice to around

$18 for a veal T-bone steak. For lunch, try the salade niçoise with grilled tuna.

ENTERTAINMENT
Generations of New Orleans club owners have thrived by promoting a combination of music and booze. From New Year's Eve through Jazz Fest, the city is a mecca for headline performers who join the talented musicians fostered in the city's creative musical environment. Look out for shows by some of the city's top performers, including the Iguanas, Dr John, and the musical dynasties of Marsalises and Neville Brothers. Also watch for brass bands such as Kermit Ruffins or the ReBirth Brass Band. The 'brass-hop' band Coolbone melds traditional New Orleans brass with hip-hop. During the summer many of the top local performers go on tour, traveling up the Mississippi River and throughout the nation and the world.

The free monthly entertainment guide *Offbeat* and the weekly *Gambit* are your best sources for reviews and information on upcoming performances. The *Times-Picayune* publishes 'Lagniappe' every Friday. For information on jazz entertainment contact the Louisiana Jazz Federation Hotline (☎ 504-522-5267). To hear a general music listing call ☎ 504-840-4040.

TicketMaster (☎ 504-522-1314, 504-522-5555) has information and sells tickets to just about all major events in the city and the Gulf South. Call its hotline to reserve tickets with a credit card. You can pick them up at the venue or TicketMaster outlets (including Tower Records on Decatur St downtown).

Bars & Clubs
French Quarter Loud rock music nearly drowns out the live jazz, Dixieland, blues, zydeco and Cajun music emanating from clubs along upper Bourbon St between Bienville and St Ann Sts. On any given night one can sample most musical styles within a few footsteps. The lifestyle along Bourbon St abruptly shifts to a gay and lesbian orientation below St Ann St, marked

by throbbing disco sounds. Clubs on the Quarter's riverfront margin cater to crowds seeking mainstream headline acts, while the smaller venues toward the Quarter's periphery offer live brass bands, Irish folk music and disco. Once you tire of the tourist frenzy, bars off Bourbon St offer an opportunity to mix with locals – they also make convenient meeting spots.

Live Music Not usually listed in travel guides are the so-called 'kitty' clubs that give musicians an opportunity to jam and pass the hat (see the Tremé district). Most guides do include the institutionalized *Preservation Hall* (☎ 504-522-2841) at 726 St Peter St between Bourbon and Royal Sts. Barbara Reid and Grayson 'Ken' Mills formed the Society for the Preservation of New Orleans Jazz in 1961, drawing visitors and musicians to their new-found hall. It attracts mostly veteran jazz musicians and you can always join the crowd on the sidewalk to listen to their sets. Entrance is $3; line up before 8 or after 10 pm to avoid long lines.

Many visitors are given the mistaken impression from a banner reading, 'Dedicated to the Preservation of Jazz,' that the *Maison Bourbon* (☎ 504-522-8818), 641 Bourbon St, is Preservation Hall. In any case, you can almost always find a seat and enjoy a Dixieland set for the price of a drink. Note that many musicians will abruptly stop playing and berate photographers who ignore signs forbidding snapshots.

It's jazz by day and rock at night at the *Famous Door* (☎ 504-522-7626), 339 Bourbon St, and the *Famous Door Jazz Cafe* (☎ 504-522-7623), 411 Bourbon St.

Some of the city's hottest spots are clustered on N Rampart St, where a few clubs swing with modern sounds from the best of New Orleans brass bands and musicians like Kermit Ruffins. Check out *Donna's* (☎ 504-596-6914), 800 Rampart St, and the *Funky Butt* (☎ 504-558-0872), 714 N Rampart St. Back in the days of Storyville bordellos, pioneer jazz musicians like Buddy Bolden played at the Union Son's Hall, known as Funky Butt Hall. (Note: Donna cooks up a mean slab of baby back ribs.)

There's barely room to move, let alone dance inside the *Funky Pirate* (☎ 504-523-1960), 727 Bourbon St, which regularly features either Big Al Carson and the Blues Masters or blues guitarist Frankie Nola, who plays loads of riffs from Jimi Hendrix and Stevie Ray Vaughn.

A few locals grumbled when Dan Aykroyd opened the *House of Blues* (☎ 504-529-2583, concert line 504-529-1421), 255 Decatur St, which features a full calendar of fine musical talent. Yet even the most closed-minded, anti-outsider New Orleanians have to admit that besides presenting a steady flow of sparkling-hot headline acts, they do a number of other things right. Among these is the acoustic blues happy hour every Friday from 4 to 8 pm, when

Gay & Lesbian Nightlife

New Orleans' gay nightlife scene is concentrated in the lower Quarter and Faubourg Marigny. All sexual persuasions have their place, from the fetish leather scene at the *Rawhide Lounge* (☎ 504-525-8106), 740 Burgundy St, to the Marigny's neon lesbian disco *Rubyfruit Jungle* (☎ 504-947-4000), 640 Frenchmen St, or *Charlene's* (☎ 504-945-9328), 940 Elysian Fields Ave, a lesbian dance club often featuring live music. You'll also find that the gay nightlife extends into a few of the mainstream clubs when lesbian groups like Stone Rainbow, Rouxmyrs or Sweet Revenge perform. After-hours on Thursday nights at the *House of Blues*, DJ Mary Pappas has a strong gay and lesbian following.

The place to find out about the night's happenings is Faubourg Marigny Bookstore (☎ 504-943-9875), 600 Frenchmen St, the South's oldest gay bookstore. Pick up a recent edition of the free *New Orleans Pink Pages*, which includes a useful bar pull-out section. More listings and maps showing bars appear in *Impact* and *Ambush* magazines. ■

domestic beers are $1. After-hours disco is another plus: on Friday and Saturday it's funk and R&B, on Sunday it's hip-hop, on Monday the House of Blues All Stars play, and it's a gay and lesbian scene on Thursday. Who cares if their Sunday Gospel Brunch does not quite equal Little Richard's performance in *The Blues Brothers*. Tickets (☎ 504-529-3480) cost between $5 and $22.

Jimmy Buffett's *Margaritaville Cafe* (☎ 504-592-2565), opposite the Farmers Market at 1104 Decatur St, books as many as three performers each day. You're likely to hear first-rate blues, jazz or zydeco, and occasionally Jimmy himself – check the recorded music-information hotline (☎ 504-592-2552). The shows have no cover charge.

Irish folk music is featured nightly at *O'Flaherty's Irish Channel Pub* (☎ 504-529-1317), 514 Toulouse St near Decatur St.

Dance Clubs Credit for breaking the New Orleans standard entertainment mold must go the large gay nightclubs on lower Bourbon St that rely strictly on DJs. Foremost are the twin sentinels of pulsing sounds: *Oz* (☎ 504-593-9491), 800 Bourbon St, and the *Bourbon Pub* (☎ 504-529-2107), 801 Bourbon St. Both are open to straights who want to dance nonstop and don't have a problem with guys in g-strings on stage.

A young, mixed crowd packs the dance floor at the *Gold Mine Saloon* (☎ 504-586-0745), 705 Dauphine St, which charges a $1 cover. Ask around here about other high-energy nightspots and unadvertised all-night rave parties.

Bars The classic hurricane is found at *Pat O'Brien's* (☎ 504-525-4823), 718 St Peter St. Its labyrinthine series of alcoves links Bourbon St and St Peter St with a grand courtyard patio. Sing in the piano bar at this continuous party while sipping on your hurricane ($5 plus $2 refundable deposit on the souvenir glass). Don't forget to get your deposit! If you purchase the glass it must be boxed as it's illegal to drink from a glass container on the streets.

Jim Monaghan's *Molly's at the Market* (☎ 504-581-9759), 1107 Decatur St, is the Irish cultural center of the French Quarter. Monaghan inaugurated the wild St Patrick's Day parade that starts at Molly's. It's a good place to get a pint of Abita or Guinness or watch TV or grab some pub food to eat in the back courtyard. You can join the diverse mix of local characters, from off-duty working class to business types – it's not just the shamrock crowd.

Happy hours from 4 to 7 pm or 2 to 5 pm feature $1 draft beers at *Haggerty's* (☎ 504-523-2337), 700 Burgundy St at St Peter St. *Fahy's Irish Pub* (☎ 504-586-9806), 540 Burgundy St, attracts a local crowd with pool, darts and Guinness on tap for $2.75 a pint.

A legend about the pirating brothers Jean and Pierre Lafitte – that they ran a blacksmith shop as a cover for their illegal trade in slaves – is the inspiration for *Lafitte's Blacksmith Shop* (☎ 504-523-0066), 941 Bourbon St, a well-worn corner bar farther down from the action. Another old bar is *Napoleon House* (☎ 504-524-9752), 500 Chartres St. It's fun to listen to the various histories recited by carriage guides as they pass by either place.

Absinthe was once regarded as 'the spirit of New Orleans.' It was outlawed in 1914 because of its poisonous effect on the nerves. Pernod, a safe liqueur flavored with anise, now acts as the poison of choice. It's served at the original *Old Absinthe House* (☎ 504-523-3181), 240 Bourbon St, and the *Old Absinthe Bar* (☎ 504-525-8108), 400 Bourbon St, which opened after federal agents raided the original during prohibition.

Oyster bars now feature food rather than drink; nevertheless, a popular spot that draws many visitors is *Acme Oyster & Seafood House* (☎ 504-522-5973), 724 Iberville St. It still features a small busy bar where you can watch a crew shuck oysters while you sip a beer. The Acme bar also marks the entrance to a bawdy section

Cooling Off

No other city in the US, except perhaps Las Vegas, has such liberal liquor laws. Bars are open around the clock and people can drink in the streets (no bottles or cans; use a 'go-cup' when leaving an establishment). A popular refresher in the French Quarter is the hurricane, which contains dark rum, 151-proof rum, orange juice, pineapple juice and grenadine, served in a large hurricane-lantern shaped glass. Frozen drinks are popular in the sweltering summer months; whole shops on Bourbon St specialize in flavored frozen daiquiris. Dixie and Abita are local breweries; Dixie is in the city and Abita is on the North Shore (see Around New Orleans, below). ■

of Iberville St, off Bourbon St toward the river, that continues to thrive away from the view of most visitors.

New Orleans' only microbrewery is the *Crescent City Brewhouse* (☎ 504-522-0571), 527 Decatur St, a brewhouse equivalent of the Hard Rock Cafe. After you order a pint (about $4) at the bar, the bartender will gladly serve a few small samplers of the other brews.

Faubourg Marigny & Bywater District

Arrive early to get good seats at *Snug Harbor* (☎ 504-949-0696), 626 Frenchmen St, the premier contemporary jazz venue in New Orleans. Views from both the floor and loft seats benefit from large mirrors on the side of the stage. It's a great place to hear the Delfeayo Marsalis Ensemble or pianist Ellis Marsalis perform with his son Jason on drums and Roland Garand on bass. Charmaine Neville's R&B act also appears frequently.

Cafe Brasil (☎ 504-947-9386), 2100 Chartres St at Frenchmen St, appeals to an alternative-lifestyle crowd that rides bicycles (parking out front) and likes to dance to bands ranging from brass to reggae.

A pillowy venue that offers a mixed bag of live music with no cover is the *Dragon's*

The Soul Queen of New Orleans
Irma Thomas, a 60s R&B sensation, started her music career by getting fired for singing on the job while she worked as a waitress at the Pimlico Club. Bandleader Tommy Ridgley stepped in and promised to help her get a record contract, and her first hit '(You Can Have My Husband, but Please) Don't Mess With My Man' was produced in 1960 by Ron Records. Some of her other big hits include 'Wish Someone Would Care' (1964 Imperial Records) and 'Time is on My Side' (1964 Imperial Records). Her latest release is *Story of my Life* (1997, Rounder Records), and her *Live, Simply the Best* album recorded in 1991 (Rounder Records) won a Grammy Award.

She still performs every weekend (if she's not on tour) at the Lion's Den, which she co-owns with her husband and manager, Emile Jackson. ∎

Den (☎ 504-949-1750) at 435 Esplanade Ave, upstairs from the Siam Cafe. Loud rock and R&B groups perform at *Igor's Checkpoint Charlie* (☎ 504-947-0979), 501 Esplanade Ave, where you can do your laundry and play pool with no cover.

A popular bar that always seems to be playing Patsy Cline on the jukebox is the *R Bar* (☎ 504-948-7499), 1431 Royal St (they also operate the 'bed and beverage' Royal St Inn). They offer $2 pints and pool, but the real attraction is the mixed gay and straight crowd that never seems to lose the Mardi Gras spirit.

Downriver from the Marigny at 2239 St Claude Ave, the *Hi Ho* (☎ 504-947-9344) hosts dirty rockabilly that draws a quirky crowd. Folks play Etch-a-Sketch, chess and X-rated Scrabble. A short drive farther down, the *Saturn Bar* (☎ 504-949-7532), 3067 St Claude Ave, is a cosmic dive where trendsetters like to slum. It's locally notorious as the setting of the obscure film *Heaven's Prisoners*.

Even farther out, *Vaughn's* (☎ 504-947-5562), 800 Lesseps St, is a friendly neighborhood bar that hosts brass bands every Thursday.

Tremé District Recording artists continue to flow out of the down-at-the-heels Tremé district's small halls. At 58 years of age, singer Wallace Johnson, a former longshoreman, recorded his first album after performing at local kitty club *Joe's Cozy Corner*, 1030 N Robertson St at Ursulines St. Joe's is a popular venue for brass, soul and R&B. Just across the street, well-known groups like the ReBirth Brass Band frequently play at the *Tremé Music Hall* (☎ 504-596-6942), 1601 Ursulines St. For down-home blues on weekends, check the sounds coming from the *C&C Club*, 1501 St Philip St. Irma Thomas puts on a great show at the *Lion's Den* (☎ 504-822-4693), 2655 Gravier St, near the Dixie Brewery.

Warehouse District *Howlin' Wolf* (☎ 504-523-2551), a first-rate club at 828 S Peters St, hosts blues, rock bands and other local acts. *Rolling Stone* magazine called the Continental Drifters (Howlin' Wolf regulars) the 'best unsigned band in the country.' Revered blues artist Snooks Eaglin is another regular, and George Porter Jr is a hit whenever he appears.

Michaul's (☎ 504-522-5517), 840 St Charles Ave near the YMCA, offers Cajun music and dance lessons as well as pricey Cajun cooking. Another Cajun music and food place is *Mulate's* (☎ 504-767-4794), 201 Julia St.

As for bars, *Vic's Kangaroo Cafe* (☎ 504-524-4329), 636 Tchoupitoulas St, is among the most popular after-work spots. Australian hospitality, hearty beers on tap and cheap food attract a sizable business crowd. Nearby, *Lucy's Retired Surfer Bar & Restaurant* (☎ 504-523-8995), 701 Tchoupitoulas St, is another place to meet before heading out to the Quarter or home to your hotel.

Lower Garden District There aren't many clubs here, mostly budget bars that rely on a local crowd and a captive audience from nearby backpacker hostels.

The *Bamboo Lounge* (☎ 504-568-1319), at 1225 St Charles Ave below the Audubon Hotel, is a new spot for debauched hipsters. Thursdays features Martini Mischief 'for the discriminating loungeoisie.'

Monaco Bob's (☎ 504-586-1282), 1179 Annunciation St, is a small club that attracts a hip young crowd. It has a weekly wet T-shirt night and live music featuring mainly R&B; out-of-town bands can be a surprise.

Uptown bar-hopping trendsetters typically drop in at the *Half Moon* (☎ 504-522-7313), 1125 St Mary St at Sophie Wright Place, but you might stay and play at the best pool tables in the area.

Igor's Lounge (☎ 504-522-2145), 2133 St Charles Ave, is a dive that never closes. It has a greasy grill, pool tables and washing machines, and serves red beans and rice for free on Monday night. On Sunday there's free barbecue at the *RC Bridge Lounge*, 1201 Magazine St.

Uptown & Garden District It's usually too crowded to see the bust of Henry Roland Byrd (1918-80), also known as Professor Longhair, at the entrance to *Tipitina's* (☎ 504-895-8477, concertline 504-897-3943), 501 Napoleon Ave at Tchoupitoulas St. The club is named after his 1953 hit 'Tipitina;' his 'Big Chief' and 'Go to the Mardi Gras' are carnival classics. Tips has long been the best music club in New Orleans, with cover charges in the $15 to $20 range for performers like pianist Dr John, whose 1972 hit 'Right Place, Wrong Time' is known worldwide; the Neville Brothers, a dynasty comprised of Charles, Art, Cyril, Aaron and relatives; and out-of-town groups like George Clinton and P-Funk. Two bars and an ATM on the lower level keep the draft Abita beer ($2.25) flowing while another bar serves

Professor Longhair

the crowd upstairs. Watch for shows at Tipitina's new 2500-capacity warehouse, 310 Howard Ave. If you can't make it to Cajun Country, Tipitina's Sunday night fais-do-do is a close second.

Le Bon Temps Roulé (☎ 504-895-8117), 4801 Magazine St, is a fun neighborhood spot to dance to R&B or just play pool when there's no band.

You can catch guitarist Carlos Sanchez and flamenco dance shows every Saturday at *Tango Tango* (☎ 504-895-6632), 4100 Magazine St. Admission costs $7. Call for information about other Latin and jazz performances.

Acoustic performers of just about any genre regularly play at the *Neutral Ground Coffee House* (☎ 504-891-3381), 5110 Danneel St at Dufosat St, a nonprofit organization dedicated to keeping the live music coming. Most nights showcase three or more performers and a few nights each month are reserved for nonsmokers – yow! There's no cover charge.

The lively *Columns Hotel* (☎ 504-899-9308), 3811 St Charles Ave, is suffused with an atmosphere of faded grandeur. You can drink inside at the old bar or outside on the portico.

Riverbend & Mid-City At the *Maple Leaf* (☎ 504-866-9359), 8316 Oak St, you can catch performances from local stars like Walter 'Wolfman' Washington, Rockin' Dopsie Jr & the Zydeco Twisters, and the ReBirth Brass Band. Don't miss acoustic blues guitarist John Mooney, or no-cover Monday nights featuring traditional piano. You can choose to work up a sweat on the small dance floor in front of the stage or you can relax at the bar in the room next door.

There are plenty of other bars and pool halls catering to college students in the area, but perhaps the most unusual bar is the hole-in-the-wall *Snake & Jake Christmas Club Lounge* (☎ 504-861-2802), 7612 Oak St, four blocks east of Carrollton Ave. It's a late-night place where swingers spend the wee hours around one of the best jukeboxes in the country.

Beyond Riverbend across the freeway, *Mid-City Lanes Rock 'N Bowl* (☎ 504-482-3133), 4133 S Carrollton Ave, reached it's exalted status as the premier venue for bowling and zydeco (Wednesday and Thursday nights) at the hands of owner John Blancher. He also features rousing brass and R&B performers. Blancher claims he was on the road to visit a religious shrine when he had an epiphany to buy the bowling alley. Now Virgin Mary guards the entrance and Blancher throws an awesome Twelfth Night party each year to celebrate the Rock 'N Bowl's success. It's one of the best places to dance in the city.

Theater
Major touring troupes typically perform at the *Saenger Theatre* (☎ 504-522-5555), 143 N Rampart St, where it's worth the admission to just see the fine restoration of the ornate 1927 theater. Student plays are frequently offered at the *University of New Orleans Performing Arts Center* (☎ 504-286-7469) and Tulane University's *Lupin Theatre* (☎ 504-865-5105). Most other theater activity picks up after the locals have packed away their carnival costumes. In addition to the following performing groups, you should also check to see what's playing at the *Contemporary Arts Center* (☎ 504-523-1216), 900 Camp St.

Le Petit Théâtre du Vieux Carré (☎ 504-522-2081), 616 St Peter St at Chartres St, is one of the oldest theater groups in the country. They offer particularly Southern fare, like 'Steel Magnolias' as well as special children's programs featuring classics from Rudyard Kipling and others.

Founded in 1986, *Southern Repertory Theatre* (☎ 504-861-8163), 3rd floor of 333 Canal Place, performs classically Southern plays.

Theatre Marigny (☎ 504-944-2653), 616 Frenchmen St, offers works that often portray humorous local themes.

The *True Brew Theatre* (☎ 504-522-2907) is in the Warehouse District at 200 Julia St. They perform seasonal classics like Dickens' *Christmas Carol* along with their own works.

Also check the playlist at *Theater 13* (☎ 504-524-3090); it's on the 13th floor of the Masonic Temple Building at 333 St Charles Ave.

Comedy improvisation is featured every Saturday night at *Movie Pitchers* (☎ 504-488-8881), 3941 Bienville St.

Classical Music
New Orleans' concert-goers are justifiably proud of the *Louisiana Philharmonic Orchestra* (☎ 504-523-6530), which is led by music director Klaus Peter Seibel. When the New Orleans Symphony collapsed financially in 1990, the musicians invested their own money to create one of only two musician-owned symphonies in the world. From September through May the symphony performs at the richly ornamented Orpheum Theater, 129 University Place, downtown. Tickets cost between $11 and $36. A special concert series at nearby plantations is extremely popular and costs only $7.

Cinema
IMAX stands for 'image maximum' films shown on a 74-foot by 54-foot screen. The *Entergy IMAX Theatre* (☎ 504-581-4629), at the foot of Canal St near the Aquarium of the Americas, shows films like 'The Living Sea' and 'Antarctica'; they're guaranteed to capture your attention. Shows air several times daily; call for a current schedule.

For first-run art and mainstream movies try the *Canal Place Cinemas* (☎ 504-581-5400), 3rd floor of 333 Canal St. The Uptown *Prytania Theatre* (☎ 504-895-4518), 5339 Prytania St, is another venue with a similar approach.

Movie Pitchers (☎ 504-488-8881), in Mid-City at 3941 Bienville Ave, usually plays films that wouldn't otherwise get exposure in New Orleans. *Zeitgeist Theatre Experiments* (☎ 504-524-0064), 740 O'Keefe St not far from the main post office, has decidedly avant-garde film offerings. Patrons at their Dog Days film program were encouraged bring their pets to the show.

SPECTATOR SPORTS
Tickets to all Louisiana Superdome (☎ 504-733-0255), 1500 Poydras St, events are available through TicketMaster (☎ 504-522-5555).

Horseracing
Perhaps the most traditional sport in New Orleans is horseracing.

Buried in the infield at the Fair Grounds Race Track (☎ 504-944-5515), 1751 Gentilly Blvd, are derby winners from an era when New Orleans was one of the best tracks in the country. Opened in 1872, the Fair Grounds is the nation's third-oldest track – the handsome gatehouse was designed by James Gallier in 1859 for an agricultural fair. The stands were rebuilt following a disastrous fire in 1993. The racing season runs from November to March, Wednesday through Sunday, with a 1:30 pm post time.

Football
The 60,000-seat Louisiana Superdome is home to the National Football League's New Orleans Saints. Barring post-season play, the Saints play nine home games from August through December. Tickets cost $22 to $50, and seats are generally available.

Baseball
With 72 home games from April to September, the minor league New Orleans Zephyrs (☎ 504-282-6777) baseball team can be seen almost every week during the summer season. Games between the Zephyrs (a Milwaukee Brewers affiliate) and other AAA clubs in the Southern League are always played in cool evening comfort – the first pitch is at 7:05 pm, except Sunday when games begin at 6:05 pm. General admission costs $5.

College Sports
College football, basketball and baseball games get plenty of attention; local teams tend to rank highly nationwide and contribute stars to the professional ranks. Attending college games is inexpensive,

refreshments are usually very inexpensive and you can often get a glimpse of the nation's up-and-comers.

The Tulane Green Wave plays NCAA Division I football at the Superdome. Regardless of which sport is played, baseball, basketball, women's or men's teams, the best and most exciting Tulane game is one against long-standing rivals Louisiana State University (LSU) from Baton Rouge.

The hottest football ticket is the New Year's Sugar Bowl contest at the Superdome. It features Southeastern Conference champions, and out-of-town fans keep the demand high for tickets ($60 to $100).

The University of New Orleans (UNO) Privateers basketball team is quite good; games are played at the UNO Kiefer Lakefront Arena (☎ 504-280-7222).

THINGS TO BUY

Most shops are open Monday through Saturday from 10 or 11 am (no matter how early the sign might indicate) to 5 or 6 pm. Bookstores (see the Information section of this chapter) are an exception – many are open daily, and booksellers tend to sleep in after keeping later hours in the evening. Of course most tourist-oriented shops are open daily – on Sunday the Flea Market in particular is a hive of activity.

International visitors should note that they can save sales tax by buying at select stores; see Taxes in the Facts about Louisiana chapter.

Shopping Malls & Districts

Besides the premier shopping and browsing areas along Royal St and in the French Market (described under French Quarter sights), several other areas may be worth a shopping stop.

The Jackson Brewery Mall (☎ 504-566-7245), 600 Decatur St, has been redeveloped into a small shopping mall best known for its convenient ATM and public restrooms. The Bayou Country General Store (☎ 504-523-3313) sells cooking supplies and cookbooks. The mall is open Sunday through Thursday from 10 am to 9 pm, and until 10 pm on Friday and Saturday.

Canal St today is largely a grimy corridor of stores. Mingling with the multitude of tax-free camera shops and drugstores are a few remnants from the days when downtown shopping was popular, such as the Maison Blanche department store (☎ 504-566-1000), 901 Canal St. Another large department store, the Krauss Company (☎ 504-523-3311), 1201 Canal St, offers budget-priced selections and can even repair your shoes if they're worn from hoofing it through the Quarter.

The Canal Place Shopping Centre is a new mall anchored by Saks Fifth Avenue at 333 Canal St at N Peters St. Featured at the mall entrance is LA Showcase (☎ 504-558-0054), offering eclectic, locally crafted furnishings. Craftspeople operate the nonprofit craft cooperative, RHINO (Right Here In New Orleans), on the lower level, showcasing the work of over 70 artists. On the 2nd level, RHINO (☎ 504-523-7945) offers handcrafted fabrics and wearable art in their Fyberspace shop. Other shops include Chanel, Laura Ashley, Brooks Brothers and Coach. A multiplex cinema and a performing arts theater are on the 3rd floor (see Entertainment).

The air-conditioned Riverwalk Mall (☎ 504-522-1555), on the riverfront upriver from the aquarium, provides a sanitized alternative to the Quarter's shops and restaurants. In fact, many Quarter shops have outlets in the mall or its food court, perhaps to keep the cash flowing during heavy rain. Stores in the mall include Banana Republic, Sharper Image and other mall favorites.

Adjoined to the Superdome at the corner of LaSalle St and Poydras Ave, the air-conditioned New Orleans Centre (☎ 504-568-0000) is yet another downtown mall with a wide selection of favorite mall shops and Lord & Taylor and Macy's department stores, as well as a food court.

In the heart of the Garden District, a small group of upscale shops, including a bookstore and a coffee shop, is housed in The Rink, a tiny complex next to the Lafayette Cemetery No 1 at the corner of Prytania St and Washington Ave. Another neighborhood center with coffee shops and bookstores is on Magazine St at Jefferson St. Dispersed along Magazine St from Washington Ave all the way to Audubon Park are many antique shops and galleries; this stretch is renowned throughout the South for its 'finds.'

At the Riverbend, fashionable shops and restaurants front a small square on Dublin St near S Carrollton Ave where it meets St Charles Ave. Student-oriented shopping is centered on Maple St, where bookstores, restaurants and coffee shops make the street lively in an otherwise quiet, residential neighborhood. Riverside of S Carrollton Ave, Oak St is an older neighborhood commercial zone intersecting with the streetcar line. It is reasonably compact for pedestrian strolls and offers a few interesting businesses like a vibrant fresh fish market, plus a few restaurants and the stellar Maple Leaf nightclub.

Specialty Stores

Specialty stores offer things you won't find back home and are worth going out of your way for. Music stores, for example, not only offer recordings but can share insights about the local music scene, which performers are in town, and the like. Here's a select sampling of some of the more unusual things you can find. Bookstores are listed in the Information section at the front of this chapter.

Music In the French Quarter, after visiting the jazz exhibit at the Old US Mint, scan the collection of CDs and tapes offered in the gift shop on the museum's ground floor. Nearby is Jazzology/Audiofile Records (☎ 504-525-1776), 1206 Decatur St.

The museum-like collection of historic rock posters and album covers at Record Ron's Stuff (☎ 504-522-2239), 239 Chartres St, is just the tip of the iceberg as his large, yet pricey, collection of Louisiana recordings (mainly LPs) fills his main store, Record Ron's (☎ 504-524-9444), 1129 Decatur St. The Louisiana Music Factory (☎ 504-523-1094), 225 N Peters St, specializes in regional music.

Uptown, over half a million records are available at Jim Russell Rare Records (☎ 504-522-2602), 1837 Magazine St, opposite Pie in the Sky Pizza. Ritual Groove, 3336 Magazine St, always has the latest posters and information on upcoming performances and offers records, tapes and CDs. Both Underground Sounds (☎ 504-897-9030), 3336 Magazine St, and Mushroom (☎ 504-866-6065), 1037 Broadway, serve the university area and sell tickets to shows at Tipitina's (see Entertainment).

Voodoo & Occult If you're not feeling well, try some *gris-gris* (worn in a sachet) to make you feel better. For yellow fever or malaria the Yoruba voodoo practitioners needed a powerful gris-gris known as High John the Conqueror *(Iopomea purga)*. A dried frog gris-gris is useful if you want to practice a little black magic on a bad neighbor. Perhaps you just need some Love Potion No 9. Zombies Voodoo Shop (☎ 504-897-2030), 723 St Peter St, which has a large selection of books on the occult, the Witch's Closet (☎ 504-593-9222), 521 St Philip St, and the Voodoo Museum (☎ 504-523-7685), 724 Dumaine St, all have potions.

Alligator Stuff We don't advocate that you help create a demand for endangered species. Although the alligator has made a comeback from near extinction, poachers could readily decimate the population again if demand rose. Hides from legally harvested 'gators are fashioned into high-value products as may be seen at Wehmeier's Belt Shop (☎ 504-525-2758), 719 Toulouse St. Preserved heads are sold from many Cajun shacks out in the swamps and at the Flea Market.

GETTING THERE & AWAY
Air
New Orleans international airport (☎ 504-464-0831) largely serves domestic passengers. The only international flights are to and from Canada and Central American countries. There is no need for gigantic tramways or moving walkways here – even

passengers fresh from Bourbon St are not likely to get lost. Baggage and ground transportation is on the lower level. See Getting Around for airport transport information.

The main information booth is at the A & B concourse, and is open from 8 am to 9 pm daily. Be sure to pick up a free copy of the excellent *New Orleans Street Map*. Brochures are available in Spanish, French, German, Italian, Portuguese and Japanese. A Travelers' Aid (☎ 504-528-9026 at the airport, 504-525-8726 in the CBD) information booth on the upper level operates daily from 9 am to 9 pm. There is a post office near concourse C, next to Whitney Bank.

There is a branch of the Whitney Bank (☎ 504-838-6432) and an ATM in the terminal near concourse C. It's open weekdays from 10 am to 5 pm. Travelex (☎ 504-465-9647), operated by Mutual of Omaha, charges a sliding service fee ($2 for amounts greater than $50; $4 for those less than $50). For the best exchange rates, wait till you get downtown on a weekday.

Bus

Greyhound (☎ 800-231-2222) operates long-distance bus services to and from New Orleans out of the Union passenger terminal (which is also the Amtrak station) at 1001 Loyola Ave.

From New Orleans there are two morning, three afternoon and four evening Greyhound buses to Baton Rouge. The travel time is under two hours and round-trip fares cost $26. Other frequently scheduled service includes Memphis ($78 roundtrip) and Nashville ($82 roundtrip). Bicycles must be boxed (boxes are not available from Greyhound) and cost an additional $10 each way.

Green Tortoise (☎ 415-956-7500, 800-867-8647) is an 'alternative' bus service that runs trips from San Francisco to Boston via New Orleans in April, May and September. Fares for the 11-day journey to New Orleans start at $380 (including meals).

See To/From the Airport in Getting Around for information on buses from Biloxi and Gulfport.

Train

Three Amtrak (☎ 800-872-7245) trains serve New Orleans, arriving and departing from the Union passenger terminal (☎ 504-528-1610), 1001 Loyola Ave. The *City of New Orleans* runs to Memphis, Jackson and Chicago. The *Crescent* serves Birmingham, Atlanta, Washington, DC, and New York City. The *Sunset Limited* runs between Los Angeles and Miami. All three offer both coach seating and sleepers. See the Getting Around chapter for fare information. Amtrak bus connections allow you to travel between New Orleans and Baton Rouge on one through-ticket. Bicycles are accepted on all trains when packed in boxes provided at the station for $7.

Car & Motorcycle

Because New Orleans sits on an isolated piece of high ground, all of the highway approaches to the city travel over lakes and bayous and are signed as hurricane evacuation routes away from the city. I-10 is the nation's southernmost east-west route, linking Jacksonville with Los Angeles via Mobile and Houston. Baton Rouge (Plantation Country) and Lafayette (Cajun Country) are also on I-10, west of New Orleans. I-10 through-travelers can avoid downtown congestion by taking the I-610 shortcut. Or you can avoid the metro area entirely by following the northern shore of Lake Pontchartrain on I-12 between Slidell and Baton Rouge.

The north-south routes, I-55 to Chicago and I-59 to Chattanooga, meet I-10 to the west and east of New Orleans on either side of Lake Pontchartrain.

On the east bank of the Mississippi River, Hwy 61 (Airline Hwy), offers an alternate route from New Orleans to Baton Rouge. Another older route, Hwy 90, crosses the Huey P Long Bridge as it follows a southern route between Mobile and the Cajun bayous south of Lafayette. I-310 enables drivers to bypass suburban Hwy 90 traffic en route to Cajun Country.

Note that there is a $1 toll to cross Lake Pontchartrain, and river crossings (bridge or ferry) outside of the city proper are $1.

Rental All national car-rental operators, along with some smaller operators, can be found in New Orleans, concentrated at the airport. If you are staying downtown and only visiting the French Quarter you do not need a car. An option for visitors planning on taking an excursion is to pick up a rental downtown when checking out of your hotel, then drop the car at the airport when you leave. Airport rates are generally better than downtown rates. Rates go up and availability lessens during special events or large conventions; a reservation ensures your choice of car and quoted rates.

Some of the larger operators with outlets in or near the downtown area are:

Agency
    7901 Earhart Blvd
        (☎ 504-486-7323, 800-321-1972)
Avis
    2024 Canal St
        (☎ 504-523-4317, 800-831-2847)
Budget
    1317 Canal St
        (☎ 504-467-2277, 800-527-0700)
Hertz
    901 Convention Center Blvd
        (☎ 504-568-1645, 800-654-3131)
Enterprise
    1939 Canal St
        (☎ 504-522-7900, 800-325-8007)
Value
    1717 Canal St
        (☎ 504-529-1222, 800-468-2583)

The lowest rates are available by renting older cars for local travel from Econo-Cars (☎ 504-827-0187), 4417 Earhart Blvd, but you must provide proof of insurance. They offer three-day rentals for $55, or a week for $120.

Bicycle

Louisiana gives bicyclists the same rights and responsibilities as motorists. However, the interstate freeways and highway bridges near New Orleans are closed to bicyclists. Instead, use Hwy 90 or Hwy 61 (see Car & Motorcycle, above, for route details). All of New Orleans' free state-operated ferries crossing the Mississippi River permit bicycles.

Riverboat

Visitors to New Orleans during Mark Twain's time arrived by boat via the Mississippi River. This once common mode of travel is still offered by a few paddlewheel riverboats and ocean-going cruise ships. Costs are high compared to other travel modes – the era of steerage passage is over. River travel is now typically offered as a package tour or excursion that includes top-end food and lodging (see the Getting Around chapter for information on the Delta Queen Steamboat Co headquartered in New Orleans).

GETTING AROUND

The flat and compact riverfront make walking and bicycling the preferred ways to get around. Like cities throughout the USA, public transit in New Orleans has deteriorated as transportation funds have been diverted to subsidize motorists. Nevertheless, visitors will find that the buses, streetcars and ferries generally serve the most popular attractions (with the glaring exception of Union passenger terminal). In fact, the streetcars and ferries are exciting attractions in themselves.

To/From the Airport

The New Orleans international airport is in Kenner, 11 miles west of the city center. Most visitors use the airport shuttle (☎ 504-522-3500), which offers frequent service between the airport and downtown hotels for $10 per passenger each way. It's cheap and comfortable, but can be time-consuming, especially if you're the last to be dropped off. Purchase tickets at the airport from counter agents in the baggage area. You can purchase a return ticket at your hotel or just pay the driver. Be sure to call a day ahead to arrange for a departure pickup, which is typically two hours prior to your flight.

If your baggage is not too unwieldy, the Louisiana Transit Company (☎ 504-737-7433) offers the cheapest ride to downtown aboard its Jefferson Transit Airport Express, route E2, for $1.10. Passengers can exit at stops along Airline Hwy (Hwy 61) and along Tulane Ave. You must flag the bus to board except at the airport's main terminal lobby stop opposite door No 5 on the upper level, and downtown on Tulane Ave at Elks Place opposite the public library. Two bikes may be carried on front racks. Buses run from 6 am to 6:30 pm. Frequency runs every 10 minutes during peak weekday hours, and every 23 minutes around midday. Weekend services run every half-hour. From 6:30 pm to midnight, buses only operate between the airport and Carrollton Ave where you can continue to downtown on the RTA No 39 Tulane bus for $1.

The Coastliner (☎ 601-432-2649, 800-647-3957) offers nine daily buses to and from New Orleans airport and the Gulfport-Biloxi regional airport for $33, or $59 roundtrip. They will carry boxed bicycles for an additional $20.

Taxis to downtown cost $21 for one or two people, or $8 per passenger for three or more persons (four passengers maximum; note that for two or more, a taxi is only $1 more than the shuttle.) The taxi stand is on the lower level outside baggage claim.

By car, the quickest way to drive between the airport and downtown is to take I-10. Coming from downtown on I-10 take exit 223 for the airport. Going to downtown take exit 234 as the Superdome looms before you. An alternative route, Airline Hwy (Hwy 61), passes through a seedy zone.

To/From Union Passenger Terminal

New Orleans provides few options for arriving bus and train passengers. Although it's tempting to walk the short distance to the French Quarter, be wary of going solo through the deserted CBD at night. Cab fare to the corner of Bourbon and Canal Sts costs about $3.50.

As implausible as it seems, local buses do not serve Union passenger terminal directly. Arriving passengers must search for the sheltered stop in front of the station across broad Loyola Ave at Howard Ave. The RTA No 17 S Claiborne Ave bus goes to the edge of the French Quarter at Canal and Rampart Sts. During the weeks

preceding Mardi Gras, a hand-lettered sign directs passengers to board one block down Loyola Ave at Julia St. For route information, call ☎ 504-248-3900 (note that posted RTA information numbers may be incorrect).

Although Union passenger terminal provides neither bicycle lockers nor secure racks, Amtrak is obligated to offer a baggage check service to passengers. You can check a bike as stored baggage by paying $1.50 per day.

Bus

The Regional Transit Authority (RTA; ☎ 504-248-3900) runs the city's bus service. The RTA office at 101 Dauphine St, 4th floor, distributes bus schedules. (The free *New Orleans Street Map*, available from information booths at the airport and downtown, shows most of the route numbers and names.) Fares are $1, plus 10¢ for transfers, except on express buses which charge $1.25. All buses require exact change. Consider purchasing an RTA Visitor Pass good for unlimited travel on buses and streetcars – three days costs $8, or it's $4 for one day. Passes are available from most hotels (ask the concierge) or by visiting the RTA office.

From the French Quarter most destinations are served by buses that stop at the intersection of Basin and Canal Sts. All stops have signs noting the route name and number – you may have to explore all four corners of an intersection to find the stop you want.

Streetcar

The RTA also operates streetcar service on two separate lines. The historic St Charles Ave Line opened as the New Orleans & Carrollton Railroad in 1835. It was the nation's second horse-drawn streetcar line and was among the first in the country to convert to electricity. Now it is one of the few streetcar lines to have survived the automobile era.

Check out the streetcar-era suburbs with their Georgian architecture and ornate churches that evolved along the tracks extending from Canal St uptown to S Carrollton Ave. Transfers to RTA buses cost 10¢ and discount visitor passes are available for frequent users.

The fare is $1 each way (exact change required) and the 13-mile roundtrip from the corner of Canal and Carondelet Sts takes 1½ hours. The line and vintage cars from the early 1920s are listed on the National Register of Historic Places. Although the St Charles Ave streetcar operates 24 hours a day with frequent services during peak hours, it only runs hourly from midnight to 4 am.

In 1988 the wheelchair-accessible Riverfront Line began operating vintage red streetcars on the old dockside rail corridor wedged between the levee and flood wall. The two-mile line runs between the Old US Mint, in the lower end of the French Quarter near the Faubourg Marigny, and the upriver convention center, passing Canal St on the way. The fare costs $1.25 (an additional quarter is required if you use an RTA transfer or Visitor Pass). It operates from 6 am to midnight.

Future expansion plans aim to construct a link on Canal St between the two streetcar lines.

Car & Motorcycle

Bringing a car to downtown New Orleans is a costly proposition, and narrow one-way streets and crowds in the French Quarter will hamper your progress. Otherwise, New Orleans is a relatively easy city to navigate your way through if you stick to the main corridors.

I-10 conveniently scoops down near the French Quarter and Superdome for easy on-off access via Rampart St or Canal St, which are the major arteries through the thickest part of town. To get Uptown, drive alongside the streetcar tracks on St Charles Ave or behind the bus that runs along Magazine St. Esplanade Ave is a handy 'back door' into the lower French Quarter with wide lanes and less competitive street parking than in the upper Quarter. Shoot for the streetcar terminus and you can park and easily access all other riverfront sights on public transit.

Downtown on-street parking is designed for short-term use. Parking meters offer 12 minutes for a quarter with a two-hour limit from 8 am to 6 pm, Monday through Friday. Exceptions are numerous and enforcement is quixotic, so even reading and obeying all posted restrictions will not ensure that you will escape a parking citation, or worse. If you park in a driveway, within *20 feet* of a corner or crosswalk, 15 feet of a fire hydrant, or on a street-sweeping day, you will need about $75 (cash or credit card) plus cab fare (do not walk) to retrieve your car from the Auto Pound (☎ 504-565-7450), 401 N Claiborne Ave.

The Dixie Parking Garage (☎ 504-522-5975), near the upper end of Bourbon St at 716 Iberville St, charges $4 for the first hour or $11 for 24 hours. Other garages concentrated in the upper area of the Quarter charge similar rates.

See Getting There & Away for information about car rental in New Orleans.

Taxi

Except when parades are blocking streets and during peak events, hailing a cab is easy in downtown New Orleans. Taxi stands are located in front of most hotels and cabs queue like predators near Bourbon St to intercept late-night revelers.

One downside to staying Uptown or visiting the nightclubs is the difficulty of hailing a cab. You will usually need to call. Also, it's best to give an address and cross streets rather than just cross streets.

Telephoned requests for a taxi are usually quickly met, yet none of the taxi services can be recommended as being completely reliable. White Fleet Cabs (☎ 504-948-6605) and United Cabs (☎ 504-522-9771) offer pickups at the airport and anywhere within New Orleans. Metairie Cab (☎ 504-835-4242) and Service Cab (☎ 504-834-1400) specifically serve the outlying suburbs. Rules are made to be broken, but don't plan on taking a taxi with a crowd of more than four people. Fares in New Orleans cost $2.10 for the flag drop plus about $1 per mile. A 15% tip should be added to the fare.

As some stranded travelers have discovered, it can sometimes be pointless to call ahead for a taxi pickup – especially during Mardi Gras or Jazz Fest. Drivers are choosy and may actually decline to pick up a passenger if the destination is a bit out of the way. During carnival parades, when travel is especially difficult, many drivers refuse to travel beyond the downtown area after being hailed on the street.

Another problem is the restricted service area of the cab companies. One passenger reported calling ahead to United Cab to schedule an early-morning ride from a rental-car return lot in Kenner to the airport terminal. No cab was waiting at the prescribed time. After making two additional calls and missing the flight, the dispatcher explained that United does not serve Kenner – except for pickups at the airport.

Bicycle

Cyclists will be pleased to find that New Orleans is flat and relatively compact. On the negative side are heavy traffic and potholes that make fat tires a near necessity. Oppressive summer heat and humidity also discourage some bicyclists.

Residents typically follow either Burgundy St or Dauphine St to quickly traverse the French Quarter between the CBD and Faubourg Marigny, where the bicycle is the transport mode of choice. Esplanade Ave is somewhat busy, but the cars can go around you as you peddle from the Quarter to the Fair Grounds or City Park. At City Park you should avoid Wisner Blvd where it crosses I-610 and instead travel through the western side of the park to Lakeshore Dr, where the Linear Bike Path runs along the lake. Roads and paths along the lake are bicycle friendly. Racers favor workouts in City Park on the Roosevelt Mall oval and along Lakeshore Dr.

Many cyclists travel from the Quarter through the Warehouse District on Magazine St. Prytania St is a good choice for crossing through the Lower Garden District. The rest of Uptown is readily traversed, from Jackson Ave to Audubon Park, on quiet residential streets like Camp

St or Chestnut St. From S Carrollton Ave, at the Riverbend, the river levee offers a continuous off-road bicycle route upriver to near the airport.

Although there are few official bike routes and trails in the New Orleans area, the *New Orleans Bicycling Map & Guide*, published by the New Orleans Bicycle Awareness Committee, is extremely useful for riding throughout town. The map can be purchased for $3 at most bike shops.

Bicycles can be rented for around $15 to $20 a day. Specializing in rentals and tours, Olympic Bike (☎ 504-522-6797), 1615 Prytania St in the Lower Garden District, also offers free pickup and delivery. Joe's Bike Shop (☎ 504-821-2350), 2501 Tulane Ave next to the Dixie Brewery, rents used bikes for $13 a day. Rental bikes are also available from French Quarter Bicycles (☎ 504-529-3136), 522 Dumaine St, and nearby in the Faubourg Marigny from Bicycle Michael's (☎ 504-945-1948), 618 Frenchmen St. Near Loyola and Tulane Universities try the Bikesmith (☎ 504-897-2453), 4716 Freret St; or GNO Cyclery on S Carrollton Ave at Willow St.

See Organized Tours for information about bicycle tours.

Walking

The compact French Quarter is ideally suited to the pedestrian. In fact, there is no better way to participate in the action along Bourbon St or appreciate the local architecture than on foot. Aside from the French Quarter, some of the other areas that are best toured on foot include the Warehouse District and its galleries centered on Julia St, anywhere along the river levee, and the Faubourg Marigny. Should a sudden thundershower catch you without an umbrella, many shops offer plastic ponchos for under a $1.

Walks through the Garden District or Audubon Park are readily served by the St Charles Ave streetcar from downtown. To leave the frenzied activities and noise behind, consider taking the ferry from Canal St to Algiers for a stroll through quiet neighborhoods or walk along the west bank levee for views of New Orleans and river shipping.

Be aware that pedestrians do not have the right of way and will find their lives in danger should they attempt to challenge motorists. Local motorists consider it a courtesy to honk at pedestrians in the street before speeding by.

Ferry
The cheapest way to cruise the Mississippi River is aboard one of the state-run ferries. Ferries operate daily between New Orleans at Canal St and the west bank community of Algiers and between Jackson Ave and Gretna. Another ferry travels between Chalmette and lower Algiers. All begin service at either 5:45 or 6 am and continue to 9 or 9:15 pm, except the ferry from Canal St which operates until 11:45 pm or midnight. In the vicinity of New Orleans the ferries are free. Boats leave Canal St and Jackson Ave on the hour and half-hour, Algiers and Gretna on the quarter-hour and three-quarter-hour, and Chalmette every quarter-hour.

Around New Orleans

You can easily see the varied attractions around New Orleans by booking tours, but you might want to rent a car to get off the beaten track. For detailed information on booking swamp tours, see the sidebar in the Cajun Country chapter.

Living in the rural fishing villages of St Bernard Parish south of the city, the Isleños are a distinctive cultural group. Their Museo de los Isleños is an interesting small-town museum. Also south of the city, the Barataria Preserve (a unit of the Jean Lafitte National Historic Park) gives travelers a chance to paddle a canoe through the wilderness of a Louisiana bayou.

Around Lac Des Allemands west of the city, Cajun Country begins with the towns of Des Allemands and Kraemer. If you can't get into the heart of that region, this is a short trip with vivid highlights.

Two state parks on the North Shore near the suburban towns of Mandeville and Covington offer tranquil respite from city heat and congestion.

East of the city, the town of Slidell is a jump-off point for pursuits on Lake Pontchartrain and on the Pearl and Bogue Chitto Rivers. Swamp and bayou paddling around here is a great getaway from New Orleans, as well as a nice stopover on excursions farther north or east.

SOUTH OF NEW ORLEANS
Below New Orleans the Mississippi River flows 90 miles to the 'bird's foot' delta where trained Mississippi River pilots board ships entering from the Gulf. Only occasional tufts of trees, on the oak-covered *chenier* mounds, jut above the swampy environment. Rather than travel for hours to Venice, the farthest downriver point accessible by automobile, you can satisfy the same end-of-the-road travel desire with Isleño fishing villages in nearby St Bernard Parish. On the way, the Chalmette Battlefield offers a brief interesting side trip.

The best way to reach Chalmette and the Isleño villages is by car or bike. From N Rampart St on the edge of the French Quarter, ride downriver on St Claude Ave to the St Bernard Hwy (Hwy 46). Chalmette is six miles from the French Quarter. Continuing on Hwy 46 to Bayou Rd, it's just over 11 miles to the Museo de los Isleños. From there it's seven miles to Hwy 300 leading to Delacroix.

Chalmette Battlefield
On January 8, 1815, General Jackson's forces engaged British attackers in the Battle of New Orleans; less than two hours later, Jackson's troops emerged with a stunning victory. Your visit to the Chalmette Battlefield and NPS Visitor Center (☎ 504-589-4430) should only take about half that time – even if you stay to watch the excellent half-hour film about the battle. The open battlefield site was once the narrowest piece of dry ground below New Orleans, but in itself it's not very

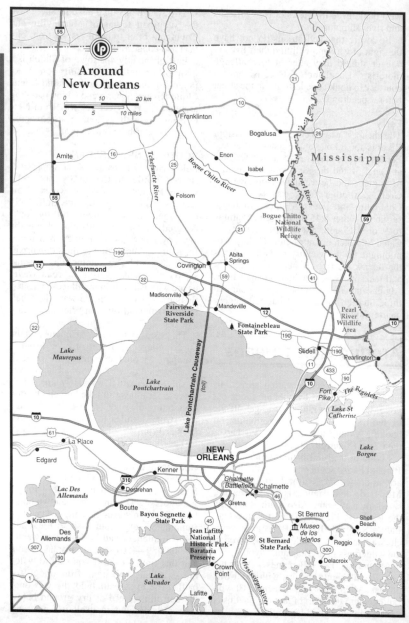

Around New Orleans

interesting. Pick up the map and description of the battle, available from the visitor center to read later. It's open daily from 8:30 am to 5 pm; the visitor center closes at 4:30 pm. Admission is free.

Isleño Fishing Villages

Following the American Revolution in 1776, Spanish officials' fear of British encroachment on their possessions in Louisiana grew. The deteriorating economic situation in the Canary Islands aided the Spanish in prompting about two thousand Isleños to settle in Louisiana. From 1778 to 1783, entire families came from the islands of Tenerife and Gran Canaria to Delacroix and other Louisiana destinations, where they could pursue fishing, trapping and moss gathering. Today, the Spanish language no longer serves as a major element in the Isleño identity; only a few of the older people still speak it.

Isleño architecture is distinctive, due in part to the repeated hurricanes that have devastated the communities and forced them to rebuild: following the widespread destruction from Hurricane Betsy in 1965 all homes were raised eight feet; after Hurricane Juan in 1985 the standard was raised to 14 feet.

To get a good feel for the community, visit the **Museo de los Isleños** (☎ 504-682-0862), on Hwy 46 in St Bernard (a town established in 1780). This small cultural center is located in a donated home that was built in 1840; on display are arts and crafts, including items from the Canary Islands, and exhibits on the Isleño way of life. Bayou Terre-aux-Boeufs is right outside, and the grounds are shaded with live oak and pecan trees. Local families and their children are likely to stop by to visit with the grandmotherly ranger, Helen Alfonso, or the exceedingly humble Irvan Perez, who devoted his energy with others in the community to start the museum in 1975. It's open Wednesday through Sunday from 11 am to 4 pm. Tours of the museum and the 15-acre grounds are offered by appointment.

Anglers line the scenic Bayou Terre-aux-Boeufs beside the narrow, winding Hwy 300

to **Delacroix**, where a water tower and string of raised houses opposite the docked fishing boats mark the settlement. You'll see herons, ibis and brown pelicans along the banks. The road ends at a footbridge to a private island. You can tell by the names on the commercial fishing boats that many are owned by Vietnamese immigrants – their more efficient shrimp net has caused much resentment around here and was recently outlawed. About the only 'cultural center' is Rudy Melerine's *Boat Dock* (☎ 504-684-3316), just below the abandoned school on Hwy 300, where you can stop for a beer and hear locals swap stories; it's open from 4:30 am to 6 pm.

The picturesque Yscloskey Draw Bridge over Bayou la Loutre leads to **Yscloskey**, with **Shell Beach** on the left. Commercial fishing boats line the bayou. Near the bridge, the *Pete Grocery* has a short-order cook.

Barataria Preserve

The Barataria Preserve, a unit of south Louisiana's ubiquitous Jean Lafitte National Historic Park, was originally settled by Isleños in 1779. It offers hiking and canoe trips into the swamp and is a good sample of the delta's environment. As such it is not a pristine wilderness; canals and other structures offer evidence of human activities, yet wild animals and plants are abundant.

The place to start is the NPS visitor center (☎ 504-589-2330), where you can pick up a map of the eight miles of hiking trails and nine miles of dedicated canoe trails, which are closed to motorized boats. There is a 25-minute introductory nature film, *Jambalaya: A Delta Almanac*. Ranger-led walks around Bayou Coquille are offered daily at 2 pm. The visitor center is open daily from 9 am to 5 pm. Trails in the preserve are open daily from 7 am to 5 pm, with extended hours during daylight savings time.

Other activities require reservations. Rangers conduct Education Center Programs on Wednesday through Friday mornings, and on Tuesday and Saturday they lead group walks and special programs. A

Sunday morning ranger-led canoe trek meets at 8:30 am. On evenings around a full moon, rangers lead moonlight canoe treks.

Earl's Canoe Rental (☎ 504-689-3271) rents canoes for use in the preserve; $25 gets a canoe that seats up to three people with drop-off and pick-up service in the preserve. You must pay at Earl's, which is one mile from the park on Hwy 3134. Earl's also has cold drinks and is open from 9 am until dusk, unless other rental arrangements are made.

You can also rent canoes to paddle on the Bayou de Familles just outside the park ($15 for two hours) at the Bayou Barn (☎ 504-689-2663), at the intersection of Hwys 45 and 3134. Cajun or zydeco bands play to lively local crowds at their dance ($3) held every Sunday from 9 am to 6 pm; add the Cajun buffet and the price is $10. The Bayou Barn is closed Mondays.

Upscale dining at *Restaurant de Familles* (☎ 504-689-7834), behind the Bayou Barn, is a special reward for paddling or hiking all day. The beautiful dining room overlooking the bayou features Creole and Cajun seafood dinners for $10 to $15. The restaurant features a bar and lounge and is closed on Monday.

From New Orleans, motorists heading to the Barataria Preserve should take Business Hwy 90 across the Greater New Orleans Bridge, to the Westbank Expressway and turn south on Barataria Blvd (Hwy 45) to Hwy 3134, which leads to the national park entrance. The trip is about 20 miles south of the city.

WEST OF NEW ORLEANS
Lac Des Allemands is considered the dividing line between the affable suburban fringe around Barataria Preserve and the relative outback of the Cajun wetlands. Kraemer and Des Allemands make an easy day trip from New Orleans for folks who want to go farther out.

Des Allemands
The approach to Des Allemands crosses the Mississippi River on I-310 and rolls down Hwy 90 into the lush bayou country.

Just 30 miles from New Orleans, the town makes an easy stop for a meal at its landmark catfish joint. At *Spahr's Restaurant* (☎ 504-758-1902), fried catfish is the specialty; it's $7.25 with French fries and toast. (They also serve it broiled.) The restaurant occupies a former gas station (look for Spahr's gas spire) and has full-length windows overlooking the Des Allemands marsh. Turn north at the sign on Hwy 90; the restaurant is two miles from the bridge.

The town hosts its annual Catfish Festival on the first weekend in July.

Kraemer
From the turn north off Hwy 90, Hwy 307 to Kraemer winds along a scenic road that barely skims the swamp surface.

Across from the drawbridge on the bayou, Zam's Swamp Tours (☎ 504-633-7881) leads swamp tours aboard motorized boats. The Cajun guides here like to play up the mock-hick schtick, but they actually are the real item – their pet 'wrestling gators' are kept in a pond. The rancid smell comes from the thousands of gator hides and heads drying in the shed nearby. (Such operations were once common throughout the Cajun wetlands, and were responsible for endangering the now prolific alligator population.) Boat tours are scheduled year round daily at 10:30 am, 1:30 and 3:30 pm – all include an alligator feeding spectacle. Tours cost $12.50 for adults, $6 children.

Edwina's Cooking Cajun (☎ 504-633-5628), next door to Zam's, serves up the gator. Her gator piquante over rice comes with potato salad ($7).

THE NORTH SHORE
There is a bounty of superb outdoor attractions on Lake Pontchartrain's North Shore. The beaches, parks, rivers and swamps give you an eyeful of wildlife and flora that are found in few other places around the world. More and more travelers are opting to stay on the North Shore rather than in New Orleans not only for these attractions but because of lower travel costs (accommodations and dining) and lower crime.

Some North Shore hotels provide guests with daily shuttle service to New Orleans' French Quarter.

The area is only 32 miles north of downtown New Orleans across the Lake Pontchartrain Causeway. If crossing a 24-mile bridge isn't your idea of a stimulating drive, take I-10 or Hwy 90 east to Slidell and connect with I-12 west. A third option is to take I-10 west to I-55 or Hwy 51 north and connect with I-12 east at Hammond. The latter takes about an hour longer, but the scenery is more varied.

Towns here include Hammond (which isn't very entertaining for visitors) at the west end of the North Shore and Slidell (covered below) at the east end, a distance of about 45 miles. In between – conveniently linked by I-12 and Hwy 190 – are Mandeville and Madisonville (which have many hotels and restaurants), Abita Springs and Covington. Fairview-Riverside State Park and Fontainebleau State Park are the highlights of this area.

The St Tammany Parish Tourist & Convention Commission (☎ 504-892-0520, 800-634-9443, ext 116), 68099 Hwy 59, Mandeville, LA 70471, is located off I-12 at exit 65. Its information covers Slidell (see Slidell & Around, below), Mandeville, Madisonville, Covington, Abita Springs and Lacombe.

Fontainebleau State Park
What a gem! This 2700-acre park sprawls along the north shore of Lake Pontchartrain in Mandeville. It has nature trails, ruins of a plantation brickyard and sugar mill, a sandy beach, a swimming pool (open in summer), a campground and lots of picnic areas. It's bordered by Lake Pontchartrain, Bayou Cane and Bayou Castine, making it an excellent spot for bird and wildlife watching. The Tammany Trace (see below) passes through here.

There are 250 improved ($12) and 90 primitive ($10) campsites with grills and picnic tables, all well spaced and nicely shaded. The bathhouses and restrooms are clean and there's a public phone. For groups, there's a separate camp area and a

lodge that sleeps nine to 13 people ($90). If you want some evening entertainment, cross Hwy 190 and enter Pelican Park, where you can watch youth and league baseball teams play on a lighted field.

To get to Fontainebleau (☎ 504-624-4443, 888-677-3668), from I-12 take exit 65, go south 3½ miles and turn left onto Hwy 190, go 2½ miles and turn right. From New Orleans, take the Causeway and exit at Hwy 190 east; continue five miles to the entrance.

Fairview-Riverside State Park
Fontainebleau's smaller neighbor has 98 acres and was donated by Frank Otis in 1961 through his will. Otis' home is the centerpiece for the park and is being renovated as an interpretive center. The rest of the park consists of picnic tables and barbecue pits under live and water oaks. This is an ideal spot for contemplating nature's bounty. It's on the Tchefuncte River, where the fishing is good for trout, bream, bass and other fish. Visitors also crab from the banks.

For camping, there's a restroom and bathhouse accompanying 85 improved sites and a large area with water for primitive camping. Fairview-Riverside (☎ 504-845-3318, 888-677-3247) is west of the causeway on Hwy 22, or four miles south of I-12.

Tammany Trace
An old railroad track was converted into this 32-mile trail (☎ 800-634-9443, ext 115), Koop Dr in Mandeville. So far nine miles have been paved, from Mandeville to Abita Springs, including a section through Fontainebleau State Park, for biking, hiking and in-line skating. An unpaved equestrian trail parallels the trace.

Organized Tours
Merle Mulkey is a walking encyclopedia of information about the North Shore, New Orleans and Louisiana. She operates St Tammany Tours (☎ 504-893-0862, 800-543-6362), 70031 Mulkey Rd, Mandeville 70471, and gives visitors the lows and

highs, everything from where Jayne Mansfield was killed while driving back to New Orleans to how the Big Easy was founded. A full-day city tour of New Orleans from the North Shore costs $32 and is worth every cent.

Places to Stay & Eat
For camping options, see Fontainebleau and Fairview-Riverside State Parks, above.

Mandeville If you plan to use Fontainebleu by day and need accommodations, try the *Mt Vernon Motel* (☎ 504-892-1041), 1110 N Hwy 190, a spiffy little 10-room hotel that was recently renovated. Rates are $33 for one bed (one or two people), $40 for two beds.

In Mandeville you can dine at the popular *Deanies* (☎ 504-626-6060), 2100 Florida Ave (Hwy 190), where they serve pecan-encrusted catfish or shrimp creole ($8). Po-boys run $4 to $6. It's open for dining or take-out Monday to Saturday from 10 am to 11 pm.

Covington There's a nice new *Courtyard by Marriott* (☎ 504-871-0244), 101 N Park Blvd in Covington, with big rooms with all the amenities. There's a lounge with a TV and fireplace, a pool and whirlpool, coin laundry and exercise room. Rates are $72/82 single/double, $82 to $109 single suites, $92 to $119 double suites. The daily full Southern breakfast buffet is all-you-can-eat for $6.

In Covington, but worth the drive, is *Licata's* (☎ 504-893-1252), 1102 N Hwy 190. The restaurant is connected to a fish market, so the seafood is fresh. It's really popular with locals, who come for the all-you-can-eat shrimp ($13) and crawfish ($11, in season November to July). Most menu items run $4 to $9. The restaurant is open Tuesday to Sunday from 11 am to 10 pm. Market hours are 10 am to 9 pm.

Abita Springs This is the home of Abita Springs bottled water and the *Abita Brewery & Brew Pub* (☎ 504-893-3143), 72011 Holly St, the oldest microbrewery and brewpub in the state. The pub serves better-than-average seafood, salads, sandwiches and steaks. On the lunch menu, the highest prices are for blackened shrimp and avocado salad ($8) and seafood muffuletta ($7). Dinner prices are equally attractive with fajitas ($6) and Louisiana barbecue shrimp ($16). The brew sampler ($4.50) features five four-ounce glasses of their beers.

Tours are given Saturday at 1 pm and 2:30 pm, Sunday at 1 pm. Kids are welcome and are served root beer. The adjoining brewpub is open Sunday to Thursday 11 am to 9 pm, Friday to Saturday 11 am to 11 pm.

Getting There & Away
Greyhound has stations in Mandeville (☎ 504-626-3350), 445 Lafitte St, and Covington (☎ 504-892-4038), 627 E Boston St. Service is from Atlanta, Baton Rouge, Jackson and New Orleans.

For shuttle service to New Orleans, see St Tammany Van Pool & Charter Service under Getting There & Away in Slidell.

Amtrak's *City of New Orleans* train stops west of Covington at Hammond (☎ 504-345-6264), NW Railroad Ave, with service from Jackson, Memphis, New Orleans and Chicago. Roundtrip fare from New Orleans to Hammond is $19 with several trains a day. Memphis to Hammond is $93 roundtrip with one train per day.

Enterprise, which will deliver one of its rental cars to you at the bus or train station, has branches in Hammond (☎ 504-345-4100), 1133 S Morrison Blvd, and Covington (☎ 504-893-0462), 600 N Hwy 190.

SLIDELL & AROUND
There's little of interest for tourists in Slidell, which is an industrial center and New Orleans bedroom community on the eastern shore of Lake Pontchartrain. However, there is terrific bird and wildlife-watching, and excellent boat tours thanks to the neighboring pristine nature preserves. The Pearl River is a winding, slow-moving river that flows along the border of Louisiana and Mississippi. It floods into the Pearl River Basin, a bottomland hardwood

forest that drains into almost 9000 sq miles of both states.

Two public areas in this basin include the Pearl River Wildlife Management Area (55 sq miles) and Bogue Chitto National Wildlife Refuge (63 sq miles). These areas offer opportunities for canoeing, hiking, fishing and camping. For boaters and canoeists, winter and spring floods provide the best conditions. For hikers and campers, summer and autumn offer the most dry land. The weather page of the New Orleans *Times-Picayune* lists water levels daily.

In addition, you can enjoy Lake Pontchartrain or the secluded bayous with pontoon boat rentals out of Slidell.

Tours to this area are easy to book from New Orleans, but if you want to spend more time and visit areas north (Bogue Chitto Refuge and Bogalusa) and west (Covington, Mandeville and Madisonville), you should rent a car.

Orientation & Information

Slidell is about 22 miles northeast of New Orleans; take either I-10 or the scenic Hwy 90 to Hwy 11 or to Hwy 190. If you take Hwys 90/190, you cross Rigolets (pronounced like the gum, Wrigley's) Harbor, a narrow channel that feeds water into Lake Pontchartrain from Lake Borgne and the Mississippi Sound near the Louisiana border. It also passes Fort Pike and puts you closest to the wildlife areas and the river, where the swamp tours depart. The city centers around Gause Blvd, exit 266 on I-10, which is where you'll find most hotels, restaurants and shopping centers. The city is bounded by Lake Pontchartrain to the south and the Pearl River to the east. I-12 cuts across east-west, I-10 north-south before it veers east to Mississippi's Gulf Coast.

To thoroughly explore the Pearl River area, consider purchasing the USGS maps for Bogalusa (Louisiana) and Gulfport (Mississippi) or a topographical map.

For a map and information about Bogue Chitto National Wildlife Refuge, contact the US Fish & Wildlife Service (☎ 504-646-7555), 1010 Gause Blvd, Building 936,

Slidell, LA 70458. For information on Pearl River Wildlife Management Area, see below.

The St Tammany Parish Tourist & Convention Commission (☎ 504-892-0520, 800-634-9443, ext 116) is at 68099 Hwy 59, Mandeville, LA 70471, exit 65 off I-12. It's open daily 8:30 am to 4:30 pm.

St Tammany Parish Hospital (☎ 504-898-4000), 1202 S Tyler St, and Slidell Memorial Hospital (☎ 504-643-2200), 1001 Gause Blvd, handle emergencies and routine care.

Boat Rental

The closest place to rent canoes is in Covington, about 20 minutes west of Slidell, at HJ Smith & Sons, a hardware store. The rate is $30 a day. There's no shuttle service, but they'll help you tie your canoe to your car. It's open weekdays from 8:30 am to 5 pm, Wednesday only to noon, Saturday 8:30 am to 1 pm.

Several marinas rent out 16 to 18-foot fishing boats for use on Lake Pontchartrain: Gilbert's Boats & Baits (☎ 504-643-5432), 4987 Pontchartrain Dr, just before the bridge to New Orleans, rents 18-foot boats ($35 with a six-horsepower motor, $40 with 15-hp). It's open daily 7 am to 3 pm. Tite's Place (☎ 504-649-4339), 4983 Pontchartrain Dr, charges $30 a day for a 16-foot skiff with a six-hp motor. The hours are daily from 5 am to 5 pm.

Slidell Marine rents 20-foot pontoon boats, which seat 10 people, for exploring Bayou Bonfouca and Bayou Liberty, two wild areas west of I-10. The rate is $85 for four hours, $150 for eight hours, plus gas. It's open Tuesday to Friday from 8 am to 6 pm, Saturday and Sunday 7 am to 7 pm.

Pearl River Wildlife Management Area

Most of the 55-sq-mile protected area is cypress and tupelo swamp and hardwood forest. It adjoins the Honey Island Swamp and the Nature Conservancy's White Kitchen Nature Preserve and is especially popular with boaters, canoeists and hunters.

The land area has a short nature trail, campground, boat ramp and abundant wildlife. The water area has gorgeous trees dripping with Spanish moss, lubbers, turtles, snakes and other reptiles, wood ducks and abundant water fowl, song birds, perch, bass, bream, catfish and crawfish. There are inlets and coves with water hyacinths, cutgrass and yellow and white water lilies with unusual and colorful floating fishing villages.

If you really enjoy the outdoors, consider bringing your own canoe or renting one in New Orleans and setting up camp here. The campground consists of a large fenced area with lots of grass and oak trees. The sites are unmarked and facilities are limited to fresh water. A wildlife officer lives next door.

The area (☎ 504-646-6440, 504-765-2360) is on Holly Ridge Dr, two miles east of Slidell. Get off I-10 at exit 266 (Hwy 190 or Gause Blvd). Take Hwy 190 east two miles to Military Rd (Hwy 1090) and turn left. Drive north one mile and go over I-10, then take the first right onto Crawford Landing Rd (the I-10 service road) and continue 1½ miles to the end of the road. Admission is free.

For additional information, contact the Louisiana Department of Wildlife & Fisheries (☎ 504-765-2800, 504-765-2360), Information Section, PO Box 98000, Baton Rouge, LA 70898.

Organized Tours Taking a Honey Island Swamp tour is a highlight of the numerous day trips you can take from New Orleans.

Most companies operate 12 to 20-passenger motorized, flat-bottom boats and cover about 10 miles. Almost all of the operators offer two prices, one if they pick you up from your hotel in New Orleans ($35 to $40), the other if you drive yourself ($20). Typically, there is a tour in the morning and another in the afternoon. Some also run evening and overnight trips.

'Up close and personal' aptly describes Mr Denny's Canoe Swamp Tours, two-hour tours of run by former school teacher Denny Holmburg (☎ 504-643-4839). Up to seven canoeists can paddle through the cypress and tupelo of Honey Island Swamp

as Mr Denny points out flora and fauna. The highlight is the Nature Conservancy's Eagle Slough, which is off-limits to power boats. In spring it serves as a rookery for anhinga, egrets, herons and other water fowl, as well as nutria and raccoons. By summer the young birds are attempting flight and the canopy is filled with chatter. Tours cost $20 adults, $12 children under 12. He also offers evening tours and two-day camping tours. Credit cards are not accepted.

Except for feeding gators marshmallows (they're not good for humans, so how could they be good for alligators), Dr Wagner's Honey Island Swamp Tours provide visitors an entertaining and educational motorized visit to the Honey Island Swamp. Dr Wagner, a wetlands ecologist and environmental consultant on south Louisiana swamps, leads many of the two-hour, 12-mile tours himself. They depart daily at 8:30 am and 1:30 pm. To arrange a tour, call ☎ 504-641-1769 (☎ 504-242-5877 from New Orleans), fax 504-641-1769, or write to 106 Holly Ridge Dr, Slidell, LA 70461. The cost is $20, or $40 for New Orleans pick up. Credit cards are not accepted.

White Kitchen Eagle Preserve
Birdwatchers have come here for decades to watch bald eagles, who have nested in the area in winter for more than 50 years. To give birdwatchers better access, the Nature Conservancy teamed up with Chevron Corporation to build a 300-foot boardwalk over the swamp at a rest stop with picnic tables. The scenery of live oaks heavy with moss, cypress and cypress knees, pickerel, marshmallow and song and waterbirds is as beautiful as the soaring eagles. Bring binoculars and a lunch.

To reach the preserve (☎ 504-338-1040) at the intersection of Hwy 190 and Hwy 90, from I-10 exit 266, take Hwy 190 east to Military Rd (Hwy 1090) and turn right. At the dead end (at the cemetery), turn left. Go five miles to Hwy 90. It's on the left.

Bogue Chitto River
The Bogue Chitto River (BO-gay SHEE-to) joins the Pearl River about 25 miles north

of Slidell. Like the Pearl, it offers lots of opportunities to canoe, hike, fish and camp.

Bogue Chitto Canoeing and Tubing Center (☎ 504-735-1173), Hwy 16 in Isabel, is a fun mom-and-pop operation that rents two-person canoes ($25 a day) and inner tubes ($6), including shuttle service. They shuttle you up river and you float or paddle down. It takes three to four hours, unless you stop at sand-bar beaches to picnic and look for wildlife.

The small campground accommodates tents ($10 or $15 with water and electricity) and RVs ($15 with hookups).

Restrooms and showers are available for day canoeists and tubers as well as campers, and there's a small store for tackle, bait, ice and beverages.

To get there take Hwy 41 north to Sun, then Hwy 16 west for seven miles to Isabel. Turn left at the Isabel store and go two blocks. For advance reservations write to 10237 River Rd, Bogalusa, LA 70427.

Places to Stay
Camping You can camp in the Pearl River Wildlife Management Area and on the Bogue Chitto River, see above.

Hotels *Budget Host Inn* (☎ 504-641-8800), 1662 Gause Blvd in Slidell, has a pool, free local calls and movies. Major interstates and restaurants are nearby. Rooms run $35/39 for a single/double.

Econolodge (☎ 504-641-2153), 58512 Tyler Dr at I-10 and Hwy 190, has 57 rooms with free cable movies. Rooms ($42/44) are basic, but clean. It's close to restaurants and the road leading to the swamp tours.

Days Inn Slidell (☎ 504-641-3450), 1645 Gause Blvd, is on the main road through town, with easy access to I-10, I-12 and I-59. It has a restaurant, pool and free in-room movies. Rates start at $55.

The recently renovated *La Quinta Inn* (☎ 504-643-9770), 794 E I-10 service road, has a pool and whirlpool, free continental breakfast and a good restaurant and lounge. The spacious rooms, which go for $62/69, have a large TV, coffeemaker, data port, free movies and free local calls.

The Ramada Inn on the I-10 service road is convenient, but noisy, and there are better places to stay.

B&Bs The best buy in the area, especially if you're traveling with more than one person, is *The Garden Guest House B&B* (☎ 504-641-0335), 34514 Bayou Liberty Rd (Hwy 433) in Slidell. For a rate of $90 to $120 a night, you get your own antique-filled three-bedroom, 2½-bath house with laundry, kitchen, a large glass-enclosed sun porch and a deck. It's located on 10-acres accented with ancient live oaks, magnolias, pines, bromeliads, ferns, palms, cycads and a large greenhouse. The owners, Bonnie and Paul Taliancich, live nearby and love to garden and collect antiques. They cater to guests' dietary needs and special interests.

The *Salmen-Fritchie House B&B* (☎ 504-643-1405), 127 Cleveland Ave in Slidell, is a picturesque turn-of-the-century house filled with antiques that has a wide wrap-around porch. They bring morning coffee to your room; a Southern breakfast is served in the dining room. Rates are $75 to $85 single, $85 to $95 double, $115 to $125 suites and $150 cottage.

Places to Eat
Slidell At *Mike Schaeffer's* (☎ 504-646-1728), 158 S Military Rd, the specialty is catfish, but shrimp, crawfish and other Louisiana favorites are also available. Lunch runs $6 to $9, dinner $6 to $12. It's open for lunch daily; dinner is served Tuesday to Saturday.

The best deal at *China Wok Chinese Restaurant* (☎ 504-641-8905), 1340 Lindberg off Gause Blvd, is the $7 all-you-can-eat buffet for lunch and dinner. It's open daily, with extended hours on Friday and Saturday.

The *Indian Village Catfish Restaurant* (☎ 504-649-5778), 115 Indian Village Rd off Hwy 190, is a ramshackle little place on the Pearl River that serves some of the best catfish in the area. Because it caters to weekend anglers and hunters, it's open only Thursday to Sunday 11 am to 8 pm.

LOUISIANA

A couple of guys got together to open *Laughing Pines Brewery & Restaurant* (☎ 504-781-2739), 1808 Front St, across from the train station. Their combined experience created this fun brewpub where the menu includes grilled pizzas, burgers, shrimp and ribs. Lunch specials are $5 to $7. It's open Monday to Thursday from 11 am to 10 pm, Friday to Saturday 11 am to midnight, Sunday 11 am to 9 pm.

Rigolets Harbor Rigolets Harbor is a small, colorful fishing community; a short bridge on Hwy 90 connects it to Fort Pike State Commemorative Area and greater New Orleans.

The view rivals the food at *Rigolets Harbor Restaurant* (☎ 504-649-5273), 52250 Hwy 90 at Hwy 433, next to Rigolets Bridge. The rustic 2nd-floor dining room has a wraparound porch and windows overlooking a marina and the Rigolets, the narrow passage between the Gulf of Mexico and Lake Pontchartrain. The menu has gator sausage gumbo, fried gator tail (a local delicacy), crawfish pie and poboys. Even the pasta dishes have a Cajun flavor. It also has a popular bar. Prices run $5 to $12, with most items around $6. It's open daily 11 am to at least 9 pm (call ahead).

Getting There & Away
Bus & Shuttle Greyhound (☎ 504-643-6545), 3735 Pontchartrain Dr, Slidell, has service from Atlanta ($71, six buses a day), Baton Rouge ($18, four buses), Jackson ($32, three buses) and New Orleans ($8, two buses).

Coastline Transportation (☎ 601-432-2649, 800-647-3957) runs nine shuttles each way between the New Orleans airport and the Mississippi Gulf Coast, stopping at Slidell ($22). The shuttle will drop you wherever you need to go, whether it be a hotel or car rental office. Reservations are suggested.

St Tammany Van Pool & Charter Service (☎ 504-641-9398) also offers New Orleans international airport and French Quarter shuttle service for about the same price.

Train Amtrak's New Orleans service includes *Crescent Line* trains that stop at an unmanned station at Slidell, 1827 Front St, connecting Atlanta, Birmingham, New York, Washington, DC, and other cities. See the North Shore for other train service in the area.

There is no local bus service, so to get from the station to your destination call Parish Cab (☎ 504-641-9479); the meter starts at $1.50 and is $1.70 per mile.

Car Enterprise (☎ 504-643-0102), 56450 Frank J Pichon Dr, will deliver a car to you at the train or bus station, and it has a branch in Covington. National (☎ 504-641-6792), 1682 Gause Blvd, also has car rental offices in Slidell.

Plantation Country

RIVER ROAD PLANTATIONS

First indigo, then cotton, rice and sugar cane brought the great wealth that fueled the construction of more than 350 opulent plantations along the banks of the Mississippi River between New Orleans and Baton Rouge. Supplies, slaves and genteel immigrants arrived by boat on the river, and sugar, lumber, rice, cotton and indigo were shipped out on the same banks. The River Road consists of two roads, one on either side of the Mississippi from New Orleans west to Baton Rouge.

Between the two cities, two-score plantations remain along the River Road, with about a dozen open to the public as historic sites. At those, expect costumed guides leading interior tours of 45 to 60 minutes, which focus on the lovely architecture, gardens and genteel lifestyle of antebellum Louisiana. Most have a gift shop, enormous moss-draped live oaks and daily hours of 9 or 10 am to 4 or 5 pm (except major holidays). Admission usually includes a guided tour of the main house and self-guided tours of the grounds. Lavish Christmastime decorations are also popular. All of the main houses on the plantations have been fully restored. (Laura Plantation is partially restored.) Some areas are under renovation, while others have been left unrestored to show the original workmanship.

With the exception of Laura, the plantation houses ignore the story of the hundreds of thousands of people who were enslaved, who made the bricks, constructed the homes, tended the fires and worked the fields that fueled the region's prosperity and created the planters' wealth. As Kathe Hambrick of the African-American River Road Museum expressed, 'Just think of how rich IBM would be if it didn't have to pay its employees.'

Historical markers point out plantations that remain private residences or have been converted to inns and eateries. Others have

HIGHLIGHTS

- The huge bonfires that illuminate the levee at Lutcher during the Christmas season
- The Creole Laura Plantation in Vacherie
- The Rural Life Museum in Baton Rouge

been replaced most noticeably by chemical companies with huge plants, belching smokestacks, tanks and unsightly grain elevators extending over the road to docks along the river.

Orientation

On both sides of the Mississippi River, the River Road runs between the mansions and the river levee in St John, St James, Ascension and Iberville parishes. Traffic crosses the river on two bridges, the Veterans Memorial Bridge between Lutcher and Vacherie and the Sunshine Bridge between Burnside and Donaldsonville ($1 toll), and a ferry runs between Reserve and Edgard between 5:15 am and 8:30 pm. The road, part of the state highway system, changes numbers frequently, but remains the River Road. (See Getting There & Away, below, for driving-tour directions of Plantation Country.) There are few accommodations other than B&Bs at plantation houses and even fewer gas stations. If you yearn to spend more time here, pick up 'Plantation Homes Along the River Road' ($3.50), a map with text and photos of plantations, churches, ruins and historic sites, by David

King Gleason. It's available at plantation houses or in advance for $3.50 plus $1.65 postage from Josie Gleason (☎ 504-275-7390), 2361 Torrey Pine Dr, Baton Rouge, LA 70816.

If you're staying in New Orleans or Baton Rouge, the best way to see the Plantation Country is by car for a day trip. Alternatively, dozens of companies offer all-day tours to the Plantation Country for $65 to $75 for three to four stops and lunch. See Organized Tours below.

Information

The following tourist offices provide brochures and information on accommodations, attractions, restaurants and local history. They can also tell you about tour companies and car rental agencies. St John Parish Economic Development Department (☎ 504-652-9569), 1801 W Airline Hwy in La Place, is open weekdays from 8 am to 4:30 pm.

St James Parish Tourist Center (☎ 504-869-9752, 800-367-7852, Net), 1988 Hwy 44 (east bank River Road) in Lutcher, is open weekdays 8 am to 4 pm in the St James Historical Society Culture & Heritage Center. The 'Great River Road Plantation Parade' brochure has a pretty good map showing the River Roads, plantations and historic sites.

Ascension Parish Tourist Commission (☎ 504-675-6550) at 6474 Hwy 22 in Sorrento is open daily 9 am to 5 pm. It covers the towns of Burnside, Darrow and Donaldsonville.

Iberville Parish Tourist Center (☎ 504-687-0641), Main St at Hwy 1, PO Box 1060, Plaquemine, LA 70765, is open daily 8 am to 4:30 pm, and it covers White Castle.

Destrehan Plantation

The tour of this 1787 plantation house begins with an interesting 20-minute video describing the mansion's designer/builder, Charles Pacquet, a free man of color, as well as its past owners and the architectural changes over the past 200 years. Former owners include Amoco, the oil corporation,

from which it was purchased by a historical society in 1971. The guided tour covers the building's construction, family anecdotes and the furnishings, most of which are period rather than original. Destrehan originally was built in a French colonial style, but was remodeled to Greek Revival from 1830 to 1840.

The plantation (☎ 504-764-9315, from New Orleans 504-524-5522), 13034 Hwy 48 (east bank River Road), is in Destrehan; it's the closest of the River Road mansions, about 15 minutes southwest of New Orleans airport. It's open daily from 9:30 am to 4 pm. Admission is $7. There's a gift shop.

San Francisco Plantation

Frenchman Edmond Bozonier Marmillion built this Creole-style house in 1856. Its name is derived from the French slang *sans frusquin*, meaning without a cent, because of the expense to build it. Edmond spared no expense, and neither did his German daughter-in-law, who took over the house with her husband, Valsin Marmillion, when Edmond died a year later and totally redecorated it. From 1974 to 1977, $2 million was spent to return the house – from the curtains and ceiling murals to the carpets and wall paint – to its original state.

Watch for details like faux marble fireplaces and faux wood moldings, underground earthenware jugs for storing perishable foods and hand-painted designs on doors and walls. The gift shop has many regional books and maps.

The plantation house (☎ 504-535-2341), Hwy 44, Reserve (east bank River Road), is open March to October daily 10 am to 4:30 pm, November to February daily 10 am to 4 pm, except Thanksgiving, Christmas, New Year's Day, Mardi Gras Day and Easter Sunday. Admission is $7 for adults, $4 students age 12 to 17, $2.75 for children age six to 11.

St James Historical
Society Culture & Heritage Center

This little gem of a museum (☎ 504-869-9752, 800-367-7852), 1988 Hwy 44 (east

LOUISIANA

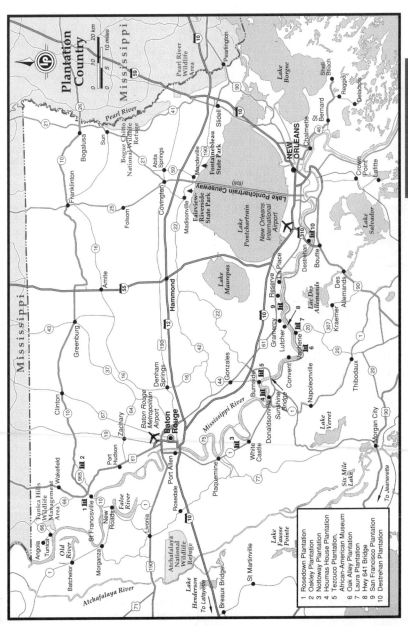

Plantation Country

0 5 10 miles
0 10 20 km

1 Rosedown Plantation
2 Oakley Plantation
3 Nottoway Plantation
4 Houmas House Plantation
5 Tezcuco Plantation,
  African-American Museum
6 Oak Alley Plantation
7 Laura Plantation
8 Hwy 641 Bridge
9 San Francisco Plantation
10 Destrehan Plantation

bank River Road), Lutcher, tells the story of River Road history, from the plantations to the lumber mills to the tobacco companies. The main building houses artifacts and documents. Furnished outer buildings are comprised of replicas and restored businesses, barns and a blacksmith shop. The center is free and open weekdays from 8 am to 4 pm.

Tezcuco Plantation & African-American Museum

Built in 1855, this mansion's Aztec name means 'place of quiet rest.' It's part of a complex that includes a gift shop, museum, restaurant, antique shop and guest cottages in historic buildings and slave quarters, three of which are original to the property. The house is furnished in period pieces that are not original.

Festival of the Bonfires

Legend has it that bonfires lit along the Mississippi River levee during the Christmas season were intended to show Papa Noel the way to the homes of good children. Another claims the fires illuminated the River Road for parishioners on their way to midnight mass.

No matter which is right, the tradition has continued since the 1880s. Just after Thanksgiving, residents in St James Parish (about 25 miles west of New Orleans) begin to erect 20-foot-tall tepee-shaped wooden structures, which they place 100 feet apart along the levee.

Throughout December, riverboats from New Orleans travel up the Mississippi to see a few bonfires. On the second weekend in December, residents stage a festival in Lutcher with bonfires, gumbo competitions, music, dancing and fun for kids. Nightly, a few bonfires can be seen until Christmas Eve, when at 6 pm the fire marshal checks the wind's direction, then gives the okay signal at 7 pm, and the entire levee lights up with bonfires stretching for 12 miles from Gramercy to Convent. As many as 50,000 spectators come to watch the fiery spectacle. ∎

The mansion (☎ 504-562-3929), 3138 Hwy 44 (east bank River Road) in Burnside, is open daily 9 am to 5 pm, except Thanksgiving, Christmas and New Year's Day. The restaurant is open 8 am to 3:30 pm. Admission is $6 for adults, $5.50 seniors, $3.25 children age four to 12.

A must-see on the mansion grounds is the African-American Museum (☎ 504-562-7703, 644-7955), started by Kathe Hambrick, a local African-American woman who after visiting Tezcuco five years ago decided that someone needed to tell the story of the slaves. Through grants and donations, she's assembled a collection of photos, recipes, documents, musical instruments, clothing, masks, tools and other items to tell the story of rural Louisiana and slavery. The most remarkable item is a 900-name list of slaves who worked on neighboring plantations. She encourages locals to come in and search for their ancestors. Exhibits change every six months. Hours are weekends 1 to 5 pm, weekdays by appointment. Admission is a $3 donation.

If you plan to stay, the mansion's B&B accommodations include cottages with kitchens, air-conditioning and rockers on the porches, but no telephones. Rates range from $55 for a one-bedroom, one-bath cottage to $150 for the two-bedroom, two-bath, kitchen, dining and living room General Suite in the plantation house. The rooms are clean, and yes, it beats driving back and forth to New Orleans or Baton Rouge if you haven't seen all the plantations. The downside is that there is zip to do at night other than go out to eat.

Houmas House Plantation

Three aspects distinguish this mansion from other River Road plantations. It's the oldest structure, having originally been built in the late 1700s as a four-room dogtrot house and added onto in 1840. Of all the plantations, it has the most formal gardens and grounds. And, although it's open to the public for tours, it's still occupied by the current owners, the nieces of Dr George Crozat, a New Orleans physician who purchased and restored it in 1940.

The furnishings are part of the doctor's personal collection.

The plantation house (☎ 504-473-7841, from New Orleans 504-522-2262), 40136 Hwy 942 (east bank River Road), is on the town borders of Burnside and Darrow. Hours are February to October daily from 10 am to 5 pm, November to January daily from 10 am to 4 pm. Admission for the 45-minute guided tour is $8, children age 13 to 17 are $6, children age six to 12 are $3. It has a gift shop.

Laura Plantation

Ten minutes into the tour of this Creole plantation a vacationing Swiss journalist commented, 'Finally, reality.' That's what many visitors say. This is the only plantation tour that doesn't gloss over the role of slaves and that covers the Native Americans who lived here before and with the Europeans.

Still under renovation, the mansion's peeled back wallpaper and exposed bricks are perhaps a metaphor for Laura's interpretation, which local historians Sand and Norman Marmillion have researched from numerous sources. These primary sources include memoirs by the first owners' granddaughter, Laura Locoul, which contains stories about relatives, women, slaves and children; 5000 pages of documents from the Archives Nationales de Paris; and not to forget the original Tar Baby stories and Br'er Rabbit legend as written by Alcée Fortier in 1894, based on interviews with Senegalese slaves at Laura. (See Louisiana Folktales sidebar.)

Family artifacts, including clothing, photo albums and business and slave records are on display. Besides the main house, there are 12 historic buildings, including another manor house, slave quarters, a Creole cottage and informal gardens. Don't miss this treasure.

Laura (☎ 504-265-7690, from New Orleans 504-488-8709, Net), 2247 Hwy 18 (west bank River Road), is in Vacherie. It's open daily 9 am to 5 pm for tours, which cost $6. These start outside on the front lawn with a discussion of the Native

Louisiana Folktales

Born in 1856, Alcée Fortier grew up on the River Road, the son of a prominent Creole family. He spent his adult years recording and teaching Louisiana folktales as a professor at the University of Louisiana in New Orleans (which became Tulane during his tenure). Most notable of the collection is the 'The Tale of the Piti Bonhomme Godron' (Tar Baby) told by the West African slaves' descendants who lived on the plantations near his home in Vacherie. The tale revolves around the antics of the mischievous clever rabbit Compair Lapin, more commonly known as Br'er Rabbit in contemporary North American folklore.

Fortier collected this and other stories during the late 19th century and in 1888 published *Bits of Louisiana Folk-lore* and *Louisiana Folk-tales*.

To commemorate the 100th anniversary of *Louisiana Folk-tales*, Laura Plantation and Sand Warren Marmillion faithfully translated from the original Creole and published the tale of 'Compair Lapin and Piti Bonhomme Godron.'

On a side note: many consider the collector of the Tar Baby stories to be Joel Chandler Harris. Well, Fortier and Harris were colleagues. They both interviewed Senegalese slaves in the 1870s and even collaborated on historical papers. Fortier published his Tar Baby collection first in the original Creole dialect for fellow historians, but Harris may be known as the collector of the stories because he was later the first to publish them in English for the general public in 1895. ∎

Americans who lived on the property. You can walk around the outside of the other buildings and the gardens on your own. Daily at 10:30 am, they give a 15-minute tour of the slave quarters that's included in the tour price. Tours in French are offered on Monday, Wednesday and Friday. The gift shop features quality arts and crafts by local artisans, souvenirs and books on history and culture.

LOUISIANA

Oak Alley Plantation

Of all the plantations, Oak Alley has the most dramatic entrance: a quarter-mile canopy of majestic live oaks from the River Road to the house. The 28 trees, 14 on each side of the driveway, predate the house by a hundred years. More symmetry awaits at the house, which is built in Greek Revival style and has 28 columns, each eight feet in diameter, surrounding it.

Oak Alley (☎ 504-265-2151, 800-442-5539), 3645 Hwy 18 (west bank River Road), is in Vacherie, just north of Laura Plantation. Admission is $7 for adults, $5 for children age 12 to 18, $3 for children six to 12. It's the most commercial in feel, with a gift shop, restaurant, B&B, seasonal dinner theater and RV parking. Overnight guests stay in beautifully decorated cottages behind the mansion, which feature full kitchen, bath, living and dining room and porches overlooking attractive gardens. Rates run $95 to $125. These are on a par with high-quality hotels (but if money is an issue, stay at the Holiday Inn in Reserve for around half the price). All cottages are nonsmoking.

Nottoway Plantation

The largest plantation house in the South has 64 rooms and 53,000 square feet. Guides don't wear costumes and deliver no drama, yet the tours are rich in personal history thanks to business records and *The White Castle of Louisiana*, the diary written by the original owner's daughter, Cornelia Randolph. The house has original furnishings and period pieces, 200 windows and 165 doors – an opening for each day of the year – and wide galleries with rocking chairs on which visitors may sit and look out onto the river. Note the elaborate hand-carved plaster frieze-work throughout.

Nottoway (☎ 504-545-2730, from Baton Rouge 504-346-8263), Hwy 1 (west bank River Road), is two miles north of White Castle. Guided tours run continuously daily 9 am and 5 pm, except Christmas. Admission is $8, children $3.

The pricey restaurant serves Cajun specialties daily from 11 am to 3 pm and 6 to 8 pm; lunch prices hover around $12 and dinner prices around $20. (For the money, you're much better off heading to the foot of the Sunshine Bridge to Lafitte's Landing Restaurant.) There's a gift shop with souvenirs, books, antique accessories and regional foods.

Several rooms on the tour as well as outbuildings serve as B&B accommodations with rates running $95 to $190 single, $125 to $190 double, $200 to $250 suites. Stays include a tour, plantation breakfast and use of a pool and gardens.

Organized Tours

Lucille and Chester Le'Obia of Le' Ob's Tours (☎ 504-288-3478, fax 504-288-8517), 4635 Touro St, New Orleans, LA 70122, offer a tour of Plantation Country, stopping at Laura Plantation, Houmas House, Tezcuco and the African-American River Road Museum. The seven-hour tour costs $75 and includes lunch at the historic Cabin Restaurant, a collection of renovated former slave quarters.

Otherwise, hotels and the visitor centers in Baton Rouge and New Orleans provide brochures for organizations that offer full-day tours through Plantation Country. Ask other hotel guests which tour they took and how they enjoyed it. Tours are packaged differently, with some full-day tours visiting two plantations and lunch, others three plantations and lunch ($60 to $75). Others offer a half-day with one stop (around $40). Many provide multilingual narration. In the narratives given between stops, some tour operators paint a rosy, less-than-realistic picture of plantation life. One tour operator out of New Orleans told his mostly European audience that the plantation slaves worked six-hour days, had weekends off and were paid. If you want your history straight up, ask a few questions before handing over your money.

Special Events

Folks from around the world come to Lutcher to see bonfires on the Mississippi River levees during the Festival of the Bonfires (see sidebar, earlier; ☎ 504-869-4303,

800-367-7852), Knights of Columbus Center, 1905 W Main St. It takes place the second full weekend in December and culminates on Christmas Eve with a massive burning of bonfires for 12 miles.

Places to Stay

Camping The closest campgrounds are a few miles east of Baton Rouge and west of New Orleans. See Places to Stay in Baton Rouge.

Motels *Holiday Inn* (☎ 504-647-8000, fax 504-647-7741), 1500 Hwy 30, Gonzales, is the largest hotel in the area. Its 172 rooms and suites overlook a large pool. There's a lounge with live and recorded entertainment and a better-than-average seafood restaurant. Rates are $64/69 single/double.

Holiday Inn (☎ 504-652-5544), 3900 Main St, La Place, is within 20 minutes of New Orleans airport at the south end of the River Road plantation tour. The complex has a busy pool in summer and a patio in the center, far enough away from rooms to keep the noise down. The restaurant, *Basille's*, features Italian and seafood dishes and serves three meals. There's a coin laundry and limited cable TV. Rates are $69/75.

Inns & B&Bs Nottoway, Oak Alley and Tezcuco allow visitors to stay overnight. (See entries for details.)

A former bank, *The White Castle Inn* (☎ 504-545-9932), 55035 Cambre St, White Castle, is on the west bank and north end of the River Road, making it a convenient beginning or ending point for a tour of the plantations. Upstairs are four guest rooms and private baths. The new owner redecorated in a sophisticated style using designer fabrics and bedding. Rates are $65 to $85 and include a traditional Southern breakfast.

Soft-spoken Rich Laurich and his wife, Dinah, own and run the *Bay Tree Plantation* (☎ 504-265-2109, fax 504-265-7076), a lovely Creole cottage that's now an antique-filled B&B on the west bank of the River Road in Vacherie. There are six

suites and bedrooms split between two houses on a four-acre parcel with informal gardens. A full Southern breakfast is included in the rate of $65 to $150.

Places to Eat

West Bank Owned and run by a family of fishermen, *B&C Seafood Market & Cajun Deli* (☎ 504-265-8356), 2155 Hwy 18 (River Road), Vacherie, between Laura and Oak Alley Plantations, specializes in boiled fresh seafood and also serves gumbo, po-boys, burgers, alligator and turtle. Prices range from $4 to $7. The deli is open Monday to Saturday 9 am to 5:30 pm, except Friday to 6:30 pm.

Lafitte's Landing Restaurant (☎ 504-473-1232), 10275 Sunshine Bridge Access Road (foot of the Sunshine Bridge), Donaldsonville, is the finest restaurant between Baton Rouge and New Orleans (and is comparable to New Orleans' best). It's owned by Chef John Folse, host of public television's *A Taste of Louisiana*. You can dine well yet inexpensively on a sausage or seafood po-boy ($6) or go for broke with seafood Teche ($19), a seafood cassoulet. The walls are lined with interesting paintings and posters by Louisiana artists George Rodrigue and Robert Rucker. It's open Tuesday to Saturday from 11 am to 3 pm and 6 to 10 pm, Sunday 11 am to 8 pm.

East Bank Get an early start and grab a shrimp and cheese omelet with toast ($3) for breakfast at *Sandwich World* (☎ 504-869-3894), Hwy 3125, Gramercy, between Destrehan and San Francisco Plantations. A freshly baked biscuit with an egg costs only 79¢. Like its name suggests, there are also sandwiches from $2 to $4. It's open Monday to Saturday 6:30 am to 8 pm.

The Stockpile (☎ 504-869-9917), Hwy 3125, Grand Point, between Destrehan and San Francisco Plantations, serves fried or broiled seafood and steaks ($8 to $16) and sandwiches ($2 to $8) in a rustic setting with antiques and interesting local memorabilia. It has pool tables and gaming machines in the bar. The hours are daily 10 am to 10 pm, Friday to 11 pm.

LOUISIANA

Bull's Corner (☎ 504-652-3544), 1036 W Airline Hwy, La Place, between Destrehan and San Francisco Plantations, is a popular restaurant and bar near a mall and movie theater. The menu features burgers (from $4), salads and Creole and Cajun dishes at $7 to $11 for lunch, $10 to $16 for dinner. It's open weekdays 11 am to 10 pm, weekends 11 am to 11 pm.

Because *Hymel's Restaurant and Bar* (☎ 504-562-9910), 8740 Hwy 44, River Road, is between Tezcuco and San Francisco Plantations, it's a stop on the tour bus circuit, but locals go because the food's good. The menu features fresh seafood boiled, broiled or fried. Lunch runs $4 to $9, dinner $4 to $15. Both include soup, salad, dessert and a beverage. It's open weekdays 11 am to 2:30 pm, also Thursday 5 to 9 pm, Friday 5 to 10 pm, Saturday 11 am to 10 pm, Sunday 11 am to 8 pm.

The Cabin Restaurant (☎ 504-473-3007), intersection of Hwys 22 and 44 in Burnside, features traditional po-boys, gumbos and fried seafood in a setting of restored slave cabins. It's right on the River Road and is popular with tour groups. Lunch and dinner run $8 to $17. The hours are Monday to Wednesday 8 am to 3 pm, Thursday 8 am to 9 pm, Friday to Saturday 8 am to 10 pm, Sunday 8 am to 6 pm. It's closed Christmas and New Year's.

Getting There & Away

It's best to get to and around the plantations by car. Trains don't run to or through Plantation Country; the closest service is in New Orleans.

Bus & Shuttle Greyhound (☎ 504-651-2570), 1514 W Airline Hwy (Hwy 61), La Place, has service from Atlanta ($71, four times a day); Baton Rouge ($12, three times); Biloxi ($24, three times); Birmingham ($65, one time); Jackson ($32, three times); Lafayette ($25, three times); Mobile ($24, three times); and New Orleans ($7, three times).

Marathon/Pontchartrain Transportation Service (☎ 504-241-0812) provides shuttles from New Orleans airport at $1.70 per

mile. Note: you'll need a car to get around once you're there.

Car New Orleans airport in Kenner would be the best place to rent a car to tour Plantation Country. All the major companies are represented, but Value-Rent-a-Car and Dollar offer the best rates. Both have off-site locations with courtesy vans to pick you up and drop you off. These agencies' cars aren't always immaculately clean due to high turnover, but you can brush the crumbs off the seat yourself for $5 to $8 less a day.

While driving around, be aware that the River Road is scenic, winding and narrow. When the chemical company employees go to and return from work, traffic is anything but leisurely. Be careful.

From New Orleans take I-10 then Hwy 48 east less than a mile to Destrehan on the east bank. Continue west on Hwy 48, which joins Hwy 61 temporarily, before reconnecting with the River Road as Hwy 44 near Reserve and San Francisco Plantation. Continue west to Tezcuco and Houmas Plantations, then backtrack a few miles to the Sunshine Bridge; travel west on Hwy 1 to Nottoway, then backtrack again to Hwy 18 and Oak Alley and Laura Plantations. From here you can cross the river on the I-310 to return to New Orleans airport or Hwy 90 to cross the Huey P Long Bridge to return to the French Quarter.

From Baton Rouge, take I-10 east to Hwy 44 south near Houmas Plantation and follow the River Road in reverse order.

BATON ROUGE

The city's name, which translates as 'red stick,' is said to derive from Native Americans who painted a cypress pole with blood to mark boundaries of hunting territories.

This Mississippi River town is the home of the state's two largest universities – Louisiana State University (LSU) and Southern – as well as the nation's tallest capitol, the fifth-largest port and the second-largest petrochemical industry. (Fortunately, the latter is concentrated on the river at the northern end of the city.) That's what

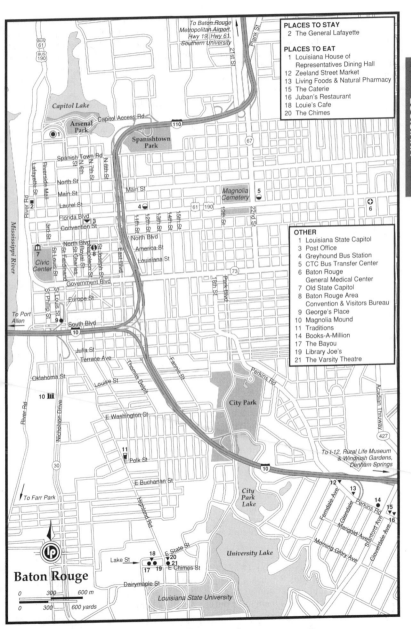

PLACES TO STAY
2 The General Lafayette

PLACES TO EAT
1 Louisiana House of
Representatives Dining Hall
12 Zeeland Street Market
13 Living Foods & Natural Pharmacy
15 The Caterie
16 Juban's Restaurant
18 Louie's Cafe
20 The Chimes

OTHER
1 Louisiana State Capitol
3 Post Office
4 Greyhound Bus Station
5 CTC Bus Transfer Center
6 Baton Rouge
General Medical Center
7 Old State Capitol
8 Baton Rouge Area
Convention & Visitors Bureau
9 George's Place
10 Magnolia Mound
11 Traditions
14 Books-A-Million
17 The Bayou
19 Library Joe's
21 The Varsity Theatre

Baton Rouge

defines Baton Rouge physically and economically. Without question, politics have defined it since the early 19th century through such controversial men as former governor and senator Huey P Long. Though there are plenty of *bons temps* to be had, the pace slows in Louisiana's state capital.

Orientation

Baton Rouge sits on the east bank of the Mississippi River. The new and old state capitols, casinos and a riverfront entertainment complex are located downtown off I-110, just north of I-10. LSU's main campus sits on the Mississippi River in the southwest corner of the city. The neighboring streets are home to parks, inexpensive restaurants, nightclubs, movie theaters and shops. Highland Rd is its main thoroughfare. Perkins Rd, a few miles north and south of I-10, has many restaurants, bookstores and shops. Ditto for College Dr and S Acadian Thruway southwest of I-10.

Information

Tourist Offices Baton Rouge Area Convention & Visitors Bureau (☎ 504-383-1825, 800-527-6843), 730 North Blvd, downtown, is open weekdays from 8 am to 5 pm. There's a smaller branch, along with a state tourism office, in the capitol lobby.

Community Connection (☎ 504-267-4221) is an easy-to-use dial-up service that offers free information about attractions, recreation, the arts and religious services.

Post The main branch (☎ 504-381-0713), 750 Florida Blvd at 7th St, downtown, is open weekdays from 8:30 am to 5 pm, Saturday 9 am to 12:30 pm.

Media *The Advocate* is the main daily newspaper. The free monthly tabloid *gris gris* is a hip guide to local entertainment, dining and lifestyle.

Bookstores Books-A-Million (☎ 504-343-9584), 3525 Perkins Rd, has a strong regional section and carries some titles in French. The hours are daily 9 am to 11 pm.

Books to Hear & Movies to See (☎ 504-926-9005), 8210 Jefferson Hwy, carries taped recordings of 2000 unabridged and abridged fiction and nonfiction titles for sale or for rent. It's open daily 9 am to 9 pm.

Libraries The Baton Rouge Main Library (☎ 504-231-3750), 7711 Goodwood Blvd at Airline Hwy, is open Monday to Thursday from 8 am to 10 pm, Friday and Saturday 8 am to 6 pm, Sunday 2 to 10 pm.

Campuses Baton Rouge has two major universities. The main part of the Louisiana State University (LSU) campus is grouped on a 650-acre plateau in the southern part of Baton Rouge. The LSU Museum Complex is the most important area for visitors. The complex features the Museum of Art (☎ 504-388-4003) and the Museum of Natural Science (☎ 504-388-2855) as well as the off-site LSU Rural Life Museum (see below). The area surrounding the campus has inexpensive eateries, nightclubs and shops. Collegiate sports fans can purchase tickets for Tiger games and events by calling the LSU athletic department at ☎ 504-388-2184, or if you're out of town, Ticketmaster at ☎ 504-761-8400.

Southern University was the founding campus for the largest predominantly black university system in the country. It spreads across the north end of Baton Rouge, on the Mississippi River a few miles west of the airport. Campus attractions include a small Gallery of Fine Arts (☎ 504-771-2070) with changing exhibitions, a Jazz Institute (☎ 504-771-4417) and guided tours (☎ 504-771-2430) arranged through the admissions office.

Medical Services For emergency and routine medical care, go to Our Lady of the Lake Medical Center (☎ 504-765-6565), 5000 Henessy Blvd at Essen Lane, or Baton Rouge General Medical Center (☎ 504-387-7000), 3600 Florida Blvd at Acadian Thruway.

Rural Life Museum & Windrush Gardens

In the middle of urban Baton Rouge, a road turns from Essen Lane and winds a mile through the Windrush Gardens and fields before reaching the Rural Life Museum. Among the 20 buildings that depict rural life in 18th to early-20th-century Louisiana is a barn with hundreds of artifacts and folk art, seven examples of folk architecture and a dozen authentically furnished structures representing plantation life. Start the self-guided tour with a 15-minute video presentation. Knowledgeable staff members provide interpretation. Allow one to two hours, depending on your interest in history, then head outside to the 25-acre gardens for a visual feast of crape myrtles, azaleas and camellias.

Craftspeople demonstrate their skills and folk musicians and storytellers perform on the first Saturday of the month. The museum (☎ 504-765-2437), 4600 Essen Lane, just south of I-10, is open daily from 8:30 am to 5 pm, except major holidays. Admission is $5 for adults, $4 seniors, $3 children five to 11 years.

Louisiana State Capitol

Three years after Louisiana governor Huey P Long had this elegant tribute to himself built, an assassin gunned him down in its halls. Long is buried on the grounds and his statue in the surrounding 27-acre park faces the building (☎ 504-342-7317), State Capitol Dr, exit 1E on I-110. Three hundred and fifty feet up, the 27th-floor observation deck affords an unsurpassed view of the city, Mississippi River and belching chemical plants in north Baton Rouge. The architectural details and works of art are exquisite. The building is open daily 9 am to 4:30 pm. The last elevator ascends at 3:45 pm. Admission is free.

Old State Capitol

Mark Twain described the old capitol (☎ 504-342-0500, 800-488-2968), 100 N Blvd, downtown, as the ugliest building he'd ever seen. The white, 150-year-old imposing Gothic structure sits on a bluff overlooking the Mississippi River and now serves as the Center for Political and Governmental History. Don't let that discourage you. Louisiana's often scandalous political history provides entertaining insight into its culture. There's a 20-minute film, interactive exhibits, multimedia presentations and exhibitions covering Huey Long's assassination, ballot boxes, campaigns and elections. The spiral staircase and stained-glass windows are noteworthy. Hours are Tuesday to Saturday 10 am to 4 pm, Sunday noon to 4 pm. It costs $4 for adults, $3 for seniors and veterans, $2 for all students.

Magnolia Mound Plantation

The Creole-style Magnolia Mound (☎ 504-343-4955) at 2161 Nicholson Dr is the oldest (circa 1791) plantation house in the Baton Rouge area. It has period furnishings, and costumed guides escort visitors. Also on the grounds, which are managed by the Baton Rouge Recreation & Park Commission (BREC), are an overseer's house, period kitchen, carriage house, vegetable gardens and gift shop.

It's open Tuesday to Saturday 10 am to 4 pm, Sunday 1 to 4 pm, except major holidays. Admission is $5 for adults, $4 seniors, $2 students over 12 years, $1 children under 12 years.

Baton Rouge Recreation & Park Commission

Baton Rouge has an exemplary recreation system, called BREC for short, that encompasses 176 parks. Among them is the new **Bluebonnet Swamp Nature Center** (☎ 504-757-8905, 273-6405), 10503 N Oak Hills Pkwy, one block off Bluebonnet Blvd. A one-mile boardwalk with two observation decks winds through an upland hardwood forest before descending to a cypress swamp. The nature center features wildlife folk art, ecology displays and exhibits of insects, alligators and mammals. Admission is $1.50 for adults, $1 seniors, 50¢ students under 18.

Snow Cones

New York has its hot dog carts, Paris its roasted chestnut hawkers, Cartagena its *perro caliente* vendors. Baton Rouge, New Orleans, and other Louisiana cities and towns, both large and small, have snow-cone stands. All summer long, snow cones (also known as snow balls) – flavored shaved ice in paper cones – are sold at small roadside shacks with signs reading 'Sno Balls,' 'SnowCones,' 'Sno Cones' and even 'Sneaux Cones.'

The vendor is armed with a machine that shaves the ice and a rack of dazzling glass bottles filled with colored flavors. He fills the paper cone with shaved ice, then generously sprinkles it with the syrupy flavoring – such as coconut, strawberry, grape, blackberry, blueberry, cherry or banana – until it's saturated with brilliant color. Bite into it with your front teeth and suck on the cool, sweet ice. There's nothing more refreshing on a hot, muggy summer day. ∎

Farr Park (☎ 504-769-7805, 766-8828), 6400 River Rd, is one of only two campgrounds (both city run) within Baton Rouge. Located near the LSU campus and the Mississippi River, it also has a horse activity center and a gym, where you often can catch a pick-up game of hoops. The campground has few trees, but offers water, electricity, restrooms, showers, picnic tables and pavilions and a coin laundry. Sites cost $10 for RVs, $3 for tents. Technically, you can't rent the horses, but you can ride indoors or outdoors Monday to Wednesday by taking a private lesson for $20 an hour or a group lesson (five people) for $15 an hour.

Greenwood Park Campground (☎ 504-775-3877), 13350 Hwy 19 at Thomas Rd, is north of downtown near the Baton Rouge Zoo (another city-owned park) and features RV ($7) and tent ($2) campsites offering water, electricity, bathhouses, restrooms and picnic tables. The wooded park, which also has tennis courts and a 30-acre fishing lake, is near golf courses and city-owned Cohn Arboretum.

Perkins Road Park (☎ 504-273-6400), 7122 Perkins Rd, has a BMX Raceway where you can bring your own bike or rent one ($2) to ride Tuesday and Wednesday 5 to 9 pm, Thursday 5 to 6:30 pm. There's racing Thursday and Saturday at 7 pm. If you prefer track riding, there's also a velodrome, where you can rent a bike ($2) Tuesday and Thursday from 5 to 9 pm.

The three-mile **Comite River Bike Trail** (☎ 504-273-6400) starting at 8900 Hooper Rd meanders along the banks of the Comite River and Cypress Bayou. The challenging course features steep, hilly terrain. **Hooper Road Bike Trail** (☎ 504-273-6400), 6261 Guynell (Sharon Hills subdivision), offers five miles of off-road riding through woods and over bluffs. Both trails are open daily during daylight hours.

Activities

See Baton Rouge Recreation & Park Commission for BMX, trail and track bicycle riding.

The Backpacker (☎ 504-925-2667), 7656 Jefferson Hwy (Hwy 73), opposite Bocage Mall, is one of the best sources of outdoor information in the South. Downstairs near the entrance is a rack of free maps and charts showing **biking, hiking** and **canoeing** trails in Louisiana and southern and western Mississippi. Upstairs is a free library of books and maps with similar information. The best of the related books is *Trail Guide to the Delta Country: Canoeing and Hiking* by a local chapter of the Sierra Club (☎ 504-482-9566), 5534 Canal Blvd, New Orleans. You can take notes at the store or purchase a copy.

The Backpacker staff can steer you to their favorite trails and help you with rentals of backpacks, sleeping bags, two- and four-person tents and canoes. The store sells equipment as well as guidebooks, maps, kayaks and just about anything else you need for outdoor adventure. It's open Monday to Friday from 10 am to 7 pm, Saturday 9 am to 6 pm.

While Alligator Bayou Tour's motorized sightseeing boats (see Organized Tours below) appeal to more sedentary visitors, their canoes provide a terrific, low-cost, high-energy way to experience Louisiana's bayous and wildlife. You can bring your own canoe ($2 map and put-in charge) or rent one from them ($5 per hour for canoe, paddle, life jacket and map) and put-in on the spot to tour Alligator Bayou, part of the pristine 13,000-acre Spanish Lake Basin, a cypress swamp with many smaller bayous, islands and lakes. Paddling is a year-round activity.

Located on the outskirts of Baton Rouge, the rental shop is open all year Wednesday to Friday from 8:30 am to 6:30 pm, weekends 7 am to 7 pm, and in summer also Monday and Tuesday noon to 5 pm.

Organized Tours

Quick-witted Mark Armstrong provides tours with local color and insights into Baton Rouge, the swamps and plantations through his Tiger Taxi & Tours (☎ 504-635-4641, 921-9199). Rates start at $22.50 an hour.

Alligator Bayou Tours (☎ 504-642-8297, 888-379-2677), 35019 Alligator Bayou Rd in Prairieville, 15 minutes from downtown, offers two-hour sightseeing tours of Alligator Bayou on a canopied pontoon boat. Wildlife is abundant. Tours depart Wednesday to Friday at 6:30 pm, Saturday at 10 am and 4 and 6:30 pm, Sunday at 4 and 6:30 pm. They cost $15 for adults, $10 for seniors and students, $8 for children. The Friday and Saturday 6:30 pm dinner cruise is $25. On Friday nights there's live Cajun music under an outdoor pavilion from 8 pm to midnight.

Places to Stay

Many of the moderate to expensive chain hotels are located just off I-10 around College Rd and Acadian Thruway exits. Less expensive chains are clustered along the north side of I-12, within a mile of I-10. Some hotels increase rates 20% to 30% on football-game weekends in fall.

Camping For information about Farr Park and Greenwood Park, see Baton Rouge Recreation & Park Commission, above.

Baton Rouge KOA (☎ 504-664-7281, 800-562-5673), 7628 Vincent Rd, Denham Springs, is seven miles east of downtown off I-12. It's a peaceful setting with lots of trees, separate pools for adults and kids, a playground, store, and picnic tables at each site, which are well shaded. Rates are $17 for tents, $23.50 for RVs with hookups. There are also a pair of small log cabins for $30 double.

If you can't get into one of the closer campgrounds or are headed north to St Francisville and prefer to take back roads, consider *Tranquility Lakes Campground & 3-D Archery Range* (☎ 504-777-4393), Hwy 16, 18 miles north of I-12. It's a low-key family-run campground on a 35-acre lake. Chickens and song birds are right at home. There's a pool, coin laundry, three bathhouses, and tennis, volleyball and basketball courts. Nonmotorized aluminum fishing boats rent for $5. Tent sites are $14 to $15, RV sites $15 for full hookups. Cabins have air-conditioning, refrigerators, baths and barbecue pits for $45; add $10 for units with a stove.

Motels & Hotels Cross the river and save at the *Motel 6* (☎ 504-343-5945), 2800 I-10 Frontage Rd, Port Allen, which has 132 rooms, a pool and free coffee. Rates are $30/36 single/double.

The General Lafayette (☎ 504-387-0421), 427 Lafayette St, downtown, is convenient to the state capitols, casinos and riverfront museums. It's an older hotel undergoing remodeling. Rates are $38/50.

The three-story *Budgetel Inn* (☎ 504-291-6600), 10555 Rieger Rd, off I-10, is in southeast Baton Rouge, two exits east of the LSU Rural Life Museum. There's a pool, and rooms have coffeemakers, free cable movies and breakfast included. Rates are $47 for one double bed, $51 for two double beds, $54 for a king bed.

Shoney's Inn (☎ 504-925-8399), 9919 Gwenadale Dr, is moderately priced and conveniently located at the intersection of I-12 and Airline Hwy (Hwy 61/190). It features attractive but smallish rooms and suites, a pool with a brick courtyard, satellite TV with free movies, a restaurant and free coffee and newspapers in the lobby. Rates are $48/56.

Wilson Inn & Suites (☎ 504-923-3377), 3045 Valley Creek Dr, off I-12, has 110 rooms with free cable movies, in-room refrigerators, free local calls, a fax and a breakfast bar. The staff is cheerful, helpful and knowledgeable. Rates for rooms are $53/58 weekday/weekend, and suites run $75/78.

The three-story *Red Roof Inn* (☎ 504-275-6600), 11314 Boardwalk Dr off I-12, has 109 rooms, each with a data port and free movies. There's free coffee in the lobby. Rooms are $51/58 single/double.

Ramada Inn (☎ 504-293-4100), 10330 Airline Hwy, off I-12, recently completed a total renovation inside and out. New rooms are clean and spacious. There's a full-service restaurant, room service and complimentary continental breakfast. The pool is in an attractive courtyard. Rates are $54/59.

Comfort Inn University Center (☎ 504-927-5790), 2445 S Acadian Thruway off I-10, has an ideal location for trips to LSU, a variety of restaurants along College Dr and Perkins Rd, and easy access to I-10, I-12 and I-110. There's a 24-hour coffee shop next door, free continental breakfast and newspaper, a pool, data port and spacious rooms. Rates are $65/75.

Embassy Suites (☎ 504-924-6566), 4914 Constitution Ave off I-10, is one of the nicest hotels in the city. It features two-room suites – each with a galley kitchen, microwave, coffeemaker and dual-line phones – an indoor pool with a sauna and whirlpool, airport shuttle, complimentary full breakfast and afternoon beverages, a restaurant and a popular lounge. Rack rate is $139, with weekend discounts.

Places to Eat
The area around the LSU campus, College Dr, W Chimes and Highland Rd, has affordable eateries with lots of atmosphere. Another hot spot is Perkins Rd on the south side of the I-10 overpass.

Budget Satisfy your appetite around the clock at *Louie's Cafe* (☎ 504-346-8221), 209 W State St, near LSU, which according to some locals is the best 24-hour eatery in town. The hash browns are a must, whether you get them plain, with cheese, chili or smothered in mushrooms, cheese and sour cream. Louie's has been feeding students, faculty and friends since 1941. It has a diner look with black and white decor, vintage 1950s-style counter with chrome, and vinyl counter stools.

Dine on seafood, po-boys, sandwiches and Louisiana specialties nightly until midnight at *The Caterie* (☎ 504-383-4178), 3617 Perkins Rd at Acadian Thruway, and *The Chimes* (☎ 504-383-1754), 3357 Highland Rd. Both also serve up live music (see Entertainment below) and are near LSU.

Grab a cup of brew and a beignet or muffin at *Coffee Call* (☎ 504-925-9493), 3010 College Dr, Village Square. It's open daily 6 am to 2 pm and also serves lunch weekdays. The menu features a variety of po-boys and a soup and salad bar.

Both locations of the *Living Foods & Natural Pharmacy*, 8875-A Highland Rd at Staring Lane (☎ 504-767-8222), and 3033 Perkins Rd just off I-10 (☎ 504-346-1886), serve hot vegetarian lunches weekdays starting around 10:30 am and ending when they run out of food. Meals are served at a small bar with stools. Soups cost around $3. The $3.50 sandwich special includes chips and a beverage.

The most expensive item on the deli menu at *Zeeland Street Market* (☎ 504-387-4546), 2031 Perkins Rd, is the club style po-boy at $7. That's just one of the reasons for its popularity. Others are mouth-watering omelets served from 7:30 to 10:30 am, fresh salads like the Zeeland Zen with tender baby greens, walnuts, sprouts and blue cheese, and a sophisticated (but not necessarily expensive) selection of wines. It's open weekdays from 7:30 am to 8 pm, Saturday 7:30 am to 3 pm.

Our Daily Bread (☎ 504-924-1215), 9414 Florida Blvd, two blocks from Cortana

Mall, serves vegetarian lunches Monday to Saturday from 11 am to 3 pm. The deli with four tables is in the back of this health-food store. It offers a menu of healthful sandwiches, including a veggie po-boy ($4 to $7), salads and a generously sized lunch special ($3.50). They bake their whole-grain breads daily. Try the cinnamon buns.

Two downtown favorites that won't stretch your wallet include the cafeteria-style *Louisiana House of Representatives Dining Hall* (☎ 504-342-0371), State Capitol Dr, exit 1E on I-110, in the basement of the new capitol. It's open weekdays from 7 am to 2 pm. The other is *Phil's Oyster Bar* (☎ 504-924-3045), 5162 Government St, which serves oysters on the half shell, po-boys, seafood and Italian dishes. Lunch specials such as red beans and rice with smoked sausage, a salad and cornbread cost $6. It's open Monday to Saturday 10:30 am to 9:30 pm.

Crawford's Seafood Restaurant (☎ 504-664-1412), 136 W Rushing Rd, Denham Springs, off I-12, claims its special batter makes its catfish the best in the South. While that's not true, it does deliver a crispy, albeit salty, fried catfish at a good price. The bigger bargain is its all-you-can-eat buffets for $5 to $6, including a beverage.

Moderate & Expensive A repeat winner of the local city magazine's 'Best Restaurant' title is *DeAngelo's* (☎ 504-762-4465), 7955 Bluebonnet Rd. It wins by serving rich pizzas (from $8) that start with home-made tomato sauce, imported cheeses, hand-tossed crusts and fresh ingredients. Then there are the freshly baked focaccia and bruschetta, the light panini with capocollo ham, the calzones and the salads. It's heaven. Hours are Monday from 10 am to 3 pm, Tuesday to Saturday 10 am to 10 pm, Sunday 10 am to 9 pm.

Louisiana Pizza Kitchen (☎ 504-763-9100), 7951 One Calais Ave, has great pizza with or without cheese. A favorite is the roasted chicken with a black bean purée, cilantro, slivers of jalapeño pepper and sliced fresh tomatoes, without cheese ($8).

Try the pastas, too. It's open Sunday to Thursday from 11 am to 10 pm, Friday and Saturday 11 am to 11 pm.

For more than 20 years *Chalet Brandt* (☎ 504-927-6040), 7655 Old Hammond Hwy at Jefferson Hwy, has been one of the best restaurants in town. The decor is Swiss and the food French, with offerings like steak au poivre and sea scallops Betsy sautéed in Pernod.

Juban's Restaurant (☎ 504-346-8422), 3739 Perkins Rd at S Arcadian Thruway near LSU, has a beautiful Creole interior. It has the feel of a well-to-do but unpretentious antebellum plantation house where dining is unhurried. At lunch, the $9 daily special is the best deal. There's also a lovely crawfish ravioli ($11). The dinner menu has grilled items as well as seafood and lamb, veal and fowl ranging from $13 to $28. It's open weekdays from 11:30 am to 2 pm and 6 to 10 pm, Saturday from 6 to 10 pm.

Entertainment

The cult film *Sex, Lies and Videotape* was filmed at *The Bayou* (☎ 504-346-1765), 124 W Chimes, and the pop band REM played here in its early days. It hasn't lost its appeal and the quality of live music remains high. Just down the block, *Library Joe's* (☎ 504-344-3935), 136 W Chimes, has a similar cachet. *The Varsity Theatre* (☎ 504-343-5267), 3353 Highland Rd, is *the* place for live music – there's a variety of acts, large and small, from rock to La Noche Latina.

While the neighborhood is questionable, there's no doubt about the quality of blues at either *Phil Brady's* (☎ 504-927-3786), 4848 Government St, or *Tabby's Blues Box and Heritage Hall* (☎ 504-387-9715), 1315 North Blvd at 13th. The clientele averages mid-30s and 40s at this Baton Rouge staple.

The Caterie (☎ 504-383-4178), 3617 Perkins Rd at Acadian Thruway, has live local talent nightly that attracts the 20- to 30-year-old crowd. The same crowd makes its way past the tattoo parlor and Plasma

Center to hang out and drink some of the 120 varieties of beer from 24 countries at the *The Chimes* (☎ 504-383-1754), 3357 Highland Rd. Both also have a following of middle-age folks who go strictly for the good food they serve (see Places to Eat).

Traditions (☎ 504-344-9291), 2183 Highland Rd at Polk St between LSU and downtown, is a big dance club with a big following of gays and lesbians, sprinkled with straights who love to dance. When the bodies get too hot, cool off upstairs in the bar. Over at *George's Place* (☎ 504-387-9798), 860 St Louis St, the clientele that shows up for the dramatic drag show is decidedly gay, but heterosexual friendly.

The Happy Note (☎ 504-924-9107), 5240 Florida Blvd, lacks class, but that doesn't bother the college frat types who hang here for the cheap beer.

Grab a few laughs at *Funny Bone Comedy Club* (☎ 504-928-9996), 4715 Bennington Ave at College Dr, which has shows Thursday to Friday at 9 pm, Saturday at 8 pm and 10 pm.

Getting There & Away

Air Baton Rouge metropolitan airport (☎ 504-355-0333), 9430 Jackie Cochran Dr north of the city off I-110, is served by major US airlines. The only direct flights would be from airline hub cities – Dallas for American Airlines, Atlanta for Delta, Houston for Continental. All roundtrip fares into Baton Rouge are over $100.

Bus Greyhound (☎ 504-383-3811), 1253 Florida Blvd at N 12th St, has daily buses to Atlanta ($83, nine buses a day); Biloxi ($34, six buses); Birmingham ($71, two buses); Gulfport ($34, six buses); La Place ($12, three buses); Lafayette ($11, 10 buses); Mobile ($47, 13 buses); New Orleans ($12, nine buses); New Orleans airport ($14, four buses); Shreveport ($31, four buses); Slidell ($18, four buses), and other cities. Generally, the same number of buses arrive from and depart to the cities. The station is on a well-lit major street a few miles east of downtown. It's easy to catch a cab from here.

Train The Amtrak Thruway Bus Service connects Baton Rouge eight times a day (five buses from New Orleans, three to New Orleans) to trains that stop in New Orleans with coordinated schedules and through-fares. It stops at the Greyhound station.

Car I-10 enters Baton Rouge from the southeast from New Orleans and west across the river from Lafayette. I-12 enters from the east and terminates at I-10. I-110, a short highway, runs north from I-10 to the city boundary before becoming Hwy 61 as it heads north towards St Francisville.

Avis, Budget, Hertz and Thrifty have counters at the airport. Rent-A-Wreck (☎ 504-381-5712), 15052 Florida Blvd, and Enterprise (☎ 504-929-7560), 8121 Florida Blvd, have offices in town. Enterprise includes a car drop-off and pick-up service, which is convenient for bus and train travelers.

Getting Around

To/From the Airport Mackie's Airport Cab Service (☎ 504-357-4883) and Yellow Cab (☎ 504-926-6400, 800-259-2227) serve the airport. A ride from the airport to downtown costs $12 to $16.

Bus The Capital Transportation City Bus (☎ 504-343-8331, 336-0821) costs $1.25, 25¢ for a transfer. Look for blue signs with the letters 'CTC.' Drivers also stop when flagged. City buses require exact change and run Monday to Saturday from 6 am to 6 pm.

The bus system revolves around a transfer station at 2222 Florida St. From there, you can pick up the North Blvd shuttle to the new and old state capitols and other downtown and waterfront attractions. The downtown shuttle costs 10¢. Buses to LSU (University line) and Southern (Scotlandville line) also run through the transfer station. A special 30-minute shuttle runs between LSU and Southern University. The shuttle departs LSU on the half-hour, Southern on the hour.

Taxi You must call for cab service. Yellow Cab (☎ 504-926-6400) serves Baton Rouge; the meter starts at $1.95 and runs $1.40 per mile.

ST FRANCISVILLE
In the early 18th century, Spanish Capuchin monks found the highland bluffs here more suitable as a burial ground than the land across the river in Pointe Coupee Parish. Soon the area took on the name of the monks' patron saint, St Francis. By the late 18th century, northern British loyalists began arriving to escape the Revolutionary War. Plantations sprang up surrounding the town.

This pretty town retains nearly 150 of its historic houses and buildings, including seven that are open to the public for tours. Its most well-known resident was John James Audubon, who lived on the 200-year-old Oakley Plantation.

St Francisville makes a pleasant day trip from Baton Rouge if you're interested in 18th and 19th-century architecture, quaint towns with antique shops, gift shops and restaurants, and cozy B&Bs in historic houses.

Pick up a brochure and map from the tourist office/historical society, then walk or drive past the historic structures. Afterward, leave downtown and head to Rosedown and Oakley Plantations.

Orientation & Information
St Francisville is about 25 miles north of Baton Rouge on Hwy 61. The highway enters the city on the southeast side, just after passing Hwy 965, which heads northeast to Audubon State Park. As Hwy 61 continues through the city, Hwy 10 cuts diagonally across the center, running northeast to Rosedown Plantation and southwest to St Francisville's historic district, where there are scores of historic buildings. Most can be found along Ferdinand St (Hwy 10) and Royal St, which forms a half-circle on the south side of Ferdinand St, as well as Johnson, Prosperity and Fidelity Sts, all of which run perpendicular to Ferdinand as it heads to the Mississippi River.

The West Feliciana Parish Tourist Commission (☎ 504-635-6330), 11757 Ferdinand St, St Francisville, is open Monday to Saturday from 9 am to 5 pm, Sunday 9:30 am to 5 pm. It's home to the West Feliciana Historical Society and has a small museum and restrooms.

Audubon State Commemorative Area & Oakley Plantation
In 1821, John James Audubon came to Oakley Plantation to teach painting to the 13-year-old daughter of owner James Pirrie. Though his assignment lasted only four months, he completed or began more than 30 paintings of birds found in the plantation's surrounding 100-acre forest. Guided tours of the house start every half hour. Self-guided tours of the grounds include a beautiful herb and vegetable garden, two slave's cabins, a working kitchen and a barn. You can picnic on the grounds or hike a short, wooded trail. Admission to Oakley Plantation (☎ 504-635-3739), on Hwy 965, is $2; free for seniors and children. It's open daily 9 am to 5 pm, except major holidays.

Rosedown Plantation
Just as at the Oak Alley Plantation on the River Road, an avenue of oak trees forms a canopy over the driveway to this antebellum mansion (☎ 504-635-3332), 12501 Hwy 10. It differs from most plantation houses in three ways: Many of the furnishings on view were purchased in the mid-19th century by the original owners, Martha and Daniel Turnbull, who were cotton planters. It still has many original outlying structures, and the European-style formal gardens with camellias, azaleas and Italian statuary command as much attention as the house.

It also serves as a B&B; see Places to Stay, below.

Bicycling
The quiet roads around St Francisville are ideal for bike outings.

Baton Rouge Bicycle Club's 23-mile ride starts at the Audubon State Commemorative Area, crosses forests and Bayou Sara, and eventually loops back to the start.

LOUISIANA

Maps of the route are available at the Backpacker in Baton Rouge; it's from the Sierra Club's *Trail Guide to the Delta Country: Canoeing and Hiking* mentioned under Activities in Baton Rouge.

Birdwatching
Naturalist and wildlife artist Murrell Butler (☎ 504-635-6214), an heir to Greenwood Plantation, leads birding tours ($10 an hour) through a 350-acre upland forest. Although there are birds year round, the best time is spring. Expect to see waterfowl as well as songbirds.

Special Events
Guides dressed in antebellum period costumes lead tours of historic plantations, houses, churches and gardens during the annual Audubon Pilgrimage (☎ 504-635-6330) the third weekend in March.

Every Sunday in October Angola Prison hosts a sell-out rodeo and arts & crafts show (☎ 504-655-4411) in Angola, 24 miles northwest of St Francisville.

Places to Stay
Camping Water, electricity and full hookups are available at the handsome *Green Acres Campground* (☎ 504-635-4903), 11907 Hwy 965. Tent ($12) and RV ($14) campers can swim in the large pool, fish in a private pond, hike a nature trail and prepare meals either on a grill or in a pavilion with a kitchen. There are clean restrooms and showers, laundry facilities and a store.

Inns & B&Bs Historic accommodations abound in St Francisville, including guest rooms in several of the houses open for tours. Rates run $65 to $150. For advance written reservations, all zip codes are St Francisville, LA 70775.

Rates for B&B accommodations at *Rosedown Plantation* (☎ 504-635-3332), 12501 Hwy 10, range from $95 to $145. Guest rooms are artistically decorated in 1835 period furnishings and are non-smoking with private baths and canopied beds. Guests may use the swimming pool

and tennis court. It's an elegant place to stay and has a gracious staff.

Butler Greenwood (☎ 504-635-6312), 8345 Hwy 61, has six lovely guest cottages scattered around oak-shaded grounds. Stays include continental breakfast, use of the pool and a tour of the owner's antebellum home. Rates for one or two guests are $100 to $110 for a one-bedroom; for two to four guests $160 for a two-bedroom. It's a quiet, civilized respite.

Guests at *Hemingbough* (☎ 504-635-6617), Hwy 965, two miles south of Hwy 61, can relax in one of eight antique-filled guest rooms or two suites with private baths and phones and explore the 238-acre grounds and lake. Its comfortable rooms and peaceful grounds combine to make it most relaxing. One or two guests pay $85 for a room, $105 for a suite.

A four-mile drive north of St Francisville takes you to *Green Springs B&B* (☎ 504-635-4232, 800-457-4978), a country house with large rooms with large beds, lovely grounds and a full Southern breakfast served on the porch. Madeline Nevill promises and delivers sophisticated country comfort. Upstairs rooms in the main house for one or two guests run $85 to $95. Half of a duplex is $120, an entire single cottage $150. The latter has a fireplace, king-size bed and double Jacuzzi.

Motels & Hotels Built in the 1920s, the *3V Tourist Court* (☎ 504-635-3120, 635-5540) at the corner of Ferdinand and Commerce Sts claims to have been the first motor court in the South. It was recently renovated and accommodations are in small cabins with kitchenettes. Rates are $50 to $65.

St Francis Hotel on the Lake (☎ 504-635-3821, 800-826-9931 in state, 800-523-6118 out of state), Hwy 61 at Hwy 10, is one of only a few accommodations here that's not a B&B, yet its wooded setting and lake give it charm. It has 100 rooms, a popular restaurant and lounge, a large pool, daily lunch buffet and free cable movies. Rates are $65 double.

Places to Eat

Magnolia Cafe (☎ 504-635-6528), 121 E Commerce St, is nothing to look at, but the food's tasty and includes pizzas, po-boys (around $5) and Mexican selections (up to $10). It's open Sunday and Monday from 11 am to 4 pm, Tuesday to Saturday 10 am to 8 pm.

Good food, local artists and their works have made *D'John's* (☎ 504-635-6982), Hwy 61 just south of St Francisville, a favorite for seafood, steaks and barbecue. Selections run $6 to $16. It's open Sunday to Friday 11 am to 9 pm, Saturday 11 am to 2 pm.

Myrtles Plantation (☎ 504-635-6276), 7747 Hwy 61, an allegedly haunted house, offers tours and serves good, moderately priced food.

Contemporary local luxury takes the form of *The Bluffs on Thompson Creek* (☎ 504-634-5088), 6495 Freeland Rd, two miles south of St Francisville, where there's a lodge, a golf course designed by Arnold Palmer and a club house restaurant that serves Louisiana specialties as well as steaks and seafood. Dine indoors or outdoors for breakfast, lunch and dinner. It's busy March to April and October to November.

Getting There & Away

There's no commercial transportation into St Francisville. You can reach it by car on Hwy 61 or I-110 from Baton Rouge from the south and from Natchez, Mississippi, from the north. Hwy 10 enters town from the west bank of the Mississippi and runs east-west across the state from the Mississippi state line.

From Baton Rouge, you can stop along the way at Port Hudson State Commemorative Area (see below). Signs indicate that Hwy 61 is a scenic highway; it's true only if you enjoy seeing roadside petrochemical plants.

AROUND ST FRANCISVILLE
Port Hudson Commemorative Area

One of the bloodiest battles of the Civil War was fought here to protect Port Hudson and control the Mississippi River. Today, the park has a museum, outdoor exhibits, picnic areas with water, grills and restrooms and six miles of wooded trails that connect battery positions and earthworks used during the battle.

The area (☎ 504-654-3775), 756 W Plains-Port Hudson Rd (off Hwy 61) is in Zachary, 13 miles south of St Francisville. It's open daily from 9 am to 5 pm. Admission is $2 for adults; seniors and children are free.

Tunica Hills Wildlife Management Area

This 3366-acre area has rugged hills, bluffs and mixed hardwood forests ideal for hiking, birding and watching wildlife. The woods are thick, and the climbs challenging due to rough footing and hills. You can hike to a ridge and look out over the Mississippi River. February and March are the best times to go, when it's cool and the spring flowers are opening.

As in many wilderness areas, beware of snakes. A state wildlife biologist described those found here as 'the prettiest and largest copperheads and rattlesnakes I've ever seen.'

Tunica Hills (☎ 504-765-2360) is located on Hwy 66 in Tunica. To get there, take Hwy 61 north from St Francisville about 3½ miles, then turn west onto Hwy 66 for 17 miles. You'll see an Exxon Country Grocery (with a friendly proprietor). Turn left a hundred yards past the grocery onto a blacktop road, which turns to gravel. Small signs are posted on an iron gate indicating the entrance. You can pick up a free map at the Backpacker (☎ 504-925-2667), 7656 Jefferson Hwy, in Baton Rouge.

Cajun Country

Cajun Country – officially 'Acadiana' – encompasses a 22-parish region of south Louisiana that fans out from its center in Lafayette to the Texas border in the west and to the Mississippi River in the east. Home to the largest French-speaking minority in the nation, the region is named for the French settlers exiled from L'Acadie (now Nova Scotia) who sought refuge in the bayou country starting in 1763.

Known around the world for its cuisine, music and spirited *bons temps*, Cajun Country consists of three distinct subregions revolving around Lafayette, the self-proclaimed Capital of French Louisiana. North and west of Lafayette is the Cajun prairie, an area of cattle ranches and rice cultivation settled by Cajuns and Creoles – now a center for Cajun and zydeco music. South of Lafayette, swinging east in an arc out to below New Orleans, is the Cajun wetlands region – a maze of bayous and swamps that held the earliest Cajun settlements. West of Lafayette is the Cajun coast – a ruggedly remote region along the Gulf of Mexico headed up by the port city of Lake Charles.

Lafayette, a worthy destination in itself, makes an easy base of operations for exploring the rest of the region. While some rural attractions might be hit-or-miss depending on the time of your visit (the best thing is to schedule your visit to coincide with a local festival), Lafayette and adjacent communities offer a guaranteed good time throughout the week year-round. You might start in Lafayette, which is a straight shot west from New Orleans via I-10 or through the wetlands region via Hwy 90 – then plant yourself in whatever town or region you take a particular liking to. The most picturesque choices are along Bayou Teche (east and south of Lafayette). The earthiest choices (author's picks) are Gibson in the wetlands and Mamou in the prairie. An odd sleeper choice is Holly Beach, near great bird-watching refuges, for travelers with time on their hands who have had too much of a good thing elsewhere.

History

The history of Acadiana begins off the Atlantic coast of Canada 16 years before the Pilgrims landed at Plymouth Rock. Here a band of French settlers founded L'Acadie, named after the legendary Greek paradise Arcadia. Acadians lived a relatively peaceful agrarian life for more than a century despite the contests France and England waged for control of the island.

HIGHLIGHTS

- Sampling crawfish and other seafood specialties, boudin, andouille sausage, smoked meats, and red beans and rice
- Enjoying local Cajun music, zydeco and swamp pop at block parties, festivals and night spots such as Richard's in Lawtell near Opelousas, El Sido's in Lafayette and Clifton's Club in Loreauville
- Mardi Gras and small-town parades and festivals
- Taking a swamp tour on board a boat for the best view of the wetlands environment

With the fateful treaty of Utrecht in 1713, the British took control and renamed the island Nova Scotia (Latin for 'New Scotland'). Thirty years later, the British decided to expel the Acadians to prevent any alliance with the French (who continued to compete with the British for other North American territories). The governor demanded that the Acadians swear an unqualified oath of allegiance to the British crown and Anglican church as a pretense for their expulsion. When the Acadians refused, deportation began in 1755.

Ten thousand Acadian men, women and children were banished from the island and forced to sail on boats that were not seaworthy. Half lost their lives. Survivors faced a diaspora the Acadians call 'le Grand Dérangement' (the Great Upheaval) that lasted nearly two decades. Thousands headed down the Atlantic Coast to American colonies, but by the most charitable accounts the colonies were unprepared to receive them. Often the Catholic peasants endured hostile treatment from Protestant settlers, and in many cases the refugees were sent away by communities that refused to accept them.

Louisiana, as a historically French settlement in North America, soon became the idealized destination for the Acadians. Between 1765 and 1785, dispersed groups of Acadian refugees from American colonies, Nova Scotia, the West Indies and France arrived in New Orleans. Though by this time the territory was governed by Spain, the Spanish welcomed fellow Catholic settlers. The refined Creoles of New Orleans, however, were less inclined toward the motley refugees, and they shunted the Acadians off to western swamplands. (Longfellow's epic, 1847 poem *Evangeline* – much revered in Acadiana – relates the tragic Acadian history from L'Acadie to Louisiana through the story of long-separated lovers. Today a 'Queen Evangeline' and 'King Gabriel' are named each year to reign over Mardi Gras festivities.)

The Acadians needed to live off the land and adapt to an environment radically different from the one they had left. They were helped by the local Houma and Chitimacha Indians, who taught their new neighbors to trap, hunt and catch fish with their bare hands (a technique still practiced today). They also learned about the sacred crawfish – a crustacean native to the bayou that figured prominently in the Chitimacha creation myth as well as in their diet. The Acadians came to endure the region's devastating floods and hurricanes.

Within a generation these exiles had so firmly reestablished themselves that they became the dominant culture in south Louisiana, absorbing other ethnic groups around them. Most of the French Creoles, Spanish, Germans, Anglo-Americans and Afro-Haitians eventually adopted Acadian traditions and language. (Besides traditional French names, such Acadian surnames as Soirez, Castille, Farris, Reed, McCauley, O'Connor and Israel illustrate the Acadian absorption of many different groups.)

During the antebellum period, as cotton ruled much of the South, it was sugar cane that came to dominate southern Louisiana. Some Acadians became planters, but most were forced off prime plantation land into backwater swamps. During the Civil War, Acadians joined Confederate forces as Union troops invaded and confiscated many plantations, and they fought in the Battle of Lafourche Crossing (not far from Houma). After the war, freed slaves joined communities of free people of color, Afro-Haitians and other Louisianians of African descent. These French-speaking blacks came to define themselves and their culture as Creole.

On the prairies north of Lafayette, Acadians and Creoles maintained Brahmin cattle ranches and developed traditions more closely associated with neighboring Texas than wetland Acadiana. (Le courir de Mardi Gras is a horseback run common on the prairies – see sidebar in the Cajun Prairie section.) On the prairies, rice replaced cotton late in the 19th century. The solid clay foundation holds the water necessary for rice cultivation.

For several generations many Acadians were largely unschooled and unlettered,

LOUISIANA

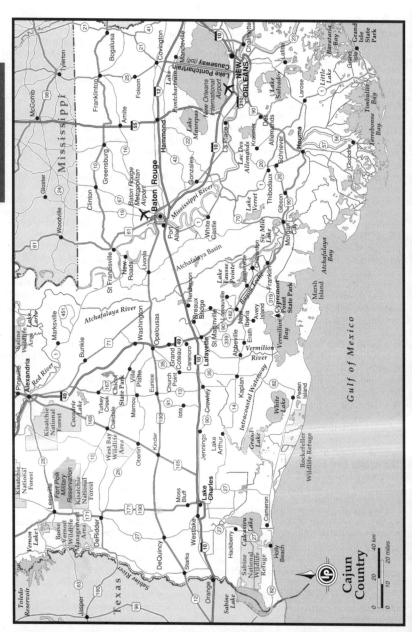

Cajun
Country

and so speaking French became associated with cultural inferiority in Louisiana. In 1916, the Heure de la Honte (Time of Shame) began. For 40 years, Louisiana's Board of Education enforced a ban prohibiting students from speaking French in school and on school grounds. The following two generations of Acadians would be disciplined for using their mother tongue. (As one old-timer recalled, 'You could *curse* on school grounds but not speak French!')

In the 1940s, WWII had a tremendous impact on local soldiers, especially those who had never been outside the region. Blacks identifying themselves as Creole often found that the army did not classify them among black troops, who received more prejudicial treatment. Acadian soldiers in France discovered that the language and culture they'd been told to forget helped them survive and made them valuable as interpreters. After the war, returning GIs immersed themselves in their own culture, sparking a drive to renew cultural pride after decades of debasement.

In 1955, local politician Dudley Le Blanc used the bicentennial anniversary of Acadian expulsion from Nova Scotia to remind the community of its enduring roots and rally them in support of their heritage. In 1964, Cajun musicians were invited to perform at the Newport Folk Festival, exposing the folk music and culture to a national audience.

In 1968, the state of Louisiana officially recognized the Cajun cultural revival by creating the Council for the Development of French in Louisiana (CODOFIL) to encourage the use of the suppressed local language. Teachers from France, Belgium and Canada were brought in to reintroduce French to schoolchildren and to inspire pride in French heritage. Efforts were not restricted to education; CODOFIL also organized a Cajun music festival to invigorate the folk music movement.

In 1901 oil was first discovered in the region, and the first oil well was dug in 1947, but the oil boom in the 1970s and subsequent bust in the 1980s had the most dramatic effect on the local economy. As in the plantation era, only a few Acadians were enriched by the oil crop. Most local oil workers were devastated when prices dropped in the 1980s; many left the region in search of jobs.

In 1973, the I-10 bridge (an engineering marvel) across the 18-mile-wide Atchafalaya Basin was completed after seven years of construction. This arduous last link of the nation's interstate network made this part of south Louisiana readily accessible to outsiders for the first time – the last 25 years have brought radical change to communities that had been relatively isolated for centuries.

From the late 1980s to the present, a renaissance of interest in Cajun music and cuisine has brought an unprecedented number of visitors to Acadiana to celebrate the crawfish once decried as 'poor man's lobster,' to speak the language once banned, and to hear the homespun accordion music many local youth had once been embarrassed to admit their families played. Cajun chefs and musicians are now internationally known and respected for their formerly maligned folk traditions.

Acadian Folklife

Until the late 20th century, the geographically isolated Acadians lived off the bounty of the land around them. To them, the swamps were enormous pantries of fish, crawfish, bullfrogs and turtles. (Alligator meat was not generally consumed before the 1970s.) In the spring, families would harvest crawfish and live on commercial fishing; net-making was an important skilled craft. When water levels dropped in summer and fall, families trapped fur-bearing animals and sold their pelts. Spanish moss – used for mattress stuffing – was harvested as their only cash crop.

The *pirogue* – a shallow skiff rowed standing up – was an indispensable means of transport in bayou country. While steamboats and railroads opened up the region somewhat, many Acadian villages remained isolated well into the 20th century, and bayous remained the primary routes for travel and commerce. Originally, pirogues were made from cypress trunks; after the cypress was clear-cut earlier this century, the boats were made of plywood or fiberglass. Small wooden pirogues remain in common use today.

Acadian vernacular architecture was also distinctive. A popular image of Cajun life is of swampers living on houseboats and pioneer cabins on swamp islands, but there were also town houses – some still standing today – that reflected European design. As easily seen at Acadian village attractions in Lafayette, the typical Acadian cottage was a 1½-story, four-room house with a front porch and steep-gabled roof. Roof supports evolved from early European design, and exposed beams also reflect French influence. Because of the heat and fear of fire, kitchens were detached and set behind the house. *Bousillage*, a mixture of Spanish moss and clay, served to insulate walls and chimneys. Unusual features on some houses included a *garconnière*, an attic reserved for young men, which had its own entrance from the front porch and another separate entrance for guests or travelers who would be put up for several days before continuing their journey. Access to the bayou was critically important, so waterside lots in town tended to be long and narrow.

A close-knit family life has been the foundation of Acadian society, and to this day celebrations surround births, marriages and deaths. An interesting facet of weddings is the Money Dance, during which participants pin money to the bride's veil. Other communal gatherings include the winter hog slaughter *la boucherie* (even some locals consider this a grisly affair) and *les coups de mains*, 'helping hands,' the Acadian equivalent of barn-raising. As devout Catholics, community spiritual life was centered in the church, though geographic isolation led to *la messe blanche* (the white Mass), prayer services conducted by laymen, and home altars once supplemented churches as a place to worship. On All Saints' Day, the above-ground crypts of ancestors were washed and decorated, and a

priest delivered Mass by candlelight in the cemetery. Shrines to the saints, particularly to St Mary, considered the patron saint of Acadians, were built throughout the region.

While most surrounding ethnic groups came to adopt Acadian traditions – isolated local Indians continue to speak a more archaic form of French – their various influences can perhaps best be recognized in the Cajun music distinct to south Louisiana. From the Indians, the Acadians borrowed wailing styles and new dance rhythms; from blacks they learned the blues; and from Anglo-Americans they picked up new fiddle tunes designed for Virginia reel dances and hoe downs. The Spanish contributed the guitar; Afro-Haitians brought in a syncopated West Indian beat; and Jewish-German immigrants imported accordions. Zydeco developed concurrently as a more blues-influenced style performed by black Creoles. With the introduction of rock 'n' roll, 'swamp pop' was born, with Cajun rhythms and French lyrics transforming American popular music. (A favorite radio oldie is 'Va Johnny Va.') Local radio programs today broadcast a great variety of authentic south Louisiana music; some programs are in French.

Cajun dances called *fais-do-do* take their name from local baby-talk for 'go to sleep.' The story goes that the nickname was inspired by mothers who wanted their babies to fall asleep at dance halls so that they could get back out and dance. A high-stepping waltz and two-step jitterbug were common dances at a fais-do-do. (The uninitiated will find that locals are happy to demonstrate traditional steps to newcomers.)

Beyond the famous crawfish of Acadiana, visitors today feast on such traditional foods as cracklins (fried pork rinds) and boudin – a sausage that can be 'blanc' or the more daring 'rouge.' Andouille sausage, jambalaya, gumbo, alligator and turtle are also found at restaurants throughout the region. (See the Sacred Mudbug sidebar on crawfish in this chapter, and the Boudin: Rouge et Blanc sidebar in the Central Louisiana chapter.)

The Sacred Mudbug

According to the mythology of the Chitimacha who still inhabit their ancestral bayou homelands, the universe was founded by the crawfish, a freshwater crustacean (the official state crustacean) native to the swamps of south Louisiana. The crawfish resembles in appearance and taste a miniature lobster – in fact, it was once nicknamed the 'poor man's lobster.' Today in Cajun Country, it's often called a mudbug (but never crayfish, the name the same critter goes by in other states).

The Acadians who settled the region in 1755 considered the crawfish humble fare. In the 1930s, crawfish were served free in local pubs to push beer sales. Commercial fishing did not begin until after WWII, when a fishery for wild crawfish was developed in the Atchafalaya Basin near Henderson. By 1980, Louisiana had 40 crawfish processing plants. Yet changing water levels in the wild produce erratic harvests, so aquaculture techniques began to be introduced in the 1960s. Pond farming began near Eunice, extending the season, increasing production and ushering in a golden age of crawfish farming. Farmers quickly discovered that crawfish make an ideal rotation crop in the rice fields. Today ponds ranging in size from hundreds to thousands of acres are flooded in fall and drained in summer. Of 30 different local species, two make up the commercial crop – the red swamp crawfish *(Procambarus clarkii)* and the white river crawfish *(Procambarus zonangulus)*.

According to LSU's Agricultural Center, the combined annual yield ranges from 75 million to 105 million pounds. The total economic impact on the Louisiana economy is estimated at $125 million annually. They also estimate that 7000 people depend directly or indirectly on the crawfish industry, nearly all in Acadiana. St Martin Parish maintains the highest yield by far, with surrounding parishes of Vermilion and Acadia vying for second place.

Foreign Competition The importance of the crawfish industry in south Louisiana makes the availability of less-expensive crawfish from China a threat to the local industry. Louisianians have pressed the federal government for an import tariff to stem the tide of the foreign alternative.

'This strikes at our culture, our food and our jobs,' Dwight Landreneau, aquaculture agent for the state's Cooperative Extension Service, told the *New York Times* in May 1997. He added, 'The crawfish industry is not major corporations. It's not Xerox. It's not Monsanto. It's individual families.' Importers counter that consumers benefit from lower prices and that the Louisiana industry is simply unready to accept that it no longer enjoys a monopoly on the product.

The International Trade Commission is currently reviewing the proposed levy, which Louisiana producers say would enable them to remain competitive.

Crawfish Boils The traditional way to enjoy crawfish in Cajun Country is at a Friday night crawfish boil, a communal gathering of family and neighbors that often includes music and dancing. Live crawfish are cooked in a vat of boiling water laced with spices along with potatoes and corn. The crawfish are often served on large tin trays, with empty trays ready for discarded shells and plenty of paper towels for clean-up. Accomplished mudbug suckers tear off the head, suck out the 'butter,' tear off the back fin, pull out the vein and squeeze out the morsel of white tail meat. The crawfish season peaks from March through May, with limited availability from January to June. ■

Ecology & Environment

The Atchafalaya (ahtch-ah-fah-LIE-ah) Basin is the predominant geographical feature of south Louisiana. The Atchafalaya River courses from around the southwest corner of Mississippi along a straight shot south to the Gulf of Mexico. As the most direct and steepest route, the Mississippi River would have long ago opted to take this course if it weren't for the Army Corps of Engineers' extraordinary efforts to confine the Mississippi to the channel around New Orleans. The corps has also contained the Atchafalaya flood plain into a basin 20 miles wide and 80 miles long by constructing earthen levees along its length down to Morgan City, where the river then pours out to the Gulf. One of the most complex managed water systems in the world, the basin drains flood waters from as many as 38 states.

The watery 134-sq-mile wilderness within is dense with the stumps of bald cypress (the official state tree) that remain from the clear-cut lumbering in the first half of the 20th century. The black willow you see all over is actually not native, nor is the water hyacinth, which was imported from Japan. Though it blooms with a beautiful lavender flower, the hyacinth is actually a nuisance that easily chokes bayous and channels. Fields of white water lilies and other aquatic plants fill the landscape.

The nutria, an aquatic mammal with webbed feet, thrives in Louisiana's bayous.

Throughout the swamp you can see alligators, frogs, turtles, snakes and an odd fur-bearing South American rodent called a nutria. Deer, raccoons, rabbits, squirrels and snakes inhabit the larger swamp islands. Herons (which have yellow legs), egrets (black legs) and ibises are commonly seen. Owls, anhingas and brown pelicans (the official state bird) are a few of the hundreds of other bird species seen in the swamp. Besides serving as breeding grounds for crawfish, swamp waters are rumored to harbor elusive giant catfish – a world record 128-pounder was caught in the basin in 1986.

Oil deposits under the basin drew interest as far back as 1901. Today the basin is dotted with oil rigs, and the petroleum industry is a mainstay of the local economy. Drilling has hastened natural erosion, contributing to environmental problems in the region.

Mismanagement of coastal lands in combination with natural forces has led to a catastrophic land-loss problem. While most places account for erosion in geological time, south Louisiana loses its land in human time. The Coalition to Restore Coastal Louisiana estimates that 25 sq miles of coastal land are reclaimed by the Gulf each year. At this rate, they suggest, Houma and New Orleans are projected to be on the coast within 50 years. In 1989 a state initiative committed petroleum taxes to try to reverse this trend.

Language

The term 'Cajun' itself is an American derivative of Acadian (which is quickly pronounced kay-DEEYN in French). Despite its faintly derogatory origin (reminiscent of Injun), the term is widely accepted by locals. (The football team of the University of Southwestern Louisiana is called the 'Ragin' Cajuns.') 'Acadian' is the most proper historical term. The 22-parish region considered Cajun Country is officially called Acadiana, an accidentally lyrical combination of homeland Acadie and Louisiana inspired by a typo that affixed an extra 'a' onto Acadian. (Some dissenting locals insist that Acadiana is more a state of mind than a geographical destination.)

The 700,000 Acadians in southern Louisiana constitute the largest French-speaking minority in the US. Acadians speak their own dialect of French that is as different from Parisian French as hard-core Southern-accented English is from British English. As would be true for such different English speakers, such varied French speakers can make themselves understood with close attention. This was actually more of an issue in the past; as French language instruction is being resuscitated after decades of suppression, people are now learning a more standard form of French. French-speaking travelers will find that bilingual folks in the tourist industry speak a more easily understood dialect than local swampers might, and that the folks most likely to speak French are old people and schoolchildren. Many printed materials are bilingual, and the area draws French-speaking travelers from Canada, France and other French-speaking countries around the world. Lafayette's Festival International de Louisiane each April celebrates French-speaking cultures around the globe. Lafayette's University of Southwestern Louisiana is a center for Francophonic studies.

Special Events

If you can plan a trip around an Acadian festival, all the better. Whether the festival focuses on food or music, there's sure to be plenty of both at every one.

January
> Lafayette holds its *Mid-Winter Fair & Rodeo* mid-month, and the *Louisiana Boudin Festival* is held in Broussard.

February
> Krewe balls, pageants and dances are held all month up to Mardi Gras, when parades and the unique Acadian *Courir de Mardi Gras* take place throughout Acadiana (see sidebar in the Cajun Prairie section).

March
> Eunice hosts the *World Championship Crawfish Étouffée Cook-off* in the latter part of the month.

Cajun Mardi Gras

Lafayette's Mardi Gras celebration is second in size only to New Orleans. Like New Orleans, Mardi Gras season in Lafayette officially opens on Epiphany, and krewes organize balls as momentum grows to Fat Tuesday. Some traditions are distinct to Acadiana: The royal couple reigning over Mardi Gras festivities is called Queen Evangeline and King Gabriel – symbolizing the long-lost Acadian lovers of Longfellow's epic poem. Lafayette hosts a five-day festival preceding Mardi Gras, with krewe parades all day the Saturday before. (See Facts for the Visitor for upcoming Mardi Gras dates.)

Small towns throughout the region host Mardi Gras parades, such as Lafayette, Carencro, Youngsville, Kaplan, New Iberia, Sunset, St Martinville, Jeanerette, Franklin, Jennings and Morgan City. A Mardi Gras Folklife Festival is held in Iota. To hear tell, some jaded folks who have had enough of carnival in New Orleans prefer the folksy parades and small town Mardi Gras celebrations throughout Acadiana. ∎

April
> Lafayette's six-day *Festival International de Louisiane* celebrates French-speaking cultures around the world with films, visual arts, theatrical performances and, of course, plenty of French-influenced food and music (around the last weekend). The city holds its *Downtown Alive* block party on Friday nights from early April through June and again from September through November. Eunice hosts the *Cajun Music Festival* mid-month.

May
> The *Zydeco Extravaganza* is held in Lafayette at the end of the month, and the *Cajun Heartland State Fair* takes place in the CajunDome mid-month. Breaux Bridge simultaneously celebrates the *Crawfish Festival* with Cajun music and the *Creole Crawfish Festival* with zydeco music early in the month. Mamou hosts its *Cajun Music Festival* late in the month.

June
> *Le Festival de Viande Boucanée* (the smoked meat festival) is held in Ville Platte near the end of the month.

LOUISIANA

July

Independence Day celebrations are held on July 4 in Lafayette, Erath and New Iberia. In Des Allemands (see the New Orleans chapter), the Catfish Festival is on. Kaplan celebrates Bastille Day on or around July 14.

August

The Cajun Music Awards Festival and Reggae Fest are held in Lafayette early in the month. The Festival of Riches in New Iberia is also held in early August. Mid-month, a shrimp festival is held in Delcambre. The Louisiana Shrimp & Petroleum Festival in Morgan City is held toward the end of the month.

September

The Saturday before Labor Day, the Southwest Louisiana Zydeco Music Festival brings together a dozen zydeco bands for a 13-hour-long concert in Plaisance, near Opelousas. Lafayette's Festivals Acadiens on the third weekend draws crowds of 100,000 to its music festival featuring Cajun and zydeco bands, its food festival and its native crafts festival featuring artisans, storytellers and boat-builders. Lafayette simultaneously hosts a Creole Family Festival at Vermilionville. The Rayne Frog Festival is in the middle of September. The Louisiana Sugar Cane Festival is held in New Iberia at the end of the month.

October

There's the Germanfest in Rayne, Cattle Festival in Abbeville (early in the month), Cotton Festival in Ville Platte, International Rice Festival in Crowley (both mid-month) and Alligator Festival in Franklin. Eunice also hosts the Cajun Prairie Folklife Festival in mid-October.

November

Abbeville's Celebration of the Giant Omelet consumes 5000 eggs early in the month. Basile holds a swine festival with contests and rides in early November. Port Barre holds its Cracklins Festival mid-month.

December

Throughout the month, Lafayette and surrounding parishes light up special decorations for Christmas, notably in Lafayette's Acadian Village and in St Martinville.

Getting There & Around

Lafayette is 129 miles west of New Orleans via I-10 (around 2½ hours) or 165 miles and up to a full day's leisurely drive along Hwy 90. The scenic route starts from I-310 west of the New Orleans airport to Hwy 90. You might detour as early as Des Allemands for food or Kraemer for a swamp tour (see the New Orleans chapter), or continue to the River Road following the levees of the Mississippi up to Thibodaux to see the Acadian Cultural Center and attractions there, meeting back up with Hwy 90 in Gibson. At Morgan City, Hwy 90 expands to a busy four-lane; the two-lane Hwy 182 is a more scenic parallel route. At New Iberia, Hwy 182 heads to Lafayette, or you might detour south to see the gardens on Avery Island or north to the pretty town of St Martinville. See South of Lafayette for these and other Cajun wetlands attractions.

Amtrak serves several towns in Acadiana, and even offers a Trails & Rails journey from New Orleans that features an NPS ranger delivering talks on the region's history and heritage.

Buses serve major cities in the region, but to discover the natural features, out-of-the-way restaurants and night life, you'll need a car. There are nice routes for bicycling, if you prepare for frequent south Louisiana rain. See Getting Around in Lafayette.

Lafayette

In 1821, a local Acadian named Jean Mouton donated a portion of his lands near the Bayou Vermilion for the construction of a church. (The church has since grown into the towering Cathedral of St John the Evangelist, reconstructed in 1918.) A settlement grew around the church, and in 1823, the Louisiana legislature created Lafayette Parish. Mouton then donated more land for a courthouse near the church, and the town of Vermilionville became the new parish seat. In 1844, Vermilionville was renamed in honor of the French Marquis de Lafayette.

Lafayette (population 100,000) has an older downtown in various stages of rehabilitation with chain sprawl along the

LOUISIANA

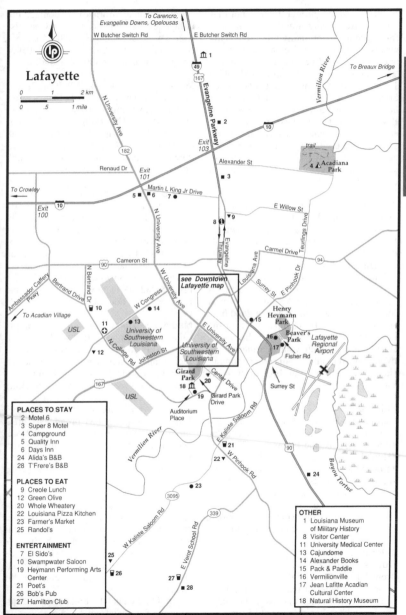

PLACES TO STAY
2 Motel 6
3 Super 8 Motel
4 Campground
5 Quality Inn
6 Days Inn
24 Alida's B&B
28 T'Frere's B&B

PLACES TO EAT
9 Creole Lunch
12 Green Olive
20 Whole Wheatery
22 Louisiana Pizza Kitchen
23 Farmer's Market
25 Randol's

ENTERTAINMENT
7 El Sido's
10 Swampwater Saloon
19 Heymann Performing Arts Center
21 Poet's
26 Bob's Pub
27 Hamilton Club

OTHER
1 Louisiana Museum of Military History
8 Visitor Center
11 University Medical Center
13 Cajundome
14 Alexander Books
15 Pack & Paddle
16 Vermilionville
17 Jean Lafitte Acadian Cultural Center
18 Natural History Museum

central four-lane through town – not that different from many American towns and, frankly, not exceptionally attractive. This makes it all the more remarkable that it manages to feel like someplace – in fact 'the Capital of French Louisiana'! With 17,000 Ragin' Cajuns at the University of Southwestern Louisiana (USL), Lafayette has a reputation as a groovy college town. If you can venture no farther than Lafayette (and this would be a shame), you can see the most civilized swamp in the world at the center of the USL campus, where signs warn 'Alligator Habitat – Keep Pets on Leashes.'

Three attractions in town shed light on Acadian heritage – the NPS Acadian Cultural Center and Vermilionville next door, and the Acadian Village across town. A trip with kids might take you to the Children's Museum downtown or to the Natural History Museum.

Lafayette's convenient position on I-10 ensures a great number of budget motel accommodations. Add to this its central location, and Lafayette makes a good base for discovering the Cajun prairie to the north and Cajun wetlands to the south. After you've gotten your bearings, however, move on to the small rural communities to experience Cajun life closer to the land.

Orientation

Lafayette is easily accessible via I-10. Most attractions are either on or accessible from exit 103A, the Evangeline Thruway (Hwy 167), which runs north and south through the center of town along two parallel one-way streets. Jefferson Blvd is the main street in the small, compact downtown. Pinhook Rd west of the Evangeline Thruway holds more sprawling suburban development southwest of the airport.

Information

Tourist Offices A short half-mile south from I-10 in between the northbound and southbound lanes of the Evangeline Thruway is a visitor center that distributes maps, guides and brochures daily until 5 pm.

For advance information, contact the Lafayette Convention & Visitors Commission (☎ 318-232-3808, 800-346-1958,. Net), Box 52066, Lafayette, LA 70505. From Canada, call ☎ 800-543-5340.

Money Local banks and ATMs are linked to national networks. Three banks offer currency exchanges: Bank One's main office (☎ 318-236-7000) at 200 W Congress St downtown; First National Bank (☎ 318-265-3377) at 600 Jefferson Blvd downtown; and Whitney National Bank (☎ 318-264-6158) at 911 Lee Ave.

Post & Communications The main post office downtown (☎ 318-232-4910), 101 Jefferson Blvd at E Cypress St, is right across the tracks east of the central commercial district. Mailboxes Etc (☎ 318-233-2139, fax 318-233-3256), 2851 Johnston St, provides mailing, packaging and fax services. Kinko's Copies (☎ 318-233-8124, fax 318-232-3001) provides photocopy and fax services 24 hours a day.

Media *The Times of Acadiana* – simply called the *Times* – is a free weekly tabloid that covers the news and events for the region much better than local newspapers. Look for it at the visitor center and select outlets – it's definitely worth tracking down.

Radio Acadie out of USL (KRVS 88.7 FM; ☎ 318-482-5668) broadcasts great programs devoted to authentic south Louisiana music. Their zydeco show is Saturday mornings; they broadcast the Liberty Theater *Rendez Vous des Cajuns* show on Saturday evenings; and they play more local music all day Sunday. Also tune in for information about upcoming events and club dates. (In fact, radio stations throughout Acadiana, unlike in most of the US, reflect the distinct musical heritage of the region. State folklorist Mike Luster says he drives through the region with one hand on the wheel and the other on the dial.)

On TV, channel 10 broadcasts a Cajun program Saturday from 4 to 5 pm.

LOUISIANA

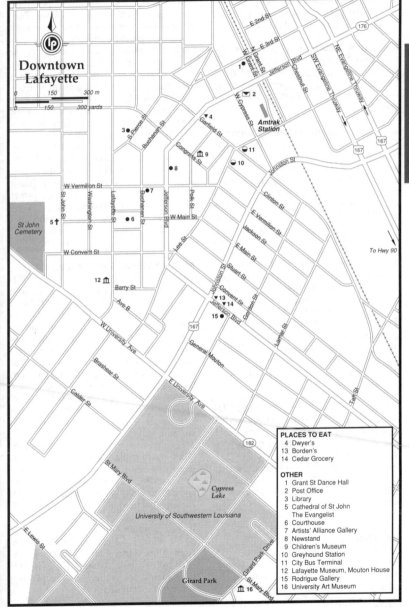

Downtown Lafayette

0 150 300 m
0 150 300 yards

To Hwy 90

PLACES TO EAT
4 Dwyer's
13 Borden's
14 Cedar Grocery

OTHER
1 Grant St Dance Hall
2 Post Office
3 Library
5 Cathedral of St John
   The Evangelist
6 Courthouse
7 Artists' Alliance Gallery
8 Newstand
9 Children's Museum
10 Greyhound Station
11 City Bus Terminal
12 Lafayette Museum, Mouton House
15 Rodrigue Gallery
16 University Art Museum

Bookstores Alexander Books (☎ 318-234-2096), 2001 W Congress St, sells new, used and rare editions along with periodicals.

Medical & Emergency Services The University Medical Center at 2390 W Congress St can be reached at ☎ 318-261-6000. The Lafayette police department can be reached at ☎ 318-261-8630; its fire department at ☎ 318-261-8700.

Jean Lafitte Acadian Cultural Center

The National Park Service (NPS) maintains three sites in Cajun Country that focus on Acadian heritage under the umbrella of Jean Lafitte National Historic Park (which also includes the Barataria Preserve around New Orleans). The Acadian Cultural Center in Lafayette is the most comprehensive of the three; the Cajun wetlands center is in Thibodaux, and the Cajun prairie center is in Eunice. All three have thoughtful, well-presented exhibits, artifacts and interpretive captions that provide an excellent introduction to regional history and cultural heritage.

Here in Lafayette, the center also screens a short film that dramatizes (and at times graphically overdramatizes) the plight of the Acadians at the hands of the British. But the exhibits and artifacts are very good, illuminating the distinct Acadian history and heritage.

Select souvenirs are sold, including handicrafts, musical instruments and CDs, along with a fine collection of books on history and cultural arts. The modern center also overlooks a small bayou that borders Vermilionville. The center (☎ 318-232-0789), 501 Fisher Rd, is open daily; admission is free. To reach it from the Evangeline Thruway, follow signs east on Pinhook Rd bordering the airport as Pinhook swings around a half-mile to Fisher Rd.

Vermilionville

This refined living history museum (☎ 318-233-4077), 1600 Surrey St, is the premier attraction in Lafayette. Within the 23-acre park, nicely landscaped walkways along a bayou and lake lead past craft shops, cabins and houses typical of Acadian villages from the mid-18th century to late 19th century. Docents in period costumes guide groups through the historic homes and explain the furnishings, architecture and folkways, while craftspeople demonstrate whittling, blacksmithing, weaving and other traditional crafts. Many guides speak from their own experience, and locals on tour may add their stories for an even more personal insight into the culture. Cajun bands perform several shows daily in the barn, and cooking demonstrations (with sample tastings) and other workshops are also scheduled. A cafe on the premises serves lunch, and a gallery sells locally made prints, cards, music boxes and woodwork. A gift shop sells souvenirs, cookware and toys. The museum is open daily. Admission is $8 for adults, $6.50 seniors, $5 students.

Acadian Village & Indian Museum

This living history village (☎ 318-981-2489) is like Vermilionville, but is more folksy, smaller and remote. You'd likely need to go out of your way to find it, but that adds to the sense of peaceful tranquillity here in the compact village. After purchasing tickets at the general store (cool drinks and shaded picnic tables available), follow a rippling brick path around a tiny bayou and over bridges to authentic restored houses, craft shops, a church and outbuildings. Ducks and farm animals roam about. Occasional Cajun music performances are held.

Located near the (artificial) mound, the **Missionary Indian Museum** is a sight in itself – huge paintings express pivotal events in local Native American history, and a historian is usually on hand to further explain. (Let him talk – it's air-conditioned!) The village and museum are open daily. Inclusive admission is $5.50 for adults, $4.50 seniors, $2 children. Follow signs from Ambassador Caffery Parkway, several miles south from I-10 exit 100. (Restaurants are available on this parkway south of the turnoff.)

Children's Museum

Carved out of the old brick Heymann's Grocery right downtown, this museum (☎ 318-232-8500), 201 E Congress St, opened in 1996 to entertain children ages two to 12 with a hands-on operating room and full-size ambulance, a mini TV studio, a recycled art station, a bubble factory and even an Acadian-style cottage with a huge blue-haired anatomical doll. The museum is open Tuesday to Saturday from 10 am to 5 pm; closed Sunday and Monday. Admission is $5 for children over age one. Free parking is available at the Polk St and Taylor St entrances. Kids will also like the giant whale mural around the corner across from Dwyer's café.

Natural History Museum

This sleek modern museum (☎ 318-268-5544), 637 Girard Park Dr, has changing exhibits on southern Louisiana's exotic natural environment and other science and nature displays. (On one visit, an interactive exhibit explored the sense of sound.) The planetarium here has a schedule of shows and telescope observation times. The museum is open daily (afternoons only on weekends), and admission is free.

University of Southwestern Louisiana

USL is the intellectual center for Acadian culture; in addition to publishing several well-respected journals on Cajun literature and history, they offer one of the country's only advanced degrees in Francophonic studies.

The highlight of a USL visit for many visitors is **Cypress Lake**, an incongruously civilized swamp in the center of campus behind the student union (short-term pay parking is available for visitors here on McKinley off University Ave).

The **University Art Museum** (☎ 318-482-5326) maintains a permanent collection of primarily 19th and 20th-century paintings by Louisiana and American artists, along with some Southern folk art and Japanese prints, in galleries in two locations on campus: in modern Fletcher Hall on E Lewis and Girard Park Dr, and in a Greek Revival plantation-style house at 101 Girard Park Dr down the street. They're open weekdays only. Admission is $2 adults, $1 seniors, no charge for those under 18.

Acadiana Park Nature Trail & Station

This 42-acre mature bottomland forest remains relatively undisturbed, and it is preserved by the city in cooperation with the Natural History Museum as Acadiana Park (☎ 318-261-8448). A subdivided three-mile loop trail winds under a canopy of hardwoods and over a 'coulee' (COO-lee, from the French word for 'pour') that streams into the Vermilion River in wet weather. The park is an oasis in the midst of urbanization for birds, fish and such larger mammals as squirrels, opossum, raccoons, rabbits, armadillos and even gray foxes. Spring is the best time for bird watching, when migratory birds return north and before the foliage grows too dense. The park is most dry in October and November when most of the flowering plants display a second bloom. From the first summer rain until fall, mosquitoes dominate the flood plain.

The treetop nature station office offers exhibits on the local habitat along with guided bird walks and monthly night hikes by reservation. It's open daily. The park is tucked south of I-10 and east of the Evangeline Thruway. Take the frontage road in front of the Northgate Mall north to Alexander; turn east and follow signs. (Camping is also available here; see Places to Stay.)

Other Attractions

On St John St downtown (look for the 10-story domed tower), the **Cathedral of St John the Evangelist** (☎ 318-232-1322) offers daily services and guided tours by request in the dramatic 700-seat Romanesque sanctuary built in 1918. The congregation dates back to 1821, before the town was founded. A huge 500-year-old live oak stands alongside.

You can see a collection of Mardi Gras costumes at the city's historic house museum. The **Lafayette Museum/Mouton House** (☎ 318-234-2208), 1122 Lafayette St, opens the antique-studded 19th-century home of the city's founder and former governor to public tours for $3 adults, $2 for seniors, students and children. They decorate lavishly at Christmastime.

The **Artists' Alliance Gallery** (☎ 318-233-7518), 125 W Vermilion St downtown, showcases the work of local artists and hosts such occasional events as a 'coffeehouse series' featuring performances by local poets, writers and musicians. The haunting stare of the regionally popular, yellow-eyed Blue Dog surrounds you at the **Rodrigue Gallery** (☎ 318-232-6398), 1206 Jefferson Blvd. The artist George Rodrigue has reproduced his pet's image on many paintings and prints.

Next to Evangeline Downs (see Spectator Sports), a highlight of the 25,000-sq-foot **Louisiana Museum of Military History** (☎ 318-235-4322) is to sit in an army tank and aim your sights at highway traffic. The museum also features hands-on weaponry, touchable control panels and climb-aboard jeeps. It's closed on Monday. Adult admission is $5, children $2.50.

Activities

The first thing a visitor to Cajun Country needs to do is to get on out into the swamp – see the sidebar on Swamp Tours in this chapter. At Lake Martin, 15 minutes east of Lafayette (see Breaux Bridge), a seven-mile trail leads around the lake (a rare opportunity for hikers to experience the swamp). For forest hikes, the Acadiana Park (see above) maintains a subdivided loop trail for a maximum three-mile hike. For short and civilized city walks, follow the nicely landscaped paths around Girard Park at Girard Park Dr and St Mary Blvd – a nice spot for picnics or naps.

For outdoor adventures, the primary resource is Pack & Paddle (☎ 318-232-5854, 800-458-4560), 601 E Pinhook Rd. This outfitter organizes biking, kayaking,

canoeing and hiking trips throughout the region, from casual Saturday morning rides out to Cajun bakeries in the countryside to elaborate six-day excursions. They rent bikes, distribute bike maps and guides and host classes in kayaking, hiking and in-line skating. They publish a free tabloid, *Outside Scoop*, listing their full slate of events; it's available in their store and around town. A particularly scenic trip is their 10-mile paddling tour 'Sunset on Bayou Teche' between Loreauville and New Iberia (around $25 for canoe or kayak, guide and transportation).

Places to Stay

Lafayette has the widest choices of accommodations in the region. Listings for Lafayette and some adjacent communities follow here, but visitors should be aware of highlights elsewhere: for houseboat adventures, see Henderson; for choice swamp cabins, see Gibson; for bottom-dollar room rates, see Mamou; and for great-value vacation cabin rental and camping, see listings for the region's state parks.

Camping *Acadiana Park* (☎ 318-261-8448), 1201 E Alexander St, has been a popular camping area for over five thousand years according to the ranger station. Today they offer 75 woodsy sites (some for tents only) for around $9 a night in a bottomland forest (see Acadiana Park Nature Trail & Station above). On higher ground but more exposed, the *KOA Kampground* (☎ 318-235-2739), I-10 exit 97 in Scott, offers 180 sites, as well as cabins and tent sites, right off the interstate, with a pool, mini-golf and playground for $19 a night. Note that frequent rains and moisture may make RV camping a surer bet than tents, though hearty locals canoe out to barely surfaced swamp islands and tent-camp in all kinds of weather.

Motels By virtue of its location off the interstate between two dry stretches to either side, Lafayette has many inexpensive, relatively new, well-tended and easily accessible budget motels to choose from.

Rooms are familiarly predictable and are all you need after a night of too much food and dancing. Most offer pools and at least continental breakfasts. There are 3500 guest rooms in town, and all the usual chains are present, such as Comfort Inn, Travelodge, Red Roof, and so on. Rates are fairly consistent from around $34 to $44 for doubles.

The best value is the new *Motel 6* (☎ 318-233-2055), 2724 NE Evangeline Thruway, nicely set back from Hwy 49, just north of I-10, with an inviting pool. Rates are $35 for a single. The *Super 8 Motel* (☎ 318-232-8826), 2224 NE Evangeline Thruway, just south of I-10, is in a more developed strip. Here you could walk to shops and restaurants, although the area is not designed for pedestrians. They also have a pool. If these two are full, there are two nonchain budget motels on either side of the same road beyond Motel 6; these are less well maintained, you pay for phone calls and neither has a pool.

The *Quality Inn* (☎ 318-232-6131), 1605 N University Ave, is an exit away (exit 101); it is out of the fray but also out of the 'zone.' Here, too, is a *Days Inn* (☎ 318-237-8880), 1620 N University Ave. Both have a pool.

Several other properties, both chain and independent, are sprinkled around town. These tend to be older facilities in nondescript areas that are less accessible to main thoroughfares but no cheaper, so the newer interstate motels are your best bet.

B&Bs If you want to make your room the main attraction, several high-end B&Bs in the region offer personalized hospitality (see also Inns & B&Bs in Facts for the Visitor). Small towns generally offer more B&B-style ambiance, but the Lafayette area has several choices as well. By the airport and railroad tracks, *Alida's* (☎ 318-264-1191, 800-922-5867), 2631 SE Evangeline Thruway (Hwy 90), offers four rooms in a 1902 Victorian for $75 and up. Resident host Doug Greenwald has been written up in the local papers for his cooking, so gourmet breakfasts are a

highlight. *T'Frere's* (☎ 318-984-9347, 800-984-9347), 1905 Verot School Rd, on a main street farther away from traffic (and very close to the zydeco Hamilton Club), also offers four rooms in a tidy 1880 two-story house. Prices of $75/90 for a single/double include a Cajun breakfast. All rooms in both B&Bs have private baths.

Places to Eat
Three restaurants in the area offer one-stop live entertainment and dancing along with full menus of regional cuisine: two in Lafayette (Prejean's and Randol's) and one 15 minutes to the east in Breaux Bridge (Mulate's). Of the three, Mulate's is hands-down the best time (see the Cajun Wetlands below). All of these are firmly on the beaten path and are a sure thing – on off nights when many nightclubs are dark, one or all of these are bound to offer good food, music and dancing.

Prejean's (PRAY-jhonz; ☎ 318-896-3247), 3480 Hwy 167N next to Evangeline Downs, has the most creative kitchen of the three. The dining room is lined with the chef's cooking trophies. The Cajun angel dish, for example, is sautéed crawfish, shrimp, artichokes and mushrooms in a cream sauce over black angel hair pasta. Entrees start around $16, or make a great tapas dinner sampling alligator, boudin balls and popcorn crawfish au jus from a dozen exotic appetizers (from $7). You can eat with the grown-ups near the band or at the bar. Prejean's is visible off Hwy 49 near Evangeline Downs; from exit 2 go north on Hwy 167 almost a mile.

Randol's (☎ 318-981-7080) at 2320 Kaliste Saloom Rd seems less notable than the other two. It offers plenty of delicious Cajun seafood and has a big dance floor, but it usually caters to a relatively quiet, suburban crowd.

The popular culinary landmark *Enola Prudhomme's Cajun Cafe* (☎ 318-896-3646), 4676 NE Evangeline Thruway in Carencro, is named for Enola Prudhomme, sister of the internationally famed Cajun chef Paul and author of several cookbooks.

Brand-name specials include eggplant pirogue, stuffed catfish and fried and blackened Cajun dishes, all served with fresh jalapeño bread. Look for the bright yellow 19th-century house off I-49 several miles north of I-10. It's also on many tourist itineraries (the parking lot is full of Saturns and Pathfinders), but has indisputably great food nevertheless. It's closed Sunday.

At the *Creole Lunch House* (☎ 318-232-8605) in the Northgate Mall, daily specials like chicken fricassee with black-eyed peas, corn, rice and gravy and a roll run you $4.50. Their specialty is Creole stuffed bread packed with ground meat, sausage and jalapeño peppers for $3. To find it, go around past the Montgomery Ward to the second parking lot and look for American Cookies; the lunch house is next door. They're open Monday through Saturday, 11 am to 6:30 pm.

For late nights or early starts, *Dwyer's* (☎ 318-235-9364), 323 Jefferson Blvd downtown, opens at 4 am for generous breakfasts and daily plate lunches served at the counter or at tables inside or out under umbrellas on the patio. Also downtown, *Cedar Grocery* (☎ 318-233-5460), 1115 Jefferson Blvd, makes good and cheap po-boys. Right down the street, the classic *Borden's* ice creamery (☎ 318-235-9291), 1103 Jefferson Blvd, dishes up fountain treats and milkshakes.

On the south side of town, the chain *Louisiana Pizza Kitchen* (☎ 318-237-5800), 1926 W Pinhook Rd, creates individual-size pizzas with such exotic ingredients as goat cheese, pesto and artichoke hearts. It's open daily from 10 am to 10 pm.

For a complete change from anything remotely local, the *Green Olive* (☎ 318-234-0004), on 2441 W Congress St out past the CajunDome, offers Lebanese specialties, including many meatless dishes. Their vegetarian combination plate includes a stuffed grape leaf, falafel, tabbouleh, lentils-and-rice mujadara and hummus with pita bread for $9 at dinner, $6 at lunch (also available as individual appetizers). Add around $2 for Lebanese beer. It's open for lunch on weekdays from 11 am to 2 pm

and for dinner on weekends from 5 to 9 pm.

A wholly vegetarian place near campus is the *Whole Wheatery* (☎ 318-269-0144), 927 Harding. For fresh produce, there's a farmers market on the corner of Kaliste Saloom and S Beadle Rds, just southwest of Pinhook.

Of course, locals don't take most of their meals in restaurants, but instead find cheap eats at markets, convenience stores and even gas stations, nearly all of which seem to keep a crock pot of hot boudin by the cash register. Check out the Shell station on the corner of Evangeline and Pinhook Rd, for example, for hot plates. If you're tired of the city altogether, a straight shot south to Erath will land you at the down-home Big John's Seafood Patio, a 20-minute ride (see the Cajun Wetlands section below).

Entertainment

To find out who's playing where, look around town for the free, weekly *Times*. Another free tabloid, *In Tune*, also carries entertainment listings. Upcoming performance schedules are also broadcast on Radio Acadie KRVS 88.7 FM.

In temperate months (April through June and again from September through October), the weekend gets started at the free *Downtown Alive!* block party on Jefferson Blvd from around 6 to 8 pm. Favorite local bands – playing everything from rockabilly and country to R&B and blues, with plenty of Cajun and zydeco music – pack the streets with revelers, stands sell beer and snacks, and the party continues at downtown bars.

For zydeco, *El Sido's* (☎ 318-235-0647), 1523 N St Antoine St, is a big welcoming cinder-block joint all yellow inside where they can usually cook up a Creole chicken plate in the kitchen out back. It's close to the interstate. The *Hamilton Club* (☎ 318-984-5583), 1808 Verot School Rd, is an old clapboard place farther out south of the airport. You can usually find a raucous scene at either one each weekend night; they seem to trade off.

The cavernous *Grant St Dance Hall* (☎ 318-237-2255), 113 W Grant St at Jefferson Blvd (off Jefferson at the tracks right downtown), books a variety of bigger acts (some nationally known) including blues, reggae, classic rock and lots of zydeco. There's lots of room to dance or stand around, depending on the band and crowd.

Bob's Pub (☎ 318-984-9540) at 104 Republic is a comfortable place to hear live blues most nights and a blues jam on Thursdays. It's in the strip mall across from Randol's on Kaliste Saloom Rd.

The popular *Poet's* (☎ 318-235-2355), tucked in the shopping center behind Pinhook and Kaliste Saloom Rds at 119 James Comeaux Rd, draws clean-cut college-plus audiences for crowd-pleasing dance music – rock 'n' blues, swamp pop, zydeco – and comedy.

Swampwater Saloon (☎ 318-269-9717), out near the CajunDome at the split of Bertrand and N Bertrand Dr, is a favorite oil worker dive for pool, hard women and swampy rock 'n' roll.

The CajunDome hosts large concerts by such national acts as Harry Connick Jr, and the Smashing Pumpkins. The Heymann Performing Arts Center (☎ 318-237-2787), at S College and Bendel Rds, hosts theatrical performances and dance. Tickets are available through Ticketmaster (☎ 800-488-5252).

Spectator Sports

The CajunDome, on W Congress St a couple miles west of downtown Lafayette, is the home of the University of Southwestern Louisiana's Ragin' Cajuns, ('Geaux Cajuns!' is their rally cry.) The CajunDome also holds major concerts, theatrical performances and fairs and festivals.

The horseracing track a mile north of I-10 on Hwy 49 is Evangeline Downs (☎ 318-896-7223), which formalizes a long-standing tradition of casual horseracing at 'bush' tracks throughout the region. Evangeline Downs is also commonly cited by locals as a landmark when giving directions.

Getting There & Away

Lafayette is most practically approached by car, but it has more varied alternatives to personal automobiles than many cities this size.

Air Lafayette regional airport (☎ 318-266-4400) is served by four major carriers and their subsidiaries: American Eagle, Atlantic Southeast, Continental and Northwest. The airport is at the Evangeline Thruway (Hwy 90) south of town.

Bus Greyhound runs bus service out of its station (☎ 318-235-1541) in a compact transit hub near the Amtrak station and city bus terminal south of Lafayette's central commercial district, at Grant St and Jefferson Blvd. (The area's not bad and a huge police station is nearby.) The station is within walking distance of an open business or two, but you would likely need a cab to your destination. Around six buses a day leave for and arrive from New Orleans, a three-hour trip ($18 one-way, $36 roundtrip).

Train Amtrak's *Sunset Limited* transcontinental route from Los Angeles to Jacksonville serves New Orleans with stops in several cities in Acadiana. The tracks roughly follow Hwy 90 from New Orleans, with stops in Schriever at an isolated outpost four miles south of Thibodaux (if the phone were busted, you'd be stranded), in New Iberia at a relatively inviting station in a developed area a short drive from the central commercial district (too long a walk with luggage), and in downtown Lafayette at Grant St and Jefferson Blvd. These stations all offer little more than a pay phone and waiting room, but taxi service is available from all. Trains run around three times weekly, so they aren't suitable for travel within Acadiana except by happenstance. Call for current schedules (☎ 800-872-7255) .

The Lafayette station is itself decrepit, but it's conveniently located right next to a huge police station and a block from transit terminals for Greyhound and city buses.

Amtrak Thruway provides coordinated service from Lafayette to Baton Rouge via Greyhound buses.

The Trails & Rails project brings NPS rangers aboard select trains to host educational programs about the region's history and heritage. Live music is often featured. At present these are offered in summertime only. Call the Jean Lafitte National Historic Park headquarters in New Orleans (☎ 504-589-4428) for more information.

Car Via I-10, Lafayette is around 2½ hours (129 miles) west of New Orleans. Via the more scenic Hwy 90, it's 35 miles longer and could take you a full day if you stopped off to eat and see a few sights along the way (and why else would you chose this route).

Once in Lafayette, note that the central stop-and-go thoroughfare, the Evangeline Thruway, slides into a full-fledged interstate freeway (I-49) as soon as you pass under the I-10 overpass. (I-49 accesses Cajun prairie towns to the north.) Hwy 90 meanders south through bayou country, at times as a four-lane bypass, at others as a two-lane slog through towns. The most scenic stretch of Hwy 90 is from the Mississippi River through Gibson. To avoid the industrialized, suburbanized stretch west of Morgan City, pop up to Hwy 182, which runs roughly parallel without the truck traffic.

Although gas stations are readily available, distances are long, and filling up at a convenient opportunity is a wise move.

Car rentals are available from Thrifty Car Rental (☎ 318-237-1282), 401 E Pinhook Rd; Enterprise (☎ 318-237-2864), 137 James Comeaux Rd; or Bruce's U-Save Auto Rentals (☎ 318-233-2120), 1413 Jefferson Blvd.

Getting Around

Again, while Lafayette offers more alternatives than many cities its size, a car is nevertheless indispensable to see the widely dispersed sights. Visitors on a bike tour or those intent on houseboating or staying at

a plantation B&B might not need a car if hosts arrange a shuttle from the airport or station.

Bus City of Lafayette Transit (COLT; ☎ 318-261-8570) runs buses from a convenient central terminal (☎ 318-237-7945) in the transit hub between the Greyhound station and the Amtrak station. Buses operate from 6:30 am to 6:30 pm Monday through Saturday (no service on many major holidays). The fare is 45¢ for adults, 30¢ for children five to 12. Routes are not designed with tourists in mind, yet a few routes serve major sights. Bus No 15 goes downtown and out to the CajunDome; bus No 25 goes to USL.

Taxi The Acadiana Cab Co (☎ 318-264-9707, 800-487-9707) provides cab and limousine service. Also try Yellow Cab at ☎ 318-237-9707. Both advertise restaurant delivery among their services.

Bicycle The outfitter Pack & Paddle (☎ 318-232-5854), 601 E Pinhook Rd at the Evangeline Thruway near the airport, rents bikes and distributes maps and guides to the more than 60 miles of marked bike routes in the region. They also organize guided trips, from casual Saturday morning rides to Acadian bakeries in the countryside to elaborate six-day trips through the Cajun prairie or to local Mardi Gras sights that include lodging and food. Call for their 'French Louisiana Bike Tours' brochure.

One scenic bike loop route runs 35 miles from downtown St Martinville through Bayou Teche country. Signs show a bicycle with the route No 31, but some signs may have been blown down by hurricanes, so it's best to follow a map.

Boat If you end up staying on a houseboat or camping at Lake Fausse Pointe State Park (see St Martinville below), you can use a motorboat to make excursions to dockside restaurants. If you can take bikes along, you can then bike from landings to nearby restaurants and sights.

The Cajun Wetlands

Southwest of Lafayette, historic Abbeville and its surrounding communities are well known for seafood restaurants and small-town festivals.

Swinging out in an arc southeast from Lafayette to the Mississippi River is the heart of the Cajun wetlands, roughly along where Hwy 90 is now. This route was once part of the Old Spanish Trail Highway network that traversed the continent from St Augustine to Los Angeles in the 1920s. The lowland area is covered with dense lush growth and cut through with a watery maze of swamps, bayous and lakes.

East of Hwy 90 are the compact towns along Bayou Teche (pronounced 'tesh') – principally St Martinville and New Iberia. This region is among the oldest settled in Acadiana and retains many historic sights. A detour from St Martinville leads to Lake Fausse Pointe State Park with its impressive campground, cabins and boat rentals. A detour from New Iberia leads to Avery Island, the home of McIlhenny Tabasco pepper sauce and an exotic garden.

South of New Iberia, Bayou Teche continues to parallel the four-lane Hwy 90, but the two-lane Hwy 182 is a scenic alternative that leads through Jeanerette and past the Chitimacha reservation before hooking back up with Hwy 90 at Centerville. Morgan City is a major industrial port on the Atchafalaya River at the leveed banks of the Atchafalaya Basin.

East of Morgan City, Gibson and neighboring Donner make an interesting stop on Bayou Black before entering the maze of bayous through and around Thibodaux and Houma.

ABBEVILLE

West of Hwy 90 south of Lafayette via Hwy 167, Abbeville holds two historic squares in its compact downtown along the Vermilion River. The visitor center (☎ 318-898-2491) is on the Hwy 14 bypass north of town at 7507 Veterans Memorial Dr, but Abbeville is not the kind of place you need a map to find your way about. Major highways lead to the center of town and around the courthouse square, a lively center of activity surrounded by storefronts constructed around the end of the 19th century.

St Magdalen Square hosts many of the town's festivals, along with theatrical performances by the local Abbey Players Theater troupe and art fairs under the oaks. The congregation of St Mary Magdalen Church on the bayou dates from 1856; the present sanctuary was built in 1910.

As the seat of cattle-producing Vermilion Parish, Abbeville is well recognized for the Louisiana Cattle Festival the first weekend in October, which features cattle shows, horse shows and plenty of local food, music and dance. The Celebration of the Giant Omelet the first weekend in November entails consuming, to hear tell, 5000 eggs. Festival highlights include the knighting of foreign guests into the Confrerie of the Worldwide Fraternity of the Omelet, an omelet-toss contest and an evening fais-do-do.

If you visit in fall, the smell of warmed sugar emanates from Steen's Syrup Mill at 119 Main St. Their syrup is a popular topping for pancakes and is available at markets and restaurants. Another five blocks south is the Riviana Rice Mill, which claims to be the oldest rice mill in the state.

But even with all these culinary landmarks, Abbeville is perhaps best known as the home of legendary oyster bars: *Dupuy's* (☎ 318-893-2336), at 108 S Main St, established in 1887, and *Blacks* (☎ 318-893-4266), at 319 Pere Megret St, open 25 years. Both restaurants, a block from one another and a block from the downtown bridge over the bayou, are closed Sunday and from May to August. *Shucks* (☎ 318-898-3311), 701 W Port St, is a newcomer to the scene with half-shell oysters priced comparably to the others at $4 a dozen, shuck'em shrimp for $6 and oyster loaf sandwiches for under $5. Find it where Hwy 167 dead-ends.

Abbeville is also the jumping-off point for the long drives into western Acadiana along Hwys 82 or 14. It might be wise to gas up before leaving.

ERATH

East of Abbeville in Erath, the **Acadian Heritage & Culture Museum** (☎ 318-233-5832), 203 S Broadway a block south of Hwy 14, holds Acadian history exhibits in three rooms within one of the oldest buildings in the area. The first room relates the local history of Erath in photographs. The second holds a replica of the Port Royal settlement in L'Acadie from 1603 to the 1755 exile. The Cajun room is devoted to a study of Acadian life in south Louisiana.

Big John's Seafood Patio on Broadview Rd is a country seafood place easily accessible from Lafayette. The 'patio' part does not mean outside; it's a term used regionally to describe a casual seafood joint. In fact, Big John's couldn't be more dark – with its floor pavement, windowless cinder-block walls and strip fluorescent lighting, it has all the charm of an interrogation room. But it's authentic – in crawfish season they serve up a heaping tin tray of boiled mudbugs with mayonnaise, ketchup and Tabasco for diners to whip up their own dip. With beers and tip, a shared tray is under $12. From Lafayette, follow Verot School Rd (Hwy 339) 16 miles south through the half-mile-jog east, and continue south another six miles to the Big John's sign on Broadview in a suburban residential district. Follow this road for a half-mile till it dead-ends in a broad field. From downtown Erath, turn off Hwy 14 north on Hwy 339 to Broadview.

Smiley's Bayou Club on Hwy 14 in downtown Erath is a traditional Cajun dance hall where famed Erath native DL Menard started out. Smiley's features live music and dancing on most Friday and Saturday nights, and in the late afternoon and early evening on Sunday. Signs prohibit same-sex dancing and the wearing of shorts.

BREAUX BRIDGE

population 7300

Nine miles east of Lafayette, the sign on the namesake drawbridge in Breaux Bridge welcomes you to La Capitale Mondiale des Ecrevisses (the Crawfish Capital of the World). The town hosts an annual Crawfish Festival – with a crawfish étouffée cookoff, crawfish-eating contests (the record is 55 pounds in 45 minutes) and even crawfish races – the first complete weekend in May. Daily admission costs around $5, or purchase a three-day pass for $10. But it's easy to find great food, great music and a good time in Breaux Bridge year round. Use I-10 exit 109 to access all sights in Breaux Bridge.

Downtown Breaux Bridge is an oldfashioned row of shops along Bayou Teche a block from the drawbridge (south of I-10). A tiny park at the water's edge commemorates the establishment of the town in the late 18th century after the Breaux family built their bridge. Street signs appear in French as well as in English. A visitor center (☎ 318-332-8500), 314 E Bridge St, can provide maps and fill you in on upcoming festival dates.

The Plantation Brown, Vermilion Red and Cypress Amber Ale served at local festivals and restaurants are made here in town at the *Louisiana Brewing Company* (☎ 318-332-2155), 1058 Oneal Dr. Home brewers Ed Boudreaux and George Harris left the oil industry to start the microbrewery a couple of years ago. There's usually someone there to show you around the operation and offer you a sample of the day's brew (call first to be sure). To find it from I-10, go south to the first stop sign; turn right onto Hwy 94 and go about three miles to Oneal Dr; turn right and follow Oneal to the end.

South of Breaux Bridge, the Nature Conservancy's **Cypress Island Preserve** at Lake Martin offers the unusual chance to see swamp wildlife from a hiking trail. A seven-mile trail atop the levee leads around the lake, which houses the largest white ibis rookery in the world. Herons and egrets also populate the preserve, along with alligators,

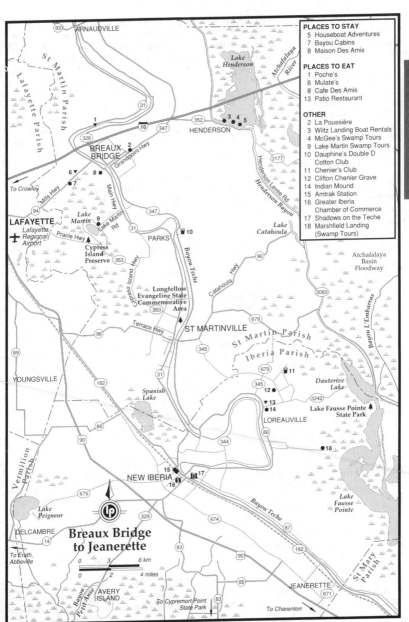

PLACES TO STAY
5 Houseboat Adventures
7 Bayou Cabins
8 Maison Des Amis

PLACES TO EAT
1 Poche's
6 Mulate's
8 Cafe Des Amis
13 Patio Restaurant

OTHER
2 La Poussière
3 Wiltz Landing Boat Rentals
4 McGee's Swamp Tours
9 Lake Martin Swamp Tours
10 Dauphine's Double D
     Cotton Club
11 Chenier's Club
12 Clifton Chenier Grave
14 Indian Mound
15 Amtrak Station
16 Greater Iberia
     Chamber of Commerce
17 Shadows on the Teche
18 Marshfield Landing
     (Swamp Tours)

Breaux Bridge
to Jeanerette

0   3   6 km
0   2   4 miles

deer, ducks and many other swamp creatures. It's a wonderfully still and peaceful place surprisingly close to all the activity. Marcus de la Houssaye (☎ 318-845-2557) leads personally guided tours here aboard a 20-foot aluminum skiff (around $20 per adult and $5 per child for a two-hour tour) and also rents canoes and jonboats – all by calling in advance. Because it's a preserve, there are no services, stores or restrooms at the lake. To reach the landing, lake and trail from I-10 exit 109, go south onto Hwy 328; go 1.7 miles and turn right onto Hwy 336-1; go three blocks and turn left onto Hwy 31 (Main Hwy); continue to Lake Martin Rd and turn right. Two miles farther on at the stop sign is the lake. The boat landing is to the right, and you can park to the right or left. The road gets tricky in very wet weather.

Places to Stay

Rocky Sonnier's *Bayou Cabins* (☎ 318-332-6258), 100 Mills Hwy west from Hwy 31, offers individual private cabins with porches set out over the bayou within walking distance of Mulate's (see Places to Eat). The cabins are rustic (rates around $50) and come with a lagniappe of boudin, cracklins and hogshead cheese from the adjacent restaurant.

At *Maison Des Amis* (☎ 318-332-5273), 140 E Bridge St, the Breaux family will put you up on Bayou Teche in their Creole cottage, which dates back to 1870 – best yet, breakfast at Cafe Des Amis is included. Rooms run from $75 to $85.

Places to Eat, Drink & Dance

In a corner storefront built in the 1920s, the *Cafe Des Amis* (☎ 318-332-5273), 140 E Bridge St, is a homey place for breakfast, serving beignets, crawfish omelets, pain perdu (French toast) and boudin-and-eggs. It is also an intimate dinner spot where you can sit under the pressed tin ceiling and hear French spoken all around. They also operate an inn (see Places to Stay).

A historical marker outside *Poche's* (po-SHAYZ; ☎ 318-332-2108), 3015-A Main

Hwy north of I-10, confirms its credentials as a legendary local charcuterie. The market specializes in boudin and cracklins (fried pork rinds) and serves daily Cajun lunch specials and weekend barbecue. It's open daily from 5:30 am to 9 pm; lunch is served only from 10:30 am to 2 pm. To find Poche's from I-10, head north two miles to Poche Bridge Rd (look for pharmacy at the corner); it's around a half-mile down to the left.

At 'the world's most famous Cajun restaurant,' *Mulate's* (MOO-lotz; ☎ 318-332-4648), 325 Mills Hwy, great Cajun bands draw crowds onto the well-worn dance floor – old people, young people, couples and women together (the bartender says it would be uncommon to see men dance together). Mulate's also offers a full selection of Cajun dishes for lunch and dinner; the house specialty is catfish. It's open daily, and there's no cover charge. To find Mulate's from I-10, follow signs south to a quick right.

One of the most infamous Cajun dance halls might just be *La Poussière* (☎ 318-332-1721), 1301 Grandpoint Hwy, where a few years back a lawsuit by two African American lawyers charging they were barred from admittance led to a change in policy. It's very traditional. The fais-do-do is Saturday night at 8:30 pm (admission $3); on Wednesday nights there's bingo. To find it from I-10 exit 109, go south to the second signal; turn left and go to the signal; take a right and go two blocks to Grandpoint Hwy; they're a half-mile down on the left.

For live zydeco, *Dauphine's Double D Cotton Club* (☎ 318-394-9616), St Louis Rd, usually has music on weekend nights. It's the Creole equivalent of a juke joint, way out in the countryside in the community of Parks. Take Hwy 31 five miles south of town to Parks; turn left onto Hwy 350; turn right onto Hwy 347; drive 600 yards and turn left onto St Louis.

HENDERSON

Henderson is the most convenient access point to the Atchafalaya Basin, a tremendous recreational resource for boating, fishing and hunting. Swamp tours, canoe and motorboat rentals, houseboats and restaurants overlooking the basin can be found on landings. To find the levee road, take I-10 exit 115, head south, and make a fairly immediate left turn onto Hwy 352. Follow this route seven miles through the small community. Across the bridge you will see the levee that encases the basin. Turn right and watch signs for landings open to the public.

This **levee road** is a sight in itself. The two-lane route (paved only as far as Lake Fausse Pointe State Park) leads around the levee for around 50 miles south to Morgan City. For most of its length, the basin is out of sight unless you drive up and over into a public landing, but there are houses, shacks and trailers to see at the basin's edge and the drive is mostly smooth. (Watch for animals – the route is remote and drivers are tempted to speed.) Canoe and motorboat rentals are available from two Wiltz Landing (☎ 318-228-7880) locations; the first one is on the levee road a mile or so south from the Hwy 352 bridge turnoff.

The family-run McGee's Swamp Tours (☎ 318-228-2384), 1337 Henderson Levee Rd, takes party boats into the basin for guided tours by Cajun old-timers who use a microphone. Tours last 1½ hours. The advantages are convenience (even I-10 through-travelers could manage this one), several tours daily most of the year (closed in January) and low prices. The disadvantage is that this portion of the swamp – practically under the I-10 bridge – is hardly the most remote. They also feed gators. Reservations are recommended. Buy tickets ($12 adults, $6 children) from the cashier inside. Their landing restaurant has a high basin view and serves seafood specialties (alligator, frog legs) along with inexpensive sandwiches (a decent catfish po-boy for $4). Boat passengers might want to pick up a cold drink (or souvenir alligator-claw back-scratcher) for the ride.

For those who want to camp, the 108-site *Frenchman's Wilderness Campground*

& RV Park (☎ 318-228-2616) is off I-10's Butte La Rose exit 121. They charge $13 for tents, $15 for hookups and $1 to use the pool (noncampers pay $4). Owner David Olivier frequently DJs Cajun music, which draws locals as well as campers to the woods for a family dance.

Houseboat Rentals
One of the most distinctive overnight experiences you can find anywhere is a night aboard a houseboat in the Atchafalaya Basin. Doug Sebatier and his wife, Diane, run Houseboat Adventures and will 'push you out' from their landing in Henderson into a protected cove for a stay aboard a comfortably cozy modern houseboat that sleeps four or six (some on futons, some with twin bunks). The boats are equipped with generators to power the TV, VCR, lights and air-conditioning, but you can skip the noise and go natural with candles, the breeze off the water and the sounds of the birds, bugs and frogs (even an alligator's roar in mating season). Boats have two-burner ranges and some have mini-refrigerators. All have porch swings for rocking away the afternoon.

Bring your own food and drinking water, and an ice chest if you have many drinks to keep cold. Judging from guest book accounts, drinking is a favorite pastime. A flashlight will also come in handy, as well as insect repellent, and of course, pack your fishing gear. They provide linens and towels, dishware, candles, matches and quick generator-operating lessons. They'll even throw in a pirogue or motorized skiff so that you can row around or motor back-and-forth to shore and nearby restaurants.

To arrange a stay with Houseboat Adventures, call the Sebatiers (who require advance reservations and your estimated arrival time) at ☎ 318-821-5898 or ☎ 800-491-4662. The peak rate from March through October is $145 a night (two-night minimum on weekends), plus a $25 towing fee. Discounts are available off-season and for three or more nights. An airport shuttle is available from Lafayette.

LOUISIANA

Swamp Tours

You haven't been to Cajun Country until you've been out in a swamp. There are dozens of different kinds of swamp tours, each with its particular advantages and disadvantages, but pretty much anything that gets you out onto the water is a good move. Many leave from the town of Henderson. Another set farther south leave from Loreauville, a smaller landing that accesses the deeper basin. Trips out into the smaller bayous and swamps are scattered in the region around Houma, from Gibson to Des Allemands.

Tours run on many different kinds of boats. The most common are party boats – open-sided pontoon boats that seat around 40. These tours are inexpensive, easy to find and most often run at regularly scheduled times year round. The disadvantage is that such big boats can't hope to nuzzle their way into the narrow shallow channels where most of the animals seek refuge. Operators who use smaller craft can get deeper into the swamp, but tours may run only seasonally or on a less predictable schedule. And prices may vary according to how full the boat is – making it comparable to party-boat costs if the boat is full, or much more costly if it ends up being a personal tour. Smaller operators require reservations.

A big philosophical dividing line between operators is whether or not they feed the alligators. Most do, throwing chicken parts or marshmallows (because they float, and seem to do the trick) to lure alligators into camera range. At least one guide even catches a small alligator for a close look before releasing it. As you might imagine, these are not the most ecologically sensitive practices, and operators who do not feed the gators make it their calling card. Another high-impact tour is aboard an airboat that buzzsaws through fields of lily pads at 40 mph making such a racket that passengers are loaned ear-protective headphones for the ride. These are popular for speed thrills and to access shallow channels, but most animals are only seen as they flee from the noise.

On any tour, cameras, binoculars, insect repellent, sunscreen, sunglasses, hats and maybe a cool drink come in handy. On deeper swamp tours, you might be more comfortable in clothing that covers your limbs, with socks and boat-worthy shoes instead of sandals. It's better to organize a tour either early in the morning or in the early evening. One reason is to avoid the heat of the day, but another is to see wildlife when it's most active.

You can also rent canoes at several locations and get out into the swamp independently, but one of the highlights of a swamp tour is having an engaging local guide who can point out wildlife, relate stories and who knows his or her way around. A guided expedition might be a better bet. Pack & Paddle (☎ 318-232-5854) in Lafayette, the premier outfitter in the region, organizes paddling expeditions into the basin, bayous and area lakes, including night rides. Group tour prices start around $20 per person, including a naturalist guide and canoe; prices increase if trips require shuttles or meals. (No meals are served to gators.) ∎

KIM GRANT

ST MARTINVILLE & AROUND

Established around 1765 as the Post des Attakapas before the first Acadians arrived, the town – renamed St Martinville – has grown to be the spiritual center of Acadiana. This is the home of the famed Evangeline Oak from Longfellow's 1847 poem *Evangeline*, about the long-lost lovers Evangeline and Gabriel, separated during le Grand Dérangement. According to the epic poem, the two were to be reunited beneath the venerable oak that stands beside the Bayou Teche below the bridge.

The quiet town carries much of the charm befitting such a legend. A quaint downtown of old wooden storefronts with wide 2nd-story galleries is centered around the manicured square surrounding the historic **St Martin de Tours Church** (☎ 318-394-7334) at 103 S Main St. The congregation dates back to the town's founding in 1765. The present sanctuary was built in 1832; a replica of the Grotto of Lourdes is built inside. A statue of Evangeline, donated by the actress who portrayed her in the 1929 silent film *Evangeline*, sits beside the church. The adjacent **Petit Paris Museum** (named for the city's moniker after aristocrats fleeing the French Revolution settled here) holds a colorful collection of carnival costumes. Guided tours of the church, museum and statues on the grounds are $5 adults, or there's a separate admission for each.

The **Longfellow-Evangeline State Commemorative Area** (☎ 504-342-8111), on Hwy 347 a mile or so north of downtown, preserves the site of an 18th-century sugar plantation. Its draw is broader than a historic house museum tour, as appealing as this one is (the state park-backed tour emphasizes the history of the decor over design). As soon as you enter the gates, huge moss-draped trees and a calm, narrow bayou offer a beautiful Acadian landscape. A farming cottage, exhibits on Acadian immigration in the small visitor center and occasional living history programs shed light on 19th-century life here.

The *Old Castillo Hotel* (☎ 318-394-4010, 800-621-3017), 220 Evangeline Blvd, is a three-story brick landmark across from the bayou and famed oak. The site of the town's first trading post, the 19th-century hotel now operates as a B&B, offering five rooms that were once classrooms when the original hotel was converted to a girl's high school run by the Mercy nuns. Room rates are $50 to $80.

Live entertainment is provided by the Romero Brothers – a stalwart pair of troubadours who pound out Cajun standards at the bayou-side park beside the oak. There are several Cajun restaurants in town, and *Danna's Bakery* (☎ 318-394-3889), 207 E Bridge, has great fig bars and pastries.

Lake Fausse Pointe State Park

Lake Fausse Pointe State Park (☎ 318-229-4764), 18 miles southeast of St Martinville on the levee road, is scenically poised on the edge of the Atchafalaya Basin. The 6217-acre park offers exceptional vacation cabins, camping and boat rentals and launch. A short nature trail explores swamp woodlands. On a summer weekend, the park is busy with families from north Louisiana with their speedboats, bicycles and camper vans. Occasional Cajun music programs are held, though for the most part the park is an island of modernity set apart from the history and heritage of the surrounding region.

Eighteen modern, spacious cabins that sleep six are built on stilts at the water's edge. They rent for $65 a night (and are often reserved months in advance). Cookware, dishware, flatware and bed linens are provided; bring your own towels. The campsites are spacious, private and set around well-tended woodlands ($10, $12 with hookups). Bring all the food you need – the closest market is a 20-mile drive. The small park store has little more than cold drinks, bait and a few miniature boxes of macaroni-and-cheese and popcorn.

Access the park through St Martinville via Hwy 96 to Hwy 679, then seven miles south along Hwy 3083 (signs are intermittent – shoot an azimuth). It is also a straight shot down the levee road from Henderson off I-10 (see also Henderson).

LOREAUVILLE

From St Martinville, Bayou Teche snakes around in a big loop before reaching the adjacent town of New Iberia. On the far end of the loop is Loreauville, a quiet little town set among cane fields at the edge of the Atchafalaya Basin. Hwy 86 traces the loop and becomes Main St downtown. An ancient Indian mound, a celebrity grave and dance hall (see the sidebar King of Zydeco) and a small town restaurant are found in this remote corner of the back-country.

Loreauville is around a 45-minute drive from Lafayette. The trip would also make a nice bike ride or boat-and-bike ride from places in the basin, such as Lake Fausse Pointe State Park.

Most **swamp tours** into the basin leave from landings around 2½ miles east of downtown. Guides with Airboats Inc (☎ 318-229-4457) run surface-skimming skiffs with huge motors out back. The advantage is that the boats can access extremely shallow channels for the chance of seeing wildlife who shirk the larger, more well-traveled deeper basin. The disadvantage is that the motor's roar is so loud that the guide provides ear protection for the ride, and instead of a running narration, the guide buzzes through the marsh, then cuts the engine and explains what just flew or dove out of view. One-hour tours run $10 per person if it's fully reserved; the minimum cost per tour is $50 (when you call, ask if you can join a largely reserved tour to keep costs low). They operate Tuesday through Sunday from February through October; boats leave from Marshfield Landing.

The *Patio Restaurant* (☎ 318-229-8281), on Main St (Hwy 86) downtown, is a good place to end up after a day in the swamp. The 18-table restaurant (look for the green tarp entrance) serves ambitious seafood plates like the stuffed-catfish Cajun delight ($14); a salad bar is also available. They open for lunch from 11 am to 2 pm every day but Monday, and serve dinner Tuesday through Saturday from 5 to 9 pm.

Also in the downtown area, an **Indian mound** attests to an ancient village that once was here. Look for it off Main St, between Bonin St and Champagne.

NEW IBERIA & AROUND

Named for the Iberian Peninsula, New Iberia was settled by the Spanish in 1779; today it claims to be the only permanent Spanish settlement in Louisiana. The town prospered on the sugar crop from surrounding cane plantations, and some plantation homes can still be seen in the area. There's an annual Gumbo Cook-off each fall; the Louisiana Sugar Cane Festival is held the last weekend in September.

Hwy 182 leads right to New Iberia's Main St, with its compact downtown set along Bayou Teche. (Main St runs one-way northbound; the southbound thoroughfare is St Peter St.) The Greater Iberia Chamber of Commerce (☎ 318-364-1836), 111 W Main St, sells parish maps for $1 and distributes brochures. A visitor center out by Hwy 90 also distributes information.

A walking tour of downtown could start at **Shadows on the Teche** (☎ 318-365-5213), 317 E Main St, an 1834 house museum open daily for tours. A walk up Main St goes by Books Along the Teche (☎ 318-367-7621), 110 E Main St, and the central plaza at the bayou across from the Chamber of Commerce. A favorite lunch spot is the *Lagniappe Too Cafe* (☎ 318-365-9419), 204 E Main St.

A cheap place to stay is the *Royal Motel* (☎ 318-369-9285), 218 W St Peter (1½ blocks from the Amtrak station). Rooms in the low-rent 1950s motel out back (the older house out front is apartments) are $34 single or double. Modern chain motels (Holiday Inn and Best Western) are out by the interstate.

The Amtrak station (☎ 318-364-9625), 402 W Washington at Railroad Ave, is in a 1910 depot. The Greyhound station is on E Main St and Darcey, around a mile south of the central commercial district.

Teche City Taxi can be reached at ☎ 318-367-1752.

King of Zydeco

Clifton Chenier (1923-87), a native of St Landry Parish, is widely credited with popularizing zydeco music. Nicknamed the King of Zydeco, Chenier toured the country with his Louisiana Hot Band, and often performed wearing a crown. The Les Blank film *Dry Wood and Hot Peppers* features Chenier on and off stage. Awarded with a Grammy and a National Endowment for the Arts Heritage Award, Chenier inspired many Creole musicians.

Chenier's landmark lament, 'Zydeco Sont Pas Sale,' is from a dance tune in both the Cajun and Creole traditions called 'Les Haricots Sont Pas Sales' – Louisiana French for 'the snapbeans aren't salty.' The quick corruption of *les haricots* into *zydeco* is how many believe the genre got its name. (Dissenters suggest the term may actually be rooted in West African languages.) The genre developed concurrently with Cajun music, and it similarly featured accordions and washboards with lyrics sung in a local French dialect. It was then called 'LaLa' music and it was accompanied by the LaLa dance (the two-step).

While such performers as Beausoleil, Queen Ida and Wayne Toups continue to bring the music of Clifton Chenier to national audiences, keepers of the zydeco flame in south Louisiana include Keith Frank, Boozoo Chavis, Walter Mouton, Chris Ardoin, Beau Jocque, and Nathan and the Zydeco Cha-chas. Each generates devoted crowds in clubs, dance halls and at festivals throughout the region.

The unmarked grave of the legendary Chenier can be found in Loreauville, east of Main St. Take Hwy 3242 toward Dauterive Lake; turn left on Landry Rd, and go 1½ miles to the cemetery. His grave is parallel to the Veret and Broussard graves.

Nearby, *Clifton's Club* (☎ 318-229-6576), formerly operated by Chenier's widow, Margaret, is still in the family. A Chenier relative still manages to pack the 700-seat remote dance hall. Schedules are unpredictable and not widely advertised; call first to see if there's a band playing. To find the club, follow directions to the cemetery then continue up Landry St a half-mile farther north, and turn left onto Crochet Lane. The club is a mile up on the right past Braquet Rd. ∎

Avery Island

A detour south of New Iberia leads through cane fields and along a small bayou to Avery Island, the home of **McIlhenny Tabasco**. A 50¢ bridge toll over a small inlet gains you admittance to the island. McIlhenny Tabasco pepper sauce factory tours (☎ 318-365-8173) are a touchstone for many gourmet travelers, but unfortunately the tour doesn't live up to the hot reputation of the product. They no longer guide visitors through the factory itself, and the exhibits and presentations in the tour room leave visitors wanting more. However, it does rate landmark status, it's a nice drive out there and you can visit the gardens.

The adjacent **Jungle Gardens** (☎ 318-365-8173) brings visitors through exotic subtropical jungle flora. Legend has it that a few of the exotic species the gardens harbored were set loose in the hurricanes and have flourished in the surrounding landscape

without natural predators. Admission for adults is $5.25 ($3.75 children).

Cypremort Point State Park

This day-use state park (☎ 318-867-4510), situated amid coastal marshlands 24 miles south of Jeanerette, is the only place near the Gulf of Mexico that can be reached by car between Grand Isle and Cameron. A half-mile stretch of landfill beach, a sailboat launch and a 100-foot fishing pier provide recreation at the 185-acre park. Admission is $2 per car, free for seniors. From Hwy 90, follow signs south on Hwy 83, then right on Hwy 319.

Chitimacha Indian Reservation

A short detour off Hwy 182 or Hwy 90 to Charenton leads to the 1260-acre reservation of the Chitimacha, the only Indians in Louisiana to retain federally recognized sovereignty over a portion of their ancestral lands. According to tribal tradition, their original territory was marked by four sacred trees: one east of Baton Rouge, one southeast of New Orleans, one near the mouth of the Mississippi, and a fourth – a great cypress – at present-day Cypremort (dead cypress) Point State Park. With the arrival of the Acadians and subsequent intermarriage, many Chitimacha began speaking French and adopted Catholicism. The estimated colonial population of 20,000 was decimated by European diseases. Today about 350 tribal members live on the reservation; total tribal membership is now around 850. Their name is derived from the Chitimacha expression *pantc pinanka'nc*, which translates as 'men altogether red.' The Chitimacha Visitor Center (☎ 318-923-4830) contains a small collection of projectile points, pottery and baskets.

The tribe's largest commercial development is the 115,000-sq-foot *Cypress Bayou Casino*, which includes two restaurants and a cocktail lounge, and is open 24 hours. A portion of the revenues from the casino are used to purchase adjacent lands to expand the reservation.

GIBSON & DONNER

West of Houma, these two tiny towns are not discernible at 60 mph along Hwy 20 around where it joins with Hwy 90. Turn in at one of the streets, however, and you will come upon these communities built along Bayou Black. Some of the best adventures in Acadiana start out in Gibson (80 miles east of Lafayette, 75 miles west of New Orleans).

Atchafalaya Basin Backwater Adventure Tours (☎ 504-575-2371), 6302 N Bayou Black Dr, is in Gibson. Jon Faslun has been running motorized boat tours along waterways that are not commercially navigable (not the open swamp) in the Great Chacahoula Swamp for more than 20 years. In 2½ hours, Faslun's tours wind through ten thousand years of natural history as he relates stories of the swamp's evolution, flora and fauna, swamp survival and swamp medicine. This is no jokey-Cajun show – Faslun's a serious swamper with a

strong respect for nature and a firm policy against feeding alligators. For basic tours he charges $50 per person with a two-person minimum; the maximum boat capacity is six. During the high season from March through May, he runs two boats daily, at 11 am and 3 pm; the rest of the year at 11 am only unless special arrangements are made (a slightly higher rate applies). Longer tours deeper into the swamp last four to five hours ($60 per person). All tours are weather permitting and reservations are essential. He also rents pirogues for $10 per person per day with a map that will direct you to an abandoned cypress mill. As with any trip into the deeper swamp, you'll be more comfortable in socks and boat-worthy shoes and in clothes that cover your limbs.

The most adventuresome of Faslun's tours are primitive camping trips into the backwater. Faslun motors campers into the deep swamp to a small island about 20 yards in diameter. Campers dine on freshly caught fish cooked over a campfire and sleep in tents underneath moss-covered willow and palmetto. (Faslun himself uses a jungle hammock, a good alternative if you bring your own.) Guided overnight camping trips including all equipment, food and transportation cost $100 per person per day ($60 if you bring your own camping gear). He can outfit up to four people. Faslun's place is on the bayou a couple blocks down from the plank bridge in 'downtown' Gibson on Caroll St (watch for the street sign and turn south off Hwy 20 a couple of miles west of Chester's).

Chester's Cypress Inn (☎ 504-446-6821), visible on Hwy 20 in Donner a couple miles east of Gibson, is the sort of metal-awning old dining hall you might expect to stumble across in a faded mountain resort like the Adirondacks – but here they serve Dixie beer and frog legs. They say that when Miss Bobbie's daddy owned it there was an orchestra and dance floor, and it has the nostalgic air of a place where the music's long gone. They're famous for their chicken – posters declare 'If the colonel had our recipe, he'd been a general' – and offer it up regular, spicy or no-batter for $6 a plate. They're only open for dinner from 5 pm, experimenting with a new Thursday through Sunday schedule.

Coming off a swamp tour on an off-day at Chester's, you might instead crawl into *Sugar Bear's*, on Hwy 20 east of Chester's, for a cold beer and a game of pool. They usually have a band or DJ on weekends.

At *Wildlife Gardens* (☎ 504-575-3676), 5306 N Bayou Black Dr in Gibson, James and Betty Provost lead visitors over the shady paths they have cut through their private swamp preserve. The couple also keeps ostriches, nutria and alligators on display in cages, and peacocks roam the grounds. It's an appealingly homespun attraction, wonderful for kids and, again, a rare opportunity to observe the swamp landscape on foot.

But the most unusual feature about Wildlife Gardens is the one-of-a-kind B&B accommodations here. The Provosts have built four small 'trappers cabins' out into the swamp. Each has its own front porch over the water, and in the morning the Provosts will feed catfish to the resident alligators from your porch. Inside, the rustic cabins are spare but comfortable, with big high beds, air-conditioning, ceiling fans and stall showers. Cabins rent for $70 for two including breakfast. Follow signs off Hwy 90 around nine miles east of the Hwy 90 and Hwy 20 intersection.

THIBODAUX

population 14,000

Thibodaux (TI-ba-doh), at the confluence of Bayou Lafourche and Bayou Terrebonne, was the most important town between New Orleans and Bayou Teche when commerce was restricted to travel by boat. The town has been the Lafourche Parish seat since 1820; the copper-domed courthouse at the corner of 2nd and Green Sts was built in 1855. Early French and German farmers in the area produced crops for the New Orleans market. Isleños arrived about 1780 on upper Bayou Lafourche. By 1800, Acadians and Americans extended down the bayou to Thibodaux. Today the entire polyglot mix proudly refer to themselves as Cajuns.

The 166-acre Nicholls State University campus is south of town. The small downtown, less charming than many bayou-side towns farther east, consists of narrow streets with more empty storefronts than open ones, with most business drawn out to the modern shopping center across the bayou. The Thibodaux Chamber of Commerce (☎ 504-446-1187), 1048 E Canal St, distributes maps and information on local events.

Jean Lafitte Wetlands Acadian Cultural Center

The Wetlands Acadian Cultural Center (☎ 504-448-1375), 314 St Mary St, which is part of Jean Lafitte National Historic Park, operates an impressive museum, gallery and gift shop. Artifacts and enlightening captions present the startling Acadian history and depict how the group adapted to the south Louisiana environment. A video focuses on one aspect of the culture – handfishing, as taught to the Acadians by local Indians – to express unusual cultural skills that have been lost due to assimilation and the loss of wetlands. You may catch demonstrations of boat-building or net-making, or a storyteller relating Acadian folk tales *(don't* request politically incorrect 'Boudreaux & Thibodaux' stories; collections of these gently self-deprecating tales are found in local shops). The center also hosts many Acadian musicians – jam sessions are scheduled on Monday nights from 5:30 to 7 pm. The center opens daily at 9 am. Closing times vary: Tuesday through Thursday at 6 pm; Friday through Sunday, 5 pm; and Monday, 7 pm. A local library upstairs maintains an exhaustive collection of reference works on south Louisiana, from volumes on Acadian crafts and local botany to cancer statistics in the industrial chemical belt along the Mississippi River. Though the center is huge, signs are intermittent. There's a nice bayou view from the deck.

Laurel Valley Village

This nonprofit history village (☎ 504-446-7456), about two miles east of town on Hwy 308 (down Bayou Lafourche), maintains antebellum plantation structures, including the best-preserved slave structures in the state. Exhibits in the General Store next to the highway describe the now-abandoned settlement that existed here in 1785. The land here is still farmed, and livestock roam the grounds. A former slave community, now consisting of 70 weathered shacks, is visible about a half-mile down Laurel Valley Rd, but there's no trespassing without a guide. A $5 donation should be enough to get a volunteer at the store to accompany you on a visit to describe the former slave community in the now-picturesque village. Posted hours at the general store are weekdays 10 am to 4 pm and weekends noon to 4 pm, but it closes if no volunteers are available (call first to confirm).

Places to Stay

Budget accommodations can be found at the *Bayou L Motel* (☎ 504-447-2683), 526 St Mary St, down from the Acadian Cultural Center. The rooms are fairly dark and verge on shabby, but they're kept clean ($28/39 single/double). The location is unglamorous but convenient; you can walk to some shops and to Politz's restaurant across the street; but there's no pool. The modern *Howard Johnson's* (☎ 504-447-9071), 201 N Canal Blvd, has a pool, a lounge actually populated by locals and a 24-hour restaurant with exceptionally poor food for any hour. Rooms are $60/62. The *Holiday Inn* (☎ 504-446-0561), 400 E 1st St, is the grand hotel in town (with pool), and it actually retains historic architectural details from a 19th-century academy once on the site (rooms $64/71).

Places to Eat & Drink

The restaurants in Thibodaux are unimpressive, but a meat market south of town is a local landmark. In town, most locals crowd into *Politz's* (☎ 504-448-0944), 100 Landry St at St Mary St, for a heaping plate of corn or flour-breaded seafood, or a broiled catfish dinner for about $11. The place to get a big platter of boiled crawfish is *Seafood Outlet* (☎ 504-448-1010), 100

St Patrick Hwy across the bayou from downtown. *Utopia Fine Foods* (☎ 504-447-4544), 601 W 3rd St, has the only espresso machine in town and serves breakfast, lunch and dinner, including a few vegetarian dishes. South of Thibodaux on Hwy 20 in Schriever, the *Bourgeois Meat Market* (☎ 504-447-7128), 519 Hwy 20, sells both boudin blanc and zesty boudin rouge (blood sausage), along with their specialty beef jerky. The tender, spicy meat strips have been likened to 'shrunken sirloin,' and the Bourgeois family ships the jerky out to meat-lovers across the states.

Despite the Cajun population, it can be difficult to hear a Cajun band on a stroll past the many popular night spots that pepper Thibodaux's old town area between W 1st and W 4th Sts. Pickup trucks identify the country and western bars; other bars cater to university students. To hear Cajun music, head north to *Dawn's Lounge* (☎ 448-2559), at 1302 St Patrick Hwy on the edge of town. On the way to Dawn's you can check the action at *Gros Place*, 710 Patrick St, a popular hangout in an ancient service station.

Getting There & Away

Greyhound runs buses from New Orleans to Thibodaux twice daily. Amtrak deposits *Sunset Limited* passengers six miles south of Thibodaux at a forlorn station outpost in Schriever, behind the railroad overpass at the junction of Hwys 20 and 24.

Thibodaux is a 60-mile drive west of New Orleans via I-10 to I-310 to Hwy 90 to Hwy 1, which follows Bayou Lafourche along a scenic route of waterside cottages for 17 miles to Thibodaux.

HOUMA

The city of Houma itself hasn't much to offer travelers besides being an urban hub between long stretches of rural Hwy 90, but it holds many attractions on the spidery routes that emanate from its commercial center along Bayou Terrebonne. While plans for a bypass remain incomplete, Hwy 90 is routed downtown along the bayou.

Patron Reptile of Acadiana

Houma and the towns surrounding it have managed to stake a fair share of the local economy on prehistoric reptiles. Swamp tours, menus, swamp cabins and camping all do better with a few alligators to be seen. Tourism dollars here quadrupled to $54.3 million in 1994 from $10.9 million in 1987 'thanks largely to so-called gator dollars,' according to a 1995 *Wall Street Journal* report.

The American alligator *(Alligator mississipiensis)* gets its name from Spanish sailors, who called it *el lagarto* – 'the lizard.' They belong to the order Crocodilia, but they can be distinguished from their crocodile cousins by snout shape and overbite. Gators have rounded snouts, where a crocodile's is pointed, and crocodiles expose a lower tooth outside the upper lip. Alligators have been known to reach 20 feet, though six to eight feet is the average. Alligators are most at home in the water, where they swim with snakelike movements. On land, they travel forward in a straight direction, sometimes surprisingly quickly – when running away from an alligator, use zigzag steps.

Alligators are most active in spring, when mating occurs. First 'bulls' fend off competing males in a show of strength: the two prehistoric giants lock jaws and thrash about until the exhausted party gives up and slinks off. The victor then begins an equally tumultuous ordeal with the female. A bull alligator's bellow – which has been compared to a lion's roar – sounds a territorial warning throughout the year, but in spring the cry has special meaning. Females follow this sound to the love den, lured also by the musky odor of the bull's emissions.

All crocodilians are egg-laying animals. After mating, females lay 40 to 60 eggs on a bank, covering them with decaying vegetation that insulates the eggs. Some 60 to 90 days later, 'clucking' cries alert the mother to uncover her nine-inch hatchlings. Nest temperature decides gender: males hatch from warmer spots, females from cooler. The babies frolic around their mother for months in an unusually familial relationship for reptiles (though alligators have been known to eat their young in hard times).

Alligators in captivity live around 40 years; in the wild they can live much longer – some beyond 100 years. They eat anything in close range that moves; their appetite subsides in winter and they hibernate the coolest weeks of the year.

Alligator is on many local menus; restaurant alligator is farm-raised, not wild. Dried and laminated alligator heads and claws are popular souvenirs. ■

The historic district is centered around the 1938 St Francis de Sales Cathedral on Church St, a block from Bayou Terrebonne. Here the church and courthouse head up a central park square, and older homes and shops are nearby. The local tourist commission operates a visitor center (☎ 504-868-2732) on Hwy 90 at St Charles St west of town.

Swamp Tours

Alligator Annie Miller's Swamp Tours (☎ 504-879-3934), on Hwy 90 eight miles west of Houma, and Cajun Man's Swamp Cruise (☎ 504-868-4625), 10 miles east, are intended to be two of the most entertaining swamp tours in the region. Alligator Annie has built a reputation feeding her gator 'babies' drumsticks for so long

that they're now trained to respond to the sound of her approaching motor. She charges $15 for adults and $10 for children. Cajun Man 'Black' Guidry serenades his passengers with his trusty dog Gator Bait at his side. He charges $15 for a ride through a scenic slice of swamp. Both tours last two hours and both operators run year round on schedules that vary by season. Call for reservations.

Places to Stay & Eat

The *Capri Court Campground* (☎ 504-879-4288), on Hwy 316 off Hwy 90 north of Houma, has a pool and offers 45 campsites at $12, with hookups $15. Weekly and monthly rates are available.

A nice budget choice is the *Sugar Bowl Motel* (☎ 504-872-4521) on Hwy 90 east across the bayou from the central commercial district. Decent 1960s roadside rooms are $34 single or double. There's also a *Red Carpet Inn* (☎ 504-876-4160), on Hwy 90 west near Houma's visitor center, which offers basic rooms for $40 with one bed, $49 with two beds, and has a pool.

Several seedier motels in town are geared toward oil workers as their most legit crowd; by appearances, it's not surprising that the local police consider them vice dens.

A-Bear's Cafe (☎ 504-872-6306), 809 Bayou Black Dr, in town, and *Dula & Edwin's Cajun Restaurant* (☎ 504-876-0271), 2821 Bayou Blue Rd, north of town near the Capri Court Campground, both offer Cajun music along with menus of Cajun specialties.

GRAND ISLE

Adventurers are always tempted to go to the end of the road in hopes that a pot of gold is awaiting discovery. There is no pot of gold at the end of Hwy 1, but it is nevertheless an interesting route that begins from Hwy 90 east of Houma and runs south along the west bank of Bayou Lafourche. As soon as you cross the high bridge over the Intracoastal Waterway, you're within view of the busy shipping channel that brings all shapes and sizes of craft down to the Gulf of Mexico. The first town sign greets visitors with *Bienvenue!*, and scattered bayou-side development for the next two hours is full of propeller repair shops, snowball stands and boarding motels for ship and derrick workers. The brimming bayou diffuses into expansive marshlands as it approaches the coast, and another tall bridge brings drivers across to Grand Isle.

The beach at Grand Isle is a narrow strip of dark, hard-packed sand largely obscured behind high dunes – nothing like the white-sand beaches along the Mississippi Gulf Coast and eastward. The community consists of humble shacks for an undemanding group of vacationers and a small year-round resident population. Rental rooms in cabins and motels are exceptionally shabby

(not funky shabby, low-down shabby) for prices starting at a pricey $50 a night. The low-rent resort is propped up by several local bars, some of which feature lingerie modeling, designed to attract the oil workers who work at refineries on the island and fishermen lured to the artificial reefs created by offshore drilling rigs.

The highlight is **Grand Isle State Park** (☎ 504-787-2559), on the far eastern tip of the island. It's the only state-owned and operated beach on the Louisiana Gulf Coast. The park provides modern bathhouses for swimmers and campers and an observation tower. A 400-foot fishing pier ($2 adults) enables anglers to fish for speckled trout, redfish, croaker and other saltwater species. Camping here is simple and straightforward – RVs pull up on the beach to the water's edge ($10 a night, no hookups). From the pier you might be able to see the ruins of Fort Livingston across Barataria Pass. The fort sits on Grand Terre Island (boat access only), which served as a base of operations for the Lafitte brothers, who organized a smuggling ring in New Orleans in the early 19th century (see the New Orleans History section). Admission to the park is $2 per car, free for seniors.

Across from the park, the Pirate's Cove Marina (☎ 318-787-3880), designed largely for the condominium dwellers gated inside, has a store for minimal supplies.

The Cajun Prairie

If the Cajun wetlands can be said to be the heart of the region, the prairie, an area north of Lafayette extending just about to Alexandria, is its soul. As the center for Cajun and zydeco music, its spoon-struck washboard rhythms seem to permeate the local life of rice cultivation, fishing camps, crawfish boils and le courir – or maybe it's just the radio, which seems to always play wonderful local south Louisiana music such as you hear nowhere else.

They have a saying here that everyone needs three places to be – home, work and a third place that may be a church or club or cafe or wherever people come together to soothe their soul. The prairie has plenty of these 'third places.'

OPELOUSAS & AROUND

The third-oldest city in Louisiana, Opelousas gets its name from an Indian tribe that once inhabited the area. The most commonly accepted translation of the name is 'Black Leg,' the origin of which is uncertain. During the Civil War, Opelousas was named the Confederate capital of Louisiana, and today it's the seat of St Landry Parish and the largest city in the prairie region. Its position at the intersection of I-49 and Hwy 190 makes it a natural thoroughfare for folks seeking out more disparate attractions, clubs, accordion factories and boudin markets across the prairie.

The historic city center revolves around the county courthouse square bounded by Market St, Court St, Landry St and Bellevue St. Nineteenth-century shops and offices surround the square. The landmark *Palace Cafe* (☎ 318-942-2142) here draws a great mix of people for Southern plate-lunch specials. Three blocks up near City Hall, the **Opelousas Museum** (☎ 318-948-2589), 329 N Main St, explains the city's Indian, Acadian and Creole history. Spring weekends kick off every Friday (except Good Friday) at 5:30 pm downtown at Bellevue and Main Sts with street concerts from late March to early May.

Zydeco Landmarks

Around Opelousas are three of the best zydeco venues in the world. North of town on Hwy 182, *Slim's Y-Ki-Ki* (☎ 318-942-6242) is a few miles up from the square. In Lawtell, find *Richard's* (REE-shardz; ☎ 318-543-6596), out in a rural stretch of Hwy 190 eight miles west of Opelousas. On weekend nights you should have little trouble finding either place; if a band is playing, the buildings are surrounded by cars, as folks come from all over to hear the likes of Chris Ardoin, Keith Frank, Boozoo Chavis, and Nathan and the Zydeco Cha-chas.

The Southwest Louisiana Zydeco Music Festival is held in Plaisance, off Hwy 167 northwest of Opelousas, around Labor Day weekend. The 13-hour Saturday concert is often preceded with a kick-off concert at one of the clubs above the night before. Call ☎ 318-942-2392 for dates.

Washington

Six miles north of Opelousas and only a few blocks from I-49, Washington retains its character as a historic steamboat port. Though settled as early as the mid-18th century, the riverfront town was not incorporated until 1835. At the head of navigation on Bayou Courtableau, and on the stagecoach line, Washington boomed with activity in the late 18th century, shipping out cotton, lumber, sugar and cattle. Wealthy merchants, brokers and steamboat captains built the antebellum houses that remain in the historic district today. In fact, 80% of the buildings in town are now on the National Historic Register, making it a wonderful place to walk around and sightsee. The tranquil town also has a few antique shops for browsing. What the historically American town lacks, however, is the full-bodied pulse of the surrounding Cajun and Creole communities – fortunately only a short drive away.

You might begin a walking tour at the **Washington Museum** (☎ 318-826-3626), at the town's only traffic light on the corner of Main St and Dejean (also the site of the town's old opera house). The museum explains the town's history and also serves as a visitor center, distributing a self-guided walking tour map that takes you along the bayou, past the cemetery (with its traditional above-ground crypts and a grotto), flea market and historic residential and commercial centers. It's open daily; closed for lunch from noon to 1 pm.

The **Hinckley House** (☎ 318-826-3906), 405 E Dejean (three blocks downriver from the museum), is open to the public as a historic house museum. It's been in the same family since the 18th century. The cypress house is constructed with wood pegs, and its original plaster walls are bound with cattle and deer hair. Several other homeowners in the historic district also open their doors for personal tours. Admission to all historic homes is $5, by advance reservation only (can be arranged at the museum).

Stop for a drink or bowl of gumbo ($8 for a meal-size bowl) at *Jack Womack's Steamboat Restaurant* (☎ 318-826-7227) on Main St, a bayou-side restaurant carved out of an 1830 steamboat warehouse. It's open Tuesday through Saturday from 5 pm, and midday Sunday from 11 am to 2 pm. There's also a deli market on Main St diagonally across from the museum.

Several B&Bs offer pampered overnight lodging in historic homes. *Camellia Cove* (☎ 318-826-7362), 205 W Hill St at St John, provides three guest rooms – two that share a bath and one with a private bath ($64 to $75) – in a circa 1825 house on two acres a block off Main St. The Johnsons offer two guest rooms in their B&B *De la Morandiere* (☎ 318-826-3510), 515 St John at the corner of Sittig; one has a private entrance ($75 per night).

The town hosts its Festival de Courtableau in March and a Heritage Festival in May.

Grand Coteau

Between Opelousas and Lafayette, the tiny community of Grand Coteau is set on an ancient Mississippi River levee (*coteau* means ridge). It features the landmark **Academy of the Sacred Heart** (☎ 318-662-5275), off Church St. Founded in 1821 by a local couple to provide Catholic education for the parish, the school has an exceptional history. The oldest school west of the Mississippi, Sacred Heart was the scene of a bona fide miracle in 1866. Today a shrine marks the place where a dying young girl saw the saintly vision of the Blessed John Berchmans, who as a result of his appearances was later canonized a saint.

During the Civil War, the school served briefly as Union headquarters for General Nathaniel Banks and 20,000 Federal

troops. As it happened, Banks had a daughter enrolled in the Manhattanville Convent of the Sacred Heart in New York (one of an affiliated network of 20 or so Sacred Heart schools in the US), and the Manhattanville superior urged the general to provide for the nuns in Grand Coteau. Banks complied with the request, and his commissary supplied the nuns with enough food to keep the school open through even the leanest times of the Civil War.

Live oak arcades of Spanish moss lead to the historic Academy building, which continues to operate as a private girl's school from grades five to 12. The original three-story building is detailed with wrought-iron balconies, green shutters and dormer windows dotting its pitched roof. The academy's formal French garden of boxwood and azaleas was laid out in 1831. Also on the grounds are a chapel and a Jesuit retreat house, built in the Spanish Mission style as a school around 1850.

Guided tours are available; it's best to call first to confirm times and the admission charge, which at the last visit was $5.

In the historic district in town, the tea room in *The Kitchen Shop* (☎ 318-662-3500), at the corner of Cherry and King Sts, offers coffee, teas and fancy pastries from 10 am to 5 pm Monday through Saturday.

Sunset

Across the interstate from Grand Coteau in Sunset, the **Chrètien Point Plantation** (☎ 318-662-5876) opens the 1830s Greek Revival house and grounds of a 10,000-acre cotton plantation to the public for guided tours and B&B accommodations. The plantation is rife with legend. One story goes that a Civil War skirmish took place here, and the master Hypolite Chrètien was able to save his property by making the sign of a Mason – when the Yankee officer recognized the sign he decided to spare the plantation. Another story tells how the mistress of the house once shot the head off a would-be thief; faint traces of the tell-tale bloodstains remain on the stairs (the same stairs, meanwhile, that are said to be the model for Tara's stairs in the film of *Gone with the Wind*). In less glorious days after the war, the house was reportedly used to house livestock and hay.

Now completely restored, the present owners provide tours daily (under $6 adults, under $3 children) and B&B lodging. Room rates start at $110 for downstairs rooms to $145 for the upstairs room with its own Jacuzzi (a favorite with honeymooners). They have a pool and tennis courts, and children are welcome.

The flip-side in lodging is available from *La Caboose* B&B (☎ 318-662-5401) at 145 S Budd St, where the Brinkhauses can put you up in their caboose and depot.

Church Point

West of Sunset and 16 miles north of I-10, the small Church Point community of 4500 is known for celebrating its French-Acadian traditions, particularly Cajun music. (It competes with Mamou for the title of Cajun Music Capital of the World.) Church Point claims to be home to more Cajun musicians than anywhere else in Acadiana, including the 'Father of Cajun Music' Iry Lejeaune. A Cajun house dance – *bal de maison* – held in Church Point every other Saturday night is broadcast over local radio stations. The Sound Center (☎ 318-684-2176), 329 N Main St, is a record store and recording studio where Cajun musicians record on the Lanor label. Handmade Cajun musical instruments are sold at Le Vieux Moulin (the Old Mill; ☎ 318-684-1200), 402 Canal St.

The town's Mardi Gras courir is held the Sunday before Mardi Gras (so folks can attend this and another celebration come Mardi Gras day). Riders assemble at the town's Saddle Tramp Riding Club (☎ 318-684-2739), 1036 E Ebey St, early in the morning, and the party starts here then moves over to watch the afternoon parade down Main Street as the riders return for more fais-do-do. The party shuts down by 6 pm to commemorate the beginning of Lent.

The town's horse-drawn Buggy Festival the first weekend in June harks back to the 1920s, when worshipers from all over rode buggies to attend Sunday services at local churches. Other traditions celebrated here include the Feast of St Joseph in March and a boucherie – communal hog slaughter – in November.

EUNICE

Eunice's Prairie Acadian Cultural Center, Liberty Theater, cultural museums and festivals make it the family-oriented center for prairie Cajun heritage. It's also the home of the famed Savoy Music Center and its Saturday morning jam session.

Eunice hosts the World Championship Crawfish Étouffée Cook-off (the last Sunday in March unless it's Easter), its own Mardi Gras courir and parade, and the Cajun Prairie Folklife Festival the second weekend in October. With a compact downtown sprinkled with shops, cafes, a cinema and a great record shop, downtown Eunice is pleasant to walk around. Drop down off Hwy 190 at 2nd St to reach the Liberty Theater and adjacent Prairie Acadian center. The Chamber of Commerce operates a visitor center, which is downtown next to the depot on Hwy 13, that distributes maps and calendars of events. The mayor's office at City Hall can also provide information.

Jean Lafitte Prairie Acadian Cultural Center

In downtown Eunice, the Prairie Acadian Cultural Center (☎ 318-457-8499), next to the Liberty Theater, is a part of Jean Lafitte National Historic Park, and it introduces the Acadian heritage particular to the prairie terrain. Well-presented exhibits reveal that more Caribbean immigrants settled here than in other parts of Acadiana, infusing the prairie with its still pronounced Creole heritage. Other artifacts relate the heritage of the region's cattle ranches, rice industry and courir de Mardi Gras. The center helps operate the Liberty Theater next door and occasionally schedules other

LOUISIANA

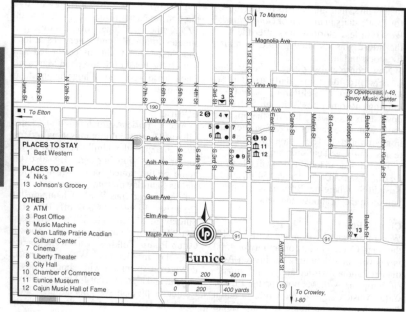

PLACES TO STAY
1 Best Western

PLACES TO EAT
4 Nik's
13 Johnson's Grocery

OTHER
2 ATM
3 Post Office
5 Music Machine
6 Jean Lafitte Prairie Acadian
   Cultural Center
7 Cinema
8 Liberty Theater
9 City Hall
10 Chamber of Commerce
11 Eunice Museum
12 Cajun Music Hall of Fame

Eunice

musical programs and craft demonstrations.
The gift shop has a nice selection of books
and handmade crafts, including Mardi Gras
screen masks and miniature wooden pirogues. The center is open daily; admission
is free.

Liberty Theater

Officially known as the Liberty Center for
the Performing Arts, the restored 1924
Liberty Theater (☎ 318-457-7389), at the
corner of S 2nd St and Park Ave, is best
known for its *Rendez-Vous Des Cajuns*, a
Saturday night performance that is simultaneously broadcast on local radio and
television stations. The *Rendez-Vous* features traditional Cajun and zydeco music
and dance in sort of a Grand Ole Cajun
Opry format. Emcee Bergen Angeley
serves as the bilingual Garrison Keillor,
with his French and English quickening
into a snappy Cajun Franglais mix like

Tex-Mex. They tell stories, talk about the
songs and share recipes. Many old-time
couples and families circle the dance floor
below the stage. The show runs from 6 to
8 pm; seating is in the orchestra or balcony. Admission is $3, children under 12
are free.

Eunice Museum

Housed in the historic train depot that put
Eunice on the map around 1893, the Eunice
Museum (☎ 318-457-6540), 220 S 1st St, at
Duson St, is chock-full of memorabilia
from the town's founding and development.
The museum contains numerous sepia
photographs, farm tools, hand-cranked
appliances, a loom, old toys, Indian artifacts and the like. The Mardi Gras courir
costumes are most interesting to see close-
up, and the depot is itself evocative. They're
closed Sunday and Monday and for lunch
from noon to 1 pm. Admission is free.

Other Musical Landmarks

The **Savoy Music Center** (☎ 318-457-9563), on Hwy 190 east, is the accordion factory of famed musician Marc Savoy. Instrumental in reviving and promoting Cajun folk music, Savoy has been acclaimed in two films about Cajun music, both by Les Blank, (*Laissez les Bons Temps Rouler* and *Marc and Ann*). Most Saturday mornings, Savoy hosts a Cajun music jam session here from 9 am to noon (a contrast to the debauched scene at Fred's at the same time – see Mamou). At other times, it's fascinating to see the artistry and variety of accordions in the shop. To find it, look for the huge Savoy Music Co sign three miles east of downtown (actually easy for eastbound travelers to miss); it's west of the Cajun Campground.

Downtown, Music Machine (☎ 318-457-4846), 235 W Walnut Ave, is a record shop that carries exclusively southern Louisiana music. The staff is extremely knowledgeable and they mail-order hundreds of titles of Cajun, zydeco, swamp pop, compilation and festival recordings. Also downtown, the tiny **Cajun Music Hall of Fame** is slowly emerging next to the depot on 1st St. Currently the walls are covered with photographs of artists who have been nominated, and the curator will drop in a tape for visitors who stop by. For the moment, admission is free.

Places to Stay

The *Cajun Campground* (☎ 318-457-5753), on Hwy 190, five miles east from downtown, offers $13 hookup sites for mostly RVs (tents $9, special area available) with a pool, small store and snowball stand surrounded by woods. (Noncampers pay $2 to swim.) It's a very authentic Cajun camping resort. *Howard's Inn* (☎ 318-457-2066), 3789 Hwy 190 east, offers singles for $33, doubles $42, in a decent two-story brick motel (no pool) three miles from downtown. The *Best Western* (☎ 318-457-2800), 1531 W Laurel Ave (Hwy 190 west), offers rooms for $61/65 single/double, including a pool and continental breakfast. B&B accommodations are available at the *Seale Guest House* (☎ 318-457-3753) on a more rural stretch of Hwy 13 south of town. The Seales offer four guest rooms in their house for $65 to $75, including breakfast.

Places to Eat

For a bite to eat downtown there's *Nik's* (☎ 318-457-4921), 123 S 2nd St, no place to commit entree dollars to, but OK for a $5 po-boy at the bar. Though *Johnson's Grocery* (☎ 318-457-9314), 700 E Maple Ave, is considered the high altar of boudin, many locals prefer the *Eunice Slaughterhouse* (☎ 318-546-6041), at the dead-end of Maple Ave and Bobcat Dr, for less mushy boudin. The Slaughterhouse is down from the high school and open 6 am to 5 pm Monday to Friday and on Saturday till noon.

A great joint open only in crawfish season is *Hawk's* (☎ 318-788-3266), 12 miles outside town at 1110 Hawkins Rd. Hawk's specializes in boiled crawfish that is first 'purged' for 24 hours – a process the owner asserts accounts for its sweet flavor. From around February through June (call to confirm), Hawk's is open Wednesday through Sunday 5 to 10 pm. It's off the beaten path; try to head out during daylight. Take Hwy 13 south from the old depot to Hwy 98; turn left (east) and continue 8 miles to Hawkins Rd. (See the Rice Belt for directions from I-10.)

MAMOU

Mamou calls itself the Cajun Music Capital of the World, and it's a humble town to make so large a claim. But you won't get any argument from anyone who's been to Fred's Lounge on Saturday morning. The place starts hopping around 8 am every Saturday, and if you arrive much later than 9, there's a chance you may not get in. Cajun Fever starts to play, beer flows, folks two-step and waltz, a basket of boudin goes around, and by 11 am they're all wearing Mardi Gras hats and parading in a rumba line out into the street. The whole thing is broadcast on KVPI 92.5 FM.

When the music's over at *Fred's* (☎ 318-468-5234), the party continues a couple doors down at *Diana's*, one of the four other bars in Mamou's block-long commercial center on 6th St. Another unusual bar is the peculiarly swank *Holiday Lounge*, seen blinking in the field west of Hwy 13 at the Mamou turnoff. Apparently it used to be the biggest gaming house on the prairie, which must account for all the Naugahyde and fake tropical flora.

Mamou was one of the first towns to revive le courir de Mardi Gras, and nowadays Mamou's celebration is the best known and most raucous of all. Crowds party in the streets all day and all night after the riders return. The town also hosts a Cajun Music Festival in May.

Mamou has two terrifically low-rent places to stay. One is the *Cazan Hotel* (☎ 318-468-7187), on 6th St downtown above the corner bar by the same name. Rooms are sparsely furnished with metal bedposts, bare floors and radiators, and doors don't close so exactly, but fortunately it's too dimly lit to tell how dingy it really is. They charge $20 a night, and fill up many weekends and during festivals. Call to reserve (ask to overlook 6th St), and check in at the bar. The other is the *Bamboo Motel* (☎ 318-468-9958), on Hwy 13 several blocks west of the downtown block.

Le Courir de Mardi Gras

A Mardi Gras spectacle unique to Cajun Country is 'le courir' – the horseback run through the countryside held in Cajun prairie towns north of Lafayette. The ritual has its roots in the medieval tradition of ceremonial begging and resembles Christmas 'mumming' in Europe and the West Indies. On Mardi Gras, bands of masked and costumed men ride from house to house 'begging' for ingredients to add to a community gumbo in exchange for singing, dancing or clowning antics. A traditional Mardi Gras song is sung in French, recalling medieval French folk music.

Typical courir costumes and characters are far different from the refined or outrageous dress of revelers in New Orleans or even Lafayette. The *paillasse* – straw man – who acts as the clown or fool wears a costume of burlap and straw decorated with other readily available materials like buttons, fabric and metallic objects. Painted and decorated screens serve as masks. Other colorful characters wear tall cone-shaped hats called *capuchon* (French for 'hood') that symbolize a mockery of the upper class. A *capitaine* oversees the melee. The same ritual carried out in Creole communities tends to be more traditional and less brawling than in Cajun communities. The tradition is a rite of passage for many young men in small communities known for their courir celebrations, such as Church Point, Eunice, Mamou, Ville Platte and Elton.

While the riders are out in the countryside, folks gather in town to await their return. After they gallop back in triumph, a communal supper is held with much more drinking and dancing. Visitors may join in the festivities – staking out a corner to watch the riders pass or joining the party. ∎

LOUISIANA OFFICE OF TOURISM

They charge $20 for equally dim motel rooms with less dark charm.

There are two restaurants: *Carl's*, across the street from Fred's, and *Jeffrey's*, near the Cazan. Jeffrey's is more of a breakfast place, with a counter and a waitress who calls you 'sha' (the Cajun endearment derived from the French *cher*). *Ortego's Meat Market* (☎ 318-468-3746), about two blocks down from Fred's, is known for its tasso beef and pork. The 24-hour *Shell station* at the north edge of town dishes out Creole plates of fried chicken and rice and beans for under $2; a few benches are available inside.

VILLE PLATTE & AROUND
Ville Platte (flat town) was named for this last stretch of level prairie bordering the rolling hill region to the north. The slight rise in elevation is perceptible and welcome. The town of 10,000 was founded by Major Marcellin Garand, who is considered responsible for initiating the jousting tournaments still held each year. This knightly *tournoi* – one of the most unusual events in a region already distinguished by such events as masked chicken runs on horseback, giant 5000-egg omelets, and annual fests honoring frogs, crawfish and petroleum – takes place during the town's Cotton Festival. Usually held the second weekend in October, the festival also features parades and the coronation of a Cotton Queen. The town also hosts a gumbo festival the first Saturday in November and Le Festival de Viande Boucanée – celebrating the local specialty smoked meats – the last weekend in June. All celebrations bring out great food, local bands and festive folks for dancing and merrymaking. The Chamber of Commerce (☎ 318-363-1878), 306 W Main St, can give you exact upcoming dates and city maps.

The town holds a landmark for local music fans: **Floyd's Record Shop** (☎ 318-363-2138), 434 E Main St, maintains the largest collection of south Louisiana music around. Owner Floyd Soileau operates a recording studio down the street and puts out records of local musicians on his home labels. Tune in to Ville Platte's KVPI at 1050 AM/92.5 FM for local Cajun music broadcasts.

A block from Floyd's is a favorite barbecue joint, the *Pig Stand* (☎ 318-363-2883), 318 E Main St. It goes beyond its popular pork barbecue to offer exotic sausages and stews with its trademark onion and garlic sauce (also sold separately). It's often open late, some nights as late as 2 am. Another culinary landmark is *Dupre's Grocery* (☎ 318-363-4186), 102 W Hickory. Dupre's makes sausages that are distributed around the state, and it sells boudin, cracklins and fresh meats (a convenient stop for Chicot State Park campers looking for something for the grill and for the ride). They sell cold beer, too. Find Dupre's off SW Railroad Ave (along the tracks), around a half-mile southwest of Main St.

In a rural area fifteen miles north of Ville Platte, *Bette's Log Cabin Catfish Kitchen* (☎ 318-461-2800), 6813 Hwy 167, in Turkey Creek, is a family restaurant that serves a seafood buffet Wednesday through Saturday from 5 pm. Typical selections include boiled crawfish (in season), crabs, baked or fried catfish, gumbo, fish stew, fried corn balls, fried okra, blackberry cobbler and Mason jar iced tea all for under $11 adults, $6 children five to 12.

South of town, pass by *Shorty's Zydeco Club* (☎ 318-363-8093), 1161 Te Mamou Rd (in a far field on the road to Mamou), on a weekend night to see if a band is playing.

State Arboretum & Chicot State Park
Here in south-central Louisiana, the state park and adjacent arboretum enter a sloping forested terrain in sharp contrast to the flat prairie to the south. The 600-acre **Louisiana State Arboretum** holds a mature forest dominated by beech and magnolia. More than two miles of nature trails wind through the woodlands and over footbridges past signs identifying native

LOUISIANA

Louisiana plants. The entrance is off Hwy 3042, 1½ miles from the main entrance to the state park.

Chicot State Park (☎ 318-363-2403), off Hwy 3042, surrounds Lake Chicot. It has cabins, a lodge, campgrounds, boat launches, fishing piers, a pool and a trail through the bottomland hardwood forest. The trail is suitable for hiking, backpacking and mountain biking.

Twenty-seven fully equipped lakefront cabins sleep four ($45) or six ($60); lodge rooms sleep groups of seven or larger ($90). They're designed for families, so some beds are twin bunks and may not be suitable for several couples traveling together. Bring your own towels. Camping is $12 a night with hookups, $10 for tents or primitive backpacking sites. Admission is $2 per car, free for seniors.

Crooked Creek Recreation Area

A local camping alternative to Chicot State Park is Crooked Creek (☎ 318-599-2661), off Hwy 3187, 12 miles west of Chicot. You can also swim in the lake here at a small beach of imported sand. It's a well-used spot for fishing, boating, water-skiing and camping. Sites are $12 for RVs, $10 for tents in a tent-only area near the lake (though unfortunately far from the bathhouse). Day-use admission is $2 per person, 50¢ for children.

THE RICE BELT

Off I-10 between Lafayette and Lake Charles is the Rice Belt of the Cajun prairie. Nineteenth-century railroad towns here hold rice landmarks and other small-town pleasures.

Note that Eunice is 18 miles north of I-10 with many more attractions (see above), including the notable Hawk's Restaurant (open crawfish season only). To reach Hawk's from I-10, exit at Rayne and head north to make a quick left after the overpass onto Hwy 98. Defy all attempts to throw you off Hwy 98 and proceed west around 6½ miles to the Hawk's sign at Parish Rd 2-7. Hawk's is less than a mile up the dirt road.

As the Frog Capital of the World, **Rayne** earns its title with whimsical frog murals on downtown walls and storefronts and a Frog Festival the second weekend in September. The festival features a frog-legs eating contest, the crowning of the Frog Queen, Frog Jockeys, a Diaper Derby, parade and traditional fais-do-do. Legs of the local mascot are served up a variety of ways at the festival and also in area restaurants.

For lighter fare, *Memere's Tea Room* (☎ 318-334-8287), 112 E Edwards St just before the tracks, serves pastries and coffee, croissant sandwiches under $4, soups and salads; it's open Monday through Friday and some weekends.

Crowley, Rice Capital of Louisiana, celebrates its primary industry at the Rice Festival the third weekend in October. More monuments to rice can be found at the Rice Museum (☎ 318-783-6842), off Hwy 13 directly north of I-10. Once the LSU rice experiment station, the museum tells the story of rice with vintage machinery and a demonstration rice mill. The **Crystal Rice Plantation** (☎ 318-783-6417), off Airport Rd south of town via Hwy 13 south, contains a historic house museum (an Acadian cottage from 1848 furnished with period antiques), an automobile museum of a half-dozen vintage cars and an aquaculture tour, which describes the crop rotations of rice and crawfish common to the region. It's open weekdays, Saturdays by appointment.

Crowley's *Rice Hotel* (☎ 318-783-0970), 125 3rd St, is a rare old downtown hotel, which has been in continuous operation since 1908. It certainly shows its age, but rooms are clean, comfortable and cheap. A double is under $40. Other motels are clustered around I-10 exit 80, including a *Best Western* (☎ 800-940-0003) or the modest *Crowley Inn* northeast of the interstate ($45/50 single/double, with a pool). The *Rice Palace* video poker casino at I-10 exit 80 is open 24 hours with meal service.

Fourteen miles northwest of Crowley, **Iota** celebrates Mardi Gras with a courir and folklife festival retaining traditions no longer found elsewhere. Here at a free open street festival downtown on Mardi Gras, a hundred riders return wearing the traditional handmade screen masks, capuchon hats and costumes. Cajun and zydeco bands, prairie Cajun food specialties and a lively dance are all part of the event. Also in town, Cajun musical-instrument maker Larry Miller (☎ 318-779-2246), on Hwy 370, will show off his work by appointment.

In **Jennings**, the Zigler Museum (☎ 318-824-0114), 411 Clara St, contains a small but select collection of works in the former home of its patron, the wife of a local industrialist. Among its most distinguished works are paintings by Audubon, Whistler and van Dyck. Admission is $2 adults; closed Monday. The museum is in the historic district downtown, which retains many old storefronts along a nine-block stretch of Main St between Hwy 90 and the railroad tracks. Right off the highway, the city's 31-acre **Oil & Gas Park** is a handy pit stop for I-10 through-travelers, with a visitors center, small lake, captive alligators, picnic tables and an oil well replica commemorating the first oil well struck near here in 1901.

Downtown, the *Boudin King* (☎ 318-824-6593), 906 W Division St, several blocks west of Hwy 26/Lake Arthur Ave, offers gumbo and fried chicken in addition to its namesake boudin. A half-mile north of the interstate on Hwy 26 at exit 64, *Donn E's* (☎ 318-824-3402) serves reasonably priced Cajun buffets daily. Several chain motels surround I-10 exit 64, including the *Holiday Inn* (☎ 318-824-5280) and the *Days Inn* (☎ 318-824-6550). The budget *Sundown Inn* (☎ 318-824-7041), a half-mile north of I-10 on Hwy 26, charges $39 double.

Worth a short detour 12 miles north of I-10 on Hwy 97, *DI's Cajun Restaurant* (☎ 318-432-5141), between Jennings and Basile, offers live Cajun music along with Cajun cooking. It's open Tuesday through Saturday from 5 pm. Cajun bands perform from around 7 to 10:30 pm these nights, with jam sessions on Wednesdays.

The Cajun Coast

The western region near the Texas border is the most remote in Cajun Country, and the terrain is more open than in the eastern wetlands. Many wildlife refuges provide sanctuary for birds migrating along the Mississippi Flyway. The city of Lake Charles provides easy-access services for interstate travelers and a great state park, but besides that it's not a highlight of the region. The appeal of southwest Louisiana lies in walks through the quiet marshlands, long range drives through arcades of live oak and a cultural outing to the 'Cajun Riviera' at Holly Beach. Though it's officially Acadiana, culturally the region borrows many traditions from neighboring Texas, so it's a bit Western, even if it is mostly marsh. If your timing's right, you might catch a fishing rodeo, an alligator harvest festival or the Fur and Wildlife Festival in Cameron in January.

LAKE CHARLES
Lake Charles is largely an industrial port, with its commercial center built on the eastern shore of the Calcasieu River south of I-10. Also here, on the southeast side of the river, visible for eastbound travelers, is a visitor center for southwest Louisiana. On the western side of the bridge is the exit for the casino area, which leads to two casinos (with more hotels on the way). The casinos provide meal service and are open 24 hours. Interstate through-travelers won't lack for services, but if you can hold on till Lafayette, you'll have plenty more choices. The modern chain lodging at interstate exits – the Motel 6, the Days Inn, the Best Western – provide the best value in terms of quality and convenience if you have to stop. The city is most useful to travelers as a jumping-off point for exploring the quiet coast – it would be wise to gas up and buy provisions here.

SAM HOUSTON JONES STATE PARK
This inviting state park (☎ 318-855-2665), 12 miles north of Lake Charles, is well

worth the detour for folks looking to camp or needing a refuge from interstate travel. The park (named for Louisiana's 37th governor, who was instrumental in securing the land) is set around a beautiful cypress pond. Visitors can paddle around the trees (canoe rentals available). The 73 campsites ($12 a night, hookups available) are set off along shell roads by the pond. Twelve waterside vacation cabins that sleep six are also available for $60 a night, but note that state park cabins are often booked far in advance (linens and dishware provided, bring towels). There's also a deer pen (two fawns roamed about on a recent visit), modern playground equipment and a trail along an old stagecoach road. Signs direct drivers from I-10.

Outside the entrance to the park is a small, friendly market and gas station beside a small marina. The market stocks a decent selection of groceries and deli food along with camping and fishing supplies.

CREOLE NATURE TRAIL

From **Sulphur** west of Lake Charles, Hwy 27 heads down to the coast then loops

back up to Holmwood. This loop has been officially designated a national scenic byway known as the Creole Nature Trail. It's far from spectacular, but it has a homely, deserted appeal. The two-lane route traverses marshland, passing refuges (prime fishing grounds); a ferry at Holly Beach crosses over the Calcasieu River to Cameron.

While it passes through several small towns (see below), provisions are minimal, and it would be good to head out with enough gas, cash, insect repellent and cold drinks for the trip. Aim your drive to end up at the *Boudin Factory* in **Sweetwater**, at the intersection of Hwys 27 and 384. It's open for $2.25 crab burgers or daily plate lunches Monday through Saturday from 9 am to 6 pm.

Sabine National Wildlife Refuge

The 196-sq-mile Sabine Refuge is the largest coastal refuge on the Gulf. Under both the Mississippi and Central Flyways, it preserves wetlands for wintering and migrating waterfowl. Snow and blue geese can be seen from November through

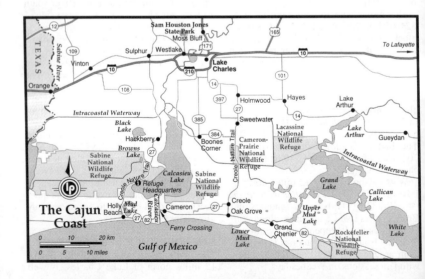

February. It is also a major nursery for marine species as well as for alligators, turtles and numerous wading, water and marsh birds. The marsh landscape is dominated by cordgrass – thin slivers of estuary streams cut through tufts of the green reeds – interspersed with cattails, water hyacinth, cypress, elm, willow and palmetto on patches of higher ground. While the marshlands are not as varied as, say, those on the southeastern Atlantic Coast of the US, they are a wide-open contrast to the forested canopy of the Cajun wetlands to the east.

At refuge headquarters on Hwy 27 (11 miles south of Hackberry), a small visitors center provides maps and distributes information on boating through 150 miles of waterways, as well as for recreational fishing, crabbing, shrimping, crawfishing and duck hunting. There's also a button-activated Cajun robot to explain the history of the area.

The 1½-mile **Marsh Trail** can be found four miles south of the center. The all-access trail enters the tranquil marsh and allows opportunities to see alligators (most visible on windless, bright, warm days) and other wildlife.

Holly Beach

Holly Beach heads up the rugged coastline called (mockingly) the Cajun Riviera. It could be considered a down-home resort, if you knew anyone who lived like this. Here they drive pickup trucks onto the sand right up to the water, set out lounge chairs on the flatbed, and wing out the doors to play music. On last visit, the beach was littered with jellyfish carcasses, which might account for the lack of people in the water. At night, they rake the beach by dragging along a skeletal box-spring from the back of a monster truck.

Many of the residences are trailers raised on story-high stilts to avoid hurricane waves. There are three bars in town, two cafés and two markets. Two establishments are apparently obligated by the federal government to post signs publicly

acknowledging that members of any race may do business there.

The bar music you'll hear over the sound of video poker machines won't be Cajun, but country – most likely an electric countrified rock. *Lagneaux's Lounge* (☎ 318-569-2242) on Hwy 27/82 might be the most colorful place to sample the local ambiance – the interior is cast in the glow of Christmas lights and silver tinsel garland. The low, white wooden building also houses the town's café and grocery. But the *Four Corners Bar* (☎ 318-569-2351), down from Lagneaux's a block from the beach, has a better view. Holly Beach hosts the Cajun Riviera Festival the second weekend in August.

In the winter, the year-round population is around a hundred. In the summer that figure swells to 10 times that amount, filling cabins, RV sites and motel rooms. Like the beach at Grand Isle, most of the accommodations are seriously below par at any price, and prices start at a hefty $50.

One oasis among the offerings is *Cajun Cabins* (☎ 318-569-2442), 2431 Gulf Beach Hwy, where the rooms themselves are off the highway on a side street. The proprietors offer five modest, clean rooms with two double beds, ceiling fans, enough light, stall showers and TVs for $55 a night. The rooms are three short blocks to the beach. For a quick overnight, towels are provided; for a longer stay, bring your own. Another choice is *Tommy's Motel & Cabins* (☎ 318-569-2426) at 404 Tarpon Ave; it's more in the thick of things near the trailer cafe.

HWY 82 SCENIC DRIVE

From the Creole Nature Trail on Hwy 27 past Holly Beach, Hwy 82 roughly follows the coast east to Abbeville. The route first crosses over the Calcasieu River aboard a free car ferry to the town of **Cameron**. Devastated by Hurricane Audrey in 1957, which killed 500 and toppled many buildings, Cameron has recovered somewhat as a commercial center for ship workers, oil workers and pilots. This is where you can find an ATM.

Beyond the turnoff for Hwy 27, the two-lane route careens through intermittent marshlands and woodlands, past sparsely populated communities and refuges. A scenic arcade of oaks follows much of the route.

In **Grand Chenier**, Mary Grovenburg offers B&B lodging at *Chateau Chenier* (☎ 318-538-2389), on Hwy 82 at the river. Rooms with private bath run $55, shared bath $45. She sometimes rents the whole house out, commonly to deep-sea fishermen, for $140 a night. The place is popular with birders, and Grovenburg can arrange for knowledgeable local guides to bring visitors (at no small cost) out into the nearby refuges and bird sanctuaries.

ROCKEFELLER WILDLIFE REFUGE

The 131-sq-mile Rockefeller Refuge provides the opportunity to see the same wildlife species and landscapes as at Sabine Refuge (see above), but in a more remote location that borders the Gulf of Mexico. The property was once owned by the McIlhennys of Tabasco fame, then sold to the Rockefeller Foundation, which later turned it over to the state of Louisiana for preservation. Aerial inventories conducted by refuge biologists list the midwinter duck population at about 400,000.

The headquarters is at the northwestern corner of the refuge outside Grand Chenier, and is open to visitors from March to December. Access on foot is for the most part restricted to weirs on artificial canals.

Central Louisiana

History

There is no Maginot Line that divides northern Louisiana from southern Louisiana. Instead, there is central Louisiana ('Cenla'), a region with pockets of both cultures – from Natchitoches with its strong, proud French heritage; to Marksville, home of the Tunica Indian tribe; to Alexandria, a city described in AJ Liebling's brilliant book *The Earl of Louisiana* as 'the political navel of Louisiana [where] Southern bilingual, French Catholic Louisiana, the land of the bougalees, shades into Northern monolingual, Anglo-Saxon Protestant Louisiana, the land of the rednecks.'

Liebling's characterization of Alexandria might well be applied to the whole region east and south of Natchitoches. Though tagged as Cenla, the culturally diverse parishes of the region have little in common beyond geographical proximity.

Much of central Louisiana is a lonely place, densely forested and sparsely populated. Beginning around 1900, lumber companies began flocking to the region, intent upon harvesting the monstrous virgin pines. Today there may be more reforestation than deforestation going on, but pulpwood trucks still clog the highway. What is left of the virgin forests is a direct result of the efforts of one woman: Caroline Dorman, the first female forester in the nation. By sheer will alone, she convinced the state of Louisiana and the USFS to establish the Kisatchie National Forest, comprised of 937 sq miles stretching over seven parishes.

On the western fringe of the region, Natchitoches is still under the sway of the French explorers who first came to the area in 1714. Under the direction of Louis Juchereau de St Denis, they established the first European settlement in what is now Louisiana, Fort St Jean-Baptiste. Three years later, the Spanish, intent upon stemming westward migration of the French,

HIGHLIGHTS

- The 'steel' magnolias and cast-iron balconies of Natchitoches
- A tour of Melrose Plantation, where women ruled the roost
- Hiking and canoeing in Kisatchie National Forest
- Kent House Plantation
- The Tunica Treasure in Marksville

built a fort just 15 miles away and named it Los Adaes. The frontier standstill ended in 1762 when France ceded Louisiana to Spain. Save a few minor conflicts, the French and Spanish never really did battle. What they did do was trade with Caddo Confederation Indian tribes like the Adaes and the Natchitoches.

Despite 40 years of de facto Spanish rule, by the time of the Louisiana Purchase in 1803, Natchitoches fancied itself to be a decidedly French town – so much so that most of the local gentry looked upon the coming of the Americans as tantamount to an invasion of vulgarians.

Today, Natchitoches still clings tenaciously to its French ancestry. Equally proud, and just as disdainful of the Anglo-Saxon Protestants in their midst, are the Franco-African people who live along the Cane River just south of Natchitoches and are known as 'Creoles of Color.'

Surrounded as it is by the Kisatchie National Forest, Natchitoches feels a bit removed from other population centers in the state. But, just 40 miles up the road is

LOUISIANA

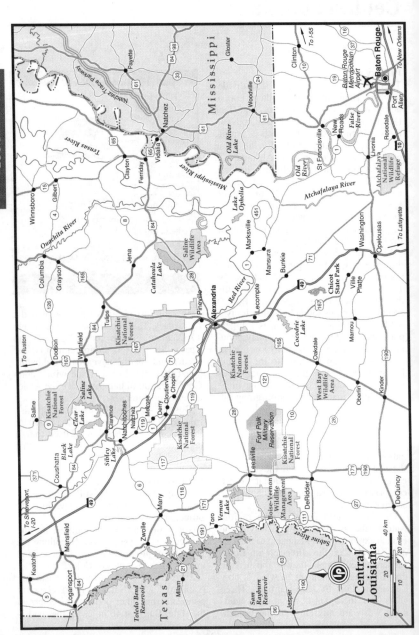

what may well be (with apologies to Mr Liebling) the epicenter of Louisiana politics – Winnfield, seat of government for Winn Parish and birthplace of the state's strongest and strangest political legacy. Once known as the 'Free State of Winn' because of its resistance to secession during the Civil War, Winn Parish remains a hotbed of rancorous populist politics where voters are more impressed by a good stump speech than promises of a tax cut.

South of Winnfield, the landscape begins to change from rolling hills to flatter, often swampy land. Though the French settled along the Red River here in 1723, the present-day French influence is not as strong as it is upriver.

By the 19th century, Rapides Parish was the economic hub of the region. But during the Civil War most of the towns along the southern stretch of the Red River were burned. It was not until WWII, when troops came to train at Camp Beauregard in Rapides Parish, that Cenla came to life again. Today only Marksville, southeast of Alexandria, seems to be thriving. There, the Tunica Indians (only recently recognized as a tribe by the US Bureau of Indian Affairs) have opened a glitzy new casino that pulls in visitors from around the region.

Flora & Fauna

This is timber farming territory. Accordingly, there are huge tracts of dense pine forests scattered about the region. The whole of the area is alive with squirrels, deer, opossum, raccoons and wild turkeys, while the waterways teem with gaspergou, gar, crappie, catfish and crawfish. On and around the bayous, lily pads and iris bogs flourish beneath moss-draped cypress trees.

Louisiana Politics – The Long Way

For years, when it came to Louisiana politics, the Long way was the only way.

Huey Long, a flamboyant and charismatic populist politician, served as governor from 1928 to 1932 before entering the US Senate in 1932. At the height of his power, he had a virtual stranglehold on the state.

With a promise to 'sock it to the rich fat cats,' Long won the undying faith of the working men and women of Louisiana, on whose behalf he embarked upon a massive series of public works programs – building hospitals, schools and highways throughout the rural parishes. But along with such good works came a good measure of graft.

Through intimidation and bribery, Huey Long squashed any challenges to his authority, until, in September of 1935, he was assassinated by a Baton Rouge physician. At the time of his death, Huey Long was poised to make a run for the US presidency.

Earl Long, while not as ambitious or as controlling as his brother Huey, was nevertheless a singular political personality. His three terms as governor during the 1940s and 1950s provided both comic relief and strong leadership. Infamous for his liaisons with strippers and affinity for strong drink, 'Uncle Earl' was at one time during his administration committed to a hospital for the insane.

For a more in-depth portrait of these men, pick up a copy of T Harry Williams' voluminous biography *Huey Long* or AJ Liebling's brilliant and witty portrait *The Earl of Louisiana*.

Or, if you're in search of the roots of these two political titans, you might want to visit the town of Winnfield, just 30 miles east of Natchitoches. Aside from the bronze statue of Huey at the courthouse and the imposing sculpture of Earl at the Earl K Long Memorial Park on Elm St, the prime attraction is the Louisiana Political Museum and Hall of Fame (☎ 318-628-5928), 499 E Main St.

Located in an old railroad depot, this cozy little museum is filled with political ephemera. Though life-size statues of the Longs dominate the room, the more interesting artifacts are more mundane, from an old voting machine to campaign buttons that read 'Vote for Uncle Earl. I ain't crazy.' Even the bathrooms are plastered with political bumper stickers. ■

Activities

Thanks to the Kisatchie National Forest, located to the northeast and southwest of Natchitoches, central Louisiana abounds with hiking and other recreational opportunities. Once you're 50 feet into these piney hills, all traces of the modern world quickly recede, for though this is beautiful country it's not highly trafficked by either tourists or locals. Or take advantage of the lakes and rivers scattered about and try canoeing along the Kisatchie Bayou. See the more detailed entry below.

Getting There & Away

Alexandria boasts a regional airport with regular connections to hub cities like New Orleans and Dallas. Train service is unavailable to and from any of the major population centers, while Greyhound buses provide service throughout the region. As a rule, a car is the preferred mode of transportation. For those traveling through the western part of the region, I-49 and Hwy 71 connect Natchitoches and Alexandria, but elsewhere you will travel circuitous (but often scenic) routes. Continuing southward, I-49 is the primary route, with the Cajun capital of Lafayette just 90 miles down the road (see Cajun Country chapter).

NATCHITOCHES

population 17,000

Despite its storied history and charming French architecture, Natchitoches (pronounced NA-kid-ish by locals) remained a sleepy little backwater with hardly a tourist on the street until, in 1988, Hollywood filmmakers arrived to make the blockbuster movie *Steel Magnolias*. Based upon the play by native son Robert Harling, the film drew a bevy of movie stars to town for the filming, including Shirley MacLaine, Darryl Hannah, Dolly Parton, Julia Roberts, Sally Field and Olympia Dukakis.

In their wake, Hollywood left Natchitoches transformed. Where before hardware stores and junk shops were clustered downtown, now there are fancy-schmancy dress shops. Before *Steel Magnolias* it was hard to find a decent hotel in town. Now there are at least 20 B&Bs ranging from opulent homes to converted duplexes.

This was once a transportation center, but Natchitoches River commerce literally dried up when, in 1825, the Red River began changing course. Now the former Red River is a tranquil lake, and the economy depends upon tourists and college students from Northwestern State University for sustenance.

Today, Natchitoches is an enchanting blend of genteel French town and thriving tourist destination. The riverfront bustles with tourists shopping for souvenirs and gawking at the elaborate wrought ironwork on Front St townhouses. But don't think that the city's rich history has been tossed aside in a grab for the almighty dollar. Natchitoches residents are dead serious about their history. Stop a local on the street to talk, and chances are that 10 minutes later you will walk away with a head full of names and dates. And, halfway through that same conversation, you can be sure that he or she will mention, in an offhand manner, that Natchitoches just happens to be older than New Orleans.

Orientation & Information

At the heart of Natchitoches is a 33-block national historic district situated along the west bank of Cane River Lake. Most west-bank commercial activity is on Front St, Washington St and Second St, while Williams Blvd (Business Hwy 1) is the core east-bank thoroughfare. Hwys 1 and 6 form a de facto perimeter around the city.

The Tourist Commission (☎ 318-352-8072) is at 781 Front St, in the heart of the historic district. They're open from 9 am to 5 pm Monday through Saturday and 10 am to 3 pm on Sunday.

ATMs are found on Church St and Second St downtown, or on Keyser Ave on the eastern edge of town.

The main post office (☎ 318-352-2161) is at 240 St Denis St.

As for newspapers, the meager *Natchitoches Times* is published daily and the Shreveport paper is widely distributed in

LOUISIANA

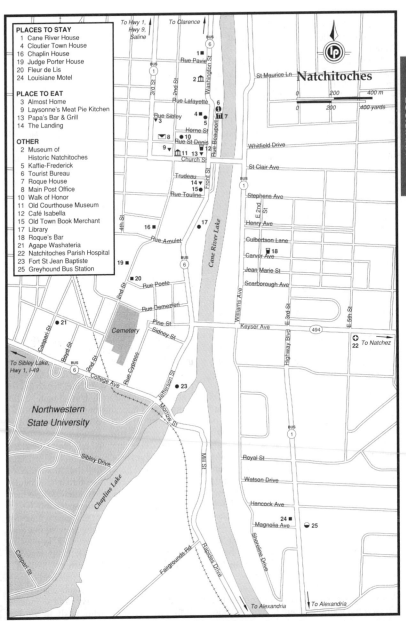

PLACES TO STAY
1 Cane River House
4 Cloutier Town House
16 Chaplin House
19 Judge Porter House
20 Fleur de Lis
24 Louisiane Motel

PLACE TO EAT
3 Almost Home
9 Laysonne's Meat Pie Kitchen
13 Papa's Bar & Grill
14 The Landing

OTHER
2 Museum of
   Historic Natchitoches
5 Kaffie-Frederick
6 Tourist Bureau
7 Roque House
8 Main Post Office
10 Walk of Honor
11 Old Courthouse Museum
12 Café Isabella
15 Old Town Book Merchant
17 Library
18 Roque's Bar
21 Agape Washateria
22 Natchitoches Parish Hospital
23 Fort St Jean Baptiste
25 Greyhound Bus Station

Natchitoches

town. If you're longing for a real newspaper, the Old Town Book Merchant (see below) sells the Sunday edition of the *New York Times*.

The main library (☎ 318-357-3280) is at 431 Jefferson St and is open weekdays from 9 am to 6 pm, Saturday until 5 pm.

The Old Town Book Merchant (☎ 318-357-8900), 512 Front St, is a cozy bookstore with a strong selection of regional history and Southern fiction. As a bonus, the helpful staff seems to always be well informed about live entertainment offerings in town. The store is open daily from 10 am to 6 pm.

For laundry, try Agape Washateria (☎ 318-357-0271), 137 Caspari St near the university. They're open daily from 8 am to 8 pm.

Natchitoches Parish Hospital (☎ 318-352-1200), 501 Keyser Ave on the east bank, offers emergency service.

Things to See & Do

No matter what the folks who run the little motorized trolley tell you, Natchitoches is best enjoyed on foot. A **walking tour** begins with a stroll down Front St between Rue Touline and Rue Lafayette; it's the ideal way to get your bearings and appreciate the Creole townhouses with their lacy cast-iron balconies overlooking the lake.

From Front St, turn away from the river and just wander the back streets. Along the way, you'll encounter a plethora of older homes ranging in style from Georgian to Victorian. On Rue St Denis between Front St and Second St, be sure and check out the **Walk of Honor**, where inscribed fleurs-de-lis are cemented into the sidewalk in tribute to everyone from Dolly Parton and John Wayne to the Dixie Debs, '1994 World Series Girls Fastpitch Softball Champions.'

At the corner of Second and Church Sts, the **Old Courthouse Museum**, a beautiful 1896 Romanesque building, hosts frequently changing exhibits but is, quite frankly, not worth the $3 admission. Across the street you will find Immaculate Conception Catholic Church, built in 1856,

while one block south at the corner of Rue Trudeau and Second St is the graceful Trinity Episcopal Church. If you continue in a south to southwesterly direction, you will become happily lost along the town's narrow back streets.

Eventually, you will want to make your way back to Front St (known as Washington St north of Rue Lafayette and Jefferson St south of Rue Touline) for a visit to the **Museum of Historic Natchitoches** (☎ 318-357-0070), 840 Washington St. Housed in a plain-as-vanilla, 1914 clapboard home, the museum has a surprisingly good collection of French colonial artifacts. Civil War (referred to, by the somewhat-biased curator, as the 'War for Southern Independence') buffs should make sure they catch a glimpse of the 1864 Natchitoches Union newspaper printed on wallpaper and the beautiful pink-and-blue flag of the 3rd Louisiana Infantry. Fans of popular music will be interested in the macabre little tribute to singer Jim Croce, who played in Natchitoches the night before dying in a plane crash.

Below the tourist offices on Rue Beauport next to the lakefront is **Roque House**, an 18th-century plantation outbuilding moved to this site to serve as a museum displaying the works of folk artist Clementine Hunter (see Melrose Plantation in Cane River Country). Unfortunately, the proprietor's hours of operation defy logic. Call them at ☎ 318-365-5555 before you make a special trip.

Just south of downtown is **Northwestern State University**, a liberal arts college founded in 1884. Now home to almost 9000 students, Northwestern was recently selected as the site for the new $20 million National Center for Preservation Technology, dedicated to the preservation of architecturally important sites throughout the nation. Those interested in Native American archaeology are encouraged to visit **Williamson Museum** (☎ 318-357-5492), 210 Keyser Hall, a research repository of over 500,000 artifacts that's open Monday through Friday from 8 am to 3:30 pm. Visitors who wish to further explore this region's rich folklife should stop by the university's Folklife Center. It houses 800 artist and subject files, 1500 audio recordings, 100 video tapes, a small but growing print library of books and periodicals and 5000 photographs. The campus hosts special lectures and concerts during the academic year; call university information (☎ 318-357-6361) for details.

Off Jackson St, near the university at 130 Moreau St on Cane River Lake, is **Fort St Jean Baptiste** (☎ 318-357-3101). Step inside the fort, and all reminders of 20th-century life vanish before your eyes. Reconstructed in 1979 from drawings made by the architect Ignace Francois Broutin in 1733, the five-acre compound features eight wood-and-mud buildings, all surrounded by a pointy wood fence. If you're lucky, one of their frontier reenactments will be taking place when you visit. One look at the actors' buckskin clothing and coonskin caps, and you'll want to join in. The fort is open 9 am to 5 pm daily.

Special Events

Call the tourist commission (☎ 318-352-8072) for more information on special events.

Each October, Natchitoches holds a somewhat subdued celebration as locals dress in colonial-period attire and open their homes for tours during the Natchitoches Pilgrimage.

On the first weekend in December, Cane River Lake is ablaze with lights as Natchitoches celebrates its Festival of Lights (☎ 318-352-8072) with boat parades and Christmas decoration competitions capped with fireworks.

Places to Stay

Camping *Hodges Gardens*, 35 miles south on Hwy 171, may be your best bet for camping (see Around Natchitoches). Otherwise drive north and east to the Kisatchie National Forest (see below), where numerous campsites await.

Motels For budget rooms, the *Lakeview Inn* (☎ 318-352-9561), on the northern edge of town at 1316 Washington St near the Hwy 1 bypass, has the cheapest rates in town. Though the exterior paint is peeling and the drapes are a little ratty, the rooms are clean and the desk clerks are accommodating. Singles are $24 and up, while doubles are $29 and up, depending upon whether the room has a refrigerator and a microwave.

Just south of town on the east bank is the *Louisiane Motel* (☎ 318-352-6401), 340 Hwy 1 south, advertised as 'The Working Man's Motel.' With rooms similar to the Lakeview priced at $32 for a single or double, this is a good second choice.

The chain motels located west of town, near the intersection of Hwy 6 and I-49, are overpriced at $45 and up. You are better off splurging and staying in one of the B&Bs in Natchitoches, where, with a little luck, you might be able to negotiate a lower rate.

B&Bs When there is an excess of something, Southerners are fond of saying, 'You can't swing a dead cat without hitting a (lawyer, junked car, pine tree – pick a noun).' In Natchitoches, that swung dead cat is likely to hit a B&B, and lucky for you. With over 20 in town, the rates are reasonable and the rooms are nice. One caveat: all rates go up approximately 25% in the month of December.

A particular favorite of ours is the *Cloutier Town House* (☎ 318-352-5242), at 8 Ducournau Square just off Front St. Built around 1820, this Creole-style townhouse fairly drips with charm and cast-iron fleurs-de-lis. With a balcony overlooking the lake, it's a great place to while away an afternoon watching the world go by. Of the two rooms available, the smaller front bedroom ($65) is the most charming. Though narrow, the room is bathed in natural sunlight, and the four-poster bed looks supremely comfortable. If you don't mind a separate bathroom, this is the best room in Natchitoches. The second room ($100) has an in-room Jacuzzi and is a bit larger. Both share a wonderful loft-like space with 30-foot ceilings and hardwood floors. A fully stocked complimentary bar awaits in the evening, as does a full breakfast in the morning.

The *Chaplin House* (☎ 318-352-2324), 434 Second St near Rue Amulet, is a more conventional B&B. This 1892 home has a wonderful front porch (called a gallery around these parts) that just begs for a book and a pitcher of iced tea. Upstairs, there is one long room built into the eaves that the owners rent for $55 to $100 a night depending upon the number of guests. As the only guest(s), you enjoy a sense of privacy that you don't find with many B&Bs. The upstairs kitchen has a microwave and refrigerator.

Established in 1983, the *Fleur de Lis* (☎ 318-352-6621), 336 Second St at Rue Poete, is Natchitoches' first B&B. This brightly painted Queen Anne Victorian home has five rooms that rent for $60 to $80 a night. The owners give guests free run of the house, encouraging them to help themselves to wine or soft drinks from the refrigerator whenever the mood strikes. In the morning, everyone sits down to a big communal breakfast before parting ways.

Though across the street from a dumpy fraternity house, the *Judge Porter House* (☎ 318-352-9206), 321 Second St, is anything but dumpy. Recently restored, this imposing 1912 home has a clean, airy feel to it. One and two-bedroom suites, complete with coffeemakers and bathrobes, are available for $95 to $160. The upstairs two-bedroom suite has a huge bathroom as well as floor-to-ceiling windows that allow access to the wraparound gallery.

For a change of architectural pace, try the *Cane River House* (☎ 318-352-5912), 910 Washington St just north of Rue Pavie. This 1923 craftsman bungalow, outfitted with period Arts & Crafts furniture, has two rooms at $70 a night, as well as a guesthouse for $75 to $95, all with private bath. The owners offer guests a choice of an early morning breakfast or a leisurely late morning brunch.

Places to Eat

It seems like every restaurant in town serves 'authentic' Natchitoches meat pies –

crusty, crescent-shaped little turnovers, stuffed with spicy ground beef, pork and onions and then fried. Once sold from street corner carts, these savory pies were on the verge of extinction when, in 1967, James Laysonne opened *Laysonne's Meat Pie Kitchen* (☎ 318-352-3353), 229 2nd St. Today, his pies are still the best. Order a Meat Pie Platter and you get a pie, dirty rice, a choice of vegetable (try the cabbage) and salad bar, all for $6. Or, if you crave vegetables, get the four-vegetable lunch with cornbread for $4. Laysonne's is open from 7 am to 7 pm Monday through Saturday.

Locals swear by *Almost Home* (☎ 318-352-2431), 729 3rd St, which offers a breakfast and lunch buffet of rib-sticking home cooking; it's open Sunday through Friday from 6 am to 2 pm.

If you're willing to drive a few miles, *Grayson's Barbecue* (☎ 318-357-0166) in Clarence is worth the trip. First-time visitors should order the mixed plate ($7), piled high with pork ribs, ham, beef, potato salad, beans and bread. If you just want a snack, order a ham sandwich on what the locals call a 'frog bun' – a fresh baked French roll. If you ask nicely, the owner might let you sneak a peek at the pits out back where that delectable hunk of ham you just ate spent the last 48 hours. On your way out the door, pick up a half-dozen chocolate or ginger cookies to go. Open Tuesday through Sunday from 8 am to 9 pm, Grayson's is at 5849 Hwy 71, just north of Hwy 84 in Clarence.

At *Papa's Bar & Grill* (☎ 318-356-5850), 604 Front St, order grilled pork chops stuffed with sausage for $9, or any of the nightly seafood specials. And if the waitress mentions something about having a few servings of catfish courtbullion left, for heaven's sake, order it; their version of this tomato-smothered dish is one of the best you'll find north of New Orleans. This comfy little spot is open Monday through Saturday from 11 am to 10 pm.

If you're in the mood for pizza, try *Beaudions's Pizza Pub* (☎ 318-356-9200), 1328 Hwy 1 South near the city limits. It packs 'em in Tuesday through Sunday from 4 pm to 2 am. The cinderblock building doesn't look like much, but the pizza is the best in these parts.

Louisiana natives will tell you that alligator makes good eating for their dogs but they wouldn't touch it. With that in mind, you should steer clear of restaurants that serve alligator in any form. One exception to that rule is *The Landing* (☎ 318-352-1579), 530 Front St. Though they serve blackened alligator, this elegant restaurant also serves some of the city's best seafood, including a great crawfish étouffée. It's open Tuesday through Saturday from 11 am to 2 pm and 5 to 10 pm, closing Sunday at 9 pm.

Also worth considering is *Monjuni's Italian Café & Grocery* (☎ 318-352-0401), 5909 Hwy 1 Bypass near Dean St just east of Sibley Lake. Though this location is not as good as the original in Shreveport, the po-boys, pastas and salads are still tasty. They're open for lunch Monday through Saturday from 11 am to 2 pm and for dinner weekdays from 4:30 to 9 pm, closing at 10 pm on weekends.

Entertainment

Café Isabella (☎ 318-357-1555), 624 Front St, a trendy little bohemian coffeehouse, is popular for its poetry readings and live acoustic music. They're open weekdays from 10 am until they feel like closing, while Saturday and Sunday they open around 11 am or noon and close around 6 pm if there's no evening entertainment. Your best bet is to call first and find out what's going on.

On the opposite end of the social spectrum is *Point Place Marina* (☎ 318-352-1707), 1209 Patrick Rd, just off Hwy 119 on the edge of Cane River Country. Set in the middle of a trailer park along the Cane River, this is the place to go when Natchitoches is feeling a bit too cutesy and contrived. Sunday is the best day to join the locals on a makeshift deck to sunbathe, drink cheap beer and watch a steady parade of water-skiers. Open daily from 10 am to 1 am.

If you're really lucky, you'll be in town on the last Friday of the month when *Roque's Bar* (☎ 318-352-6586), 235 Carver Ave, comes alive to the sounds of a blues jam. On most other days, a lively group of older gentleman – most of them proud 'Creoles of Color' – hold forth at this bar they call home. The beer is cheap ($1 for a 16-ounce Schlitz), and first-time visitors shouldn't be surprised when one of their bar-mates picks up the tab.

Things to Buy

Kaffie-Frederick (☎ 318-352-2525), 758 Front St, open since 1863, is a treasure trove of upscale hardware and home furnishings. They stock the largest selection of little red wagons you have ever seen. Open weekdays from 7 am to 5 pm and Saturday from 7 am to 4 pm.

For life's essentials there is a WalMart (☎ 318-352-5607) at 925 Keyser Ave near Williams Ave, on the east side of Cane River Lake.

Getting There & Away

There are no air or train services that connect with Natchitoches.

Buses arrive and depart from the Greyhound station (☎ 318-352-8341) at 325 Cane River Shopping Center just off Business Hwy 1 south. Six buses come through daily headed to and from Shreveport (two hours away) and Alexandria (one hour) with connecting service throughout the region.

Though you won't need a car around Natchitoches, you will need one to explore the Cane River Country and Hodges Gardens south of town or Briarwood nature preserve north of town.

AROUND NATCHITOCHES
Hodges Gardens

Drive 27 miles west of Natchitoches on Hwy 1 and then turn south for 12 miles on Hwy 171 to reach Hodges Gardens (☎ 318-586-3523). In the 1940s, AJ Hodges reclaimed 4700 acres of land as a tree farm and experimental arboretum. Where turn-of-the-century workers left an abandoned rock quarry, Hodges fashioned formal gardens and a 225-acre lake.

Today the gardens are encircled by a 10-mile loop road that offers access to forested hiking trails as well as 60 acres of formal terraced gardens. The gardens are a maze of switchback, paved trails skirted by babbling brooks. Occasionally, a deer will sprint across the path ahead of you.

Fishing boats are available for rental at $30 a half day and $50 for a whole day. The catch is catfish, bass and bream, and you must bring your own tackle.

Campsites rent for $16 with a tent pad, electricity and water, or $7 with none of these amenities, but be aware that admission fee, $6.50, is still charged.

Across the street is **Emerald Hills Golf Resort** (☎ 318-586-4661), a low-slung 1950s-style motel with nicer rooms for $45/50 single/double. A round of golf is $21 on the weekdays and $29 on the weekends.

Briarwood

Also known as the Caroline Dormon Nature Preserve, Briarwood (☎ 318-576-3379) is as remote and rustic as Hodges Gardens is accessible and well groomed. Established by Dormon (see History) as a center for the study of horticulture, the preserve is open during the months of April, May, August and November, but only on Saturday from 9 am to 5 pm and Sunday from noon to 5 pm. It's located about 37 miles north of Natchitoches via Hwy 84 east and Hwy 71 north, and three miles south of Saline on Hwy 9.

CANE RIVER COUNTRY

Once you've spent any time driving through Louisiana and Mississippi, columned plantation houses begin to draw about the same amount of attention as double-wide mobile homes. They're everywhere.

From bayou-front palaces to hill country showplaces, these homes all begin to look the same. And, should you choose to tour one of these mansions, chances are that some hoop-skirt-wearing guide will regale

you with a tall tale of brave Southern belles defying 'Damnyankee' looters – all in the name of saving 'the old home place.' If you saw *Gone With the Wind*, you know the shtick.

The Cane River country, just south of Natchitoches, is different – far different. Sure, there are some fairly typical plantations along the 30-mile stretch of Hwy 119 that leads to Cloutierville. But the monotony of all those white columns is broken by two outstanding attractions: Melrose Plantation, home of folk artist Clementine Hunter and Creole dowager Marie Therese Coincoin; and the Bayou Folk Museum, residence of Kate Chopin, who wrote an early feminist novel titled *The Awakening* in 1899.

South from Natchitoches, the highway hugs the bank of the Cane River Lake, and you'll pass locals dipping fishing poles into the lazy river or whiling the afternoon away on front gallery (around these parts, a porch is termed a gallery) rockers.

Along the western bank of the lake you pass four plantations in quick succession: Oaklawn, Cherokee, Beau Fort and Oakland, all suitably white and predictably unimpressive. Drive a bit farther on this two-lane meandering blacktop and you begin to notice that this is not just a land of wealth. Poor folks live here, too. Their jauntily painted shotgun houses and hard-listing trailers are proof-positive of their claim to this land.

Melrose Plantation

Just north of the Hwy 119 intersection with Hwy 493 is Melrose Plantation (☎ 318-379-0055), a fascinating complex of three main buildings and various outbuildings dating as far back as 1790. Though the 'big house' looms large from the road, the most compelling features are the Africa and Yucca Houses, which are found out back. The plantation is open daily from noon to 4 pm.

The **Yucca House**, built around 1796, was the original dwelling on the plantation, but it is perhaps best known as the guest-house where, in the early to mid-20th century, hostess Cammy Henry offered lodging to artists and writers like William Faulkner and John Steinbeck. This is where folklorist Lyle Saxon lived while writing about Louisiana and where artist Francois Mignon stayed for 32 years after being invited for only six months.

The **Africa House**, of Congo-style construction, is just about the most African-looking building you are likely to see in the US. This two-story structure, capped by an enormous roof with a 12-foot overhang, looks like a squat brick mushroom. The ground floor once served as a jail for slaves, and the top floor is where folk artist Clementine Hunter, a longtime employee of the plantation, painted a vivid, colorful 50-foot mural depicting life as she knew it on the plantation. Though Hunter was a prolific artist (she died at the age of 101 in 1988), and many of her paintings are on display in museums across Louisiana, this is her masterwork. To see this work alone is worth the price of admission.

More so than the architecture or art, Melrose Plantation is unique as a place where women rather than men were the dominant forces. From Cammy Henry and Clementine Hunter back to Marie Therese Coincoin, the home bears the imprint of a long line of forceful, enterprising and artistic women. Foremost among them was perhaps Coincoin. Born a slave in 1742, she became the mistress of a Frenchman named Metoyer, to whom she gave 10 children.

By 1778 Metoyer had granted Coincoin her freedom and a parcel of land, including what is now Melrose Plantation. For years Coincoin worked the land with slaves of her own, eventually earning enough money to purchase the freedom of her children not already freed by Metoyer. At the time of her death in 1816, the family owned over 1200 acres of land and almost a hundred slaves. Though the plantation was later lost due to mounting debt, her heirs and those of Metoyer still live in the Cane River area

Clementine Hunter

today and proudly boast of their lineage as Creoles of Color (see sidebar).

Magnolia Plantation
Eight miles of narrow roadway separate Melrose from the town of **Cloutierville**. Along the way, you pass Magnolia Plantation, which, with 27 rooms, is one of the largest plantation homes in the area. It is beautiful from the road and makes a nice stop if you're interested, but don't tarry so long that you miss the Bayou Folk Museum a little farther south.

Bayou Folk Museum
The Bayou Folk Museum (☎ 318-379-2233), just off Hwy 1 on the eastern edge of Cloutierville, is housed in the plantation

home once managed by author Kate Chopin. The museum features few mementos of Chopin's life but is nevertheless an interesting place to visit for an hour or so. Fans of Chopin are probably most familiar with her novel *The Awakening*, which depicts a woman's sexual and emotional coming of age, but they may be less familiar with her colorful work *Bayou Folk*, for which the museum is named.

Wander from room to room, taking in the museum's enjoyable collection of ephemera and oddities, including a cross-emblazoned cookie cutter once used by the local Catholic church when making communion wafers. Those with more morbid tastes should ask to see the hand-hewn coffins stacked up in the attic.

With a little luck, you will get the same guide we did: when queried about a bright, almost surreal painting in one of the front rooms, she said, 'Oh, Father Albert must have done that after taking LSD.'

The two-story house, built around 1806, is nothing grand, but it's surrounded by a variety of outbuildings that bear a look, including a doctor's office. Jammed full of antique medical equipment, the building was moved to the site in 1938, while a nearby blacksmith shop was added recently.

On your way out, catch a glimpse of Chopin's well-worn copy of Thomas Hardy's *Jude the Obscure*, displayed in a showcase on the bottom floor. The museum is open Monday through Saturday from 10 am to 5 pm, Sunday from 1 to 5 pm. Admission is $5 for adults, $3 students, $2 children six to 12.

KISATCHIE NATIONAL FOREST

It's not hard to stay off the beaten path in Louisiana. Outdoor enthusiasts can explore a vast wilderness, which, thanks to its dispersal across the state, is never more than an hour's drive from any of the region's population centers. Though attempts made

---

The Contentious Definitions of Creole

Indiscriminate use of the term Creole can get you in a lot of trouble when in Louisiana. Ask any two natives who or what is Creole, and most likely the only thing they'll agree on is that, whether you are referring to people, architecture or food, Cajun and Creole are not synonymous.

From there, it gets kind of murky.

When the term came into frequent use in the 18th century, it was used to refer to people of European parentage who were born in the colonies. By the 19th century, usage had expanded to embrace all things and peoples that were native to Louisiana. Then, people born of mixed European and African ancestry began claiming the mantle of Creole, much to the consternation of aristocratic natives of pure French ancestry, who felt it was theirs. And, to further confuse the matter, many people began to use the term 'Creole' to refer to the architecture and foods of New Orleans.

Today, the debate rages on. Only around Natchitoches and Cane River Country are you likely to find a consensus among residents as to who is and who is not a Creole. There, the term is most often used to refer to *gens de couleur libre*, translated from the French as 'free people of color.'

These Creoles of Color, as they are also known, trace their origins to the union of a slave, Marie Therese Coincoin, and the scion of a noble French family, Claude Thomas Pierre Metoyer, whose 10 children have produced as many as 10,000 descendants. Long a wealthy people (during antebellum days, many owned plantations worked by slaves), these Creoles still consider themselves neither white nor black but a distinct race, a Creole race. Theirs is an insular community, as constrained by the dictates of society and parentage as any you might encounter. Centered along the Cane River at Isle Brevelle, this micro-culture is one of the most unique you will encounter during your travels in the Deep South. ∎

during the 1920s to save some of the area's virgin forest failed, what remains is as densely forested and remote an environment as you are likely to encounter in the state. While roaming under cover of immense longleaf pine trees, you will encounter bears, opossums, deer and other animals, but you'll rarely see another group of hikers, for this is truly a wilderness and humanity's imprint is rarely seen.

Spanning 937 sq miles in northern and central Louisiana, Kisatchie National Forest, the only national forest in Louisiana, is comprised of two main districts: **Kisatchie**, with headquarters in Natchitoches (☎ 318-352-2568), and **Winn**, where the headquarters are in the town of Winnfield (☎ 318-445-9396). Four other districts, not covered here, are **Catahoula**, with headquarters in the town of Pollock (☎ 318-765-3554); **Evangeline**, headquartered in Alexandria (☎ 318-445-9396); **Caney**, with headquarters in Homer (☎ 318-927-2061); and **Vernon**, with headquarters in Leesville (☎ 318-239-6576).

The national forest offers campgrounds, automobile tours, canoeing and hundreds of miles of hiking trails. Camping is permitted anywhere in the forest all year long, unless posted otherwise – with one notable exception. During hunting season, which is from October through April, visitors to the Catahoula and Kisatchie districts should only camp where designated. Fees are charged for use of a few facilities, but in all cases rates are reasonable. Camping permits, with the above noted exception, are not required.

The following is a sampling of the variety of recreational opportunities available in the two main districts. For more detailed information, or to obtain maps, contact the Kisatchie Supervisor's office (☎ 318-473-7160), 2500 Shreveport Hwy, Pineville, LA 71360.

Located between the cities of Natchitoches and Alexandria, the Kisatchie Ranger District is home to the **Longleaf Scenic Byway**, a 17-mile route that runs from Hwy 117 in the west, connecting with Hwy 119 and ending at an intersection with I-49, just west of the town of Derry.

Along this narrow, blacktop road are eight campgrounds, ranging from rustic to improved. One of the most beautiful is the *Kisatchie Bayou Campground*, where sandy, level campsites are arrayed along the waterfront. To get there, turn off Hwy 117 in the direction of Middle Branch Overlook onto Forest Service Rd 321, then turn left onto Forest Service Rd 366. Also worth noting here are the pockmarked red–cockaded woodpecker trees just east of the turn off for Middle Branch Overlook. These pines, infected with red-heart decay, are the favorite haunt of these endangered birds.

Five miles south on Hwy 117, at the corner of Hwy 118, is the Kisatchie General Store (☎ 318-239-0119), where all the world seems to stop for bait, food and directions. In addition to renting canoes ($20 per day including shuttle) and providing shuttle service for floats down Kisatchie Bayou ($7 to $10 for shuttle only), they also have facilities for hot showers. They're open daily from 6:30 am to 8 pm.

Located between the cities of Natchitoches and Winnfield, Winn Ranger District is home to a spectacular, short hiking trail and a newly christened National Scenic River Corridor. **Dogwood Trail**, located off Hwy 84 near Natchitoches, approximately one mile west of Hwy 477, is a 1.3-mile hiking trail that is at its best during the spring when the dogwoods are in bloom. Along this loop trail are signs identifying common plants, making this an ideal hike for children.

Beginning near the town of Saline and running about 20 miles south to Saline Lake is the **Saline Bayou National Scenic Corridor**, a tranquil little waterway that is ideal for a lazy day of canoe paddling on the glassy waters. Developed campsites are available off Forest Service Rd 513 at Cloud Crossing Recreation Area. Call the Winn Ranger Station (☎ 318-628-4664) for more information.

LOUISIANA

ALEXANDRIA

population 50,000

Local chamber-of-commerce types like to call Alexandria the Crossroads of Louisiana. After visiting this compact city on the banks of the Red River, you might be inclined to agree that crossroads is a fitting moniker. With a few notable exceptions, Alexandria is truly a place one passes through en route to somewhere else.

Established, along with its cross-river neighbor Pineville, as a trading center in the mid-18th century, Alexandria prospered as the seat of government for Rapides Parish until, on May 13, 1864, Union General Nathaniel Banks burned almost every structure in town. By the early 1900s, Alexandria was reborn as a center for the Louisiana timber industry, as thousands of men flooded the area searching for work in the sawmills and lumber camps.

In 1941, Rapides and its surrounding parishes played host to the largest peacetime military maneuvers in the history of the nation as over 500,000 troops under the leadership of General George Patton and Colonel Dwight Eisenhower (among others) engaged in war games and planning for battle in Europe.

Today, Alexandria is fighting for its economic life. In 1992, the area's largest employer, England Air Force Base, closed. Though doomsayers were quick to predict Alexandria's demise, local business leaders and civic organizations banded together. Now, just a few years later, the base has been turned into an industrial park and retirement village, while the downtown area, on the wane since the 1970s, is slowly coming alive as a cultural and recreational center.

Orientation & Information

MacArthur Dr is the great octopus of a highway that encircles Alexandria. Also known as Hwy 71, this limited-access, four to six-lane road is at the core of city life, with its tentaclelike frontage roads ensnaring the whole of Alexandria in its grasp. As N MacArthur Dr, MacArthur Dr, and S MacArthur Dr, it is a much busier and more useful thoroughfare than I-49, which runs north and south through the eastern flank of downtown. Once you've mastered MacArthur, you've got Alexandria licked.

The local visitors center (☎ 318-443-7049) is at 1470 MacArthur Dr.

ATMs are found all along the MacArthur Dr frontage roads, especially near Alexandria Mall, just east of the traffic circle. Also try downtown along 3rd St and in the 3700 block of Jackson Ave.

The main post office (☎ 318-487-9402) is downtown at 515 Murray St.

Though both B Dalton and Waldenbooks operate bookstores at Alexandria Mall, the best bookseller in these parts is Books-A-Million (☎ 318-448-5116), 3660 North Blvd. Complete with a coffee shop, this large and well-stocked chain store is open daily from 9 am to 11 pm.

The Rapides Parish Library (☎ 318-445-2411) is downtown at 411 Washington St, at the corner of 4th St.

Emergency services are provided by the Huey P Long Medical Center (☎ 318-473-6280), 352 Hospital Blvd, Pineville; Rapides Regional Medical Center (☎ 318-473-3111), 211 4th St; and St Francis Cabrini Hospital (☎ 318-448-6750), 3330 Masonic Dr.

Kent House

Owing to its location in a middle-class neighborhood just off MacArthur Dr, it's difficult to suspend a sense of 20th-century disbelief when on a visit to Kent House (☎ 318-487-5998), 3601 Bayou Rapides Rd. Rumor has it that this home, completed in 1800, was spared destruction during the Civil War in deference to its owner, who, like marauding Union General Sherman, was a member of the Masonic order.

Though the big house is a wonderful example of French colonial architecture, the collection of outbuildings recently moved to the property are more interesting. Among the structures are a blacksmith shop, two slave cabins, and a kitchen where open-hearth cooking demonstrations

LOUISIANA

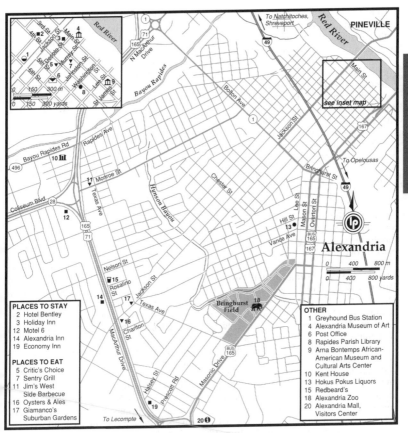

PLACES TO STAY
2 Hotel Bentley
3 Holiday Inn
12 Motel 6
14 Alexandria Inn
19 Economy Inn

PLACES TO EAT
5 Critic's Choice
7 Sentry Grill
11 Jim's West
   Side Barbecue
16 Oysters & Ales
17 Giamanco's
   Suburban Gardens

OTHER
1 Greyhound Bus Station
4 Alexandria Museum of Art
6 Post Office
8 Rapides Parish Library
9 Arna Bontemps African-
   American Museum and
   Cultural Arts Center
10 Kent House
13 Hokus Pokus Liquors
15 Redbeard's
18 Alexandria Zoo
20 Alexandria Mall,
   Visitors Center

are held every Wednesday from October through April. The guides are happy to answer questions about the antique farm equipment on display, taking special delight in pointing out a hand-rocked butter churn that local school children often mistake for a television set. Also of interest is the massive brick sugar mill where employees boil up a mess of syrup each November. Open Monday through Saturday from 9 am to 4 pm and Sunday from 1 to 4 pm, Kent House charges $5 admission for adults, with reduced prices for students and children.

Hotel Bentley

As much a sight to see as a place to spend the night, the Hotel Bentley (☎ 318-448-9600), 200 Desoto St, has, since its opening in 1908, achieved near mythical status in Alexandria. Desk clerks relish telling the (apocryphal?) story of lumber magnate Joseph Bentley, who, when refused a room at the Rapides Hotel because of his shabby dress, built the Bentley and pledged that no one (and one would assumes this included people of color) would ever be refused service in his hotel.

Dubbed the Biltmore of the Bayous, the Bentley is an imposing neoclassical building with massive columns that looks like it belongs on Park Ave in New York instead of on a narrow street in a fourth-tier Southern city.

Inside, a marble fishpond and fountain are at the center of the lobby beneath a domed ceiling with stained-glass inserts. All in all, it's a fine spot to cool off on a hot summer day or to warm yourself on a cold one. Though the Bentley still impresses, it is no longer at the center of social life in Alexandria. Long gone are the days when Louisiana Governor Earl Long kept a suite of rooms here or when leaders like General George Patton used the hotel as a head-quarters while planning WWII military offensives. (History buffs hungry for more should be sure to read the two historical markers out front.)

Arna Bontemps African-American Museum & Cultural Arts Center

The center (☎ 318-473-4692), 1327 3rd St, is more a cultural clearinghouse than a museum. Though the facility is housed in Bontemps' boyhood home (circa 1890), visitors only get to see a few books and lesser personal effects of this author, poet and scholar. Bontemps made his mark during the Harlem Renaissance of the 1920s alongside luminaries like Richard Wright and Zora Neale Hurston, but he is perhaps best known as an author of children's litera-ture. Open Tuesday through Friday from 10 am to 4 pm; admission is free.

Other Attractions

Founded in 1906, **Louisiana College**, 1140 College Dr in Pineville, is a Baptist-supported liberal arts school set on an 81-acre tract covered by native pines, oaks and dogwoods. At the center of the campus is the attractive columned facade of Alexandria Hall. Though home to only 1000 students, the college offers a surprising array of perfor-mances and lectures. Call ☎ 318-487-7011 for more information on campus events.

Though it was recently closed for reno-vations, the **Alexandria Museum of Art**

(☎ 318-443-3458), 933 Main St, may be worth a look. The museum features an extensive collection of Louisiana folk art. If the construction site is any indication, the building should prove to be an attrac-tion in and of itself.

The wooden boardwalks that encircle the 500 animals at the **Alexandria Zoo** (☎ 318-473-1143), 3016 Masonic Dr, provide a good afternoon's diversion. Though this compact little park doesn't measure up to those you see in larger cities, this one is recently renovated and, at $2 for adults, $1 for children, a comparative bargain. The zoo is open daily from 9 am to 5 pm.

For a glimpse of one the most arresting neon signs we have ever seen, drive by **Hokus Pokus Liquors** (advertised as 'the house of many spirits') near the Alexandria Zoo at 2130 Lee St, and watch the straw-hatted spook flap its neon wings. You won't be the first person to drive out of the way to view the sign. In order to catch a glimpse of this wonderful piece of neon Americana, Governor Earl Long used to make a detour down Lee St on his way to the Hotel Bentley. If the tales they tell about Uncle Earl are true, he probably picked up a bottle or two while he was in the neighborhood.

Special Events

The Louisiana Nursery Festival (☎ 318-346-2575) brings bargain-hunting plant lovers to the area during the third weekend in March.

The annual Cenlabration takes place along the Red River in Alexandria each Labor Day weekend. Call the chamber of commerce (☎ 800-551-9546) for more information.

The Louisiana Pecan Festival is held the first weekend in November in nearby Colfax. Call the local chamber of commerce (☎ 318-627-3711) for more information.

Places to Stay

As with most things in Alexandria, the budget motels are strung out along MacArthur Dr. On the cheap side, there are three decent choices – all with swimming pools. The *Alexandria Inn* (☎ 318-473-2302), 1212 MacArthur Dr, features simple, spare rooms for $29/34 single/double. Just up the road is the newly renovated *Economy Inn* (☎ 318-448-3401), 3801 Halsey St, with rooms at $34/46. At these rates, the best buy might be the *Motel 6* (☎ 318-445-2336), 546 MacArthur Dr, where the rooms go for $30 and up.

Downtown, at 701 4th St, is the comparatively upscale *Holiday Inn* (☎ 318-442-9000), where rooms rent for $60 to $70 a night. With a business center and complimentary shuttle service, this motel is preferred by many businesspeople.

Despite all the hoopla (see above), a night's stay at the *Hotel Bentley* (☎ 318-448-9600), 200 Desoto St, is really not that expensive. But be aware, though the lobby of this grand old hotel still shines, the rooms are beginning to look a little dowdy. And if you're looking for a swimming pool, you're out of luck. Still, at $69/79, it may be worth the splurge.

Places to Eat

The best restaurant in Alexandria is actually 15 miles down the road, just north of Lecompte on Hwy 71. Open since 1928, *Lea's* (☎ 318-776-5178) serves simple Southern fare to a loyal cadre of regulars who make the pilgrimage for some of the best pies (boysenberry was one of the eight or so offered on our last visit) and baked ham you will find in the South. Lea's is open Tuesday through Friday from 7 am to 6 pm, weekends 7 am to 7 pm.

In Lafayette, *Brocatto's* (☎ 318-473-4396), 3140 S MacArthur Dr, is a local favorite. This cinderblock building turns out good po-boys (try the fried oyster version), burgers and plate lunches, but the most popular meal is a breakfast of biscuits and gravy accompanied by scrambled eggs and a dollop of grits for around $4. It's open from 6:30 am to 2 pm weekdays.

Just across the bridge in Pineville is *Lee J's* (☎ 318-487-4628), 208 Main St. Its lunchtime buffet ($5) offers you a choice

JOHN T EDGE

Best neon in town, LP 'Road Awards,' 1998

of meat (fried chicken comes highly recommended), three vegetables and cornbread in a cheerful little building with lots of windows. It's open weekdays from 11 am to 2 pm.

Open since 1956, *Jim's West Side Barbecue* (☎ 318-443-9607) at 3336 Monroe St looks like a barbecue shack should – clean, functional and smoky. They serve high-quality smoked sirloin beef, ham and sausage accompanied by near perfect potato salad. Sandwiches are less than $2. They're open from 10:30 am to 7 pm.

For a taste of nostalgia try the *Sentry Grill* (☎ 318-442-4475), 1002 3rd St. Located in an old downtown drugstore, this vintage diner serves good, greasy breakfasts and better plate lunches for $4 to $5. It's open Monday through Friday from 7:30 am to 3 pm, Saturday 7:30 am to 1 pm. Also downtown and economical is *Critic's Choice* (☎ 318-442-3333), 415 Murray St.

The owners serve a variety of sandwiches Philadelphia-style, which means that the meat is sliced thin and everything is blanketed in cheese, onions and peppers.

For the best seafood in town, head to *Robbie G's* (☎ 318-443-8621), 5859 Jackson St. Though they've only been open since 1996, this no-frills restaurant has quickly developed a reputation for boiling good, spicy crawfish ($8). Po-boys and fried seafood platters are also offered. Robbie G's is open for lunch Tuesday through Saturday from 11 am to 2 pm. They open for dinner on weekdays from 4 to 9 pm and close later on the weekends.

Oysters & Ales (☎ 318-448-4890), 3425 Jackson St, a New Orleans–style restaurant festooned with Mardi Gras beads and painted lurid shades of green and purple, serves an all-you-can-eat po-boy lunch buffet with your choice of shrimp, oysters, catfish and roast beef for $6. For dinner try the crawfish étouffée; the restaurant is open Monday through Saturday from 11 am to 10 pm, Sunday from noon to 7 pm.

Bangkok Restaurant (☎ 318-449-1950), 3648 North Blvd, a hybrid Chinese, Thai and Japanese restaurant, serves economical noodle dishes and soups ($5) as well as more elaborate fish entrees daily from 11 am to 10 pm. For the best of what this kitchen has to offer, choose exclusively from the Thai dishes.

During the hot summer months, one local we met likes to cool off by resting his head on the cool black and yellow tile bar at *Giamanco's Suburban Gardens* (☎ 318-442-6974), 3322 Jackson St. When the summertime temperature is nearing 100°F, the bar is indeed cool to the touch, but the real reason to visit this funky (almost tacky) restaurant is to taste Alexandria's best Italian food. Among the specialties are oysters on the half shell ($6), chicken liver spaghetti ($5) and pollo à la Michelle ($10) – chicken rolled in Italian spices, wrapped in foil and then deep fried. In business since 1951, Suburban Gardens is open Tuesday through Saturday from 4 to 10:30 pm.

Entertainment

It's not easy to find an evening's diversion in Alexandria. Though performances are held here infrequently, *Café Au Lait* (☎ 318-448-1802), 2312 MacArthur Dr, is worth a try for poetry readings and acoustic music. Most of the customers, however, seem to be more interested in drinking coffee and surfing the Web on the computers scattered about the room.

On Monday nights, the place to go is *Redbeard's* (☎ 318-448-8429) at 1133 MacArthur Dr. This weekly blues jam attracts musicians from around the region from 9 pm to 1 am. During the rest of the week, the place is packed with regulars playing pool, watching the big screen television or drinking beer on the back patio.

Spectator Sports

If you happen to be in town from May through September, plan a trip to Bringhurst Field (☎ 318-473-2237), 1 Babe Ruth Dr, home of the *Alexandria Aces*, a AA baseball team in the Texas-Louisiana minor league. You really haven't seen a pro baseball game until you've experienced the intimacy of a small ballpark like this one.

Things to Buy

If you're in search of a souvenir (or if you're just out of clean clothes), pick up a T-shirt from Lea's restaurant (see above) in Lecompte. Made of heavy cotton and emblazoned with a picture of one of their famous pies, they're a bargain at $8.

Alexandria Mall (☎ 318-448-0227), 3437 Masonic Dr, should suffice for more mundane shopping needs; it's open daily from 10 am to 9 pm.

Getting There & Away

They may call it Alexandria international airport, but with the exception of military flights, all service is regional. Located at 1303 Billy Mitchell Blvd off England Dr, the airport is served by Delta, American, Continental and Northwest airlines with connecting flights to hub cities Houston, Dallas, Memphis and Atlanta.

Ferriday – What a Genepool!

Located just across the Mississippi River from Natchez, Mississippi, Ferriday is a town in conflict with itself. Here, bars and churches compete for the same clientele. And, in this small town, much of that clientele is related.

Firebrand Sun Records rock 'n' roller Jerry Lee Lewis, country music singer Mickey Gilley and adulterous televangelist Jimmy Swaggart all hail from Ferriday, and though they have taken different paths to stardom, each is a strange and oddly similar amalgam of secular and sacred – of Saturday night and Sunday morning. The town of Ferriday operates a museum devoted to their favorite sons on Hwy 65, two miles north of town, but to be frank, it is a bit sterile. Housed in a former bank building, the displays give you an idea of what these men have done, but no rationale as to why.

Questions are better answered by a trip to the **Lewis Family Museum** (☎ 318-757-2460, 757-4422), 712 Louisiana Ave, and its next-door neighbor, **Terrell's Drive Thru**, a liquor store. Owned by Jerry Lee's sister Frankie Jean, this cultural compound is the wackiest and most wonderful spot we've encountered north of New Orleans.

You enter the museum through what was once the garage of a ranch-style brick home. Soon after paying the $6 admission, Frankie Jean launches into a rapid-fire recitation of her family history, talking unashamedly about her father's moonshine still, her brother's antics and her cousin Jimmy's infidelities.

Pictures of Jerry Lee, Jimmy Swaggart and Mickey Gilley cover nearly every surface in the house. Baby portraits and bibles are displayed alongside framed, handwritten sermons written by Jerry Lee 'during his religious phase.'

The dining room table is covered with publicity photos and mementos. Look closely for the check from Elvis A Presley to Frankie Jean in the amount of $10,403.99. Ask her about it, and she will tell you, 'Oh, Elvis, he was all on drugs; he thought I was a Chevrolet salesman.'

Give yourself a good hour or so to take it all in. And, when you've had enough, jump back in your car and get in line at Frankie Jean's drive-through liquor store. Even if you are a teetotaler with a taste for nothing stronger than a Coca-Cola, this tin hut, brimming with alcohol and kitsch, is worth a look. Terrell's offers over 40 different shots as well as a variety of mixed drinks, beer and wine – all of which can be consumed in the privacy of your own car. According to Frankie Jean, the only folks in town who don't patronize her store are the Baptists.

The museum is open daily from 1 to 8 pm; admission is by donation. The liquor store is open from 9 am to midnight. ■

Greyhound (☎ 318-445-4524), 530 Jackson St, provides bus service to the larger cities in the region, but a car is the preferable mode of transportation whether traveling around town or between cities in the region.

MARKSVILLE

population 6000

The farther south and west you travel in Louisiana, the closer you come to the mythical Acadiana, home of the Cajuns. Once you're south of Alexandria, the only sure way to tell whether you're in Cajun Country is to look for the crock pots. If you walk into a convenience store and spy a crock pot full of boudin sausage next to the cash register, then you are in Cajun Country. No crock pot? No Cajun.

Marksville, seat of government for Avoyelles Parish, is on the cusp of crock pot territory. Founded in 1783 as a French outpost, the city boasts of a long and proud French heritage. Of equal, if not greater, influence has been the continuing Native American presence in the area.

Marksville affords travelers a great introduction to both ancient and modern Native American culture. Today, you may tour the ancient burial mounds of the

LOUISIANA

Boudin: *Rouge et Blanc*

'What's a seven-course Cajun meal?' asks the old joke. 'A six-pack of beer and a link of boudin.'

Boudin (pronounced boo-DAN) is Cajun convenience food, pure and simple. Spend any time driving the backroads of the state and you will begin to notice the little signs that dot the landscape: 'Hot Boudin & Cold Beer.'

Of the two types available – rouge and blanc – boudin blanc is by far the most popular. Ground pork and liver is cooked, seasoned with (among other things) cayenne pepper, combined with rice, and then stuffed into sausage casings. As for the rouge version, it acquires its distinctive coloring and its name through the addition of pig's blood. It's not for the squeamish.

After being steamed or boiled, the sausage is eaten out of hand. A nibble is taken from the top of the link and then the sausage is pushed up from the bottom, in the same manner that you would extract toothpaste from a tube. It takes a little getting used to, but by your fourth link, you'll be an old hand at it.

And, yes, boudin goes fine with a cold beer. ∎

Marksville culture, view the reclaimed 'Tunica treasure' or try your luck at a local casino owned by the Tunica-Biloxi Indians.

If these Native American sites don't interest you, jump back in your car and drive 90 miles south to Lafayette – you'll find a crock pot on every counter.

Orientation & Information

Marksville is a fairly compact town. Hwy 1 (known as Tunica Dr within the city limits) runs from the northeast corner of town to the southeast corner, where the Tunica reservation and casino are located, while Preston St runs from its intersection with Tunica Dr on the south end of town to the northern suburbs. Downtown Marksville lies in the wedge between the two roads.

The chamber of commerce (☎ 318-253-0284) is at 242 W Tunica Dr, near the corner of Cottage St. Though touted as a tourist attraction, the house (circa 1800) does not impress.

ATMs are found on Tunica Dr and on Main St.

The post office (☎ 318-253-9502) is at 207 N Monroe St.

The library (☎ 318-253-7559) is at 104 N Washington St and is open weekdays from 8 am to 5 pm, Wednesday until 6 pm.

Avoyelles Hospital (☎ 318-253-8611), out on Hwy 1192 on the northern outskirts of town, offers emergency service.

Marksville State Commemorative Area

When it comes to funding, this site (☎ 318-253-8954), 700 Martin Luther King Dr, gets short shrift compared to Poverty Point, a Native American site in the northeast corner of the state (see Northern Louisiana chapter). The Marksville facility makes do with displays and signage that the curator confesses to have retrieved from the attic. That said, there is a certain charm to the yellowed and water-stained map she encourages visitors to run their hands up and down, feeling for the little bumps that represent Indian mounds and their distribution across the Mississippi River Valley.

Dubbed the Marksville culture (a variant of the better-known Hopewell culture centered in Ohio and Illinois) by the archaeologists who discovered the site in the 1920s, this complex society originated around two thousand years ago in this area. Archaeologists believe that the extant mounds were probably used for burial ceremonies rather than defensive purposes.

Along an old river bed in what is now a lower-middle-class neighborhood are five mounds of varying height, bordered by a lower half-moon-shaped earthwork. Though the site encompasses 39 acres, given a couple of hours, you can hike around and see most of the mounds. And, if you're lucky, your introductory site overview will be given by the same guide that we encountered.

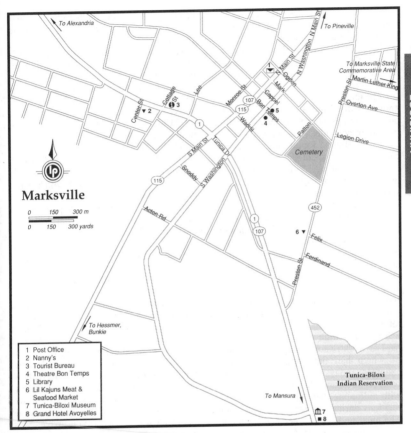

Marksville

0   150   300 m
0   150   300 yards

1 Post Office
2 Nanny's
3 Tourist Bureau
4 Theatre Bon Temps
5 Library
6 Lil Kajuns Meat &
   Seafood Market
7 Tunica-Biloxi Museum
8 Grand Hotel Avoyelles

LOUISIANA

Though her love for the site was obvious, she couldn't help poking a little fun at herself and the condition of the visitors center.

On some Saturdays the museum sponsors classes where you can learn how to make pottery in the same manner that the Marksville inhabitants once did. The site is open daily from 9 am to 5 pm. Admission is $2 for visitors between the ages of 12 and 62.

Tunica-Biloxi Museum

Just down the road from the Marksville State Commemorative Area is another burial mound of more recent construction. Home to the Tunica-Biloxi Museum (☎ 318-253-8174), on Hwy 1 just south of town, this mound was built in the late 1980s for the symbolic re-interment of some 200,000 artifacts that were looted from graves in the Tunica Cemetery at Trudeau. Most of the objects are from the 18th century when the Tunica traded with French settlers in the area. There is even a story that some of the coins and china that are part of the treasure were given to the Tunica by King Louis XV in appreciation of services provided to French explorers.

The Tunica tout the artifacts as the world's largest collection of Indian and European artifacts from the colonial period in the Mississippi Valley, but the story behind their recovery and the Tunica nation's concurrent ascendance is also interesting.

Until the summer of 1968, what is now known as the 'Tunica treasure' lay buried on the grounds of the Trudeau Plantation near St Francisville. That summer, Leonard Carrier of Bunkie found the centuries-old cache and then spent the next two years digging for more. By 1974, Carrier had unearthed enough artifacts to sell to a consortium of museums including the Peabody and the Smithsonian.

Carrier's gains, though, were short-lived. By 1976, he was embroiled in a lawsuit brought by the Tunica who were seeking return of the artifacts, which they claimed he had robbed from their ancestral graves. Over the next nine years litigation crawled at a snail's pace, but in March of 1985 a federal court ruled that the artifacts did indeed belong to the Tunica and must be returned.

Since that time the Tunica have been hard at work restoring the artifacts, many of which had deteriorated since being exhumed. Today, much of the collection has been restored and shares exhibition space with a diorama that depicts French-Indian relations during the early colonial period. The museum is open weekdays from 8 am to 4:30 pm and charges $2 admission.

Special Events
Nearby Bunkie has a Corn Festival (☎ 318-346-2575) the second weekend in June each year, while the burg of Mansura sponsors the Couchon de Lait Festival, where locals roast pigs and make cracklins on the second weekend in May. Call the Mansura chamber of commerce (☎ 318-964-2887) for more information.

Places to Stay
Unlike many towns with casinos, you can still find relatively inexpensive accommodations in Marksville. That said, rates are generally 20% higher on the weekends and during other times when the casino is crowded.

The best deal is the *Terrace Inn* (☎ 318-253-5274), 915 Tunica Dr W, a nice, inviting little motel with a pool and free shuttles to the casino. The Terrace charges $35/45 for singles/doubles. If they're all booked up, try the *Ranch House Motel* (☎ 318-253-9507), 5406 Hwy 1, but the rooms aren't as nice, and at $40 to $50, they're no bargain.

Directly adjacent to the casino off Hwy 1 is the *Grand Hotel Avoyelles* (☎ 318-253-0777), a newer luxury hotel with a large outdoor pool and over 200 rooms for $60 to $90 a night. During slow periods you may be able to wrangle a better deal from the desk clerk.

Places to Eat
The best meal in Marksville requires a little advance planning, but it's more than worth the effort for a taste of John Ed LaBorde's gooey, cheesy crawfish bread. *Panaroma Foods* (☎ 318-253-6403), 815 Tunica Dr W, has built a national reputation through appearances at the New Orleans Jazz & Heritage Festival every spring, where tens of thousands flock to John Ed's little stand for a taste of his stuffed bread creations ($4). Though most of his business is geared toward local catering, if you call 20 minutes in advance, they will have a crusty, hot sandwich waiting when you arrive. Most mornings they also serve hot cinnamon pecan rolls. All food is packaged to go, and they are open weekdays from 6:30 am to 5 pm, Saturday from 7:30 to 11 am.

For good, but a tad livery, boudin, fresh pork cracklins and generous plate lunches, try *Lil Kajuns Meat & Seafood Market* (☎ 318-253-4191), 334 S Preston St. This spotlessly clean market serves the best Cajun food in Marksville; open weekdays from 9 am to 3 pm. Locals vouch for *Nanny's* (☎ 318-253-6058), 333 W Tunica Dr, which features a bounteous steam table piled high with vegetables and fried meats for around $5. And, if you want more than a pecan roll from Panaroma Foods for breakfast, they bake a good biscuit. Nanny's is open Monday through Friday from 5:30 am to 10 pm, Saturday from 7 am to 11 pm, Sunday from 8 am to 2 pm.

Entertainment

If locals are to be believed, when it comes to entertainment, the *Grand Casino Avoyelles* (☎ 318-253-1946) is the only game in town. Located just south of the Tunica-Biloxi Museum on Hwy 1, this gambling hall, when approached in the heat of a Louisiana summer, looks as though it is floating on a sea of steaming black asphalt. Inside, the usual assortment of T-shirt-clad tourists clutch plastic cups as they pop quarter after quarter into the slot machines. At least the profits from this casino benefit the local Tunica Indian tribe. Travelers in search of musical entertainment will be disappointed, though, for the casino rarely features well-known entertainers like the larger casinos in Mississippi do.

Getting There & Away

Travel via bus or air is best arranged through nearby Alexandria, which is just 30 miles up the road. Or you might try flying in and out of Lafayette, 90 miles south. Despite the popularity of the new casino, it's hard getting to, from or around Marksville without a car.

Northern Louisiana

Stretching from the rich, alluvial soil of Mississippi Delta cotton country in the east to the comparatively arid, mineral-rich lands of the west, northern Louisiana resists encapsulation.

Make no mistake: northern Louisiana is as far removed, culturally and historically, from New Orleans and the Cajun Country of southwest Louisiana as Paris, Texas, is from Paris, France. But you would never know it for the profusion of roadside billboards advertising Cajun-this and New Orleans-that.

History

Though drive-through daiquiri stands now dot the landscape, this remains a land apart, where Baptist churches, not neighborhood taverns, are the favored meeting spots, and locals tout a history that begins not with the first European settlement in the 1700s, but with early Native American inhabitants of what is now known as Poverty Point around 2000 BC.

At its height, the Poverty Point culture was the center of a network of more than one hundred communities scattered throughout present-day Louisiana, Mississippi and Arkansas. The earthworks visible today hint at a culture that flourished long before

Rome and Athens, only to collapse inexplicably around 750 BC.

By the time the area was first settled by Europeans in 1786, the eastern portion of the region had already played host to French hunters and trappers for over 50 years. The founding of Fort Miro on the Ouachita River in the late 18th century established this European presence.

Until the 1830s, a huge logjam on the Red River stifled westward expansion, but by 1838, Captain Henry Shreve had broken through the 165-mile floating barrier, opening the area to trade with New Orleans. By 1863, Shreve's frontier-town namesake, Shreveport, was the Louisiana capital of the Confederate States of America.

During the early days of the Civil War, northern Louisiana remained on the fringes of the fiercest fighting, a positioning that led to one of the most bizarre acts of the war. In an attempt to bypass the strategic Confederate stronghold of Vicksburg, Mississippi, General US Grant tried to dig a canal on the Louisiana side of the Mississippi River to connect Lake Providence to the lower Mississippi River by way of a series of oxbow lakes and bayous. Despite Grant's failure, Union troops captured Vicksburg soon thereafter.

HIGHLIGHTS

- In Monroe, the Ouachita River, a Bible museum, and formal gardens and 5¢ Cokes at the Emy-Lou Biedenharn Foundation
- The corn-fed college town of Ruston
- A former frontier town, Shreveport is as Western as it is Southern
- Poverty Point, one of the most important (and most interesting) Native American archaeological sites in the country

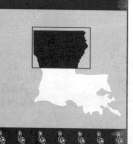

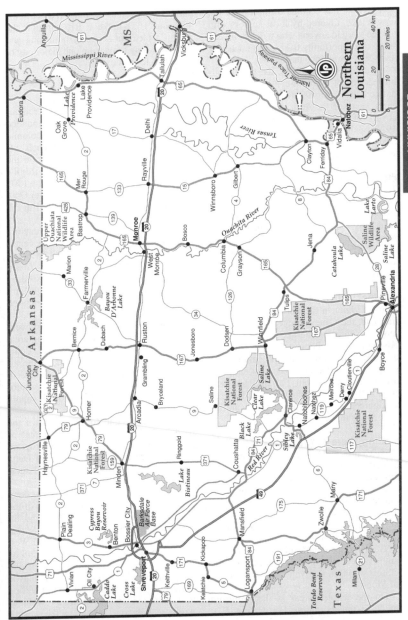

And what has become of the canal? It's now a lake, favored by local anglers who tell the story to anyone who will listen, relishing the opportunity to cast a line where a Yankee general once floundered.

As in antebellum times, the boom-and-bust cycles of a cotton-centered economy defined life in northern Louisiana in the early years of the 20th century. The discovery of natural gas in 1916 and oil in 1920 pushed the booms higher and the busts lower. Today, boom-and-bust cycles still define the region's economy.

Flora & Fauna
The area has a diverse topography bursting with native plants and animals. Be on the lookout for deer, opossum, armadillos and wild pigs while traveling in the region's forests. On and around the bayous and lakes, cypress knees jut from the water and, in some spots, moss hangs heavy from the trees.

Outdoor Activities
Above Homer in the northwestern part of the state, the Caney Ranger District is the most far-flung of the six sections of the Kisatchie National Forest. It offers camping and hiking trails in a desolate and remote setting. World-class mountain biking trails await you at Lincoln Parish Park near Ruston. Farther east, the Ouachita River is recognized as one of the most beautiful waterways in the US.

Getting There & Away
Both Monroe and Shreveport boast regional airports with regular connections to hub cities like New Orleans and Dallas.

Greyhound buses provide service throughout the region, as does a local company, Trailways. Most routes are along the primary north-south highway corridors, so reaching smaller towns by bus can be problematic.

Train service is unavailable to and from any of the major population centers; the closest stop is in Lafayette, 180 miles south of Monroe.

On the whole, a car is the preferred mode of transportation. Fortunately, I-20

and I-49 (as well as the older Hwys 80, 71, 171 and 165) make a trip through the region a pleasant series of hour-long and half-hour-long tours from one major city or attraction to the next.

MONROE
population 90,000
Though West Monroe (formerly Trenton) is a relatively new railroad town, founded in 1880, Monroe proper traces its colonial origins to Don Juan Filhiol, a French soldier who wrangled a land grant from the Spanish King in 1785. Under Filhiol's direction, Fort Miro was built, and by 1805 it served as the seat of government for Ouachita Parish (pronounced WATCH-ih-tah or WASH-ih-tah).

Due to its location on the Ouachita River, Fort Miro was a major trading center during the 1800s. It was not until 1819 and the arrival of the first steamboat, *James Monroe*, that area residents, impressed by the majesty of the vessel and caught in a sweeping tide of nationalism, renamed their city Monroe.

The early years of the 20th century were kind to Monroe and the surrounding area. In 1916, according to local legend, Louis Lock flipped a half-dollar coin in the air and drilled his first well where it landed. By 1924, the Monroe gas field was producing three-quarters of the world's supply of natural gas.

Around the same time, just down the road in Tallulah, the US Department of Agriculture began a crop-dusting program that would result in the founding of Delta Airlines, now one of the world's largest commercial air carriers.

Today, the economic boom seems long gone. Where the beautiful mansions of the moneyed elite lined Monroe's Grand St, ramshackle homes now adjoin jails that once served as schools. Monroe and West Monroe now appear, at first glance, to be nothing more than a tangle of concrete off-ramps and elevated highways. Well, maybe at second glance, too. But if you're willing to skip around town, there are a few things worth seeking out, including the world's

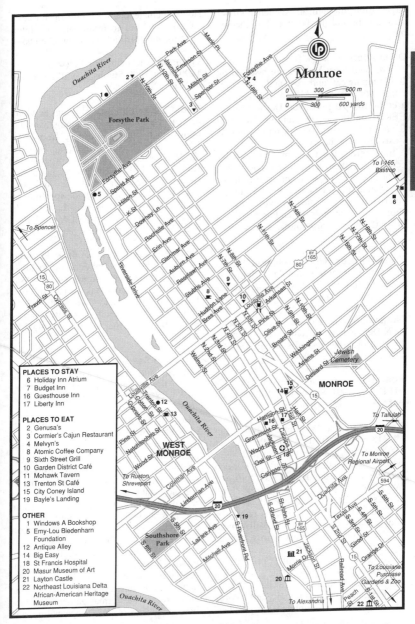

Monroe

To I-165, Bastrop

To Spencer

Forsythe Park

Ouachita River

Jewish Cemetery

MONROE

WEST MONROE

To Tallulah

To Monroe Regional Airport

To Ruston, Shreveport

To Louisiana Purchase Gardens & Zoo

Southshore Park

To Alexandria

PLACES TO STAY
6   Holiday Inn Atrium
7   Budget Inn
16 Guesthouse Inn
17 Liberty Inn

PLACES TO EAT
2   Genusa's
3   Cormier's Cajun Restaurant
4   Melvyn's
8   Atomic Coffee Company
9   Sixth Street Grill
10 Garden District Café
11 Mohawk Tavern
13 Trenton St Café
15 City Coney Island
19 Bayle's Landing

OTHER
1   Windows A Bookshop
5   Emy-Lou Biedenharn Foundation
12 Antique Alley
14 Big Easy
18 St Francis Hospital
20 Masur Museum of Art
21 Layton Castle
22 Northeast Louisiana Delta African-American Heritage Museum

LOUISIANA

largest Bible museum, an excellent regional art museum and the perfect chili cheese-burger.

Orientation

Monroe and West Monroe are bisected by I-20, running east and west, and I-165, running north and south. Monroe is situated in a crook formed by Bayou Desiard (deys-EERD) on the north and the Ouachita River on the west. West Monroe sprawls westward from the river.

In Monroe, most commercial activity centers upon the riverfront areas, on N 18th St, on N 6th St, and in the maze of frontage roads along the interstates. West Monroe's riverfront area is packed with antique shops and restaurants, extending westward down Cypress St, also known as Hwy 80.

Information

Tourist Offices The visitors bureau (☎ 318-387-5691) for Monroe and West Monroe is located off I-165, just south of I-20, at 1333 State Farm Dr.

Money A profusion of ATMs can be found on N 18th St and Louisville Ave in Monroe. In West Monroe, best bets are on Cypress St and Thomas Rd.

Post The main post office (☎ 318-387-6161) is at 501 Sterlington Rd near the intersection with Desoto St.

Bookstores The Windows A Bookshop (☎ 318-361-9004), near Forsythe Park at 609 Park Ave, is a pleasant, if small, shop with a knowledgeable staff. It's open Monday to Saturday from 10 am to 6 pm. While there, pick up a copy of John Dufresne's *Louisiana Power & Light*, a portrait of the fictional Fontana family of Monroe; this quirky, wacky, well-written novel is one of the most highly praised Southern works in years.

In the rear of the Atomic Coffee Company (see Places to Eat), 1012 N 4th St, is Serendipity Books (☎ 318-388-4202), a cluttered closet of used books and records stacked among a jumble of old couches.

Hours fluctuate, but it's usually open week-days from 7 am to midnight, with later opening and closing hours on weekends.

Libraries The main library (☎ 318-327-1490) is at 1800 Stubbs Ave at the corner of N 18th St.

Media The best musical offerings in Monroe can be found, oddly enough, on the radio. Each Sunday morning from 8 to 10 am Sister Pearlie Tolliver, *the Jewel of the Dial*, broadcasts a gospel program on KYEA 98.3 FM. Mike Luster, a fan of her show and the director of the Louisiana Folklife Festival, spins a wide spectrum of Louisiana music on his own show, *Creole Statement*, broadcast on KEDM 90.3 FM, Saturday nights from 7 to 9 pm.

Medical Services St Francis Hospital (☎ 318-327-4171), 309 Jackson St at St John St; Columbia Hospital (☎ 318-388-7875), 3421 Medical Park Dr just off Hwy 165 N in Monroe; and Glenwood (☎ 318-329-4760), 503 Mcmillan Rd off Thomas Rd in West Monroe, all offer emergency service.

Things to See & Do

Atlanta is not the only town that Coca-Cola built. After making a fortune as the first bottler (in 1894) of the omnipresent caramel-colored sugar water, Joseph Biedenharn moved his family from Vicksburg to Monroe. While in Monroe, Biedenharn's business interests continued to thrive, but his achievements were overshadowed by the artistic vision of his daughter Emy-Lou Biedenharn, creator of a singular cultural complex that now includes Elsong Garden & Conservatory, the Biedenharn Home and a Bible museum, all administered by the **Emy-Lou Biedenharn Foundation** (☎ 318-387-5281), 2006 Riverside Dr.

In 1939, with much of Europe embroiled in war, Miss Emy-Lou abandoned a successful international opera career to return home. While in Europe, she had become enamored of the formal gardens and biblical antiquities of the European elite, and upon her return to Monroe she set out to replicate such an environment. By 1947 her vision of a European garden began to take shape in the backyard of her family home.

Today, visitors stroll the manicured lawn that once served as a ballet stage and gawk at the wrought iron orchestra boxes amid a riot of colorful flowers. After touring the hothouse conservatory, the Plants of the Bible garden, and the Japanese pavilion, you are likely to forget you are in the backyard of a large rambling house in a nice but somewhat ordinary neighborhood in the middle of Louisiana.

Though the 45-minute escorted home tour can be a bit pedantic, the museum and gardens are worth an hour or two. Especially interesting is the current display of contemporary handmade Bibles by renowned artists like Jim Dine. Admission is free. Before you leave, pop a nickel in the Coke machine and fish out an icy-cold, 6½-oz bottle (subsidized courtesy of the Biedenharn family fortune).

Just north on Riverside Dr at Forsythe Ave is **Forsythe Park** (☎ 318-329-2440), a well-manicured green space with tennis courts, a swimming pool, a nine-hole golf course and public boat launch.

Across town at 503 Plum St is the **Northeast Louisiana Delta African-American Heritage Museum** (☎ 318-323-1157), a study in austerity compared to the Biedenharn complex. Housed in a converted shotgun house, the museum is open Tuesday, Thursday and Saturday from 10 am to 5 pm, offering numerous outreach programs as well as a small exhibit on the African-American experience in Louisiana.

A drive along Riverside Dr or down Grand St affords a view of the Ouachita River levee as well as a collection of grand and once-grand homes. Among the former is the turreted, red-brick **Layton Castle** (☎ 318-322-4869), 1133 S Grand St, built in 1814 and available for group tours by prior arrangement.

The **Masur Museum of Art** (☎ 318-329-2237) at 1400 S Grand St at Morris Dr is also worth a look. Exhibits take full advantage of the intimate spaces of the former mansion, and wandering from room to room you have a chance to view the collection of contemporary Southern artists. The museum is open Tuesday to Thursday from 9 am to 5 pm; Friday to Sunday it opens at 2 pm. Admission is free.

The **Louisiana Purchase Gardens & Zoo** (☎ 318-329-2400), on Bernstein Dr just southeast of downtown, are open daily from 10 am and charge admission of $2 to $3.25. Recently refurbished, though still a bit worn around the edges, they do a good job of displaying the flora and fauna of the surrounding region without neglecting the more exotic leopards and zebras. The Bayou Safari boat trip ($1) provides a pleasant orientation to the park.

Special Events

Monroe is home to one of the state's best events: the annual Louisiana Folklife Festival, held the second week in September. Not only do you get a chance to hear some of the state's best musicians play everything from Cajun fiddle music to swamp pop to zydeco, but you also get a chance to learn more about the culture of the state – all made that much more palatable by bounteous supplies of cold beer. Call the festival office (☎ 318-329-2375) for more information.

The annual Black Heritage Parade (☎ 318-387-5691) features gospel music and marching bands. It's held the fourth Saturday in February.

Places to Stay

Camping *Shilo Resort* (☎ 318-345-5981), 7300 Frontage Rd off I-20 east of Monroe, offers tent sites with water for $12 and small cabins for $20. The compound features a small, stocked lake, a swimming pool, a hot tub and mini-golf.

Motels Numerous chain motels are grouped around I-20 exits 114, 117 and 118.

Nothing special but at least well situated are the *Guesthouse Inn* (☎ 318-323-4451), 610 Lea Joyner Ave, with a pool and adjacent restaurant for $38/45 single/double, and the slightly grungy but appealingly inexpensive ($28/35) *Liberty Inn* (☎ 318-325-0621), 401 Grammont St near the corner of Catalpa St. Both of these are off I-20 exit 117.

The cheapest bed in town can be had in West Monroe at the *Canary Motel* (☎ 318-325-7383), 3002 Cypress St (Hwy 80), for $22 a night. The rooms are scruffy, but the grounds are well tended and the parking lot is well lit.

The best deal is the *Budget Inn* (☎ 318-322-8161), 2115 Louisville Ave (Hwy 80) near N 21st St, where the tidy rooms go for $25/30, and the swimming pool is clean.

The *Holiday Inn Atrium* (☎ 318-325-0641) at 2001 Louisville Ave is what passes for a luxury hotel around these parts. Rooms cost $73/78 single/double. Amenities include a Jacuzzi, pool, restaurant and complimentary in-town transportation.

Those in search of B&B accommodations should travel 15 miles south to *Boscobel Cottage Bed & Breakfast* (see Around Monroe).

Places to Eat

Health-conscious shoppers should check out the aptly named *Health Food Store* (☎ 318-325-2423), 801 Natchitoches St at 4th St in West Monroe.

The best meal in the area may well be one of the cheapest. The *Hollywood Snack Bar* (☎ 318-322-7984), at 1810 Bernstein Park Dr just a few blocks east of the zoo, serves hearty breakfasts and traditional African-American plate lunches ($5 to $6), featuring oxtails, chittlins, mustard greens, black-eyed peas and cornbread. It's open weekdays from around 8 am to 4 pm.

For a taste of the hip side of Monroe, pick up morning coffee and pastries at the stylish *Atomic Coffee Company* (☎ 318-388-4202), 1012 N 4th St.

For lunch, do like the locals and get a side order of gravy to dip your fries into at *Melvyn's* (☎ 601-325-2055), 200 18th St at Forsythe Ave. Open Monday to Saturday from 11 am to 10 pm, they also serve some of the best burgers in Louisiana.

If you're in search of really cheap eats, seek out *City Coney Island* (☎ 318-322-9159), 519 Desiard St, for good and greasy chili dogs.

In West Monroe, try the *Trenton St Café* (☎ 318-322-1444), 322 Trenton St, for po-boys on fresh-baked French bread and weekday plate lunches.

The *Hob Nob* (☎ 318-396-9101) is on the western outskirts of West Monroe at 5076 Cypress St near the intersection with Thomas Rd. A loyal cadre of regulars packs into this ramshackle roadhouse to eat oysters, gumbo and other local specialties Monday through Saturday from 11 am until 10 pm (until midnight on Friday and Saturday). The beer is always cold, and on Wednesday nights in season, the crawfish are cheap ($9 for three pounds).

Better yet, grab a seat at the bar or in one of the booths that line the back wall of the *Mohawk Tavern* (☎ 318-322-9275), 704 Louisville Ave near N 8th St. Among the stuffed fowl and 1950s-era beer advertising you can savor Monroe's best bowl of gumbo, nut brown and pungent, with still-crunchy shrimp ($6). The Mohawk is open Tuesday to Saturday from 11 am to 9 pm, until 10 pm on the weekends.

Also popular and economical is *Cormier's Cajun Restaurant* (☎ 318-322-0414) at 1205 Forsythe Ave. Great boiled crawfish, boudin, and red beans and rice are served on picnic tables in front of this shed of a building facing Forsythe Park.

West of Windows A Bookshop at 815 Park Ave, *Genusa's* (☎ 318-387-3083) is Monroe's most attractive Italian restaurant and features the town's best wine list. Especially good are the portobello mushrooms, tomato-and-pesto salads and grilled fish dishes. Though dinner ($10 to $20 per person) is the main meal served Monday through Saturday from 5 to 10 pm, they are open for lunch weekdays from 11 am to 2 pm.

In a recently renovated bungalow home, the *Garden District Café* (☎ 318-387-1414), 605 Louisville Ave near N 7th St, features an eclectic menu of gussied up Southern cooking and an astonishing variety of martinis (15 types).

For reasonably priced pasta and pizza in a publike atmosphere, try the *Sixth Street Grill* (☎ 318-323-0010) at 1026 6th St.

Entertainment
Monroe is not exactly the live music capital of Louisiana, though the *Sixth Street Grill* (see above) books college rock and folksy acts most weekends, while the *Big Easy*, 500 Desiard St, hosts blues jams and open mic nights on a regular basis.

Bayle's Landing (☎ 318-322-8278) is a popular fish house at 113 S Riverfront Rd in West Monroe, known more for the ambiance than the food. It's a great spot to sip a beer and take in a sweeping view of the Ouachita River.

Your best bet might be taking a drive out along Bayou Desiard to the *Cypress Inn* (☎ 318-345-0202), 7805 Desiard St, to have a drink or two and feed leftover hushpuppies (provided free of charge) to the turtles. The view of the moss-shrouded cypress trees is magnificent.

Things to Buy
Along a four-block stretch of Trenton Ave near the waterfront in West Monroe is an area known as **Antique Alley**, comprising 25 or so antique stores, restaurants, art galleries and tchotchke shops of varying degrees of quality and appeal.

With more than 80 stores, Pecanland Mall, 4700 Millhaven Rd, should suffice for mundane shopping needs.

Getting There & Away
Monroe regional airport (☎ 318-329-2461), east of town on Hwy 80, has a few more connecting flights than the norm owing to the city's still strong ties to Delta Airlines. Delta provides jet service six times a day to Dallas and Atlanta, while Continental, Northwest and US Airways provide commuter air service three times a day. US Airway's service to Baton Rouge and New Orleans might be of most use to travelers.

Greyhound (☎ 318-322-5181) has bus service to and from Jackson, Mississippi, scheduled three times a day; its service to and from Chicago, Dallas and Atlanta is offered just once or twice a day. Trailways offers service to Baton Rouge twice a day.

Monroe's bus depot is at 830 Martin Luther King Dr (Hwy 165) on the east side of Monroe near the intersection with Roberta Dr. All tickets are sold at this location. The only problem with bus service is that once you arrive in Monroe, you really need a car to get around.

JOHN T EDGE

Old cotton gin sign, rural Louisiana

AROUND MONROE

Traveling east from Monroe, the landscape becomes flatter – and bleaker. You're in the Mississippi Delta now, a former swampland reclaimed with slave labor in the mid-1800s. The few surviving plantations – their main houses blinding white and columned – look like relics from a long-forgotten past, plopped down in the midst of acre upon acre of cotton fields, now tended by monstrous machines. Driving through the flat, open fields, past row upon regimented row of crops, you can't help but think of the slaves who once worked these same fields. Where did those who attempted escape from their masters hide in a land so vast and open?

Fifty miles northeast of Monroe on Hwy 65 (via Hwy 165 N and Hwy 2 E), **Lake Providence** is, quite frankly, a dump. Long a thriving settlement before Shreveport or Monroe, it is the oldest Louisiana town north of Natchitoches. Today few vestiges of the town's cotton-enriched glory days remain, save the infamous Grant's Canal and the recently opened, but not yet completed, Louisiana Cotton Museum.

The historical marker for **Grant's Canal** (see History, above) is directly across Hwy 65 from the local visitors center on the northern edge of town. There is an elevated walkway that meanders out into the oxbow lake and affords a view of what remains of the canal. One mile farther north on Hwy 65 is the **Louisiana Cotton Museum** (☎ 318-559-2041), open Tuesday through Friday from 9 am to 4 pm. Local civic boosters have great hopes for this museum, which is in an early-1900s farmhouse. They hope to restore a church and plantation commissary that will share the grounds with a working 1920s-era cotton gin.

Eight miles farther north on Hwy 65 is the **Panola Pepper Corporation**, maker of less well known but, to this jaded palate, better sauces than Tabasco down in New Iberia. The company brews a wide variety of pepper sauces, including a zippy Worcestershire and a blistering Habernero sauce. Tours of the plant may be arranged by calling Jennie at ☎ 318-559-1774. A gift shop sells Panola Pepper products at a deep discount.

By the way, ignore the tourist-targeted come-ons for **Transylvania**, 10 miles south of Lake Providence. There's nothing to see or do save a tchotchke-filled general store and a water tower emblazoned with a bat.

A 15-mile drive south of Monroe along the Ouachita River on Hwy 165 brings you to a wide place in the road known as Bosco, home to *Boscobel Cottage Bed & Breakfast* (☎ 318-325-1550). Nestled under a mess of pecan trees near the river levee, this tin-roofed, converted dogtrot house is a comfortable, quiet retreat, convenient to both Monroe and Columbia. Only a few hundred feet off the highway on Cordell Lane, Boscobel has three well-furnished rooms priced at $75 a night as well as a former chapel, priced at $95 a night. Rooms are equipped with coffeemakers and well-stocked refrigerators, but purposefully no TV. Guests wake each morning to the chirping of crickets and a great breakfast of garlic cheese grits and other Southern delights prepared by the charming cook, Miss Berta, who warns adventurous guests to stay off the levee during the rainy season, 'cause there's a right smart of snakes when the water's up.'

Just one mile north of the hamlet of Columbia (see below) on Hwy 165 is the **Martin Homeplace Folklife Museum** (☎ 318-649-6722). Antique farming equipment, kitchen utensils and frayed but beautiful quilts are displayed throughout the 1880 home. If you happen to be in town on a Thursday, stop by for a delicious Southern luncheon for only $5.

About 30 miles south of Monroe is the hamlet of **Columbia**, once a thriving steamboat landing on the Ouachita River. Today the town's Main St is more likely to be bustling with tourists than roustabouts. The main attraction is a two-block section of Main St, now restored to its Victorian glory. Stop by the **Shepis Museum** (☎ 318-649-2138), 107 Main St, and take a gander at the Italianate carved-stone structure built in 1916. The museum, open from 10 am to 4:30 pm Tuesday through Friday and 10 am to 3 pm on Saturday, features a wide range of exhibits from modern art to antiques.

Three doors down at 101 Main St is the *Watermark Saloon* (☎ 318-649-0999), 101 Main St, named after a stain left on an interior wall by the 1927 flood. This saloon, the oldest on the Ouachita River, is a comfortable, well-worn old haunt with high ceilings, wood floors and a great view. Live music is featured on most Saturday nights. Just down the road a few blocks is the *Bayou Tavern* (☎ 318-649-7922). Though the inside is painted a garish pink, the exterior of this modular building is worth your attention. Assembled in 1927 as a distribution station for Standard Oil, this shiny, tin box, perched on the bank of a small waterway, is now a restaurant and bar, serving good gumbo and plate lunches. If you are curious about the building, seek out the owner, Mr Wayne, and he'll be happy you tell you its story. Located at 415 Kentucky St, the Bayou Tavern is open from 10 am to midnight, Monday through Saturday.

POVERTY POINT

The community at Poverty Point was once the hub of a network of more than a hundred Native American communities scattered throughout a region encompassing present-day Louisiana, Mississippi and Arkansas. From 2000 to 750 BC, Poverty Point inhabitants enjoyed a particularly sophisticated lifestyle, benefiting from a trading network that reached as far north as what is now Minnesota.

Today, many archaeologists consider Poverty Point culture the premier pre-Columbian civilization in the southeastern US, and they flock to this site. In fact, there are often more archaeologists milling about the place than tourists.

What both archaeologists and tourists come to see are a remarkable series of earthworks and mounds arrayed along what was once the Mississippi River and is now known as Bayou Macon. Though somewhat eroded over time, the series of six concentric ridges that define the parameters of the village are still impressive when

viewed from the two-story observation tower. Stretching over three-quarters of a mile in diameter, the ridges, thought to be originally 8 to 10 feet in height, are purported to be the foundations for village dwellings.

Six earthen mounds, most of which are located outside the ridges, are also scattered about the 1500-acre site. With so much area to traverse, you'll have to make a few choices if you only want to spend a few hours looking around.

Upon arrival consider devoting a half-hour to the film, which gives a good introduction to the people of Poverty Point. (Granted, the film is a little too concerned with what grand folks archaeologists are.) Then you might spend 30 minutes or so wandering around the display area. The displays of clay balls used for cooking are especially interesting. Many of these balls are on display along with molded owl and bird figures, not to mention intricate female torsos, wrought from the same clay.

After this introduction, board a shuttle (six person minimum) for a tour of all the mounds, or take a brief hike out to the most spectacular mound – a bird-shaped one measuring 700 by 800 feet at its base and rising 70 feet. The roundtrip hike will take you 30 or 45 minutes and from there you can take hikes out to the more remote mounds.

Located 50 miles northeast of Monroe on Hwy 577, one mile north of Hwy 134, Poverty Point (☎ 318-926-5492) is open daily from 9 am to 5 pm. Admission is $2.

RUSTON
population 21,000

Just 35 miles south of the Arkansas border, Ruston is the seat of government for the hill country parish of Lincoln. Lincoln Parish was one of two 'Reconstruction parishes' (Grant Parish is the other) created by radical Republican politicians during Reconstruction, and it has always been perceived as a bit different from its hill-country neighbors.

The town of Ruston was founded in 1884, when entrepreneur Robert Russ

LOUISIANA

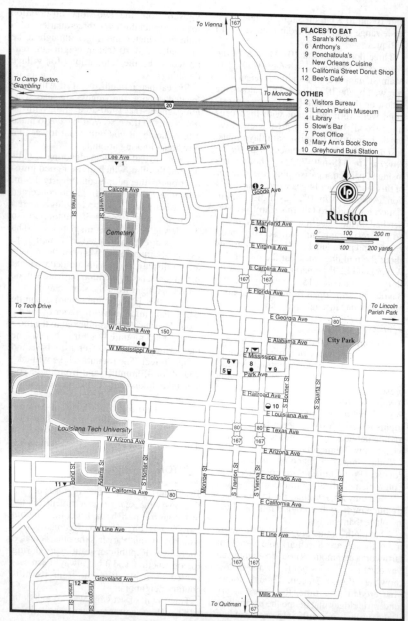

PLACES TO EAT
1 Sarah's Kitchen
6 Anthony's
9 Ponchatoula's
   New Orleans Cuisine
11 California Street Donut Shop
12 Bee's Café

OTHER
2 Visitors Bureau
3 Lincoln Parish Museum
4 Library
5 Stow's Bar
7 Post Office
8 Mary Ann's Book Store
10 Greyhound Bus Station

Ruston

convinced the Vicksburg, Shreveport and Pacific Railroad to lay track through a 640-acre site that he owned. Russ's Town, later renamed Ruston, literally sprang up overnight as settlers flooded there, first living in tents and other temporary shelters.

By 1890, with the organization of a Chautauqua Society, Lincoln Parish had become the educational capital of northern Louisiana. A 2000-seat tabernacle was built near Ruston, where society members played host to noted educators, philosophers and politicians, including populist William Jennings Bryan. Though the tabernacle no longer stands, the educational legacy endures.

Today, both Grambling State University and Louisiana Tech University are anchors of Lincoln Parish's economic, social and educational life. Those in search of a bucolic college town are forewarned: Ruston and surrounding Lincoln Parish are not places of great scenic charm. There are no green lawns shaded by live oaks here. But the area does offer a few spots worth checking out, including one of the best – and oddest – restaurants that you will ever visit, and like most things in Ruston, it's only a short detour off the highway.

Orientation

I-20 forms a northern border for Ruston, with most commercial activity clustered to the south along two main arteries: Tech Dr and Trenton St/Vienna St. Trenton and Vienna Sts run one-way through the middle of town (southward and northward respectively), while Tech Dr runs through the Louisiana Tech campus on the west side of town.

Information

The visitors bureau (☎ 318-255-2031) is at 900 N Trenton St. ATMs are easily found downtown, either on or just off Trenton St. The main post office (☎ 318-255-3791) is downtown at 501 Trenton St.

Mary Ann's Book Store (☎ 318-255-0845), 130 Park Ave, has a small assortment of books. The public library (☎ 318-251-5030) is at 509 W Alabama Ave, while the Louisiana Tech library (☎ 318-257-3555) is just off Tech Dr.

Most motels lack laundry facilities. Try Soap Opera (☎ 318-251-9614) at 1612 Farmerville Hwy.

Lincoln General Hospital (☎ 318-254-2456) offers emergency service.

Things to See & Do

Although it is first and foremost a restaurant, **Sarah's Kitchen** is a must for anyone traveling anywhere near Ruston. For a description of this cafe-cum-folk-gallery environment, see the restaurant description below.

Most towns bury their dirty laundry deep. Not so with the good folks of Ruston, who have thrown their support behind efforts to restore **Camp Ruston** (☎ 318-247-3721), a prisoner-of-war compound from WWII set to open as a museum in 1998. Just a few miles outside the city limits at 2101 Walnut Ave, the camp once housed 4000 prisoners, most of whom were Germans and Italians. Many of the original buildings are intact and efforts are underway to collect arts and crafts produced by prisoners during their incarceration.

The **Lincoln Parish Museum** (☎ 318-251-0018) is a comparatively conventional tourist attraction. The home, built in 1886, displays the usual assortment of local treasures assembled to tell the story of the local, moneyed elite. That said, the narrative murals painted along the wainscoting bear a peek. Reminiscent of a lesser Thomas Hart Benton, the works tell the history of Lincoln Parish in a series of somber-hued vignettes.

For sports lovers, **Lincoln Parish Park** (☎ 318-251-5156) down Hwy 33 is worth seeking out. Heralded by enthusiasts as 'one of the best locations for mountain biking anywhere,' the park offers a 10-mile trail suitable for both beginners and experienced riders. As a blend of old jeep trails and fire lanes, the track has several challenging jumps including the 120-foot Tomac Hill. Each fall, the park hosts the X Terra race, drawing mountain bike racers from around the country. In addition to the

LOUISIANA

mountain bike trails, camping, fishing and picnic facilities are available (see below).

Louisiana Tech University is a tangle of concrete walkways and five-story buildings that hardly looks inviting. Founded in 1895 as an industrial school, the university now enrolls over 10,000 students in what many consider the state's finest school for math and science. If you're in town during the fall, call campus information (☎ 318-257-0211) for a schedule of home football games. Louisiana Tech usually fields a good football team (former NFL star Terry Bradshaw is an alumnus), as does its neighbor Grambling State, and Tech often has a good women's basketball team as well.

Grambling State University was founded in 1901 by Charles P Adams, an emissary sent by Booker T Washington of Tuskegee Institute. It's just five miles west of Ruston off Lincoln Ave in the town of Grambling. Originally conceived as an industrial school, Grambling State now offers a broad range of undergraduate and graduate degrees, including well-respected programs in sports administration and early childhood education.

Though the surrounding town of Grambling appears to be in shambles, the university bustles with about 8000 students. Unfortunately, there is little for a visitor to see, save the stadium where coach Eddie Robinson leads the Grambling Tigers to victory. Robinson is, at present, the winningest football coach (over 500 wins) in the history of college athletics. Call campus information (☎ 318-247-3811) for a schedule of fall home football games and other campus events.

About 13 miles north of Ruston off Hwy 167 at the intersection of Hwys 151 and 152 near the hamlet of Dubach is the **Autrey House Museum** (☎ 318-251-0018). Though hours are advertised, call in advance to schedule an appointment to view this restored dogtrot house, built in 1849. Typical of planter homes in the hill country, this log home has an open central hall, built to catch the cooling breezes, flanked by two rooms on both the east and

west sides and an ironstone chimney on the east side. Though few interior furnishings are present, the house is a fine example of the fast-vanishing dogtrot style and thus worth the trip for any architecturally curious traveler weary of white-columned Georgian mansions.

Special Events

Ruston hosts an annual peach festival during the first weekend in June to celebrate the area's acclaimed crop. Activities include a cooking contest, concerts by almost famous or once-famous country singers and an arts-and-crafts fair. Call the Ruston Visitors Bureau (☎ 318-255-2031) for more information.

More compelling are the annual Chuck Wagon Races held the first weekend in July in nearby Dubach. Everyone turns out to watch locals race through the Louisiana backwoods at breakneck speeds before setting up camp and cooking a frontier-style meal. Call ☎ 318-777-3955 for details.

Places to Stay

Camping Primitive ($6) and improved ($12) campsites are available at *Lincoln Parish Park* (see above).

Motels The cheapest place in town is the *Lincoln Motel* (☎ 318-255-4512), 1104 Georgia Ave. The rooms are nothing special, but at least they're clean. They're also reasonably priced at $22/28 for singles/doubles. Also on the cheap side, though not as well situated, is the *Pines Motel* (☎ 318-255-3268). Located at 1705 California Ave, the Pines charges $25/35.

Along the three I-20 exits is a cluster of chain motels including the *Comfort Inn* (☎ 318-251-2630) off exit 86 at 1801 N Service Rd. This newly built motel features an outdoor pool and 60 comfortable rooms complete with refrigerators and microwave ovens.

Places to Eat

Every day, thousands of motorists whiz by *Sarah's Kitchen* (☎ 318-255-1226), unaware of the quirky cuisine just a few blocks off I-20. Instead of wolfing down a burger at some highway hash house, seek out this inestimable eatery at 607 Lee Ave in a neighborhood of tidy clapboard homes.

Sarah is a stickler for fresh foods. On any given day she offers four to five meats and 13 to 15 fresh vegetables. Turnip greens, black-eyed peas, okra and tomatoes and yams are menu mainstays. If you're lucky, Sarah will be serving her special sweet-and-sour squash, a hybrid she developed in her own backyard.

As good as the food is, the surrounding gardens and restaurant decor may be the prime attractions. The makeshift fence is constructed of old radiators, and cast iron stoves are overflow with plants. Inside, every surface of the ramshackle, wooden building is covered with mementos of Sarah's culinary career. African tribal art is stacked in a dark corner. Yet, all is overshadowed by Sarah's visionary paintings. Sarah's is open from 11 am to 7 pm daily.

Bee's Café (☎ 318-255-5610), 805 Larson St, serves a fine plate lunch in comparatively conservative surroundings, but the real reason to go is for Bee's breakfast. For around $3 you get a belly-busting plate of eggs, grits and homemade biscuits. Bee's is open Monday through Friday from 5 to 9 am and 11 am to 3 pm.

Also worth a visit for breakfast is the *California Street Donut Shop* (☎ 318-251-0770) open 24 hours a day at 803 W California St, on the southern edge of the Louisiana Tech campus.

Ponchatoula's New Orleans Cuisine (☎ 318-254-8683), 109 E Park Ave, serves great boiled crawfish (in season), good gumbo and pleasingly sloppy roast beef poboys to a college crowd. They're open from 11 am to midnight Monday through Saturday and from 11 am to 2 pm on Sunday.

Locals flock to the *Boiling Point* (☎ 318-255-8506) for incendiary boiled crawfish and cold beer in a rather institutional setting. Located at 2017 Farmerville Hwy, one mile north of I-20, the Boiling Point is open weekdays from 11 am to 9 pm.

In search of a little more atmosphere? Try *Anthony's* (☎ 318-255-9000), where the tables are covered with checkered cloths and the lighting is soft and romantic. Especially good is the pizza Margherita ($8) with fresh tomatoes, basil and mozzarella, or the Tuna Sorrentino ($9), a yellowfin tuna steak topped with olives and served in a tomato cream sauce. Anthony's, located at 109 N Trenton St, is open daily from 11 am to 9 pm, but keep in mind that they close a little earlier on Sunday and stay open a little later on Friday and Saturday.

Entertainment

Ponchatoula's (see above) offers occasional live music as does the *Trenton Street Café* (☎ 318-251-2103), 201 N Trenton St, a brass, fern and brick bedecked place.

If you want a little local color with your beer, *Stow's Bar* (☎ 318-255-9949) at 210 W Park Ave can't be beat. Before opening as a bar in 1975, the graceful old building served as both a hotel and hospital. Today, locals wearing cowboy hats share the scuffed old bar with frat boys out for a night on the town. Around 9 pm on the weekends things take a decided turn toward hipness, when a disk jockey takes over, spinning alternative tunes for the pleasure of the dancers in what once was the lobby of the old hotel.

During the academic year, Louisiana Tech University sponsors a variety of lectures, recitals, sporting events and plays. Call ☎ 318-257-4427 for information. For those in search of more 'down-home' entertainment, a 20-mile drive south down Hwy 146 is warranted. On Hwy 4 southeast of Chatham, the *Super Bee Speedway* (☎ 318-249-4595) hosts dirt track stock-car races every Saturday night at 8 pm.

Things to Buy

For life's necessities, the phalanx of strip malls along the interstate highway frontage roads should suffice. Out on California Ave, Louisiana Tech Farm Sales (☎ 318-257-3550) offers farm-fresh milk, cheese, chickens, flowers and other products at very reasonable prices.

Getting There & Away

Both Shreveport (45 miles west) and Monroe (30 miles east) have regional airports with fairly frequent service.

Greyhound (☎ 318-255-3505), 118 W Louisiana Ave, offers four eastbound buses daily toward Jackson and four westbound buses daily toward Shreveport.

SHREVEPORT

population 350,000

Is Shreveport a Southern or Western town? Ask that question of five locals and you're liable to get five different answers. Advocates of a Southern appellation point out that the city once served as the Louisiana state capital during the Civil War and that Shreveport residents were so fiercely loyal to the Confederacy that they held out against federal forces for nearly seven weeks after Lee's surrender at Appomattox.

Advocates of a Western heritage point to the city's origins as a frontier town founded in 1839 – four years after the land was 'purchased' from the Caddo Indians for

$80,000 and just one year after Captain Henry Shreve cleared the 165-mile Red River logjam, opening the area to trade. They might also mention the aborted 1873 bid to annex Shreveport and lands west of the Red River by overzealous Texans. Or they might quote AJ Liebling, who posited that 'Shreveport is a dilution of Texas.'

More recent history is a bit less contentious. Until the discovery of oil, the Shreveport area economy depended upon farming, forestry and transportation. But by 1905, Shreveport and neighboring hamlets like Mooringsport had become boom towns, complete with saloons, brothels and hard-drinking oil men, intent upon making a fortune in exploration and speculation. Though much of the oil extraction has since shifted to offshore sites in the Gulf of Mexico, the area immediately surrounding Shreveport still has many smaller wells.

The oil boom brought more than economic wealth to the Shreveport area. Though now decimated by the interstate highway system that bisects the city, there was a time when Shreveport boasted strong immigrant and African-American cities within the city.

Racin' Round 'n' Round

Today, stock-car racing is the nation's most well attended sport. From New England to California and almost everywhere between, hundreds of thousands of fans gather on Sunday afternoons to cheer on their favorite drivers to victory. Until recently, the sport and its fans were shunned by the national media. Thought to be the province of the poor and uneducated, stock-car racing warranted little attention and little corporate sponsorship. Perhaps the public perception was a legacy of the early days of the sport when the great drivers were often part-time racers and full-time 'moonshiners' who learned how to take a curve at 100 mph while evading government tax collectors intent upon stemming the distribution of homemade liquor.

Legend has it that the sport had its Southern beginnings one afternoon in the 1930s when a group of moonshine runners met in an old pasture to decide, once and for all, who had the fastest car. The first race, hardly an organized affair, was attended by the drivers alone, but as news spread and the races continued, spectators began to come and a sport was born. By the early 1950s, the sport began moving from dirt tracks to high-banked paved raceways, and races began to be regulated by a governing body, NASCAR, the National Association for Stock Car Auto Racing.

In today's rural South, dirt-track ovals dot the landscape, and on Saturday evenings, the packed dirt tracks come alive with local folks who have modified their Chevrolets, Dodges and Fords in pursuit of the cash prizes and bragging rites that are the spoils of the victor. ■

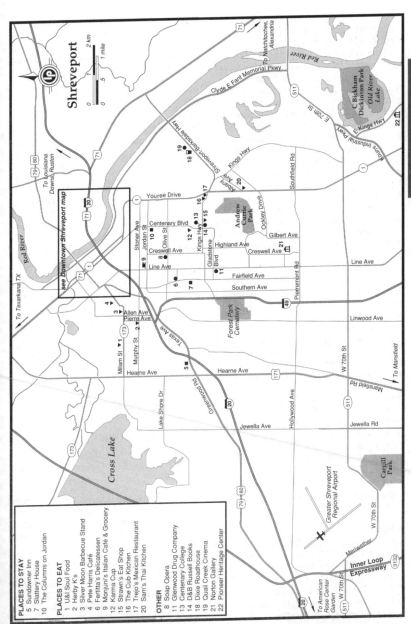

Shreveport

LOUISIANA

see Downtown Shreveport map

After decades as a transportation center, Shreveport's river port went into decline after WWII. Downtown businesses were closed and boarded; riverfront warehouses stood empty. Today, downtown Shreveport is undergoing something of a renaissance. With the opening of three casinos and the refurbishment of the old warehouses along the Red River, local boosters are quick to proclaim the riverfront revitalization a success. Yet the first-time visitor might well wonder whether it's a bit too early to tell.

Just across the Red River from Shreveport is Bossier City, established as a trading post in the early 1840s. Home since 1933 to Barksdale Airforce Base, Bossier City retains the rough, rowdy feel of a military town. Unless you want to gamble at the city's two casinos or its thoroughbred racetrack, there's not much reason to cross the bridge.

Orientation

This city is considered part of the greater 'Ark-La-Tex' region, which comprises northwest Louisiana, southwest Arkansas and northeast Texas.

On the west bank of the Red River is Shreveport. Despite its fairly compact downtown, the city is best appreciated for its suburban enclaves, fanning east and west along Line Ave, the city's toney shopping corridor. The city is bisected by I-49, running north and south, and I-20, running east and west. All is encircled by a perimeter highway known as I-220 on the north side of town but labeled the Inner Loop on the south side.

East of the Red River, Bossier City sprawls eastward along two major corridors, Hwy 80 and I-20, with Barksdale Airforce Base accessible off I-20 via North Gate Rd.

Information

Tourist Offices The Shreveport visitors center (☎ 318-222-9391) is downtown at 629 Spring St. The visitors center (☎ 318-226-8884) for Bossier City is at 100 John Wesley Blvd. Both locations have ample information on either city and are open weekdays from 9 am to 5 pm.

Money ATMs are easily found in downtown Shreveport near Texas Ave; in suburban Shreveport along Line Ave and Ellerbee Rd; and in Bossier City along Hwy 80.

Post Shreveport's main post office (☎ 318-677-2222) is at 2400 Texas St.

Bookstores Shreveport doesn't have a good, independent, general-interest bookstore. Your best bet for new books is the warehouselike Books-A-Million (☎ 318-688-4488) at 8932 Jewella Ave in the suburbs. For used hardbacks D&B Russell (☎ 318-865-1685) at 129 Kings Hwy near Centenary College has a great selection of Louisiana fiction and nonfiction works. They are open Monday through Friday from 10 am to 6 pm, opening an hour earlier on Saturday.

Libraries Shreveport's Memorial Library (☎ 318-226-5897) is downtown at 424 Texas St. Housed in a beautiful turn-of-the-century building, it is open Monday through Thursday from 9 am to 9 pm, closing at 6 pm on Friday and Saturday. On Sunday, the library is open from 1 to 5 pm. During the summer months all hours are shortened.

Media The *Times* newspaper covers Shreveport, Bossier City and Ark-La-Tex.

Laundry Most motels lack laundry facilities. Soap Opera at 1915 Creswell Rd (☎ 318-424-8048) is conveniently located off Kings Hwy.

Medical Services Bossier Medical Center (☎ 318-741-6021), Columbia Highland Hospital (☎ 318-798-4343) and Willis-Knighton Health Center (☎ 318-752-7500) offer emergency services.

Downtown

Flowers are the focus at the **Barnwell Garden & Art Center** (☎ 318-673-7703), 601 Clyde Fant Parkway in downtown along the riverfront. Though the enclosed

LOUISIANA

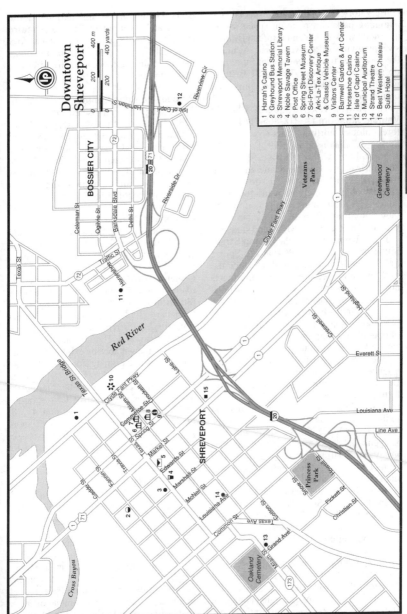

Downtown Shreveport

0   200   400 m
0   200   400 yards

BOSSIER CITY

SHREVEPORT

Red River

Cross Bayou

Veterans Park

Greenwood Cemetery

Oakland Cemetery

Princess Park

1 Harrah's Casino
2 Greyhound Bus Station
3 Shreveport Memorial Library
4 Noble Savage Tavern
5 Post Office
6 Spring Street Museum
7 Sci-Port Discovery Center
8 Ark-La-Tex Antique
   & Classic Vehicle Museum
9 Visitors Center
10 Barnwell Garden & Art Center
11 Horseshoe Casino
12 Isle of Capri Casino
13 Municipal Auditorium
14 Strand Theatre
15 Best Western Chateau
   Suite Hotel

conservatory is nothing very special, the adjoining park is a pleasant space for an afternoon walk or jog and affords visitors a sweeping view of the Red River. At night, the park is the best vantage point for gazing up at the neon-bathed **Texas St Bridge**, which has 3000 feet of red, pink and orange neon.

The **Ark-La-Tex Antique & Classic Vehicle Museum** (☎ 318-865-0661), just three blocks north of the river at 601 Spring St, is housed in a 1921 Moorish-style building with expansive tile floors and intricate woodwork. Scattered among the cars is an interesting assortment of curious objects, including antique juke-boxes and fire-fighting equipment, all on view daily from 10 am to 5 pm. Admission is $4 for adults, $3 for seniors and students.

Just down the street is the **Spring Street Museum** (☎ 318-424-0964) at 525 Spring St. Originally built as a bank in 1865, the building now features a grandmother's attic-style assortment of local treasures, augmented by special exhibits. If you are interested in the history of Shreveport, this is a worthy stop. Call first for current hours of operation. Admission is $2 for adults, $1 for students and children.

One block closer to the river is a small science museum for children, the **Sci-Port Discovery Center** (☎ 318-424-3466). Exhibits that teach how wind forms dunes and drifts in the desert pale in comparison to the see-through toilets in the bathrooms. Located at 528 Commerce St, the museum is open weekdays from 9 am to 5 pm, Saturday from 10 am to 5 pm and Sunday from 1 to 5 pm. Admission is $2 for children and $3 for adults.

Three blocks southeast along Texas St from the Spring Street Museum, look for the statue of Huddie 'Leadbelly' Ledbetter, famed bluesman and writer of standards like 'Goodnight Irene.' It's near the Memorial Library.

Two downtown performance venues worth at least driving by are the art-deco **Municipal Auditorium** (☎ 318-673-5100), 705 Grand Ave, original home of the *Louisiana Hayride* program where Elvis Presley made his national radio debut; and the opulent **Strand Theatre** (☎ 318-226-1481), 619 Louisiana Ave, built in 1925 as the flagship for a national theater chain. Both occasionally offer live performances.

Pioneer Heritage Center

This living history museum (☎ 318-797-5332) looks out of place among the 1970s architecture and flat green lawns of Louisiana State University, but it's worth a visit. It's only open on Sunday from 1:30 to 4:30 pm, but if you can make it, the six turn-of-the-century buildings offer a great glimpse of frontier life.

Centenary College

Established in 1825, Centenary College is a liberal arts school with strong arts and classics departments. The compact campus, nestled on the corner of Kings Hwy and Centenary Blvd, is home to a small but relatively progressive student body. **Meadows Museum of Art** (☎ 318-869-5169), 2911 Centenary Blvd, the prime campus attraction, displays a remarkable collection of Indochinese and Haitian paintings and sponsors frequent touring exhibitions. Open Tuesday through Friday from noon to 4 pm and weekends from 1 to 4 pm, the museum is free and open to the public. During the academic year, the university hosts a variety of lectures and performances; call ☎ 318-869-5011 for schedules. A student sponsored film series is also shown while classes are in session. See Entertainment below for details.

Norton Gallery

As you turn off Line Ave onto a meandering, suburban street, you will become quickly convinced that you've taken a wrong turn. Surely this can't be the way to the Norton Gallery? But there it is, in a cul-de-sac at the end of a narrow street in a thoroughly inauspicious, middle-class neighborhood. Built in 1966, the contemporary, columned building features 20 exhibition rooms, showcasing a collection that spans from European sculptures by

Rodin to American naturalist illustrations by Audubon. Though the smaller, alcove-like galleries display everything from 19th-century dolls to vintage rifles, the most impressive collections are housed in the Remington Gallery, where the American artist's sculptures and paintings of the Old West are displayed alongside a collection of his personal letters and illustrations.

The museum (☎ 318-865-4201), 4747 Creswell Ave, charges no admission and is open Tuesday through Friday from 10 am to 5 pm; on Saturday and Sunday it opens at 1 pm.

American Rose Center Garden

Shreveport scored a coup in 1974 when the American Rose Society moved its head-quarters and gardens from Columbus, Ohio, to a 118-acre plot on the west side of town. Today, the garden (☎ 318-938-5402) boasts over 20,000 rose bushes scattered among 64 gardens. The manicured path-ways that wind through these piney hills, past burbling fountains and mountainous banks of yellow, red and white roses, are breathtakingly beautiful. Celebrity roses (the Dolly Parton, Minnie Pearl, and Bar-bara Mandrell among them) are scattered throughout the park as are a bounty of blooming azaleas, dogwoods and other colorful flowers and trees.

The grounds are worth a good hour or two. Though spring is the best time to visit, there's always something in bloom except in December and January. For the $4 admission you are also entitled to use the playgrounds, sheltered picnic areas and barbecue pits. Open from 8 am to 5 pm weekdays and 9 am to dusk on Saturday, the garden is just west of Shreveport off I-20 at exit 5.

Special Events

Around New Year's Day, the Independence Bowl (☎ 318-221-0712) tests the mettle of two college football teams in an NCAA post-season playoff. It's held at the state fairgrounds in Shreveport.

In nearby Blanchard, a Poke Salad Fes-tival is held the Saturday before Mother's

Day to celebrate this wild green that many Southerners prize. Activities include a rather campy parade as well as the usual assortment of arts-and-crafts booths. Call the festival organizer (☎ 318-746-7056) for more information.

In October the city of Shreveport's pre-mier event, the Red River Revel, is a big street party held along the river down-town. Expect performances by well-known country and Louisiana musicians. For details call the visitors center.

Places to Stay

Camping Comfortable, clean campsites are hard to find around Shreveport. But if you're willing to drive 15 miles north, *Cypress Black Bayou Park* (☎ 318-965-0007), 135 Cypress Park Dr off Airline Dr, has 73 lakeside sites for $12 a night as well as rustic cabins that sleep four for $45 a night.

Motels A typical cluster of chain motels can be found at the Airline Dr exit in Bos-sier City and the Monkhouse Dr exit in western Shreveport. Other than that, it's slim pickings for the traveler in search of budget accommodations. Since the arrival of the casinos, cheap, independently owned lodging has become increasingly difficult to find.

The best bet for the budget traveler may be the *Sundowner Inn* (☎ 318-425-7467), 2134 Greenwood Rd. With a location just off Texas Ave, the motel is convenient to downtown and the interstate. Don't expect opulence at $35/45 for singles/doubles. The rooms are clean, but the desk staff can be gruff and the grounds are not well tended.

In the downtown area, the *Best Western Chateau Suite Hotel* (☎ 318-222-7620) is ideally situated, just four blocks from the riverfront at 201 Lake St. Recently remod-eled, the hotel features an outdoor pool and fitness center as well as complimentary air-port and bus station transportation. Rooms are $89 for up to three people, while suites are $109. It's an extra $10 for each addi-tional guest.

LOUISIANA

In the Highland historic district (an area of graceful older homes, bounded on the north by Murphy St and on the south by Kings Hwy), a number of B&Bs are worth considering. *The Columns on Jordan* (☎ 318-222-5912), 615 Jordan St, is on the fringes of the neighborhood and thus a little less expensive than many of the neighboring B&Bs. For $85 a night, guests enjoy breakfast prepared to order on the verandah beneath the looming white Doric columns.

The *Slattery House* (☎ 318-222-6577), 2401 Fairfield Ave, is a 1903 Victorian home with a wonderful deck out back where you might be tempted to while away the afternoon sitting in one of their comfortable Adirondack chairs. Rooms are $85 to $150, including a full breakfast.

Places to Eat

Start your day with good coffee at the *Karma Cup* (☎ 318-221-9700), 2710 Centenary Blvd, a hip little coffeehouse across from Centenary College. Open Monday through Saturday from 8 am to midnight and Sunday from 10 am to 7 pm, this cubbyhole of a cafe, plastered with local art, serves a variety of vegetarian breakfast, lunch and dinner specials for $3 to $5.

Another good breakfast spot is *Strawn's Eat Shop* (☎ 318-868-0634), east of Centenary Blvd on Kings Hwy. It's been in business since 1944. Though they serve a full breakfast menu, your best bet for breakfast (or an afternoon snack) is a $1.50 slice of one of their rich strawberry, banana or chocolate pies, topped with gravity-defying meringue. Strawn's is open Monday through Saturday from 6 am to 8:30 pm, while they open at 7 am on Sunday.

For a quick, cheap bite on the run, try *Fertitta's Delicatessen* (☎ 318-424-5508), 1124 Fairfield Ave. Open since 1925, this ancient looking store is one of the best places in town for lunch. Famous for their 'Muffy' sandwiches (a muffuletta-inspired deli sandwich of bologna, ham, cheese and olive salad), Fertitta's is open weekdays from 9:30 am to 5:30 pm.

If simplicity is what you're after, stop by at the *Silver Moon Barbecue Stand*

(☎ 318-222-9832) at 1418 Milam St. At this smoke shack open since 1926, they serve barbecue pork ribs and beef brisket, doused in a searing vinegar sauce and wrapped in butcher paper along with a few slices of cottony white bread. You won't find better barbecue in all of northern Louisiana. And, at $5 per half-pound of ribs, you won't find a better deal.

Yearning for a taste of home cooking? Stop by *U&I Soul Food* (☎ 318-425-5175) just down the street at 1804 Milam St where oxtails, corn, okra and greens are the favorites of a loyal, local clientele. Housed in a squat brick building, the place isn't much to look at but the food is great.

Serving similar food but to wealthier folks is *Pete Harris Café* (☎ 318-425-4277), 1335 Milam St, touted by its owners as the oldest African-American owned restaurant in the US. Though the food is still tasty, the new location is a rather cavernlike expanse of gray carpet and grayer walls. Best bets are the smothered chicken livers and the stuffed shrimp for $5 to $7. They're open seven days a week from 8 am to 2 am, sometimes staying open until 3 am on Friday and Saturday nights.

Shreveport doesn't have many restaurants that feature food from foreign lands That said, two eateries are worth noting: *Trejo's Mexican Restaurant* (☎ 318-861-4367) at 3044 Youree Dr features more than the usual assortment of Tex-Mex dishes. Try the enchiladas in mole sauce (spicy and chocolate-based) at $6 or, for the same price, the eggs scrambled with chorizo (sausage). For Thai food, seek out *Sam's Thai Kitchen* (☎ 318-868-8424) at 3815 Youree Dr, open Monday through Friday for lunch and Monday through Saturday for dinner until 9 or 10 pm. Their catfish dishes come highly recommended.

If you're in search of a truly unique dining experience, try *Herby K's* (☎ 318-424-2724), 1833 Pierre Ave. In a derelict neighborhood where most of the other businesses have been either burned up or boarded up long ago, this Shreveport institution endures. Famous since 1936 as the home of the Shrimp Buster – a 'sandwich' of four shrimp perched atop buttered French bread and served with a side of special sauce ($9) – Herby K's is as appreciated for the eccentricities of its ribald staff as for its frosty cold fishbowls of beer and delicately fried soft-shell crabs. Grab a seat at one of the shaded picnic tables in the beer garden or one of the four interior booths and relax. You've found the best seafood in Shreveport. The restaurant is open from 11 am to 9 pm Monday through Thursday and 11 am to 10 pm on Friday and Saturday.

Hundreds of bunches of plastic grapes hang from the ceiling at *Monjuni's Italian Café & Grocery* (☎ 318-227-0847), 1315 Louisiana Ave, a strange amalgam of dark Italian grotto and 1950s malt shop. It's open Monday through Saturday from 10:30 am to 9 pm (10 pm on the weekends). On Sunday they serve brunch from 11 am to 2 pm. The food is great. Try the meaty lasagna ($7) or shrimp and fettuccine in a cream sauce ($10) – they're made with fresh pasta. The muffulettas and po-boys are first rate as well.

If you want to splurge and you're more concerned with wonderful food than a swank atmosphere, try the *Cub Kitchen* (☎ 318-861-6157) at 3002 Girard St. Although the restaurant is an offshoot of a popular but dumpy bar, don't think for a moment that these folks aren't serious about good food. All steaks are cut to order and include a baked potato and salad for prices ranging from $13 for a rib eye to $19 for a New York strip. Nightly specials that pair a steak with quail or soft shell crabs are good bets. Reservations are suggested for Friday and Saturday nights when the restaurant is open until 11 pm, but are not needed Monday through Thursday when they are open from 6 to 10 pm.

Entertainment

For the best independent, foreign and documentary films Shreveport has to offer, call the *Centenary College Film Society* (☎ 318-869-5184) and ask for their current schedule. *Quail Creek Cinema* (☎ 318-865-1683) at 808 Shreveport-Barksdale Hwy, seems to be the only commercial venue for independent films.

If you're in search of live music, don't expect too much from the clubs on the riverfront; they tend to feature bad cover bands doing Tony Orlando and Dawn tributes. Instead, go a few blocks west of the river to the *Noble Savage Tavern* (☎ 318-221-1781), 417 Texas St across from the public library. Thursday through Saturday nights from 8 pm to midnight they feature bluegrass, blues and other roots music in a narrow brick-walled room with high ceilings. Cover charges are usually in the $3 to $5 range.

For the best in college rock, head to the *Dixie Roadhouse* (☎ 318-868-2400), 820 Shreveport-Barksdale Hwy. The interior is a bit cutesy and contrived, but the musical offerings are usually pretty sound.

Soon after it opened in 1939, the garrulous group of old codgers who gathered to drink at this local dive rechristened it the *Cub Lounge* (☎ 318-868-9118), 3002 Girard St. The story goes that upon leaving home for an evening of drinking, one fellow would tell his teetotaling wife that he was headed to the Christian Union Building. After a while, everyone began to refer to the bar by the three initials. This bar is imminently comfortable and its patrons warm and welcoming. Under the same ownership (and roof) as the Cub Kitchen (see above), the Cub Lounge is open Monday through Saturday from 7 am to 2 am.

If you're intent upon gambling, there are three casinos to choose from. *Harrah's Casino* (☎ 318-424-7777) is on the Shreveport riverfront. *Horseshoe Casino* (☎ 318-742-0711), 711 Horseshoe Blvd, and *Isle of Capri Casino* (☎ 318-678-7777), 711 Isle of Capri Dr, are in Bossier City. Of the casinos, Harrah's seems the best.

Spectator Sports

Want to watch fast cars go round and round and round? Try *Boothill Speedway* (☎ 318-938-3566), at 9144 Greenwood Cemetery Rd in Greenwood, 12 miles west of Shreveport. Every Saturday night at 8 pm,

March through November, stock-car drivers from around the country come to race at this, the South's fastest quarter-mile dirt track.

If horses are more your thing, the *Louisiana Downs Racetrack* (☎ 318-747-7223) is at 8000 Texas Ave E in Bossier City.

Things to Buy
From fine wines to fancy duds, Line Ave is Shreveport's prime shopping street. In the 4800 block are Pierremont Mall and Uptown Shopping Center, both chock-a-block with nicer stores. Worthy of special mention is the Glenwood Drug Company (☎ 318-868-3651), 3310 Line Ave, a strange hybrid of antique store, gift shop, pharmacy and English tea room.

Getting There & Away
Greater Shreveport regional airport features frequent flights to hub cities. Delta offers service seven times a day to and from Atlanta, while Continental offers eight trips a day to and from Houston. American offers commuter service 10 times daily to Dallas. All the major rental car companies are on site. Transportation to and from downtown is best accomplished by taxi, but be forewarned, the fare can top $25.

Greyhound (☎ 318-221-4205), 408 Fannin St near Texas St, offers 20 morning and afternoon buses heading to New Orleans (eight hours), Dallas (four hours) and Jackson (five hours).

Sportrans, the citywide bus system, is of little use in visiting the city's widely dispersed attractions. Again, it's best to have a car.

AROUND SHREVEPORT
To get an idea of how much the area's economy owes to the oil business, take a drive up Hwy 1 toward Oil City. As you pass through Mooringsport and across Caddo Lake, the surrounding farm fields begin to be dotted with little oil wells. By the time you reach Oil City, 30 miles or so up the highway, the roadside is thick with pumping wells.

Just off Hwy 1, on Land Ave in downtown Oil City, is the **Caddo-Pine Island Oil & Historical Society Museum** (☎ 318-995-6845): Amid rusting, junked oil derricks, antique tools and tractors sits a small-frame building that houses a collection of oil industry ephemera and Native American items. It's open weekdays from 9 am to 5 pm and charges a $1 admission.

Mississippi

Facts about Mississippi

Long scorned for its lamentable civil rights history and its low ranking on the list of nearly every national indicator of economy and education, Mississippi is a state most people feel content to malign without first-hand experience. The observable Mississippi, however, is much more complex and compelling.

The Delta in the northwest corner of the state comes closest to what people might imagine Mississippi to be – endless miles of cotton fields and shotgun shacks. Today the landscape also includes huge Vegas-style casinos. Most travelers are drawn down Hwy 61 to discover the legendary landmarks and juke joints that have made the Delta the homeland of the blues. Blues lovers might want to schedule a trip around one of the region's major music festivals.

Northeast Mississippi holds the Magnolia State's most famous musical pilgrimage site. Elvis Presley was born in Tupelo in 1935, and today his humble birthplace and hometown museum provides a personal glimpse into the origins of the King of Rock 'n' Roll. Oxford, home of William Faulkner and the University of Mississippi, is the state's literary epicenter. Starkville, home to Mississippi State University, is the funkier college-town alternative.

Central Mississippi holds the state capital at Jackson, where the old downtown commercial center remains a ghostly remnant long since forsaken for suburban sprawl along modern freeways. Some clubs, motels and hairstyles appear fixed in amber from decades back. To the east in Philadelphia, memorials remember the three civil rights workers killed by the Ku Klux Klan here in 1964, and nearby the Choctaw Indian nation thrives on ancestral lands.

In Southwest Mississippi, the Natchez Trace Parkway delivers travelers to a compact corner of the state with much dramatic history and scenery. Refined antebellum mansions in Natchez, ancient Indian mounds, leisurely bike loops and renowned barbecue stands make this an easy region to visit.

The Gulf Coast is perhaps the most surprising part of Mississippi. Here you'll find wilderness islands with live oaks, lagoons and deserted beaches along Gulf stream waters. A ferry sails out to one of the islands; more adventurous travelers can take a sea kayak to remote islands for primitive camping. On the mainland, coastal towns hold a small art colony, Vietnamese markets and more casinos. Carnival is celebrated locally as a lively family affair.

History

De Soto was the first European to encounter the Mississippi River, in the Delta region, in 1540. The first European settlement was founded on the coast in 1699 by Pierre Le Moyne, Sieur d'Iberville, in what is now Ocean Springs. France established a fort at Natchez in 1716. The territory between these original French Catholic settlements was contested between France and England until the English predominated in 1763 and began moving Protestant emigrants from Atlantic colonies. Spain laid claim to coastal lands ceded from France – this West Florida region stretched to the Mississippi River – until overtaken by American troops in 1798. The Mississippi Territory was created that same year, carved out of Choctaw and Chickasaw territory treaty-by-treaty. The territory became a state in 1817. In 1861, Mississippi was the second state to join the Confederacy, and its native son Jefferson Davis was named Confederate president. During the Civil War, the port at Vicksburg was the target of an elaborate Union campaign and siege.

Over the next century after Reconstruction, Mississippi was to gain for itself an overarching reputation for repression of the civil rights of its black population. In the 1960s, Dr Martin Luther King Jr called

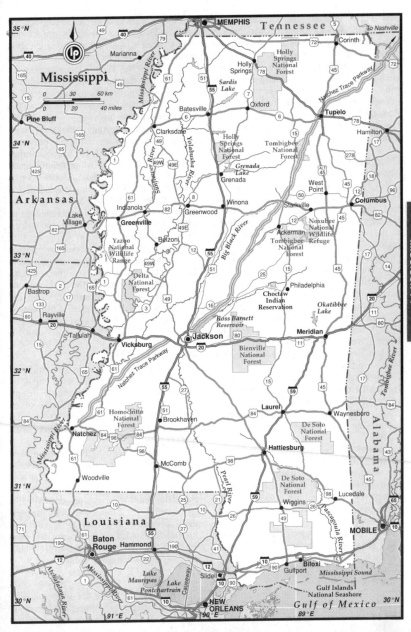

MISSISSIPPI

Mississippi 'a desert state sweltering with the heat of injustice and oppression.' In 1963 University of Mississippi professor James Silver described it 'as near to approximating a police state as anything we have yet seen in America.' Some of the most lamentable events of the time occurred in Mississippi, including the murders of Medgar Evers, Emmett Till, and Goodwin, Chaney and Schwerner (see the Central Mississippi chapter).

Geography

The state of Mississippi occupies 47,233 sq miles (including 420 sq miles of inland water surface) and is bounded by Louisiana and Arkansas at the Mississippi River, western Tennessee to the north, Alabama to the east, and the Gulf of Mexico in the south.

The two most distinct geographical features are the Delta and the Gulf Coast. In the northwestern corner of the state, the Mississippi Delta forms a leaf-shaped alluvial basin that is around 85 miles across at its widest point and 200 miles long. The Gulf Coast stretches 44 miles from the Pearl River at the Louisiana line to the Alabama border, and includes 27 miles of white-sand beaches.

Northeastern Mississippi runs from the loess hills that form the eastern boundary of the Delta across the fertile Black Prairie region to the uplands shared with Alabama along the Tombigbee and Tennessee rivers.

Central Mississippi, which is dominated by the state capital, Jackson, slopes from the northern uplands through a sandier prairie region and down to the Piney Woods region of southern Mississippi.

Southwestern Mississippi, like the Delta, features alluvial soils banked by loess hills in a narrow corridor along the river. To the east, these give way to a hilly farming region stretching to the Piney Woods.

Government & Politics

The self-proclaimed 'Mississippi Miracle', Governor Kirk Fordice, is Mississippi's first Republican governor since 1873, and the first this century to be elected to consecutive terms. (That is not all that's miraculous about 'King Kirk' – he narrowly escaped death in a mysterious car accident on election day in 1996.) The governor takes credit for bolstering the state economy, though dissenters point to the thriving casinos, which Fordice opposed on moral grounds, as the true reason for the upswing.

Mississippi's attorney general Michael Moore has led the nation in pursuing claims against powerful tobacco companies to reimburse the state for tobacco-related health care costs. Moore won a settlement in 1996, setting precedent for other states to follow. Moore has now taken his campaign to the national stage to press for nationwide action to reduce teenage smoking.

Perhaps no two facts about government and politics in Mississippi are more powerfully juxtaposed than these – that the state legislature didn't ratify the 13th amendment outlawing slavery until 1995, and that Mississippi today has a greater proportion of African-American elected officials than any other state in the nation.

Population & People

Mississippi's population is 2.57 million, most of which is rural. The most populous city is the capital, Jackson, with around 395,000 people. Of the state's 10 other cities with populations over 20,000, the largest is the coastal town of Biloxi, with 46,000 people.

Mississippi has the highest proportion of African-American residents of any state – around a third of its population. Yet this proportion is not spread evenly throughout the state; numbers may vary dramatically by region. For example, the Delta, historically a cotton-producing area, is today around 80% African American. By contrast, the population of the Gulf Coast remains overwhelmingly white.

Information

Tourist Offices There are welcome centers on nearly all major interstate freeways. You can also request information from the

Mississippi Division of Tourism, PO Box 1705, Ocean City, MS 39566 (☎ 800-927-6378). In the UK, you can contact the Mississippi tourist office at ☎ 01462-440784; there are no walk-in facilities.

Taxes The statewide sales tax is 7%. Places to stay frequently carry additional lodging taxes, which vary by city.

Driving Laws The minimum driving age is 15. Motorcycle helmets are required across the state. Highway speed limits reach a maximum of 70 miles per hour.

Drinking Laws The minimum drinking age is 21 years.

Gambling The minimum age for gambling is 21 years.

State Parks & Forests Information about fishing and hunting regulations and state parks is available from the Department of Wildlife, Fisheries and Parks (☎ 601-362-9212), PO Box 451, Jackson, MS 39205. National forest information can be obtained from the Forest Service, 100 W Capitol St, Suite 1141, Jackson, MS 39269; call ☎ 601-965-4391 or the national toll-free camping reservations number at ☎ 800-280-2267. A multitude of other national, state and local authorities oversee other natural areas in Mississippi; see destination chapters for more information.

MISSISSIPPI

The Mississippi Delta

The alluvial plain known as the Mississippi Delta stretches for 200 miles along the mighty river in northwestern Mississippi. The Delta is buttressed by the loess hills to the east and high river levees to the west. Yet the feeling that you're sinking down into something as you enter and climbing back out of it as you leave is only partly due to geography.

The landscape within is disturbingly flat and nearly treeless. Its forests were cleared more than a century ago to make way for millions of acres of knee-high cotton fields, interrupted only occasionally by tin gins and pockets of cypress swamp. In summer, the Delta sun scorches the cotton bolls till they pop open like kernels of corn on an open flame. After the harvesters tear through in October, tendrils of white fibers cling to barren stalks as blood red as manzanita, and 40-foot bales of cotton are stored at the side of the road.

The descendants of the cotton aristocracy remain in a clean white universe of town houses, academies, cotillions and country clubs – but this is noticeable only on a second look. At first glance, the Delta appears to be the poorest place you've ever seen – 'the South's South' – with whole families living out of tiny shotgun shacks insulated with newspaper. The Delta has the highest proportion of households without electricity or indoor plumbing in the nation. So, without air-conditioning or cool showers, most folks around here are used to working at a slower, more relaxed pace in an effort to conserve energy during the unrelenting summer heat. You might call it 'Delta time.'

It comes as no surprise that the Mississippi Delta is known throughout the world as the birthplace of the blues. Blues music, drawn from African beats, emanated from the hard living the Delta extracted from its workers. As hauntingly compelling as the Delta itself, blues music shaped the foundation for the most popular musical movement of this century. Today, visitors come from as far as Germany and Japan to make the blues pilgrimage tour – to search for Robert Johnson's elusive grave, and to pass the notorious plantations of Parchman Penitentiary and Dockery Farms. And to a blues fan, there is nothing like hearing this music in its natural context.

History

The Portuguese explorer Hernando de Soto came through the Delta area in 1541 as he searched for gold; blazing a trail of massacre across the southeast. The Choctaw remained on the land for more than two

---

HIGHLIGHTS

- Cruisin' down Hwy 61, hitting the Delta Blues Museum and juke joints along the way
- The small-town, real-life blues and slow pace of life in this unassuming and remote corner of America
- Belzoni, the Catfish Capital of the World
- Civil War history at Vicksburg's National Military Park & Cemetery

centuries after de Soto, even while their nation gradually lost territory to European immigration in the south. The northern part of Mississippi was the last to 'fall' to the Europeans, through questionable treaties and finally by banishment of all Indian nations in 1835.

Recurrent flooding of the alluvial basin made this region sparsely populated until a levee system was built before the Civil War. The levees were strategically destroyed during the fighting, but rebuilding started in 1884. With flooding controlled, the railroads moved in, providing ready access for northern hardwood industries to clear-cut and ship out millions of acres of trees. Cotton production expanded into the newly cleared land. Towns shot up and the population quadrupled between 1870 and 1920. This post-war cotton kingdom was as dependent on the single crop as before the war, though sharecropping replaced slavery as a labor system. Immigrant laborers – Chinese, Italians, Jews, Lebanese, Syrians and Irish among them – were replaced by African Americans. In 1910 the population of Tunica County was over 90% black, and neighboring counties were not far behind.

The boll weevil tore through around 1914, devastating the cotton industry and sending many people north to Memphis, then on to Chicago and other northern cities to look for work. The Depression followed, and then in 1943 the first cotton-picker machine was introduced, supplanting thousands more laborers. The 'Great Migration' eventually drew more than five million blacks out of the South.

The harsh and plaintive lives of sharecroppers were reflected in their music. Workers sustained themselves with work songs based on African rhythms. These work chants – old slave songs and spirituals – evolved into the mournful sound known as the blues. The sound gained wider exposure when music researchers from the Library of Congress came to the Delta to document the folk music.

Recently, the stagnant cotton-dependent economy in the Delta has been prodded by the growth of the catfish industry. The

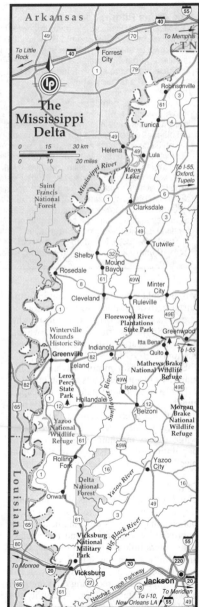

The Blues Pilgrimage

The Mississippi Delta was the incubator for famed blues artists, from Charley Patton, WC Handy and Robert Johnson to BB King, Ike Turner and John Lee Hooker. Most visitors are drawn to the region to hear live blues in rugged roadside juke joints, where the beer is pulled from a Coleman ice chest and late-night dancing gets down and dirty.

Blues pilgrimage sites – a headstone here, a crossroads there, handprints in concrete, the scene of a famous lyric, a small park named for a hometown artist made good – are modest, yet moving in context. And the search itself is a good way to explore the Delta, its music and its heritage.

Whereas in New Orleans or Memphis live music can be heard every night, live music in the Delta is usually only heard on weekend nights. A good way to be sure of hearing the blues is to schedule a trip around a regional music festival (make motel reservations).

The Delta region hosts three major blues festivals annually. The Sunflower River Blues Festival in Clarksdale is held the first weekend in August, the Mississippi Delta Blues Festival is held in Greenville the third weekend in September, and, across the river in Arkansas, Helena's King Biscuit Blues Festival is held the second weekend in October. Smaller events include BB King's Homecoming the first weekend in June, when the artist returns to his hometown of Indianola; the Mississippi Crossroads Festival in Greenwood held the last Saturday in May; and the Bentonia Blues Festival held in Bentonia the first Saturday in July. Just east of the Delta, the Northeast Mississippi Blues and Gospel Folk Festival is held the second Saturday in September – see Holly Springs.

The Delta Blues Museum in Clarksdale – a major arts touchstone – opens Saturdays from 10 am to 2 pm as well as weekdays from 9 am to 5 pm. ∎

Mississippi Delta leads the nation in farm-raised catfish production, and Belzoni is known as the Catfish Capital of the World. Soybeans, rice, sorghum, wheat, peanuts and cattle also diversify the local economy.

Despite these minor advances, the majority of Delta residents remain mired in a depressed economic state. The per capita annual income is only around $7000 – half the national average. Over a third of the housing is officially substandard. And while Blacks maintain 35% of the entire population of Mississippi, in the Delta blacks outnumber whites two to one.

Climate

The Mississippi Delta has the same subtropical climate as the rest of the region, but is perhaps more stultifying because it's unbroken by any breeze, and the treeless plain offers little relief from the sun. Consider this fact seriously if traveling from June to September. The rest of the year has mild temperatures, requiring no more than a warm sweater or light jacket in the coldest months.

Ecology & Environment

The ecology of the Delta region has been shaped by human engineering. From the alluvial plain, the fertile growing region was created by containing the flow of the great river behind batteries of levees. The forests were cleared and the swamps drained for farmland – predominantly cotton fields. These days cotton grows alongside soybean fields and earthen catfish ponds.

Small pockets of nature are preserved as wildlife refuges, primarily for migrating waterfowl. Tiny patches of cypress swamps still dot the landscape.

Dangers & Annoyances

For many visitors accustomed to travel in the US, the Delta region may resemble the Third World. No matter how friendly local encounters may be, just the sight of tenant shacks, shantytown communities, and ghostly, dilapidated business districts spells danger to many travelers. While standard rules apply – maintain an awareness of your surroundings, don't flaunt (or don't take) valuables, and lock cars and doors – special conditions warrant special precautions. For example, if your car is hailed or approached by anyone other than the police, continue to the next town instead of stopping. Drivers of snazzy rental cars planning a lot of nighttime driving around the region may want to consider renting a cellular phone (available from many major rental car companies) for added security. Be aware that guns are prevalent in the region. Unnecessary encounters with local law enforcement are best avoided.

Accommodations

Given the distances, heat, subtropical wildlife (particularly fire ants) and the prevalence of guns, camping would not be the best option for an overnight stay. For these same reasons, RV camping would be more attractive than tent camping. Again, being equipped with a cellular phone might not be a bad idea.

On the flip side of caution, going through the Delta on a motorcycle with nothing more than a jungle hammock (if you can find two trees) would be an excellent adventure.

There are several chain motels and cheaper non-chains in each of the major cities in the Delta. During festivals, you'll need advance reservations.

Getting There & Around

There is virtually no local public bus transit available in the region. You could localize your trip to the Delta and stay only in Clarksdale (not a bad way to really get a feel for the place), but to see the disparate sights you'd need a car. Though it's completely flat for easy bike touring, there's the heat to contend with, and visitors on foot or bike stand out like Martians.

Northern Delta

MEMPHIS TO CLARKSDALE

Coming south from Memphis, as soon as you cross the state line you'll see cotton fields stretching out to the horizon, dotted

MARION POST WALCOTT

A slower pace of life (Gunnison, Mississippi, 1939)

with gins, cabins, idle farm equipment and cypress swamps. The area seems like the middle of nowhere and it might appear as if there's nothing around should you want a meal, a place to stay or a little music. However, with a little scouting, you'll find a few interesting stops.

As soon as you enter Tunica County, this landscape is interrupted by huge Vegas-style casinos with their mammoth signs blinking on and off. There are eight or nine now, with more on the way. The casinos operate 24 hours a day, and many offer accommodations and around-the-clock meals as well.

At the ghost town crossroads in **Robin-sonville**, a stones' throw from Hwy 61, the proprietor, 'Big Man,' serves generous burgers, the original fried pickles (an acquired taste) and $3 beers in a souvenir mug at the *Hollywood* (☎ 601-363-1126), an old roadhouse with plank floors and high ceilings that occasionally features live entertainment. (It's mentioned in Mark Cohn's 1977 song 'Blues Walking.')

In the town of **Tunica**, behind the gas pumps at the *Blue & White* (☎ 601-363-1371), a roadhouse on Hwy 61, the coffee shop serves meals from 5 am. *Campbell's Barbecue* a few doors up also has food, and is open early for breakfast biscuits. The *Hotel Marie* (☎ 601-363-0100, 800-363-6307), 1195 Main St, is a surprisingly nice old-fashioned but refurbished hotel in the middle of forlorn downtown Tunica (rates start around $50 a double).

A turn west off Hwy 61 at Hwy 49 leads to **Lula**. Among the five or so storefronts 'downtown' is the Wash Bucket, which features a mural of blues greats as homage to Charley Patton's song about Lula, 'Dry Well Blues.' A quarter-mile or so south is the junction of Hwy 49 and Moon Lake Rd.

Follow Moon Lake Rd south and enter a tranquil cove of trees surrounding the misty lake. **Moon Lake** is an old-time escape for Delta families, and it's easy to imagine couples boating, boys fishing and lazy afternoons after Sunday dinner. The center of all this activity was the Moon Lake Club, which figures prominently in

several works by Mississippi playwright Tennessee Williams, who frequented the place as a boy. Today *Uncle Henry's Place* (☎ 601-337-2757), 5860 Moon Lake Rd, continues to offer guest rooms ($70 a double, including breakfast) and serves Southern dinners in the old lodge (entrées start at $10.75). The casino described by Williams now resembles little more than a basement rec room, and no longer permits gambling.

The most distinctive of the modern casinos reinvigorating the Mississippi's gambling tradition is the *Lady Luck* 'Rhythm & Blues' casino on Hwy 49 right at the Mississippi River bridge. While most casinos drain the local economy, at least this one promotes and hires local musicians.

Across the river in Arkansas, **Helena** is the home of the King Biscuit Blues Festival held the second weekend in October. This major regional festival is named after the radio program 'King Biscuit Time,' which is aired on KFFA 1360 AM; it was originally hosted by Sonny Boy Williamson and sponsored by the local distributors of King Biscuit Flour. The **Delta Cultural Center** in the renovated rail depot downtown is open daily till 5 pm; admission is free. The *King Biscuit Times* reports on the blues scene (for subscriptions and souvenirs call ☎ 800-637-8097).

CLARKSDALE

Clarksdale is the heart of the Delta, and its Delta Blues Museum is the major touchstone of a blues heritage tour. It's the birthplace of musical greats such as Jackie ('Rocket 88') Brenston, Sam Cooke, 'Son' House and 'Little Junior' Parker. Right on famed Hwy 61, it's also a convenient base for exploring the Delta. It evokes all of that raw anti-charm that makes the region so compelling.

Clarksdale hosts the Sunflower River Blues and Gospel Festival during the first weekend in August, and also Muddy Waters Day on the first Saturday in April and Robert Johnson Day on the first Saturday in May.

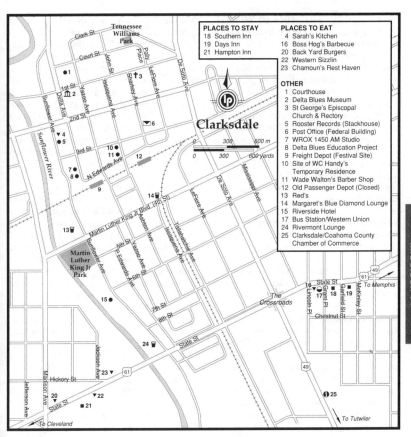

PLACES TO STAY
18 Southern Inn
19 Days Inn
21 Hampton Inn

PLACES TO EAT
4 Sarah's Kitchen
16 Boss Hog's Barbecue
20 Back Yard Burgers
22 Western Sizzlin
23 Chamoun's Rest Haven

OTHER
1 Courthouse
2 Delta Blues Museum
3 St George's Episcopal
   Church & Rectory
5 Rooster Records (Stackhouse)
6 Post Office (Federal Building)
7 WROX 1450 AM Studio
8 Delta Blues Education Project
9 Freight Depot (Festival Site)
10 Site of WC Handy's
   Temporary Residence
11 Wade Walton's Barber Shop
12 Old Passenger Depot (Closed)
13 Red's
14 Margaret's Blue Diamond Lounge
15 Riverside Hotel
17 Bus Station/Western Union
24 Rivermont Lounge
25 Clarksdale/Coahoma County
   Chamber of Commerce

Clarksdale

MISSISSIPPI

Orientation

Hwy 61, known here as State St, skirts the old downtown area. The central business district occupies several square blocks at the junction of the railroad tracks and the Sunflower River. This is where you'll find the Delta Blues Museum, Rooster Records and the Freight Depot (site of the annual blues festival).

Across the tracks is a rough-looking part of town along Martin Luther King Jr Blvd (formerly 4th St). Here many stores are closed and boarded up, but there are several places to eat, juke joints and lots of people hanging out.

Information

Tourist Office The Clarksdale/Coahoma County chamber of commerce (☎ 601-627-7337), 1540 DeSoto Ave (Hwy 49), can direct you to established chamber members, but they rarely can recommend what most people come to see, which is essentially what's regarded as the underbelly of their community.

Money Several banks downtown have ATMs that hook up to major networks, and will cash traveler's checks inside. There is a Western Union office in the bus station at 1024 State St.

Post The main post office (☎ 601-627-7834) is located in the Federal Building downtown.

Bookstores The Delta Blues Museum sells a small number of titles on the region as well as on music. Look for *Living Blues* magazine, *Blues from the Delta* by William Ferris, *Lost Highway* by Peter Guralnick and *The Land Where Blues Began* by Alan Lomax.

Laundry Clarksdale has several laundromats, but if you can stop in Lula (20 miles north), the Wash Bucket features a wall mural of blues greats.

Medical & Emergency Services The Northwest Mississippi Regional Medical Center (☎ 601-627-3211) is at 1970 Hospital Dr.

The local police can be reached at ☎ 601-621-8151, and the local fire station at ☎ 601-627-8444.

Delta Blues Museum

The blues museum (☎ 601-627-6820, Net), 114 Delta Ave at 1st, upstairs at the Carnegie Public Library, opened in 1979 to commemorate the artists who transformed the popular music of the 20th century. A state map identifies hundreds of blues recording artists who have sprung from the Delta and elsewhere in Mississippi. The collection of artifacts – ZZ Top's guitarist's 'MuddyWood' guitar (see South of Clarksdale), an effigy of Muddy Waters, photos of juke joints in action – is modest, but there are detailed historical notes. Look for the diagram outlining the roots of sacred and secular musical styles in the US, from field hollers to hip hop. The library contains specialized periodicals and volumes for researchers.

The museum sells recordings and a small number of select titles on regional themes as well as on music. There are plans to move the museum to expansive quarters down at the Freight Depot, pending renovations. Admission is free.

Rooster Records

Jim O'Neal, co-founder of *Living Blues* magazine, operates Rooster Records (☎ 601-627-2209), 232 Sunflower Ave, from a steamboat shack (also called Stackhouse) on the banks of the Sunflower River. Out of cardboard boxes stacked on the floor he sells original recordings by local artists, including Rooster's great compilation tape *Coahoma the Blues* with tracks by Wade Walton and other local blues artists. The people at Rooster are usually an excellent source of information about music playing around town. Their homespun *Delta Blues Map Kit* sells for $7.50 in 'cash, stamps or in exchange for Charlie Patton 78s.' Voodoo followers should note that they also sell the red flannel mojo bags (around $4) you might have seen pinned up in corners of rooms around town, and pricey John the Conqueror roots (around $30) to get your mojo workin'.

Empress of the Blues

The recording career of jazz singer Bessie Smith (1894-1937) came to an abrupt end at the Riverside Hotel on September 26, 1937. Traveling from Memphis for an appearance in Clarksdale, Smith was in a car accident north of town and brought to the black clinic, now the Riverside Hotel. A popular legend implied that she was sent here only after being refused admittance at the whites-only hospital, but this is now widely considered to be untrue.

Born in Chattanooga, Tennessee, Smith was, at her peak in the 1920s, the highest paid black entertainer of her day. She recorded 156 songs, including 'T'aint Nobody's Bizness If I Do,' 'St Louis Blues,' and 'Nobody Knows You When You're Down and Out.' Her singing style influenced Billie Holiday, Mahalia Jackson and Janis Joplin. In fact, Bessie Smith's grave went unmarked until Janis Joplin bought a gravestone for it. ■

Top: Medric Martin Store, Franklin, LA   **Bottom:** Thibodeaux Courthouse, LA

JOHN T EDGE

JOHN T EDGE

DAVE G HOUSER

Top Left: Man with handcrafted bike accessories, Alexandria, LA

Top Right: Marksville State Commemorative Area, Marksville, LA

Bottom: Richard Cataloa Sr demonstrates his Cajun pirogue in Bayou Vermilion at Vermilionville Living History Museum, LA

Other Blues Sights

The **Riverside Hotel** (☎ 601-624-9163), 615 Sunflower Ave, now a dilapidated boarding house operated by the venerable Mrs Hill and her son (bluesy characters from way back), is where Bessie Smith died in 1937 after a car accident on Hwy 61 (see sidebar, Empress of the Blues). Here also in 1951, James Cotton wrote 'Rocket 88' – the song widely considered the first rock 'n' roll release.

The studios of **WROX 1450 AM** (☎ 601-627-7343), 125 3rd St, broadcast 'Clarksdale Saturday Night' from 6 to 10 pm, featuring DJ Early 'Soul Man' Wright, one of the first African-American DJs in the South – he's been playing blues programs since 1947. Next door, the **Delta Blues Education Project** (☎ 601-627-4070), 291 Sunflower, aims to ensure the continuance of blues music through children's education.

The **Freight Depot**, on the tracks between Sunflower and Yazoo, is where the Sunflower River Blues Festival is held every year on the first weekend in August. The old **passenger depot** at Issaquena (now awaiting renovation) is where WC Handy left for Memphis with the seeds of the Beale St Blues in his bag. Marked by a plaque, the site at the southwest corner of 3rd and Issaquena was Handy's home from 1903 to 1905.

Walton's Barber Shop, in the cement-block building with blue trim on Issaquena a block from the tracks, is where famed blues barber Wade Walton practices his craft. The interior is decorated with photos of Wade with Ike Turner and BB King. If you're lucky, he'll eke out a rhythm for you by slapping the razor against the strap.

Tennessee Williams Sights & Events

Mississippi's famous playwright Tennessee Williams, born in Columbus, spent much of his childhood here in Clarksdale at the rectory of St George's Episcopal Church at 1st and Sharkey, where his grandfather served as rector for 16 years. A park in the city's affluent residential area around John and Court Sts is dedicated to the artist.

Clarksdale hosts the Tennessee Williams Festival the second weekend in October, featuring presentations by friends and scholars, theatrical performances, house tours and an opening dinner at Moon Lake's former casino, 20 miles north (see the Memphis to Clarksdale section).

Organized Tours

Ad hoc blues tours may be arranged locally through Rooster Records; contact Jim O'Neal at ☎ 601-627-2209, or write to the Mississippi Delta Blues Society, Box 1805, Greenwood, MS 38935-1805, for local blues tour information.

Giving Back to the Delta

The Delta is a very poor region, and local community organizations put donations of time and money to good use.

Concerned Citizens organizes a free lunch program for children on Saturdays, and they could always use an extra set of hands; contact Joe Holmes at ☎ 601-627-1156. The Clarksdale affiliate of Habitat for Humanity (☎ 601-624-8984) is dedicated to improving substandard housing in the region, and the Georgia-based organization is planning a major Delta initiative.

Blues musicians often devote their lives to their craft without the standard perks of employment such as health care. Blues Aid (☎ 501-338-3501), c/o Sonny Boy Blues Society, PO Box 237, Helena, AR 72342, organizes concerts and other fund-raisers to provide these services to musicians and their families.

Making an offering in exchange for any impromptu concerts is another way to support the community. For a blues barber, you might request a shave and leave a big tip; for a front porch recital, purchase a recording if available; and cash is rarely refused if discreetly offered.

Attending Sunday church services earns neatly dressed visitors local respect. If you decide to attend, be prepared for lengthy services (around 11 am to 1 pm) and heart-rending gospel music. It's a good idea to have something for the offering plate. ■

MISSISSIPPI

Places to Stay

In Clarksdale, the new, high-end budget motel franchise *Hampton Inn* (☎ 601-627-9292), 710 State St, has an attractive, comfortable lobby and an inviting pool that seeps from indoor to outdoor. The *Days Inn* (☎ 601-624-4391), 1910 State St, is decent enough, though it's a drop in quality from the Hampton and less well-kept than most Days Inns (several police cars swept through on a recent visit). Rooms are $48/53 for a single/double.

A good budget choice would be the *Southern Inn* (☎ 601-624-6558), on Hwy 61 next to the Days Inn. Basic rooms with private bath and TV are $34/45.

Though the famed Riverside Hotel (see Other Blues Sights, above) is open to overnight guests, it operates more as a rooming house. At $25/40 a night with old shared facilities in a run-down cabin, it's not a good value compared to local motels offering comfortable, clean lodging with modern bathrooms.

Places to Eat

Chamoun's Rest Haven (☎ 601-624-8601), 419 State St, is a rare opportunity for Lebanese specialties, such as stuffed kibbie (a sort of fried meat loaf packed with roasted pine nuts), stuffed cabbage and grape leaves ($8 for a combo plate), and spinach pie, tabbouleh and hummus.

Boss Hog's Barbecue (☎ 601-627-5264), 1410 State St, is the culinary equivalent of a juke joint and has finger-lickin' good barbecued food. It's open Wednesday through Saturday from 11 am to 2 am. *Sarah's Kitchen* (☎ 601-627-3239), 224 Sunflower, serves dinners along with live entertainment

MARION POST WALCOTT

Jitterbugging with police (Clarksdale, Mississippi, 1939)

on some weekends – fried chicken plates or catfish strips are $4. *Back Yard Burgers* (☎ 601-624-9292), 849 State St, is a modern chain that dishes out chili for under $3 a bowl. The barber Wade Walton recommends the buffet at *Western Sizzlin* (☎ 601-627-4381), 707 State St.

Entertainment

Beyond the few major scheduled festivals, musical events are often spontaneous. Information spreads by word of mouth – ask around. Watch for posters that appear around town announcing a concert that very night.

On any given night, chances are that only one juke joint will feature live entertainment, whether it's *Sarah's Kitchen*; *Red's* (☎ 601-627-3166), 395 Sunflower Ave; *Margaret's Blue Diamond Lounge* (☎ 601-627-4060), 381 W Tallahatchie Ave; or the *River Mount Lounge* (☎ 601-627-1971) at 911 Sunflower Ave. Larger shows are held at the city's auditorium.

Getting There & Away

Bus Greyhound (☎ 601-627-7893), 1604 State St, runs buses to several cities in the region. Clarksdale has a small, clean, well-lit modern bus station right on Hwy 61. About five buses a day travel between here and Memphis ($16), and about two buses a day travel to New Orleans ($65). There's a Western Union office at the station.

Car & Motorcycle Hwy 61 is memorialized in blues songs as the route that brought musicians from the Delta north to Chicago and south to New Orleans. Note that traces of 'Old Hwy 61' can be found alongside the modern highway; this was the original route 60 years ago. The 'new' highway – construction continues to make it a modern four-lane highway – bypasses the center of town.

Though it bypasses Clarksdale, the Great River Road (Hwy 1) along the Mississippi is another intriguing rural route through typical Delta landscapes of cotton and shantytowns. The river itself is obscured by levees.

Getting Around

Edward's Transportation Service (☎ 601-624-5965) advertises car rentals from their office on 1811 State St. Local taxi service is available from Jerry's Cab Co (☎ 601-624-9288).

SOUTH OF CLARKSDALE

Seven miles south of Clarksdale is **Stovall Farms**, formerly a huge plantation where Muddy Waters lived and worked. His wooden shack was cannibalized by ZZ Top guitarist Billy Gibbons for the 'Muddy-Wood' guitar now among the collection at the Delta Blues Museum.

Fifteen miles southeast of Clarksdale is **Tutwiler**. Here at the abandoned-looking tracks a mural of WC Handy recounts the story of Handy's first exposure to the blues in 1903 at the train depot that was once here. Handy carried this sound to Memphis, where he popularized the Delta blues sound. Blues trivia: the song Handy first heard in Tutwiler made reference to 'where the Southern cross the Dog,' which was local code for the intersection of the Southern and Yazoo-Delta (also known as 'Dog') railroads farther south in Moorhead.

The same Tutwiler mural also shows the way to the nearby grave of Sonny Boy Williamson (also known as Aleck Miller, 1908-65) adjacent to the Whitfield Church. The great harmonica player's marker (adorned with his photo, a regional custom) is often strewn with blues harps, cans of beer, and other mementos.

South of Tutwiler on Hwy 49, **Parchman Penitentiary** has been the home of many a bluesman, and has been the subject of several songs, including Bukka White's 'Parchman Farm Blues' and Miles Davis' 'Going on Down to Parchman Farms.' The 'Midnight Special' heard in many blues lyrics recalls the weekend train from New Orleans that brought visitors to the prison. Vernon Presley, father of the King, once did time here for passing a bad check. The only self-supporting penitentiary in Mississippi, Parchman used its unpaid (overwhelmingly black) labor pool to produce cotton.

MISSISSIPPI

Picking up Hwy 61 is **Shelby**; the *Do-Drop Inn* here at Third and Lake Sts is a locally famed juke joint, along with the *Windy City Blues Cafe* across the street. Just south, you reach the historic community of **Mound Bayou**. This rare independent African-American town was founded in 1887 by Isaiah Montgomery, who was once enslaved on the plantation belonging to the brother of Jefferson Davis, the president of the Confederacy.

Cleveland, the home of the Fighting Okra of Delta State University, is where the elite meet to eat. Set slightly back off Hwy 61 just north of the Hwy 8 junction (and easy to miss), the modest exterior of *KC's Restaurant* (☎ 601-843-5301) masks a fancy nouveau deco interior. The restaurant serves duck confit and wild game accompanied by a 47-page wine list. Their six-course fixed price menu is a minimum $69 per person; obviously this place is not for everyone.

A few miles east on Hwy 8 between Cleveland and Ruleville is **Dockery Farms**, once a huge plantation where some music historians say the Delta blues was born. Early bluesman Charley Patton worked here, along with his teacher Henry Sloan, who was said to have been playing the blues as far back as 1897. Patton's 'Pea

Muddy Waters

Vine Blues' refers to Dockery's Pea Vine railroad. In **Ruleville** proper, a section of Front St known as Greasy St features several blues clubs.

Southern Delta

Hwy 82 links the southern Delta towns of Greenville, Leland, Indianola, Itta Bena and Greenwood.

GREENVILLE
population 40,648

The largest city in the Delta, Greenville has a reputation for being more liberal than its neighbors. Here in 1946, Hodding Carter won a Pulitzer Prize for editorials in his family's *Delta Democrat Times* urging racial moderation. At the time his lone voice in the staunch segregationist Delta helped set the tone for the community. Civil War chronicler Shelby Foote is also from Greenville.

The Mississippi Delta Blues Festival, a major regional music festival, is held the third weekend in September off Hwy 454 south of town. Made famous by Little Milton in 'Annie Mae's Cafe,' *Perry's Flowing Fountain* (☎ 601-335-9836), 928 Nelson St, anchors a rough strip of blues clubs downtown.

At the crossroads of Hwy 82 and the Great River Road (Hwy 1), Greenville supports miles of eyesore neon along both of these six-lane strips. The *Ramada Inn* and the new *Holiday Inn Express* are on Hwy 82. The bottom-end *Levee Inn* (☎ 601-332-1511) has rooms for $29 single or double and is on Hwy 82 east of Hwy 1. The *Budget Motel* (☎ 601-334-4591) is on Hwy 1, a few doors down from Hwy 82, and has rooms for $50 single or double.

Doe's Eat (☎ 601-334-3315), 502 Nelson St at Hinds St, has been a culinary landmark since 1941 – even former Arkansas governor Bill Clinton has sampled their generous steaks and skillet-fried potatoes. It's open Monday through Saturday from 5:30 to around 10 pm; during the day they serve take-out tamales. A *Morrison's Cafeteria* is on Hwy 1 about a mile south of Hwy 82.

At the river, several casinos operate around the clock. At the Hwy 82 bridge, there's a state welcome center (☎ 601-332-2378) inside the *River Road Queen* paddle boat building at Hwy 82 and Reed Rd.

North of town off Hwy 1, **Winterville Mounds State Historic Site** preserves an ancient set of 15 Indian mounds, including one that measures six stories high. Admission to the museum is $1 for adults and 50¢ for children; it's closed on Monday and Tuesday.

There's a regional airport (☎ 601-334-3121) in Greenville, served by Northwest Airlink.

LELAND

Between Hwy 61 and Greenville, visitors are greeted as they cross over Deer Creek with the announcement that this is the birthplace of Kermit the Frog. A tiny visitor center here overlooks the creek and displays photographs of Jim Hensen (the Muppet's creator), his Delta childhood and early Kermit and Muppet characters. At Christmas, local boy scouts and civic organizations assemble festive floats which they decorate with electric lights and plant in the water along Deer Creek.

INDIANOLA

Indianola and the surrounding Sunflower County have produced much of what is famous and infamous in Mississippi. The musician BB King, the chef Craig Claiborne and the civil rights heroine Fannie Lou Hamer all hail from here. Also the repressive Citizens Council (a white-collar Klan) was born here in 1954.

In 1983, when local leaders invited both whites and blacks to a reception they sponsored for BB King, it made national news. Today the 'Beale Street Blues Boy' is honored with a namesake street and a park (on Roosevelt St). His handprints and footprints are sunk unceremoniously into the sidewalk at the corner of Second and Church (currently there's no street sign; it's

> If you've been singing the blues as long as I have, it's kind of like being black twice.
> – Riley (BB) King

across from Court St), a block up from the main drag on Front St.

The town hosts the BB King Homecoming on the first weekend in June, when King returns to town to play at the outdoor festival along with local musicians. Afterwards he customarily retreats to the sleek interior of *Club Ebony* (☎ 601-887-9915), 404 Hannah Ave. To find the club from downtown, take Second St out to Depot, turn right and drive across the tracks. According to locals snacking at *Our House*, a somewhat frilly bakery cafe on Front St at Second, even the white folk turn up to hear him here. Live local music is featured most weekends.

GREENWOOD

The seat of Leflore County, Greenwood is named after Greenwood Le Flore, the half-Acadian, half-Choctaw negotiator of the treaty of Dancing Creek. This infamous treaty banished the Choctaws to Oklahoma, and enriched Le Flore with a 15,000-acre estate and hundreds of slaves. Greenwood is second only to Memphis as the largest cotton market in America.

The county came to national attention in 1955, when the white men who'd confessed to the abduction and murder of 14-year-old Emmett Till (in supposed retribution for eyeing a white woman) were acquitted in about an hour. Byron de la Beckwith, convicted murderer of Medgar Evers, also hails from these parts.

The local convention and visitors bureau (☎ 800-748-9064) is at 1902 Leflore Ave. Greenwood has two mainstream attractions. **Cottonlandia** (☎ 601-453-0925), on Hwy 82 west of town, is a quirky cinderblock museum that houses not only the industry exhibits you'd expect from its name, but also a large annotated collection of Indian beadwork and projectile points, stuffed swamp critters, costumes and ankle bracelets from a celebrated local belly dancer, and Victorian furnishings belonging to the notorious Le Flore. The museum is open daily; admission is $2 for adults. Further west on Hwy 82, the **Florewood River Plantation State Park** maintains 'living history' exhibits on this restored antebellum plantation. Admission is $3.50 for adults and $2.50 for children.

The birthplace of Walter 'Furry' Lewis, Greenwood is now home to the Mississippi Crossroads Festival, which is held on the last Saturday in May. The Mississippi Delta Blues Society leads pilgrimage tours (send inquiries to Box 1805, Greenwood, MS 38935-1805).

In town, Grand Boulevard is an affluent residential district with turn-of-the-century homes. Several restaurants offer fine dining. *Yianni's* (☎ 601-455-6789), 506 Yalobusha, serves upscale Greek entrées for around $12 along with $4 cheeseburgers in a glamorous setting. *Lusco's* (☎ 601-453-5365), 722 Carrollton Ave, serves steaks and seafood in private rooms that have become locally legendary.

The Greyhound bus station is in the center of the commercial district at Church and Main Sts and is better kept than the train station. Greenwood is an Amtrak stop on the *City of New Orleans* route; the train station is in a run-down part of town. A one-way fare between Memphis and Greenwood is $35; a one-way fare between Jackson and Greenwood is $25.

BELZONI

The undisputed Catfish Capital of the World, Belzoni is surrounded by the catfish ponds that are altering the face of the Delta and, ultimately, catfish.

Catfish have always been a local staple food, although they used to have a bad reputation as bottom-feeders. By feeding the farmed catfish with floating meal, the industry hopes to turn around this cultural prejudice – meanwhile, it's changing the nature of the breed itself. Besides overcoming inbred instincts to scavenge, the farmed fish are also taking on a new

appearance, with the shape of their mouths becoming more fishily pointed, a departure from their pan-jawed relatives in the wild.

You can learn these and other catfish facts from the sleek and modern **Catfish Visitor Center** (☎ 800-408-4838), 111 Magnolia St, a lavishly renovated depot that's the jewel of downtown Belzoni. Beyond the video and trivia, there are catfish and industry-related paintings and sculptures inside and out – it's definitely worth a visit. Free recipe books are available upon request. Their World Catfish Festival, which features the 'world's largest fish fry,' a catfish-eating contest and the crowning of a catfish queen, attracts 20,000 fish fans on the first Saturday in April (second Saturday if Easter is the first Sunday).

You can sample the local specialty at *Alison's* (☎ 601-247-4487), 107 E Jackson, a half-block away from the visitor center. It's a comfortable family place with booths and tables that serves plates of fried catfish, hushpuppies, French fries and lemon cake for $5. There are also burgers and salads. On the flip side, *Little Wimp's Barbecue* (☎ 601-247-9933), Martin Luther King Blvd several blocks up from Jackson, is a popular hole-in-the-wall barbecue joint with a few tables inside. A tamale trailer parks nearby.

Ten miles north in Isola, *Teter Bo's*, on the west side of Hwy 19, serves a generous luncheon buffet for around $5.

SOUTH TO VICKSBURG

South of Hwy 82, Hwy 61 is a quiet rolling run that skirts the Delta National Forest. A ranger station in **Rolling Fork** (poorly signed, look for the green pickup trucks outside an eight-doored complex on the east side of Hwy 61, just past the Hwy 16 turnoff) distributes forest maps, trail maps, and hunting, fishing and camping information.

The tiny crossroads at **Onward**, where Hwy 1 (the Great River Road) rejoins Hwy 61, is famous for its historical marker commemorating how President Theodore Roosevelt earned his famous nickname.

Robert Johnson at the Crossroads

Born in Hazelhurst in 1911, Robert Johnson is the most legendary of all Delta blues musicians. It's said he got his talent from having sold his soul to the devil down at the crossroads (folks here like to speculate on which crossroads it was). This legend is recounted in *Folk Beliefs of the Southern Negro* by Newbell Niles Puckett (Patterson Smith, 1968):

If you want to make a contract with the devil...Take a black cat bone and a guitar and go to a lonely fork in the roads at midnight. Sit down there and play your best piece, thinking of and wishing for the devil all the while. By and by you will hear music, dim at first but growing louder and louder as the music approaches nearer... After a time you feel something tugging at your instrument...Let the devil take it and keep thumping along with your fingers as if you still had a guitar in your hands. Then the devil will hand you his instrument to play and will accompany you on yours. After doing this for a time he will seize your fingers and trim the nails until they bleed, finally taking his guitar back and returning your own. Keep on playing; do not look around. His music will become fainter and fainter as he moves away...You will be able to play any piece you desire on the guitar and you can do anything you want to in the world, but you have sold your eternal soul to the devil and are his in the world to come.

Johnson left only 29 songs – *Sweet Home Chicago*, *Me and the Devil Blues* and *Crossroads Blues* among them – when he died outside a Greenwood bar in 1938. They say it was poison administered by a jealous husband, and that Johnson was on all fours 'baying like a hell hound' moments before he died. To this day no one can say for certain where he's buried.

The Pilgrimage Southwest of Greenwood, there are two memorials to Robert Johnson off Hwy 7, south of Itta Bena.

Robert Johnson's gravestone (whether or not it marks his actual grave is unknown) is in Quito, a tiny settlement that straddles Hwy 7, five miles south of Itta Bena (no sign identifies it as Quito). After you pass the small bridge at the start of town, turn right (west) onto the first dirt road and continue to the Payne Chapel Methodist Baptist Church. You'll find Johnson's modest marker near the swamp.

Robert Johnson's memorial is around two miles farther south off Hwy 7 (north of Morgan City). Turn off Hwy 7 at the sign for Mathews Brake National Wildlife Refuge and you'll find the small Mount Zion MB Church nestled in a thicket less than a quarter of a mile up the road. Johnson's memorial takes the shape of a small obelisk and is inscribed with the titles of his songs. It's often adorned by offerings left by his fans. ∎

Apparently the president was hunting nearby when an aid tried to make the task easier by capturing a cub for the President to shoot. His refusal at such easy prey earned him the nickname 'Teddy.' The Onward Store here features mechanical dancing bears (two bits a dance), bear skins and a little roadhouse saloon room with a country-music jukebox.

VICKSBURG

population 20,908

Vicksburg stands on a high bluff overlooking a bend in the Mississippi River. Its strategic location made it a prime target during the Civil War. As Union troops worked their way northward from the Gulf of Mexico and southward from Illinois, overpowering Confederate defenses one by one, Vicksburg became the final Confederate stronghold. President Lincoln considered Vicksburg the key to Union victory, declaring 'the war can never be brought to a close until that key is in our pocket.' The price of that key was one of the longest sieges in American military history.

After several unsuccessful attempts to capture the city by storm, Union General Ulysses S Grant decided to lay siege by encircling the Confederate lines of defense around the city. Federal gunboats north and south of town further cut off communications and supplies. The city held out for 47 days – still painfully recalled in the local collective memory – until its official surrender on July 4, 1863. (The Fourth of July was until relatively recently only celebrated by African Americans in Vicksburg.) The national military park tells the story of the entire campaign; its cemetery contains the graves of 17,000 Civil War soldiers. The few antebellum houses that survived the onslaught (one is a luxurious B&B) are best seen during the town's house tours in spring and fall; several of the mansions are open year-round as historic house museums.

Orientation & Information

Located right off I-20, Vicksburg's major sights are readily accessible from exit 4B

(Clay St), and tourist services are plentiful. The national park makes a particularly easy detour for through-travelers as it's under a mile from the freeway.

Vicksburg's old, slow downtown stretches along several cobblestone blocks of Washington St and overlooks the river. There are several lavish casinos on the water at the foot of Clay St that operate 24 hours.

There is a visitor center across from the entrance to the national park, and the offices of the local convention and visitors bureau (☎ 601-636-9421, 800-221-3536, Box 110, Vicksburg, MS 39181) are at the corner of Clay and Washington Sts, downtown by the river.

National Military Park & Cemetery

The Vicksburg national military park (☎ 601-636-0583), under a mile north of I-20 on Clay St, preserves 1858 acres where the Union army laid siege to Vicksburg. From the visitor center inside the gates (where they show an introductory film), a 16-mile driving tour through the rolling wooded hills leads past historic markers explaining emplacements and recounting key events in the campaign. Audio-tape tours bring the landscape to life (rentals available for $4.50).

The McRaven House on the grounds of the park served as Union headquarters for the occupation. The house is legendary as the home to the ghost of Union General McPherson; as recently as 1991 an Episcopalian priest was called in to perform a rite of exorcism – but so far, no luck.

The cemetery, in which nearly 17,000 Union soldiers are buried, is in the far north end of the park. Nearby, a museum houses the remains of the Union's iron-clad gunboat the USS *Cairo*, sunk in the Yazoo River by an electrically detonated mine (the first boat in history to be sunk in this way).

The visitor center and *Cairo* museum are open daily except Christmas. Admission is $4 per car. Inquire about guided tours (fees are extremely reasonable), Civil War reenactments in May and July, and other special events.

Other Attractions

About a dozen historic house museums in town are clustered in Vicksburg's Garden District, on Oak St south of Clay, and also in an attractive residential district between 1st St E and Clay (follow the signs). Admission is usually around $5. During the fortnight-long pilgrimages (popular with lovers of interior design) in late March, early April and mid-October, multiple-house tickets are available; contact the local tourist board for exact dates and prices.

Biedman's **Museum of Coca-Cola Memorabilia** (☎ 601-638-6514), 1107 Washington St, occupies the 1890 building where Coca-Cola was first bottled. The displays include a circa 1900 soda fountain and restored 1890 candy store with ice-cream floats and penny candy treats for sale. It's open daily.

The US Army Engineer **Waterways Experiment Station** (☎ 601-634-2502), 1909 Halls Ferry Rd, features a scale model of the Mississippi River, where some of the town's 3500 riparian engineers try to maintain domination over the mighty Mississippi.

On Washington St, north of downtown, is **Margaret's Grocery** on the left-hand side around three miles up; look for the sign: 'All is welcome – Jews and Gentiles – Here at Margaret's Gro & Mkt and Bible Class.' When the Reverend Dennis and his wife, Margaret, started the grocery, he promised to build her a castle, and he's been working on it ever since, concrete block by block, wooden spire by spire. Stop by for a little something and you'll be treated to one of the reverend's favorite orations as well.

Eight miles east in **Bovina**, Earl's Art Shop (☎ 601-636-5264), is an homage to popular advertising, including a five-foot-high pack of Kool and colorful cardboard jukeboxes. To get there, take the Bovina exit, pass the Texaco station, cross the tracks, and continue around the bend. Admission is $2. If you can't make it to Bovina, examples of Earl's art are displayed in Vicksburg at the **Attic Gallery** on Washington St south of Clay.

Places to Stay

Travelers may require reservations during popular pilgrimage weeks, and the lowest rates are available from November to February.

Several private campgrounds offer sites designed primarily for RV travelers. *Battlefield Campgrounds* (☎ 601-636-2025), 4407 Frontage Rd, is by I-20; the *Isle of Capri RV Park* (☎ 601-631-0402), 720 Lucy Bryson St, is adjacent to the Isle of Capri casino on the riverfront.

At the bottom end, the *Hillcrest Inn* (☎ 601-638-1491) at 40 Hwy 80, offers rooms starting at $24/28 a single/double. The *Park Inn International* (☎ 601-638-5811, 800-359-9363), on the I-20 Frontage Rd off exit 4B, is an almost incongruously luxurious road motel, with a wicker-filled lobby and ceiling fans; rates range from $35/45 to $57/67, including a breakfast buffet.

The town's grand B&B is *Cedar Grove* (☎ 601-636-1000, 800-862-1300), 2300 Washington St (enter off Oak St). It's an 1840 Greek revival mansion on four acres with landscaped gardens overlooking the river. A Union cannonball is still lodged in the parlor wall, and the house retains many original antiques and gas-lit chandeliers. Their 24 guest rooms all have private baths; rates range from around $85 to $160 and include breakfast.

Places to Eat

A traditional Southern feast – including pork tenderloins, fried okra, pecan pie and the like – is served at *Walnut Hills* (☎ 601-638-4910), 1214 Adams St at Clay. The soul-food equivalent is the hole-in-the-wall *Kitchen in the Garden*, 802 5th St North at Main St. It's open weekdays only, from 11 am to 2 am. *Burger Village* (☎ 601-638-0202), 1220 Washington St at Clay downtown, is a local alternative to the many fast-food choices out by the interstate; they also serve breakfast all day. Many riverfront casinos offer round-the-clock meals and ample buffets at lunch and dinner.

MISSISSIPPI

Getting There & Away

Bus Greyhound (☎ 601-638-8389) operates a regional bus service from its station at 1295 S Frontage Rd.

Boat Vicksburg is a stop on riverboat tours along the Mississippi River conducted by the Delta Queen Steamboat Company; most originate in New Orleans (see Getting Around).

Getting Around

Drivers should note that waist-high white stone posts at intersections serve as street signs. Driving any faster than a crawl makes the signs easy to miss. The city tries to supplement these by suspending street numbers from traffic signals in the centers of intersections. In addition, posted signs direct drivers to major attractions.

Northeastern Mississippi

History

The Indian mounds and village sites off the Natchez Trace north of Tupelo tell the story of the area's oldest inhabitants. In fact, the trace itself – now an interstate parkway – was originally an Indian footpath. When Spanish explorer Hernando de Soto passed through in 1540, the Chickasaw dominated the northern Mississippi and central Tennessee area. The two sides clashed in battle and de Soto was driven west. Two centuries later, the Chickasaw were armed by the British to fight the combined forces of the French and Choctaw in the French & Indian War in 1736. The Chickasaw prevailed in what came to be called the Battle of Ackia, fought near Tupelo.

Civil War battles were also fought in the region for control of strategic railroad lines which supplied Atlanta. The Battle of Brices Cross Roads pitted Confederate General Nathan Bedford Forrest against Union General Samuel Sturgis on June 9, 1864 – a Confederate rout. (The field where they fought is preserved as a historic site.) The next month, Union General William T Sherman sent in General Joseph Mower to 'follow Forrest to the death, if it costs 10,000 lives and breaks the Treasury.' Mower and 14,000 troops advanced from Tennessee against Forrest's forces moving north from fortified defenses in Oklalona, and the two armies met in Tupelo on July 15. Though the Union held off additional Confederate attacks and temporarily secured the railroad, neither side could claim complete victory in the Battle of Tupelo. A commemorative monument on W Main St in downtown Tupelo is all that remains of the engagement.

The next major invasion of northeastern Mississippi was by the federal agencies that descended on the area in the first half of the 20th century. The US Army Corps of Engineers constructed the Tennessee-Tombigbee Waterway (the 'Tenn-Tom') to

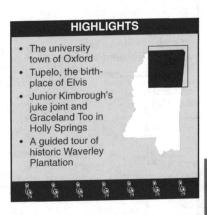

HIGHLIGHTS

- The university town of Oxford
- Tupelo, the birthplace of Elvis
- Junior Kimbrough's juke joint and Graceland Too in Holly Springs
- A guided tour of historic Waverley Plantation

direct the waters of the Tennessee and Tombigbee Rivers from the state of Tennessee clear down to the Gulf of Mexico. The federal Appalachian Regional Commission, USDA Soil Conservation Service, Tennessee Valley Authority (TVA), NPS, USFS, and even NASA have had a hand in shaping the economic development of the extreme northeastern corner, historically one of the poorest regions in the state.

Adjacent to the west runs a sliver of the Black Belt, the fertile crescent that sweeps through the South. As the home of many of the largest cotton plantations, the Black Belt is also historically the source of the South's greatest wealth. To the north, the hill country contains some of Mississippi's most scenic countryside – a gently rolling terrain of well-watered forests and cropland. Oxford – the state's literary and intellectual epicenter, and home to the University of Mississippi campus – is the heart of the region.

Flora & Fauna

The northeastern corner of the state contains the westernmost reaches of the Southern Appalachian forest in a thickly wooded upland area that is historically one

331

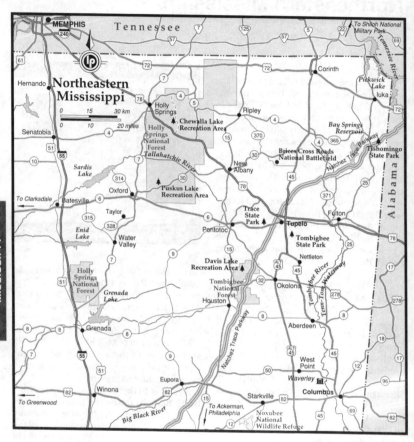

of the least developed in the state. You will see the small mammals most commonly associated with the South – opossums, armadillos, squirrels, raccoons and bats, though legends of elusive panthers at large still circulate. The Tombigbee and Holly Springs National Forests, and Noxubee National Wildlife Refuge provide access to remote public areas.

Hiking

Access to public land – especially national forests and state parks – is readily available throughout the region. Most locals are drawn to lakes and reservoirs that have swimming beaches; these recreation areas frequently offer trails as well.

For a nice selection of woodland hiking trails, visit Tishomingo State Park (☎ 601-438-6914), which straddles the Natchez Trace just in from the Alabama line. A trail network of several loop routes crosses over a swinging wooden bridge, up to rock bluffs, and to a tiny box canyon with a little waterfall. The park sponsors float trips down Bear Creek (canoe rentals available) and also offers a swimming pool, cabins, and a 62-site campground with hookups.

Farther off the beaten path, the Noxubee National Wildlife Refuge south of Starkville occupies a graceful, compelling landscape of quiet woods and small lakes. Its trail network includes old plank roads that once traversed its swampy corners. (See Starkville, Hiking & Biking.)

TUPELO

population 30,685

Incorporated in 1870 and named after the native Tupelo gum tree, Tupelo is rather proud that it was the first city in the nation to provide electric power to its citizens through the TVA. It was once a railroad hub; today it supports itself through manufacturing. More upholstered furniture is manufactured in and around Tupelo's Lee County than anywhere else in the world. Yet humble Tupelo is notorious around the world as the birthplace of the King of Rock 'n' Roll, Elvis Presley. Presley's dirt-poor origins here figure largely in the Elvis mystique.

Elvis and his family left Tupelo for Memphis when he was 13; he returned to his hometown in 1956 to play the Mississippi-Alabama Fair and Dairy Show to crowds so wild the National Guard was called in to contain them. Elvis returned again to the fair the following year for a benefit concert with proceeds going to the city's purchase and restoration of his birthplace, which attracts nearly 100,000 visitors each year.

Tupelo is no city you'd want to go out of your way to visit, beyond paying your respects to the King at his birthplace. But because it's the largest city in these parts, and strategically positioned at several major crossroads, you might need to use its resources.

Orientation

The Natchez Trace Parkway, which is headquartered in Tupelo, and Hwy 78 intersect northeast of downtown Tupelo. Elvis Presley's birthplace is farther east off Hwy 78, and the short detour is well signposted.

Downtown Tupelo, however, is oddly challenging to navigate for a city this size due to an access freeway that connects Hwy 78 with Hwy 45. You pretty much just need to stick to Gloster St to find motels, restaurants and other services along its length, with the greatest concentration around the intersection of Gloster and McCullough. The older downtown area, indicated by the old blue-and-yellow neon arrow at Gloster and Main (an intersection known as 'Crosstown') is about a mile east of this intersection.

Information

Tourist Offices The city's visitor center (☎ 601-841-6521, 800-533-0611) is at 399 E Main St, but chances are if you've found it you already know all you need to about Tupelo. There's a Natchez Trace Parkway visitor center (☎ 601-680-4025, 800-305-7417), right on the parkway north of Hwy 78 that distributes maps and displays historic exhibits.

Money There are ATMs at the shopping malls (see Things to Buy), at banks along Gloster St and downtown.

Post The central post office (☎ 601-841-1286) is on Main St between the landmark Crosstown arrow on Gloster St and downtown.

Bookstores In operation since 1907, Reed's (☎ 601-844-1355), at 111 Spring St downtown, hosts events by Southern writers. At the Barnes Crossing shopping complex north of town, Books-A-Million stocks a wide selection of periodicals (including national and international papers), regional

A nocturnal animal with bad eyesight, the armadillo fares poorly on roads and freeways.

interest books, children's books and toys, and has a cafe open in the evening. It's big but tucked away – find the Hampton Inn and it's directly east.

Medical & Emergency Services The emergency room of the Northeast Mississippi Medical Center can be reached at ☎ 601-841-4157.

Dangers & Annoyances Standard urban precautions apply. Tupelo is a conservative town – don't pull any highjinks that will draw too much attention from local authorities.

Birthplace of Elvis Presley

Off Veterans Blvd in what was once the outskirts of town, the shack that was Elvis Presley's birthplace now stands as a shrine to the King of Rock 'n' Roll. The 15-acre park complex (☎ 601-841-1245), at 306 Elvis Presley Blvd, includes a museum and chapel. None of his music is played anywhere on site – this is ground too sacred for such earthy sounds.

The 450-sq-foot **shotgun shack** was built by Vernon Presley and his brother with a borrowed $180. In the front room in 1935, Elvis and his stillborn twin, Jesse, were born on January 8 at 4:35 am. A guide stationed inside collects $1 per person (50¢ for children under 12) and explains that the Presleys lived here until Elvis was three, when the house was repossessed.

The **museum** (admission $4 for adults, $2 for children) displays the private, intensely personal collection of items Elvis gave to Janelle McComb, a lifelong family friend of the Presleys. In addition to the jump-suits and baby pictures of Lisa Marie, on display are the gifts McComb gave to Elvis, including an Elvis-tear-stained poem penned by McComb (smeared reproductions available at the gift shop).

A tiny **chapel** (free admission), oriented to overlook the shack, contains Elvis' own bible, donated by his father.

The shack and museum are open Monday to Saturday from 9 am to 5 pm (till 5:30 pm from May through September) and Sunday from 1 to 5 pm.

Other Elvis Sights

Elvis is immortalized all around town – everyone seems to have their own story of who cut the King's hair or who taught Elvis his first chord.

Elvis bought his first guitar in 1946 for $12 at **Tupelo Hardware** (☎ 601-842-4637) at 114 W Main St, downtown across from the railroad tracks – his first choice was a rifle, but his mother wouldn't go along with that. Elvis attended grades one to five at **Lawhon School**, down Elvis Presley Dr from his birthplace. His fifth-grade teacher here entered Elvis in a talent contest held at the **fairgrounds** west of town (off W Main at Mulberry Alley) – the King won second prize for a rendition of 'Old Shep.' Elvis earned A grades in music at **Milam Junior High School** at Gloster St and Jefferson St (a block north of the Crosstown arrow). The Presleys attended the **First Assembly of God** church at 909 Berry St at Adams.

The only Elvis shrine that serves quarter-pounders, the Crosstown **McDonald's** (☎ 601-844-5505) at 372 S Gloster St, across from the Gloster Creek Village mall, contains photo collages and descriptive captions on the life of Elvis, along with a tiny collection of memorabilia.

Tupelo Museum

'Fossilized Crocodile Found in Mississippi May Be the Lost Link' is the first exhibit to greet you at the Tupelo Museum (☎ 601-841-6438), a rambling, eclectic collection of Indian dioramas, sepia photographs of the 'tornador' that swept through town killing 210 in 1936, a Model T, a mannequin in an iron lung, a Swedish massage therapy office, a deflated Teddy Roosevelt effigy in a wheelchair, and homey postcards from the moon. Don't make this your first stop in Mississippi; season yourself first. The museum is a quick half-mile or so west of the Natchez Trace off Hwy 6 next to a park; there are few other services to speak of. Admission is $1 for everyone over 12, 50¢ for kids. It's open weekdays 8 am to 4 pm, weekends 1 to 5 pm.

Places to Stay

Camping Two state parks on either side of town, Tombigbee to the east and Trace to the west (well signposted from nearby highways), provide campsites for $11 ($7 for seniors) per night. Trace also offers swimming, fishing and trails. See Around Tupelo, below. The *Elvis Presley Lake Campground* north of Elvis' birthplace is another possible (but untried) option.

Motels You might want to avoid the two budget motels most readily fallen into off the highways – namely, the *Trace Inn* off the Natchez Trace (catering to leisure travelers) and the *All-American Inn* off Hwy 45 (full of truckers). These are isolated and less desirable than the cluster of motels at the overpass rise at Gloster St and McCullough.

The cheapest place in town is the *Commodore Motel* (☎ 601-844-7455) on Business Hwy 78 about a half-mile east of Elvis' birthplace, with rates from $19 (cash only). The *Village Inn* (☎ 601-842-4903), 1013 N Gloster, across the overpass from the Ramada, is a decent budget option ($32/38 for a single/double) with a nice pool and old-fashioned court-like layout; the owners smoke. The plain *Scottish Inn* (☎ 601-842-1961), 401 N Gloster, down a half-mile or so from the Ramada has decent small rooms for $35 (single or double); nonsmoking rooms are available. The *Ramada Inn* (☎ 601-844-4111), 854 N Gloster, is the grand hotel in these parts – it anchors a stretch of a half-dozen budget motels. The Ramada has a nightclub, restaurant, nice pool and rooms for $47/57.

Places to Eat

Jefferson Place (☎ 601-844-8696), 823 Jefferson, is a Tupelo institution run out of a big old house just a block northwest of the Crosstown arrow, off Gloster St. The bar-and-grill serves steaks and sandwiches to a local crowd from 11 am to midnight every day but Sunday. A *Morrison's Express* cafeteria at the Barnes Crossing Mall (☎ 601-840-4317) is easy to get to from Hwy 78 (follow the signs to the food court; it's back by the cinemas). A bigger *Morrison's Cafeteria* (☎ 601-844-5895) is at the Gloster Creek Village mall on Gloster St a half-mile or so down from the Crosstown arrow.

Entertainment

It's a shame that in the hometown of Elvis you can't hear some good rockabilly, but Tupelo is not that kind of town – though it does host an Elvis Presley tribute week in August.

The *Tupelo Coliseum* hosts major events, including concerts by nationally known performers, rodeos, the Harlem Globetrotters and Disney on Ice. The night we arrived, 2000 people were turned away – the 10,000-seat arena was packed to hear the Franklin Graham Crusade (Christian evangelist Billy Graham's heir apparent).

Things to Buy

The Elvis Presley Museum at his birthplace sells a small collection of Elvis-branded cold-drink covers, key chains and the like, but the choicest pieces are the handcrafted guitar-shaped decoupage Elvis clocks for a pricey $35. Postcards proclaiming 'From Tupelo to Graceland!' tell the whole story.

Two shopping malls – the newer one at Barnes Crossing north of town off Hwy 78, and Gloster Creek Village on Gloster St south of the Crosstown arrow – provide many department stores and specialty shops, as well as banking services, food courts and cinemas.

Getting There & Away

Though there is a regional airport and a municipal bus station, the best way to get to Tupelo is by car; that way you can make a quick getaway after seeing the town's few sights.

Greyhound (☎ 601-842-4557, 800-231-2222) deposits passengers at a decent bus station downtown at 201 Commerce St, directly across from the Tupelo Coliseum. Buses arrive from and depart to Memphis

MISSISSIPPI

four times daily. The trip takes from two to three hours and costs $24/22 weekend/weekday. One bus a day travels between Oxford and Tupelo for $9 and takes 1¼ hours.

Hertz, Budget and other national car rental companies are located at the airport.

Getting Around
Taxi services are available from City Taxicab (☎ 601-842-5277) or Tupelo Cab Co (☎ 601-842-1133).

AROUND TUPELO
Two state parks on either side of town – **Tombigbee** to the east and **Trace** to the west – offer camping (see Tupelo, Places to Stay) and hiking. Trace has a 600-acre lake for swimming and reportedly great bass fishing, and a large backcountry area with trails littered with historic debris. Horses and bikes are allowed on some trails.

Two historic sites adjacent to the Natchez Trace Parkway are within five miles north of Tupelo. The closer one is the site of a **Chickasaw village**. An information kiosk overlooking a small field tells the story of the nation that once controlled the territory from central Mississippi to central Tennessee. A **mound site** a mile or so up the trace reveals the earthworks constructed by Chickasaw ancestors.

At **Brices Cross Roads**, around 12 miles northwest of Tupelo, a monument, a small cemetery and an empty field commemorates the Confederate victory here in 1864. More Civil War sites – earthworks, the Battery Robinette battle site, and a historic house used as headquarters for both sides – are found farther north in the city of **Corinth**. (If you go, stop to eat at the old drug store lunch counter at *Borrum's*, 604 Walron St downtown.)

Twenty miles up Hwy 78, **New Albany** is the birthplace of writer William Faulkner. The 'Faulkner family trail' traces the local travels of Faulkner and his family (for more information call ☎ 601-538-0014, 534-1010). Special remembrances are held on the late author's birthday (September 25). See Oxford for more Faulkner sights.

OXFORD
population 9984
Here's where you *really* want to go in northern Mississippi. Driving in, it feels different from any other Southern town. It's bustling and prosperous without the familiar extremes of wealth and poverty. The stately courthouse square continues to be the center of community activity without interruption, keeping things to a friendly human scale – folks walk or ride bikes. Galleries, bookstores and cafes reveal the local literary bent. Suburban sprawl is confined to the outskirts, out of sight.

Oxford is home to the University of Mississippi and a lively intellectual community. The university's acclaimed Center for the Study of Southern Culture presides over the rumination of Southernalia, from cornpone and Elvis cults to high culture. The university's blues archives hold the largest collection of blues recordings and publications in the world.

Things weren't always so pretty here. Many remember the university for some very ugly riots in 1962 that accompanied the enrollment of James Meredith, the first student to integrate the school that is widely considered 'the bastion of the Old South.' Troops were called in, and the price of the protest against Meredith's admission was the death of French journalist Paul Guihard and Oxford resident Ray Gunter. While a Confederate soldier monument occupies a preeminent spot on the campus, efforts are underway to construct a civil rights memorial.

The history that's easier to talk about stretches back to 1837, when the town was founded. The university opened a decade later. During the Civil War, Oxford was captured by Union soldiers and most of its buildings were burned to the ground. The few structures that remain (including the 1838 Barksdale House, now a B&B) are treasured. But the era that's closest to the town's heart is the early 20th century, when William Faulkner mythologized the region in his famous stories set in Yoknapatawpha County. His graceful Southern

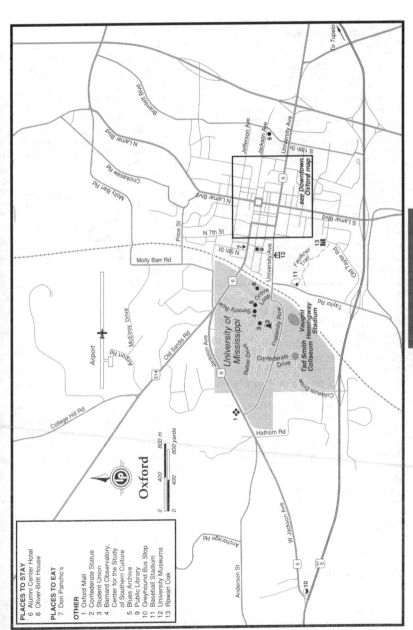

MISSISSIPPI

Oxford

0   400   800 m
0   400   800 yards

PLACES TO STAY
6 Alumni Center Hotel
8 Oliver-Britt House

PLACES TO EAT
7 Don Pancho's

OTHER
1 Oxford Mall
2 Confederate Statue
3 Student Union
4 Barnard Observatory,
   Center for the Study
   of Southern Culture
5 Blues Archive
9 Public Library
10 Greyhound Bus Stop
11 Baseball Stadium
12 University Museums
13 Rowan Oak

The Endangered Rebel

The University of Mississippi, whose nickname 'Ole Miss' is derived from the pet name for the mistress of a plantation, is facing an identity crisis. Its widely recognized symbols – white-haired mascot 'Colonel Reb' and its Rebels sports teams – are under attack. Like much Old South imagery, these symbols are treasured by some as sources of Southern pride, and are offensive to others because of their relationship to slavery. Yet what does the University of Mississippi stand for if not tradition? To purists, any proposed changes to the university's mascots are seen as tantamount to asking the pope to update the Church's stand on birth control.

Students seem divided on the issue. 'It's long overdue,' said one woman graduate student. Her companion was not so sure: 'If you willingly change your tradition when it becomes unpopular, what are traditions good for?' The university officially disassociated itself from the Confederate battle flag 14 years ago, but a sea of them still wave at home football games. Though 'Dixie' was once the sporting Rebel's fight song, the school has officially dropped that too.

In the last few years, states across the South have had to question their use of Confederate symbols and Old South nostalgia. Georgia and South Carolina have debated removing the 'Stars and Bars' from state flags. In 1997, Virginia dropped its 'Old Dominion' anthem because its lyrics of plantation life are now considered racist. Most likely the University of Mississippi will follow suit, but it will be a hard sell either way. The university has employed the services of alumnus Harold Burson (class of '40) of New York's Burson-Marstellar (the world's largest public-relations agency), to make the transition as gentle as possible. ■

---

home – Rowan Oak, built in 1844 – provides a personal glimpse into the life of the Bard of Mississippi.

Orientation & Information

The city is centered around Courthouse Square, which is bisected by Lamar Blvd. The campus (technically in its own town of University) is a short mile or so west of the town square at the head of University Ave. You can get almost everywhere on foot or on bikes (rentals available, see Getting Around). There's a visitor center on the square in the yellow house next to City Hall. Or you can contact the Oxford Tourism Council (☎ 601-234-4680, 800-758-9177), 111 Courthouse Square, Oxford, MS 38655, for more information. For Oxford's online sites, see the Internet directory. Square Books is an excellent bookstore; see Things to Buy, below.

University of Mississippi

From 80 students enrolled in 1848, the University of Mississippi has grown to an enrollment of 10,000 in 10 colleges and professional schools, including liberal arts,

medicine and law. Today its enrollment is 11% black.

The attractive 2500-acre campus contains several 19th-century buildings shaded by magnolias and dogwood. Some of the most popular activities on campus are sporting events featuring the Ole Miss Rebels and Lady Rebels.

The university's **Center for the Study of Southern Culture** occupies the 1857 Barnard Observatory building on Grove Loop. Established in 1977, the center runs degree programs in Southern studies. Its faculty members, directed by William Ferris (author of *Blues from the Delta* and co-author of the *Encyclopedia of Southern Culture*), are preeminent scholars in Southern lore. Its publications include the magazines *Living Blues* and *Mississippi Folklife*. The center hosts special events to examine and celebrate Southern culture (see Special Events). Past conferences have delved into the cult of Elvis and Southern culinary traditions. The center's welcoming offices (☎ 601-232-5993) usually have an exhibit of some kind on display (and we're eager to see them expand their small Southern kitsch collection upstairs, which presently includes vials of alleged Elvis sweat). Inquire about steamboat trips, Delta blues tours and cultural programs and seminars.

The university's **blues archive** (☎ 601-232-7753) contains the largest collection of blues recordings and publications in the world, including BB King's personal collection. It aims to archive and provide materials for serious researchers (by advance notice) – unfortunately for the casual visitor, there's really nothing to see but a few posters and locked stacks of tape and vinyl. Nevertheless, it remains a touchstone on the blues pilgrimage. It's in the modern Farley Hall across from the center. (Blues-lovers should tune in to WUMS 92.1 FM for the Hwy 61 blues program hosted by Scott McCraw – currently on Sunday evenings.)

The papers and mementos of native sons William Faulkner (including his Nobel citation) and James Meredith are displayed at the **John D Williams Library** (☎ 601-232-5858). It's behind the Greek revival lyceum.

On University Ave at 5th, outside the campus gates, the **University Museums** building (☎ 601-232-7073) contains several collections of ancient, decorative, fine and folk arts worth a look. Admission is free.

Faulkner's Home & Grave

The grounds and old house at Rowan Oak on Old Taylor Rd (☎ 601-232-7237) gracefully evoke the spirit of the Nobel laureate William Faulkner, who bought the property in 1930 and lived here until his death in 1962. The university acquired it in 1974 from Faulkner's daughter, and now opens it to the public. Built in 1840, the sparsely furnished house is set down an arcade of oak and cedar. Here the writer produced his Snopes trilogy – *Sanctuary*, *Light in August*, and *A Green Bough* – along with *Absalom, Absalom!* and *A Fable* (the story outline for which remains sketched on the wall of Faulkner's office). Rowan Oak is open Tuesday through Saturday from 10 am to noon and 2 to 4 pm, and Sunday

The Oxford of Mississippi

I discovered that my little postage stamp of native soil was worth writing about and that I would never live long enough to exhaust it. It opened up a gold mine of people, as I created a cosmos of my own.
– William Faulkner

Since William Faulkner immortalized his home town and the surrounding county – which he called the city of Jefferson and Yoknapatawpha County in his books – Oxford has maintained its reputation as a literary center. Faulkner's home of Rowan Oak is today a spiritual center for literary pilgrims and aspiring writers (its curator Cynthia Shearer is a novelist herself). On the centenary of his birth, September 25, 1997, the city installed a statue of Faulkner on the courthouse square.

Square Books, meanwhile, is the heart of Oxford's literary community, and the best bookstore within several states. Within two stories of warping plank floors that once belonged to a drugstore (the sign remains outside), Square Books packs stacks of titles and specializes in Southern writers and themes. It schedules a full calendar of author readings, and their patio cafe overlooking the courthouse is a gathering place for writers and readers. See Things to Buy, below.

Titles worth searching for include the Center for Southern Culture's *Living Blues* magazine, and the *In Search of Elvis* conference papers, and the bimonthly *Oxford American*, published by popular novelist John Grisham, who maintains a family compound nearby. ∎

from 2 to 4 pm only (closed on Monday and major holidays). Admission is free.

The **Faulkner Trail**, a 10-minute walk, leads through Bailey's Woods (adjacent to Rowan Oak) towards the university's baseball stadium.

Faulkner's **grave** is about a half-mile northeast of Rowan Oak at the cemetery on Jefferson Ave at 16th. Go down 16th to the base of the hill; the family grave is several steps in from the worn pull-out.

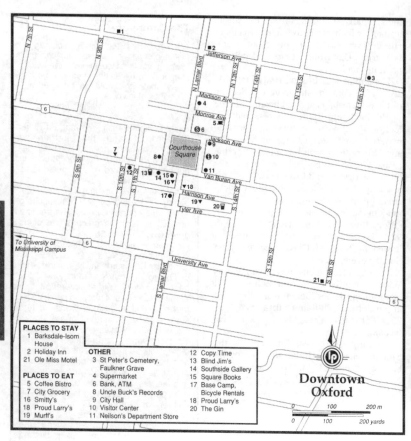

PLACES TO STAY
1 Barksdale-Isom
   House
2 Holiday Inn
21 Ole Miss Motel

PLACES TO EAT
5 Coffee Bistro
7 City Grocery
16 Smitty's
18 Proud Larry's
19 Murff's

OTHER
3 St Peter's Cemetery,
   Faulkner Grave
4 Supermarket
6 Bank, ATM
8 Uncle Buck's Records
9 City Hall
10 Visitor Center
11 Neilson's Department Store

12 Copy Time
13 Blind Jim's
14 Southside Gallery
15 Square Books
17 Base Camp,
   Bicycle Rentals
18 Proud Larry's
20 The Gin

Downtown
Oxford

Special Events

The university's Center for the Study of Southern Culture sponsors the annual Conference for the Book in April and the Faulkner Conference in August. The city of Oxford hosts a Double Decker Arts Festival with plenty of local music on the last Saturday in April.

Places to Stay

Camping You can camp at two lake recreation areas around 10 miles outside town; rates are around $5 a night for primitive

sites. The USFS *Puskus Lake* campground is northeast off Hwy 30, and the Army Corps of Engineers maintains several campgrounds around the *Sardis Lake* reservoir northwest off Hwy 314.

Motels & Hotels The low-end establishment downtown is the *Ole Miss Motel* (☎ 601-234-2424), 1517 University Ave, a few blocks away from the square but still within easy walking distance. Modest singles/doubles are $30/35, and the family who runs it say they may be able to pick folks up at the Greyhound stop. Several budget motel franchises can be found around exits off the Hwy 6 bypass.

Right on campus, the *Alumni Center Hotel* (☎ 601-234-2331), 172 Grove Loop, provides 89 guest rooms with private bath for $49/57 a single/double.

The high-end motel downtown, the *Holiday Inn* (☎ 601-234-3031), 400 N Lamar Blvd, is conveniently located not far from the square. It provides 123 rooms with private bath for $56/63, with pool, restaurant and lounge.

Inns A comfortably worn choice is *Oliver-Britt House* (☎ 601-234-8043), 512 Van Buren Ave (three blocks from the square); rates are around $45 for a single, add $10 for doubles and on weekends.

At the high end is *Barksdale-Isom House* (☎ 601-236-5600, 800-236-5696), 1003 Jefferson Ave. Lavishly appointed rooms with private bath occupy the refined 1835 two-story house a block north of the square. Rates between $120 and $150 include a full Southern breakfast.

Places to Eat

Smitty's (☎ 601-234-9111), 208 S Lamar Blvd, is a homey cafe that serves Southern breakfasts (from $3 beignets to all-out $9 country plates of ham, eggs and grits) and daily luncheon buffets ($5) to a crowd of regulars and old-timers. It's open daily for all three meals. The *Bottletree Bakery* (☎ 601-236-5000), 923 Van Buren Ave, serves pastries and espressos in an arty interior just off the square. *Coffee Bistro* (☎ 601-281-8188), 107 N 13th St, features live entertainment some nights and is open to midnight and often beyond. The cafe at *Square Books* spills out onto the balcony overlooking the square.

At *City Grocery* (☎ 601-232-8080), 1118 Van Buren Ave, the spicy house specials include shrimp and cheese grits, a barbecue shrimp salad, and other nouveau Southern specialties served at freshly papered tables inside an old brick grocery. Lunch entrees are around $8 to $10; it's more expensive for dinner (there's a good wine selection

too). For a great cheap meal of chicken and rice or fried catfish, there's *Don Pancho's* (☎ 601-238-2736), 512 Jackson Ave, a tiny five-table place tinged with flavors from the Dominican Republic.

Proud Larry's (☎ 601-236-0050), 211 S Lamar Blvd, serves thick burgers, pizza, and daily pasta specials, and there's live entertainment nightly. *Murff's* (☎ 601-234-7588), 1212 Harrison Ave, is a popular blue-collar watering hole that also serves tamales and bar food.

A few far-flung restaurants are a good excuse for a drive outside town. Eight miles east on Hwy 334, the *Yocona River Inn* (☎ 601-234-2464) serves up good crawfish pie. It's open for dinner Thursday through Sunday. On Old Taylor Rd, the *Taylor Grocery & Restaurant* (☎ 601-236-1716) is a classic catfish house open Thursday to Sunday from 5:30 to 10 pm.

Entertainment

Good live entertainment – blues, bluegrass and roots rock can be heard nightly, which is impressive for a town this size. Be aware that the entertainment calendar closely follows the academic calendar – things may shut down around spring break, for example. The free entertainment weekly *Oxford Town* lists what's happening where; it's distributed at the tourist office and other places downtown. You can catch readings at Square Books.

Blind Jim's (☎ 601-234-6147), 1112½ Van Buren Ave, features blues some nights, and at last visit, a live Tuesday-night radio broadcast hosted by the bluegrass-country-jug band the Sincere Ramblers. Check listings for what's going on at *Proud Larry's* and *Murff's* (see above), and also at the *Gin* (☎ 601-234-0024), on Harrison Ave off Lamar Blvd.

Things to Buy

More of a cultural center than a mere place to shop, Square Books (☎ 601-236-2262), 160 Courthouse Square, is one of the best bookstores in the South. Used titles are down the street at Off Square Books. They're open until at least 9 pm most nights.

Also around the square, Southside Gallery (☎ 601-234-9090) exhibits contemporary arts and craftwork, including folk art.

One of the oldest stores in the nation, Neilson's Department Store (☎ 601-234-1161) started as a trading post out of a log cabin in 1839; nowadays it sells Villager blouses to sorority co-eds from its 1897 building.

At Uncle Buck's Records (☎ 601-234-7744) look for the local label Fat Possum Records (☎ 601-236-3110), which records many Delta blues musicians. It's also a good place to inquire about bands playing locally.

Getting There & Away
Greyhound (☎ 800-231-2222) runs a scheduled service from 2612B W Jackson Ave (across from Shoney's restaurant). From Oxford to downtown Memphis it's around $20 one-way.

Getting Around
No local bus service is available. There is one taxi in town; call ☎ 601-238-9988.

HOLLY SPRINGS
population 7261
Holly Springs' citizenry is proud of its Confederate civic organizations and the annual pilgrimage that visits its antebellum homes. In addition, the town has found itself notorious for a funky juke joint and a very peculiar Elvis shrine. Oh, and *USA Today* named its Phillips Grocery as having the best hamburgers in the country. The Blues & Gospel Folk Festival in town on the second Saturday in September is also a good reason to visit.

Stop at the chamber of commerce (☎ 601-252-2943), off the square at 154 S Memphis St (follow signs), for information about house tours, the local history museum and the golf course.

Phillips Grocery (☎ 601-252-4671) serves good burgers and fried okra. It's very close to the downtown square but tricky to find. To get there, follow Van Dorn a half-mile east from the square; at

the lights, you must turn left to continue along Van Dorn. Phillips is a block up at the tracks

Junior Kimbrough's juke joint is among the few which can be counted on to host live entertainment regularly. Sunday nights are your best bet. With luck you'll find the man himself, blues musician Junior Kimbrough. Recorded on Fat Possum Records of Oxford, the 58-year-old 'hellfired virtuoso' released *All Night Long* in 1993, which the *Washington Post* acclaimed as 'the best Delta blues album in nearly 40 years.' 'It isn't just music,' wrote Tower Records' *PULSE!* in a review of Kimbrough's 1994 *Sad Days Lonely Nights* release. 'It conjures the slow grind of sex in the summer heat, mesmerizing the neighbors who come to his juke joint for $1.25 beers and dancing.'

To get there, exit off Hwy 7 to Holly Springs and travel 10 miles west along old Hwy 4 to Kimbrough's wooden shack.

Graceland Too
Paul MacLeod, by all evidence the world's most devoted Elvis fan, has dedicated his life and his son's – Elvis Aaron Presley MacLeod – to tracking the course of Elvis' live and posthumous career. MacLeod Sr has turned his house into a shrine wallpapered with Elvis posters, memorabilia and likenesses – including the blurry lines of his own and his son's (slicked black hair, muttonchops, tuxedo shirts) next to the King's. The father imitates Elvis with little encouragement and tells stories about the used carpet he allegedly got from the jungle room at Graceland – he sells tiny swatches of it in dime-store picture frames for around $10; folks have asked to be buried with their used Elvis carpet swatch, so he says.

This faux Graceland (☎ 601-252-7954), 200 Ghoulson Ave at Randolph, is open most afternoons, but will open its doors at nearly any hour of the day or night for pilgrims. It's $5 a visit – after three visits you're proclaimed a lifetime member and are entitled to have a Polaroid taken of you in a leather jacket with the MacLeods standing by your side (they have walls of such snapshots). You'll find it two blocks east and one block south of Courthouse Square (follow Hwy 4 east; when it makes a 90-degree turn at the landmark Christ Episcopal Church, you're a block away).

STARKVILLE
population 18,458
If Oxford becomes too civilized for you, head to Starkville, the home of Mississippi State University. (In Mississippi, eldest sons attend Ole Miss; the rest go to State.) It's a laid-back Southern town – nowhere near quaint – with a diverse population, nearby wilderness, a great gallery, bookstore, beatnik cafe, historic hotel and inn, and the best public radio station in Mississippi. (Driving around the conservative heartland twisting the dial between Christian broadcasting and country-music stations, it's a shock to pick up ska on WVDS 91.1 FM.)

Orientation & Information
Signs to downtown lead drivers to the small Main St strip with shops, restaurants and the landmark State House Hotel at Jackson St. Farther east, Main St turns into University Dr, which leads to the campus. You will find the Starkville Visitors and Convention Council (☎ 601-323-3322, 800-649-8687) at 322 University Dr. It has maps, brochures and other information. The wonderful Book Mart (☎ 601-323-2844) on 120 E Main stocks local-interest publications, along with the *New York Times*. There's a laundry on University Dr next to the Bulldog Deli.

Mississippi State University
Founded in 1878, Mississippi State University (☎ 601-325-2450) enrolls around 14,000 students in 10 colleges and professional schools annually. Its attractive campus features several 19th-century brick buildings and is near the Noxubee Wildlife Refuge to the south. The university's home team, the Bulldogs, excels in basketball (advancing at one point to the Final Four in the NCAA tournament), and their football and baseball games are also popular. The popular novelist John Grisham is a celebrated alumnus.

On campus, besides the usual stadiums, auditoriums and halls featuring sporting competitions, college theater, films and art exhibits, there's also a wine-making lab, a drive-through rose garden, an entomological collection and cheese for sale at the campus dairy. The **Templeton Music Museum** (☎ 601-325-8301) displays old Victrolas and ragtime-era antiques.

Main St Gallery & Studio
Carved out of an old-fashioned gas station, this gallery (☎ 601-320-9550), 111 W Main St, specializes in Southern folk art – among the best of such galleries in the Deep South. Coke-bottle lamps and candelabras, cigar-box dressers and globes covered with folk wisdom are among its eccentric collection, which also includes canvases and textiles by master-trained artists. A pottery studio next door shows the resident artist at work. It's closed on Sunday and Monday.

Hiking & Biking
Several trails and old roads in the Noxubee National Wildlife Refuge (☎ 601-323-5548) south of town attract hikers and mountain bikers, as well as naturalists and university biologists. From the university's veterinary school, follow the country road towards Oktoc southeast for around eight miles to Bluff Lake Rd. Trail maps are available at the headquarters in the center of the refuge, across the Noxubee River.

Places to Stay
The *University Motel* (☎ 601-323-1421), Hwy 82 west, is a rundown motel in a rundown block, but it's cheap and only a block from Main St; rates are $24/35 for a single/double. The *Regal Inn* (☎ 601-323-8251), Hwy 82 east, is an attractive low-key motel with an outdoor pool; rooms are $35/40.

The *State House Hotel* (☎ 601-323-2000, 800-722-1903), at the corner of Main and Jackson Sts, is a rare find. It's a 1925 hotel handsomely restored (but not persnickety) with all modern conveniences and a restaurant with a great buffet, and it's in the center of the downtown area. Rooms start at $45.

For B&B lodging, the *Caragen House* (☎ 601-323-0340), 1108 Hwy 82 west, provides guest rooms in a white villa down a long gravel drive just a mile or two out of town. Rooms start at $85 a night, including a full breakfast.

Places to Eat

Easy Street (☎ 601-324-2834), 122B N Jackson St (between Main St and Hwy 82) is a funky hangout that serves coffee and pastries. The *City Bagel Cafe* (☎ 601-323-3663), 511 University Dr, is the local Starbucks equivalent and has a nice patio. The *Bulldog Deli* (☎ 601-324-3354), 702 University Dr, makes generous sandwiches next door to a laundromat and across from *Flo & Eddie's* (☎ 601-324-6000), 801 University Dr, which is a nice sit-down restaurant. *Rosey Baby* (☎ 601-324-1949), 100 S Jackson St, operates out of the old depot across the tracks; it serves Cajun food with a zydeco soundtrack and occasionally hosts live entertainment. The Waverley dining room of the *State House Hotel* (☎ 601-323-2000), on Main St at Jackson St, serves a great buffet lunch for around $5.

WEST POINT

population 8489

West Point has an old downtown area where the most visible industry is the manufacture of Big Yank camouflage fatigues. Along a rundown strip of abandoned storefronts, *Anthony's* (☎ 601-494-0316) 116 W Main, is a regional landmark for food and blues. Owner Leo McGee started the Howlin' Wolf Blues Society, which sponsors a blues night here at Anthony's on the first Saturday of every month. Folks come from as far as Memphis to hear the likes of famed Delta musicians such as Mojo Buford and RL Burnside (make reservations). Inside the old grocery store, plates of fettuccine Alfredo and Greek pizza are served at booths and red-and-white checkerboard tables while old ceiling fans overhead stir the air; there's a bar too. Also inquire about the Howlin' Wolf Blues Fest.

WAVERLEY PLANTATION

Between West Point and Columbus, on the banks of the Tombigbee River, lies an antebellum plantation house that's a legend in itself. Waverley (☎ 601-494-1399) was one of the biggest plantations in the pre-Civil War South. It was a self-contained community of 50,000 acres and 1200 residents, a thousand of whom were enslaved Africans. In its demise it was occupied by two spinster brothers; on the death of the surviving brother in 1913 the estate was fought over by extended family members and sat vacant for 50 years. Everyone in town has a story of wandering through the abandoned old mansion in their youth. The house nevertheless managed to hold on to its three floors of carved balconies, marble mantels, molten-gold leaded windows, ceiling-high mirrors, and other exquisite architectural details. In 1962, the family finally decided to sell. The current owner has stocked it with period antiques and opens it to tours with a young friend of the family whose steadfast Southern perspective is a tour in itself. The house is stunning; its highlight is a three-story-high octagonal gallery.

It's open daily from 9 am to 5 pm. Admission is $5 for the house tour, with reduced admission to visit the grounds only.

COLUMBUS

population 23,799

The Victorian home and birthplace of the famous author Tennessee Williams is now the Mississippi Welcome Center (☎ 800-327-2868), on Main St at 3rd St.

The town's many antebellum houses make it a popular destination for annual house tours in spring (the pilgrimage), during which over a dozen historic homes are on display. Another historic highlight is **Friendship Cemetery**. By marking the graves of Union soldiers in this cemetery, locals inspired the national observance of Memorial Day. During the pilgrimage, a costumed Confederate officer tells tales of famous crypt residents by candlelight.

The historic campus of the **Mississippi College for Women** is also in Columbus, with many grand old brick buildings. The college counts writer Eudora Welty among its distinguished alumnae.

Riverhill Antiques (☎ 601-329-2669), at 122 3rd St S, occupies two Victorian houses side by side (across from the Welcome Center) and is jammed with antiques from refined crystal and china to wooden implements and dusty architectural details.

Columbus is on the 234-mile **Tenn-Tom Waterway**, a canal system linking the Tennessee and Tombigbee Rivers to the Gulf of Mexico. The waterway is lined with recreation areas, swimming beaches, campgrounds and marinas along its length, and is popular for recreational boating. Call the Tenn-Tom Development Authority (☎ 601-328-3286), which is headquartered in Columbus, for waterway maps, recreation directories and other information.

Central Mississippi

The rolling midlands of central Mississippi lie between the northern hills and coastal plain. Besides the sprawling state capital at Jackson and its urban attractions, the rest of the region is largely agricultural. National forests remain interspersed among croplands, woods and small rural towns.

One of the most scenic ways to see the region is along the Natchez Trace Parkway, which travels its most quiet stretch between Jackson and Tupelo. A detour along Hwys 15 and 16 to Philadelphia lands travelers in an intriguing area full of Choctaw mythology and civil rights history.

Most travelers only see Meridian from the frontage roads off I-20, but a few quick detours inland offer a break from the monotony of interstate travel. The midland region south of Meridian attracts the fewest visitors of any area in the state, despite the Checker Hall of Fame located outside Hattiesburg.

History

The Nanih Waiya Mound at the northeastern Neshoba County line is the legendary birthplace of the Choctaw nation that dominated the Mississippi region before European settlement. In the early 1800s, a succession of treaties with the Europeans substantially reduced Choctaw territory (see Choctaw Country, below).

In 1817 the Mississippi Territory was admitted to the Union as a state, with its capital in Natchez. Four years later, the legislature appointed a commission to find a more central place for a state capital on Choctaw land the US had recently appropriated. It recommended the site of a trading post overlooking the Pearl River known as LeFleur's Bluff, near the Natchez Trace and close to the geographic center of the state.

JACKSON

population 395,000

Previously known as LeFleur's Bluff (after a French-Canadian fur trader), Mississippi's capital city was renamed to honor the US national hero of the time, General Andrew Jackson. The grand Greek revival capitol, built in 1832, remains open today as a state museum; the legislature moved into an equally grand capitol patterned after the national Capitol in 1903.

During the Civil War, Jackson was put to the torch on three separate occasions by Union troops under the direction of General William Tecumseh Sherman. The few public buildings spared by Sherman – the capitol, the governor's mansion and city hall – are treasured landmarks today. The city earned the nickname Chimneyville for what remained standing.

Jackson is the home of Jackson State University, the largest of three historically African-American colleges in the state; the other two are Millsaps College and the University of Mississippi Medical Center.

Although Jackson is Mississippi's largest city by far (the second-largest city, Biloxi, is nearly one-eighth its size), most modern development has eschewed the commercial center in favor of sprawling

---

HIGHLIGHTS

- The civil rights exhibit in the State Historical Museum, and the Mississippi Agriculture & Forestry Museum, both in Jackson
- Jackson's nightspots, including the Sun-n-Sand Motel, Hal & Mal's and the Subway Lounge
- A backroads trip to the Choctaw reservation

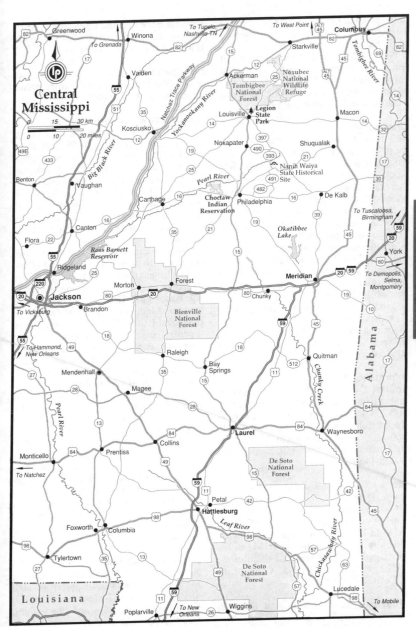

suburban areas to the north. While most of the population lives in the suburbs, they hold little appeal for travelers.

What is appealing is the ghost town that remains of downtown, which is quickened only by official state business, a few worthwhile museums, a legendary nightclub and a classic motel frozen in the 1950s.

Orientation

Jackson's downtown area consists of a short stretch of Capitol St, from the Amtrak station to the old capitol, and a few blocks to either side. Capitol St dead-ends into State St, a useful thoroughfare to more points of interest nearby.

The city's grandest attractions – the Agriculture & Forestry Museum and Sports Hall of Fame – are clustered north of downtown, a quarter-mile east of I-55, exit 98B. LeFleur's Bluff State Park nearby is nicely situated around a wooded lake. The small but inviting zoo and Myrnelle Gardens are both off I-220, exit 2.

Suburban expansion stretches north to Ridgeland. Here you will find predictably modern suburban development and access to recreation around the Ross Barnett Reservoir.

Information

Tourist Office The Jackson Convention and Visitors Bureau (☎ 601-960-1891, 800-354-7695) has an information desk at the Agriculture & Forestry Museum (☎ 601-960-1800); or write to them for advance information at PO Box 1450, Jackson, MS 39215-1450.

Money Of the half-dozen banks downtown, Deposit Guaranty National Bank (☎ 601-354-8211), 200 E Capitol St, offers foreign currency exchange and a 24-hour ATM (a Delta Airlines desk is also here). Freeway travelers can find ATMs in the Northpark Mall off I-55 just south of the I-220 junction; take the I-55 County Line Rd exit east to the mall.

Post Jackson's post office (☎ 601-968-0520) is at 401 E South St.

Medical Services The University of Mississippi Medical Center (☎ 601-984-4000) is located at 2500 N State St.

Emergency The police can be reached at ☎ 601-960-1926; the fire department can be reached at ☎ 601-960-1392.

Agriculture & Forestry Museum

The 'Ag Museum' (☎ 800-844-8687) is directly east of I-55's exit 98B, at 1150 Lakeland Dr. This complex offers thoughtful and attractive indoor and outdoor exhibits on agriculture and forestry and how they have been historically intertwined with the state's population and environment. The exhibits also reveal the state's cultural and ecological history. Kids will like it.

Enter by crossing the bridge past the crafts store to the main building: a 35,000-sq-foot hangar that houses farm machinery, including crop-dusting airplanes and vintage cotton gins. There's a fire observation tower and Indian exhibits, too. Outside, a re-created 1920s Mississippi town features a general store (drinks, penny candy and souvenirs available), gas station, church, school, newspaper office, doctor's office, and gardens down a dusty gravel walk. An 1860s farmstead is complete with cabins, farm animals and a sawmill. Carousel and pony rides are also available. A boardwalk with a swinging bridge leads through the woods out back.

Admission is $4 for adults, $2 for children aged from six to 18, and 50¢ for those under six (special events such as hog barbecues and harvest festivals may carry an additional fee). During the summer it's open Monday to Saturday from 9 am to 5 pm and Sunday from 1 to 5 pm; it's closed on Sundays from Labor Day to Memorial Day.

Sports Hall of Fame

Next door to the Agriculture & Forestry Museum, the new Mississippi Sports Hall of Fame (☎ 601-982-8264) has 21,500 sq feet of sports statistics and biographies, touch-screen video displays and tributes to

Mississippian athletes such as Jerry Rice, Brett Favre, Archie Manning and Dizzy Dean. Virtual golf, fast-pitch baseball and hockey penalty shots are among the interactive exhibits. Admission is $5 for adults and $3.50 for children and seniors. It's closed on Mondays.

State Historical Museum (Old Capitol)

The State Historical Museum (☎ 601-359-6920) is located in the beautifully restored 1833 capitol building on State St at the head of Capitol St. (The current capitol is another elegant domed building several blocks west.) Unless you have a taste for political portraits, military statues and restored legislative chambers, it's worth spending all your time in the 20th-century history exhibit, packed into a small room on the first floor. It features careful interpretations of Mississippi's ignominious history, along with looping vintage black & white film footage of civil rights clashes. The Eudora Welty photo exhibit on the mezzanine provides a rare personal glimpse of Jackson's famous storyteller.

The gift shop has a selection of local-interest books, as well as magnolia-studded

MISSISSIPPI

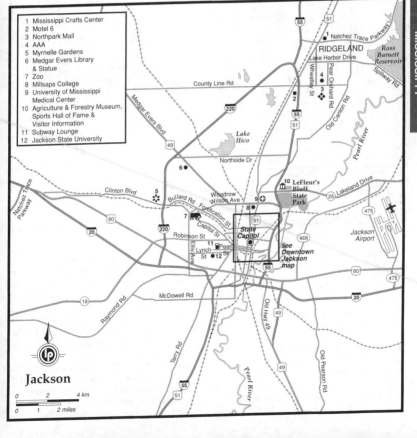

1 Mississippi Crafts Center
2 Motel 6
3 Northpark Mall
4 AAA
5 Myrnelle Gardens
6 Medgar Evers Library & Statue
7 Zoo
8 Millsaps College
9 University of Mississippi Medical Center
10 Agriculture & Forestry Museum, Sports Hall of Fame & Visitor Information
11 Subway Lounge
12 Jackson State University

Jackson

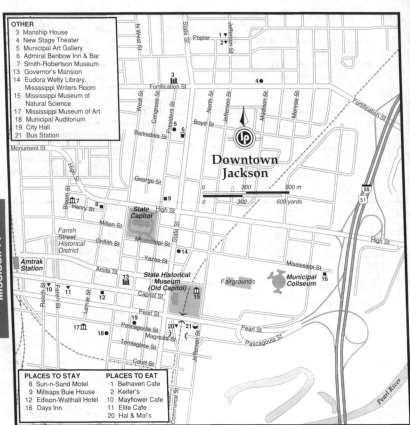

Downtown Jackson

OTHER
3 Manship House
4 New Stage Theater
5 Municipal Art Gallery
6 Admiral Benbow Inn & Bar
7 Smith-Robertson Museum
13 Governor's Mansion
14 Eudora Welty Library,
   Missssippi Writers Room
15 Mississippi Museum of
   Natural Science
17 Mississippi Museum of Art
18 Municipal Auditorium
19 City Hall
21 Bus Station

PLACES TO STAY
8 Sun-n-Sand Motel
9 Millsaps Buie House
12 Edison-Walthall Hotel
16 Days Inn

PLACES TO EAT
1 Belhaven Cafe
2 Keifer's
10 Mayflower Cafe
11 Elite Cafe
20 Hal & Mal's

souvenirs. The museum is open weekdays from 8 am to 5 pm, Saturday 9:30 am to 4:30 pm, Sunday 12:30 to 4:30 pm. It's closed on major holidays. Admission is free. You can park around the back; go all the way around the hill and approach from Amite St.

Mississippi Museum of Art

The state's art museum (☎ 601-960-1515), 201 E Pascagoula St, displays a small bright collection of large contemporary works including New Orleans surrealists and Georgia O'Keeffe and Andy Warhol.

There is also photography, folk art, outdoor sculpture, a great kids' room and a nice gift shop. Admission is $3 for adults and the museum is closed on Mondays and major holidays. A sophisticated little alfresco cafe on the premises serves elegant lunches, but no one seems quite sure if you can just go in to eat without paying museum admission; give it a try.

The museum is part of a modern complex housing a **planetarium** (call ☎ 601-960-1550 for show schedule), performing-arts organizations and the city auditorium. See Entertainment for more information.

Mississippi Museum of Natural Science

This appealing natural-history museum (☎ 601-354-7303), near the old capitol, examines the diverse habitats found throughout the state – cypress swamps, Delta bottomland, Gulf Coast islands, abandoned farms and spring gardens. They have nice native fish aquariums, and a lively kid-centered educational environment overall. Admission is free.

African-American Heritage Sites

The **Smith Robertson Museum** (☎ 601-960-1457), 528 Bloom St, serves as a cultural center and museum for Jackson's African-American community. The 1894 building, named after a prominent city alderman, housed Jackson's first public school for African-American children. The spacious galleries now hold roving exhibits of photographs and contemporary artwork most dramatically displayed in the small skylit atrium.

It's open weekdays from 9 am to 5 pm, Saturday mornings and Sunday afternoons. Admission is $1 for adults and 50¢ for those 18 and under. It's only a couple of blocks from the new capitol but a little tricky to find – follow signs off High St and look for the two-story building with the high-fenced parking lot in the front.

The center of the black community is a stretch of **Farish St** north of Capitol St. Its

And Justice Shall Prevail

In 1963, Medgar Evers was field secretary for Mississippi branch of the National Association for the Advancement of Colored People (NAACP). Evers led economic boycotts of white-owned businesses that perpetuated segregation, and assembled information on the Citizens Council, a segregationist band suspected of coordinating repressive acts against blacks throughout the state. Shortly after midnight on June 12, 1963, Evers was shot with a high-powered rifle as he stepped out of his car in the driveway of his home at 2332 Margaret Walker Alexander Dr in northwest Jackson (private, exterior views only). His family ran from the house and Evers was rushed to the University of Mississippi Medical Center, where he died within the hour. He was 36 years old. Evers was buried with military honors in Arlington National Cemetery outside Washington, DC.

Byron de la Beckwith, an ardent segregationist from Greenwood, was tried twice for the murder in 1964, but both times the jury was deadlocked. In 1975 Beckwith was sentenced to five years in prison for his role in attempting to bomb the Jewish Anti-Defamation League's headquarters in New Orleans. While in Louisiana prison he boasted of killing Evers.

In the late 1980s, Evers' family pushed for the case to be reopened, and in 1991 Evers' body was exhumed in a search for new evidence. Finally in 1994, de la Beckwith was convicted of the murder of Medgar Evers. Maryanne Vollers relates an account of the murder in her book *Ghosts of Mississippi*, and the Hollywood version of the story is based on her work.

After her husband's death, Myrlie Evers joined the sisterhood of widows whose husbands became martyrs to the cause of civil rights – a triumvirate that included Coretta Scott King and Betty Shabazz (the now-deceased widow of Malcolm X).

A life-sized bronze statue of Medgar Evers stands outside the neighborhood library renamed in his honor on Medgar Evers Blvd (Hwy 49) at Sunset Dr (south of Northside Dr, accessible from I-220 or I-55). ■

heyday was in the early 1900s, when it served as the hub of black political, economic, social, religious and cultural development for the state. Today, though the district has deteriorated and is no longer a thriving commercial center, some Victorian architecture remains. The renovation of the old Alamo Theater into an entertainment complex might help bring about the neighborhood's renaissance. The area's historic significance continues to be celebrated annually at the Farish St Festival on Labor Day weekend. The weekly *Jackson Advocate* (☎ 601-948-4122), headquartered at 300 N Farish St, carries news on the local black community.

In addition, those on a black heritage tour would not want to miss the civil rights exhibit at the State Historical Museum or Jackson State University. See also the sidebar on Medgar Evers.

Historic Buildings

The new capitol, designed in the image of the national Capitol in Washington, DC, and decorated with an interior nearly as lavish, has been the seat of state government since its completion in 1903. Note the monumental statue at its High St entrance dedicated to the women of the Confederacy.

The residence of Governor Kirk Fordice and his wife, Pat, the 1842 Greek revival **Governor's Mansion** at 300 E Capitol St, is open to visitors via a guided tour on the half-hour Tuesday through Friday from 9:30 to 11:30 am only.

Manship House (☎ 601-961-4724), 420 E Fortification St preserves the 1857 'cottage villa' of ornamental painter and mayor Charles Manship. It's humble and charming compared to standard plantation house museums, and is one of the few antebellum houses that survived the war. Donations are encouraged; it's closed on Sunday and Monday.

The **Municipal Art Gallery** (☎ 601-960-1582) displays contemporary works by Mississippian artists in an 1860s house at 839 N State St. On the first Sunday of the month, the gallery hosts a public opening of its new exhibitions.

> And then her mother's high-heeled slipper threw her off balance and she fell to the sidewalk in a great howling tangle of soiled white satin and torn pink net, and still nobody looked at her. I wonder if she is not, now, a Southern writer.
>
> – Tennessee Williams

Mississippi Writers Room

A small shrine-like room in the city's **Eudora Welty Library** (☎ 601-968-5811), 300 N State St, is dedicated to Mississippi-born writers and poets, including heavy-hitters Eudora Welty, William Faulkner and Tennessee Williams along with Richard Wright *(Black Boy)*, Shelby Foote *(The Civil War: A Narrative)*, Larry Brown *(Big Bad Love)* and hundreds of others. Author portfolios are collected in notebook binders; audio and video recordings are available by request. Admission is free.

Jackson Zoo

The small, compact Jackson Zoo (☎ 601-352-2580), Capitol St at Ellis Ave, provides an intimate look at exotic and local species in well-designed woodland habitats that also highlight the local flora. The well-maintained facility includes an impressive barn and playground area. There is also a concession stand and a train ($1 per ride). Admission is $4 for adults and $2 for children aged three to 12. The zoo is open daily from 9 am to 6 pm in summer and till 5 pm the rest of the year. From I-220, exit 2, continue 1½ miles east to the zoo. On the opposite side of the freeway, you'll find fast-food chains and Myrnelle Gardens.

Myrnelle Gardens

Amid highway traffic a half-mile west of I-220's exit 2, is Myrnelle Gardens (☎ 601-960-1894), 4736 Clinton Blvd. The gardens' appeal creeps up on you as you wind into the beautifully sculpted landscape scented with magnolia and wisteria. Once inside the small refuge, all you hear are songbirds, fountains and occasional

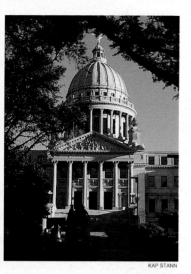

Top Left: State capitol, Jackson, MS
Bottom Left: Living history, downtown Jackson, MS

Top Right: Local architecture, Biloxi, MS
Middle Right: Dunleith Mansion, Natchez, MS
Bottom Right: The mighty Mississippi

RICK GERHARTER

KAP STANN

RICK GERHARTER

RICK GERHARTER

Top: Ocean Springs, MS
Middle Left: Cabin that's seen better days,
   Natchez Trace Parkway, MS

Bottom Left: Pass Christian, MS
Bottom Right: Biloxi, MS

jumping fish or diving frogs. Seek out the shady swings, the small Zen sand garden and the vine-covered arched bridges. The gardens are wheelchair-accessible. Admission is $2 for adults and 50¢ for children under 12.

Activities

LeFleur's Bluff State Park (☎ 601-987-3985) preserves a wild little pocket of woods right near the heart of the city. Its many modern facilities include a swimming pool, tennis courts, a nine-hole golf course, and nature trails and camping. There's a small admission charge of around $2 per car to enter the park; enforcement appears slack in the off-season.

Boating and fishing are popular activities at the 33,000-acre Ross Barnett Reservoir (☎ 601-354-3448), adjacent to the Natchez Trace Parkway north of town. Marinas, piers and picnic areas are located around its banks. Rapids (☎ 601-992-0500), a water park with a 215-foot twisting whip slide, wave pool and float rides, is one mile east of the spillway on Spillway Rd. Admission is around $9 for adults. Concessions and picnic tables are available.

Special Events

For more information on the city's festivals, contact the Convention and Visitor's Bureau (see Information, above). Jackson's main festivals include:

January
    The *Martin Luther King Day* celebration is held around the 15th.
February
    The three-week *Dixie National Rodeo & Livestock Show* is held the last week in January and the first two weeks in February.
March
    Mal's St Patrick's Day Festival & Parade is held around the 17th
April
    Zoo Blues and the *International Red Beans & Rice Festival* are held on the second weekend.
May
    The *Jubilee Jam Arts & Music Festival* is held the third weekend of the month; there's also the *Mule Festival*.

June
    The *Crawfish Festival* is held mid-month.
July
    Behold the *Hog Wild* cook-off the second weekend in July.
August
    The *Scottish Heritage Festival* is held late in the month.
September
    The *Farish Street African-American Heritage Festival* occurs at the end of the month.
October
    Held over 10 days, the *Mississippi State Fair* can be counted on for fun in the early part of the month.
November
    The *Pioneer & Indian Festival* at the crafts center on the Natchez Trace (Ridgeland) is at the end of the month.
December
    The *Chimneyville Crafts Festival* is held the first weekend, while *Starry Safari* at the zoo and *Christmas* at the old capitol are celebrated throughout the month.

Places to Stay

Camping Tucked into LeFleur's Bluff State Park (☎ 601-987-3985), near the heart of the city at 2140 Riverside Dr, is a nicely wooded lakeside campground, right off I-55 (exit 98B) within a mile of the Agriculture & Forestry Museum complex. The park also has its own golf course. Cozy sites are $11, and it's $14 for a hookup (30 RV sites).

Hotels & Motels The place to stay in Jackson is the *Sun-n-Sand Motel* (☎ 601-354-2501), a relic of 1950s road hotels at 401 N Lamar St, a block from the capitol.

The Etymology of 'Redneck'
An exhibit at the State Historical Museum traces the use of the pejorative term 'redneck' to the red neckties worn in 1902 by an emergent breed of Mississippian politicians who supported the interests of small farmers and laborers. The term evolved to describe this laboring white class. Today it is considered an offensive ethnic slur. ∎

MISSISSIPPI

It's all orange and turquoise, with Polynesian touches and a great trapezoidal pool with sun deck. The proprietor chain-smokes beside a sign that scolds 'No locals permitted without prior consent of owner.' See Entertainment, below, for details on the lounge. The parking lot is encased with barbed wire. Room rates are $30/35 for a single/double.

At the other end of the spectrum, the *Edison-Walthall Hotel* (☎ 601-948-6161, 800-932-6161), 225 E Capitol St, is the capital's preeminent hotel, with an elegant dark wood lobby, restaurant and bar, an atrium pool and less elegant but comfortable motel-like singles/doubles (you may opt to overlook the pool) starting from $60/70. It offers complimentary van service to/from the airport and within a three-mile radius. There is an American Airlines desk within the hotel.

Of course, probably 95% of the people who stay in Jackson never even venture to the downtown area, staying in scores of franchise motels lining the freeway exits. All brands are represented, including the budget *Motel 6* (☎ 601-956-8848) off I-55 at 6145 I-55 N. Rates are around $36 for a single.

B&Bs The *Millsaps-Buie House* (☎ 601-352-0221), 628 N State St downtown near the capitol, offers B&B accommodations in 11 guest rooms with private bath (singles/doubles from $85/100) within a refined 1888 Victorian mansion furnished with antiques and period reproductions.

Places to Eat
Downtown The *Mayflower Cafe* (☎ 601-355-4122), at 123 Capitol St behind the giant flashing neon sign, is a local institution run by two aging Greek brothers, one of whom walks around chewing on an unlit cigar. Southern plates come slathered with thick gravy and French dressing (don't go for the food). Safest bets are breakfast (from 7 am), Greek salads, pie, coffee and conversation. The *Elite Cafe* down the block is the same breed; their servers have a surlier reputation.

For stylized meals downtown, the cafe at the *Museum of Art* (see above) serves sophisticated gourmet lunches with nice wines. The *Edison-Walthall Hotel* restaurant (see Places to Stay) caters to the power-lunch crowd. The cafe outside the *Agriculture & Forestry Museum* makes a convenient stop.

Off the Interstate There are a couple of places easily accessible from the interstate that are nice local alternatives to freeway food. You may not need to go farther than *Hal & Mal's* (see Entertainment below).

Or try *Keifers* (☎ 601-355-6825), 705 Poplar St, which serves excellent Greek food to a mixed crowd who pack into patio seats or the amply planted interior for fresh, inexpensive meals. From I-55's Fortification St exit, proceed west (toward downtown) uphill to the State St signal; turn right and continue a block or so to Poplar and turn right – it's downhill on the right.

There is a *Morrison's Cafeteria* (☎ 601-956-0016) in Northpark Mall (see Things to Buy).

Entertainment
The *Clarion-Ledger*'s Weekend entertainment guide is distributed with the Thursday edition. Blues fans can tune in WMPR 90.1 FM for great music and announcements of local blues events.

At *Hal & Mal's* (☎ 601-948-0888), 200 S Commerce St, owner and music promoter Malcolm White has covered the walls with autographed glossies of recording stars and other famous patrons. They serve a full slate of bar food, burgers, salads, Mississippi catfish and quiche to a well-mixed crowd. It's a great place to hear music. Hidden above the Pascagoula St underpass, it's tricky to find, but very close to the old capitol and convenient from the Pearl St freeway exit. Drive south on State St away from the capitol dome landmark and slowly bypass the Pascagoula St underpass, but turn left immediately onto the adjacent alley marked Magnolia St. At the end of the alley, you'll see Hal & Mal's to your left. Or ask anybody.

For a weirder time, you could search out the downstairs lounge at the *Sun-n-Sand* (see Places to Stay). The retro lounge is authentic right down to the vinyl barstools, and the clientele of big-hair divorcees, off-duty cops and good old boys. Descending further still, the local *Admiral Benbow Inn* (☎ 601-948-4161), 905 N State St, is a motel with a rugged country bar; the sign 'remove all headgear' attests to the bar's popularity with bikers.

The *Subway Lounge* at 619 W Pearl St out toward Jackson State, hosts live low-down blues in an intimate space carved out of the basement of the old Summers Hotel. Weekend shows start at midnight. As one drummer put it in *Living Blues* magazine, the Subway is 'about the only place where middle-class whites and inner-city blacks can meet with some kind of common humanity' in Jackson.

As for the classical arts, Jackson hosts an international ballet competition every four years in June; future competitions are scheduled for 1998 and 2002. Contact *Mississippi Ballet International* (☎ 601-355-9853) for details.

The *New Stage Theater* (☎ 601-948-3531), 1100 Carlisle St, is the state's only professional theater company. It produces a full season of works and screens art and alternative films on Monday nights.

The Museum of Art complex houses a cluster of performing-arts organizations, including the *Mississippi Opera* (☎ 601-960-2300) and the *Mississippi Symphony Orchestra* (☎ 601-960-1565). Both host local performances.

Spectator Sports

The Jackson Generals (☎ 601-981-4664), a AA-minor league farm team for the big-league Houston Astros, play professional baseball at Smith-Wills Stadium on Lakeland Dr across from the Sports Hall of Fame.

Things to Buy

The nonprofit Craftmen's Guild of Mississippi operates two stores in the metropolitan region selling quilts, jewelry, woodwork and a great variety of handicrafts. The guild offers an exceptional collection of traditional Choctaw arts and crafts, including baskets made of cane, white oak or pine needles; beadwork; dolls; and clothing (including children's sizes). The guild also hosts crafts fairs in fall and at Christmas, with demonstrations and Choctaw cultural arts. It's based within the Agriculture & Forestry Museum complex, where their Chimneyville Crafts Center (☎ 601-981-2499) offers retail sales (no museum admission required to shop; closed on Sunday). The Mississippi Crafts Center (☎ 601-856-7546) is located right on the Natchez Trace Parkway in Ridgeland, north of Jackson, and is open daily.

Small selections of handcrafted souvenirs are sold in the gift shops of the State Historical Museum and the Museum of Art downtown.

Northpark Mall, off I-55 just south of the I-220 junction north of town, offers a range of stores and has ATMs.

Getting There & Away

Jackson is easily accessible by car, bus, train or plane, but for tourists it's more of a hub for through-travel than a destination in itself.

Air Jackson airport (☎ 601-939-5631), 10 miles east of downtown, off I-20, is served by Delta, American, Northwest and United Airlines.

Bus Greyhound (☎ 601-353-6342) operates many routes from a modern station at 201 S Jefferson St at Pearl St. It's conveniently downhill from the old capitol and across from the stadium in a decent area. Facilities include lockers, a snack bar and a well-lit waiting area.

Several buses leave and arrive daily along well-traveled routes to New Orleans and Memphis. Express buses are sometimes available at no extra cost. A trip to New Orleans takes four hours and costs around $36 one-way. To Memphis, the five-hour trip costs $39.

Train Amtrak's *City of New Orleans* train stops right in downtown Jackson along its route between Chicago and New Orleans (other stops include Memphis and Greenwood in the Mississippi Delta). One-way fares are comparable to buses, yet Amtrak offers discounts for roundtrip tickets.

The run-down station (☎ 601-355-6350) on Capitol St at Mill St is surrounded by dilapidated buildings, but it's only a long block to the edge of the commercial district (walk down Capitol St away from the railroad overpass) and five blocks to its heart. Use extra caution after dark.

Car & Motorcycle South of Jackson, I-55 is a very straightforward stretch of freeway to New Orleans, well punctuated with gas stations, restaurants and chain motels. If you're looking for local color, the two-lane Hwy 51 runs a parallel route that for many years served as the well-traveled thoroughfare between Memphis and New Orleans.

Natchez Trace Parkway drivers should note that it's disjunctive around Jackson from Ridgeland north of town to Clinton west of town. Posted signs divert through-travelers along I-55, I-220 and I-20. North of Ridgeland, the trace runs a scenic stretch along the Ross Barnett Reservoir before the long, quiet ride to Tupelo. South of Clinton, many attractions make this among the most interesting stretches of the trace (see Southwest Mississippi).

Bicycle A resource for Natchez Trace bicyclists who need equipment or service is the Indian Cycle Shop (☎ 601-956-8383), 1060 E County Line Rd in Ridgeland. Unfortunately, they do not rent bikes.

Getting Around

If you arrive by train, you could walk to several hotels, restaurants and city sights, but to see disparate attractions you need a car. As in many Southern cities, the limited bus transit is not a practical option.

AROUND JACKSON

From Jackson's northern suburb of Ridgeland, the interrupted **Natchez Trace Parkway** picks up again at the Mississippi Crafts Center. A long quiet stretch of the highway begins with a view of the Ross Barnett Reservoir and heads north to Tupelo. (See Northeastern Mississippi for sights in Starkville and north of there).

Around 15 miles north off Hwy 49 in **Flora**, the Petrified Forest (☎ 601-879-8189) provides a self-guided tour past petrified logs to an earth-science museum.

Around 30 miles north off I-55 in **Vaughan**, the Casey Jones Museum (☎ 601-673-9864) occupies a restored railroad station near the site of the 1900 train crash that killed Luther 'Casey' Jones. The folk song that dramatized this event created a posthumous hero out of Jones. Exhibits detail the history of railroads in Mississippi. Admission is $1 for adults and 50¢ for children aged three to 11.

Canton

The central Mississippi town of Canton is 25 miles north of Jackson. The exit from I-55 leading to downtown Canton goes past a row of shops so shabby it might tempt hesitant travelers to retreat.

However, further investigation of the town will uncover its tidy square, with a Greek revival centerpiece, and residential district of Victorian homes. It is so beautifully Southern it looks like a movie set – which Canton was, for the film adaptation of John Grisham's *A Time to Kill* in 1995. Sets remain on view today; inquire about this and house tours at the visitor center (☎ 800-844-3369) in the former Triolio Hotel, west of the courthouse. Sharing space in the Triolio is Allison's Wells School of Arts & Crafts, a center for traditional Southern arts dating back to the late 19th century. Artisans from here and all over display their wares at the **Canton Flea Market** held only twice a year on the second Thursdays of May and October.

One of the most unusual things in town is a monument to black Confederates. Slave owner William Hill Howcott erected a small obelisk in the 1890s to honor his slave Willis (Howcott), 'a colored boy of rare loyalty and faithfulness whose memory I cherish with deep gratitude,' as well as 'the good and loyal servants who followed the fortunes of the Harvey Scouts during the Civil War.' To find the memorial from the square, turn up N Liberty St and go two blocks to E Academy St (with the Piggly Wiggly supermarket at the corner). Turn left; the memorial is half a block past Lyon St, between two houses in a row of shotgun shacks.

PHILADELPHIA EXCURSION

Central Mississippi hides a sordid past among an unsentimental landscape of cropland, chicken farms, clear-cut forests, trailers, shacks on stilts and cinder-block churches. Near Philadelphia, the Neshoba County seat, the Mississippi Band of the Choctaw Indians continue to work their ancestral lands, while civil rights memorials remember the 1963 murder of Goodwyn, Chaney and Schwerner (see sidebar). This patch of Southern backcountry and its lamentable legacies evoke the Gothic tales of Southern writers like Faulkner and O'Connor. Drivers can construct a triangular detour off the Natchez Trace Parkway with Hwys 16 and 15.

On Hwy 16, a short detour southeast of Carthage brings you to **Bryan's Grocery**, about four miles outside town. To get there turn left off Hwy 16 onto Hwy 35; follow this road south for a couple of miles to the Hwy 488 turnoff; turn left and continue east a couple of miles to **Freeny**, where you'll find the 1929 general store. It sells standard staples (canned goods, tackle, flea-market china, soda in a tank of ice and gas out front) along with barrel-sized Choctaw baskets (not easily found on the reservation) and, surprisingly, tortillas, *queso*, avocados and Virgin Mary nightlights. (A large Mexican community has settled in the area since the chicken production farms expanded.)

Continue east on Hwy 488 past megacoops to Hwy 427 and go north toward Edinburg to pick up Hwy 16 east. Continue about 13 miles to the town of **Philadelphia.**

Greek for the City of Brotherly Love, Philadelphia is notorious as the place where three civil rights activists were killed in 1963. Downtown Philadelphia appears little changed since that time – the men still

gather at Dot's Cafe for grits, you can sample the latest in Christian music at the River of Life bible store, the Muffler Mansion still claims there's 'No Muff Too Tough' and the local radio station announces the daily menu of school lunches. The highlight of the annual Neshoba County Fair (one of the few remaining campground fairs in the US) is its horse races.

A mile or two south of town off Hwy 19S there's a *Days Inn* (☎ 601-650-9794), the lower-priced *Claridge Inn* and a buffet at *Western Sizzlin*.

A detour off Hwy 15 into downtown **Louisville** brings drivers to the **American Heritage 'Big Red' Fire Museum** (☎ 601-773-3421) on Business Hwy 15, a block north of Main St (Hwy 14). It's open by appointment from 10 to 11 am and 3 to 4 pm on weekdays only. Bill Taylor can show you around his private collection of 19 antique fire engines, which he's been busy restoring since his retirement.

North of Louisville, Hwy 15 crosses the rolling woods of the **Tombigbee National Forest**. At Choctaw Lake, the USFS maintains an 18-site campground (☎ 800-280-2267 for reservations) set on a wooded hill of pine and dogwood overlooking the lake ($7, or $11 with hookups). The campground and swimming beach ($3 per car per day) are both open from late spring to early fall. The ranger station (☎ 601-285-3264) directly north distributes information and maps on the area's hunting, fishing, horseback riding and hiking trails.

At Louisville on Hwy 25, or at **Ackerman** on Hwy 12, travelers can turn east to get to the college town of Starkville. Otherwise, continuing north on Hwy 15 will bring travelers back to the Natchez Trace. For continued coverage on this route see the Northeastern Mississippi chapter.

CHOCTAW COUNTRY

Through a number of treaties, the Choctaw nation ceded more than 63,000 sq miles of land to the US government in the early 1800s. The Treaty of Dancing Creek (1830) saw Indian removal when half-Indian half-Acadian Greenwood LeFlore signed away the last of the Choctaw territory (an action that enriched LeFlore with a 15,000-acre estate). Most of the remaining Choctaw Indians were exiled along the Trail of Tears in 1837, all except the Mississippi Band of the Choctaw. It took many years of struggle with state and federal authorities before they regained control of small portions of their ancestral lands. Reservation status was granted in 1918.

Today, the industrious Choctaw reservation (population over 8100) is a major employer in the region. In fact, it's one of the 10 largest employers in Mississippi as a

Remembering Chaney, Goodman & Schwerner

In the summer of 1964 James Earl Chaney, Andrew Goodman and Michael Schwerner were invited by local churches to help organize literacy campaigns (literacy was then a prerequisite to vote) and voter-registration drives in Philadelphia. While driving on a country road the night of June 21, the three young men – two white, one black – were arrested on a traffic violation and taken to jail in Philadelphia. They were later released, chased through the Mississippi countryside by sheriff's deputies and armed Klansmen, caught, and shot dead. Their bodies were hidden in an earthen dam outside town.

The FBI was called in to investigate, and President Lyndon Johnson pulled in a troop of sailors to aid the search for the missing men. A local lead eventually helped authorities locate their bodies. The men accused of the murder were set free by the judge's 'not guilty' verdict in the Neshoba County Courthouse in Philadelphia. Six of the men later faced federal charges and were imprisoned for violating the civil rights of the three activists. (Hollywood's version of the story is told in the film *Mississippi Burning*.)

On June 21, 1989, the 25th anniversary of the killings, former Mississippi Secretary of State and Philadelphia native Dick Molpus (who was 14 at the time of the murders) made an eloquent speech at an ecumenical service attended by the families of the victims:

We deeply regret what happened here 25 years ago. We wish we could undo it. We are profoundly sorry that they are gone. We wish we could bring them back. Every decent person in Philadelphia and Neshoba County and Mississippi feels that way...We acknowledge that dark corner of our past. But we also take pride in the present, and we are hopeful about the future...If James Chaney, Andy Goodman and Mickey Schwerner were to return today, they would see a Philadelphia and a Mississippi that, while far from perfect, are closer to being the kind of place the God who put us here wants them to be. And they would find – perhaps to their surprise – that our trials and difficulties have given Mississippi a special understanding of the need for redemption and reconciliation and have empowered us to serve as a beacon for the nation...Fear has waned – fear of the unknown, fear of each other – and hope abides.

The tribute was delivered at the Mt Zion Methodist Church, the church whose firebombing in 1964 had prompted the three young men to come to Philadelphia, and the last church the three visited before their murder. A simple granite memorial and historical marker stands out front. The church holds a memorial service every year to educate children about the sacrifices made to obtain equal rights.

Mt Zion is 10 miles east of the courthouse: travel east on Hwy 16 for 3½ miles to Hwy 482 (turn left at the sign 'Yesteryear Shack'); go north six miles to Hwy 747; turn right and the church is under a mile farther on.

The Mt Nebo Missionary Baptist Church, which had invited the three activists, maintains a memorial out front with photos. It's right downtown but tricky to find. From the courthouse, go west on Hwy 16 to Lewis Ave (see Gun 'n' Pawn at the corner); turn right on Lewis Ave and continue to Border St; turn right and go to Martin Luther King Jr Dr and turn left; go 350 yards to Adams St (see Gill's Cafe on the corner); turn right and continue 350 yards to Mt Nebo on the corner of Adams and Carver. The memorial is out front.

In both the Jewish and African traditions, it is often customary to leave small stones to remember the dead. Donations to maintain the memorials are also accepted. ∎

UNIVERSITY OF MISSISSIPPI SPECIAL COLLECTIONS

A game of Choctaw stickball

MISSISSIPPI

manufacturer of parts for the Ford Motor Company and also a contributor to the American Greetings card company. The reservation consists of eight communities centered west of Philadelphia, off Hwy 16.

The **Choctaw Museum of the Southern Indian** (☎ 601-650-1685), a mile or two north of Hwy 16 (follow the signs to Choctaw Industrial Park), tells the ancient story of the Choctaw. In a small room, traditional beadwork, drums and costumes are on display, along with maps that show the reduction of tribal territory. You can buy a copy of the Lord's Prayer in Choctaw, baskets, pottery and jewelry. It's free and open daily till around 4 pm (closed Sunday mornings).

The annual four-day Choctaw Indian Fair, a variation on the ancient green corn ceremony, is celebrated starting in the early morning of the second Wednesday after July 4. Here at the grand gathering of the *okla* – the people – you can see traditional dances, crafts and stickball competitions.

From the surrounding hardscrabble landscape of clapboard and cinder block, the

Silver Star Casino Resort (☎ 800-656-5251) on Hwy 16 looms on the horizon like a mirage – seven stories of flashy neon and bright lights (picture an Indian reservation with valet parking). The Mississippi Band of Choctaw Indians operates the resort, which includes a high-rise hotel (with rates starting from $69 for a single). Its steak and seafood restaurant *Phillip M's* (open for dinner only) is renowned as far as Jackson, and the adjacent buffet restaurant offers a good-value meal for $6. The casino also hosts big-name entertainment – Loretta Lynn was appearing when we passed through.

Casino revenues have enabled the reservation to buy new fire engines and police cars, and to build a new elementary school. Soon the Lady Warriors – 1997 state basketball champions – will have a new gym at Choctaw Central High School.

Nanih Waiya Mound

Thirty miles northeast of the reservation's casino, in the corner of Neshoba County off Hwy 393, is Nanih Waiya Mound, the legendary birthplace of the Choctaw nation. The steep 40-foot-high mound is across from a ranger office (☎ 601-773-7988), a cypress swamp and restrooms protected by barbed wire. Camping is not permitted. The gates are closed on Sundays.

Nearby, a historical marker at a Choctaw cemetery commemorates the Treaty of Dancing Rabbit Creek, which in 1830 forced the Choctaw to surrender the last 10 million acres of ancestral homeland. (Today's 22,000-acre reservation was later recouped.) The marker is along a gravel road that turns south off Hwy 14 at the tiny community of Mashulaville in southwestern Noxubee County.

MERIDIAN
population 41,036

Meridian is a common stop for interstate through-travelers after long dry stretches either side of town. Most services line freeway exits; the greatest concentration is either side of exit 153 (22nd Ave). Nearly every major motel chain is represented, and there are a few other bottom-end options. Of these, the *Astro Hotel* (☎ 601-693-3210), 2101 S Frontage Rd (on the southeast side of exit 153), has rooms for $19 a night and is decently kept. A *Morrison's Cafeteria* (☎ 601-693-6326) in the Village Fair Mall on the northwest side of exit 153 makes a convenient stop.

A short detour downtown can break the monotony if you've been doing a lot of driving. *Weidmann's* (☎ 601-693-1751), 210 22nd Ave, is a half-mile north of I-20 exit 153, over the tracks. This Meridian institution serves seafood and prime rib (entrees from $13 to $15) as well as simple breakfasts ($3.50 for poached eggs), sandwiches (oyster po-boy $7.50) and salads. It's the kind of place that has buttermilk on the menu. It's open daily from 6 am to 10 pm.

If you end up with more time in town, Highland Park at 41st Ave and 19th St (the far side of town from I-20) holds two of the city's biggest attractions: an **antique carousel** (☎ 601-485-1801) still in operation, and the **Jimmie Rodgers Museum** (☎ 601-485-1808), dedicated to the father of country music known as the Singing Brakeman.

The museum occupies an old depot with a locomotive outside. Inside, a collection includes railroad equipment from the steam-engine era and Rodgers' original guitar. Admission is $2 for adults and free for children under 10. It's open Monday to Saturday from 10 am to 4 pm and Sunday from 1 to 5 pm. The Jimmie Rodgers Memorial Festival features a week-long tribute to country music; it's held during the last full week in May.

The Amtrak route from the Atlantic coast to New Orleans stops in Meridian, but it's no city you'd consider designing a stopover around. The train station (☎ 601-693-6471) is at 1901 Front St. The Greyhound station (☎ 601-693-1663) is at 212 21st Ave.

The town of **Chunky**, 10 miles west, is home to the Chunky Rhythm & Blues Festival, held the third Saturday in July. It takes place in the middle of a secluded wooded area and features well-known bands. The Great Chunky River Raft Race courses three miles down from Boyette's Fish Camp on the first Saturday in June.

HATTIESBURG & AROUND

Home of the University of Southern Mississippi, Hattiesburg makes an OK stop for through-travelers. There are some quaint sandwich shops and diners as well as an upscale coffee bar across Main St from the courthouse. The landmark Mrs Curry's Boarding House restaurant is now closed. (Take our word for it – posted signs warn that trespassers will be shot – 'No Kidding.')

East of Hattiesburg in Petal, the **Checker Hall of Fame** (☎ 601-582-7090) features one of the world's largest game boards. With luck you might challenge resident expert Guichio the monkey to a game. The museum is housed in a half-brick, Tudor-style mansion complete with pool, fountains, walled garden and guard tower. International tournaments are played here occasionally. Admission is free. To find it from Hattiesburg, take Hwy 11 north to Hwy 42; go east one mile.

Turn right onto Central St; turn left onto Main St and pass the shopping center. Main St turns into Leesville Rd; look for Lyn Ray Rd and turn right to checkerland.

A long detour west of Hattiesburg leads to *Leatha's Bar-B-Que Inn* (☎ 601-736-5163), in Foxworth, near Columbia. It's a hidden treasure with barbecued chicken, pork or beef (from $7.50, large plates $13.50). The miracle sauce is served unceremoniously in a coffee mug with a spoon onto fold-out tables and chairs covered in plastic. Leatha's is 'right with God,' so no alcohol is served. Leatha's is open Thursday to Saturday from 11:30 am to 11:00 pm. The turnoff for Leatha's is off Hwy 98 between the Hwy 35S junction to the west and the Pearl River bridge to the east. This Foxworth service road leads to a stop sign; turn right, then make an immediate left onto Leatha Rd. Cross the tracks and continue on an eighth of a mile to Leatha's on the left – look for the large smoker.

Southwestern Mississippi

The loamy brown hill region of southwestern Mississippi takes its name from the aboriginal nation – the Natchez – that flourished here. The Natchez District stretches from the Louisiana line through the city of Natchez north to Vicksburg. After the coast, this region was among the first settled by Europeans. A grand plantation culture grew here along the bluffs of the Mississippi River. Hwy 61 from Louisiana north through Natchez is today spotted with arcades leading to antebellum homes, many open for public tours and as historic inns.

The city of Natchez itself is full of historic homes. This, along with a compact downtown area, and residents accustomed to visitors, makes it an inviting, easy destination. North of town is the Natchez Trace, an ancient Indian route that became the overland route for Mississippi River traders. Today the trace is a streamlined national scenic parkway and a popular bicycle-touring route that leads through forest, pasture, Indian mounds and ghost towns. Short detours lead to small Southern towns, plantation ruins, a historic African-American college and Civil War battle sites.

East of the Natchez District bluffs, the land changes around the I-55 corridor. With soil too thin to support cotton cultivation, this area historically produced vegetables, fruits and nuts. Today travelers know I-55 best as the long, generally indistinct stretch endured on a trip to or from New Orleans. While facilities at highway exits are ample for through-travelers, drivers with time to kill might want to detour off onto the parallel stretch of Hwy 51. Be prepared for the typical two-lane delays, like getting stuck behind a slow-moving cabbage truck, though you're never far from meeting back up with the four-lane freeway. Before the interstate, Hwy 51 was the primary route north and south. As such,

HIGHLIGHTS

- Historic house tours and gracious antebellum style in Natchez
- A drive or bike ride along the scenic Natchez Trace Parkway
- A backroads trip along Hwy 61

it's a stretch of road nearly as revered in local legend as Hwy 61 further west. Towns off Hwy 51 are typical Southern hamlets. Small downtown strips are still lively for the most part.

History

The Natchez civilization – distinct from the predominant Mississippian culture that dominated the South – reached its height in the mid-15th century. It was centered on the banks of what is today St Catherine's Creek, south of downtown Natchez. The restored Grand Village of the Natchez attests to their unique culture, one that bears striking resemblance to the Inca culture that was reaching its zenith in southern Peru around the same time.

Like the ancient Inca, the Natchez built an aristocratic society, in which their leader, the Great Sun, was believed to descend from the sun god both civilizations worshiped. Both the Inca and Natchez considered the sun their male deity, the moon their female deity and the stars the children of the sun and moon.

Relations between the French settlers and the Natchez deteriorated as the French began laying claim to ancestral lands. The Natchez carried out a surprise attack in

362

1729, massacring the French garrison at Fort Rosalie on the bluff. The French retaliated with a devastating attack on the Grand Village in 1730, and as a consequence the Natchez nation was vanquished.

The French possession of Natchez transferred to British control in 1763 as a result of the Seven Years' War, but only lasted until 1779, when the Louisiana territory came under Spanish control. On March 30, 1798, the Spanish garrison was evacuated, and Natchez was named the seat of the US's Mississippi Territory. As the Choctaw and Chickasaw were pushed off their lands in the rest of Mississippi, European settlers from Atlantic states moved in and expanded cotton cultivation. The port of Natchez grew rich on cotton exports, and large plantations flourished in the region.

Other trade came downriver on flatboats. Tradesmen would customarily sell the whole lot, right down to the boat lumber, and return upland on foot along the old Chickasaw Trace. In 1801, a treaty granted the US a right-of-way, and the wagon route became known as the Post Road. Today the Natchez Trace Parkway follows the route of the original footpath from Natchez to Nashville. With the advent of the steamboat era, the road was supplanted by river traffic, which brought unsavory elements to river towns. Natchez-under-the-Hill is today a quiet reminder of that rowdy era.

During the Civil War, Natchez – a town that reportedly never flew the Confederate flag – surrendered without a fuss (which accounts in large part for the survival of many of its antebellum structures). Yet Union General Ulysses S Grant's campaign to capture the strategic port of Vicksburg further north brought Yankee troops to the Natchez District.

After several unsuccessful attempts to capture Vicksburg by storm, Grant decided to lay siege by encircling the Confederate

MISSISSIPPI

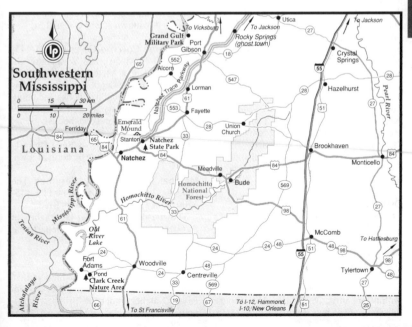

lines of defense around the city. Grant's troops swung south, crossed the river at Grand Gulf (now a state park) and continued through southwestern Mississippi to Jackson before approaching Vicksburg. The siege ended with Vicksburg's surrender on July 4, 1863.

The region was also distinguished during the civil rights era. In Port Gibson in 1966, the local African-American community organized a grassroots voter registration drive and an economic boycott of white merchants who were reserving certain jobs and privileges for whites. Three years into the boycott, the merchants sued, and the case dragged on for 13 years until 1982, when the US Supreme Court unanimously affirmed the right of peaceful protest through economic boycott.

NATCHEZ
population 20,000
Natchez is a beautiful antebellum town on a high bluff overlooking the Mississippi River. It has the charm of a small town and the kind of sophistication you usually find only in much bigger cities. Yet the town rarely feels overwhelmed with tourists, even during the 'pilgrimage' seasons, when dozens of local homes are opened to elaborate public tours.

Opulent antebellum architecture and historic interior design are the main attractions. Only one plantation home – Melrose, run by the National Park Service (NPS) – retains the slave quarters as a reminder of the source of its original affluence.

By logical extension, you can also find a wonderful range of historic B&B accommodations in Natchez.

Orientation
The compact downtown area (officially a national historic district) occupies the bluff overlooking the river north of the bridge. The old depot on Canal St at State St serves as the center of tourist activity. House museums and historic inns, restaurants, shops and a bike-rental outlet are all within this attractive district. More house museums are a short drive away.

Information
Tourist Offices Four visitor centers provide maps and information. The city visitor center in the old depot on Canal St at State St also houses the Natchez Pilgrimage Tour office (☎ 601-446-6631, 800-647-6742). The convention and visitors bureau (☎ 601-446-6345, 800-647-6724) is on S Canal St at Hwy 84. These two offices handle requests for advance information.

The Mississippi State Welcome Center at 370 Seargent Prentiss Dr (the Hwy 61/84 connector) distributes local, regional and statewide information. The NPS office of the Natchez Historic District (☎ 601-442-7047) is at 504 S Canal St, but the NPS-maintained Melrose Plantation on Melrose Ave is better suited for drop-in visitors.

Money Several banks downtown have ATMs and cash traveler's checks. Currency exchange is available at Deposit Guaranty Bank (☎ 601-445-2600, 800-748-8501), 320 Franklin St.

Post The main post office (☎ 601-442-4361) is downtown at 214 N Canal St.

Bookstores Cover to Cover (☎ 601-445-5752, 800-398-5656), 208 Washington St, operates out of a Victorian house a half-block south of the depot downtown. It has an impressive collection of books, including some on local history as well as specialty guides, biographies and cookbooks.

Laundry Brown's Duds-N-Suds (☎ 601-446-7094) is at 624B Hwy 61 north of town.

Medical & Emergency Services The Natchez Community Hospital (☎ 601-445-6200) is at 129 Jefferson Davis Blvd.

The fire department can be reached at ☎ 601-442-3684; the police department can be reached at ☎ 601-445-5565.

Natchez-under-the-Hill
A restored bawdytown half-hidden in a mysterious cove along the Mississippi River, Natchez-under-the-Hill was originally the commercial center of town. Once

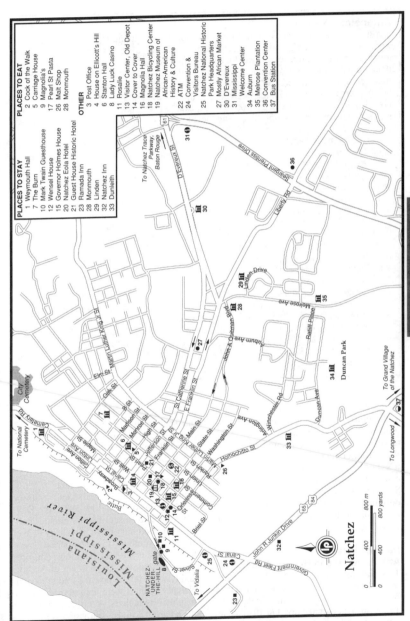

MISSISSIPPI

PLACES TO STAY
1 Weymouth Hall
7 The Burn
10 Mark Twain Guesthouse
12 Wensel House
15 Governor Holmes House
20 Natchez Eola Hotel
21 Guest House Historic Hotel
23 Ramada Inn
28 Monmouth
29 Linden
32 Natchez Inn
33 Dunleith

PLACES TO EAT
2 Cock of the Walk
5 Carriage House
9 Magnolia's
17 Pearl St Pasta
26 Malt Shop
28 Monmouth

OTHER
3 Post Office
4 House on Ellicott's Hill
6 Stanton Hall
8 Lady Luck Casino
11 Rosalie
13 Visitor Center, Old Depot
14 Cover to Cover
16 Magnolia Hall
18 Natchez Bicycling Center
19 Natchez Museum of
   African-American
   History & Culture
22 ATM
24 Convention &
   Visitors Bureau
25 Natchez National Historic
   Park Headquarters
27 Mostly African Market
30 D'Evereux
31 Mississippi
   Welcome Center
34 Auburn
35 Melrose Plantation
36 Convention Center
37 Bus Station

Natchez

Antebellum Natchez

In 1899, Natchez historian Gerard Brandon IV foretold the future of the city of Natchez when he said 'Yet hither must Mississippians ever come, as to the cradle in which the infant state was rocked. Hither will Pilgrims journey to visit our historic shrines, and to drink from the primal springs of a glorious past.' Visitors today can see antebellum style that would make Margaret Mitchell proud, thanks largely to the preservation efforts of two garden clubs – the Natchez Garden Club (now headquartered on the House on Ellicott Hill) and the Pilgrimage Garden Club (at Stanton Hall) – and to the oil money that supported many grand restorations. The local tourist industry, worth $35 million, draws around 450,000 visitors annually.

Each pilgrimage season, around two dozen historic homes are open to ticket-holders over the course of three weeks. Tour guides in antebellum costumes are stationed in each room to provide detailed descriptions of the furnishings, decor, architecture and family of residence. Other special events, including nighttime entertainment, coincide with the pilgrimage.

Pilgrimages are scheduled in spring (generally mid-March to mid-April), October and the second half of December. Tours operate daily from 8 am to 5:30 pm.

Tour passes are required and are not available at houses. Obtain tickets in advance by phone (☎ 800-647-6742 for information and reservations) or at the pilgrimage office (☎ 601-446-6631) in the old depot at Canal at State St. You can buy a morning or afternoon tour pass to see the properties open that day. It costs $18 per person for a half-day tour. They take credit cards.

More than a dozen historic house museums are open for public tours year-round. For visitors with the time to visit only a few, the most outstanding houses are the House on Ellicott's Hill, Longwood, Melrose, Rosalie and Stanton Hall. Most are open daily, and admission is generally $4 or $5. As noted, many operate as luxurious inns.

Elderhostel (☎ 617-426-8056) operates an educational program open to people 55 years and older and their companions which delves into Natchez history and tours homes. The cost is $370 for the week-long program; the cost includes all fees, meals and lodging. For more information write to: 75 Federal St, Boston, MA 02110-1941.

the legitimate businesses moved higher up to the bluff, this section retained a reputation for lusty riverboat vices. Today's reconstructed version resembles an Old West frontier stage set – strangely though, it's peopled with folks that somewhat resemble the original cast of characters. Several picturesque cafes, saloons and popular family restaurants overlook the river, the bridge and the riverboat casino down the hill.

Natchez Museum of African-American History & Culture

This 2nd-floor museum (☎ 601-445-0728), 307A Market St, recounts local African-American history from the 1880s to the 1950s in a personal way. On display are period kitchens, costumes and accounts of the nightclub fire that killed dozens of community members. It's presently only open Wednesday to Saturday from 1 to 5 pm. Donations are requested.

Grand Village of the Natchez

This archaeological park and museum (☎ 601-446-6502), 400 Jefferson Davis Blvd, contains a set of small mounds and a reconstructed hut or two in a shady glen off Hwy 61, south of town (suburban homes bank the ancient site). The museum, operated by the state's Department of Archives and History, relates how the traditions of the Natchez Indians were unique from those of neighboring nations. A trail crosses through the adjacent woods. Admission is free.

Auburn (☎ 601-442-5981), 400 Duncan Ave at Auburn Ave, is a city-operated 1812 landmark set in the midst of Duncan Park, which offers swimming, golfing, tennis and nature trails.

The Burn (☎ 601-442-1344), 712 N Union St, is a three-story Greek revival mansion built in 1836; the gardens are notable for rare varieties of camellias. It's also an inn.

D'Evereux (no phone listed), D'Evereux St, is a Greek revival mansion built around 1840.

Dunleith (☎ 601-446-8500), 84 Homochitto St, is an 1856 Greek revival 'temple' built around colonnaded galleries. Situated within a 40-acre park with many antebellum outbuildings, the house operates as an inn.

Governor Holmes House (☎ 601-442-2366), 207 S Wall St, downtown, was the home of the last governor of the Mississippi Territory and the first governor of Mississippi when it became a state in 1817. It's also an inn.

House on Ellicott's Hill (☎ 601-442-2011), N Canal St at Jefferson St, a restoration project of the Natchez Garden Club, is the oldest property open for tours. Andrew Ellicott raised the American flag on this hill in 1798 in defiance of Spain, and the small two-story house was built the following year.

Linden (☎ 601-445-5472), 1 Linden Dr off Melrose Ave, has been the rambling Federal-style home of the Conner family since 1849; it is now open for house tours and as an inn.

Longwood (☎ 601-442-5193), 140 Lower Woodville Rd, is an unfinished, grand, octagonal house with Oriental accents; construction was begun in 1860, disrupted by the Civil War and never completed.

Magnolia Hall (☎ 601-442-6672), 215 S Pearl St, is a Greek revival mansion built in 1858.

Melrose Plantation (☎ 601-446-5790), 1 Melrose Ave, is a grand plantation estate operated by the NPS. Rangers lead tours of the plantation house ($5), and visitors can wander the grounds themselves at no charge. The slave quarters hold exhibits on the history of slavery.

Monmouth (☎ 601-442-5852), John A Quitman Blvd, is a monumental mansion; it's open to the public for tours and also has an inn and restaurant.

Rosalie (☎ 601-445-4555), S Broadway St at Canal St, is situated atop the river bluff downtown near the depot. Named after the nearby site of Fort Rosalie, the statuesque brick mansion served as Union Army headquarters during the Civil War.

Stanton Hall (☎ 601-442-6282), High St at Pearl St, is an 1857 palatial mansion and home to the Pilgrimage Garden Club. The Cottage Restaurant offers fine dining and hosts performances.

Weymouth Hall (☎ 601-445-2304), 1 Cemetery Rd, is an 1855 Greek revival mansion overlooking the river; it's also an inn. ∎

MISSISSIPPI

Activities

Horse-drawn carriage tours leave from the depot visitor center downtown. Fares cost around $8 for adults and $4 for children.

Two hundred-acre Duncan Park (☎ 601-442-5955) at Auburn and Duncan Aves provides a swimming pool, 18-hole golf course, tennis courts and a nature trail (the Auburn house museum is also here).

Places to Stay

Natchez is an ideal place to splurge on accommodations – few cities of this size in the South offer a greater range of meticulously furnished historic houses open as inns. Note, however, that some historic properties won't allow young children, and that some request no children of any age.

Camping Shady sites in a wooded, hilly campground are available at *Natchez State Park* (☎ 601-442-2658), 10 miles north of town at the foot of the Natchez Trace. The facilities are adequate and electricity is available.

Hotels & Motels The bottom-end *Natchez Inn* (☎ 601-442-0221), 218 John R Junkin Dr, just down from the Ramada, offers basic rooms for $30 with one bed or $35 with two beds. There are another couple of low-end motels across the river in Vidalia, LA, within a mile of the bridge.

The *Natchez Eola Hotel* (☎ 601-445-6000, 800-888-9140), 110 Pearl St, maintains a graceful lobby, restaurant and courtyard that stem from its days as the town's preeminent hotel. Its six stories of guest rooms, however, are an uneven mix of modern and well worn. Nevertheless, some rooms overlook the river, all kids are welcome, and it's the least expensive hotel or motel within walking distance of downtown. Its twin rooms are $55, while doubles are $60.

There are several chain motels on highway corridors north and south of town. Of these, the *Ramada Inn* (☎ 601-446-6311) overlooks the Mississippi River. The circa 1960s property is otherwise unimpressive, but it has a pool. Rates start at around $60 for a single.

Historic Inns & B&Bs Natchez offers a variety of inns and B&B lodgings in grand, beautifully restored historic houses. Though they differ slightly in style, setting and perks, they are all top end (starting at around $90 a night single or double), high-quality accommodations furnished with antiques, with an emphasis on gracious Southern hospitality. Most include an elaborate breakfast; very few have pools.

The local tourist board lists 32 inns and B&Bs in town (request their full-color brochure *Bed & Breakfast Natchez Style*

The riverboat era brought great prosperity to Natchez.

by calling ☎ 800-996-2824). You can make reservations through Historic Inns of Natchez (☎ 800-256-4667) or Natchez Pilgrimage Tours (800-256-4667).

The *Guest House Historic Hotel* (☎ 601-442-2366), 201 N Pearl St, is nicely set between the commercial and residential district downtown. It offers 16 rooms in a two-story 1840 house. Room rates start from $95 and include breakfast.

Five inns in Natchez are landmark sights in themselves (see the sidebar 'Antebellum Natchez', earlier): *The Burn* (☎ 601-442-1344), 712 N Union St, with seven rooms and a pool; *Dunleith* (☎ 601-446-8500), 84 Homochitto St, with 11 rooms (starting at a perplexingly steep $130); *Governor Holmes House* (☎ 601-442-2366), 207 S Wall St, with four rooms in a Georgetown-style place downtown; *Linden* (☎ 601-445-5472), 1 Linden Dr off Melrose Ave, with an animated host related to the original owners, offering seven rooms in a country setting; *Monmouth* (☎ 601-442-5852), 36 Melrose Ave, with 25 rooms in perhaps the grandest inn, is also known for its restaurant (which serves non-guests, too); and *Weymouth Hall* (☎ 601-445-2304), 1 Cemetery Rd, with four rooms.

A less expensive B&B in the center of the downtown action is *Wenzel House* (☎ 601-445-8577), an 1888 two-story Victorian house at 206 Washington St. Room rates start at $75 for a double.

The bottom-end *Mark Twain Guesthouse* (☎ 601-446-8023), under the hill at 33 Silver St, provides 2nd-floor rooms in the rough-and-ready riverfront below the bluff (a short hike up to downtown). A non-view room costs $55 a night, while rooms with a view go for $65 to $75 (with discounts for two or more nights and for two adjoining rooms for families).

Places to Eat
Several places to eat in and around the depot visitor center offer reasonably priced, family-friendly meals in cute settings. There's an open-air Mexican food spot right in the depot, a soda fountain cafe

and ice-cream parlor across the street, a log-cabin tamale place down Canal St at Silver St, and a barbecue place up Canal St about a block north of the depot.

The *Malt Shop* (☎ 601-445-4843), a local pit stop for burgers and delicious shakes, is on Homochitto St at Martin Luther King Jr St.

At the bluff, *Cock of the Walk* (☎ 601-446-8920), at 200 N Broadway, is a casual Southern restaurant serving fried catfish and skillet cornbread. Downtown, *Pearl St Pasta* (☎ 601-442-9284), 105 S Pearl St, serves fresh pasta and vegetables, and has a 2nd-story balcony. Tucked under the hill with an attractive river-view patio is *Magnolia's* (☎ 601-446-7670), 49 Silver St, for surf-and-turf.

A historic inn, *Monmouth* (☎ 601-442-5852), John A Quitman Blvd, serves a fixed-price five-course dinner with high-style plantation ambiance for $35 a person. It's a good way for budget travelers to experience Natchez without an overnight B&B stay, if formal dinners are your style. The *Carriage House* (☎ 601-445-5151), on the grounds of Stanton Hall at 401 High St, is a lunch place that also hosts dinner shows during pilgrimages.

Entertainment
The *Lady Luck Casino* (☎ 800-722-5825) operates around the clock on a riverboat at the bottom of Silver St below town.

Stanton Hall hosts dinner theater occasionally; check around for other live performances, especially during pilgrimage weeks.

Things to Buy
The Mostly African Market (☎ 601-442-5448), 125 St Catherine St, displays and sells handcrafted artwork. Purchases support a children's summer program. It's open afternoons only, from Wednesday through Sunday.

The larger historic houses have gift shops selling magnolia-studded souvenirs, cotton-boll wreaths, corn-husk dolls and the like.

Getting There & Away
The closest major airports are in Jackson (115 miles northeast of Natchez) and Baton Rouge, Louisiana (100 miles south of Natchez on Hwy 61). It's not advisable to use either, as you can fly into New Orleans and drive to Natchez along a scenic route through Louisiana's Plantation Country (see that chapter). Without stops, this drive will take about as long as it would take to fly, and the car rental may be less expensive. As well, the Natchez Trace Parkway, which begins here (see below), provides further car-touring options.

Bus service is available from the Greyhound station (☎ 601-445-5304) at 103 Lower Woodville Rd. One bus daily runs between Jackson and Natchez. The bus is routed through Vicksburg; the trip takes 2¾ hours from Jackson to Natchez and costs $21 one-way.

The Delta Queen Steamboat Company runs cruises up the Mississippi River that stop in Natchez; see Cruises under Getting There & Away for more information.

Getting Around
Downtown attractions are easily seen on foot. Outlying attractions are within a short drive or comfortable bike ride (depending on weather). Bike rentals are available from the extremely resourceful and knowledgeable folks at the Natchez Bicycling Center (☎ 601-446-7794), 334 Main St (closed Sunday), who provide maps of local and regional bike trips of varying lengths. It costs $14 to rent a bicycle all day; no rentals to children under 12.

The Natchez Transit System (☎ 601-445-7568) operates local buses, but more practical for sightseers are the trolleys (☎ 601-442-5082). For double-decker bus tours (☎ 601-445-9300), or carriage tours, inquire at the depot. For a cab, call ☎ 601-442-7500.

NATCHEZ TRACE
The Natchez Trace began centuries ago as a footpath between the homeland of the

MISSISSIPPI

Natchez Indians and the game-rich Cumberland River valley. As native nations established villages in the vicinity of the trace, the path became an important trade route. Early European explorers such as de Soto traveled along the trace, and French explorers set up trading posts at its northern and southern endpoints.

Use of the trace expanded tremendously with increasing white settlement in the late 18th century – as settlers brought their trade downriver, they discovered it was more sensible to sell the whole lot, boat lumber and all, and return north on foot rather than struggle upriver. When a treaty granted the US a right-of-way in 1801, the route became a post road, and was later widened to serve as a military road. It was along here that Major General Andrew 'Old Hickory' Jackson marched homeward after the Battle of New Orleans. With the advent of the steamboat era, the road was supplanted by river traffic. Gradually the road began to revert to nature, with a brief revival during the Civil War.

Modern interest began in 1909 when the Daughters of the American Revolution initiated a program to mark the route of the old trace, and the Department of the Interior began to consider it for a national historic route in 1934. Today it's a scenic stretch of meandering two-lane road through woodlands and pasture. Pull-outs and short detours lead to Indian mounds, ghost towns, plantation ruins, Civil War battle sites and snippets of the original footpath.

See Car in the Getting Around chapter for a map of the trace.

Natchez to Port Gibson

The parkway is around 10 miles north of downtown Natchez via Hwy 61. Mile posts at the side of the road mark distances from a planned southern terminus at Natchez; for the moment the parkway starts at around eight miles up. Detailed map brochures listing all sites are available from several ranger offices along the route. The smooth wide parkway (which prohibits commercial traffic) is popular for bicycle touring. For local bike rentals, see Getting Around in the Natchez section. For organized bike tours and important tips on traveling the trace, see the Getting Around chapter.

There is much to see within the first 20 or so miles on and around the trace. **Emerald Mound** (a short turn-off west about 10 miles from Natchez), one of the largest Indian mounds in the southeast, was built around 1400 AD. Interesting not only for its imposing size and proximity to the trace, it is also somewhat jarringly juxtaposed with a surrounding community of trailer beauty shops and patchwork shacks. East at this same turn-off past a country store, **Natchez State Park** provides a 24-site wooded campground (less impressively maintained than NPS campgrounds) and fishing at a small lake.

Back along the parkway, the exposed **loess bluffs**, approximately 12 miles from Natchez, reveal the local geology. The **Mt Locust** ranger station, a few miles on, is in a historic inn built in 1783.

A very scenic 20-mile driving or biking loop starts at Mt Locust. Bicyclists can park at Mt Locust and ride north along the trace for five miles to Hwy 553. A turn west along Hwy 553 leads past Springfield Plantation, a general store (note the crossroads and stay left), Christ Church, Oak Grove and Cedars plantation houses (all homes are private), and through rolling countryside before winding back toward the trace. At the shack 200 yards west of the trace, a 1½-mile loop leads to Emerald Mound. Rejoining the trace, it's another three miles north to return to Mt Locust.

Another longer loop follows Hwy 552 to several sights and the town of Port Gibson. At **Windsor Ruins**, only the statuesque columns are left from this evidently once-grand plantation home. Further west the road leads past **Alcorn College**, considered the first land-grant college for African Americans in the country.

In **Port Gibson**, a small exhibit in the county administration building (☎ 601-437-4994, 510 Main St, open weekdays only) attests to the town's civil rights movement. A local African-American boycott of white merchants begun in 1966 led to a Supreme Court decision in 1982 affirming the right of peaceful protest through economic boycott. The exhibit was produced by Mississippi Cultural Crossroads (☎ 601-437-8905), a community organization that operates out of 507 Market St. A colorful children's mural across the street from the Mississippi Cultural Crossroads celebrates multiculturalism. A parallel route to main street runs through an attractive residential district of well-tended historic homes and churches. They say General Grant thought it 'too pretty to burn' when he came through in May 1863. As a result, many antebellum structures remain standing today.

While in Port Gibson, stop at the one-table *Pappy's Bar-B-Q* (☎ 601-437-4300), 1003 Market St, for generous plates of chicken or ribs with two side orders (from $4.25). It's in the tiny red shack down the hill near the supermarket.

A detour off the trace 10 miles northwest of Port Gibson, **Grand Gulf Military Park** (☎ 601-437-5911) commemorates the scene of a Civil War bombardment in April 1863. The Union fleet had hoped to clear the way for a crossing here, but after five hours of battle with no relief, continued further south to find another way across. A 42-site campground offers sites for $11; hookups are available.

North of Port Gibson

From Grand Gulf Military Park, northbound travelers will find diversions at **Sunken Trace**. Here you're able to walk through a deeply eroded stretch of the original route, the **Grindstone Ford** site, where aboriginal artifacts have been found. There is a beautiful picnic spot at **Owen Creek Waterfall**.

Rocky Springs, a major rest stop, provides a nicely wooded NPS campground (free; first come, first served; 22 sites), hiking routes along the original trace, and a ranger station, all around the site of a **ghost town**. In 1860, Rocky Springs was

a prosperous community of more than 2500, with a church, post office and several stores. Devastated by the Civil War, yellow fever, the boll weevil and land erosion, today the people and stores are gone. The Methodist church, however, remains open and draws descendants out to pay respects at its cemetery.

Off the trace near Utica, the cultural heritage of Jews in the South is explored at the **Museum of the Southern Jewish Experience** (☎ 601-362-6357), off Hwy 18 northeast of Utica (by appointment only).

See the Central Mississippi chapter for information on the trace north of Jackson.

WOODVILLE & AROUND

From Natchez, Hwy 61 south finds its way to Woodville; travelers will find this is also a route to and from Louisiana's Plantation Country (see that chapter).

An attractive courthouse square sits at the center of little Woodville, a natural stop along the pleasant Hwy 61 drive, 35 miles south of Natchez. Around the square you'll find a free local history museum (☎ 601-888-3998), at the corner of Bank St and Depot St, and the *L&M Bakery-N-Deli* (☎ 601-888-3600), 121 Boston Row, with simple meat-and-three plates. Off Hwy 24 east, the **Rosemont Plantation** (☎ 601-888-6809) opens the boyhood home of Confederate President Jefferson Davis (open summers, only on weekdays except during Natchez pilgrimages in spring and fall). B&B lodgings are offered in a cottage on the property.

West of Woodville, Pinckneyville Rd leads to one of the most beautiful natural areas in the state. Follow signs to the **Clark Creek Nature Area**, 13 miles away in the hamlet of Pond. Here winding trails traverse 1200 acres of loess bluffs and hardwood forest, past huge boulders and limestone outcroppings, and under waterfalls (one is 40 feet high). To find the trailhead, look for Pond's large white general store and turn west on the road that goes past the store to Fort Adams. The parking lot and trailhead are to the left. (Note that there is no restroom here and the store does not maintain a public restroom.)

In this corner of the state stands the linchpin of all lower Mississippi River navigation. The Old River Project here attempts to keep water channeled around Baton Rouge and New Orleans, when it would much rather run the quicker, steeper route through the Atchafalaya basin. Hydrologists fear it's just a matter of time before mother nature has her way – with dreaded consequences for communities downriver.

Gulf Coast

The Gulf Coast is nothing like the rest of Mississippi and it never has been. The Native American nations on the coast developed their own traditions based on the area's unique coastal environment.

Its colonial history is also different. The influence of French and Spanish settlement has been retained in a character more cosmopolitan than the rough-and-ready country inland.

Just the way it's situated, the Mississippi Gulf Coast receives a breeze that the nearby city of New Orleans lacks, and for that reason it has been a popular summer resort area for affluent New Orleanians since the city was founded. But the coast's primary traditional means of income has always been the seafood industry, with most schooners and canneries based in Biloxi.

In the early 1990s the coast became the target of big casino owners from Las Vegas. Since the first casino opened in 1992, a dozen huge casinos (with more on the way) have come to dominate the sleepy fishing villages and old family resorts. At first the casinos seemed a dismal local addition, but they soon began to draw busloads of Midwesterners, conventioneers and even church groups.

And so these days the coast sports an interesting mix of people, including Southern-speaking Vietnamese, Irish (in heritage) fishermen, and pant-suited gambling grandmothers.

The Gulf shore has a long, narrow white-sand beach that extends 26 miles and looks over several wild islands. The greatest excursion in the region is 10 miles offshore, where barrier islands are preserved as the Gulf Islands National Seashore. A ferry runs frequently from Gulfport to West Ship Island; the others can be reached by private boat, charter, or, for the truly adventurous, sea kayak.

If your view is limited to the I-10 corridor, you'll miss the whole coast. If you

HIGHLIGHTS

- Biloxi's George E Ohr Arts & Cultural Center and Mardi Gras festivities
- Deserted beaches, warm waters and wilderness camping on the Gulf Islands

have time, drop down to Hwy 90 for some local scenery, including cheap motels and pawn shops around Waveland, and exclusive boutiques, a quaint harbor and nestled Davis Bayou in Ocean Springs.

Orientation

Biloxi is the center of the vacation action. Across the bay, Ocean Springs is where you'll find the nicest residential community, with a great beach and small harbor. West of Biloxi and Ocean Springs, there's Gulfport, an industrial city that's being developed as a casino resort, and a few finds here and there, including a big state amusement park. East of Biloxi and Ocean Springs, there's a smaller more low-key state park in Gautier, and the industrial city of Pascagoula, dominated by the refinery at the Alabama state line.

Information

The Mississippi Gulf Coast Convention and Visitors Bureau (☎ 888-467-4853) distributes maps, events calendars, and information on lodging and attractions by mail or from its offices at 135 Courthouse Rd in Gulfport. The Biloxi visitor center is in a Victorian cottage right on Hwy 90 at the town green.

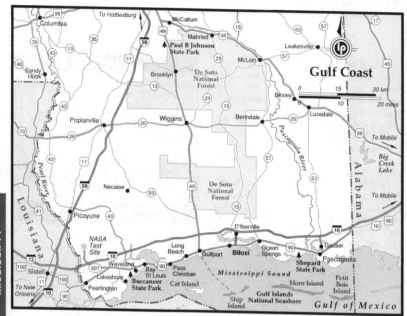

Special Events

January

Fort Maurepas Living History Weekend takes place in Ocean Springs toward the end of the month; for information call ☎ 601-255-4142.

February

Mardi Gras festivities and parades are celebrated along the coast throughout the month. *Mardi Gras* (Fat Tuesday) is celebrated the night before Ash Wednesday to herald the Lenten season.

March

Biloxi hosts the *Cajun Country Crawfish Festival* (☎ 601-388-8010).

April

In the latter part of the month, the *Reenactment of the Landing of d'Iberville* takes place in Ocean Springs; call ☎ 601-872-2766.

May

Pass Christian Tour of Homes takes place the first weekend; call ☎ 601-452-0063.

June

In Biloxi, the *Coliseum Fair and Expo* is mid-month; call ☎ 601-388-8010.

July

On the July 4 weekend, Waveland hosts a *Crab Festival* (☎ 601-467-6509).

August

The low-key *Literary Lecture Series* (☎ 601-872-3164) in Ocean Springs is month-long.

September

The *Mississippi Gulf Coast Blues Festival* (☎ 601-388-8010) is held at the Coliseum in Biloxi the first weekend. *Anything That Floats but Isn't a Boat Regatta* (☎ 601-938-6612) in Pascagoula is the last weekend of the month, or the first weekend in October.

October

Fort Maurepas Living History Weekend, the second of the year is held the second weekend (see January). The *Gautier Mullet Festival & Cook-Off* (☎ 601-497-1294) is held in that town. In Ocean Springs, the *Storytelling Festival under the Oaks* (☎ 601-872-8109) is held the second weekend. *Beauvoir's Fall Muster* (☎ 601-388-1313) is held the third weekend of the month in Biloxi. The town also hosts the *Mad Potter's Ball* and the *Ohr Fall Arts Festival* (☎ 601-435-6308) on the last weekend in October.

November

Mississippi Coast Jazz Society Jazz Festival (☎ 601-432-1600) is held in Biloxi around mid-month.

December

Christmas on the Water boat parade (☎ 601-435-6320) can be witnessed off Biloxi's coast.

BILOXI & GULFPORT

Biloxi gets its name from the Native Americans who lived on these shores at the time of European contact. The French came ashore in 1699, actually landing next door in Ocean Springs but establishing settlements here and on the Gulf Islands. The town claims to be the second-oldest enduring settlement in the US, after Florida's St Augustine.

In addition to being home to two casinos and an industrial port, Gulfport is the jumping-off point for ferry trips to West Ship Island (see Gulf Islands National Seashore).

Information

The visitor center (☎ 601-374-3105) on Hwy 90 next to the town green distributes maps of the downtown historic district and information on historic homes that are open to the public. Spanish Trail Books (☎ 601-435-1144), 781 Howard St, is a wonderful bookstore selling new and vintage books. It's run by knowledgeable local guides.

Museums & Other Attractions

The last home of Confederate President Jefferson Davis, **Beauvoir** (☎ 601-388-1313), 2244 Beach Blvd (Hwy 90), opens its 52-acre seaside estate to public tours. The property includes his restored 1851 home, two museums, a cemetery and nature trails. It's open daily from 9 am to 4 pm in winter or 5 pm in summer. Admission is $7.50 for adults, $7.50 for seniors, $4.50 for children.

The **lighthouse** (☎ 601-435-6293) on Hwy 90 was built in 1848 and remains a well-loved local landmark. It has a tradition of female lighthouse-keepers. It's open by appointment.

The **George E Ohr Arts & Cultural Center** (136 George E Ohr St, ☎ 601-374-5547) commemorates the 'Mad Potter of Biloxi,' an eccentric artist who named his six kids Clo, Oto, Flo, Zio, Ojo and Geo. His pots look pretty contemporary today, even though they were made at turn of the century. The stylish, modern Ohr house features works by local artists as well as Ohr's pottery. It also sponsors children's art activities. Admission is $2, and free for those under 12.

At Point Cadet, off Hwy 90, is the **Seafood Industry Museum** (☎ 601-435-6320). Admission to see the old photos, nets, crab pots, cannery equipment and boat parts is $2.50 ($1.50 for children six to 16 and seniors). It's open Monday through Saturday from 9 am to 4:30 pm, and Sunday from noon to 4 pm.

There's a **Mardi Gras Museum**, but visiting a museum about Mardi Gras is a lot like reading about dancing. Better to catch the celebration, or attend any local parade or festival – they all seem to include the bead-wearing and candy-throwing associated with the pre-Lenten holiday.

The **Marine Education Center & Aquarium** (☎ 601-374-5550) at Point Cadet next to the Isle of Capri Casino features a 42,000-gallon tank. Admission is $3.50 for adults, $2 for children. It's open Monday to Saturday from 9 am to 4 pm.

At Gulport's small craft harbor, trained bottle-nosed dolphins and sea lions perform shows at the **Marine Life Oceanarium** (☎ 601-863-0651).

Activities

The 26-mile-long beach is nice for sunbathing, castle-building and swimming; the gentle Mississippi Sound is clean enough and warm.

You can rent skiffs out to Deer Island, an undeveloped stretch of sand (with some shade) a half-mile out from the Biloxi Small Craft Harbor (☎ 601-436-6592). Check here too for charter boats that will take you fishing or give you access to the islands farther offshore. Boat tours are available aboard shrimp boats and Biloxi schooners leaving from Point Cadet; the old sailing ships were used for shrimping in the early days of the industry. Inquire at the visitor center in Biloxi.

There are 18 golf courses on the coast, and many hotels offer golf packages.

Places to Stay

Camping The *Biloxi Beach Campground* (☎ 601-432-2755), 1816 Beach Blvd/ Hwy 90, is a private campground in the center of the action. It maintains a comfortably worn lot under tall shady trees.

Motels & Hotels Motels line the coast around Biloxi. Most are modest budget motels, and nearly every motel chain is represented. The casino hotels are the newest and fanciest (some with boudoir-style red tuffets, flocked wallpaper and ornate chandeliers), and prices are reasonable (they expect to make their money back in the casino). There is a surprisingly small difference between the price of a room in a casino hotel and a room in beach motel, but prices vary considerably by season. Rates in the high summer season might be double what they are in winter, though there's less fluctuation at the casino hotels. Prices quoted here are generally for

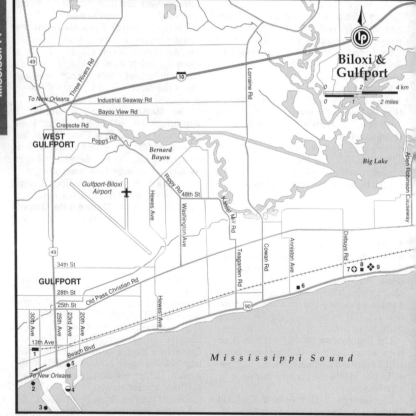

the spring and fall seasons; call the hotels for date-specific prices.

There are a few cheapies in town, but be wary of shattered windshield glass in the parking lot, decrepit Cadillacs, Confederate flag decals and the like. A decent low-end choice that seems family-friendly is the *Deep South Motel* (☎ 601-896-7808); the pool appears well kept but was unfortunately closed for the season at last visit. Rooms start from $29.

Most hotels and motels in Biloxi are right by the water on Hwy 90. Stoplights are infrequent, so, although summertime traffic slows to a crawl, cars may also race by at 60 mph – enough to frazzle a parent's nerves. For that reason, lodging near lit pedestrian crossings is your safest bet; this also generally assures cafes or stores will be nearby.

The *Budget Inn* (☎ 601-388-5111) is a charmless motel in a busy stretch, but it's on the beach side of the highway. Rooms start from $55. The *Biloxi Beach Resort* (☎ 601-388-3310) is a well-established 'motor hotel' kind of place that looks like it keeps the same families returning every year. Rates start from $65.

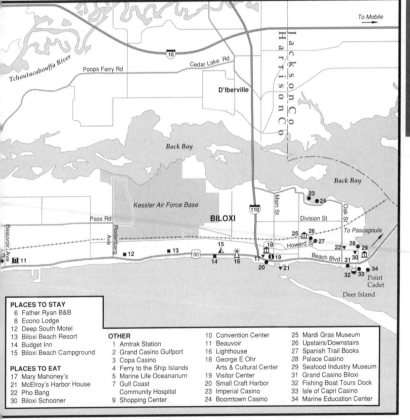

MISSISSIPPI

PLACES TO STAY
  6 Father Ryan B&B
  8 Econo Lodge
 12 Deep South Motel
 13 Biloxi Beach Resort
 14 Budget Inn
 15 Biloxi Beach Campground

PLACES TO EAT
 17 Mary Mahoney's
 21 McElroy's Harbor House
 22 Pho Bang
 30 Biloxi Schooner

OTHER
  1 Amtrak Station
  2 Grand Casino Gulfport
  3 Copa Casino
  4 Ferry to the Ship Islands
  5 Marine Life Oceanarium
  7 Gulf Coast
    Community Hospital
  9 Shopping Center
 10 Convention Center
 11 Beauvoir
 16 Lighthouse
 18 George E Ohr
    Arts & Cultural Center
 19 Visitor Center
 20 Small Craft Harbor
 23 Imperial Casino
 24 Boomtown Casino
 25 Mardi Gras Museum
 26 Upstairs/Downstairs
 27 Spanish Trail Books
 28 Palace Casino
 29 Seafood Industry Museum
 31 Grand Casino Biloxi
 32 Fishing Boat Tours Dock
 33 Isle of Capri Casino
 34 Marine Education Center

Father Ryan B&B (☎ 601-435-1189) operates out of a lovely historic house (with tours available for non-guests). It charges $80 for a double, and this includes a generous Southern breakfast.

The *Econo Lodge* (☎ 601-863-9350), 40 E Beach Blvd/Hwy 90 in Gulfport offers basic motel accommodations, with beach restrooms conveniently across the way. Rooms start from $49.

The *Grand Casino* (☎ 800-946-2946) in Gulfport is less grand than the one in Biloxi but right on the beach with a 400-room hotel (rates range from $79 to $109 for a double).

The *Copa Casino* (☎ 601-863-3330) operates out of a Love-Boat-style cruise ship in Gulfport's harbor.

Places to Eat

The *Biloxi Schooner* on 139 Howard St at the foot of Myrtle St (☎ 601-374-8071) should be your first stop. It's an old diner with paneling lined with old black & whites of fishing schooners in their 1940s heyday, and it has orange booths, a 10-seat counter and a great jukebox. It's the most reliable place for fishermen's breakfasts (from $4), po-boy lunches (from $4.50) and seafood plates at dinner (from $11). It's across the street from the Palace Casino on the Back Bay, and down the street from a fabulous Vietnamese market. It's closed on Sunday.

You won't find many authentic Vietnamese restaurants in the South, so it's well worth finding *Pho Bang* (☎ 601-374-7666), 295 Howard St at Oak, about a half-mile west of the Biloxi Schooner. Pho Bang serves good rice-noodle soups ($4.50 a dinner bowl) with shrimp and meat, along with other traditional specialties. It's open daily to 8 pm.

Locals send visitors to *Mary Mahoney's* (☎ 601-374-0163), off Hwy 90 near downtown Biloxi, which serves expensive seafood for lunch and dinner in butlered antebellum style within a 1737 mansion. For a more casual setting, eat in the tavern out the back. There's also a cafe here open 24 hours serving café au lait and beignets around the clock.

McElroy's Harbor House seafood restaurant (☎ 601-435-5001) is on the pier at the scenic Biloxi Small Craft Harbor. Daily lunch specials start at $6; the dinner menu includes mullet and broiled shrimp for $9. It's also open for breakfast.

Casinos serve all-you-can-eat buffets at reasonable prices, which is a great value for big appetites. The *Copa Casino* has a seafood buffet for $7. In general, casinos offer short-order food and snacks nearly around the clock. The casinos also have big fancy restaurants, but you pay mostly for decor; service isn't appropriate for the prices. That said, the Grand Casino's *Crab House* is supposed to have a great gumbo.

Entertainment

Nationally known entertainers perform on the Mississippi Coast, and there are plenty of events such as beach concerts, dance contests and auto shows. Ticket prices are reasonable and many events are free. The *Grand Casino* in Biloxi has a snazzy theater, and most casinos have smaller stages with comedy and cabaret-style performances. The *Convention Center* also puts on large concerts and other special events.

Locals who ignore the casino scene hang out at the *Upstairs/Downstairs* lounge (☎ 601-374-5291), 785 Vieux Marché Mall off Howard St, which features local blues acts.

Things to Buy

Mary Mahoney's (see Places to Eat) has a gift shop selling dainty items such as fine lace aprons and Aunt Jemima thimbles. The George E Ohr Arts & Cultural Center sells locally made crafts, Christmas ornaments and lots of pottery.

Getting There & Away

Air The only airport on the coast is the Gulfport-Biloxi regional airport (☎ 601-863-5951) in Gulfport, which offers nonstop flights to a limited number of cities (including Atlanta, Dallas, Tampa and Memphis) with Delta Airlines, Continental Express and Northwest Express.

The closest major airport is in New Orleans, which may be cheaper than flying to the regional airport, and is a drive of under two hours to Biloxi.

Train Amtrak stops in Biloxi (at a somewhat forlorn outpost with a platform only) and at a full-fledged train station (complete with waiting room, parking lot, cabs outside) in downtown Gulfport.

Boat Passenger ferries to West Ship Island (see Gulf Islands National Seashore) depart from the Gulfport Yacht Harbor; see Gulf Islands National Seashore.

Getting Around

Biloxi is perfectly flat and suited to bike touring, as long as you don't mind competing with highway traffic; call the Gulf Coast Bicycle Club (☎ 601-388-0096) for more information.

Casino shuttles run between many of the motels and casinos.

GULF ISLANDS NATIONAL SEASHORE

The national seashore preserves four barrier islands 12 miles off the eastern Mississippi coast: West and East Ship Islands, Horn Island and Petit Bois Island. The national seashore also encompasses the Davis Bayou on the mainland in Ocean Springs (where you'll find the ranger station), and property further east in Florida. The two most notable islands are the historic West Ship, serviced by regular ferries, and Horn Island, a wilderness favored by adventurers and accessible only by private boat.

Coastal Casinos

The Vegas-style casinos that have grown to dominate the Mississippi coast are huge theme parks on the water. There is currently 600,000 sq feet of casinos, and this is expected to top one million in the near future. Casinos must technically be 'offshore' to permit legal gambling, even if that means they are constructed on barges no farther than a broad leap from land.

The most action is at Point Cadet, a nice vantage point where the Mississippi Sound spills into Biloxi's Back Bay. On the Mississippi Sound side is the Isle of Capri and the Grand Casino Biloxi. On the Back Bay, there's the Palace, Boomtown and the Imperial. A short drive farther west along the sound there's Treasure Bay and the President close together, then a long stretch about 20 miles to Gulfport, where there's another Grand Casino and the Copa Casino.

The casinos are open 24 hours, and their prices for entertainment, lodging and food tend to be very reasonable (they expect they'll make up the difference at the gaming tables and slot machines). Their lavish buffets are your best bet for a cheap meal.

Here's the rundown of casinos now in operation.

Grand Casino Biloxi (☎ 800-946-2946), 265 Beach Blvd, Point Cadet – the 'grand dame' of the coast's casinos, it features a large theater as well as a posh casino and a 500-room hotel (rates for a double range from $79 to $139).

Isle of Capri Casino (☎ 800-843-4753), 151 Beach Blvd, Point Cadet – features jungly waterfalls, parrots, Flintstone-foam rocks and the 367-room Crowne Plaza Hotel (double rates range from $119 to $139).

Palace Casino (☎ 800-725-2239), 158 Howard Ave, north of Point Cadet on Biloxi's Back Bay – more subdued than most and a nice spot; no hotel.

Boomtown (☎ 601-435-7000, 800-627-0777), 676 Bayview Ave on the Back Bay – Western-style and goldrushy; no hotel.

Treasure Bay (☎ 800-747-2839), 1980 Beach Blvd – a black pirate ship appealing to younger gamblers; no hotel.

The narrow islands are ringed with white-sand beaches and blue-green Gulf waters. The smaller ones aren't much but dune, while the larger ones host a maritime forest of oak and pine studded with lagoons. You'll want to pack sunscreen and insect repellent when you explore these islands.

Ship Islands

What was once a single island was split in two by Hurricane Camille in 1965. Though officially named West Ship and East Ship Island, folks still expect it'll patch itself together, so they continue to use the singular Ship Island. West Ship is the most accessible and historic of all the Gulf Islands. An old island family runs ferry

> **West Ship Island Ferry Schedule**
> Passenger ferries leave the Gulfport Yacht Harbor for hour-long rides to and from West Ship Island every season except winter. Fares are $14 roundtrip for adults, and $7 for children aged three to 10 (discounts for seniors and members of the military). For information call Pan Isles (☎ 601-864-1014, 800-388-3290); times and fares are subject to change. Note that weather conditions may affect schedule. No camping is permitted on the island.
>
> **Spring** (first Saturday in March to second weekend in May)
>
> Saturday & Sunday
>   Departs Gulfport   9 am, 12 noon
>   Departs Ship Island   2:40 pm, 5:40 pm
>
> Monday to Friday
>   Departs Gulfport   9 am
>   Departs Ship Island   2:40 pm
>
> **Summer** (second weekend in May to first Tuesday in September)
>
> Daily
>   Departs Gulfport   9 am, 12 noon
>   Departs Ship Island   2:40, 5:40 pm
>
> **Fall** (first Tuesday in September through the last Sunday in October)
> Same as the spring schedule

services to the island from Gulfport (see the ferry schedule for fares, times and contact information).

The island's most distinctive feature is **Fort Massachusetts**. Early in the Civil War, the Confederates seized the unfinished fort. After federal troops regained control in 1861, they finished construction and used the island as a prisoner-of-war camp and staging area for the capture of New Orleans. An African-American Confederate troop was housed here during the war. You can take a ranger's tour or wander around on your own.

You can sunbathe, swim and hike around the island (less clothing required as you head east). There's a shop that sells hot snacks, candy and cold drinks along with other supplies such as sunscreen and insect repellent. They also rent out umbrellas and beach chairs (but these aren't cheap); there are decent beach showers and restrooms. No camping is permitted on West Ship Island.

By advance arrangement, the ferry company can provide transportation to East Ship Island (bring water and food) for $100 minimum or $50 per person during the standard ferry season. It's more expensive in winter. Camping is permitted on East Ship Island.

Horn Island Wilderness

The jewel of the Gulf Islands National Seashore is Horn Island, a 3650-acre strip of pristine wilderness with pine and palmetto forests, lagoons attracting over 280 bird species, and 13 miles of deserted beach – an ideal destination for hikers, sun worshipers and backpacker campers.

You can hike 30 miles around the island, and there are several opportunities to cut through the half-mile-wide interior (beware of mosquitos in forested areas). The best places to camp are at the breezier tips. No ferry serves the island, and though a ranger is stationed there, no public services are available.

To get out there, you can either kayak or charter a boat across the Mississippi Sound. To kayak, rangers recommend starting from Shepard State Park (☎ 601-497-2244) in Gautier, east of the mainland NPS ranger station. There are several chances to quit along the way if you get into trouble. For boat charters, the park has licensed four environmentally conscious captains. One of these, Patrick Peterson, transports day-trippers and campers for a minimum of $100, or $50 per person, on his fast boat *Conspira Sea*. He can provide all camping equipment for up to six people, and he will guide you and prepare meals for your party for an additional fee. Peterson, who is also the environment reporter for the local newspaper, has raised his voice against drilling rigs that would encroach on the unspoiled view around Horn Island.

Coastal painter Walter Anderson's images of Horn Island can be seen at his namesake gallery in Ocean Springs and at the ranger station just north at Davis Bayou.

Davis Bayou

The NPS ranger station for the national seashore is on the mainland east of downtown Ocean Springs at a beautiful spot called Davis Bayou. It has a nice visitor center with a film introducing barrier-island ecology; some paintings by Walter Anderson; and a deck and boardwalk overlooking the scenic marshland.

There is a pretty campground; the sites aren't too private and we saw a lot of RVs, but they're well spaced and surrounded by forest.

The ranger station distributes comprehensive information on camping on the wilderness islands, including boat charters; ask for their brochure.

OCEAN SPRINGS

Ocean Springs is a nice residential community tucked south of Hwy 90. Over the railroad tracks you'll find the old depot converted into boutiques and shops, the compact downtown strip and renowned art museum down Washington St. It's a short drive or bike ride to the nice and quiet beach, or to the picturesque harbor, with its small fishing fleet and yacht cove.

The **Walter Anderson Museum of Art** (☎ 601-872-3164), at 510 Washington Ave, features Anderson's paintings of the Mississippi coast (particularly the Horn Island wilderness). Anderson painted in a compellingly whimsical way with a pastel palette – a style that's often been compared to Van Gogh and Picasso. Its worth a stop. Admission is $3 for adults and $1 for children (free for those under six). The museum is open daily, but closed on major holidays.

For camping on the coast, the NPS campground (☎ 601-875-9057) at Davis Bayou on the national seashore is off Hwy 90. This 51-site campground charges $14 per night. Hookups are available.

Shearwater Pottery (☎ 601-875-7320) displays and sells locally crafted works; it's open weekdays only.

The *Breakroom* (☎ 601-872-1256) in Ocean Springs, just over the bridge from Biloxi off Hwy 90, is an inviting roadhouse that features live entertainment on weekends and Christmas lights year-round.

WEST OF BILOXI & GULFPORT

The town of **Long Beach** is home to the University of Southern Mississippi's Gulf Coast campus and also features historic buildings and tall old trees, including the Friendship Oak – folks meeting under it are said to be friends for life. *Catfish Charlie's* (☎ 601-832-9195), in Long Beach, has a huge hillbilly-inspired dining hall (and plenty of shining BMWs and Tauruses in the parking lot) decorated with old license plates and farm implements. Its catfish plate and fried chicken plate are under $10. The iced tea is very sweet, and bottomless. There is a giant two-story-high rocking chair out in front.

In **Pass Christian** (pronounced pass kristi-ANN) you can see attractive antebellum houses facing the Gulf. This was a favorite resort for families from New Orleans and many attractive houses and shady old oaks have survived centuries of hurricanes.

In **Bay St Louis**, the NASA Space Center (☎ 601-688-2370) offers guided

MISSISSIPPI

tours of the satellite facility. At night, you might want to check out the *Dock of the Bay* (☎ 601-467-9940) downtown; the house band features a former member of the band Blood, Sweat & Tears.

In **Waveland**, a short drive south of Hwy 90 takes you across the railroad tracks (caution: no crossing gates) to **Buccaneer State Park** (☎ 601-467-3822). The park features water slides, a campground, a pier and a nice stretch of beach. Camping is available for $8, $11 with hookups.

EAST OF OCEAN SPRINGS

North of Gautier, the **Mississippi Sandhill Crane National Wildlife Refuge** (☎ 601-497-6322), preserves the habitat of an unusual species of sandhill crane. While most varieties of sandhill crane are migratory birds that interbreed, the particular Mississippi sandhill crane native to this isolated habitat does not migrate, nor does it interbreed. As a result, encroaching coastal development severely threatens its survival, and this patch has been preserved to protect the endangered species. The preserve also benefits the endangered local red-cockaded woodpecker population. A very short nature trail stretching into the refuge allows visitors to wander in to

catch a glimpse of the long-legged cranes, listen for the woodpecker cries and observe the coastal piney woods in their natural state.

Shepard State Park (☎ 601-497-2244), 1024 Graveline Rd in Gautier, is nestled in a quiet corner of the coast. The 400-acre park provides hiking and biking trails and a wooded campground ($8, no hookups available). It's also an ideal put-in point for sea kayak trips across the Mississippi Sound out to the Horn Island Wilderness.

At the mouth of the Pascagoula River, **La Pointe-Krebs House** (☎ 601-769-1505), 4602 Fort St (formerly known as the Old Spanish Fort) in Pascagoula, is believed to be the oldest standing European structure in the Mississippi Valley. Joseph de la Pointe, who at 12 years old was a member of the original d'Iberville expedition of 1699, settled down among the Pascagoula Indians. His estate on Krebs Lake included a carpenter's shop built around 1721. This shop, which later served as a house and became fortified, was known as the Old Spanish Fort and remains standing. Its walls are whitewashed with ground oyster shells over *bousillage*, a mixture of Spanish moss and clay commonly used for insulation at the time. The house underwent extensive restoration in 1996. A nearby cemetery holds generations of residents of the historic house, and a museum on the grounds displays a mixture of pre-Columbian artifacts and memorabilia from the early 19th century and the Civil War period. Admission is $3 (seniors $2, children $1). It's open daily.

DE SOTO NATIONAL FOREST

The De Soto National Forest is the largest forest in Mississippi. It's a great place for backpacking, camping, hiking, swimming, fishing and canoeing. Its greatest attractions are within the Black Creek ranger district (☎ 601-928-4422), which is headquartered in Wiggins. The ranger's office distributes forest maps and information.

At Black Creek, adventurers can canoe down 21 miles of officially 'wild and

> ### River of Love
> The legendary Pascagoula River near the Alabama border has been nicknamed the 'Singing River' for the mysterious sounds folks say emanate from its depths. The story goes that a young Biloxi Indian princess, though betrothed to a chieftain within her own warrior tribe, instead fell in love with a young man of the peace-loving Pascagoula tribe. After running off with her love, the jilted Biloxi fellow ran a raid on the Pascagoula. The Pascagoulas vowed to save the young couple or die trying. The relentless Biloxi attack pushed the community to the river and to their deaths. It's the death chant of the Pascagoula that's said to account for the strange sounds heard at the river. ■

scenic' river and hike along the 41-mile Black Creek Trail. The trail passes along the white sandy banks of the tannin-stained creek and under the shade of magnolias, sweet bays, sweet gums, tulip trees and oaks. It passes an ox-bow lake studded with cypress, crosses 82 bridges over streamlets and ravines, and swings off into the rolling piney woods. It is not uncommon to see deer, wild turkeys, owls, great blue herons and beavers along the stream.

A good place to start the trail is near **Paul B Johnson State Park** (☎ 601-582-7721), beside the national forest between Wiggins and Hattiesburg. Find the entrance to the trail off Hwy 49, four miles south of the state park. Keep your eyes out for a service road to the east, where a small brown sign for Ashe Nursery and Black Creek Seed Orchard leads a mile or so down Yeaton Spur Rd past the nursery and orchard to the USFS-signed parking lot.

The state park makes a nice base. It offers a lake with swimming and paddle boats, campgrounds ($11 drive-up, or primitive tent sites for $7), and 16 cabins that are fully furnished with linens and basic cookware and dishware. Black Creek hikers may prefer to park in the secured state parking lot instead of the unsecured USFS lot – first obtain permission for overnight parking at the desk, and be aware that not everyone around here knows about the trail.

Black Creek Canoe Rentals (☎ 601-582-8817), in Brooklyn, outfits expeditions ranging from a five-mile day trip to a 25-mile three-day launch. (Bring all your own food, though a store nearby offers an opportunity for last-minute purchases.) The folks here probably know more about creek and trail conditions than even the forest service. The canoe shop has operated here since 1977 with a USFS special-use permit. A fee of $20 per day includes life vest, paddles and shuttle service (advance reservations and deposits required). It's on Carnes Rd east of Hwy 49 – the turnoff is about 6½ miles south of the state park (northbound drivers should watch for the large yellow-and-black sign).

Red-cockaded woodpecker

LUCEDALE & AROUND

Around 20 miles west of the Alabama state line off Hwy 98, Lucedale evokes that small-town Southern feel that is fast disappearing throughout the region. The famed back-scratching post downtown is rumored to have been there for at least a hundred years. But what draws most people through town is a visit to the home-spun biblical shrine **Palestinian Gardens** outside town.

At Palestinian Gardens (☎ 601- 947-8422), in nearby Bexley, visitors are guided through a to-scale model of the Holy Land. A Reverend Jackson constructed the site, and though he passed on six years ago, the site is maintained by the Reverend Don Bradley and members of his family and congregation. The folks here take a good deal of pride in their knowledge of biblical history. March and April are probably the best months for a visit, as the azaleas, magnolias and wisteria are in full bloom. Bring a picnic lunch; no food is available in the park (though a grocery nearby sells provisions). The gardens are open Monday to Saturday from 8 am to 6 pm and Sunday from 1 to 6 pm. Admission is $2.50 for adults and $1.50 for children. To get to the gardens, look for Carolyn's Grocery at N Bexley Rd, turn right and drive 3½ miles to the first available right turn at a stop sign. Turn right here onto Palestinian Gardens Rd.

Pilgrims might want to stop at the *Landmark Cafe* (☎ 601-766-9619), on Main St in downtown Lucedale, for breakfast or lunch. The Landmark offers Cajun kebabs and 'Old-World-style' po-boys. The oyster loaf and fried onion ring combo is distinctly Southern.

Alabama

Facts about Alabama

Alabama can't shake its reputation. It's thought of more for its past – 'rednecks,' rebels, segregation, discrimination and public officials who made the news for all the wrong reasons – than its present. There's no denying the importance of the events of the past. Indeed, they have helped Alabamians move closer toward racial harmony. Not just by removing the 'Whites Only' and 'Colored Restrooms' signs, but by telling a more complete history. It's impossible for visitors to miss the extra effort that is made to try to correct the wrongs of the past. Guides in museums, historic houses and parks acknowledge the contributions made by Native Americans and African Americans as well as European Americans. Visitors learn that before Hernando de Soto 'discovered' Alabama, there were sophisticated Native American cultures that created beautifully embellished pottery, held elaborate ceremonies, created an alphabet and constructed large earthen mounds. African Americans were not simply slaves. They built many of Alabama's historic houses, painted many of its masterpieces and fueled the cotton empire.

History

According to historians, Alabama maintained its traditional white racial and political traditions longer than any Southern state other than Mississippi, severely retarding its development. However, in the last few decades, Alabama has experienced much political and social turmoil and change.

Telling evidence of the seismic political change that Alabama has undergone is the political transformation of former Governor George Wallace. Once the very symbol of the system of white supremacy, Wallace underwent an about-face from staunch segregationist in the 1960s to supporter of biracial politics in his successful fourth-term campaign in 1982.

In recent decades, Alabamians (and other Southerners) have gradually reversed their historic allegiance to the Democratic Party, particularly in presidential elections. The Democrat's hold on the state started to erode gradually beginning in 1948 with the formation of the States' Rights Party, or Dixiecrats, who protested the national Democratic Party's adoption of a liberal civil rights plank in its platform. Then, in 1964, Barry Goldwater won 49% of the Southern vote and carried Alabama and four other Deep South states. With the exception of Jimmy Carter in 1976, no Democratic presidential candidate has carried Alabama since John F Kennedy in 1960.

Following President Lyndon Johnson's signing of the Voting Rights Act of 1965, the percentage of Alabama's eligible black registered voters rose from 23.5% to 65.4% in five years. The white vote also soared during that period, from 78.7% to 96.9%. The rate of increase in electoral participation was highest among females, blacks and poor Alabamians.

Long viewed condescendingly and inaccurately for its largely rural 'redneck' population that didn't wear shoes and ate dirt, Alabama shifted from a predominantly rural to urban population for the first time in its history in the early 1970s. Outsiders flooded in and by the early 1990s the state had grown to be the 22nd largest. However, the black population decreased from 40% to 25% as blacks continued to leave the state. They left rural areas where the number of farms and factories had declined sharply. Similarly, coal and iron mining and the automobile industry downsized, costing black workers thousands of high-paying union jobs. Ironically, the number of African Americans elected to public office, including judges, mayors and members of Congress, soared to more than 700, higher than ever before.

ALABAMA

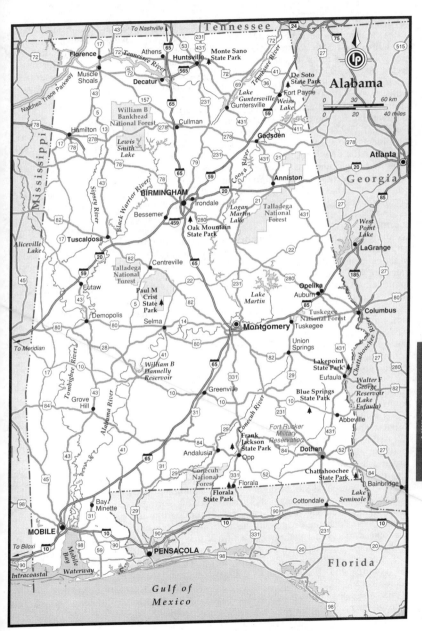

Government & Politics

In 1994 Alabamians elected Forrest H 'Fob' James Jr as their 55th governor. He is the only governor in the state's history to be elected first as a Democrat (1979-83) and then re-elected as a Republican (he switched parties in April 1994). The governor serves a four-year term and can serve more than one term (but not more than two consecutive terms). Governor James addresses his constituents every Monday evening on a statewide radio show, 'Fob James Live.'

The state legislature has 35 senators and 105 representatives elected for four-year terms. Alabama has two US senators, seven representatives and nine electoral votes.

Economy

Economic factors have contributed substantially to the state's changing attitudes. As the economies of moderate neighboring states grew, Alabama suffered major economic setbacks during the racial turmoil of the 1950s and 1960s.

In the 1960s, two-thirds of Alabama's rural farmland, mostly cotton plantations, was converted to forests for lumbering, making wood (and related goods) the state's leading agricultural product. Poultry production also saw significant increases. By the 1970s Alabama was the biggest lumber producer in the South and the third-largest poultry producer in the country. In the 1980s, mills gave way to malls. The traditional textile and steel industries were eclipsed by service industries, light manufacturing, the aquaculture of catfish, construction and, in Huntsville, aerospace and high-tech industries.

The 1970s and 1980s brought roller-coaster economics to a state whose economic ranking among the 50 states was already 47th. Alabama's per capita income was one of the lowest nationwide, a fifth of the population lived below the poverty line, infant mortality was the highest in the country and 12.5% of the people couldn't read.

Alabama's population is now at 4.2 million, but the economic situation for schools, health care and the state's poor remains bleak. Many Alabamians blame politicians, whom they say have refused to pass meaningful tax and educational reforms. In turn, politicians blame the taxpayers for resolutely defeating local attempts to raise taxes for education.

Geography

At its widest point, Alabama measures 210 miles. Its length is 329 miles. There are 53 miles of coastline and nearly 1000 miles of inland waterways. Thirteen major rivers crisscross the state, carving it into seven distinct physiographic regions. These rivers helped determine the state's history. Native Americans settled fertile river valleys, giving the state one of the richest Indian histories in the country; Hernando de Soto and other Europeans explored the state by river; and the more than 1000 miles of navigable inland waterways allowed cotton to be sent to the port of Mobile, where it was shipped to markets around the world.

Recognizing the importance of navigable waterways, attempts were made as early as 1871 to improve navigation along 457 miles of the river system with the use of locks and dams. Alabama's rivers continue to influence the economy. The system moves more than 15 tons of goods each year, including coal, iron and manganese ores, petroleum products, limestone, sand and gravel, logs, chemicals, steel products, sulfur and agricultural products.

Alabama has a geographical diversity unparalleled for a state of its size. Moving south from the rugged foothills of the Appalachians, the waterfalls, canyons and mountain lakes give way to the hilly, richly forested central highlands, before turning into the gently rolling hills of the Black Belt farm country and the lowlands that grow wiregrass and crops. These gradually yield to the marshes, bays and white sandy beaches of the Mobile and Tensaw delta and the Gulf Coast. The highest point is Cheaha Mountain (2407 feet) in the northeast.

Alabama's ecological diversity ranks behind only California and Florida. Forests, primarily pine, cover about two-thirds of the state. More than three hundred types of wildflowers are native. Azaleas, in resplendent bloom throughout the state in March and April, were brought to Alabama in the late 1700s from France. Alligators inhabit the delta swamps and wetlands north and east of Mobile and geese, ducks and other waterfowl winter in the river wetlands of Decatur. Dauphin Island is on the migratory flyway, making it an ideal spot for bird-watching.

Alabama and many of its rivers, counties and towns take their names from the Native Americans who lived here for thousands of years. Alabama, from the Alibamu Indians, means 'clearer of the thicket.'

Spectator Sports

Sports, especially college football, have attained religious status in Alabama thanks to the University of Alabama's Paul 'Bear' Bryant and his team, the Crimson Tide, which won six national championships between 1961 and 1979. Bryant, along with Auburn Tiger's Ralph 'Shug' Jordan, made a national name for Alabama in sports. Though Bryant died in 1983 and Jordan was replaced by Pat Dye, who won or shared four conference championships during the 1980s with players like Vincent 'Bo' Jackson, the Alabama sports tradition continues with Gene Stallings at University of Alabama and Terry Bowden at Auburn. Getting tickets to college football games is always difficult and next to impossible for bowl games and when Auburn and cross-state rival University of Alabama face off.

Race car fans have much to cheer about. The Talladega Superspeedway claims some of the fastest track times in racing history and fans regularly fill the stands to see homeboys like Bobby Allison, Neil Bonnett and Red Farmer take the checkered flag.

Off the field and track, Alabamians pay homage to its saints of sports at three major attractions: the International Motorsports Hall of Fame in Talladega, the Alabama Sports Hall of Fame in Birmingham, and the Paul Bryant Museum in Tuscaloosa.

Arts

Historically a state with a large rural population, it should not be surprising that much of Alabama's best art comes from the countryside. Folk artists received their greatest recognition in 1994 when Crane Hill Publishers published *Revelations: Alabama's Visionary Folk Artists*, a glossy, in-depth look at the state's distinctive culture through art.

The Art of Southern Living is a weekly, half-hour TV program about Alabama's artists and writers.

Music Alabama boasts a long, impressive musical tradition, from Florence's WC Handy (the 'father of the blues') to the contemporary rock of Muscle Shoals' Fame Studios, from Hank Williams Sr to the group Alabama. The state's musical excellence is reflected in the Alabama Music Hall of Fame in Tuscumbia and the Alabama Jazz Hall of Fame in Birmingham.

Literature For a good overview of 19th and 20th-century literature from Alabama, consider reading *Many Voices, Many Rooms: A New Anthology of Alabama Writers* (1997) edited by Philip D Beidler. It showcases the rich literary heritage of the state and is a companion volume to Beidler's earlier work, *The Art of Fiction in the Heart of Dixie: An Anthology of Alabama Writers* (1987).

Margaret Walker Alexander is considered one of the foremost voices in black fiction and poetry. She is the author of numerous books, including the classic, 'For My People' (1937), which celebrates African-American history and culture. *Jubilee* (1966), the story of her enslaved great-grandmother's life, received its greatest recognition when Alexander sued – and lost – Alex Haley for taking parts from her book for *Roots*.

The existentialist novels of Birmingham's Walker Percy include *The Moviegoer* (1961), *The Last Gentleman* (1967), *Love in the Ruins* (1971), *Lancelot* (1977) and *The Second Coming* (1980). Many of his books deal with the alienation found in

ALABAMA

a technologically oriented society. His last work was the collection of essays *Signposts in a Strange Land* (1991).

Helen Norris Bell drifts from novels to short stories to poetry. She's received numerous prestigious literary awards, and the *Christmas Wife* (1985) and *The Cracker Man* (1992) were made into films. Although she often writes about Alabama and the South, her work also covers foreign locales, including Poland and Vietnam. Critics often compare her writing style to that of Henry James.

Race is a common theme in Alabamian literature for white and black writers. One of the most poignant examples is the work of novelist, critic and biographer Albert Murray, who grew up in the South during the 1920s. His first book, a collection of essays called *The Omni-Americans: New Perspectives on Black Experience and American Culture* (1970), was republished in 1983 as *The Omni-Americans: Some Alternatives to the Folklore of White Supremacy*. It was primarily for this work, which deals with the dilemmas of race and American identity and asserts that the similarities between American blacks and whites are more striking than their differences, that he was inducted into the American Academy of Arts and Letters in 1997.

Bill Butterworth, writing under his own name as well as many pseudonyms (WEB Griffin, Alex Baldwin, Webb Beech, Walker E Blake, James McM Douglas, Eden Hughes, Edmund O Scholefield and Patric J Williams), has published more than 100 books, landed on the *New York Times* best-seller list 19 times and sold an estimated $25 million worth of books. While his work covers a wide range, he's best known for his military stories, including the 12-book *MASH* series in the 1970s.

Few critics took note when Winston Groom received the Southern Library Association Best Fiction Award in 1980 for *As Summers Die*, but recognition eventually came to Groom when his 1986 book, *Forrest Gump*, became a popular motion picture.

Born in Monroeville in 1957, Mark Childress started as a journalist but turned to writing novels in 1982. *Crazy in Alabama* (1993), his most celebrated work, delivers two parallel stories set in the bitter, racially charged 1960s South.

Sculpture Frank Fleming creates whimsical bronze sculptures of animals. These include his *Storyteller* in Birmingham's Five Points South and similar allegorical pieces outside the Montgomery Museum of Fine Arts.

Lonnie Holley is known as the 'Sand Man' because of his carved sandstone sculptures. When his sister's children died in a house fire in 1978, he used kitchen utensils to carve their names in sandstone because there wasn't enough money to buy tombstones. He experimented with sandstone carving and a year later the work of this young black man caught the attention of the Birmingham Museum of Art. He also paints and creates assemblages out of junk. The Rockford Art Museum, Meadow Farm Museum and Birmingham Museum of Art are among the museums showcasing his work.

Not yet as well known, but equally fine, are artists Leah Webb, who works in stone and occasionally bronze; the duo of Tony Buchen and Jeralyn Goodwin, who as artists-in-residence at the historic Sloss Furnaces, created many metal sculptures; and Robert Taylor, who creates insect sculptures that look like the real thing.

Architecture The Civil War destroyed many major towns, but a few escaped with their architectural heritage intact. Major historic districts with antebellum and turn-of-the-century buildings exist in Huntsville, Decatur, Mobile, Mooresville, Opelika and Eufaula. Montgomery's Old Alabama Town, a re-created historic village, has examples of most architectural styles found around the state, from early dog-trot design (a house with two rooms on either side of an open passageway) to an antebellum mansion.

Painting The work of Sister Gertrude Morgan, a former street missionary, features biblical themes. Born in Lafayette in 1900, she moved to New Orleans in the late 1930s. She aimed to spread the gospel through art, working with whatever media she could find, including styrofoam trays, jelly glasses, and oblong strips of cardboard stitched together and painted to make fans. Her work is in the National Museum of American Art, among other locales.

Considered one of the state's finest artists, Gary Chapman, a professor of art at the University of Alabama, Birmingham, paints large-scale conceptually based figurative oil paintings. His work is suggestive of classical chiaroscuro paintings and is on display at the Museum of Fine Arts in Montgomery, the Birmingham Museum of Art and the Mobile Museum of Art.

The work of Woodie Long, a former house painter turned folk artist is now extremely popular among collectors. In the 1980s while his wife, Dot, an accomplished watercolor artist, took lessons, he stayed home and played with her art supplies, creating colorful, childlike memory paintings that depict his childhood in a sharecropping community in Plant City, Florida. His work is primarily in New York City galleries and in private collections. In the early 1980s he moved to Andalusia, Alabama, where he still lives and works.

Information
Tourist Offices Alabama Bureau of Tourism & Travel (☎ 334-242-4554, 800-252-2262), 401 Adams Ave, PO Box 4927, Montgomery, AL 36103-4927. Alabama has eight welcome centers along the interstate highways, just inside the state line. They're open 24 hours a day, with restrooms and vending machines, but they are staffed only from 8 am to 5 pm. The state publishes two free comprehensive guides: *Alabama: The Official Vacation Guide for the State of Alabama* and *Alabama's Black Heritage*. Local convention and visitor bureaus and chambers of commerce

also dispense tourism information. The state bureau provides a list. In addition, many visitor offices have Internet web sites. See the Internet directory at the back of this book for details.

Time Alabama operates on Central Standard Time, with the exception of three towns – Lanett and Valley, located at the Alabama/Georgia border on I-85, and Phenix City, also on the border on Hwys 431 and 80. They run on Eastern Standard Time. Daylight-saving time (one hour ahead of standard time) goes into effect throughout the state at 1 am on the first Sunday in April and ends at 2 am on the last Sunday in October.

Taxes There's a statewide sales tax of around 8%. It varies slightly by county. Hotels must collect an additional 4% occupancy tax.

Liquor Laws The legal drinking age is 21 years. Beverage sales stop at 2 am on Sunday – except in private clubs and the cities of Huntsville, Birmingham, Montgomery and Mobile – and restart at 12:01 am on Monday. Dry counties do not sell alcohol. There are 26 dry counties (out of 67) in Alabama. A few cities, including Clanton, Guntersville, Decatur, Enterprise, Florence, Jasper, Bridgeport and Scottsboro, are wet even though they are in dry counties. There are 22 counties that only serve draft beer. You may not transport more than one case of beer and three quarts of liquor or wine into or through a dry county. It's illegal to bring alcoholic beverages purchased outside the state into Alabama. Driving with blood-alcohol level of 0.08% or higher is illegal. Refusal to take a breath test when stopped may result in a 90-day suspension of your driver's license.

State Parks The Alabama Department of Conservation & Natural Resources operates 24 state parks with a wide range of facilities. Most have campsites, and many

ALABAMA

have rustic cabins and resorts or lodges. The mountain parks have hiking, biking and horseback-riding trails, including the 102-mile Pinhoti Trail in northeast Alabama. Lake, river and Gulf-front parks have marinas and are great places for fishing. In addition, there are four national forests, a national monument and four national wildlife refuges. Order the free *National Forests in Alabama Pocket Visitor Guide* by calling ☎ 334-832-4470 or writing to 2946 Chestnut St, Montgomery, AL 36107. The $30 annual day-use permit for all of Alabama's national forests (except the Clear Creek area of William Bankhead National Forest) will save you money if you plan to visit the forests for more than 10 days. Parks have decent trail maps. If you're planning on a hiking vacation, consider Patricia S Sharpe's *Alabama Trails* and topographical maps available at ranger stations for about $4.

There are many caves in north-central and northeast Alabama. However, most are on private property and require permission to explore. Due to the high number of accidents, permission is rarely granted unless you are a member of a recognized speleological organization. Contact the National Speleological Society (☎ 205-852-1300), Cave Ave, Huntsville, AL 35810, for information about caving and grottos in Alabama.

The Army Corps of Engineers manages Alabama's extensive river system with locks and dams that have created numerous lakes that provide fishing, water sports, camping and hunting. Parks and a limited number of marinas rent nonmotorized aluminum boats for less than $10 a day. Motorized fishing and power-boat rentals are practically nonexistent. John H Foshee's *Alabama Canoe Rides and Float Trips* is the best source book for a canoeing vacation. Rentals are limited and cost $25 to $45 a day, including shuttle. Canoeing and rafting on many rivers is dependent on adequate rainfall and dam releases. Be sure to call in advance to check water levels.

In spite of condominiums and vacation homes built roof to roof in parts of Gulf Shores and Orange Beach, much of the shoreline remains natural, with white sandy beaches and graceful sand dunes dotted with sea oats.

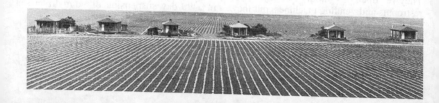

Birmingham

Birmingham (population 908,000) is the largest city in Alabama. It's also the state's most cosmopolitan city, with abundant cultural and outdoor activities and a rich dining and nightlife scene. Parks and green spaces dot the urban landscape, and farms surround the suburbs that surround the city. The University of Alabama is the city's largest employer.

When coal, iron ore and limestone – the ingredients for making pig iron and steel – were found beneath its soil in the late 19th century, Birmingham quickly grew from a small farming town at a railroad intersection into the South's foremost industrial center, earning it the moniker, the 'Magic City.' Money flowed and thousands came to get rich. Saloons, prostitution, gambling and crime raged, and the city took on a new nickname, 'Bad Birmingham.'

Simultaneously, Jim Crow legislation began segregating the city, peaking in 1915 with zoning ordinances that restricted where blacks could live and work. A year later, it was here that the Ku Klux Klan organized its first klavern in Alabama. Within 10 years it had 18,000 members, and by 1925 it had a stronghold on county politicians.

In the 1950s, blacks, especially returning servicemen, began verbalizing dissatisfaction with the status quo. Tension increased. Birmingham voted in 1954 to maintain segregated sports, shutting out professional teams from other cities which had white and black players. It became known as America's most segregated city.

White businesspeople who recognized that segregation was limiting business advocated change. Some were also worried about the impact of declining steel prices on Alabama's one-industry economy and urged diversification. Intransigent politicians refused to listen. By the 1960s race relations were smoldering and the steel industry was going into a tail spin.

HIGHLIGHTS

- The Civil Rights Institute
- The wide open spaces of Oak Mountain State Park and Tannehill Historical State Park
- The Birmingham Museum of Art's collection of masks, effigies and pre-Columbian artifacts
- The view of the city and surrounding valley at night from Vulcan Park

---

Racial tension erupted in 1963 when the commissioner of public safety, Eugene 'Bull' Connor, turned fire hoses and dogs on students marching for civil rights near Kelly Ingram Park. At the same time, he turned a blind eye to more than 50 racially motivated bombings, including the bombing of the 16th St Baptist Church, which killed four little girls. The press renamed the city 'Bombingham' and the 'Tragic City.'

Faced with disaster, newly elected politicians forced change. Within 10 years the city council was integrated and the economy had diversified. The result was greater racial harmony and a new mayor, this time black, elected in 1979. Today, Mayor Richard Arrington is serving his fifth term and the medical, banking, retail and manufacturing industries fuel the economy.

Orientation

Birmingham sits at the southern edge of the Appalachian Range, giving the city a dramatic topography, through which an interstate network weaves. It's laid out in a numerical grid with streets running north-south, avenues east-west. The railroad

ALABAMA

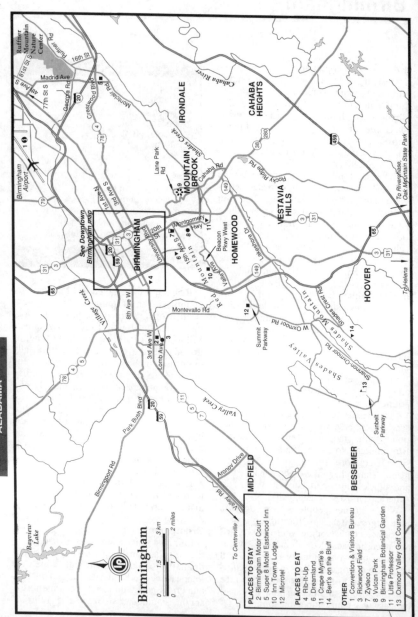

Birmingham

0   1.5   3 km
0   1   2 miles

PLACES TO STAY
2 Birmingham Motor Court
5 Super 8 Motel Eastwood Inn.
10 Inn Towne Lodge
12 Microtel

PLACES TO EAT
4 Rib-It-Up
6 Dreamland
11 Crape Myrtle's
14 Bert's on the Bluff

OTHER
1 Convention & Visitors Bureau
3 Rickwood Field
7 Zydeco
8 Vulcan Park
9 Birmingham Botanical Garden
11 Little Professor
13 Oxmoor Valley Golf Course

tracks divide the city north and south. The central north-south thoroughfare is 20th St. The wide boulevard runs from downtown's Linn Park south through Southside and Five Points South, then over Red Mountain. The major attractions are downtown. The best dining and nightlife are in Southside, either on or a few blocks off 20th St. The historic civil rights district lies between 6th Ave N and 2nd Ave N, 15th St N and 19th St N. The historic 4th Ave business district sits along 3rd, 4th and 5th Aves N between 15th and 18th Sts N.

Information

Tourist Offices There are convention and visitors bureaus in three locations. The main office (☎ 205-458-8000, 800-458-8085) is at 2200 9th Ave N and has a souvenir shop; the university branch (☎ 205-458-8001) is at 1201 University Blvd, and there is also an office at the airport (☎ 205-458-8002), on the lower level. The Historical 4th Ave Visitors & Information Center (☎ 205-328-1850), 319 17th St N, provides information and walking tours around 4th Ave, a historic black business district.

Post The main post office (☎ 205-521-0302), 351 24th St N, opens Monday at 4:30 am and remains open 24 hours a day until Saturday at 4:30 am. It's closed on Saturday and Sunday.

Media Birmingham has two daily newspapers, the morning *Birmingham Post-Herald* and the afternoon and Sunday *Birmingham News*. There's a combined edition on Saturday. The weekly *Birmingham World* has served the black community since 1930. The monthly tabloid-size *black & white* is the best source for cultural and entertainment happenings. *Birmingham* is a slick monthly magazine published by the chamber of commerce.

Bookstores Little Professor (☎ 205-870-7461), 2717 18th St S, Homewood, has a cafe and a large selection of books and international magazines. Everything in Lodestar (☎ 205-939-3356), 2020 11th

---

Bad Birmingham

During Birmingham's wild frontier days, there were more licenses issued for 'sin' businesses – pool halls, liquor outlets and tobacco shops – than regular businesses, and those were the establishments that bothered to file. Things got so bad in 1907 that a newspaper reported that more people were murdered in this town of 30,000 residents than 'in all of Great Britain with its 40 millions.' The number of arrests peaked at 11,814 that year. ■

Ave S, Southside, is related to women and women's issues. Books-A-Million has four locations, including Eastwood Mall (☎ 205-591-0573), 7703 Crestwood Blvd, each with large regional and periodical sections. Two bookstores specialize in African-American fiction and nonfiction: Yamini's Books (☎ 205-322-0037), 1417 4th Ave N, and the Civil Rights Institute Book Shop (☎ 205-328-9696), 520 16th St N.

Libraries Birmingham's central library (☎ 205-226-3600), 2100 Park Pl next to the Jefferson Courthouse, is comprised of two buildings linked by a crosswalk. The exquisite South Linn-Henley Research Library (☎ 205-226-3665), built in 1927, houses historic maps, archival manuscripts and photographs relating to regional and state history, genealogy records and numerous collections. Its contemporary partner contains the usual books, magazines and videos. The library is open Monday and Tuesday from 9 am to 8 pm, Wednesday to Saturday from 9 am to 6 pm, and Sunday from 2 pm to 6 pm.

Campuses Birmingham's biggest campus is the University of Alabama (UAB; ☎ 205-934-4011). It sprawls over Southside between 11th and 20th Sts S and 5th and 10th Aves S. Campus street signs have UAB above the street name.

Medical Services There are half a dozen hospitals, including the University of

Alabama Hospital (☎ 205-934-4011), 619 19th St S, and Hill Crest Hospital (☎ 205-833-9000, 800-292-8553), 6869 5th Ave S.

THINGS TO SEE

Birmingham Civil Rights Institute

The tribute to civil rights on display at the Civil Rights Institute (☎ 205-328-9696), 520 16th St N, downtown, will move your soul. Start with the 12-minute film introducing Birmingham from its founding to the 1920s. The Barriers Gallery shows the conditions of segregation and discrimination between 1920 and 1954 that led to confrontation. Audio, video, photography and artifacts are used to tell the story of the civil rights movement. Historic film footage shows police letting dogs loose on peaceful demonstrators. There's the actual charred shell of a bus that was burned during the Freedom Rides and the door from Reverend Martin Luther King Jr's Birmingham jail cell. The Human Rights Gallery explores the international scope of discrimination. The gift store has a broad selection of souvenirs and books. The institute is open Tuesday to Saturday from 10 am to 5 pm, and Sunday from 1 to 5 pm. Admission is $3 for adults, $2 for seniors, and $1 for college students with ID; children and those under 17 years go free.

Kelly Ingram Park

This park on 6th Ave N at 16th St N, downtown, was the site of one of Alabama's most disturbing racial incidents. Former police commissioner Eugene 'Bull' Connor guaranteed himself a page in the history books when he fired water hoses and let loose police dogs on peaceful civil rights protesters, many of whom were children, while the international press recorded it. Bull is gone, but you're reminded of his intransigence through sculptures of Martin Luther King, police dogs attacking children and children jailed with the inscription 'I am not afraid' on their cell door. It's across the street from the Civil Rights Institute and 16th St Baptist Church. Inscribed stones at the entrance to the park read, 'A Place for Revolution and Reconciliation.'

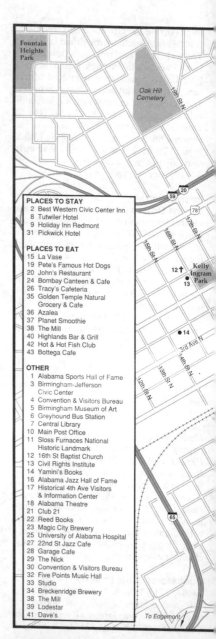

PLACES TO STAY
2 Best Western Civic Center Inn
8 Tutwiler Hotel
9 Holiday Inn Redmont
31 Pickwick Hotel

PLACES TO EAT
15 La Vase
19 Pete's Famous Hot Dogs
20 John's Restaurant
24 Bombay Canteen & Cafe
26 Tracy's Cafeteria
35 Golden Temple Natural Grocery & Cafe
36 Azalea
37 Planet Smoothie
38 The Mill
40 Highlands Bar & Grill
42 Hot & Hot Fish Club
43 Bottega Cafe

OTHER
1 Alabama Sports Hall of Fame
3 Birmingham-Jefferson Civic Center
4 Convention & Visitors Bureau
5 Birmingham Museum of Art
6 Greyhound Bus Station
7 Central Library
10 Main Post Office
11 Sloss Furnaces National Historic Landmark
12 16th St Baptist Church
13 Civil Rights Institute
14 Yamini's Books
16 Alabama Jazz Hall of Fame
17 Historical 4th Ave Visitors & Information Center
18 Alabama Theatre
21 Club 21
22 Reed Books
23 Magic City Brewery
25 University of Alabama Hospital
27 22nd St Jazz Cafe
28 Garage Cafe
29 The Nick
30 Convention & Visitors Bureau
32 Five Points Music Hall
33 Studio
34 Breckenridge Brewery
38 The Mill
39 Lodestar
41 Dave's

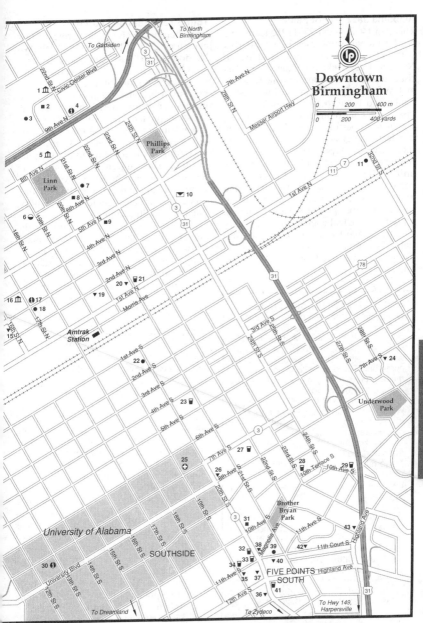

Downtown
Birmingham

0   200   400 m
0   200   400 yards

ALABAMA

Alabama Jazz Hall of Fame

This hall (☎ 205-254-2731),1631 4th Ave N, downtown, showcases jazz musicians with ties to Alabama: Dinah Washington, Nat King Cole, Duke Ellington, Avery Parrish, James Reese Europe, Erskine Hawkins and WC Handy, to name a few. Push a button and listen to Washington's velvety voice. She's one of many great jazz singers, conductors, performers and dancers you can learn about and hear in exhibits and interactive displays. Other exhibits cover the history of jazz. You'll be touched by artifacts like ticket stubs and posters from performances in the 1940s, 1950s and 1960s. The pink walls and art deco-patterned carpet give the place a vibrant, jazzy feel. The hall is in the historic Carver Theatre, where live performances are still held. Donations are accepted. It's open Tuesday to Saturday from 10 am to 5 pm, and Sunday from 1 to 5 pm.

Batter Up at Rickwood Field

What do Ty Cobb, Satchel Paige, Jackie Robinson, Willie Mays, Pie Traynor, Babe Ruth, Hank Aaron, Willie McCovey, Carl Yastrzemski, Reggie Jackson and Dizzy Dean have in common? The only ballpark in which all these great names played baseball was Birmingham's Rickwood Field.

Opened in 1910 by AH 'Rick' Woodward, a railroad and mining engineer, it's America's oldest baseball park. It served as the home field for the Birmingham Barons of the Southern Association and the Black Barons of the Negro National League. Never did the two meet, because city ordinances prohibited blacks and whites from playing together. It was also the park of the Oakland A's farm team. Professional ball left in 1989, but school and community teams still wind-up on the mound.

A multimillion dollar effort is underway to restore the venerable park to its glory days, and with it will come a museum commemorating the two old leagues and Southern baseball.

Rickwood Field (☎ 205-783-6333, 205-783-6332) is at 1137 2nd Ave W. ■

16th Street Baptist Church

Long before the civil rights protests, this church (☎ 205-251-9402), 1530 6th Ave N, downtown, was known as 'Everybody's Church,' and served as the center of black community life. During the protests it become a gathering place for meetings and marches. When racial terrorists exploded the bomb that blew up this institution and killed four little girls on September 15, 1963, Birmingham was flung into a whirlwind of social change. The church was rebuilt and today serves as a house of worship and historical landmark. Of the 100,000 visitors each year, most come for the history, but the church's stained-glass windows are worth seeing. The window at the center rear of the church depicts black Christ on a cross. It was a gift from the people of Wales. It's open Tuesday to Friday from 10 am to 4 pm. Tours are given on Saturday and by appointment. Services are held on Sunday at 11 am. Donations are welcome.

Alabama Sports Hall of Fame

Jesse Owens, Paul 'Bear' Bryant, Joe Namath, Hank Aaron and Jennifer Chandler are just a few of the inductees in this hall (☎ 205-323-6665), at 2150 Civic Center Blvd, devoted to sports legends with Alabama ties. Visits start with a 17-minute video highlighting the athletes and describing the hall. The most interesting parts are the personal artifacts donated by the athletes: Bo Jackson's Heisman trophy, Kenny Stabler's $100,000 Hickok belt, numerous athletes' Olympic gold medals and Joe Louis' fighting robe. Interactive touch-screen videos test your knowledge of sports trivia. Collegiate football occupies a lot of the space. The museum is woefully weak on women inductees primarily because the number of women competing in sports in Alabama has always been low. There's a gift shop. The hall is open Monday to Saturday from 9 am to 5 pm and Sunday from 1 to 5 pm. Admission is $5 for adults, $4 for seniors, and $3 for students.

Birmingham Museum of Art

The Birmingham Museum of Art (☎ 205-254-2565), 2000 8th Ave N, in the Southeast, has 30 galleries on three floors and a multilevel sculpture garden almost the size of a football field. Much of the permanent collection focuses on European decorative arts. The 1400-piece Wedgwood Collection is the largest in the country. Other collections feature pieces from Africa, Asia, North America and pre-Columbian Latin America. The gift shop is loaded with unusual items. The Terrace Cafe overlooks the sculpture garden and pedestrian thoroughfare, making it a great place to linger over coffee and a roasted portobello sandwich ($6.50) or crabcake ($12). The cafe hosts a jazz brunch on the first Sunday of the month. There are free museum tours four times a day on Tuesday, Thursday and weekends. It's open Tuesday to Saturday from 10 am to 5 pm, and Sunday from noon to 5 pm; closed on Monday, Thanksgiving, Christmas and New Year's Day. Entry is free.

Sloss Furnaces
National Historic Landmark

The mighty smokestacks of this massive workhorse of the 'Pittsburgh of the South' (☎ 205-324-1911), 20 32nd St N, just east of downtown, belched smoke for nearly one hundred years, supplying pig iron to feed Birmingham's steel foundries until the American steel industry buckled in the 1970s. Now it serves as a museum of industry and it's also a much-favored site for concerts, festivals and special events. There is a 10-minute show on the history and technology of iron and steel in Birmingham, and tours, often led by former employees, are also available. If you feel an unexpected chill while you're there, consider yourself visited by the ghost of Theo Jowers, a former employee who died when he fell into one of the furnaces. It's open Tuesday to Saturday from 10 am to 4 pm, and Sunday from noon to 4 pm. Tours are given on weekends at 1 pm, 2 pm, 3 pm and by appointment at other times. Admission is free.

Five Points South

A delightful sculpture by Frank Fleming called 'Cecil's Fountain,' in honor of humanitarian Cecil Johnson Roberts, is the focal point of this popular historic area, south of downtown at the intersection of 20th St S and 11th Ave S. It depicts a ram reading a book to an audience of animals. The neighborhood developed in the 1880s as one of Birmingham's first streetcar suburbs, and its heart was Five Points Circle, a major streetcar intersection. Now it has shops, restaurants, breweries and nightclubs housed in art deco buildings. The area is on the National Register of Historic Places. It has the safest ATM in town, right outside the door of the South Precinct Police Station. To reach Five Points South, take city bus No 39 (Homewood) from downtown and Homewood hotels.

Vulcan Park

Vulcan, the mythical god of fire and metalworking, towers over Birmingham from a 124-ft observation tower in Vulcan Park (☎ 205-328-6198). The park is on Montgomery Hwy, just south of Five Points South, at the top of Red Mountain. Built for the 1904 World's Fair in St Louis, the 55-foot statue is the largest iron figure ever cast. A loin cloth covers his front, but his buttocks are exposed in what locals refer to as 'Moon over Homewood,' Homewood being the small community south of the statue. The view from the observation tower is fantastic. Go at night, when the city lights up. There's a snack bar, souvenir shop and picnic area. Ask about the color of the torch he holds. It's open daily, except Christmas and Thanksgiving, from 8 am to 10:30 pm. Admission is $1.

Birmingham Botanical Garden

This 67-acre garden (☎ 205-833-8264), 2612 Lane Park Rd, about two miles southeast of Five Points South, was built on a former Native American campsite. Now it features flower beds, sculpture gardens, a conservatory housing tropicals and exotics, cactus and succulents, camellias, and orchids and ferns. The garden is open from

ALABAMA

sunrise to sunset. Sunday afternoon tours (☎ 205-939-4001), rain or shine, cover subjects like bonsai, herbs, wildlife and gardening for allergy sufferers; call in advance to book your place. It's a learning center as well, with gardens such as the Bruno Vegetable Garden, offering ideas for gardeners interested in edible landscapes, and the Thompson Enthusiast Garden, illustrating ways to garden in small spaces. There's a restaurant and gift shop. Admission is free.

Ruffner Mountain Nature Center

This 538-acre nature center (☎ 205-833-8112), at 1214 81st St S, lies within the city, only eight miles east of downtown. From downtown, the closest city bus, No 17 (Naples), drops you about five blocks away. The southern upland forest is home to native plants and animals, springs and unusual geological formations. Besides the seven miles of hiking trails, locals are attracted by the beautiful vistas the mountain affords. The best trail for views is Hawk's View Overlook (three miles roundtrip). The longest is Five Mile Trail. There's a wildflower garden at the trail head, rock quarries that show fossilized remains and some mining ruins. On weekends there are often special programs like night hikes and animal look outs. The trails and the nature center are open Tuesday to Saturday from 9 am to 5 pm, and Sunday from 1 to 5 pm. It's free, but donations are encouraged and special programs have a nominal charge.

ACTIVITIES

Alabama Small Boats (☎ 205-424-3634), 2370 Hwy 52, Helena, runs **canoeing** and **kayaking** trips. Most trips put in at Riverchase landing, just south of Birmingham, for the 10-mile paddle down the Cahaba River, the longest free-flowing river in Alabama. Highlights are the bluffs that climb 30 to 60 feet and the abundant birds and other wildlife, including turtles, fish, foxes, turkeys, herons, king fishers, ducks, geese, beavers and, on rare occasions, otters and deer. Trips depart year-round unless the water is too high or too cold, or the weather is bad. There's no white water on these peaceful nature outings. The best time to go is March to October. One-day rental is $25 for kayaks or $30 for canoes. The best deal is a three-day weekend rental for $60. Shuttle service up the river is an additional $10 per boat, but there's a discount for three or more people. Shuttles depart Tuesday to Saturday at 8 am, 9 am and 10 am; call a day in advance to reserve a seat.

Other Cahaba River outfitters include Bulldog Bend Canoe Park (☎ 205-926-7382), 65 Bibb County Rd, Centreville, which also offers camping and swimming. Cahaba Outfitters (☎ 205-969-1991), 4137 White Oak Dr, Birmingham, offers flatwater and white-water excursions.

There's no shortage of **golf** links within easy reach of metropolitan Birmingham, which boasts seven public and 15 private courses. See Oak Mountain State Park in Around Birmingham for information. Oxmoor Valley (☎ 205-942-1177), 110 SunBelt Parkway, part of the Robert Trent Jones Golf Trail, has three courses built around the forested hills and lakes. Greens fees are $64.

For details of where to go **horseback riding**, see Oak Mountain State Park in Around Birmingham .

SPECIAL EVENTS

In late January or early February the Southern Voices conference (☎ 205-444-7888) features notable regional writers and playwrights. On the second weekend in May, 20,000 spectators turn out to watch floats and dog owners with their costumed best friends celebrating the annual Do-Dah-Day, which benefits the Birmingham Humane Society. Father's Day weekend brings Birmingham's biggest bash with some 250,000 folks at Linn Park for the three-day City Stages music festival (☎ 205-251-1272) headed by big-name musicians and local talents. The first weekend in August has another biggie, the Heritage Festival (☎ 205-324-3333), celebrating the African-American community.

On the first weekend in October (unless a football game is scheduled), local and national jazz, blues and gospel artists turn up the heat at Sloss Furnaces during the Birmingham Jam (☎ 205-323-0569), a celebration of Southern culture and foods. From December 15 to 21 the Alabama Theater (☎ 205-252-2262) features a week of classic holiday movies, including *White Christmas*.

PLACES TO STAY
Camping
For camping at Oak Mountain State Park, see the park listing in Around Birmingham. The new *Birmingham South KOA Kampground* (☎ 205-664-8832), 222 Hwy 33, is luxurious by most standards. It has 125 tent and RV sites with full hookups, heated pool and spa, bathhouse, camp store, grills, cabins, phones on some sites, hiking and TV in one and two-room cabins. From Birmingham take I-65 south to exit 242 (Hwy 52). Go west on Hwy 52 to the first stoplight, which is Hwy 33, and turn north. The campground is on the right.

Hotels
Birmingham Motor Court (☎ 205-786-4397), 1625 3rd Ave W, west of downtown, has basic, inexpensive rooms and not much else. Singles/doubles are $25/$32.

A restaurant and pool put the *Super 8 Motel Eastwood Inn* (☎ 205-956-3650), 1813 Crestwood Blvd, a notch above your basic motel. The rooms are clean. It's east of downtown, near Ruffner Mountain Nature Center. Singles/doubles are $46/51.

The 102-room *Microtel* (☎ 205-945-5550), 251 Summit Parkway, Homewood, has queen beds, desks with modems, free coffee and cable movies. It's south of Southside, near Vulcan Park, halfway between downtown and Oak Mountain State Park. Rooms are $42 to $46.

Inn Towne Lodge (☎ 205-942-2031), 400 Beacon Parkway W, Homewood, offers bargain daily and weekly rates and lots of amenities. Rooms have a microwave, fridge, coffeemaker and fully equipped kitchen. There's an on-site laundry, pool

and complimentary continental breakfast. It's south of Southside, near George Ward Park and Vulcan Park. Ask for the corporate rate, which is $49 a night for a single/double or $168 a week.

The *Holiday Inn Redmont* (☎ 205-324-2101), 2101 5th Ave N, is in a historic building downtown within a few blocks of the civic center and major cultural attractions. The large rooms have refrigerator, cable TV, valet parking, airport shuttle, access to a health club, and a sidewalk cafe and restaurant. Single/doubles start from $99/$109.

Best Western Civic Center Inn (☎ 205-328-6320), 2230 Civic Center Blvd, offers good value. It's a great location for visiting downtown attractions and has spacious rooms, modems, swimming pool, complimentary breakfast and free parking. Rates are $135 to $165 for a single or double.

The *Tutwiler Hotel* (☎ 205-322-2100), 2021 Park Pl N, is Birmingham's historic grande dame. Built in 1911, it retains much of its old-world style. The rooms are spacious, especially the corner suites, and well appointed. It has a restaurant, valet parking, morning newspapers, a pub and health club. It's situated near downtown attractions, freeways and bus routes. Rooms run from $142 to $172; however, if it isn't full, rates can go as low as $89.

The lovely art deco *Pickwick Hotel* (☎ 205-933-9555, 800-255-7304), 1023 20th St S, is in Five Points South, within walking distance of some of the best restaurants, clubs and shops in the city. The rooms are bright and well appointed and the staff is cheerful. Continental breakfast is included, and so is a nightly wine and cheese reception, afternoon tea, daily newspaper and coffee. Standard/suite rates are $89/$119.

The *Wynfrey Hotel* (☎ 205-987-1600, 800-996-3739), 3000 Riverchase Galleria, I-459 at Hwy 31, offers modern luxury and services associated with a four-star hotel. It joins the glass Riverchase Galleria, the biggest mall in Alabama, and charges $99 to $185.

PLACES TO EAT
Downtown
Pete's Famous Hot Dogs (☎ 205-252-2905), 1925 2nd Ave N, has been feeding budget-minded customers in this tiny space since 1915. Pete is long gone, but his nephew still serves hot dogs for $1.10. Burgers and dogs with cheese cost $1.40. It's open daily from 10:30 am to 7 pm.

At *Rib-It-Up* (☎ 205-328-7427), 830 1st Ave N, near Arlington mansion, diners can eat in, drive through or take out lip-smackin' good barbecue beef, pork and chicken along with traditional Southern sides, salads and desserts. Sandwiches are $2 (regular) to $5 (jumbo). Complete dinners cost $3.50 to $7. There's no liquor. It's open Monday to Thursday from 10:30 am to 9 pm, and Friday to Saturday from 10:30 am to midnight.

La Vase (☎ 205-328-9327), 328 16th St N, in the historic black district, serves home-style soul food that sticks to your ribs. It's a meat and vegetable place with a choice of fried or baked chicken, pot roast, meat loaf or beef ribs with two sides. Portions are very generous and inexpensive at $5 to $6. For dessert, opt for the sweet-potato pie or pound cake. Skip the cobbler. It's open Sunday to Thursday 11 am to 7 pm, and Friday and Saturday to 8 pm.

John's Restaurant (☎ 205-322-6014), 112 21st St N, has been serving seafood to downtown customers long enough to be considered a landmark. Try the signature coleslaw. It's open Monday to Sunday from 11 am to 10 pm.

Southside
Dreamland (☎ 205-933-2133), 1427 14th Ave S, only serves pork ribs. Before you ask for something else, look at the servers' T-shirts that read 'No Slaw, No Beans, No Potato Salad. Don't ask.' The 'sandwich' ($5.50) is four ribs served with two slices of white bread on the side. It's open Monday to Thursday from 10 am to 10 pm, Friday and Saturday from 10 am to midnight, and Sunday from noon to 9 pm.

Pull up a stool at the juice bar at *Planet Smoothie* (☎ 205-933-7200), 1100 20th St S, for a healthy fresh fruit smoothie ($3 to $4), natural juice and low-fat sandwich ($3). It's open Monday to Saturday from 10 am to 9 pm and Sunday from noon to 8 pm. There's more good-for-you food around the corner at the *Golden Temple Natural Grocery & Cafe* (☎ 205-933-6333), 1901 11th Ave S. It's open Monday to Friday from 8:30 am to 7 pm, Saturday from 9:30 am to 5:30 pm and Sunday from noon to 5:30 pm.

Tracy's Cafeteria (☎ 205-252-7370), 729 20th St S, is another option for an inexpensive breakfast or lunch. Workers from neighboring medical facilities and the university keep it busy, so arrive before the noon rush. Lunch with a side, dessert and beverage will set you back about $5. It's open on weekdays from 7 am to 2:30 pm.

Bombay Canteen (☎ 205-322-1930), 2839 7th Ave S, is one of the best-value places in town. Entrées run from $6 to $8, and salads from $3.50 to $6. The 'big easy' crabcake sandwich with Louisiana lump crab meat on a toasted onion roll with roasted red pepper aioli is superb and sells out early. Veggies are cooked al dente. It's open weekdays from 11 am to 2 pm.

The Mill (☎ 205-939-3001), 1035 20th St S, is a bakery, brewery and eatery. Sit inside or take a table on the patio overlooking the Five Points South intersection. The wild mushroom and peppercorn meat loaf ($10) is a favorite. Sandwiches, served with one side, are around $6. Meals come with soup or salad and a loaf of freshly baked bread on a saucer of olive oil sprinkled with red pepper flakes and parmesan. Draft beers come fresh from their brewery. The bakery opens at 6 am with a line waiting for 15 kinds of doughnuts and 12 kinds of big, fluffy muffins ($1.50). It serves food Sunday to Wednesday from 6:30 am to 10 pm and Thursday to Saturday from 6:30 am to midnight.

Azalea (☎ 205-933-8600), 1218 20th St S, is an attractive restaurant with courteous service and a menu that's difficult to classify. The rosemary-garlic roasted chicken with Tillamook cheddar cheese grits and andouille sausage succotash ($16) is upscale traditional Southern cooking, but there are also Italian specialties. It's open Monday to Thursday from 11 am to 11 pm, Friday and Saturday from 11 am to midnight, and Sunday from 10:30 am to 10 pm.

Birmingham's upscale restaurants include the *Bottega Cafe* (☎ 205-933-2001), 2240 Highland Ave; the *Bombay Cafe* (☎ 205-322-1930), 2839 7th Ave S; the *Highlands Bar & Grill* (☎ 205-939-1400), 2011 11th Ave S; and the *Hot & Hot Fish Club* (☎ 205-933-5474), 2180 11th Court S.

Over the Mountain

You won't be considered rude if you read a book while dining at *Crape Myrtle's* (☎ 205-879-7891), 2721 18th St S, Homewood. This small cafe in the Little Professor bookstore serves up memorable soups, salads, sandwiches and home-cooked veggies for lunch and dinner. Checks average $5.50 for lunch and $8 for dinner. It's open Monday to Friday from 11 am to 8 pm, and weekends from 11 am to 3 pm (2 pm on Sunday).

Bert's on the Bluff (☎ 205-823-1217), 591 Shades Crest Rd, Hoover, serves country cooking in a cafeteria-style setting. The food is good and cheap. A veggie sampler costs around $3. It's open weekdays from 11 am to 8 pm.

ENTERTAINMENT

Everything, from Broadway plays to heavy-metal concerts, is staged at the *Birmingham-Jefferson Civic Center* (☎ 205-458-8400), 1 Civic Center Blvd between 9th and 11th Aves N. The University of Alabama (☎ 205-934-4011) presents theatrical performances, concerts and lectures at various venues.

Nightclubs

With a large population of students, Birmingham has nightlife that goes on and on and on. Check the monthly *black & white* for listings. Many of the most popular clubs are in Southside.

The Garage Cafe (☎ 205-322-3220), 2304 10th Terraces S, is a local favorite that always has good music and great deli sandwiches. During the 1920s it functioned as a garage for the wealthy folks who lived in the Highlands. Out back is the courtyard shop of architect Fritz Woehly, who collects antique architectural fittings. When there's no band, there's piped music, usually good jazz. Note the beautiful wooden doors and magnificent wisteria covering the courtyard.

It's generally acknowledged that *Dave's* (☎ 205-933-4030), 1128 20th St at Highland Ave, serves the best martinis in town. However, if the thing with the twist isn't your thing, choose one of 18 beers on tap and 60 bottled imports and microbrews, premium wines by the glass or a slew of other offerings. It's one of the most popular bars in town. Just ask the folks waiting in line outside to get in.

The rock music at *The Nick* (☎ 205-252-3831), 2514 10th Ave S, is live. The crowd is everything from creased blue-jean chic to really hard-core bikers. It's an aural experience of the best kind. Come to hear the latest, greatest really-into-the-music-scene bands, both local and touring.

Five Points Music Hall (☎ 205-322-2263), 1016 20th St S, books touring and local bands and can hold up to 1,000 people. If you don't like crowds, you won't like it here. There's a dance floor that's hot on Thursday nights, and pool tables. Enter through the back.

It's a toss-up whether people go to *Zydeco* (☎ 205-933-1032), 2001 15th Ave S, for the 76 varieties of imported and micro beers plus 13 on tap, for the Cajun-style crawfish or for the live music held Thursday to Sunday. It's a big place with two floors and a patio. You should go even if there's no live act. It claims to have the best jukebox in town.

The *22nd St Jazz Cafe* (☎ 205-252-0407), 710 22nd St S, is *the* small, dark, intimate spot to go to when you want to grab a bite to eat and hear live jazz and blues. It occasionally has flamenco music and dancers, and has a New York jazz club ambiance. It's open Wednesday to Saturday from 5 pm until it closes.

When you feel like dancin', head over to *Studio* (☎ 205-324-4500), 1036 20th St S,

ALABAMA

where Birmingham's beautiful people go. It has a great sound system. Another favored dance stop is *Club 21* (☎ 205-322-0469), 117 21st St N, which has a mixed straight and gay clientele.

The *Comedy Club* (☎ 205-444-0008), 1818 Data Dr, features live performances by well-known and aspiring stand-up comedians. Call ahead for tickets.

Brewpubs
Magic City Brewery (☎ 205-328-2739), 420 21st St S, was the first of Birmingham's brewpubs and is a hot spot with the white-collar working crowd. You can eat from a full menu, listen to music some nights or take a tour to see how the four flavors of suds are made. *Breckenridge Brewery* (☎ 205-327-3723), 1908 11th Ave S, serves everything from sandwiches to pasta, and has rich desserts and award-winning beer. *The Mill* (☎ 205-939-3001), 1035 20th St S, took third place in the 75th World Beer Championship in 1997 for its smoky mountain brown porter.

Theater
The University of Alabama's Department of Theatre performs at the *Bell Theatre* (☎ 205-934-3237), 700 13th St S. Southern Playworks, a joint UAB and Birmingham Festival Theatre series with works by Southern playwrights, also performs at the Bell Theatre. The *Birmingham Festival Theatre* (☎ 205-933-2383) is in Five Points South and has performances of unusual works. *Birmingham Children's Theatre* (☎ 205-458-8899), a professional not-for-profit theater group, has been performing for children for 50 years. Each season has several plays, each aimed at different age groups. If you have kids in tow, don't miss this one. The Alabama Symphonic Association (☎ 205-933-2336) presents performances by the *Opera Birmingham* (☎ 205-322-6737) and *State of Alabama Ballet* (☎ 205-252-2475).

Cinemas
The *Alabama Theatre* (☎ 205-252-2262), 1817 3rd Ave N, is a great movie house that's been completely restored to its original 1920s glamorous self. Along with concerts on its historic Wurlitzer organ, it shows first-run and art films and presents special events. It's open for tours on weekdays from 9 am to 4:30 pm.

THINGS TO BUY
Numerous antique shops are open along 7th Ave S between 29th St S and 23rd St S. The most notable antique stop is Reed Books (☎ 205-326-4460), 107 20th St S, where good stuff is stacked everywhere. Within the chaos, there is order, at least in the mind of owner Jim Reed. While most of the stuff is out-of-print books, magazines, calendars and ephemera, there are other collectibles as well.

Your best stop for fun and functional souvenirs is the Birmingham Shop (☎ 205-458-8000), 2200 9th Ave N, in the convention and visitors bureau. They have pens, books, cassettes, mugs and T-shirts. The Sloss Furnaces National Historic Landmark shop (☎ 205-324-1911), 20 32nd St N, carries more serious stuff to take home. Keeping with its industrial theme, it carries hand-wrought works of metal by local artists.

GETTING THERE & AWAY
Air
Birmingham international airport (☎ 205-595-0533), about five miles northeast of downtown, offers 140 flights daily, with nonstop service to 21 cities.

Bus
Greyhound (☎ 205-252-7120), 619 19th St N, north of downtown, serves a score of cities, including Atlanta ($26 one-way; seven daily); Biloxi ($58; two daily); Gadsden ($14; two daily); Guntersville ($23; two daily); Huntsville ($17; four daily); Jackson ($47; six daily); Memphis ($38; five daily); Montgomery ($16; four daily); Nashville ($27; five daily) and New Orleans ($62; three daily).

An Amtrak bus service connects Birmingham with Montgomery, Bay Minette and Mobile.

Train
Amtrak (☎ 205-324-3033), 1819 Morris
Ave, downtown, pulls in daily from New
York ($173 one-way) and New Orleans
($47 one-way), connecting Washington,
DC; Atlanta; Tuscaloosa; Meridian and
New Orleans.

GETTING AROUND
Bus
You can get around town, on weekdays
only, on buses ($1) operated by Metro Area
Express (☎ 205-521-0101), called MAX
for short, and around the central business
district on trolley-like buses (50¢) run by
DART. The Ride Store (☎ 205 328-7433)
ticket center serves both.

City bus (☎ 205-521-0101) No 20 (Zion
City) departs 10th Ave and 50th St, about
five blocks from the airport, weekdays
only, between 6:10 am and 5:23 pm. The
fare is $1.25.

Car
Avis (☎ 205-592-8901), 2023 5th Ave N,
and Budget (☎ 205-322-3596), 2301 3rd
Ave S, have offices in Birmingham. Hertz
(☎ 205-591-6090), National (☎ 205-592-
7259) and Thrifty (☎ 205-595-1900) rental-
car agencies have ticket counters at the
airport; they're downstairs next to the baggage claim area.

Taxi
For taxi service call Airport Taxi Cab
Company (☎ 205-833-8294, 888-712-8294)
or Yellow Cab (☎ 205-252-1131). Taxis to/
from the airport cost about $10 for one
person and $5 per additional person.

AROUND BIRMINGHAM
Though the city has many green spaces,
it's only a short drive outside the city to
two of the state's best parks and low mountains covered with forests.

Oak Mountain State Park
At nearly 10,000 acres, Oak Mountain
(☎ 205-620-2524) is Alabama's largest
state park. It has a lot going for it. Make
sure you don't miss **Peavine Falls** and

the Alabama Wildlife Rescue Center's
Treetop Nature Trail.

To reach Peavine Falls, hike the two-mile
trail to the top of Double Oak Mountain or
drive the four-mile circuitous dirt road to the
summit. Turn-outs on the road give great
views of Birmingham and Jefferson County.
Park at the top and hike downhill half a
mile to the falls, where you can sit atop
boulders for a view of the south valley.

The Treetop Nature Trail is a quarter-
mile elevated boardwalk that joins six ele-
phant-size cages housing injured and
aging raptors. The wildlife center (☎ 205-
663-7930) overlooking the trail has nurs-
eries and areas where you can watch
volunteers and staff members care for
injured animals.

The golf course (☎ 205-620-2522, 205-
620-2520), surrounded by wooded rolling
hills, has a driving range, pro shop, snack
bar and putting green. Green fees for nine
holes start at $9, or for 18 holes it's $13.
Cart fees range from $13 to $29, but it's a
very walkable course, so you can use a
pull cart ($3). No club rentals. Tee times
start at 7 am. Players renting park cabins
get a discount on golf/accommodation
packages.

The staff from the stables (☎ 205-663-
4030) offers guided rides through the
park's wooded rolling hills. A 90-minute
ride costs $22, a 35-minute ride is $12, and
a 20-minute ride is $10. Children can rent a
pony for $5. Reservations are essential on
weekends and in summer.

There is also a demonstration farm,
BMX and hiking trails, a lakeside beach, a
marina, a crafts center and tennis courts.

There are 131 campsites open year-
round. RV sites ($13) have electricity,
water and sewer. Tent sites ($9.50) have a
grill and picnic table. There's a bathhouse,
two laundries, a store, a playground and
plenty of shade. Ten fully equipped two-
bedroom, one-bath cabins surrounding a
45-acre lake accommodate up to eight
people and cost $95 a night. Rentals come
with a flat-bottom boat, life preservers and
a paddle. Reservations are advised, especially in summer and on weekends. There

is a two-night minimum on weekends, and a three-night minimum on major holidays. The park day-use fee is $1 per person, and 50¢ for seniors. The park information center is 15 miles south of Birmingham in Pelham. Take I-65 south to exit No 246.

Tannehill Historical State Park

Once a smoky, smoldering ironworks, this park (☎ 205-477-5711, fax 205-477-9400), 12632 Confederate Parkway, McCalla, 23 miles southwest of Birmingham, is now a serene escape. Go for the history, but you'll come away remembering the beauty of 1500 acres of tall pines and low green pastures. Amid all this nature are a dozen historic, rustic buildings transported from other parts of the state. There's hiking, camping, exploring galore, or you can sit on a rocking chair on the wooden porch of the Furnace Master's Restaurant and watch the creek flow. You can also visit the museum, ride a horse or miniature train, or talk to craftspeople in a restored cabin. On the third Saturday of each month from March to November, shoppers and traders come to Tannehill Trade Days.

Many of the hiking trails follow the historic roadways of the region, including the three-mile 1815 Stage Coach Rd, the two-mile Slave Quarters Trail, and the 2½-mile Iron Rd. All trails pass through forest with abundant wildlife and native plants.

Primitive camp sites are $7, or $11.50 with water and electricity ($3 extra for sewage). Four cabins are available for up to six or eight people; they cost $60 to $80 a night, $5 for each additional person. Bring your own linen. No credit cards are accepted.

The day-use fee for adults is $2, and $1 for children aged six to 12. It's between Birmingham and Tuscaloosa on I-59/20. Take exit No 100 (Bucksville) and follow the signs for two miles.

Northern Alabama

The northern third of Alabama, nestling in the foothills of the Appalachian Range, is covered by mountains, valleys, lakes and forests. The highest point in the state is here at Cheaha Mountain (2407 feet), but the most significant feature of the region topographically and economically is the Tennessee River. It enters the state in the northwest corner where Mississippi, Alabama and Tennessee converge, then dips south about 55 miles before turning north in a lopsided 'V' and exiting the state in the northeast corner near the intersection of Alabama, Georgia and Tennessee.

During the 1930s the Tennessee Valley Authority (TVA) built dams along the river to control flooding and to bring electricity to the poorest section of the state. In the process the 'Great Lakes of the South' were created. There are numerous parks and wildlife refuges areas surrounding the lakes, making outdoor recreational opportunities plentiful.

The most scenic area of the region is the northeast around the Little River Canyon, the deepest gorge east of the Mississippi River, near Fort Payne. The most populous city is Huntsville, famous for its space industry.

This chapter begins in Huntsville, goes west to Decatur and the Shoals, then travels southeast through the Bankhead National Forest to Cullman. It continues southeast to Anniston and Gadsden, then finishes in northeast Alabama in Guntersville, Fort Payne and Scottsboro.

HUNTSVILLE

population 170,000

This well-to-do aerospace community has the highest per capita income of any metropolitan area in the southeast. It had its high-tech beginnings in the 1950s when Senator John Sparkman brought in a group of German scientists to develop rockets for the US army. The US space program took off, attracting international aerospace-related businesses. Not surprisingly, programs at the University of Alabama Huntsville and Alabama A&M University focus on science, engineering and technology. However, the community also actively supports the arts through numerous cultural organizations and events. Huntsville has a lively club scene, making it a virtual paradise for night owls. Diners will find a pleasing combination of good ol' country cooking and international fare.

HIGHLIGHTS

- 'Roughing it' in the city by hiking in Huntsville's Monte Sano State Park, where more than 15 miles of trails pass breathtaking lookouts and waterfalls
- The view of Huntsville from Burritt Park at the summit of Round Top Mountain
- Cook's Natural Science Museum in Decatur
- Hiking the trails of Wheeler National Wildlife Refuge and watching birds from its two-story observation tower
- Touring the hip, interactive Alabama Music Hall of Fame

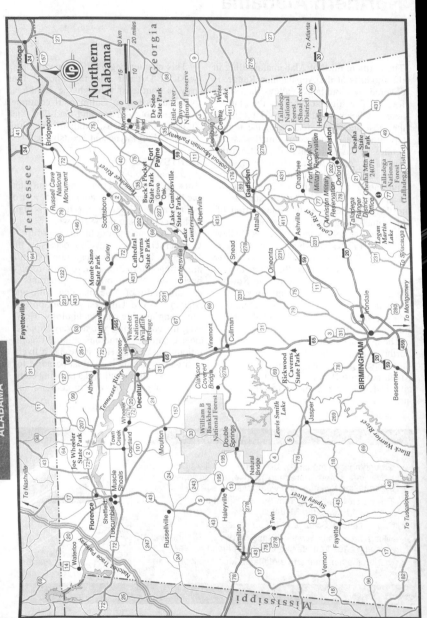

History
Huntsville was named after pioneer John Hunt, who settled here in 1805 following the removal of Creek and Chickasaw Indians. By 1819, the year Alabamians met here to petition the US Congress for statehood, it was the largest town in the Alabama Territory. Wealthy merchants and planters built lavish houses in the Twickenham area, which today has the largest collection of antebellum houses in the state. During the Civil War many residents flew Union flags over their houses, sparing Huntsville the destruction wrought on other cities in Alabama. Throughout the 1940s and 1950s it served as the Tennessee Valley's cotton-trading center. Cotton remained the primary industry and Huntsville remained a sleepy northern town of fewer than 20,000 people until the 1950s.

Orientation
Huntsville lies in the Tennessee River Valley between the Tennessee and the Tennessee River. Foothills of the Appalachian Range surround it on three sides. It lies 17 miles east of I-65. The I-565 and Hwy 72 connect I-65 with Huntsville, bringing travelers from the north, south and west. Hwys 72, 231 and 431 draw traffic from the east.

Huntsville addresses reflect the city's layout in a quadrant: NW, SW, NE, SE. The Twickenham and Old Town historic districts lie northeast of downtown, off I-565's exit 19. A new tourist trolley provides inexpensive transportation to some major attractions.

Information
Tourist Offices The convention and visitors bureau (☎ 205-551-2230, 800-772-2348, Net), 700 Monroe St, Von Braun Civic Center, is open Monday to Saturday from 9 am to 5 pm and Sunday from noon to 5 pm. The Huntsville airport branch is open Monday to Saturday from 8:30 am to 5:30 pm and Sunday from 12:30 to 6 pm.

Post The main post office (☎ 205-539-9686), 615 Clinton Ave, is open Monday to Friday from 8:30 am to 5 pm.

Bookstores Books-A-Million (☎ 205-883-1942, 205-536-1940), 975 Airport Rd SW, and 1001 Memorial Parkway NW, has a strong regional section.

Libraries The main branch of the public library (☎ 205-532-5940), 915 Monroe St, is open Monday to Thursday from 9 am to 9 pm, Friday to Saturday from 9 am to 6 pm, and Sunday from 2 to 6 pm.

Media The *Huntsville Times* is the local daily. Thursday's 'Out and About' section features entertainment and events. Many newsstands carry Birmingham, Nashville and Atlanta dailies. The alternative *Rant Magazine* covers the entertainment scene for serious night owls. Alabama A&M broadcasts university-related events open to the public on WJAB (90.9 FM). WLRH (89.3 FM) is an NPR affiliate.

Medical Services Huntsville Hospital (☎ 205-517-8020), 101 Sivley Rd SW, and Crestwood Hospital (☎ 205-882-3100), 1 Hospital Dr, off Airport Rd, provide medical care.

US Space & Rocket Center
This is a combination science museum and theme park without the hype. The center (☎ 205-837-3400, 800-637-7223), 1 Tranquility Base, exit 15 off I-565, shows IMAX films on a 67-foot domed screen, space demonstrations, exhibits of training suits worn by astronauts and a moon rock from Apollo XII, as well as half a dozen simulators and rides such as the Space Shot, which launches passengers on a 4G, 45-mph ride into weightlessness. Cheery flight-suited young men and women stationed around the center assist visitors and run shows. Be sure to volunteer at 'Outpost in Space: the International Space Station' so you'll get to experience how astronauts will sleep, eat, bathe and use the bathroom in microgravity when the real station is launched in the 21st century. An optional guided bus tour goes to NASA's Marshall Space Flight Center, stopping at the space station module

ALABAMA

Monte Sano State Park

Moores Mill Rd

Meridian St

Chase Rd

Bankhead Pkwy

Nolen Rd

Monte Sano Blvd

Burritt Drive

Carl T Jones Drive

Whitesburg Drive

Airport Rd

Madison St

see Downtown Huntsville map

Pulaski Pike

Governors Drive

Brahan Spring Park

Byrd Spring Lake

To Green Mountain Park

Jordan Lane

Bob Wallace Ave

Patton Rd

Sparkman Drive

Oakwood Rd

Wynn Drive

Boardwalk

Rideout Rd

University Drive

To Burgreen Black Cotton Gin

Redstone Arsenal
(NASA Marshall Space Flight Center)

Huntsville

MADISON

Old Madison Pike

Huntsville-Decatur Hwy

Arlington Drive

Wall Triana

To Huntsville International Airport

PLACES TO STAY
2 Dogwood Manor
4 Hampton Inn
5 Huntsville Amberley Suite Hotel
6 Budgetel Inn
10 Econo Lodge
15 Days Inn
16 Ramada Inn Space Center
18 Huntsville Marriott

PLACES TO EAT
3 Ol' Heidelberg
8 Caribbean House Restaurant
9 Fogcutter
12 Jamo's Juice & Java and More
13 The Mill
20 Cafe Berlin
22 Green Bottle Grill

OTHER
1 Alabama A&M University
7 University of Alabama Huntsville
11 Books-A-Million
14 Burritt Museum & Park
17 US Space & Rocket Center
19 Huntsville Botanical Gardens
21 Books-A-Million
23 Crestwood Hospital

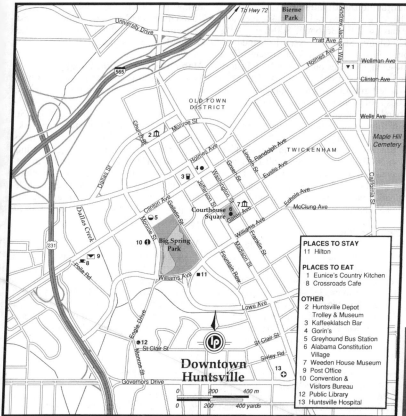

Downtown Huntsville

PLACES TO STAY
11 Hilton

PLACES TO EAT
1 Eunice's Country Kitchen
8 Crossroads Cafe

OTHER
2 Huntsville Depot
  Trolley & Museum
3 Kaffeeklatsch Bar
4 Gorin's
5 Greyhound Bus Station
6 Alabama Constitution
  Village
7 Weeden House Museum
9 Post Office
10 Convention &
  Visitors Bureau
12 Public Library
13 Huntsville Hospital

assembly building and neutral buoyancy simulator, where astronauts train for space walks. Three gift shops, a snack bar and cafeteria are on the premises. The US Space & Rocket Center is open daily from 9 am to 5 pm (until 6 pm in summer). Admission is $14 (children $10), including a tour, or it's $9 (children $6) for the exhibit only.

Huntsville Botanical Gardens

This garden (☎ 205-830-4447, fax 205-830-5314), 4747 Bob Wallace Ave, is so well designed that architectural elements like arbors, pavilions, ponds and brick-work blend naturally into the woods, creeks and hollows. Gravel and wood-chip paths follow the gentle curves of the terrain, leading to specialty gardens of annuals, day lilies, herbs, ferns and vegetables. From November to April the gardens are open Monday to Saturday from 9 am to 5 pm, and Sunday from 1 to 5 pm. From May to October they're open Monday to Saturday from 8 am to 6:30 pm, and Sunday from 1 to 6:30 pm. Admission is $2.50 (seniors $2, students and children $1).

Huntsville Depot Museum

The state's oldest railroad passenger terminal (☎ 205-535-6565, 800-678-1819), 320 Church St, served as a prison and hospital during the Civil War. Today, it's a museum focusing on Huntsville's history and the transportation industry. The Civil War left graffiti written by soldiers and the ghosts of a young woman and her boyfriend, a Confederate prisoner, who were killed by a single bullet while embracing. It's open Monday to Saturday from 9 am to 5 pm. Hours change on holidays and in winter. Tours depart every half-hour until 4 pm. Full adult admission is $6 (seniors $5, children $3.50). Save by buying a combination pass to the museum and Constitution Village.

Depot Trolley

A motorized replica of a 1920s trolley plays an interesting taped narrative as it winds through the antebellum Twickenham and Victorian Old Town historic districts on a 30-minute tour. Get off and reboard anywhere along the route. The free brochure *Historic Huntsville Walking Tour* augments the tour, which departs weekdays every 30 minutes from 10 am to 12:30 pm and 1:30 to 4:30 pm. Board the trolley outside the Huntsville Depot Museum. Adult fares cost $2 (seniors and children $1). Huntsville Depot Museum visitors pay half-price.

Alabama Constitution Village

More than 175 years ago 44 men met here to draw up the state's constitution. Today, it's a living history village (☎ 205-535-6565, 800-678-1819), 404 Madison St, with costumed guides performing tasks typical of the period and leading tours through reconstructed buildings, including Constitution Hall. It's open Monday to Saturday from 9 am to 5 pm, except in winter and on holidays. Tours depart every half-hour until one hour before closing. The gift shop is worth a stop. Admission is $6 (seniors $5, children $3.50).

Weeden House Museum

Poet and artist Maria Howard Weeden, better known as Howard Weeden, was born, lived and died in this Federal-style house (☎ 205-536-7718), 300 Gates Ave, downtown, which was built in 1819. The comprehensive collection of Weeden's art work on display garners the most attention. Her *Shadows on the Wall* appeared in 1898

Shadows on the Wall

When the book *Shadows on the Wall* by Howard Weeden appeared in 1898, the nation's press descended upon Huntsville to find the artist and poet *Mr* Weeden. The person they were seeking was, in fact, an unmarried woman named Maria Howard Weeden.

Weeden had shown an early interest in art and was taking instructions before her 10th birthday. She was shy and sickly, but had a strong belief in her talents as an artist. She wanted to travel the world to find subjects for her art, but her health prevented it, so, instead, she sought subjects from her own backyard, a decision that made her famous.

Her first 'backyard' work was a painting of a 'negro's' head to illustrate Sarah Pratt McLean Green's poem 'De Massa ob de Sheepfol.' Visitors told her, 'Your negro head is so good that you should throw away all your colors except brown.' From then on, she painted many likenesses of her friends' cooks, coachmen and mammies.

Unlike artists Edward W Kemble, who created 'Kemble's Coons,' and Arthur B Frost, who illustrated 'Uncle Remus' stories, Weeden chose not to caricature blacks, but rather to capture their kindly, loyal, proud spirit in words and pictures. Her work was shown and applauded in Berlin and Paris, then eventually published in book form by well-known New York publishers, including Doubleday.

Weeden died of tuberculosis in 1905 at the height of her popularity. Her works are in private collections and museums around the country, including the Weeden House Museum and Burritt Museum in Huntsville. ■

to great literary acclaim. It featured 11 poems and portraits of blacks as they appeared on plantations after the Civil War. It's open Tuesday to Sunday from 1 to 4 pm. Admission for adults and seniors is $2 (children $1).

Burritt Museum & Park

Much like an eagle's aerie, the beautiful Burritt Museum (☎ 205-536-2882), 3101 Burritt Dr, exit 17B off I-565, overlooks the city from the summit of Round Top Mountain. The 11-room mansion was the home of Dr William Henry Burritt, a physician and inventor who left it and 167 acres to the state. Early medical equipment, art work and pottery are exhibited. There's also a historic park with renovated 19th-century log buildings and a nature park with great trails that crisscross the estate. For a vigorous two to three-hour challenge, hike the trail that connects Burritt Park with Monte Sano State Park. The office has trail maps. The park is worth a visit if only for the commanding view of Huntsville.

The nature park is open April to September from 7 am to 7 pm, and October to March to 5 pm. From March to December the mansion and historic park are open Tuesday to Saturday from 10 am to 4 pm, and Sunday from noon to 4 pm (except Thanksgiving and the day after). Admission is charged only at the historic park and is $3 (seniors $2, children $1).

Monte Sano State Park

Monte Sano (☎ 205-534-3757) at 5105 Nolen Ave is one of Alabama's most attractive parks. Its name means 'mountain of health' and the park is a popular mountain retreat. There's a two-acre Japanese garden, an amphitheater and a slew of outdoor activities. More than 15 miles of trails cover the mountain with remarkable elevation changes, lookouts, waterfalls and training walls for rock climbing. You can easily spend a day here and go back for more. It's open daily from 8 am to 5 pm. The fee is $1.

The setting makes it a great place to stay. The campground has 20 primitive tent sites

> ## It's Cotton-Pickin' Time
>
> Throughout the 19th and well into the 20th century, cotton was picked by hand. Then it was ginned, pressed into a bale, weighed, marked and finally sent to a port city like Decatur, Montgomery or Mobile, where it was shipped to a mill. Burgreen Black Cotton Gin, west of Huntsville, is a thriving cotton gin that allows visitors a glimpse of the modern cotton industry. You can see how cotton is processed, then go out into the field and hand-pick a boll of cotton, a step that mostly is done by machine nowadays. The gin is open for visits from September to November. Visitors should set up an appointment with Dewanda Black (☎ 205-232-2875), 29484 Huntsville Browns Ferry Rd, Madison. From Huntsville, take Hwy 72 west to the Limestone Flea Market; turn left on Burgreen Rd and continue straight ahead for 1¼ miles. The firm runs a restaurant, *Wendells B&B* (☎ 205-232-2955), next door; note that the 'B&B' stands for Burgreen and Black, not bed and breakfast. Catfish is the favorite dish, unless it's the weekend, when the rib-eye special steals the show. Lunch costs $5.50 and dinner is $10. ∎

and 85 improved tent and RV sites, including 20 with full hookups. Primitive sites are $6, improved sites $11 to $12. There are 14 fully equipped rustic cabins that rent for $45 a night.

Hiking

You'll find plenty of excellent hiking within the city and just beyond its limits. The combined trails in Monte Sano State Park and Burritt Park offer more than 25 miles of challenging and relaxing hiking (see the park entries). Twelve miles south of downtown on South Shawdee Rd, Green Mountain Park (☎ 205-883-9501) features the lovely wooded 1½-mile Madison County Nature Trail. The park also has two other trails and a 16-acre lake with a covered bridge. It's open weekdays from 7 am to 7 pm, and weekends from 8 am to 7 pm; entry is free.

ALABAMA

Special Events
The city's biggest event, Panoply of the Arts (☎ 205-533-6565), is a three-day outdoor arts festival held the last weekend of April. In April and December the Huntsville Pilgrimage Association (☎ 205-533-5723, 800-772-2348) conducts tours of historic houses in the Twickenham and Old Town districts. The Indian Heritage Festival is celebrated the third Saturday in October. The Tennessee Valley Jazz Society (☎ 205-858-0409) sponsors the five-day Jazz-N-June outdoor concert series the first weekend in June. The Big Spring Jam (☎ 800-772-2348) attracts more than 100,000 folks to Big Spring Park, with national musicians performing on the last weekend in September.

Places to Stay
Camping For camping at Monte Sano State Park see the park entry.

Ditto Landing (☎ 205-882-1057, 800-552-8769), Hobbs Island Rd off Hwy 231, occupies 60,000 acres along the Tennessee River. The campground is densely wooded and there are 26 improved sites with hookups. The rate is $10 a night.

Hotels & Motels Rooms at the *Econo Lodge* (☎ 205-534-7061), 3772 University Dr NW, near Hwy 231/431, are furnished in somber colors, but it has free movies, a pool with patio tables and lounge chairs, and complimentary coffee in the lobby. Rooms cost $30/45 for a single/double.

The three-floor, 102-room *Budgetel Inn* (☎ 205-830-8999), 4890 University Dr NW, serves complimentary continental breakfast. There's a pool and rooms have modem data ports. You'll pay $40/42 for a single/double.

Rooms at the *Ramada Inn Space Center* (☎ 205-772-0701), 8716 Hwy 20W, Madison, are larger than usual and there's a nice pool, tennis court, seafood restaurant and lounge. It's near the airport. The rate is $40/50.

Days Inn (☎ 205-772-9550), 102 Arlington Dr, Madison, offers complimentary continental breakfast, airport shuttle, free

movie channel, VCR rentals and an outdoor pool. It's conveniently located between the airport and US Space Center. Its singles/doubles are $46/52 and suites cost $75.

The 164-room *Hampton Inn* (☎ 205-830-9400), 4815 University Dr NW, is within two miles of the US Space Center and offers complimentary continental breakfast and privileges at a nearby health club. Relax in the whirlpool or outdoor pool in summer. Rooms have free movies and modem ports. Single/doubles are $54/56.

Though it's oriented toward business travelers, the *Huntsville Amberley Suite Hotel* (☎ 205-837-4070), 4880 University Dr NW, has an at-home feel. It's loaded with amenities including fitness center, pool, sauna, restaurant, lounge, ministore, coffeemakers and hair dryers, and there's an airport shuttle. The rate is $71/83.

Its location next to the US Space Center makes the *Huntsville Marriott* (☎ 205-830-2222), 5 Tranquility Base, exit 15 off I-565, popular with business and family travelers. It has attractive rooms and suites, free movies, a cafe, fancy restaurant, lounge, games room, pool, sun deck and fitness center. Singles are $109 and one-bedroom suites are $275. Some discounts apply.

Rooms in one wing of the *Hilton* (☎ 205-533-1400), 401 Williams Ave, surround an attractive atrium, while others overlook a pool. The property is downtown across from Big Spring Park. There's a restaurant, piano bar, exercise center and a popular nightclub. Room rates range from $79 to $125. Ask about off-peak discounts.

Inns & B&Bs *Dogwood Manor* (☎ 205-859-3946), 707 Chase Rd, is a restored historic home that's a 10-minute drive from downtown Huntsville. Three guest rooms have queen-size beds and private baths. Two rooms have a fireplace. There's an upstairs sun porch, a library and a new bridal suite. A full breakfast is included in the $75 rate (honeymoon suite $85).

Places to Eat
Northwest Huntsville You'd have to go to Germany to get schnitzels, sauerbratens and

wursts more authentic than those at *Ol' Heidelberg* (☎ 205-922-0556), 6125 University Dr NW. Expect to pay around $8 for lunch and $6 to $15 for dinner. It's open Sunday to Thursday from 11 am to 9 pm, and Friday and Saturday from 11 am to 10 pm.

The first thing you notice at *Fogcutter* (☎ 205-539-2121), 3805 University Dr NW, is the low lighting and solid furniture. Things have been this way since the 1970s when it opened. The fare – good steaks and seafood – hasn't changed either, making it one of Huntsville's most popular restaurants. Lunch is $10 to $12, dinner $20 to $25. It's open Monday to Friday for lunch and dinner, Saturday for dinner only, and Sunday for brunch (11 am to 3 pm) and dinner.

University While not strictly vegetarian, *Jamo's Juice and Java and More* (☎ 205-837-7880), 413 Jordan Lane, is the closest you'll find in Huntsville. A bowl of Sherpa rice (red lentils, rice and barley) is served plain ($2) or with big bang vegetarian chili or vegetables ($3.50). There's live entertainment Thursday, Friday and Saturday nights. You can eat in or take-out. It's open Monday to Thursday from 7 am to 9 pm, Friday from 7 am to midnight, Saturday 9 am to midnight, and Sunday from 9 am to 9 pm.

The small, laid-back *Caribbean House Restaurant* (☎ 205-837-1474), 2612 Jordan Lane, features authentic island-style foods like jerk chicken, roti and curries. Vegetarians will feel right at home as there are lots of vegetable sides and vegan dishes. Checks average $5.50 and you can eat in or take-out. It's open Sunday from 11:30 am to 7 pm, Monday to Thursday from 11 am to 8 pm and Friday from 11 am to 3 pm.

Downtown & Environs Only the oldest Huntsvillians can remember when *Eunice's Country Kitchen* (☎ 205-534-9550), 1006 Andrew Jackson Way, wasn't serving biscuits and gravy, country ham, and grits and eggs. It's a make-yourself-at-home place where you pour your own coffee. Lots of celebs, politicians and families pass through these doors. Full breakfast costs $3.50 to $6,

and hamburgers are $2. It's open Wednesday to Monday from 5 am to noon.

The *Crossroads Cafe* (☎ 205-533-3393), 721 Clinton Ave, Market Square Mall, has can't-be-beat prices on hot and cold delistyle sandwiches. They even serve peanut butter and jelly ($1.50). With chips and a soft drink, a satisfying meal will cost $3.50 to $5. Food is served weekdays from 11 am to midnight, and weekends from 6 pm to midnight.

The Mill (☎ 205-534-4455), at 2003 Whitesburg Dr at Governors Dr, combines a bakery, eatery and brewery into a popular meeting spot. Salads range from $3 for a small caesar to $6 for southwest chicken. Soups are $1 a cup or $2.50 a bowl. It's open daily 6:30 am to 10 pm.

Southwest Huntsville The *Cafe Berlin* (☎ 205-880-9920), 975 Airport Rd, Westbury Square, is a little piece of Europe. It has German music and, of course, German fare on the menu, albeit adjusted a little lighter for American palates. The chicken Berlin is a consistent favorite. Locals and business travelers keep it busy. Checks average $10 to $15 for lunch, and up to $25 for dinner. It's open Sunday to Thursday from 11 am to 9 pm, and Friday and Saturday from 11 am to 10 pm.

The *Green Bottle Grill* (☎ 205-882-0459), 505 Airport Rd, Westbury Square, is where Huntsvillians dine on special occasions. The à la carte menu sometimes features venison and grilled yellowfin tuna. Lunch checks range from $10 to $15, dinner checks from $35 to $55. There's an impressive wine list. It's open for lunch Monday to Friday and for dinner Monday to Saturday.

Entertainment

The *Alabama Film Makers Co-op* (☎ 205-539-3456), shows art and documentary films and videos, often presented by the filmmaker. Locations vary.

The hot rock *Crossroads Cafe* (☎ 205-533-3393), 721 Clinton Ave, Market Square Mall, brings in local, regional and national acts on Friday and Saturday nights with a

ALABAMA

cover of $3 to $6, plus some good local solo acts and bands from Tuesday to Thursday. It has exceptional made-to-order sandwiches.

In other cities, *Gorin's* (☎ 205-534-3848), 101 Washington St NE, serves ice cream and light fare. Huntsville's Gorin's is as much about music as it is treats. This intimate cafe/club has live entertainment on Wednesday, Friday and Saturday from 9 pm. Acts are primarily rock. Thursday is open-mike night. On Sunday local bands rule the stage. The cover charge varies.

Kaffeeklatsch Bar (☎ 205-536-7993), 103 Jefferson St N, features rock and blues. The groups are primarily touring acts, but some good local talent also performs. It's the home of Microwave Dave and the News and is the place for serious music fans, especially blues listeners. Great pizzas are served nightly. Shows start at 8 pm on weekdays, 9 pm on weekends. Occasionally there's a $5 cover charge.

The *Main Stage Players* (☎ 205-539-7529), Round the Corner Theater, 214 Holmes Ave, stage several original productions of high-caliber community theater a year. There are evening performances Wednesday to Saturday at 8 pm and matinees on Sunday at 2 pm.

Huntsville's *Community Ballet Association* (☎ 800-277-1700) puts on company productions and hosts guest dance troupes. The *Huntsville Symphony Orchestra* (☎ 205-539-4818) presents classical, pop and chamber series. The *Huntsville Community Chorus Association* (☎ 205-533-6606) also hosts a season of concerts and musicals. The *Tennessee Valley Jazz Society* (☎ 205-858-0409) presents concerts, lectures and special events. The *Huntsville Opera Theater* (☎ 205-881-4796) performs three full-length operas each season. The city has an active arts council (☎ 205-533-6565), which provides fine-arts information and an extensive calendar.

Getting There & Away

Air Huntsville international airport (☎ 205-772-9395), at 1000 Glenn Hearn Blvd, Madison, just west of Huntsville exit 7 on I-565, is served by American, Delta, Northwest, US Airways and several commuter lines.

Bus Greyhound (☎ 205-534-1681), 601 Monroe St NW, serves Atlanta ($33; three daily), Birmingham ($16; three), Chattanooga ($51; four), Decatur ($10; four), Mobile ($59; three), Montgomery ($41; three), Nashville ($24; four) and New Orleans ($74; two).

Car Taking I-65 and I-565 you can drive to Huntsville from Birmingham or Nashville in a little over two hours, or Decatur in 30 minutes. More scenic, slower US and state highways link Huntsville with the same cities as well as Cullman, on Hwy 31, which is an hour south, and the Shoals, on Hwy 72, an hour west.

Alamo, Avis, Budget, National and Hertz have rental counters at the airport. The following have offices in town: American (☎ 205-772-3176), 8884 B Hwy 20W, Madison; Avis (☎ 205-772-9301, 205-539-8483), 3154 University Dr; Thrifty (☎ 205-772-9653), 9300 Hwy 20W; and Enterprise (☎ 205-971-0025), 6125 University Dr.

Getting Around

Bus Huntsville Shuttle System (☎ 205-532-RIDE, 205-532-7433) provides public transportation hourly on nine routes Monday to Friday from 6 am to 6 pm. The one-way fare is $1 for adults and 50¢ for seniors and students; free transfers are provided. A new tourist trolley serves downtown attractions, the Von Braun Civic Center, the botanical gardens and the US Space Center. The fare is $1 or $2 for a one-day pass.

A shuttle service, Executive Connection (☎ 205-772-0186), has a counter at the airport near baggage claim. Rates to downtown are $15 to $20. Travelers with reservations are served first.

Taxi Huntsville Cab (☎ 205-539-8288) and United Deluxe Cab (☎ 205-536-3600, 205-534-9213) offer taxi services. Taxis from the airport cost around $15 to $20.

Top Left: Old Alabama Town shotgun house, Montgomery, AL
Bottom: Museum of Fine Arts, Montgomery, AL

Top Right: Statue of Noccalula at Noccalula Falls Park, Gadsden, AL

Top Left: Talladega Scenic Drive, Talladega
National Forest, Heflin, AL
Bottom: De Soto Falls, De Soto State Park,
Fort Payne, AL

Top Right: Oak Mountain State Park, Birmingham, AL
Middle Right: Tennessee River, Decatur, AL

MOORESVILLE

Incorporated in 1818, Mooresville, six miles east of Decatur and 14 miles west of Huntsville, predates Alabama's admission to the Union (1819). Disney recognized that not much had changed in Mooresville over the years; the studio filmed the movie *Tom & Huck: The Adventures of Tom Sawyer and Huck Finn* here. Towering trees, small gardens, green lawns, picket fences and historic houses cover the town's 160 acres. The only public building is the post office, which still uses the original boxes dating from 1840.

In May of every odd-numbered year, residents don period costumes for a festival and give walking tours of the town, but you can take a self-guided tour at any time. Start at the old **Stagecoach Inn & Tavern** (1825), said to be the oldest in the state. It's the first building on your left as you enter town off I-565. This is not its original location. Among the other notable structures are **McNiell House** (1825), on the corner of Piney and Market St, where President Andrew Johnson served as a tailor's apprentice when he was a young man, and the **Church of Christ**, where General James Garfield – later the 20th US president – preached sermons while the Union army was camped nearby. A tourist office brochure describes significant houses. It's available from Alabama Mountain Lakes Tourist Association (☎ 205-350-3500, 800-648-5381, fax 205-350-3519, Net), 25062 North St, PO Box 1075, Mooresville, AL 35649; and the Decatur convention and visitors bureau (☎ 205-350-2028, 800-524-6181), 719 6th Ave SE, PO Box 2349, Decatur, AL 35602.

DECATUR

population 52,000

The creation of the TVA greatly influenced Decatur, which sits on the south bank of the Tennessee River. Wheeler Dam, part of the TVA system, created the 104-sq-mile Wheeler Lake reservoir, which brought industry and recreation to Decatur's front door. Textile and chemical companies looking for power, labor and river access first arrived in the 1950s and continue, along with agribusiness, to drive the economy of this town. A score of Fortune 500 companies have plants here, mainly on the west side. The dam also created wetlands, 54 sq miles of which are Wheeler National Wildlife Refuge on the town's right flank. Residents know when winter and spring arrive by the quacking and honking of tens of thousands of ducks and geese migrating to and from the refuge. The migration peaks between mid-December and mid-January.

History

Decatur was created on the south bank of the Tennessee River in the early 1820s to honor US naval commodore Stephen Decatur for his bravery in the War of 1812. Prosperity came with the opening of the Old State Bank in 1833 and the arrival of the Tuscumbia railroad, both of which proved almost fatal during the Civil War when Union and Confederate forces recognized Decatur's strategic importance and took turns burning it. When the fighting was over, only four buildings remained, but the town was quickly rebuilt.

Orientation & Information

The I-65 skirts Decatur on the east, bringing travelers from the north and south. Drivers from the east and west enter the city on Hwy 72/Hwy 20. Street addresses reflect the town's division into four geographic areas: NW, NE, SE and SW. Moulton St divides the town north and south and the railroad tracks divide it east and west. Sixth Ave is the same as Hwy 31.

The convention and visitors bureau (☎ 205-350-2028, 800-524-6181, Net) is at 719 6th Ave SE (Hwy 31). Books-A-Million (☎ 205-350-3535), 1682 Beltline Rd SW (Hwy 67), Beltline Plaza, has a large regional section. It's open from 9 am to 11 pm daily. Wheeler Basin Regional Library (☎ 205-353-2993) is at 504 Cherry St NE. The *Decatur Daily* and dailies from Birmingham and Atlanta are available on newsstands. Decatur General Hospital (☎ 205-341-2000), 1201 7th St SE, handles medical emergencies and routine care.

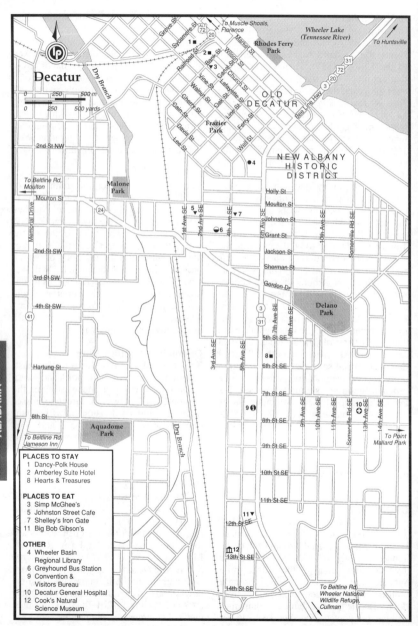

Decatur

To Muscle Shoals, Florence

Wheeler Lake (Tennessee River)

To Huntsville

Rhodes Ferry Park

OLD DECATUR

NEW ALBANY HISTORIC DISTRICT

Malone Park

Frazier Park

To Beltline Rd, Moulton

Delano Park

Aquadome Park

To Beltline Rd, Jameson Inn

To Beltline Rd, Wheeler National Wildlife Refuge, Cullman

PLACES TO STAY
1 Dancy-Polk House
2 Amberley Suite Hotel
8 Hearts & Treasures

PLACES TO EAT
3 Simp McGhee's
5 Johnston Street Cafe
7 Shelley's Iron Gate
11 Big Bob Gibson's

OTHER
4 Wheeler Basin Regional Library
6 Greyhound Bus Station
9 Convention & Visitors Bureau
10 Decatur General Hospital
12 Cook's Natural Science Museum

ALABAMA

Historic Districts

The city has two historic districts, Old Decatur and New Albany Historic District, with buildings dating from 1829 to 1939. If you like architecture, this is a great place to see many fine buildings. You can walk the six square blocks of New Albany Historic District, stopping for lunch along the way or picnicking in Delano Park at 10th Ave and Gordon Dr.

It's better to drive through Old Decatur and then picnic at Frazier Park, on the corner of Line and Cherry Sts, or Rhodes Ferry Park, at Canal St on the Tennessee River. The latter has a pavilion and benches, where you can eat and watch river traffic pass.

Most of the buildings on both tours are private homes, but a few are B&Bs, restaurants, churches or businesses. Walking tours are detailed in the brochure *A Walking Tour of Historic Decatur*, available free from the convention and visitors bureau. Roughly, the districts lie between the river and Railroad St, Lee St, 1st Ave, Gordon Dr (Hwy 24) and Somerville Rd. Hwy 31 (6th Ave) runs through the middle.

Cook's Natural Science Museum

John Cook started collecting bugs when training the employees at his pest-control company 35 years ago. Word of the collection spread and children and teachers dropped by to see the insects. Overwhelmed by visitors, Cook built this science center (☎ 205-350-9347), 412 13th St SE, in 1980 and expanded it to include insects, birds, animals, seashells, coral, stones and fossils. Animals are displayed in a natural setting with an informative description. There are interactive exhibits as well. The most amusing exhibit is the collection of mousetraps; the most beautiful is the semiprecious stones and geodes; and the most unusual, a display on the damage that insects and rodents inflict. Opening hours are 9 am to 5 pm (closed noon to 1 pm), Monday to Saturday, and 2 to 5 pm on Sunday. It closes for one week in September for cleaning. Admission is free.

Point Mallard

One of the loveliest spots along the river is this 750-acre city-owned water and recreation theme park (☎ 205-350-3000, 800-669-9283) at 1800 Pt Mallard Dr. While it's open year-round, the busiest time is Memorial Day to Labor Day, especially at the 30-acre aquatic center, which has a sandy beach on Flint Creek, waterslides, an Olympic-size swimming pool and a wave pool.

The campground (☎ 205-351-7772, fax 205-351-7951) has 210 improved sites in a wooded area. Tent and RV sites cost $12 and have electricity and water. RVs pay an additional $1 for sewer and $2 for air. There's a laundry, bathhouse and grocery store. This is a family place with lots of children running around.

Wheeler National Wildlife Refuge

This 34,500-acre refuge was established in 1938 as a wintering home for ducks, geese and other migratory birds. It encompasses wetlands, bottomland hardwoods, pine uplands, agricultural fields and backwater embayments on both sides of the Tennessee River from Huntsville to the Elk River. From mid-December to mid-February as many as 120,000 ducks and geese winter here. The rest of the year local waterfowl and tardy migrants visit. Early morning and late afternoon are the best times to see the birds.

The visitor center (☎ 205-350-6639), Hwy 67, two miles west of I-65, shows a 10-minute video and provides a map showing the refuge's walking trails, boat landings, fishing piers and boardwalks. There is also a fascinating working beehive at the visitor center. The observation tower on Flint Creek is a two-story wooden structure with floor-to-ceiling observation windows on each floor. The 1½-mile Flint Creek Environmental Trail crosses marsh and woodlands.

From October to February the visitor center is open daily from 10 am to 5 pm; the rest of the year it's open Wednesday to Sunday from 10 am to 5 pm. Trails are open from sunrise to sunset year-round. Entry is free.

Activities
The 25-yard indoor swimming pool at
Aquadome Park (☎ 205-351-7793), 5th
Ave at 8th St SW, is open weekdays from 1
to 3 pm and weekends from 1 to 4 pm.
Admission is 75¢ (children 50¢). Jay's
Landing Marina (☎ 205-350-4722) rents
out pontoon boats ($130 a day) on Wheeler
Lake from May to September. There's
hiking at Wheeler Wildlife Refuge and
Point Mallard Park. There are golf courses
at Point Mallard Park (☎ 205-351-7776)
and Cedar Ridge (☎ 205-353-4653).

Special Events
On Memorial Day weekend the Alabama
Jubilee Hot-Air Balloon Festival lifts off
with races, an arts and crafts show and
entertainment. Held on Labor Day weekend
at Point Mallard Park, the September Skirmish is a Civil War re-enactment with more
than 200 soldiers. On the second Saturday
in December, owners of four houses in the
historic district open them to the public for
candlelight tours.

Places to Stay
Camping See the Point Mallard Park entry
for details.

Hotels & Motels The *Economy Inn*
(☎ 205-353-8194), 3424 6th Ave SE (Hwy
31), is a basic hotel with few frills other
than a pool. Singles/doubles are $26/32.

The *Knights Inn* (☎ 205-355-0190, 800-
660-0730), 3429 6th Ave SE (Hwy 31), is
an older property but was recently renovated and offers good value for budget-
minded travelers. There's a pool and a bar
and grill that serves sandwiches, hamburgers and fried foods. Singles/doubles
are $36/38.

The *Jameson Inn* (☎ 205-355-2229),
2120 Jameson Place SW (just off Beltline
Rd/Hwy 67) has clean, nicely decorated
rooms, some with reclining chairs. Amenities include free *USA Today* on weekdays,
continental breakfast and coffee, and use of
an exercise room and pool. The basic rate
is $55/59, but discounts and specials some-
times drop the rate to $45/49.

The *Amberley Suite Hotel* (☎ 205-355-
6800, 800-288-7332), 807 Bank St NE,
has large rooms, plus suites with microwaves, refrigerators, coffeemakers and hair
dryers. There's a pool, fitness room, whirlpool, sauna, restaurant, deli store (with
imported beers and snacks to go) and
lounge. It's a comfortable, no-nonsense,
business-oriented hotel. Rates are $65/75.

Inns & B&Bs *Dancy-Polk House* (☎ 205-
350-3601), at 901 Railroad St, one of
Decatur's best known landmarks, was
built in 1829. It's beautifully restored and
furnished with antiques and has a display
of Civil War artifacts. It's across from the
railroad tracks. Singles and double rooms
are $59.

Hearts & Treasures (☎ 205-353-9562,
pager 205-351-3558), 911 7th Ave SE, has
an inviting porch and five guest rooms with
antique furnishings. Three have private
baths, while two have a sink and toilet, but
share a shower and whirlpool bath. Owner
Lukie Pressley provides fluffy bathrobes
for the trip down the hall. There's no
smoking. Rates, which include a big breakfast, are $60/72 for a single/double.

Places to Eat
There are fast-food chains on Beltline Rd
(Hwy 67) and 6th Ave (Hwy 31).

McCollum's Catfish & Seafood (☎ 205-
353-9321), 2057 Gordon Terry Parkway
(Hwy 24), serving delicious, inexpensive
seafood, chicken and steaks, has been in the
same location for 35 years. Lunch and
dinner prices start at $4. A small fish platter
with two fillets, potatoes and trimmings
costs $7. It's open Tuesday to Saturday
from 8 am to 9 pm. Locals like to drop by
early for coffee, but no breakfast is served.

Simp McGhee's (☎ 205-353-6284), 725
Bank St NE, in the Old Decatur historic
district, specializes in seafood. You can get
shrimp half a dozen ways, fish too. The
Cajun shrimp sauté is spicy but not overly
hot. Expect to pay $15 to $22. It's open for
dinner Monday to Saturday.

What sets *Big Bob Gibson's* (☎ 205-350-
6969), 1715 6th Ave SE (Hwy 31), and

2520 Danville Rd SW (☎ 205-350-0404), apart is the hickory-wood pit barbecue used to cook the beef, pork, chicken and turkey. Choose between three barbecue sauces: traditional red (tangy and spicy), white (tart and peppery) and dry (hot and dry). The prices are pretty good, too. Sandwiches cost around $2. It's open daily from 9:30 am to 8:30 pm; drive through or eat in.

The very popular *Johnston St Cafe* (☎ 205-350-6715) is in an unpretentious location in a basement at 115 Johnston St SE in the New Albany Historic District. Order a lunch to go and picnic in the park. Dinner features the likes of stuffed prawns and Szechuan rack of lamb, and prices range from $12.50 to $18. It's open Monday to Wednesday from 8 am to 5:30 pm, and Thursday to Saturday from 8 am to 10 pm.

Shelley's Iron Gate (☎ 205-350-6795), 402 Johnston St SE, is in a Queen Anne-style brick house converted into a restaurant. Choose from sandwiches, salads and casseroles, and eat inside or on the porch. Checks average $7 to $8. It's open Monday to Saturday from 11 am to 2 pm.

Getting There & Away

Air Huntsville international airport (☎ 205-772-9395), 1000 Glenn Hearn Blvd, is served by major carriers.

Bus Greyhound (☎ 205-353-5554), 215 Grant St SE, provides transportation from Decatur to Atlanta ($47; five times a day), Birmingham ($17; four), Huntsville ($10; five), Memphis ($58; four), Montgomery ($36; four), Nashville ($28; four) and other cities.

Executive Connection (☎ 205-772-0186, see Huntsville Getting There & Away) provides airport shuttles to Decatur for $18 to $32, depending on where you need to go.

Car From Huntsville, Decatur is a pleasant, scenic 30-minute drive west on I-565, passing parts of the Wheeler National Wildlife Refuge, Mooresville and cotton fields that are at different times copper-colored (when they're plowed), verdant (before the bolls open) and snowy (once

the bolls open). From the Shoals east on Hwy 72/20, the 45-minute drive is equally beautiful, as most of the trip passes farms and small towns such as Courtland and Wheeler. A slightly longer but scenic trip from the Shoals is to take Hwy 72/2 west along the Tennessee River's north bank, passing through Joe Wheeler State Park, then heading south across the river on Hwy 31 or I-65 into Decatur. The most leisurely route from Birmingham is on Hwy 31 north, which parallels I-65 most of the drive. Stop in the small Rickwood Caverns State Park or Cullman along the way. On I-65 the trip takes two hours. On Hwy 31 estimate three hours without stops.

The major rental-car agencies have counters at Huntsville airport. Enterprise (☎ 205-340-1550) has an office at 3325 Hwy 31S and Hertz (☎ 205-353-9110) is at 2410 Beltline Rd SW.

Getting Around

Bus Morgan County Area Transportation System (MCATS; ☎ 205-351-4652) offers local bus services on demand for $1 per trip ($8 for a book of 10 tickets). It operates weekdays from 8 am to 4 pm. You'll need to call the day before to make your booking.

Taxi Two cab companies provide service: Cater Cab (☎ 205-350-2202) and River City Yellow Cab (☎ 205-350-6949).

DECATUR TO THE SHOALS

The Shoals are west of Decatur on Alt Hwy 72/Hwy 20. The countryside is beautiful and has historic landmarks worth visiting. In spring the landscape is limeade green with plots of deeply plowed copper-colored soil waiting to be planted with cotton. By late summer the landscape is a checkerboard of green and white, referred to as summer snow.

Wheeler Plantation

This 50-acre plantation (☎ 205-637-8513), 12280 Hwy 20 (Hwy 72), Wheeler, is 15 miles west of Decatur. It's the former home of General Joseph 'Fightin' Joe' Wheeler,

ALABAMA

a congressman and one of the youngest generals in the Confederate Army. The plantation is undergoing much needed renovation, but the main house is open for tours. Resident curator Melissa Beasley stops mowing the lawn or cutting kudzu away from the 12 historic buildings to lead tours. On tours of the outside, you'll be joined by Beasley's two big black dogs and painted pony, one of the many horses that graze in the front pasture. There's a Christmas open house and a fall Civil War re-enactment. It's open Monday to Saturday by appointment, because Melissa is usually outside working, and Sunday from 1 to 5 pm. Admission is $4 for adults and $2 for children.

If you're heading east, grab a bite to eat at local favorite *Sonny's BBQ* (☎ 205-355-5590), located on Hwy 72/Hwy 20, four miles east of the plantation, on the north side of the road. Wheeler is in Lawrence County, a dry county, so no alcohol is served at restaurants.

Courtland

Midway between Decatur and the Shoals, just off Hwy 72/20, Courtland is a small town almost untouched by time. When cotton-planters from Virginia and the Carolinas arrived around 1818, they found good soil and a major waterway nearby. The planters built grand houses reflecting the style of their native states. Within one square mile, there are 27 early houses that belonged to merchants and cotton farmers, along with Victorian, colonial revival and bungalow-style houses and buildings. You can see them all on a driving tour outlined in a free brochure available from the Decatur convention and visitors bureau and the Courtland town hall (☎ 205-637-2707, fax 205-637-9336), 361 College St. Stop to walk through the cemetery, which has intricately carved angels, Greek Revival obelisks and other unusual funerary sculptures.

The lovely Federal-style *McMahon-Trotter House* (☎ 205-637-2137) at 833

Cotton Fever

Following the 1816 Treaty of Fort Jackson and the cession of Indian lands to the US, Alabama's cotton rush began. Like the California gold rush of 1849, tens of thousands of fortune hunters poured into the state, clearing land, planting, and making fortunes selling cotton to English and American mills. By 1849 Alabama was the country's leading cotton producer, holding a 23% market share.

Indeed, cotton was king in Alabama, but the king was ruthless. Overplanting depleted nutrients from the land and it was labor intensive – between 1820 and 1860 Alabama's population rose from 127,000 to 964,000, with nearly half being slaves who worked the fields.

The Civil War was a major setback for the cotton industry. By the end of the war, the economy was a disaster. Believing cotton would pull them out of postwar economic ruin, Alabama's farmers rushed to plant more cotton and returned to a single-crop economy. Large landowners instituted sharecropping and tenant farming to replace the slave labor force. However, this new form of bondage proved no less cruel. It left the poor black and white sharecroppers and tenant farmers struggling and indebted, and made merchants, bankers and large landowners rich. For the next 45 years cotton reigned again.

It wasn't until 1911 that cotton was dethroned. It took the boll weevil less than five years to bring down the cotton industry, permanently altering the Southern economy. ■

Hamilton St is a two-room B&B owned and restored by Ben and Barbara Wilson. Single/double rates here are $55/60. The *Krout House* (☎ 205-637-6383), 551 Tennessee St, serves a good meat-and-three lunch.

Joe Wheeler State Park

If you're looking for outdoor water activities, this park overlooking Wheeler Lake on the north side of the Tennessee River is loaded with them. You can swim, boat and, if you're so inclined, fish for your dinner.

The park is divided into three areas. The main area near Rogersville is like a country club. It has tennis courts, a lodge, a marina with boat rentals, a large L-shaped pool and a golf course with pro shop and restaurant. The nice campground is in a wooded area off the golf course. This is also where you'll find picnic areas, grills, the beach, and hiking and nature trails. The second area, on nearby Elk River, has a group lodge, fishing-boat rentals and a bait-and-tackle store. The third area, 12 miles away on the south side of the river, is more rustic and has cabins, tennis courts, a boat launch, hiking trails and playgrounds. Boat rentals cost $5 an hour for canoes and paddle boats, $30 a half-day for power boats, and $90 a half-day for pontoon boats. Day-use fees are $1 for adults and 50¢ for children. It's free for overnight guests.

The park offers a range of accomodation options. The campground has improved ($14.50) and primitive ($9) sites. Both have water and shade. The lodge, with singles from $54, doubles from $61 and suites from $86, overlooks the lake. The rustic cabins (from $52.50) sleep four to eight and are completely furnished. For camping reservations call ☎ 205-247-1184; for lodge reservations call ☎ 205-247-5461, 800-544-5639; and for cabin reservations call ☎ 205-247-0145.

The park lies on both sides of the river off Hwy 101. The main park and campground are on the north bank. The rustic cabins are on the south bank. To reach the rustic cabins, drive five miles west from Courtland on Alt Hwy 72/Hwy 20 and turn right on Hwy 101. It's on the left before you cross the river. To reach the main park and campground, continue across the river over Wheeler Dam, then turn right onto Hwy 72. They're five miles east on the right.

THE SHOALS

Four cities on the Tennessee River make up the area known as the Shoals: Florence, Sheffield, Tuscumbia and Muscle Shoals. The combined population is 64,830.

From the early days of exploration, boat pilots feared the river's treacherous 37-mile stretch of craggy rapids known as Muscle Shoals. Wilson Dam, completed in 1924, improved navigation, created recreational areas and brought inexpensive electricity to the poorest section of the US. The availability of cheap labor and power opened the door for industrialization during the 1930s and 1940s.

In the late 1960s, 1970s and into the 1980s, the Shoals made a name for itself in the music industry. It started in 1966 when Rick Hall of Fame Recording Studios and Quin Ivy of Quinvy Studio got Atlantic Records to release Percy Sledge's hit, 'When a Man Loves a Woman.' That hit was followed by hits from Wilson Picket, Aretha Franklin, the Rolling Stones, Paul Simon and many others. *Newsweek* reported that Muscle Shoals was to R&B what Nashville was to country. The music business has slowed since its platinum days, but local studios still produce records.

The Tennessee Valley Authority and several large apparel and textile manufacturers are the biggest employers.

Orientation

The four cities straddle the Tennessee River in the northwestern corner of Alabama. Florence, in Lauderdale County, lies on the north bank, while Tuscumbia, Muscle Shoals and Sheffield, in Colbert County, are on the south. They are connected by Hwy 43/72 in the west and Hwy 133, which crosses the river over Wilson Dam, in the east.

ALABAMA

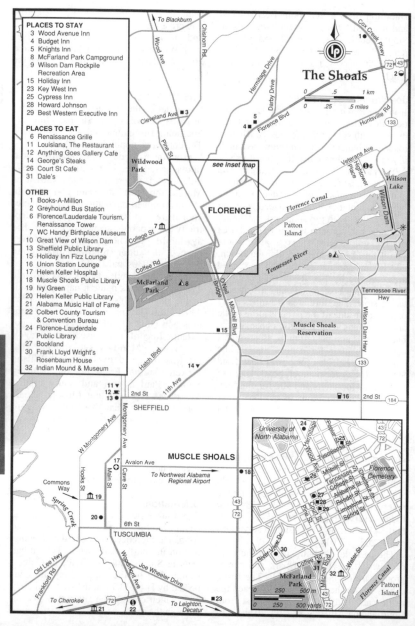

PLACES TO STAY
3 Wood Avenue Inn
4 Budget Inn
5 Knights Inn
8 McFarland Park Campground
9 Wilson Dam Rockpile
   Recreation Area
15 Holiday Inn
23 Key West Inn
25 Cypress Inn
28 Howard Johnson
29 Best Western Executive Inn

PLACES TO EAT
6 Renaissance Grille
11 Louisiana, The Restaurant
12 Anything Goes Gallery Cafe
14 George's Steaks
26 Court St Cafe
31 Dale's

OTHER
1 Books-A-Million
2 Greyhound Bus Station
6 Florence/Lauderdale Tourism,
   Renaissance Tower
7 WC Handy Birthplace Museum
10 Great View of Wilson Dam
13 Sheffield Public Library
15 Holiday Inn Fizz Lounge
16 Union Station Lounge
17 Helen Keller Hospital
18 Muscle Shoals Public Library
19 Ivy Green
20 Helen Keller Public Library
21 Alabama Music Hall of Fame
22 Colbert County Tourism
   & Convention Bureau
24 Florence-Lauderdale
   Public Library
27 Bookland
30 Frank Lloyd Wright's
   Rosenbaum House
32 Indian Mound & Museum

The Shoals

FLORENCE

see inset map

ALABAMA

SHEFFIELD

MUSCLE SHOALS

To Northwest Alabama
Regional Airport

TUSCUMBIA

University of
North Alabama

Florence
Cemetery

McFarland
Park

Patton
Island

Muscle Shoals
Reservation

Wilson
Lake

Wilson Dam

Tennessee River

Patton
Island

Florence Canal

Information
Tourist Offices Colbert County Tourism and Convention Bureau (☎ 205-383-0783, 800-344-0783, fax 205-383-2080) is at 719 Hwy 72W, near Woodmont Dr, in Tuscumbia. It covers Muscle Shoals, Sheffield and Tuscumbia. Florence/Lauderdale Tourism (☎ 205-740-4141, 888-356-8687, fax 205-740-4142, Net) is at 1 Hightower Place. It covers Florence.

Bookstores Books-A-Million (☎ 205-766-2210), 302 Cox Creek Parkway, Florence, and Bookland (☎ 205-766-1163), 114 N Court St, Florence, have good selections of regional books.

Campuses The beautiful University of North Alabama (☎ 205-765-4100, 800-825-5862) campus on Wesleyan Ave was designed by Frederick Law Olmsted, who also designed New York's Central Park.

Guided tours of the campus are given daily from 9 am to 2 pm on the hour and also by appointment.

Libraries There are four public libraries in the Shoals region: Florence-Lauderdale Public Library (☎ 205-764-6563), 218 N Wood Ave, Florence; Helen Keller Public Library (☎ 205-383-7065), 511 N Main St, Tuscumbia; Muscle Shoals Public Library (☎ 205-386-9212), 1000 E Avalon Ave, Muscle Shoals; and Sheffield Public Library (☎ 205-386-5633), 316 N Montgomery Ave, Sheffield.

Media The *Times Daily* covers the Shoals. The *Colbert County Reporter* is distributed on Tuesday in Tuscumbia, and the *Courier-Journal* is available on Tuesday in Florence.

Medical Services For medical care go to Helen Keller Hospital (☎ 205-386-4095), 1300 S Montgomery Ave, Sheffield; Columbia Medical Center Shoals (☎ 205-386-1600), 201 W Avalon Ave, Muscle Shoals; or Eliza Coffee Memorial Hospital (☎ 205-767-9191), 205 Marengo St, Florence.

Frank Lloyd Wright's Rosenbaum House
Elderly Mrs Rosenbaum, the original owner, still occupies this house (☎ 205-764-5274), 601 Riverview Dr, Florence, and gives lively tours, explaining that it was designed and built in 1940 by architect Frank Lloyd Wright. It's the only Wright structure in the state and it's the best example of a Usonian do-it-yourself house in the country. The house sits on a two-acre lot overlooking the Tennessee River. Tours are by appointment, preferably one day in advance. Admission is $10 (seniors and students $7).

WC Handy Birthplace Museum
WC Handy, the man known as the father of the blues for his 1912 song 'Memphis Blues,' was born and raised in this humble two-room wood cabin (☎ 205-760-6427), 620 W College St, Florence, in 1873. Inside is a lifetime of photos, paintings and treasures. A tape of Handy's music and a narrative play in the background. A second building houses the Black Heritage Library, filled with journals, photos and books. Especially interesting are photos of Corporal Lawson Coffee along with his original enlistment and discharge papers from the 110th Regiment of the US Colored Infantry. The museum is open Tuesday to Saturday from 10 am to 4 pm. Admission is $2 (children 50¢).

Indian Mound & Museum
At first glance this museum (☎ 205-760-6427), S Court St, Florence, at the river's edge, looks ho-hum, but it's packed with artifacts dating back 10,000 years. Many of the items come from the Mississippian-era mound outside the museum door, but others come from surrounding areas. Be sure to climb the steps up to the mound. The museum is open Tuesday to Saturday from 10 am to 4 pm. Admission is $2 (children 50¢).

Renaissance Tower
There's a splendid view of the Shoals, Wilson Dam and the Tennessee River and

Valley from the top of this 300-foot observation tower (☎ 205-764-5900), 1 Hightower Place, Florence. A restaurant occupies the top floor, giving diners the best view during lunch and after 5 pm. The rest of the day visitors are welcome to walk around while they look. It's open Monday to Saturday from 10 to 11:30 am and 1:30 to 5 pm, and Sunday from 11 to 11:30 am and 1:30 to 5 pm. Admission is $1. The *Renaissance Grille* serves meals from 11:30 am to 1:30 pm and after 5 pm.

There's a small, moderately interesting **aquarium** on the second level that's open Monday to Saturday from 10 am to 5 pm, and Sunday from 11 am to 5 pm. Admission is $4 (seniors $3, students $3.50, children $2). The tower is closed on Christmas day and Thanksgiving. Outside, the **Hall Memorial Native Plant Garden** has short trails and a picnic area.

Wilson Dam & Lock

Wilson Dam (☎ 205-386-2451), Hwy 133 in Muscle Shoals, was completed in 1924 in a neoclassical style. You can get a good view of the dam on the south side of the river by driving north on Hwy 133. Follow the unmarked road on the right just past the boat ramp and TVA powerhouse – it leads to a parking lot and lookout area with benches. For a view from the north side, continue across the dam and take the first left into a parking lot, where you'll find a lookout and the Wilson Lock. Walk down to the lock. The visitor's welcome center is temporarily closed, call when you're in town to see if it has reopened.

Ivy Green

Blind and deaf since the age of 19 months, Helen Keller learned to speak, read and write with the help of teacher Anne Sullivan. She graduated from Radcliffe College and became a world-famous writer, spending her life touring the world to lecture on behalf of blind people. Keller lived in this 1820s white clapboard house (☎ 205-383-4066) on a 640-acre wooded tract at 300 W North Commons, Tuscumbia, from her birth in 1880 until she left for college. Hundreds of family items, furnishings, and awards for her later achievements fill the house. Out back is the original pump where Sullivan taught her to associate words with things and where Keller spoke her first words in 1887. The play *The Miracle Worker*, which chronicles her studies with Sullivan, has been performed here annually since 1961 on Friday and Saturday nights in June and July. Ivy Green is open Monday to Saturday from 8:30 am to 4 pm, and Sunday from 1 to 4 pm, except major holidays. Admission is $3 (children $1).

Alabama Music Hall of Fame

The Music Hall of Fame (☎ 205-381-4417, 800-239-2643, Net), Hwy 72, Tuscumbia, is a grand salute to the music and artists of Alabama and should not be missed. From the Ronald McDowell paintings of artists at the entrance to the actual bus the group Alabama used on tours, memories will come pouring back. There's Toni Tenille's self-embroidered bell-bottom jeans, Jim Nabor's Gomer Pyle uniform, and stage clothes from Emmylou Harris and Jimmy Buffet. If you yearn to be a star, stop by the recording studio, where you can select a music track and record a personal cassette ($10) or make a video recording ($15). Induction awards held every other year are open to the public. It's open Monday to Saturday from 9 am to 5 pm, and Sunday from 1 to 5 pm, with longer hours in summer. Admission is $6 (seniors and students $5, children $3).

They Gave Their Lives

The Army Corps of Engineers constructed Wilson Dam from 1918 to 1924 to supply power to munitions factories in WWI. During construction, an accident occurred and concrete crashed down on 20 men. Unable to remove the concrete, officials left the bodies buried at the bottom of the dam. A memorial marker is located at the lookout at Wilson Lock. ■

Special Events

The Helen Keller Festival, held at Ivy Green (☎ 205-383-4066), is a three-day celebration with music, arts, crafts and a parade held the last full weekend in June. The first Sunday in August, the five-day WC Handy Festival, sponsored by the Music Preservation Society (☎ 880-472-5837, 205-766-7642), fills the air with the music of big-name entertainers and jam sessions. More major musicians come to town the second weekend of September for Harvest Jam, hosted by the Alabama Music Hall of Fame. Also in September, the Festival of the Singing River celebrates Native American culture with arts, cultural demonstrations and food. Troops assemble in mid-May for the Recall LaGrange Civil War re-enactment along the Tennessee River. Folks and their best friends can have a howling good time on Labor Day at the Coon Dog Cemetery Celebration. The annual Trail of Tears Commemorative Motorcycle Ride in September features arts, crafts and live music entertainment.

Places to Stay

Camping *McFarland Park Campground* (☎ 205-760-6416), Hwy 20 just west of Hwy 157, on the Tennessee River, Florence, is a city park with a boat ramp, improved and primitive camping, picnic areas and a fishing pier. It's open for camping from April 1 to November 30. Sites cost $7 for tents, or $10 for RVs.

The primitive campsites at *Wilson Dam Rockpile Recreation Area* (☎ 205-386-3451), Rockpile Recreation Rd, off Wilson Dam Hwy, Muscle Shoals, overlook the Wilson Dam from a bluff. The campground has 50 sites on gravel, 25 of which are located along the bluff over the river. Two trails provide good views of the river. The rate is $11 per night for tents and RVs. It's not staffed; you pay on the honor system.

Hotels & Motels The *Budget Inn* (☎ 205-764-7621), 1238 Florence Blvd, Florence, is real basic, but clean. There's coffee in the office and cable TV. The single/double rate is $25.50/31.50.

It's a Dog's Afterlife

Sometimes a man is a *dog's* best friend, as in this case, in which Key Underwood loved his coon dog, Troop, so much that he buried him in a special place near their favorite hunting ground. Since that day in September 1937, more than 100 other coon dogs have been laid to rest beside him. Sparing no expense, some owners have topped their canine's final resting place with elaborate gravestones. In honor of this special breed, there's a monument depicting two coon dogs baying up a tree. The annual Labor Day Coon Dog Cemetery Celebration features music, buck dancing, a liars' contest and barbecue.

To get to the cemetery, head west out of Tuscumbia on Hwy 72 for about seven miles, then turn left on Hwy 247, continue 12 miles, turn right and follow the signs. ■

Knights Inn (☎ 205-764-5421), 1241 Florence Blvd, Florence, has few amenities – a pool, complimentary breakfast and movie channel – but the rooms are clean and the prices reasonable. Singles/doubles start from $33/38.50.

Microwaves and refrigerators are available on request at *Howard Johnson* (☎ 205-760-8888), 400 S Court St, Florence. *USA Today*, a movie channel and continental breakfast are free. The staff are cheery and helpful. Singles/doubles are $44/49.

The *Best Western Executive Inn* (☎ 205-766-2331), 504 S Court, Florence, has a restaurant, pool and lounge. There's complimentary coffee all day and breakfast until 10 am. Some rooms have data ports and refrigerators. Singles/doubles are $51/56.

The two-story *Key West Inn* (☎ 205-383-0700), 1800 Hwy 72, Tuscumbia, is built in a tropical style and has pastel-colored furnishings. Continental breakfast is included in the rate of $45/50 a single/double.

Service is attentive at the *Holiday Inn* (☎ 205-381-4710), 4900 Hatch Blvd, Sheffield. The hotel is set back from the highway in the middle of a thicket of trees. There's an exercise room, outdoor pool, indoor whirlpool, lounge and restaurant. Rooms are spacious, and amenities include modem ports with surge protectors, coffee machines, irons and boards, hair dryers and showers with water massagers. Rates are $73 to $76, single or double.

Inns & B&Bs Located in the quiet downtown historic district, the *Cypress Inn* (☎ 205-760-1131, fax 205-760-1137), 414 N Poplar St, Florence, has two guest rooms with large picture windows, claw-foot tubs with showers, queen-size beds, telephones, TVs and antique furnishings. There's a sun room and a porch with rockers. Breakfast is included. Rooms are $65 to $75.

Wood Avenue Inn (☎ 205-766-8441), 658 N Wood Ave, Florence, is a lovely three-story Queen Anne-style house decorated in Victorian fluff, antiques and collectibles. There's a fireplace in most rooms. The five rooms have private baths, some of which are claw-foot tubs. Full breakfast is included. Rooms cost $60 to $90, single or double.

Places to Eat
Florence The *Renaissance Grille* (☎ 205-718-0092) at 1 Hightower Place wraps around the 300-foot observation tower, commanding sweeping views of the valley, river and dam. Weekday lunch specials such as burgers, salads and sandwiches cost $5 from 11 am to 4 pm. À la carte items are more expensive.

The large, bright *Court St Cafe* (☎ 205-767-4300), Mobile St at Seminary St, caters to students and young professionals. The menu features weekday all-you-can-eat specials including chicken, ribs and linguine ($7.50 to $12.50), plus menu items of fish and steaks. It's open daily for meals from 11 am to 10 pm; the popular bar is open till 11 pm. It's close to the university.

If you're looking for a simple setting with good food, try *Dale's* (☎ 205-766-4961), 1001 Mitchell Blvd, Florence.

Steaks and seafood make up the bulk of the menu. It's a casual place popular with local families. To get there cross O'Neil Bridge and take the first turn left onto the service road; Dale's is on the right. Dinner checks range from $9 to $18.

Sheffield *Louisiana, The Restaurant* (☎ 205-386-0801), 406 N Montgomery Ave, is known throughout the Shoals for its Creole and Cajun food. It's open Tuesday to Friday for lunch and dinner, and Saturday for dinner only. Lunch checks average $8, while dinner checks are about $16.

Customers lunch with art at *Anything Goes Gallery Cafe* (☎ 205-383-4161), 400 N Montgomery Ave. Original art by owner Jared Briscoe is displayed throughout the restaurant. Muffins, bagels and baked goods are available for breakfast. Lunch costs about $10. It's open 7 am to 4:30 pm.

George's Steaks (☎ 205-381-1531), 1206 11th Ave (Jackson Hwy), has been feeding locals steaks, as the name suggests, and seafood for two generations. There's also a good wine list. Dinner checks average $15 to $20.

Entertainment
The Shoals' cinemas include Carmike's *Capri Twin* (☎ 205-767-0211), in Regency Square Mall, and *Hickory Hills Cinema* (☎ 205-766-7700), Florence Blvd, Hickory Hills Shopping Center.

On Thursday nights, the *Holiday Inn Fizz Lounge* (☎ 205-381-4710), 4900 Hatch Blvd, Sheffield, hosts 'songwriter's night,' showcasing a different songwriter each week. It's a virtual who's who of music. The *Union Station Lounge* (☎ 205-383-4602), 524 E 2nd St, Muscle Shoals, presents live rock and blues acts Tuesday and Thursday to Saturday. It has pool tables and there are pool tournaments on Monday and Friday nights.

Getting There & Away
Air Northwest Alabama regional airport (☎ 205-381-2869) on TE Campbell Dr,

Muscle Shoals, is served by Northwest Airlink with three flights a day to and from Memphis. For service from other areas, the nearest airport in Alabama is Huntsville international (☎ 205-772-9395) at 1000 Glenn Hearn Blvd, 70 miles east.

Bus Greyhound (☎ 205-764-2313), 500 E Tennessee St, Florence, serves Atlanta ($51; two daily), Birmingham ($27; two), Huntsville ($14; one), Memphis ($34; two), Nashville ($36; one) and other cities in the Deep South.

Executive Connection provides an airport shuttle service from Huntsville (see Huntsville Getting There & Away) for $75.

Car There are two pleasant drives from the Shoals east to Decatur and Huntsville. See Getting There and Away for Decatur. The most scenic route south to William B Bankhead National Forest is along Hwy 43, then Hwys 5 and 13 to Hwy 278 east. The route passes through Russellville, one of Alabama's best areas for canoeing; the historic town of Haleyville; and the natural wonder at Natural Bridge.

Hertz is the only rental agency at the Northwest Alabama regional airport. The major agencies have counters at Huntsville and Memphis airports. Companies with offices in the Shoals include Enterprise Rent-A-Car (☎ 205-767-0292), 2801 Florence Blvd, Florence; Ford Rent-A-Car (☎ 205-386-7800), 2800 Woodward Ave, Muscle Shoals; and U-Save Auto Rentals (☎ 205-389-8509), 4108 Jackson Hwy, Sheffield.

Getting Around

Bus Public transportation is provided by Dial-a-Ride (☎ 205-314-0047). You need to call at least 24 hours in advance. There is no regularly scheduled service.

Taxi Express Cab Company (☎ 205-764-1010), Haney's Taxi Company (☎ 205-764-0121) and Yellow Cab of Florence (☎ 205-766-1000) provide taxi services.

WATERLOO

The picturesque town of Waterloo overlooks the Tennessee River in the northwest corner of Alabama. Incorporated in 1819, it served as an important river city and was the port of embarkation along the Trail of Tears in the 1830s, when more than a thousand Native Americans boarded ships that were headed for reservations in Oklahoma. A historical marker commemorates the tragedy.

In 1863 General William Sherman crossed the river into Waterloo and set up camp. One of his soldiers, Joseph Marion Newman, loved the town and returned after the war. His granddaughter donated the family house and personal items to the town in 1995 and these are now on display at the Edith Newman Culver Memorial Museum (☎ 205-767-6081) on Main St. Exhibits and artifacts fill the house. From April to October it's open Wednesday to Friday from 11 am to 4 pm, Saturday from 10 am to 5 pm, and Sunday from 1 to 5 pm. From November to December it's open Saturday from 10 am to 5 pm and Sunday from 1 to 5 pm. Admission is $2 (seniors and students $1). Take Hwy 20 (Savannah Hwy) to County Rd 14 (Waterloo Rd), then continue 25 miles to Waterloo and turn left onto Main St.

The Trail of Tears

Alabama's most famous motorcycle route is the Trail of Tears corridor, which stretches 200 miles from Ross Landing in Chattanooga, Tennessee, to Waterloo, Alabama, tracing the official 'Indian Removal Act of 1830' route that 1070 Native Americans were forced to walk before they were transported by boat to reservations out West. While the corridor is open year-round, an annual motorcycle ride is held in September to honor the Native Americans who suffered and died en route. There are historic markers and signs along the way, which follows much of what is now Hwy 72. ■

The annual Trail of Tears Commemorative Motorcycle Ride in September ends in Waterloo with an arts, crafts and music festival.

THE SHOALS TO CULLMAN
Natural Bridge
Nature created the Natural Bridge (☎ 205-486-5330) millions of years ago. At 60 feet high, 148 feet long and 33 feet high, the sandstone rock span is the longest natural bridge east of the Rockies. Although the park covers 100 acres, most of the terrain is rugged, so the nature trails are limited to a few miles surrounding the bridge. There's also a picnic area and gift shop. The park is on Hwy 278, one mile west of the intersection of Hwy 5 and Hwy 278, 12 miles south of Haleyville and 13 miles southwest of Double Springs. It's open daily from 8 am to sunset. Admission is $2.50 (children $1.50).

You can stay nearby at the *Natural Bridge Motel* (☎ 205-486-5261), Hwy 278 at Hwy 5. Singles and doubles are $31 at this basic, 20-room motel. There's a restaurant and gas station down the hill.

William B Bankhead National Forest
If you're looking for a park that offers outdoor diversity, this is it. Operated by the USFS, this 281-sq-mile park has forests, numerous hiking and horseback-riding trails, high bluffs, waterfalls, calm and white water, gorges, wildlife, wildflowers, Native American relics and five distinctive recreation areas, including the **Sipsey Wilderness** area for serious hikers. The Sipsey River offers a challenging six to eight-hour canoe trip with a put-in at Hwy 33 and a take-out at Hwy 278. The river flows rapidly from fall to spring, but you have to paddle in summer.

In the Grayson area east of Bee Branch, you can also check out the historic **Pine Torch Church**, thought to be the oldest log church in the state. In the Bee Branch area is a 500-year-old, 150-foot poplar tree purported to be the largest tree in Alabama.

The ranger station (☎ 205-489-5111) is one mile north of Double Springs on Hwy

33. You can reach all the recreation areas from there. It's open Monday to Friday from 7:30 am to 4 pm. At other times, check the map on the wall outside the station for directions to the other recreation areas. The free *National Forests in Alabama Pocket Visitor Guide* can be ordered by calling ☎ 334-832-4470 or writing to National Forests in Alabama, 2946 Chestnut St, Montgomery, AL 36107. It has a map and gives detailed directions for reaching recreation areas in Bankhead and other national forests.

There's primitive and improved camping at Brushy Lake ($5; 13 sites), Clear Creek ($11 or $12; 102 sites), Corinth ($20; 50 sites) and Houston ($8; 86 sites). The Sipsey Wilderness area has no designated sites, so check with the ranger station before camping. Rates are the same for tents or RVs. Corinth was recently renovated and all sites now include water, sewer and electricity.

There's a $3 day-use fee in all areas of the park. Campers at Clear Creek and Corinth must pay the day-use fee in addition to camping fees. For long stays, consider the $30 annual pass valid at all Alabama national forests except Clear Creek.

It's a big park. Brushy Lake is 27 miles north of the ranger station on scenic winding roads, so allow yourself enough travel time, especially at night.

Double Springs
Double Springs is a speck on the map 26 miles west of Cullman on Hwy 278, but two things make it a major tourist stop: it's on the edge of the William B Bankhead National Forest and it's in the heart of Winston County, famous for its role during the Civil War. Playwright Lanny McAlister was taken by the way this pertinacious county fought secession and declared itself neutral, so he wrote the two-hour musical, *The Incident at Looney's Tavern* and the sequel, *Aftermath & Legacy of the Incident at Looney's Tavern*. More than 20,000 visitors a year come to see the performance held in an amphitheater cut out of a hillside

overlooking Bankhead National Forest. There's a raft of other distractions around the theater, but with the exception of the excursion and dinner cruises on a riverboat on Smith Lake, you can do without them. For tickets and information call the office (☎ 205-489-5000, 800-566-6397, fax 205-489-3500). To reach the theater, take I-65 to exit 308 (Hwy 278) at Cullman, then drive west 29 miles on Hwy 278. It's on the left. Performances are held June through August, with shows on Thursday, Friday and Saturday at 8:15 pm. Tickets cost $18 for adults, $16 for seniors and $9 for children. Admission to the other attractions is separate. The boat cruise is $20/10 with/without dinner (seniors $19/9, children $15/5).

There's a restaurant on site, but the nearest hotels are in Cullman and Haleyville.

CULLMAN
population 14,642

This town takes its name from Colonel John G Cullmann, a German refugee who founded it in 1873. You can see his likeness in a 15-foot bronze statue by contemporary Birmingham sculptor Branko Medenica; it's in front of the Cullman County Museum. You can't miss it or the church steeples – they're everywhere. Even more numerous are the chicken coops. Cullman is the top poultry producer in the country.

Orientation & Information

Cullman is four miles east of I-65 on Hwy 278, which cuts through east-west from William B Bankhead National Forest.

The chamber of commerce (☎ 205-734-0454), 211 2nd Ave NE, is open Monday to Friday from 8 am to 5 pm.

Ave Maria Grotto

Brother Joseph Zoettl, a Benedictine monk, may not have described himself as an artist, but clearly his work, the Ave Maria Grotto (☎ 205-734-4110), St Bernard Abbey, 1600 St Bernard Dr SE, off Hwy 278, is Southern folk art at its best. Between 1912 and 1958 he collected scrap materials from friends around the world to construct 125 well-known religious sites in miniature. The shrines are in the three-acre garden in the abbey's grounds. Some of the shrines – Shrine of Peter, Lourdes, Noah's Ark, the Tower of Babel and Hanging Gardens of Babylon – stand alone. Others are

ALABAMA

The Free State of Winston

History books and movies like *Gone with the Wind* give the impression that everyone in the South sided with the Confederacy. Not true. Winston County, a small county in northwest Alabama, became known as the Free State of Winston when it declared itself neutral during the Civil War. During delegate elections for the secession convention, Charles Sheats ran and won on a platform of 'vote against secession, first, last, and all of the time.' He and 22 other delegates refused to sign the secession resolutions. He returned home and held a county meeting in Looney's Tavern on July 4, 1861, with more than 2500 residents in attendance. The meeting concluded that if it were possible for states to leave the union even though they did not have the 'right' to do so, a county, by the same reasoning, could cease to be part of a state. In the end they didn't secede, but instead refused to take up arms against the Union or the Confederacy and asked to be left alone. However, when the Confederate cavalry arrived in Winston County a few months later and arrested and shot men over 18 years old for violating the Conscript Act, residents took up arms on the side of the Union.

You can get more information about the area's history from the Haleyville Area Chamber of Commerce (☎ 205-486-4611), 1200 21st St, Haleyville; it's open Monday to Friday from 8 am to noon and 1 to 4 pm. The Winston County Tourist Association (☎ 205-486-8653), Route 4, Box 285, Haleyville, AL 35565, responds to mail and telephone requests for information. ■

complete towns covering a small hill. The last of the shrines on the path was made after Brother Joe died. The grotto is open daily from 7 am to dusk, except Christmas day. Admission is $4.50 (children $3).

Cullman County Museum

This small but earnest museum (☎ 205-739-1258), 211 2nd Ave NE, located in a replica of Cullmann's house, chronicles the history of the county beginning with the days when Native Americans were here. A wall of historic photographs shows how the city grew and changed. The original house Colonel Cullmann built in the 1870s burned down in 1912. The museum is tastefully done and the staff are knowledgeable and helpful. They also give tours of Weiss Cottage, the oldest home in the city, by appointment. The museum is open Sunday from 1:30 to 4:30 pm and weekdays from 9 am to noon and 1 to 4 pm, except Thursday, when it closes at noon. Admission is $1 (children 50¢).

Clarkson Covered Bridge

Stretching 277 feet across Crooked Creek, Clarkson Covered Bridge (☎ 205-739-3530), County Rd 1043, is the largest covered truss bridge in the state. It's an attractive bridge, with timbers forming a lattice design. It's open only to pedestrian traffic and is used mostly by visitors to the county park that lies 50 feet below. The park has nature trails, picnic tables, restrooms and a reproduction log gristmill and miller's house. Located 10 miles west of town, it's a little difficult to find. From I-65 take Hwy 278 west about 7 miles and turn right at Jones Chapel Rd (there's a small sign). Turn left after a half-mile onto County Rd 1043. The bridge is a mile down the road. It's open daily from dawn to dusk and entry is free.

Lewis Smith Lake

This 33-sq-mile lake shaped like a large rack of antlers has 500 miles of shoreline. It's noted for its bass and is thus primarily used by fishing and boating enthusiasts. However, it's good for other activities, including water-skiing and swimming. The adjoining Smith Lake Park (☎ 205-739-3530), 416 County Rd 385, has a pool, beach area, picnic facilities and campground. The campground is open from April to October. The park's day-use fee is $1.

The park's campground has almost 200 improved and primitive campsites. Rates for tents/RV are $10/13 a night for two campers, and $2 for each additional person. It's open from April to October. From Birmingham take exit 304 off I-65 and turn left on Old Hwy 69. The first park sign is five miles down the road.

Places to Stay

For camping at Smith Lake Park see the lake entry above.

Good Hope Campground (☎ 205-739-1319), 300 Super Saver Rd, south of Cullman, is a small, basic campground with 38 primitive and improved campsites for tents and RVs. The rate is $10 a night, and it's open year-round. From Huntsville take exit 304 off I-65 and turn left. It's the first street on the left.

The *Days Inn* (☎ 205-739-3800, fax 205-739-3800), 1841 4th St SW, provides simple, clean accommodations and there's a pool and restaurant. Singles/doubles are $39/46.

Places to Eat

The *All Steak Restaurant* (☎ 205-734-4322), 414 2nd Ave SW (Hwy 31), has been serving customers for more than 60 years. The menu includes chicken, fish and fresh vegetable dishes. Breakfast costs around $3.50, lunch specials are about $4.50, and dinner starts at $5.50. Desserts and breads are homemade. Warm, sweet orange rolls are a house specialty. It opens daily at 6:30 am and closes at 9 or 10 pm (4 pm on Sunday).

Getting There & Away

Greyhound (☎ 205-734-2921) 1003 Logan Rd, offers services from Birmingham ($13; four times a day) and Huntsville ($14; three).

Enterprise (☎ 205-739-9227), 1400 2nd Ave NW, rents cars. For an alternate, more rural route to Huntsville and Birmingham, try Hwy 31, which parallels I-65.

ANNISTON
population 27,097

Today's Anniston grew out of an industrial town with textile mills and blast furnaces laid out in the late 1800s by Northern industrialists. Many of its original churches and buildings remain. The army established a presence here at Fort McClellan shortly after WWI and remains the largest employer.

Orientation & Information

Anniston is located just off the I-20. From there Hwy 431/Hwy 21 runs north-south through the middle of Oxford, then Anniston. It's called Quintard Dr until Hwy 431 and Hwy 21 split at the north end of Anniston, near the Natural History Museum. Most hotels, restaurants and attractions are on or near Quintard Dr. From the southern edge of town, cross streets run alphabetically from T to A, then change to numbered streets from 1st to 55th.

The convention and visitors bureau (☎ 205-237-3536, 800-489-1087), 1330 Quintard Dr, is open Monday to Friday from 8 am to 5 pm. Books-A-Million (☎ 205-835-5331), 900A Quintard Dr, at Hwy 78, Oxford, has a large selection of regional titles. The main library (☎ 205-237-8501), 108 10th St E, is open Monday to Friday from 9 am to 6:30 pm, Saturday from 9 am to 5 pm, and Sunday from 1 to 5 pm. The *Anniston Star* is the local daily. The Northeast Alabama Regional Medical Center (☎ 205-235-5121), 400 10th St E, handles routine and emergency care.

Anniston Museum of Natural History

The first thing you notice at this terrific museum (☎ 205-237-6766), 800 Museum Dr, is a prehistoric 'bird,' with a 30-foot wingspan, suspended from the ceiling. Farther inside are interesting displays of animals, plants, minerals and mummies. Good lighting and sound effects enhance the exhibits. Don't miss the bird collection with beautiful hand-painted habitats. Nature continues outside in the wildlife garden and on the 'bird of prey trail,' which runs about 1½ miles through the

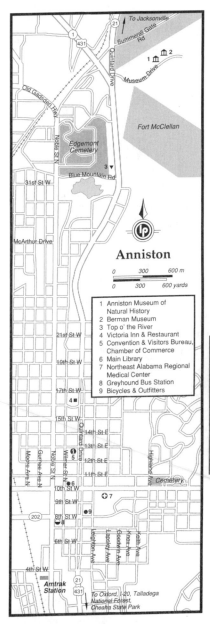

Anniston

1 Anniston Museum of
   Natural History
2 Berman Museum
3 Top o' the River
4 Victoria Inn & Restaurant
5 Convention & Visitors Bureau,
   Chamber of Commerce
6 Main Library
7 Northeast Alabama Regional
   Medical Center
8 Greyhound Bus Station
9 Bicycles & Outfitters

ALABAMA

woods. The North Route bus (see Getting Around) stops here. The museum is open Tuesday to Friday from 9 am to 5 pm, Saturday from 10 am to 5 pm, and Sunday from 1 to 5 pm. Admission is $3.50 (seniors $3, children $2.50).

Berman Museum

This fascinating museum (☎ 205-237-6261, 205-238-9055), 840 Museum Dr, houses Farley and Germaine Berman's private collection of 1500 weapons and 2000 works of art. For more than 70 years the couple sought rare objects, including bronze sculptures by Western artists Frederic Remington and Charles Russell and a royal Persian scimitar encrusted with 1295 rose-cut diamonds, 60 carats of rubies and a large emerald.

It's open Tuesday to Friday from 9 am to 5 pm, Saturday from 10 am to 5 pm, and Sunday from 1 to 5 pm. Admission is $4.50 ($3.50 for seniors, military and disabled visitors, $2.50 for children). The North Route bus stops here.

Activities

Bicycles & Outfitters (☎ 205-237-1406), 831 Quintard Dr, has access to a 4000-acre reserve with BMX trails and is tied in to the major **biking** clubs in the region. If you want to know where to ride or if you need a partner, see Terry Grizzard, the owner. He also repairs and sells bike equipment. When not biking, Terry runs **canoeing** expeditions and drives canoe-renters ($30 a day) to a put-in. While several rivers in the area make great outings, he prefers Choccolocco Creek for its abundant wildlife. For the best deal, rent on Saturday morning. It's closed on Sunday, so you bring the canoe back Monday morning and pay for only one day. Small groups of up to six people can get an escorted 4½-hour canoe outing for $90. Everything but food is included. It's open Monday to Saturday from 9:30 am to 6 pm. It's closed the week of July 4th.

Scott's Bikes (☎ 205-435-2453), 101 Ladiga St SE, Jacksonville, just north of Anniston, rents bikes and canoes. The bikes ($15 to $20 a day) are hybrids, suitable for easy off-road trails and street riding. The canoe ($30 a day) is a 16-foot, almost flat-bottomed model made for shallow creeks. There's no shuttle service. Shop hours are Monday to Friday from 10 am to 6 pm, and Saturday from 9 am to 5 pm.

Places to Stay

The *Howard Johnson* (☎ 205-835-3988), Hwy 78 at Hwy 21 in Oxford, has only 44 rooms, so the heated outdoor pool isn't crowded. There's also a whirlpool, playground, coin laundry and barbecue and picnic area. Rooms have a coffeemaker, refrigerator and free movies. Continental breakfast is included. Rooms cost $35 to $48, single or double.

The *Holiday Inn* (☎ 205-831-3410), at Hwy 78 and Hwy 21 in Oxford, has lots of extras. There's a nice outdoor pool and whirlpool, and a playground. It has a popular lounge and restaurant and is well situated for trips to Cheaha State Park and Lookout Mountain Parkway. The rates are $52/72 for singles/doubles, but can go as low as $45.

The staff at the *Lenlock Inn* (☎ 205-820-1515, 800-234-5059), 6210 McClellan Blvd in Anniston, go out of their way to make guests comfortable. There's a pool, sauna, picnic area and laundry, plus free movies and coffee. Family suites have king-size or water beds. Honeymoon suites have canopy beds. Single rooms start at $36, doubles at $41.

The *Super 8 Motel* (☎ 205-820-1000), 6220 McClellan Blvd in Anniston, has 43 clean rooms with refrigerators and free movies. The property, which is opposite Fort McClellan, has a pool and gazebo, coin laundry and picnic area. Continental breakfast is included in the rate of $38/43 single/double.

The *Victoria Inn* (☎ 205-236-0503), 1604 Quintard Dr in Anniston, is part old, part new. The main house, which is more than 100 years old, has three rooms decorated with antiques ($129 to $169). The balconied annex rooms overlooking the garden and pool are $74, but rates go lower when things are slow. The rate includes a better-than-average continental breakfast Monday to Saturday and a hot country breakfast on Sunday.

Places to Eat

Brad's Bar-B-Que (☎ 205-831-7878) at 1809 Hwy 78 in Oxford is a nondescript place with tables and booths, but the barbecue sandwiches, ribs and chicken are good. Expect the usual sides of fried okra, slaw and beans, as well as cobblers and pies for desserts. Daily specials cost around $4.50 with fries, but you can pay as little as $2 for a small barbecue sandwich. It's open Monday to Saturday from 11 am to 9:30 pm.

China Luck Restaurant (☎ 205-831-5221), 503 Quintard Dr in Oxford, has tasty daily lunch specials for $4 to $5. Dinner will set you back $6 to $12. The egg rolls and fried rice are worth a try. The hours are Monday to Saturday 11 am to 2:30 pm, Sunday 11:30 am to 3 pm, Sunday to Thursday 4:30 to 9:30 pm and Friday to Saturday 4:30 to 10:30 pm.

Top o' the River (☎ 205-238-0097), 3220 McClellan Blvd in Anniston, is a family-run fish house specializing in catfish. A catfish dinner starts at $9, with sides. Chicken, steak and oysters are also available. People have been coming here from Georgia and Alabama for almost 20 years. It's open Sunday from 11:30 am to 9 pm, Monday to Thursday from 5 to 9 pm, and Friday and Saturday from 4 to 10 pm.

Hickory wood gives the chicken and pork at *Betty's Bar-B-Q* (☎ 205-237-1411), 401 S Quintard Dr in Anniston, its good flavor. It's a huge place with a loyal following. Expect to pay $5 to $6 for a plate with sides at lunch or dinner; you can takeout or eat in. It's open Monday to Thursday from 10:30 am to 8:30 pm, and Friday and Saturday to 9 pm, except major holidays.

The 24-hour *Alabama Show Palace* (☎ 205-831-0689) restaurant and bar, 1503 Hillyer Robinson Industrial Parkway, is 'home of the $5 steak.' On Thursday night you get all the sirloin steak you can eat for $5. It comes with a potato. Add $2 for

salad. The rest of the week steaks start at $5, but you're limited to one. There's also grilled shrimp and burgers.

Le Mamas (☎ 205-237-5550) at 1208 Walnut Ave in Anniston blends dining with history in the old L&N Freight House built around 1885. There are different specials daily, but you can always get hickory-smoked chicken and pork. It's one of Anniston's favorite restaurants for lunch. It's open Monday to Friday from 11 am to 2 pm.

Anniston's best restaurant is the *Victoria Restaurant* (☎ 205-236-0503), 1604 Quintard Dr, in the Victoria Inn. The setting is casually elegant and furnished with antiques. Only dinner is served and the menu features seafood, pasta, pork and chicken. Expect a bill of $14 to $22. The lounge is a popular after-work stop for local business people. It's open Monday to Thursday from 6 to 9 pm, and Friday and Saturday to 10 pm.

Getting There & Away

Birmingham and Atlanta airports are the closest. See those cities for information on shuttles.

Greyhound (☎ 205-236-6306), 12 8th St W, serves Atlanta ($21; six daily), Chattanooga ($24; five), Nashville ($51; five) and New Orleans ($69; three).

Amtrak (☎ 800-872-7245), 126 4th St W, serves Anniston from the East and West Coasts, with connections in Atlanta, Birmingham, New Orleans, Baton Rouge, Meridian, and other Deep South cities. Anniston is an unstaffed station.

The following car rental agencies have offices in Anniston: Avis (☎ 205-831-2600), 429 S Quintard Dr; Enterprise (☎ 205-237-9644), 1030 S Quintard Dr; and Rent-A-Wreck (☎ 205-831-2917), Hwy 21.

Getting Around

The local bus service, Anniston Express, operates three lines. All depart from Trolley Central at Gurnee Ave at 14th St E on the hour. The North Anniston line runs from Trolley Central along Quintard Dr north to Fort McClellan, stopping at the entrance to Museum Dr at about five minutes after the hour. The East Anniston line runs south on Quintard, then east on Greenbrier Rd to commercial, industrial and residential areas on the east side of the city before returning. The West/South line goes west on 14th St for several blocks, then returns and heads south on Noble St and Constantine Ave into Hobson City before returning. It passes the chamber of commerce. Fares are $1 (military personnel 75¢, seniors, disabled and kids 50¢). Transfers are free.

AROUND ANNISTON
Talladega National Forest

The Talladega National Forest near Anniston has two parts: the northern Shoal Creek District, with its headquarters (☎ 205-463-2272, fax 205-463-5385) on Hwy 46 at Gray Rd, Heflin, and the southern Talladega District, with its headquarters (☎ 205-362-2909, fax 205-362-0823) at 1001 N St (Hwy 21). There's also another section of the forest in central Alabama.

Activities include swimming, fishing, hiking, scenic drives, camping, horseback riding, boating and mountain biking. The two highest points in the state, Cheaha Mountain (2407 feet) and Dugger Mountain (2140 feet), provide hikers with challenges. The 102-mile Pinhoti Trail is the park's main hiking route and the state's longest and most popular trail. It winds through rugged pine forests, into hollows and along rock bluffs and streams. Six other trails range from two to 18 miles long. The park staff continues to clear the trails of trees felled by Hurricane Opal in 1995. Warden Station Horse Camp and Turnipseed Camp, two primitive areas, offer more remote hiking, camping and horseback riding.

Some of the best fishing is at Highrock and Morgan Lakes. There are five other lakes. Swimmers can cool off in Coleman Lake.

For an overview of the park, drive the 26-mile Talladega Scenic Dr, which begins near Heflin and climbs to Cheaha Mountain.

It's especially beautiful – and busy – during spring and fall. Take Hwy 78 east to Hwy 281. The drive takes 40 minutes each way, longer if you stop to ooh and aah at the lookouts. The haze in the valley in summer is a product of tree respiration.

You can stay in a campground (for a fee) or 'disperse camp' (no fee) off most of the hiking trails. There are three campgrounds. The somewhat isolated *Lake Chinnabee Recreation Area* (Talladega) is open April 15 to November 15 and has eight sites ($5). *Coleman Lake Recreation Area* (Shoal Creek) has 39 sites ($12) and is open April 15 to November 15. The *Pine Glen Recreation Area* (Shoal Creek) offers year-round camping at 35 sites ($3).

To reach the Shoal Creek District ranger station, take the I-20 to Hwy 9 north to Heflin and turn right onto Shoal Creek Rd (Hwy 46). To reach Talladega District, take the I-20, or Hwy 231 or 280, to Hwy 21; pass through Sylacauga and continue north to the ranger station. Office hours are Monday to Friday from 7:30 am to 4:30 pm at Shoal Creek, to 4 pm at Talladega. Host volunteers at the recreation areas handle weekend and late arrivals.

Cheaha State Park

As if Talladega National Forest didn't offer enough natural beauty, in the middle of it sits this gilded lily, a 2719-acre state park with headquarters (☎ 205-488-5111) at 19644 Hwy 281. Hiking is the primary attraction, as several of the park's short trails connect with the Pinhoti Trail (see Talladega National Forest). There's also a nature center, a wildflower garden, a pool and a lake where you can go swimming, fishing and boating. A small museum dedicated to the Civilian Conservation Corps, which cleared many of the state's parks in the 1930s, is open on weekends next to the Bunker Tower, where a climb of the 62 steps to the observation platform affords a delicious breeze and a 360-degree view from the highest point in Alabama (2407 feet). There's also a great view from the end of Bald Rock Trail, a one-mile loop on the north side of the park. The Mountain

Express, Cheaha's mountain-bike trail, was designed by professionals and is considered one of the state's best. Paddle-boat rentals on Cheaha Lake cost $5 per hour. Water activities are limited to May to August.

The campground (☎ 205-488-5111) has primitive (tents $5 to $7) and improved sites (tents and RVs $12; $2 more on major holidays and in October, when the fall foliage puts on a show). There is a camp store, restaurant and nature center. The 30-room lodge with a pool and restaurant was recently renovated and charges $56 to $61. Fully furnished cabins go for $53 to $76 and sleep one to eight people. Newly renovated chalets cost $86 and sleep one to six. Call ☎ 800-846-2654 for lodge, cabin and chalet reservations.

The day-use fee is $1 (seniors and disabled visitors 50¢).

Places to Eat

Randall's Cafe (☎ 205-463-5512), Hwy 46 at Evans Bridge Rd, Heflin, is opposite the Shoal Creek Ranger Station. It features huge portions of good rib-stickin' country cooking. The chicken with dressing ($4.50) comes with two sides (try the sweet potatoes), a dollop of cranberry sauce and cornbread. A chicken fillet sandwich with fries is $4. Beverages are limited to sodas and sweet tea. It's open Monday to Friday from 6 am to 2 pm.

The *Barb-B-Que Hut* (☎ 205-463-7555), Hwy 78 at Cavender St, Heflin, about a mile north of I-20, has barbecue sandwiches from $2 and burger plates for $5. There's catfish and memorable pecan pie, too. It's a worn-down, seen-better-days place, but the food's good. The hours are Monday to Saturday from 8 am to 8 pm. Eat in or take-out.

GADSDEN

population 52,500

The town was founded in the mid-19th century on the Coosa River and claims many firsts. William Lay built the nation's first hydroelectric plant here in 1899. In 1929, Goodyear opened its first Southern rubber plant, which became the largest tire and tube plant in the world. Heavy industry remains the primary source of income. Situated at the southern end of the scenic Lookout Mountain Parkway, it also attracts tourist dollars.

Orientation & Information

Gadsden lies just east of the I-59. Waterways, including Coosa River, Big Wills Creek, Black Creek and Neely Henry Lake, define it as much as the roads. Meighan Blvd (Hwy 431) is the main east-west corridor. Hwy 411 splits it north-south. The streets running off Meighan Blvd on each side of the river increase numerically, starting with 1st St. The suburb of Attalla lies on the west border. The Gadsden-Etowah Tourism Center (☎ 205-549-0351), 90 Walnut St (Hwy 411S), downtown, is open Monday to Friday from 8 am to 5 pm, and weekends from 9 am to 5 pm.

Noccalula Falls Park

The 90-foot falls (☎ 205-549-4663), 1500 Noccalula Rd (Hwy 211), at this city-owned park were named after a Native American maiden who killed herself by jumping into them rather than submit to an arranged marriage. There's a statue of her above thundering falls, as well as a pioneer village, botanical garden, minigolf course, playground, restaurant and campground. For a quick overview, stroll around the falls, hike down the stairway to the gorge through Fat Man's Squeeze, then take the miniature train that circles the park. It's open from 9 am to sunset. Admission is $1.50 (children $1). The train ride is an additional $1 (children 50¢).

Noccalula Falls Campground (☎ 205-543-7412), bordering the park, is heavily treed and has well-spaced sites and a nice outdoor pool. Tent and RV rates are $10 for primitive sites, $12 with electricity and water, $15 with full hookups.

Alabama Princess

The *Alabama Princess* (☎ 205-549-1111), The Boardwalk, Hwy 411 at Moragne St, is a replica of a stern-wheel paddleboat. It

ALABAMA

plies the waters of the Coosa River on a narrated 1½-hour sightseeing cruise at 2 pm on weekends from May to October. It's a pleasant way to see the river and the area's dramatic terrain. Admission is $6.50 (seniors $6, kids $3.50). There's an evening dinner cruise ($25) on Saturday at 6 pm.

Special Events

The third Thursday, Friday, Saturday and Sunday of August the annual 450-mile Outdoor Sale (☎ 205-549-0351) takes place as residents along Lookout Mountain Parkway set up roadside booths to sell everything from collectibles to junk. The annual Turkeytown Pow Wow & Green Corn Festival (☎ 205-549-0351) celebrates the region's Cherokee heritage during the third weekend of September.

Places to Stay

Camping For Noccalula Falls Campground see the park entry.

At *Willow Coosa Point* (☎ 205-892-2717, 800-566-9906), 138 Willow Point Dr, Ohatchee, tent and RV campers can choose from 11 shaded sites and 60 waterfront sites. There's a swimming area, marina, camp store, 270-foot pier and boat ramps and rentals. A flat-bottom boat costs $15 a day. Add $10 for a trolling motor and battery. It's a pleasant, family-oriented area just south of Gadsden, off Hwy 77. Tent and RV sites are $15 a night ($25 on major holidays, when there's a two-night minimum stay).

Hotels & Motels You can get a clean, basic room at the *Redwood Inn* (☎ 205-543-8410), 101 E Meighan Blvd (Hwy 431), Gadsden. There's a pool and the managers are helpful. Several chain restaurants are nearby. St traffic can be noisy. Singles/doubles are $30/32.

The *Econo Lodge* (☎ 205-538-9925), 507 Cherry St NE, Attalla, has a bar and grill, an outdoor pool and free continental breakfast. It's next to the I-59. Rooms are $42 to $55, single or double.

Service at the *Super 8* (☎ 205-547-9033, 800-800-8000), 2110 Rainbow Dr (Hwy 411), Gadsden, is cheerful and helpful. The rooms are newly remodeled. There's also a pool and free continental breakfast. Singles/doubles are $40.50/45.

Most of the spacious rooms in the *Gadsden Inn & Suites* (☎ 205-543-7240, 800-637-5678), 200 Albert Rains Blvd, Gadsden, have a river view. All of them have a coffeemaker and free movies and continental breakfast. Rooms are $49 to $59, single or double.

Places to Eat

Thee Grill (☎ 205-546-7788), 135 N 7th St at Henry St, is a trip back to the '50s in food and decor. It serves burgers, dogs, fries, chicken fingers and barbecue along with terrific shakes and malts. It's open Monday to Thursday from 7 am to 3 pm, Friday and Saturday from 7 am to 10 pm, and Sunday from 7 am to 2 pm.

Mi Casita (☎ 205-547-9824) at 644 Walnut St is a popular regional chain serving Mexican specialties. It's open weekdays from 11 am to 10 pm and weekends from noon to 10:30 pm.

At the *Warehouse* (☎ 205-547-5548), 315 S 2nd St, you get a traditional Southern meat-and-four for lunch for $5. The dinner menu is more contemporary, with steaks, chicken and pasta starting around $9. Ask about the specials. It's open Monday to Saturday for lunch and dinner.

Things to Buy

There's no escaping antiques, collectibles and good ol' junk at the Mountain Top Flea Market (☎ 205-589-2706, 800-535-2286), 11301 Hwy 278, six miles west of Attalla at mile marker 101. It boasts more than 1000 dealers. It runs on Sunday from 5 am to around 2 pm.

Getting There & Away

The closest airports are in Birmingham, Atlanta, Huntsville and Chattanooga.

Greyhound (☎ 205-547-4959), 1511 W Meighan Blvd, has services from Atlanta

($24; one a day), Chattanooga ($47; one), Jackson ($56; one), Memphis ($56; two) and Nashville ($47; one).

Enterprise Rent A Car (☎ 205-494-9008) has an office in town at 200 W Meighan Blvd.

If you head north on the Lookout Mountain Parkway you'll see spectacular scenery along Little River Canyon. The first few miles along Hwy 211 and County Rd 89 pass through small farming communities. You can continue north to Fort Payne – and as far as Chattanooga – on the parkway or take the more scenic Hwy 176 loop along the rim of the canyon before returning to the parkway at Fort Payne on Hwy 35. Trees and wide shoulders keep you well away from the edge, except at the lookouts. Don't take the branch of Hwy 176 that heads southwest. It's a treacherous, winding gravel road that isn't maintained.

FORT PAYNE

population 14,000

This small community in the valley below Lookout Mountain and Sand Mountain grew out of a stockade that held Cherokees before their forced removal to Oklahoma. Today, it's best known as the home of the country group Alabama and for its sock mills.

Orientation & Information

Located west of the Little River Canyon National Preserve and southwest of De Soto State Park, Fort Payne can be reached quickly via I-59 or by taking the scenic Lookout Mountain Parkway. You can also take Canyon Rim Dr (Hwy 176) and turn west onto Hwy 35. Gault Ave (Hwy 11) is the main thoroughfare. Most streets that cross it ascend numerically north and south from 1st St.

Contact the De Kalb County Visitor Association (☎ 205-845-3957), 2201 J Gault Ave N, for information; it's open Monday to Friday from 9 am to 4 pm. The post office (☎ 205-845-0434) is at 301 1st St SE. De Kalb Baptist Medical Center (☎ 205-845-3150) is at 200 Medical Center Dr.

De Kalb County is dry. Unless otherwise posted, you may bring liquor into hotels and campgrounds. Some restaurants allow you to bring it in discreetly. Ask in advance.

Alabama Fan Club & Museum

This museum (☎ 205-845-1646) at 101 Glenn Ave SW is a tribute to Fort Payne's country music home boys and features videos of the group and lots of personal memorabilia. It's open Monday to Saturday from 8 am to 4 pm, and Sunday from noon to 4 pm (in winter only until 3 pm). There is also a gift shop selling souvenirs.

Fort Payne Depot

This enterprising little museum (☎ 205-845-5714), 105 5th St NE, is a good place to go when you can't enjoy the parks because of rain. Built as a railway station in 1891, it's now a history museum with regional artifacts from Native Americans and European settlers. A train car has railroad memorabilia. It's open Monday, Wednesday and Friday from 10 am to 4 pm, and Sunday from 2 to 4 pm.

Activities

The closest place for wild **caving** is at Russell Cave National Monument, about 40 miles north. This county has numerous caves, but most are on private property and require permission to explore. Due to the high number of accidents, permission is rarely granted unless you are a member of a recognized speleological organization. Contact the National Speleological Society (☎ 205-852-1300, fax 205-851-9241), 2813 Cave Ave, 35810, based in nearby Huntsville, for information about caving and grottos in Alabama. Dues start at $20 a year. Lookout Valley Grotto, PO Box 435, Valley Head, AL 35989, is a new spelunking group in the area.

For folks who want to experience nature without frills, Rebecca and Bill Adams of Adams Outdoors (☎ 205-845-2988), 6102 Mitchell Rd NE, Fort Payne, provide a number of outdoor activities, including

ALABAMA

rafting trips down the Little River from late winter to early June (the rest of the year the river is too low), **rappelling** and introductory caving ($60 for two people), environmental activities ($5 to $15 per person) and map interpretation for orienteering. Escorted rafting trips cost $25 per person (minimum of two people) or $10 to $15 unescorted (with shuttle). They also arrange horseback riding and wagon rides. Their 70-acre spread has rustic cabins, shelters and campsites (see Places to Stay, Camping).

Organized Tours

Ms Jackie's Open-Air Tours (☎ 205-845-7773), 518 Hwy 35, Fort Payne, provides a 2½-hour close-up view of the canyon, forest, Fort Payne and Cherokee Rock Village, a large rocky outcrop atop Lookout Mountain. The tours ($42 for adults, $25 for kids) leave at 1 pm and are for two to three people.

Places to Stay

Camping For De Soto State Park see the park entry.

You can walk to Little River Falls from *Ms Jackie's Campground* (☎ 205-845-7773), 518 Hwy 35E at Hwy 176, which has primitive/improved tent sites for $7/9 and RV sites ($12.50 to $15), showers and restrooms, a gift shop and a no-frills deli that serves hot dogs, barbecue, picnic sandwiches and refreshing Hawaiian shaved ices. The campground's office is open Monday to Saturday from 11 am to 9 pm and Sunday from 1 to 5:30 pm. The deli is open Monday to Saturday from 11 am to 6 pm and Sunday from 1 to 5:30 pm.

Adams Outdoors (☎ 205-845-2988), 6102 Mitchell Rd NE, Fort Payne, in the woods near De Soto State Park, rents rustic furnished two-bedroom cabins for up to eight people ($65 to $70) and secluded one-room cabins ($50 to $60). There are also screened weather-proof huts with sleeping gear, water and electricity ($20 to $30), and tent sites ($10).

Also tucked in the forest near De Soto State Park is 13-acre *Knotty Pine Resort* (☎ 205-845-5293), 1492 County Rd 618, Fort Payne, which has tent ($7 to $9) and

RV ($10 to $13) sites as well as cabins. Fully furnished four and six-person cabins ($65 to $90) have fireplaces, TVs, heating, air-con, grills and full and king beds; more rustic four-person cabins ($30 to $38) have no bathrooms, but have heat and AC, ceiling fans, queen and bunk beds. There's a two-night minimum on weekends (three nights on major holidays).

Hotels & Motels The nicest feature of the *Quality Inn* (☎ 205-845-4013), I-59 at Hwy 35, is the kidney-shaped pool with a separate pool for kids. Singles/doubles cost $40/45.

The *Best Western Motel* (☎ 205-845-0481), 1828 Gault Ave N, is one of the few commercial properties in the area. It has spacious rooms with a data port and sofa bed, free movies and continental breakfast, an outdoor pool and a restaurant. Restaurant hours are convenient for getting an early start: daily 5 am to 8:30 pm. Rooms are priced at $45/54 single/double.

Places to Eat

Mi Casita (☎ 205-845-2999), 3800 Gault Ave N, and 1104 Gault Ave S, Suite E (☎ 205-845-4520), serves traditional Mexican foods. The fajitas are pretty good and the lunch buffet (north location only) is a bargain at $5. Both locations are open Monday to Friday from 11 am to 9 pm and Saturday from noon to 9 pm. The north location also is open on Sunday from noon to 9 pm.

Peking Gourmet (☎ 205-845-1606), 2605 Gault Ave N, has a 30-item buffet ($5 lunch, $7 dinner) including desserts. Very filling combination plates that include an egg roll, fried rice and crabmeat cream cheese cost around $4 at lunch and $7 to $8 at dinner.

Western Sizzlin (☎ 205-845-6111), 2200 Gault Ave N, is a regional chain that serves steaks, seafood and chicken. The buffet is the best deal. It features meat, fish, veggies and macaroni with cheese on weekdays from 11 am to 4 pm for $5; after 4 pm and on weekends the buffet is $7. It's open Sunday to Thursday from 10:30 am to 10 pm and Friday and Saturday to 11 pm.

AROUND FORT PAYNE
Little River Canyon National Preserve
The Little River flows through Little River Canyon, which is about 16 miles long, three-quarters of a mile at its widest and 400 to 700 feet deep. More than 14,000 acres around the river and canyon are part of the preserve, which was established in 1992. Its headquarters (☎ 205-845-9605) are at 2141 Gault Ave N, Fort Payne. Hwy 176 (Canyon Rim Dr) follows the west rim of the canyon for 22 miles. While you're driving, the views of the waterfalls, canyon and wildflowers are the attraction. Once you're out of the car, hiking, rock climbing and white water await.

At the north end of the preserve is De Soto State Park (see the park entry). In the middle are the dramatic 60-foot Little River Falls, accessed by an easy hike at the turnoff at Hwys 176 and 35. At the south end and on the opposite side is Canyon Mouth Park, a day-use area with a 1½-mile hiking trail, swimming area, bathrooms, picnic tables and grills. Don't miss the lookouts on either side of Bear Creek, from where you can see Grace's High Falls, one of the highest cascades in Alabama. Trailheads are well marked along the rim road, particularly at the lookouts. Eberhardt Point – formerly Canyonland Park – has picnic tables, a great view of the canyon and a popular put-in for canoes, kayaks, rafts and tubes. Hike down the canyon 20 minutes to reach the water.

To reach Canyon Mouth Park, you'll need to drive northeast along the canyon rim, then cross the canyon at Hwy 35E and turn south onto Hwy 273. Day-use hours are 7 am to sunset.

De Soto State Park
The best way to explore Lookout Mountain and Little River Canyon is from this 5000-acre park, which has many facilities, including hiking trails, tennis and volleyball courts, a nature center, store (☎ 205-845-5075), restaurant, campground, lodge and chalets. The park's headquarters (☎ 205-845-0051, fax 205-845-3224) are at 13883 County Rd 89, Fort Payne. Most of the trails pass through woodlands dotted with waterfalls and interesting rock formations. In May and June rhododendrons and mountain laurels bloom. The seasoned hiker can try the 12-mile De Soto Scout Trail, which starts at a nearby boy scout camp and passes through thick brush and rugged terrain. There is no mountain biking on trails. The outdoor pool is free for visitors staying in the lodge, cabins and chalets, but costs $2 for campers and day-use visitors. North of the park store are De Soto Falls, where a cascade plummets 100 feet into a rugged gorge.

Primitive sites at the campground (☎ 205-845-5075, 800-252-7275) go for $6.50, or $12 with water and electricity ($14 with full hookups). Sites are well spaced and shaded. The fully equipped two/four/six-person rustic cabins are $61/66/71.50. Rates at the 25-room lodge range from $54 to $57. The A-frame chalets go for $79. Call or write to the park office (☎ 205-845-5380, 800-568-8840, 800-252-7275), 265 County Rd 951, Fort Payne, AL 35967, for cabin, chalet and lodge reservations.

Mentone
A few miles north of Fort Payne on Hwy 11 or County Rd 89, is this quaint 19th-century health resort that still attracts visitors looking for a fresh-air vacation. Most of the 500 residents are either retired or involved in tourism. There are numerous B&Bs, inns, summer camps, craft and antique shops and even a dude ranch. It's within five minutes of De Soto State Park and 15 minutes of Little River National Preserve.

Places to Stay Almost a dozen B&Bs operate in the area, with prices starting at $60 a night. Some places are seasonal. *Mentone Springs Hotel* (☎ 205-634-4040), 1 Hotel Square, Hwy 117 at County Rd 89, has seven rooms with fireplaces) and a restaurant. The *Mountain Laurel Inn* (☎ 205-634-4673, 800-889-4244), 624 County Rd 948, is a rustic house back in the

ALABAMA

woods, next to the Mentone chapel. The contemporary *Raven Haven* (☎ 205-634-4310), Hwy 117 at mile marker 3, has four rooms overlooking 10 acres. The farm house and cottage at *Valhalla* (☎ 205-634-4006), 672 County Rd 626, sit on 20 acres and offer modern conveniences in a country setting. The *Mentone Inn* (☎ 205-634-4836, 800-455-7470), Hwy 117 at County Rd 89, has a wide porch where you can eat break-fast or relax, period furnishings from the 1920s and 1930s, a deck and 12 rooms.

On 1000 acres atop Lookout Mountain is *Cloudmont Ski & Golf Resort and Shady Grove Dude Ranch* (☎ 205-634-4344), 721 County Rd 614, the only place in Alabama where you can ski. You can also play golf, fish, hike and ride horses on 100 miles of trails. Accommodations range from A-frame chalets ($60 to $65) to a rustic bunkhouse ($10 per person, minimum $40) that sleeps nine. The affable, sometimes politically incorrect owner, Jack Jones, opened the place as a boys' camp in 1947, then turned it into a resort in 1970.

Places to Eat Besides the three restau-rants below, there are half a dozen large and small eateries around the intersection of Hwy 117 and County Rd 89.

Dessie's Kountry Chef (☎ 205-634-4232), 5951 Hwy 117S, is owned by Dessie Newberry, voted best cook in De Kalb County in 1995. While her rib eye ($10) and two-breast chicken ($8) are excellent, it's the catfish that folks love. Fried to a golden brown, it's flavorful and tender and comes whole, as a fillet or in strips ($7). Everything comes with sides. Weekday lunch specials and sandwiches are below $5. It's open Monday, Wednesday and Thursday from 10 am to 7:30 pm, Friday and Saturday to 8:30 pm, and Sunday from 11 am to 2 pm; it's closed Tuesday.

The *Cliffs* (☎ 205-634-3040), 15861 County Rd 89, features soups and salads ($3 to $4), pastas, chicken, seafood and steaks ($8 to $10.50). It's open for dinner only and is closed Sunday and Monday. Reservations are advised.

Cragsmere Manna (☎ 205-634-4677), 17871 County Rd 89, has an eclectic menu of vegetable, seafood and chicken dishes and pasta. Checks average $15 to $25. It's open Friday and Saturday from 5 to 9 pm. Reservations are advised.

Valley Head

Blink and you might miss this little town west of Mentone on Hwy 117. Once a Cherokee Indian village, it now has about 700 inhabitants. There are many original turn-of-the-century buildings.

The most visible building in town is **Winston Place**, a historic mansion (☎ 205-635-6381) on Hwy 117 at Railroad Ave. It's open for tours and as a B&B. Built in 1831, it's situated on 25 acres on which once stood the Cherokee Council Tree, a giant black Spanish oak where Sequoyah, the Cherokee chief and scholar who devel-oped a system of transcribing the Cherokee language, taught his newly invented alphabet. Also called George Guess, he was born around 1770. He served with the US army in the Creek War (1813-14), was an accomplished artist and lived until 1843.

The tree was felled in a storm a few years ago and only the stump and a his-torical marker remain. Admission is $5 (students $3).

Sequoyah Caverns (☎ 205-635-0024) on Sequoyah Rd are known as the Looking Glass Caverns because of the perfect reflections cast in pools of water inside. Enthusiastic guides point out formations that resemble animals and famous people while explaining how the caves were found and formed. Tours are 45 to 60 minutes long and go deep into the caves. It's very tasteful – no flashy colored lights or music. Bring a sweater. It's damp, especially after it rains, and the temperature stays around 60°F. Admission is $7 (children $4). Out-side the caverns is a park with bison, deer, ducks and peacocks.

The nice campground has lots of trees, a pool and a store. RV and tent sites are $14 with electricity and water, or $15 with full hookups.

RUSSELL CAVE
NATIONAL MONUMENT
In the northeastern corner of Alabama, on Hwy 72, is **Bridgeport**, home of Russell Cave National Monument.

Tours with a ranger (☎ 205-495-2672, fax 205-495-9290) are limited to a few hundred feet beyond the entrance to the cave, 3729 County Rd 98, which functions mostly as an archaeological museum about the Native Americans who lived in and around the cave from 7000 BC to 1000 AD. The museum displays pottery shards, arrowheads, and bone fish hooks and needles. You'll also see videos, demonstrations of weapons, and a 10-minute spelunking slide show.

There is wild caving through seven miles of primarily horizontal passageways. Spelunking groups of three or more adults can obtain a permit to enter the caves from 8:30 am to 1:30 pm, returning by 4:30 pm. Request a list of required equipment and rules in advance. There's no wild caving during or right after rain storms.

The monument is open daily from 8 am to 5 pm, except Thanksgiving, Christmas and New Year's Day. There's good signage for the monument in Bridgeport. From Hwy 72 go west on County Rd 75, then travel north four miles on County Rd 98.

BUCK'S POCKET STATE PARK
This 2000-acre jewel of a park (☎ 205-659-2000), 393 County Rd 174, is off the beaten path but close enough to De Soto State Park and Guntersville State Park to attract serious outdoor enthusiasts. Four hundred feet above the floor of the gorge, the Jim Lynn Overlook affords a stunning view of the surrounding valley. Drive up by taking the first right in the park or hike up the two-mile Canyon Trail from the campgrounds below.

The two campgrounds beside Little Sauty and South Sauty Creeks are very peaceful and beautiful. There are 40 improved tent and RV sites ($12), 10 primitive sites ($8) and four backpacking sites, all wooded and spacious. There are 15½ miles of interesting trails.

To get to the park take Hwy 227 west into Grove Oak from Hwy 75. The park is well signposted from Grove Oak.

GUNTERSVILLE
population 8743
Continue south from Buck's Pocket State Park on Hwy 227 for 21 miles into Guntersville, a picturesque community at the south end of Lake Guntersville. It's the seat of Marshall County and though it's rapidly growing – there's been a 25% population increase since 1990 – it boasts one of the lowest crime rates in the southeast. The economy is driven by light manufacturing and tourism to the lake, mountains and nearby state parks.

Orientation & Information
Guntersville is located on Hwy 431, which cuts north-south through town one block from the lake. As it crosses the River Bridge (also known as Veterans Memorial Bridge) from the north, it's called Gunter Ave and runs one-way. To go north, take Blount St, which runs along the lake. The local chamber of commerce (☎ 205-582-3612, fax 205-582-3582), 200 Gunter Ave, just south of the River Bridge, is open Monday to Friday from 8:30 am to 5 pm, and Saturday from 10 am to 4 pm. The Guntersville-Arab Medical Center (☎ 205-593-8310) is at 2505 Hwy 431, in Boaz.

Activities
Town Creek Fishing Center (☎ 205-582-8358), 7966 Hwy 227, has a bait-and-tackle shop and rents out 14-foot two-seat canoes for $17 a day, $10 a half-day or $3 per hour. It also has nonmotorized flat-bottom boats for $10 a day or $7.50 a half-day. From March to October it's open Monday to Thursday from 8 am to 5 pm, and Friday to Sunday from 7 am to 7 pm.

Guntersville Boat Mart (☎ 205-582-2038), 3374 Hwy 69, rents large pontoon boats for around $150 a day. Half-day rentals are less. It's open daily from 9 am to 5 pm. Vaughn's Recreation Center (☎ 205-582-4821), Hwy 431, also has pontoon

ALABAMA

boats for $150 a day. It's open daily from 8 am to 5 or 6 pm.

Captain Lynn Williams of Sailyn, Inc (☎ 205-572-0455, 205-582-8511), at the Anchorage Marina, Hwy 431, two miles north of the River Bridge, offers 2½-hour sailing excursions on Lake Guntersville on the *II Smooth*. The $40 charge includes a stop for a swim, hors d'oeuvres and non-alcoholic drinks (you can bring your own liquor), and there's a great view of the sunset. Sailing lessons are also available.

You can fish on your own from the parks or marinas or hire a guide for about $90 a half-day or $150 a full day. Among the guide services is Lake Guntersville Fishing Guides (☎ 205-778-7464, 205-582-5463, 800-645-1585), 487 Camp Ney-A-Ti Rd, Guntersville.

Swimming is permitted along the shoreline, and there is a beach at Lake Guntersville State Park.

Lake Guntersville State Park

This beautiful park (☎ 205-571-5444), 7966 Hwy 227, on the slope of Little Mountain, has 5909 acres of meadows and forests on the edge of Guntersville Lake. It's six miles northeast of Guntersville and is better described as a resort. It has camping, a fancy restaurant and lodge, chalets and cottages, a large pool, golf course, sandy beach, nature center, boating and fishing, lighted tennis courts and a convention center. If hiking is your thing, you'll like it here – there are 19 trails to choose from. The moderately challenging three-mile Tom Beevil Trail passes half a dozen old home sites, patches of wild azaleas and huge old oak trees. The ranger station has a good descriptive flyer of all trails and an interpretive brochure for the Tom Beevil trail. Bald eagles nest in the area in winter. You can rent flat-bottomed boats with oars for $7.50 a half-day or $10 all day.

On holidays and busy weekends, people crowd into the improved campsites ($14). During those times, opt for either a primitive campsite ($7) on the lakefront or choose a nearby private campground. The cottages and chalets cost $98 and sleep up to four people. The lodge rooms are $50 to $58 for a single and $54 to $60 a double; two-room suites are around $95.

Places to Stay

Camping For camping at Lake Guntersville State Park see the park entry.

The 80-acre *Siebold Campground & Marina* (☎ 205-582-0040), 54 Siebold Creek Rd, off Hwy 79, is a TVA campground leased to private operators who live on site. The camp is set among towering pines and there are 94 improved tent and RV sites, each with a grill and picnic table. The rates are $18 on the water or $15 away from the water. There is a camp store and a marina.

The privately owned *Town Creek Campground* (☎ 205-582-8358), 7966 Hwy 227, on the north edge of Lake Guntersville State Park, has 10 primitive sites with the use of restrooms and a bathhouse ($7), 100 primitive sites with the use of portable toilets ($3.50), and 42 improved sites ($12) with a grill, water, electric and use of restrooms and bathhouse. The campground also offers canoe and boat rentals and has four fishing piers.

Hotels & Motels The *Lakeview Inn* (☎ 205-582-3104), 2300 Gunter Ave, has 24 basic rooms, some with a view of the lake. There are free movies. Singles/doubles are $28/35. It's just up the street from several restaurants.

The *Super 8 Motel* (☎ 205-582-8444), 14341 Hwy 431S, overlooks Lake Guntersville and has large rooms with refrigerators, microwaves and ceiling fans. Movies and continental breakfast are free. Singles/doubles are $38/42. Pick up a coupon to receive a 10% discount at the Pizza Hut next door.

At *Mac's Landing Lodge & Marina* (☎ 205-582-1000), 7001 Val Monte Dr, on the east side of the lake, half a mile off Hwy 431, the balconied rooms overlook the outdoor pool and the lake or the mountains. Rooms are average size, except suites, which have kitchenettes. There's a lounge, pier and free movies. Rooms are

$57 to $61 single or double, and suites are $90 to $150.

For *Lake Guntersville Lodge* see the park entry.

Places to Eat

The best bargain is the folksy *Bruce's Restaurant* (☎ 205-582-8261), Hwy 431, three miles north of Guntersville Bridge in Claysville, with an all-you-can-eat buffet of traditional Southern foods. The $6 price tag includes a drink. It's only open Friday and Saturday from 10:30 am to 9 pm and Sunday from 10:30 am to 8 pm.

Wanda's Restaurant & Ice Cream Parlor (☎ 205-582-5842), 392 Gunter Ave, serves traditional Southern breakfasts, sandwiches and burgers and 16 flavors of ice cream. It's open Monday to Saturday from 7 am to 4 pm.

Pasquale's Pizza & Pasta (☎ 205-582-0227), 754 Hwy 431, serves thin and thick-crust pizzas ($1.50 to $16.50) and traditional Italian specialties and sandwiches ($2.50 to $6). All-you-can-eat specials on weekdays at lunchtime and on Monday nights are around $4. It's open Monday to Thursday from 11 am to 9 pm and Friday and Saturday from 11 am to 10 pm.

Neena's Lakeside Grill (☎ 205-505-0550), in the Holiday Inn, 2140 Gunter Ave, specializes in prime rib (from $9), but also has seafood, chicken and pasta in an upscale waterfront setting. It's open Monday to Thursday from 6 to 9 pm and Friday to Sunday from 6 to 10 pm. The fried shrimp ($11) and shrimp scampi ($13) are both good.

Crawdaddy's Seafood Shoppe (☎ 205-582-0484), 5000 Webb Villa, features fresh Gulf shrimp, crabs and oysters, plus a few beef dishes. It's open Wednesday to Friday from 4:30 to 10 pm, and Saturday from 11:30 am to 10 pm; it's also open for lunch on Friday if it's a holiday weekend.

Getting There & Away

The Huntsville airport is 40 miles northwest of Guntersville. Executive Connection (☎ 205-772-0186, see Huntsville Getting There & Away) provides airport shuttles to Guntersville for $65 to $75.

Central Alabama

Central Alabama is crisscrossed by major and minor rivers that over the centuries have deposited nutrients, creating a rich, black soil ideal for planting cotton. Called the Black Belt, the region was named for the swath of fertile soil that cuts across the state. The rivers later served as important arteries for transporting cotton to Mobile's port.

In the early 1980s, part of the region's river system was dammed by the Army Corps of Engineers as an alternate route for river traffic traveling south to the Gulf of Mexico. They created the Tennessee-Tombigbee Waterway, a 234-mile transportation artery with 10 locks and a lift of 341 feet that connects the Gulf with the 16,000-mile inland waterway system. In the process, it created numerous recreational opportunities and wildlife refuges. The region also has seven state parks and a national forest.

Spectator sports, especially football, dominate the culture of central Alabama as the state's fiercest rivals – two of the best teams in the country, Auburn University and the University of Alabama at Tuscaloosa – are on opposite sides of the region.

Along with Montgomery, the current capital, three of the previous four state capitals are here: Cahawba, Selma and Tuscaloosa. The region is rife with Civil War and civil rights history and antebellum structures.

This chapter starts in Auburn and Opelika, then follows I-85 west through Tuskegee National Forest and Tuskegee before reaching Montgomery, in the middle of the state. It continues west on Hwy 80 to Montgomery, Selma and Demopolis before heading north on Hwy 43 and I-20/59 to Tuscaloosa.

AUBURN & OPELIKA

Nearly two-thirds of Auburn's population of 35,000 is made up of students from Auburn University (AU), the state's largest university and the city's main employer. Many campus events are free and open to the public. The university is best known for its outstanding athletic programs, especially football and basketball. The town's population swells to 85,000 on football weekends.

Campus and town life revolve around the original 1280-acre tract at the corner of College St and Magnolia Ave, called Toomer's Corner. After a winning home football game, the town converges on this corner to cover an old oak tree with toilet paper. The mayor boasts that Auburn is the country's only town with a budget for cleaning up toilet paper.

Neighboring Opelika, the county seat, has a lively historic business district with

ALABAMA

HIGHLIGHTS

- Montgomery's civil rights memorial designed by Maya Lin and honoring 40 martyrs of the movement
- The art collection at Gulf States Paper Corporation in Tuscaloosa, especially the paintings of wild birds by Basil Ede
- Moundville Archaeological Park's Mississippian-era Indian mounds, archaeological museum and nature trails
- The George W Carver Museum in the Tuskegee Institute National Historic Site
- The town of Selma, rich in African-American history

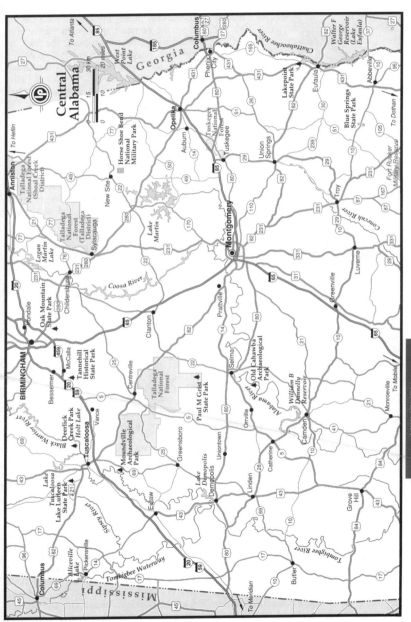

shops and restaurants as well as a historic residential district of restored 19th and early 20th-century houses.

Orientation

The twin cities of Auburn and Opelika are in east central Alabama. Auburn is situated west of Opelika. Pepperell Parkway (Hwy 29) is the main road linking Auburn and Opelika. You can walk around the campus and downtown Auburn, but you'll need a bus or car to reach Opelika, and a car or taxi to reach Chewacla State Park.

Information

Tourist Offices The convention and visitors bureau (☎ 334-887-8747, 800-321-8880) is at 714 E Glenn Ave in Auburn.

Post There are post offices at 300 Opelika Rd, Auburn, and 500 S 7th St, Opelika.

Bookstores & Libraries The best selection of regional books can be found at Books-A-Million (☎ 334-887-1888), 1716 Opelika Rd, Auburn. Auburn Public Library (☎ 334-887-4997), 161 N Ross St, and the university's RB Draughon Library (☎ 334-844-1738), at S College St and West Thach Ave, provide a quiet place to read newspapers, magazines and books.

Campuses You can pick up a parking pass at the AU police department (☎ 334-844-4901) in the Dawson Building at Donahue Dr and Thach Ave. Several original campus buildings date from 1880, including Samford Hall, the chapel and Langdon Hall. For a map and tour information contact the admissions office (☎ 334-844-4080), AU Room No 202, Martin Hall, W Thach Ave at Mell St. Free guided tours are offered Monday to Friday from 8 am to 4 pm (except between 11:45 am and 12:45 pm).

Chewacla State Park

This 696-acre park (☎ 334-887-5621), 124 Shell Toomer Parkway, off I-85's exit 51, lies on Auburn's southwest border. Its centerpiece is the 26-acre Chewacla Lake, surrounded by woodland and unusual rock formations. A dogwood-lined road climbs from the entrance to a green picnic area and nature trails overlooking the lake. In summer, people gather on the green for picnics and impromptu concerts. Two trails lead from the top down to Chewacla Falls, where hikers stop to sit on huge boulders for a view before continuing along the lake's shoreline. The first trail is a paved road used by park maintenance. The other is a dirt road that takes about an hour to walk. In addition to a mountain-biking trail, there's a tree-identification hiking trail and four other trails. Other amenities and activities include tennis courts, fishing, a large lakefront beach and playground, a bathhouse, picnic grills and pavilions, paddle boats ($5 an hour) and canoes ($4 an hour), motor boats ($4 an hour or $7.50 per day) and a swimming area with a floating diving platform.

Primitive tent sites are $9 and there are 36 improved tent sites and full hookup RV sites, which cost $12. Restrooms and showers are nearby. The five rustic lakefront cabins cost $42 to $56, except on football weekends, when the rate is $68 to $79. There's a two-night minimum on weekends and three-night minimum on holidays.

The park is open daily from dusk to dawn. The day-use fee is $1 for adults and 50¢ for children.

Toomer's Drugs

This combination drug store and soda fountain (☎ 334-887-3488), on Toomer's Corner at 100 N College St, Auburn, has been a meeting place since 1896. Sweet, tart, freshly squeezed lemonade is available Monday to Friday from 9 am to 6 pm, and Saturday from 9 am to 1 pm.

Lovelace Athletic Museum

This orange and blue shrine (☎ 334-844-4750) to AU's athletic heroes, at Donahue Dr and Samford Ave, caters to the MTV generation with high-tech multimedia and interactive displays. Among the notable players and coaches are Bo Jackson, Charles Barkley, Vickie Orr and Rowdy Gaines. For the nonsports oriented it's only

Top Left: Big Lucky Carter, Memphis, TN   **Top Right:** Beale St, Memphis, TN
Bottom: Sun Studio, Memphis, TN

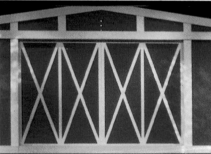

Top: Music shops and museums surrounding Nashville's Music Row

Middle Left: Pops Davis, a popular Beale St character, Memphis, TN

Bottom Left: Original log cabin used by the Andrew Jackson family 1804-21, The Hermitage, Nashville, TN

Bottom Right: Opryland USA, Nashville, TN

mildly interesting, but those who love sports shouldn't miss it. For the biggest thrill, go on game day. It's open Monday to Friday from 8 am to 4:30 pm, and when games are held, Saturdays from 9 am to 6 pm and Sundays from 9 am to 3 pm; entry is free.

Golf
Auburn boasts six public golf courses, including the Grand National (☎ 334-749-9042, 800-949-4444), 3000 Sunbelt Parkway, Opelika, a 54-hole stop on the Robert Trent Jones Golf Trail. Green fees are $39 to $49, plus $15 for a cart.

Special Events
Thirty homes along 8th and 9th Sts in Opelika's historic district celebrate Christmas Victorian style, with vintage decorations and old-fashioned Santas. There's free live music in Opelika Municipal Park (☎ 334-705-5560), 1102 Denson Dr, during the Summer Swing Concert Series held June to August on Tuesday evenings.

Places to Stay
On football weekends (September through November) room rates can double or triple. Rates also increase, but not as dramatically, during special events.

Camping For camping at Chewacla State Park see the park entry.

Leisure Time Campgrounds (☎ 334-821-2267), 2670 S College St, Auburn, is a privately owned campground with 60 gravel sites ($10 for a tent, $18 for an RV) with full hookups. There are showers, restrooms and a laundry. It's about 1½ miles from the university and only a stone's throw from Chewacla State Park. Management is helpful and friendly.

Hotels & Motels Auburn's *Econo Lodge* (☎ 334-826-8900, 800-553-2666), 2145 S College St, has a microwave and refrigerator in each room. It's new, clean and simple. Singles/doubles are $46/52.

The *Days Inn* (☎ 334-749-5080, 800-325-2525), 1014 Anand Ave, Opelika, has

DIANE MARSHALL

James Echols at Toomer's Drugs

an indoor heated pool, plus many in-room amenities, including microwave, small refrigerator, safe and hair dryer. Continental breakfast is included in the single/double rate of $45/49.50.

The *Golden Cherry Motel* (☎ 334-745-7623), 1010 2nd Ave, Opelika, has budget accommodations. It's under new management and was recently remodeled. You get a basic room with TV, radio, air-con and free movies for $27.

Shoney's Inn (☎ 334-742-0270, 800-222-2222, fax 334-742-0299), 1520 Columbus Parkway, Opelika, charges $45 for a room with TV, refrigerator, safe and coffee-maker; there's free continental breakfast and use of the fitness room, sauna, Jacuzzi and pool.

The *Holiday Inn* (☎ 334-745-6331, 800-465-4329, fax 334-749-3933), 1102 Columbus Parkway, Opelika, just completed a major renovation, so everything's spotless and bright. It has its own restaurant and pool. Singles go for $50 to $80 and doubles are $55 to $85.

Inns & B&Bs *Heritage House Bed & Breakfast* (☎ 334-705-0485), 714 2nd Ave, Opelika, is a family-run historic house built in 1914. The ceilings are 11 feet high, giving the house an open, spacious feeling. There's no smoking. Room rates are $65 to $85 (depending on room size), including breakfast.

Crenshaw Guest House (☎ 334-821-1131), 371 N College St, is a restored Victorian house in Auburn's historic district. In warm weather the front porch swing and backyard gardens beg you to stay. It's close to the campus and downtown. Each room has a phone, TV, VCR and cassette player. There's no smoking. Singles range from $48 to $65 and doubles from $58 to $75. There's a two-night minimum stay on football weekends.

Places to Eat
Auburn Typical of college towns, Auburn and Opelika offer a lot of low-priced eateries, including several with all-you-can-eat buffets for under $5. Those who want fine food won't feel left out either.

If you're on a tight budget, you can't beat the all-you-can-eat buffet at *Cici's Pizza* (☎ 334-821-2600), Flint's Crossing Shopping Center, 1550 Opelika Rd. On offer are rigatoni with tomato sauce, pizza, garlic bread, salad and a choice of pies for dessert – all for $3 for adults, or $2 if you're under 10 years old (free for those under three). A big-screen TV keeps you entertained.

Mr Gatti's Pizza (☎ 334-826-0981), 236 South Gay St, Auburn, feeds students at a bargain price. The all-you-can-eat buffet features spaghetti, pizza, salad and dessert. Lunch and dinner cost around $4.50. You can watch TV on three big-screen TVs, one of which is always tuned to cartoons.

The *Coffee Banque* (☎ 334-887-1005), 101 N College St, in the old Bank of Auburn, is a university hangout. The only vestiges of its stuffy origins are the polished wood, brass rails and some wing chairs. Patrons drink coffee, tea, Italian sodas and micro beers while munching on bagels, breakfast pastries and sandwiches. There's live folk or blues entertainment on Friday nights. It's open seven days a week, 24 hours a day, except in winter, when the hours are 7 am to 4 am.

Behind the Glass (☎ 334-826-1133), 168 E Magnolia Ave, is a fun, artsy combination bookstore, art gallery, boutique and restaurant. A delicious buy is the BTG beans ($4), which has black beans in a tomato base, served over rice. It comes with bread and a choice of toppings. Sandwiches ($4.50) come with pasta salad or chips or you can order a smaller sandwich with soup. Lunch and dinner are served daily.

Denaro's (☎ 334-821-0349), 103 N College St, is huge, seating almost 150 for its Italian and seafood specialties. You can eat in the restaurant, outside on the deck or in the sports lounge. The latter fills quickly when there's a football or basketball game on. It offers dinner only and is closed on Sunday.

Ivy's (☎ 334-821-8200), in the Auburn University Hotel and Conference Center,

241 S College St, caters to university business visitors and the parents of students. It serves three meals a day, specializing in black Angus beef and seafood for dinner. You get your money's worth at the Sunday buffet brunch ($10 adults, $6 children). It's open Monday to Thursday 6:30 am to 2 pm and 5 to 9 pm, Friday and Saturday 6:30 am to 2 pm and 5 to 10 pm, Sunday 11 am to 2 pm.

Opelika Everything at *Venable's* (☎ 334-745-0834), 913 S Railroad Ave, is available to eat in or take out. 'Picnic in the park' ($6) is sliced smoked turkey, baked ham and cheese, lettuce and tomato on a roll, and potato salad. Soup and salad ($5.50) and a vegetable plate ($6) are other options. It's open weekdays from 11 am to 2 pm.

The *Warehouse Bistro* (☎ 334-745-6353), 105 Rocket Ave, is arguably the best restaurant in town. The menu changes seasonally, retaining the basic steaks, seafood and fowl, but altering the sauces and cooking method. The á la carte menu's entrée prices run from $16 to $21. It's open Tuesday to Friday from 11 am to 2 pm and 6 to 9 pm, and Saturday from 6 pm to 9 pm. Locals stop at the *Food Factory*, the bistro's gourmet deli, for moderately priced take-out lunches, dinners and desserts.

Entertainment
Nightclubs With a large population of students, Auburn-Opelika has numerous late-night entertainment spots with live music. Check the *Auburn Plainsman* for listings.

Neon's (☎ 334-502-0514), 136 W Magnolia Ave, Auburn, has plenty of dance space. Live bands, usually progressive rock, play on Thursday from 7 pm to 3:30 am, and a DJ spins '70s and '80s dance music on Friday and Saturday from 9 pm to 3:30 am for a mostly college-age crowd. It also serves food. The cover is $4 for those over 21 years, $6 if you're under 21 years.

Denaro's (☎ 334-821-0349), 103 N College St, attracts an impressive crowd on Friday and Saturday nights who come to hear live rock and folk music. There's a $4 to $5 cover.

The *Hideaway Country Lounge* (☎ 334-749-3334), 1002 Columbus Parkway, Opelika, features a super country music band that throws in a bit of countrified rock and pop. The crowd's a mix of ages, and everybody seems to have a foot-stomping good time. Entry is restricted to those who are 21 years or older. Admission is free for women on Thursday; otherwise there's a $4 cover. It's open Thursday and Friday from 9 pm to 2 am, and Saturday from 8 pm to midnight.

The *War Eagle Supper Club* (☎ 334-821-4455), 2061 S College St, Auburn, is tuned in to the music scene. Well-known bands ($4 to $5), local and from Atlanta, play two to three nights a week, beginning on Wednesday or Thursday. There's an acoustic act ($3) on Sunday. Doors open on Thursday at 10:30 pm, on Friday and Saturday at 11 pm, and on Sunday at 9 pm.

Theater Auburn University's *Telfair Peet Theatre* (☎ 334-844-4154), Samford Ave at Duncan Dr, presents five plays from September to May plus a Halloween special called StageFright. Tickets are $8 to $12, except for StageFright, which costs $3.

Spectator Sports
Call the university's sports ticket office (☎ 334-844-4750) to buy tickets for football, basketball, baseball and gymnastics.

Things to Buy
Original creations by local artisan Jan Jones, including Victorian Santas dressed in turn-of-the-century velvet robes, are sold at Southern Crossing (☎ 334-741-0015), 813 S Railroad Ave, Opelika, a cooperative of local craftspeople.

Getting There & Away
Atlanta airport (☎ 404-530-6600), 6000 S Terminal Parkway, in Georgia, is the region's major airport. Montgomery's Dannelly airport (☎ 334-281-5040), 4445 Selma Hwy (Hwy 80), is served by Delta, US Airways and Northwest Airlink.

ALABAMA

Greyhound (☎ 334-887-8231), 802 Opelika Rd, Auburn, makes two trips a day to
and from Atlanta. The fare is $22/$44 one-
way/roundtrip Monday to Thursday, or
$24/$47 Friday to Sunday. There's also
service to Birmingham ($23; one daily),
Dothan ($27; one), Huntsville ($41; one),
Mobile ($49; two), Montgomery ($13;
two) and New Orleans ($69; two).

Dixie Excursions (☎ 334-887-6295,
800-322-5382) operates a shuttle service
between Atlanta's airport and Auburn-
Opelika. Rates are $39/70 one-way/round-
trip to or from a hotel, or $45/80 to or from
a residence.

Major rental agencies have counters at
Atlanta and Montgomery airports. Budget
(☎ 334-826-9036), 2305 S College St,
Auburn; Enterprise (☎ 334-826-0227), 1550
Opelika Rd, Auburn; and Thrifty (☎ 334-
826-2125), 615 Opelika Rd, Auburn, have
offices in town.

Getting Around
LETA, Lee County Transit Authority
(☎ 334-887-0875) operates public buses
from Auburn University to Auburn and
Opelika. The fare is $1.

Auburn Taxi (☎ 334-821-2221) provides
a 24-hour service.

With thousands of students and terrain
that's mostly flat save for gently rolling
hills, Auburn and Opelika are ideal for bicycling. However, nobody rents out bicycles.

TUSKEGEE
population 12,300

Tuskegee derives its name from the Native
American village Taskigi. It came to national
attention around the turn of the century with
the Tuskegee Institute as the most prestigious school in the country for blacks. In the
1940s blacks made another historic first
when Tuskegee Army Air Field, now Moton
Field, called the 'Cradle of Black Aviation,'
trained black pilots to fly in WWII. To show
support for black aviation, first lady Eleanor
Roosevelt came to Tuskegee and flew with
black pilot trainer, Charles Anderson. Part of
its not so illustrious history involves the
scandalous 40-year Tuskegee syphilis experiment started in 1932 and secretly conducted
jointly by US, state, county and private
physicians. Treatment was withheld from
more than 400 black men so the government
could monitor the effects of the disease.

Tuskegee Airmen
In 1940, the Army Air Corps and the NAACP battled over the army's refusal to admit
blacks into its aviation program. A separate but equal unit was suggested, but the Army
Air Corps still objected. Black civil rights leaders also opposed a separate unit – referring
to it as 'the Jim Crow air corps' – and called for an integrated armed forces. Despite
increasing government pressure, the Army Air Corps refused to integrate its forces, but
it did activate the all-black 99th Pursuit Squadron at newly established Tuskegee Army
Air Field a year later.

To show support for the program, first lady Eleanor Roosevelt went to Tuskegee and flew
with black training instructor CA 'Chief' Anderson. The first class graduated March 7, 1942.

Under black colonel Benjamin Davis Jr, the unit flew P-40 fighter missions in North
Africa in 1943. The next year other black units joined the 99th to form the 332d Fighter
Group, which participated in Allied campaigns in North Africa and Italy, conducted
strafing and bomber escorts for the air force, and flew support for the British army.

Black pilots flew more than 15,000 sorties and destroyed 261 enemy aircraft, the first
by Lieutenant Charles Hall, who downed a Focke-Wulf Fw-190 on July 21, 1943. He was
the first black awarded the Distinguished Flying Cross. Tuskegee pilots further distinguished themselves in combat and produced two generals, Benjamin O Davis Jr and
Chappie James.

In 1948, President Harry Truman signed Executive Order 9981 calling for equal
opportunity in the armed forces. Some Tuskegee airmen went on to fly in the postwar
integrated air force. ■

ALABAMA

Orientation & Information

The I-85 runs east-west north of town. Hwy 80, also east-west, cuts diagonally through the middle of town. Tuskegee University and other major attractions lie off Old Montgomery Rd between the two roads. Macon County's chamber of commerce (☎ 334-727-6619) is at 121 S Main St. The post offices are at 401 N Elm St and Old Shorter Rd. The *Tuskegee News* is the daily paper. The closest hospital is East Alabama Medical Center (☎ 334-749-3411), 20 miles east in Opelika at 2000 Pepperell Parkway.

Tuskegee Institute
National Historic Site

The National Park Service runs this site (☎ 334-727-3200, 334-727-6390) at 1212 Old Montgomery Rd, which chronicles the Tuskegee Normal and Industrial Institute (now Tuskegee University) started by Booker T Washington as an educational institute for blacks. The museum honors Washington and George W Carver, who headed the school's agriculture department. Exhibits and a 30-minute video of Carver's 40-year achievements reveal his genius as a scientist, inventor and humanitarian. Downstairs, there's a theater and exhibit on the Tuskegee airmen. On the hour, a ranger leads tours across the street to the Oaks, Washington's home. The house, which was an engineering marvel in its day, was built with bricks made by Tuskegee students. At a time when most homes were still being lit with candles or gas and had outdoor bathrooms, the Oaks was built with electric lights and five bathrooms, including one with a shower. Students also made most of the furnishings. You can request a tour of the greenhouse, where Carver worked. The gift shop has books and reprints of some of Carver's agricultural bulletins. It's open daily from 9 am to 5 pm and entry is free.

Tuskegee University

The university (☎ 334-727-8011), Old Montgomery Hwy, was founded when a

Booker T Washington

former slave and his former owner struck a deal with the state to provide $2000 to educate blacks. With the grant, Booker T Washington created the Tuskegee Normal and Industrial Institute.

Washington, an astute politician, earned donations from Andrew Carnegie, John D Rockefeller and Collis P Huntington, all of whom had buildings named in their honor. When Washington died in 1915, the school had 161 buildings on 268 acres. The architect RR Taylor, the first black graduate of MIT, designed many of the buildings. Highlights of the campus include the **Chappie James Center** (☎ 334-727-8387, 800-277-1700), which honors General Daniel 'Chappie' James, a graduate of Tuskegee Institute and the first black to become a four-star general. Cadets give tours of the museum, which is dedicated to James and African Americans in aviation. It's open daily from 9 am to 5 pm and by appointment; entry is free.

Down the street, opposite the Kellogg Conference Center, is the **Booker T Washington Monument**, a striking statue called

ALABAMA

Veil of Ignorance that depicts Washington lifting ignorance from a fellow African American who holds an open book, and the graves of Carver and Washington.

Tuskegee National Forest

This 11,050-acre park is divided into several areas, each featuring a different activity. Taska Recreation Area, located 5½ miles east of Tuskegee on Hwy 80, has picnic tables and a reproduction of the cabin where Booker T Washington was born. Hikes along the 8½-mile Bartram National Recreation Trail wind through dense woodland. The trail is named after naturalist William Bartram. You can hike or horseback ride on trails in the Bold Destiny/Bedford V Cash Memorial Trail area and watch migrating birds at the Tsinia Wildlife Viewing Area.

The park headquarters (☎ 334-727-2652) is at 125 National Forest Rd 949, off Hwy 80, three miles north of Tuskegee, and is open Monday to Friday from 7:30 am to 4 pm. Entrance is free.

Special Events

On the second Saturday in May the George W Carver Crafts Festival promotes Carver's accomplishments with arts, crafts, bands and games. On the third Saturday in October the Sweet Potato Festival features farm-fresh produce, arts and crafts, and music. On Memorial Day, Negro Airmen International (☎ 334-724-0602) sponsors a three-day fly-in to Moton Field, which attracts black pilots worldwide.

Places to Stay

Accommodations in Tuskegee are limited. For budget-to-moderate-priced rooms drive 16 miles west to Shorter. The *Days Inn Shorter* (☎ 334-727-6034), I-85 exit 22, has 100 basic rooms with in-room safes, free movies, a pool and continental breakfast. Rates are $46/52 for singles/doubles.

Tuskegee University Kellogg Executive Conference Center (☎ 334-727-3000, 800-949-6161), E Campus Ave at Nurses' Home Rd, caters to the university's business travelers and parents of students. It

has a restaurant, fitness center, an indoor pool and airport shuttles. Rooms are elegantly decorated and have TVs, modem ports, boutique toiletries and hair dryers. The single/double rate of $90/100 is flexible (as low as $70) when it's not full.

Places to Eat

The *Lake Front Eatery* (☎ 334-724-0016), 902 Marina Dr, is one mile east of downtown. Drive along the marina until you reach the blue and white trailer at the edge of Lake Tuskegee. Sandwiches cost $3 to $5.50 and snacks and platters cost $3.50 to $7. It's open daily from 11 am to 7 pm.

The restaurant in the *Tuskegee University Kellogg Executive Conference Center* (☎ 334-727-3000, 800-949-6161) is the best place to eat in town. The menu features soups, salade niçoise, succulent and crispy fried chicken, Southern specialties and pasta. Expect to pay $6 to $10 for lunch and $14 to $20 for dinner. It's open daily from 11 am to 2 pm and 5 to 9 pm.

Getting There & Away

The closest airport is in Montgomery (☎ 334-281-5040), 4445 Selma Hwy (Hwy 80). Avis, Budget, Hertz and National rental cars are available there. Greyhound (☎ 334-727-1290), 203 Martin Luther King Hwy, downtown, has buses to Atlanta ($28; seven daily), Birmingham ($27; six), Mobile ($42; six) and Montgomery ($9; three).

MONTGOMERY

population 320,183

Although Alabama's capital, Montgomery, retains a provincial feel, since the mid-19th century its primary business has been the administration of the state government. Other major employers are the cattle, dairy and lumber industries, manufacturing and a large military presence at Maxwell Air Force Base.

The small-town atmosphere belies the artistic sophistication behind two of its major attractions: the Alabama Shakespeare Festival and the Montgomery Museum of Fine Arts, both of which draw visitors from around the southeast.

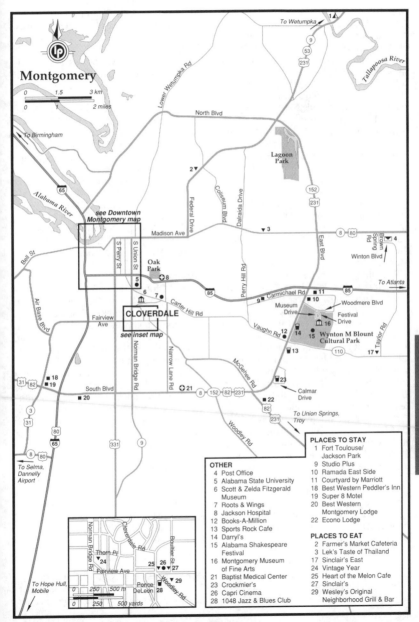

Montgomery

0   1.5   3 km
0   1   2 miles

To Wetumpka
To Birmingham
To Atlanta
To Selma, Dannelly Airport
To Union Springs, Troy
To Hope Hull, Mobile

see Downtown Montgomery map

CLOVERDALE
see inset map

Lagoon Park
Oak Park
Wynton M Blount Cultural Park

Tallapoosa River
Alabama River

Lower Wetumpka Rd
North Blvd
Madison Ave
Federal Drive
Coliseum Blvd
Dalraida Drive
East Blvd
Brown Spring Rd
Winton Blvd
Carmichael Rd
Museum Drive
Woodmere Blvd
Festival Drive
Vaughn Rd
Taylor Rd
Carter Hill Rd
Perry Hill Rd
Fairview Ave
Norman Bridge Rd
Narrow Lane Rd
McGehee Rd
Calmar Drive
South Blvd
Woodley Rd
Air Base Blvd
Bell St
S Perry St
S Union St

Cloverdale Rd
Thorn Pl
Fairview Ave
Boultier St
Ponce DeLeon
Woodley Rd
Norman Bridge Rd

0   250   500 m
0   250   500 yards

ALABAMA

PLACES TO STAY
1   Fort Toulouse/ Jackson Park
9   Studio Plus
10 Ramada East Side
11 Courtyard by Marriott
18 Best Western Peddler's Inn
19 Super 8 Motel
20 Best Western Montgomery Lodge
22 Econo Lodge

PLACES TO EAT
2   Farmer's Market Cafeteria
3   Lek's Taste of Thailand
17 Sinclair's East
24 Vintage Year
25 Heart of the Melon Cafe
27 Sinclair's
29 Wesley's Original Neighborhood Grill & Bar

OTHER
4   Post Office
5   Alabama State University
6   Scott & Zelda Fitzgerald Museum
7   Roots & Wings
8   Jackson Hospital
12 Books-A-Million
13 Sports Rock Cafe
14 Darryl's
15 Alabama Shakespeare Festival
16 Montgomery Museum of Fine Arts
21 Baptist Medical Center
23 Crockmier's
26 Capri Cinema
28 1048 Jazz & Blues Club

History

At this bend in the Alabama River an Alibamu Indian village existed for hundreds of years. In 1817, as part of Montgomery County, which had been created by the Mississippi Territorial Legislature, the land was sold. The first two buyers were Andrew Dexter, an attorney, and a year later General John Scott. They founded Montgomery.

As the northernmost point that large boats from Mobile could travel up the river, it became an important port for shipping cotton out of the Black Belt. In 1846 the Alabama legislature moved the state capital to Montgomery. In 1861 it became the first capital of the Confederacy.

Excitement came in March 1910 when Orville and Wilbur Wright built an airfield and opened a new school of aviation. That summer, two students flew the first night flights in history. Today the field is part of Maxwell Air Force Base.

Rumblings of black dissension over restrictive Jim Crow laws came in the 1940s, when Edgar Nixon, a Pullman car porter, and fellow blacks asked to register to vote. But it wasn't until the mid-1950s that Montgomery's pot of discontent started to simmer. It began with Rosa Parks' arrest for not giving up her bus seat to a white man. For the next 381 days blacks boycotted city buses. On December 21, 1956, the US Supreme Court finally ordered the desegregation of Montgomery buses.

By the 1960s Montgomery was boiling. On May 20, 1961, Freedom Riders arriving at the Greyhound bus station were beaten by Ku Klux Klansmen, who were later tried and sentenced. In 1963 George Wallace was elected governor on a platform of continued segregation. He made his famous segregation speech on the capitol steps. A year later Dr Martin Luther King Jr marched to the capitol and spoke out against segregation.

Out of Montgomery's racial strife came the Southern Poverty Law Center in 1971, headed by civil rights attorney Morris Dees. The center, which teaches tolerance and protects the legal rights of the poor and minorities, sponsored the civil rights memorial that is located outside its offices.

Orientation

Montgomery sprawls across seven hills overlooking the Alabama River. Many of its attractions are downtown and can be reached on foot. The I-65 runs north-south along the western edge of town, connecting Birmingham and Mobile. The I-85 starts at I-65 and splits the city in half as it heads east to Atlanta. Hwy 80 skirts the city's southwest corner, heading west to Selma. Most of downtown's north-south streets are one-way. The four-lane (sometimes six-lane) ring road around Montgomery is known as the Boulevard. Depending on where you are, it's called North, East, South or West Boulevard. Hotels, restaurants and shopping malls line it, especially between Vaughn and Woodley Rds.

Information

Tourist Offices The convention and visitor center (☎ 334-262-0013, 334-240-9455), 401 Madison Ave at N Hull St, downtown, is in the Thompson Mansion. It's open Monday to Friday from 8:30 am to 5 pm, Saturday from 9 am to 4 pm, and Sunday from noon to 4 pm. It has a small gift shop and puts out a comprehensive monthly events calendar and discount coupon book. On weekdays downtown parking is difficult. Pick up a free pass that allows you to park in reserved spots marked 'Visitor Permit Parking Only' while visiting the attractions around the capitol.

Post The main post office (☎ 334-244-7624), 6701 Winton Blvd, is open weekdays from 7 am to 7 pm and Saturday from 8 am to 4 pm. The downtown post office (☎ 334-244-7576) is at 135 Catoma St at Montgomery Ave. It's open Monday to Friday from 7:30 am to 5:30 pm, and Saturday from 8 am to noon.

Bookstores Books-A-Million (☎ 334-272-5580), 2572 East Blvd, has many local-interest books as well as a large selection

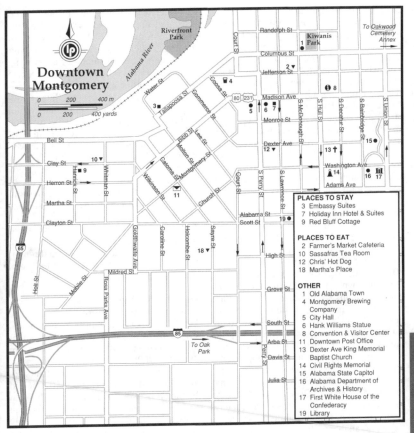

Downtown Montgomery

Scale
0   200   400 m
0   200   400 yards

PLACES TO STAY
3 Embassy Suites
7 Holiday Inn Hotel & Suites
9 Red Bluff Cottage

PLACES TO EAT
2 Farmer's Market Cafeteria
10 Sassafras Tea Room
12 Chris' Hot Dog
18 Martha's Place

OTHER
1 Old Alabama Town
4 Montgomery Brewing Company
5 City Hall
6 Hank Williams Statue
8 Convention & Visitor Center
11 Downtown Post Office
13 Dexter Ave King Memorial Baptist Church
14 Civil Rights Memorial
15 Alabama State Capitol
16 Alabama Department of Archives & History
17 First White House of the Confederacy
19 Library

ALABAMA

of international newspapers and magazines. It also has a cafe.

Roots & Wings (☎ 334-262-1700) at 1345 Carter Hill Rd champions African-American culture through the sale of books, cards, calendars, magazines and recordings. There's an art gallery and a theater for readings, lectures and storytelling.

Libraries The main branch of the city's public library (☎ 334-832-1394) is at 445 S Lawrence St.

Media The *Montgomery Advertiser* is the city's daily paper. Its Thursday 'Go' section is a guide to local entertainment. The Alabama Jazz and Blues Federation Hot Line (☎ 334-261-0300) lists the area's jazz and blues events.

Medical Services The Baptist Medical Center (☎ 334-288-2100), 2105 E South Blvd, and Jackson Hospital (☎ 334-293-8000) at 1235 Forest Ave, provide emergency and routine medical care.

Civil Rights Memorial

This stirring monument, 400 Washington Ave in the Southern Poverty Law Center, honors those who died during the civil rights movement. Created by artist Maya Lin, who designed the Vietnam Veterans Memorial in Washington, DC, the memorial is a circular black granite 'clock' with the names and dates of death of 40 martyrs of the movement. Water flows over it and an adjacent wall of granite is inscribed with the words that Dr Martin Luther King Jr often quoted from the Bible: 'Until justice rolls down like waters and righteousness like a mighty stream.' The memorial is open 24 hours a day and entry is free.

Old Alabama Town

Docents with a keen interest in history lead tours (☎ 334-240-4500, 888-240-1850) through the town's 19th-century Lucas Tavern and Ordeman-Shaw townhouse at 301 Columbus St. Visitors then listen to recordings while walking through the town, which contains examples of 19th-century architecture, including a furnished cotton gin, a doctor's office and a one-room school. On the second Saturday of the month, local musicians of all ages gather with acoustic instruments for an impromptu three-hour jam session. Don't miss it. Artisans demonstrate skills from woodcarving to dulcimer making. The tours run Monday to Saturday from 9 am to 3 pm, and Sunday from 1 to 3 pm. Tickets (adults $7, children $2) are available at the reception center on the corner of Columbus and McDonough Sts, which also has a gift shop filled with souvenirs, books and crafts.

Alabama State Capitol

Nicknamed Goat Hill, because goats once grazed here, the capitol (☎ 334-242-3935), on Bainbridge St at Dexter Ave, is the second built on the site. The first capitol was built in 1847 but was consumed by fire two years later. The current building was erected in time for the November 1851 legislative session. A guided tour includes the three-story spiral staircase built by Horace King, a former slave and

carpenter who later served in the legislature, and the chambers where delegates voted to form the Confederate States of America. The steps leading from Dexter Ave have witnessed some of history's big moments. Here, Jefferson Davis accepted the oath of office as president of the Confederacy in 1861. A century later, Governor George Wallace spoke the fateful words, 'Segregation now! Segregation tomorrow! Segregation forever!' in defiance of federal orders to integrate Alabama's colleges. Three years later, Dr Martin Luther King Jr delivered the speech in which he said 'Segregation is on its deathbed, and the only thing uncertain about it is how costly the segregationists and Wallace will make the funeral.'

It's open Monday to Friday from 9 am to 5 pm, and Saturday from 9 am to 4 pm. Tours lasting 45 minutes are given throughout the day, except from noon to 1 pm. Admission is free.

Dexter Ave King Memorial Baptist Church

Dr Martin Luther King Jr began his involvement in the civil rights movement while serving as pastor at this church from 1954 to 1960. Inside, a mural depicts his life. Tours are given Monday to Thursday at 10 am and 2 pm, Friday at 10 am, and Saturday every 45 minutes from 10:30 am to 12:45 pm and by appointment. You can walk through unescorted only on Saturday from 1:30 to 2 pm. It's closed for services on Sunday. The church is at 454 Dexter Ave, downtown.

Alabama Department of Archives & History

At 624 Washington Ave, these are the oldest state-funded archives (☎ 334-242-4363) in the country. Within the walls of the elegant building is a vast storehouse that tells the story of Alabama through exhibits and art displays. Here, too, are the original state constitution, legislative acts, official letters from governors, microfilmed newspapers from every county, photographs, maps and illustrations. Visitors may use the Reference

Room, where an introductory film explains how the material is arranged. If you're here on the third Thursday of the month, attend ArchiTreats: Food for Thought, a free lecture series covering Alabama's history. The archives are open Monday to Friday from 9 am to 5 pm and Saturday from 9 am to 5 pm (closed on major holidays). There's no admission charge.

First White House of the Confederacy
In 1861, Jefferson Davis, president of the Confederate States of America, and his wife, Varina Anne Howell, took up residence in this house (☎ 334-242-1861). Originally on Washington Ave, it was moved to its current location across from the capitol in 1919. It is furnished with furniture and family belongings from the Davis' home in Mississippi, and the 2nd-floor bedrooms are decorated as they were when the Davises lived here. There's a small Confederate museum. It's open Monday to Friday from 8 am to 4:30 pm (closed on state holidays) and entry is free.

Wynton M Blount Cultural Park
On a sunny day it seems that all of Montgomery heads for this lovely 250-acre green space on the east side of town, just off I-85. The park serves as a backdrop for the **Montgomery Museum of Fine Arts** (☎ 334-244-5700), 1 Museum Dr, and the **Carolyn Blount Theatre**, home of the Alabama Shakespeare Festival (see Theater in the Entertainment section below).

The permanent collection focuses on 19th and 20th-century American art and southeast regional art. The print collection features more than a century of masters ranging from Picasso to Dürer. Kids feel right at home in ArtWorks, a hands-on interactive gallery, art studio and learning center. In addition, the museum exhibits 10 to 15 temporary shows a year. There's a museum shop and a cafe overlooking the lake. It's open Tuesday to Saturday from 10 am to 5 pm, Thursday to 9 pm and Sunday from noon to 5 pm (closed major holidays). There's no admission charge. The closest bus service is the No 18, which

runs from Central City and along the Boulevard and stops about a mile away.

Hank Williams Statue & Memorial
Country-music fans will remember the day in 1953 when Hank Williams died in the back seat of his Cadillac at age 29. Born in nearby Mt Olive, Williams is remembered in two places in Montgomery. A life-size bronze statue stands in the shadow of tall trees at the base of a fountain and pool in Lister Hill Plaza, on Perry St, a half-block south of Madison Ave (behind the Holiday Inn). The site is opposite City Hall and the old City Auditorium, where he performed and where his funeral service was held – more than 20,000 people stood outside the auditorium during the service. Williams and his wife, Audrey, are buried in Oakwood Cemetery Annex (Upper Wetumpka Rd, just north of downtown). A large memorial with a sculpture of his ever-present hat marks the graves. The cemetery is open dawn to dusk.

Scott & Zelda Fitzgerald Museum
The writers Zelda (née Sayre) and F Scott Fitzgerald lived at 919 Felder Ave from 1931 to 1932. Zelda was born in Montgomery and spent most of her life there. Part of the house is open as a museum (☎ 334-264-4222, 334-262-1911), and a 25-minute film of the couple's life in Montgomery is shown. It's open Wednesday to Friday from 10 am to 2 pm, weekends from 1 to 5 pm, and by appointment.

Organized Tours
Alabama Anne's Tours (☎ 334-277-2526, 800-531-0502 outside Alabama) provides sightseeing excursions for individuals and groups. The Landmarks Foundation (☎ 334-240-4500) offers a self-driving tour with a book and cassette. The self-driving tour booklet costs $3 and the audio cassette is $7.

Special Events
The city's biggest bash is Jubilee Cityfest (☎ 334-834-7220), an arts and entertainment festival celebrated on Memorial Day

ALABAMA

weekend. Desta (☎ 334-244-5700, 334-271-5300), derived from an Ethiopian word meaning celebration, is a festival showcasing African-American arts and culture. It takes place at museums, theaters and lecture halls from January through March. The *Montgomery Symphony* (☎ 334-262-5182, 334-240-4004) and *Montgomery Ballet* (☎ 334-409-0522, 334-265-4664) present outdoor performances throughout August at Wynton M Blount Cultural Park. National and international musicians meet in September for the annual Alabama Jazz and Blues Federation River Jam (☎ 334-240-5052) on the waterfront. The Alabama Indian Pow Wow (☎ 334-242-2831) presents Native American dancing, crafts and entertainment on the last weekend in October in Garrett Coliseum.

Places to Stay

Camping The *Montgomery KOA* (☎ 334-288-0728), 250 Fisher Rd, Hope Hull, has over 100 sites. It's four miles south of Montgomery. Take exit 164 (Hwy 31) off I-65. The fee for two persons is $22 for an RV site with all utilities or $17 for a tent site with electricity and water; it's $1 for each extra person.

Historic *Fort Toulouse/Jackson Park* (☎ 334-567-3002), Fort Toulouse Rd, Wetumpka, has a 39-pad campground with water and electricity. There's a bathhouse, boat launch and picnic area. Be sure to visit the fort and arboretum and to hike the nature trails. Follow Hwy 231 to Fort Toulouse Rd and turn left. Sites cost $8 for tents or $10 for RVs.

Hotels & Motels The *Super 8 Motel* (☎ 334-284-1900), 1288 W South Blvd, is near the junction of the I-65, Mobile Hwy and the airport road (Hwy 80). Rooms are basic but clean and have in-room coffee and free movies. Some have refrigerators. There's a pool. Singles/doubles are $33/39.

The *Best Western Peddler's Inn* (☎ 334-288-0610), 4231 Mobile Hwy (Hwy 31), has a pool, and there are coffeemakers and free movies in all the rooms; refrigerators and microwaves in some. The on-site restaurant is moderately priced. Singles/doubles are $38/44.

The *Best Western Montgomery Lodge* (☎ 334-288-5740), 977 W South Blvd, has a pool and lounge, coin laundry and free movies. The rooms are clean and comfortable and some have microwaves, refrigerators and coffeemakers. Singles/doubles are $41/50.

The *Econo Lodge* (☎ 334-284-3400, 800-424-4777), 4135 Troy Hwy, has 45 rooms; all have modem ports and free movies. It's close to major shopping malls, popular restaurants and the Alabama Shakespeare Theater. Single/double rooms are $45/50.

Ramada East Side (☎ 334-277-2200), 1355 East Blvd, is within a mile of the Alabama Shakespeare Theater. It has a pool and deck, and rooms come with a complimentary continental breakfast. The popular lounge serves grilled burgers, sandwiches, fries and chicken wings. Single/double rooms are $53/62.

Studio Plus (☎ 334-273-0075), 5115 Carmichael Rd, is a new property geared toward long-term stays. The rooms are clean, spacious and have full kitchens and a dining area. There's voice mail, an on-site coin laundry and membership at a nearby health club. It's near the Alabama Shakespeare Festival and I-85. The room rate is $49 a night, or $45 a night on a weekly basis.

Holiday Inn Hotel & Suites (☎ 334-264-2231, 800-611-5868), 120 Madison Ave, occupies the former Madison Hotel downtown and is within a few blocks of Old Alabama Town, the capitol and other attractions. It's undergoing a much-needed major renovation. Rooms open onto an attractive atrium with plants and a piano bar. There's an outdoor pool, whirlpool, fitness center, two lounges and restaurant serving a complimentary hot buffet breakfast. Singles/doubles are $87/97.

Embassy Suites (☎ 334-269-5055, fax 334-269-0360), 300 Tallapoosa St, downtown, on the Alabama River, in front of historic Union Station and Riverfront Park, is in one of the most attractive locations in town. Its tastefully decorated suites are often full. Amenities include two phones, voice mail, modem port, complimentary made-to-order breakfast and newspaper, indoor pool, fitness room, sauna and a wine and cheese reception each evening. Locals frequent Montgomery's, the open-kitchen restaurant. The rate is $109 for a single or double.

Easy access to I-85 and the Boulevard make *Courtyard by Marriott* (☎ 334-272-5533, fax 334-279-0853), 5555 Carmichael Rd, popular. It's about a mile from the Alabama Shakespeare Festival. The rooms are clean, comfortable and have modem ports. There's an outdoor pool, exercise room, coin laundry, courtyard garden, lounge and restaurant. The suites have small refrigerators. Rooms are $86 for a single or double.

Inns & B&Bs *Red Bluff Cottage* (☎ 334-264-0056, fax 334-262-1872), 551 Clay St, was built as an inn and has four guest rooms, all decorated with antiques. The upstairs porch affords good views of the Alabama River and capitol. Singles/doubles are $55/65, including full breakfast.

The *Lattice Inn* (☎ 334-832-9931), 1414 S Hull St, is a comfortable, cozy getaway. There are two guest rooms furnished with antiques. It also offers a one-bedroom cottage for four, two modern rooms that can be made into a suite, and a pool, deck and off-street parking. Room rates range from $65 to $85.

Places to Eat

There are restaurants scattered throughout the city, but three areas give you multiple options: downtown, Cloverdale and the Boulevard.

The hot dogs at *Chris' Hot Dog* (☎ 334-265-6850), 138 Dexter Ave, are plump and juicy. This place has been a Montgomery institution since 1917. It's open Monday to Thursday and Saturday from 8:30 am to 7 pm, and Friday from 8:30 am to 8 pm.

On weekday mornings the *Farmer's Market Cafeteria* (☎ 334-262-1970) at 315 N McDonough St buzzes with customers coming for Southern breakfasts ($4). The lunch menu features country cooking – fresh vegetables and fried chicken, catfish and barbecue. It's inexpensive and good. Expect to pay about $5.50 for lunch. It's open weekdays from 5:30 am to 2 pm. There's another branch (☎ 334-271-1885) at 1659 Federal Dr.

At *Martha's Place* (☎ 334-263-9135), 458 Sayre St, bureaucrats, business people and tourists rub elbows over some of the best Southern cooking in town. Expect down-home cornbread, black-eyed peas, and greens cooked with chunks of meat. Lunch, the only meal served, costs about $5.50. It's open Monday to Friday from 11 am to 3 pm and there's a Sunday buffet from 11 am to 3 pm. It's closed on Saturday.

People go to the *Sassafras Tea Room* (☎ 334-265-7277), 532 Clay St, for the food. The atmosphere, river view and good service are extras. There's a short menu of mostly chicken and pasta, and freshly made desserts such as buttermilk pie. Dinner entrées cost $8 to $15; lunch is priced at $4 to $5.50. It's open for dinner on Friday and Saturday from 6 to 9 pm, and for lunch Sunday to Friday from 11 am to 2 pm.

Lek's Taste of Thailand (☎ 334-244-8994), 5421 Atlanta Hwy, has a good reputation. Every ingredient, from the seafood to the spices, is fresh. Lunch checks average $5, while dinner checks are around $10. It's open Monday to Thursday from 11 am to 2:30 pm and 5 to 9:30 pm, Friday to 10:30 pm, and Saturday from 11 am to 10:30 pm.

Even without the good food, *Sinclair's* (☎ 334-834-7462), 1051 E Fairview Ave, would probably be a popular meeting place. People come to drink and dine indoors and outside on the patio. The menu features an eclectic selection of soups, salads, chicken, pasta and seafood. Lunch checks average about $6, while dinner costs around $10. There is also *Sinclair's East* (☎ 334-271-7654) at 7847 Vaughn Rd.

At *Heart of the Melon Cafe* (☎ 334-269-5000), 1031 E Fairview Ave, dinner starts with freshly baked biscuits and muffins. Chef/owner Alexine Saunders' creativity is reflected in dishes that build on traditional Southern cooking: roasted chicken breast with corn grits casserole and warm black-eyed-pea salad ($10), and meatloaf with caramelized onions, mashed potatoes and sautéed greens ($7). Lunch entrées are $5 to $9. Spend $10 or more and get two movie tickets for the price of one at the Capri Theater next door. It's open Tuesday to Saturday from 11 am to 2 pm and 5 to 9:30 pm, and there's Sunday brunch from 11:30 am to 2 pm.

Wesley's Original Neighborhood Grill & Bar (☎ 334-834-2500), 1061 Woodley Rd, is another Cloverdale favorite. It's two restaurants in one. The grill serves everything from nachos and pizza to fine roasted foods. It serves lunch Sunday to Friday from 11 am to 2 pm and dinner daily from 5:30 to 10 pm. The bistro's dinner menu features fine upscale options. Sunday brunch has made-to-order eggs and some favorite fish specialties. Lunch checks average $7, while dinner will cost about $15 at the grill or $25 at the bistro. There's live entertainment on weekends.

The bistro-style *Vintage Year* (☎ 334-264-8463), 405 Cloverdale Rd, has a menu that blends Southern favorites with light, fresh, trendy ingredients. There's roasted chicken with mashed potatoes and vegetables ($12) and grilled smoked double pork chop with grits and greens ($15). The salad of mixed greens, roasted tomatoes, grilled onion, parmesan cheese and herb vinaigrette ($6) is big enough for a meal. It has a great wine list. Reservations are suggested. It's open Tuesday to Saturday from 6 to 9 pm.

Entertainment

Nightclubs & Bars *Crockmier's* (☎ 334-277-1840), 5620 Calmar Dr, off East Blvd, is popular with a variety of ages. Some come for the food, others come to unwind in the trendy lounge where there's live music on weekends. Most acts are local or regional, but occasionally they bring in a group from elsewhere. On those nights there's a $3 to $5 cover.

There's live jazz seven nights a week at *1048 Jazz & Blues Club* (☎ 334-834-1048), 1048 E Fairview Ave, Cloverdale. The acts range from the Alabama Jazz Federation Jazz Jam to soloists. There's a full bar and snacks are available. When there's a cover, it's usually $3.

Darryl's (☎ 334-277-1885), 2701 East Blvd, has acoustic rock on Sunday and there's no cover charge. *Wesley's Original Neighborhood Grill & Bar* (☎ 334-834-2500), 1061 Woodley Rd, Cloverdale, showcases rock and R&B acts with a $3 cover. It's also a good place to grab a bite to eat.

You can dine on burgers, salads and sandwiches while listening to music at the *Sports Rock Cafe* (☎ 334-260-0061), 5060 Vaughn Rd. The *Montgomery Brewing Company* (☎ 334-834-2739), 301 Columbus St, downtown, brews its own ales and lagers to wash down pasta, steaks and great gumbo. It's all served up with blues and rock on weekends. There's no cover.

Theater The *Alabama Shakespeare Festival* (☎ 334-271-5353), 1 Festival Dr, is internationally acclaimed. As well as Shakespeare's plays, which are performed from March through July, the company stages international classics and youth productions. There are two theaters, the 750-seat Festival Theater, where the acoustics are fabulous, and the 225-seat Octagon Theater. Don't miss the backstage tours ($5) given on weekends at 11 am and Theatre in the Mind, a free lecture on each play given by directors, actors and others involved, held on Saturday at noon. Nightly (except Sunday) performances begin at 7:30 or 8 pm; weekend matinees start at 2 pm. Tickets cost $15 to $26. Discounts are available for students, members of the military and seniors. Children's productions cost $16 for adults and $11 for children. Local hotels give theater discounts to guests.

Cinemas The *Capri Cinema* (☎ 334-262-4858), 1045 E Fairview Ave, Cloverdale, shows newly released nonmainstream and classic films. It teams up with Heart of the Melon Cafe for two-for-one tickets (see

Places to Eat). Nonmembers pay $5.50, members pay $4 and children pay $2.

Matinees cost $3 at the *Eastdale 8* (☎ 334-277-5164), 5501 Atlantic Hwy, in the Eastdale Mall; *Carmike 8* (☎ 334-272-6421), 1755 Eastern Bypass; and *Twin Oaks 4* (☎ 334-271-6778), 2759 Eastern Bypass.

Getting There & Away
Air Montgomery's Dannelly airport (☎ 334-281-5040), 4445 Selma Hwy (Hwy 80), is served by Delta, US Airways and Northwest Airlink. It's 15 minutes from downtown on Hwy 80 and I-65.

Bus Greyhound (☎ 334-286-0658), 950 W South Blvd, serves Atlanta ($29; nine buses daily), Auburn ($13; two daily), Baton Rouge ($71; five), Biloxi ($51; three), Birmingham ($16; four), Huntsville ($39; three), Memphis ($58; three), Meridian ($34; one), Mobile ($27; five), New Orleans ($51; six), and Tuscaloosa ($23; five).

Train Amtrak (☎ 800-872-7245) service is provided by chartered bus from Mobile ($27 one-way) and Birmingham ($15). From there you can catch trains to Atlanta ($52) and beyond. It's faster and cheaper to take a bus to New Orleans than to connect with Amtrak trains through Mobile and Birmingham. The office is at 335 Coosa St, downtown.

Car Avis, Budget, Hertz and National car-rental agencies have counters downstairs next to the airline ticket counters. Enterprise (☎ 334-277-4300), 137 East Blvd and 617 S Decatur St; National (☎ 334-213-4530), 645 East Blvd; and Snappy Car Rental (☎ 334-277-6600), 131 Eastdale Rd S, have branches in town.

Getting Around
The Montgomery Area Transit System (MATS; ☎ 334-262-7321) provides public transportation on weekdays from 6 am to 9:30 pm; there's a limited service on weekends. The fare is $1.50.

The airport shuttle service (☎ 334-279-6662) runs vans between Atlanta airport

and Montgomery. The rate per person is $90 roundtrip/60 one-way, and it's $60/40 for each additional passenger.

The Checker-Deluxe Cab Company (☎ 334-263-2512), the Original Queen Cab Company (☎ 334-263-7137) and the Yellow Cab Company (☎ 334-262-5225) all provide taxi services. A taxi downtown from the airport is about $11 for one person and $1 for each additional passenger.

SELMA
population 27,000

Modern Selmians in this small town like to boast that theirs is a two-part history: part Civil War and part civil rights. With more than 1250 buildings, Selma's historic district is the largest and second oldest in the state. The city has 88 churches, primarily Baptist. The economy is driven by tourism, neighboring industrial paper and textile plants and light manufacturing.

History
Located on the Alabama River, Selma's excellent transportation arteries – both rail and water, were important in moving cotton to markets. Known as the 'Queen City of the Black Belt,' its one-time wealth is evidenced by the scores of grand antebellum homes that remain even after more than 600 buildings, both industrial and residential, were burned in 1865 by federal troops following the Confederate defeat in the Battle of Selma.

The defeat was crucial for the Union. Nearly half of the munitions used by the Confederacy were manufactured at the Selma Navy Yard and Ordnance Works. The Brooke cannon, the most powerful muzzle-loading cannon ever produced, and the iron-clad Confederate ship *Tennessee*, which fought in the Battle of Mobile Bay, were built here.

After the Civil War, Selma quickly rebuilt, but an even bigger adversary proved to be the boll weevil. When the weevil arrived in 1914, the county produced 64,000 bales of cotton. Two years later, production had plunged nearly 80% to 14,200 bales.

ALABAMA

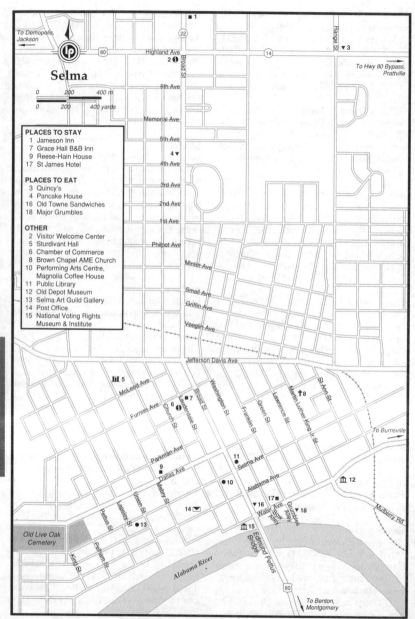

Selma

0   200   400 m
0   200   400 yards

PLACES TO STAY
1 Jameson Inn
7 Grace Hall B&B Inn
9 Reese-Hain House
17 St James Hotel

PLACES TO EAT
3 Quincy's
4 Pancake House
16 Old Towne Sandwiches
18 Major Grumbles

OTHER
2 Visitor Welcome Center
5 Sturdivant Hall
6 Chamber of Commerce
8 Brown Chapel AME Church
10 Performing Arts Centre,
   Magnolia Coffee House
11 Public Library
12 Old Depot Museum
13 Selma Art Guild Gallery
14 Post Office
15 National Voting Rights
   Museum & Institute

To Demopolis,
Jackson

Highland Ave

6th Ave

Memorial Ave

5th Ave

4th Ave

3rd Ave

2nd Ave

1st Ave

Philpot Ave

Minter Ave

Small Ave

Griffin Ave

Voeglin Ave

Jefferson Davis Ave

McLeod Ave

Furniss Ave

Parkman Ave

Dallas Ave

Selma Ave

Alabama Ave

Old Live Oak
Cemetery

Alabama River

To Hwy 80 Bypass,
Prattville

To Burnsville

To Benton,
Montgomery

Mulberry Rd

Edmund Pettus
Bridge

Broad St
Range St
Church St
Union St
Lauderdale St
Washington St
Franklin St
Green St
Lawrence St
Martin Luther King Jr St
St Ann St
Pettus St
Pettus St
Mabry St
Lapsley St
Broad St
Grumbles Alley
Water St
Bowl Alley
King St
Pettus St

ALABAMA

The majority of Dallas County's population has always been black due to the demand for cotton workers. As a major inland port in the Black Belt, Selma was an obvious choice for a slave-trading post. Writer John Hardy in *Selma: Her Institutions and Her Men* (1879) describes the atmosphere:

> Large droves, some hundreds daily, were brought to the town by men…whose business it was to trade in negroes. Several large buildings were erected in town especially for the accommodation of negro traders and their property…On the ground floor, a large sitting room was provided for the exhibition of negroes on the market, and from among them could be selected blacksmiths, carpenters, bright mulatto girls and women for seamstresses, filed hands, women and children of all ages, sizes and qualities. To have seen the large droves of negroes arriving in the town every week, from about the first of September to the first of April, no one could be surprised that the black population increased in Dallas County, from 1830 to 1840, between twelve and thirteen thousand.

During Reconstruction, blacks here made many political firsts. Selma elected three black leaders to the US House of Representatives, state senate and state judicial bench.

Ironically, it was voting rights for blacks that brought Selma international infamy nearly a hundred years later on Bloody Sunday, March 7, 1965. The media captured on film state troopers and mounted deputies beating and gassing African Americans and white sympathizers as they knelt to pray on Edmund Pettus Bridge, on their way to the state capital to demonstrate for voting rights. President Lyndon Johnson intervened and the march was rescheduled two weeks later under the protection of the federalized Alabama National Guard.

The marches, which had been preceded by two years of violence against blacks and white sympathizers as they demonstrated and attempted to register voters, ended when President Johnson signed the Voting Rights Act of 1965 and sent federal registrars and observers to Alabama.

Orientation

Hwy 80 enters the city from the east at the historic Edmund Pettus Bridge, then runs north-south as Broad St, splitting the city. The main residential community and historic district lie west of Broad St, and the commercial and historic waterfront are to the east. At the northern end of the city, Hwy 80 turns west as Highland Ave, which is lined with fast-food eateries, chain motels, supermarkets and shopping centers.

Information

The Selma chamber of commerce (☎ 334-875-7241, 800-457-3562 in Alabama) is at 513 Lauderdale St. The best calendar of events is the chamber's *In Selma*. The visitor welcome center (☎ 334-875-7485), 2207 Broad St, is open daily from 8 am to 8 pm and provides a wealth of information in a small gift shop with books and reprints of newspapers from the Civil War and days of the voting rights demonstrations. The post office (☎ 334-874-4678) is at 723 Alabama Ave.

For medical help turn to the Columbia Four Rivers Medical Center (☎ 334-418-4100), 1015 Medical Center Parkway, and the Vaughan Regional Medical Center (☎ 334-418-6000), 1050 W Dallas Ave.

The public library (☎ 334-874-1720) is located in the center of town at 1103 Selma Ave. The *Selma Times Journal* is the city's daily.

Edmund Pettus Bridge

Marchers assembled here for the Selma-to-Montgomery voting rights marches. It also was the site of Bloody Sunday. It spans the Alabama River at Water Ave and Broad St.

National Voting Rights Museum & Institute

The objects in this small museum (☎ 334-418-0800), 1012 Water Ave, near the Edmund Pettus Bridge, make powerful statements, starting with messages on the 'I Was There Wall,' which have been left by reporters, witnesses and the men, women and children who marched on Bloody Sunday and returned three decades later to relate their experiences. Hanging on other walls are original signs reading 'We Serve Colored,' 'Colored Section in Rear,' and 'White Only.' The Footprints for Freedom room houses photos of Bloody Sunday. Other rooms cover earlier periods of African-American history, including women's suffrage in Alabama. The institute sponsors an anniversary reenactment of the Selma-to-Montgomery march held each year during the Bridge Crossing Jubilee. It's open Tuesday to Saturday from 1 to 5 pm. Admission is $4 for adults, $2 for children.

Old Depot Museum
If you're limited to one stop in Selma, make this it. Few museums of this size have such a rich and important collection. The reason? It serves as the Selma-Dallas County Museum of History and Archives (☎ 334-874-2197), 4 Martin Luther King St. Among the artifacts are Native American arrowheads, tools, a bow-and-arrow case that belonged to Geronimo and US army muskets that were found bent around the skulls of buried warriors. The large Civil War collection includes letters from Andrew Jackson pardoning citizens who fought for the Confederacy, musket balls weighing up to 32 pounds and made in the Selma Navy Yard, uniforms and weapons.

The Work Project Administration (WPA) murals painted by Felix Gaines, one of a few African-American artists who painted for the WPA, are exceptional. The other standout is the Keipp Collection, 46 turn-of-the-century black & white photographs of African Americans living and working on a local plantation. The photographs, which were found in a bag in an old house, constitute a rare and unique collection. When the museum isn't crowded, request a personal tour by associate curator Russ Martin. Curator Jean Martin is a veteran journalist and a fountain of knowledge about the county and state. It's open Monday to Saturday from 10 am to 4 pm and by appointment on Sunday. Entry is $4 for adults, $3 for seniors and $2 for children.

Brown Chapel African Methodist Episcopal Church
This church (☎ 334-874-7897) at 410 Martin Luther King St was founded in 1866 and claims to be the first African Methodist Episcopal (AME) church in the state. It served as a meeting place throughout the civil rights struggle and was a starting point for the voting rights marches in 1965. Outside the red brick building are two monuments, one honoring those who died in the struggle and one of Dr Martin Luther King Jr. Inside, the Martin Luther King Room has mementos of the movement. Tours are given by appointment.

Sturdivant Hall
This Greek revival neoclassic antebellum mansion (☎ 334-872-5626), 713 Mabry St, is furnished with antiques donated by Robert Sturdivant, a wealthy businessman who left the city $50,000, and local residents, including Clara Weaver Parrish, an artist who designed stained glass for Louis C Tiffany. Among the museum's treasures are furnishings and personal items that belonged to the original owners; portraits of US Vice-President William Rufus King and his wife painted by Nicola Marschall, the artist who designed the Confederate flag; and a gold clock featuring a statue of George Washington. The home has numerous innovative architectural details, including jib windows that also serve as doors. It's open Tuesday to Saturday from 9 am to 4 pm, and Sunday from 2 to 4 pm. Admission is $5 for adults.

Old Live Oak Cemetery
'There is Glory in Graves,' reads the inscription on the Confederate Monument in the middle of this historic cemetery (☎ 334-875-7241) on Dallas Ave at King St. The cemetery derives its name from the 80 live oaks and 80 magnolias that were planted in 1879. Today, the century-old trees laced with Spanish moss shade the elaborate headstones and tombs dating back to 1829. Celebrated Selmians buried there include US Vice-President William Rufus King. It's open weekdays from dawn to dusk and entry is free.

Organized Tours

Along with tourist brochures, the chamber of commerce offers half a dozen cassette-and-brochure driving and walking tours, covering ghosts, historic homes, African-American heritage and history. It also arranges for visitors with an interest in civil rights to meet people who witnessed the voting rights drives. Pick up a free copy of *Selma's Ghost Tour*. It explains the ghostly legends behind Sturdivant Hall, Grace Hall and the cemetery.

Special Events

Two of Selma's biggest events are the three-day Historic Selma Pilgrimage tours of historic homes on the third weekend of March and the four-day Civil War Reenactment of the Battle of Selma (☎ 334-875-7241) with more than 2000 participants in late April. Selma's other unique events are the Bridge Crossing Jubilee (see National Voting Rights Museum above), which is held the first weekend in March, and the Tale Tellin' Festival held Friday and Saturday nights in October.

Places to Stay

Camping See Around Selma for campsites at Paul M Grist State Park, William B Dannelly Reservoir and Six Mile Creek Park & Campground.

Hotels & Motels The restored historic *St James Hotel* (☎ 334-872-3234), 1200 Water Ave overlooking the Alabama River, has 42 guest rooms, a restaurant and shops. In its heyday, this was a popular 1st-class hotel frequented by steamboat passengers. Note the lovely grill work around the balcony. Singles/doubles cost $85/92.

With 60 spacious rooms, a pool, movie channel and complimentary breakfast and newspaper, the *Jameson Inn* (☎ 334-874-8600), 2420 N Broad St (Hwy 80), offers good value. Singles/doubles are $57/62.

Best Western (☎ 334-872-1900), 1915 W Highland Ave (Hwy 80), is clean and comfortable; some of the larger rooms have kitchenettes. Rates are $48/55 for a single/double.

The two-story *Holiday Inn* (☎ 334-872-0461), 1806 W Highland Ave (Hwy 80), has a pool, complimentary continental breakfast, movie channel, restaurant and laundry service. Ask for a room off the highway. Singles/doubles are $50/58.

B&Bs *Grace Hall Bed & Breakfast Inn* (☎ 334-875-5744), 506 Lauderdale St, is a totally restored antebellum home dating from 1857. It has six rooms – three in the main house and three in an annex. Guests receive a tour of the mansion and full breakfast. The property has over one acre of gardens and 1000 square feet of porches. Double rooms cost $79 to $99 and singles are $69 to $89.

Owner Shannon Laramore describes the *Reese-Hain House* (☎ 334-875-6041), 722 Dallas Ave, as a 'Bed & Help Yourself.' It's her way of giving guests space, but it doesn't mean guests aren't pampered. This spunky 73-year-old who talks and waves her hands a lot leaves guests a continental breakfast to eat at their leisure and supplies snacks for later in the day. Guests have their own kitchen, but she cleans the dishes after they've gone. The rooms are beautifully decorated and cost $55 a night.

Places to Eat

There are surprisingly few restaurants for a city this size. The real problem is on Sunday evening. A church-going town, Selma closes up on Sunday afternoon. Plan to have an early dinner or go to a fast-food eatery.

Quincy's (☎ 334-874-4067), 1798 E Highland Ave (Hwy 14), is one of the few places open for dinner on Sunday evenings. It's a chain that serves all-you-can-eat buffet foods. It's open daily from 11 am to 10 pm.

Old Towne Sandwiches (☎ 334-872-3827), 1124 Water Ave, serves sandwiches, soups and salads on a wide-screened porch overlooking the Alabama River. It serves meals Monday to Friday from 9 am to 3 pm and Saturday from 10 am to 2 pm.

Many locals make the *Pancake House* (☎ 334-872-2736), 1617 Broad St, a regular morning stop. Eat in or take out breakfast or lunch. Try the fresh pies.

At *Major Grumbles* (☎ 334-872-2006), 1 Grumbles Alley, diners eat in what was once a cotton warehouse on the riverfront. Daily specials include red beans and rice, chicken gumbo soup, and burgers, salads and sandwiches. Lunch for two, including dessert, tax and tip costs about $14. It's open Monday to Saturday from 11 am to 11 pm.

Tally-Ho (☎ 334-872-1390), Mangum St, is Selma's best restaurant, serving seafood and steaks from $11 to $16. The building was originally a log cabin. Hours are Monday to Saturday from 5 to 10 pm. It's a bit hard to find. Take Broad St north and cross Highland Ave, after which Broad St splits. It becomes N Broad St as you veer left. Continue on N Broad St, then turn left onto Mangum St. The restaurant is on the right. You can eat in or take out.

Entertainment

Housed in the restored Walton Theatre, the *Performing Arts Centre* (☎ 334-875-5157), 1000 Selma Ave, is a combination theater and art gallery.

The new *Magnolia Coffee House* (☎ 334-874-2145), in the Performing Arts Centre, is a comfortable place to meet and listen to live blues, folk and contemporary music while sipping café au lait and nibbling on biscotti and ice cream. There is an outdoor courtyard. It's open Friday and Saturday from 8 pm to midnight.

Things to Buy

The Selma Art Guild Gallery (☎ 334-874-9017), 508 Selma Ave, offers a small but quality selection of paintings, pottery and photography by local and regional artists. People on smaller budgets can purchase beautiful note cards. The gallery holds a juried art show in March. It's open Wednesday to Saturday from 10 am to 4 pm and by appointment.

Getting There & Away

Montgomery's Dannelly airport (☎ 334-281-5040), 4445 Selma Hwy (Hwy 80), offers the closest air service. From there it's an easy 40-mile drive on Hwy 80.

Greyhound (☎ 334-874-4503), 434 Broad St, has buses from Selma to Atlanta ($47; one a day), Birmingham ($23; three a day), Mobile ($33; one), Montgomery ($12; two) and Tuscaloosa ($17; two).

Enterprise (☎ 334-874-91040), 1107 Dallas Ave, and Clean Machine Rentals (☎ 334-872-8054), 1505 W Highland Ave, provide car rentals in Selma.

Getting Around

Selma's taxi companies include Deluxe Cab (☎ 334-872-0021, 334-874-9287), 1020 Griffin Ave, and Eastside Cab Company (☎ 334-872-4480), 103 Division St.

AROUND SELMA
Paul M Grist State Park

Located 15 miles north of Selma on Hwy 22, the Paul M Grist State Park (☎ 334-872-5846) is a 1080-acre park surrounding a 100-acre lake. There's plenty to do here, including boating, canoeing, hiking, swimming and fishing. There are three trails, the longest a three-mile loop with rolling elevation, streams and woods with lots of wildlife. Canoes and pedal boats can be rented for $5 an hour, while flat-bottom boats cost $7.50 per day. Other facilities include a gym, lodge, pool, beach and picnic areas.

Camping costs $12.50 for sites with full hookups, or $6.50 for tent sites. All campers can use the showers and restrooms. Pets are allowed if on a leash.

The day-use fee is $1 for adults or 50¢ for seniors and those aged six to 12 years.

William B Dannelly Reservoir

The 22,000-acre reservoir snakes 105 miles southwest on the Alabama River. It's part of the Alabama River lakes system set up by the Army Corps of Engineers to provide power. The benefit for recreation is enormous, with a score of parks, boat ramps, fishing areas and marinas. One of the most popular parks is **Roland Cooper State Park** (☎ 334-682-4838, 334-682-4050), near Camden, a 236-acre spot noted for its beautiful scenery, fishing and golf. Nonmotorized boats for fishing or lazing about cost $6/$12 for a half/full day. Two mostly flat hiking trails run 1½ miles through woods. Deer, squirrels and wildlife are abundant, and bald eagles nest in the area. There are 46 improved ($12.50) and 13 primitive ($7.50) shady sites, and rest-rooms and a bathhouse. The improved sites have a picnic table, barbecue and fire ring. In addition, there are five cabins that can be rented for $42 to $62 a night. On weekends in summer the campground fills up early. There's no day-use fee.

The park is about 35 miles south of Selma on Hwy 41; the turn-off is six miles northeast of Camden. If you're traveling from Mobile or Montgomery on I-65, turn west onto Hwy 10 at Greenville and continue 45 miles to Camden.

Only six miles south of Selma, *Six Mile Creek Park & Campground* (☎ 334-875-6228), at 6484 Dallas County Rd 77, is also on the reservoir. It's a beautiful spot, with moss-draped oaks overhanging the river banks. Recreation is limited, but the campground is nice. Its 31 sites have water and electric hookups, grills, picnic tables and campfire rings. Facilities include showers and toilets, a boat ramp and a dump station. It's $12 a night, plus a $1 to $2 reservation fee for the first night only.

Old Cahawba Archaeological Park

From 1820 to 1826 Cahawba served as Alabama's state capital and was an important river town. Today, it has more significance to archaeologists than legislators. Located at the confluence of the Alabama and Cahaba Rivers, it was subject to flooding, making it unsuitable as the capital. In 1826 the capital – and most of the population – moved to Tuscaloosa. Cahawba became a major railroad stop and distribution center for cotton shipped down the Alabama River. During the Civil War, the rail lines were dismantled and the town was used as a prison for Union soldiers. In 1866, floods sent the remaining population scurrying to Selma's bluffs. The town had been abandoned for nearly 100 years when historians and archaeologists from the Alabama Historical Commission uncovered Cahawba's history and created the park.

The welcome center has photos of the former capital and provides visitor maps of the old town. Signs explain the significance of different sites. There's a short nature trail, picnic tables and grills, restrooms and a boat launch on the William B Dannelly Reservoir.

On the second Sunday in May the county celebrates the town's heritage with the Old Cahawba Festival. For information about the town and festival, contact the welcome center (☎ 334-872-8058), 9518 Cahaba Rd. The Selma chamber of commerce also provides information on Old Cahawba. From Selma, take Alabama Hwy 22 west for 8½ miles. Turn onto County Rd 9 and drive 5 miles, then turn left on County Rd 2 into Old Cahawba. The visitor center is open daily from 9 am to 5 pm, the park from 9 am to dusk.

DEMOPOLIS

population 7500

The town's location at the confluence of the Tombigbee and Black Warrior Rivers is its best asset. A 1700-foot dam with locks holds in 10,000-acre Lake Demopolis, which provides recreation, fishing and transportation. Unfortunately, nobody rents out boats, but there are areas for bank fishing, including two riverfront parks with camping. Most visitors make the trip from Selma to see the town's two antebellum mansions. Manufacturing, lumber and paper products and agriculture are the chief industries.

Orientation & Information

Demopolis lies north of Hwy 80 and south of the river. Visitors arriving on Hwy 43 from the north enter the city in the historic downtown area, near the major attractions. Those arriving on Hwy 43 from the south and Hwy 80 from the east or west should continue to Cedar Ave and turn north. Cedar runs through the heart of Demopolis. With a few exceptions, the center of the town is laid out in an orderly grid with most east-west streets named after famous political and military figures, primarily from Alabama.

The chamber of commerce (☎ 334-289-0270), at 102 E Washington St, provides visitor information Monday to Friday from 8:30 am to 5 pm. The post office (☎ 334-289-0405) is at 100 W Capitol St. The *Demopolis Times* is published Wednesday and Saturday. For medical help drive to Bryan W Whitfield Memorial Hospital (☎ 334-289-4000), 105 Hwy 80 at Cedar Ave.

Things to See & Do

General Nathan Bryan Whitfield, a Renaissance man of sorts, had no architectural training, yet he designed **Gaineswood** (☎ 334-289-4846), 805 Whitfield St E, in 1842. For 18 years he supervised its construction by his slaves, some of whom were accomplished carpenters and plasterers. The golden yellow mansion features intricate plaster medallions and friezes, jib windows, two glass-paned cupolas and three styles of columns. Tours of two floors take 45 minutes. It's open Monday to Saturday from 9 am to 5 pm and Sunday from 1 to 5 pm (closed state holidays). Admission is $5 for adults and $2 for children aged six to 12.

Like many other antebellum mansions, **Bluff Hall** (☎ 334-289-1666), 405 N Commissioners Ave, was built by slaves. Unlike many others it has the feel of a place where people really lived, not a museum. Planter Allen Glover gave it to his daughter as a wedding gift in 1832. It sits on a bluff overlooking the Tombigbee River, hence its name. Many of the furnishings on display belonged to the original family. The

Whistling Walkways

The covered path between an antebellum mansion and its working kitchen was called the 'whistling walkway,' because slaves had to whistle while carrying the food to the house. It was impossible, the owners surmised, for the servant to nibble on the food if they were whistling. ■

gift shop is equally special, with baskets, woodwork and pottery handmade by local and regional artisans. It's open Tuesday to Saturday from 10 am to 5 pm, and Sunday from 2 to 5 pm. Admission is $5 for adults and $1 for students.

Foscue Creek Park (☎ 334-289-5535), 1800 Lock & Dam Rd, is popular with the fishing crowd, but also has a few short nature trails, picnic areas, a boat ramp, a playground and a softball field. Open year-round, it has a campground and there is free day use from sunrise to sunset. It's two miles west of downtown.

Special Events

The 25-year-old Christmas on the River festival (☎ 334-289-0270) attracts up to 50,000 people who come to watch a flotilla of barges and boats decorated with Christmas lights parade up the Tombigbee River under a sky ablaze with fireworks.

Places to Stay

Camping The US Army Corps of Engineers (☎ 334-289-3540) operates two improved campgrounds within 15 miles of Demopolis. Camping fees at *Foscue Creek Park* are $12 a night per tent. Many sites are on the river's edge. All have water and electricity, picnic table, lantern holder, grill and fire ring. Locals describe the corps' small *Forkland Park* (☎ 334-289-5530) as 'way out in the woods,' which is perfect if you like the great outdoors undeveloped. There are 42 shaded sites ($12) carved between towering oaks, pines and dogwoods on a peninsula between McConnico Creek and Taylor Creek. The park's position off the main waterway adds to the solitude. All sites have water and electricity and there's a boat ramp, bathhouse and laundry.

From Demopolis, take Hwy 80 west to Hwy 43 and then travel north for 12 miles. Turn left at the park signs, which are almost invisible at night, and drive a mile down the dirt road.

Hotels & Motels The folks at *Best Western Mint Sunrise* (☎ 334-289-5772), 1034 Hwy 80, go out of their way to make guests comfortable – a 'pampering kit' with toiletries and sweets is provided for female guests. Rooms have a refrigerator and a coffeemaker. It's $42 for a single or double.

The *Riverview Inn* (☎ 334-289-0690), 1301 N Walnut Ave (Hwy 43), overlooks the Tombigbee River and Demopolis Yacht Basin. There are refrigerators, microwaves, a coin-operated laundry and electrical hookups for boats. Rooms are $36 for a single or double.

The *Days Inn* (☎ 334-289-2500) at 1005 Hwy 80E has in-room microwaves, refrigerators, coffeemakers and hair dryers. There's a small fitness room and pool. A continental breakfast is included in the room rate of $40/45 a single/double.

Places to Eat

Mr G's Pizza (☎ 334-289-4149), 602 N Walnut Ave, is the humble hands-down favorite for Italian food. Salads, sandwiches and lunch specials are $3 to $5.50. You can eat in or take out. It's open Monday to Thursday from 10 am to 10 pm, Friday and Saturday from 10 am to 11 pm, and Sunday from 11 am to 10 pm.

Seafood is the primary fare at the *Jolly Roger* (☎ 334-289-8103), 1303 N Walnut Ave. You can eat indoors or on the dock over the Tombigbee River. There's an outdoor barbecue on Thursday. Sandwiches and lunch specials range from $4 to $10, with most dishes around $5. Dinners with two sides average $10. It's open Tuesday to Saturday from 11 am to 10 pm.

The rustic *Red Barn* (☎ 334-289-0595), 901 Hwy 80E, is a favorite among locals. Grilled catfish ($8.50) comes with cornbread, vegetables, rolls and a choice of fries, baked potato or rice, and dinners include a trip to the salad-and-soup bar. Resist the cobbler for dessert; it's disappointing. The Red Barn is open Monday to Saturday from 5 pm to 10 pm.

You can satisfy a sweet tooth at *Nevil's Bakery* (☎ 334-289-9990), 1012 Hwy 80E, with a slice of pie for 75¢ or a Mounds cookie, loaded with chocolate chips and coconut for 30¢. It's open Monday to Saturday from 6 am to 6 pm.

Getting There & Away

Greyhound (☎ 334-289-4837), 1610 S Cedar Ave, provides bus services from Atlanta ($53; one a day), Birmingham ($41; one) and Montgomery ($23; one).

TUSCALOOSA
population 157,732

Choctaw and Creeks lived here until settlers displaced them in the early 1800s. The town's name comes from two Choctaw words: *tuska*, meaning 'black,' and *lusa*, meaning 'river.' Tuscaloosa was the state capital from 1826 to 1846 and has been the home of the University of Alabama (UA) since 1831. Say its name and most Alabamians will think football, specifically, UA's Crimson Tide team. While the university is a major influence, economically, physically and emotionally (grown men here cry when UA loses a football game), the main sources of revenue are lumbering and paper production and light manufacturing, led by Mercedes Benz, JVC and Gulf States Paper Corporation.

Orientation

Most of the town sits on the south bank of the Black Warrior River, but part of it stretches north across the river to Lake Tuscaloosa. It's sister city, Northport, lies on the river's north bank, north and west of Tuscaloosa. UA sprawls along the river's south bank in the heart of the city.

The town is laid out in an easy-to-follow numerical grid. Numbered avenues run north-south and numbered streets run east-west. River Rd runs east-west along the south bank. University Blvd runs parallel to River Rd a few miles south as it cuts through the middle of campus and ends at 28th Ave at the west end of town. On its east end it joins I-59/20, the road to Birmingham. I-359 enters the city from the south and becomes 25th (northbound) and 26th (southbound) Aves as it crosses the river to and from Northport. McFarland Blvd (Hwy 82) crosses I-59 and runs parallel to I-359 on the east side of town, skirting the eastern edge of the university before crossing the river.

ALABAMA

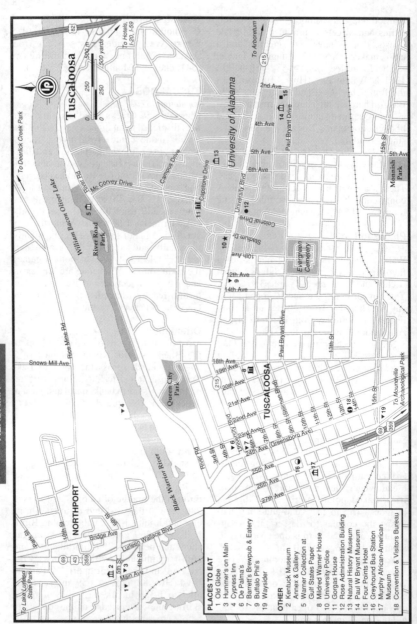

PLACES TO EAT
1 Old Globe
3 Hummer's on Main
4 Cypress Inn
6 De Palma's
7 Barrett's Brewpub & Eatery
9 Buffalo Phil's
19 Waysider

OTHER
2 Kentuck Museum
5 Warner Collection at
   Annex & Gallery
   Gulf States Paper
8 Mildred Warner House
10 University Police
11 Gorgas House
12 Rose Administration Building
13 Natural History Museum
14 Paul W Bryant Museum
15 Four Points Hotel
16 Greyhound Bus Station
17 Murphy African-American
   Museum
18 Convention & Visitors Bureau

Information

The city's convention and visitors bureau (☎ 205-391-9200, 800-538-8696) is located in historic Jemison-Van de Graaf House at 1305 Greensboro Ave (24th Ave). The daily *Tuscaloosa News* has a morning and evening edition. For medical emergencies in Tuscaloosa, go to DCH Regional Medical Center (☎ 205-759-7111), 809 University Blvd E; in Northport, choose Northport/DCH (☎ 205-339-4500), 2700 Hospital Dr.

University of Alabama

This 1000-acre riverfront campus (☎ 205-348-6010) sprawls across main city thoroughfares in the center of Tuscaloosa, making it easy to get around. You can pick up a free parking pass and campus map at the university police office in Gorgas Hall, at Stadium Dr and University Blvd, or in Room 152 in the Rose Administration Building. Free campus tours depart from Room 151 in the Rose Building on weekdays at 10 am and 2 pm and Saturdays at 10 am. For reservations call ☎ 205-348-5666 or ☎ 800-933-2262.

The **Paul W Bryant Museum** (☎ 205-348-4668), 300 Paul Bryant Dr, is a tribute to the legendary coach and his winning football team, University of Alabama's Thin Red Line (also known as Crimson Tide). It traces the history of UA football from its first game in 1892 and is full of Bryant's personal items, including his trademark black and white hat, as well as team uniforms, sweaters, shoes and helmets. Scores of trophies attest to Bryant's success (won 323 games, lost 85 and tied 17) that made him the winningest college football coach in history. Interactive exhibits and dioramas take you to the field for play-by-play action. It's open daily from 9 am to 4 pm. Admission is $2 for adults, and $1 for seniors and students.

Gorgas House (☎ 205-348-5906), Capstone Dr at Colonial Dr, was erected in 1829 and is the oldest existing structure built by the state. Guests originally entered by climbing the paired curving stairways to the 2nd-floor balcony – the main floor was built above ground level to avoid flooding. The house has lots of family items. Free tours are given Tuesday to Friday from 10 am to 4 pm, Saturday to 3 pm, and Sunday from 2 to 4 pm.

The **Natural History Museum** (☎ 205-348-9742), 6th Ave at Capstone Dr, is in a beautiful French beaux-arts building. The ground-floor exhibits cover Native Americans, and the stunning 2nd-floor gallery features a mineral and rock collection. It's open Monday to Friday from 8 am to 4:30 pm, and Saturday from 1 to 4 pm.

The 60-acre **arboretum** (☎ 205-553-3278) on Arboretum Way has flora and fauna representing every ecological zone in the state. There's a greenhouse, wildflower garden, meadow, bog, and nature trails. It's free, as are most of its programs. Take University Blvd east to McFarland Blvd and turn south. At 15th St turn east and go 3½ miles to the junction with Loop Rd.

Warner Collection

One of the finest private art collections in the world is at the **Gulf States Paper Corporation** (☎ 205-553-6200), 1400 River Rd NE. The corporate office, where the collection is housed, is a work of art itself.

Buford Boone

While African-American civil rights leaders headed the battle for equality in Selma and Montgomery, it was a white newspaper editor, Buford Boone, who took up arms in Tuscaloosa. On May 19, 1954, two days after the US Supreme Court handed down its landmark decision on *Brown* v *the Board of Education*, Boone wrote an editorial supporting compliance at Tuscaloosa's University of Alabama campus and throughout the state. In it he blamed district court judge George Wallace for being the 'chief architect of an atmosphere of violence.' Boone eventually won the Pulitzer Prize for his editorial, 'What a Price for Peace.' He died 27 years later to the day that his editorial was written. ∎

ALABAMA

It's designed as a traditional Japanese temple complete with Japanese gardens in back. In essence, there are two collections of art, artifacts and sculpture: works by early and contemporary American artists and works from the Pacific Islands, Africa and Asia. The paintings of wild birds by Basil Ede are exquisite. Free tours are given Monday to Friday at 5:30 and 6:30 pm, on Saturday hourly from 10 am to 4 pm, and on Sunday hourly from 1 to 4 pm.

Part of the collection is at **Mildred Warner House** (☎ 205-345-4062), 1925 8th St. Originally a two-room cabin built in 1822, it was expanded in the 1830s. While the house is interesting architecturally and the antiques are lovely, they pale in comparison to the art collection inside. The collection is open weekends from 1 to 5 pm.

Murphy African-American Museum

The city's first licensed black mortician, William J Murphy, lived in this 1920s cottage (☎ 205-758-2861) at 2601 Paul Bryant Dr (10th St) at Lurleen Wallace Blvd S (26th Ave). It's filled with many original pieces of furniture. Several exhibits capture how life was for middle-class and well-to-do African Americans in the first half of the century. It's open by appointment only.

Special Events

The Moundville Native American Festival, held in the Moundville Archaeological Park (☎ 205-371-2572; see Around Tuscaloosa), features crafts, storytellers, music and a market the last week in September. More than 30,000 visitors show up for the Kentuck Festival (☎ 205-758-1257), one of the South's premier crafts events; it's held on the third weekend in October.

Places to Stay

Camping See Lake Lurleen State Park, Moundville Archaeological Park, and Deerlick Creek Park in Around Tuscaloosa.

Hotels & Motels Many hotels line McFarland Blvd (Hwy 82) from I-59 north to the university. They're also clustered along Skyland Blvd, which runs parallel to and just south of I-59.

The *Executive Inn* (☎ 205-759-2511), 1780 McFarland Blvd N, is located on the north bank of the river and is basic, clean and inexpensive. It has a pool, free continental breakfast on weekends and free coffee daily. The staff are helpful. The single/double rate is $30/$39 Monday to Thursday and $40/45 on weekends.

The *Super 8 Motel* (☎ 205-758-8878), 4125 McFarland Blvd E, offers clean rooms with few extras other than cable movies and complimentary coffee in the lobby. It's $38/43 for a single/double.

The *Sleep Inn* (☎ 205-556-5696, 888-556-5696), 4300 Skyland Blvd, gives you good value for your money. It's at the south end of town near I-59. The rooms have

---

The Face in the Window

Henry Wells, a young black man, was accused of burning down the Pickens County Courthouse in 1876. Two years later he was arrested on flimsy evidence and charged with the burning and other crimes. To protect him from a lynch mob of angry townspeople, the sheriff hid him in the garret of the newly rebuilt courthouse. The mob saw him in the window and advanced toward the building. The frightened man stood looking out at the crowd. He yelled down, claiming his innocence and swore that he would haunt them if they killed him. An instant later, a flash of lightning illuminated Wells' face in a pane of the window and his anguished look was imprinted on the pane. There are two versions of the story: in one, Wells is killed by the lightning; in the other he is murdered by the mob. Whatever happened, the terrorized face remains under the eaves on the north side of the courthouse to this day, in spite of repeated scrubbing of the window, and hailstorms that have broken surrounding panes. ■

queen beds, hair dryers, coffeemakers, movie channels and VCRs with video rental in the lobby. Singles/doubles are $39/51, including complimentary continental breakfast.

The *Holiday Inn* (☎ 205-553-1550), 3920 McFarland Blvd E, has a restaurant, lounge and pool. Some rooms are suites. Rooms range from $55 to $65.

The *Four Points Hotel* (☎ 205-752-3200, fax 205-343-1139), 320 Paul Bryant Dr, has an outdoor patio and a pool. It's on the university campus next to the Paul Bryant Museum. Single/double rooms are $94/$99, with a complimentary newspaper thrown in.

Terrific service earned the *Hampton Inn* (☎ 205-553-9800), 600 Harper Lee Dr, a rating as one of the top five Hampton properties in the country. There's a pool, complimentary breakfast bar and convenience store. Rooms are clean, quiet and spacious and cost $59/65.

Best Western Park Plaza Motor Inn (☎ 205-556-9690), 3801 McFarland Blvd E, has a pool, whirlpool and movie channel. The single/double rate is $60/64, including breakfast.

Rooms are a bit bigger than usual at the *Courtyard by Marriott* (☎ 205-750-8384), 4115 Courtney Dr, which has a pool, whirlpool and lounge serving drinks and appetizers. The rate is $72 for a single or double, including breakfast. It's at the intersection of I-59 and I-359.

Places to Eat

The small *Waysider* (☎ 205-345-8239), 1512 Greensboro Ave, downtown, is the place for breakfast. Start with light, fluffy biscuits, add eggs or pancakes, bacon, grits. It's all good and breakfast will cost about $4. It's open Tuesday to Saturday from 5 am to 1:30 pm.

Buffalo Phil's (☎ 205-758-3318), University Blvd at 12th Ave, is a popular student food stop for wings, burgers and pasta. Lunch costs around $6.50, while dinner ranges from $6.50 to $11. Lighted candles on the tables dress it up at night, but it has a casual, comfortable bar feel.

A jazz band performs on Friday nights, except in summer, and occasionally there's live entertainment on Saturday nights. It opens daily at 11 am and meals are served till 11 pm. It closes at 2 or 3 am, except Sundays, when it closes at 9 pm.

Barrett's Brewpub & Eatery (☎ 205-366-0380), 2325 University Blvd (at Greensboro Ave), is Tuscaloosa's only brewpub. Suds are $3 a pint or $9 a pitcher, except for the nightly special, which is $1.50/$4.50. Upstairs it's fancy, with lunch at $7.50 to $10, and dinner for $15 to $25. Downstairs in the bar area, you can grab a pizza, burger or salad for half that while watching sports on the tube.

De Palma's (☎ 205-759-1879), 2300 University Blvd, serves fine Italian food. The crowd is young and middle-aged professionals. Favorites include pasta de Palma (an angel hair and cream creation) and pizzas. Expect to pay $10 at lunch, and $15 to $20 at dinner.

The original *Dreamland Barbecue* (☎ 205-758-8135), 6531 15th Ave E, is on the south edge of town in Jerusalem Heights. Founder John Bishop has retired, but it's still run by his family and they still serve just pork ribs ($4.50 for a sandwich, $8 for a plate). It's open Monday to Thursday from 10 am to 9 pm, and Friday and Saturday to 10 pm.

Hummer's on Main (☎ 205-345-2119), 433 Main Ave, Northport, has yummy, healthy, fresh salads and breads. The owner, Janet Graham, bakes honey wheat, rye and sourdough breads ($5 a loaf) daily. She imports rare European cheeses and makes to-die-for pasta ($4.50) and chicken salads ($5.50). Locals come here when they want to take home something special. Her combination deli-restaurant seats 20 indoors and another dozen outdoors. It's open Tuesday to Saturday from 11 am to 2 pm.

Located on a bluff overlooking the Black Warrior River, the *Cypress Inn* (☎ 205-345-6963), 501 Rice Mine Rd, Northport, has the best view in town for lunch and dinner. Lunch is $5 to $6.50 and the menu includes catfish, shrimp with mushrooms and two cheeses, and vegetarian pasta.

Dinner costs $11 to $17. It's open every day for dinner, and lunch is served Sunday to Friday.

The *Old Globe* (☎ 205-391-0949), 430 Main Ave, Northport, serves spicy Cajun red beans and rice ($7) for lunch. For dinner, try the mix of seafood, vegetables and tropical fruits in the Caribbean island stew ($15). It's a nice setting as well. Meals are served Tuesday to Saturday from 11 am to 3 pm and 5 to 10 pm, Friday and Saturday to 11 pm.

Spectator Sports
Tickets to watch the Crimson Tide roll over its opponents in the Bryant Denny Stadium usually sell out to season-ticket holders. However, you can buy tickets ($26) for games at the beginning of the season. If you're in the area, call the ticket office (☎ 205-348-6111) or stop by the stadium. You might get lucky.

Things to Buy
The Kentuck Museum Annex & Gallery (☎ 205-758-1257), 503 Main Ave, Northport, features changing exhibitions of fine American crafts and folk art, primarily by Southern artists. Choose from glass, textiles, wood and pottery. It's open Monday to Friday from 9 am to 5 pm, and Saturday from 10 am to 4:30 pm.

Getting There & Away
The closest airport, Birmingham international (☎ 205-595-0533), is 57 miles east.

Amtrak's *Crescent* travels once a day each way between New Orleans ($46/$92 one-way/roundtrip) and New York ($346/$173), with stops including Meridian, Birmingham, Anniston and Atlanta.

Greyhound (☎ 205-758-6651), 2520 Stillman Blvd, has services from Atlanta ($41; four daily), Birmingham ($13; six), Huntsville ($33; three), New Orleans ($56; two), Selma ($17; four), Jackson ($36; five) and Meridian ($21; five).

Major car-rental agencies have counters at Birmingham international airport. Rental companies with offices downtown include Budget (☎ 205-349-1300), 115 Greensboro

Ave, and Enterprise (☎ 205-349-4446), 610 Skyland Blvd E.

Getting Around
Tuscaloosa County Transit Authority provides public transportation Monday to Friday from 5 am to 6 pm. Rides cost 80¢ and transfers are 20¢. Exact change is required.

The Deluxe Radio Cab Company (☎ 205-758-9025), the Radio Cab Service (☎ 205-758-2831) and Tuscaloosa Radio Cab Service (☎ 205-349-3669) provide taxi services.

AROUND TUSCALOOSA
Lake Lurleen State Park
Named after Alabama's only woman governor, this 1625-acre park (☎ 205-339-1558) hugs the shoreline of its 250-acre lake. Swimming, fishing and boating are good reasons to visit in warm months. Fall foliage is the best reason to go when the weather turns chilly. Nonmotorized boats can be rented for fishing or just exploring and rent for $7.50 a day. Canoes and small boats cost $5 an hour. Three easy trails wind five miles through the surrounding forest and along the lake's edge. There's also a store, marina, bait and tackle shop and nature center with seasonal programs.

The campground has 91 improved sites ($12). The day-use fee is $1 (children 50¢). The park is 12 miles northwest of Tuscaloosa. Take Hwy 82 west, turn right on County Rd 21 and continue two miles.

Deerlick Creek Park
The Army Corps of Engineers operates this popular 300-acre park (☎ 205-553-9373) 12 miles east of town on 3200-acre Holt Lake. The lake has biking and hiking trails, two marinas, campsites, play areas, picnic areas and grills, boat rentals and a good beach. The paved bike trail is flat, but the hiking trails, the longest about a mile, follow the steep rise and fall of the terrain. Beech Tree Hollow is a favorite as it cuts through dense woods.

Wildlife is abundant year-round. Summer is the busiest time, but birdwatchers prefer

November through February, when they can spot bald eagles that winter on the bluffs surrounding the lake.

The campground has 40 improved and six primitive sites, a bathhouse and restrooms. Site rates are $8 with water and $12 with water and electricity. The drive to the park is convoluted, but brown park signs clearly mark the route once you're on Rice Mine Rd. From I-20/59 take Hwy 82 west to Rice Mine Rd E (County Rd 30). Go five miles, then turn right onto New Watermelon Rd (County Rd 87), which crosses Lake Tuscaloosa. Go about four miles and turn right onto Lake Nichol Rd (County Rd 42), which crosses Lake Nichol. It's another four miles to Deerlick Rd (County Rd 89), where you turn right. The road dead-ends at Deerlick Creek Park and Campground.

Mercedes Benz Visitor Center

This new museum (☎ 205-507-3537), east of town at 1 Mercedes Dr, Vance, traces the company's 112-year history through exhibitions and half a dozen original and replica versions of the first motorized carriages. There are rare and vintage cars, and displays on changes in auto development, including racing, safety innovations and exhaust systems. It's open year-round, except on major holidays, Monday to Friday from 9 am to 5 pm, Saturday from 10 am to 5 pm. Entry is $4 for adults, and $3 for seniors and kids. This is the only Mercedes Benz factory outside of Germany that allows visitors into production areas. Call for a tour reservation.

Moundville Archaeological Park

The university's 320-acre park (☎ 205-371-2572), 15 miles south of Tuscaloosa on the Black Warrior River, contains 26 archaeologically important Mississippian-era Indian mounds and is not to be missed. There is a reconstructed mound with dioramas of Indian life, as well as the **Jones Archaeological Museum** (☎ 205-371-2234), which displays excavated artifacts and a replica of an Indian village. There's much more here than archaeology. An elevated wooden nature trail winds past wildflower fields, native plants, two preserved mounds and the river. The park opens daily from 8 am to 8 pm, and the Jones Museum opens daily from 9 am to 5 pm, except on major holidays. Admission for adults is $4, and for seniors and students it's $2.

It's a great place to camp if you like nature, culture and history. Within the park, there are 31 campsites with water and electricity, a bathhouse and restrooms, picnic areas and grills. The rate for tents and RVs is $10 a night ($8 for seniors). Take I-20/59 south to exit 71 and then follow Hwy 69 for 13 miles to the park entrance.

ALABAMA

Mobile & the Gulf Coast

The southwest corner of the state has beaches, rivers, estuaries, bays, a delta and pine-covered barrier islands. These topographical features attracted explorers, who traveled from the Gulf up the bay and then continued inland on the rivers. Ownership of the region bounced between European countries before the US claimed it for the Louisiana and Alabama Territories.

The coastline stretches 52 miles along the Gulf of Mexico. The tidal shoreline of bays, inlets and estuaries extends 607 miles, from Weeks Bay to Heron Bay, much of which is environmentally protected marshland. The two spits of terra firma on either side of Mobile Bay are connected by a ferry service between Dauphin Island's Fort Gaines in the west and Pleasure Island's Fort Morgan in the east.

This chapter begins in Mobile, heads east across Mobile Bay on I-10, travels south along the bay's eastern shore on Hwy 98 through Fairhope and Point Clear, then turns west on Hwy 98 to Foley. It then moves south on Hwy 59 to explore the beaches along Pleasure Island on the Gulf of Mexico. Continuing west along Hwy 180 to Fort Morgan State Park, it crosses Mobile Bay on the ferry to Dauphin Island before heading north on Hwy 193 past Bellingrath Gardens and back to Mobile.

MOBILE
population 196,300

In 1702 Jean Baptiste Le Moyne, Sieur de Bienville, constructed Fort Louis de la Mobile north of Mobile. Good-time folks that they were, the French held their first Mardi Gras celebration two years later. In 1711 Le Moyne moved the French capital of Louisiana to the site of modern-day Mobile and built Fort Condé. The French named the city and county after the Maubila Indians of the area. Maubila means 'paddling Indians.'

Over the next hundred years it passed from French ownership to British, then to Spanish and finally into American hands; it was incorporated in 1814. Throughout the 1800s, Mobile's deep bay and strategic location at the mouth of the Mobile and Tensaw Rivers ensured it a special place in Alabama's history. Cotton and, later, timber from all over the state were shipped from Mobile to ports around the world. Wealthy Mobilians built lavish homes and filled them with imported finery.

Mobile remained an important Confederate port until the last days of the Civil War, when Admiral David Farragut defeated the Confederate ships defending it. During WWI and WWII the shipyards

---

HIGHLIGHTS

- A two-hour swamp tour through the Mobile-Tensaw Delta
- The Mobile Bay ferry crossing between Fort Morgan and Fort Gaines
- A visit to the Biophilia Nature Center, followed by an afternoon sailing the back bays of Pleasure Island and searching for dolphins
- Gulf State Park's nature trails, white-sand beach, and freshwater lakes where you can see alligators submerged among the reeds
- A walk along Fairhope's beach, pier and bluffs

and port built and repaired vessels and shipped military supplies.

Today, Mobile continues its reign as a major seaport and shipbuilding center. It's a lively, elegant city with many green spaces and Spanish moss-draped oaks making canopies over wide boulevards. On many spring mornings, fog rolls in and blankets the city, but generally it lifts by midday. Dining and nightlife are upbeat and progressive. Mardi Gras continues as well, although Mobile's version is smaller, safer, and saner than its New Orleans counterpart.

Orientation

Called the Port City, Mobile sprawls across the northwest corner of Mobile Bay. The I-10 enters the city across the seven-mile causeway over Mobile Bay. It then cuts diagonally across the city, heading southwest to Mississippi. The I-65 originates in the southeast corner of the city and runs northeast to Montgomery. Hwy 90 crosses I-10 on the south side, picks up Hwy 59 and continues south to Bellingrath Gardens. Hwy 193 originates on the south side at exit 17 off I-10 and continues south to

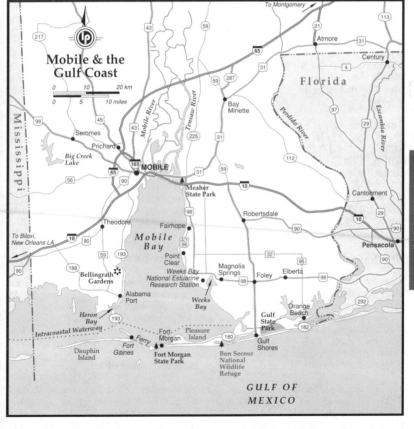

Dauphin Island. A ring road encircles downtown Mobile. Government St becomes Government Blvd when it meets Hwy 90 west of downtown. The area just west of downtown where Government St and Airport Blvd meet is called the Loop.

Information

Tourist Offices For information by mail, contact Mobile Convention & Visitors Corp (☎ 334-415-2000, 800-566-2453, fax 334-415-2060), PO Box 204, Mobile, AL 36602. To pick up information go to Fort Condé at 150 S Royal St; it's open Monday to Friday from 8 am to 5 pm.

Post The main post office (☎ 334-694-6108) is at 250 St Joseph St, downtown. It's open Monday to Friday from 8 am to 4:30 pm. The Bel Air Mall branch (☎ 334-478-8513), 3410 Bel Air Mall, on Airport Blvd at I-65, is open Monday to Friday from 8 am to 8 pm and Saturday from 9 am to 5 pm.

Bookstores Barnes & Noble (☎ 334-450-0845), 3250 Airport Blvd, and Books-A-Million (☎ 334-471-3528), in Bel Air Mall and at 3960 Airport Blvd, have good regional sections.

Libraries The central library (☎ 334-434-7073), 701 Government St, is open Monday to Thursday from 9 am to 9 pm, and Friday and Saturday from 9 am to 6 pm.

Media The *Mobile Register* is the local daily, while the *Inner City News* and *Mobile Beacon* are minority weeklies. The local National Public Radio affiliate is WHIL FM radio at 91.3.

Medical Services The University of South Alabama Hospital (☎ 334-471-7000), 2451 Fillingim St, handles emergencies and provides medical services.

Historic House Museums

Guides in period costumes lead visitors around **Oakleigh** (☎ 334-432-1281), 350 Oakleigh Place, an 1833 Greek revival mansion on 3½ acres. The museum is filled with fine American and European furnishings and Mardi Gras memorabilia. In contrast, Cox-Deasy House is a more modest Creole cottage built in 1850 on the grounds. The gift shop carries works by regional artisans. Admission is $5 ($4.50 for seniors and AAA members, $3 for children aged 12 to 18 and $2 for children six to 11).

Bragg-Mitchell Mansion (☎ 334-471-6365), 1906 Springhill Ave, west of downtown, is one of the finest examples of antebellum architecture on the Gulf Coast. Admission is $5 ($3 for students).

Mobile's first official jail is now the beautiful **Condé-Charlotte House** (☎ 334-432-4722), 104 Theatre St, downtown. Exhibits reflect the many flags that flew over it. Admission is $4 ($2 for children).

Richards-DAR House (☎ 334-434-7320), 256 N Joachim St, downtown, was built in 1860 and is one of Mobile's best examples of Italianate architecture. Fine details make this house worth seeing. Admission is $4 ($1 for children).

If you plan to visit the Bragg-Mitchell, Oakleigh, Condé-Charlotte and Richards-DAR house museums, save money by purchasing a pass for $14.

Museum of the City of Mobile

This museum (☎ 334-434-7569), 355 Government St, downtown, in an Italianate townhouse built in 1872, should be the first stop for visitors. A puzzle of 100,000-plus artifacts from different periods give a picture of Mobile's history. There are antique carriages, model ships, paintings, documents, maritime antiques, arms and a Civil War collection. The Mardi Gras exhibit has everything from lavish ball gowns to historic photos. It's open Tuesday to Saturday from 10 am to 5 pm, and Sunday from 1 to 5 pm. Entry is free.

Mobile Museum of Art

This museum (☎ 334-343-2667), 4850 Museum Dr, Langan Park in west Mobile, focuses on American art, in particular, works by well-known 19th-century landscape painters and pieces from the 1930s

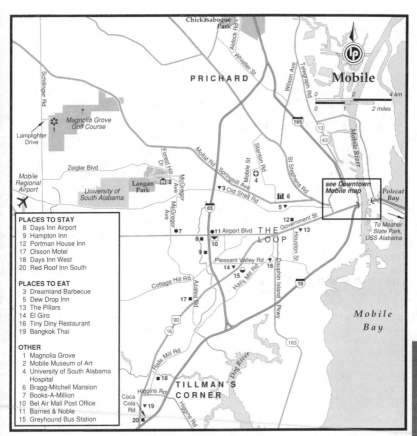

PLACES TO STAY
8 Days Inn Airport
9 Hampton Inn
12 Portman House Inn
17 Olsson Motel
18 Days Inn West
20 Red Roof Inn South

PLACES TO EAT
3 Dreamland Barbecue
5 Dew Drop Inn
13 The Pillars
14 El Giro
16 Tiny Diny Restaurant
19 Bangkok Thai

OTHER
1 Magnolia Grove
2 Mobile Museum of Art
4 University of South Alabama Hospital
6 Bragg-Mitchell Mansion
7 Books-A-Million
10 Bel Air Mall Post Office
11 Barnes & Noble
15 Greyhound Bus Station

and 1940s. The contemporary crafts collection is worth a peek. Exhibitions from the main museum's permanent collection are displayed in the downtown branch (☎ 334-694-0533), 300 Dauphin St. This is also where you'll see works by regional artists. Admission to both museums is free, except for special exhibits. The main museum is open Tuesday to Sunday from 10 am to 5 pm. Bus No 4 from downtown to Crighton stops three blocks away on Zeigler Blvd at Forest Hill Dr. The downtown museum is open Monday to Friday from 8:30 am to 4:30 pm.

National African-American Archives & Museum

Housed in the Davis Ave branch of the Mobile Public Library, which was constructed in 1930 for black residents, this small but interesting museum (☎ 334-433-8511), 564 Martin Luther King Ave, downtown, has books and portraits of famous African-Americans, as well as a room covering the history of the Colored Carnival. It's also the headquarters of the National Hank Aaron Fan Club, which displays memorabilia from this baseball player, a Mobile native. It's open Monday to Friday from 8:30 am to 5 pm, Saturday from noon to 4 pm and Sunday from 2 to 4 pm.

Fort Condé
'Soldiers' in French military uniforms greet visitors at this partially reconstructed fort (☎ 334-434-7304), 150 S Royal St at Church St, downtown, which now serves as a museum and the city's visitor center. Originally built in 1711 to guard the capital of the Louisiana Territory, it was completely torn down in 1820 to make way for the city's expansion. In the 1970s, when the George Wallace Tunnel was built, they tore down the small businesses that were near the fort's original site to make way for the road and to rebuild the fort. Today's fort is about a quarter of its original size. Live demonstrations of musket and cannon fire are given. It's open daily from 8 am to 5 pm, and entry is free.

Exploreum Museum of Science
This dynamic, interactive museum (☎ 334-476-6873), 1906 Springhill Ave at the same location as Bragg-Mitchell Mansion, is loaded with hands-on exhibits. There are permanent and temporary exhibitions. The museum is due to move downtown (65 Government St) in July 1998. It's open Tuesday to Saturday from 9 am to 5 pm. Admission is $4 for adults and $3 for children. Entrance fees vary, depending on the special exhibits.

USS *Alabama* Battleship Memorial Park
The battleship USS *Alabama* (☎ 334-433-2703, 800-426-4929), winner of nine WWII battle stars, is at 2703 Battleship Parkway. Personal items and period music transport you back to the 1940s before you climb aboard the USS *Drum*, a WWII submarine alongside, to explore a sailor's working life under the sea. The indoor aircraft pavilion contains historic planes and a jet simulator. For those who tire of looking at hardware, a rose garden and boardwalk overlook the wetlands. There's also a restaurant, picnic area and gift shop. Take exit 27 off the I-10 causeway or from the eastern shore, exit 30. It's open daily from 8 am to sunset, except at Christmas. Admission is $8 ($4 for children); there's a $2 parking fee.

Golf
Magnolia Grove (☎ 334-645-0075), 7000 Lamplighter Dr, is Mobile's representative on the Robert Trent Jones Golf Trail.

Organized Tours
You might feel uneasy riding into the swamps on a 22-passenger boat named *Gator Bait* (☎ 334-460-8206) until you realize that Captain Gene Burrell has a sense of humor and is devoted to protecting wildlife. He tells amusing, informative stories on his two-hour cruise through the Mobile-Tensaw Delta, the largest inland delta in the US. You'll also see shell mounds and hear about the history of Native Americans in the delta. Don't miss this.

The boat departs from the Chickasaw Marina Tuesday to Saturday at 10 am and 2 pm. It's $20 for adults and $10 for children. Take I-65 north to exit 13 (Hwy 158 E), continue two miles to Hwy 43 and turn south. Chickasaw Marina is half a mile down the road.

Special Events
Mardi Gras, also known as carnival, begins two weeks before Ash Wednesday or 40 days before Easter. Call the visitor center (☎ 334-415-2000, 800-566-2453) for information. Throughout March there are driving tours along the streets showing the most colorful azaleas. Maps are available at Fort Condé. The first weekend in October, BayFest features three days of big-name entertainers, food and stuff for kids. Contact the City of Mobile Special Events Office (☎ 334-470-7730) for details. For more than 45 years, the Mobile Piano Ensemble (☎ 334-645-2366) has presented a concert played by top-caliber musicians in early October. The city sponsors First Night Mobile, a nonalcoholic New Year's celebration with more than 100 musical, theatrical and dance performances outdoors on December 31. Call City of Mobile Special Events Office for information (see above).

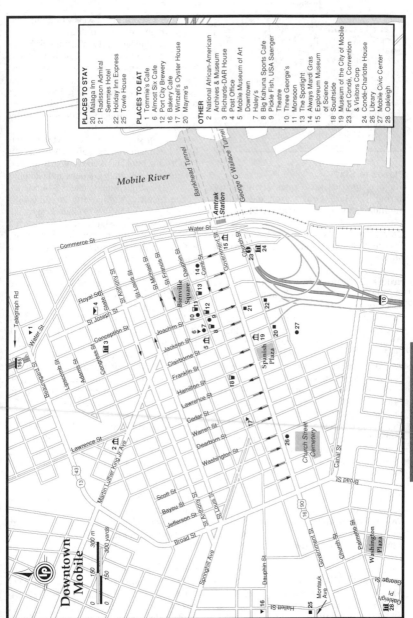

Downtown Mobile

Mobile River

Bankhead Tunnel

George C Wallace Tunnel

Amtrak Station

PLACES TO STAY
20 Malaga Inn
21 Radisson Admiral
     Semmes Hotel
22 Holiday Inn Express
25 Towle House

PLACES TO EAT
1   Tommie's Cafe
6   Almost Six Cafe
12 Port City Brewery
16 Bakery Cafe
17 Wintzell's Oyster House
20 Mayme's

OTHER
2   National African-American
     Archives & Museum
3   Richards-DAR House
4   Post Office
5   Mobile Museum of Art
     Downtown
7   Haley's
8   Big Kahuna Sports Cafe
9   Pickle Fish, USA Saenger
     Theatre
10 Three George's
11 Monsoon
13 The Spotlight
14 Always Mardi Gras
15 Exploreum Museum
     of Science
18 Southside
19 Museum of the City of Mobile
23 Fort Condé, Convention
     & Visitors Corp
24 Condé-Charlotte House
26 Library
27 Mobile Civic Center
28 Oakleigh

ALABAMA

Let the Good Times Roll!
There's a lot more to Mardi Gras than parades. There are balls, feasts and float parties. While most balls are private affairs, many events are open to the public – visitors included – at prices ranging from $3 to $25. Forget about getting a baby-sitter: there also are events designed expressly for young children. Check with the visitor center (☎ 334-415-2000) for details. ■

Places to Stay
Some properties raise rates significantly during the Mardi Gras season and require minimum stays of two to three nights.

Camping For camping at Meaher State Park and Chickasabogue Park see Around Mobile.

Hotels & Motels *Holiday Inn Express* (☎ 334-433-6923), 255 Church St, is the best buy downtown, but since it's opposite the Civic Center, you have to reserve early or get lucky. The rooms are comfortable, clean and have coffeemakers and free movies. There's an outdoor pool, free parking and complimentary continental breakfast. The single/double rate is $54/59.

The six-floor *Days Inn Airport* (☎ 334-344-3410) at 3650 Airport Blvd, West Mobile, is popular with business travelers on a budget. It offers complimentary continental breakfast, bar, pool, and refrigerators on request. The single/double rate is $59/63.

Hampton Inn (☎ 334-344-4942), 930 S Beltline Hwy (I-65 near Airport Blvd), is ideally situated for forays into Mobile, Dauphin Island and Bellingrath Gardens. It has an outdoor pool, free cable movies, an exercise room and complimentary continental breakfast. Singles are $45 to $51, while doubles range from $55 to $61.

You get far more than you'd expect for your money at *Olsson Motel* (☎ 334-661-5331, 800-332-1004, 800-351-1023 in Alabama), 4137 Government Blvd (Hwy 90 W), a 25-room, family-run operation. It's clean, the staff are courteous, and it's

cheap. It's seven miles west of downtown. Single/double rooms cost $26/31.

If you plan an early morning drive to Bellingrath Gardens and Dauphin Island, the *Red Roof Inn South* (☎ 334-666-1044), 5450 Coca Cola Rd, Tillman's Corner, is a good choice. It's clean and has bargain rates as well as free movies, complimentary coffee and modem data ports. Single/double rooms are $36/48.

Days Inn West (☎ 334-661-8181), 5480 Inn Rd, Tillman's Corner, off I-10, has a coin laundry and pool and is conveniently located for trips to Bellingrath Gardens and Dauphin Island. The single/double rate is $44/53.

The historic *Malaga Inn* (☎ 334-438-4701, 800-235-1586), 359 Church St, is *the* place to be during Mardi Gras because it's downtown on the parade route. Rooms, which are nicely furnished, open onto a balcony overlooking a courtyard with a fountain. There's a fine restaurant and small pool. Singles are $69, doubles are $79 and there's a corporate rate of $59. It's a bargain for its location.

The *Radisson Admiral Semmes Hotel* (☎ 334-432-8000, 800-333-3333), 251 Government St, is a renovated historic hotel. There's a restaurant, an outdoor pool and whirlpool, plus privileges at a nearby fitness center. Singles/doubles are $99/109. Weekend discounts may drop the rate to $79 for a single or double.

Inns & B&Bs Felix and Carolyn Vereen run the *Towle House* (☎ 334-432-6440), 800-938-6953, fax 334-433-4381), 1104 Montauk Ave, as if they were welcoming friends. The two-story house in the Old Dauphin historic district has one room with a private bath. The two rooms that share a bath are usually only rented to people who know each other. A full breakfast awaits guests in the morning and there are drinks in the afternoon. It charges a flat rate of $85 a night, $75 a night for two nights, or $70 for three nights or more.

The *Portman House Inn* (☎ 334-471-1703, 800-471-1701, fax 334-471-1718), 1615 Government St, has nine rooms with modem data ports and free movies. Some rooms have a refrigerator and microwave. Continental breakfast is included and in the evening cocktails with hors d'oeuvres are served. Rates vary according to room location and season. Single rates are $109 to $189 and doubles range from $119 to $209.

Places to Eat
Seafood is a major feature of the local cuisine. You'll find less of it fried here than in other cities in Alabama. Airport Blvd and neighboring streets west of I-65 have many chain restaurants.

Downtown *Tommie's Cafe* (☎ 334-432-4159), 416 N Water St, is owned by a Greek family and has been in business since 1916. The dishes, which are mostly seafood, are good, as is the service. There are specials nightly. Expect to pay $7 to $9.

The atmosphere at the *Bakery Cafe* (☎ 334-433-2253), 1104 Dauphin St, is casual chic. There are trendy selections such as gourmet salads, grilled vegetables, duck tart and walnut rosemary chicken. Lunch costs around $6, and dinner is about $14.

Mayme's (☎ 334-438-4701), 359 Church St, is an elegant restaurant in the Malaga Inn serving New World cuisine. The dining room opens onto a courtyard where a jazz group plays on Thursday and Friday. Dinner costs around $20 to $25.

Almost Six Cafe (☎ 334-438-3447), 6½ N Jackson St, has a menu with lump crab fritters, baked brie and seafood gumbo. Specials change daily. The wine list has depth.

Oysters are the star feature at *Wintzell's Oyster House* (☎ 334-432-4605), 605 Dauphin St, where you can get them fried, on the shell, baked, in a loaf, Bienville, Rockefeller, on a sandwich, and so on. Lunch specials are $7 with fries. Dinners are $10 to $17.

Port City Brewery (☎ 334-438-2739), 225 Dauphin St, has a menu that features grazing foods. Dine in or on the balcony, and don't miss the barbecued shrimp. The beer is brewed in vats right in front of your eyes.

Elsewhere If you instantly want to feel at home, try the *Dew Drop Inn* (☎ 334-473-7872), 1808 Old Shell Rd. This 70-year-old diner is best known for its hot dogs with sauerkraut and onions, but it also serves tasty sandwiches and seafood loaves. You can get lunch for $6.

Some of the best Mexican food in town is served at *El Giro* (☎ 334-478-9886), 2518 Government Blvd, the Loop. It has all the traditional favorites, and you can eat in or take out. It's busy on weekdays at lunch. Checks average $6/10 for lunch/dinner.

Tiny Diny Restaurant (☎ 334-476-3880), 2159 Halls Mill Rd, The Loop, isn't tiny and is reminiscent of a diner. It's been in business forever and is particularly popular for breakfast and lunch. It's worth a trip just for the pie. Breakfast, lunch and dinner all cost about $5.

The *Pillars* (☎ 334-478-6341), 1757 Government St, the Loop, is a Mobile institution long regarded as one of the best restaurants in town. The setting, a restored historic mansion, is very elegant. The menu is continental. Breads are baked on the premises. Expect to pay $15 to $30 for dinner.

It's true. *Dreamland Barbecue* (☎ 334-479-9898), 3314 Old Shell Rd, just east of I-65, has come to Mobile with a branch that serves slaw. Honest. (This from the man who brought you ribs first in Tuscaloosa and then Birmingham with a motto of 'No Slaw, No Beans, No Potato Salad. Don't ask.')

The food is super at *Bangkok Thai* (☎ 334-666-7788), 5345 Hwy 90, Tillman's Corner, and servings are generous, so make sure you're hungry. Expect to pay $7 for lunch, and up to $16 for dinner.

Entertainment
Dauphin St, home of many of the city's most popular night spots and restaurants, rarely sleeps. Instead, it takes early morning cat naps so it can start partying all over again.

The Mobile Arts Council (☎ 334-432-9796) publishes a quarterly schedule of events and answers questions about fine arts exhibits.

Nightclubs & Bars For the best nightlife in one area, hit downtown's Dauphin St, where you'll find *Southside* (☎ 334-438-5555), 455 Dauphin St, which labels itself a music hall; *Haley's* (☎ 334-433-4970), 278 Dauphin St, which has a jukebox with good tunes; *Pickle Fish* (☎ 334-434-0000), 251 Dauphin St, which also serves sandwiches, pizzas, beignets and breakfast; the *Spotlight* (☎ 334-438-4405), 155 Dauphin St, a gay-friendly club with shows on Fridays; and *Big Kahuna Sports Cafe* (☎ 334-433-0500), 273 Dauphin St, which has big-screen TVs showing sports events.

Theater & Dance The *Mobile Ballet* (☎ 334-661-2244) has two seasons, spring and fall; it also puts on performances of the *Nutcracker* every December. Broadway touring companies perform in the *USA Saenger Theatre* (☎ 334-433-2787), 6 Joachim St S. The *Mobile Theatre Guild* (☎ 334-433-7513), 14 N Lafayette St, is an award-winning community theater that presents five plays a year between October and May.

Cinema Catch the latest flicks at *Carmike 10* (☎ 334-660-0104), 4900 Government Blvd, and *Village VI* (☎ 334-471-6205) theaters, 411 Bel Air Blvd.

Things to Buy
Mardi Gras favors, including balloons and beads, are popular in and out of season at Always Mardi Gras (☎ 334-433-6273), 50 S Royal St. Three George's (☎ 334-433-6725), 226 Dauphin St, has been making chocolates and candy since 1917.

Getting There & Away
Air Mobile regional airport (☎ 334-633-0313), 8400 Airport Blvd, is served by Continental Express, Delta, Northwest Airlink and AirTran Airlines. It's an easy trip to downtown along Airport Blvd, which runs east-west through the middle of Mobile.

Bus Greyhound (☎ 334-478-6089), 2545 Government St, provides services from Atlanta ($38; five daily), Baton Rouge ($47;11), Birmingham ($36; three), Biloxi

($16; five), Gulfport, Mississippi ($17; five), Montgomery ($28; five), New Orleans ($26; 11) and Pensacola ($16; eight).

Train Amtrak (☎ 334-432-4052, 800-872-7245), 11 Government St, provides train services to Miami ($147/294 one-way/roundtrip) and Los Angeles ($240/480) and points in between on its *Sunset Limited*.

Car The best way to get in and out of Mobile is on the interstates. You can drive the 169 miles to Montgomery in just under three hours. If you prefer a much more leisurely drive, take I-65 north about 20 miles north of Mobile to exit 37 (Bay Minette), where you can pick up Hwy 31. The narrow road snakes its way through scenic countryside and many small towns. I-10 west heads to New Orleans – a three-hour, 153-mile drive across the southwest corner of Alabama and Mississippi. Going east, I-10 crosses Mobile Bay then connects with Hwy 98 south to the eastern shore towns of Fairhope and Point Clear (one hour).

Boat Private boats can travel to Mobile on the Intracoastal Waterway and the Tenn-Tom Waterway.

Getting Around
Bus Mobile Transit Authority (MTA; ☎ 334-344-5656) provides public transportation throughout the metropolitan area Monday to Saturday from 6 am to 6 pm. The fare is $1.25 plus 10¢ for transfers. Mobile Bay Transportation (☎ 334-633-5693, 800-272-6234) shuttles cost $15 from the airport to downtown. There's no bus service.

Car Major agencies have counters at the airport. Avis (☎ 334-432-7766), 2241 Michigan Ave, and Enterprise (☎ 334-661-4446), 3720 Cottage Hill Rd, have offices in town.

Taxi Checker Yellow Cab Service (☎ 334-476-7711) and Mike Cab (☎ 334-457-9448) provide taxi services.

AROUND MOBILE
Meaher State Park
This overlooked state park (☎ 334-626-5529), two miles west of Spanish Fort on Hwy 90, covers 1327 acres in the wetlands of Mobile Bay. Most folks come to picnic, birdwatch and hike the two nature trails, one of which is a 1200-foot elevated boardwalk over the delta. This is a super spot, especially if you like waterfowl and marshes. There's a fishing pier, a boat ramp and restrooms.

It has isolated primitive camping ($7); choose your own site in the woods. Day use for adults is $1 and 50¢ for seniors and children.

Chickasabogue Park
This 1200-acre park (☎ 334-452-8496), 760 Aldock Rd, Prichard, is a good place to see marshland flora and fauna within minutes of downtown. It has swimming and canoeing ($4 per hour, $15 a day), but the best part is the 11 miles of combination biking and hiking trails divided into three sections, one of which offers challenging terrain.

The 57-site campground has a bathhouse, laundry, camp store and grills. Improved sites cost $9 (water and electricity) and $12 (full utilities). Take I-65 to exit 13 (Hwy 158 W) and follow the signs.

It's open 7 am to sunset for day use, which costs $1 for adults and 50¢ for students. It's free for seniors and kids under six years.

Bellingrath Gardens
The best place to start at this garden (☎ 334-973-2217, fax 334-973-0540), 12401 Bellingrath Gardens Rd, near Theodore, is where it all began. Walk along the Bayou Observation Platform, an elevated looped walkway across the Fowl River wetlands. It shows what the adjacent area looked like before Walter D Bellingrath, a wealthy Coca-Cola bottling distributor, transformed it into a 65-acre landscaped garden, anchored by more than 250,000 azaleas. In spring there is a riot of bright colors. 'Azalea trail maids,' dressed in the finest period Southern froufrou, lead visitors around the gardens. Camellias, another mainstay, show their stuff in winter. There are numerous specialty gardens to explore as well as the Bellingrath's furnished 15-room home. There's also a cafe, gift shop and 45-minute riverboat sightseeing cruise. The gardens are open daily from 8 am till one hour before dusk. Admission to the gardens is $7, and it's an extra $7 for the riverboat cruise or house tour ($12 for both). The dinner cruise will set you back $27.50.

FAIRHOPE
population 9600
In early 1894 a group from Iowa formed a colony modeled on the concept of a single tax proposed by economist Henry George. George believed that a single tax on land would be sufficient to finance all government expenses. The colonists wanted to create an environment where everyone had 'fair hope' for the future. They chose a bluff overlooking Mobile Bay and bought land that residents leased at an annually appraised rental that equalized the varying advantages of different tracts.

In 1908 a separate municipality called the City of Fairhope was established to perform administrative duties and maintenance. The colony donated the current beachfront park, the pier, the park lands on the bluff, and Henry George Park to the new municipality. It quickly became a resort town, with wealthy Mobilians arriving by boat to vacation in bayfront cottages and hotels along the bluff.

ALABAMA

Want a Great View?
Drive north on Alt Hwy 98 (S Mobile St) between Point Clear and Fairhope. The view of Mobile Bay from the bluffside highway is spectacular. On a clear day you can see Mobile. At Cliff Dr, pull into the parking lot, walk down the wooden steps to the Fairhope pier or continue north to Fairhope Ave and turn left to the pier and marina parking lot. ∎

Today, the cottages are gone, but Fairhope remains a popular getaway that attracts independent thinkers, artists and well-to-do northern retirees. Its a small town where people pass you on the street and say hello. Tourism and light manufacturing fuel the economy.

Orientation
From Mobile take I-10 east to Hwy 98, then follow Alt Hwy 98 and head south 10 miles. Park the car and walk. Fairhope Ave runs east-west and divides the town into north and south addresses. As it reaches the bay, it turns south and becomes S Mobile St (Alt Hwy 98). Section St and Greeno Rd (Hwy 98) run north-south. Section St at Fairhope Ave marks the center of town, where the streets are lined with shops and restaurants.

Information
The chamber of commerce (☎ 334-928-6387), 327 Fairhope Ave, provides visitor information. The welcome center (☎ 334-928-5095), N Section St at Fairhope Ave, has clean restrooms and is open daily from 8 am to 9 pm or 10 pm, but is staffed only from 9 am to 4 pm. The public library (☎ 334-928-7483), 161 N Section St, is open Monday to Saturday. It shows free classic films on Thursdays at 3 pm. Page & Palette (☎ 334-928-5295), 32 S Section St, has many books covering local, regional and state interests. The *Baldwin Press Register*

is published daily. For emergency care go to Thomas Hospital (☎ 334-928-2375), 750 Morphy Ave.

Fairhope Municipal Pier & Beach
Besides a terrific beach, this prime piece of real estate at Fairhope Ave and S Mobile St (Alt Hwy 98), a few blocks from downtown, has a pier with a restaurant, park, rose garden, benches, picnic pavilions and restrooms. It's a great place to watch the sunset or just sit back and slow down.

The pier never closes and is free. The beach is open daily from dawn to dusk. It costs $8 to park at the beach, so park in town and walk.

Fairhope Single Tax Corporation
The folks in this office (☎ 334-928-8162), 336 Fairhope Ave, welcome visitors with questions about their unique form of taxation. Besides answering questions, they'll let you use their library, which is filled with books on the theory and economics of single taxation. It's open Monday to Friday from 8 am to 5 pm.

The Bell Building
Originally built as a public school, this building at 440 Fairhope Ave was the home of the Marietta Johnson School of Organic Education from 1920 to the 1940s. Today, one wing houses the **Marietta Johnson Museum** (☎ 334-990-8601), exhibiting books written by Johnson, arts and crafts

Learning the Organic Way
In 1907 Marietta Johnson, a local teacher, started a school of progressive ideas and named it the Marietta Johnson School of Organic Education. It grew so quickly from its original six pupils that she bought 10 acres of land and the Bell Building, which had formerly housed the town's public school. By 1920 there were 10 buildings and 220 students.

The school didn't charge fees. Johnson's aim was to develop the whole individual. There were no grades, books, desks or homework, yet students were well disciplined. She taught outside under the trees and sometimes in classrooms.

Students were grouped by age. Younger students concentrated on history, geography, literature, language, music, folk dancing, numbers, handwork and free play. High-school students learned English, languages (including Latin), history, math, arts and crafts, music, folk dancing and science. Many went on to first-rate colleges.

She supported the school through donations and by writing and lecturing in the United States and Europe until her death in 1938. ∎

made by the students and photographs of students and teachers. There's often a former student around to talk about the old days. It's open Sunday to Friday from 1 to 5 pm and is free.

The **Fairhope Historical Museum** (☎ 334-990-8601) is housed in another wing. Though small, it's chock full of important personal and public artifacts and photographs of the area. The staff is knowledgeable and enjoys relating local history. It's open Sunday to Friday 1 to 4 pm and is free.

Minamac Wildflower Bog

Between April and September this lakeside five-acre preserve (☎ 334-945-6157), at 13199 MacCartee Lane, is a riot of color as some 300 varieties of native wildflowers bloom. Walking paths allow you to get close to 'exotic' natives such as carnivorous pitcher plants and endangered species. The bog is named after the nature-lovers who own it, Min and Mac MacCartee. It's five miles east of Fairhope. Tours are given Monday to Saturday by appointment only. There's a nominal fee.

Organized Tours

The best way to gain insight into Fairhope and Mobile's eastern shore is through a tour with Jan Weiler of Landmark Tours (☎ 334-928-0207), 22873 Hwy 98. Every Sunday she leads a two-hour 'jubilee' (see sidebar) tour of the area for only $10. It's a great deal. Seating is limited to 15. Personal tours are $50 an hour, or $200 for half a day.

Special Events

The city hosts a three-day arts and crafts festival (☎ 334-928-6387) in mid-March with 200 artisans from around the country, concerts and food.

Places to Stay

Camping For camping at *Safe Harbor Resort*, see Fairhope to the Gulf Coast.

Hotels & Motels An older property, the *Barons Inn* (☎ 334-928-8000), 701 S Mobile Ave, has a commanding location across from Mobile Bay. The rooms have

> ### Jubilee!
> Jubilee is a rare phenomenon in which crabs, fish, shrimp, rays and other sea life swim to the shallow waters along the eastern shore of Mobile Bay. Local residents put out the call for 'jubilee!' and run to the shore with lanterns and flashlights and buckets and baskets to collect the live seafood. By morning, all the creatures have gone back to sea. The exact date is not predictable, but it generally occurs two to five times a year between June and September. An eight-page booklet called *Jubilees* explains the phenomenon. It's available at Page & Palette in Fairhope. ∎

king beds. There's a lounge and restaurant next door. Singles/doubles are $45/50. Five miles north of Fairhope, the *Eastern Shore Motel* (☎ 334-626-6601), 29070 Hwy 98, offers basic, but clean, budget accommodations. It's an older property near the highway. There's a restaurant next door. Single/double rooms are $32/39.

Holiday Inn Express (☎ 334-928-9191), 19751 Greeno Rd, is a new property with a pool, playground and access to a fitness center. Rooms have a coffeemaker and free movies. The complimentary continental breakfast is better than usual. It's off the road near a wooded area, so rooms are quiet, at least until 8 am, when housekeeping starts vacuuming. Single/double rates are $66/72.

Inns & B&Bs Fairhope has about two dozen B&Bs. The chamber of commerce and welcome center provide lists.

The *Porches Bed & Breakfast* (☎ 334-928-4754, 800-631-2810, fax 334-928-4793), 19190 County Rd 13, is aptly named after its 3500-sq-ft of wraparound porch. High ceilings make the place feel open, airy and spacious. Most chefs would die for the kitchen where Sandy Levin and husband Eddie prepare guests a country breakfast. They serve refreshments from 3 to 4 pm on the porch, where you can sit and watch sheep graze on the five-acre hobby farm. In a word, it's fabulous. Rates are $75 to $85 for a suite. In the heart of downtown, the historic *Church St Inn* (☎ 334-928-8976), 51 S Church St, is within easy walking distance of restaurants, galleries, shops and attractions. The house is decorated with antiques and has three guest rooms, each with a private bath. There's a fireplace, living room and front porch with rockers. The rate is $85 for a single or double.

Places to Eat
Though the name suggests a limited menu, *Jus' Gumbo* (☎ 334-928-4100), 2 S Church St, serves additional regional specialties including red beans and rice ($3 small, $5 large) and po-boy sandwiches ($3.50 half, $5.50 whole). It's a popular, funky little place that features live music on Tuesday and Friday nights. It's open Monday to Saturday from 11 am to 6, 8 or 10 pm or whenever the band stops.

Mary Ann's Deli (☎ 334-928-3663), 7 S Church St, serves soups, sandwiches and salads. Specialties include a salad of mixed greens, vegetables and grilled chicken topped with homemade dressing (bottled and available for purchase).

Every town has a *Julwin's* (☎ 334-990-9372), 411 Fairhope Ave, a home-style restaurant that's been open as long as anyone can remember. The potato salad and chicken salad are memorable. The restaurant is open Monday to Thursday from 6 am to 8 pm, Friday and Saturday from 6 am to 3 pm and Sunday from 6 am to 2 pm.

Gambino's (☎ 334-928-5444), Alt Hwy 98, overlooks Mobile Bay and serves traditional Italian dishes, steaks and seafood. Be forewarned, there's karaoke in the lounge three nights a week. It's open for lunch and dinner Monday to Saturday and for dinner only on Sunday.

It's a long drive to *Pelican Pointe Grill* (☎ 334-928-1747, 334-928-4414), at the end of County Rd 1, but you won't be disappointed. The drive is scenic and the food is dynamite. Try the combo platter ($16), a half-pound of royal red steamed shrimp and half a rack of barbecue ribs served with corn, potato and vegetable relish. The grill

affords a terrific view of the bay and has live entertainment, weather permitting, outside on Sundays from 3 to 8 pm. Lunch costs $8 to $10, and dinner is $16 to $20. It's open Monday to Friday from 5 to 9:30 pm, Saturday from noon to 10 pm, and Sunday from noon to 9 pm.

Yardarm Restaurant (☎ 334-928-8322), Fairhope Municipal Pier, 1 Fairhope Ave, specializes in fresh seafood. It's open Tuesday to Saturday for lunch and dinner.

Aubergine (☎ 334-928-9541), 315 De La Mar Ave, is Fairhope's fanciest restaurant. A typical dinner might feature turtle soup with sherry ($5), grilled salmon with herb pecan crust ($16) and a drop-dead dessert like tarte Tatin with crème anglaise ($4.50). It's open Tuesday to Saturday for lunch and dinner.

Entertainment
The rustic *Judge Roy Bean* (☎ 334-626-9988), 508 Main St, Daphne, has been the eastern shore's best spot for music for 20 years. They bring in good local, regional and national acts Thursday to Sunday from 9 pm to closing. Sometimes the names get as big as the Neville Brothers. There's popcorn to nibble, good wines and beers and a mascot goat that wanders around the place. The cover is $3 to $5. It's open Tuesday to Sunday from 4:30 pm until it closes.

Things to Buy
Cathi Ginder Designs (☎ 334-928-6834), 152 S School St, sells whimsical hand-painted dinnerware and accessories. It's open Tuesday to Saturday from 11 am to 5 pm. Tom Jones' Pottery (☎ 334-928-2561), County Rd 33, is in Clay City, named for the rich clay deposits and long-time manufacture of bricks and tile. You can tour the store and pottery and watch him work. The studio is seven miles southeast of Fairhope, between Fairhope Ave (County Rd 48) and Marlow Rd (County Rd 32). It's open Monday to Saturday from 9:30 am to 5 pm.

Getting There & Away
Air Travelers have a choice of two nearby airports: Mobile (☎ 334-633-4510) and

Pensacola, Florida (☎ 904-435-1745). It's about an hour's drive from either.

Bus The closest Greyhound (☎ 334-478-9793) station is at 2545 Government Blvd in Mobile. Mobile Bay Transportation (☎ 334-981-9811 ext 411 for Pensacola service, 334-633-5693 for Mobile) provides airport shuttles to and from Fairhope and Mobile ($38) and Pensacola ($57) airports. Rates are one-way and are for two passengers.

Train The closest Amtrak stations are in Mobile (☎ 334-432-4052), 11 Government St, and Bay Minette (☎ 800-872-7245), 100 E Railroad St.

Car The major car-rental agencies have service counters at the Mobile and Pensacola airports.

Boat Private boats can come south via the Tenn-Tom Waterway or north from the Intracoastal Waterway.

Getting Around

There's a scenic five-mile bike ride from the Fairhope Municipal Pier south along Alt Hwy 1 (Mobile St) to the Grand Hotel in Point Clear.

FAIRHOPE TO THE GULF COAST

Alt Hwy 98 follows the eastern shore five miles south to Point Clear, then turns east and rejoins Hwy 98. At Foley, 13 miles east, it intersects Hwy 59, which runs south to the Gulf Coast and north to the farming communities of Robertsdale and Loxley. Hwy 98 continues east 14 miles past farms, vegetable stands and feed stores around Elberta before arriving at the Florida border.

Point Clear

They say that prevailing winds make this the coolest spot on the eastern shore. Wealthy families knew that years ago when they built vacation homes here along the waterfront. Today, the historic district contains 28 homes constructed between 1850 and 1930. On a hillside near Point Clear more than 300 soldiers are buried in the Confederate Rest Cemetery. The death records were kept in the Grand Hotel, which burned down in 1961, leaving the identity of the soldiers a mystery.

There's public access to the shore via Zundel Rd; a walkway runs north to the rebuilt Grand Bay Hotel.

Point Clear Polo Club (☎ 334-928-1710) hosts free informal international matches on an 80-acre field. Matches are held on Sunday at 3 pm from April to June and September to November. Everyone is welcome. There's a three-day benefit match in October at which the beer-and-pretzel crowd gathers on one side of the field, the hats-and-champagne on the other.

The Punta Clara Kitchen (☎ 334-928-8477, 800-437-7868), Alt Hwy 98, is a confectionery business four miles south of Fairhope and a mile south of the Grand Hotel. While nibbling on preservative-free fresh pralines, fudge and toffee, you can watch sweets being made or wander through the owners' house museum, which is filled with antiques and heirlooms. It's open Monday to Saturday from 9 am to 5 pm, and Sunday from 12:30 to 5 pm.

Marriott's Grand Hotel (☎ 334-928-9201), Alt Hwy 98, is the third Grand Hotel on this location – the two previous properties were destroyed by fire and neglect. The sprawling bayfront resort provides every creature comfort, with an atmosphere of laid-back elegance. There are two restaurants in the hotel, another at the golf course and a cafe by the pool. The 'grand dining room,' with a fabulous view out over Mobile Bay, puts on a lavish buffet breakfast ($20 for hotel guests, slightly more for visitors) and lunches ($12). Depending on the season, weekday

ALABAMA

ROBERT RABURN

Back to Nature at the Biophilia Nature Center

Eight years ago Carol Lovell and her husband, Fred Saas, an architect and boat captain, bought 20 acres of dirt with a pond. Unlike most of their farming neighbors, they weren't dreaming of making a fortune from soybeans, strawberries or other crops. They wanted to take the land back to nature. Over the years, they've planted 7000 trees and 300 species of native wildflowers and in the process have created a living environmental classroom they call the Biophilia Nature Center. Many of the trees they planted eight years ago are now very tall and provide a habitat for wildlife. The center raises butterflies from eggs, keeps frogs and has a 9½-foot alligator. It also operates an environmental library and bookstore. The center (☎ 334-987-1228) is at 12695 County Rd 95, a quarter-mile south of Hwy 98 and three miles east of the Elberta stoplight. It's open Wednesday to Sunday from 8 am to noon. There's no admission fee, but donations are appreciated. ■

rates for one or two guests range from $94 to $154; weekend rates from $104 to $219.

Weeks Bay

Weeks Bay National Estuarine Research Reserve (☎ 334-928-9792), 11300 Hwy 98, 12 miles south of Fairhope and 21 miles northwest of the Gulf Coast, has a small but interesting museum on the area's wildlife and there's an elevated boardwalk nature trail to the waterfront. Drawers in the classroom house stuffed birds, animal skeletons and other goodies to look at. The staff are super about answering dumb questions. Bring insect repellent in summer.

The hours are Monday to Saturday from 9 am to 5 pm, and Sunday from 1 to 5 pm; the museum is closed on state and federal holidays. Admission is free.

The *Safe Harbor Resort* (☎ 334-928-2629, 800-928-4544, Net), 11401 Hwy 98, Weeks Bay, is opposite the Weeks Bay Reserve. It's a 115-acre park with a bathhouse, clubhouse and four fishing ponds. It has 105 campsites, some on the waterfront. Primitive sites cost $10 a night, while improved sites are $20. Guests have free use of canoes. Bring insect repellent in summer.

The same folks own *Baywatch Marina & Sunset Grill* (☎ 334-990-9907), 11525 Hwy 98, next door. It's a nice little place to eat with indoor and outdoor seating and a menu of sandwiches, salads, burgers and a few seafood items. Lunch costs $7 to $9, and dinner is $10 to $14. The food's OK and the view is great. It's open Monday to

Friday from 11 am to 10 pm, and weekends from 7:30 am to 9 pm.

Foley & Elberta

The **Baldwin County Museum** (☎ 334-986-8375), 25521 Hwy 98E, Elberta, is a tribute to the county's farming heritage, with exhibits of old hand tools and farm equipment, pottery and antique quilts. It's open Friday and Saturday from 10 am to 5 pm and Sunday from 1 to 5 pm. Admission is $3 ($1 for children, $7 for families).

Sweet Home Farm (☎ 334-986-5663), 27107 Schoen Rd, Elberta, is run by a couple who produce cheese from cows' milk the old-fashioned way. You can buy Romano, Asiago and about a dozen other natural, aged cheeses. From Elberta it's two miles east on Hwy 98. Watch for the sign on the left. Follow the dirt road for five miles, then turn right. It's open Wednesday to Saturday from 10 am to 5 pm.

Katy's Bar-B-Que (☎ 334-943-7427), 602 S McKenzie St (Hwy 59), Foley, serves meats that are slowly smoked over pecan wood. Katy's 'special SOB' ($5) is barbecued meat with red onions and coleslaw served between two thick slices of Texas toast. It comes with a side. Expect to pay $7 for lunch and $10 for dinner. It's open Monday to Saturday from 8 am to 9 pm, and Sunday from 11 am to 3 pm.

At *Sweetie Pies* (☎ 334-943-8119), 109 S McKenzie St (Hwy 59), Foley, a crowd lines up at 11:15 am for generously filled made-to-order sandwiches ($4.50), soups and salads. The food is good, but the pies are really special. Choose from 21 different pies made daily. Pies are $2.50 a slice or $7.50 to $10 for a whole one. It opens weekdays from 7:30 am to 2 pm. Eat in or take out.

GULF COAST

Pleasure Island stretches 32 miles along the Gulf Coast from Florida to Fort Morgan, on Mobile Bay. When the Intracoastal Waterway was created, it separated the coastal area from mainland Alabama, creating the island. There are two small towns: Orange Beach (population 3500) and Gulf Shores (population 5000). The island has several freshwater lakes and wide, white-sand beaches backed by rolling dunes dotted with sea oats. Hurricane Frederic wiped out almost everything on the island in 1979, but residents and developers rebuilt with a vengeance.

Today, miles of the shoreline are covered with beachfront houses with unsightly 'For Rent' signs outside, condominiums and hotels. Fishing from the Gulf State Park Pier and jetties and on charter boats is a favorite pastime here. A few companies offer sailing excursions. During the summer, traffic is heavy and restaurants are busy.

Orientation

From Foley, Gulf Shores Parkway (Hwy 59) runs south 12 miles before dead-ending at Hwy 182, which runs east along the shore to the Florida border and west about six miles to the dunes. If you're coming from the Florida Panhandle, take Hwy 292 to Hwy 182. It's a little tricky, but the scenic drive passes through the Gulf resorts in both states. Two miles north of the shore, Hwy 180 runs 22 miles west to land's end at Fort Morgan State Park and the ferry that crosses Mobile Bay to Fort Gaines and Dauphin Island.

Information

Tourist Offices The Alabama Gulf Coast Convention & Visitors Bureau Welcome Center (☎ 334-968-7511, 800-745-7263) at 3150 Gulf Shores Parkway is open

Monday to Friday from 8 am to 6 pm. The Orange Beach Welcome Center (☎ 334-974-1510, 800-982-8562), 26650 Perdido Beach Blvd (Hwy 182), is open Monday to Friday from 8 am to 5 pm, and weekends from 9 am to 5 pm.

Post Orange Beach post office (☎ 334-981-4131), 25940 John M Snook Dr, is open Monday to Friday from 8 am to 4 pm, and Saturday from 9 to 11:30 am. At Gulf Shores the post office (☎ 334-968-7000), 2149 W First St, is open Monday to Friday from 8:30 am to 4:30 pm and Saturday from 9 am to noon.

Libraries The Gulf Shores library (☎ 334-968-1176), 221 W 19th Ave, is open Monday to Thursday from 9 am to 9 pm, Friday from 9 am to 5 pm, and Saturday from 9 am to 1 pm. Hours at the Orange Beach library (☎ 334-981-2923), 25940 John M Snook Dr, are Monday and Tuesday from 10 am to 8 pm, Wednesday, Thursday and Friday from 10 am to 6 pm, Saturday from 10 am to 2 pm.

Media The *Islander*, the local newspaper, is published Wednesday and Saturday.

Medical Services The closest hospital, South Baldwin Hospital (☎ 334-952-3400 in an emergency), is 12 miles north in Foley at 1613 N McKenzie St (Hwy 59).

Gulf State Park

Look at the buildings crowding the beach nearby and you'll be thankful that the state owns 6150 acres and 2½ miles of beach and dunes on both sides of Hwy 182. Visitors love Gulf State Park (☎ 334-948-7275), 20115 Hwy 135, and it's the state's second largest. There's an 825-foot fishing pier, beachfront resort hotel, nature center, boat launch, playground, games room, camp store, golf course and pool, as well as biking and hiking trails, campgrounds and cabins, tennis courts and three lakes with canoe rentals. In winter lots of retirees come in RVs. Of the four trails, the longest is 1½-mile Middle Lake, but all trails connect to form 3¾ miles of easy walking on flat, sandy-bottom paths or old pavement. As you pass the lakes, try to spot the alligators. In the stands of live oaks, saw palmettos and saw grass, look for woodpeckers, squirrels and other small animals.

The park's 2½-mile beach has lifeguards and a beach pavilion with picnic areas and restrooms. Admission is $2 per car, $1 for park overnight guests and seniors, and $8 per van.

The park has an enormous campground with 468 sites, all with water, electricity, a picnic table and grill. Most sites are shaded, and many are on the lakefront. The tent sites are $12, full hookup RV sites are $20 and RV sites with water and electricity are $17.50. Rates are lower from November to March. Nearby are 16 fully equipped rustic lakefront cabins. From June to August they are rented by the week only. Reservations are advised. Off-season rates start at $44 a night ($54.50 in the high season) and $261 a week ($327 high season).

The park headquarters is open Monday to Friday from 8 am to 5 pm and Saturday from 8 am to 4 pm. Sunday hours vary.

Bon Secour National Wildlife Refuge

This 6000-acre refuge (☎ 334-540-7720), 12295 Hwy 180, is scattered across five parcels of coastal land ranging from beach dunes to rolling pine-oak woods. Bird-watchers are given a visual feast in spring and fall with the arrival of migrating birds, and wading birds can be seen the entire year. Monarch butterflies, sea turtles and wildflowers also thrive here. There are three hiking trails: Pine Beach, a four-mile roundtrip; Gator Lake, also four miles, which leads to the beach; and Jeff Friend, a one-mile wheel-chair accessible loop near the lagoon. The office opens Monday to Friday from 7:30 am to 4 pm, trails open dawn to dusk. There's no charge.

Fort Morgan State Park

This brick fortress (☎ 334-540-7125) on Hwy 180 was constructed in 1834 to guard the entrance to Mobile Bay. During the Battle of Mobile Bay, the fort's Confederate guns were no match for the Union fleet. You can poke around the fort, which has terrific water views, then enter the museum, which has displays of photographs, uniforms, artifacts and weapons dating from the War of 1812 to WWII. In August a re-enactment draws crowds. The fort is open daily from 8 am to sunset, and the museum is open from 9 am to 5 pm, except Thanksgiving, Christmas and New Year's Day. Admission is $3 (students and children $1).

Activities

Beaches The Gulf's long, wide beaches have fine white sand and rolling waves that are especially good for body surfing. When the surf's too rough, officials put out red flags. Never swim in red-flag conditions.

The beaches at Fort Morgan, Gulf Shores and Orange Beach (Cotton Bayou and Perdido Beach) have parking ($2 at some), restrooms and showers. There's also a small beach with beautiful views of the back bay and the Gulf across from the Alabama Point Bridge on the northeast end of the island. To avoid the madding crowds in summer, locals head west six miles to the end of Hwy 182 at Pine Beach, an isolated stretch of sand, dunes and water. There are no facilities.

For the beach at Gulf State Park, see above.

Bicycling If you go in to rent a bike at Surf N Cycle (334-974-BIKE, 334-974-2453), 23059 Perdido Beach Blvd, Orange Beach, you may find yourself still there an hour later talking to owner George O'Neal, who runs a serious bike shop and has a serious wit. He rents, sells and services bicycles and surfing gear. Bike rental costs $3.50 an hour, $12 a half-day, $19 a full day, and $74 a week. Rent after 3 pm and keep it until 10 am the next day for just the full-day rate. For an even better bargain, rent after 3 pm on Saturday and keep it until the shop reopens on Monday at 10 am and pay only the full-day rate.

Boating On nice days, locals like to catch the Mobile Bay ferry (☎ 334-540-7787) from Fort Morgan to Fort Gaines, just for the ride or for a picnic. The fare is $1 each way. Cars and pickups cost $15 one-way/23 roundtrip (motorcycles $6/12, RVs $25/50). The ferry departs daily every 90 minutes from 8 am to 6:30 pm. Occasionally it breaks down and doesn't return for hours or until the next day.

Sailing on the 50-foot double-mast ketch yawl *Daedalus* (☎ 334-987-1228) is more than a fun day out on the water. It's also a learning experience. Captained by environmentalist Fred Saas and his wife, Carol Lovell, the boat explores the bayous and back bay waters of Perdido Bay in search of wildlife and nature. Dolphins are usually sighted. The boat is docked at 6816 S Bayou Dr, Robert's Bayou, Elberta. Three-hour sails cost adults $25, seniors over 60 years $15 and children $13. Call for reservations.

You can catch shrimp (in season), search for dolphin and explore the inlets of Perdido Bay and Bayou St John on *Three's Company* (☎ 334-981-3525), a shaded six-passenger 25-ft sloop. Captain Lee Lindblom has been running the three-hour excursions for 10 years. He charges $25 a person.

Fishing Local waters are home to snapper, grouper, trigger fish, cobia and other saltwater species. Fishing permits are required and cost $6 to $24.50. Most of the offshore fishing is done over artificial reefs, but there's also fishing in the back bays. One of the most well-known marinas and fishing outfitters is Zeke's (☎ 334-981-4044, 800-793-4044), which operates 22 offshore and five back-bay boats. A party boat holding up to 60 people costs $35 per person for a four-hour trip; six-passenger charters start at $390.

Golf The best golfing bargain on the coast is Gulf State Park (☎ 334-948-4653), off Hwy 182 on County Rd 2, Gulf Shores, where the greens fees are $20 to $22. Kiva Dunes (☎ 334-540-7000), 815 Plantation Dr, Fort Morgan Rd, Gulf Shores, is a gorgeous 18-hole beachfront course 10 miles east of Fort Morgan. The greens fee is $67.

The Battle of Mobile Bay

One of the most exciting battles of the Civil War took place at Mobile Bay between Confederate admiral Franklin Buchanan, commander of the ironclad *Tennessee*, and US admiral David G Farragut, who commanded the wooden *Hartford*. On the morning of August 5, 1864, Farragut approached the mouth of the bay with 14 wooden ships, four ironclads, 2700 soldiers and 197 guns. Waiting inside the bay was an under-matched Buchanan with his ironclad, three wooden ships, 427 soldiers, 22 guns and, at the mouth of the bay, torpedoes and guns at Confederate-controlled Fort Morgan and Fort Gaines.

Federal ships, led by the ironclad *Tecumseh* charged the channel two abreast. Guns from the forts blazed. A torpedo immediately sunk the *Tecumseh* and smoke and fire clouded the air. The federal fleet faltered. Tied to the mainmast rigging of his ship, Farragut looked forward and shouted the order, 'Damn the torpedoes! Go Ahead!' (historical accounts dispute the often quoted 'Damn torpedoes! Full speed ahead!').

Three hours later, with the Confederate fleet all but destroyed, Farragut's fleet faced the *Tennessee* alone in the bay. Heavily damaged, unable to maneuver and surrounded, Buchanan surrendered. ∎

Special Events

Union and Confederate re-enactors gather at Fort Morgan in August for the annual Civil War Living History of the Battle of Mobile Bay (☎ 334-540-7125). The annual four-day National Shrimp Festival (☎ 334-968-6904), now in its 27th year, takes place in October. Nearly 100 songwriters gather in November for the annual International Songwriters Festival (☎ 334-980-5116), with performances held all over the Gulf Coast.

Places to Stay

Camping For camping in Gulf State Park see the park entry.

ALABAMA

The *Southport Campground* (☎ 334-968-6220), Intracoastal Canal Bridge on Hwy 59, Gulf Shores, has 113 improved and primitive sites with a bathhouse and fishing pier. Primitive tent sites are $11, or $13 with water and electricity. RV sites with sewer and cable TV cost $17.

Hotels & Motels *Days Inn* (☎ 334-981-9888, 800-237-6169), Hwy 182, has rooms overlooking the Gulf and an indoor heated pool. Rates range from $45 to $250, depending on the season; continental breakfast is included.

The *Gulf State Park Resort Hotel* (☎ 334-948-4853), Hwy 182 E, is a full-service beachfront resort with a pool and restaurant. All rooms are on the beach and have a balcony. Rooms are $49 to $99, depending on the season. Suites are $99 to $199. There's a three-night minimum on holiday weekends.

Callaway Cottages & RV Court (☎ 334-968-7969), 17790 Hwy 180, two miles west of I-59, has attractive cottages with screened porches on a heavily treed tract that overlooks the water. There's a boat launch, swimming area and convenience store and the setting is peaceful. There are 20 RV spaces with hookups and sewer. Weekly cottage rates are $275 for a one bedroom or $350 for a two bedroom. RV sites are $12 nightly or $150 monthly. There are no tent sites.

Gulf Pines Motel (☎ 334-968-7911), 245 E 22nd Ave, Gulf Shores, has a pool and some units have kitchenettes. Pets are allowed. Rates vary seasonally from $29 to $64 for a single or double.

The *Hampton Inn* (☎ 334-974-1598, 888-485-3726), 22988 Perdido Beach Blvd, Orange Beach, has 96 rooms on the beach. Rates vary by season; doubles are $59 to $130 ($89 to $154 with beach views) and it's $10 less for singles.

Perdido Beach Resort (☎ 334-981-9811, 800-634-8001), 27200 Perdido Beach Blvd (Hwy 182), Orange Beach, is a first-class resort with luxury rooms, indoor and outdoor pools, lighted tennis courts, and a fitness center and sauna. There are two lounges with live entertainment and the resort has the best restaurant in town. Rates are for singles or doubles with a partial view are $125/155, or with full beach view $135/159 in the off-season/summer.

West Palms Beachfront Hotel (☎ 334-948-4888), 533 West Beach Blvd, Gulf Shores, charges $60 to $145 single or double, depending on the season; free continental breakfast is included.

Gulf Shores Plantation (☎ 334-540-5000, 800-554-0344), Hwy 180, 13 miles west of I-59, is typical of the oceanfront condo resorts in the area. It's loaded with activities and amenities. What sets it apart is its location about halfway between Gulf Shores and Fort Morgan, away from the beach crowds. In the low season, rates range from $79 for a studio that sleeps four to $155 for a three-bedroom suite that sleeps 10. The range is $119 to $265 in high season.

B&Bs *Romar House B&B* (☎ 334-981-6156, 800-487-6627), 23500 Perdido Beach Blvd (Hwy 182), Orange Beach, is a romantic, rambling beach house with five rooms, one suite and a cottage, each with a private bath. Rooms are attractively decorated and there's a whirlpool, TV room, bar, and wraparound porch where you can watch the waves roll in. Full breakfast is included. The rooms are $79, $89 and $120, depending on the season.

Vacation Rentals Agencies and owners rent out condos and beachfront houses. Before you send in a deposit, ask the local Better Business Bureau (☎ 334-433-2434, 800-544-4714) if any complaints have been filed against the agency. Also ask the convention and visitors bureau for a list of reputable companies. Most beach houses have a three or four-night minimum in winter, spring and fall; seven nights in summer. Condos have three-night minimums. A $150 to $300 deposit is normal, up to $1000 for larger homes. Deposits are refunded by mail one to two weeks after departure. The total rent is due at check in. Weekly rates range from $289 to $525 for a two-bedroom, two-bath house a block from the beach.

Places to Eat

Meals at the *Gulf State Park Resort Restaurant* (☎ 334-948-4853), 21250 E Beach Blvd off Hwy 182, Gulf Shores, are a bargain. The breakfast buffet ($5.50) features fruit, biscuits and gravy, grits, French toast, eggs, bacon, sausages and home fries. The lunch buffet ($6) changes daily, but is equally filling and inexpensive. Dinner buffets and specials are $7.

Coconut Willie's Restaurant & Oyster Bar (☎ 334-948-7145), 312 E Beach Blvd (Hwy 182), serves terrific po-boys ($6). Lunch specials during the week are $6 to $7. The menu leans heavily toward seafood, but there's also chicken, steak and baby back ribs. It's open daily from 11 am to 10 pm.

Gulf Shores Steamer (☎ 334-948-6344), 124 W 1st Ave, off I-59, Gulf Shores, offers nothing but steamed seafood. The best buys on the lunch menu are grilled red snapper at $6 and steamed shrimp at $7. Everything comes with corn, potato and coleslaw. Daily specials are $4.50 to $7. Try the turtle cheesecake. In summer, expect to wait one to two hours for dinner, or, better yet, call ahead for a take-out order. Its sister act, *Ribs & Reds Gulf Shores Steamer II* (☎ 334-948-3241), 128 West 1st Ave, serves steamed and fried seafood as well as ribs. Opening hours at both are Sunday to Thursday from 11 am to 9 pm, and Friday and Saturday from 11 am to 10 pm.

Papa Rocco's Pizza (☎ 334-948-7262), Gulf Shores Parkway (Hwy 59) at 6th Ave, has pizza, pasta and an oyster bar. Oysters come raw, baked or Cajun. Spaghetti with sausage is $5.50 and a large seafood primavera pizza costs $17. There's live entertainment nightly and a jukebox. Sunday and Wednesday are all-you-can-eat spaghetti nights. Alas, it's dark and cigarette smoke quickly fills the small room. It's open daily from 11 am to midnight for meals but its bar stays open later.

Not to be confused with the aforementioned restaurant, *Papa's Place* (☎ 334-948-7799), 317 Gulf Shores Parkway (Hwy 59), serves pizza only as a special.

The rest of the menu features Italian specialties like spaghetti with sausage or meatballs ($6 small, $7 large). It's open daily with varying hours. It recently opened a dance club with a DJ. There's a quiet lounge area and a pool room.

The bohemian *Gulf Coast Coffee Merchant* (☎ 334-948-7878), 701 Bayou Village, Gulf Shores, is a cafe overlooking a bayou. Italian-style sandwiches ($5 to $6.50) made with focaccia bread are served Monday to Saturday from 10:30 am to 4 pm. Twice a month there's entertainment ($4 cover charge). They also offer beer, wine and liquor. It's open Monday to Saturday from 8 am to 10 pm. In summer it's also open on Sunday from 10 am to 4 pm.

At the *Bayside Grill* (☎ 334-981-4899), 27842 Canal Rd (Hwy 180), Orange Beach, in the Sportsman Marina, you can dine outdoors on a wide porch or indoors and look out picture windows. Good music goes with the good food. The menu emphasizes seafood prepared Southern and New Orleans style. The panéed catfish ($11) is a local favorite. Reservations are a must in summer.

Few places can beat the *View* (☎ 334-948-8888), 1832 West Blvd (Hwy 182), 9th floor of Gulf Shores Surf & Racquet Club, for watching the sun set or for the food. The menu changes often, but there's always fresh seafood, lamb, pork and beef prepared in a New World style. Dinner costs $14 to $23. It's open Monday to Thursday from 5:30 to 9 pm, and Friday and Saturday to 10 pm.

The *Oar House* (☎ 334-540-7991), 1577 Hwy 180 W, serves grilled, fried and blackened seafood, as well as steaks, kebabs and chicken. It's one of the few places where you can get grilled oysters. It's a long drive, but if you're heading toward the ferry, make a stop. Lunch costs around $6 and dinner is about $12. It's open Tuesday to Sunday from 11 am to 9 pm, with live entertainment featured Friday to Sunday.

When locals want good seafood, a laidback atmosphere and a good view, they go to *Zeke's Restaurant* (☎ 334-981-4001),

12887 Perdido Beach Blvd (Hwy 182), Orange Beach. The bar's a popular meeting place. Lunch costs about $7 and dinner is around $17. It's open for lunch and dinner everyday, with Sunday brunch available from 10:30 am to 3 pm.

Entertainment
Nightclubs *Florabama* (☎ 334-980-5119 in Alabama, 904-492-3048 in Florida), straddles the Florida and Alabama state line. In summer and during spring break, the crowd borders on unmanageable. Since opening in 1961, the club has added patios, bar rooms, game rooms, lounges and a liquor store. As many as three bands can play at the same time on indoor and outdoor stages. It's open daily from 9 am to 2:30 am.

The *Pink Pony Pub* (☎ 334-948-6371), 137 E Beach Blvd, (Hwy 182), at Hwy 59, Gulf Shores, is at the east end of a public beach. Locals like it. It's a good place to meet, grab a burger or po-boy and listen to live music. It opens 11 am until it closes.

Nolan's (☎ 334-948-2111), 508 E Beach Blvd (Hwy 182), is a popular spot for dining and dancing. It attracts a more mature audience than most beach dance halls. There's live music Tuesday to Saturday evenings. The food selection includes Lebanese salad and Greek-style fish dishes. The kitchen is open Monday to Thursday from 5 to 10 pm and Friday to Saturday from 5 to 11 pm. Dancing goes on until no one is left standing.

Live Bait (☎ 334-974-1612), 24281 Perdido Beach Blvd (Hwy 182), Orange Beach, is a fun joint that attracts a youngish crowd. It's also a decent restaurant, serving mostly seafood and popular short-order specials. The kitchen is open daily from 11:30 am to 10 pm. On Thursday, Friday and Saturday the bar stays open late and there's live entertainment.

Cinema There are two cinemas in the area: *Canal St Theater* (☎ 334-981-6796), Hwy 180 E, Orange Beach, and *Foley Cinema* (☎ 334-971-1144), Hwy 59 N.

Things to Buy
Alvin's Island Tropical Department Store (☎ 334-948-3121), 100 W Beach Blvd, Gulf Shores, is a behemoth store that carries beach stuff and decorative items. There's a smaller version farther east at 24949 Perdido Beach Blvd, Orange Beach. It's open Sunday to Thursday from 9 am to 7 pm, and Friday and Saturday from 9 am to 10 pm, with extended hours in summer.

Getting There & Away
Air Pensacola regional airport (☎ 904-435-1746), 2430 Airport Blvd, Pensacola, Florida, is served by Delta, Continental, Northwest Airlink, US Airways and several commuter airlines. The 45-mile drive to Gulf Shores and Orange Beach takes just over an hour. In summer, double that time if you take the scenic route. Mobile regional airport (☎ 334-633-0313), 8400 Airport Rd, is served by Continental, Delta, Northwest Airlink and Airtran Airlines. It's just over an hour by car to Gulf Shores and Orange Beach.

Bus The closest Greyhound station is in Pensacola (☎ 904-476-4800), 505 W Burgess St, with services from Atlanta ($41; daily), Birmingham ($53; four), Jackson ($56; two), Mobile ($15; seven), Montgomery ($56; four) and New Orleans ($27; four). Mobile Bay Transportation (☎ 334-981-9811 ext 411 from Pensacola, 334-633-5693 from Mobile) provides an airport shuttle service to Mobile ($88 one-way) and Pensacola ($42) airports. Call in advance.

Train The closest Amtrak (☎ 800-872-2745) stations are in Mobile at 11 Government St; Bay Minette at 100 E Railroad St; and Pensacola at 940 E Heinburg St.

Car Except when summer and spring-break vacationers bring traffic to a standstill, driving along the Gulf Coast is a pleasure. There's mile after mile of beautiful beach along Hwy 180 out to Fort Morgan (allow half an hour) and Hwy 182 to the Florida border. Heading inland from the shore on

Hwy 59 is commercial for the first 20 minutes, then the scenery is open fields and farms.

Boat The Mobile Bay ferry (☎ 334-540-7787) runs daily except for one to two weeks in December when it shuts down for maintenance. Poor weather and breakdowns also limit service. Call before making the long drive to the port. From Dauphin Island, on the west side of the bay, ferries depart every 1½ hours from 8 am to 5 pm. On the east side, they leave Fort Morgan State Park every 1½ hours from 8:45 am to 5:45 pm. One-way fares are $1 for walk-ons, $6 for motorcycles, $25 for RVs and $15 ($23 roundtrip) for cars and pickup trucks. It departs from the east end of Dauphin Island and the west end of Hwy 180, 22 miles west of Gulf Shores. The crossing takes about half an hour.

Private boats can travel the Intracoastal Waterway to the Gulf Coast. There are numerous marinas with slips.

Getting Around

Bus BRATS Bus Service (☎ 334-947-2728) is a local public transportation system covering Baldwin County, which includes the Gulf Coast, eastern shore and Bay Minette, Elberta, Foley, Robertsdale and Weeks Bay. Within the city in which you are picked up the fare is $1 each way; elsewhere the fare depends on how far you're going. It's $10 to Mobile. All service is by reservation at least 24 hours in advance.

Car Major rental agencies have counters at the Mobile and Pensacola airports and offices in Gulf Shores and Orange Beach. Gulf Shores Aero (☎ 334-968-6380), Enterprise (☎ 334-943-3888), Mobile Bay Transportation (334-981-9811) and Moyer Ford (☎ 334-943-1661) also have branches in Gulf Shores and Orange Beach.

Taxi Blue Dolphin Taxi (334-952-0222) will take you around town or to Pensacola airport. From the airport to Gulf Shores it's $65 and to Orange Beach it's $55. Gulf

Shore Shuttle (☎ 800-968-3514) and Blue Marlin Taxi (☎ 334-968-6243) also have cab services.

DAUPHIN ISLAND

This 14-mile-long island, Alabama's longest natural barrier island, has a colorful history. Six flags have flown over it, starting with the French, then English, Spanish, Republic of Alabama, Confederacy and, finally, the US. For a short while, it was even the capital of French Louisiana under Governor Cadillac, hence the street named in his honor. The French originally called it Massacre Island, after the large number of bones found here. It's geologically striking, with 30 to 40-foot bluffs and low sand dunes along the Gulf of Mexico. On the migratory flyway, the island is a bird sanctuary. About 1200 people live on the island year-round. In spring that figure jumps to 7000. Summer visitors drive the population to 15,000. The beaches, the ferry, Fort Gaines, camping and fishing are the main attractions for visitors.

Orientation & Information

The island stretches along the narrow tip of land squeezed between Mississippi and Mobile Bay. It's reached by taking Hwy 193 south from I-10 for 35 miles to a 3½-mile bridge from the mainland. You also can arrive by crossing Mobile Bay on the ferry from Fort Morgan in Gulf Shores. Most streets on the island run north-south and are organized alphabetically from east to west. Bienville Blvd runs east-west, the length of the island. The chamber of commerce (☎ 334-861-5524) has visitor information. The post office (☎ 334-861-5162), 1011 Levente St, is open Monday to Friday from 9 am to 4 pm and Saturday 9 to 10 am.

Fort Gaines

The cannons, tunnels and bastions that proved no match for Admiral Farragut during the Civil War still remain (see the Battle of Mobile Bay sidebar). Visitors can explore the entire fort, which was built out of brick. An excellent museum (☎ 334-861-6992) at the east end of Bienville Rd houses

ALABAMA

military artifacts from the mid-19th century to 1946, the period the fort was used. There's a brochure outlining a self-guided walking tour. The fort is open daily from 9 am to 5 pm (except Christmas and New Year). The entrance fee is $3 (children $1).

Audubon Bird Sanctuary

A freshwater lake punctuates this 160-acre sanctuary (☎ 334-861-2120), E Bienville Blvd near the ferry landing, where trails pass through pine and palmetto forests, marsh and sand dunes. Some lead to the beach, while others circle the lake. It's especially popular for watching migrating birds and butterflies in spring and fall. Locals say the east end of the swamp has the best birding. It's open from dawn to dusk.

Indian Shell Mound

This shell mound on Cadillac St is one of the state's best examples of early Native American mound building. Paths crisscross the mound, which was used by the Woodlands Indians. You can visit the mound on your own, but you'll enjoy it more if you take a free tour with Don Bland from the Department of Conservation office (☎ 334-861-2882) located behind the mound. Ask him about the hoof marks on the limbs of the live oaks growing on the mound. Tours are given from 8 am to noon and 1 to 5 pm.

The Estuarium

The Dauphin Island Sea Lab (☎ 334-861-2141), 101 Bienville Blvd, recently opened a new 10,000-sq-foot exhibit hall featuring the four main native habitats of the Mobile estuary. The hall complements the new Living Marsh Boardwalk, where visitors can go outside and explore the estuary up close. The boardwalk has interpretive signage that explains the history and evolution of marshes and barrier islands.

Activities

Beaches Behind the wooden picnic pavilions on the sand dunes that you see from

the road is the beach at Dauphin Island Park & Pier (☎ 334-861-3607 park, 334-861-6972 pier), Bienville Blvd at Penalver St. Climb the steps over the dune to reach the beach and 850-ft-long pier. The pier shop has bait and tackle, equipment rental, and sandwiches and snacks. It costs $3 (children $1) to stroll or to fish from the pier. The white, sandy beach with dune grasses, rock outcroppings and stands of pine trees is free. It's officially closed for swimming because of a swift current that's causing erosion and drownings. The beach behind Fort Gaines is another option. Use the restrooms near the ferry.

Bicycling Dauphin Island is a great place to bicycle. For now, the bicycle path along Bienville Blvd runs between Audubon St and Narvaez St, but eventually it will extend the length of the island.

Boating You can cruise the waters around Dauphin Island on the 41-foot motor yacht *Let It Be*, which is run by Island Cruises' (☎ 334-861-4499), Dauphin Island Marina. The tour takes you to see the Sand Island lighthouse, shell mounds, the spot where the first Yankee ironclad was sunk and you'll get a waterside view of Fort Gaines. Captain Jim Hall tells great stories during the two and three-hour cruises, which range in price from $25 to $35.

Fishing You can fish from the Dauphin Island Pier (see Beaches) and the East End Pier (it's free), or you can hire a charter or join a party boat. The East End Pier is near the ferry landing and the mouth of Mobile Bay. For organized deep-sea fishing, locals recommend Captain Mike Thierry (334-861-5302), Dauphin Island Marina, who operates the *Island Star* party boat ($65) and *Lady Ann* charter boat.

Special Events

The second weekend in January signals Fury on the Gulf, a simulated battle of the surrender of Fort Gaines to Confederate forces when Alabama seceded from the Union. The Dauphin Island Sailing Regatta, held on the last weekend in April, is the largest one-day sailing event in the country. The Dauphin Island Spring Festival features three days of fun at Fort Gaines the first or second weekend in April.

Places to Stay

Camping The *Fort Gaines Campground* (☎ 334-861-2742), 109 Bienville Blvd, has 150 improved sites. There are walking trails, a lighted boardwalk to a secluded beach, and picnic pavilions and grills. Tent sites with water and electricity cost $11. RV rates are $15 with full hookup, or $14 without sewer.

Hotels & Motels The best place to stay is the *Harbor Lights Inn* (☎ 334-861-5534, 800-743-7132), 1506 Cadillac Ave. The owners have taken a run-down, two-story hotel and turned it into a cozy, laid-back beach getaway. The six rooms, all of which are two-bedroom suites with cable TV, phones, full kitchen and living and dining room, open in front and back onto balconies or patios. The back overlooks grass and marsh. Guests may use the inn's crab traps and barbecue. The beach is a few hundred feet away. Rates vary with the season, but range from $47 to $62, with one free night with a week's stay.

The *Gulf Breeze Motel* (☎ 334-861-7344) at 1512 Cadillac Ave is a family-owned business offering 19 rooms and apartments. In the low season singles/doubles are $37/37 ($42/52 in the high season). Apartments cost $47/62 in the low/high season.

Places to Eat

The best place to grab a bite to eat on the island is *Sea Food Galley* (☎ 334-861-8000), 1510 Bienville Blvd, serving breakfast, lunch and dinner, with a seafood buffet ($13) on Friday and a fish and grits all-you-can eat ($7) on Wednesday. *Barnacle Bill's* (☎ 334-861-5255), 1518 Bienville Blvd, has pizza and sandwiches and operates the restaurant at the Isle Dauphine Golf Club, the *Grill* (☎ 334-861-3201), 100 Orleans Dr. It has a nice view of the water and serves dinner on weekends and brunch on Sunday. Off the island, at 14750 Dauphin Island Parkway (Hwy 193) in Codine, is *Ellen's Place* (☎ 334-873-4612). It serves seafood (including lobster), po-boys and steaks. The *Seahouse Club* (☎ 334-861-3049), 650 La Moyne Dr, features steak and a pretty good flounder stuffed with shrimp and crab meat.

Things to Buy

Shopping on the island is limited, but the Treasure Trove (☎ 334-861-5919), Bienville at Le Moyne Blvd, has lots of interesting souvenirs. Its sister store, just 200 feet down the block, is the Shipwreck Emporium (☎ 334-861-6055), 918 Bienville Blvd. It sells yummy fudge, chocolates, specialty foods and gifts. Six artists sell their work at Pelican Palette (☎ 334-861-7271), 1606 Bienville Blvd, a cooperative. While some of the work has a marine or island theme, most varies widely in media and subject. Five of the artists paint and one is a potter. The gallery is open everyday, except Wednesday, from 10 am to 5 pm.

ALABAMA

Southeastern Alabama

Bordered by the Florida Panhandle to the south and the Chattahoochee River and Georgia to the east, the Wiregrass Region was named after the area's stiff, wiry native grasses with long wire-like spikes. Around here wiregrass is rare now, having disappeared with the pine forests that were farmed for timber and removed to make room for farmland, and now the region is a prosperous farming area. There are five state parks here, of which four have lakes primarily used for bass fishing, but also for boating and swimming, and a wildlife refuge.

Dothan, in the southeast corner of the state, is the region's largest city. Most traffic passes through on Hwy 231 from central and northern Alabama on the way to Florida beaches, located only 72 miles south of Dothan.

This chapter starts in Eufaula and runs parallel to the Chattahoochee River along the 55 miles of Hwy 431 to Dothan. This is the lower section of a tourist corridor called the Chattahoochee Trace, which showcases communities and attractions in Alabama and Georgia along both sides of the river (see Facts about Alabama for details).

HIGHLIGHTS

- The neoclassical Shorter Mansion and Italianate Fendall Hall in Eufaula
- Eufaula National Wildlife Refuge
- The Wiregrass Museum of Art in Dothan

EUFAULA

population 13,200

Eufaula's early prosperity in the 1830s was linked to its location on the Chattahoochee River, which allowed cotton to be shipped to Gulf ports and on to world markets. When cotton's importance diminished, Eufaula turned to textiles, lumber and other industries. Today, the economy is enhanced by recreation on Lake Eufaula, created after the 1963 construction of the Walter F George Lock and Dam on the river. The Seth Lore and Irwinton Historic District has more than 700 buildings on the National Register of Historic Places and is the second largest in Alabama.

Orientation & Information

Hwy 431, south from Auburn and Opelika and north from Dothan, is the main road (Eufaula Ave) through town. It passes Lakepoint Resort State Park and the historic district.

The Eufaula/Barbour County Chamber of Commerce is at 102 N Orange Ave, PO Box 1055, Eufaula, AL 36027. It's open Monday to Friday from 9 am to 5 pm.

The Historic Chattahoochee Commission (☎ 334-687-9755) is at 211 N Eufaula Ave.

Lakeview Community Hospital, 820 W Washington St, provides medical care.

Seth Lore & Irwinton Historic District

A self-guided walking and driving tour that passes by 61 of Eufaula's 700 historic structures begins and ends at **Shorter Mansion** (☎ 334-687-3793), 340 N Eufaula Ave, which houses the Eufaula Heritage Association and Eufaula Museum. Tours of the neoclassical house are given Monday to Saturday from 10 am to 4 pm and Sunday 1 to 4 pm.

Two other houses are open for tours. **Fendall Hall** (☎ 334-687-8469), 917 W Barbour St, was the first Italianate house built in Eufaula. Its most striking aspect

ALABAMA

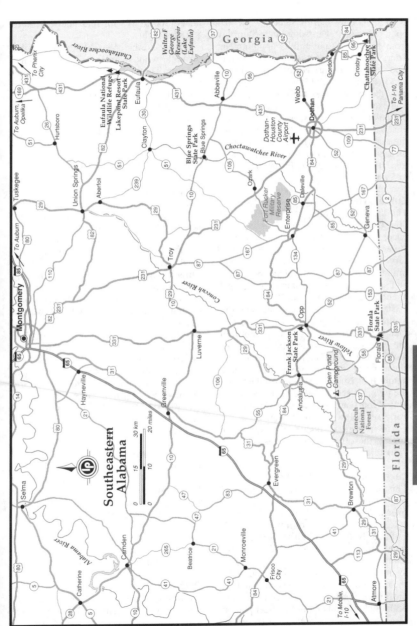

Southeastern Alabama

is its elaborate interior stencil work. It's open Monday, Thursday and Saturday from 10 am to 4 pm and by appointment. Tours cost $3 and last about half an hour. The interior of **Hart House** (☎ 334-687-9755), 211 N Eufaula Ave, has hardly changed since it was built in 1850. It's a fine example of Greek revival architecture. Part of the building is used to house the Historic Chattahoochee Commission, and the rest is sparsely furnished with original pieces. Allow 20 minutes for a self-guided tour. It's open Monday to Friday from 8 am to 5 pm; entry is free.

Eufaula National Wildlife Refuge

The 11,598-acre refuge (☎ 334-687-4065), 509 Old Hwy 165, encompasses land, water and marsh along the Chattahoochee River and Walter F George Reservoir and serves as a winter home to thousands of migratory waterfowl, resident wood ducks and small wildlife. In summer, get a peak at endangered wood storks.

Start a visit at the refuge office to pick up a map and birding checklist to see how many of the 281 species you can spot from the elevated observation platform overlooking the river. The park also features a seven-mile wildlife drive. A half-mile nature trail is another easy introduction to the park. To see the refuge from the water, rent a Jon boat at Lakepoint Resort State Park (see below) and boat over.

The refuge is open daily sunrise to sunset; the office is open weekdays from 7:30 am to 4 pm.

Lakepoint Resort State Park

This state park (☎ 334-687-8011, 334-687-6676), 104 Lakepoint Dr, is spread out over gently rolling hills and a 70-sq-mile lake on the north edge of town, next to the Eufaula National Wildlife Refuge. The focal point is Lake Eufaula, offering fishing – primarily for bass – boating and swimming. To explore the lake and part of the neighboring refuge, you can rent three-passenger Jon boats ($30 for four hours, $50 for eight) and eight-passenger pontoon

boats ($60 to $75 for four hours, $100 to $115 for eight).

Nature trails cover about five miles through woods and around the campground. They're working on re-opening former equestrian trails as challenging hiking trails. You can play tennis and golf, or listen to a naturalist talk about fish and wildlife at the nature center.

The lodge/restaurant/lounge has a large swimming pool and sits on a hill overlooking the beach and lake. Accommodations vary widely; see Places to Stay.

Tom Mann's Fish World

Think big. This tribute to fishing claims that it has the world's largest freshwater aquarium: 38,000 gallons, which translates to 40 feet long by 20 feet wide by eight feet deep. The setting is as natural as if you stuck your head underwater in Lake Eufaula and looked around. Really big largemouth bass swim inches from your face. Ten smaller aquariums (1400 gallons) contain fish native to Alabama waters. There is also an indoor stream and waterfall, and outside a 10-acre lake stocked with catfish that you can view through an underwater tunnel. The fishing tackle/gift shop next door has good prices.

Admission to Tom Mann's Fish World (☎ 334-687-3655), 1951 N Eufaula Ave (Hwy 431), is $2.50 for adults, $1.50 seniors and students. Hours are daily from 8 am to 5 pm.

Special Events

Eufaula's three biggest events are the Watchable Wildlife Weekend at Lakepoint Resort State Park (☎ 334-687-6676) the second weekend in March; the three-day Spring Pilgrimage (☎ 334-687-3793) historic home tours on the first weekend in April; and the Indian Summer Arts and Crafts Festival (☎ 334-687-6664) on the second weekend in October.

Places to Stay

Camping *Lakepoint Resort State Park* (see above) has tent ($13 for primitive sites, $14 for improved) and RV ($15.50) camping on the edge of the woods.

Hotels The 42-room *Best Western Eufaula Inn* (☎ 334-687-3900), 1337 S Eufaula Ave, has a pool, free movies and is near restaurants. Rates are $32/38 for a single/double. The 92-room *Holiday Inn* (☎ 334-687-2021), 631 E Barbour St, east of downtown, has a restaurant, lounge and courtyard pool. The rate is $42 to $54 single or double. Rooms with a lake view are higher. *Days Inn* (☎ 334-687-2021), 1521 S Eufaula Ave, has 45 rooms, a pool and fitness center. The $38/45 rate includes continental breakfast.

Lakeside Motor Lodge (☎ 334-687-2477), 1010 N Eufaula Ave, is a waterfront lodge with 48 rooms ($35 to $38) and cabins ($65), a boat dock, pool, fireplace and restaurant.

At *Lakepoint Resort State Park* (see above), the rustic concrete and wood lodge, with small wildlife dioramas in the lobby and a game room, has 101 rooms, most of which have two double beds and a balcony overlooking Lake Eufaula. Rates are $58 in spring and summer, $49 in fall and winter. Furnished lakefront cabins have a fireplace, and feature two ($75) or four ($136) bedrooms.

B&Bs *Kendall Manor Inn* (☎ 334-687-8847), 534 W Broad St, combines history with accommodations. Six rooms with private bath are beautifully decorated in antiques in this house in the historic district. Climb the tower for a fabulous view. Breakfast is included in the $75 to $95 rate.

Places to Eat
Good, simple food is what *Willy T's* (☎ 334-616-0075), 126 State Dock Rd, is all about. Try the chicken fingers snack ($3), while the burgers, coleslaw and baked potatoes are memorable, too. Don't miss the pie. It's open Monday to Saturday from 10 am to 9 pm.

Lakepoint Resort State Park (see above), serves three meals. Lunch features sandwiches, salads and burgers from $3 to $6.

The dinner menu offers mostly steaks and salads, from $4 to $14.

According to local sources, the best place to eat is the *Airport Restaurant* (☎ 334-687-3132) on Hwy 431 about four miles north of town. It's next to the state trooper station. The Speights family has owned it for 21 years, and matriarch Betty Speights runs it, doing everything from cooking and waiting tables to keeping the books. Hand-cut steaks (try the rib eye) and fresh seafood make up most of the menu, which also includes a fresh salad bar and freshly made soups. Prices range from $10 to $15. The dining room is open Tuesday to Saturday from 5 to 10 pm, the lounge from 3 pm to closing.

Getting There & Away
Greyhound (☎ 334-687-9558), 1486 S Eufaula Ave (Hwy 431), has once-a-day service to Atlanta ($34); Birmingham ($36); Dothan ($13) and New Orleans, ($69); twice-a-day service to Jackson ($69) and Mobile ($49).

DOTHAN
population 55,792
Alibamu and Creek Indians inhabited the region until the late 1800s. The first white settlers came to the area then known as Poplar Head to harvest timber. By 1885 it was the largest town in Houston County and was incorporated as Dothan. Along with timber, cotton was a main industry, and when the boll weevil arrived, Dothan turned to peanuts. Today, one-fourth of the country's peanuts come from Houston County.

Orientation
Dothan is 16 miles west of the Georgia state line and 15 miles north from the Florida state line. Hwy 84 (Main St) runs east-west and divides Dothan north and south. Hwy 231 (Montgomery Hwy/Oates St) splits the city east and west. Most hotels are in the 2000 and 3000 block, or southeast and southwest quadrants, of Ross Clark Circle, a road that rings the city.

ALABAMA

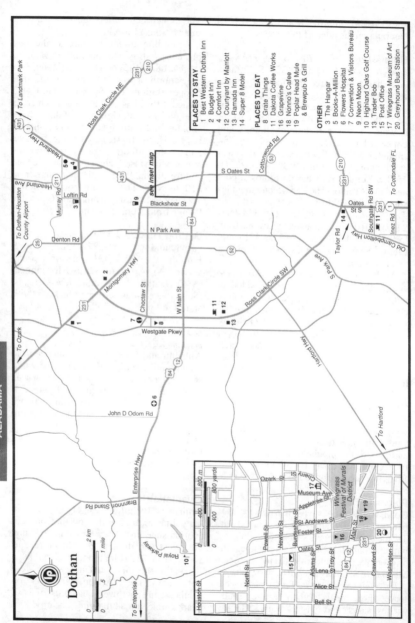

Dothan

To Landmark Park

Headland Hwy
Headland Ave
To Dothan-Houston County Airport
Murray Rd (211)
Loftin Rd
Montgomery Hwy
Choctaw St
To Ozark
Denton Rd
Ross Clark Circle NE
S Oates St
Blackshear St
N Park Ave
Cottonwood Rd
Ross Clark Circle SW
S Park Ave
Taylor Rd
Oates St S
Old Campbellton Hwy
Southgate Rd SW
Inez Rd
To Cottondale FL
W Main St
Westgate Pkwy
Hartford Hwy
To Hartford
John D Odom Rd
Enterprise Hwy
Brannon Stand Rd
Royal Parkway
To Enterprise

see inset map

2 km
1 mile
.5
1
0

800 m.
800 yards
400
0

PLACES TO STAY
1   Best Western Dothan Inn
2   Budget Inn
4   Comfort Inn
12 Courtyard by Marriott
13 Ramada Inn
14 Super 8 Motel

PLACES TO EAT
8   Grate Things
11 Dakota Coffee Works
16 Grapevine
18 Nonno's Cafee
19 Poplar Head Mule
    & Brewpub & Grill

OTHER
3   The Hangar
5   Books-A-Million
6   Flowers Hospital
7   Convention & Visitors Bureau
9   Neon Moon
10 Highland Oaks Golf Course
15 Trader Bob
17 Post Office
    Wiregrass Museum of Art
20 Greyhound Bus Station

Ozark St
Cherry St
Museum Ave
Appletree St
Wiregrass Festival of Murals District
St Andrews St
Burdeshaw St
Newton St
Foster St
Powell St
Oates St
Adams St
Lena St
Alice St
Bell St
North St
Holatch St
Troy St
Main St
Crawford St
Washington St

ALABAMA

Information

The Dothan Area Convention & Visitors Bureau (☎ 334-794-6622; 888-449-0212, Net), 3311 Ross Clark Circle NW, PO Box 8765, Dothan, AL 36304, is open Monday to Friday from 8 am to 5 pm, Saturday 9 am to 5 pm, Sunday 1 to 5 pm.

The post office (☎ 334-794-8567), 307 N Oates St, is open Monday to Friday 8 am to 4:30 pm, Saturday 8 am to noon.

Books-A-Million (☎ 334-712-1341), 3489 Ross Clark Circle NW, has a large regional section. Dothan News Company (☎ 334-792-6572), 182 N Foster St, carries books and domestic and international newspapers and magazines.

Do South is a monthly entertainment guide for Dothan and surrounding areas.

Flowers Hospital (☎ 334-793-5000), 4370 W Main St, provides medical care.

Wiregrass Museum of Art

A recent multimillion dollar renovation augmented this inspiring little museum (☎ 334-794-3871), 126 Museum Ave (formerly College St), near the Civic Theater. Emphasis is on 19th and 20th-century art, but there's an interesting collection of decorative arts downstairs. No matter what your age, go upstairs to the Children's Gallery. This is really cool stuff, especially Ed Tannenbaum's *Recollections II*, an interactive computer art installation. Hours are Tuesday to Saturday from 10 am to 5 pm, Sunday 1 to 5 pm; plan to spend an hour here. A $1 donation is suggested. The gift shop sells works by Alabama artists, including those on exhibit.

Wiregrass Festival of Murals District

Eventually, the city plans to have 30 murals depicting the history, life, culture and industry of Alabama's Wiregrass region. Six have been completed downtown. *De Soto's First Encounter with the Wiregrass Natives* is on E Main St at Museum Ave; *The Abduction of Elizabeth Stewart Dill* is on E Main St, west of St Andrews St; *Johnny Mack Brown* and *Chief Eufaula, Creek Indian Removal* are on S St Andrews St, north of E Main St; *Mules in the Wiregrass*

is on S St Andrews, north of E Main St, on the Poplar Head Mule Co building; and *Salute to the Peanut Industry* covers a wall in the municipal parking lot at E Main St and S St Andrews St.

Call The Downtown Group (☎ 334-793-3097) to arrange a guided walking tour ($3).

Landmark Park

This small family-oriented park (☎ 334-794-3452) combines history, culture and nature in an outdoor setting. There's a living history farm where a typical day in the 1890s unfolds on the fields and in a farmhouse, blacksmith shop and other buildings. Wildlife exhibits, short trails and an elevated boardwalk through the woods get visitors eye-to-eye with nature. Free evening concerts take place every other Thursday in June and July. November's Fall Folklife Festival is a big regional event. It's open Monday to Saturday 9 am to 5 pm, Sunday noon to 6 pm. Adult admission is $1, children 50¢. To get there, take Hwy 431 N to 430 Landmark Dr, 2½ miles north of Ross Clark Circle.

Golf

Highland Oaks Golf Course (☎ 334-712-2820), 904 Royal Parkway, is part of the Robert Trent Jones Golf Trail.

Special Events

Pick up maps at the visitor center showing the streets with the most vibrant displays during the Azalea-Dogwood Trail & Festival (☎ 334-793-0191) throughout March. More than 100,000 people attend the nine-day National Peanut Festival (☎ 334-793-4323) starting the first weekend in November. On the second Saturday in May, the outdoor Down-home Jazz Festival (☎ 334-983-3521) features national and local entertainment at the Olympia Spa located south of the city.

Places to Stay

The Budget Inn (☎ 334-793-7645) at 1964 Montgomery Hwy NW, provides clean, basic accommodations with cable. The staff is cheerful, but speaks little English

ALABAMA

and often has trouble communicating. Rates for singles/doubles are $24/32.

At the 120-room *Best Western Dothan Inn* (☎ 334-793-4376), 3285 Montgomery Hwy NW, you can relax by the pool or sun and barbecue deck. Continental breakfast and airport shuttle service are free. The rooms ($49/53) are clean, but drab.

The 44-room *Super 8 Motel* (☎ 334-792-3232), 2215 Ross Clark Circle SW, gives you a lot of bang for the buck. It has a pool, free movies, an exercise room, kitchenettes and a honeymoon suite with a whirlpool. Rooms are $45/50.

The *Olympia Spa Golf Resort* (☎ 334-677-3321), 7410 Hwy 231 S, is a good buy even if you don't play golf. It has 96 rooms, a pool, mineral pool, restaurant and lounge, health club and an 18-hole golf course. It's seven miles south of downtown. The rate is $42 to $48, single or double.

Rooms at the *Comfort Inn* (☎ 334-793-9090), 3593 Ross Clark Circle NW, are spacious and clean. There's a pool and a gym and room rates include movies and continental breakfast with fresh Krispy Kreme donuts. There's a chain restaurant across the parking lot and a shopping center behind. Rooms are $63/68.

Courtyard by Marriott (☎ 334-671-3000), 3040 Ross Clark Circle SW, features an indoor heated pool, an exercise room, an on-site restaurant for breakfast and a lounge. The staff is helpful and cheerful. The rate is $68/75.

The *Ramada Inn* (☎ 334-792-0031), 3011 Ross Clark Circle SW, is the largest of Dothan's chain hotels. It has a pool, airport shuttle, restaurant and popular lounge (see Entertainment). The breakfast buffet is included with the room rate ($50/56), as are health club privileges.

Places to Eat
Northwest A great place for lunch is *Grate Things* (☎ 334-793-2038), 139-6 Westgate Parkway NW. Their pasta, chicken and shrimp salads are good and they're huge. Don't miss the muffins. Nothing on the menu is more than $7. It's open weekdays from 9 am to 5 pm for dining or take-out.

Downtown *Nonno's Cafee* (☎ 334-712-0007), 160 S St Andrews St, is one of Dothan's hot, fun downtown restaurants. It's original, it's good, it's a bargain. Nonno's 'Pick-a-Pasta' and 'Chooze-a-Sauce' are all-you-can-eat. If you have a favorite dish that's not on the menu, the chef will try to make it. There's an espresso bar and a wood-burning brick oven for pizzas. Hours are Monday to Thursday from 11 am to 10 pm, Friday and Saturday 11 am to 11 pm.

The *Grapevine* (☎ 334-678-6271), 111 W Troy St, serves Mediterranean and Greek specialties. Salads are generously sized. For lunch try risotto with chicken, sausage and spring vegetables in a light tomato broth ($7.50). The dinner menu features hot, hearty dishes like seafood and shellfish stew ($15) and moussaka ($10). There's a selection of fresh made pastries and desserts. Hours are weekdays 11 am to 2:30 pm, Monday to Saturday 5 to 10 pm.

Southwest The two locations of *Dakota Coffee Works*, 121 Southgate Rd SW (☎ 334-702-8785), and 3074 Ross Clark Circle SW (☎ 334-677-1718), are upbeat java joints that sell imported beans and coffee. They're popular for sandwiches, soups, the '$5 Lunch Special' and for a cup of brew with pastries. Opening hours are Monday to Thursday from 8 am to 10 pm, Friday from 8 am to midnight, Saturday from 9 am to midnight, Sunday 10 am to 10 pm.

South Dothan *Gabe's Covered Bridge Restaurant* (☎ 334-677-7776), 7990 S County Rd 33, Crowley Farm Park, seven miles south of downtown, is in a wooded country setting and has a porch with rocking chairs, huge stone fireplace and pretty good food. Locals go for the catfish ($7 to $10). It's open Tuesday to Friday from 4 to 10 pm, Saturday and Sunday 11 am to 10 pm.

Brewpubs The *Poplar Head Mule & Brewpub & Grill* (☎ 334-794-7991), 115 S St Andrews, has four varieties of freshly brewed drafts, a restaurant and live entertainment Tuesday and Thursday to Saturday. There's a complete menu from sandwiches to grilled shrimp. The kitchen is open Monday to Thursday from 11 am to 10 pm, and Friday and Saturday till 11 pm. The brewpub is open Monday to Saturday from 11 am to the wee hours.

Entertainment
Theater *Opus Nostrum* (☎ 334-671-1117) at the Basketcase Cafe, 228 S Oates St, presents a variety of comedy and drama. Call for a schedule. Tickets ($17 plus gratuity) include performance and a meal.

Nightclubs *The Hangar* (☎ 334-794-1518), 4129 Ross Clark Circle NW, is a local institution that hosts local, regional and national acts on Thursday, Friday and Saturday nights. There's also an outdoor pool and deck.

Trader Bob (☎ 334-792-0031), 3011 Ross Clark Circle SW, at the Ramada Inn, features live music on Wednesday, Karaoke Tuesday and Saturday ($2). Friday at 9 pm is a live dinner comedy act ($15 with dinner, $3 without).

Neon Moon (☎ 334-702-8274), 1186 Montgomery Hwy, is a combination night spot and restaurant with live music Tuesday to Saturday 5 pm till the wee hours.

Getting There & Away
Air Dothan-Houston County Airport at Napier Field (☎ 334-983-8100), is served by Atlantic Southeast Airlines and Northwest Airlink.

Taxi, Taxi (☎ 334-793-8294) supplies transportation to Dothan.

Bus The Greyhound station (☎ 334-792-1191), 285 S Foster St, has buses that serve Atlanta ($41, four times a day), Birmingham ($41, four), Huntsville ($53, three), Mobile ($47 to $53, five), Montgomery ($23, four), Panama City, Florida ($21, one), and Pensacola ($36, three).

Car Enterprise (☎ 334-792-6868), has an office at 2838 Montgomery Hwy.

The roads leading in and out of Dothan are highways and county roads. From Eufaula, Hwy 431 follows the Chattahoochee River before bending southwest through farmland. Allow 1½ hours for the 60-mile drive. Hwy 84 from Enterprise and Fort Rucker passes through many little towns and takes 45 to 60 minutes. The 90-mile drive to Montgomery on Hwy 231 takes about two hours.

Getting Around
AAA Cab (☎ 334-794-6359), City Cab (☎ 334-792-2138), and Taxi, Taxi (☎ 334-793-8294) serve the city.

AROUND DOTHAN
State Parks
While most of the region south, east and west of Dothan is farmland and small farming communities, there are four state parks. Although they provide peaceful respites, getting to and away from them is time consuming as they're all on back roads. If your interest lies in a laid-back vacation crawling from park to park, these are for you.

The main attraction of **Blue Springs State Park** (☎ 334-397-4875), 2595 Hwy 10, six miles west of Clio, is a large freshwater pool popular with locals. Other features include a tennis court, picnic facilities and a snack concession. It has 50 improved tent and RV campsites ($11) and a separate primitive camping area ($5). There's a bathhouse and restrooms. Park hours are 8 am to 7 pm. The day-use fee is $1/50¢ for adults/kids and seniors.

Frank Jackson State Park (☎ 334-493-6988), Hwy 331 in Opp, has 2050 acres, half of which is a lake stocked with bass, catfish and crappie. Besides fishing, there's a swimming beach and picnic areas. The two wooded trails cover a mile. Camping is pretty decent here with bath and restroom facilities. Most of the 26 improved tent and RV campsites are waterfront. Sites are $8, $10 and $15. For day use, the park is open 6 am to 9 pm; the fee is $1/50¢.

Florala State Park (☎ 334-858-6425), off Hwy 331, Florala, is the smallest park in the system, but that doesn't account for the adjoining 400-acre Lake Jackson, where park visitors spend most of their time swimming – which is pretty good – fishing and water-skiing. The campground has 23 improved tent ($8) and RV ($13) sites, half of which are waterfront. There's a bathhouse, coin laundry and restrooms. The park is open for day use from 8 am to 5 pm.

Chattahoochee State Park (☎ 334-522-3607), 250 Chattahoochee State Park Rd, in Crosby, is as far southeast as you can go without leaving the state. It's a gorgeous, heavily wooded 600-acre park that gets little use but warrants more if only for the eight hiking trails that cover seven mostly flat miles. Wildlife, from turkeys to gopher tortoises, is abundant. You can rent a nonmotorized flat-bottom boat ($5, $2 for campers) to fish for bass and bream. The primitive camp sites ($5) are nestled between moss-draped trees. The primitive campground has grills and tables, a boat launch and pavilion. Showers and permanent restrooms are planned. The day-use fee is $1. It's open 7 am to dark.

Conecuh National Forest

This USFS area (☎ 334-222-2555), Hwy 29 and Hwy 55 south of Andalusia, is 90 miles west of Dothan. It has three distinct recreation areas. **Conecuh Trail** draws hikers from around the Southeast to hike 20 miles through deep forest, along bottom lands, across creeks and around Open Pond. For shorter hikes, take the trail's five-mile or 12-mile loop. The **Blue Pond Recreation Area** has the best swimming.

To get here, take Hwy 29 south from Andalusia for 10 miles, then turn south onto Hwy 137 for four miles, then east on USFS Road 347 for one mile. **Open Pond** is the trailhead for Conecuh Trail. There's no swimming, but tent ($5) and RV ($10) camping is here.

There's a $2 day-use fee. The ranger station, which is open weekdays 8 am to 4 pm, is just south of Andalusia on Hwy 29.

Army Aviation Museum

If you got goose bumps watching the helicopter scene accompanied by 'Ride of the Valkyries' in *Apocalypse Now*, you'll love this museum (☎ 334-255-2893), Building 6000, Andrews Ave, Fort Rucker, 23 miles west of Dothan, which houses the world's largest collection of choppers. Dioramas show situational uses of helicopters, while exhibits tell stories of development and history. A few interactive displays challenge your coordination skills. The gift shop is loaded with military and aviation stuff. It's open daily 9 am to 4 pm, except major holidays. From Dothan take Hwy 84 west 22 miles to Daleville, turn north on Hwy 85, then drive two miles.

Tennessee

Facts about Tennessee

Tennessee is like three different states in one. Memphis anchors the western Tennessee bottomland to the Mississippi Delta, with its history of cotton production and riverboat trade. Tennessee's capital, Nashville, is also the unofficial capital of middle Tennessee, a fertile plateau that serves as the liaison between the state's two disparate ends. Eastern Tennessee, with Knoxville as its urban center, is an Appalachian region that aligns with the Great Smoky Mountains.

The western and eastern reaches of the state are dissimilar in topography, history, racial makeup and culture. The east was settled by hardscrabble Scots and Irish who carved small farms out of the Cherokee wilderness. Their reputation for independence goes back to the Revolutionary War, when many remained Tories. As early as 1797, eastern Tennessee distinguished itself from its Southern neighbors with calls for an abolition society, and the area grew to be one of the strongest centers of abolitionist sympathy in the nation.

Elihu Embree, an early member of eastern Tennessee's manumission society, founded the first periodical in the US devoted to abolition. At the outset of the Civil War, while the ratio of slaves to the white population was three to five in western Tennessee, and one to three in middle Tennessee, it was one to 12 in eastern Tennessee.

In the west, plantation society expanded north from the Gulf and westward from Virginia and the Carolinas as entrepreneurial landowners established large slave-worked cotton plantations. While western Tennessee supported secession from the Union, eastern Tennessee was staunchly pro-Union and remained so even after Tennessee eventually seceded. After the Civil War, the Ku Klux Klan was founded in 1868 by former Confederate soldiers (led by Grand Cyclops General Nathan Bedford Forest) in Pulaski in an effort to control the

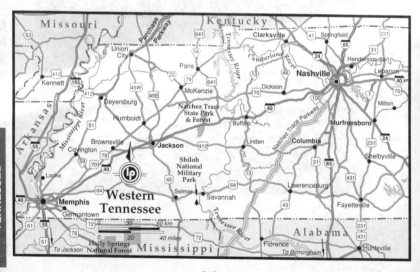

512

large numbers of freed slaves in western Tennessee.

We cover Memphis and Nashville in this guide. Both have made tremendous contributions to the cultural heritage of the Deep South – most notably in their music. Today, Memphis and Nashville are as different from one another as blues music is from country music, and the distinct genres are apt metaphors for the nature of each city.

Information
Tourist Offices
The Tennessee Department of Tourist Development (☎ 615-741-2158, 800-836-6200, TDD 615-741-0691), PO Box 23170, Nashville, TN 37202, distributes statewide tourist information.

The bicycle coordinator at the Tennessee Department of Transportation (☎ 615-741-2848), James K Polk Bldg, Suite 700, Nashville, TN 37243-0349, distributes state-sanctioned bike route maps.

Taxes
Sales tax is 6% in Tennessee; additional accommodations taxes vary from around 3% to 5%. Shelby County (where Memphis is located) adds a 2.25% sales tax, for a total of 8.25%; lodging taxes are added on top of this.

Driving & Liquor Laws
The legal drinking age is 21. No alcohol sales are permitted on Sunday morning. Tennessee has strict laws on Driving Under the Influence (DUI). A driver convicted of DUI with a child in the car may be charged with a felony offense.

Children under four are required to ride in a car seat.

State Parks
The central office for Tennessee State Parks (☎ 615-532-0001) is at 401 Church St, 7th floor, Nashville, TN 37243-0446. Fishing regulations can be obtained from the Tennessee Wildlife Resources Agency (☎ 615-781-6500), PO Box 40747, Nashville, TN 37204.

Memphis

Named for the ancient Egyptian capital on the Nile, Memphis on the Mississippi is best known for the rise and fall of two men who led vastly different movements.

The King of Rock 'n' Roll, Elvis Presley, rocketed to fame here in the late 1950s; his Graceland estate draws more than 700,000 visitors to town each year. And it was here, on April 4, 1968, that the Reverend Dr Martin Luther King Jr was assassinated on the balcony of the Lorraine Motel downtown, a site now preserved in his honor as the National Civil Rights Museum. The site is infused with all the solemn decorum one would expect for a fallen hero. Strangely perhaps, so is Graceland.

But in general the city takes its cues from something that happened much earlier. In the early 1900s, WC Handy's 'Beale Street Blues' established Memphis as the home of the blues. Today, the dockside city retains a certain soulful grittiness from a history replete with cotton, riverboats and blues. The blues continue to resonate from clubs on the new and improved Beale St – the city's answer to Bourbon St – and in rugged dives around town.

The Memphis-based courier company Federal Express is the city's largest employer, with 23,000 employees. Memphis is also the home of the first supermarket (Piggly Wiggly opened here in 1916), the original Holiday Inn, and site of the first Welcome Wagon, founded here in 1928. Almost half of the US cotton crop continues to float through Memphis.

For all its big city trappings, Memphis (population 1,056,135) is really more of a big town. Its major sites are easily seen in a few days, its roads are easy to navigate, and you'll probably find yourself running into the same people that you met days earlier.

History

Three thousand years ago, the loess bluffs on the eastern shore of the Mississippi

River were occupied by Native American tribes (see Chucalissa Archaeological Site & Museum, below, for a glimpse of how village life was around 1500 AD).

In 1541, the locals came in contact with the troops of Hernando de Soto when he first encountered the great Mississippi River. The town was abandoned soon thereafter (Chucalissa is a Choctaw word for abandoned) and the area came under Chickasaw domination.

The earliest European settlement on the site of Memphis was the French Fort Assumption established in 1739. In 1818 a US treaty edged the Chickasaw nation out of western Tennessee, and Andrew Jackson helped found the settlement he named Memphis. The city was incorporated in 1826 and prospered on the expanding cotton trade of the fertile Mississippi Delta directly south. Early in the Civil War a Union fleet defeated Confederate naval forces at the Battle of Memphis, and federal troops occupied the city.

Though there was little physical destruction, recovery from the war was hampered by a crippling yellow-fever epidemic in 1878 that claimed more than 5000 lives. The disproportionate toll on the white population was attributed to a genetic predisposition,

514

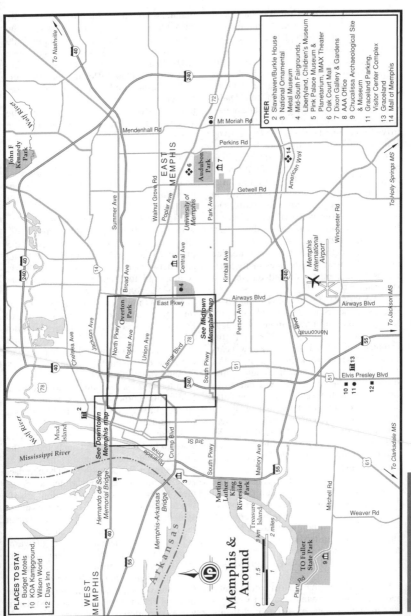

OTHER
2 Slavehaven/Burkle House
3 National Ornamental
   Metal Museum
4 Mid-South Fairgrounds,
   Libertyland, Children's Museum
5 Pink Palace Museum &
   Planetarium, IMAX Theater
6 Oak Court Mall
7 Dixon Gallery & Gardens
8 AAA Office
9 Chucalissa Archaeological Site
   & Museum
11 Graceland Parking,
   Visitor Center Complex
13 Graceland
14 Mall of Memphis

PLACES TO STAY
1 Budget Motels
10 KOA Kampground,
   Wilson World
12 Days Inn

Memphis &
Around

TENNESSEE

and surviving whites virtually abandoned the city. The following year Memphis officially declared bankruptcy and its city charter was revoked until 1893.

The black community took over daily operations and brought the town back to its feet. A former slave named Robert Church became a prominent landowner, civic leader and millionaire by buying real estate at bargain rates. Emigrants from the Delta arrived great numbers and the city thrived as the center of the cotton trade.

In its heyday in the early 1900s, a long stretch of Beale St was the hub of social, civic and business activity for the large African-American community not only in Memphis but across the mid-South. The street gained a provocative reputation for drinking, gambling and other shady pastimes associated with riverboat towns. In the Depression the district began its decline and over the next few decades many businesses closed; others moved out to East Memphis.

In the early 1950s, music visionary Sam Phillips opened Sun Studio and began producing records by now-famous blues legends such as Howlin' Wolf and Rufus Thomas. This paved the way a few years later for white rockabilly artists. For Phillips to record both black and white musicians indiscriminately was radical in the South at the time, as was equally renowned local WHBQ disc jockey Dewey Phillips who played the records cut at Sun. Following Sun's lead, more studios began springing up around Memphis, recording soul music, R&B, and rock that peaked in the 1960s and '70s.

With the civil rights movement of the 1960s came integration, which prompted the affluent white population to move, and expanded suburban development east. In 1968, city sanitation workers walked out on strike and Martin Luther King came to town to lend his support. He was assassinated in Memphis on April 4 (see sidebar).

By the 1970s the historic downtown had been largely abandoned and Beale St was in such a state of disrepair that city planners hoped to bulldoze the whole strip. Objections by preservationists grew loud enough for the city to commit $500 million to restoration instead of complete redevelopment. A new entertainment district was sculpted out of the old commercial buildings and storefronts along the few central blocks of Beale St. Plans for more riverfront development demonstrate a renewed commitment to revitalizing downtown Memphis.

Orientation

Downtown Memphis runs along the east bank of the Mississippi. Riverside Dr and a promenade run parallel to the river below the bluff, with a nice view of river traffic and bridges, particularly at night with the I-40 bridge lights making the shape of the letter 'M.' The civic and financial centers are clustered in a compact area between I-40 and Confederate Park. A monorail to Mud Island departs from the civic center off Front St.

The two main east-west thoroughfares through downtown are Union Ave and Poplar Ave, which start at the river and run east through midtown till they cross and change names in East Memphis. Downtown streets generally run east-west, avenues run north-south.

In the northeastern area of downtown, a funky little corner around N Main St and North Parkway called 'the Pinch' retains a few historic dives.

A short walk south (or train-trolley ride) leads to the tourist district anchored by the Peabody Hotel and centered in the Beale St strip between 2nd and 4th Sts. The compact zone around the Peabody Hotel is convenient to the Greyhound bus station, a half-block east across 3rd St. Public parking is available on a side street off 2nd St between the Peabody and the Beale St strip.

East of here there's a district of warehouses and muffler shops too long, uninteresting and suspect to walk through, but it's interrupted by a few finds like the Kudzu Cafe and the landmark Sun Studio. A huge medical center forms the eastern border of what's considered downtown.

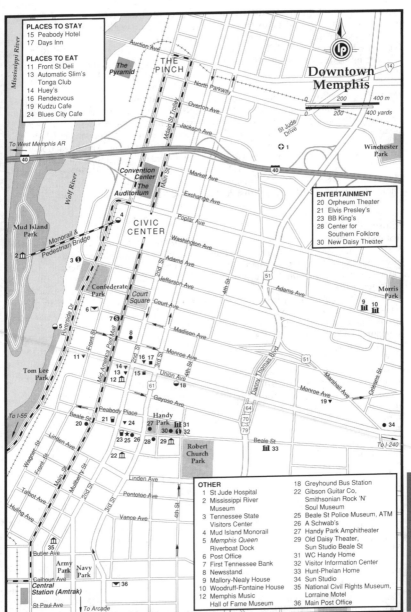

PLACES TO STAY
15 Peabody Hotel
17 Days Inn

PLACES TO EAT
11 Front St Deli
13 Automatic Slim's
   Tonga Club
14 Huey's
16 Rendezvous
19 Kudzu Cafe
24 Blues City Cafe

Mississippi River

To West Memphis AR

The Pyramid

THE PINCH

Auction Ave

North Parkway

Overton Ave

Jackson Ave

Main St Trolley

Downtown Memphis

St Jude Drive

Winchester Park

Wolf River

Convention Center
The Auditorium

Market Ave

Exchange Ave

Poplar Ave

CIVIC CENTER

Main St

Mud Island Park

Monorail & Pedestrian Bridge

Washington Ave

Adams Ave

Jefferson Ave

ENTERTAINMENT
20 Orpheum Theater
21 Elvis Presley's
23 BB King's
28 Center for
   Southern Folklore
30 New Daisy Theater

Adams Ave

Morris Park

Confederate Park

Court Square

Court Ave

Madison Ave

Monroe Ave

Danny Thomas Blvd

Monroe Ave

Marshall Ave

Orleans St

Riverside Dr

Front St

Mid-America Ped Mall

Union Ave

Gayoso Ave

Tom Lee Park

To I-55

Beale St

Peabody Place

Handy Park

Linden Ave

Wagner St

Front St

Main St

Mulberry St

Robert Church Park

Beale St

To I-240

Linden Ave

Pontotoc Ave

Vance Ave

Talbot Ave

Huling Ave

Army Park

Navy Park

Butler Ave

Calhoun Ave

Central Station (Amtrak)

St Paul Ave

To Arcade

OTHER
1 St Jude Hospital
2 Mississippi River
   Museum
3 Tennessee State
   Visitors Center
4 Mud Island Monorail
5 Memphis Queen
   Riverboat Dock
6 Post Office
7 First Tennessee Bank
8 Newsstand
9 Mallory-Nealy House
10 Woodruff-Fontaine House
12 Memphis Music
   Hall of Fame Museum

18 Greyhound Bus Station
22 Gibson Guitar Co,
   Smithsonian Rock 'N'
   Soul Museum
25 Beale St Police Museum, ATM
26 A Schwab's
27 Handy Park Amphitheater
29 Old Daisy Theater,
   Sun Studio Beale St
31 WC Handy Home
32 Visitor Information Center
33 Hunt-Phelan Home
34 Sun Studio
35 National Civil Rights Museum,
   Lorraine Motel
36 Main Post Office

TENNESSEE

Midtown runs from the medical center to the East Parkway and holds the city's Overton Square and Cooper-Young neighborhoods. From here, East Memphis spreads out with miles of increasingly affluent suburban development.

Maps It's easy to get through town following major routes, but a decent map is necessary to navigate complex freeway interchanges (see Getting Around). Auto club members can get maps at AAA (☎ 901-761-5371), 5138 Park Ave (in East Memphis, around a mile west of I-240). Gas stations sell maps and car-rental companies, hotels and visitor centers distribute free maps.

Information
Tourist Offices The new Tennessee State Visitor Center on Riverside Dr makes an easy and scenic first stop for maps, event calendars and information. It's open around the clock.

The visitor information center (☎ 901-543-5333, TDD 901-521-6833), 340 Beale St, is open daily and distributes maps, brochures and city bus schedules.

Visitors may call or write for information from the Memphis Convention and Visitors Bureau (☎ 901-543-5300), 47 Union Ave, Memphis, TN 38103.

The 24-hour Memphis information hotline can be reached at ☎ 901-753-5847. A translation service can be reached at ☎ 901-372-7373.

Online there are two sites for visitor information (see the Internet directory at the back of this book).

Money ATMs are distributed throughout the city. Currency exchanges are available at the Memphis international airport and at the downtown headquarters of the First Tennessee Bank (☎ 901-523-4444), 165 Madison Ave.

Post The main post office (☎ 901-521-2119), 161 E Calhoun Ave, is near the train station. More convenient is the branch at 1 N Front St (☎ 901-576-2013) at the foot of Madison Ave downtown. There is a post office at Watkins St and Union Ave, midtown.

The Mail Center (☎ 901-725-9173), at 1725B Madison Ave, midtown, is equipped to send packages via UPS or Fed Ex.

Travel Agencies An American Express office – the American and International Travel Service (☎ 901-345-8920) – is near the airport at 2741 Nonconnah Blvd.

In addition to the Amtrak station downtown, you can purchase train tickets at Gulliver's Travel (☎ 901-794-9950) in the Mall of Memphis east of the airport at the I-240 Perkins Rd exit.

Travel services are also available at AAA (see Maps above).

Bookstores Memphis has several wonderful bookstores. Davis-Kidd (☎ 901-683-9801), 387 Perkins Rd Extended at Poplar Ave, near the Oak Court Mall, offers the most comprehensive selection, with many periodicals and out-of-town newspapers. Davis-Kidd also has a cafe and hosts author events.

Burke's Bookstore (☎ 901-278-7484), 1719 Poplar Ave, established in 1875, has rare collectibles among its new and used literary selections, and features author readings and book signings.

Meristem (☎ 901-276-0282) is a feminist bookstore at 930 S Cooper St in the Cooper-Young neighborhood.

For periodicals, there's a newsstand convenient to downtown at the corner of 2nd St and Monroe Ave, one block north of Union.

Libraries The Memphis/Shelby County Public Library and Information Center (☎ 901-725-8895), headquartered at the main library, 1850 Peabody Ave at McClean Blvd, two blocks south of Union Ave, operates 23 branch libraries around town.

Books Look for Robert Gordon's *It Came from Memphis*, which comes with an accompanying CD. It describes the city's kookier side with a cast of midget wrestlers, wasted rock stars and grizzled bluesmen.

Drive-in movies, cemetery stalking and the favorite local pastime – recounting what Memphis once was – are described in the *Lowlife Guide to Memphis: Memphis on $12.96 a day*. It's produced and distributed by Shangri-la Records (☎ 901-274-1916, Net), 190 Madison Ave.

Media The *Commercial Appeal* is the daily newspaper in Memphis. Expanded entertainment listings appear in the Friday and Sunday editions.

The free weekly *Memphis Flyer*, distributed at many outlets around town, covers news and entertainment from an alternative perspective. The free monthly *Triangle Journal News* covers news and entertainment of special interest to the gay community; it's distributed at the main library, Squash Blossom market and around town.

The nonprofit community radio station WEVL 89.9 FM plays a tremendous variety of local music, including blues, rockabilly, bluegrass, swamp pop and soul classics. More blues can be heard on KMZN 107.1 FM and WAVN 1240 AM. You'll find the local NPR affiliate at 91.1 FM.

Medical & Emergency Services For the police, call ☎ 901-528-2222. For the Sexual Assault Resource Center (a program so responsive it's considered a national model), call ☎ 901-528-2161.

Major city hospitals are located at Union Ave near I-240. The Methodist Hospital (☎ 901-726-7000) and Baptist Memorial Hospital (☎ 901-227-2727) here are two of the city's largest employers. St Joseph's Hospital staffs a 24-hour information line providing health advice at ☎ 901-577-3000.

A nationally recognized center for pediatric medicine, St Jude's Children's Research Hospital (☎ 901-495-3300) was established by actor Danny Thomas (note Danny Thomas Blvd).

The Memphis Center for Reproductive Health (☎ 901-274-3550), 1462 Poplar Ave at McNeil, staffs its phone lines 24 hours a day to answer medical questions.

THINGS TO SEE & DO

Peabody Hotel

Not only a grand hotel, the Peabody, off Union Ave between 2nd and 3rd Sts, is the town's social hub with its own quirky traditions. At 11 am every day, the Peabody's famous ducks descend in the elevator from their penthouse apartment and file across a red carpet to cavort in the lobby's marble fountain – the story goes that a general manager's prank in the 1930s started the tradition. (The ducks' retreat commences at 5 pm sharp.)

The hotel complex includes a tourist information booth, pricey and formal restaurants, cafes and shops, and a Gray Line tours ticket agent; downtown tour operators park outside. See also Organized Tours and Places to Stay.

Beale Street

Though only one of the original stores remains from Beale St's heyday in the early 1900s, you can still get a taste for the old commercial strip from the brick

---

The Original Memphis Bluesman

'The seven wonders of the world I have seen, and many are the places I have been. Take my advice, folks, and see Beale Street first'
— WC Handy

In 1909 William Christopher Handy, a young band leader and trumpet player from Florence, Alabama, wrote a campaign song for Memphis mayoral candidate EH Crump. 'Boss' Crump won and the song was an instant success, not so much for its lyrics as for its new sound – a tune composed of 'blue notes' that caught on with the public. The song was retitled 'Memphis Blues' and became the first blues song published. Handy followed it up with 'St Louis Blues,' which established him as the Father of the Blues. His statue stands at WC Handy Park on Beale St. The turn-of-the-century shotgun shack in which he once lived is at 352 Beale St today ($2 adults, $1 children). ∎

storefronts, cobblestones and, of course, its legendary blues.

The two-block strip of Beale between 2nd and 4th Sts is now the city's entertainment district. The swanky clubs, restaurants, souvenir shops and neon signs lead critics to call it a Disneyfied blues theme park. But it's hard to argue too vehemently against independent, locally owned and operated, safe, comfortable places to hear masterful live music.

The **Orpheum Theater**, on Beale at Main St, has been restored to its 1928 glory. A grand opera house was built here in 1895 but it was later destroyed by fire.

The Elvis statue at the corner of 2nd Ave heralds **Elvis Presley's**, a nightclub and restaurant. It's carved out of the famous clothier shop Lansky's, where Elvis bought the outfit he wore for his notorious performance on the *Ed Sullivan Show* (when the cameras only showed him from the waist up). Diagonally across the street at **BB King's**, the 'Beale St Blues Boy' himself occasionally performs at his namesake club, which was once the Colored Business Exchange building.

Between 2nd and 3rd Sts, the **Walk of Fame** features musical notes embedded in the sidewalk with the names of blues artists. The Beale St substation **Police Museum** exhibits criminalia such as the extradition order for convicted Martin Luther King assassin James Earl Ray. Owned by the same family since 1876, the landmark **A Schwab's** dry-goods store is the only original still operating on Beale St. Schwab's fills three floors with voodoo powders, 99¢ neckties, handcuffs, clerical collars, saucepans and the largest selection of hats in town. Its motto is justifiably 'if you can't find it at A Schwab's, you're better off without it!' The rest of the block is filled with restaurants, shops, clubs and pubs. A ghostly façade held up on steel girders is all that remains of the Gallina Hotel.

Between 3rd and 4th Sts, the **WC Handy statue** overlooks a park with an amphitheater that hosts outdoor concerts. (This is where Memphians ring in the New Year.)

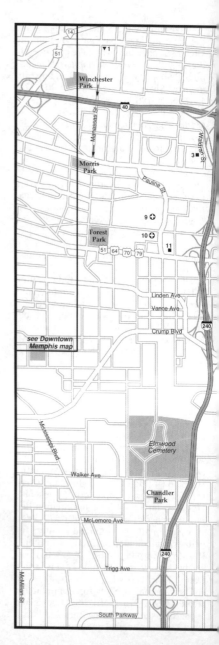

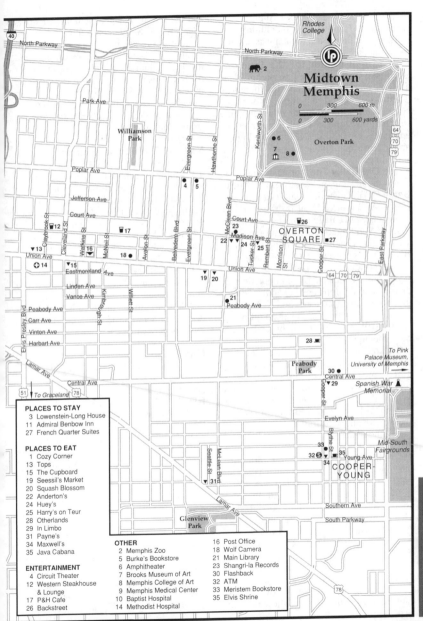

PLACES TO STAY
3 Lowenstein-Long House
11 Admiral Benbow Inn
27 French Quarter Suites

PLACES TO EAT
1 Cozy Corner
13 Tops
15 The Cupboard
19 Seessil's Market
20 Squash Blossom
22 Anderton's
24 Huey's
25 Harry's on Teur
28 Otherlands
29 In Limbo
31 Payne's
34 Maxwell's
35 Java Cabana

ENTERTAINMENT
4 Circuit Theater
12 Western Steakhouse
      & Lounge
17 P&H Cafe
26 Backstreet

OTHER
2 Memphis Zoo
5 Burke's Bookstore
6 Amphitheater
7 Brooks Museum of Art
8 Memphis College of Art
9 Memphis Medical Center
10 Baptist Hospital
14 Methodist Hospital
16 Post Office
18 Wolf Camera
21 Main Library
23 Shangri-la Records
30 Flashback
32 ATM
33 Meristem Bookstore
35 Elvis Shrine

At the far end of the block is the shotgun shack where Handy raised six children.

Though at first you'd think it was nothing more than a cafe with some unusual gifts, the nonprofit **Center for the Study of Southern Folklore** (see Entertainment) is a major cultural touchstone for the entire South. It's situated in a former dry-goods store. Today's funky decor represents fine folk traditions and includes music and arts and crafts on exhibit and for sale. Inquire about performances, local tours and film screenings.

The **Old Daisy Theater** has exhibits on blues music and it houses **Sun Studio Beale St** (the historic studio is a drive out Union Ave), where 'You Be the Star!' by recording souvenir karaoke tapes. Hourly tours of Sun Studio cost $5 (children under 12 free) and include free parking behind Beale St. It's open noon to 8 pm daily.

The **New Daisy Theater**, across the street, has art deco backdrops depicting the district's honky-tonk heyday and continues to hold big-name concerts and shows.

The visitor center at the east end of the strip distributes city maps, brochures and bus schedules.

Tucked in behind Beale St at 3rd St is the Gibson Guitar plant, where many of the guitar models made famous by local recording stars are now manufactured. Within the plant, the Smithsonian Institution's **Rock 'n' Soul Museum** examines the social and cultural history that produced the music of the Mississippi Delta.

Memphis Music Hall of Fame Museum

The nonprofit Hall of Fame (also called the Music & Blues Museum; ☎ 901-525-4007), at 97 S 2nd St, illustrates popular music's roots – from African rhythms through slave chants, blues, gospel, R&B, soul and rock 'n' roll – with 7000 sq feet of artifacts (such as the shoeshine box belonging to bluesman Furry Lewis), instruments and costumes (including Elvis' karate suit and Isaac Hayes' 10-inch platform shoes). You can hear vintage recordings through headsets, and black & white TV sets show rare film

and television footage, including *St Louis Blues*, Bessie Smith's only film.

Admission seems high at $7.50 for adults, but it's a studiously researched and nicely maintained collection. Select music-related books and other souvenirs can be purchased at the gift shop, which is open Monday to Thursday from 10 am to 6 pm, Friday and Saturday to 9 pm and Sunday from noon to 6 pm.

National Civil Rights Museum

This must-see museum (☎ 901-521-9699), 450 Mulberry St five blocks south of Beale St, is housed in the Lorraine Motel where Reverend Dr Martin Luther King Jr was fatally shot on April 4, 1968. The exterior of the turquoise 1950s motel remains much the same as it was at that time; the Cadillacs parked below the balcony were there when Dr King was struck down.

Documentary photos chronicle key events in civil rights history that led to the end of official segregation in the US.

Admission to the museum is $5 ($4 students and seniors, $3 children six to 12, kids under six free). It's closed Tuesday.

Mud Island

Above the new Tennessee State Welcome Center, cross the Wolf River via a monorail and elevated walkway to 52-acre Mud Island Park (☎ 901-576-7241, 800-507-6507). The park has an impressive to-scale bas-relief reproduction of the lower Mississippi River culminating in a 1.3-million-gallon Gulf of Mexico. You can wade in the miniature river and swim in the Gulf! There are also river exhibits, a WWII bomber, and restaurants.

Open from mid-April through October, it's closed Mondays in spring and fall, but open daily in summer from 10 am to 7 pm. The beach and pool are not open Mondays in summer. Adults pay $8 for all attractions, or $4 for admission to the grounds only (children four to 11, seniors 60 and over and the disabled pay $6, or $3 for grounds only). You can catch the monorail on Front St between Poplar and Adams Aves.

A Conspiracy to Kill Martin Luther King?

In the spring of 1968, Martin Luther King came to Memphis to lead a march supporting striking city sanitation workers. Late in the afternoon on April 4, King was fatally shot on the balcony of the Lorraine Motel. Rioting and sporadic violence across the nation followed the murder, and the city's (as well as the nation's) recovery was slow and painful.

King's accused killer was a 40-year-old petty burglar named James Earl Ray. Ray pleaded guilty in 1969, yet three days later he recanted his guilty plea. Nevertheless, he was sentenced to 99 years in prison without a trial. Ray has continually asserted his innocence for the past 30 years, though now he is an old man and suffering from terminal liver disease. He says the rifle found near the murder scene was put there by conspirators who wished to frame him.

Recently lawyers for Ray have renewed his request for a jury trial, with the claim that new ballistics-testing technology can prove that the rifle believed to be the murder weapon did not kill King. Though prosecutors contend that new test results would not be enough to overturn Ray's guilty plea, in 1997 a state appeals court cleared the way for new ballistics tests.

The case for a trial has won the support of the King family. King's widow, Coretta Scott King, and son Dexter testified before Shelby County Criminal Court's Judge Joseph Brown in February 1997, saying they want Ray to get a new trial to resolve whether King was the victim of a conspiracy or a lone gunman. Dexter King, who met with Ray in a Nashville prison, has said he believes Ray was a pawn in a murder conspiracy. ■

Sun Studio

The 'most famous recording studio in the world,' Sun Studio (☎ 901-521-0664), 706 Union Ave near Marshall Ave straddling downtown and midtown (see Downtown Memphis map), is the nursery where rock 'n' roll was born. Starting in the early 1950s, owner Sam Phillips recorded blues artists like Howlin' Wolf, BB King and Ike Turner, followed by the Sun rockabilly dynasty of Jerry Lee Lewis (see Northern Louisiana chapter), Carl Perkins, Johnny Cash, Roy Orbison and, of course, Elvis Presley. In 1952, Sun produced Jackie Brenston's classic 'Rocket 88' – widely regarded as the first rock 'n' roll release. In 1955, Sun cut Elvis' first hit, 'Don't Be Cruel.'

The tiny room with its warped tiles remains active today – contemporary artists such as Ringo Starr, U2 and Def Leppard have all come to Memphis to record on its hallowed ground. The 30-minute 'tour' (you stand around) starts hourly and includes vintage audio clips; it costs $8 (free for children under 12). Sun is open daily from 10 am to 6 pm and has extended hours in summer. A cafe, gift shop, memorabilia exhibit and free parking are adjacent.

TENNESSEE

Graceland

The Graceland estate was home to Elvis Presley for 20 years; he died here and is buried on the grounds outside the house. Before Elvis bought the property, the estate was part of a 500-acre farm that belonged to the Toof family; it was named Graceland after a female relative. In the spring of 1957, at age 22, Elvis purchased the house and grounds for $100,000. After Elvis' death in 1977, the estate passed to his father and grandmother (now deceased) and his daughter, Lisa Marie Presley. Priscilla Presley (who divorced Elvis in 1973) opened Graceland to tours in 1982.

According to the brochure, 'from the cool elegance of the all-white living room to the playful decor of his famous 'jungle den,' Elvis' brilliant personality is evident throughout' – but you can see for yourself. Cobalt-blue drapes with gold fringe, peacock stained glass, avocado-green kitchen appliances, a 15-foot couch, yellow vinyl, a stone waterfall and green shag carpeting on the ceiling make Graceland a museum of 1970s aesthetics.

A tour of Graceland (☎ 901-332-3322, 800-238-2000, TDD/TTY 901-344-3146, Net) on Elvis Presley Blvd (Hwy 51), begins with the visitor plaza across the street. Here you'll find tour ticket sales, accessory museums, cafes, far-too-tasteful souvenir shops, and even a post office that stamps mail with a Graceland postmark. A free 22-minute film airs on the hour and half-hour in the plaza.

In busier seasons, you must wait for an assigned hour for a tour of Graceland itself, or call for reservations. From the visitor plaza, vans transport ticket-holders across the street to the mansion. The tour is a recording narrated by Priscilla Presley, which is something of a disappointment since Graceland begs for a personal guide. Seven languages are offered on tape.

The mansion tour alone is $10. In the visitor plaza, the car museum tour is $5; the 'Sincerely Elvis' memorabilia collection is $3.50; and the aircraft collection is $4.50. There are discounts for seniors and children. Admission for the whole package is $18.50 for adults, $17 for seniors and $11 for children seven to 12. The whole package is colossal and possibly too mind-bending for the uninitiated; the house tour alone might do it (though the cars and planes are cherry).

Parking costs an additional $2, but is free for the disabled.

The complex is open daily from 8 am to 6 pm from Memorial Day to Labor Day and 9 am to 5 pm the rest of the year. It's closed on major holidays. The mansion alone is closed Tuesdays from November to February.

During candlelight vigils, which are held on the anniversary of his death (August 15), worshippers (including many impersonators) stand in line for hours for

Elvis the Pelvis

Born in Tupelo, Mississippi, Elvis Presley (1935-77) began his recording career in Memphis at Sun Studio in 1954. By 1956, he had become an international superstar. His record sales account for more than any other individual or group in recording history – an estimated billion units sold.

Yet Elvis was much more than an entertainer. Rising from dirt-poor Southern roots to become a household name around the globe made him a working-class hero. Since his death by cardiac arrest at age 42 (legend has it he died on the toilet while reading The Scientific Search for the Face of Jesus), he has become mythologized as a cultural icon – some adherents claim to have been healed by appealing to the spirit of Elvis or by attending the shrine that his Graceland estate has become. Free walk-up visits to the grave at Graceland are permitted early in the morning year-round. (For a house tour, it's pricey, but for spiritual healing it's a bargain.) Graveside guests must leave 30 minutes before the first tour. ■

the opportunity to parade up the drive and around the King's tomb in the Meditation Garden. On or around January 8 (Elvis Presley Day in Memphis by proclamation) other special events commemorate Elvis' birthday. The mansion is specially decorated at Christmastime.

Since Graceland is a quick $7.50 cab ride from the airport, you could conceivably visit on a layover in wintertime, when it's less crowded (but not on a Tuesday – it's closed). Cabs from downtown to Graceland cost $18 to $20.

Historic House Tours

The two-story Federal-style **Hunt-Phelan Home** (☎ 910-344-3166, 800-350-9009), 533 Beale St just east of Danny Thomas Blvd, served as headquarters for Union general Ulysses S Grant after the city's Civil War surrender in 1862. It was also used as a hospital for Union soldiers. As attractive and historic as it is, tours are expensive and grandly overproduced. A cloyingly theatrical recorded tour, modern visitor center and a gift shop detract from the antebellum appeal of the artifacts, furnishings and architecture. Admission is $10 for adults ($9 for students and seniors, $6 for children five to 12, under five free). It's open daily from spring to fall; in winter it's closed Monday and Tuesday. A freemen's schoolhouse on the premises is currently being restored.

Architecture buffs will also be interested in the restored turn-of-the-century houses in the tiny **Victorian Village** district on Adams Ave. Two homes are open to public tours: Woodruff-Fontaine House (☎ 901-525-2695) at 680 Adams Ave, and Mallory-Neely House (☎ 901-523-1484) at 652 Adams Ave.

Slavehaven/Burkle House (☎ 901-527-3427), 826 N 2nd St at Chelsea Ave, north of downtown, will interest students of history and African-American heritage. With its trap doors and tunnels, it's thought to have been a way station for runaway slaves on the Underground Railroad. Tours are given Monday through Saturday from 10 am to 4 pm.

E Pluribus Elvi

Dedicated to hard-working Elvis impersonators from around the world, the First Church of the Elvis Impersonator at 2170 Young St in the city's bohemian Cooper-Young neighborhood maintains a 'multi-media kind of kinetic installation art kind of shrine thing' that lights up and plays music around the clock – only 25¢ per blessed vista. Inside, Elvis impersonators officiate at the King-festooned wedding chapel. ∎

Pink Palace Museum & Planetarium

The original Pink Palace (☎ 901-320-6320), 3050 Central Ave, was built here in 1923 as a residence for Piggly Wiggly founder Clarence Saunders. It reopened in 1996 as a natural and cultural history museum with fossils, Civil War exhibits, restored WPA murals and an exact replica of the original Piggly Wiggly, the world's first self-service grocery store. Museum admission is $5.50 ($4 for children three to 12); unless you come on Thursday when it's free. Museum hours are Monday to Wednesday from 9 am to 5 pm, Thursday to Saturday till 9 pm, and Sunday noon to 5 pm. Winter hours are Monday to Wednesday from 9 am to 4 pm, later on Thursday and Saturday, and Sunday from noon to 5 pm.

A planetarium has regular shows ($3.50/2.50 adults/kids) and features a special Elvis laser show in August. Admission to big-screen films at the IMAX theater on site is $5.75/4.25.

Brooks Museum of Art

Within Overton Park (a greenway surrounded by stately homes), the city's fine arts museum (☎ 901-722-3500), off Poplar near Kenilworth St, fans out from its gracious central rotunda into three floors of handsome galleries. Peruvian effigy vessels from 250 BC, a 1st-century Greco-Roman marble torso of Pan, a Florentine *tondo*, a Duncan Phyfe dining table, a Picasso pitcher and spray-paint art are among its varied collection.

TENNESSEE

Admission to the museum is $4 ($2 students and seniors). It's open some evenings; closed on Mondays and major holidays. The museum's restaurant overlooks the park. They have a nice gift shop too.

Dixon Gallery & Gardens

The Dixon Gallery (☎ 901-761-5250), 4339 Park Ave, houses an impressive collection of impressionist and postimpressionist paintings by artists such as Monet, Degas, Renoir and Cezanne. There are 17 acres of woodland and landscaped gardens. Admission Tuesday to Sunday is $5 ($4 seniors, $3 students and $1 children under 12). On Monday, only the grounds are open and admission is half-price.

Chucalissa Archaeological Site & Museum

At the Chucalissa archaeological site (☎ 901-785-3160), situated on a remote bluff south of downtown Memphis (off Mitchell Rd, west of Hwy 61), the Department of Anthropology at the University of Memphis maintains a reconstructed 15th-century Native American village atop ancient moundworks unearthed during construction of the nearby state park. Around the central plaza once used for ceremonies, dances and ball games, the thatched houses belonging to the chieftain, shaman and skilled craftsmen sit on elevated earthworks that also served as burial grounds.

Museum exhibits, crafts demonstrations and a knowledgeable staff tell the story of the sophisticated Mississippian civilization that once dominated the southeastern US. Though the floodlit mannequin dioramas and red-painted concrete floors are distracting, Chucalissa nonetheless provides easy access to an authentic Mississippian site. An archaeological highlight is an enclosed cutaway trench revealing the sequential layering of one ancient mound. Admission is $3 ($2 for seniors and children). It's closed Mondays.

A spring powwow is held on Mother's Day weekend, and a Choctaw festival featuring native dances, crafts and foods is held the first weekend in August.

Other Attractions

Grand Egyptian porticos decorated with colorful hieroglyphics flank the entrance to the **Memphis Zoo** (☎ 901-276-9453) at the northwest corner of midtown's Overton Park. Inside, 400 animal species inhabit Indiana Jones-worthy habitats such as Peruvian rain forest, African veldt and a Jamaican cavern. Admission is $7 ($5.50 for seniors, $4.50 for children aged two to 11). Parking costs $2 per car. The zoo is open daily. **Overton Park** itself is one of the largest urban parks in the country. It features a small art museum, and concerts are held in an amphitheater.

The swank **Children's Museum** (☎ 901-320-3170), 2525 Central Ave at Hollywood (at the Mid-South Fairgrounds), entertains kids with a tree house, miniature store and bank, fire engine and performances. Admission is $5 ($4 for seniors and children).

Also at the fairgrounds, **Libertyland** is an old-time amusement park with a huge old wooden roller coaster and dozens of other rides open seasonally. Admission is $7 ($4 after 4 pm).

At the **National Ornamental Metal Museum** (☎ 901-774-6380), an outdoor sculpture garden overlooks the Mississippi River. More metallurgical arts are on display inside – from jewelry to architectural trimmings – along with metalsmiths at work. Admission is $2 ($1 for seniors, students and children). It's closed Monday. To get to Metal Museum Dr from downtown, take I-55 exit 12C.

Two state parks offer a wide range of activities, including camping. South of town is **TO Fuller State Park** (☎ 901-543-7581), situated on a remote bluff off Mitchell Rd west of Hwy 61. The park has an 18-hole golf course and swimming pool, and is also home to the Chucalissa archaeological site (see above).

Thirteen miles north of town, 14,500-acre **Meeman-Shelby State Park** (☎ 901-876-5215) offers more than 20 miles of hiking and horse trails. Horse and boat rentals are available. There is also an Olympic-size pool.

ORGANIZED TOURS

Riverboat rides aboard the *Memphis Queen* (☎ 901-527-5694) depart from the foot of Monroe Ave at Riverside Dr. Sightseeing tours (1½ hours) start at $10 for adults; you'll pay more for sunset dinner, moonlight music or Sunday brunch cruises.

The Gray Line (☎ 901-346-8687, 800-948-8680) offers the most foreign-language bus tours around town. It has a pick-up and drop-off service from most hotels and there are 10 tour packages ranging from three to eight hours.

Horse-drawn carriage tours downtown (☎ 901-527-7542) depart from Beale St, outside the Peabody Hotel on Union Ave, and a few other downtown locations. A half-hour tour costs around $25 for two passengers, with additional charges for longer rides.

The nonprofit Center for Southern Folklore (☎ 901-525-3655), on Beale St, can provide cultural-heritage walking tours of the neighborhood. Call for more information.

Outdoors Inc (☎ 901-722-8988), 1710 Union Ave, is a good resource for outdoor adventures such as canoeing, kayaking and hiking.

SPECIAL EVENTS

Check special-events listings in the entertainment supplements in Friday and Sunday's *Commercial Appeal*. Also see listings in the free weekly *Memphis Flyer*.

January

By city proclamation, January 8 is *Elvis Presley Day*; the King's birthday is celebrated at his Graceland home. On or around January 15 (usually the third Monday in January), *Martin Luther King Jr's Birthday* is celebrated with a national holiday and a city tribute.

February

Beale St hosts a *zydeco festival* and ethnic activities are scheduled to coincide with *Black History Month*.

March

The rowdy little Pinch district celebrates *St Patrick's Day* on March 17.

April

The anniversary of Martin Luther King's death is marked with a *Memorial March* on April 4. *Africa in April* is a big ethnic festival. Beale St hosts a *spring festival* block party.

May

Memphis in May is the major citywide festival held mid-month; it includes a barbecue cook-off and the *Beale St Music Festival*. On Mother's Day weekend (late May or early June) the *Spring Powwow* is held at Chucalissa.

June

Juneteenth is celebrated on or around June 19 at Slavehaven/Burkle House and at the *Freedom Festival* in Douglas Park. BB King's club celebrates its anniversary this month.

July

On July 4, *Independence Day* fireworks can be seen exploding over the Mississippi River from Mud Island Park. The Center for Southern Folklore hosts the *Memphis Music & Heritage Festival*, a major cultural event with fabulous roots music. It runs for three days at Court Square downtown and is usually held the second weekend of the month.

August

The August 15 anniversary of the death of Elvis sparks city-wide events. On the official tour, Graceland hosts a candlelight vigil to the grave. On the unofficial tour, the P&H Cafe (see Places to Eat) hosts the *Dead Elvis Ball*. The Memphis College of Art sponsors the annual *White Trash/Black Velvet* show for which artists submit black velvet masterpieces; food is awarded for the 'dish most likely to be Elvis' favorite.' The *Memphis Blues Festival* is usually held this month.

September

The *Mid-South Fair* brings amusement park rides and a carnival atmosphere to the fairgrounds for 10 days. The *Cooper-Young Festival* is a street party. Beale St hosts a *Labor Day* festival.

October

The *International Blues Talent Competition* highlights new talent on Beale St. *Native American Day* at Chucalissa features children's activities.

TENNESSEE

November

Mid-month, the *WC Handy Birthday Celebration* pays tribute to the original Beale St bluesman. At the end of the month, *Starry Night*, a popular drive-through extravaganza with colored lights benefits the Metropolitan Inter-Faith Association. Graceland dresses up for the holidays and stays that way till around Epiphany in early January. The Victorian Village is also specially decorated.

December

Christmas celebrations and decorations remain (see above). The traditional *New Year's Eve* celebration turns Beale St into a giant street party; while the Peabody's gala costs $225 per couple.

PLACES TO STAY

Memphis has 106 hotels and motels. The most distinctive are the high-end Peabody, the moderate motels around Graceland with 24-hour Elvis movies, and the one low-end hostel.

Camping

The *KOA Kampground* (☎ 901-396-7125), 3691 Elvis Presley Blvd, is practically across the street from Graceland. Amenities include a pool. Its year-round campsites cost $19, more with hookups. Cabins are also available.

South of town, *TO Fuller State Park* (☎ 901-543-7581), on a remote bluff off Mitchell Rd east of Hwy 61, has a 53-site campground, 18-hole golf course and pool. Sites cost $11 per night; there are no hookups.

Thirteen miles north of town, *Meeman-Shelby State Park* (☎ 901-876-5215) offers hiking trails, a pool and boat rentals. Its 50-site campground charges $11 a site; there are no hookups. Six fully equipped two-bedroom lakeside cabins (linens provided) sleep six people each and cost $65.

Hostels

The independent hostel at the *Lowenstein-Long House* (☎ 901-527-7174), 217 N Waldran St, provides dormitory lodging on the 3rd floor of a ramshackle Victorian house off Poplar Ave near I-240. Beds cost around $9. It's extremely casual (no curfew or lockout, work exchange negotiable, 'free beer') and has the ambiance of a hip flophouse. It also has private rooms for $33/30 with/without TV.

Motels

A half-block from Graceland, the *Days Inn* (☎ 901-346-5500, 800-329-7366), 3839 Elvis Presley Blvd, features a guitar-shaped swimming pool and 24-hour in-room Elvis movies; rates start at $77 (single or double). Behind Graceland's parking lot, *Wilson World* (☎ 901-332-1000, 800-945-7667), 3677 Elvis Presley Blvd, also offers Elvis movies and a lobby with the same faux elegance of Graceland. There's free popcorn and an airport shuttle is available. Rooms cost $51 and up.

The downtown *Days Inn* (☎ 901-527-4100), 164 Union Ave, is only two blocks from Beale St, across from the Peabody. Rooms cost around $65/70 for a single/double; there's no pool.

A bottom-of-the-barrel choice for budget doubles is the *Admiral Benbow Inn* (☎ 901-725-0630, 800-321-2949), 1220 Union Ave, which offers rooms for $37 (single or double) in an extremely shabby old building. It's centrally located at the medical center off I-240 in an area that's charmless but walkable.

The best, most modern budget motel options are across the river in West Memphis, Arkansas. Nearly a dozen can be found in a pit-stop gulch at I-40 exit 279, including the *Motel 6* (☎ 501-735-0100, 800-466-8356); it has a pool and charges $37/43 a single/double.

Hotels

The landmark *Peabody Hotel* (☎ 901-529-4000, 800-932-2639) at 149 Union Ave is the most exclusive place to stay in Memphis. Rates start at $130/160 for a single/double room and climb from there (Romeo & Juliet suites range from $595 to $1000 per night, $30 per extra person). The hotel has no pool.

Another option is the *French Quarter Suites Hotel* (☎ 901-728-4000, 800-843-0353), 2144 Madison Ave, in the walkable Overton Square district – suites run from $110 (single or double) and include a breakfast buffet and airport shuttle. There is an outdoor pool.

With rates starting from $35, the tidy and small *Skyport Inn* (☎ 901-345-3220) within Memphis international airport terminal A, is a bargain and tremendously convenient for quick layovers. The hotel claims its 44 rooms are soundproof. Free guest parking is included.

PLACES TO EAT
Memphis is famous for its barbecue: pork is the meat of choice, specifically chopped pork shoulder, often served as a barbecue sandwich. You shouldn't leave Memphis without a ritual stop at the Rendezvous, Cozy Corner or Payne's. Cozy Corner owner Raymond Robinson explains the subtleties of local barbecue: 'Memphis barbecue is different than any other. Hell, in Carolina, they cut it up in chunks. Here, we either slice it, chop it or pull it, and that makes all the difference.' Advice from the owner of the Rendezvous: 'Don't go into a barbecue place unless you can see the smoke.'

See also Entertainment, below, for more places to eat.

Downtown
While the *Arcade* (☎ 901-526-5757), 540 S Main St, has served traditional Southern fare since 1919, it's recently been rehabilitated by a New Orleans chef who has added exotic dishes such as eggplant pizza to the menu. It's hard to find many places that serve breakfast downtown; in addition to the Arcade, try the *Days Inn coffee shop*, or the Peabody Hotel's *Cafe Expresso* for pastries and coffee.

Tucked in an alleyway off Union Ave across from the Peabody Hotel, the *Rendezvous* (☎ 901-523-2746) has been in operation for 30 years. It sells five tons of barbecue ribs ('wet' or 'dry') every week.

Blues City Cafe (☎ 901-526-3637), 138 Beale St, is an easy choice for a casual lunch or dinner on the strip, though it's often packed. The *Front Street Deli* (☎ 901-522-8943), 77 S Front St at Union Ave, was featured in the movie *The Firm* and makes good sandwiches; eat in or take your sandwich down to the water. A local favorite, *Huey's* (☎ 901-525-4839), 77 S 2nd St at Union Ave, is a casual pub with burgers, beer and live entertainment.

Automatic Slim's Tonga Club (☎ 901-525-7948), 83 S 2nd St, serves pan-scorched, slow-roasted and oil-drizzled entrées of yellowfin tuna, jerk duck and voodoo stew in an arty interior. Dinner is served Monday to Saturday; entrées are priced at around $15. Lunch is served weekdays for about half the price of dinner.

In an isolated industrial zone east of downtown, the *Kudzu Cafe* (☎ 901-525-4924), 603 Monroe Ave near the intersection with Marshall Ave, occupies an old brick storefront not far from Sun Studio's original location. It serves burgers, tamales and sandwiches for under $4. It occasionally hosts live bluegrass concerts. The cafe at *Sun Studio* is also a nice stop for cheap diner meals and vegetable plates; breakfast is served all day.

South of downtown, *Ellen's* (☎ 901-942-4888), 601 S Parkway E at Macmillan, serves its specialty – fried pork chops – along with soul food and barbecue in a well-worn corner joint with yellow barstools and orange and blue booths.

Midtown
Squash Blossom (☎ 901-725-4823), 1801 Union Ave west of McLean Blvd, offers wonderful natural foods and diverse exotic fare to eat-in or take-out. Organic produce, packaged kappa maki to go, herbs and vitamins are also available. The gourmet supermarket *Seessel's*, next door, also has designer groceries.

A daily slate of comfort food at *The Cupboard* (☎ 901-276-8015), in a shopping strip at 1495 Union Ave at Cleveland St, includes dishes like fried catfish filet and meatloaf with turnip greens, fried green tomatoes, corn pudding and plum cobbler for around $6.50. It's open weekdays from 11 am to 8 pm, weekends till 3 pm. Across from Methodist Hospital, *Tops* (☎ 901-725-7527), 1286 Union Ave at Claybrook St, is part of the local chain of cheap and decent barbecue joints.

In Overton Square, a drive down Madison Ave takes in all the neighborhood's offerings. *Anderton's* (☎ 901-726-4010), 1901 Madison Ave at McClean Blvd, has been a Memphis institution since 1945, serving seafood specialties. At the ship-shaped bar, pull up a captain's chair and order a cocktail.

You can eat inside or out at *Harry's on Teur* (☎ 901-725-6059), 2015 Madison Ave, a tiny old favorite for pecan-smoked sausages and 'jimbolaya,' now under new ownership. Another *Huey's* (☎ 901-726-4372), 1927 Madison Ave, serves as the neighborhood pub with occasional live music.

In the compact Cooper-Young district 4½ miles east of downtown, several restaurants, cafes and a deli are all within two blocks of the intersection of S Cooper St and Young Ave. At the corner, *Maxwell's* (☎ 901-725-1009), 948 S Cooper St, serves eclectic Mediterranean fare to an equally eclectic crowd of suits, weight-lifters and hippies. Caribbean cuisine with many fish specialties is served in a colorful, cozy storefront at *In Limbo* (☎ 901-726-4999), 926 S Cooper St. *Java Cabana* (☎ 901-272-7210), 2170 Young Ave, home of the Elvis shrine, serves regular joe along with java shakes, quiche and pie. Inquire about wedding services. It opens daily at 1 pm and closes at 11 pm or midnight. Another coffee shop, *Otherlands* (☎ 901-278-4994), 641 S Cooper, attracts an under-21 crowd.

A short drive from Cooper-Young, *Payne's* (☎ 901-272-1523), 1762 Lamar Ave at Seattle St, serves barbecue to customers in rusty pickups and old Cadillacs all day long. The infamous *Cozy Corner* (☎ 901-527-9158), 745 North Parkway near Danny Thomas Blvd (Hwy 51), in the middle of a strip mall, serves its trademark dry-rub pulled pork or barbecue Cornish game hens under multicolored fluorescent lights while the jukebox plays Aretha Franklin. It's closed Sunday and Monday.

Near Graceland

There's not much to recommend near Graceland, though the regional chain cafeterias along Elvis Presley Blvd (Hwy 51) offer a low-priced, large-selection alternative to fast food and pricey on-site Graceland eateries. Try the *Piccadilly Cafeteria* (☎ 901-346-5522), in the Southland Mall at Elvis Presley Blvd and Shelby Dr south of Graceland, or *Luby's Cafeteria* (☎ 901-398-3966), 3420 Elvis Presley Blvd north of Graceland.

ENTERTAINMENT

For entertainment listings, pick up the free *Memphis Flyer* newspaper at many outlets around town (restaurants, clubs, street corners) or the Friday and Sunday editions of the *Commercial Appeal*. Several restaurants listed above, such as Huey's, are also popular spots for live entertainment.

Beale St features live blues mostly on weekend nights, when the two-block street is closed to traffic. The scene often becomes one giant block party, with streetside stands selling giant stalks of beer. Occasional festivals (see Special Events) bring free outdoor concerts to WC Handy Park.

There's a lot of music to choose from at clubs, saloons and theaters on Beale St. Cover charges for most clubs are only a few dollars, but since you can take your drink with you on Beale, bar-hopping is part of the scene and charges add up quickly. Many folks listen from outside.

The fancy *Elvis Presley's* (☎ 901-527-9036), 126 Beale St, operates out of the King's old clothiers, Lansky's. At *BB King's* (☎ 901-524-5464, 800-443-8959), the man himself occasionally performs. Both aim for a swank, supper-club atmosphere. You can call ahead to find out who's playing and to buy tickets. Elvis Presley's also features gospel brunches on Sunday.

The city's *Center for Southern Folklore* (☎ 901-525-3655), 209 Beale St, sworn to 'preserve, defend and protect the music, culture, arts and rhythms of the South,' hosts popular local performers such as Mose 'Boogie Woogie' Vinson.

You can sit in the Elvis booth at *Western Steak House & Lounge* (☎ 901-725-9896), 1298 Madison Ave, midtown; if you're lucky you'll catch an impersonator performing.

At the *P&H Cafe* (☎ 901-726-0906), 1532 Madison Ave, matriarch Wanda Wilson, a colorful local character notorious for her costumes and drama, hosts the annual Dead Elvis Ball each August. Inquire here about sideline city or Delta blues tours given in Cadillac style. The hole-in-the-wall *Backstreet* (☎ 276-5522) at 2018 Court Ave, north of Madison at Morrison St, draws a largely gay male crowd.

The *Orpheum Theater* (☎ 901-525-7800), 203 S Main St at Beale St, a vaudeville palace built in 1928 and restored with a $5 million facelift, hosts Broadway shows and major concerts. The *Circuit Theater* (☎ 901-726-4656), 1705 Poplar Ave in Overton Square, is the city's alternative theater.

Ballet Memphis (☎ 901-763-0139), *Memphis Symphony Orchestra* (☎ 901-324-3627) and *Opera Memphis* (☎ 901-678-2706) appeal largely to the affluent East Memphis crowd, with prices and decorum to match.

A vibrant visual arts community supports and encourages young artists anchored by the Memphis College of Art in Overton Square. Look for the free quarterly *Number* for exhibit round-ups, reviews and gallery listings in town and across the region.

SPECTATOR SPORTS

The Memphis Chicks (☎ 901-278-1687) are a minor league farm team for Major League Baseball's San Diego Padres. The Chicks play at Tim McCarver Stadium, 800 Homerun Lane. The Memphis River-Kings (☎ 901-274-9009) play Central Hockey League ice hockey at the Mid-South Coliseum at Libertyland. The nationally ranked University of Memphis Tigers (☎ 901-678-2331) play basketball in the Pyramid.

The city hosts the St Jude Liberty Bowl Football Classic each year in January at the stadium at Libertyland.

THINGS TO BUY

Disappointingly, Graceland offers only a tasteful assortment of high-ticket Elvis-emblazoned mementos for sale (but check out the pink Cadillac phone and the Elvis-meets-Nixon postcards). Still, a comprehensive collection of Elvis tapes and videos is available here. An independent souvenir shop north of the visitor center sells float pens, customized nail clippers, and Elvis clocks with swinging hips.

Sun Studio has a small but select collection of souvenirs, books and records.

A Schwab's (☎ 901-523-9782) at 163 Beale St is where you'll find the oddest assortment of housewares, clothing and hardware – the mezzanine is a museum of

The Full Gospel Tabernacle & Reverend Al Green

Some of the most soulful music in town is not heard on Beale St or at any club in town. It's at the Full Gospel Tabernacle presided over by the soul artist Reverend Al Green. Reverend Green's powerful oratory is backed up by electric guitar and a formidable choir. Visitors are welcome to attend the 2½-hour Sunday service at 11 am. Etiquette tips for the uninitiated: dress neatly, place at least $1 per adult in the offering tray and don't leave early. Don't take kids who are unaccustomed to lengthy services.

To get to the church (☎ 901-396-9192), which is in Whitehaven, drive four traffic lights south of Graceland on Elvis Presley Blvd; turn right at Hale Rd and drive a half-mile west to 787 Hale Rd. ■

TENNESSEE

antique general store paraphernalia. It's closed Sunday.

Flashback (☎ 901-272-2304), 2304 Central Ave, revives art deco and 1950s style with its pristine collection of vintage clothing and colorful decor – it's a combination thrift store and museum. Shangri-la Records (☎ 901-274-1916, Net) at 1916 Madison Ave distributes its *Lowlife Guide to Memphis*; it also maintains a 1970s kitsch museum and sells books and records.

Look up *R Crumb Draws the Blues* and other animated classics at Memphis Comics (☎ 901-452-1304), 665 S Highland.

The Mall of Memphis, off I-240 at Perkins Rd exit near the airport, fulfills mundane needs and has an ice rink and cinemas.

There's a Wolf Camera on Union Ave at Willet St, midtown.

GETTING THERE & AWAY

Memphis is a hub for air and train travel and is also easily accessible by interstate freeway. You can even arrive by boat on an excursion cruise from New Orleans. See the Getting There & Away chapter for more information on flights and fares.

Air

Memphis international airport (☎ 901-922-8000) is 20 minutes southeast of downtown via I-55. It is served by Northwest, American, Delta, TWA, United, US Airways and 25 regional carriers.

KLM Royal Dutch Airlines has direct nonstop flights to Amsterdam.

See Getting Around, below, for airport transportation information.

Bus

The Greyhound (☎ 901-523-1184) route between Memphis and Nashville is served by 12 buses daily; the trip takes three to four hours and costs $30 one-way. The route between Memphis and New Orleans is served by four buses daily. The trip takes eight to 10 hours and costs $50 one-way.

The central bus station at 203 Union Ave is in a fine part of downtown next door to the Radisson Hotel and a half-block from the Peabody Hotel.

Train

An ambitious and sorely needed renovation of central station on S Main St, downtown, aims to restore the 191,000-sq-foot building to its original 1914 splendor by 1998. In addition to improving Amtrak passenger comfort and convenience, the renovated station is slated to include retail and office space. It connects with the Main St trolley (see below).

Amtrak (☎ 901-526-0052) runs a passenger service through Memphis on the *City of New Orleans* from Chicago. See the Getting There & Away chapter for details.

Car

Car-rental agencies are represented at the airport by a bank of courtesy (free) phones near baggage claim. You can call for availability and competitive rates, and each agency will send a shuttle van to take you from the airport to their office. Agencies include Alamo, Avis, Budget, Dollar, Enterprise and National, along with Rent-A-Wreck (☎ 901-525-7878), which is open weekdays only and weekends by appointment. (Note that on one recent Liberty Bowl weekend in January, many rental agencies were completely out of cars – it wouldn't hurt to reserve in advance.)

Boat

Delta Queen (☎ 800-513-5028) riverboat excursions up the Mississippi start in New Orleans and make several stops, including Memphis. See the Getting Around chapter for details.

GETTING AROUND
To/From the Airport

The airport is about 20 miles from downtown via freeways, and transportation options are limited. Taxis leave from outside baggage claim and cost $25 one-way to downtown. Many hotels provide free shuttle service for guests (so it may pay to add $50 to your lodging budget rather than spending it on a roundtrip taxi fare).

Public transit is cheap, but extremely troublesome. Catch the No 32 bus outside baggage claim (the far island, beyond where taxis and shuttles stop). The bus first heads east then stops in midtown, necessitating a transfer to a bus going downtown. Buses are infrequent. The fare is $1.10; transfers cost 10¢.

Most travelers rent cars to get to their destination. The quickest route downtown is via I-55 – but note that to travel west from the airport, you need to follow signs to I-55 north.

Bus

Bus service around metro Memphis is operated by Memphis Area Transit Authority (MATA; ☎ 901-722-7100) and follows a network of travel patterns and schedules of little use to visitors. The few bus shelters or benches (long waits standing exposed to the sun) are uncomfortable. That said, useful bus routes are the No 32 to/from the airport and the No 2 route which runs between downtown and the Cooper-Young district via the Madison Ave strip of restaurants, bars and shops in Overton Square. Fares are $1.10; transfers are 10¢.

Trolley

The Main St trolley (☎ 901-274-6282) runs vintage trolley cars from the Amtrak station on S Main St up through a pedestrian-only cobblestone strip called the Mid-America Mall; they then loop around the Pyramid and riverfront. It previously ran such a short distance that for the $40 million price tag it was considered a local joke, but its expanded service makes it a more viable form of transit for downtown destinations. The fare is 50¢ (25¢ at lunchtime).

Car & Motorcycle

The I-40 and I-55 freeways intersect in Memphis, though not all too cleanly, with junctions complicated by the bypass route I-240. In Memphis, I-40 goes north (while signs still direct you east), I-55 grazes downtown, and the bypass I-240 runs straight through midtown.

Memphis would be a nice town to blast around on a motorcycle. (See Elvis' car and motorcycle collection at Graceland to sense the town's devotion to big wheels.)

Taxi

Taxis are relatively expensive and not widespread beyond downtown, but for short, specific jaunts they can be a less costly alternative to renting a car. The fixed fare from the airport to downtown is $25; from the airport to Graceland costs $7.50. Downtown to Graceland it's $18 to $20. The standard fare is $2.90 for the first mile, $1.40 for each additional mile.

Call Checker Cab (☎ 901-577-7777) or City Wide Cab (☎ 901-324-4202).

Bicycle

Memphis is a very easy city to bicycle around. Excepting the oppressive summertime heat, conditions are generally conducive to bike touring – it's a city of manageable size with streets that are wide, flat and decently maintained, without big-city traffic or tempers. But cycling is not in the local culture and there are no bike lanes or other special provisions for riders. The phone directory lists no rentals available.

AROUND MEMPHIS

Easy excursions from Memphis are forays down Hwy 61 into the Mississippi Delta, particularly Clarksdale (see the Mississippi Delta chapter). Casinos in Tunica County, Mississippi, draw many city folk from Memphis. The lively college town of Oxford and odd attractions in Holly Springs (particularly Graceland Too) are an hour's drive away.

Those on the Elvis tour would want to check out the King's birthplace in Tupelo. For attractions and information about Tupelo, Oxford and Holly Springs, see the Northeastern Mississippi chapter.

Not far from the Mississippi border, 100 miles east of Memphis, **Shiloh National Military Park** (☎ 901-689-5275) commemorates one of the Civil War's most significant – and most bloody – battlefields. Nearly 400 soldiers are buried here in the national cemetery. The visitor center shows a film describing military strategy and distributes self-guided auto tour maps of the monuments and fields marking

TENNESSEE

troop positions. Admission is $2 per person or $4 per family.

The least time-consuming route for casual visitors would be to explore the park as a diversion from the Natchez Trace Parkway, either from northeastern Mississippi or from Nashville. To drive between Memphis and Nashville and visit the park might take two days, but is completely worthwhile for Civil War buffs or families interested in seeing the Tennessee countryside.

Nashville

Nashville (population 532,838) is a great town with friendly people, cheap food, lots of wonderful music heard for next to nothing at homey country dives, and an unrivaled assortment of tacky souvenirs. Business is booming, the streets are clean and unemployment is at an all-time low. Interestingly, whether it's because the US is moving towards the South or because the South is moving towards the rest of the country, Nashville seems more than ever like an all-American city – and one of the most guileless cities you're ever likely to visit.

As Country Music Capital of the World, Nashville (pronounced NASH-vul) carries a certain down-home glamour. Banners and billboards announce new recording stars and record releases like accolades in a high school yearbook, and streets are named after country celebrities such as Roy Acuff and Chet Atkins. City folk wear cowboy hats and read the music industry rag *Billboard* over a short stack at the Pancake Pantry.

While famous for country music, Nashville supports a sophisticated and diverse music scene – you can even hear soulful blues at tony cafes where discriminating patrons wear black and the men have ponytails. No one suffers a lousy sound system.

Northwest of the city off Briley Parkway is the huge Opryland theme park, including a modern 4400-seat home for the Grand Ole Opry. Franchises fill in the surrounding Music Valley district with motels, fast food, a KOA Kampground and relaxed nightclubs. Boats travel between Opryland and downtown to get people out on the water and to bring money and audiences to the city center, which hangs on to its honky-tonk character despite the presence of Planet Hollywood.

History
The ancient mound-builders and the wandering Shawnee of Algonquin stock occupied these Cumberland River bluffs

centuries ago. Nashville was settled by Europeans in 1779 as Fort Nashborough (the name was changed to Nashville five years later). The legendary Daniel Boone had a hand in the deal, and his Wilderness Road brought immigrants over the Appalachians from Virginia, the Carolinas and northeastern states. Nashville developed rapidly as a trade and manufacturing center; it was chartered in 1806 and named state capital in 1843.

Its vital position on the Cumberland River (linking it to the Mississippi navigation system) and at the crossroads of important rail lines made it a strategic point during the Civil War. As federal troops advanced upriver, the state legislature (which held Confederate allegiances) picked up and moved to Memphis, and within the week Nashville surrendered to Union troops. Andrew Jackson (a native Tennessean) was appointed military governor and installed Union loyalists to occupy and impose martial law on Nashville from 1862 to 1865. In 1864, as a last-ditch attempt to regain control of Nashville and cut off rail lines supplying Union General Sherman's campaign against Atlanta, Confederates attacked the occupied city. The two armies clashed in

TENNESSEE

Nashville & Around

TENNESSEE

1 Sakota-African Heritage
   Museum
2 Radio Cafe
3 Hermitage Golf Course
4 The Hermitage
5 Brown's Diner
6 Cheekwood Museum of Art
   & Botanical Gardens
7 Belle Meade
8 Green Hills Mall
9 Bluebird Cafe
10 Travelers Rest
11 Nashville Wildlife Park
   at Grassmere
12 Loveless Cafe

the bloody Battle of Nashville, and Confederate General Thomas Hood's troops were destroyed. The Union occupation was fortunate for Nashville as it saved many of the city's historic structures, a few of which are now open for tours.

The city's economic recovery after the Civil War was hampered by two major cholera epidemics that killed about a thousand people and caused thousands more to flee. The Centennial Exposition in 1897, for which the reproduction of the Greek Parthenon was built, signaled the city's eventual recovery.

Nashville's Maxwell family established the world-recognized Maxwell House coffee business here, and Teddy Roosevelt himself proclaimed it 'good to the last drop' at the Maxwell House Hotel downtown. The Maxwell estate is now a fine-arts center and botanical garden open to the public.

Eventually, Nashville became famous around the globe for the rocketing popularity of its live radio broadcast *Barn Dance* – later nicknamed the 'Grand Ole Opry' – which began in 1925. The city was quickly proclaimed the Country Music Capital of the World and recording studios and production companies established themselves along Music Row just west of downtown.

Fisk University, established in 1885, has played a distinguished role in Nashville's African-American history. The struggling black college was partially financed by the successful benefit tours by the Fisk Jubilee Singers, who popularized traditional black spirituals in the 1870s across the US and in Europe. Today, the campus boasts the first permanent building erected for the higher education of blacks in the US, Jubilee Hall. In the 1960s, Fisk students led sit-in demonstrations at lunch counters downtown, encouraged an economic boycott and marched on city hall to demand desegregated facilities. Their successful nonviolent protests served as a model for civil rights demonstrations throughout the South. Author WEB Du Bois is among its distinguished alumni.

In the 1970s, Nashville's patron Gaylord Enterprises invented the Oprylandia empire and shaped the city's country-music tourist business by moving the Grand Ole Opry, renovating the Ryman Auditorium, sending boats up and down the river and contributing to the economic revitalization of the downtown riverfront. Besides the entertainment business and the city's $2-billion-a-year tourist industry, Nashville also relies on its health-care industry and Nissan plant as economic mainstays.

Orientation

Nashville is constructed on a rise along the Cumberland River. The capitol sits at its highest point; from there a busy, compact downtown of narrow one-way streets and high-rise office buildings slopes eastward to Broadway, the city's central artery. The circle of flags at the bottom of the bluff at Riverfront Park marks the head of Broadway – avenues change from north to south at this divide. Renovation of the historic commercial buildings along 2nd Ave and Broadway has created a tourist destination out of a larger section of downtown called 'the District,' but locals don't seem to mind and continue to frequent favorite dives and rib joints clustered around Planet Hollywood and the Hard Rock Cafe.

Music Row is a commercial district south of I-40, less than a mile from downtown.

In the rest of sprawling Nashville, it's hard to pinpoint what constitutes a neighborhood, but a few are easily discernible. Elliston Place is a compact stretch of bohemian alternative culture about a mile west of downtown and north of West End Ave. South of West End Ave here is the Vanderbilt campus.

South of Vanderbilt, Hillsboro Village is an inner-city suburb on 21st Ave S south of Blakesmore (two miles north of I-440, about 1½ miles south of downtown). After this things get a bit vague.

West End is what you hear to describe the cluster of restaurants along Broadway and West End Ave on either side of the university; you might also hear 'around

TENNESSEE

GERMANTOWN

Jefferson Street Bridge

Cumberland River

Spring St N
Jefferson Street
Exit (85B)

31W
41

Spring St

Douglas Park

Downtown Nashville

0   200   400 m
0   200   400 yards

Monroe St

Madison St

▼1

Jefferson St

8th Ave N

▼2

Tennessee Bicentennial Mall

Harrison St

12
ALT 41

3 🏛

Robertson Pkwy

Gay St

Gay St

Public Square

Victory Memorial Bridge

431 41

31B

Main St

N 1st St

Woodland St

Woodland St 2nd St

N 1st St

▼4

24
65

Steps

State Capitol

5

9 ▼

Deaderick St

Union Arcade

8 🏛

10

7

6

Legislative Plaza

Charlotte Ave

7th Ave N

8th Ave N

5th Ave N

George L Davis Blvd

Printers Alley

3rd Ave N

2nd Ave N

Union St

Woodland St Bridge

11 ▼

THE DISTRICT

12

13

14 ▼

15

16

Riverfront Park

Site of Future Arena

Shelby Ave

Shelby Ave

Shelby St Bridge

Commerce St

Convention Center

17 21

20   22

19   23   24

18

Broadway

70

31

2nd Ave S

1st Ave S

3rd Ave S

4th Ave S

McGavock St

Demonbreun St

Franklin St

Howell Park

Hermitage St 24

70

⊕ 30

Church St

40

12th Ave N

25

27

26

28

29

Clark Place

Shirley St

8th Ave S

10th Ave S

7th Ave S

6th Ave S

5th Ave S

Peabody St

Lea Ave

South Park

65

40

To West End Ave

Industrial Blvd

13th Ave S

26

6

La Fayette St

Elm St

31 ▼

Division St

Fort Negley Park

65

Fort Negley Park

General Hospital

PLACES TO STAY
6   Days Inn
7   Hermitage Hotel
27 Union Station Hotel

PLACES TO EAT
1   Mad Platter
2   Farmers Market
4   Gerst Haus
6   Huddle House
11 Caffe Milano
15 Hard Rock Cafe
22 Jack's Barbecue
24 Merchants
25 Station Inn
26 Pie Wago
27 Arthur's
31 Arnold's

OTHER
3   Museum of Tobacco
     Art & History
5   Library
8   Tennessee State Museum,
     Performing Arts Center
9   Transit Mall
10 Bourbon St Blues & Boogie Bar
12 Fort Nashborough
13 River Taxis to Opryland
14 Wildhorse Saloon

16 Ace of Clubs
17 Ryman Auditorium
18 Nahville Arena,
     Visitor Center Tower
19 The Turf, Music City Club
20 Tootsie's Wild Orchid Lounge
21 Robert's Western World
23 Ernest Tubb's Record Store
25 Station Inn
28 Post Office
29 Greyhound Bus Station
30 General Hospital

TENNESSEE

Vanderbilt'. In a no man's land east of Elliston Place, Lucy's Record Store on Church St at 17th Ave N (see Entertainment) appears to be the center of a tiny struggling punk village, with a tattoo parlor, vegetarian restaurant and Pakistani market nearby.

Across the river in East Nashville, there is a funky historic area called Edgefield that has a tiny commercial strip.

Of course many tourists never set foot in downtown Nashville and confine their visit to the Opryland complex off the Briley Parkway, out by the airport. Here the prefabricated Music Valley holds a tourist ghetto of budget motels, franchise restaurants, outlet stores and a KOA Kampground.

Most folks live in the wide reaches of the suburbs, off the pikes that fan out from downtown. The southern suburb of Green Hills, easily reached off I-440 exit 3, provides easy access south to the landmark Bluebird Cafe, or north to Hillsboro Village. The city's historic house museums – the Hermitage, Cheekwood and Belle Meade – are farther out on the pikes.

Maps A good map is indispensable for navigating around the metro area because of the complex interstate interchanges. If you rent a car, ask for a complimentary map. AAA distributes maps free to members; its offices are easily found about a quarter-mile north of I-440 exit 3 at 21st Ave. Gas stations often sell comprehensive street maps. Visitor information centers distribute free maps that are less comprehensive but adequate.

Information
Tourist Offices The central visitor center is in the space-age tower adjacent to the new arena at Broadway and 5th Ave. There's also a welcome center (☎ 615-741-2158) at the airport. For tourist information online, see the Internet directory at the back of this book.

The Nashville Convention & Visitors Bureau (☎ 615-259-4730), 161 4th Ave N, Nashville, TN 37219, maintains a tourist hotline at ☎ 615-259-4700.

Money ATMs can be found throughout the metro area. Foreign money exchanges operate at the First American Bank (☎ 615-748-2941) downtown and at the airport (☎ 615-275-2660), and American Express (☎ 615-385-3535) is at 4400 Harding Rd.

Post The main post office (☎ 619-885-1005) is at 525 Royal Parkway. More convenient is the Broadway branch (☎ 619-225-9447) downtown at 901 Broadway. The Mailroom Inc (☎ 619-256-6776) at 31 Music Square W, packs and mails packages via US mail, UPS or FedEx. They will also pick up packages.

Travel Agencies AAA (☎ 615-297-7700) provides travel planning services at 2501 Hillsboro Rd. American Express also offers travel services (see Money, above).

Bookstores The greatest variety and selection is found at Davis-Kidd Booksellers (☎ 615-385-2645), 4007 Hillsboro Pike in the Green Hills shopping complex (a mile or so south of I-440 exit 3, on the right); they also have a cafe. Specializing in Southern history, Elders Books (☎ 615-327-1867), 2115 Elliston Place, is a great place to browse for old and new titles. Tower Books (☎ 615-327-8085) at 2404 West End Ave (around 24th Ave) is part of a national chain with a good selection. The Vanderbilt University Bookstore 615-423-4369, in the university's Rand Hall, is well stocked and has a wide range of titles.

Libraries The main library (☎ 615-862-5800) at 225 Polk Ave heads up 17 branch libraries throughout the city and Davidson County.

Media The *Tennessean* is the morning newspaper and the *Nashville Banner* is published weekday afternoons. The free alternative weekly *Nashville Scene* covers local entertainment and news, and is distributed at newsstands, restaurants and shops throughout the city. Also look for *No Depression*, an alternative country-music magazine.

TENNESSEE

A great variety of periodicals can be found at Mosko's newsstands (one on Elliston Place) and at Music City newsstands on Music Row and downtown at 2nd Ave N and Commerce. Ernest Tubb's record stores also have music-related publications.

Fisk University's radio station at 88.1 FM is a refreshing alternative to the many similar-sounding country stations. The local NPR affiliate is at 90.3 FM.

Country music's cable television network, the Nashville Network (TNN), bases its studios at Opryland. TNN's *Wildhorse Saloon* program is filmed at the dance hall of that name on 2nd Ave at Broadway.

Campuses West of downtown, Nashville is dominated by the huge central city campus of Vanderbilt University, including its large medical center. Fisk University has a humble campus northwest of downtown. Both universities have art collections worth checking out. Tennessee State University, George Peabody College and Belmont College are also in Nashville.

Cultural Centers The International Cultural Association of Nashville (☎ 615-361-2587) works hard to promote ethnic and cultural diversity. It hosts a festival in town each April.

The Center for Lesbian and Gay Community Services (☎ 615-297-0008) is at 703 Berry Rd.

Laundry You can find a combination laundry-pub, Harvey Washbanger Eat Drink Do Laundry (☎ 615-322-9274), at 106 29th Ave N, right off West End Ave. More laundries can be easily found on 21st Ave S, around a mile north of I-440 exit 3, not far from Hillsboro Village.

Medical & Emergency Services To contact the police call ☎ 615-862-8600. The Tennessee Highway Patrol can be reached at ☎ 615-741-2060.

Health care is a key industry in Nashville. Besides the county's General Hospital (☎ 615-862-4000) at 72 Hermitage Ave, major medical centers are operated by the Baptist Hospital and Vanderbilt University.

Planned Parenthood (☎ 615-321-7216) is at 412 DL Todd Blvd (which connects with 18th Ave N) north of Charlotte Ave and south of Fisk University.

Dangers & Annoyances Nonsmokers should note that Nashville is an extraordinarily smoker-friendly town.

THINGS TO SEE & DO

Downtown
Walking Tour Downtown Nashville is compact and pleasant to walk around. Tall office buildings and modern halls dominate without overwhelming the city's historic structures. Pay parking is easily found in lots south of Broadway. Carry quarters for parking meters and unstaffed lots.

At downtown's western end, built on the highest point above Charlotte Ave, the 1845 Greek revival **state capitol** remains the area's principal landmark. The architect William Strickland is buried in its northeast corner, and the tomb of President and Mrs James K Polk is outside on **Capitol Hill**. Steep stairs on its northern side lead down to the **farmers market** and the **Tennessee Bicentennial Mall** at downtown's back door.

Facing Charlotte Ave, the capitol overlooks stately government buildings surrounding the **Legislative Plaza**. The plaza's cherry trees bloom with white blossoms in early spring. The city-block sized **Performing Arts Center** downhill to the east also houses the **Tennessee State Museum**. The underground museum spills out onto Union St, off which you'll find the city's banks and hotels, most notably the 1910 **Hermitage Hotel** at 6th Ave N.

Union St leads east to 1st Ave N and the western end of **Riverfront Park** on the Cumberland River. The park runs between the bridges at Woodland St and Shelby Ave, providing a landscaped promenade planted with trees and busy with walkers, couples, families, and horse-drawn carriages stalling car traffic along First Ave. In the park, just south of Davis Blvd, a

Quick Country Music Primer

Country music is big business: it's the nation's most popular radio format – with 2600 stations. Record sales have quadrupled in the 1990s to $2.1 billion. Yet the sound-alike pop style that dominates radio isn't indicative of the variety of country music you can find, nor is it country music's cutting edge. In Nashville, you can hear first-hand what's new as well as a diverse range of styles. The following is the lowdown on the evolution and sub-genres of country and western music.

Bluegrass This acoustic style of country music evolved out of old-time southeastern string band music that originated in the Appalachian mountains. Bluegrass (named for the Bluegrass hills of Kentucky) makes use of the fiddle, guitar, mandolin, five-string banjo, bass and dobro guitar. Early practitioners such as Bill Monroe and his Blue Grass Boys began to define the style in the mid-1940s, leading the way for the Stanley Brothers and Flatt & Scruggs in the 1950s. Bluegrass was discovered by national audiences in the next decade's 'back-to-the-land' era and is now perpetuated at bluegrass festivals across the South and across the country. In Nashville you can hear it live at the Station Inn.

Cowboy The 'western' in country and western music comes from cowboy music originating in the American West. The first cowboy songs were the traditional occupational folksongs of cowboys on Western rangelands in the late 19th and early 20th century. In the 1920s, authentic cowboys such as Jules Verne Allen and Carl T Sprague made the first recordings of the style. The style exploded with the popularity of Western movies featuring singing cowboys in the '30s, including Gene Autry's *Singing Cowboy* in 1936. While the standard contemporary country and western spin has faded from popularity, twangy cowboy laments are being resurrected in new retro-style recordings.

Cajun The Acadians – Cajuns – emigrated from Canada to southern Louisiana in the late 18th century and brought with them their French folk-music heritage (see the Cajun Country chapter in Louisiana). Cajun folk music evolved when it was mixed with the fiddle, guitar and German accordion encountered in Louisiana. Artists began recording as early as the 1920s, but the style had little impact until 1946 when Harry Choate's hit recording 'Jole Bon' drew wider audiences. A revival in the 1980s popularized swingier Cajun zydeco music.

Western Swing Originating in the 1930s with Texan fiddler Bob Wills and fellow band-leader Milton Brown, western swing music featured a heavily bowed fiddle with guitars, electric mandolin and big band instruments. The dance music is a hybrid of south-western fiddle music, big-band swing, country and blues. Its popularity peaked in the 1940s and '50s, but the style had a resurgence in the 1970s with acts such as Asleep at the Wheel and Merle Haggard.

Honky-Tonk From the roadside saloons and dance halls of the South just prior to WWII, Ernest Tubb and Hank Williams brought drinking ballads preoccupied with broken relationships and the wilder side of life. Temporarily eclipsed by rock 'n' roll in the 1950s, the style has enjoyed a resurgence since the '60s with performers such as George Jones and Buck Owens.

Rockabilly Elvis Presley was at the forefront of this new genre with his first recordings, which combined the country music and gospel he'd grown up hearing with the blues he heard on Beale St in Memphis. Carl Perkins and Roy Orbison also wrote and recorded classic rockabilly.

Contemporary Influenced by Willie Nelson's 'outlaw' movement, Loretta Lynn and the urban-cowboy genre in the early 1980s, today's mainstream country music is dominated by Garth Brooks look-alikes and sound-alikes who suit the marketing demographics of white baby boomers outgrowing rock 'n' roll. On the flip side is the innovative retro country-punk of Nashville's BR5-49 and artists on the Dead Reckoning label; these performers are the cutting edge of the modern Nashville sound. A good sampler of alternative country is the CD *Nashville: the Other Side of the Alley* (Bloodshot Records). ■

TENNESSEE

stockade surrounds **Fort Nashborough**, a 1930s replica of the city's original outpost. Just north of Broadway, river taxis run from the dock out to Opryland, a scenic hour's ride away (see Getting Around). Across the river, just north of Shelby Ave, a new football stadium (due to open in 1999) is being built to house the relocating Houston Oilers.

The historic 2nd Ave N business area was the center of the cotton trade in the 1870s and 1880s, when most of the Victorian warehouses were built (note the cast-iron and masonry facades). Today it's the heart of the area known as the District. Modern interiors house shops, restaurants, underground saloons and nightclubs, including the Wildhorse Saloon (see Entertainment). From 2nd Ave N, walk two blocks south on Commerce St to **Printers Alley**, a narrow cobblestone lane that's been known for its nightlife since the 1940s. Here the Bourbon St Blues & Boogie Bar anchors a set of nightspots and restaurants.

A walk along Broadway from Riverfront Park leads past an old feed-and-seed at 1st Ave and Broadway, the Hard Rock Cafe, an Ernest Tubb's record outlet, the Hatch Show Print shop, several western-wear stores and Planet Hollywood. On 5th Ave N (with another entrance on 4th Ave N), the Ryman Auditorium has reopened as a performance venue. A scenic, seedy cowboy ghetto along 'Lower Broad' between 4th and 5th Aves has country bars, adult bookstores and barbecue joints behind the glamorous Ryman. Tootsie's Wild Orchid Lounge on the north side is the best known of the dives (you can charge souvenirs to American Express), and you can buy snakeskin boots and chewing tobacco between acts at Robert's Western World next door.

West of 5th Ave, the boxy **Convention Center** and the new **Nashville Arena** can be spotted on Broadway by the astro tower cone that houses a visitor center.

Ryman Auditorium Called 'the Mother Church of Country Music,' the Ryman Auditorium (☎ 615-254-1445) at 116 5th Ave N was home to Grand Ole Opry for 31 years. Riverboat captain Thomas Ryman built this huge gabled brick tabernacle in 1890 and dedicated it to spiritual music after he 'got the call'. At his death in 1904 the hall was named in his honor and made available for a wide variety of performances. The most famous became known as the Grand Ole Opry after a radio announcer introduced the Saturday night Barn Dance with 'For the past hour we have been listening to music taken largely from the Grand Opera, but from now on we will present the Grand Ole Opry.'

In 1974 the Opry was moved to the Opryland complex on Hwy 155. In 1994, after an $8.5 million renovation, the Ryman reopened as a performance venue.

The auditorium is best seen during performances, which vary. The graceful interior is evocative even when there's no show on, but admission is steep for a self-guided tour of an empty theater. Adults pay $5.50 ($2.25 for children four to 11). It's open daily from 8:30 am to 4 pm.

Tennessee State Museum Housed on three floors of the Performing Arts Center building downtown on 5th Ave N and Union St, this museum (☎ 615-741-2692) traces the state's history from the effigy pots and engraved gorgets of ancient tribes through pioneers, pillories, daguerreotypes, sabers and Confederate dollars. Exhibits document Tennessee's strong abolitionist movement that began in 1797, as well as the Ku Klux Klan. It's open Monday to Saturday from 10 am to 5 pm and Sunday from 1 to 5 pm. Admission is free.

The state's **military museum**, located in the classical War Memorial Building across 6th Ave, covers conflicts from the Spanish-American War to WWII. Admission is free.

Museum of Tobacco Art & History Well signed behind the capitol south of the farmers market, this museum (☎ 615-271-2349), 800 Harrison St, is a free advertisement

TENNESSEE

promoting the refined smoking arts. It has everything from artful glass vases and ivory snuff boxes to cigar-store Indians.

West End & Around

Music Row Music Row consists of two parts. One is the country-music strip occupying Music Square south of the Hall of Fame. This is where you'll find all the platinum-studded offices of the production companies, agents, managers and promoters that run Nashville's music industry. The other is the tourist strip on Demonbreun St (pronounced di-MUN-bree-un) south of the Hall of Fame.

Country Music Wax Museum The wax museum, 16th Ave south of McGavock, heads up a thick row of 'museums' and souvenir shops devoted to the likes of Hank Williams Jr and George Jones. Record your own songs, sing karaoke or browse around for guitar-shaped fly swatters, hillbilly outhouse toothpick holders, Elvis cookbooks, and playing cards with 52 dated photos of big-hair country-music stars. Admission is $5.50 for adults, $2 for children six to 12. There is also an Ernest Tubb record outlet and a newsstand.

Country Music Hall of Fame The lavish, devotional hall of fame is a great introduction to Nashville and to the evolution of country music. It's chock full of artifacts, including Garth Brooks' trademark hat, Gene Autry's string tie and the original handwritten lyrics to 'Mamas Don't Let Your Babies Grow Up to be Cowboys' behind glass. The *pièce de résistance* is Elvis Presley's custom Cadillac with a convertible cover that lifts up at the press of a button to reveal the gold-plated interior. The Hank Williams Jr room, beautiful Gibson guitars and vintage film clips and recordings are also highlights. Admission is $9.95 ($4.95 for children six to 11). It's open daily from 9 am to 5 pm year-round (8 am to 6 pm in the peak summer season).

A tour of **RCA Studio B**, down the street at 4 Music Square E and a trolley shuttle ride there and back are included in the price of admission. Studio B is revered in musician's circles for producing the 'Nashville sound.' The 1950s-style studio, now again in use after renovation, is touted to have launched more hit records than any other recording studio in the country. When Elvis recorded a Christmas album here in the dog days of summer, they had to truck in a tinseled tree and turn up the air-con before the session would go smoothly.

Hillsboro Village Stretching along several blocks of 21st Ave S from S Blakemore to Acklen Aves, Hillsboro Village qualifies as a neighborhood. It's home to the famed Pancake Pantry (see Places to Eat), an unassuming breakfast spot that's an industry hangout and has been the backdrop for several music videos. Rounding out the area are several upscale restaurants off Belcourt, the old Belcourt Theater (now a cinema), the refined Provence cafe and funky Fido cafe, a very odd hardware store (more like an electronic flea market) and several more practical shops.

To reach this neighborhood from downtown, turn left at the Broadway split to stay on Broadway and you'll end up here. From the freeway, take I-440 exit 3 and follow 21st Ave north a mile or so.

Centennial Park The highlight of the Centennial Exposition held here in 1897 was the full-scale plaster reproduction of the Greek **Parthenon**, which still stands today. Inside is a giant 42-foot statue of the Greek goddess Athena. Admission is $2.50 ($1.25 for seniors and children). Mythology books, busts and pop-up Parthenons are available in the subterranean gift shop.

Centennial Park is the city's most popular spot for urban recreation; it's off West End Ave.

University Galleries Between Hillsboro Village and Elliston Place, Vanderbilt University maintains a fine arts gallery (☎ 615-322-0605) on campus at 23rd and West

PLACES TO STAY
12 Quality Inn

PLACES TO EAT
6 Owl's Nest
7 Mosko's
8 Red Hot & Blue
10 Elliston Place Soda Shop
16 Noshville
18 Bound'ry
20 Pancake Pantry
21 Sunset Grill
22 Bongo Java, Fido's

OTHER
1 Van Vechten Gallery
2 Baptist Hospital
3 Lucy's Record Store
4 Country Music Wax Museum
5 Ernest Tubb's Record Store
7 Exit/In
9 Elders Books
11 Country Music Hall of Fame
13 Harvey Washbanger Eat Drink
    Do Laundry
14 Tower Records & Books
15 Fine Arts Gallery
17 Great Escape
19 RCA Studio B
23 Belmont Mansion

Jefferson St

Meharry Medical College

Fisk University

Watkins Park

Jackson St

Herman St

Charlotte Ave

Patterson St

State St

Church St

Hayes St

West End Ave

ELLISTON PLACE

Parthenon

Centennial Park

Vanderbilt University

West End Ave

Scarritt College

George Peabody College

Edgehill Ave

Horton St

Music Row

Music Circle N

Music Circle S

Grand Ave

To Downtown

Broadway

McGavock

Demonbreun

Division St

Chet Atkins Pl

South St

To Cheekwood Museum of Art & Botanical Gardens

West End & Around

0   200   400 m
0   200   400 yards

S Blakemore Ave

Belcourt Ave

Acklen Ave

HILLSBORO VILLAGE

Wedgewood Ave

To I-440, Green Hills

Belmont College

TENNESSEE

End Aves. It's free and open afternoons only.

The small **Van Vechten Gallery** (☎ 615-329-8720), at the corner of DB Todd Blvd and Jackson St at Fisk University (see West End & Around map), houses more than 100 paintings collected by Alfred Stieglitz and donated by his widow, Georgia O'Keeffe. O'Keeffe's work is displayed along with paintings by Picasso, Renoir and Cezanne. Admission is free, but donations are encouraged. It's closed Mondays and university holidays.

While you're here, visit Fisk's African art collection in the **Aaron Douglas Gallery** on campus. Visitors might also want to see Jubilee Hall on Meharry Blvd.

Music Valley

The **Opryland Hotel** heads up this suburban tourist zone about 10 miles downriver from downtown Nashville. It is accessible via Hwy 155 (Briley Parkway) exit 12B. Some tourists never leave this self-contained nucleus of hokey attractions, franchise motels, fast food and outlet stores. The Opryland Hotel is a sight in itself and shouldn't be missed (see Places to Stay). It costs $5 to park at the hotel; no street parking is available without a long walk.

The **Music Valley Car Museum** (☎ 615-885-7400), 2611 McGavock Pike, displays the 1981 DeLorean owned by George Jones; Elvis' limo; and a Cadillac that once belonged to Dolly Parton. **Music City Wax Museum** (☎ 615-883-3612), 2515 McGavock Pike, features 50 wax statues of country stars in original costumes. Its Sidewalk of the Stars features the handprints, footprints and signatures of 250 stars. The **Willie Nelson Museum** (☎ 615-885-1515), 2613A McGavock Pike, features the artist's gold and platinum records and guitars. Each of the museums charges $3.50 ($1.50 for children six to 12).

The Opryland Hotel operates shuttle buses which run between the hotel, Opryland USA and the KOA Kampground at the far end of Music Valley Dr; drivers will generally drop you at any destination in

between. The fare is $3.50 roundtrip for adults. Buses leave every 20 to 30 minutes, but schedules are uncertain. If you're in Music Valley and have a boat to catch from an Opryland USA dock, you may be better off walking back rather than depending on the shuttle bus. If your car is parked at the $5 Opryland USA parking lot, you may not want to move your car and face another $5 parking fee at the Opryland Hotel. The paved, all-access, well-lit path between Opryland USA and the Opryland Hotel is under a mile.

The giant **Opryland USA theme park** (☎ 619-889-1000) and the adjacent Grand Ole Opry House (☎ 619-889-3060), 10 miles from downtown off Hwy 155 (Briley Parkway) exit 11, are Nashville's best-known attractions. The country-music-themed park features 24 rides, including roller coasters. It frequently hosts concerts by nationally recognized country-music artists. Several restaurants and cafeterias provides meals. It's all squeaky clean fun for families and ardent country-music fans. Admission is $29 ($19 for children four to 11). The theme park is open only from April to October and from Thanksgiving to New Year's Day.

The **Grand Old Opry House** seats 4400 when it hosts the Grand Ole Opry show, which moved to these digs in 1974 from its home in the Ryman Auditorium. Performances are held on Friday and Saturday nights year-round (see Entertainment). Guided tours backstage are offered once a day by reservation for around $8.

Several museums across the plaza from the Grand Old Opry House are open year-round without an admission charge (beyond the parking fee). The Grand Ole Opry Museum tells the story of the Opry with wax characters in colorful costumes – don't miss Patsy Cline's classic 1950s rec room diorama. The Minnie Pearl Museum and Roy Acuff Museum are housed in a mock-Victorian village nearby. (Souvenirs include replicas of Minnie Pearl's famous $1.98 hat for $3.95.)

The CBS-owned Nashville Network (TNN, ☎ 615-883-7000) broadcasts from

TENNESSEE

studios at Opryland USA. Visitors can see a live taping of the 'Prime Time Country' show for free. Reserve tickets in advance.

River taxis run along the Cumberland River between downtown Nashville and the Opryland USA dock (see Getting Around). Paddleboat rides are available aboard the four-deck *General Jackson* (☎ 615-889-6611) for around $32 to $55 ($21 to $43 for children), depending on whether it's a lunch or dinner cruise.

For all the above attractions, drivers are charged $5 per car to park; there is no street parking. A day-use pet kennel is available for $1.

The Hermitage

The historic home of Andrew Jackson, the Hermitage (☎ 615-889-2941), is northeast of town off Lebanon Pike at Old Hickory Blvd. Not only is the graceful mansion one of Nashville's prized historic house museums, but the Hermitage serves as a monument to the state's most famous political figure. Starting his national political career as Tennessee's single representative even before Tennessee had officially gained statehood, Jackson went on to become the seventh US president. The modern visitor center introduces the life of Andrew Jackson with a short film.

The 1821 mansion was built in Federal style and Grecian columns were added in the 1830s. It is nicely set among gardens. The big house was once the center of a self-sufficient cotton plantation of 1500 acres worked by 150 slaves.

Admission is $8 ($7 for seniors, $4 for children six to 12, under six free). Special events held here include a jazz and blues concert series from May to August (see Special Events). Also on the premises, a cafeteria serves an appealing buffet for around $6.

Other Antebellum Houses

In addition to the Hermitage, three other antebellum houses are open to the public.

The **Belle Meade Plantation** (☎ 615-356-0501), 5025 Harding Place, is an 1853 Greek revival mansion that was once the centerpiece of a 5300-acre plantation and thoroughbred stud farm. Admission is $7 ($2 for children six to 12, under six free).

The **Belmont Mansion** (☎ 615-460-5459), 1900 Belmont Blvd, dates from 1850. The villa was built as a summer home for Adelicia Acklen, who was one of the wealthiest women in America at the time. Admission is $6 ($2 for children six to 12, under six free).

Travelers Rest (☎ 615-832-8197), 636 Farrell Parkway (I-65 Harding Place exit), restores the plantation home and

Music Valley

1 KOA Kampground
2 Fiddlers Inn North
3 Music Valley Wax Museum
4 Willie Nelson Museum
5 Music Valley Car Museum
6 Ernest Tubb's Record Store
7 Grand Ole Opry House
8 Opryland USA
9 *General Jackson* Dock
10 River Taxis

outbuildings constructed as early as 1799 by Andrew Jackson's presidential campaign manager. Admission is $5 ($3 for children six to 11); it's closed on Monday.

Sakofa-African Heritage Museum
This museum (☎ 615-726-4894) opened in 1997 to showcase African art, sculpture and artifacts dating from 1441. Admission is $5 ($3 for seniors, free for children under 11). The museum is located at 101 French Landing; take I-265 Metrocenter exit, go north four blocks and turn left.

Cheekwood Museum of Art & Botanical Gardens
The grand 1920s mansion of the Cheek family, heirs to the Maxwell House coffee fortune, is open to the public as a fine-arts museum and botanical garden. The three-story neo-Georgian home is a work itself – its lapis lazuli mantel is a highlight. Exhibits range from Worcester porcelain to Warhol and include stone carvings by local self-taught artist Will Edmondson (1883-1951), the first African American with a solo show at New York's Museum of Modern Art.

The lovely 55-acre gardens host classical concerts by Vanderbilt musicians in summer. An outdoor sculpture trail is planned.

Cheekwood (☎ 615-356-8000) is at 1200 Forest Park Drive; drive south from downtown on West End Ave and follow the signs. Admission is $6 ($5 for seniors and students, $3 for children, under six free). It's open daily. A refined restaurant in a modern outbuilding overlooks the wooded grounds.

Nashville Wildlife Park at Grassmere
The Nashville Wildlife Park (☎ 615-833-1534) is at 3777 Nolensville Pike, one mile from I-65 and two miles from I-24. It's a 'walk-through' park where visitors can spot cougars, black bears and gray wolves. Admission is $6 ($4 for seniors and for children three to 12). Parking is an additional $2. It's open daily spring to fall from 9 am to 6 pm and in winter from 10 am to 5 pm.

Patsy Cline

Nashville Zoo
The Nashville Zoo (☎ 615-370-3333) is north of Nashville in Joelton at 1710 Ridge Rd Circle, off I-24 W exit 31. The zoo houses leopards, lions, white tigers and red pandas, but as a habitat it's seen better days. It's scheduled to move into the wildlife park property at Grassmere in 2001. Admission is $6 ($4 for seniors and for children three to 12). Parking is an additional $2. It's open year-round.

Parks & Activities
Six miles of easy to moderate hiking trails are located in the 1000-acre **Radnor Lake State Natural Area** (☎ 615-373-3467). It's nestled in the steep Overton Hills six miles south of downtown (directly west of I-65). The scenic sanctuary surrounding the 85-acre lake is considered Nashville's Walden Pond.

Parkland largely surrounds **J Percy Priest Reservoir**, 10 miles east of downtown. The district manager's office (☎ 615-889-1975), on the north shore west of the dam on Bell Rd (easily accessible from

TENNESSEE

I-40 exit 221, Old Hickory Blvd), distributes maps of a dozen recreation areas around the lake. There are campsites and the lake is perfect for swimming and fishing (fishing licenses are required for anyone over 12).

All around the dam, the **Hermitage Recreation Area** is developed as a resort; you can rent boats (☎ 615-399-7661) or sailboats (☎ 615-883-0413). For camping and cabins see Places to Stay.

Adjacent to Hwy 100 to the south, **Percy Warner Park** and **Edwin Warner Park** offer hiking and golfing (☎ 615-352-9958) in the wooded hills. They're close to the landmark Loveless Cafe and the northern terminus of the Natchez Trace Parkway. The Natchez Trace itself is one of the most popular bicycle touring routes in the US (see Around Nashville).

Golfing is extremely popular and there are dozens of courses in the area. Recording moguls often play the Hermitage Golf Course (☎ 615-847-4001), 3939 Old Hickory Blvd.

A mile south of Opryland, east of Hwy 155, the **Wave Country** (☎ 615-885-1052) water park offers a wave pool, slides and floats. It's open in summer only. Admission is $5 ($4 for children, four and under free). Admission is half-price after 4 pm.

In town, the Centennial Park Sportsplex (☎ 615-862-8490), off West End Ave, offers a swimming pool, tennis courts and an ice skating rink.

Vertical Inline (☎ 615-327-3696), 2318 West End Ave, rents in-line skates and is open daily. Cumberland Transit (☎ 615-327-4093), 2807 West End Ave, rents bicycles and in-line skates; it's closed Sunday.

SPECIAL EVENTS

January

A commemoration of the Battle of New Orleans takes place at the Hermitage on January 8, with a ceremony at Andrew Jackson's tomb.

February

Mid-month a musical extravaganza highlights new and emerging talent at various venues around town.

March

The *Music City Blues Celebration* is held downtown in early March; admission is charged. On *Andrew Jackson's Birthday*, March 15, the Hermitage hosts a wreath-laying ceremony.

April

In mid-April the annual *Tin Pan South* music festival showcases songwriters; it's held at the Ryman and other venues.

May

Each Thursday evening from May to September the city hosts free concerts at Riverfront Park. In early May, the *Tennessee Crafts Fair* brings more than 150 artisans to Centennial Park. A rite of spring for the horsey set, the *Iroquois Steeplechase* features races and picnics in early May at Percy Warner Park. From late May to mid-August, the *Tennessee Jazz & Blues* concert series is held on the grounds of Belle Meade Plantation and the Hermitage. On Memorial Day weekend, Opryland hosts the *Gospel Jubilee*; admission is charged. In late May, *Summer Lights in Music City* is a downtown outdoor festival of arts, music, dance and theater.

June

In mid-June the *American Artisan Festival* at Centennial Park brings craftspeople from 35 states to display their wares. The *Celtic Music & Summer Solstice Celebration* revels in Scottish and Irish music, dance and culture at Travelers Rest, generally on Father's Day. The *TNN Country Music Awards* (the 'People's Choice' of country music) bring national stars to Opryland mid-month; a steep admission is charged. The *International Country Music Fan Fair* at the fairgrounds and at Opryland draws 24,000 fans to more than 35 hours of concerts by 100 artists mid-month. In late June, Chet Atkins hosts *Musician Days* concerts to celebrate the session musician.

July

On July 4 the *Independence Day* celebration at Riverfront Park is a family event with food and fireworks (no alcohol). In mid-July, Cheekwood's *Little Spoleto* festival has dance, music and children's activities; admission is charged.

August

In mid-August the *Music City Pig Fest* at the National Guard Armory features a barbecue cook-off, Tennessee winetasting, hog-calling and pony rides.

September

In early September the *Civil War Encampment* at Travelers Rest re-enacts Union occupation; admission is charged. The *Tennessee State Fair* brings livestock, midway rides and arts and crafts to the fairgrounds; admission is charged. In late September, the *African Street Festival* at the Tennessee State University campus features poetry, rap, reggae, blues, jazz and gospel music along with ethnic foods and fashions. The *Italian Street Fair* is a big block-party fundraiser for the symphony. Opryland hosts another *Gospel Jubilee*.

October

In mid-October an *Oktoberfest* is held in the tiny Germantown historic district. A mid-month *storytelling festival* at the Hermitage relates traditional and contemporary Southern, African and Native American stories. In late October a *Pow Wow* at the Hermitage Landing Recreation Area brings Native Americans from many different nations together for traditional dances and cultural arts.

November

Starting in late November, *Christmas* celebrations are scheduled at the Opryland Hotel, Belle Meade and the Belmont Mansion – most run through early January.

December

In early December, the *Christmas Parade* enlivens downtown. Also in early December, *Trees of Cheekwood* showcases elaborately designed Christmas trees.

PLACES TO STAY

The most distinctive lodgings in Nashville are high end, including the Opryland Hotel and historic hotels downtown. There are also a handful of deluxe hotels downtown and out in West End.

Camping & Cabins

The *Opryland KOA Kampground* (☎ 615-889-6611, 800-562-7789), 2626 Music Valley Dr, occupies 27 acres at the tail end of the commercial strip between the river and highway north of Opryland (shuttles run for $3.50). The campground actually trails off into woods, providing some spacious shady sites. It has 25 cabins, country-music shows, a swimming pool and weekly church services. Full hookup sites cost $33 per night ($20 for tents); kids stay free.

The Army Corps of Engineers maintains several campgrounds around J Percy Priest Lake about 12 miles east of downtown. *Seven Points* (☎ 615-889-5198), off I-40 exit 221, Old Hickory Blvd, offers swimming and is open from April to November; sites cost $16 to $20 with or without hookups (premium for lakeside sites).

Hermitage Landing (☎ 615-889-7050), off the same exit, has 147 campsites in its extensively developed private resort and recreation area. Camping is $20. It also rents out 20 cabins that each sleep six for around $70 a night; these are available May to Labor Day.

Motels

There's a cluster of budget motels and fast-food joints north of downtown west of I-65 exit 87B. Note that I-65 between here and downtown is often congested.

Two low-end, well-tended options that serve a minimal continental breakfast are the 150-room *Knights Inn* (☎ 615-226-4500, 800-843-5644), 1360 Brick Church Pike, offering singles/doubles for around $28/38, and the *Hallmark Inn* (☎ 615-228-2624), 309 W Trinity Lane, with rooms for $25/38. Next door, the new *Motel 6* (☎ 615-227-9696), 311 W Trinity Lane, has a pool and overlooks a pawn shop; it charges $28/32.

The *Downtown Days Inn* (☎ 615-329-7466), 711 Union St, charges $60/66 for rooms near the capitol and above the 24-hour Huddle House cafe. You could walk all over downtown from here.

On Music Row, the *Quality Inn* (☎ 615-242-1631) at 1407 Division St charges $49/59 for rooms next to the Country Music Hall of Fame. If you stay here you could get by without a car, traveling on foot and by taxi. Perhaps its greatest asset is its country lounge featuring the LeGarde Twins.

Motels in the Music Valley tourist ghetto around Opryland are designed primarily for families visiting the theme park. When the park is open (April to September) they're more expensive than similar facilities elsewhere, but they're heavily discounted in the off-season. At the low end, with a pool, *Fiddlers Inn North* (☎ 615-885-1440), 2410 Music Valley Dr, charges around $32/37 a single/double in the off-season, $60/70 at other times.

Motels near the airport are convenient for through-travelers but too far from the city center to conveniently visit Nashville. Among the cheaper options is the *Red Carpet Inn* (☎ 615-228-3487), 1902 Dickerson Rd; rates are $28/33 off-season, $38/43 at other times.

Hotels

The gargantuan *Opryland Hotel* (☎ 615-889-1000), 2800 Opryland Dr, looks like a sentimentally designed space colony – 'a cross between a Victorian hothouse and a shopping mall' according to author Bill Bryson. Covering nine acres, the self-contained Opry-sphere features cascading waterfalls, boat rides, magnolia trees three stories tall and elevated walkways above the rainforest canopy. For most of its guests, it's Eden – the hotel's wedding consultants have their own telephone exchange. Rates start at around $209. Parking costs $5. It's under a mile to the theme park and the river taxi dock; shuttles are available for $3.50 roundtrip.

The *Union Station Hotel* (☎ 615-726-1001, 800-331-2123), 1001 Broadway, was built in 1900 and grandly restored in 1986. It's a limestone fortress with castley buttresses, and its exclusive restaurant is one of the city's best. Rooms start at $139 a single or double. It's centrally located if you're getting around by car, but too isolated for walking.

The elegant *Hermitage Suites Hotel* (☎ 615-244-3121, 800-251-1908), 231 6th Ave N, has housed the power brokers doing business downhill from the capitol since the 1920s (it underwent restoration in 1995). The suites start at $149. Even if you don't stay overnight, let the uniformed Beefeater show you into the lobby bar. You can walk all over downtown from here.

PLACES TO EAT

The farmers market, along 8th Ave N at Jefferson St, has the greatest variety of cheap food in one spot. Though the market here behind Capitol Hill dates back 30 years, it now occupies a swank modern building with lots of air and light next to a wide lawn. Ethnic markets sell exotic goods such as jackfruit, curries, tomatillos and pickled okra, along with fresh produce. Food stands offer gyros, empanadas, muffulettas, Reubens and more. A branch of the popular local *Swett's* cafeteria serves meat-and-three plates for under $5.

The *Mad Platter* (☎ 615-242-2563) at 1239 6th Ave N two blocks north of the farmers market at Monroe St, is tucked away in the tiny Germantown historic district of colorful Victorians and brick walkways, an inviting respite from the congestion on the other side of the hill. It serves an upscale eclectic menu; grilled salmon with artichoke pesto is $21.50.

For upscale dining in downtown proper, the classic *Merchants* (☎ 615-254-1892), 401 Broadway, overlooks the lower Broad scene from the dark wooden central bar and window tables all around. For trendier elegance, *Caffe Milano* (☎ 615-255-0073), 174 3rd Ave N, attracts sophisticates. In Union Station, *Arthur's* (☎ 615-255-1494), 1001 Broadway, serves $55 fixed-price dinners to the *Town & Country* set.

The true taste of Nashville can be best found in cinder-block cabins in the industrial zone south of Broadway. Meat-and-three spots spoon out heaping portions of mashed potatoes and gravy, turnip greens and cornbread dressing along with your choice of daily specials such as roast beef, fried whole catfish, meatloaf or fried oysters for around $5. Look for the line outside *Arnold's* (☎ 615-256-4455), 605 8th Ave S at Division, or the *Pie Wagon* (☎ 615-256-5893), 118 12th Ave S at Demonbreun – both are open weekdays only for breakfast and lunch. *Jack's Barbecue* (☎ 615-254-5715), 334A Broadway, dishes out hole-in-the-wall 'cue. Try the turkey plate.

The *Elliston Place Soda Shop* (☎ 615-327-1090), 2111 Elliston Place, serves soda fountain treats along with meat-and-three plates; it's open 6 am to 7:45 pm daily except Sunday. You can find table-service barbecue at *Red Hot & Blue* (☎ 615-321-0350), 2212 Elliston Place; at *Mosko's* (☎ 615-327-3562), 2204 Elliston Place; and at the *Owl's Nest* coffeehouse (☎ 615-321-2771), 205 22nd Ave N.

Farther west the bungalow Sylvan Park neighborhood tucks away the *Sylvan Park Restaurant* (☎ 615-292-9275) at 4502 Murphy Rd. There is another branch downtown at 221 6th Ave N.

A cluster of restaurants on Broadway beyond the West End split includes the *Bound'ry* (☎ 615-321-3043), 911 20th Ave S, with a nouveau South menu that features Memphis manicotti and Southern Thai chicken. Open for breakfast, lunch and dinner, *Noshville* (☎ 615-329-6675), 1918 Broadway, offers New York deli specialties (lox, borscht, pickles) to eat in its crisp chrome interior or take out.

In Hillsboro Village, anchoring the neighborhood and the city's culinary scene, is the classic *Pancake Pantry* (☎ 615-383-9333), 1796 21st Ave S (look for the line down Belcourt Ave). Silver dollars, Georgia peach pancakes and blintzes are among the dozens of variations that arrive steaming and dusted with powdered sugar.

You can order up Fruit Loops and Pez at *Fido's* (☎ 615-385-7959), 1812 21st Ave S, a Bongo Java affiliate housed in the old Jones Pet Shop. The world-famous 'NunBun' – a cinnamon roll that bears the likeness of Mother Theresa – is shellacked at its sister *Bongo Java* store (☎ 615-385-5282), 2007 Belcourt Blvd.

Nearby, *Sunset Grill* (☎ 615-486-3663), 2001 Belcourt Ave, is an industry hangout (dubbed 'Nashville's Spago') with tall menus describing phyllo and gorgonzola-encrusted entrées with complete nutritional labeling and an annotated wine list.

Johnny Cash – the Man in Black

Continue south on 21st Ave a half-mile beyond Hillsboro Village to *Brown's Diner* (☎ 615-269-5509), 2102 Blair Blvd at 21st Ave S, for burgers in what appears to be a long-abandoned train car.

ENTERTAINMENT
Many talented country, folk, bluegrass, Southern rock and blues musicians and songwriters play smoky honky-tonks, blues bars, seedy storefronts and organic cafes for tips. Also, see who's playing in the Ryman Auditorium. The *Tennessean* has entertainment listings in Friday and Sunday editions; the *Nashville Banner* has entertainment listings in Thursday's edition. The free alternative weekly *Nashville Scene* covers local entertainment and is distributed throughout the city.

For high production values (and prices to match), the Gaylord Opry conglomerate delivers the traditional *Grand Ole Opry* (☎ 615-889-6611) at Opryland USA year-round on Friday and Saturday evenings for around $17 a seat, with discounts in the

TENNESSEE

upper balcony. They also present 'New Country' dance music at the *Wildhorse Saloon* on 2nd Ave at Broadway; there is a $6 cover charge on weekends.

The 'lower Broad' cowboy gulch on Broadway between 4th and 5th Aves has five clubs that range from respectable to low-down. The crown jewel is *Robert's Western World* (☎ 615-256-7937), 416 Broadway; in fact, it's the only place you need to go. The club, with its long wooden bar and vinyl booths, has been carved out of an old western-wear clothing store. The walls are lined with cowboy boots in exotic leathers and colors.

In *Tootsie's Wild Orchid Lounge* (☎ 615-726-7937), 422 Broadway, lower Broad's most venerated dive, customers have carved their names and initials onto nearly every inch of wall – and a great deal of vinyl too. Cowboys perform upstairs and down and, as it gets later, often out into the street as well. Hold onto your drinks when the band plays 'Rocky Top, Tennessee.'

Across the street, *The Turf* and *Music City Club* are more hard-core, neighboring the adult bookstore, and home to winos all day long.

The classic venue for bluegrass is the *Station Inn* (☎ 615-255-3307) over the hill at

402 12th Ave N. Robert's has plans to open the place next door as the Bluegrass Inn.

Caffe Milano (☎ 615-255-0073), 174 3rd Ave N, is a fancy supper club for big-name performers who want an intimate crowd. Chet Atkins is a regular here and it's also played host to Peter Frampton, Mary Chapin Carpenter, Yo-Yo Ma, Johnny Cash and Emmylou Harris.

The classic down-home place to hear some of the city's most talented musicians is the small, unassuming *Bluebird Cafe* (☎ 615-383-1461), 4104 Hillsboro Rd, in a strip shopping mall in suburban Green Hills (2½ miles south of I-440 exit 3). Singer-songwriters who sell off their commercial hits to big names save their heartfelt, soulful pieces for performances here. There are often two shows on weekend nights; the early show is often free, while there's a cover charge for the later one.

The *Radio Cafe* (☎ 615-262-1766), 1313 Woodland St at N 14th St (two miles east of downtown), 1¼ miles from the I-65 overpass), is a small club that hosts surprisingly good live entertainment nightly (closed Sunday).

Rock and alternative music is played at the *Ace of Clubs* (☎ 615-254-2237), 114 2nd Ave S, a popular dance club downtown on the other side of Broadway, and at *Exit/In* (☎ 615-321-4400) on Elliston Place north of 23rd Ave N.

Lucy's Record Store (☎ 615-321-0882), 1707 Church St, admits all ages to shows in the back of its storefront. Its motto reads 'no racist, sexist, or homophobic shit tolerated.'

The *Lava Lounge* (☎ 615-329-3666), 1719 West End Ave, features swing dancing.

Bourbon St Blues & Boogie Bar (☎ 615-242-5837), 220 Printers Alley, is the city's premier blues venue.

On Saturday and Sunday nights at the *Gerst Haus* (☎ 615-256-9760), 228 Woodland St at 1st St N (across the river at I-65 exit 85), you can munch on Wiener schnitzel while listening to accordion music performed by a fellow in lederhosen with faces painted on his knees.

BR5-49

As the big red boot sign outside declares, Robert's Western World is the home of BR5-49, Nashville's retro-country group that is forging new ground for old country. Named after a phone number on a skit from the old TV show *Hee Haw*, BR5-49 features Gary Bennett and Chuck Mead as lead vocalists and guitarists, Don Herron on steel guitar, mandolin, dobro guitar and fiddle, Smilin' Jay McDowell on bass and Hank Wilson on drums. The group performs wearing string ties, neckerchiefs and shirts that snap shut. Their CD *Live at Robert's* includes their 'Hillbilly Thang' and an X-rated anthem for a lost *Andy Griffith Show* episode. ∎

TENNESSEE

The massive *Tennessee Performing Arts Center* downtown (☎ 615-242-6460) hosts larger Broadway-type shows.

Vanderbilt University's *Blair School of Music* (☎ 615-322-7651) is renowned for its concerts.

SPECTATOR SPORTS
The Nashville Kats (☎ 615-254-5287) play arena football at the new Nashville Arena. The Houston Oilers – with a new name yet to be determined – are expected to relocate in 1999 to Nashville's new stadium on the other side of the river, across from Riverfront Park. The Nashville Nighthawks (☎ 615-259-7825) play NHL professional hockey at the Municipal Auditorium. The Nashville Sounds (☎ 615-242-4371) play at Greer Stadium; they're a AAA minor-league team for baseball's Chicago White Sox.

Nashville Speedway USA (☎ 615-726-1818) auto races run at the Tennessee State Fairgrounds.

THINGS TO BUY
Besides the sequined denim vests, American flag ties and garters emblazoned with Jack Daniels insignia that you can find at Music Row, western wear is sold all over town. The nightclub Robert's Western World still sells boots. A select collection of vintage western wear is sold at Ranch Dressing (☎ 615-259-4863), 17th Ave S at Broadway.

Shop for records, along with comic books and video games, at Great Escape (☎ 615-327-0646), 1925 Broadway at Division St, or at Ernest Tubb's (☎ 615-255-7503), 417 Broadway. Tubb also has outlets on Music Row and in Music Valley.

Fusion (☎ 615-227-0200), 1022 Woodland St, is a neat weird vintage decor shop in the Edgefield neighborhood a mile east of the I-65 overpass (on the way to the Radio Cafe).

A variety of things, including cheap socks ($2 per bundle), watches, swap-meet sunglasses, low-grade and low-cost clothes and linens, is sold at the farmers market on 8th Ave N at Jefferson.

GETTING THERE & AWAY
Air
Nine major carriers operate out of Nashville international airport (eight miles east of downtown off I-40), including American, Continental, Delta, Northwest, Southwest and United. Not a major hub, Nashville can be more expensive to fly into than neighboring Memphis.

Continental, Northwest and Delta have roundtrip flights to New Orleans for as low as $100, though $200 is the average fare. Delta and United have roundtrip fares to Atlanta for around $200.

Bus
Greyhound operates a busy station at 200 8th Ave S, between Demonbreun St and Clark Place (a two-block walk to Broadway).

Greyhound serves Memphis ($30/57 one-way/roundtrip, eight buses daily, four hours), Atlanta ($41/79, eight buses, six hours), Birmingham ($25/50, seven buses, 4 hours) and New Orleans ($42/82, nine buses, 12 to 15 hours).

Car
Major car-rental companies are represented at the airport; their courtesy phones are near baggage claim.

The most scenic way to approach Nashville is along the Natchez Trace Parkway, which begins in Natchez, Mississippi, and terminates just south of Nashville off Hwy 100; see Nashville Excursions.

GETTING AROUND
Downtown is easily manageable on foot, and a river taxi is the best way to get from there to Opryland. But for most other attractions and districts, it's easiest to get around by car. Bicycling is possible – the streets are wide and flat, and drivers are courteous – but bikes are a rare sight in town. See Activities for bike and in-line skate rentals.

To/From the Airport
MTA bus No 18 connects the airport and the downtown transit mall (Shelter C) for

TENNESSEE

$1.35. It runs roughly every hour on weekdays, but has only four departures daily on weekends. Call ☎ 615-862-5950 for exact schedules.

Many hotels have complimentary shuttles for airport service; use courtesy phones near baggage claim and wait at the island outside.

Gray Line (☎ 615-275-1180, 800-669-9463) operates an airport express to major downtown and West End hotels for $9/15 one-way/roundtrip. Buy a ticket at the Gray Line counter one floor below baggage claim.

A cab fare is $14 to $17 to downtown, plus 50¢ for each additional passenger.

Car rental is available at the airport, see above.

Bus

The Metropolitan Transit Authority (MTA; ☎ 615-862-5950) operates city bus service. The fare is $1.35; exact change is required. Besides the No 18 airport route (see above), another useful route is No 3 West End, which runs frequently from downtown out to Cheekwood and Percy Warner Park.

All routes originate and terminate at the transit mall downtown at Deaderick and 4th Ave N, a block and a half from the capitol.

Trolley

MTA also operates a trolley-like shuttle between major tourist sites at the riverfront and out to Music Row. The fare is 95¢ (dollar bills accepted, no change given). In the summer season, trolleys pass every 12 minutes or so.

Taxi

Call Allied Taxi (☎ 615-244-7433) or Music City Taxi (☎ 615-262-0451, 800-359-9692). Fares start at $1.50; add $1.50 for each additional mile.

Car

In town, city streets are wide and drivers are generally courteous. Downtown is tricky to navigate with all the narrow one-way streets; it's best to park the car in a lot south of Broadway or a garage north of

Broadway and wander around on foot. The I-40 Broadway exit is the most direct route downtown – from I-65 take the Woodland St exit.

The three interstate freeways around Nashville – I-40, I-65 and I-24 – combined with bypass routes I-440 and I-265 and the Briley Parkway, create a complicated maze of intersections. While this provides ready access to much of Nashville, it's difficult for newcomers to navigate. Note particularly that directions may be given to cities that are unfamiliar and irrelevant to your metro route (to Birmingham or Chattanooga, Memphis or Paducah), that freeways split off abruptly, and that heavy 18-wheeler traffic can block vital signs and increase anxiety on the curved highways. Map out your route carefully to avoid wrong turns.

River Taxi

Opryland USA operates river taxi service (☎ 615-889-6611) along the Cumberland River between downtown and the Opryland theme park aboard two 57-foot passenger boats for $12 roundtrip ($9 for children four to 11). Tickets may be purchased at Opryland ticket booths, at the Ryman Auditorium, or by phone. Schedules vary by season and according to the weather. Boats dock downtown south of Fort Nashborough at Riverfront Park and at Opryland USA.

Considering how vital rivers have been to the development of Southern cities, this is one of the few opportunities to travel one. This is also a peaceful alternative to congested freeway traffic.

AROUND NASHVILLE

Surrounding Nashville beyond the broad suburban development are middle-Tennessee's forested hills cut by creeks and tributaries of the Cumberland River.

Sixteen miles northeast of Nashville in the town of Goodlettsville, the **Museum of Beverage Containers & Advertising** (☎ 615-859-5236) displays 25,000 beer and soda cans – reportedly the largest such collection in the world.

In Hurricane Mills, 70 miles west of Nashville, **Loretta Lynn's ranch** (☎ 615-296-7700), off I-40 exit 143, is a museum to the 'Coal Miner's Daughter' housed in a restored old gristmill. Visitors can tour the downstairs of Lynn's antebellum home and see a re-creation of her childhood home. In summer the ranch is crawling with country-music fans. There are pedal boats and camping ($13 to $18) is permitted. Admission is $10.50.

About 25 miles southwest of Nashville off Hwy 100, drivers pick up the **Natchez Trace Parkway**, which leads 450 miles southwest to Natchez, Mississippi, along what was an old Indian route and later a traders' footpath. This northern section is one of the most attractive stretches of the entire route, but slow going (speed limit 50 mph, many bicyclists) as the road meanders through woods and around curves overlooking beautiful Tennessee pastureland. (For details on the entire trace, see Scenic Routes in the Getting Around chapter.)

To find the entrance to the trace, look for the *Loveless Cafe* (☎ 615-646-9700) at 8400 Hwy 100. Still operating as a cafe (but no longer a motel), the 1940s roadhouse serves ample portions of Southern country cooking to city folk out for a day's drive. It's open daily from 8 am to 9 pm (closed 2 to 5 pm Monday to Saturday). On the weekend, make reservations or there's a long wait.

Southeast of Nashville past Murfreesboro (the geographic center of the state, marked by an obelisk), in Milton off Hwy 96, **Manuel's Cajun Country Store** (☎ 615-273-2312) on Main St features Cajun music and dancing on most Friday nights. In summer, the kitchen serves up fried alligator and has Wednesday night crawfish boils.

Glossary

AAA – American Automobile Association

antebellum – the period prior to the Civil War (Latin for 'before the war')

arpent – a French unit of land measurement equal to about 0.84 acres

Acadia – East Canadian region located between the St Lawrence River and the Atlantic Ocean and including New Brunswick and part of Maine; it was settled by the French between 1632 and 1713

andouille – a French sausage made with tripe; the Creole version is ground pork in a casing made from smoked pig intestines (or chitterlings); sausages made entirely of chitterlings are called *chitlins*

Arts & Crafts – an architecture and design movement that gained popularity just after the turn of the 20th century; the style emphasizes simple artisanship and functional design; also known as American Craftsman

Bama – short for Alabama and also for the University of Alabama

banquette – a diminutive form of 'banc', meaning bench, applied to the early wooden boardwalks; it's sometimes used today to refer to sidewalks in New Orleans

batture – a sedimentary deposit on the inward side of a riverbend or other sluggish section on the river side of the levee crest; often covered with a tangled mass of trees and shrubs

bayou – a natural canal of marshy water that is a tributary of the main river channel (from the Choctaw 'bayuk')

beignet – a deep-fried pastry that is New Orleans' version of the doughnut; it's typically sweet and covered with powdered sugar, but there are also savory versions, usually flavored with herbs or crab meat

boudin – Cajun sausage filled with a mixture of pork, pork liver and rice

bousillage – the mud and Spanish moss mixture sometimes used as a wall filler in *colombage* construction

briquette entre poteaux – similar to English half-timber construction and using bricks to fill the wall space between posts

brown and white cooking – slang for 'meat and potatoes'

café au lait – mixture of coffee and steamed milk

Cajun – a corruption of *Acadian*; Louisianans descended from French-speaking colonists exiled from *Acadia* in the 18th century; may also apply to other rural settlers who live amid Cajuns

calliope – a keyboard instrument fitted with steam whistles

carnival – a festival held just before Lent; in New Orleans, locals often refer to Mardi Gras as carnival

carpetbagger – a derogatory name given to itinerant financial or political opportunists, particularly Northerners in the reconstructed South, who carried their possessions in heavy cloth satchels; their Southern accomplices were branded as 'scalawags'

cataract – a waterfall

chantilly – a dessert topping of whipped cream sweetened with sugar and possibly a liqueur

chenier – a beach ridge formed above swamp deposits, typically covered with *live oaks* (from the French word 'chène', oak)

chicken-fried – a breaded and deep-fried piece of meat, usually steak or pork chops, served with gravy

chicory – a relative of endive used as a coffee substitute; Creole coffee is typically a blend of coffee beans (60%) and roasted chicory root (40%)

chitlins – chitterling (pig intestine) sausages; see *andouille*

Code Noir – the Black Code adopted by the French administration in 1724 that regulated the treatment and rights of free people of color and slaves; free people of color were accorded the rights of full citizenship except that they could not vote, hold public office or marry a white person

cold drink – A soda; when you visit someone's home, they'll offer you a cold drink

colombage – a type of construction using heavy timbers (horizontal, vertical and diagonal) with mortise and tenon joints

concession stand – a stand selling snacks, drinks and ice cream, and operating on a tract of land granted by the government or other authority

Confederacy – the 11 Southern states that seceded from the United States in 1860 and 1861

corvée – slave or statute labor; plantation owners were expected to provide corvée to maintain levees or public roads adjacent to their land

courir de Mardi Gras – a horseback run through Cajun prairie country during Mardi Gras; bands of masked and costumed men ride from house to house singing and dancing in exchange for ingredients used to cook a community gumbo

cracklins – fried strips of pork skin and fat, considered a snack food

Creole – a term was first coined in the early 18th century to describe children born of French immigrants in Louisiana, and, later, the children of the slaves of these immigrants; after the Civil War the term encompassed free Creoles of color; these days persons descended from any of the above cultures are considered Creole

CSA – Confederate States of America

dirty rice – white rice cooked with small quantities of chicken giblets or ground pork, along with green onions, peppers, celery and herbs and spices

dressed – a 'dressed' po-boy sandwich comes with lettuce and tomato

entrée – the main course of a meal

entresol – the mezzanine-like area of low rooms between the ground floor and the first floor; in many French Quarter buildings the entresol was used for storage

étouffée – a spicy tomato-based stew that typically includes crawfish or shrimp and is served with rice

factor – person or firm offering short-term loans in exchange for accounts receivable; many 19th-century sugar and cotton factors were concentrated in the port of New Orleans

fais-do-do – a Cajun house dance

feed-and-seed – a store selling livestock feed and crop seed

filé – ground sassafras leaves used to thicken sauces

frottoir – a metal rubbing board used for percussion, especially in zydeco music

gallery – a balcony

gens de couleur libre – the name given to free people of color during the antebellum period; after the Civil War they were known as Creoles of color

go-cup – a plastic container provided for patrons at bars so that they can transfer their beverage from a bottle or glass as they leave; in New Orleans it is legal to drink alcoholic beverages in the street, but it's illegal to carry an open glass container

Grand Dérangement – the great dispersal of Acadians that followed the 18th-century colonial wars between England and France; about 10,000 Acadians were deported from Nova Scotia by the English in 1755

gris-gris – magical objects having curative, protective or evil properties; used in the Yoruba religious practice of voodoo

grits – coarsely ground *hominy* prepared as a mush and served with breakfast throughout the South; it picks up the flavor of whatever is ladled over it, often butter or gravy

gumbo – traditionally an African soup thickened with okra and containing seafood or chicken; Cajun gumbos are often made with a *roux*, while Creole gumbos use *filé* powder

hominy – hulled and dried corn kernels, usually boiled and eaten as *grits*

hookup – a facility at an RV campsite that connects a vehicle to electricity, water, sewer and even cable TV

hushpuppy – a down-home bread substitute served with many Southern meals; made from deep-fried balls of cornmeal and onion

improved campsite – a campsite providing electricity and water *hookups*, hot showers and other facilities

jambalaya – a one-dish meal of rice cooked with onions, peppers, celery, ham, sausage and whatever else is on hand

Ku Klux Klan – an organization, founded in 1866, that espouses white supremacy; although outlawed by the Federal government in 1870, it has secretly conducted a campaign of violence against blacks, Jews and others whom they accuse of betraying the white race; often abbreviated to KKK

krewe – a group whose members participate in the Mardi Gras parades; membership is hereditary

lagniappe – a small gift from a store owner or friend; literally, a 'little something extra'

laissez les bons temps rouler – to have fun; literally, 'let the good times roll'

levee – a raised embankment that prevents a river from flooding

live oak – an evergreen oak indigenous to Mexico and the US

Lundi Gras – the Monday before Mardi Gras

making groceries – grocery shopping

Mardi Gras – 'Fat Tuesday', the day before Ash Wednesday; the carnival period leading up to Lenten fasting, usually celebrated with masquerade balls and costume parades

marsh – Wetland area predominantly covered with grasses rather than trees

meat-and-three – a set-price meal that includes a meat dish plus three side orders of vegetables

meunière – a cooking style where food, usually fish, is seasoned, coated lightly with flour and pan-fried in butter; it's served with a lemon-butter sauce

mirliton – an indigenous pear-shaped vegetable with a hard shell that is cooked like squash and stuffed with either ham or shrimp and spicy dressing

mojo – a voodoo charm

moon pie – a chocolate-covered marshmallow-filled treat that is often thrown by people on floats to observers during Mardi Gras parades

muffuletta – an enormous sandwich of ham, hard salami, provolone and olive salad piled onto a loaf of Italian bread liberally sprinkled with olive oil and vinegar

mulatto – a person of mixed black and white ancestry

NPR – National Public Radio; a noncommercial, listener-supported broadcast organization that produces and distributes news and cultural programs via a network of loosely affiliated radio stations throughout the USA

NPS – National Park Service

pain perdue – New Orleans' version of French toast; French for 'lost bread'

parish – an administrative subdivision in Louisiana that corresponds to a county in other US states

picayune – something of little value

pirogue – a dugout canoe traditionally carved by burning the center of a log and scraping out the embers; modern pirogues are shallow-draft vessels often made from plywood

po-boy – a submarine-style sandwich served on fresh French bread; in New Orleans fried oysters, soft-shell crabs, catfish and deli meats are offered as fillings

praline – a dessert made from caramelized sugar and nuts

primitive campsite – a campsite usually providing drinking water, a fire pit and a vault toilet; also called an unimproved campsite

quadroon – a person who is one-quarter black

R&B – abbreviation for rhythm & blues; a musical style developed by African Americans that combines blues and jazz

Reconstruction – the postwar period (1865-77) during which the states of the *Confederacy* were controlled by the federal government before being readmitted into the *Union*

red beans and rice – a spicy bean stew with peppers and a hunk of salt pork or *tasso*; often served with a piece of *andouille* sausage

Redneck Riviera – an unflattering nickname for the Gulf Coast beaches

rémoulade – a mayonnaise-based sauce with a variety of ingredients such as pickles, herbs, capers and mustard; crawfish or shrimp rémoulade is often a cold noodle salad

réveillon – a traditional Creole Christmas Eve feast

roux – a mixture of flour and butter or oil that is slowly heated and then used as a thickener in Cajun soups and sauces

RV – recreational vehicle; also known as 'motor home'

second line – the partying group that follows parading musicians; also a traditional New Orleans song and dance originally played during carnival and usually used as a last dance at parties and weddings

swamp – a permanently waterlogged area that often supports trees

tasso – highly spiced cured pork or beef that's smoked for two days; small quantities are used to flavor many Creole and Cajun dishes

Union – of or relating to the United States of America during the Civil War

USFS – United States Forest Service

Vieux Carré – the original walled city of New Orleans bounded by Canal St, N Rampart St, Esplanade Ave and the Mississippi River (French for 'old square')

what and what – Southern idiom meaning 'whatever' or 'it doesn't matter'; for example, Do you want a red cupcake, blue cupcake, or what and what?

WPA – Works Progress (later Works Projects) Administration; a Depression-era program established to increase employment by funding public works such as road building and the beautification of public structures (especially post offices)

y'at – refers to people with heavy New Orleans accents; these people say the greeting 'Where y'at?' with a broad 'a'

zydeco – fast syncopated black Creole dance music influenced by Cajun, Afro-American and Afro-Caribbean cultures; it is often a combination of R&B and Cajun with French lyrics; bands typically feature guitar, accordion and *frottoir*

Internet Directory

Following is a comprehensive listing of websites and online services that will help you plan your travels in the Deep South.

MISCELLANEOUS

Access-Able Travel Source
www.access-able.com

AmeriCan Adventures
email in US: amadusa@attmail.com
email in UK: amaduk@attmail.com

Council Travel
Info@ciee.org
www.ciee.org/travel/index.htm

Hotmail
www.hotmail.com

Lonely Planet Publications
www.lonelyplanet.com

Mobility International USA
miusa@igc.apc.org

The Mudcat Cafe:
Online Magazine of Blues and Folk
www.deltablues.com

The National Association for the
Advancement of Colored People
www.naacp.org

National Legal Aid & Defender
Association
www.nlada.org

National Park Service
www.nps.gov

RocketMail
www.rocketmail.com

Seattle Times Martin Luther King
website
www.seattletimes.com/mlk/

Southern Poverty Law Center
www.splcenter.org

TrekAmerica
www.trekamerica.com

Y'all: The Webzine of the South
www.yall.com

AIRLINES

Air Canada
www.aircanada.ca

Air France
www.airfrance.fr

American Airlines
www.amrcorp.com

British Airways
www.british-airways.com

Continental Airlines
www.flycontinental.com

Delta Air Lines
www.delta-air.com

KLM Royal Dutch Airlines
www.klm.nl

TWA
www.twa.com

United Airlines
www.ual.com

Virgin Atlantic Airways
www.fly.virgin.com

OTHER TRANSPORTATION

Amtrak
www.amtrak.com

Greyhound
www.greyhound.com

LOUISIANA

Lafayette Convention & Visitors
Commission
lcvc@worldnet.att.net
www.travelfile.com (search: Lafayette LA)

Laura Plantation
lauraplantation.com

Louisiana Department of Culture,
Recreation & Tourism
www.louisianatravel.com

St James Parish Tourist Center
www.stjamesla.com

Greater New Orleans Free-Net
www.gnofn.org

New Orleans Connection
www.neworleansla.com

New Orleans Metropolitan Convention & Visitors Bureau
www.nawlins.com

New Orleans Public Library
www.gnofn.org/~nopl

***Times-Picayune* Destination New Orleans**
www.neworleans.net

Preservation Resource Center
www.prcno.org

MISSISSIPPI

Choctaw Reservation
www.choctaw.org

Clarksdale Online
www.clarksdale.com

Delta Blues Museum
www.deltabluesmuseum.org

Oxford Visitor Information
www.ci.oxford.ms.us

University of Mississippi
www.olemiss.edu

ALABAMA

Alabama Bureau of Tourism & Travel
info@touralabama.org
www.touralabama.org

Alabama Department of Archives and History
www.asc.edu/archives/agis.html

Alabama Mountain Lakes Tourist Association
info@almtlakes.org
www.almtlakes.org

Alabama Music Hall of Fame
alamhof@hiwaay.net
www.alamhof.org

Alabama State's Directory of Alabama City Internet Addresses
www.state.al.us/city_dir/cities.html

Alabama State Website: AlaWeb
www.state.al.us

Alabama Web Directory: V-Ten Online
www.vten.Com

Auburn-Opelika
www.auburn-opelika.com

Decatur Convention & Visitors Bureau
www.decaturcvb.org

Dothan Area Convention & Visitors Bureau
dothancvb@mail.ala.net
www.dothanalcvb.com

Fairhope Visitor Information
www.cofairhope.com

Florence/Lauderdale Tourism
dwilson@floweb.com
www.flo-tour.org

Gulf Shores Visitor Bureau
www.gulfshores.com

Safe Harbor Resort
www.safeharborresort.com

Huntsville Convention & Visitors Bureau
www.huntsville.org

Montgomery Area Visitor Center
www.montgomery.al.us

Selma and Dallas County Chamber of Commerce
www.olcg.com/selma/

Tuscaloosa Convention & Visitors Bureau
www.tcvb.org

US Space & Rocket Center: Space Camp
www.spacecamp.com

TENNESSEE

Elvis Presley/Graceland
www.elvis-presley.com

Memphis Mojo music information
www.memphismojo.com

Memphis Visitor Information
www.memphistravel.com

Nashville Convention & Visitors Bureau
www.nastn.citysearch.com

Shangri-la Records
www.shangri.com

Index

SIDEBARS

LONELY PLANET TRAVEL ATLASES

Lonely Planet has long been famous for the number and quality of its guidebook maps. Now we've gone one step further and produced a handy companion series: Lonely Planet travel atlases–maps of a country produced in book form.

Unlike other maps, which look good but lead travelers astray, our travel atlases have been researched on the road by Lonely Planet's experienced team of writers. All details are carefully checked to ensure the atlas corresponds with the equivalent Lonely Planet guidebook.

The handy atlas format means no holes, wrinkles, torn sections or constant folding and unfolding. These atlases can survive long periods on the road, unlike cumbersome fold-out maps. The comprehensive index ensures easy reference.

- full-color throughout
- maps researched and checked by Lonely Planet authors
- place names correspond with Lonely Planet guidebooks –no confusing spelling differences
- legend and traveling information in English, French, German, Japanese and Spanish
- size: 230 x 160 mm

Available now:

Chile & Easter Island • Egypt • India & Bangladesh • Israel & the Palestinian Territories • Jordan, Syria & Lebanon • Kenya • Laos • Portugal • South Africa, Lesotho & Swaziland • Thailand • Turkey • Vietnam • Zimbabwe, Botswana & Namibia

LONELY PLANET TV SERIES & VIDEOS

Lonely Planet travel guides have been brought to life on television screens around the world. Like our guides, the programs are based on the joy of independent travel, and look honestly at some of the most exciting, picturesque and frustrating places in the world. Each show is presented by one of three travelers from Australia, England or the USA and combines an innovative mixture of video, Super-8 film, atmospheric soundscapes and original music.

Videos of each episode–containing additional footage not shown on television–are available from good book and video shops, but the availability of individual videos varies with regional screening schedules.

Video destinations include: Alaska • American Rockies • Australia (Southeast) • Baja California • Brazil • Central Asia • Chile & Easter Island • Corsica, Sicily & Sardinia • East Africa, Tanzania & Zanzibar • Ecuador & the Galápagos Islands • France • Greenland & Iceland • Indonesia • Israel & the Sinai Desert • Jamaica • Japan • La Ruta Maya • Morocco • New York City • North India (Varanasi to the Himalayas) • Pacific Islands • South India • Southwest China • Turkey • Vietnam • West Africa • Zimbabwe, Botswana & Namibia

The Lonely Planet TV series is produced by:
Pilot Productions
Duke of Sussex Studios
44 Uxbridge St
London W8 7TG UK

Lonely Planet videos are distributed by:
IVN Communications Inc
2246 Camino Ramon
California 94583, USA

107 Power Road, Chiswick
London W4 5PL UK

Music from the TV series is available on CD & cassette.
For ordering information contact your nearest Lonely Planet office.

PLANET TALK

Lonely Planet's FREE quarterly newsletter

We love hearing from you and think you'd like to hear from us.
When... is the right time to see reindeer in Finland?
Where... can you hear the best palm-wine music in Ghana?
How... do you get from Asunción to Areguá by steam train?
What... is the best way to see India?

For the answer to these and many other questions read PLANET TALK.

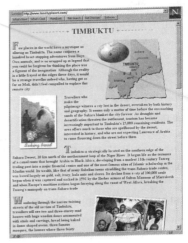

Every issue is packed with up-to-date travel news and advice including:

- a letter from Lonely Planet founders Tony and Maureen Wheeler
- travel diary from a Lonely Planet author–find out what it's really like out on the road
- feature article on an important and topical travel issue
- a selection of recent letters from our readers
- the latest travel news from all over the world
- details on Lonely Planet's new and forthcoming releases

To join our mailing list contact any Lonely Planet office .

Also available: Lonely Planet T-shirts. 100% heavyweight cotton (S, M, L, XL)

LONELY PLANET ONLINE

Get the latest travel information before you leave or while you're on the road

Whether you've just begun planning your next trip, or you're chasing down specific info on currency regulations or visa requirements, check out Lonely Planet Online for up-to-the-minute travel information.

As well as travel profiles of your favorite destinations (including maps and photos), you'll find current reports from our researchers and other travelers, updates on health and visas, travel advisories, and discussion of the ecological and political issues you need to be aware of as you travel.

There's also an online travelers' forum where you can share your experience of life on the road, meet travel companions and ask other travelers for their recommendations and advice. We also have plenty of links to other online sites useful to independent travelers.

And of course we have a complete and up-to-date list of all Lonely Planet travel products including guides, phrasebooks, atlases, Journeys and videos and a simple online ordering facility if you can't find the book you want elsewhere.

www.lonelyplanet.com *or* **AOL keyword: lp**

LONELY PLANET PRODUCTS

Lonely Planet is known worldwide for publishing practical, reliable and no-nonsense travel information in our guides and on our web site. The Lonely Planet list covers just about every accessible part of the world. Currently there are eight series: *travel guides, shoestring guides, walking guides, city guides, phrasebooks, audio packs, travel atlases* and *Journeys*–a unique collection of travel writing.

EUROPE

Amsterdam • Austria • Baltic States & Kaliningrad • Baltic States phrasebook • Britain • Central Europe on a shoestring • Central Europe phrasebook • Czech & Slovak Republics • Denmark • Dublin • Eastern Europe on a shoestring • Eastern Europe phrasebook • Finland • France • French phrasebook • Germany • German phrasebook • Greece • Greek phrasebook • Hungary • Iceland, Greenland & the Faroe Islands • Ireland • Italy • Italian phrasebook • Lisbon • London • Mediterranean Europe on a shoestring • Mediterranean Europe phrasebook • Paris • Poland • Portugal • Portugal travel atlas • Prague • Romania & Moldova • Russia, Ukraine & Belarus • Russian phrasebook • Scandinavian & Baltic Europe on a shoestring • Scandinavian Europe phrasebook • Slovenia • Spain • Spanish phrasebook • St Petersburg • Switzerland • Trekking in Greece • Trekking in Spain • Ukrainian phrasebook • Vienna • Walking in Britain • Walking in Italy • Walking in Switzerland • Western Europe on a shoestring • Western Europe phrasebook

NORTH AMERICA

Alaska • Backpacking in Alaska • Bahamas • Baja California • Bermuda • California & Nevada • Canada • Chicago • Deep South • Florida • Hawaii • Honolulu • Los Angeles • Mexico • Mexico City • Miami • New England • New Orleans • New York City • New York, New Jersey & Pennsylvania • Pacific Northwest USA • Rocky Mountain States USA • San Francisco • Seattle • Southwest USA • USA phrasebook • Washington, DC & The Capital Region

CENTRAL AMERICA & THE CARIBBEAN

Bahamas, Turks & Caicos • Central America on a shoestring • Costa Rica • Cuba • Eastern Caribbean • Guatemala, Belize & Yucatán: La Ruta Maya • Jamaica

SOUTH AMERICA

Argentina, Uruguay & Paraguay • Bolivia • Brazil • Brazilian phrasebook • Buenos Aires • Chile & Easter Island • Chile travel atlas • Colombia • Ecuador & the Galápagos Islands • Latin American Spanish phrasebook • Peru • Quechua phrasebook • Rio de Janeiro • South America on a shoestring • Trekking in the Patagonian Andes • Venezuela

Travel Literature: Full Circle: A South American Journey

AFRICA

Arabic (Moroccan) phrasebook • Africa on a shoestring • Africa The South • Cape Town • Cairo • Central Africa • East Africa • Egypt & the Sudan • Egypt travel atlas • Ethiopian (Amharic) phrasebook • Kenya • Kenya travel atlas • Malawi, Mozambique & Zambia • Morocco • North Africa • South Africa, Lesotho & Swaziland • South Africa travel atlas • Swahili phrasebook • Trekking in East Africa • West Africa • Zimbabwe, Botswana & Namibia • Zimbabwe, Botswana & Namibia travel atlas

Travel Literature: The Rainbird: A Central African Journey • Songs to an African Sunset: A Zimbabwean Story

ISLANDS OF THE INDIAN OCEAN

Madagascar & Comoros • Maldives & Islands of the East Indian Ocean • Mauritius, Réunion & Seychelles

Also Available: Travel with Children • Traveller's Tales

MAIL ORDER

Lonely Planet products are distributed worldwide. They are also available by mail order from Lonely Planet, so if you have difficulty finding a title please write to us. North American and South American residents should write to Embarcadero West, 155 Filbert St, Suite 251, Oakland CA 94607, USA; European and African residents should write to 10A Spring Place, London NW5 3BH, UK; and residents of other countries to PO Box 617, Hawthorn, Victoria 3122, Australia.

NORTH-EAST ASIA

Beijing • Cantonese phrasebook • China • Hong Kong • Hong Kong, Macau & Canton • Japan • Japanese phrasebook • Japanese audio pack • Korea • Korean phrasebook • Mandarin phrasebook • Mongolia • Mongolian phrasebook • North-East Asia on a shoestring • Seoul • Taiwan • Tibet • Tibet phrasebook • Tokyo

Travel Literature: Lost Japan

MIDDLE EAST & CENTRAL ASIA

Arab Gulf States • Arabic (Egyptian) phrasebook • Central Asia • Central Asia phrasebook • Iran • Israel & the Palestinian Territories • Israel & the Palestinian Territories travel atlas • Istanbul • Jerusalem • Jordan & Syria • Jordan, Syria & Lebanon travel atlas • Lebanon • Middle East • Turkey • Turkey travel atlas • Turkish phrasebook • Trekking in Turkey • Yemen

Travel Literature: The Gates of Damascus • Kingdom of the Film Stars: Journey into Jordon

INDIAN SUBCONTINENT

Bengali phrasebook • Bangladesh • Delhi • Goa • Hindi/Urdu phrasebook • India • India & Bangladesh travel atlas • Indian Himalaya • Karakoram Highway • Nepal • Nepali phrasebook • Pakistan • Rajasthan • Sri Lanka • Sri Lanka phrasebook • Trekking in the Indian Himalaya • Trekking in the Karakoram & Hindukush • Trekking in the Nepal Himalaya

Travel Literature: In Rajasthan • Shopping for Buddhas

SOUTH-EAST ASIA

Bali & Lombok • Bangkok • Burmese phrasebook • Cambodia • Ho Chi Minh • Indonesia • Indonesian phrasebook • Indonesian audio pack • Jakarta • Java • Laos • Lao phrasebook • Laos travel atlas • Malay phrasebook • Malaysia, Singapore & Brunei • Myanmar (Burma) • Philippines • Pilipino phrasebook • Singapore • South-East Asia on a shoestring • Thailand • Thailand's Islands and Beaches • Thai phrasebook • Thailand travel atlas • Thai audio pack • Thai Hill Tribes phrasebook • Vietnam • Vietnamese phrasebook • Vietnam travel atlas

ANTARCTICA

Antarctica

AUSTRALIA & THE PACIFIC

Australia • Australian phrasebook • Bushwalking in Australia • Bushwalking in Papua New Guinea • Fiji • Fijian phrasebook • Islands of Australia's Great Barrier Reef • Melbourne • Micronesia • New Caledonia • New South Wales & the ACT • New Zealand • Northern Territory • Outback Australia • Papua New Guinea • Papua New Guinea phrasebook • Queensland • Rarotonga & the Cook Islands • Samoa • Solomon Islands • South Australia • Sydney • Tahiti & French Polynesia • Tasmania • Tonga • Tramping in New Zealand • Vanuatu • Victoria • Western Australia

Travel Literature: Islands in the Clouds • Sean & David's Long Drive

THE LONELY PLANET STORY

Lonely Planet published its first book in 1973 in response to the numerous 'How did you do it?' questions Maureen and Tony Wheeler were asked after driving, bussing, hitching, sailing and railing their way from England to Australia.

Written at a kitchen table and hand collated, trimmed and stapled, *Across Asia on the Cheap* became an instant local best seller, inspiring thoughts of another book.

Eighteen months in South-East Asia resulted in their second guide, *South-East Asia on a shoestring*, which they put together in a backstreet Chinese hotel in Singapore in 1975. The 'yellow bible', as it quickly became known to back-packers around the world, soon became the guide to the region. It has sold well over half a million copies and is now in its 9th edition, still retaining its familiar yellow cover.

Today there are 240 titles, including travel guides, walking guides, language kits & phrasebooks, travel atlases and travel literature. The company is the largest independent travel publisher in the world. Although Lonely Planet initially specialized in guides to Asia, today there are few corners of the globe that have not been covered.

The emphasis continues to be on travel for independent travelers. Tony and Maureen still travel for several months of each year and play an active part in the writing, updating and quality control of Lonely Planet's guides.

They have been joined by over 70 authors and 170 staff at our offices in Melbourne (Australia), Oakland (USA), London (UK) and Paris (France). Travelers themselves also make a valuable contribution to the guides through the feedback we receive in thousands of letters each year and on our website.

The people at Lonely Planet strongly believe that travelers can make a positive contribution to the countries they visit, both through their appreciation of the countries' culture, wildlife and natural features, and through the money they spend. In addition, the company makes a direct contribution to the countries and regions it covers. Since 1986 a per-centage of the income from each book has been donated to ventures such as famine relief in Africa; aid projects in India; agricultural projects in Central America; Greenpeace's efforts to halt French nuclear testing in the Pacific; and Amnesty International.

'I hope we send people out with the right attitude about travel. You realize when you travel that there are so many different perspectives about the world, so we hope these books will make people more interested in what they see. Guidebooks can't really guide people. All you can do is point them in the right direction.'

– Tony Wheeler

LONELY PLANET PUBLICATIONS

Australia
PO Box 617, Hawthorn 3122, Victoria
☎ (03) 9819 1877 fax (03) 9819 6459
e-mail talk2us@lonelyplanet.com.au

USA
155 Filbert St, Suite 251
Oakland, California 94607
☎ (510) 893 8555, TOLL FREE (800) 275 8555
fax (510) 893 8563
e-mail info@lonelyplanet.com

UK
10A Spring Place, London NW5 3BH, UK
☎ (0171) 428 4800 fax (0171) 428 4828
e-mail go@lonelyplanet.co.uk

France
71 bis rue du Cardinal Lemoine, 75005 Paris
☎ 01 44 320620 fax 01 46 347255
e-mail 100560.415@compuserve.com

World Wide Web: www.lonelyplanet.com

H A

MILWAUKEE
& MADISON

THOMAS HUHTI

DOWNTOWN MILWAUKEE

Lake Michigan

Juneau Park

Milwaukee Lakeshore State Park

McKINLEY MARINA

MILWAUKEE JEWISH MUSEUM

COAST GUARD STATION

WAR MEMORIAL / CALATRAVA ADDITION

MILWAUKEE ART MUSEUM

BETTY BRINN CHILDREN'S MUSEUM

DISCOVERY WORLD AT PIER WISCONSIN

MUNICIPAL PIER

VISIT MILWAUKEE

SUMMERFEST

SHANK HALL

KNICKERBOCKER ON THE LAKE

COUNTY CLARE

LINCOLN CENTER

ASTOR HOTEL

POINTS EAST PUB

SANFORD

SKYLIGHT THEATRE

MILWAUKEE COUNTY HISTORICAL CENTER

MSOE

ELSA'S

PABST THEATER

MILWAUKEE REPERTORY THEATRE

KARL RATZSCH'S OLD WORLD RESTAURANT

GRAND EXCHANGE

IRON BLOCK

PFISTER

SAFE HOUSE

IROQUOIS BOAT DOCKS

HISTORIC THIRD WARD AND RIVERWALK

WATER STREET BREWERY

EDELWEISS BOAT TOURS

MILWAUKEE HISTORIC TURNER'S

USINGER'S SAUSAGE

MCPA

KING & I

BUTCH'S CLOCK

THE FONZ STATUE

VISIT MILWAUKEE

PURE

SHOPS AT GRAND AVENUE MALL

RIVERWALK BISTRO

MILWAUKEE ALE HOUSE

EISNER MUSEUM OF ADVERTISING AND DESIGN

MILWAUKEE INSTITUTE OF ART AND DESIGN

BROADWAY THEATRE CENTRE

SLIM McGINN'S

CAROLINES

HAVE A NICE DAY CAFÉ

MADER'S

WYNDHAM HOTEL

HYATT REGENCY

MIDWEST AIRLINES CENTER

BRADLEY CENTER

MILWAUKEE THEATRE ARENA

HILTON

POST OFFICE

AMTRAK / GREYHOUND

HARLEY-DAVIDSON MUSEUM

IRON HORSE HOTEL

MILWAUKEE COUNTY COURTHOUSE

MILWAUKEE PUBLIC MUSEUM / IMAX

BADGER BUS DEPOT

GESU CATHOLIC CHURCH

MARQUETTE UNIVERSITY

HAGGERTY MUSEUM OF ART

ST. JOAN OF ARC CHAPEL

MARQUETTE INTERCHANGE

PABST MANSION

AMBASSADOR HOTEL

DREAM DANCE / POTAWATOMI BINGO CASINO

Menomonee River

0.5 mi
0.5 km

DOWNTOWN MADISON

Lake Mendota

Lake Monona

James Madison Park

★ CARILLON TOWER
★ WASHBURN OBSERVATORY
OBSERVATORY DR
★ MEMORIAL UNION
■ "OLD RED GYM"

■ MEMORIAL LIBRARY
★ CHAZEN MUSEUM OF ART
UNIVERSITY AVE
■ UNIVERSITY OF WISCONSIN-MADISON CAMPUS

▼ CAMPUS INN
▼ STEEP & BREW
■ KABUL
N FRANCES ST
▼ UNIVERSITY INN
PUBLIC PARKING
PUBLIC PARKING
S FRANCES ST

EDGEWATER HOTEL
■ MANSION HILL INN

LANGDON ST
N HENRY ST
N GILMAN ST
GORHAM ST
N CARROLL ST

PUBLIC PARKING
■ PLAZA TAVERN
ORPHEUM THEATER
HIMAL CHULI
CHAUTARA
■ WASABI
▼ AVOL'S
ANGELIC BREWING CO

STATE ST
W JOHNSON
W DAYTON ST

DOTTY DUMPLING'S DOWRY

WISCONSIN AVE
N PINCKNEY ST
E GORHAM ST
N JOHNSON
E DAYTON ST
N HAMILTON ST

NEW MADISON CHILDREN'S MUSEUM (2010)
CONCOURSE HOTEL
WISCONSIN VETERAN'S MUSEUM ★
★ STATE CAPITOL

MADISON CHILDREN'S MUSEUM
HOUSE OF WISCONSIN CHEESE
Madison Arts District (Madison Museum of Contemporary Art)
WISCONSIN HISTORICAL MUSEUM ★
STATE HISTORICAL SOCIETY MUSEUM ★

BLUE MARLIN
CAFE MONTMARTRE
THE OLD-FASHIONED
L'ETOILE
HARVEST

WEBSTER ST
BUTLER ST
HANCOCK ST
FRANKLIN ST
BLAIR ST
HAMILTON ST

PUBLIC PARKING
PUBLIC PARKING

N BLOUNT ST
BLOUNT ST
MAIN ST
N WASHINGTON ST

151
▼ HIGH NOON SALOON
■ CVB
BANDUNG ▼
COME BACK INN ■
ESSENHAUS ▼
SARDINE ▼
CARDINAL BAR ■
HI MADISON HOSTEL ■

W MAIN ST
E WASHINGTON ST
E MIFFLIN ST
FAIRCHILD ST

ARGUS
OPUS LOUNGE
ANCORA COFFEE ROASTERS
MARIGOLD KITCHEN
GREAT DANE BREWPUB
RESTAURANT MURAMOTO
THE MAJESTIC
POST OFFICE
HILTON MADISON

KING ST
NOLEN DR
Capital City Trail

PUBLIC PARKING
PUBLIC PARKING

E WILSON ST
E MAIN ST
S HAMILTON ST

INN ON THE PARK
HYATT PLACE
GENNA'S
TORNADO CLUB
PARADISE
SHAMROCK
LIBRARY
STATE TOURISM OFFICE
FAIRCHILD ST
S HENRY ST
S FAIRCHILD

PUBLIC PARKING

BROOM ST
DOTY ST
BASSETT ST
BEDFORD ST

W DOTY ST
W WASHINGTON AVE
W MAIN ST
MIFFLIN ST CO-OP
W MIFFLIN ST

WILSON ST

JOHN NOLEN DR
151

■ MONONA TERRACE

GREYHOUND/ BADGER BUS DEPOT
MAIN STREET DEPOT

S PARK ST
S FRANCES ST
S BASSETT ST
REGENT ST

KOHL CENTER

▼ HONG KONG CAFE
UW VISITOR CENTER ★

© AVALON TRAVEL

N

0   200 yds
0   200 m

Contents

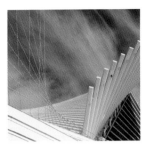

Discover
Milwaukee & Madison

Milwaukee and Madison. Call them the Heart and Soul of Wisconsin. Mind and Body. *Yin* and *yang.* Though which is which is delightfully debatable.

The two sibling cities perfectly realize the scope of what the state is and so much more. Cows? Sure. Naïve country folk? Well, you'll hear "gosh" a lot and have perfect strangers chat you up at bus stops and restaurants. When the two cities reveal their true Midwesterness is when you'll be most appreciative. You'll be utterly befuddled when, at a four-way stop-sign, a local will wave everyone through while waiting patiently – proof that urban can be lovely and polite.

The state capital is personified in its earnest politicos, earth-friendly neo-hippies, and overworked grad students. In Madison, everything is worthy of a community watchdog committee. The people of Milwaukee, on the other hand, roll up their sleeves and get to work; they don't have to debate – things are, after all, "cooler by the lake." Milwaukee and Madison have a contentious relationship at times – like any siblings – but they have many things in common, including being woefully overlooked and underappreciated by outsiders.

Aw-shucks humble, these two cities would never think to brag on their superlatives, yet there are many. Madison and its surroundings are perennial winners in "Best Places to Live" rankings and Milwaukee was even named "America's Sexiest City" recently. Together they help keep Wisconsin in the top five most livable states.

Surrounding both cities are splendid sights. For your picture book clichés, moo-cow farmlands provide the best agricultural tourism of the state, especially south and west of Madison (Monroe and New Glarus). Anachronistic tiny towns such as Cedarburg and Mineral Point seem straight out of a 19th-century daguerreotype. Even the North Woods resort experience can be found at Lake Geneva, the place where generations of Chicagoans have relaxed for the summer.

Whatever you're looking for, these two cities have got *it*. And, assuredly, *it* always comes with a handshake and a smile.

Planning Your Trip

▶ WHERE TO GO

Milwaukee

Dash the images of blue-collar-dom, as it's but one piece of the puzzle. This low-key citizenry is darned (and rightly) proud of cultural and architectural gems, of which the new Harley-Davidson Museum is the most recent respected addition. (And, of course, the Miller Brewing megacomplex.) You'll not find a lovelier littoral (and riverine) scene anywhere to pedal or stroll. Dressed-to-the-nines locals arrive via Harleys to eateries feted by international media (or to a pub serving bratwurst). And everyone there oozes Midwestern friendliness.

downtown Milwaukee

and the University of Wisconsin bookend much of what the city offers. Madison was "green" before it was a word; nature lovers will find no better chance to walk amid native state flora than at the UW's Arboretum and the Olbrich Botanical Gardens.

Vicinity of Madison

Madison is an exploding city, population-wise, yet you'd hardly know it by venturing into the outskirts (cows outnumber people still). How about a drive learning about the state's dairy industry in Fort Atkinson or its aboriginal history at author fave Aztalan State Park? Cheese (Swiss especially) around New Glarus and Monroe? Badgers in historic Mineral Point?

But definitely, visit the mighty Wisconsin River. First in Frank Lloyd Wright Country, or Spring Green.

Madison's Monona Terrace in the morning light

Vicinity of Milwaukee

Foraying beyond Milwaukee, you will find villages, like Cedarburg, that time seems to have forgotten, classic lakefront loveliness in Port Washington, superb wildlife viewing at Horicon Marsh, and a magnificent retreat at Holy Hill. Experience the best mountain biking in southern Wisconsin at Kettle Moraine State Forest or tour the state's settlement period at Old World Wisconsin. Don't miss the posh but humble southern retreat region around Geneva Lake or the quaint downtowns of Great Lake cities Kenosha and Racine.

Madison

The Island Surrounded by Reality. Madison is a vibrant and fetching city plopped among a quartet of jewel-like lakes—upon one of which sits the eye-catching Monona Terrace. The city hums with the push and pull between the state government—the grand State Capitol

IF YOU HAVE...

- **TWO DAYS:** Visit Milwaukee and Madison.
- **FOUR DAYS:** Add side trips to Geneva Lake or Old World Wisconsin near Milwaukee, and Spring Green or Monroe near Madison.
- **ONE WEEK:** Add Horicon Marsh, Watertown, Port Washington, and Cedarburg.
- **TWO WEEKS:** Add Racine, Kenosha, Janesville, and Beloit.

autumnal colors in southern Wisconsin

▶ WHEN TO GO

This is a four-season kind of place—there is something for everyone no matter if it is winter, spring, summer, or fall. That said, most visitors do come between Memorial Day and Labor Day. All accommodations, restaurants, and attractions will be open during this time; prices will also rise precipitously in more popular spots (and many lodgings will require a two- or three-night minimum stay). Another peak season is from late September through late October, when throngs arrive to witness fall's splendorous colors. (Between Labor Day and late September, you can often get great rates and, if cold weather comes early, great colors!) Winter in general sees fewer visitors except for snowmobilers and skiers, and areas popular with those types will not have lower rates. Other places may shut down entirely November through April. Pretty much nobody comes here March 1 through early April—grim, gray, muddy, and windy, and this is a native Cheesehead speaking. Then again, it's dirt, dirt cheap!

icy scene along Harrington Beach State Park, north of Port Washington

► BEFORE YOU GO

Transportation

It's arguable whether most travelers arrive by car (usually via Chicago or Minneapolis) or plane (in which it'll be Milwaukee or Madison, the former probably offering more competition and thus lower fares). I've met only a couple who've arrived by bus (definitely via Chicago or Minneapolis). My favorite way to get here is from Michigan across Lake Michigan via one of two car/passenger ferries: an express to/from Milwaukee and a slower, steam-driven ferry from Manitowoc, WI, a couple of hours north of Milwaukee.

Good bus service exists between (and within) Madison and Milwaukee; outside of these, however, you're for the most part on your own, meaning bring your own wheels or rent a car.

gorgeous fall colors at the University of Wisconsin

What To Take

You can buy most anything you need in the state, even in the village outposts (though this does not include spare parts for your laptop), but one thing you don't want to be caught without is mosquito repellent. Trust me. A face net for blackflies and skeeters wouldn't be a bad idea if you plan on delving into the woods (or even camping).

Regarding clothing, Wisconsin is a place where most consider L. L. Bean dress-up clothing. Heels, ties, and fancy skirts are fine for clubbing in Milwaukee or Madison, but you'll be absolutely conspicuous in all but the most chichi restaurants anywhere else (hey, Badger sweatshirts are perfectly fine in even the most famous supper clubs).

Weather is often the deciding factor. Dress appropriately for the weather at all times—that includes wearing a hat. Do not come to Wisconsin in winter without a good pair of gloves or mittens. Inuit-worthy mittens are something you'll be ever so grateful for on a sleigh ride or while you await a tow truck. A good pair of boots is also a necessity; some people carry a heavy-duty pair in the car at all times, in case of an emergency.

Always remember the mantra near Lake Michigan: cooler near the lake. This means it may be warm in the sun during the day, but once the sun goes down the temperature might drop precipitously compared to towns inland. (Thus, it is never a bad idea to have a pocket-sized windbreaker handy, even in summer.)

Given the state's somewhat iffy weather, it's paramount to prepare your car for any possibility by winterizing your vehicle. Carry an emergency kit with booster cables, sand or gravel (in a pinch, try sandpaper strips or your car's floor mats), flares, candles, matches, a shovel and scraper, flashlight and extra batteries, blankets (space blankets are excellent), extra heavy clothing, high-calorie nonperishable food, and anything else you might need if you have to spend the night in a snowbank. I cannot emphasize how important it is—I've stumbled upon people stuck in a snowy ditch and been amazed that, had someone not stumbled along, they were woefully unprepared to spend a winter night in the car.

Explore Milwaukee & Madison

▶ THE BEST OF MILWAUKEE AND MADISON

This author has spent half his life midway between the two cities, and the second half in one of the cities, and he still hasn't come close to seeing everything. So, you get the idea that one must balance the ideal with the realistic. A week and a half (ish) would allow you to see *most* of the highlights without pushing too much.

This *counterclockwise* (roughly) trip presumes arrival by car from the south via Chicago, the way most travelers arrive.

Days 1-2

Try to start on a weekend, when more stuff is going on. (If not, that's OK; it'll still be a lovely couple of days.) A made-in-Milwaukee weekend? First, on your way up from the Windy City, drive along the Lake Michigan coast along WI 32 and enjoy the picturesque vistas of downtown Kenosha and pick up some Danish *kringle* in Racine for some great roadfood. (Alternatively, head northwest out of Chicago and visit the Lake Geneva area and, possibly, Old World Wisconsin before cruising into the Beer City.) Start off Friday evening with a dinner of German food and then retire (you'll need to, given the food's, er, density). Feel your soul

Milwaukee Riverwalk scene

the Milwaukee Art Museum's Calatrava addition, from Wisconsin Avenue

Madison's Lake Monona

Wisconsin State Capitol

recharge as the sunrise illuminates your walk to the winged Santiago Calatrava addition to the Milwaukee Art Museum. After a stroll/bike/drive north along the grand lakefront to the museums overlooking the north end atop the bluff line, it's time for lunch in the funky Brady Street area. In the afternoon, try to wander the Riverwalk before a dinner at one of Milwaukee's legendary fish fries.

On day two, try to hit any outlying site—a tour of Miller Brewing or the new Harley-Davidson museum (or, for the nature/recreation-minded, a visit to the Schlitz Audubon Center) before returning downtown for a wander through the immense Milwaukee Public Museum.

Day 3

Pick one of the following. Northward, strike northward for postcard-perfect Cedarburg or continue a bit farther to Port Washington. Alternatively, head northwest to Holy Hill and, later, Horicon Marsh and overnight.

Day 4

On day four, from wherever you are, make your way to Watertown and start the Highway 26 History Route (not an official name—just what I think it is) south to Fort Atkinson. From here it's a lovely drive along US 12 to Madison, where you simply must see

your first sunset at the UW Memorial Union Terrace with a beer before or after dinner.

Day 5

Start with a stroll at sunrise along the John Nolen recreation path along Lake Monona (you may want to bike this later!). Wander through the nothing-else-like-it Monona Terrace Convention Center. Take in the gargantuan, stately Wisconsin State Capitol. Grab lunch at a food cart and hang alfresco with the Capitol crowd. Start trekking the Museum Mile, which will definitely fill out the first day's activities.

Day 6

Arise the next morning and grab coffee and a scone at the University of Wisconsin's Memorial Union. Stroll along the gorgeous lakefront path to Picnic Point. Backtracking via the campus, this author would later stop at Babcock Hall for some famed ice cream! Now, sack out on Bascom Hill with the class skippers. After lunch, visit the grand Olbrich Gardens.

If you're a type-T personality, on day two, you could alternatively give your feet a break along the greatest city bike trail in the state (no argument here, please). From Monona Terrace ride counterclockwise along Lake Monona all the way to the Capital City Trail. Continue on this trail through splendid, bucolic countryside all the way to bike-friendly Seminole Highway. Turn right and keep riding to the magnificent UW Arboretum and stretch the legs on some trails or take a nap under the blossoms. From here, turn left at the other end of the arboretum to the fun Vilas Zoo. From here, you're just a hop up to the student district.

Day 7

Either spend a day on the Dane County day-trips detailed within the pages and then overnight one more night in Madison or hit the Trollway to Mt. Horeb and see what the mustard is going on before driving south to New Glarus and doing some yodeling. (If you're a road warrior you'll have time for a limburger-onion sandwich farther south in Cheesetown, a.k.a. Monroe.)

Day 8

Head west for Mineral Point and find out what the deal with "Badger" is (hint: it ain't the animal and an aside: all county—not state roads leading to Mineral Point are gorgeous). You'll need a full day of history-learnin' and shoppin', trust me.

Day 9

Choose one of the following: a full day of Frank Lloyd Wright touring in Spring Green or a full day freaking out at the insanely fun House on the Rock nearby. (Trust me—doing both would be sensory overload.)

Day 10

Spend the day following the Wisconsin River, along the way watch for eagles in Sauk Prairie, visit many of the unique natural sights in the area, such as Blue River Sand Barrens, Avoca Prairie, Devil's Elbow, or catch a glimpse of the Baraboo Range from Ferry Bluff.

RUSTIC ROAD TRIPPING

Travel media have consistently voted Wisconsin one of the greatest road-touring states in the country. Much of this comes from natural beauty; a good deal also comes from the fact that many rural roads, originally known as farm-to-market roads, seem to have changed little (other than

the ubiquitous farm country sign

having pavement) in a century and a half.

Within the regions of this book you'll find more than two dozen fantastic roads that cannot be rivaled. **Near Milwaukee**, the communities with this author's favorites include Cedarburg (#52), Mequon (#65), Burlington (#42), Lake Geneva (#11 and #29), and Horicon Marsh (#106). **Near Madison,** this author's favorites are near Fort Atkinson (#84), Interstate 90/94 (#49), and especially Green County in its basic entirety!

Options for serpentine blue highways are infinite; thankfully, the Department of Transportation has highlighted more than 90 of the state's best back-roads trips in an effort to preserve the lightly traveled avenues into the real Wisconsin. A road trip on one of these roads is a phenomenal way to view the countryside and the culture. Every single Rustic Road of the state is guaranteed to offer an amazing palette of colors **mid-September-late-October.** Pick up the book *Wisconsin's Rustic Roads*, which outlines these routes and is available free from tourist centers or by visiting the website of the **Wisconsin Department of Transportation** (dot.wi.gov/travel/scenic/rusticroads.htm).

► MADISON WEEKEND

Madison in a weekend is a snap because everything is within walking distance and there's zilch traffic getting to the few spots outside the center.

Day 1

If you can get here early enough, here's the rule: sunrise at the Monona Terrace Convention Center, followed by a tour of the place and then a visit to the extraordinary Wisconsin Capitol. (If you're here April through November, budget an extra hour for a stroll around the Dane County Farmer's Market on the Capitol Square!)

Lunch across the street at the Wisconsin-in-a-menu Old Fashioned before walking State Street along Museum Mile. You're going to do a lot of shopping along the way, so expect this to take up the rest of the day.

Rest up and prepare for dinner at one of the country's top 50 restaurants—L'etoile, followed by an evening performance at the Overture Center for the Arts in one of its myriad theaters.

For a memorable place to lay your head, choose between the ornate but cozy historic Mansion Hill Inn or the only-in-Madison Arbor House, an Environmental Inn.

Day 2

For breakfast, classic heartland stick-to-(and overload)-your-ribs fare at Mickey's Dairy Bar on the west end of downtown, or, if you're closer to downtown, Marigold just off the Capitol Square.

You can spend the rest of the morning at the UW Madison campus and still not see it all. Your best bet is to walk the Lakeshore Path from the Memorial Union Terrace west to Picnic Point, then backtrack along the bluffs overlooking the lake, taking in any of the university's sights along the way.

Lunch anywhere along State Street, an

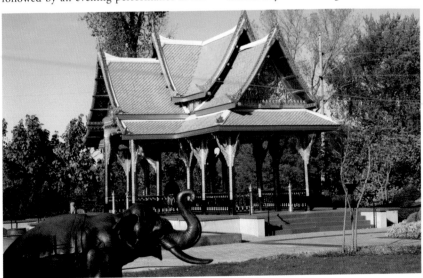

Thai pavilion at Madison's Olbrich Botanical Gardens

SPORTS: THE PACKERS AND BEYOND

Even the nosebleed seats at Miller Park are grand.

To preface, an admission: truly, when you say "sports" in Wisconsin, you really mean the Green Bay Packers. However, denizens of southern Wisconsin have to have something to go nuts about when the Packers aren't playing, and Milwaukee and Madison have their own passions.

MILWAUKEE

Milwaukee is a true anomaly – a small-market big city with three professional sports teams. The true sports heartbeat of the city revolves around its beloved **Milwaukee Brewers** baseball team. Despite being near the bottom in market-size, the Brewers in 2008 finished in the top five in attendance (over three *million* fans). The Brewers play in one of the most amazing stadiums, the retro-mod **Miller Park,** which is a must to visit. And above all, you must attend a game because of the tailgating. Yup, 40,000 people show up five hours before game time loaded with *trailers* full of barbecue and picnic supplies. Many people tailgate even if they don't have tickets!

MADISON

Madison, on the other hand, literally bleeds red and white. Cardinal red, that is, for the University of Wisconsin Badgers and its myriad sports

teams. Do try to be in Madison on a Saturday when the Badgers' football team plays; you will be overwhelmed by the oceans of red-garbed humans moving about the city. Another classic experience is to see a UW basketball or hockey game at the **Kohl Center,** a place where opponents honestly fear playing, given the absolutely thunderous – but always polite – crowds.

MORE BANG FOR THE BUDGET

However, a couple of other options exist. In Milwaukee, the **Marquette University Golden Eagles** basketball team is nationally-ranked and as of late, much more exciting than the woeful Milwaukee Bucks of the NBA. Madison's favorite summertime team now is the **Madison Mallards,** a member of an independent pro baseball league – it's a real treat for families: dirt cheap with tons of goofy entertainment. Do consider a game in Beloit (south of Madison), watching the **Beloit Snappers** wallop somebody. The Snaps are a Class A member of the Minnesota Twins organization, are always a league leader, and follow that great minor-league baseball tradition of offering tons of excitement and entertainment for rock-bottom prices. (Their snapping-turtle logo is a perennial winner of favorite team logo contests.)

international smorgasbord of eateries. After a day of rest, head for either the Olbrich Botanical Gardens or the University of Wisconsin Arboretum (I'd do both, in a hurry.) Hurry back to the Memorial Union for the loveliest sunset in the city before driving to the west side for a steak at Smoky's Club, the most classic Midwestern steak house/supper club in town.

Following that, a final stroll about the downtown for a nightcap. I'd head for Fresco, atop the Madison Museum for Contemporary Art; chic but comfortable, with superb views of nighttime Madtown.

▶ OUT ON THE TOWN IN MILWAUKEE

Milwaukee is more spread out than Madison, obviously, but a weekend in the Beer City is still a nice mix of lovely walking and relatively pain-free driving.

Day 1

First stop for any visitor is the city's Historic Third Ward and Riverwalk for lots of shopping and noshing.

For lunch, try the Riverwalk Bistro which has a splendid patio.

In the afternoon, Drink in the exteriors of the Milwaukee Art Museum and then go in for its fine holdings; if time, bop over down

the, er, lakepath to the Discovery World at Pier Wisconsin.

After a rest, you'll head for Milwaukee Historic Turner's for fish fry or any of their other wonderful eclectic dishes. After dinner take in a show at the Pabst Theater or Marcus Center for Performing Arts (MCPA).

The classic Milwaukee hotel is the Pfister; if you have the dough, it's worth the splurge.

Day 2

You've got to be up to see the sunrise over Lake Michigan; it's spectacular, anywhere

Milwaukee's historic Pabst Theater

SAY CHEESE!

You'll be driving down a country road and from out of nowhere a simple hand-lettered sign may say, "Cheese Curds Today" and point toward what looks for all the world like nothing more than a whitewashed barn.

Do stop in, because it's possibly one of a dying breed – a farm-run cheese operation. Yet don't fret – while more and more gleaming copper-kettle high-tech operations are taking over, Wisconsin's countryside is still home to many, many dozens of smaller operations, many of which have been in operation since the mid-19th century. And most of these offer viewing platforms/observation windows, if not outright tours. (And once in a while, they'll let you pick up an implement to help churn!) All, naturally, will have retail shops!

The **Wisconsin Milk Marketing Board** (wis-dairy.com) has an endless list of diminutive cheese operations where you can poke your head in for a visit. If I were to choose one place to go, it'd be Monroe, south of Madison, home to a number of operations. South but still closer to Madison in Monticello you can find a couple of classic operations. Most typical of new operations is tiny **Bleu Mont Dairy,** in Blue Mounds, west of Madison, where all the cheese is organic and made from all-chemical free raw milk, and where all power comes from the sun, wind, and cow!

Cheese is everywhere you go in Wisconsin!

along the lake You'll be hungry afterwards, so head for a healthy breakfast thereafter at Beans and Barley.

Then head for the worth-a-whole-day Milwaukee Public Museum/IMAX and, if you have time, the Harley-Davidson Museum. Lunch along the lake again at Bartollotta's Lake Park Bistro.

In the afternoon, after a rest up, take in a tour of what made Milwaukee famous at Miller Brewing. Throw in a coffee along Brady Street before dining at Karl Ratzsch's Old World Restaurant, for a taste of what German food can be at its best.

For a quiet final evening drink, head for Jefferson Street or, for a bit more, er, fervor, concentrate on Water Street.

▶ A FAMILY ROAD TRIP

Got kids? Well, load 'em up—Wisconsin has plenty to offer kids of all ages.

Day 1

Kids love to help the post office deliver mail on the mail boats in Geneva Lake! If that doesn't wear them out, take them along the fabulous Lakeshore Trail around the lake and see if they're not snoring like sawmills that night!

Day 2

Kids have tons to do—churn butter, feed animals—while learning something at Old World Wisconsin. Alternatively, let 'em get their ya-ya's out on the trails at the Kettle Moraine State Forest-Southern Unit.

Day 3

Drive east to Milwaukee and let the kids go nuts at the Discovery World at Pier Wisconsin. There's plenty for 'em to see but

Kids love the critters at the Vilas Zoo!

even better there's more for 'em to get their hands on and learn with.

Day 4

Head to Madison and let your wallet take a break at the family fun (and free) Vilas Zoo before heading to the downtown area for the Madison Children's Museum and some legendary ice cream at the world famous Babcock Hall at the University of Wisconsin.

Building Boom Table at the Madison Children's Museum

WISCONSIN'S BEST BREWS

Say "Wisconsin" and you think of cheese. And beer. Where some of the mightiest of Milwaukee's brewing empires have fallen, other great options have appeared across the state. The following is by no means comprehensive, just the author's favorites.

MILWAUKEE AND VICINITY
Well, this is the "Beer City" after all, so all of your time could technically be spent here. But do venture out of city limits to experience historic as well as modern-day breweries.

- **Miller Brewing:** One cannot bypass a tour of this beer powerhouse.
- **Microbreweries** and **Brewpubs:** The city has about a half-dozen microbreweries.

Enjoy a handcrafted brew with a view in Madison.

Try **Water St. Brewery,** a popular microbrewery new on the Milwaukee scene.

- **Sprecher Brewery:** Head north of downtown Milwaukee five miles to **Glendale** to visit this longtime microbrewery; it's got great beer but this author raves about the tasty root beer!
- **Brewery Works:** Everyone comes to **Cedarburg** for its Victorian charm, you can also get wonderful beer in an 1840s brewery.

MADISON AND VICINITY
The Madison area has it's own fair share of can't miss brew stops.

- **The Great Dane Brewpub:** Simply everyone mingles for outstanding beer, grub, and atmosphere at this downtown Madison standard.
- **Memorial Union Terrace:** Possibly the most unforgettable Madison experience can be had here at the University of Wisconsin quaffing a Wisconsin brew as you people watch while the sun sets over Lake Mendota.
- **Grumpy Troll Brewpub:** The Military Ridge State Trail in **Mount Horeb** is one of the best biking trails in the state, and near its terminus is this outstanding brewpub.
- **Brewery Creek Brewing Company:** While learning Wisconsin history in amazing **Mineral Point,** sample historic beers in a historic structure.
- **New Glarus Brewing Company:** Probably the best beer brewed in Wisconsin (save the letters, please) is in the tiny Swiss town of New Glarus .You have to try the Spotted Cow.
- **Minhas Craft Brewery:** Formerly called the **Joseph Huber Brewing Company,** this brewery is a bedrock of local taverns across southern Wisconsin.

MILWAUKEE

Drop any glib stereotype that you want—Milwaukee's heard 'em all (and shrugged 'em off and gone back to work). The largest city in a state that itself has trouble overcoming associations of hayseeds stepping over cowpies, Milwaukee is used to patiently waiting for outstaters to overcome their ingrained blue-collar imagery of belching smokestack effluvia. (Even the wacky Badgers down I-94 in the capital can't escape it. While Madison denizens picture Milwaukeeans as beer-and-bowling knuckleheads, Milwaukeeans see Madisonians as time-warp radicals convinced that they live at the center of the universe.)

Milwaukee is in fact a (surprising) mosaic of modestly sprawling metropolis, upwardly mobile financial center, hard (as hell) working industrial linchpin, and amalgamation of

funky Old World neighborhoods. All of which happen to lie in a gorgeous Lake Michigan setting. Milwaukee is thus one of those cities about whom impressed first-time visitors have been known to say, "I never would have thought . . ."

Milwaukee *is* decidedly more lunch box than bento box, but that's only one piece of this wondrous mosaic. The city still rates in the top five percent in the nation in arts, attractions, and recreation. Even with a half million denizens, it has an awfully low-key, rootsy feel to it. The lingua franca in the city's older neighborhoods is often a mother tongue peppered with accented English. You'll often hear people speak of *gemütlichkeit* (warmth, hospitality) in Milwaukee, and it's by no means hyperbole. Even the *Utne*

© THOMAS HUHTI

HIGHLIGHTS

◖ Historic Third Ward and Riverwalk: Milwaukee's most historic commercial district is gentrified but not tacky with shops, a farmers market, cafés, museums, grand architecture, and a cool riverwalk (page 29).

◖ Milwaukee Art Museum: Its stunning, sail-like addition by Santiago Calatrava was trumpeted in international media in 2001; don't forget the fantastic collections inside the building (page 33).

◖ Discovery World at Pier Wisconsin: Wow. This lakefront addition is architecturally and educationally a magnificent exclamation point (literally, from above, and figuratively) on the city's massive downtown works projects (page 34).

◖ Pabst Mansion: It drops most visitors' jaws – yes, this indeed was the Beer City, and the brewery families spared no expense showing off their riches (page 35).

◖ Milwaukee Public Museum/IMAX: This phenomenal museum – which pioneered the concept of walk-through exhibits – has the nation's largest number of exhibits, so many a day is needed to stroll through them all (page 36).

◖ Villa Terrace: Smashing terraced gardens and renowned art collections make this museum unparalleled in the Midwest (page 39).

◖ Miller Brewing: It soldiers on in the grand tradition of Milwaukee brewing. This megacomplex simply must be seen to be believed. Moreover, it's a definite point of pride for Milwaukeeans (page 42).

◖ Harley-Davidson Museum: The new Hog Heaven. Made in America with steel and pride. 'Nuff said (page 42).

◖ Summerfest: Otherwise known as the Big Gig, it's the granddaddy of U.S. festivals – an 11-day blowout of music, food, and fun, with zillions of people partying heartily (page 51).

LOOK FOR ◖ TO FIND RECOMMENDED SIGHTS, ACTIVITIES, DINING, AND LODGING.

Reader and its readers chose it as "America's Top Underrated City"!

Bottom line? Hang out here long enough and you'll appreciate it.

Oh, and a climatic by-the-way: In every weather report, you'll hear the tagline "cooler near the lake." The Great Lakes establish their own microclimates and influence inland areas for miles. Temperatures along littoral stretches endure much less extreme fluctuations than you find in inland communities. The lake is best appreciated during the dog days of summer, when its breezes take some of the swelter out of the weather. On the beaches, even during August, sweaters are not unheard of in late afternoon. (Metaphorically, it's fairly well established that the city is, in fact, much, um, "cooler," as well.)

A popular local forecasting method is to espy the tear-shaped light atop the Wisconsin Gas Company building downtown: Yellow means cold, red means warm, blue means no change, and any color flashing means precipitation is predicted.

PLANNING YOUR TIME

Any visit, if possible, should be planned around **Summerfest** in late June/early July—12 hours here aren't enough and you'll sleep for a day after, but it's a hell of a great time.

HISTORY

The Mascoutin and Fox Indians were the first to live in the tamarack swamps along the Milwaukee, Menomonee, and Kinnickinnic Rivers. Their various successors included the Potawatomi; thus, it was most likely they who, around 1675, welcomed the initial French voyageurs, Jesuit Black Robes, and renegade beaver-pelt traders paddling south. The city's name purportedly originates in an Algonquian language: *Mahn-a-waukee, Millioki,* and any number of other conjectures have all been translated as, roughly, "gathering place by the waters," a fitting appellation.

Wealth-copping fur traders built the first cabins in the malarial mucklands in the 18th century. Northwest Fur Company trader Jacques Vieau is generally credited with erecting the first shack along the Menomonee River in 1795; he was soon followed by Yankee speculators. The United States duped the Potawatomi and Menominee into ceding all lands east and north of the Milwaukee River in 1831; a couple of years later, all Native American lands in southeastern Wisconsin were gone.

The Bridge War

The first of Milwaukee's famous native sons, Solomon Juneau—the city's first permanent European—arrived around 1820 and grabbed erstwhile Native lands. Juneau, George H. Walker, and Byron Kilbourn built rival communities in and around the rivers near Lake Michigan, and none of the three could deflate his ego enough to cooperate on creating one city. For years, bad blood lingered until finally the internecine squabbles escalated into claim-jumping and city sabotage in what became known as the Bridge War. Irate east-siders considered actually going to war with the west side and at one point even buried a cannon pointed across the waters at Kilbourntown. (Attentive visitors can still discern traces of the Bridge War on a walk of the downtown streets and bridges.)

Immigrants

A steady tide of settlers streamed into the area. The first of three massive waves of German immigrants occurred in 1836. By the 1880s, 35 percent of Milwaukee would be German-born, making up 70 percent of Milwaukee's total immigrant population and contributing to its status as the most ethnically rich area in the country. (It was even dubbed the German Athens.) The ethnic mosaic includes Poles, Serbs, Italians, Irish, African Americans, Dutch, Scandinavians, Bohemians, and Hispanics; in the 2000 census, more than 50 ethnic groups were represented. Milwaukee had the country's first Polish-language newspaper, and the German publishing industry there rivaled any contemporary press group.

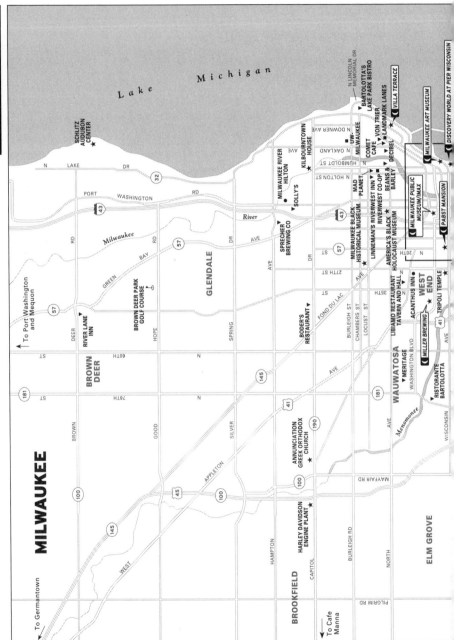

MILWAUKEE

Lake Michigan

SCHLITZ AUDUBON CENTER

N LAKE DR

PORT WASHINGTON RD

Milwaukee

River

GLENDALE

BROWN DEER PARK GOLF COURSE

RIVER LANE INN

BROWN DEER

BODER'S RESTAURANT

GREEN BAY RD

HOPE

FOND DU LAC

SPRING

60TH

76TH

GOOD

SILVER

APPLETON

WEST

HAMPTON

CAPITOL

BROWN

PILGRIM RD

BURLEIGH RD

MAYFAIR RD

NORTH

WISCONSIN

BROOKFIELD

ELM GROVE

To Germantown

To Port Washington and Mequon

To Cafe Manna

ANNUNCIATION GREEK ORTHODOX CHURCH

HARLEY DAVIDSON ENGINE PLANT

Menomonee

WAUWATOSA

RISTORANTE BARTOLOTTA

MERITAGE

MILLER BREWING

WASHINGTON BLVD

WEST END

ACANTHUS INN

TRIPOLI TEMPLE

LIBIAMO RESTAURANT TAVERN AND HALL

AMERICA'S BLACK HOLOCAUST MUSEUM

LINNEMAN'S RIVERWEST INN

MILWAUKEE BLACK HISTORICAL MUSEUM

MILWAUKEE PUBLIC MUSEUM/IMAX

PABST MANSION

BEANS & BARLEY

RIVERWEST CO-OP

MAD PLANET

DECIBEL

COMET CAFE

VON TRIER

LANDMARK LANES

UW-MILWAUKEE

KILBOURNTOWN HOUSE

MILWAUKEE RIVER HILTON

SOLLY'S

SPRECHER BREWING CO

N DOWNER AVE

N OAKLAND AVE

N HUMBOLDT ST

N HOLTON ST

N LINCOLN MEMORIAL DR

BARTOLOTTA'S LAKE PARK BISTRO

VILLA TERRACE

MILWAUKEE ART MUSEUM

DISCOVERY WORLD AT PIER WISCONSIN

27TH ST

35TH

20TH

BURLEIGH ST

CHAMBERS ST

LOCUST ST

MILWAUKEE

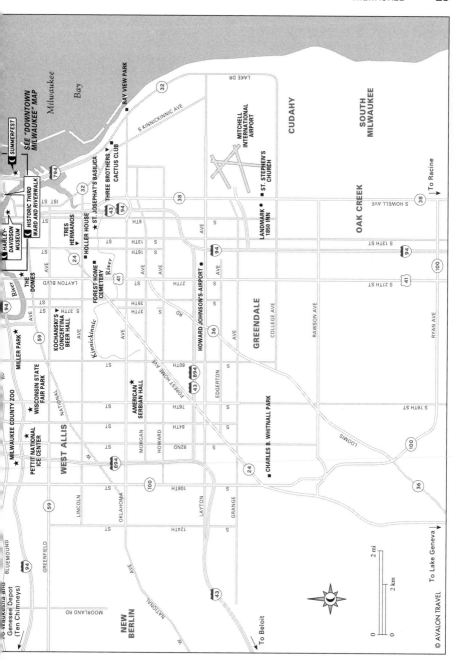

SEE "DOWNTOWN MILWAUKEE" MAP

SUMMERFEST

HARLEY-DAVIDSON MUSEUM ★

HISTORIC THIRD WARD AND RIVERWALK ★

BAY VIEW PARK ■

Milwaukee Bay

S KINNICKINNIC AVE

THREE BROTHERS ▼
CACTUS CLUB ■
★ ST. JOSEPHAT'S BASILICA

TRES HERMANOS ★
HOLLER HOUSE ■

THE DOMES ★

FOREST HOME ■ CEMETERY

KOCHANSKI'S ▼ CONCERTINA BEER HALL

Kinnickinnic River

MILLER PARK ★
WISCONSIN STATE FAIR PARK ★

MILWAUKEE COUNTY ZOO ★
PETTIT NATIONAL ICE CENTER ★

WEST ALLIS

AMERICAN ★ SERBIAN HALL

HOWARD JOHNSON'S-AIRPORT ●

MITCHELL INTERNATIONAL AIRPORT

ST. STEPHEN'S CHURCH ■
LANDMARK ● 1850 INN

CUDAHY

SOUTH MILWAUKEE

GREENDALE

OAK CREEK

CHARLES B. WHITNALL PARK ■

NEW BERLIN

To Waukesha and Genesee Depot (Ten Chimneys)

BLUEMOUND
GREENFIELD
LINCOLN
OKLAHOMA
LAYTON
GRANGE
MOORLAND RD
NATIONAL
MORGAN
HOWARD
NATIONAL
COLLEGE AVE
RAWSON AVE
RYAN AVE
LOOMIS
LAKE DR
S KINNICKINNIC AVE
LAYTON BLVD
FOREST HOME AVE

To Beloit
To Lake Geneva
To Racine

0 2 mi
0 2 km

© AVALON TRAVEL

American Made

The Civil War provided Milwaukee's biggest economic boon. Milwaukee's deepwater harbor provided both an outlet for goods and an inlet for immigrant labor. More than 3,300 tanneries, meatpacking plants, and machine and ironworks became industrial stalwarts, and through the 1870s Milwaukee remained the wheat-milling and transport capital of the world. Nowadays, though Milwaukee has shed a bit of its rough exterior, more than 20 percent of the population is still employed in manufacturing, and the city has retained the moniker "machine shop of America."

Socialist Central

Immigrant labor gave Milwaukee its trademark socialistic overtones. Workers—many of them enlightened freethinkers from Germany fleeing oppression—organized the first trade and labor unions and played a direct role in the establishment of the country's first unemployment compensation act. In 1888, Milwaukee elected the first socialist ever elected in a major city. Socialist mayor Dan Hoan once said, after refusing to invite the king of Belgium to the city, "I stand for the common man; to hell with kings." Socialists were later elected to a few county posts, and Milwaukee eventually sent the first socialist to the House of Representatives. Milwaukee labor unions and their strikes are legendary in the Midwest. They were among the initial and definitely most vociferous proponents of workplace reform; by the mid-1880s, up to 15,000 workers at a time would stage demonstrations, and in 1886 militia groups fired on crowds in the eastern European enclave of Bay View, killing five immigrant laborers.

20th Century

World War I was not a particularly good time for German-heavy Milwaukee, but worse was the Prohibition that followed. The Beer City switched to root beer, the socialists organized quasi-WPA relief agencies that predated the Depression, and everybody held on tight. (Interestingly, at 12:01 A.M. on the day

Prohibition was officially repealed, Milwaukee somehow managed to ship 15 million bottles of beer!)

After World War II, as African Americans migrated to factory jobs along the Great Lakes, Milwaukee's African American population reached 17 percent within three decades. Unfortunately, Milwaukee remained one of the nation's most segregated cities, as riots and marches of the 1960s pointed out.

Slowly but surely, the lucrative factory days waned, and the central city declined. Exhaustive machinations to overhaul the downtown began in the mid-'80s, and a careful gentrification—no sickening ersatz tourist-shakedown sheen—has real history. Still, that's not to say Milwaukee isn't striving for a new image: A zillion dollars invested in infrastructure and tourism has kept the city squarely in the media—national and beyond—spotlight. In all, tourism in Milwaukee generates around $2 billion, accounting for more than 20 percent of the state economy.

NEIGHBORHOODS AND HISTORIC DISTRICTS

"Indeed, it is not easy to recall any busy city which combines more comfort, evidences of wealth and taste and refinement, than this town on the bluffs," an impressed easterner once observed more than a century ago.

You *will* find neighborhoods and architecture to pique your interest, even today.

The Convention and Visitors Bureau offers detailed brochures covering all Milwaukee neighborhoods; it also has lists of tour companies, including **Historic Milwaukee Inc.** (828 N. Broadway, 414/277-7795, historicmilwaukee.org), which offers an astonishing number of strolling tours ($7), for many of which you needn't make reservations.

Yankee Hill

Yankee Hill makes other grand Milwaukee neighborhoods appear raffish. This grande dame enclave arose north of East Mason Street to East Ogden Avenue and west off the lakefront to North Jackson Street. Originally owned by Milwaukee's first resident, Solomon Juneau, this became the city's center of government, finance, and business. Churches are everywhere, along with lovely old row houses and town houses as well as examples of Victorian Gothic, Italianate, and every other 19th-century architectural predilection.

Juneautown

Juneautown constituted the east side of the 19th-century internecine Milwaukee wars. This high-and-dry real estate enjoyed a prime location from the river to Lake Michigan and developed into the effective heart of the original city. Today, both Water Street and Wisconsin Avenue atavistically claim the title of most-happening area in the city. Original architectural gems such as the Milwaukee City Hall, Pabst Theater, Iron Block, and funky old Milwaukee Street are still chockablock with baroque Victorian buildings. **St. Mary's Church** (836 N. Broadway, at the corner of E. Kilbourn Ave. in Juneautown) is precisely the same age as Milwaukee. Made of Cream City brick in 1846, it is the oldest Catholic church in the city. The Annunciation painting above the altar was a gift from King Ludwig I of Bavaria.

Kilbourntown

Kilbourntown went up as a direct, contemporary rival to Juneautown. Speculator Byron Kilbourn refused to align his bridges with Juneautown's, the consequence of which is apparent today. Low-lying and marshy, there wasn't much going for the land, other than location—spreading west from today's Old World 3rd Street, the community was an important transit point to Madison. Other than North Old World 3rd Street, much of the architecture was razed for megaprojects. Highlights in Kilbourntown include the Mediterranean revival Riverside Theater along West Wisconsin Avenue; the Germania Building on West Wells Street, once the site of a German-language publishing empire and notable for its carved lions and copper-clad domes (endearingly

dubbed "Kaiser's Helmets"); the odd-shaped Milwaukee County Historical Center; the legendary Turner Hall; the Milwaukee Public Museum; Milwaukee Public Library; and the enormous Grand Avenue Mall.

Brady Street

Brady Street spans a land bridge connecting the Milwaukee River and Lake Michigan. Another major overhaul of the local architecture has restored this area, originally Milwaukee's version of Little Italy. There's also an appreciable quotient of hipsters and misunderstood geniuses lining coffeehouse windows (an *unreal* array of java joints is here!). The refurbishing has nice touches, such as the etching of Brady Street history into the sidewalk concrete.

Bronzeville

Bronzeville, an erstwhile African American cultural and entertainment center that has faded, has begun a Brady Street gentrification to make it hip and happening. The district runs from North 4th Street to North 7th Street, using America's Black Holocaust Museum (in danger of closing at the time of writing) and the Wisconsin Black Historical Museum as touristic cornerstones.

Now this has not come without a bit of controversy. As black Milwaukeeans have migrated from just this district, some say "Bronzeville" and any gentrification is being done without enough African American input in design or execution; or, in other words, it'll be just another trendy district of chi-chi-dom and not much about the black experience in the city—serious in a city in which 38 percent of the population is African American.

Walker's Point

Immediately north of the Allen-Bradley clock, between 1st and 2nd Streets on West National Avenue, is a stretch of Milwaukee that kinda smacks of a Depression-era photo during the day but by night becomes one of the city's most underappreciated tip-the-elbow neighborhoods. This small, formerly marshy peninsula at the confluence of the Milwaukee and Menomonee Rivers was settled by George Walker, who knew that when the swamplands were drained, he would have an overland route between the east and west sides of the city. Walker's Point is also one of the most ethnically mixed neighborhoods in Milwaukee. German, Scandinavian, British, Welsh, Irish, Serb, Croatian, and Polish settlers came in originally, and Hispanics and Southeast Asian immigrants have arrived more recently.

Activated in 1962, the **Allen-Bradley clock,** the second-largest in the world—but the largest four-faced clock in the world, according to the *Guinness Book of World Records*—has octagonal clock faces twice the size of the clocks of Big Ben in London. The hour hands are 15 feet 9 inches long and weigh 490 pounds; the minute hands are 20 feet long and weigh 530 pounds. It's still crucial as a lake navigation marker. Stop by **Tivoli Gardens** to see another good example of gentrification. An original alfresco produce market was renovated into a *biergarten* by Schlitz Brewing Company and in the past decade was redone yet again, but without undoing the better aspects of its design.

North Point District

Virtually all of the Northpoint District is on the National Register of Historic Places. This longtime exclusive community lies west of North Lincoln Memorial Drive and south of East Park Place to East Woodstock Place,

tracing the northern stretch of Milwaukee's coastal bight. The North Point Watertower occupies the central radial point, and the northern section is bookended by Lake Park.

East of here along the lakefront is **Lake Park,** designed by Frederick Law Olmsted, planner of New York City's Central Park and San Francisco's Golden Gate Park. Prehistoric Native American burial mounds are here. At the top of North Avenue is the **North Point Water Tower,** a Victorian Gothic structure dating from the 1870s and one of the few extant water towers like it in the United States.

West End

A case can be made that the West End rivals Yankee Hill's opulence. West End became the city's first residential suburb, between North 27th Street, North 35th Street, West Wisconsin Avenue, and West Vliet Street. Yankee bluebloods and prominent German American families competed in building the most opulent mansions. Highland Boulevard was at one time referred to as "Sauerkraut Boulevard." District by district preservation efforts have restored lots of the original grandeur. Three historic districts are now within the West End. Highlights of the area include the Tripoli Shrine Temple on West Wisconsin Avenue, Central United Methodist Church on North 25th Street, Harley-Davidson's corporate headquarters, and Miller Brewing Company.

autumn stroll in Lake Park

© WISCONSIN DEPARTMENT OF TOURISM

Sights

No guidebook gush—lots of Milwaukee awaits. The city comprises 96 square miles in a big rectangle backing off the lake. Note that much freeway "gentrification" (sorely needed) is on-going, so be patient! The U.S. government says Milwaukee is likely to suffer L.A.-esque traffic death by 2020—prepare for gridlock at rush hours already. (On a positive note, in August 2008, the city finished the first major highway project, the leviathan Marquette Interchange south of downtown; this hundreds-and-hundreds-of-millions-of-dollars project actually came in *early* and *under budget*. Ah, that good old-fashioned Midwestern work ethic!)

Beware: Jaywalking is illegal and strictly enforced in Milwaukee, especially during lunchtime hours. You *will* be ticketed; don't even try it. On the other hand, the police dole out equal numbers of tickets to drivers who don't give way to pedestrians, so it works out.

From the west, I-94 is the primary thoroughfare; I-894 skirts the southern and western fringes north to south, and I-43 meets I-94 at the Marquette interchange downtown and then heads north.

Off the freeways, most of the sights—save the Historic Third Ward or outlying sights—are concentrated in a rough square bounded by WI 145 to the north, I-43 to the west, I-794 to the south, and the big old lake to the east. The Milwaukee River splits the square down the middle and separates the city into its east and west sections. The river is also the line of demarcation for street numbering, so if you bear in mind where the river is, you should be fine.

A comprehensive skywalk system connects the Midwest Airlines Convention Center, the Federal Plaza, and the Shops at Grand Avenue. When it was built, one stretch, the Riverspan, was the only skywalk in the United States built over a navigable riverway, here the Milwaukee River.

Milwaukee Angels

Bless the city of Milwaukee for its angels—not seraphims, but civic altruists walking the

walkways, biking the streets, or staffing little info kiosks. Officially called public service ambassadors (PSAs around here), they'll happily guide you wherever you're going or find someone who can help—as the unofficial eyes and ears of emergency services, they also help make the city safe. An admirable service from the city, quite honestly.

DOWNTOWN
◖ Historic Third Ward and Riverwalk

Until the mid-1980s, this was a zone in distress. The one-time bustling ethnic warehouse district suffered a catastrophic conflagration in 1892 in which more than 500 buildings burned (only one was left standing), displacing thousands of immigrants. Though the area was rebuilt, the earlier verve was always missing. Halfway through the 1980s, however, that started to change. Antique stores and art

© THOMAS HUHTI

You'll find great shopping along Milwaukee's Riverwalk.

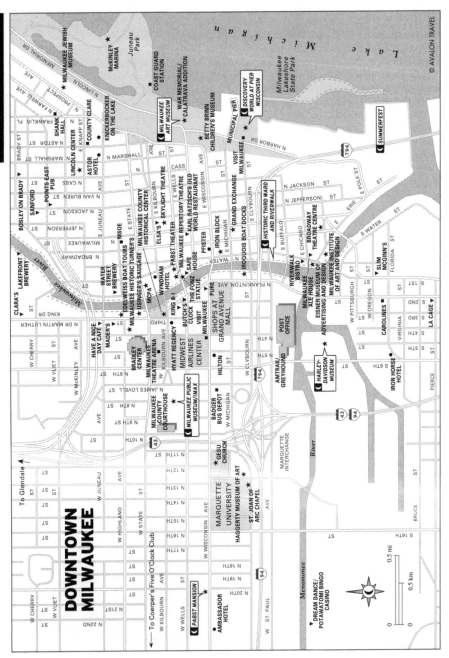

© AVALON TRAVEL

galleries are the norm now, among cafés, upscale shops, and a few longtime holdovers. It's also the fruit and vegetable district, quite a sight in the morning as the trucks roll through. A quick tour via www.historicthirdward.org before arrival would help.

The unofficial "off-Broadway" area of the city, the Third Ward has the **Broadway Theatre Center** (158 N. Broadway, 414/291-7800), which smacks of an 18th-century European opera house; within you'll find four venerable artistic institutions: Skylight Theatre; Milwaukee Chamber Theatre; Renaissance Theaterworks; and Milwaukee Shakespeare Theatre.

The well-regarded **Milwaukee Institute of Art and Design** (273 E. Erie St., 414/276-7889, www.miad.edu) is housed in an old terminal, rebuilt in the days after the ward fire. *Many* galleries (generally open during sessions 10 A.M.–5 P.M. Tues.–Sat., till 7 P.M. Thurs.) display student work.

Run by the MIAD, the around-the-corner **Eisner Museum of Advertising and Design** (208 E. Water St., 414/203-0371, www.eisner-museum.org, 11 A.M.–5 P.M. Wed. and Sat., till 8 P.M. Thurs., noon–5 P.M. Sat., 1–5 P.M. Sun, $5 adults) is only the second facility related to

this subject in the country, and the only one owned by an art school. Extensive exhibits include the automobile in advertising, beer in ads (natch), along with a half dozen rotating exhibits. (Trust me, at least one of these exhibits on famous ads will make you chuckle nostalgically.) You can even record your own radio commercial!

The riverwalk in the Third Ward includes the **Public Market,** a year-round farmers market, replete with anachronistic warehouse-style buildings and early-20th-century facades. It's not just a farmers' market—you'll find artisan and ethnic foodstuffs, artists, the occasional busker, cooking classes, and a lovely second-floor patio/garden to rest, snack, or sip. No way space here allows for a *complete* rundown of what they offer, so thwack your way to www.milwaukeepublicmarket.org to get the lowdown.

Old World 3rd Street and Water Street

North of I-794 is another modestly gentrified zone along both sides of the Milwaukee River. To the east is Water Street, the happening mélange of microbreweries, sports pubs, dance clubs, restaurants, and cultural attractions. To

© THOMAS HUHTI

Milwaukee's Historic Third Ward

IT'S *FREEZING* HERE. WHAT DO I DO?

Well, if you're staying in the Residence Inn Downtown or the Hyatt Regency, you never have to wear a coat as they're part of downtown's **skywalk system.** The former is connected to the three-block complex of the Grand Avenue shopping center, so you've got that going for you. The latter is connected merely to the Midwest Airlines convention center but there's also a city information office there, and the solicitous folks there will have loads of ideas to escape the cold (though they might inwardly think: *Whaddaya mean, cold?*). (Many people don't realize the Midwest Airlines Center does have over $1 million in art on display, too.)

BUT SERIOUSLY, NOW – IT'S COLD.

OK, here are the top places to forget about the cold:

Milwaukee Public Museum: Rainforest exhibit. Need I say more?

Discovery World: Come here and think of unfrozen water when you see the aquariums (plus, it's so big you'll be here all day).

The Domes: You're inside a ginormous set of greenhouses, one of which is devoted to tropical flora.

Harley-Davidson Museum: Nothing reminds you of spring like Harleys.

I LIKE WINTER. WHAT CAN I DO?

Everyone will tell you that you have to go to the **Pettit National Ice Center** (listed within) since it's the Olympic Training Center, blah blah. It's awesome and has daily skating, but it's far west of downtown and, come on, it's indoors.

The best way to get a cold lick in the face is to just walk along the Lake Michigan shoreline. Go ahead – see what lake-effect means (and wind chill).

Seriously, for the best all-round winter experience, head for **Whitnall Park** (listed within). First off, it's got miles of semi-groomed trails (but no rentals, and they're hard to find downtown), warming huts, and concessions. Even better, however, is the outstanding tobogganing at this park; they even ice down one sucker of a trail – wow! You can rent a toboggan here for $6.50 per hour. The trails are lit at night, as well.

No time for that? No problem. At 920 North Water Street downtown you can head for Red Arrow Park's **Slice of Ice** for some outdoor ice skating. The park offers a nice rooftop viewing platform, skate rentals, a warming house and next door is a Starbucks!

a couple enjoys a beautiful post-snow walk

© THOMAS HUHTI

the Milwaukee Art Museum's Calatrava addition

the west is Old World 3rd Street, with more classic Milwaukee edifices, original old hotels and factories, the Bradley Center (where the Milwaukee Bucks play, among many other activities), and more restaurants. The riverwalk here includes **Pere Marquette Park,** with a gazebo, pavilion, and boat dock for tours, along with permanent decks and slips over the water.

Also along North Old World 3rd Street is **Usinger's** (1030 N. Old World 3rd St., 414/276-9100, 8:30 A.M.–5 P.M. Mon.–Sat.), known as the Tiffany of sausage makers. In a city raised on *fleisch,* Usinger's has been the carnivore's heaven since 1880 and partially explains the occasional odd olfactory sensation downtown—the sweet scent of wood smoke mingling with the smell of brewer's yeast. *Food and Wine* has dubbed Usinger's bratwurst the best sausage in America.

Lakefront

Milwaukee sits on the deepest harbor on the western edge of Lake Michigan. For miles, the city rolls like a sideways wave along the lake. You can drive the entire lakefront on WI 32 or bike most of it on separate county park bike paths. You pass nine beaches along the way; the most popular include **South Shore**

Beach along South Shore Drive, **McKinley** and **Bradford Beaches,** both along North Lincoln Memorial Drive; and **Grant Beach,** in South Milwaukee. At Veterans Park near downtown you can rent paddleboats, hydrobikes, and sailboats.

Lincoln Memorial Drive is what most visitors see, and most visitors start precisely at the Milwaukee Art Museum; it stretches about three miles from north of the Summerfest grounds along green space to Lake Park at the tip of a modest promontory. Three miles of park, park, and more park.

South of the Milwaukee Art Museum and the Discovery World at Pier Wisconsin crown jewels is one of Wisconsin's newest state parks—**Lakeshore State Park**—a nearly 20-acre parcel of land adjacent to the Summerfest grounds with beaches, fishing, and trails linking it to *the rest of the state.*

◖ Milwaukee Art Museum

Among the tops in the Midwest for visual arts museums is the Milwaukee Art Museum (700 N. Art Museum Dr., 414/224-3200, www .mam.org, 10 A.M.–5 P.M. Tues.–Sun., till 8 P.M. Thurs., $8). The museum holds one of the United States' most important and extensive collections of German Expressionist art—not unimportant, given the city's Teutonic link (the museum is ranked third in the *world* in German art). The museum now houses well over 20,000 paintings, sculptures, prints, and decorative art. Other noteworthy exhibits include a panorama of Haitian art and the repository of Frank Lloyd Wright's Prairie School of Architecture. Pieces date back as far as the 15th century, and the permanent displays are impressively diverse—Old Masters to Warhol through the Ash Can School. The Bradley Wing houses a world-renowned collection of Modern Masters.

MAM is actually one piece of the vast **Milwaukee County War Memorial Center,** a complex comprising several parts of the immediate lakefront and assorted buildings throughout the city. The complex was originally already a landmark, designed by Eero Saarinen. But it's right here at the MAM that a few years ago the city really put itself on the map. A massive, $50 million architectural enhancement to the museum by international designer Santiago Calatrava is, with zero exaggeration, breathtaking. Or stunning. Or any other superlative you choose. Whatever the description, do not miss it. The addition—gull-like wings, which can be raised or lowered to let sunlight in, soaring above the complex—features a suspended pedestrian bridge linking it to downtown. So important is this addition that no less than *Time* magazine named it "building of the year" in 2001.

Discovery World at Pier Wisconsin

Simply overwhelming—in the best possible sense—is this ultra-high-tech (and fetchingly designed) conglomeration of every single science known, all done in an accessible, fascinating manner. Seriously, it's an unbelievable place. Discovery World (500 N. Harbor Dr., 414/765-9966, www.discoveryworld.org, 9 A.M.–4 P.M. weekdays except Mon., 10 A.M.–5 P.M. weekends, $17 adults) is a freshwater education center—limnological as well as natural/human history. (It's the best

freshwater educational experience in the U.S., hands down.) It's got 120,000 square feet—including two massive fresh- and saltwater aquariums—of exhibits (more than 200 ultimately), all of them the cutting-est of cutting edge. (And it's not just biology—students have exhibits from communications technology to astronomy, most of it active rather than passive.) In 2008 the center unveiled a new exhibit to the innovations, musically or music technology, of local boy Les Paul. The center hopes for this exhibit to become permanent—it all depends on the fate of the planned Les Paul museum/complex in his hometown of Waukesha, west of Milwaukee.

A cool by the way—one of this author's favorite experiences is to experience the whole complex via the on-site Segways!

Either moored outside or off on some research jaunt is the *Denis Sullivan,* a floating classroom and the only Great Lakes schooner recreation anywhere. Yes, you can sail on it and it's amazing, but do check out the website for these regular but un-oft occasions.

Local Architecture

A block from the Milwaukee Public Museum, the distinctive **Milwaukee Public Library** (814 W. Wisconsin Ave., 414/286-3032, free tours 1:30 P.M. Sat.) is an impressive 1895 edifice. You can find it by looking for the dome. Inside, a spacious rotunda displays well-preserved original detail work. The city sank more than $10 million into a post-millennium preservation effort, and the results—graceful century-old design, ambient light, Old World detailing—are admirable (the staircase alone is worth a view!). Oh, and free wireless access too.

In the 200 block of East Wells Street, **Milwaukee City Hall** (414/286-2266, 8 A.M.–4 P.M. weekdays, free) is a navigational aid for first-timers, with its can't-miss-it Flemish Renaissance design (and also because many remember it from the television sitcom *Laverne and Shirley*). Antechambers there display Old World craftsmanship. The 10-ton bell in the tower now rings only for special occasions, and it rocks the entire downtown when it does. A $44 million restoration project is also to restore the gorgeous edifice's luster.

On the southeast corner of Water Street and Wisconsin Avenue, the antebellum **Iron Block** is the only example of cast-iron architecture left in Milwaukee, and one of three in the Midwest.

Wisconsin's one-time status as leading world grain producer explains the lavish interiors of the **Grain Exchange** (225 E. Michigan St.). In the Mackie Building, the three-story exchange was built in 1879 (the first centralized trading center in the United States); recent touchups resulted in atavistic Victorian opulence—gold motifs and enormous paneled murals adorn the 10,000-square-foot room.

Breweries, Past and Present

Milwaukee was once home to dozens of breweries churning out the secret sauce of *gemütlichkeit*. The pungent malt scent can still pervade, and beer does remain a cultural linchpin. In 2007, plans were finally set to renovate the long-dormant Pabst brewery into a gentrified residential/commercial district; purportedly, the *loooooong*-awaited **Museum of Beer and Brewing** (www.brewingmuseum.org)—c'mon, how can Milwaukee not already have this?—signed a letter of intent to locate there.

Though Pabst, once the sixth-largest (and oldest) U.S. brewer, lives on in name (it's popular in China, of all places), it's no longer made in the United States. Schlitz—the "Beer that Made Milwaukee Famous"—has just made a reappearance, though it's not brewed in Milwaukee. Miller is the lone megabrewing holdout though Milwaukeeans flipped their collective wig a bit in 2008 when, after a merger with Coors, it was decided to relocate the corporate headquarters to—gasp, of all places, oh the betrayal!—Chicago (worry not, the big ol' brewery itself ain't goin' anywhere).

Microbreweries and brewpubs are picking up the slack in a very large fashion.

Lakefront Brewery (1872 N. Commerce St., 414/372-8800, www.lakefrontbrewery.com, tours at 3 P.M. most days except Sun., $5) started as a kitchen experiment for some

Milwaukee brothers and now puts out 2,000 barrels annually. Tours take in Larry, Moe, and Curly on the tanks, a cheeky start. Lakefront brews include specialty beers such as pumpkin- and cherry-flavored varieties; it's even got New Grist, a gluten-free variety. This generally is voted best brewery tour by local media. The brewery also has a boat dock and lies on the riverwalk.

A few friends have howled that a certain author has been remiss not mentioning **Milwaukee Ale House** (233 North Water St., 414/226-2336, 11 A.M.–10 P.M. Mon.–Thurs., till 1 A.M. Fri./Sat., till 9 P.M. Sun., $6–15) and its brews are excellent—even better sipped by its great riverside location with double-decker *biergarten*. Great live music here. Local tidbit: This building was once a saddlery and, later, the place where the Hula Hoop was invented!

North of here find Milwaukee's original brewpub at **Water Street Brewery** (1101 North Water St., 414/272-1195, food served 11 A.M.–9 P.M. Mon.–Sat., $5–15). It's got great brews and a good fish fry, but if for no other reason stop by to see the amazing beer memorabilia collection (some 60,000 items).

But if you're in Milwaukee, ya gotta check out something original, eh? Beerheads should check out the original interiors of **Landmark 1850 Inn** (5905 S. Howell Ave., 414/769-1850), on the grounds of the airport (one of the great original "taps," or corner bar; the ex-Pabst Brewery taproom, reborn as **Slim McGinn's** (338 S. 1st St., 414/271-7546); and, newest, **Libiamo Restaurant Tavern & Hall** (221 W. Galena St., 414/271-1155), an Italian restaurant with lunch and dinner nightly—good enough, but it was built from the famous Brown Bottle Taproom of the original Schlitz Brewery.

◖ Pabst Mansion

Look what vats full of money once got you at the Pabst Mansion (2000 W. Wisconsin Ave., 414/931-0808, www.pabstmansion.com, 10 A.M.–4 P.M. Mon.–Sat., noon–4 P.M. Sun., closed Feb., $8 adults), the must-see

© THOMAS HUHTI

the legendary Pabst Mansion

architecture stop in the city. Built 1890–1893 of those legendary cream-colored bricks, it was the decadent digs of Captain Frederick Pabst, who slummed as a steamship pilot while awaiting his heirship to the Pabst fortune. The Flemish Renaissance mansion, unique in a city that didn't have much like it, is staggering even by the baroque standards of the time: 37 rooms, 12 baths, 14 fireplaces, 20,000-plus feet of floor space, carved panels moved from Bavarian castles, priceless ironwork by Milwaukeean Cyril Colnik, and some of the finest woodwork you'll likely ever see. An adjacent pavilion, now the gift shop, was the Pabst showcase at the World's Columbian Exposition in Chicago in 1893 but was later renovated to resemble St. Peter's Basilica.

◖ Milwaukee Public Museum/ IMAX

Among the most respected nationally and number one nationwide in exhibits is the Milwaukee Public Museum (800 W. Wells St.,

414/278-2702, www.mpm.com, 9 A.M.–5 P.M. Mon.–Sat., from noon Sun., $11 adults.). It initiated the concept of walk-through exhibits in 1882 and total habitat dioramas (with a muskrat mock-up) in 1890; today, its "Old Milwaukee" street life construct is quite possibly Milwaukee's most visited tourist spot. The museum's multilevel walk-through Rain Forest of Costa Rica—featuring its own 20-foot cascade—wins kudos and awards on an annual basis. Among the catacombs of displays on archaeology, anthropology, geology, botany, ethnography, and more are its jewels of paleontology: the world's largest dinosaur skull and a 15-million-year-old shoveltusk elephant skeleton obtained from the Beijing Natural History Museum.

The museum constantly reworks itself to allow some of the six million-plus pieces in storage to see the light of day. One heartwarming display that one hopes will always draw throngs of visitors is the skeleton of beloved Samson, the 600-pound gorilla and longtime resident of the Milwaukee County Zoo, who died in 1981. The Live Butterfly Garden has become another popular exhibit with the general public and especially with this author's relatives. Its new planetarium (in a $17 million IMAX theater) is a big deal, as it is the only place on earth to have such advanced computer projection systems.

When waltzing in, stop and examine the leviathan mammoth (it's a reconstruction—the original is used for research) in the lobby. Calling the museum home as of 2008, the Big Dude (a Hebior woolly mammoth, and this is my name for the big fella) was found in Kenosha County (WI), and is the most complete ever found in North America. More importantly, butchering marks on the skeleton dated to 14,500 years ago, putting a major dent in the Clovis Theory, which posits that humans shouldn't have been here at that time. Archaeologists and paleontologists come from around the world to study this bad boy as he helps rewrite the history books.

Take walking shoes, as the three floors—

and you'll want to see every one—will wear you down.

Other Museums

Across from the arts museum in O'Donnell Park, the **Betty Brinn Children's Museum** (929 E. Wisconsin Ave., 414/291-0888, www .bbcmkids.org, $5) has been rated by *Parents* magazine in the top 10 for best museums for families. Kids become artists, walk through the human body, grow a garden, or even work at their own TV station—but most just love to ride the choo-choo. Hours are 9 A.M.–5 P.M. daily, noon–5 P.M. Sunday, closed Monday September–June.

The triangular **Milwaukee County Historical Center** (910 N. Old World 3rd St., 414/273-8288, www.milwaukeecountyhistsoc .org, 9:30 A.M.–5 P.M. weekdays, 10 A.M.–5 P.M. Sat., and 1–5 P.M. Sun., free) features fascinating explicative displays on the city's legendary Bridge Wars and roiling socialism. A painting alcove displays works of the Panorama painters—an obscure Milwaukee specialty.

Across the river from here, the Milwaukee School of Engineering's **Grohmann Museum** (1000 N. Broadway, 414/277-7501, www.msoe .edu/manatwork, hours vary, free admission) is new and houses over 700 paintings and sculptures. All of these—and here's the cool part—comprise the world's largest collection focused on work. Yes, on the concept of working. Fascinating.

Marquette University

Though the university's namesake was not particularly enamored of the Great Lake coastline, this Jesuit university was founded in 1881 and christened for the intrepid explorer. (The university purportedly even has bone fragments from the Black Robe.) The university (Wisconsin Ave., 414/278-3178, www.marquette.edu) has regular event updates.

The primary attraction here is the **St. Joan of Arc Chapel** (10 A.M.–4 P.M. Mon.–Sat. and noon–4 P.M. Sun.), an inspiring, five-century-old relic from the Rhone River Valley of France. Transported stone by stone, along with

another medieval chateau, it was reassembled on Long Island in 1927 by a railroad magnate (the French government put the kibosh on cultural relocation after this). It was lovingly redone by some of the nation's premier historic architects and renovators and remains the only medieval structure in the Western Hemisphere where Mass is said regularly. Stories regarding St. Joan and the chapel may or may not be apocryphal; she is said to have kissed one of the stones while worshiping in the chapel during the war between France and England, and that stone has been colder than the surrounding ones ever since. The chapel may be closed weekends when school is out.

Another treasure of architecture here is the Brobdingnagian Gothic 1894 **Gesu Church.** The vertiginous heights of the spires are enough, but the gorgeous rose stained glass, divided into 14 petals, is equally memorable.

Also on campus is the **Haggerty Museum of Art** (530 N. 13th St., 414/288-1669, www .marquette.edu/haggerty, 10 A.M.–4:30 P.M. Mon.–Sat., noon–5 P.M. Sun. and Thurs. evening, free). It is easily one of the city's most challenging galleries and worth it for anyone jaded by excessive exposure to the old masters. It's multicultural and multimedia with a modernist bent. The priciest piece is the Bible series of more than 100 hand-colored etchings by Marc Chagall.

One fascinating item at the **Marquette University Memorial Library** (1415 W. Wisconsin Ave.) is the world-renowned J.R.R. Tolkien Collection—more than 10,000 pages for *The Lord of the Rings* alone, but also thousands of other documents. Given the magnitude of the Hollywood opus's popularity, which rekindled all sorts of interest in the original work, this collection is seeing a phenomenal increase in attendance. Hours vary by semester and are reduced in summer.

Freebies

Bless Milwaukee—there's always free stuff! The Marcus Center for Performing Arts (see *Entertainment and Events*) has a riverside tent with free cultural performances Tuesday

THE BEER CITY

It's hit the skids to a certain extent, but in a state that conjures images of beer halls and morning quaffs, Milwaukee was the place that gave rise to the stereotype. King Gambrinus, the mythical Flemish king and purported inventor and patron of beer, would no doubt have called the city home.

THE BEGINNINGS AND THE RISE

The first brewery in Milwaukee wasn't started by a German. In 1840, Richard Owens and two other Welshmen founded a lakefront brewery and began producing mostly ales. Germans got into the act not much later with Herman Reuthlisberger's brewery in Milwaukee – and the city's character was never the same. In 1844, Jacob Best started the neighborhood Empire Brewery, which later became the first of the megabreweries, Pabst. The same year saw Milwaukee's first beer garden – that all-inclusive picnic/party zone with lovely flower gardens and promenades so essential to German culture – open, and this was two years before the city's charter was approved! The next half decade saw the establishment of the progenitors of Milwaukee's hops heritage – in order, Blatz, Schlitz, and the modern leviathan, Miller.

Without question, the primary beer spur was massive immigration. Most influential were the waves of German immigrants, who earned Milwaukee the nickname "German Athens" by the 1880s. Breweries and state beer consumption rose and fell in direct proportion to the level of Teutonic immigration. Further, when the government levied a whiskey tax of $1 per barrel, tavern patrons immediately began asking for beer instead.

Another factor in Milwaukee's brewery success was location; Wisconsin was a world agricultural player in herbs, hops among them. In addition, Milwaukee's plethora of natural ice gave it an edge over other U.S. brewers. The Great Chicago Fire of 1871 also helped by devastating virtually all of Milwaukee's competition. Breweries sponsored their own salons throughout the city. The city became famous for production and consumption; by the Civil War, there was one tippler's joint for every 90 residents – and *during* the war, the breweries doubled their production yet again. At one time, there were nearly 600 breweries in the state. This led temperance cru-

afternoons and evenings in summer. Pere Marquette park has **free concerts** Tuesday and Wednesday evenings; Cathedral Park Square at Jefferson and Wells features free live jazz Thursday evenings.

NORTH OF DOWNTOWN
Charles Allis Art Museum

Southwest of Lake Park and overlooking Lake Michigan, the Charles Allis Art Museum (1801 N. Prospect Ave., 414/278-8295, www.cavtmuseums.org, 1–5 P.M. Wed.–Sun., $5 adults) is in a Tudor mansion built by the first president of Allis-Chalmers, a major city employer. It has a superb collection of world art, fine furniture, and nearly 1,000 objects d'art dating back as far as 500 B.C. and covering the entire world. The museum's posh interiors feature Tiffany windows, silk wall coverings, and

© THOMAS HUHTI

Charles Allis Art Museum

sader Carrie Nation to declare in 1902, "If there is any place that is hell on earth, it is Milwaukee. You say that beer made Milwaukee famous, but I say that it made it infamous."

The brewers' vast wealth allowed them to affect every major aspect of Milwaukee society and culture; ubiquitous still are the brewing family names affixed to philanthropic organizations, cultural institutions, and many buildings. So popular was Pabst beer that it could afford to place real blue ribbons on bottles by hand; so pervasive were the beers that Admiral Robert Peary found an empty Pabst bottle as he was nearing the North Pole.

THE DECLINE
At the industry's zenith, untold numbers of large breweries were in operation in Milwaukee. Perhaps 60 at the peak, the number dwindled to only a dozen or so after Prohibition, and today there is just one, Miller.

In the 1950s, Milwaukee could still claim to produce nearly 30 percent of the nation's beer; as of now, the number is less than 5 percent.

Microbreweries and brewpubs (not the same thing) have inevitably cut into the megabrewery markets: The fickle tastes of aging yuppies and the protean nature of trendy youth don't bode well for tradition. Today, the nation boasts more than 2,500 different beers. And yet microbrews are a throwback of sorts. The first beer brewed in Milwaukee came from neighborhood brewers, most of which put out only a barrel a week, just enough for the local boys. As the major breweries gained wealth, they gobbled up large chunks of downtown land to create open-atrium *biergartens* and smoky *bierhalls*, in effect shutting out the smaller guys.

Most telling of all may be the deconstruction of yet another Wisconsin stereotype: Cheeseheads, despite being born clutching personalized steins, do not drink more beer per capita than any other state — that honor goes to Nevada. (C'mon, though, it's all tourists on benders, right?)

It ain't for Milwaukeean lack of trying; in 2006 *Forbes* called Milwaukee "America's Drunkest City." A much-battled plan to redevelop the former Pabst brewery into a residential/commercial district finally went under way.

loads of marble. Guided tours are available most Sundays. A special extra: Every Friday night local bands play and your museum entrance ticket gets you in.

◖ Villa Terrace
Within walking distance of the Charles Allis Museum, the lavish 1923 Mediterranean Italian Renaissance Villa Terrace (2220 N. Terrace Ave., 414/271-3656, www.cavtmuseums.org, 1–5 P.M. Wed.–Sun., $5 adults) houses an eclectic collection of decorative arts, including art and handcrafted furniture from the 16th through the 20th centuries. A four-year Garden Renaissance program involved the restoration of a variety of botanical collections (organically melding interiors and exteriors), one of the country's only existing examples of Italian Renaissance garden art and design.

America's Black Holocaust Museum
America's Black Holocaust Museum (2233 N. 4th St., 414/264-2500, www.blackholocaustmuseum.org, 9 A.M.–5 P.M. Tues.–Sat., $5 adults) is an exposé of nearly three centuries of de facto ethnic cleansing. (The museum's Milwaukee location is ironic, given Milwaukee's history of segregation.) The museum's founder witnessed friends' lynchings in the 1930s; he survived one himself.

Quite honestly, this is an unforgettable museum. Disturbing, yes, but necessary.

It was therefore a pain to see that at the time of writing in summer 2008, the museum had closed its doors to "reconfigure operations," code for they are in economic dire straits due to a lack of a moneyed foundation. Hopefully it will reopen; it would be a shame for the city to lose this unforgettable museum.

Wisconsin Black Historical Society Museum

Just to the northwest of the Black Holocaust Museum, the Wisconsin Black Historical Society Museum (2620 West Center St., 414/372-7677, noon–5 P.M. Mon.–Fri. and 9 A.M.>–2 P.M. Sat., $5) presents a modest but thorough examination of the African American experience in Milwaukee. This is the place to discover the city's thriving Bronzeville area from the 1930s to the 1950s, but black culture here dates way back to 1835 when Solomon Juneau arrived on a ship. Also on board was a man named Joe Oliver, the first African American resident of what would be the city (with Juneau's money and help). (An interesting by the way: Late that year, also with Juneau's help, Oliver became the first African American to cast a legal vote in the Wisconsin Territory.)

Jewish Museum of Milwaukee

The city's newest museum (1360 N. Prospect Ave., 414/390-5742, www.jewishmuseummilwaukee.org, 10 A.M.–4 P.M. Mon.–Thurs., till 2 P.M. Fri., noon–4 P.M. Sun., $5 adults) examines the immigration and life of Milwaukee's Jewish residents over waves of immigration. The highlights are the exhibits detailing the crucial role the city played in Jewish history in the 19th and 20th centuries, right up to the point where Milwaukee native Golda Meier became Israel's fourth prime minister.

University of Wisconsin-Milwaukee

UWM is second in enrollment only to the main campus in Madison; it's well known for its civil engineering program. The **Golda Meir Library** (2311 E. Hartford Ave., 414/229-6282, www.uwm.edu, 8 A.M.–5 P.M. weekdays, free) houses the **American Geographical Society Collection,** a priceless collection of more than half a million maps, atlases, logbooks, journals, globes, charts, and navigational aids, including what is reportedly the world's oldest known map, dating from the late 15th century.

Sprecher Brewery

The beers of Sprecher (701 W. Glendale Ave., Glendale, 414/964-2739, www.sprecherbrewery.com, $3), one of the original Milwaukee microbrews, can be found just about anywhere in Wisconsin and beyond. The brewery also makes killer root beer and cream soda and has one of the city's favorite microbrewery tours, given its oompah music in a heavily Bavarian-themed lager cellar. Tours (reservations required) are offered at 4 P.M. Friday and at 1, 2, and 3 P.M. Saturday year-round, with occasional weekday tours in summer.

Kilbourntown House

Constructed during a Greek revival craze in the 1840s, Kilbourntown House (4400 N. Estabrook Pkwy., 414/273-8288) is no longer in Kilbourntown, one of the city's original enclaves. Precariously close to demolition in 1938, it was instead moved to Estabrook Park (just northwest of UWM off Capitol Drive) and restored by the WPA. Inside, the collection of mid-19th-century furniture and decorative art is impressive. Hours change often.

Schlitz Audubon Nature Center

On the far north side of the city, in Bayside, Schlitz Audubon Nature Center (1111 E. Brown Deer Rd., 414/352-2880, www.sanc.org, 9 A.M.–5 P.M. daily, $4) abuts the edge of Lake Michigan on the grounds of an erstwhile Schlitz brewery horse pasture. A six-mile network of trails winds along the beach and through diverse prairie, woodland, and wetland. An observation tower with parapet offers lake views. Check out the interpretive center's new $5.5 million renovation, giving it many environmentally friendly features, such as recirculated rain water, sustainable wood resourced from Aldo Leopold's homestead, solar power panels, and low-flow toilets; inside, it sports lots of cozy wood interiors and plenty of natural lighting.

Whitnall Park

One of the larger municipal parks in the United States at 600-plus acres, Charles B. Whitnall Park (5879 W. 92nd St., Hales Corners, 414/425-7303, free) is the cornerstone of Milwaukee County's enormous park system. So unusual is the acreage here that in 2002 it was dedicated as the cornerstone of the state's proposed Oak Leaf Birding Trail, which will eventually have 35 separate parks and forests to view crucial avian habitat. Lush landscaped gardens are found inside the park at **Boerner Botanical Gardens** (414/425-1130). Forty acres of roses, perennials, wildflowers, and more thrive here; the 1,000-acre arboretum surrounding the gardens includes the largest flowering crabapple orchard in the United States. Tour the gardens 8 A.M.–sunset daily mid-April–October; a garden house is open till 7 P.M. in summer; the rest of the year, hours are significantly reduced. Entry is free, though parking costs $4.

Also in Whitnall Park is the **Todd Wehr Nature Center** (9701 W. College Ave., 414/425-8550, 8 A.M.–4:30 P.M., parking $3), designed as a living laboratory of eco-awareness, with nature trails and an ongoing mixed-grass prairie restoration.

SOUTH OF DOWNTOWN
Churches

Just south of downtown, the first Polish basilica in North America is the city's **St. Josaphat's Basilica** (Lincoln Ave. at S. 6th St., 414/645-5623, tours by appointment but public welcome to Masses). Parishioners built the structure out of salvaged rubble from the Chicago Federal Building. The capacious dome is modeled after St. Peter's in Rome; inside is a rather astonishing mélange of Polish iconography and hagiography, relics, stained glass, and wood carvings.

South of here, the only thing remaining of a Teutonic settlement in New Coeln (founded in 1840), **St. Stephen's Church** (5880 S. Howell Ave., just west of Mitchell International Airport), now resides in Milwaukee and houses a collection of famed wood carvings.

Beer Corner

The only-in-Milwaukee award goes to **Forest Home Cemetery** (2405 W. Forest Home Ave.) and its designated sector of eye-catching monuments to the early Milwaukee brewing giants: Blatz, Pabst, Best, and Schlitz rest in peace beneath the handcrafted stones. Kooky or spooky, heritage is heritage. You can usually enter the

Boerner Botanical Gardens

cemetery weekdays until around 4 P.M. and on Saturday mornings.

Mitchell International Airport

Mitchell International Airport has its **Mitchell Gallery of Flight** (5300 S. Howell Ave., 414/747-4503, www.mitchellgallery.org, 8 A.M.–10 P.M. daily, free) housing a number of aircraft, including a zeppelin. More appealing is the retrospective of the iconoclastic and innovative military aviation pioneer Billy Mitchell, a Beer City native.

Speaking of the airport, a unique, free way to kill time waiting for your plane to depart is to drive your rental car along Layton Avenue to near South Kansas Avenue (the north side of Mitchell International Airport). You'll find a small, relatively unknown viewing area to watch planes take off and land.

WEST OF DOWNTOWN
◖ Miller Brewing

King of the hill (besides Harley Davidson) in Milwaukee is megabrewer Miller (4251 W. State St., 414/931-2337, www.millerbrewing.com, tours Mon.–Sat., hours vary, free). This slick, modern operation is the very antithesis of a neighborhood brewer. Frederic Miller apprenticed and served as a brewmaster at Hohenzollern Castle in Sigmaringen, Germany, before striking out for the United States in 1855 at age 28 and starting a small brewery. His original Plank Road Brewery, bought from the son of the Pabst progenitor and not to be confused with Miller's shrewdly named contemporary brewing operation, put out 300 barrels per year—no mean feat, but nothing stellar. Today, Miller—now owned by whatever corporate entity merged with it recently, Coors most recently—is the second-largest brewery in the nation, with six satellite operations and a total production of *45 million* barrels a year (the warehouse is the size of five football fields). Brewery visits start with a mammoth-screen multimedia history and devotional to Frederic Miller. Hour-long tours then depart, taking in the ultra-high-tech packaging center, the hangar-size shipping

center, and, finally, the brewhouse. Tours end at the Caves Museum, a restored part of Miller's original brewery in which kegs of beer were cooled before the advent of refrigeration. Historic brewing equipment and memorabilia are on display. The ineluctable Bavarian hut dispenses free samples (to those 21 and over, natch) and features an antique stein collection and ornate woodwork. Miller is considering its own **brewing museum** at its west-side corporate headquarters.

◖ Harley-Davidson Museum

I ain't seen it published elsewhere yet, so I hereby call dibs on "Hog Heaven" for the name of this, the Mecca of Made-in-America and the cathedral for the ethos of a place—the massive, 130,000-square-foot Harley-Davidson Museum (Canal and South 6th Sts., 414/343-4235, www.h-dmuseum.com, 9 A.M.–6 P.M. Thurs.–Tues., 9 A.M.–8 P.M. Wed., $16 adults). This $30 million project features an interactive museum and exhibits on the history, culture, and lifestyle engendered by the company and its slavishly devoted riders. You know the highlight: bikes owned by the famous, at the moment the most popular being Elvis Presley's old beaut. Best of all—they work 365 days a year here, true blue-collar style.

If you get there off-hours, or if you don't/can't drop the coin to enter, do stop by to check out the fantastic grounds (which spread some 20 acres) and exquisite building architecture—all the exterior chrome and its chic yet tough design will have you shopping for leathers. Better—the west wall is glass, so you can get a gander inside.

Note that the shop keeps shorter hours November–April (though it is still open seven days a week).

Harley-Davidson Engine Plant

Hogs and Ultra-Glides are not actually assembled *in toto* in the Beer City, yet visitors can view one crucial aspect of the motorcycle-manufacturing process at the Harley-Davidson engine plant, which also assembles transmissions (11700 W. Capitol Dr., Wauwatosa, 414/535-

3666, www.harleydavidson.com). The plant produces Sportster and Buell engines. Even if you know zilch about motorcycles, it's kind of a thrill to walk down a Harley assembly line. Free hour-long tours are generally offered between 9:30 A.M. and 1 P.M. but get there early to snag a free ticket!

The best way to experience Harley otherwise is to be around for Harley riders' conventions, when literally 100,000 Harleys descend on the city to fete the metallic beasts. It's an indescribable experience to see the parade of Harleys roaring down I-94 toward Miller Park on their way to a Brewers game—the Beer City becomes a tented Hog City for a glorious summer-long celebration.

Annunciation Greek Orthodox Church

"My little jewel—a miniature Santa Sophia" is how Frank Lloyd Wright described the final major work of his life—the Annunciation Greek Orthodox Church (9400 W. Congress St., Wauwatosa, 414/461-9400). Its imposing rondure is a landmark to Milwaukee architecture—a dramatic inverted bowl into which Wright incorporated symbolic golds and blues and the Greek cross. The blue-tiled dome rises 45 feet above the floor and spans 104 feet. During the most recent update the congregation was involved in a heated dispute as to whether the original murals should be changed to more, er, "religious" themes. Individual tours are not possible.

Other Churches

The progressive **Central United Methodist Church** (639 N. 25th St., 414/344-1600, tours by appointment 8:30 A.M.–4 P.M. Mon. and Wed., till 1 P.M. Fri., free) is partially enclosed by earth and incorporates radical energy-saving and solar-energy measures (the tower holds solar panels).

It's not a church per se, but the **Tripoli Shrine Temple** (3000 W. Wisconsin Ave., 9 A.M.–4 P.M. weekdays, free) is worth a look, if only for the oddly appealing Taj Mahal nature of the place. It was built during a period of

"fantasy architecture" and was indeed based on the Taj Mahal of India. The main dome is 30 feet in diameter and is flanked by two smaller domes. Camels, lanterns, and floral designs are some of the artwork decorating the interiors.

International Clown Hall of Fame

Sounds odd, but Wisconsin was once a major hotbed of the circus life; in fact, southern Wisconsin was the wintering site of numerous circuses. (If you're in Wisconsin and into circuses, you simply must check out diminutive Baraboo, about an hour north of Madison, and its superlative Circus World Museum.) Several regional collections of clowns have been combined into one thrilling display at the **International Clown Hall of Fame** (State Fair Park, 414/290-0105, 9 A.M.–5 P.M. Mon.–Sat., $2). Figure big shoes, little cars, spinning bowties, and scads of make-up, all for kids, big or small. Semi-regular clown shows—incredible fun for the urchins—are on offer, though it's best to phone ahead for precise times.

Milwaukee County Zoo

Though its innovative designs have been mimicked nationally and internationally for the past four decades, none have quite duplicated the charm or ingenuity of the Milwaukee County Zoo (10001 W. Bluemound Rd., 414/256-5411, www.milwaukeezoo.org). The animals' five global environments, grouped in specific continental areas with a system of moats, create apparent juxtaposing of predator and prey. Almost 5,000 specimens live here, many of them also residents of the endangered species list. Perennially popular are the polar bears and other aquatic leviathans viewable through subsurface windows. Newest additions? Giraffes and sting rays! (Seriously, this author was practically pushing kids out of the way to get to the giraffe observation deck to feed 'em!) In a century-old barn is a dairy complex—an educational look at milk production. Zoomobiles ($3) roll about the expansive grounds, and mini-trains ($1.50) also chug around. On occasion, you can even hop aboard an elephant or a spitting camel. Animal shows take place

HOG HEAVEN

Beer may have made Milwaukee famous, but to some, Milwaukee-born Harley-Davidson — the bikes, the slavishly devoted riders, and the company — truly represents the ethos of Milwaukee: blue-collar tough, proud, and loyal. Anyone who witnessed Harley's 2003 centennial Anniversary Reunion in Milwaukee knows what it's all about. A quarter million Harley riders invaded the city in a thunderous cacophony, effectively shutting down the interstates and then taking over the lakefront festival grounds and Miller Park for a Brewers game.

THE COMPANY
William S. Harley and Arthur Davidson, boyhood friends in Milwaukee, were fascinated by the bicycle (and German motorbike) craze around the turn of the 20th century. In 1903, they rigged a single-cylinder engine (the carburetor was a tin can) and leather-strap

a Harley homecoming

© WISCONSIN DEPARTMENT OF TOURISM

drive chain onto a thin bicycle frame — with no brakes. Thus began the first putterings of the company known for roaring.

Within three years they were getting a dozen orders a month; the company incorporated in 1907, bringing in additional family members, and within a decade became the largest motorcycle maker in the world. The Harleys' reputation for sound engineering and thus endurance — the first motorcycle lasted 100,000 miles — made them popular with the U.S. Postal Service and especially police departments. In the first Federation of American Motorcyclists endurance test, a hog scored above a perfect 1,000 points, leading to Harley dominance in motorcycle racing for decades. Constant innovations, such as the first clutch, also fueled success.

But it was during World War I that Harley gained the U.S. government's devotion — Harleys with sidecars equipped with machine guns also pursued pesky Pancho Villa into Mexico in 1917. Europeans found a great enthusiasm for the machines, too, after the Great War; within five years, 20 percent of the company's business was exported.

Further, no motorcycle maker could claim the innovation or the zeal with which Harley-Davidson catered to its riders. Original dealers were instructed to employ the consumers in as much of the process as possible. Harley-Davidson open houses were legendary. *The Enthusiast,* the company's newsletter, is the longest-running continuously published motorcycle organ anywhere.

THE BIKES
The company hit eternal fame with the goofy-looking, radically designed Knucklehead in 1936, when a public initially dismayed by the bulging overhead valves (hence the name) soon realized its synthesis of art and engineering — it has been called the most perfect

motorcycle ever made. The Sportster, introduced in 1957, also gets the nod from aficionados – it's called the Superbike. In the 1970s, the Super Glide – the *Easy Rider* low-rider's progenitor – singlehandedly rescued the company. The modern Softail and Tour Glides are considered by Harley-Davidson to be the best ever engineered.

GOOD TIMES, BAD TIMES

By the 1940s, two-thirds of all U.S. bikes were Harley-Davidsons. By the 1950s, swelled by demand, Harley managed to push out its main competitor, Indian Motorcycle. But somewhere along the line, something happened, and the company took it on the chin. Harleys had been derisively dubbed "Hardly Ablesons" because of their tendency to break down and the maddeningly high requirement of patience and maintenance – or so said owners of archrival Indian Motorcycles.

When AMF (American Machine and Foundry) took control of the company in 1969, sales were plummeting. Some blame incompetent corporate oversight, others blame a toxic image problem brought on by Hollywood. Whatever the cause, sales hit the wall, morale of the company's workforce hit an all-time low, and things got so bad that manufacturing was doled out to separate factories around the country.

In 1981, a group of about 30 Harley employees (most of them longtime vets of the original company but some from AMF) bought the company back and virtually reinvented it. With top-of-the-line products, brilliant marketing, and a furious effort at regaining the trust of the consumer, Harley-Davidson moved steadily back into the market. By the late 1980s, the company was again profitable against Japanese bikes. The effects are manifest: There's a veritable renaissance of the Harley craze, an extensive waiting list for bikes (all 75,000 produced in a year are spoken for up to a year in advance), and Harley groups tooling even the streets of Hong Kong. More than half of Harley owners are senior citizens, married, college educated, and have high incomes. Some of Harley-Davidson's highest-profile proponents have included the late Malcolm Forbes and Jann Wenner, founder and publisher of *Rolling Stone*.

The contemporary Harley-Davidson headquarters sits very near the site of that shed/workshop that cobbled together the first bike. The bikes aren't assembled here anymore – just transmissions and engines – but the company remains firmly committed to its downtown location. It has programs encouraging employees to live in the neighborhood and is one of the most in-touch corporations in town. Its 2008 grand opening of a new Harley-Davidson Museum cements it as a Milwaukee brand forever.

© THOMAS HUHTI

a genuine Harley-Davidson

throughout the day; the Oceans of Fun sea lions and harbor seals show is a scream.

It's open 9 A.M.–5 P.M. Monday–Saturday, 9 A.M.–6 P.M. Sunday and holidays May–September, till 4:30 P.M. the rest of the year. The rides and animal shows have varied schedules. Admission is $9 adults; parking is $6. All rides and activities within are extra. Admission rates are lower October–May.

The Domes

Though it's officially the **Mitchell Park Horticultural Conservatory** (524 S. Layton Blvd., 414/649-9800, www.countyparks.com, 9 A.M.–5 P.M. daily, $4.50 adults), everybody knows this complex as "the Domes." You'll know why once you take a gander at the conical seven-story, 148-foot-tall glass-encased buildings. The capacious interiors, totaling about 15,000 square feet, are isolated into arid desert, traditional floral, and tropical rainforest biospheres. One is landscaped up to half a dozen times annually. Outside, the conservatory, ringed with more sunken gardens, is the only structure of its type in the world.

Waukesha

Farther west of Wauwatosa, the suburb Waukesha has proposed two potentially intriguing museums. The first, a museum dedicated to local-boy-done-good Les Paul (he is the musician and designer of the same-named famed electric guitar), has plenty of memorabilia but no home save for the exhibit (which may become permanent) at Discovery World in downtown Milwaukee. At the time of writing, the city had raised about one-third of the $3 million it needs to create the museum; we'll see how it goes.

Also bandied about has been a museum dedicated to the Cold War in Hillcrest Park, site of a former Nike missile radar guidance silo.

Till then, Les Paul memorabilia and displays are at the **Waukesha County Museum** (101 W. Main St., 262/521-2859, www.waukeshacountymuseum.org, 10A.M.–4:30P.M. Tues.–Sat., $3), along with three stories of historical flotsam—the dolls are nice.

the distinctive Domes

Ten Chimneys

And then, a few minutes' drive west of Waukesha brings you to "Broadway's Retreat" in the Midwest—Ten Chimneys (S43 W31575 Depot Rd., Genesee Depot, 262/968-4161, www.tenchimneys.org), the erstwhile home of the Great White Way's legendary Alfred Lunt and Lynn Fontaine. From its creation as a haven for artists in the 1920s, it welcomed legions of actors, writers, singers, and film stars, all seeking spiritual rejuvenation in a bucolic retreat. Having fallen into disrepair, it was nearly razed before an extraordinary renovation effort saved it. The 2003 reopening gave the public a jaw-dropping view of an entirely unknown piece of U.S. cultural history. Inside, the exquisite detailing and furnishings are almost an afterthought, so caught up are visitors by mementos sent to Fontaine and Lunt from Helen Hayes, Noel Coward, and Charlie Chaplin, among others. The sublime 18-room main house sits perched above 60 acres of rolling moraine topography; nearby are a "quaint" eight-room cottage and Swedish-style log cabin, and a dozen other buildings. Not simply a memorial to a bygone era, Ten Chimneys is a living artists' retreat again—sponsoring workshops, collaborations, teacher-training programs, and public classes.

Tours are available, but don't count on an impromptu visit; officially it's open to the public 10 A.M.–4 P.M. Tuesday–Saturday May 1–October 31, but if a special event is taking place you may not get in. The place is also pricey: $35 for a full estate tour, $30 for a main house tour only. Twilight tours are available Friday evenings and it has awesome dinner packages.

Germantown

Well, what do you think you're gonna find here, given the name? Northwest of Milwaukee is this town with a great German crossroads hamlet, the erstwhile **Dheinsville,** whose nearly two dozen buildings have been painstakingly renovated into a historic park. The highlight for most is the on-site Bast Bell Museum (262/628-3170, 1–4 P.M. Wed.–Sun. Apr.–Oct., $5), featuring the state's largest bell collection (one a gargantuan half-tonner); it also, oddly, sports a fire-fighting collection, including a cool working 1929 fire engine. This author's favorite is the Wolf Haus, an 1854 *fachwerke* (half-timber building)—it's the oldest of its kind in the region. The whole shebang is a block east of U.S. 145 on Holy Hill Road (though you can't miss it).

Entertainment and Events

Milwaukee is a city with something for everyone, culturally speaking. Events? Got 'em in boatloads here; indeed, throw a dart at a calendar and you'll hit an enormous festival of some sort. Nightlife? Well, Milwaukee's in the top 10 nationwide for number of places to drink per capita—though this doesn't translate to a thriving music or dance scene here. Most surprisingly to most visitors is the city's respected cultural arts and attractions; you'll definitely leave impressed by that.

NIGHTLIFE

Milwaukee is no Manhattan, but there's a lot more music and nightlife than people realize. Then again, it's also the city where sheepshead (a native card game) tournaments might get equal billing with live music in the same bar. Milwaukee has more than 5,000 bars, in keeping with tradition, so there's something out there for everyone.

You know how it goes: These places come and go. The ones in here show staying power. The free weekly *Shepherd Express* gives a rundown of most of the clubs; fairly thorough is the Friday edition of the *Milwaukee Journal-Sentinel.*

Nightlife Districts

Stretching along the Milwaukee River, aptly named **Water Street** draws a preponderance of Marquette students and lots of downtown business types. Nightlife varies from a microbrewery to sports bars and dance clubs. The **Water Street Brewery** (1101 N. Water St., 414/272-1195) is one of the popular newer microbreweries in town but similar to others with gleaming copper kettles on display. Get the best bar food around at **Rosie's Water Works** (1111 N. Water St., 414/274-7213).

More and more shops, boutiques, and restaurants are moving into the **Walker's Point** neighborhood. Nightspots here vary from a pub with a sand volleyball court outside to a Teutonic watering hole, dark sippers' pubs, and a whole lot more. Walker's Point is also the home of Milwaukee's oldest LBGT dance club, **La Cage** (see *LBGT*). (It's also the largest in Wisconsin.)

Bar/restaurants such as **Elsa's on Park** (833 N. Jefferson St., 414/765-0615), **Louise's** (801 N. Jefferson St., 414/273-4224), and others, all in the same area, have given **North Jefferson Street** and environs the feel of a subdued scene—all in the ritzy section of town full of boutiques, galleries, and the like. These are the clubs for you if you want to avoid the fun but occasionally wild contingent on Water Street.

Dance Clubs

These come and go, but as of these keys thwacking, the hottest place seemed to be **Decibel** (1905 North Ave., www.decibelmke .com), the place where you can act like a VIP (or see one). Indeed, even in the depths of winter you'll see fashionistas stepping gingerly from limousines dressed head to toe in up-to-the-minute wear. The dance floor is hot, but you can escape the low-frequency thumping in the DeepBar, a relaxing vodka lounge.

One with the most staying power locally is the live music/dance club **Mad Planet** (533 East Center St., 414/263-4555), a perennial winner of local awards for best dance club. In addition to hosting touring national acts, they have regular dance parties that always turn into a mix of all local subcultures; here, goths mix with punks. Get there early or phone in advance, since they fill up quickly.

Yeah, I know it's a chain, but **Have a Nice Day Cafe** (1101 N. Old World 3rd St., 414/270-9650) is a fun retro haven for those stuck in the '70s. You can't help but get groovy with the smiley faces plastered everywhere, and their signature goldfish bowl drinks will help you get into the, er, groove.

Rock

Shank Hall (1434 N. Farwell Ave., 414/276-7288) offers a constant barrage of prominent local, regional, and national acts. It was once a stable, so the interior isn't exactly a delight when the lights come up. More good spots for local rock or regional alternative acts and mostly college crowds include **Points East Pub** (1501 N. Jackson St., 414/272-0122) and the acoustically atrocious **Rave** (2401 W. Wisconsin Ave., 414/342-7283). Many readers of local websites and other media have voted the live music—genres and atmosphere—at **Milwaukee Ale House** as tops.

Not here on a weekend? Fret not, for the **Cactus Club** (2496 S. Wentworth Ave., 414/482-0160) has music every single night, often national acts. Look for more local flavors at **Club Brady** (1339 E. Brady St., 414/278-0188).

Latin

Real-deal no-frills Mexican food brings in throngs to **Tres Hermanos** (1332 W. Lincoln Ave., 414/384-9050), but you also can't beat the dancing to live Tex Mex and Norteña music Friday and Saturday nights.

Blues and R&B

It used to be all blues all the time (in a scuzzy kind of way) at the **Up and Under Pub** (1216 E. Brady St., 414/276-2677); under new owners it's gotten a freshening up and added a nice variety of rock, roots, and more. Along the river, the **Milwaukee Ale House** (233 N. Water St., 414/226-2337) has nightly roots rock and R&B–infused acts.

The Riverwest neighborhood is a prime spot. A small neighborhood tavern unconcerned with decor, **Linneman's River West Inn** (1001 E. Locust St., 414/263-9844) has blues and some folk.

Jazz

Serious jazzers should head for the **Jazz Oasis** (2379 N. Holton Ave., 414/562-2040) or a local institution, **Caroline's** (401 S. 2nd St., 414/221-0244), just south of downtown, where you go for the music and atmosphere, not necessarily the decor.

World Music and Eclectic

International flavors—musical and otherwise—are on offer in a comfortable setting at **Nomad World Pub** (1401 E. Brady St., 414/224-8111), part coffee shop, part unpredictable drink-pouring bar where you can get betel nuts while listening to world beat music, sometimes live.

Regular Irish music—along with Irish fare—is available at **County Clare** (1234 N. Astor St., 414/272-5273), set in a retro guesthouse.

Taps, Taverns, and More Nightspots

The **Safe House** (779 N. Front St.—look for the "International Exports" sign, 414/271-2007) is a bar-restaurant done to the hilt in espionage decor. The drinks have spy names, you may be asked for a password, etc. ad nauseam. It's a ritual watering hole for Milwaukee first-timers; others think it's the biggest joke in town. The bathrooms are certainly unique (especially the ladies room—check and see!).

Along bopping North Farwell Avenue, **Von Trier** (2235 N. Farwell Ave., 414/272-1775) could pass for a German *bierhall* with its long heavy wooden bench seating and a summertime *biergarten*. In true Bavarian and Wisconsin style, there's a buck's head affixed to the wall. A block away on North Avenue, **Vitucci's** (1832 N. Ave., 414/273-6477) is a quieter place and a personal favorite watering hole—one Milwaukee fave since 1936.

At **Landmark Lanes** (2220 N. Farwell Ave., 414/278-8770), in the bowels of the Oriental Landmark Theater, there's bowling—this is Milwaukee, after all—but mostly it's a happening young nightclub with three separate bars, pool tables, and dartboards. The place has been around forever, and it's great.

A British-style waterside place, **John Hawk's Pub** (in the basement at 100 E. Wisconsin Ave., 414/272-3199) offers an oak bar and cozy fireplaces as well as live music-blues or rhythm and blues. (Food has gotten mixed reviews.)

If you're looking for a more upscale place, try the **Hi-Hat Lounge** (E. Brady and Arlington Sts., 414/220-8090). With cool jazz wafting in the background it's got a classy but not showy feel and an older, sophisticated crowd.

Too many neighborhood taverns to count exist in Milwaukee, and everybody's got a different recommendation. The since-1908 **Wolski's** (1836 N. Pulaski St., 414/276-8130) is a corner tavern that defines a Milwaukee tippler's joint. You're an unofficial Beer City denizen if you drive home with an "I closed Wolski's" bumper sticker on your car!

THE FONZ, BRONZED

In 2008, the character of Arthur Fonzarelli, a.k.a "the Fonz," on the hit 1970s TV show *Happy Days* was chosen by *Entertainment Weekly* magazine and TV Land (they'd know!) as the 32nd most recognized TV icon of all time. (It's amazing – this author grew up absolutely adoring the show and even when he gives a thumbs-up "Ayyyyyy!" a la the Fonz to his friends' kids, they get it without having seen the show, a fairly good mark of iconic status!)

Milwaukeeans certainly took pride in this, as the fictional show was set in "happy" 1950s Milwaukee; a spin-off show, *Laverne and Shirley*, was also set here.

The characters, the plots, all heartwarming of course, but it was always the Fonz who we all wanted to be: a Harley rider with a heart of gold, good with all the ladies but a stand-up guy to his buds, most of whom were geeks.

So at some point a handful of years ago, somebody in Milwaukee said, "You know what? This downtown rejuvenation is great, but let's have some fun with this public art." Thus, the memorializing of the Fonz in statue form was born in downtown Milwaukee.

This being modern U.S. culture, naturally it took about a handful of years of hand-wringing, "discussion," online bitching, etc. ad nauseam. "Oh, but it cheapens the idea of art, blah blah blah." But finally, the hoi polloi won the day and on August 19, 2008, it happened: the casts of *Happy Days* and *Laverne and Shirley* and umpteen thousands of their local friends unveiled the statue (gotta say – the color of the jeans don't match my mental image of the ones my Fonz wore, but whatever) downtown along Milwaukee's Riverwalk (east side, just south of Wells Street).

If nothing else, consider it a memorial to nostalgic memory of a bygone era. If it's still up and running, check out all the hoohah at www.bronzethefonz.com!

LGBT

The longtime standard for the LGBT community is **La Cage** (801 S. 2nd St., in Walker's Point, 414/672-7988). Four bars, a half dozen dance floors, and frenetic video screens all have helped keep this a shaking place for years.

CULTURE AND THE ARTS

In Rand McNally's *Places Rated,* Milwaukee hit the top 5 percent of big cities for cultural attractions and the arts. Since the 1990s, more than $100 million has been poured into downtown arts districts. Per capita, Milwaukeeans donate more to the arts than any U.S. city besides Los Angeles. Four dozen cultural organizations call the city home—23 theater companies alone.

Rundowns for all cultural activities can be found in the Friday and Sunday editions of the *Milwaukee Journal-Sentinel. Milwaukee Magazine* also has a comprehensive monthly compendium.

Cultural Centers

The **Pabst Theater** (144 E. Wells St., 414/286-3663, www.pabsttheater.org), an 1895 Victorian piece of opulence that still today seems as ornate as ever, is a majestic draw in its own right (free public tours are given at noon on Saturdays if show schedules don't conflict), but it also continues to attract national acts of all kinds. The **Marcus Center for Performing Arts (MCPA)** (929 N. Water St., 414/273-7121, www.marcuscenter.org) has a regular season of theater, symphony, ballet, opera, children's theater, and touring specials. It is the home of the Milwaukee Symphony Orchestra, the Milwaukee Ballet Company, the Florentine Opera Company, and much more.

A detailed, painstaking postmillennial restoration of the **Milwaukee Theatre** (500 W. Kilbourn Ave., 414/908-6000, www.milwaukeetheatre.com), a historic 1909 gem, has created a state-of-the-art facility for concerts and theatrical productions.

Theater

The city has nearly two dozen theater

companies performing in many locations. The **Skylight Opera Theatre** (414/291-7800, www.skylightopera.com) and **Milwaukee Chamber Theatre** (414/276-8842, chamber-theatre.com) are residents of the lovely Broadway Theatre Centre downtown. The Chamber Theatre's language-centered contemporary plays are always a challenge.

The nation's only African American professional theater group is the **Hansberry-Sands Theatre Company,** which performs at the Marcus Center (929 N. Water St., 414/273-7121, www.marcuscenter.org).

The **Milwaukee Repertory Theater** (108 E. Wells St., 414/224-1761, www.milwaukee-rep.com) is part of an international network of cooperating organizations and offers classical, contemporary, cabaret, and special performances September–May.

Music

The **Milwaukee Symphony Orchestra** (700 N. Water St., 414/291-6010, www.milwaukeesymphony.org) is one of the nation's top orchestras. No less than *New Yorker* magazine, with an all-too-typical coastal undercurrent of surprise, described it as "virtuoso."

A low-cost alternative is the **Wisconsin Conservatory of Music** (1584 N. Prospect Ave., 414/276-5760, www.wcmusic.org), which offers performances of faculty, students, and guest artists.

A personal favorite is **Present Music** (1840 N. Farwell Ave., 414/271-0711, www.presentmusic.org), a group commissioning and performing eclectic, challenging works from modern composers.

Dance

Milwaukee has a thriving modern dance culture; New York City companies make regular visits to do performances in numerous sites around the city. The classics aren't ignored. Ranked among the top ballet companies in the country is the **Milwaukee Ballet Company** (504 W. National Ave., 414/643-7677, www.milwaukeeballet.org), whose December production of *The Nutcracker* always packs the house.

dancers at the Holiday Folk Fair

Nationally renowned is Milwaukee's modern **Ko-Thi Dance Company** (414/442-6844, www.ko-thi.org), committed to the preservation and performance of African and Caribbean arts. Wildly popular shows are held in spring and fall at the Pabst Theatre.

Visual Arts

In addition to the magnificent art museums, Milwaukee has a worthy art scene to check out. Your first stop should be at one of the visitors centers to pick up *artscene* (www.artscenemilwaukee.com), a comprehensive guide to each and every spot offering visual arts in the city, with a superb map to boot.

EVENTS

Another term of endearment for Milwaukee is the City of Festivals. Almost every week of the year brings yet another celebratory blowout feting some cultural, ethnic, or seasonal aspect of the city—and sometimes for no reason at all. The city's festival rundown is one large database. Show up any weekend from late May to early November and you're guaranteed something to do at a festival grounds in town.

The short list: German Fest, the largest multiday festival in the country (July); Bavarian Folk Fest (June); Oktoberfest; Polish Fest (June); Lakefront Festival of Arts (July); Festa Italiana (July); Bastille Days (July); Greek Festival (July); Mexican Spring Festival–Cinco de Mayo (May); Mexican Fiesta (August); Irish Fest (August); African World Festival (August); Serbian Days (August); Indian Summer (September); Asian Moon Festival (September); and Holiday Folk Fair (November).

The largest party of all is early August's **Wisconsin State Fair,** at the fairgrounds west along I-94. This fair of all fairs features carnivals, 500 exhibits, livestock shows, entertainment on 20 stages, and the world's greatest cream puffs.

Summerfest

This is the granddaddy of all Midwestern festivals and the largest music festival in the world (so says the *Guinness Book of World Records*). For 11 days in late June, top national musical acts (as well as unknown college-radio mainstays) perform on innumerable stages along the lakefront, drawing millions of music lovers and partiers. Agoraphobics need not even consider it. Shop around for discount coupons at grocery stores and assorted businesses, or consider a multiday pass, available at businesses all around town.

SHOPPING

There's more to shopping in Milwaukee than the requisite cheddar cheese foam wedge hat and cheese and bratwurst gift packs. (Though these should, of course, be on your list!)

Shops at Grand Avenue Mall and Environs

Virtually everyone starts at the economic (as well as geographic) heart of Milwaukee, the Grand Avenue Mall—a synthesis of old and new. Originally built in 1915 as the Plankinton Arcade, much of its architecture was retained when the four-block area was gentrified into a lower level of shops and an upper level of sidewalk cafés and people-watching heights. (Best of all, it has interconnected walkways between the mall and outlying downtown locations, to keep you out of the snow and cold!)

From here, neighborhoods reach out for your wallet. To the immediate north, North Old World 3rd Street has mostly good restaurants but a few long-standing shops, the highlight of which has to be Usinger's (see *Sights*). Sausage as a souvenir—is that a Milwaukee gift or what? Other highlights include Ambrosia Chocolates and, of course, the Wisconsin Cheese Mart.

Other Shopping Districts

The **Historic Third Ward,** which likes to call itself the "SoHo of the Midwest," **Jefferson Street,** and **East Brady Street** areas offer the most compelling strolls for shoppers. All are blocks-long areas of carefully gentrified Old World–feeling streets filled with art and antique galleries, specialty shops, and oodles of places to grab a cup of java or a quick bite in a chic setting to recharge the purchasing battery.

Sports and Recreation

Milwaukee has been rated in the top 10 percent of like-size U.S. cities for recreational opportunities in and around the city. Don't forget that the Beer City is major league. No exaggeration—it supports three professional teams along with a minor league hockey team.

RECREATION

Looking for something more aerobic? Consider the more than 150 parks and parkways and 15,000 acres of greenland. Milwaukee has more park area per person than any metropolitan city in the United States. The place to inquire first is the Milwaukee County Parks System (414/257-6100, www.countyparks.com).

Hiking and Biking

The following is but a thumbnail sketch of what the county has to offer.

The **Oak Leaf Trail** is the diamond of all Milwaukee-area trails. One name but

comprising multiple loops, this beauty wends through all the parkways and major parks of the county, topping out at longer than 100 miles (the main section for most is an easy loop around the lakefront)! The trail begins along Lincoln Memorial Drive between Ogden Avenue and Locust Street. Signs from here point your way, though note that not *all* myriad loops are well marked (or even marked). The most popular subroute is a 13-mile marked route, the **Milwaukee '76 Trail,** starting from O'Donnell Park and stretching along the lakefront from the Charles Allis Museum and through east-side historic districts. As the Oak Leaf trailhead is along the lakefront, the best thing to do is explore the littoral scenery after huffing and puffing all day. At 2400 North Lincoln Memorial Drive is the city's most popular beach—**Bradford Beach.**

Henry Aaron State Trail, a new addition to the state's reputable system, is a six-mile path

Biking is a great way to explore Milwaukee's many parks.

leading from the lakefront, through historic districts, and ending in the near-west suburbs, much of it following the Menomonee River.

Other popular multiuse trails run along the Menomonee River between Good Hope and Bluemound Roads, along the Milwaukee River from Good Hope Road to the lakefront near McKinley Marina, along the Root River from Greenfield Avenue to Loomis Road, and along the south lakefront through Cudahy and South Milwaukee.

Find great ski trails at a number of parks, including Schlitz Audubon Nature Center, Whitnall Park, and, believe it or not, the zoo.

Bike and in-line skate rentals and personal watercraft (and kayaks) are usually available along the lakefront at **Milwaukee Bike and Skate Rental** (www.milwbikeskaterental.com) in Veterans Park. Just north of McKinley Marina, **Welker Water Sport Rentals** (414/630-5387) rents personal watercraft and kayaks.

The county's website has maps of the Oak Leaf Trail and others, or you may request them.

Charter Fishing

Milwaukee leads the state in charter operations and salmonoids taken. On a scintillating summer day, the marina and harbor areas of Milwaukee appear to be discharging a benevolent, whitewashed D-Day flotilla.

The Convention and Visitors Bureau can provide more detailed information on specific charter operations. Investigating charter operators before sailing can save quite a lot of personality friction; the boats are not that big, and you are the one who'll have to sit out on the big lake with the skipper all day.

Bowling

A joke: Wisconsin's the only state where you can factor your bowling average into your SAT score. The city's *81* regulation bowling centers can take care of your bowling jones, but better, a couple of neighborhood joints have old-style duckpin bowling. The **Holler House** (2042 W. Lincoln Ave., 414/647-9284) has the two oldest sanctioned bowling lanes (Lanes 1 and 2) in the United States. A tradition of sorts here is to "donate" your bra to the rafters on your first visit! A true Milwaukee treasure is long-standing **Koz's Mini Bowl** (2078 S. 7th St., 414/383-0560), with four 16-foot lanes and orange-size balls; the pin setters still make $.50 a game plus tips. An aside: Koz's was actually a WWII–era house of ill repute; the lanes were simply a cover to keep locals from asking questions.

A couple of bars on Water Street even have *virtual* bowling; now what is up with that?

Ice Skating and Hockey

The **Pettit National Ice Center** (500 S. 84th St., off I-94, 414/266-0100, www.thepettit .com) is the only one of its kind in the country and one of only five of its scope in the world. National and international competitions are held here regularly. The public can enjoy the 400-meter ovals and two Olympic-size hockey rinks throughout the day for $6; you can even jog on a running track. Tours cost $3.

Golf

Milwaukee is often mentioned for its nearly 20 golf courses within a short drive. Most prominent in the near vicinity is **Brown Deer Park** (7835 N. Green Bay Rd., 414/352-8080), site of a PGA tour event, the U.S. Bank Championship; for a public course, it's amazing. Whitnall and Oakwood Parks also have excellent courses.

Camping

The best public camping is a half hour to the west in **Kettle Moraine State Forest** (262/646-3025, open year-round); it's very popular and is often booked, so arrive/reserve early. The nearest private campground is southwest of Milwaukee along I-43 in Mukwonago at **Country View Campground** (S110 W26400 Craig Ave., 414/662-3654, $23–24). Country View is open mid-April–mid-October and offers a pool, playground, hot showers, and supplies. RVs can camp at the Wisconsin State Fairgrounds, west along I-94 in West Allis, but it's crowded and cacophonic with freeway traffic.

SPECTATOR SPORTS
The Brew Crew

Milwaukee remains something of an anomaly—the smallest of the small markets. And most markets of comparable size support just one major league franchise, not three, as Milwaukee does.

Debate over a proposed $200 million (ultimately $400 million) retractable dome stadium for the Brewers raged before the bill to pay for it was finally passed—some say rammed through—in an epic all-night session of the Wisconsin Legislature that cost at least one legislator his job in a recall election (and the death of three workers in a horrific accident during construction). Whatever your take on it, the stadium is absolutely magnificent. It has been described as the most perfect synthesis of retro and techno in the world—do check it out.

Baseball season runs early April–late September, and obtaining tickets is sometimes an issue, especially on weekends or whenever the archenemy Chicago Cubs come to town. This true-blue Brew Crew fan is exhausted (from 162 games of stress) but overjoyed to report that on the day of this chapter's writing, the Brewers had just won a trip to the playoffs for the first time in 26 years!

For ticket information, call 414/902-4400 or 800/933-7890, or log on to www.brewers.com.

Milwaukee Bucks

Except for a woeful hiccup from 2006 to 2008 (last place, and deservedly so!), the Bucks are generally an upper-tier team in the NBA Eastern Conference. Tickets are rarely now hit or miss, but unless the Los Angeles Lakers are in town, you can usually land them. The Bucks offer great deals on their Bonus Nights, when certain seats (and not all of them at nosebleed elevation) are dirt cheap—by NBA standards, anyway. For ticket information, call 414/276-4545 or log on to www.bucks.com.

OTHER SPORTS
Milwaukee Wave

Also in the major leagues, though a bit out of the mainstream, are the professional indoor soccer Milwaukee Wave (414/224-9283, www.milwaukeewave.com), four-time champions of Major Indoor Soccer League. They are impressive otherwise as being the oldest continuously operating professional soccer team in North America.

Milwaukee Admirals

Also playing in the Bradley Center are the Milwaukee Admirals (www.milwaukeeadmirals.com) of the American Hockey League. The AHL is a bruising minor-league quasi-farm system of the National Hockey League (NHL), and if you follow hockey now and again you'll see retread veterans or up-and-coming college players on the rosters.

College Athletics

The local hometown Division 1A Golden

THE BREW CREW

Not a baseball or even a sports fan? Matters not; a Brewers game is a cultural necessity. Consider the following:

TAILGATING

Nobody but nobody parties before a ball game like Wisconsinites, and Milwaukeeans (and Green Bay Packers fans) have perfected the pregame tailgate party. The requisite pregame attraction is the meal of beer, grilled brats, and potato salad, eaten while playing catch in the parking lot. (The *Guinness Book of Records* recognized the Brewers' erstwhile home, Milwaukee County Stadium, as the site of the world's largest tailgate party – the new Miller Park has nearly double the party area!) And the food inside the stadium is superb: NBC Sports commentator emeritus Bob Costas has deemed the stadium's bratwurst tops in the major leagues.

AND IT'S THE BRATWURST BY A, ER, NOSE...

But this is not the best reason to go to a game. The Brewers have the coolest stunt in pro sports: the **Sausage Race.** Just after the halfway point of the game, while the field is being tailored, ground-crew members stick themselves into big, clunky sausage outfits – a hot dog, a Polish sausage, an Italian sausage, a bratwurst and, as of 2007, a Mexican *chorizo* – and lumber around the field to a thrilling finish at home plate. It's so popular that opposing players beg for the opportunity to be a Milwaukee sausage for the day; other teams ask the Brewers to bring the costumes along when they go to other cities.

© THOMAS HUHTI

Nobody tailgates like Wisconsin sports fans.

Eagles of **Marquette University,** the perennially popular basketball team, also play at the Bradley Center. Top-notch, the program is consistently ranked in the top 20 nationally.

The **University of Wisconsin-Milwaukee Panthers** are known for excellence in Division 1A sports, including basketball and especially soccer.

Milwaukee Mile

At Wisconsin State Fair Park, the Milwaukee Mile has been a legendary racing stop since 1903 (making it the oldest in the world); it's the only facility that offers stops from all three of the series held in the United States: NASCAR, Champ Car World Series, and Indy Racing League.

Accommodations

Most travelers will find lodging in downtown Milwaukee much better than they may have expected, given the historic grace of many buildings (yet there are plenty of bargains in chain hotels for the budget conscious). The only real reason to locate yourself away from the city center is if you need a dirt-cheap place; for this, the farther away from downtown, the cheaper the room.

A good trick is to check the Visit Milwaukee website (www.visitmilwaukee.org) for constant package deals at local hotels, even in peak seasons.

Note: All rates given are a) what they themselves have provided and b) merely the lowest on offer during peak season.

DOWNTOWN

Downtown Milwaukee is full of gracefully aging anachronisms, some wearier than others. The central area has also seen a boom in new lodgings. One hint: Given Wisconsin's winter, you may wish to note whether your accommodation is linked via the downtown **skywalk system.** Just a thought.

Under $50

Downtown? Are you serious? Forget about a hotel, but 35 miles north of town in Newburg you can find a hostel (4382 Hickory Rd., 262/675 6755, www.wellspring@hnet.net); rates are $20 per night.

Another not-too-far-away hostel is in Kettle Moraine State Forest in Eagle (608/931-2201, $25).

$50-100

Once again—good luck. First place to check is the 1920 art deco **Astor Hotel** (924 E. Juneau St., 414/271-4220 or 800/558-0200, www.theastorhotel.com, $99 and up), which has character (and characters strolling about) through and through, down to the original fixtures. Rooms have a retro elegance to them. Nice views of the lake can be had from its promontory; the interiors sport regional artwork. Complimentaries include breakfast, newspapers, shuttle service, business center, and passes to a nearby fitness center. The lounge is a popular place for jazz music.

If these are full, Best Western, Holiday Inn, Courtyard by Marriott, Ramada Inn, and Howard Johnson chain options also exist downtown and generally have rooms for rates similar to—if not slightly lower than—the Astor's.

$100-150

The historic apartment/condo building housing **(Knickerbocker on the Lake** (1028 E. Juneau Ave., 414/276-8500, www.knickerbockeronthelake.com, $125) overlooks Lake Michigan on a bluff just northeast of the funky Brady Street area; you're near parks and historic neighborhoods everywhere—a great location. Enter and espy original marble floors and vaulted ceilings. Rooms—each individually designed—are detailed with antiques but also have modern amenities such as air-conditioning, Internet access, and more; some rooms have smashing deck views, fireplaces, or other extras. Well-regarded restaurants on-site. For the price, it's a deal.

The **☖ Hilton Milwaukee City Center** (509 W. Wisconsin Ave., 414/271-7250 or 800/445-8667, www.hiltonmilwaukee.com, $100–240) is perhaps the best example of restored charm downtown. This incarnation features limestone ashlar, pink granite, and buff terra-cotta; it's Milwaukee's sole Roaring '20s art deco–style hotel, right down to the geometric marble motifs in the lobby. If Lake Michigan's too chilly, fear not, for in addition to a recreation center, the hotel now sports an island-themed water recreation area with water slides and a real sand beach.

Over $150

Generating lots of well-earned buzz is **☖ Hotel Metro** (411 E. Mason St., 414/272-1937, www .hotelmetro.com, $159 s, $259 d), a posh but cute boutique hotel in an erstwhile art deco office building. Glass sinks from Wisconsin's Kohler Company are among the noticeable design highlights of the 65 oversize suites replete with steeping tubs or whirlpool baths; downstairs is a chic, seen-on-the-scene bar. The art deco stylings include environmentally friendly practices such as bamboo-wood floorings and wood from sustainable forests. It's also got one of the best cafés in Milwaukee. Among the service highlights—bicycles for guests!

The granddaddy of Milwaukee hotels—called the "Grand Hotel" in fact—is the **☖ Pfister** (424 E. Wisconsin Ave., 414/273-8222 or 800/558-8222, www.thepfisterhotel .com, $244 s, $264 d), built in 1893. This posh city-state–size behemoth oozes Victorian grandeur. The somewhat overwhelming lobby is done with such ornate intricacy that the hotel organizes regular tours of its displays of 19th-century art. Its state-of-the-art recreation facility outshines most health clubs. The laundry list of attractive features and service accolades could fill a phone book.

WEST OF DOWNTOWN

Those options listed here are nonchain lodgings and those inside the western suburbs. If you're simply searching for a clean, cheap place, heading north or south from downtown gives you more (and better) choices. If you're looking for western accommodations, the suburbs of Wauwatosa, Elm Grove, Brookfield, and Waukesha (all along I-94 West) have plenty of chain motels and hotels; however, they'll likely push $100 in peak season. If you travel north off I-94 along U.S. 45 just east of the zoo, you'll come across a half dozen chain (and nonchain) motels, all with equally fine rooms at greater value.

$50-100

Adjacent to the Ambassador Hotel, its sister hotel is the more business travel–oriented (but equally worthwhile) **Executive Inn** (414/342-0000, www.execinn.com, from $69). There are similar amenities here with the bonus of a fitness center.

$100-150

For a B&B, try the 1897 Queen Anne **Acanthus Inn** (3009 W. Highland Blvd., 414/342-9788, $85–120), a 10-room historic mansion that has retained most of its original design. Period lighting and artwork add a nice touch.

Resurrected from the doldrums (and helping the neighborhood do the same) is the **Ambassador Hotel** (2308 W. Wisconsin Ave., 414/342-8400, http://ambassadormilwaukee. com, $129), just outside the western fringes of downtown. Inside a remodeled 1927 art deco structure ($12 million and counting sunk into upgrades), right down to the terra-cotta exterior), this boutique hotel is a new fave. Historic meets state-of-the-art. I just love to sip a martini in its Envoy Lounge. As it's on Wisconsin Avenue, you can't beat the transportation options to downtown, either.

NORTH OF DOWNTOWN

Most lodging choices are found off I-43 along Port Washington Road; virtually all are chain lodgings and range $65–150 single or double. Best overall rooms and location are at the **Hilton Milwaukee River Inn** (4700 N. Port

Washington Rd., 414/962-6040 or 800/445-8667, www.milwaukeeriver.hilton.com, $101), with well-appointed one-bedroom rooms and a gorgeous, quiet river location. The excellent restaurant has an even better river view.

SOUTH OF DOWNTOWN

If you've got an early-morning flight or are just looking for something cheap close to downtown, head south. At least two dozen lodgings are scattered about, most along South Howell Avenue, West Layton Avenue, and South 13th Street, and all save one are neon-light chain options. Of these, close enough to get you off to your plane early is **Howard Johnson** (1716 W. Layton Ave., 414/282-7000 or 800/446-4656, $69).

Over $150

Any hotel that aims to, as they say, mingle business suits with biker leathers and boots is gonna raise a few eyebrows, but **The Iron Horse Hotel** (500 West Florida Street, 414/373-4766 or 888/543-4766, www.theironhorsehotel.com, $225 and up) is an I'll-be-damned near success in that. Honestly—a biker boutique hotel, and appropriately a stone's throw from the new Harley Davidson Museum. Truth be told, it was just opening (a bit behind schedule) at the time of writing but already looked smashing, with loft-style rooms loaded to the gills with chic-but-tough (naturally) design and everything designed, indeed, for someone waltzing in with biker boots or a biz laptop (or, these days, both).

Food

Milwaukee boasts a large array of cuisine—a pan-ethnic food heaven spanning the gamut from fish fries in cozy 120-year-old neighborhood taprooms to four-star prix fixe repasts in state-of-the-art gourmet restaurants. So dash those thoughts of casseroles and meat-and-potatoes monotony—gastronomically, you'll be surprised by Milwaukee.

DOWNTOWN
Fish Fries

In Milwaukee, you'll find a fish fry everywhere—even at the chain fast-food drive-through and Miller Park during Friday-night Brewers games. Dozens of neighborhood taverns and bars still line up the plank seating and picnic tables with plastic coverings on Friday nights. The tables are arrayed with tartar sauce and maybe pickles (you'd better like coleslaw, because that's what you get as a side dish). Most fish fries come in under $7 for as much as you can stuff in. The most unreal fish fries are found south and west of downtown. Or head for a Catholic church; Milwaukee's got 275 parishes, so you'll find a good one.

Founded in 1833, the oldest civic and cultural organization in Milwaukee, **Turner Hall** (1034 N. 4th St., 414/276-4844, 11 A.M.–midnight Sun.–Thurs., till 1 A.M. Fri. and 2 A.M. Sat., $6–18), presents a defining Milwaukee dining experience. Once-dingy interiors were lovingly restored, and the reborn ◖ **Milwaukee Historic Turner's** is refreshingly warm and wondrously bright, allowing a look at the classic Old World interiors: stained glass, photographs, murals, and century-old memorabilia. And yes, it's still got the legendary fish fry, although it's a menu item now and not quite the socializing buffet of before. Along with the fish fry is an eclectic array of appetizers, sandwiches, creative salads and pastas, and a few traditional German dishes.

Also inside is the **Heritage Tourism Center,** with rotating exhibits and information on ethnic areas and multicultural events along the Lake Michigan Settlement Trail and in Milwaukee.

Coffee Along Brady Street

Those with a java fixation should head

immediately for the Brady Street area (www
.bradyst.com), where you'll find an inordinate
number of coffee shops of every possible variety. A highlight is the **Brady St. Pharmacy**
(1696 N. Astor St., 414/272-4384), a real-deal
old-school pharmacy with a lunch counter and
steaming coffee—eavesdrop on the Italian
from the neighborhood denizens!

Tea Shop
Watts Tea Shop (761 N. Jefferson St., 414/291-
5120, 9 A.M.–4 P.M. daily, tea 2:30–4 P.M.)
heads the list for afternoon tea and homemade
everything, from scones to chicken salad. The
shop is ensconced in the ritzy Watts store, purveyor of prohibitively fragile china, silver, and
crystal.

Steak Houses
The rule of thumb in town was always that
the farther west one strayed from downtown,
the better the ambience and steaks—no longer true. Staying in the Hilton Milwaukee
City Center? Go no farther than your establishment's **Milwaukee Chop House**
(633 N. 5th St., 414/226-2467, 5–10 P.M.
Mon.–Sat., $18–68); in addition to luscious
steaks, the bone-in rib eye is likely the best
in Milwaukee.

Some Milwaukee friends howled to include
Butch's Clock Steak House and Martini Bar
(414/347-0142, dinner nightly except Sun.,
$20–40) for its backhash to bygone days atmo-
sphere; others wailed equally for the new and
cool (elegantly chic) **Yanni's** (540 E. Mason
St., 414/847-9264, lunch/dinner weekdays,
dinner daily except Sun., $9–45).

On the river and closer to the Historic Third
Ward is the new and superb **Riverwalk Bistro**
(223 N. Water St., 414/272-4200, lunch/din-
ner daily except Mon., from $7)—world cui-
sine on a riparian patio.

Seafood
Milwaukee's newest place for creative and solid
seafood is **Bosley on Brady** (815 E. Brady St.,
414/727-7975, 4–10 P.M. Tues.–Sat., till 8 P.M.

FISH FRIES

Cuisine experience number one in Wisconsin
is a Friday-night fish fry. Its exact origins are
unknown, but it's certainly no coincidence
that in a state contiguous to two Great
Lakes, featuring 15,000 glacial pools, and
undergoing three successive waves of German Catholics, followed by Italian, Irish, and
Polish Catholics (Catholics don't eat meat on
Fridays during Lent), people would specialize
in a Friday-night fish-eating outing.

Fish fries are myriad. Corner taverns,
family restaurants, diminutive cafés and
greasy spoons, supper clubs, and even local
churches and VFW posts all have their own
take on the tradition. Milwaukee does it bigger and better than anywhere else – it's so
popular that even the local fast-food restaurants have them; the American Serbian Hall
serves 2,500 people at a drive-through; Chinese, Mexican, and other ethnic restaurants
get in on the act; and even Miller Park has
fish fries at Friday Brewers games.

Everybody has an opinion on who has
the best fish fry, but, truthfully, how many
ways can you deep-fry a perch (or one of
the other species variants – haddock, walleye pike, and cod)? Those with an aversion
to deep-fried food can usually find one
broiled option.

Generally set up as smorgasbords (sometimes including platefuls of chicken, too),
the gluttonous feasts are served with
slatherings of homemade tartar sauce and
a relish tray or salad bar. The truly classic
fish-fry joints are packed to the rafters by
5:30 P.M. – and some even have century-old
planks and hall-style seating (the kind of
place where you gaze at the tartar sauce
on the table and wonder really how long it's
been sitting out, unrefrigerated).

Consider yourself truly blessed if you get
to experience a smelt fry. This longtime tavern tradition has pretty much disappeared;
in the old days, smelt – milk-dipped, battered, and even pickled – were *the* thing.

Go immediately to www.classicwiscon-
sin.com and hit the link to "Fish Fries" – a
list of reviews is maintained.

Sun., $17–33)—seafood with a Key West attitude (it says).

Just north of downtown, the 🅒 **Roots Restaurant and Cellar** (1818 N. Hubbard St., 414/374-8480, lunch/dinner/brunch, $10–45) is to be praised for following an ethos of sustainability in ingredients. (It's also one of the few vegan-friendly places in town.) Better—it's got phenomenal food: classy upstairs, more casual downstairs. And great deck views. All in all, this is the place the author treats his friends to.

Fine Dining

Nouvelle cuisine is done magnificently at 🅒 **Sanford** (1547 N. Jackson St., 414/276-9608, 5:30 P.M.–9 P.M. Mon.–Thurs., 5 P.M.–10 P.M. Fri.–Sat., $30–70), one of the state's most original and respected innovators of cuisine and definitely a place to cook up an excuse for a splurge. It's feted by national foodie media and garnered a wall full of awards—*Gourmet* magazine in 2006 once again named it one of the United States' top 50 restaurants and in 2008 chef Sanford D'Amato was named one of the 20 outstanding chefs in the country by the James Beard Awards.

Something you'd never expect? How about a remarkable meal in a Milwaukee casino? Read on, for the elegant and creative fare at Potawatomi Bingo Casino's 🅒 **Dream Dance** (1721 W. Canal St., 414/847-7883, 5–9 P.M. Tues.–Thurs., 5–10 P.M. Fri.–Sat., $26–125) is worth the trip even for the nonslots players. Mouthwatering steaks and outstanding venison highlight a lengthy, creative menu, all of which celebrate the history and cuisine (and seasons) of Wisconsin. Chef Jason Gorman was nominated by the James Beard Award as "Best Chef: Midwest." Even better—in 2008 the casino polished off a quarter-billion dollar renovation, and they spared no expense for a redesign of the dining rooms—wow.

Most of the more sybaritic Milwaukee accommodations offer excellent dining. Of note might be the Knickerbocker on the Lake, which features two well-realized restaurants.

The **Knick** (1028 E. Juneau St., 414/272-0011, 11 A.M.–3 P.M. weekdays and 5 P.M.–midnight daily, also 9 A.M.–3 P.M. Sat., till 5 P.M. Sun., $5–22) has casual to elegant, traditional to cutting-edge fare, all well done. Also in the hotel is the coolly elegant but quite relaxed **Osteria del Mondo** (5–10 P.M. Mon.–Thurs. and Sun., 5–11 P.M. Fri.–Sat., $16–32).

Vegetarian and Health Food

For takeaway health food, a number of co-ops and natural-foods stores are in the downtown area. The largest is **Outpost Natural Foods** (100 E. Capitol Dr., 414/961-2597), easily mistaken for any other megagrocery store save for the organically grown veggies, dietary-restriction sections, and juice bar—there are also a good bakery and deli. This author's favorite, however, is definitely the vegan-friendly **Riverwest Co-op** (733 E. Clarke St., 414/264-7933, 7 A.M.–9 <H>p.m. Mon.–Fri., 8 A.M.–9 P.M. weekends, $4–8), especially for a quick, healthy breakfast (and a smoothie in mid-morning). The veggie Korean *bibimbop* is damned fine, as are the Saturday night vegan pizzas.

Not a veggie restaurant per se, but a Slow Food movement follower and one where you'll find the best from-scratch food in town without a hell of a price mark-up is the great **Comet Café** (1947 N. Farwell Ave., 414/273-7677, 10:30 A.M.–10 P.M. Mon.–Thurs., till 11 P.M. Fri.–Sat., from 9 A.M. Sat.–Sun., $6–12). Your carnivore friend can have the traditional mom (well, Milwaukee mom, anyway) meatloaf with beer gravy, while your vegan friend can have the vegan Salisbury steak. Everyone's happy!

German

Rollicking, boisterous, and full of lederhosen, **Mader's** (1037 N. Old World 3rd St., 414/271-3377, 11:30 A.M.–9 P.M. daily, till 10 P.M. Fri.–Sat., from 10:30 A.M. Sun., $18–24) has held its position as *the* German restaurant for the hoi polloi since 1902. Purists sometimes cringe at the over-the-top atmosphere (it's packed to the rafters with German knickknacks, not to mention tour buses idling outside), but the cheeriness is unvanquishable. Try the *knudel* (which doesn't taste as if it came out of a box), Rheinischer sauerbraten, oxtail soup, or Bavarian-style pork shank. Mader's also serves a Viennese brunch on Sunday.

However, ◖ **Karl Ratzsch's Old World Restaurant** (320 E. Mason St., 414/276-2720, 11:30 A.M.–2 P.M. and 4:30–9 P.M. weekdays, 4:30–10 P.M. Sun., entrées $8–30) is superbly realized and this author's fave Milwaukee experience. This decidedly more upscale multiple-award winner is split into two levels. The lower level features a bar with an extensive stein collection and impressive dark interior woodwork. The menu is copious and decidedly carnivorous—sauerbraten, braised pork shank, *rouladen, käse spätzle,* special strudels, and even some vegetarian offerings. Not Teutonic-centered? Even the fish fry is among Milwaukee's best! A pianist tickles the keys nightly.

Italian

The city's best purveyor of *alta cucina* is **Osteria del Mondo** (1028 E. Juneau Ave., 414/291-3770, 5–10 P.M. Mon.–Thurs. and Sun., till 11 P.M. Fri.–Sat., $16–32). The restaurant also has an atmospheric Italian wine bar and thoroughly relaxing patio.

Mimma's Cafe (1307 E. Brady St., 414/271-7337, 5–11 P.M. Fri.–Sat., till 10 P.M. otherwise, $11–19) constantly gets national write-ups for its cuisine—more than 50 varieties of pasta and weekly regional Italian specialties.

You want this author's favorite picnic fixings? Find 'em right on Brady Street. Grab some cheese and/or sausage from the venerable, six-decade-strong **Glorioso Brothers** (1020 E. Brady St., 414/272-0540), then head a block up to **Peter Sciortino's Bakery** (1101 E. Brady St., 414/272-4623) to get Milwaukee's best bread.

COURTESY OF KARL RATZSCH'S RESTAURANT

Karl Ratzsch's Old World Restaurant

French

Milwaukee…French food? Absolutely. You can find diminutive eateries fashioned after casual Paris restaurants to Gallic-oriented hot spots whose fare and style rival those of much larger metropolises. Starting it all was **Bartolotta's Lake Park Bistro** (see *Fine Dining* under *North of Downtown*). The owners of Milwaukee's prestigious Sanford restaurant also opened the more casual but still creative and outstanding **Coquette Cafe** (316 N. Milwaukee St., 414/291-2655, 11 A.M.–10 P.M. Mon.–Thurs., till 11 P.M. Fri., 5–11 P.M. Sat., $7–17), modeled after a French or Belgian brasserie. Hearty yet chic—a wonderful combination. ñ

Latin American

Cempazuchi (1205 E. Brady St., 414/291-5233, 11:30 A.M.–10 P.M. Tues.–Sat., 5–9 P.M. Sun., $11–19) wavers not a bit from edition to edition. A pan-Mexican menu features superbly realized dishes, from succulent moles to light Veracruz seafood dishes.

African

Very central is the **African Hut** (1107 N. Old World 3rd St., 414/765-1110, 11:30 A.M.–10 P.M. daily, $6 and up), whose specialty is *lumumba,* peppered wings. Or absolutely anything with peanut sauce is divine.

Asian

Milwaukee's got a couple of recommended Indian restaurants. **Dancing Ganesha** (1692-1694 N. Van Buren St., 414/220-0202, 11 A.M.–2 P.M. and 5–10 P.M. weekdays, 5–9 P.M. Sun., $7–19) offers an extensive list of less-than-usual items on its menu. (Turkey? Yup, and it's mouthwatering.)

Venerable **Izumi's** (2150 N. Prospect Ave., 414/271-5278, 11:30 A.M.–2 P.M. and 5–10 P.M. weekdays, 5–10:30 P.M. Sat., 4–9 P.M. Sun., $6–26), run by a Japanese chef/owner well trained by years of experience in Milwaukee Japanese eateries, tops the choices in town. The food here is impeccably well thought out and executed; this author's fave has to be its chef's remarkable take on the Milwaukee fish fry!

For Thai food, it's nearly impossible to walk away unsated from **The King and I** (838 N. Old World 3rd St., 414/224-7076, 11 A.M.–2 P.M. Mon.–Sat., 5–9 P.M. daily, $16–45), always but always recommended by locals—citizens, media, and foodies. The lunch buffet is gargantuan and well worth it!

NORTH OF DOWNTOWN
Milwaukee's Best Burger

Strong words, eh? But you will absolutely not find a better burger or old school eating experience (double horseshoe counter!) than **Solly's Grille** (4629 N. Port Washington Rd., 414/332-8808), dishing up their famous Butter Burger—they claim to have started it—since 1936, along with tried and true real deal Americana fare—three squares a day. The ambience is wondrous and if you can stomach the "cheesehead burger" (ahem, that'd be 0.67 pound sirloin, stewed and raw onions, mushrooms, Swiss and American cheeses from Wisconsin…plus fries), you're a true local.

Coffee Shops

The **Fuel Café** (818 E. Center St.)—great name—is exceedingly young, hip, and alternative; you'll find cribbage players and riot grrls. The decor is mismatched rummage-sale furniture with an arty flair, and the service bills itself as lousy. It isn't—and there's a great menu of coffee drinks, bakery items, salads, sandwiches, even Pop Tarts! Try the Kevorkian Krush, three shots of espresso and mocha.

Custard

Frozen custard is an absolute must of a Milwaukee cultural experience; the dozens of Milwaukee family custard stands were the inspiration for Big Arnold's Drive-In on the 1970s TV show *Happy Days.* In an informal poll, 20 questions determined a dozen different recommendations for where to experience frozen custard. Most often mentioned (but you really can't go wrong anywhere): **Kopp's** (5373 N. Port Washington Rd., 414/961-2006), which does custard so seriously that it has a flavor-of-the-day hotline.

Vegetarian and Health Food

A longtime standby for a low-key and decidedly body-friendly meal is **Beans and Barley** (1901 E. North Ave., 414/278-7878, 9 A.M.–9 P.M. Mon.–Sat., till 8 P.M. Sun., $4 and up). Very much a hip (though low-priced) eatery, it's housed in what smacks of an old grocery store warehouse encased in glass walls from an attached grocery and small bar. Everything from straight-up diner food to creative vegetarian is on the menu, with Indian and Southwestern options. Juices and smoothies, too.

Soul Food

Mr. Perkins (2001 W. Atkinson Ave., 414/447-6660, 5:30 A.M.–6 P.M. daily, $5 and up) is the place to go for soul food, with tons of down-home specialties—collard greens, catfish, chitterlings, fried apples, turkey legs, and the like, as well as homemade sweet potato pie and peach cobbler like you'll find nowhere else.

Fine Dining

An exquisitely restored 19th-century park structure houses (**Bartolotta's Lake Park Bistro** (3133 E. Newberry Blvd., 414/962-6300, 11 A.M.–9 P.M. weekdays, 5–10 P.M. Sat., 11 A.M.–2 P.M. and 5–9 P.M. Sun., entrées $7–12). Opened by a prominent local restaurateur and housed in an exquisitely restored century-old park pavilion, this bistro has, with each edition of this book, somehow managed to remain rock-solid as a dining highlight. Its French cuisine is superb and, if nothing else, the view from the drive along the lake is worth the time. It's a popular Sunday brunch spot. Best of all—the interiors are airy, offering plenty of privacy between tables. Chef Adam Siegel was named a finalist for the James Beard Awards as "Best Chef: Midwest" in 2008.

The regular airmail cod-cheek delivery is a bit gimmicky, but the seafood is recommended by most Milwaukeeans at **River Lane Inn** (313 W. River Lane, Brown Deer, 414/354-1995, 11:30 A.M.–2 P.M. weekdays, 5–10 P.M. Mon.–Sat., $15–28). Try to sit on the lovely patio—great view and a sense of privacy.

A newer, fantastic restaurant in the far northern suburbs is **The Riversite** (11120 N. Mequon Rd., Mequon, 262/242-6050, 5–10 P.M. Mon.–Sat., $19–31), which features remarkable seasonal cuisines to supplement classics—excellent steak and lamb. Of note here are the unusually capacious dining areas—a popular place but one where you're not elbow-to-elbow. The chef here was yet another finalist as the best chef in the Midwest in 2008, according to the James Beard Awards.

SOUTH OF DOWNTOWN
Fish Fries

For the most one-of-a-kind fry *anywhere,* head for (**American Serbian Hall** (53rd and Oklahoma, 414/545-6030, $10), recognized as the largest in the nation. On Friday night, this hall serves more than a *ton* of Icelandic-style or Serbian baked fish to more than 2,500 people (make that two tons on Good Friday). The operation got so big that a drive-through has been added, which serves an additional 1,200 patrons. Unreal—watching cars backed up for miles while next to the complex waiting patrons (many chattering in Serbian) engage in fun-spirited bocce ball games.

This author loves the side dishes of beans and rice, *ensaladas,* and the Puerto Rican batter on the fish at the **United Community Center's Café el Sol** (1028 S. 9th St., 414/384-3100, $9).

Custard

The south side has perhaps the most legendary in the city. An institution since the early '40s is **Leon's** (3131 S. 27th St., 414/383-1784); it's got the best neon. The **Nite Owl Drive In** (830 E. Layton Ave., 414/483-2524) has been dishing up ice cream and doling out burgers by the same family for a half century; even Elvis loved to eat here. All have ice cream from a buck or so.

Mexican

You'll find the most substantial Mexican menu (not to mention a most unpretentious atmosphere) at **Tres Hermanos** (1332 W. Lincoln Ave., 414/384-9050, 11 A.M.–10 P.M.

Sun.–Thurs., 11 A.M.–midnight Fri.–Sat., $9–20), specializing in seafood in virtually every form—particularly a soup that'll knock your socks off. Rootsy, live Tex Mex and Norteña music on weekends.

Milwaukee's southeast side is a haven for unpretentious authentic Mexican eateries; some Mexican grocers have lunch counters in the back or sell delectable tamales ready for takeout. **Conejito's** (4th and Virginia Sts., 11 A.M.–midnight daily) is a neighborhood bar-restaurant with authentic atmosphere and real-deal Mexican food from $4. The same is true at **Jalisco's,** which has numerous locations (one at 2207 E. North Ave.) but whose original (9405 S. 27th St., 414/672-7070, $5), after perishing in a fire, has a slick new rebuild to go with its great food. Jalisco's restaurants (7 A.M.–3 A.M. Sun.–Thurs., 24 hours Fri.–Sat.) serve creative burritos as big as your head.

Serbian

Enjoy top-notch Serbian food in a delightful Old World atmosphere at **◖ Three Brothers** (2414 S. St. Clair St., Bay View, 414/481-7530, 5–10 P.M. Tues.–Thurs., 4–11 P.M. Fri.–Sat., and 4–10 P.M. Sun., $11 and up). The 1897 turreted brick corner house, an original Schlitz brewery beer parlor, was turned into a restaurant by the present owner's father, a Serbian wine merchant. Not much has changed—the high paneled ceilings, original wood, dusty bottles on the bar, mirrors, and mismatched tables and chairs. All of it is charming. The food is heavy on pork and chicken, lots of *paprikash* and stuffed cabbage. The signature entrée is *burek,* a filled phyllo dough concoction the size of a radial tire; you wait a half hour for this one. The restaurant is difficult to find—this neighborhood is the real Milwaukee—you'll likely wind up asking for directions from a horseshoe club outside a local tavern. Take Superior to Bay View and then take a left on Russell; that should get you to St. Clair. The views from Bay View's side streets are absolutely splendid.

One little-known place for Serbian in south Milwaukee is **Fritz's Pub** (20th and Oklahoma, 10 A.M.–1 A.M. Mon.–Tues., 7 A.M.–1 A.M. Wed.–Sat., closed Sun.), with a decent selection of Serbian-style sandwiches.

Polish

◖ Polonez (4016 S. Packard Ave., St. Francis, 414/482-0080, 11 A.M.–3 P.M. Tues.–Fri., 5–9 P.M. Tues.–Sat., 11 A.M.–8 P.M. Sun., $5–17) is a longtime Milwaukee favorite and it *rocks.* Since previous editions of the book, it has transformed geographically and atmospherically—it's now a white-tableclothed fine-dining (but very casual in feeling) experience. The pierogi and cutlets are phenomenal, as is the very good *czarnina* (a raisin soup with duck stock, duck blood, and fruits—seven soups daily). The Sunday brunch is unrivaled; this author could go weekly for the rest of his life and not tire of it!

Indian

Rock-bottom pricing (most of the million choices under $5), outstanding takeout, and mesmerizing smells—you can't beat local unknown **Bombay Sweets** (3401 S. 13th St., 414/383-3553, 11 A.M.–8 P.M. daily).

WEST OF DOWNTOWN
Fish Fry

A good bet is **Tanner Paull Restaurant** (6922 W. Orchard St., 414/476-5701, 4–9 P.M. Fri., $9), in an American Legion Post (how cool!). A half ear of corn is among the unique sides at this place, the first to offer all-you-can-ram-in fish fry in the Beer City.

Steak Houses

◖ Coerper's Five O'Clock Club (2416 W. State St., 414/342-3553, 5:30–9:30 P.M. Tues.–Sat., entrées $19–32) has been around forever and is so popular for steaks you absolutely need a reservation. It has the largest portions in town, all simmered in the eatery's legendary meat juice, and old-fashioned touches such as relish trays, but some have opined that its quality doesn't always match its legendary tradition.

Some locals say the best steaks aren't even in Milwaukee itself but in Wauwatosa at **Mr. B's, a Bartolotta Steak House** (17700 W. Capitol Dr., Wauwatosa, 262/790-7005, 5:30–9:30 P.M. Mon.–Sat., till 8 P.M. Sun., $16–37), run by one of Milwaukee's most successful restaurateurs. The steaks are grilled over hardwoods; Italian entrées are also available.

Italian

Hmm, the name Bartolotta in Wauwatosa seems to be omnipresent. Yes, 🄲 **Ristorante Bartolotta** (7616 W. State St., Wauwatosa, 414/771-9710, 5:30–9:30 P.M. Mon.–Thurs., 5–10 P.M. Fri.–Sat., and 5–8:30 P.M. Sun., $16–28) is a warm and friendly eatery run by a legendary Milwaukee restaurateur—definitely worth the trip. Bartolotta certainly rivals Mangia of Kenosha, the other great Wisconsin Italian eatery.

Indian

If you're an aficionado of southern Indian food, you're generally out of luck. But Milwaukee has **Tandoor** (1117 S. 108th St., West Allis, 414/777-1600, 11:30 A.M.–3 P.M. and 5–10 P.M. daily, $8–15), and it's a godsend. India's extraordinarily diverse cuisine is represented in toto here, divinely.

Vegetarian

Loads of restaurants in Milwaukee can accommodate vegetarians, but we all know that that generally means a couple of pasta entrées or something done the same way only they don't throw in the meat. This author's favorite vegetarian restaurant (it's also vegan friendly) is far west of downtown in Brookfield, but worth the drive; it's **Café Manna** (3815 North Brookfield Rd., Brookfield, 11 A.M.–9 P.M. Mon.–Sat., $6–15). This author would die right now for their Jamaican lentil burger (and he is an avowed carnivore).

Information and Services

Visit Milwaukee (400 W. Wisconsin Ave., 414/908-6205 or 800/554-1448, www.visitmilwaukee.org, 8 A.M.–5 P.M. weekdays, 9 A.M.–2 P.M. Sat. in summer, weekdays only the rest of the year) is in the Midwest Airlines Center. Additional offices are at Mitchell International Airport (414/747-4808) and by Discovery World at Pier Wisconsin (414/273-3950).

The local sales tax totals out at 5.6 percent. You'll pay a 9 percent tax on hotel rooms in addition to the sales tax, 3 percent on car rentals, and a 0.025 percent tax on food and beverage purchases.

Media

The *Milwaukee Journal-Sentinel* is a morning daily. The Friday paper has a complete listing of weekend cultural events, music, clubs, and movies. Fans of alternative views pick up weekly copies of the free *Shepherd Express,* which is also a good source of local arts and nightlife info. The local monthly repository of everything Milwaukee

is *Milwaukee Magazine.* For online help, check www.onmilwaukee.com or www.info-milwaukee.com, and www.metromilwaukee.org, which are generally the best of the half dozen or so web guides. Another one might be www.cityonthelake.com, though the first few are better.

By the time you read this, pretty much every coffee shop in downtown Milwaukee will have Internet access, though most of them are WiFi but not necessarily with their own terminals.

Listen to the eclectic, student-run **WMSE** at 91.7 FM—it might surprise you. Local standby has always been WTMJ (620 AM) for news and talk radio.

Milwaukee LGBT Center (315 W. Court St., www.mkelgbt.org) is a good local organization for the lesbian, gay, bi, and transgendered community.

Bookstores

The bookstores-per-capita quotient is pretty high here. Two blocks north of Grand Avenue Mall, **Renaissance Book Shop** (834 N.

Plankinton Ave., 414/271-6850) has an amazing six stories of books. It even has a second place at the airport!

GETTING THERE
By Air
General Mitchell International Airport (5300 S. Howell Ave., 414/747-5300, www .mitchellairport.com) is southeast of downtown, near Cudahy. It's best reached by traveling I-94 south and following the signs. From downtown, head south on 6th Street North; it should get you to WI 38 (Howell Avenue). Named for a native-son Army Air Corps general who was run out of the armed forces for his outspokenness, it's not bad as airports go. Nearly 100 cities are reached direct from Milwaukee; more than 225 flights per day depart.

A genuine treat for Milwaukee-bound travelers is the chance to experience what is doubtless the nation's best domestic carrier, Milwaukee-based **Midwest Airlines.** Travelers who try Midwest Airlines vow they'll never step aboard another cattle carrier again. How can you compete with double-wide leather seats throughout the whole cabin, exquisite meals, and genuinely solicitous service? (The prices are competitive, too!) Nonstop flights are available to all major and minor airports in the nation. The airline offers excellent package deals including airfare, car rental, and accommodations from a dozen major U.S. cities. For information on Midwest Airlines, call 414/570-4000 or 800/452-2022, or visit www.midwestairlines.com.

Milwaukee County Transit System **buses** run to the airport; almost any bus can start you on your way if you ask the driver for transfer help. A taxi from downtown costs $15–20 and takes 20 minutes. Airport limousines cost half that.

For all ground transportation questions, call the airport's hotline, 414/747-5308.

By Bus
Greyhound (414/272-9949) is at 606 North James Lovell but should be in the renovated Amtrak depot by the time you read this. Buses leave up to a dozen times daily for Chicago; buses also go to Minneapolis, Madison, and

certain points in central Wisconsin. A few other intercity coaches have offered service to similar areas, but their consistency in scheduling leaves much to be desired.

Up the street from the Greyhound station is the **Badger Bus** hangout (635 N. 7th St., 414/276-7490). Buses leave this location for Madison seven times daily. Badger Bus also leaves from Mitchell Field International Airport and heads to downtown Milwaukee before leaving for Madison six times a day.

The Southwest Airlines of bus service— **MegaBus** (www.megabus.com/us)—started in 2006 between Milwaukee and Chicago, as well as Minneapolis. Fares are a couple of bucks (at best—they're usually around $20, as bus companies have begun hidden-fare games like the airlines—but there are no ticket offices, terminals, or sometimes even service. It is imperative to check the website for pick-up information.

By Train
Amtrak service between Milwaukee and Chicago is oft-debated but never seems to die. With a multimillion dollar facelift to its terminal (done by the time you read this, one hopes), it looks to be good to go for a long time.

At present, seven trains operate daily, with hefty fares of $21 one-way on off-peak weekdays, $31 on the weekend. Service to Minneapolis is less imperiled; one train still leaves daily. The Amtrak station (433 W. St. Paul Ave., 414/271-9037) will also house Greyhound.

Discussions have been endless about whether to link Chicago's Metra service through Kenosha and Racine to Milwaukee and, possibly, outlying suburbs; it would be slower than Amtrak but also much cheaper. Other experimental train service west toward Madison will likely, sad to say, never be realized.

By Boat
Long-debated high-speed ferries from Milwaukee to Muskegon, Michigan, are finally running with **Lake Express** (866/914-1010, www.lake-express.com). Three round-trips make the zippy 2.5-hour run across the lake:

leaving Milwaukee at 6 A.M., 12:30 P.M., and 7 P.M. Rates (one-way/round-trip) are fairly reasonable: $50/85 adults, $24/40 children under 16. Add $59 for your car. Service starts in early May and tapers off in late October. The terminal is in Milwaukee's south-side neighborhood of Bay View. A passenger-only hovercraft service between Milwaukee and Chicago, with a possible stop in Racine, has been proposed from this new pier.

GETTING AROUND
Taxis

Taxis are all metered and have a usual drop fare of around $3 for the first mile and about $1.50 for each additional. **American United Taxicab** (414/220-5010) is the state's largest operation and has computer-assisted dispatching with GPS-aided guidance.

Buses

The **Milwaukee County Transit System** (414/344-6711, www.RideMCTS.com) operates loads of buses. (Save 25 percent by buying a 10-pack of tickets.) The system also has good options for trolley tours and for easy ways to take in a Milwaukee Brewers game at Miller Park, among others.

Rental Cars

Every major rental-car agency is represented at Mitchell International Airport and many have a half dozen or so representatives throughout the city. There is a 3 percent tax on car rentals.

Organized Tours

Increasingly popular are Milwaukee River (and occasionally Lake Michigan harbor) cabin cruiser tours, some also offering dining cruises.

The venerable *Iroquois* boat tours of Milwaukee Boat Lines (414/294-9450, www .mkeboat.com, 1 P.M., 3 P.M., and 6 P.M. late-May–Sept. 1, $14 adults) departs from the Clybourn Street Bridge on the west bank of the Milwaukee River and offers scenic narrated tours. Naturally there are also a few live music tours as well.

Equally venerable are cruises aboard the *Edelweiss* (414/276-7447, www.edelweissboats. com). It would take about a page and a half to list all of the tours they offer, but hey, your average beer-and-a-brat cruise runs about $16!

Rent your own as well but more, ahem, "social" sunset cruises (need an ID!) are offered at **Riverwalk Boat Tours and Rental** (Pere Marquette Park, 414/283-9999, www .riverwalkboats.com). This operation has a fave three-hour brewery tour taking in three local microbreweries on weekends ($25), along with a host of other public tours. You can also rent your own two-person boat ($15 per hour) or pontoon boat ($55 per hour).

At the Municipal Pier, south of the Milwaukee Art Museum, the replica 19th-century schooner *Denis Sullivan* is Wisconsin through and through, with all lumber culled from northern Wisconsin forests; it is more than 130 feet long with three 95-foot native white pine masts. Technically it's a floating classroom, part of the new nonprofit Pier Wisconsin project, but its pricey tours ($25 children, $50–55 adults) are available to anyone interested in maritime history and ecology. They're also jaw-droppingly spectacular, not to mention better-than-any-book educational. For sailing schedules, which vary year to year (and by season), call 414/276-7700 or visit www .discoveryworld.org.

You can do it yourself by hopping aboard an old-fashioned **trolley** ($1) from Milwaukee County Transit System (414/344-6711, www.RideMCTS.com). Schedules have varied quite a bit, but service has generally been Wednesday–Sunday, summer only. Note that Summerfest, Brewers games, and other sights outside the downtown are not served (the city has special summer shuttles for these).

Perhaps the most Milwaukee way to tour the city would be aboard a rumbling Harley-Davidson. Organized group tours no longer operate, but **House of Harley** (6221 W. Layton Ave., 414/282-2211, www.houseofharley.com) has the blessings of Harley-Davidson to rent brand-new motorcycles.

VICINITY OF MILWAUKEE

Spend enough time in Milwaukee and it's easy to forget that you are in America's Dairyland, or that you're in a state famed for carpets of forest and 16,000 residual glacial pools (lakes, that is). Indeed, leave the outskirts of Milwaukee in any direction and before long the population density decreases in direct proportion to the number of miles driven; simultaneously, quizzical Holsteins appear along the winding roads.

Heading north you'll also find villages that time seems to have forgotten and superb classic lakefront loveliness. Northwest of the city highlights include some of North America's grandest wildlife viewing at **Horicon Marsh** and a true retreat at **Holy Hill.**

Go west, oh traveler, and find the best mountain biking in southern Wisconsin and a walk-through of the state's geological history at **Kettle Moraine State Forest** and a walk-through of the state's settlement period at **Old World Wisconsin,** along with perhaps the greatest concentration of milk-bearing moo-cows.

Even if you bear south, that oft-overlooked compass point, toward (or from) the Windy City you've got, er, great Great Lake downtowns of **Kenosha** and **Racine;** and the posh but humble southern retreat region around **Geneva Lake.**

PLANNING YOUR TIME

The Vicinity of Milwaukee could easily be explored within a day in any direction—that is, a day for the north, or a day for the

HIGHLIGHTS

◖ Cedarburg: To Milwaukee's north is a gem of an anachronism, a preserved village with charm and lots of shops (page 71).

◖ Holy Hill: Recharge your soul at this cathedral towering over surrounding forests and farms (page 76).

◖ Horicon Marsh: It's unforgettable when, quite literally, millions of birds take flight on their epic migrations (page 77).

◖ Old World Wisconsin: This is one of the United States' most expansive and detailed collections of settlement structures (page 81).

◖ Geneva Lake: A haven for tourists from the south for generations, it's got one of the loveliest lake-path strolls anywhere (page 85).

◖ Racine Art Museum (RAM): The fetching, retro-chic RAM holds the United States' most superlative collections of folk arts (page 95).

◖ Golden Rondelle Theater: Racine's gem is an unmistakable piece of Frank Lloyd Wright art (page 95).

LOOK FOR ◖ TO FIND RECOMMENDED SIGHTS, ACTIVITIES, DINING, AND LODGING.

VICINITY OF MILWAUKEE

south, a day for the southwest, etc. Granted, you could easily make it a couple days anywhere or, for example, combine the route to Chicago with Lake Geneva and environs.

For the north, take one day and head up the lakeshore, then return to Milwaukee via the Horicon Marsh, Holy Hill, and Kettle Moraine State Forest-Southern Unit.

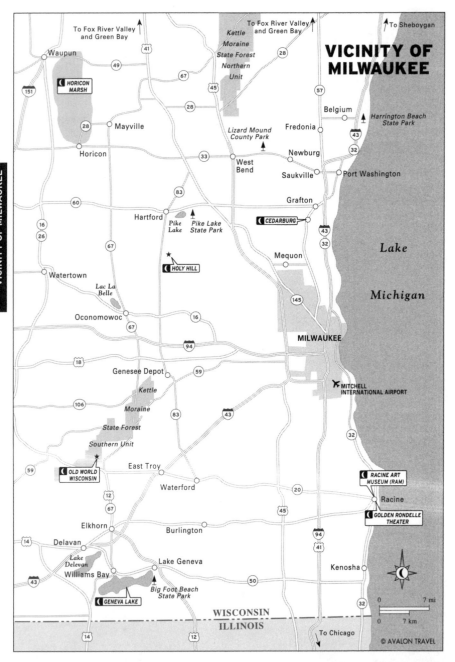

Old World Lake Country

North of Milwaukee along WI 32 you've got one of the loveliest little sidetrips in the state, taking in Cedarburg, a tiny town that time seems to have forgotten (well, except for the zillion tourists and relevant infrastructure), and one of this author's favorite lake towns, Port Washington, where the views and fish fries are legendary.

◖ CEDARBURG

What candy-facade original-13-colony spots such as Williamsburg are to the East Coast, Cedarburg is to Old World Wisconsin. It's been seemingly preserved in a time vacuum, thanks to local residents who successfully fought off wholesale architectural devastation from an invasion of Milwaukeeans looking for an easy commute. Cedarburg, about a half hour north of downtown Milwaukee, was originally populated by German (and a few British) immigrants, who hacked a

community out of a forest and built numerous mills along Cedar Creek, which bisects the tiny community, including the only worsted wool mill and factory in what was then considered the West. Those mills, and more than 100 other original Cream City–brick buildings, have been painstakingly restored into the state's most concentrated stretch of antiques dealers, shops, galleries, bed-and-breakfasts, and proper little restaurants. Stop at the visitors center for an excellent booklet on historic-structure walking tours. **Landmark Tours** (P.O. Box 771, Cedarburg, WI 53012, 262/375-1426) leads group tours through Cedarburg and Ozaukee County.

Sights

The heart and soul of the town is **Cedar Creek Settlement,** an antebellum foundation mill once the village's center of activity but now a several-blocks-long hodgepodge of

Cedarburg covered bridge

shops, restaurants, and galleries. The **Cedar Creek Winery** (10 A.M.–5 P.M. Mon.–Sat., 11 A.M.–5 P.M. Sun.) is also on the premises; tours take in the aging cellars. West of the main drag (Washington Rd.), Portland Road features one of the original structures in Cedarburg, the enormous, five-story **Cedarburg Mill**, now home to yet another antique shop. Along Riveredge Drive is the **Brewery Works** (262/377-8230, 1–4 P.M. Wed.–Sun.), a restored 1840s brewery housing art studios and the Ozaukee County Art Center. Whether or not you see working artisans is hit or miss.

North of town three miles is the last extant **covered bridge** in the state, dating from 1876; to get there, head to the WI 143/60 junction on Washington Avenue (well, another one does exist near Waupaca, though there's debate about whether it counts). This is an excellent bike tour. Southeast of Cedarburg via Hamilton Road is the original settlement of **Hamilton,** with another picturesque creekside mill.

The town has a great **Performing Arts Center** (262/376-6161), with a full slate of visiting artists and performances. **Cedarburg Cultural Center** (262/375-3676) has regular jazz and folk performances along with art exhibits. The local **visitors center** (262/377-9620 or 800/237-2874, www.cedarburg.org) is here; very friendly and useful staffers will point you in the right direction. A small **general store museum** is also in the complex.

Accommodations and Food

Gorgeous lodging options exist; nobody comes here to stay in a *motel*. The **Stagecoach Inn and Weber Haus Annex** (W61 N520 Washington Ave., 262/375-0208 or 888/375-0208, www.stagecoach-inn-wi.com, $85–150) is a historic inn and pub on the old Milwaukee–Green Bay stagecoach line. Nine lovely rooms are in the main inn; three are in a restored 1847 frame building across the street where you can stroll in a private garden. Six suites have whirlpools; two have gas fireplaces. Rumors say a benign, black-garbed apparition wafts through the inn.

Get classic Wisconsin German tavern fare or the casually upscale cuisine found at most gentrified enclaves such as this. Newest is the **Anvil Pub** (Cedar Creek Settlement, 262/376-2163, 11 A.M.–3 P.M. and 5–10 P.M. Mon.–Sat., $6–24), with casual-to-ambitious cuisine in a wondrous old renovated blacksmith's shop. Do try the house sandwiches served on homemade bread.

It's a chichi name and menu at **Cream and Crepe Café** (Cedar Creek Settlement, 262/377-0900, 10 A.M.–8 P.M. Tues.–Sat., till 5 P.M. Sun.–Mon., $4–10), but the crepes are delectable, as is the creekside dining area.

Galioto's Vintage Grille (1221 Wauwatosa Rd., 262/377-8085, 11 A.M.–2 P.M. Mon.–Fri., 5–9 P.M. Mon.–Thurs., 5–10 P.M. Fri.–Sat., 4–8 P.M. Sun., $7–26) is a smashing eatery housed in an erstwhile classic Wisconsin country tavern. The superb renovation features original beams and flickering flames in an original fireplace. The well-done dishes focus on creative comfort food—the pork chops are legendary.

PORT WASHINGTON

Forty minutes north of Milwaukee is Port Washington, a littoral Lake Michigan community that links up with east-central Wisconsin. Port Washington put itself into the history books with its quixotic anti–Civil War draft riots, when mobs took over the courthouse and trained a cannon on the lakefront until the army showed up and shooed the rabble-rousers home. Part Great Lake fishing town and part preserved antebellum anachronism, Port Washington, a declination backing off the lake, is known for its enormous downtown **marina** and fishing charters. (The marina came about due to the North Harbor, which was the first man-made harbor in the United States, first dredged in 1870.

Sights

You can stroll along the breakers, snapping shots of the art deco **lighthouse,** now a historical museum and National Historic Site renovated and opened to the public in 2002—the

WHEN YOU'RE DONE ANTIQUING . . .

Most folks get their sweat on simply via lovely gingerbread-espying – or antique buying – strolls in Cedarburg, yet running smack through downtown is the fantastic 30-mile-long **Ozaukee Interurban Trail,** a multi-use recreation trail that takes you through some of the county's cutest communities and most pastoral of agrarian swaths. (Perhaps this was why the county was named the second-best place in the United States to raise a family by *Forbes* magazine.) Just try counting all the octagon barns along the way – in summer you can buy fresh fruit to munch along the way from roadside stands.) It technically starts just north of downtown Milwaukee, but Cedarburg lies smack in the middle and makes a great starting point.

You could head south toward Milwaukee via Mequon, where you should really stop at **Libby Montana** (5616 Donges Bay Road, 262/242-2232,) for a ginormous buffalo burger and, south and west of there, the **Trinity Creek Wildlife Area** a restored wetland great for birding.

Alternatively, you could also pedal north all the way to Port Washington (covered elsewhere in this chapter) via **Grafton,** which has, at 12th and Falls Road, one of the most unique historical markers you'll see in the area. Here, during the late 1920s and early 1930s, in a little town in Wisconsin, 25 percent of

all Delta blues, gospel, soul, and other music was recorded and pressed by Paramount Records – some for the first time (you can still see the foundations and rusted power wheel of the disc press in the old chair factory used by the company). Who knew, eh? Music greats are celebrated with statuary and memorials in downtown's Paramount Plaza. (Regular free music concerts downtown in summer!) A tad more mundane – but still historically relevant, and fun for the kiddies – is **The Family Farm** (328 W. Port Washington Rd., 262/377-6161, 9 A.M.-4 P.M. Wed.-Sat., from 11 A.M. Sun., May-Oct., $6.50), a nearly 50-acre former homesteading site with renovated buildings and, better, antique farm machinery and tons of farm animals; try the wagon rides!

North of town a few miles is a great bridge over the Milwaukee River. Continue on to **Lion's Gorge,** a 79-acre secluded area with great hiking and views of (along with access to) Lake Michigan.

The trail actually runs all the way north to Sheboygan County via **Belgium,** home of Wisconsin's proud Luxembourger immigrant heritage. The largest Luxembourg festival outside Europe is held here annually the second week of August (gotta try the *mustreipen* or blood sausage!). A Luxembourg cultural center is also being built.

Grand Duchy of Luxembourg paid for it (all the Belgians and Luxembourgers hereabouts). The site is also home to the **Port Washington Historical Society Museum** (311 Johnson St., 1–4 P.M. in the summer). The **Eghart House** (same hours) on Grand Avenue at the library is done up in turn-of-the-20th-century style.

Also along Grand Avenue, what's known as the **Pebble House,** site of a tourist center (800/719-4881, www.portwashingtontourism.com), was painstakingly arranged of stones scavenged from the beaches along the lake. Franklin Street, dominated by the thrusting spire of St. Mary's Church and various castellated building tops, rates as one of the most

small town–like of any of the Lake Michigan coastal towns. Upper City Park, on a bluff overlooking the water, affords wondrous views of the lake and horizon.

Port Washington claims to hold the **world's largest fish fry** annually on the third Saturday of July, though it's got a couple of in-state rivals for that title.

Farther north is **Harrington Beach State Park,** unknown to most outside of the Milwaukee area, which is too bad. It's got great lake and limestone bluff views, an abandoned limestone quarry and quarry lake, and hiking trails, some a bit treacherous. A new campground here relieves a serious need for public

© WISCONSIN DEPARTMENT OF TOURISM

Harrington Beach State Park, Lake Michigan

camping along Lake Michigan's southern shore-line. The only campground with yurts is here! (They've also gone beyond making it accessible to making it downright easy here—a shuttle bus runs to and from the park highlights.)

One sidetrip nugget that nobody ever seems to know of is to head north of Port Washington via WI 32, then north on Highway H to Fredonia, where north and west along Highway I you'll find the **Stony Hill School,** the birthplace of Flag Day. Continuing on to Waubeka brings you to the **National Flag Day Foundation Americanism Center** (third Sunday after-noon of each month; free admission), which celebrates all things flag-oriented.

West of Port Washington you could head to Saukville, where, heading west yet again via Cedar Sauk Road or WI 33 you could visit the **Cedarburg Bog,** a 2000-acre Mesozoic bog (the southernmost in the state), with a University of Wisconsin research station.

Accommodations

Redone B&Bs are sprouting up regularly, including the huge shingle Victorian **Port Washington Inn** (308 W. Washington St., 877/794-1903, www.portwashingtoninn

.com, from $140), a gorgeous structure that gets kudos for its environmentally sound prac-tices—the gardens are lovely.

Posh, posh, posh rooms are at the 1902 **Port Hotel** (101 E. Main St., 262/9473, www.the-porthotel.com, $150), a splendid redone-to-the-nth beauty with probably the nicest rooms—the priciest rooms have spectacular lake views—between Milwaukee and Door County to the north. Most rooms even have fireplaces! Dinner here is also recommended.

Food

Plenty of good food is available in Port Washington—every place will have a decent fish selection, if not a particular specialty. The **Smith Bros. Coffee House** (100 N. Franklin St., 262/268-2767, 11 A.M.–10 P.M., $5–7) re-placed an absolutely gorgeous century-and-a-half fish shanty started by the eponymous brothers. A fire and a resultant sale of the building had locals and tourists bemoaning the loss of a treasure; well, it's different, but the place still has a wondrous old-timey feel to it—and the coffee is good. **Bernie's Fine Meats Market** (9:30 A.M.–5:30 P.M. Mon.–Fri., 9:30 A.M.–4 P.M. Sat., closed Sun.) on

North Franklin is a good place to scout out Wisconsin-style smoked meats—especially sausage varieties.

Fantastic is the newest: **Wind Rose Wine and Martini Bar** (262/284-4800, 5–9 P.M. Sun.–Tues., 5–10 P.M. Fri.–Sat., dinner daily $16–24). Superb steaks and salmon in a Midwest-chic environment—the place is tastefully decorated and musicians tinkle the ivories and twiddle the strings in the background.

It would, however, be difficult to beat the lighthouse views at **Newport Shores** (407 E. Jackson St., 262/284-6838, $6–16). It would furthermore be hard to beat the cheeriness of the staff—or the fish fry (fish lovers will absolutely find something to chow on here). Hours are complicated, but basically lunch and dinner daily (till 10:30 P.M. Fri. and Sat.), with a luscious Sunday brunch as well.

WEST BEND

West Bend lies 15 minutes west of Port Washington. You may know this busy manufacturing center as the point of origin of dozens of small kitchen appliances. There's a lot of parkland, too, in the city limits, much of which is connected via flower-laden multi-use trails along the Milwaukee River.

The **Museum of Wisconsin Art** (300 S. 6th Ave., 262/334-9638, 10 A.M.–4:30 P.M. Wed.–Sat., from 1 P.M. Sun., $5) boasts the largest holding of early-19th-century to early 20th-century Wisconsin art. In addition to the works of Milwaukee-born German Carl von Marr, an antique dollhouse spans an entire room. This is a real-deal museum and local and state authorities have big plans for it—as a matter of fact, by 2010 it was scheduled to move into lovely new $12 million digs designed by the same architects that did the Discovery World complex in Milwaukee. The new museum will double present holdings, which would allow new wings for contemporary Wisconsin art. (One of the coolest ideas is to use "visible storage," so that even pieces that aren't on permanent display can be temporarily viewed—what a grand idea!)

The **Old Courthouse Museum** (320 S. 5th Ave., 262/335-4678, 11 A.M.–5 P.M. Wed.–Fri,

9 A.M.–1 P.M. Sat., 1–4:30 P.M. Sun., free) is in a funky old 1880s county jail and courthouse, both worth a trip right there. Walk-throughs of the main floor and the cellblock of the old jailhouse are great fun.

An aside about those kitchen appliances. The West Bend Company has untold thousands of original appliances in storage, with no repository to show them, choosing to keep them locally (rather than in Madison at the State Historical Society) in hopes that the historical museum might find a wing for them. The Smithsonian has gushed about the collection, saying it far surpasses its own.

North of town on WI 144 and Highway A is the awe-inspiring **Lizard Mound County Park,** along with Aztalan State Park, one of the state's most important archaeological sites. The Mississippian Indians here predated Aztalan's by perhaps 500 years and built amazingly detailed earthworks in geometric and animal forms. Well worth a trip.

If, following your visit to Lizard Mound County Park, you haven't sated your nature needs yet, then head due north to the **Kettle Moraine State Forest–Northern Unit,** a node

lookout tower, Kettle Moraine State Forest

on the Ice Age National Scenic Trail and one of the most perfectly realized geographical primers in Wisconsin. The best place to start is to head north of West Bend via WI 45, then east on WI 67 to the **Henry Reuss Interpretive Center** (920/533-8322, generally 8:30 A.M.–5 P.M. Mon.–Sun. in summer but can vary), which has great exhibits, a panoramic view from its deck, and a nearby lookout tower.

From here, all roads are gorgeous (in fact, about 120 miles of this parks segments are subsumed by the Wisconsin Rustic Roads network—meaning they're jaw-drop lovely); just find a road with an acorn-shaped sign and off you go—it'll be splendid. At the north end of the park is the **Wade House and Jung Carriage Museum** (Hwy. T and WI 23, 920/526-3271, $10 adults), which sits along the oak plank road that stretched from Sheboygan to Fond du Lac. The state historic site is a wondrous, detailed reconstruction of the 1848 sawmill—not the post and beam work—and is one of the few like it in the United States. Environmentally friendly construction was used—as in the original. Also on-site is the painstakingly restored Greek revival home of the Wades' in-laws.

Perhaps the biggest draw is the impressive **Wisconsin Jung Carriage Museum** (10 A.M.–5 P.M. daily May–Oct.), with the state's largest collection of hand- and horse-drawn vehicles (many rideable). In early September the state's largest Civil War reenactment takes place here.

Holy Hill and the Horicon Marsh

It isn't actually odd to juxtapose these two wondrous, life-recharging spots, for both accomplish the same thing—a retreat from the madness of the rat race, a place to ponder, a place to re-ground oneself in the connection between the earth and the sky.

◖ HOLY HILL

Even recovering Catholics might appreciate a side trip to Holy Hill, with the neo-Romanesque church dominating the skyline, simply because, as one visitor noted, there is simply nothing like the sound of Holy Hill's

© WISCONSIN DEPARTMENT OF TOURISM

a rustic road near Holy Hill

bells tolling through the Wisconsin countryside. In 1855, a disabled mendicant hermit experienced a "cure" atop the 1,340-foot bluff and established Holy Hill as a pilgrimage site. One of the church spires, 180 steps up, affords commanding views of variegated kettle moraine terrain and, on clear days, the downtown Milwaukee skyline. A $5 million (plus) renovation replaced the roof with Vermont slate that matches the surrounding hills; the priceless interiors were painstakingly reappointed.

Then again, some say, get there while you can. The nearby town of Erin is showing every sign of suburbia, so much so that Scenic America has placed Holy Hill on its 10 Most Endangered Landscapes list.

Around the church are 400 heavily wooded acres crossed by the National Ice Age Scenic Trail; the grounds also contain a half-mile trail and a grotto. The monastery has guest rooms and retreat facilities; reservations are required. There is also a cafeteria open weekends year-round and daily June–October; the Sunday brunch is another nice reason to visit. To get there, head 30 miles north of Milwaukee via U.S. 41/45, then west on WI 167. For more information, call 262/628-1838.

HARTFORD

Little Hartford is a few miles north of Holy Hill via WI 83. It's worthy of a stop just to see the art deco interiors and smashing pieces of auto history at the **Wisconsin Automotive Museum** (147 N. Rural St., 262/673-7999, 10 A.M.–5 P.M. Mon.–Sat. and noon–5 P.M. Sun. in summer, less the rest of the year, $8 adults). The museum displays more than 80 antique automobiles, motorcycles, farm equipment, and other engine-driven machines in pristine condition, including Wisconsin-produced Nash automobiles and high-caliber Kissels, which were built in Hartford 1906–1931.

East of town is **Pike Lake Unit,** a relatively unappreciated chunk of glacial terrain. The large park—once a state park, now melded into the Kettle Moraine State Forest—is dominated by 1,350-foot-high Powder Mountain. (Well,

actually, it's a "kame"; that's all right, the lake is a "kettle!") A brand-new 160-foot-high tower makes for wonderful views. The park has close to a dozen miles of trails on six primary loops. A stretch of the National Ice Age Scenic Trail cuts through the park on Highway CC one-quarter mile south of WI 60 and leaves near Glassgo Road.

◖ HORICON MARSH

One of nine nodes of the National Ice Age Reserve, the Horicon Marsh is divided into two parts: the National Wildlife Refuge in the north and the Horicon Marsh Wildlife Area in the southern tier of the greenery. Spreading over 32,000 acres, the marsh was formed by the Green Bay lobe of the Wisconsin Glacier beginning around 70,000 years ago. The result was a shallow glacial lakebed filled with

© AVALON TRAVEL

silt—the largest freshwater marsh in North America, often called the "Little Everglades of the North." (And it's the largest cattail marsh in North America.)

The marsh was populated originally by no-madic Paleo-Indians, who hunted animals right along the edge of the receding ice floes. In turn, Hopewellian tribes, mound builders, Potawatomi, and Winnebago all lived in or around the marsh. Europeans showed up and began felling the region's deciduous forests. A dam was later built to facilitate floating tim-ber logs on the Rock River and to create mill power. The water levels rose nine feet, resulting in the world's largest man-made lake. Around the time of the Civil War, far-thinking con-servationists succeeded in having the dam re-moved and reconverting the marsh to wetland. It became a legendary sport-hunting paradise; private clubs removed whole wagonloads of birds after hunts.

Around the end of the 19th century, agricul-tural interests once again lobbied to drain the marsh and reestablish farming. What couldn't be drained off was going to be used for profit-rich muck farming or moist-soil agriculture. The efforts failed, though the dikes the compa-nies built still exist in a gridlike pattern today. Citizens' groups finally organized in the 1920s to call for legal designation of the marsh as a refuge. In 1927, the state legislature passed the bill, which officially protects the lower one-third; the federal government still maintains the upper two-thirds.

The marsh has a few Indian mounds along the east side, accessible by a driving route, as well as a four-mile-long island, an educational barn, and plenty of fishing.

But birds are the big draw. Annually, more than one million migrating Canada geese, ducks, and other waterfowl take over the marsh in a friendly—if histrionic and cacophonic—invasion. The geese alone account for three-quarters of the total.

The marsh has an established 30-mile-long **Wild Goose Parkway,** a drivable loop that takes in the whole of the marsh and offers some spec-tacular vistas. There are innumerable pulloffs with educational displays. The gates open 8 A.M.–3 P.M. weekdays and some Saturdays mid-April–mid-September.

Wildlife

Wetlands, upland grassy fields, and deciduous woodlands harbor a panorama of flora and fauna. The deep marshes are flooded every year except during severe droughts; water levels can rise four feet—crucial for nesting waterfowl, especially diving ducks, grebes, and fish-eat-ing fowl. The denser vegetation brings security in nesting, breeding, and rearing young. Even wild rice grows again in the great marsh.

Some of the more than 260 species of birds include mallards, blue-winged teals, coots, ruddy ducks, cormorants, herons, and terns. The marsh is the largest nesting area east of the Mississippi River for redhead ducks, al-most 3,000 of which show up each year. Birds are most often spotted during spring and fall migrations. Rookeries—particularly one on Cotton Island—attract egrets, herons, and cor-morants. In 1998, for the first time in more than 100 years, trumpeter swans returned to the marsh. No state has spent more time or money to bring trumpeter swans back to native areas, and after years of preparation, a dozen swans were released. The goal is to have 20 nesting pairs eventually.

What of those honking geese? They come from the watery tundra near Hudson Bay in northern Canada. Some begin arriv-ing by mid-September, with a gradual in-crease through October and sometimes into November. Upon arrival, they establish a feed-ing pattern in surrounding fields, eating waste corn and grass. Picture-perfect mass takeoffs occur right around sundown. The geese re-main until dwindling temperatures freeze their water supply.

Recreation and Tours

The Horicon Marsh Wildlife Area, in the southern half of the marsh, has several estab-lished **canoe trails** through the wetlands, Mieske Bay, and along the east branch of the Rock River.

More than six miles of **hiking trails** are accessible on the south side of WI 49. The trails spin deep into the marsh, occasionally on boardwalks, sometimes shrouded by cattails. A two-mile hiking trail starts near the foot of Conservation Hill at the north end of Palmatory Street in Horicon. One Mile Island is also accessible for wildlife watching; to get there, follow WI 33 through town to the boat landing at the end of Nebraska Street, where a hiking trail leads a half mile out to the island and Main Ditch.

Canoes can be rented at the **Blue Heron Landing,** WI 33 at the bridge in Horicon, also the place to get aboard a **pontoon boat tour** of the marsh with **Blue Heron Tours** (920/485-4663, www.horiconmarsh.com). Tours run daily at 1 P.M. May–September, weekends only in the off-season. A one-hour tour is $10 adults. A special two-hour tour, taking in the largest heron and egret rookery in Wisconsin, is twice the price. Canoe and kayak tours can also be arranged.

Tons of special events take place throughout the year. One of the best in North America is early May's **Bird Festival;** check www.horiconmarshbirdclub.com for information.

Marsh Haven Visitors Center

Three miles east of Waupun along WI 49 is the marsh's **visitors center** (920/342-5818, 10 A.M.–4 P.M. weekdays, 9 A.M.–5 P.M. weekends, $1). It has a theater, art displays, exhibits on the natural history of the marsh—including a live display of birds—and trail access from the parking lot.

Marsh Headquarters

The DNR Headquarters (920/387-7860) of the Horicon Marsh Wildlife Area is along WI 28, open weekdays. The National Wildlife Refuge Headquarters (920/387-2658) is open weekdays.

Plans are under way to create a unique public-private partnership to establish a $5 million addition to the headquarters building for a new education center, hiking trails, and wildlife-viewing area. Plans include features such as a 6,500-square-foot education center between Horicon and Mayville.

Horicon

The small town of Horicon has camping ($8), its own hiking trails, and Indian caves under the bluff line at **Ledge Park,** east of town via WI 28 and Raasch's Hill Road. Truly a spectacular place to hang out, it's the western edge of the Niagara Escarpment, which stretches all the way up to Niagara Falls. There's also the **John Deere Horicon Works** (203 E. Lake St., 920/485-4411, free admission), producing distinctive green and yellow lawn-care tractors along with snow throwers and other essentials. Plant tours are offered during the week before 10 A.M. by appointment.

Horicon also has an access trail to the **Wild Goose State Trail,** a 30-mile multipurpose trail skirting the western edge of the marsh all the way north to Fond du Lac. Brief sections of the trail allow horses, ATVs, and snowmobiles. Trail passes, which are available at the Marsh Headquarters, are required.

Waupun

Even with a maximum-security prison casting a shadow over the town, Waupun somehow manages to maintain an attractive, if somewhat subdued, downtown. (It was described by the old WPA Wisconsin guidebook as "almost oppressively pleasant.") Noteworthy are its five life-size bronze statues scattered throughout town, presented to Waupun by a late industrialist/sculptor, some of whose own sculptures are also seen about. One of the life-size statues, on Madison Street, is the first casting of James Earl Fraser's *End of the Trail,* part of a series commemorating the genocidal expansionism of the frontier.

Geese are everywhere in Waupun, both as decoration and physically during migration. The city fetes all those geese the first week of October during **Wild Goose Days.** Great ethnic festivals in Waupun include the **Klompen Fest,** a Dutch fair in June in which townsfolk literally "klomp" through town and scrub the streets in one particularly memorable parade; and **Volksfest,** a German blowout the first week of September.

Waupun has an access trail leading east to the Wild Goose State Trail.

Mayville

East of the marsh in the town of Mayville—whose city water has been judged by certain scientists as some of the best tasting in the United States—is the **White Limestone School** (N. Main St., 920/387-3474, www .mwlm.org, 1:30–4:30 P.M. first and third Sun. May–Oct., free admission), known mostly for its collection of rural Wisconsin photographs taken by Edgar Mueller. The local historical society operates the **Hollenstein Wagon and Carriage Factory** (11 N. German St., 920/387-5530), an old factory that once produced wagons. Several wagons are on display. The factory is free and open 1:30–4:30 P.M. every second and fourth Sunday.

One of the best inns in Wisconsin—for eating and sleeping—the **(Audubon Inn** (45 N. Main St., 920/387-5848, www.auduboninn.com, from $120) dates from 1897 and you'll feel you're in bygone days when you enter.

KETTLE MORAINE STATE FOREST–SOUTHERN UNIT

The Kettle Moraine State Forest-Southern Unit is sibling to the northern tier. Debate continues—gets a bit bristly at times—over plans to acquire sufficient private lands to link the two (and the Ice Age National Scenic Trail), creating a green buffer against Lake Michigan suburban expansion and, thus, preventing the destruction of southern Wisconsin's glacial topography. The Wisconsin DNR hoped to add more than 16,000 acres by 2010 or it may be too late (at last look in late 2008 it didn't seem that that number was do-able).

The state's oddball glacial heritage pops up everywhere—residual kames, eskers, and

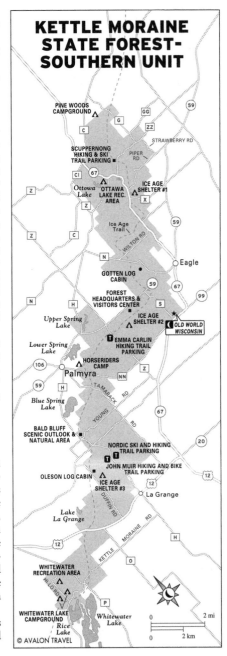

KETTLE MORAINE STATE FOREST– SOUTHERN UNIT

the eponymous kettles and moraines. Also within the forest are weatherbeaten homestead log cabins, now one-eyed and decaying in the tall grass, and a handful of bluff-line panoramas taking in all the glacial geology. In 2002, the forest literally returned to life. Original prairie seeds dormant for 150 years bloomed again; the resurgence happened because of agricultural lands lying fallow long enough. With time DNR hopes to bring back 5,000 acres of phoenixlike seeds, which would make it the largest natural prairie area east of the Mississippi River.

At 21,000 acres, much smaller than its northern counterpart, the forest is packed, especially on weekends. But it does have a whole lot more trail mileage than the north.

The **KMSF Headquarters** (S91 W39091 WI 59, 262/594-6200, 8 a.m.–4:30 p.m.) has detailed maps of the whole shebang.

Recreation

You'll hear cyclists muttering about the parking lots being chockablock with autos, but those same whiners seem to forget innocent hikers, who can barely take a step without checking for gonzo mountain bikers. Yes, Kettle Moraine is popular, so be prepared.

The forest offers 160(!) miles of trails, some hiking, some biking, some both; most of these are groomed for cross-country skiing in winter. The National Ice Age Scenic Trail cuts through the park from the Pine Woods Campground to Rice Lake—about 30 miles (usually cut into four segments). Mountain biking is allowed on the **Emma Carlin** and **John Muir Trails.** Emma Carlin Trails offer a blend of open and wooded areas, winding through apple and walnut groves and affording vistas of Lower Spring Lake and, on a good day, Holy Hill. The rough but popular John Muir Trails boast incredible blooms of pasque flowers in spring and some of the best biking—diverse, challenging, and designed specifically for mountain bikes. (Look at the twists and turns of the blue loop's southernmost point, stretching into a mature

hardwood forest, and you'll see the outline of a squirrel.)

Camping

Primitive camping is allowed at three Adirondack backpacking shelters along the Ice Age Trail—free, registration necessary. The forest also has four campgrounds, some with walk-in sites. There is also a fully accessible camping cabin. For tranquility, head directly to **Pine Woods Campground;** not only does it have the most isolated, shaded campsites, but it also has 32 sites where radios are banned (a godsend—respite from the yahoos)! You can also get to boat-in campsites; check at the ranger station.

Food

Impressive is **Union House** (262/968-4281, dinner from 4:30 p.m. Tues.–Sat., $17–32), in Genesee Depot. Great heartland fare buttressed by unique entrees such as quail—lots of wild game, actually.

Supplies and Rentals

La Grange General Store (N1242 WI 59, 262/495-8600, www.backyardbikes.com) is a welcome little gem dispensing a luscious array of deli, café, and natural-food items. You can also get items such as buffalo burgers, organic chicken from Oconomowoc farms, and other meats from local producers. It also rents mountain bikes and cross-country skis.

◀ OLD WORLD WISCONSIN

Say "Eagle, Wisconsin," and even natives say, "Where?" But say, "Old World Wisconsin" and everybody's eyes light up. City-size Old World Wisconsin, a 575-acre outdoor museum run by the state historical society, comprises more than 65 immigrant structures relocated from around the state and organized here into Polish, Danish, Norwegian, Yankee, Finnish, and not one but two German homesteads. Its collection of original log and wood buildings is the largest in the

FOLLOWING GLACIERS

Wisconsin's epic Ice Age National Scenic Trail is a 1,200-mile course skirting morainic topography left behind by the state's four glacial epochs. It's also an ongoing project, started in the 1950s and still being pieced together. When county chapters have finally cobbled together enough municipal, county, and state forest land with donated private land for right-of-way, Potawatomi State Park in Door County will be linked with Interstate State Park on the St. Croix National Scenic Riverway via one continuous footpath.

ICE AGE NATIONAL SCENIC TRAIL

A GEOLOGICAL PRIMER

Glaciation affected all of the Upper Midwest, but nowhere is it more exposed than in Wisconsin. Southwestern Wisconsin's Driftless Area is also the only purely unglaciated region on the planet surrounded by glacial till. The ultimate glacial period, the Wisconsin, began 25,000 years ago and crawled across two-thirds of the state northwest to southeast. The glaciers ad-vanced and retreated, their lobes carving the state's topography.

THE ICE AGE SCIENTIFIC RESERVE

Technically, the trail is but a segment of the Ice Age National Scientific Reserve, established

United States and considered the best. Newer are reconstructed buildings and a cemetery from Pleasant Ridge in Grant County in southwestern Wisconsin (five miles south of Lancaster); this was among Wisconsin's first African American communities. The complex is so big that trams ($2) make a circuit continuously.

Walking the whole route is about 2.5 miles; to save your legs, nature trails cut through woods or across meadows. The Aldo Leopold Trail System includes nine ecological zones; another cultural history trail wends past more extant architectural gems and doubles as cross-country ski tracks on winter weekends. (Rentals available on-site.) Sleigh rides are also offered.

Despite this, attendance has been plummeting. New proposals to incite interest include relocating an original Wisconsin by congressional fiat in 1971 after decades of wrangling by forward-thinking ecologist Ray Zillmer of Milwaukee.

The reserve's nine units are scattered along the advance of the glacial periods and highlight their most salient residuals. Numerous other state and county parks, equally impressive geologically, fill in the gaps. Kames, eskers, drumlins, moraines, kettles, and all the glacial effects are highlighted in the units on the east side of the state. From Devil's Lake west, the magnificence of bluffs, dells, and gorges carved by meltwaters of the glaciers becomes apparent.

THE TRAIL

As of 2006, around 700 miles of trails had been established either by the National Park Service, county chapters, or state parks. The longest established stretches come in the Chequamegon and Nicolet National Forests, along the Sugar River Trail in southwest Wisconsin, through the Kettle Moraine State Forest, and along the Ahnapee State Trail in the Door Peninsula. Hiking the whole thing is possible, though it takes about three months and oodles of patience attempting to circumvent cityscapes where segments have not yet opened.

Camping is a problem along the route if you're outside an established park or forest. Do not trespass to camp, or attempts to finish the trail will suffer as private landowners balk at helping inconsiderate trekkers.

INFORMATION

View the National Park Service's website (www.nps.gov/iatr) or contact the Ice Age National Scenic Trail (608/441-5610, www.iceagetrail.org) in Madison. The latter can direct you to county authorities – the best source of information on trekking the trail.

© WISCONSIN DEPARTMENT OF TOURISM

hiking on the Ice Age National Scenic Trail

beerhouse here, constructing a Native American village, and even loosing buffalo and elk on-site!

Very popular is the **Clausing Barn Restaurant,** an octagonal 1897 barn designed by a Mequon immigrant. It offers casual cafeteria-style dining with an emphasis on heritage cuisine; it's open until 4 or 4:30 P.M. except on Fridays in summer,

when it *sometimes* stays open until 9 P.M. for its fish fry.

The complex (262/594-6300, www.wisconsinhistory.org) is open 10 A.M.–4 P.M. weekdays, 10 A.M.–5 P.M. Saturday, noon–5 P.M. Sunday in summer, shorter hours May–November. Admission is $14 adults. A ticket purchased after 3 P.M. can be used the following day.

Lake Geneva and Environs

Interstates 90 and 94, along with the Illinois state line, form a tight quadrilateral in southeastern Wisconsin. Bisecting this neatly is I-43, and just south of the region's midpoint is Wisconsin's southernmost lakes playground, the gateway resort city of Lake Geneva (not to be confused with the lake itself, Geneva Lake!).

It's visited by quite a few Windy City summertime refugees who'd prefer not to tackle the five-hour drive all the way to the northern woods. About 60 percent of annual visitors call Chicago home; another quarter come from Milwaukee. In the town and around the entire perimeter of the lake are eye-catching anachronistic residences, cautious development (a modicum of tacky ersatz New England does exist), a state park, and sites of historical interest.

History

The lake was originally settled by Potawatomi Indians on its western cusp. Big Foot State Park is named for a Potawatomi chief—bleakly ironic since the Potawatomi were forcibly relocated to Kansas. Humble, somnolent days of milling lasted until the Iron Rooster steamed into town on freshly laid tracks, carrying Chicago's elite for a summertime respite. The Great Fire of 1871 cemented the city's status as a getaway when it became a retreat for Chicago's refugees. So many magnificent estates lined the shores it was dubbed "Newport of the West," a moniker still applicable today.

A note: Lake Geneva is one piece of the Geneva Lake area mosaic. Actually composed of four lakes—Delavan, Comus, Como, and Geneva—the area forms a rough triangle with the city of Lake Geneva to the east, Delavan 10 miles to the west, and little Fontana to the south on the western cusp of Geneva Lake. Williams Bay is also included, along the northern perimeter of Geneva Lake. Lakeless little Elkhorn lies to the north, outside the immediate area.

Geneva Lake cruise boat at sunset

© WISCONSIN DEPARTMENT OF TOURISM

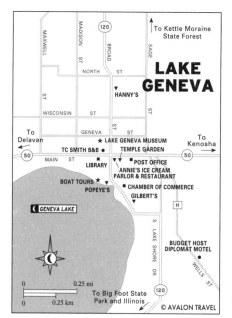

To Kettle Moraine State Forest

LAKE GENEVA

◖ GENEVA LAKE

With a surface area of 5,262 acres (7.6 miles long by 2.1 miles wide) and a depth of 135 feet, Geneva Lake is one of the larger lakes in southern Wisconsin. Spring-fed, it was carved out by the Michigan glacier during the ultimate glacial epoch. Today one can't help but love its loopy mix of restored Victorian and low-key resort, natural splendor, and most of all, its accessibility in circumference to the public.

The coolest activity in southern Wisconsin? Lake Geneva residents still get their mail delivered by boat, just as in the '30s. Visitors can also hop on the mail boat, the *Walworth II,* in operation for more than 100 years, seven days a week in summer.

Just opened as this was being typed is **Black Point Estate,** one of those opulent lake mansions, now reopened to tourists after a massive $1.2 million restoration. (Bless the family for this—they could have sold it off for bazillions in subdivision cash.) One state historian has called it the most perfect example of summer mansion in the state. In order to see it, you

should arrive the way residents here always did: by boat. (Though note that you'll need to climb about 100 stairs to scale the bluff from the dock.) Boats for lake/estate tours (11 A.M. and 1 P.M. daily in high season, $34 adults) depart Gage Marina in downtown Lake Geneva. For more information, call 800/558-5911 or go online to www.gageboats.com.

Then again, busy-as-a-bee types with itchy feet absolutely insist the most fun is a 26-mile-long **footpath** that circles the lake via linked ancient Native American footpaths. (Truly remarkable, given the century the place has been a tourist haven.) You can reach it at any park along the lakefront. Along the way, the path passes those same gargantuan summer homes (palatial manors), a state park, and loads o' natural beauty. Ultimately, the one big typical draw is **Yerkes Observatory,** which has the world's largest refractor telescope. The observatory, now obsolete (though lovely from the outside), has been shopped around by its owner, the University of Chicago. One plan included—gulp—building a luxury resort around it (it was quashed due to public outcry).

The easiest—and thus most popular—way to experience it is on a tour in either a replica Mississippi paddle wheeler or lake steamer from **Geneva Lake Cruise Lines** (Riviera Docks, 262/248-6206 or 800/558-5911, www.cruiselakegeneva.com). Tours leave six times daily mid-June–early September, less otherwise. Full tours range from one hour up to just under three hours and cost $20–50 adults; the higher-cost tours are daily luncheon cruises, Thursday–Friday dinner cruises, or the Sunday brunch cruise. In peak summer season boats seem to depart constantly. Other boats in the cruise line include genuine lake steamers, including one still using a steam engine from the early 1900s, the only large steamboat left in Wisconsin.

SIGHTS

For a great freebie, head for the **library** (9 A.M.–8 P.M. Mon.–Thurs., 9 A.M.–6 P.M. Fri., 9 A.M.–1 P.M. Sat., closed Sun.) which has comfy chairs and a four-star view of the lake. You can also peruse detailed county guidebooks on historical structures and local history. Also, at the corner of Mill and Main Streets is the fairly decent **Geneva Lake Historical Museum,** chock-full of mansion and boat history of the area. Beyond that, head immediately for **Big Foot Beach State Park,** where you'll find sublimely cool waters for dipping.

ENTERTAINMENT AND EVENTS

The third weekend of August, the community has **Venetian Nights,** when the town and lake turn into an ersatz Venice with torch-lit boat rides and lots of fireworks.

For six decades, the **Belfry Theatre** in Williams Bay (414/245-0123) has been the home of entertainment for the lakes region, generally a Branson, Missouri-type review. A full slate of cultural entertainment is also offered by **Aurora University** (866/843-5200, www.aurora.edu).

RECREATION
Boating

The Geneva Lake region has more marinas than you can imagine, including **Gordy's** (262/275-2163) in Fontana, with ski boats, ski schools, sailboats, and cruises.

Golf

Who said marinas? The list of golf courses is the size of a small phone book. Noteworthy is **Geneva National** (262/245-7010), four miles west of Lake Geneva town on WI 50. Rated in the state's top 10 by *Golf Digest,* it's got championship courses designed by Arnold Palmer and Lee Trevino. Fees are extravagant.

Camping

Just outside of Lake Geneva to the south along WI 120, **Big Foot Beach State Park** features great swimming and picnicking. The short trails make for easy strolls and great cross-country skiing. It has too many campsites, however, for a 270-acre park.

ACCOMMODATIONS

Dozens of motels, hotels, inns, bed-and-breakfasts, and resorts line Geneva Lake and fill downtown Lake Geneva town as well as the small communities surrounding the lake—you need to call ahead for summer weekends.

$50-100

Wells Street has most of Lake Geneva's motels and hotels. Expect to pay a minimum of $60 for a single in the high season (summer). Good has always been the **Budget Host Diplomat Motel** (1060 Wells St., 262/248-1809 or 800/283-4678), an award-winning property with an outdoor pool. The decor is pleasant, and some rooms have waterbeds and/or refrigerators.

$100-150

The sybaritic rooms at the **❨ French Country Inn** (WI 50 W, 262/245-5220, www.frenchcountryinn.com, $135–275) are some of the most lovingly restored and touchingly detailed in the area. Partially constructed in Denmark and shipped stateside more than a century ago to serve as the Danish pavilion in the 1893 World's Fair, the house later did time as a Chicago rumrunner's joint during Prohibition. All rooms have TV and air-conditioning; some have fireplaces. There are a swimming pool and a modest but reputable French country-style dining room serving excellent steaks, fresh fish, and from-scratch cooking.

Over $150

The **Abbey** (Fontana, 262/275-6811 or 800/558-2405, www.theabbeyresort.com, from $150) is an enormous spread of 13 parlors and 140 villas, some fireplace suites, and standard rooms. Amenities include indoor and outdoor pools, a health club, waterskiing, tennis, bicycling, and golf. It has four restaurants, four lounges, and, perhaps its most attractive offering, a sybaritic European spa. It has recently undergone a $40 million facelift, so who knows what'll await you?

Bugs Moran used to hang out at the **Waters**

Edge of Lake Geneva (W4232 West End Rd., 262/245-9845, www.watersedge.com, from $150) in the 1920s and '30s. Seven suites full of antiques—each with its own private deck—are available in a bucolic, quiet setting.

The multidiamond, polystarred ◖ **Grand Geneva** (US 12 and WI 50, 262/248-8811 or 800/558-3417, www.grandgeneva.com, $189-319) is worth every penny if every media outlet is to be believed. A three-story lodge with more than 300 rooms, its amenities include indoor tennis, a 36-hole golf course, driving range, boat and ski rentals on-site (a downhill ski mountain is adjacent), bicycles, skeet shooting, a recreation room, indoor exercise facilities, massage therapists, weights, whirlpools, sauna, and steam room. Its private land holdings include almost 1,500 acres of diverse meadow and forest, along with its own lake.

Central to Lake Geneva, a block off Broad Street, is the **T. C. Smith Inn B&B** (262/248-1097 or 800/423-0233, www.tcsmithinn.com, $165-245). It may not be very quiet (or cheap), but it's got the most authentic historical feel—an eclectic mélange of architectural styles in an 1845 mansion set amidst a formal courtyard, gardens, and a waterfall. The posh interiors feature oriental carpets, antiques, artwork, original gasoliers, and an original trompe l'oeil (a still-life painting designed to give the illusion of reality), as well as fireplaces everywhere. Pricey, but you get breakfast in bed!

FOOD
Cafés
On the corner of Dodge and Broad Streets, salt-of-the-earth ◖ **Hanny's,** obvious for its huge neon sign, is a spacious family-style restaurant. In business since around World War II, it's got the cozy charm of a classic. The food tastes old-fashioned homestyle—it still uses the original buttermilk pancake recipe. For a couple of bucks, you can fill your stomach and meet the locals. Hanny's is open daily for lunch and dinner. Best of all, it stays open 24 hours Friday and Saturday.

The best option for dessert—for a half century—is **Annie's Ice Cream Parlor and Restaurant** (712 Main St., 262/248-1933, $3-5). The interior is done up in late-19th-century style, and the light menu offers fresh sodas, lots of waffles, salads, quiches, and big sandwiches.

Waterfront
Legions keep coming back to **Popeye's** (Broad St. and Wrigley Dr., 414/248-4381, lunch and dinner daily, $5-11) for fare from the roaster, which smokes chicken, pork, and lamb (each on a different day). The menu also features Yankee pot roast, Middle Eastern salad, liver and onions, pot pies, and veggie burgers. Adjacent is **Scuttlebutt's** (262/248-1111, 7 A.M.-9 P.M. daily, $5-15), another American joint with, interestingly, some Swedish specialties.

Supper Clubs and Steak Houses
An institution on the lake is the tavern downstairs at **Chuck's** (lunch and dinner daily, weekends for breakfast) on Lake Avenue in Fontana. The menu isn't ambitious enough to be a supper club, but who cares when you can wolf down your one-third-pound burger and gander at the famed "seven-mile view" across the lake?

Worth a side trip just for the ambience is **Fitzgerald's Genoa Junction Restaurant** (772 Hwy. B, 262/279-5200, $7-13) in Genoa City approximately 10 minutes southeast of Lake Geneva. Housed in a historic octagon house, the supper club is famed for fish boils Friday; ribs, fish boil, and chicken on Wednesday and Saturday; and fish, ribs, and chicken Sunday. It's open 5-9 P.M. Monday–Saturday and 3-7 P.M. Sunday.

Continental and Fine Dining
In a reconverted Victorian farmhouse loaded with classic woodwork, a baker's dozen hand-carved fireplaces, and more, ◖ **Gilbert's** (327 Wrigley Dr., 262/248-6680, 5-9 P.M. Tues.–Sat., $15-28) is a four-star place oozing with heritage. More, its American regional with world cuisine uses organic products, free-

range meats, and line-caught fish (superior in taste, foodies say); a concerted effort is made to make vegetarians also feel welcome. Ninety percent of what it uses is organic. Upstairs, the kids can romp in a Victorian playroom or even play with a sitter ($10). In short, this great eatery misses no detail.

Most of the resorts have their own restaurants. Of note is **The Abbey** in Fontana, which has three. **La Tour de Bois** is a continental fine-dining room under the resort's legendary A-frame; **The Monaco** features Wisconsin specialties and a great Sunday brunch.

Chinese

In 1998 when this restaurant moved from Madison to Lake Geneva, Madisonians were beside themselves with grief. Rightly so. Arguably the most important Chinese restaurant (this Sinophile thinks it is) in Wisconsin, **◖ Temple Garden** (724 W. Main St., 262/249-9188, lunch and dinner daily, $6–14) shouldn't be missed for Middle Kingdom cuisine. The Tibetan-Taiwanese owners are masters of Chinese cuisine and nothing is overlooked. Let the experts guide you here; you won't be sorry.

INFORMATION

The **Lake Geneva Chamber of Commerce** (201 Wrigley Dr., 262/248-4416 or 800/345-1020, www.lakegenevawi.com) is well versed in helping tourists out.

VICINITY OF LAKE GENEVA
Elkhorn

This trim village up US 12 northwest of Lake Geneva lies splayed around a somnolent tree-shaded square. Settled by speculators in the 1830s, it was named by a U.S. Army colonel who espied a set of elk antlers in a tree. It is a picturesque place; in fact, it's sometimes called "Christmas Card Town"—and you'll know why if you show up anytime around Christmas. It's the kind of place where local businesses list their home phone numbers as well as their business phones. The oldest municipal band in the state, established in the

1840s, still toots it out summer Friday evenings at Sunset Park. This seems singularly appropriate, because five primary industries of the town are related to the manufacture of musical instruments.

One rumor running rampant around Elkhorn concerns the existence of a large-eared, werewolf-type beast said to prowl the surrounding forests. During the last century, many sightings have been reported; the local humane officer once even had a file labeled "werewolf."

While in Elkhorn don't miss **Watson's Wild West Museum** (off US 12/67—look for the sign, 414/723-7505, 10 A.M.–5 P.M. Tues.–Sat. May–Oct., $5 adults). This is the lifelong labor of love of the proprietor, who's got a serious Western obsession. Over 35 years, his collection has grown to museum-worthy proportions. Branding irons seem to be a specialty, but there are also thousands of assorted knick-knacks. The interiors are done up to resemble an 1880s general store and dance-hall saloon. The owner may even show up dressed like Wyatt Earp. New are lunch and dinner specials with musical variety shows.

The **Webster House Museum** (9 E. Rockwell St., 262/723-4248, 1–5 P.M. daily mid-May–Oct., $5 adults) once served as the territorial land office and later the home of composer Joseph P. Webster, who penned more than 1,000 songs, including "The Sweet By and By."

Delavan

Delavan's two lakes are great reasons to visit—excellent fishing on Delavan Lake—but for nonhydrophiles, Delavan is also home to a bit of clown history. For about 50 years in the 19th century, Delavan was the headquarters for most of the country's traveling circuses, including the prototype of P. T. Barnum's. Local cemeteries at the end of 7th Street are full of circus performers and workers dating from this time; Tower Park is chock-full of colorful circus memorials and statuary.

Visitors can wander about trails at the **arboretum** north of town along the shores of

Lake Comus. Delavan Lake was once one of the most polluted in Wisconsin, heavily soiled by phosphorous runoff; however, an aggressive rehabilitation campaign has turned it into one of the southeast's cleaner lakes. In fact, in 2002 the state established the **Turtle Valley Wildlife Area** just north of town. Restored from fallow farmland, these 18,000 acres are a good example of Wisconsin's aggressive wetlands restoration programs. Hike through dark peat... and mint!

Believe it or not, Delavan is becoming known for Mexican food. **Hernandez El Sarape** (212 S. 7th St., 262/728-6443, lunch and dinner daily, $2–6) has excellent versions of food from San Luis Potosí state.

It's worth the trip to **Millie's** (N2484 Hwy. O, 414/728-2434, $5–8) for the delectable Pennsylvania Old World–style, from-scratch cooking—not to mention the expansive, farm-like setting. It's open 8 A.M.–4 P.M. Monday–Saturday, and daily in July and August.

From Milwaukee to the Windy City

KENOSHA

Though its history was one of smokestacks and work whistles and its primary employer for decades was an automobile plant, Kenosha *definitely* belies any blue-collar stereotype. In fact, *Reader's Digest* once declared it the second-best "Family Friendly City" in the United States. (Sheboygan, Wisconsin, was first.) The southernmost Lake Michigan port in Wisconsin, it offers endless stretches of inspiring littoral parkland (the city owns eight out of 10 lakefront plots) and an appealing array of early-20th-century buildings, anchored by a downtown revitalized by green space, a promenade, a farmers market, and electric streetcar lines.

New Englanders first inhabited this region in 1835. Farming dominated, but a harbor and docks made it a permanent lake port (though it would never rival Milwaukee or Racine).

By the 20th century, more than 100 modest-to-large factories employed a quarter of the city's population (then around 21,000). Kenosha remains an industrial linchpin for Wisconsin today, even though car manufacturing has dipped of late. The hardy city of more than 90,000 is also gaining a reputation as a center for fishing and shopping.

Sights

Streets run gridlike east-west, avenues north-south. The major arteries into town are:

WI 50 (75th Street), WI 158 (52nd Street), and WI 142S.

At the turn of the millennium, Kenosha beaverishly set out to redo its downtown lakefront—spectacularly—into **HarborPark.** This is truly one of the freshest-looking Lake Michigan city stretches anywhere.

Southport Lighthouse

© WISCONSIN DEPARTMENT OF TOURISM

VICINITY OF MILWAUKEE

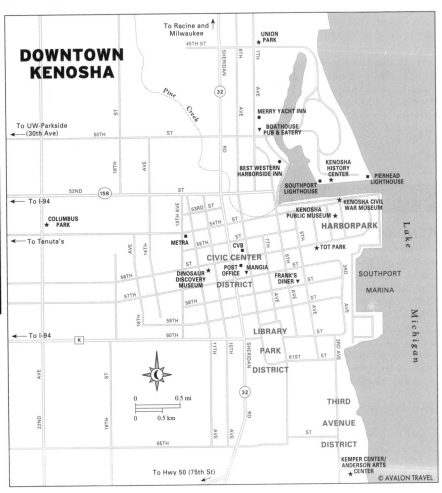

The cornerstone, as it were, is definitely the **Kenosha Public Museum** (56th St. at 1st Ave., 414/262-4140, www.kenoshapublicmuseum .org, 9 A.M.–5 P.M. Tues.–Sat., noon–5 P.M. Sun.–Mon., free). Its most exciting exhibit is on the Schaeffer Mammoth, the oldest butchered mammoth found in the Western Hemisphere; the bones date to 12,000 years ago, and it helped prove human existence during that era—no small detail. More recent archaeological digging in the county, along with sites in Virginia and Pennsylvania, has caused scientists to rethink traditional Siberian land-bridge theories of paleonatives to North America. Definitely check it out!

From here it's about 30 seconds to the **Civil War Museum** (5400 First Ave., 262/653-4140, 9 A.M.–5 P.M. Tues.–Sat., from noon Sun.–Mon., $5) focusing on the role of Wisconsin and neighboring states (and Indiana) during the war. The galleries and immersive exhibits are truly amazing, giving as real an experience as a 21st-century person can have for what it was like without heading for a Civil

War reenactment (I particularly like the train one can board, which is just like the one the soldiers would have clambered onto).

Across the channel next to gorgeous **Southport Lighthouse** (itself slated for a grand reopening in 2008) is the **Kenosha History Center** (220 51st Pl., 262/654-5770, www .kenoshahistorycenter.org, 10 A.M.–4:30 P.M. Tues.–Fri., till 4 P.M. Sat., noon–4 P.M. Sun., donations). The permanent collections include decorative and folk arts, toys, and artifacts of the previous century, and there's a Victorian ensemble and exhibits on ethnocultural highlights of the past three centuries. An interesting exhibit highlights Kenosha's impact on America's early transportation industry; it was a major automobile manufacturing center.

The Library Park District, between 59th and 62nd Streets and 6th Avenue and Sheridan Road, was once the site of homes on the Underground Railroad, now marked by a plaque. It was patterned after New England communities with village commons (and was originally even called the Commons). In addition to the mishmash of architectural styles, visitors can view the birthplace of Orson Welles at 6116 7th Avenue.

East of the Library Park District and fronting the lake between 61st and 66th Streets, the **3rd Avenue District** is the most popular historic stroll, featuring most of the ornate mansions of the wealthy early-20th-century citizens.

Within the 3rd Avenue District, **Kemper Center** is a complex of historical structures that sits inside one of seven gorgeous county parks. This, the largest at 18 acres, is the only one in the nation listed in its entirety on the National Register of Historic Places. The Gothic revival and Italianate antebellum hall was originally a school for girls but now serves as a multipurpose center for the city. Its grounds include an arboretum with more than 100 species of flora (including more than 100 types of roses and a flower and herb garden designed for those without sight). Open by appointment only, 262/657-6005, one mansion is open to the public 1–4 P.M. weekends March–October. Also in the park is the impressive French Tudor

Anderson Arts Center (121 66th St., 1–4 P.M. Tues.–Sun., grounds open dawn till dusk, free), featuring local and regional artists.

Northwest of the Library Park District, roughly between 55th and 58th Streets and 8th and 11th Avenues, the **Civic Center District** during the late 19th century was the first district to undergo massive experimental civic rejuvenation. As part of a "City Beautiful" campaign, this district has been credited with effecting political reform. Even the post office is a neoclassical revival gem. Highlights now include the county courthouse, a miniature Statue of Liberty in Civic Center Park, and the Kenosha Area Convention and Visitors Bureau. In 2006 the city unveiled its new, kid (of all ages)-friendly **Dinosaur Discovery Center** (5608 10th Ave., 262/653-4460, www.dinosaurdiscoverymuseum.org, noon–5 P.M. Tues.–Sun., free). The usual fab hands-on stuff makes it fun; this author loves the on-site working paleontology lab.

Sportfishing

In most years, Kenosha sportfishing rates number one in the state in terms of fish caught per hour, especially trout and salmon. You'll

Land a lunker on Lake Michigan.

find the greatest opportunity to catch all species of coho salmon, rainbow trout, king salmon, brown trout, and lake trout. Contact the **Kenosha Charter Boat Association** (800/522-6699, www.kenoshacharterboat .com) for all details.

Trails

The **Pike Trail** runs 14 miles south along Lake Michigan to the Illinois border and through **Chiwaukee Prairie** (near Carol Beach), the only unbroken stretch of mixed-grass prairie in Wisconsin. The prairie is home to more than 400 native plant species, including the endangered pink milkwort. The area is now protected as both a National Natural Landmark and a State Natural Area. The trail also goes north to Racine. Eventually one will be able to bike from the Illinois border north through Milwaukee to Cedarburg, Grafton, and who knows how much farther north?

Camping

The closest decent public campground is at the 4,500-acre **Richard Bong State Recreation Area** (262/878-5600), along WI 142, a mile west of WI 75 in Brighton, about 25 minutes northwest of Kenosha. One of the oddest state parks in Wisconsin, it's named after a famed WWII ace and was slated to be an Air Force base. Therefore, it's not surprising that you'll see hang gliders, parasailors, and remote-controlled planes buzzing around. Dozens of ponds and lakes dot the recreation area, and 15 miles of trails wind through diverse terrain.

Accommodations

Most of Kenosha's hotels and motels are along I-94 west of town, along WI 50 (75th Street), and on 122nd and 118th Avenues. Cheaper options are north along WI 32 between Kenosha and Racine.

A step up in price but a unique lodging is the **Merry Yacht Inn** (4815 7th Ave., 262/654-9922, $50). The quaint little place was built into an old firehouse.

You'll get great views at the **Best Western Harborside Inn** (5125 6th Ave., 262/658-

3281, $109–199), right on the lake. It has 110 rooms, an indoor pool, Jacuzzi, whirlpool, wading pool, and restaurant with lounge and nightclub.

Food

While Racine is Danish to the core, Kenosha is distinctly Italian. Travelers who neglect to visit **Mangia** (5517 Sheridan Rd., 262/652-4285, $9–30) are missing the most memorable dining experience in southeastern Wisconsin, and some say the state. It's regularly praised by culinary scribes *from around the globe* but hasn't rested on its laurels. One of the finest simple restaurants in the state, this basic trattoria pushes out unbeatable wood-fired pizzas and exquisitely done pastas, meats, seafoods, and roasted entrées. Pay attention, now: Hours are 11:30 A.M.–2 P.M. Monday–Friday, 5–9 P.M. Monday–Thursday, 5–10 P.M. Friday–Saturday, 4–9 P.M. Sunday.

Some, however, say the most nostalgic Kenosha Italian experience comes from long-time fave **Tenuta's Deli** (3203 52nd St., 262/657-9001, 9 A.M.–9 P.M. Mon.–Sat., until 6 P.M. Sun., $4–9). A good place to stop if you're in a hurry, it's got a smattering of pastas, salads, and ready-made entrées. It's also an outstanding Italian grocery store.

This author, long favoring scuffed newsprint-on-Formica-kind-of-eating, has always adored **Frank's Diner** (508 58th St., near HarborPark, open 7 A.M.–2 P.M. daily), a place where auto-factory workers coming off shift and misunderstood genius writers pour each other's coffee. It's housed in the oldest continually operating lunch car diner in the United States (pulled here by six horses!). Forget the train car aspect; this is simply roots eating, plain and simple, in a warm and welcoming Midwestern atmosphere.

There's not much left of the wonderful Bohemian cooking style, a pastiche of German, Polish, and Serbian cuisine, but Kenosha has **Little Europe at Timber Ridge** (6613 120th Ave., 262/857-9073, $7–11), along a frontage road near I-94. The many styles of pork are the specialty, but you can get hearty stews, dumplings,

Travel through downtown Kenosha aboard an electric streetcar.

and a wonderful Bohemian meat loaf. It's only open Thursday–Sunday, 11–10 A.M. till whenever everybody leaves at night.

Oh, yeah, if you catch a lunker, take it to the **Boat House Pub and Eatery** (4917 7th Ave., 262/654-9922), where the staff will grill it for you!

Information and Services
You'll encounter solicitous and chatty folks at the Kenosha Area Convention and Visitors Bureau (812 56th St., 262/654-7307 or 800/654-7309, www.kenoshacvb.com), which is open banker's hours weekdays.

A Wisconsin Travel Information Center (262/857-7164) is near Kenosha on I-94 north of the Illinois state line.

Transportation
Kenosha is connected to Milwaukee by **Wisconsin Coach Lines** (877/324-7767, www.wisconsincoach.com), which runs numerous buses daily. The bus stops in Kenosha at the Metra station, among other places. En route to the Beer City, you can get off in Racine or at Mitchell International Airport, and there are numerous stops in downtown Milwaukee.

You can also hop aboard Wisconsin Coach Lines' **Airport Express,** which goes north to Milwaukee via Racine and south to Chicago (but it stops way out west of town).

Metra (312/322-6777, www.metrarail.com) offers train service between Kenosha and Chicago's Madison Street Station. Trains depart the METRA Commuter Rail Center (5414 13th Ave., 262/653-0141) up to eight times daily.

Kenosha's utterly cool electric streetcar rumbles through the downtown area to the Metra train station and back; best, it whips through two of the historic districts. And costs all of a quarter!

RACINE
Like its de facto sister city to the south, Kenosha, Racine, suffers somewhat from its association with manufacturing. A few sections do show their age and their blue-collar roots. But the stereotypical drab image of gritty soot clinging to building facades simply doesn't hold up. The city lakefront, once a true-to-form, ugly-as-hell mill town with a horizon of gas tanks and brown sloughs, was mostly razed in the early 1990s and spruced up to the point of meticulousness. Now, it's full of landscaped parks and plenty of public

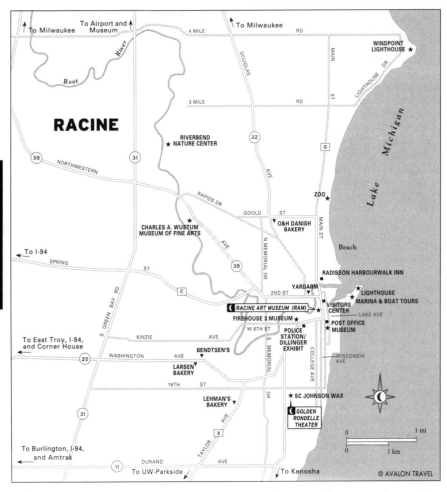

boat launches, and the city sports the largest marina on Lake Michigan—more than 100 acres. (Sections when you're coming in, yeah, smack a bit of Rust Belt.)

Ethnically, while in the early 20th century the city boasted the nation's most appreciable Bohemian influence, it is now known for its Danish contingent—it's got the largest Danish population outside of Denmark—and West Racine is even referred to as "Kringleville," for the pastry produced in huge numbers by local bakeries.

Racine has one of the most productive charter operations on Lake Michigan; it also has the largest marina on the Great Lakes—more than 100 acres. Six different species of salmon and trout cohabit near three reefs lying outside the harbor.

The Root River, named by early Native Americans for its gnarled, knife-resistant roots, so unimpressed French voyageurs in the 1670s that they up and decamped. Potawatomi, Winnebago, Menominee, and Sauk Indians were the only inhabitants until white settlers arrived in 1820 to set up trading outposts.

Within a half decade, the population climbed to 300, and in 1841 the town incorporated under the name Racine ("root" in French). Like Kenosha, Racine was plagued by the maddeningly shifty river mouth and resultant sandbars, so citizens had to dig out and construct the first piers in 1843–1844. Initially, lake traffic was the lifeblood of the city. Later, agricultural-implement manufacturing was among the first economic supplements to shipping, and by the mid-1850s small factories were producing more than 20 wares. By the turn of the 20th century, Racine was a leading national figure in farm-implement and wagon production.

Sights
❰ RACINE ART MUSEUM (RAM)
The impressive Racine Art Museum (RAM) (441 Main St., 262/638-8300, www.ramart .org), in a scintillating, chic edifice (yet meshed superbly with its 1860s structure) in the city center, is, with little hyperbole, one of the best in the Midwest. Holding one of the top three collections (more than 4,000 pieces) of Works Progress Administration's traditional arts and crafts in the United States, it is rivaled only by the Smithsonian and the American Craft Museum in New York. As an aside, this building, once a bank, was the place John Dillinger robbed in 1933. (Another bookend piece of architecture nearby is the new Johnson building, which, incidentally, uses environmentally sound construction methods, including salvaged wood from Lake Superior sunken timber.) RAM is open seasonally, generally 10 a.m.–5 p.m. daily except Monday. Admission is $5.

❰ GOLDEN RONDELLE THEATER
It's hard to miss the globular-shaped (with 90-foot arching columns) Golden Rondelle Theater (1525 Howe St., 262/631-2154) on the city's south side. The most distinctive of Racine's architectural landmarks, it was unveiled at the New York World's Fair in 1964–1965, where the short documentary about the theater, *To Be Alive,* riveted the crowds and garnered an Oscar for best documentary short subject. After the fair, Taliesin Associate

© THOMAS HUHTI

Racine's Golden Rondelle Theater

RACINE KRINGLE

Racine is still lovingly called Kringleville, for good reason. Almost all travelers leave town with white wax-paper bags stuffed with *kringle,* a flaky, ovoid kind of coffeecake filled with a variety of fruits and almond paste or pecans. Family bakeries vie annually for top honors of best *kringle,* and they still make it the Old World way – some taking three days to prepare the dough alone. Aficionados who have written in with advice say: 1) pecan kringles are best; and 2) always go for the thinnest slice on the plate, since it always has the most filling.

O&H Danish Bakery (1841 Douglas Ave., 262/637-8895) does the most advertising and probably ships the most *kringles,* but most readers have opined that **Larsen Bakery** (3311 Washington Ave., 262/633-4298, 6 A.M.-5 P.M. Mon.-Fri., 6 A.M.-4 P.M. Sat.) or **Bendtsen's** (3200 Washington Ave., 262/633-0365) have the best.

(By the way, another Danish highlight is *aeblewskiver,* a lovely spherical waffle.)

Architects was commissioned to bring the theater to Racine and incorporate it near the SC Johnson Wax administration building, also designed by Wright. Free tours of the SC Johnson administration building depart the theater at various times on Fridays only; *reservations are necessary.* The Great Workroom in the administration building is worth the entire tour.

OTHER MUSEUMS

Much of RAM's art was moved from the **Charles Wustum Museum,** which still displays regional art. Housed in a historic 1856 Italianate farmhouse on a 13-acre spread of park and formal garden, this is an excellent art outreach facility. The museum (2519 Northwestern Ave., 262/636-9177, free) is open 10 A.M.-5 P.M. Tuesday–Saturday.

A former fire station full of antique equipment constitutes the **Firehouse 3 Museum**

(700 6th St., 262/637-7395, 1–4 P.M. Sat., free), right downtown and easily visited.

The **Dillinger Exhibit** isn't a museum but a fun look at the bad old days of cops and robbers. On November 20, 1933, four brazen robbers held up a downtown Racine bank, stole $27,700, and relieved a security guard of his machine gun. When Dillinger was finally taken down in Arizona, the gun was recovered—complete with Dillinger's signature on the stock. It's now on display in the Racine Police Department lobby (730 Center St.).

WINDPOINT LIGHTHOUSE

Many visitors associate Racine with the eye-catching red beacon atop the breakwaters across from Reefpoint Marina. Racinians would likely rather be associated with Windpoint Lighthouse, north of town between Three Mile and Four Mile Roads. Believed to be the oldest (built in 1880) and tallest (112 feet) lighthouse on the Great Lakes, it is still in use today. You can't go inside, but you can stroll the grounds at most hours of the day.

SCENIC DRIVES

The city of Racine boasts a historic chunk of roadway for **scenic drives.** Three Mile Road, beginning at 108th Street and running east to 80th Street, was laid out in the early part of the 19th century and has remained virtually untouched (and unwidened). It still has old oaks and rail fences at its verges and makes a beautiful tour.

State Rustic Roads are everywhere you look. One heads north of town along Honey Lake Road, Maple Lane, and Pleasant View Road to Highway D and WI 83, passing along the way a woodland preserve, dairy farms, and marshes with muskrat houses. Backtrack to Highway DD and it picks up with another Rustic Road adjacent to the **Honey Creek Wildlife Area.** This route also passes the **Franklyn Hazelo Home,** which is on the National Register of Historic Places. Southeast of Burlington off WI 142 via

Brever Road or Wheatland Road, a Rustic Road passes under an expanse of oak and black walnut trees. Highlights include old barns, an old farmhouse, marshes, and lots of great fishing along the Fox River, accessible from Hoosier Creek Road.

Northeast of Waterford via WI 164 and WI 36 is Loomis Rustic Road, originally an 1840 territorial road that's little changed. Along the way, you'll pass Colonel Heg Memorial Park, commemorating Wisconsin's highest-ranking Civil War officer. A park museum describes the region's settlement by Norwegians, and an 1830s cabin sits nearby.

BURLINGTON
The best road trip destination is the town of **Burlington,** about 25 miles west of Racine. For a town of only 8,900 people, it's sure got a bunch of damn liars. The home of the world-famous Burlington Liar's Club, it hosts an annual yarn- and fib-spinning festival and also distributes a brochure about the town's **Tall Tales Trail.** Also called Chocolate Town USA (a Nestlé plant is here), Burlington has many streets named after candy bars. And, of course, the **Chocolate Experience Museum** (113 E. Chestnut St., 9 A.M.–5 P.M. weekdays, 10 A.M.–2 P.M. Sat., free admission).

The **Spinning Top Exploratory** (533 Milwaukee Ave., 262/763-3946, www.topmuseum.org, $5) has more than 1,500 examples of yo-yos, tops, and anything else that revolves. *With reservations only,* you get a tour featuring videos, demonstrations, and game-playing, as well as a look at prototype tops used in a feature film on the subject.

North of Burlington along WI 36 is Waterford, site of the **Hoppe Homestead Family Dairy Farm** (33701 Hill Valley Dr., 262/534-6480, www.hoppehomestead.com). This century-old dairy farm invites visitors to do any of the many chores—milking included—or just enjoy hay and wagon rides. Farm tours are available May–October; tours are generally weekends and cost $5. There are also sleigh rides.

Accommodations
The only over-the-water hotel on southern Lake Michigan is a goodie. The **Radisson Harbourwalk Inn** (223 Gaslight Circle, 262/632-7777 or 800/333-3333, $139 s, $149 d) has rooms affording gorgeous lake views, and suites with whirlpools on balconies. Boaters can dock at slips and the restaurant on-site is well regarded. Extras include 24-hour room service, in-room coffeemakers, airport transportation, and more.

Food
The **Yardarm** (920 Erie St., 262/633-8270, 11 A.M.–10 P.M. Sun.–Thurs., 11–midnight Fri.–Sat., from $6) has fish fries nightly. It's generally got great food overall, actually. Incidentally, people keep telling me about the burgers at the Yardarm, though the fish is always too good to pass up. Ribs too!

Not a greasy spoon per se, **Kewpee** (520 Wisconsin Ave., 262/634-9601, 7 A.M.–6 P.M.) rates a nod as the best burger joint in perhaps all of southern Wisconsin. Devotees regularly come from as far away as the Windy City. Decades old (it started in 1927), this erstwhile teen hangout doesn't have much in the way of ambience now. It's as fast as fast grub gets, but you can't beat the burgers or malts. It's standing-room-only at lunchtime. Selections from a buck.

The **Corner House** (91251 Washington Ave., 262/637-1295, 5–10 P.M. daily, $7–16) serves enormous tender roasts and exquisite prime rib. Around since World War II, this is the institution of institutions.

The Summit (6825 Washington Ave., 262/886-9866, lunch and dinner daily, $6–18) is a wonderful place. This restaurant has marvelous lunches and dinners in a casual atmosphere, but you might want to check out its incredible Sunday brunch, if only for the extraordinary array of *kringle* available.

Information and Services
The Racine County Convention and Visitors Bureau (345 Main St., 262/884-6400 or

800/272-2463, www.visitracine.org) is open regular business hours (with weekend hours in summer).

Transportation

There's no Amtrak service directly to Racine, but trains do stop at 2904 Wisconsin Street in Sturtevant to the west. Racine city buses travel to Sturtevant. Kenosha's Metra trains still haven't been extended north to Racine though everyone wants them.

Airport Express (877/324-7767, www .wisconsincoach.com) makes stops in Racine on its routes to and from Chicago's O'Hare Field and Milwaukee's Mitchell International Airport.

Wisconsin Coach Lines also stops in Racine on its run between Milwaukee and Kenosha.

Buses stop at the **Racine Transit Center** in the 1400 block of State Street.

Ferry service proposals (Racine to Ludington, Michigan) have been bandied about for years, but there's nothing yet.

To get around, ya gotta take the trolley around! One buck gets you as far north as Reefpoint Marina and as far south as 7th Street. The trolleys run daily Memorial Day–Labor Day (usually); on Friday and Saturday, the city has at times offered "pub and grub" runs stopping at restaurants and bars downtown till late. For more information, call 262/637-9000.

MADISON

Madison—the Mad City, Madtown. "Mad" as in "crazy," rather than "angry" (unless it's something political, or social, or environmental). Ah, Madison, what a hoot this nutjob city is, a Sybil city, a city that is whatever it feels that it is, that day in that neighborhood—passionately.

A Wisconsin governor's aide once quipped, "Madison is 60 square miles surrounded by reality." (Please hold off on any disputing email—first of all, local librarians helped track down the number; furthermore, I *know* it's now somewhere around 77 square miles!) His precision inarguable, it has become a proud bumper-sticker slogan in the city. Madison may be reminiscent of other leftist hot spots such as Berkeley and Ann Arbor, but the salad days of revolution are long gone. Financial institutions are rather more conspicuous than cubbyhole

political storefronts, and corpulent lobbyists now definitely outnumber radicals, at least near the State Capitol. The student population rarely raises a fuss anymore, unless to celebrate UW sports teams' championships or holidays (Halloween and the end of classes in May are infamously rowdy party times) in beer-soaked student hoo-hah fests (tear gas for drinking, not for war protesting).

Still, the capital is a wacky place. Octogenarian Progressives mingle with aging hippies and legions of university professors, and corporate and Capitol yuppies don't seem out of place. The student-body omnipresence is a given—everyone in Madison is considered a de facto student anyway. It remains the "Madtown"—one agreeable, engaging, oddball mix.

© SUZANNE TUCKER/123RF

HIGHLIGHTS

◖ **State Capitol:** Similarities in size and design were a deliberate in-your-face to the powers that be in D.C., so typical for the state (and city) where maverick progressivism is a way of life (page 103).

◖ **Monona Terrace:** Whether a jewel of Wisconsin's capital or a memorial to an egomaniac, this striking white edifice melds the land and water distinctly (page 105).

◖ **University of Wisconsin-Madison Campus:** This city-state has it all: a weekend's worth of museums; the Memorial Union, a nightlife institution in the Mad City; gorgeous lakeside trails; and the best napping spots in the city (page 108)!

◖ **University of Wisconsin Arboretum:** The entire city population gets its blood working here, though few realize how amazing its flora actually are, an enormous preservation and restoration project to re-create the landscape of the state in its virgin form (page 111).

◖ **Olbrich Botanical Gardens:** It's often outshined by the carpets of wildflowers of the University of Wisconsin Arboretum, yet its own holdings are magnificent. Even the King of Thailand donated a gorgeous Thai pavilion under which to sit and gaze at the beauty (page 111).

LOOK FOR ◖ TO FIND RECOMMENDED SIGHTS, ACTIVITIES, DINING, AND LODGING.

No guidebook hype—Madison is a lovely town, ensconced erratically on an isthmus between two lakes. You'll find endless patches of green, a low-key downtown, a laid-back way of life, and a populace appreciably content if not downright enjoying themselves. Civic pride runneth over. No surprise, then, that after years of being a bridesmaid, Madison was finally named by *Money* magazine in 1996 as the best place to live in America; it would repeat the honor two years later and pretty much never leave the top five—in any national poll. (Just google "Madison" and "best" and see how many media have celebrated the city.)

Not coincidentally, then, Madison is populated by droves of people who came for college and never left (this humble author included). And those who left pretty much only did so for job reasons or, rarely, the winters finally did them in.

PLANNING YOUR TIME

You can do Madison quickly or slowly. Luckily, most of the sights are spread out along the downtown, so they're walkable (take good shoes). If your time is limited, you're going to be limited to walking from lake to lake, Wisconsin Capitol to the University of

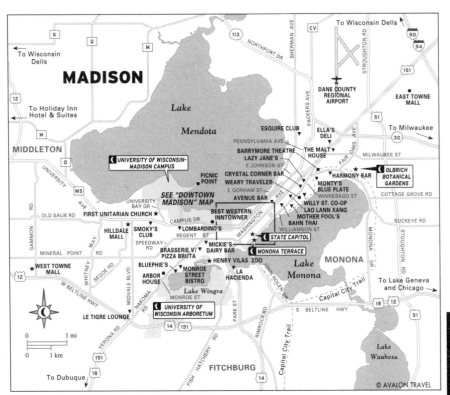

MADISON

To Wisconsin Dells

To Holiday Inn
Hotel & Suites

*Lake
Mendota*

MIDDLETON

To Wisconsin
Dells

DANE COUNTY
REGIONAL
AIRPORT

EAST TOWNE
MALL

To Milwaukee

ESQUIRE CLUB

ELLA'S
DELI

BARRYMORE THEATRE
LAZY JANE'S

THE MALT
HOUSE

UNIVERSITY OF WISCONSIN–
MADISON CAMPUS

PICNIC
POINT

CRYSTAL CORNER BAR
WEARY TRAVELER

HARMONY BAR

OLBRICH
BOTANICAL
GARDENS

SEE "DOWTOWN
MADISON" MAP

AVENUE BAR

MONTY'S
BLUE PLATE

FIRST UNITARIAN CHURCH

BEST WESTERN
INNTOWER

WILLY ST. CO-OP
LAO LANN XANG
MOTHER FOOL'S
BAHN THAI

HILLDALE
MALL

SMOKY'S
CLUB

LOMBARDINO'S

STATE CAPITOL

WEST TOWNE
MALL

BRASSERIE V/
PIZZA BRUTA

MICKIE'S
DAIRY BAR

MONONA TERRACE

*Lake
Monona*

MONONA

BLUEPHIE'S

HENRY VILAS ZOO

ARBOR
HOUSE

MONROE
STREET
BISTRO

LA
HACIENDA

To Lake Geneva
and Chicago

Lake Wingra

UNIVERSITY OF
WISCONSIN ARBORETUM

LE TIGRE LOUNGE

0   1 mi

0   1 km

*Lake
Waubesa*

FITCHBURG

To Dubuque

© AVALON TRAVEL

Wisconsin campus. You can do it in a day if you push it. More good news: Madison has ridiculously light traffic, so no worries about that. The bad news, however, is that given the city's circuitous, topographically-meandering streets, you can expect to lose that extra time getting lost a lot.

ORIENTATION

The downtown spreads along a narrow isthmus between two large lakes, which doesn't bode well for traffic (though you're always within eight blocks of lakeside prettiness, I guess).

Traffic can be maddeningly circuitous (this combined with all the small hills can make winter driving a terrifying experience). Always keep an eye on the Capitol. Also keep in mind that east and west in street names are

approximations—it's actually closer to northeast and southwest. *All east-west streets use the Capitol as the dividing point.*

The main thoroughfare down the throat of the isthmus is East Washington Avenue (U.S. 151); it leads directly to, and then around, the massive state Capitol, which is connected to the university by State Street.

The main artery between east and west Madison is the white-knuckled swells of the Beltline: U.S. 12/14 and 151/18 (or any combination thereof). It's unlikely you'll be able to avoid the Beltline altogether; just avoid rush-hour peaks.

Like everywhere else, parking sucks here. Either not enough or expensive; worse, parking sentinels are thought to be omniscient. Pay attention to snow emergencies (broadcast on

MADISON

MADISON LINGUISTIC PRIMER

The whole weird Wisconsin linguistic thing is covered in the introduction (for example, "bubbler"); here are a few specific to Madtown:

- **East Wash:** East Washington Avenue
- **West Wash:** Take a guess.
- **Willy Street:** Williamson Street on the Near East Side
- **The Union:** The University of Wisconsin's Memorial Union
- **The Terrace:** the outdoor seating area in back of the Memorial Union
- **The Rat:** Der Rathskeller, the main drinking/live music spot of the Memorial Union
- **Bucky:** any UW team that's playing ("Bucky kicked butt last night.")
- **The Beltline:** I call it Hell, this, the mixing of Highways 18/151/12/14 and the only major east-west thoroughfare in town. You'll experience a white-knuckled terror or turtle crawl.
- **The East Side:** Democrats, hippies, and Subarus
- **The West Side:** Republican, sprawl-mall hell, SUVs

local radio stations) and alternate side parking rules (for street cleaning). You park incorrectly on some streets and the tow truck will be waiting for the clock to strike the second they can haul your car away; you're lucky if you get only a $25 ticket. If you're towed, add $60 to the ticket price or $120 during a snow emergency!

HISTORY

Perhaps appropriately for such an enclave of iconoclasm, Madison did not even exist when it was picked as the capital site. Judge James Duane Doty lured legislators away from the original capital—tiny Belmont—with offers of free land in what were no doubt termed lush river valleys to the northeast. Territorial legislators, probably dismayed by the isolation of Belmont, fell over themselves to pass the vote. Not one white person lived in the Madison area at the time.

Four Lakes

Originally dubbed "Taychopera" (Four Lakes), these marshy lowlands were home to encampments of Winnebago Indians. The first whites trekking through the area—most heading for lead mines in the southwest—remarked upon it in journals as a preternaturally beautiful, if wild, location. One early soldier wrote that "the country…is not fit for any civilized nation of people to inhabit. It appears that the Almighty intended it for the children of the forest."

It remained that way until 1837, when a solitary family set up a rough log inn for workers who arrived to start construction on the Capitol. (Bars doubled as the first churches, this being Wisconsin.) A half decade after it became the capital, only 150 or so people called this semiwilderness home.

After Statehood

In 1848, the territory became a state, just as finishing touches were being added to the Capitol. The population had mushroomed to more than 700, yet there was still not even a semblance of established roads. At this point a munificent Milwaukee millionaire, Leonard Farwell, showed up and, most likely aghast at the beastly conditions, started on major infrastructure work.

When the railroad arrived in 1854, the city had a rollicking population of just under 7,000.

Civil War spending allowed the city's finances to expand rapidly; a decade after the end of the hostilities, Madison had nearly 500 factories of all sorts. By the 20th century, more than 19,000 inhabitants lived in Madison. Still, despite the numbers, wild animals gamboled through the remaining thickets, and one contemporary Eastern visitor remarked that Madison resembled nothing much more than an exaggerated village, down to a village's mannerisms and conduct.

WATCH YOURSELF

Please accept a local's apology in advance. While on the one hand, *most* Madisonians are some of the politest folks you'll ever meet (Wisconsin, actually, was #2 in the country in a recent Oxford University study), you have to remember that we also think we're the center of the universe. And thus, when many of us are driving, pedaling, or walking, we will simply not pay any attention to anyone else. *All* here are culpable: pedestrians, bikers, drivers. When you're driving, bikers will fly through a stop sign in front of you; when you're biking, pedestrians will walk across a red light in front of you and give you a sniff if you even look like you may question it; when

walking, you're fair game (no matter what the signs say).

Now, I know a lot of people are going to dispute this, but yes, we all do it. I also know that many people will laugh and say, "Dude, you should come to..." True. However, the goat-getter is the hypocrisy mixed with self-righteousness. We honestly believe we're Mr. and Ms. Polite, yet when we're riding our bikes, stop signs just don't apply to us. We may growl at you to stop at a stop sign on your bike, but we don't have to use our turn signals. Or give a pedestrian right of way in our car. Grr. (Even the cops – one of the best, most patient police forces I've ever witnessed worldwide – never give you right of way!)

20th Century

Madison in the first half of the 20th century is noteworthy for a dearth of juicy history. One historian said of most of Madison's past, "The historian finds little of stirring interest; and that little almost always the reflex of the legislature." From the boozy, brawling first legislators, Madison has always had a sideshow accompaniment to its vast cultural arenas. This was perhaps never more manifest than in the 1960s, during implosions over the Vietnam War, when Madison truly became the Mad City—one of the nation's foremost leftist concentrations.

Overtones of radicalism still exist, but the city really doesn't seem to get *too* worked up about much anymore. (As said, we just organize a community action neighborhood committee potluck and sit around and discuss it to death.) Everyone's too busy biking around the lakes or people-watching on State Street (if not hustling for that graduate seminar).

Sights

DOWNTOWN AND ISTHMUS
◖ State Capitol

Standing atop the most prominent aerie in Madison, the stately white bethel granite Wisconsin State Capitol (608/266-0382, www.doa.state.wi.us) is the largest in the country and definitely one of the most magnificent. Designed by George Pesi, who also designed the New York Stock Exchange, it sits a stately 300 feet above an already high moraine—a beacon for lost out-of-towners. Crowning it is the three-ton gilded bronze statue *Wisconsin*, a golden lady with a badger on her head! The

current building (the first two burned) was constructed over 11 years and cost $7.25 million—$.25 per state resident per year of construction. (Never again would something like this be possible on the public nickel.) It resembles the nation's Capitol from afar: The powers that be in D.C. took this as a sign of homage but then realized plans were to build Wisconsin's Capitol taller than D.C.'s. So ours had to become shorter, though its volume is greater (holds more beer, of course). The interior features 43 different types of stone from eight states and six foreign countries, including

MADISON

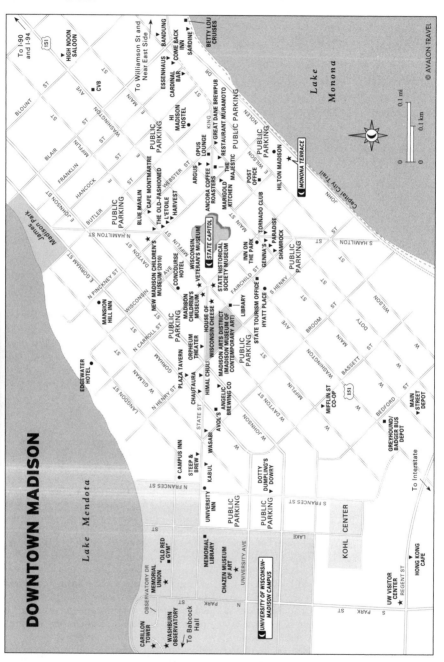

DOWNTOWN MADISON

© THOMAS HUHTI

Wisconsin State Capitol, viewed from Monona Terrace

semiprecious marble nonexistent today. The mosaics, imported and domestic hand-carved furniture, massive murals, and hand-stenciling make the building priceless. Interesting Capitol tidbit: The Capitol always wins local surveys for cleanest public bathrooms. If you don't arrive in time for a tour, the observation deck is also generally open, with superb views! The building is open 8 A.M.–6 P.M., with free tours hourly 9–11 A.M. and 1–3 P.M. Monday–Saturday, Sunday also in summer.

◀ Monona Terrace

Garish white whale or architectural cornerstone? You be the judge of Monona Terrace Community and Convention Center (608/261-4000, http://mononaterrace.com). Madisonians may never come to terms with their decades-old love-hate relationship with it. Supporters hoped that the structure, which some call Frank Lloyd Wright's masterpiece, partially atop Lake Monona on pylons, would draw attention (and moneyed conventioneers) to Madison; critics moaned that it was yet

another civic white elephant—and a monument to someone they considered an egotistical SOB. (This author was just P.O.'d that his bike path was gone for two freaking years. Big deal, you say? Never, ever mess with Madison's biking community—they'll critical mass your butt and tie up traffic in protest.) Not to mention that it didn't really, well, "fit" the skyline much when approaching the city from the southwest along the lake (I know, I know, heresy; it certainly is better than the electric company's smokestacks jutting from behind it.) Whatever, when it was finally approved (after about six decades of typical Madison arguing) by a thumbnail-narrow margin in a referendum, you couldn't help noticing that Wright's hoped-for design included much, much more than was finally constructed, and only three years after it opened its structures already required repairs. (Sorry, but that's *so* Frank Lloyd Wright, even admirers would have to admit!) But even opponents admit that nothing like it exists in a city of comparative size. Most visitors simply wander about, taking in the views; a photography gallery highlighting Wright's work is inside, as is the **Madison Sports Hall of Fame.** If you get a chance, get a glimpse of it from a canoe in the early morning sun. Wow.

The building is open 8 A.M.–5 P.M. daily. The rooftop garden area is open till 10 P.M. Sunday–Thursday, till midnight Friday and Saturday. Guided tours ($3) are available at 1 P.M. daily. Free concerts are offered often during summer.

State Street and Museum Mile

Bookended by the Capitol on one end and the university on the other, State Street is a quasi-pedestrian mall (buses and taxis are allowed, and you need to be fully aware of bicycles, baby strollers, in-line skaters, and cars running red lights on cross streets when walking). It's full of shops, boutiques, coffeehouses, restaurants, bookstores, museums, cultural centers, and much of the downtown's character. People-watching along these seven blocks is a long-standing tradition.

The **Madison Arts District** takes up the

MADISON

© THOMAS HUHTI

Frank Lloyd Wright's Monona Terrace Community and Convention Center is enormous.

100 block of State Street along with a few blocks on either side of it for a zone of galleries, art spaces, museums, and performance venues. It was brought about by the amazingly generous donation of $50 million—later increased—by a local Madtown philanthropist. This being Madison, it didn't come without vocal opponents. Did Madison really need another arts venue for wine-sipping yuppies? Why gut a youth center (where is that now, anyway?) for it? Why not more support for local artists or arts education for youth? The original plans had, quite unbelievably, planned on gutting the memorable Oscar Mayer Theater inside the Civic Center. The plans were later scaled back, but not enough for some.

Six museums and a couple of other highlights lie along State Street and Capitol Square. On the State Street corner of Capitol Square, the **State Historical Museum** (30 N. Carroll St., 608/264-6555, www.wisconsinhistory.org, 9 A.M.–4 P.M. Tues.–Sat., noon–5 P.M. Sat., $4) lets you stroll through commendable, challenging permanent multimedia exhibits that detail the state's geological, Native American, and European settlement history. The lower level is a gallery area featuring revolving exhibits; three more floors feature boatloads of historic

exhibits. They were just finishing a mockup of a fur trade–era post last time I popped in—wanted to go home and dig out my old coonskin cap. Free public programs occur at 10:30 A.M. every Saturday. This museum also has unquestionably the best bookstore for Wisconsin titles and a great gift shop (the latter something I rarely mention).

Kitty-corner from the historical museum, the **Wisconsin Veterans Museum** (30 W. Mifflin St., 608/267-1799, www.museum.dva .state.wi.us) has two impressive main galleries of exhibits, dioramas, and extensive holdings tracing Wisconsin's involvement in wars from the Civil War to the Persian Gulf conflict. Even Mexican border campaigns are detailed. Main attractions are the mock-ups of battles and cool aircraft hovering overhead. Children will love the submarine periscope sticking out of the gallery's roof, which allows for a true panoramic view of downtown Madison. Hours are 9 A.M.–4:30 P.M. Monday–Saturday year-round and noon–4 P.M. Sunday April–September; admission is free.

The kid-centric **Madison Children's Museum** (100 State St., 608/256-6445, www .madisonchildrensmuseum.org) is housed in this old triangular corner edifice. (However, it

IT'S COLD HERE. WHAT CAN I DO?

You've got four lakes and you always seem to be standing next to one, so wind is an issue here. State Street, the city's main pedestrian thoroughfare, is a damned wind tunnel (but the city's absolute worst corner for winter wind is the Pinckney Street/Mifflin Street corner opposite the State Capitol – walk there at your peril). Then again, here are some options:

Memorial Union: Zillions of nooks and crannies to lounge and pass the time (and it's always warm in there, to me anyway) – many of these spots have great lake views, especially at sunset.

Monona Terrace: Kinda garish carpeting, but it's got nice open spaces and the sunshine absolutely streams in in the mornings (best spot for sunrises in Madison, actually).

University of Wisconsin Arboretum's McKay Center: This solar-heated treasure is a wondrous place to read and ponder. (But come on, you're in the midst of natural splendor – at least hit one trail, snow be damned!)

Olbrich Botanical Gardens: Tropical forest. Ahhh.

I LIKE WINTER. WHAT CAN I DO IN MADISON?

Here are the best things to do if you've got some free time in Madison and ain't afraid of the snow and cold:

Ice skate at Vilas Park: Madison's got loads of parks to skate on, but this is your best bet because you can rent skates at the warming house, then head from the lagoons onto Lake Wingra and into the Arboretum (being very careful of ice conditions, natch), and when you're done, visit the zoo! (Saturday or Sunday morning? See me and my buds at the lagoons playing hockey – stop by and say hi!)

Cross country ski at Elver Park: It ain't the best but it offers rentals and 10 kilometers of trails.

Hike to Picnic Point for a winter sunrise or sunset: The air positively shimmers over the lake.

Walk the UW Arboretum Trails: Just you and nature in the middle of a city – amazing.

© YUKI TAKANO

Winter doesn't stop kite-flying fans.

was slated for a new home a few blocks away off the intersection of Pinckney, Mifflin, and Hamilton Streets by mid-2010 so check before you go.) Visitors can romp through and get their hands on a variety of traditional and computer-oriented activities. Significant is the display regarding Madison's lake environment. Hours are 1–6 P.M. Monday, 9 A.M.–4 P.M. Tuesday–Friday, 9 A.M.–5 P.M. Saturday, noon–4 P.M. Sunday. Admission is $4, free to all the first Sunday of every month.

One block nearer the university from the children's museum is the distinctive Madison Civic Center and, within it, the **Madison Museum of Contemporary Art** (211 State St., 608/257-0158, www.mmoca.org). The prominent gallery window is always attracting the attention of passersby, most staring quizzically at the art or, occasionally, the performance artist trapped inside. The small galleries are interspersed through three floors of the civic center complex and feature contemporary art—mostly paintings and some photography. The museum has done an admirable job in its eclectic temporary exhibitions. A good gift shop is here. It's open 11 A.M.–5 P.M. Tuesday–Friday (till 9 P.M. most Fridays), 10 A.M.–5 P.M. Saturday, 1–5 P.M. Sunday; admission is free.

The complex also houses the Overture Center for the Arts, which hosts modern and classical music, touring shows, and Broadway plays. The Isthmus Playhouse inside is a thrust-stage venue.

The remaining museums operate under the auspices of the University of Wisconsin. The first one listed here is only one block off the end of State Street (for the others see *University of Wisconsin-Madison Campus*). As State Street runs its final block and melds with the Library Mall, walk past the bookstore and a church and then bear left down a cul-de-sac. The **Chazen Museum of Art** (800 University Ave., 608/263-2246, www.chazen .wisc.edu) contains almost 17,000 holdings, the oldest dating from 2300 B.C. The open, airy design features three levels of permanent collections, including Egyptian and Greek porcelain, a Roman cask, Japanese prints, Indian figurines, Russian icons, early European and American art, and a somewhat moody roomful of Renaissance church art. The top floor showcases modern American artists. All of this was being expanded greatly at the time of writing; by its planned 2009 grand reopening it should be a whole lot bigger. The museum is open 9 A.M.–5 P.M. Tuesday–Friday, from 11 A.M. weekends, and admission is free.

◀ University of Wisconsin-Madison Campus

Bascom Hill on the "other" end of State Street affords a view similar to the one from the State Capitol rise. Crowning this is Bascom Hall, one of the original buildings of the university, established in 1848. North Hall, down the hill toward the lake, was the campus's original building and served until 1850 as a one-room university. A statue of a relaxed Abraham Lincoln sits in a tiled courtyard between Bascom and North Halls; the tiered hill is a favorite sack-out spot for students between (or skipping) classes. From a handful of students and wild animals in 1848, the university has grown to 1,000 acres and more than 50,000 students and faculty; it is a world-renowned institution in a host of fields.

Since its inception, UW has imbued the fabric of the community to a larger extent than even the state government has. The campus sprawls gorgeously for nearly two miles along the southern cusp of capacious Lake Mendota.

The nucleus of campus is **Memorial Union** (800 Langdon St., 608/262-1331, www.union .wisc.edu). Perched beside Lake Mendota, it's a must-stop for any visitor. Have but one night in the Mad City? You'll never forget relaxing by the lakeside on the Union Terrace, sipping a refreshment in one of the legendary Union rays-of-the-sun metal chairs as the sun lazily sets behind musicians performing on a stage. (So associated with the UW is the Union Terrace that even T-shirts now sport the multicolored chairs—and they've had to chain 'em down 'cuz people kept stealing 'em!)

A **visitors information center** (608/263-

Bascom Hill chillin', a Madison tradition

2400 or 608/265-9500, www.vip.wisc.edu) is available in the "Old Red Gym" next to the Union; it's open 8 A.M.–5:30 P.M. weekdays, 11 A.M.–2:30 P.M. weekends. Guided tours depart weekdays at 3 P.M. and weekends at noon. Technically, the main visitors center (608/262-4636) is about a 10- to 15-minute walk south of here at 21 North Park Street; it's got a lot more information for your basic, non-mom-and-dad-of-student traveler and even better, it's got a drive-thru window! It's open 9 A.M.–4:30 P.M. weekdays, 11 A.M.–2 P.M. Saturday.

For both visitors centers, please keep in mind that university activities—and by this I definitely mean *football games*—will affect hours and availability of tours, so phone first!

Not far from Bascom Hall is a **carillon tower** with 56 bells and sporadic Sunday afternoon performances. It's one of just three in the state, and it's—they say—the 25th largest in the nation.

Up the hill from the tower is **Washburn Observatory** (1401 Observatory Dr., 608/262-9274), one of the first observatories to use radio astronomy. It's open at 9 P.M. the first and third Wednesday of each month April–October (every Wed. mid-June–late July); the rest of the year, it opens at 7:30 P.M. Note that it's open only if skies are at least 75 percent clear. If for nothing else, hike up to the observatory to drink in the views of Lake Mendota. You're sitting on Observatory Hill, and you can still espy some effigy mounds used by Native Americans.

(Behind the observatory, check out the President's Burr Oak, which is over 300 years old.)

A hundred yards away from the Union along Observatory Drive, at the corner of Babcock Drive, is **Allen Centennial Gardens,** a conglomeration of 22 gardens on a 2.5-acre Victorian estate that once belonged to the university deans. They're for multidisciplinary research but they're still gorgeous (and, yes, educational). Another gem is just below Birge Hall on Bascom Hill; **Botany Garden** has nearly 1,000 plants arranged in evolutionary sequence.

The **UW Geology Museum** (1215 W. Dayton St., Weeks Hall, 608/262-2399, www

.geology.wisc.edu, 8:30 A.M.–4:30 P.M. weekdays, 9 A.M.–1 P.M. Sat., free) is rather small but has large exhibits, including a scaled version of a limestone cave, a 30-some-foot-long dinosaur, and a mastodon skeleton. Of course, you'll also view the detritus of millions of years of the machinery of fossilization, meteorites, and minerals. Kids like the walk-through limestone cave reconstruction.

Less enthralling for the urchins is the **Physics Museum** (Chamberlin hall, 1150 University Ave., 8 A.M.–4 P.M. weekdays, free). At least in the beginning, until they see that it's mostly hands-on. Yup, they can experiment with lots of fun stuff (though not, sadly, electricity when I was there).

One retreat from throngs of folks that most people don't know about isn't really a museum. But **Wisconsin State Herbarium** (430 Lincoln Dr., 608/262-2792, www.botany.wisc .edu, 7:45 A.M.–4:30 P.M. weekdays, free), in front of Bascom Hall atop Bascom Hill, is the nucleus of the botany department and its greenhouses are wonderful. The staff asks that you phone first, just to be sure someone knows you're coming.

Ditto the **UW Zoological Museum** (250 N. Mills St., 608/262-3766, 8:30 A.M.–noon and 1–4 P.M. weekdays, closed July and Aug., free), with exhibits of hundreds of species on the first and fourth floors.

Lots of UW's other departments offer tours; it's best to call ahead and verify it is possible. Or log on to www.vip.wisc.edu for a full list of offerings.

This is the Dairy State, after all, so when you need to refuel, there is *only* the **Babcock Hall Dairy Plant** (1605 Linden Dr., 608/262-3045, 9:30 A.M.–5:30 P.M. weekdays, 10 A.M.–1:30 P.M. Sat., free), where you can get up-close-and-personal looks at the creation of UW's famed ice cream; the department also makes cheese and other dairy-related products. Personal fave is the legendary fudge-bottom pie, but walking away without an ice cream cone is a cardinal sin! Biotechnology is a new addition to the **agricultural campus.** The aesthetics of the **Dairy Barn** (1915 Linden Dr.) aren't to be missed. Designed in 1898 by a UW professor, its cylindrical style became a world standard. Tours focusing on the university's crucial role in Midwestern agriculture, biotechnology, and veterinary science can be arranged through the information center at the Old Red Gym.

Where State Street ends and the university begins stands the **Memorial Library.** Ranking in the top five nationwide for its collection (it holds more than five million volumes), it also has a few areas with rare books. A plan to add floors to the library raised a hullabaloo, since it would block the view of the Capitol.

Bus lines (many lines free within campus areas) serve just about everything.

Picnic Point: A lakeshore path runs from the popular terrace of the Memorial Union, bypasses dormitories, boathouses, beaches, and playing fields, and winds up at yet another of the university's gorgeous natural areas—Picnic Point. This narrow promontory jutting into Lake Mendota is split by a screened gravel path and is popular with hikers, joggers, and bikers. You can walk to the tip in under 20 minutes; along the way there are offshoot roads and trails as well as firepit picnic sites. The views of the city merit the stroll/jog.

OUTSIDE OF DOWNTOWN
Henry Vilas Zoo

Still delightfully free to the public is Henry Vilas Zoo (702 S. Randall, 608/266-4732, www.vilaszoo.org, 9:30 A.M.–5 P.M. weekdays, till 8 P.M. some weekends in summer; children's zoo open summers only). For a city of Madison's size, the array of 800 wild animals, representing almost 200 species, is quite impressive, with constantly expanding facilities, especially for big cats and primates. The Herpetarium and Discovery Center offers hands-on entertainment for kids; they can also get free rides and various entertainment Sunday mornings in summer. This is perennially voted tops in town (along with the UW Memorial Union) as the best free-bie around.

(University of Wisconsin Arboretum

The UW Arboretum is one of the most expansive and heavily researched of its kind in the nation. Its 1,260 acres comprise stretches of natural communities from wetland to mixed-grass prairie; the restoration work on some is unique—designed to resemble Wisconsin and the Upper Midwest before settlement. More than 300 species of native plants flower on the prairies, some of which are the world's oldest restored tallgrass prairie and the site of the first experiments (in the 1940s) on the use of fire in forest management. The deciduous forests include one virgin stand dating to the time of European settlement in the lower half of the state. Flowerphiles the world over come here to sit beneath the fragrant lilac stands! In the deciduous forests along Lake Wingra, Native American burial mounds dating as far back as A.D. 1000 can be found. Best of all are the more than 20 miles of trails and fire lanes. *Note that no bicycles or in-line skates—or dogs, darn it—are allowed.*

The **McKay Center** (608/263-7888, www.uwarboretum.org) is a solar-heated visitors center—the first to use solar in Wisconsin—plunked in the midst of the arboretum, surrounded by 50 acres of ornamental gardens and shrubs. It has free guided tours at 1 P.M. Saturdays and every other Sunday, along with family tours every other Sunday. It's generally open 9:30 A.M.–4 P.M. weekdays, 12:30–4 P.M. weekends. The trails and landscaped areas are open 7 A.M.–10 P.M.

First Unitarian Church

Frank Lloyd Wright has left his mark on Madison in more ways than the Monona Terrace center. Several residences in town show his handiwork, and one structure he designed that attracts many viewers is the First Unitarian Church (900 University Bay

© THOMAS HUHTI

winter at the University of Wisconsin Arboretum

MADISON

Dr.), distinctive for its acclivitous triangles. In the 1940s the brouhaha over choosing Wright to design this church would mirror the sniping that took place over the Monona Terrace Convention Center a half-century later. In 2008, at the time of writing, the church had *just* unveiled a 21,000-square-foot, $9 million addition, and it's sublime, adding some graceful rondure to the original angular geometry, not to mention a host of cutting-edge design and construction implementations (geothermal heating, mowing-free landscaping, high-tech glass, and more). Even if you've already seen the original, do check it out again.

(Olbrich Botanical Gardens

Along Madison's east side, these mammoth gardens feature a tropical forest conservatory (608/246-4550, www.olbrich.org) with waterfall inside a 50-foot glass pyramid, along with a botanical education center and seemingly endless gardens covering almost 15 acres. The rose and herb gardens are particularly impressive; the rose displays include approximately 600 bushes. Concerts (free every Tues. in summer), plant sales, and educational events are held throughout the year. This author's friends love Yoga in the Gardens on Monday afternoons and Thursday mornings. A nice thought is the accessible tram car that buzzes about the different areas (summers and spring/autumn weekends).

A highlight for the center—and, incidentally, the place where many of these pages were dutifully scribbled in a morning ritual by yours truly—is a magnificent Thai-style pavilion, donated in part by the royal family of Thailand in recognition of the close relationship between the UW-Madison and Thailand. Peak season hours given here are April–September. The conservatory is open 10 A.M.–4 P.M. daily, 10 A.M.–5 P.M. Sunday. Admission to the conservatory is $1; admission is free 10 A.M.–noon Wednesdays and Saturdays. The gardens are open 8 A.M.–8 P.M. daily. Admission to the gardens and Thai pavilion is always free.

© THOMAS HUHTI

the Thai pavilion at Olbrich Botanical Gardens

DAWN PATROL, OR, THE INSTITUTION

Visiting friends in Madtown over the weekend? Well, don't party too hearty Friday night, 'cuz you ain't sleepin' in Saturday. No matter how hung over or work-week-weary we are, arising early for a stroll around the Capitol at the Dane County Farmers Market (www.madfarmmkt.org) – the largest of its kind in the United States – to pick up goat cheese, salmon, and organic produce (and java) is an absolute must.

More than 200 farmers line Capitol Square April-October and dispense everything you could possibly imagine. (A younger sibling market sprouts up around noon Wednesdays two blocks southeast along Martin Luther King Jr. Drive and there are also a couple of others in town.)

Key word: organic – though not exclusively; everything, however, must be grown/raised in Wisconsin. The only-in-Madison juxtapositions include an organic herb farmer, a free-range-chicken vendor, a Hmong family selling vegetables, jugglers, local politicos pressing the flesh, and a heckuva lot of political or social organizations of many bents. Add to this zillions of gapers circling counterclockwise (most hauling SUV-size baby strollers). Agoraphobics won't take to it at all. An absolute fave is **Ingrid's Lunch Box,** a food cart that has the best food in the city coming from a cart (especially the crepes).

Just *try* to beg off when your friends shake you awake!

Nightlife

The city's best nightlife is downtown and on the east side; cultural draws are downtown, period. The west side is mostly a zone where Hooters is a draw within megamall sprawl.

Check the free local paper *Isthmus* (www .thedailypage.com) for club happenings. You can also check out a few other free weeklies about, such as *77 Square,* but *Isthmus* is best.

DOWNTOWN
Memorial Union
It's free, open to all ages, and a local tradition: an alfresco music mélange Thursday–Saturday on the Memorial Union's outdoor terrace (800 Langdon St., 608/262-1331, www.union.wisc .edu). The whole place really gets bopping Friday and Saturday—the music cranks up and the beer starts flowing. During inclement weather, the whole shebang moves indoors to the cavernous Rathskeller (an acoustic death zone). Technically, you are supposed have a UW ID *and* valid driver's license to buy beer here, but it's often overlooked especially if you look like a parent; the heavy-handed staff cards for underage drinkers often here, unlike in the old days.

Bars and Pubs
Madison—mostly thanks to the UW, one thinks—pretty much always tops the *Princeton Review* for top party school in the United States (though Texas came out on top in the two most recent surveys); the city definitely leads in binge-drinking. Read: tons and tons of watering holes.

The closer you are to the university, the greater the population of students in the raucous bars. Agoraphobics need not even consider venturing into them, but at least Madison's legendary drink specials keep things cheap (and you can actually see a list of all the city's drink specials daily at www.sconnie.com). The Capitol Square area, a mere seven blocks from the university, has a much lower undergrad quotient; you'll be rubbing elbows with lots of suit-and-tie government wannabe-powers-that-be as much as backward-hatted soused undergrads.

It's mostly students at the well-lit and capacious **Plaza,** just off State Street at the corner of Johnson Street, known for its tangy burgers. Two floors of twenty-somethings—the upper level looks for all the world like a house party—socialize at **Genna's** (608/255-4770) across from the Capitol along West Main Street. A half block away is the dimly lit **Paradise Lounge** (608/256-2263), once home only to serious rumrats but now a hangout for the black-and-flannel crowd. A few doors down is the **Shamrock Bar** (117 W. Main St.), one of Madtown's four—only!—gay bars.

Lots of Capitol suits enjoy good pub grub at the **Argus** (123 E. Main St., 608/256-4141), an antebellum building with pressed-tin coffered ceilings; at night, legions of the netherworld mingle with the late-going yuppies.

Another string of bars—nay, *sports bars*—chock-full of students is found along Regent Street down from Camp Randall stadium. The hordes of students generally don't stray as far as the subdued **Greenbush Bar** (914 Regent St., 608/257-2874), an excellent Italian neighborhood eatery and *the* place in the area for a glass of wine or a scotch.

If you find yourself waiting for a Greyhound bus, wander over to the **Main Street Depot** (627 W. Main St., 608/257-4100), housed in the town's original phone company building. This has always been a great spot for nursing a drink in an unobtrusive local tavern.

Away from the Student Crowd
The *best* views in the city come at **Fresco** (608/663-7374), perched atop the Madison Museum of Contemporary Art. Sit in a chic sofa encased by glass with a panorama of the city. Great opulent drinks at great prices before 10 P.M.

You'll find jazz groups (and occasionally folk or even unplugged roots rock), local art and photography on the wall, and a light sandwich menu at **Cafe Montmartre** (127 E. Mifflin St., 608/255-5900) (call it "Momo" and fit right in); this brick-walled subterranean wine bar has an atmosphere most amenable to sipping and chatting.

For a few years now **Opus Lounge** (116 King St.) has been the place to attempt to be "scene;" pricey drink concoctions and global fusion appetizers are the thing here.

Oompah

Get your personalized mug filled with one of more than 250 beers and join in a boisterous bout of singalong or polka with lederhosen- and dirndl-clad help at the **Essenhaus** (514 E. Wilson St., 608/255-4674, 4–10 P.M. Tues.–Thurs., till 11 P.M. Fri.–Sat., 3–9 P.M. Sun.). A local tradition is to imbibe a boot of beer—a prodigious amount. Oh, yeah, it is a German restaurant, too, for the sauerbraten deprived.

If that gets too much, the **Come Back Inn** (608/258-8619), a huge adjoining tavern, is a great place to quaff a tap—for all the world like a subterranean German *bierhall*.

Live Music

Once again, *Isthmus* has the best rundown for live music; however, you may also wish to check out this website, which shows promise for keeping up with local music: www.madtownlounge.com.

Two of the state's legendary hole-in-the-wall venues for music burned down. After a brief period of mourning—and a huge crevasse in the music scene—a few places have picked up the slack. You can always find something at the affably run **High Noon Saloon** (701A E. Washington Ave., 608/268-1112). It was opened by a legendary Madison alt-club owner after her equally legendary alt-club burned down. Absolutely head here if you're around on a Tuesday night; the Rockstar Gomeroke extravaganza features a hilarious and tight-as-hell local band (the Gomers) who do live karaoke—Black Sabbath to Dylan or whatever you want. A Madison institution. (The

also play "Happyoke" for Friday happy hours sometimes.)

Fans of alternative rock head for **The Annex** (1206 Regent St.) along the sports bar row of Regent Street.

At the **Majestic** (115 King St.) you may find live music, you may find hot and heavy dancing, you may find hip-hop, you may find a Packers game projected onto the big screen—it was formerly a grand movie theater, so the interiors are fascinating.

Dance Clubs

A perennially fave dance club is **The Cardinal** (418 E. Wilson St., 608/251-0080), heavy on Latin music but you may find a jazz/martini fete or even a fetish night.

OUTSIDE OF DOWNTOWN
Near East Side

The Near East Side begins four or five blocks east of the Capitol, downhill along East Wilson Street to the hairy junction of about six or seven roads at the cusp of Lake Monona. Here, legendary Williamson Street ("Willy Street") begins. Willy Street and its neighborhoods are a pleasant hodgepodge of students and families, with an up-and-coming array of restaurants, clubs, bars, and shops, all still recalling the 1960s salad days, when these blocks were the hippified enclaves of revolution and fighting The Man. The cornerstone is the **Crystal Corner Bar** (the Crystal) at the corner of South Baldwin and Willy Streets (608/256-2953); this neon-lit bar is a hot blues (especially blues), roots rock, Cajun, and R&B spot in town (though it doesn't have as much music as it used to).

Up the road to the west is funky **Mother Fool's Coffeehouse** (608/259-1301), with eclectic music regularly. (Though head yet another block or two west and you'll see **Escape Java Joint** (916 Williamson St.), which is a bit more anarchic in its artistic offerings—hopefully you'll be there during their film parties or outdoor screenings. Continuing east of the Crystal, you'll find one of the greatest neighborhood bars in Madison: **Mickey's** (1524 Williamson,

608/251-9964). It's famous for rock-bottom beer prices, coasters made from well-worn carpeting, and large crowds. Well, somewhat shockingly, over the last couple of years the place has begun to offer food that is decidedly nearing gastropub level. Worry not, however, it's still retained its amazing local feel.

Regular eclectic big-name music acts—roots rock, alternative, hip-hop, folk, international—appear at the neighborhoody **Barrymore Theatre** (2090 Atwood Ave., 608/241-2345), recognizable for its distinctive-hued dome. This old vaudeville hall (which also hosts film festivals) has an endless schedule, so something is bound to be in town. (Nearby is the fabulous local watering hole **Harmony Bar.**)

Some would argue it's a bit far east to be in the Near East Side, but the new **Malt House** (2609 E. Washington Ave., 608/204-6258) warrants going the extra mile, with the largest and most eclectic beer selection in town (owned and run by a beer connoisseur extraordinaire). Now, many places make that claim, but what sets this place apart is that it is—gasp—sans jukebox, TVs, or stupid open mic nights. That's right, it's a place where you can enjoy a unique brew and actually hear your partner. Love the old, old wooden bar top, too—the oldest in the city (pre–Civil War).

Folkies definitely should head to the hippified Near East Side. Most acoustic music will be found at Mother Fool's or, inside the Wil-Mar Center, the **Wild Hog in the Woods** (953 Jenifer St., 608/257-4576), which regularly welcomes folk artists and holds barn dances and the like.

West Side

The west side of Madison may be a dreary slice of strip-mall hell, but **Le Tigre Lounge** (1389 S. Midvale Blvd., 608/274-0944) is a time trip back to the Rat Pack. West-side friends, defending the honor of their geography, have also insisted I include **J. T. Whitney's** (674 S. Whitney Way, 608/274-1776), a brewpub, so I will. And I will add that the beer is certainly creative.

A bit closer to downtown along Old University Avenue, **Blue Moon Bar and Grill** (2535 University Ave., 608/233-0441), once a classic Wisky tavern, spruced itself up into a cool art deco B&G without losing any of its charm. Burgers are legendary here, but the clam chowder is also luscious.

MADISON

Entertainment and Events

A cornerstone of local culture is the **Overture Center for the Arts** (201 State St., 608/258-4141, www.overturecenter.com), home to ten artistic groups as well as the Madison Museum of Contemporary Art and a few other galleries with local and regional arts. In the center's three theaters you're guaranteed to have something on offer while you're in town—classical to ballet to a touring Broadway musical. The center is generally open regular business hours (and shorter Saturday hours) for your own perusal, but Wednesdays at 2 P.M. and Saturdays at noon you can take a 90-minute tour ($3) that gets you into all venues and—usually—backstage areas.

THEATER

The University of Wisconsin's **Vilas Hall** (821 University Ave., 608/262-1500) has two theaters presenting university dramatic and musical productions throughout the year. The long-standing **Broom Street Theatre** (1119 Williamson St., 608/244-8338, www.broomstreet.org) is the Midwest's oldest year-round experimental theater group. Note, of course, that it isn't actually on Broom Street!

A refurbished movie theater is now the **Bartell Theatre** (113 E. Mifflin St., 608/294-0740, www.madstage.com), which also features many of the same local and regional theatrical groups as the Overture Center, including the **Madison Theatre Guild** (608/238-9322).

CLASSICAL MUSIC

The popular **Madison Symphony Orchestra** (608/257-3734) performs a dozen or more times during the year. On campus, the **UW-Madison School of Music** (608/263-9485) has a year-round slate of performances by faculty, students, and visiting musicians; the Chazen Museum of Art has a popular Sunday Afternoon Live series in autumn and winter.

FREEBIES

Grab a picnic basket and head for the Capitol Square Wednesday evenings for free concerts put on by the **Wisconsin Chamber Orchestra.** Though the weather is incessantly bad for these concerts, they are wildly popular. The **Memorial Union** at the UW is the most popular place to be Thursday–Saturday for its free concerts.

For family-themed freebies, always check the local *Isthmus;* you'll find tons on offer locally.

EVENTS

In June there is **Cows on the Concourse,** a fun way of highlighting Wisconsin's dairy industry; you can get up close and personal with dairy cows (statues, actually, though real ones have made appearances), as they're scattered all over the Capitol area.

July's biggie is the now-annual **Rhythm and Booms** choreographed fireworks display on the Fourth—it's the largest in the Midwest and definitely a treat. Later that month, the **Art Fair on the Square** is a huge draw—one of the largest events in the Midwest and one of the largest juried art fairs in the country; the **Dane County Fair** also brings many visitors. October brings the world's largest dairy show, the **World Dairy Expo,** a big-time international event, with agriculturalists and scientists from all over the globe coming to check up on any new dairy industry progress; regular folks can get a lifetime of knowledge about dairy.

SHOPPING

Depends what you're looking for. Locals will probably tell you to head for East Towne

© YUKI TAKANO

Cows on the Concourse (Go Brewers!)

Mall or West Towne Mall. Six of one, half a dozen of the other; but they're malls, right?

Likely 99 percent of visitors to Madison purchase something on State Street, since you can't help but walk it. Many times. Actually, State Street nowadays is about half bars, a quarter restaurants, and a few odds and ends clothing, gift, and the odd, er, "smoking" shops. To be a true-red Wisky, visit any purveyor of T-shirts and lids and buy a "Sconnie" shirt; Sconnie is the brainchild of two genius-slacker UW students who are now making a killing doling out this moniker of Badgerland. Check out their website (www .sconnie.com) for a hilarious rundown of what it means to be a Badger, along with great souvenir items.

At the exact other end of State Street, a block from the Capitol, check out **House of Wisconsin Cheese** (www.houseofwisconsincheese.com, 9 A.M.–8 P.M. daily), which sells not just cheese but every other imaginable thing grown or produced in the state, much of it shippable elsewhere. Of course you also get all your tongue-in-cheek type stuff here too: foam cheeseheads, cow

Take your pick of Wisconsin cheeses!

tipping T-shirts, Holstein-colored coffee cups and the like.

Madison otherwise doesn't have any real gallery districts and the like, but the two—discussed many times elsewhere in the book—you may want to check out are the Monroe Street area (think chi-chi) and the Near East Side along Williamson Street (think renegade art, aging hippies, hemp clothing, etc.).

Sports and Recreation

You may notice that Madisonians spend all their time jogging, biking, 'blading, skiing, or participating in some other cardiovascular exercise. In fact, this may be why *Outside* magazine has declared Madison a dream spot to live.

RECREATION
Bicycling

No doubt about it, cycling is king in Madison. *Bicycling* and *Outside* magazines in 2006 called Madison the best biking city in North America. Second only to Seattle in number of bikes per capita, Madison pedals virtually everywhere it goes. There are—quite seriously—bike traffic jams on certain routes in peak hours since

15–*20* percent (no joke) of the citizenry commute by bicycle. Mad pedalers will happily discover 25 miles of established pathway on trails and more than 110 miles of interconnected routes along city streets, bike paths, and parkways.

The most popular path is the **Lake Monona Loop,** easily accessible along John Nolen Drive, which passes the Monona Terrace Convention Center along the lake; it's about 12 miles long and cruises through residential neighborhoods. A caveat: The route is marked much better if you go clockwise from the Monona Terrace, though the best lake views come if you start counterclockwise.

Many head over to the UW Arboretum for a

lovely ride. Note that the arboretum's unpaved trails are for feet only. That's all right, as there are loads of bike racks to lock up and hit the side trails. When you need a break, just lounge with the rest of us amongst the colors on the fields of grass.

Here's an outstanding way to combine the two: the Capital City State Trail (trail pass required). You can reach it from the Lake Monona loop where the lakeshore path bisects the Beltline Highway at Waunona Way; signs point you along a spur underneath the overpass 300 yards to the official trailhead. Follow this through Fitchburg and then turn right on Seminole Highway (bike-friendly) and continue to the entrance of the arboretum.

Should you wish to keep on the Capital City State Trail, it stretches west from Lake Monona all the way to Verona, where it links with the existing Military Ridge State Trail, a grand journey. (Better, it will in the future lead all the way to Illinois and down along Madison's isthmus before heading east to Cottage Grove to link with the Glacial Drumlin State Trail, allowing one to bicycle all the way to Milwaukee.) The Madison segment is part of a visionary project dubbed E-Way, a corridor encompassing more than 3,200 acres for ecological, educational, and recreational use. It isn't just a trail—it's an established "necklace" of linked islands of educational or environmental importance. Madison environmentalists lobbied and fought hard for 25 years to see it established.

All that would be a full day's work. A much easier ride is to start at the UW's Memorial Union, from where a path leads along Lake Mendota to Picnic Point. Gorgeous sunrises.

Budget Bicycle Center (1230 Regent St., 608/251-8413) and **Yellow Jersey** (419 State St., 608/257-7733) both rent bikes. The former also is part of a unique program for travelers to the city; for a $40 bike deposit and $20 lock deposit, you get a bike, and when you return both, you get everything back. All bike shops also stock maps of city bicycle routes, as

WINTER HARDY, SUMMER WEAK

Wisconsinites love to show off our toughness, especially in winter. We take great pride in amazing outsiders when we walk around a sub-freezing (or even sub-zero) day sans hat, gloves, rational footwear, or even decent jacket. (This author's January dog park jacket is often a thick flannel shirt with a Packers sweatshirt, and it's perfectly fine.) We scoff at snow. We turn down the thermostat. (Well, most of us – this author's fiancée points out she loathes it, but she's an outsider.)

However, watch us mention it quite a bit when the mercury tops 75° Fahrenheit. If it gets over 80°, we begin to get nervous. If it's 85° and even a whiff of humidity, we won't shut up about it. Reach the dreaded 90° mark with humidity and we won't want to leave the house. Hit 100 degrees (thank God it's rare enough or I'd skedaddle to Canada) and the governor practically has to call a state of emergency.

So, please, if you're from somewhere hot and/or humid, please keep this in mind. If we're joshing you come winter, you'll have plenty of time to exact revenge in summer.

does the visitors center along East Washington Avenue (but the best maps—free!—are at the Streets office of the City-County building, opposite the post office).

Hiking

Any cycling trail in the city is also open to hikers. The UW Arboretum has the most bucolic trails, some of them quite superb for an urban area. Picnic Point is your best second choice. The city otherwise has 6000 acres of parkland—that's a hell of a lot for a city this size. What this author generally does is tool around in his car with his pooch, circling the downtown lakes and sniffing out (literally) the tiny little "nook parks" (I call 'em) along the lakeshore. You'll be amazed how many there are, some as tiny as your living room. The city's website (www.ci.madison.wi.us) has a great page of all parks.

Cross-Country Skiing

Madison has about 20 miles of groomed trails for cross-country skiing. Parks include Warner Park (1511 Northport Dr.), Monona Golf Course (111 Dean Ave.), Olin-Turville (1155 E. Lakeside St.), Elver Park (1301 Gammon Rd.), and Odana Golf Course (4635 Odana Road). An excellent county park west of town via U.S. 12 and WI 19 is **Indian Lake County Park.** There's a $2 day-use fee to ski at county parks.

Fontana Sports (251 State St., 608/257-5043) rents skis though call first to make sure.

Golf

Madison has four public courses, of which **Yahara Hills** (6701 E. Broadway, 608/838-3126) is the least crowded. **Odana Hills** on the west side is so crowded at times it's like Disney World.

An outstanding course is the University of Wisconsin golf center, **University Ridge Golf Course** (7120 CR PD, 608/845-7700), a championship par-72 course with the tightest slingshot fairways you'll find in town. If you're a Tiger wannabe, this is where you should make a reservation.

Canoeing and Water Sports

Canoeing magazines also rave about the city; a couple of my friends commute to work by kayak. This comes as little surprise since the city spreads amidst four lakes, the larger two of which—Mendota and Monona—are connected by the Yahara River, a superb ribbony urban stream passing through locks and a series of smaller lakes. The Yahara connects to the Rock River, which itself flows through southern Wisconsin. Factoring in tributaries of the Rock leading westward to the Ol' Miss, technically, you could paddle all the way to the Big Easy!

Hoofer's, part of the UW's Memorial Union, rents sailboarding equipment, boats, canoes, and sailboats, and also gives lessons.

Camping

The nearest public campground is **Lake Kegonsa State Park,** approximately 15 miles southeast off I-90 on Highway N. It's not a particularly breathtaking park, but it's large and the lake is nice.

SPECTATOR SPORTS
Badger Nation

The UW is what draws the sports nuts to Madison. The university is NCAA Division 1A in all sports, and the cardinal red–garbed citizenry is gaga over the Badgers. Camp Randall Stadium on a football Saturday is an experience you'll not soon forget. At the end of the third quarter, the *entire* student section—and it's huge—starts jumping and screaming with the hit hip-hop song "Jump Around"; the place actually shakes. (A more mundane but equally great tradition is for the band to roll out the barrel, as it were, and perform post-game.) If the opponent is a Big 10 foe, forget about a ticket, but for early-season games an occasional ticket may be available.

Ditto the excitement with the perennial Western Collegiate Hockey Association champion (and six-time national champion—latest in 2006) Badgers, who play at the spanking new Kohl Center (one of the best hockey facilities in the United States); the fans here may be more rabid than the football legions. (The blasting of "Sieve!" at opposing goaltenders after scores is truly cacophonous.)

The men's and women's basketball teams have both had a renaissance in the 1990s; no longer doormats, both regularly get to their respective tournaments. For information on ticket availability, call the ticket office at 608/262-1440.

Lesser-known UW sports are well worth the money, particularly track, cross-country, and men's and women's soccer, consistently ranked in the nation's top 20.

MADISON

Madison Mallards

Wildly popular is this independent baseball league team (www.mallardsbaseball.com) with college players on summer break. Cheap seats, generally competitive baseball, and the usual zany promotions of minor league baseball that are as much fun as the games. They play at Warner Park on the north side of town and you can have a great evening for less than twenty bucks.

Accommodations

Listings here are but highlights, and chain affiliations are generally eschewed. One bright spot in Madison is that comfortable digs can be had for under $100—though not necessarily anywhere near the university or Capitol, and most definitely not when something government- or university-affiliated is going on (often).

DOWNTOWN
Under $50

Madison's **HI Madison Hostel** (141 S. Butler St., 608/441-0144, www.madisonhostel.org, $18 members, $21 nonmembers), a year-round facility, is central, progressive, and very well run. Six-bed dorms and one- to three-person rooms book out in summer so try to make reservations.

$50-100

In peak periods it's getting tough to find anything even close to downtown for less than $100. But here's something no one else seems to know about: stay at the you're-gonna-go-there-anyway **UW Memorial Union** (800 Langdon St., 608/262-1583, www.union.wisc.edu/guestrooms, $75–102). Perfectly comfortable rooms with a couple of double beds; higher-end rooms have lake views. And in the morning, just roll downstairs to grab some java at the cafeteria and hang out on the terrace with everyone else.

Otherwise, depending on the season, you *may* find sub-$100 prices (like, $99) with an inspiring view at the **Best Western Inn on the Park** (22 S. Carroll St., 608/257-8811, $99), which sits opposite the magnificent Capitol. Nothing flashy, but decent.

Same ownership but closer to the university, just off State Street, is **University Inn** (441 N. Frances St., 608/257-4881 or 800/279-4881, $99); again, nothing flash but you're right in the heart of things.

$100-150

Gorgeous vistas of a more natural bent are found at the **Edgewater** (666 Wisconsin Ave., 608/256-9071, www.theedgewater.com, $119), plopped on a small bluff overlooking Lake Mendota a handful of blocks east of the university campus. Smallish but decent rooms, though keep in mind this place is over a century old and so, you know, building codes for pipes and such weren't what they are now. Not many extras—health club privileges mean a bit of a hike—but hey, it's got a swimming beach! The dining room is popular with locals for the sunsets as much as the food. Just an FYI: Literally on the day this text was being finalized, owners had announced plans to completely refurbish the aging piece of art-deco eye candy, adding rooms and hoping to give it a more public access feel. Just a thought now, but keep an eye on it—it may turn into something special.

The towering (for the Mad City, anyway) **Madison Concourse Hotel and Governor's Club** (1 W. Dayton St., 608/257-6000, www.concoursehotel.com, $119) certainly can boast some of the most reputable dining and seen-on-the-scene options in town.

A spiffy boutique hotel with European stylistic flair just off the State Street corridor is the **Campus Inn** (601 Langdon St., 608/257-4391, www.thecampusinn.com, from $135)—very distinctive and more than one traveler has raved about the service.

Recommended without hesitation is the **Mansion Hill Inn** (424 N. Pinckney St., 608/255-3999, www.mansionhillinn.com, from $145), an opulent 1858 Romanesque revival on the National Register of Historic Places. Set snugly along a quiet residential street close to downtown, this ornate piece of Victoriana features a distinctive gabled roof and wrought-iron railings encircling the etched sandstone facade. Inside, the opulence is breathtaking, with thrusting round-arched windows, ornate cornices, hand-carved marble, spiral staircase, and a wraparound belvedere. All surrounded by Victorian gardens. The eight rooms vary from Empire style to a Turkish nook, Chinese silk, an Oriental suite, a room done up as a study, and more.

$150 and Up

A new Hyatt Place—a two-room suite hotel—is being built a few blocks southwest of the State Capitol in an erstwhile hospital; the plans look distinctive.

Otherwise, the newest hotel in town, with smashing views, is the **Hilton** (9 E. Wilson St., 608/255-5100, from $150), a stone's throw from the Monona Terrace Convention Center. The higher-priced rooms have great lake views and the restaurants come recommended.

OUTSIDE OF DOWNTOWN

Accommodation zones—mostly chain or mom-and-pop operations, not bad but simply unremarkable—are strung along the Beltline (U.S. 12, 14, 18, 151), the artery linking east and west Madison. Another concentration of motels is found at the junction of U.S. 151 and U.S. 51 and east along U.S. 151 (East Washington Avenue) to East Towne Mall—the major commercial section of the east side. Others are spread a bit more widely around West Towne Mall on the west side. The cheapest room you'll find is around $45 in the low season but be forewarned some of these are downright scuzzy.

$100-150

Given Madison's progressive environmentalism, it's little surprise to find the **Arbor House–An Environmental Inn** (3402 Monroe St., 608/238-2981, www.arbor-house.com, $125–230). Its renovation using all recycled materials, from the frames to the beams to the tiling is but a start; it is about as environmentally progressive as it gets. Highly respectable and superb location on the near west side—directly across from the arboretum and within walking distance of the chichi shop zone of Monroe Street. The extras here—canoeing to sauna, massage, and babysitting, to name a few—run a full page long.

West of the university but still within a brief walk is the **Best Western InnTowner** (2424 University Ave., 608/258-8321, $125–245). Standard rooms are fine; the pricier rooms on the top floors have recently been redone—smashingly, with some architectural and design awards having been won for the effort.

The west side is home to tons of mall zones, and strung along the Beltline are dozens of motels and hotels. Families generally head directly for the **Holiday Inn Hotel and Suites-West** (1109 Fourier Dr., 608/826-0500, $135), as it's home to Madison's only full-fledged indoor water park. The kids go nuts on the water slides or in the game room; parents relax in the grand piano bar. Some rooms have kitchenettes.

Food

Given the cosmopolitan-minded citizenry that apparently doesn't like to stay home and cook, you'll find something you like.

Supper Clubs

It may be one of the hearts of the state, but you'd hardly know it by downtown Madtown's lack of a real-deal supper club. This is truly galling. Oh, a couple do exist *just* outside of the Capitol/university area and isthmus, but even locals quibble over whether, due to atmosphere or fare, those are truly deemed supper clubs. Readers' opinions on this matter are most welcome.

DOWNTOWN
Quick Bites

A Madison dining tradition is to buy a box from a food cart—Thai, Chinese, African, Cuban, Jamaican, barbecue ribs, vegetarian, and a whole lot more—and sprawl on the mall

Dane County farmers market

at the university end of State Street or at the Capitol Square. You'll find half a dozen carts at either end; usually for around $5 you can fill up and munch with the ever-friendly squirrels. Best people-watching-cum-meal experience in the city! (This author's favorite appears only Saturdays during the Dane County farmers market—the little red cart housing the sublime food from **Ingrid's Lunch Box.**)

Burgers, Brewpubs, and Brats

Dotty Dumpling's Dowry (317 N. Frances St., 608/259-0000,11 A.M.–1 A.M. daily, $4) always wins local surveys for burgers, which really are sublime creations (if a bit pricey). Some Madison radicals frequent the place simply because the owner put up a Pyrrhic battle against the city when it wanted to buy his former location for the city's new arts district. He lost, but Madison's antiestablishment thinks it's worth paying a few bucks for his Himalayan piles of legal bills.

Yet when his tummy's carnivore regions start barking, this author heads up State Street to the corner of Johnson and cuts over to the **Plaza Grill** (11 A.M.–11 P.M. daily, $3–6), a popular nighttime hangout that serves the legendarily tangy Plazaburgers—a slider of a sandwich if ever there was one.

The Great Dane (123 E. Doty St., 608/284-0000, 11 A.M.–11 P.M. daily, $7–16) is a brewpub occupying what was Madison's landmark Fess Hotel. The interior upstairs is fairly spacious, but it's best known for its great courtyard. The catacomb-like downstairs is a great place for moody swilling. The Great Dane has been ranked in the top 10 brewpubs in the nation in terms of beer consumption; no surprise in a university town in Wisconsin. The food is exceptional, way above basic pub grub, and the place has got a new billiards hall and cigars for aficionados.

It's nearly raucous inside, but stick the brats, burgers, and other pan-Wisconsin-produced fare at **❰ The Old-Fashioned** (23 N.

Pinckney St., 608/310-4545, 11 A.M.–9 P.M. Mon.–Fri., 4 P.M.–1 A.M. Sat.–Sun., $5–28) on china on a white tablecloth and it'd pass for fine dining. It's my fave restaurant in town to explain what it is a "typical" cheesehead eats. (And a shout out to the Fendt's Brothers sausages; they're from your humble author's hometown and bring back fond childhood memories every time he eats there.)

Cafés

Not really a café per se but unclassifiable otherwise is the **Grand Lobby Café and Lounge** in the lobby of the Orpheum Theater (216 State St., 608/255-2594, 11 A.M.–2 P.M. and 5:30–10 P.M. Tues.–Fri., 9 A.M.–1 P.M. and 5:30–10 P.M. Sat., 10 A.M.–2 P.M. Sun., $6–12). It's a totally cool take on breakfast, lunch, or dinner, in the stately interiors of a grande dame of Madison. Some items are quite creative; the Sunday brunch is great.

Praise the universe, we now have something other than greasy eggs at a casual place downtown. Extremely understated but heads above others of similar ilk is **⟨ Marigold Kitchen** (118 S. Pinckney St., 608/661-5559, 7–10:30 A.M. and 11 A.M.–3 P.M. weekdays, 7 A.M.–2 P.M. Sat., $4). This bustling bistro does unique takes on breakfasts (the breakfast sandwich is probably this author's favorite city meal) and lunch—personalized sandwiches like you've never experienced.

Coffeehouses

State Street is crawling with the places. One venerable institution is **Steep and Brew** (544 State St., 608/256-2902, hours vary with UW semesters). An initiator of the coffee generation in Madison, it's got a cubbyhole lower level and a cozy—if a tad noisy—upper level, with muted lighting and artwork adorning the walls. Live music is offered, too.

An excellent option is **Ancora Coffee Roasters** (112 King St., 608/255-2900, hours vary by UW semesters), which has the best interior of any coffee shop downtown. Warm and naturally lit, this is a place to relax with a latte.

Fish Fries

Madison doesn't necessarily live and die for the fish fry, but some good ones are here. Check out www.madisonfishfry.com for some locally recommended places.

Generally voted the best fish fry in Madison is an institution, **⟨ The Avenue Bar** (1128 E. Washington Ave., 608/257-6877, 11 A.M.–10 P.M. weekdays, 8 A.M.–10:30 P.M. Sat., 8 A.M.–9 P.M. Sun., $6), with a number of tables along its huge bar and a newer hall decorated in a pastiche of Badger memorabilia and farm implements. It does a fish boil every day that is worth a try. (OK, OK, it's a bit of a hike if you're walking from the Capitol Square area, but it's close enough.)

Greasy Spoons and Diners

Come 7 A.M., I've been stopped more than a few times in the Capitol vicinity by weary out-of-towners looking for a place with chipped mugs. Well, for chipped mugs, you're gonna have to head to **Willaby's** (6 A.M.–1:30 P.M. Mon.–Fri., 6 A.M.–3 P.M. Sat., and 7 A.M.–3 P.M. Sun.), 15 or so blocks east on Williamson Street. Seriously. Everything else downtown is kinda fruits and nuts.

Still, the most classic downscale Madison breakfast place has to be **Mickie's Dairy Bar** (1511 Monroe St., 608/256-9476, lunch and dinner daily except Mon.), doling out awesome breakfasts (luscious pancakes) and malts since the '40s. The atmosphere is super here and the decor real-deal, down to the aging napkin dispensers and anachronistic knickknacks everywhere (the café's name harks back to the establishment's days as one of the largest milk and bread retailers in the city). Try the Scrambler or the Frisbee-size flapjacks.

Custard and Ice Cream

Madison has caught the custard bug so prevalent in Milwaukee and now has varieties rivaling its bigger brother. Personal favorites include **Michael's Frozen Custard,** with lots of locations, and **Culver's,** found throughout southwestern Wisconsin (the latter's butterburgers are also something to write home about!).

But for the obligatory Wisconsin experience, a true Homer Simpson moment to say "Mmmm," head directly for the UW campus and **◀ Babcock Hall,** where the university cooks delectable batches of its own proprietary ice cream, which is also served at the Memorial Union.

Vegetarian and Health Foods

Pick pretty much any restaurant in downtown Madison and it'll have vegetarian friendly food—though, oddly, no purely vegetarian restaurant existed at the time of writing (www.vegmadison.com is a good source of info, as is www.veganmadison.com). What yours truly does is grab a lunch to go from the **Willy St. Co-op** (1221 Williamson St., 608/251-6776, 8 A.M.–9 P.M. daily), which is technically on the Near East side.

Asian and Middle Eastern

Without question the best new restaurant in town is **◀ Restaurant Muramoto** (225 King St., 608/259-1040, 11:30 A.M.–2 P.M. weekdays, 5–10 P.M. Mon.–Sat., till 9 P.M. Sun., $7–15). Creative pan-Asian with Japanese at its heart, nothing here disappoints—a cliché but it's true. Even the service has been far, far above the usual college-town-lethargic, with servers who may still be preoccupied by their master's degree thesis but still do a damn good job.

But you'll never go wrong with the superb sushi (so says this author's Japanese fiancée) at **Wasabi** (449 State St., 608/255-5020, 11 A.M.–2:30 P.M. Tues.–Sat., 4:30–10 P.M. Tues.–Sun., $4–18), which had been for years pretty much the only place to get great—not good—Japanese cuisine.

With overtones of Mediterranean and Middle Eastern cuisine, **Kabul** (541 State St., 608/256-6322, 11 A.M.–10 P.M. Mon.–Thurs. and 11 A.M.–11 P.M. Fri.–Sat., $6–15) is unique in Wisconsin—most likely the only Afghan restaurant. It's well worth it, and you can dine outside in summer.

Wisconsin's only Indonesian restaurant is **Bandung** (600 Williamson St., 608/255-6910, 11 A.M.–2 P.M. Mon.–Sat., 5 P.M.–9 P.M.

Mon.–Thurs., 5 P.M.–10 P.M. Fri., 4 P.M.–8 P.M. Sun., $5–15). The Indonesian food is solid, but Bandung also has Thai choices; every month special dinners and Indonesian dance are presented.

Do not miss **◀ Caspian Cafe** (610 University Ave., 608/259-9009, 11:30 A.M.–5 P.M. Mon.–Thurs., till 8 P.M. Fri., noon–3 P.M. Sat., $4–9). Its inexpensive creative Persian cuisine—always with a smile—is hands-down this author's favorite quick meal in the Mad City.

The Madison institution for Nepali cuisine has always been **Himal Chuli** (318 State St., 608/251-9225, 11 A.M.–9 P.M. Mon.–Wed., 11 A.M.–9:30 P.M. Thurs.–Sat., noon–9 P.M. Sun.), a great little place with a menu that will never let you down. Lovers of Himalayan food were orgasmic when the owners opened the equally delightful **Chautaura** (334 State St., 608/255-3585, 11 A.M.–9 P.M. Mon.–Wed., 11 A.M.–9:30 P.M. Thurs.–Sat., and noon–9 P.M. Sun., $7–14), which serves Nepali with heavy overtones of Indian and even Tibetan—at higher prices, mind you, given the expansive space. Both of these places are open Monday–Saturday for lunch and dinner.

Steak House

Grazing vegetarians—a dominant sociopolitical force locally—must have been a bit taken aback by the resurgence of the true carnivorous experience downtown. Steak houses with a true-blue throwback, '50s martinis-and-slabs-era feel now exist, highlighted by the **Tornado Club** (116 S. Hamilton St., 608/256-3570, 5:30–10:30 P.M. daily, $17–36). This might be the best nouveau take on the old supper club in town. Steaks are the highlight, but the Friday pan-fried perch are a wonderful option for those non-red-meat lovers. Sunday, wonderfully, is homestyle chicken dinner night.

Fine Dining

If you're in town for only one night, the place to choose has always been **◀ L'Etoile** (25 N. Pinckney St., 608/251-0500, 6–8:45 P.M. Mon.–Thurs., 5:30–9:45 P.M. Fri.–Sat., $20–35), on Capitol Square directly opposite the

Capitol. The creative regional fare has garnered nationwide raves and placed the owners in the national cuisine spotlight—in 2006 named one of the United States' top 50 restaurants by *Food and Wine.* The restaurant is a supporter of local produce merchants and uses organic ingredients; it also truly strives to reach that esoteric netherworld of the harmony of cuisine, art, and culture. Simply put, the menus are incredible gastronomic representations of the geography and ethos of this place.

No places at L'Etoile? Problem solved: Walk two doors south to the equally well-realized ❰ **Harvest** (21 N. Pinckney St., 608/255-6075, 5:30–10 P.M. Mon.–Thurs., 5:30–11:30 P.M. Fri.–Sat., $16). The burgeoning slow-food movement—French and American, with local organic ingredients—inspires the culinary experience at this, one of southern Wisconsin's best.

Making a name for itself is the newer ❰ **Sardine** (617 Williamson St., 608441-1600, 5–10 P.M. Tues.–Thurs., 5–11 P.M. Fri.–Sat., 9 A.M.–9 P.M. Sun., $6–20). It may not consider itself a fine dining establishment (as in posh), but the seafood in a capacious lakeside dining room is really something special. (Except for getting into the parking lot; it's at a mish-mash of roads and can be crazy—I always approach from along John Nolen Drive.) The skate here is sublime.

Way up the price scale is the crisp ❰ **Blue Marlin** (101 N. Hamilton St., 608/255-2255, 11:30 A.M.–2:30 P.M. and 5:30–10 P.M. Tues.–Sat., 5:30–10 P.M. Sun., $8–40), a white-linen place with fresh grilled swordfish, salmon, tuna, crab, and more—even a San Francisco fish stew. The classic, century-old aesthetics are hard to beat. For seafood, this is the place.

NEAR EAST SIDE AND WEST SIDE
Supper Club
At 61 years and counting, **Esquire Club** (1025 N. Sherman Ave., 608/249-0193, 11 A.M.–10 P.M. daily, light dinner menu Mon.–Thurs., from $6), you can pretty much guess, knows what it's doing. What it does is real-deal supper club fare in a *real* supper club environment. Utterly unpretentious and serving the same families for generations, this is the kind of place the author remembers of family nights out to supper clubs. They also offer fish fry Wednesdays in addition to Fridays.

Cafés
Best place to take guests when they show up unannounced on a Saturday morning for the farmers market is ❰ **Monty's Blue Plate** (2089 Atwood Ave., 608/244-8505, 7 A.M.–9 P.M. Mon.–Thurs. and Sun., till 10 P.M. Fri.–Sat., $5–9), an upscale diner on the Near East Side with deliciously art deco cool blue interiors. You'll find the best synthesis of American meat and potatoes with trendy off-the-beaten-menu items. The chefs are equally adept with meat loaf and tofu and scrambled egg Mediterranean surprise.

It doesn't feature the usual artery-clogging bar food; hell, it isn't even pub grub. **The Harmony Bar** (2201 Atwood Ave., 608/249-4333, food 11 A.M.–midnight weekdays, till 8:45 P.M. Fri.–Sat., $4) is the most perfect approximation of a very casual neighborhood bar that happens to have great food. An early 20th-century east-side tavern and fish-fry server extraordinaire, the current incarnation is a comfortable tavern with one of the best jukeboxes in town and a menu varying from homemade pizzas to walnut burgers. The back room features mostly blues and roots rock on Friday and Saturday.

Music, great beer selection, but even better pan-world food—try the Bad Breath Burger—are at the simply-always-packed **Weary Traveler** (1201 Williamson St., 608/442-6207, 11:30 A.M.–1 A.M. Tues.–Sun., $5–12). While there, keep yer eyes peeled for a ginormous-headed yellow lab looking in the window, begging sad-eyed for food; that'd be yours truly's Bobo, and this is his favorite spot in Madison. (Don't believe his eyes, by the way—he uses them peepers to his great advantage!)

Two blocks east of here you can also catch yours truly quite a few mornings getting a scone and massive healthful breakfast and sitting on an upstairs sofa at **Lazy Jane's** (1358 Williamson St., 608/257-5263, 7 A.M.–3 P.M. weekdays, 8 A.M.–2 P.M. weekends for breakfast only). You can go with seitan scramble; you can go with heart-stopper eggs and sausage—everyone's welcome. And it truly is like eating in someone's living room. Be prepared to stand in line.

Family-Friendly

The wildly popular **Ella's Deli** (2902 E. Washington Ave., 608/241-5291, 10 A.M.–11 P.M. Mon.–Thurs., 10 A.M.–midnight Fri.–Sat., from $3) is a kosher deli and ice-cream parlor—though traditionalists quibble with the revered "deli" moniker (they cavil, this author says). This Near East Side location is very family-friendly—a wild descent into circus kitsch, complete with a carousel outside.

Cajun

A longtime favorite is the takeout only **New Orleans Take-Out** (1920 Fordem Ave., 608/241-6655, 11 A.M.–9 P.M. Mon.–Sat., $5 and up), with the hottest dirty rice you'll find in Madison and some delectable sweet potato pie.

Laotian

The food will clear your sinuses, but the spices don't dominate the wondrously simple but rich fare at **Lao Laan-Xang** (1146 Williamson St., 608/280-0104, $6–16), which has good specials—and delivers! It also serves a traditional Laotian brunch on Saturday that is a godsend if you're sick of eggs and bacon. Hours are complicated, but essentially lunch and dinner daily, with that additional Saturday brunch.

WEST AND SOUTH OF DOWNTOWN

If you can find the University of Wisconsin's Camp Randall Stadium—the football stadium—head south along Monroe Street to find any number of quality restaurants. **Mickie's Dairy Bar** (1511 Monroe St., 608/256-9476, lunch and dinner daily except Mon.) at the north end of the street is close enough to walk and is where this pub-and-grub stroll can start.

This street has not one but two quality gastropubs. (I'm not going to get into the occasional heated verbal sparring match that is the discussion over the difference between gastropub and brasserie—or even bistro; let's just say it's fantastic food in an *unpretentious*—honestly—pub or even neighborhood bar setting. Everyone claims to do that, but few actually achieve high-quality food without any forced chi chi-ness.) **Brasserie V** (1923 Monroe St., 608/255-8500, 11 A.M.–11 P.M. Mon.–Thurs., till midnight Fri.–Sat., 9 A.M.–3 P.M. Sun., $5–17) and **Monroe Street Bistro** (2611 Monroe St., 608/441-5444, 11 A.M.–11 P.M. Mon.–Sat., $5–15) both fit the definition precisely.

An admission: This author loathes pizza. Well, to be honest, it's the cooked tomato—a horrible thing to do to a wonderful fruit—that leaves him gagging. Thus, the whole avoid-the-pizza thing. (University town greasy Frisbee pizzas don't help things either.) What a surprise, then, to eat at **Pizza Brutta** (1805 Monroe St., 608/257-2120, 11 A.M.–9 P.M. Mon.–Thurs., till 10 P.M. Fri.–Sat., $8–13) and absolutely rave about it. Sublime crust and the crafting of sauce and toppings are nearly artistic. Honestly—a great thing.

Vegetarian

Not officially vegetarian but one that has enough respect for noncarnivores on its menu to warrant a visit is **Bluephie's** (2701 Monroe St., 608/231-3663, 11 A.M.–9 P.M. weekdays, 8 A.M.–10 P.M. weekends, $6–15), which is very similar to Monty's Blue Plate diner on the Near East Side—meat and potatoes with an amazingly skilled update.

The west side has one of the largest natural-food store chains in the country, **Whole Foods** (3313 University Ave., 608/233-9566, 8 A.M.–10 P.M. daily).

Italian

Well, the decor can be a bit garish, what with fountains and all, but Madisonians absolutely remain rock solid behind **Lombardino's** (2500 University Ave., 608/238-1922, 5–9 P.M. or 10 P.M. Tues.–Sun., $6–21), with a seasonally adjusted menu of freshly prepared high-quality Italian fare.

Mexican

The title of top Mexican eatery now belongs to 🅒 **La Hacienda** (515 S. Park St., 608/255-8227, 8 A.M.–3 A.M. daily, 8 A.M.–4 A.M. weekends, $4–12). Owned by the same Milwaukee family that has given southeast Wisconsin the outstanding Jalisco restaurants, La Hacienda has spartan decor as stereotypically Mexican-restaurant as any you'll find, but the service is always friendly. The menu is an encyclopedic traipse through home-style Mexican, down to a great daily *comida corrida,* menudo, huge burritos, sweetly tart mole sauce, and a killer *chile de arbol* sauce. The lunch specials are good deals and, best of all, it doesn't close until way, way late every day.

Thai

Diminutive **Sa Bai Thong** (2840 University Ave., 608/238-3100, 11 A.M.–9 or 10 P.M. Mon.–Sat., 5–9 P.M. Sun., $5–15) is arguably the best Thai restaurant in the state. Ensconced drearily in another of those endless strip-mall hells on the near west side, its menu really isn't extensive, but the food is generally done to perfection. It's so popular it has recently expanded into the suite next door.

Japanese

Best Japanese—well, Japanese and creative Japanese—is at **Sushi Muramoto** (546 N. Midvale Blvd., 608/441-1090, 11 A.M.–10 P.M. daily, $10–20) in Hilldale Mall on Madison's Near West Side. This is actually the second spot opened by a master chef who also has a flagship restaurant downtown. His signature miso black cod is basically what a culinary experience is meant to be.

Fish Fry

From the west side of town, it may be better to swing toward Middleton, where **The Stamm House at Pheasant Branch** (6625 Century Ave., 608/831-5835, 5–9 P.M. Tues. and Thurs., 5–10 P.M. Wed. and Fri.–Sat., 4–9 P.M. Sun., $6) is a popular supper club housed in a century-old farmhouse. The place is absolutely jam-packed and very festive; given the crowds, service can be spotty, but the atmosphere is unbeatable.

Steak Houses

Ah, 🅒 **Smoky's Club** (3005 University Ave., 608/233-2120, 5–10 P.M. Mon. and Wed.–Sat., $12–35). One of a dying breed, it's a real charcoal-killer place. The classic supper club-cum-steak house, Smoky's is the type of place where the waitresses have been bustling for four decades and the bartender will remember your drink on your second visit. Big 10 sporting teams make pilgrimages here when they're in town. The decor is simple but homey, and the atmosphere most definitely frenetic. Reservations are essential.

Best bet for a prime rib (you can damn near cut it with a fork)—according to a UW Meat Sciences staffer—is **Fitzgerald's** (3112 W. Beltline Hwy., 608/831-7107, $8–26), also good for steaks and seafood. It's open weekdays for lunch, daily for dinner, with a Saturday brunch. Popular? This place had to put in a pickup window!

Information and Services

Visitor Information

The Greater Madison Convention and Visitors Center (615 E. Washington Ave., 608/255-2537 or 800/373-6376, www.visitmadison.com, 8 A.M.–5 P.M. Mon.–Fri.) is not well located if you're on foot. They operate information desks at the airport (basically noon–10 P.M., from 10 A.M. Friday) (though I've never seen anyone there when I arrive) and at the Overture Center for the Arts in the Madison Arts District (10:30 A.M.–5 P.M. Mon.–Fri.).

The Wisconsin Department of Tourism (608/266-2161) operates a visitors center (on the second floor, if you can find it) a block west of the Capitol on West Washington Avenue, though it's seasonal and honestly doesn't have all that much—ask the workers though, who are wondrously helpful.

Bookstores

Madison is an amazing place for a bookworm, with more than 50 bookshops. The country's largest **Barnes and Noble** (7433 Mineral Point Road, 9 A.M.–11 P.M. Mon.–Sat., 10 A.M.–9 P.M. Sun.) megastore (outside of New York City's original) is on the west side, with more than 150,000 titles in stock.

You'll find more than half a dozen bookstores by strolling along State Street. Three blocks or so down State Street from the Capitol, a left on Gorham Street takes you to the great selection at **Avol's** (10 A.M.–9 P.M. Mon.–Sat., noon–5 P.M. Sun.). The granddaddy, though, has always been **Paul's** (9 A.M.–7 P.M. Mon.–Sat., noon–5 P.M. Sun.), at the far end of State Street, just off the Lake Street corner; it's been around since the '50s.

Newspapers

Until 2008 Madison was one of the few remaining two-paper towns in the country. The *Capital Times* was the lefty paper and *Wisconsin State Journal* more conservative and a bit denser in news coverage. The *Cap Times*

bit the dust as a paid daily and reinvented itself as a twice-weekly freebie; it also produces the arts/culture/food/social life freebie *77 Square*. Its website (www.captimes.com) also has news content. You may also see a copy of *Madison Magazine* (www.madisonmagazine.com) lying around.

Neither of these really compares to the free weekly *Isthmus* (www.thedailypage.com) distributed en masse throughout the downtown on Thursday, when Madisonians dutifully trek to java shops for a scone and a folded *Isthmus* with their lattes. A civic watchdog, it's got the most energetic writing and especially kicks in entertainment and food scribblings. This is the best resource on entertainment, movies, clubbing, and other nightlife.

DID YOU SEE *THE ONION* TODAY?

First off, if you don't know what *The Onion* – gasp – is, then immediately head for www.theonion.com and check it out.

Done wiping your tears of laughter (or swallowing your indignation at the shameless humor)? OK, then, a good piece of trivia is that this famed weekly satirical newspaper – which pretty much half of those 40 and under in its satellite cities cannot live without – got its start in a cubbyhole office near the UW campus. Yup, it kinda fits. Its headquarters is now in – sheesh – New York City (we think they've gotten too big for their britches and will come crawling back), but there is still a presence here.

Every Thursday, keep an eye out for the green newspaper machines; there's yer *Onion*, with its satire and, better, fantastic arts writing, along with pretty good rundowns of local live music, eats, and more.

Websites and Internet Access

For the best all-around coverage of the city, check the *Isthmus* website: www.thedailypage .com. Even locals use their directory page on the website; if you have a question, it'll be here. Otherwise, you never know what you're gonna get from www.dane101.com, a local umbrella page of absolutely everything in the county.

Virtually all the downtown coffee shops have wireless Internet access, yet if you don't have your own laptop, you're pretty much out of luck. The **public library** (608/266-6300, www.madisonpubliclibrary.org, 9 A.M.–9 P.M. Mon.–Thurs., 9 A.M.–6 P.M. Fri., 9 A.M.–5 P.M. Sat., 1 P.M.–5 P.M. Sun., Apr.–Oct., shorter hours Nov.–Mar.) is one block west of the State Historical Society Museum on the Capitol Square and has free Internet terminals—but a small wait. Note that the library's hours change rather often.

Other Media

A delightful mélange of progressivism, half-assed professionalism, at times near-anarchy, and great music, **WORT** (89.9 FM) is a local community-sponsored station. It's the only place to hear jazz, blues, genuine alternative rock, Latin, and experimental music, along with hefty doses of community issues. There's little else like it in town, as you'll soon discover.

GETTING THERE
By Air

The **Dane County Regional Airport** (608/246-3391) has more than 100 nonstop flights daily to more than a dozen U.S. cities, though as a minor airport, Madtown at times gets bumped off some carriers' schedules. Nonstop flights are available to Atlanta, Chicago (Midway or O'Hare Airports), Cincinnati, Cleveland, Dallas/Fort Worth, Denver, Detroit, Memphis, Minneapolis, Milwaukee, Newark, and St. Louis.

City buses run to the airport. The closest bus stop is a couple of hundred yards after you walk left out the doors of the airport along International Lane.

A taxi ride from the airport to downtown costs $12 minimum.

By Bus

The local intercity **bus station** (2 S. Bedford St., 608/255-6771) is about six blocks west of the State Capitol on West Washington Avenue. The station also houses **Greyhound** (800/231-2222), offering numerous daily departures to all points; the schedule changes regularly.

The depot is also home to **Badger Bus** (www.badgerbus.com), which has up to eight daily departures to Milwaukee 7 A.M.–10:30 P.M., some via Mitchell International Airport. For a quick and cheap ($19 one-way) trip to downtown Milwaukee, this is hard to beat. Buy online for a cheaper ticket.

Badger Bus, by the way, also departs from the Memorial Union (below), but not on Sundays.

Those heading to downtown Chicago via O'Hare Field can either go in a Greyhound or, better, head for Memorial Union on campus, where the **Van Galder** bus (608/257-8983 or 800/747-0994) leaves up to eight times daily 2 A.M.–6 P.M. for O'Hare—four of these continue to downtown Chicago's Union Station and the Best Western Hotel. A one-way ticket downtown is $23, $21 to O'Hare. The Van Galder also makes stops in Janesville and Beloit.

Megabus (www.megabus.com) offers rides to Chicago (average price $26) and Minneapolis ($25 average). This formerly el cheapo option is no longer that; furthermore, there is no terminal, so you have to hop aboard far, far outside of downtown at a commuter parking lot near the interstate.

GETTING AROUND
Taxis

Three taxi services operate in Madison. The most common choice is **Badger Cab** (608/256-5566), since it operates a shared-ride (read: cheaper) service. If that's not an option, **Madison Taxi** (608/258-7458) and **Union Cab** (608/242-2000) are both fine.

MADISON

a water tour of Lake Mendota

© JEFF MARTIN

Buses

Madison buses generally run 6 A.M.–10 P.M. or 11 P.M., though this varies by line, often quite a bit. If in doubt, always head to Capitol Square, around which spins just about every bus in town.

Rental Cars

National (608/249-1614) is at the airport (as are all other major car-rental agencies); it also has satellites closer to downtown. Find **Enterprise** (608/833-3467) at half a dozen offices in town.

Organized Tours

A couple of places offer water tours of Madison lakes, including **Betty Lou Cruises** (608/246-3138, www.bettyloucruises.com, Thurs.–Sun. summers, $25–40), which has dining and sightseeing trips, including a very popular Pizza and Beer cruise.

Easier and just as fun (not to mention cheaper) are the **pontoon boat rides** from Madison School-Community Recreation (MSCR, 608/204-3027, www.mscr.com), offered on both Lakes Mendota and Monona May–late September.

VICINITY OF MADISON

Milwaukee may be surrounded by bucolic loveliness, but Madison itself is bucolic—it practically has cows and tractors inside the city. And that means go about 100 feet outside the city and you're truly in the land of Pleasantville. Indeed, it would be hard to find a state capital with a more glorious and variegated host of sights to see within a short drive.

To the east, how about a drive learning about the state's dairy industry in **Fort Atkinson** or its aboriginal history at author fave **Aztalan State Park?** Along the way, take the tiny town tour outlined below and see how downright cute the county around Madison is (and why it's perennially listed as one of the best places to live in the United States).

You can hardly go wrong heading south, itself a drift into state European settlement… and the state's dairy heritage. Learn about the history of the state's cheese-centric dairying (Swiss cheese especially) around **New Glarus** and **Monroe.** If that weren't enough, historic **Mineral Point** is a cute-as-a-button anachronism you won't soon forget.

And definitely don't miss the mighty Wisconsin River, Frank Lloyd Wright Country, and **Spring Green.**

HIGHLIGHTS

Hoard Historical Museum and Dairy Shrine: What would a visit to America's Dairyland be without a visit to this temple to the moo-cow state (page 138)?

Aztalan State Park: Lake Mills's isolated, picturesque gem is one of the state's archaeological treasures (page 139).

Octagon House: Watertown's one-of-a-kind behemoth was the site of America's first kindergarten (page 141).

Mount Horeb Mustard Museum: Ditto most of the previous, only for mustard (page 142)!

New Glarus: Here you'll find a little slice of Switzerland in America (page 145).

Mineral Point: You could be in the 1850s in the place that gave us the name "Badger" (page 151).

The Lower Wisconsin State Riverway: It doesn't get much lovelier than a drive (or canoe) along this beauty (page 154).

Spring Green: Artists live in a bucolic town synonymous with Frank Lloyd Wright and his inspiring Taliesin (page 158).

The House on the Rock: Sensory overload of equal parts kitsch and pack rat's dream comes from one man with a singular vision (page 162).

LOOK FOR **(** TO FIND RECOMMENDED SIGHTS, ACTIVITIES, DINING, AND LODGING.

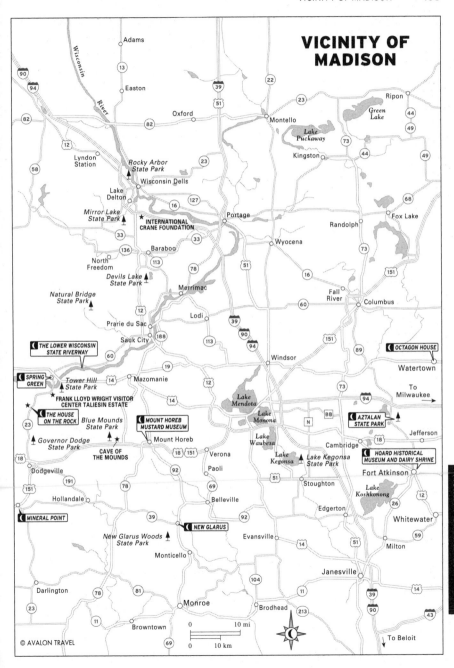

VICINITY OF MADISON

Adams
Wisconsin River
13
Easton
90
94
39
22
23
Ripon
Green Lake
44
82
Oxford
Montello
49
Lake Puckaway
12
82
49
Lyndon Station
58
302
73
Kingston
44
Rocky Arbor State Park
23
127
Fox Lake
68
Wisconsin Dells
Lake Delton
16
Mirror Lake State Park
33
INTERNATIONAL CRANE FOUNDATION
Portage
Randolph
136
Baraboo
33
North Freedom
113
78
Wyocena
73
Devils Lake State Park
Merrimac
51
16
151
Natural Bridge State Park
12
60
Fall River
Columbus
Prairie du Sac
Lodi
39
Sauk City
188
90
151
89
THE LOWER WISCONSIN STATE RIVERWAY
60
113
94
Windsor
OCTAGON HOUSE
19
73
SPRING GREEN
14
Mazomanie
12
94
To Milwaukee
Watertown
Tower Hill State Park
FRANK LLOYD WRIGHT VISITOR CENTER TALIESIN ESTATE
14
Lake Mendota
AZTALAN STATE PARK
THE HOUSE ON THE ROCK
Blue Mounds State Park
MOUNT HOREB MUSTARD MUSEUM
Lake Monona
BB
N
23
Jefferson
Governor Dodge State Park
Mount Horeb
Lake Waubesa
Cambridge
HOARD HISTORICAL MUSEUM AND DAIRY SHRINE
18
CAVE OF THE MOUNDS
18
151
Verona
Lake Kegonsa
Lake Kegonsa State Park
Fort Atkinson
Dodgeville
92
Paoli
51
Lake Koshkonong
12
151
191
78
69
Stoughton
Hollandale
Belleville
Edgerton
Whitewater
26
MINERAL POINT
39
92
59
NEW GLARUS
Evansville
14
Milton
51
New Glarus Woods State Park
Monticello
104
Janesville
14
Darlington
78
81
11
39
23
Monroe
Brodhead
90
43
11
213
To Beloit
Browntown
69
0   10 mi
0   10 km
© AVALON TRAVEL

Small Town Trips

CAMBRIDGE

A perfect day trip from Madison, Cambridge lies along U.S. 12/18 to the east. Actually a mosaic of communities around the minor resort-area nucleus of Lake Ripley, Cambridge is now mostly associated with its myriad pottery shops, antique stores, and quaint architecture. (One magazine called it the number-one small town shopping destination in the Midwest; *Midwest Living* magazine adores the place, always picking it in its Top 100 places to visit—not just the Midwest, either.) Yet the architecture is not at all cloyingly artificial—it's worth a gander. The **Cambridge Antique Mall** (608/423-9952) packs 25 dealers into a century-old church complex.

Nonbrowsers can head to the innumerable parks, including Ripley Park on the west end of Lake Ripley. Better is the **Cam-Rock Park System,** consisting of three parks with tons of trails around small ponds and lakes. The Glacial Drumlin Trail passes north and west in Deerfield.

STOUGHTON

From Cambridge take Highway B south to Highway N and follow signs to Stoughton. Towheaded Norskis dominate the landscape and ethos here—everything affixed with the word "Viking." Their mid-May hootenanny Syttende Mai celebration fetes anything and everything Norwegian, and it's a treat. Many people pass through town on their way to/from the state park to the north. Should it be you, just keep tooling along U.S. 51 till you get to their proudly refurbished **railroad depot** downtown, which is the home of their tourist information center (522 E. Main St., 888/873-7912, www.stoughtonwi.com). They have information on the historic districts in town; they will definitely point out the town's **opera house,** one of very few operating upper-floor theaters in the country. (This author personally

loves the other kind of theater in town—a cinema/café with burgers, pizza, and such—great idea, that.) Then, it's probably on to the 1858 First Universalist Church. Not enough historic structures for you? Then just head seven miles south on WI 138 to **Cooksville,** with a whole slew of 1850s buildings.

EDGERTON

This diminutive town lies about 15 minutes southeast of Stoughton via Highway N (the scenic route). Whiz through the fields surrounding Edgerton and you'd swear you were in North Carolina or eastern Virginia by the odor of tobacco on the air. Edgerton is Wisconsin's "Tobacco City," the tobacco-growing and distribution center. Thus it makes sense that the **Tobacco Heritage Days** are held here in mid-July. Interesting to note that for a few years there, apparently PC-dom had run amok (they likely thought filtering down from Madison) and the name had been changed (dropping the, er, "T" word). Well, that's been done away with and it's back to tabacky, proudly. Well, the tobacco-spitting contest has been discontinued, but that's another matter entirely.

Otherwise, you can check out Rascal's home here too in a new museum. Rascal, as in the raccoon of the eponymous classic children's book, which was written by local Sterling North, whose home (409 W. Rollin St., 608/884-7589, 1–4:30 P.M. Sun., $3) is pretty much as the family left it. Great if you're of the age to recall that wondrous book—apparently a true-ish story (he really did keep a raccoon in his room!).

You can find information about tobacco or anything else here at the local chamber of commerce (20 S. Main St., 608/884-4408, www.edgertonwisconsin.com), in yet another restored railroad depot. (Local shops may also have tobacco memorabilia.) The chamber of commerce office is adjacent to local historical society displays.

EVANSVILLE

From Edgerton, head south and west via Highways F and M to Evansville, with one of the state's largest and best-preserved examples of mid-19th century to early-20th century architecture (of all styles). Stop by the city hall for a fantastic walking tour brochure. Along the way you're most certainly going to buy something at one of the antique shops, artist galleries, and craft shops sprouting up here.

This author generally just heads to the **Real Coffee al Gusto** (18 E. Main St., 608/882-0949), a great coffeehouse with fabulous—eclectic as hell—live music offerings. You may hear Tom Waits wannabes; you may get a string quartet.

MONTICELLO

The country roads leading southwest to Monticello from Evansville are classic Wisconsin cow country (keep it slow, as there are plenty of ribbony twists out there!). Eventually you arrive in Monticello, and it's got the *de rigueur Our Town* look and feel to it, a Norman Rockwell painting come alive. The old drugstore is now a local museum, but we ain't here for historical diorama. I hope it's eating time since it's got **(The Dining Room** (209 N. Main St., 608/938-2200, 5–9:30 P.M. Wed.–Sat., $20–30), one of southern Wisconsin's finest spots for cuisine (the food, the atmosphere, and the locale). Superb.

If you need to hang your hat, check out the **Little Sugar River Farm** (Schneeberger Rd., 608/862-2212, www.littlesugarriverfarm.com, $220) for a grand retreat—a guest-farmhouse (and architecturally award-winning) on an organic farm surrounded by 2000 acres of wildlife refuge.

BELLEVILLE

More great folks, more great architecture. But I love Belleville, cuz it's sort of Area 51 North. Yup, one weird autumn in 1987 dozens of UFO sightings happened here—to cops, local rumrats, and decent citizens alike. UFO freaks descended on the place; the town made national news. But nothing since. Still, what the hell, they still have regular parties in October's **UFO Days.**

From Belleville, you could head south toward New Glarus and Monroe, or, if you're in a hurry, head back to Madison via the following stop.

Paoli

North of Belleville, you pass through some ready-made Sunday drive country and charming towns, including the quaintest of them all, Paoli. Known mostly for its somnolent waterside small-town appeal, and now, due to its renovated, grand 1864 **Paoli Mill,** it's full of shops. Next door the Artisan Gallery(6858 Paoli Rd., 608/845-6600, www.artisangal.com) is an outstanding gallery of 125 Midwest artisans working in virtually every medium.

AMERICA'S DAIRYLAND

Surprise, surprise: Dairying was not the first gear in the state's agricultural machine – wheat was. Wisconsin was a leading world wheat producer and exporter through the 1870s. Chronic pest plagues, tiring soils, financial panics, and lunatic overproduction (among others) doomed the wheat industry.

Wisconsin cheese had an inauspicious beginning, to say the least. The state's initial forays into home butter- and cheesemaking were derisively called Western Grease. Wisconsin cattle were initially hybrids of hardier species bred essentially for an ability to withstand the elements. Milk production was an extra but hardly a necessity.

THE BIRTH OF A STEREOTYPE

In the 1850s, transplanted New York farmers organized the first commercial cheesemaking factory systems. In addition, the first experiments in modern herd management and marketing were undertaken. One New Yorker, Chester Hazen, opened a cheese factory in Ladoga and in 1864, its first year, produced 200,000 pounds. Within a half decade, the state had nearly 50 factories, and in some spots the demand for milk outstripped the supply.

Immigrants followed up. Mostly Germans and Swiss populated the southern regions of the state, finding the topography reminiscent of home and the glacial till profoundly fecund (one spot of Dane County has been termed the world's richest agrarian soil).

Old World pride mixed with Yankee ingenuity created an explosion of Wisconsin dairying. The first dairy organizations were founded after the Civil War; a dairy board of trade was set up in Watertown in 1872. The state's dairies shrewdly diversified the cheesemaking and took the western markets by storm. By the 20th century, a stereotype was born: Jefferson County, Wisconsin, was home to 40,000 cows and 34,000 people.

W. D. HOARD

A seminal figure in Wisconsin's rise to dairy prominence was William D. Hoard, an otherwise unknown dabbler in lumber, hops, and publishing. In 1870, Hoard published the first issue of *The Jefferson County Union*, which became the mouthpiece for southeastern Wisconsin farmers. The only central source for disseminating information, the paper's dairy columns transmogrified into *Hoard's Dairyman*. It was the most influential act in Wisconsin's dairy industry.

Hoard had never farmed, but he pushed tirelessly for previously unheard-of progressive farm techniques. Through Hoard, farmers learned to be not so conservative, to keep records, and to compare trends. Most significantly, Hoard almost singlehandedly invented the specialized, milk-only cow. He became such a legend in the industry he was elected governor in 1889.

The University of Wisconsin followed Hoard's lead and established its College of Agriculture's experimental stations in 1883. The renowned department would invent the butterfat test, dairy courses, cold-curing processes, and winter feeding.

HOW YOU GONNA KEEP 'EM DOWN ON THE FARM?

Dairying in Wisconsin is a $19 billion industry, accounting for a tenth of the state's total economic output (and 40 percent of all agricultural jobs). It is more crucial to the state's economy than citrus is to Florida or potatoes are to Idaho.

Nearly three-tenths of all the butter and cheese in the United States is produced in Wisconsin. It produces 2.2 billion pounds of milk per year on average; that's fourth highest of any nation in the world. And as for quality, at the 2008 United States Cheese Competition, Wisconsin cheeses took 91 awards to California's 46. Ha. Wisconsin cheesemakers have won 33 percent of World Cheese Championship first prizes; California, less than 5 percent.

Look, Wisconsin is the only state to require a master's license to make cheese! (Others point out that 90 percent of state milk is used for cheese and small herds on family farms raised stress free – on good soil – will produce quality milk.)

Wisconsin has 26.4 percent of the U.S. cheese market today, at 2.4 billion pounds annually, while California has 23.4 percent (experts had predicted California would eclipse Wisconsin by 2005, but as of 2008 the gap has actually grown, with Wisconsin still putting out 30 million pounds more). Wisconsin keeps its lead in specialty cheeses, which is Wisconsin's main cheese industry today. It leads in every cheese type except mozzarella. Wisconsin has 650 varietals, California less than half of that.

And yet, things have been far from easy.

In 1993, the unspeakable occurred: California edged ahead of Wisconsin in whole-milk output – egads. California's dairy output is now hovering around 10 percent more per annum than Wisconsin's. Further, Wisconsin has seen its family dairy farm numbers dwindle from post-WWII figures approximating 150,000 to 17,500 in 2005; at one grim point the state lost an average of 1,000 dairy farms annually. This hurts when 99 percent of your farms are family owned. Apparently, "America's Dairyland" is a title under siege.

Badger State politicians on Capitol Hill blame the dairy problems on outdated – nay, absurd politically uneconomic insanity – federal milk-pricing guidelines, which pay other states higher rates than Upper Midwest farmers. Eau Claire, Wisconsin, is the nucleus; the

farther you get from that point, the higher the price – up to $3 more per 100 pounds (milk paying a farmer $1.04 per 100 pounds in Wisconsin fetches a South Florida farmer $4.18!). Wisconsin farmers even resurrected "milk strikes," dumping milk in protest. In 2004, six states sued California for forcing out-of-staters to sell in the state at a deflated price. No dice – in fact, recent legislation has even strengthened the system and solidified regulations favoring corporate farms.

Not to be completely apocalyptic, Wisconsin, though in a decline, is in little danger of completely losing its cultural underpinnings of rural Americana. Supplying so much of the cheese in the United States still equals a huge market – and predicted U.S. cheese consumption rises will help. And Badger farmers are finding ways to stem the wave of disappearing farms. One innovative program involves rural villages' banding together, pooling resources, and buying family farms to keep them operational. In 2005 (and right through 2007) the numbers of cows in the state actually rose for the first time in decades.

Economists also say that California's cheese industry is dangerously tied to the stock market, since many of its consumers are Double Income No Kids types – every time the stock markets hiccup, California's markets quake, but not Wisconsin's. (Wisconsin's have been around for more than a century.) California cheesemakers, also, are mostly huge factory operations, as opposed to small family operations in Wisconsin. Seventy-five percent of Wisconsin cheesemakers grew up in an operation in which a grandparent had worked in the industry; only 20 percent of California's cheesemakers can say that.

One thing Wisconsin will never have to worry about is water – something that California agriculture constantly has to face, and projections paint a fairly dire picture for enormous farm operations in the Golden State.

And don't forget about that quality issue.

Thus, it may not be able to compete in whole numbers, but on a per capita basis, Wisconsin is still America's Dairyland.

© THOMAS HUHTI

This is your Wisconsin countryside!

Highway of Wisconsin History (WI 26)

The name, Highway of Wisconsin, is not official, just what it truly is to this author. Running north-south, WI 26 roughly bisects the Madison and Milwaukee areas nicely. Along its length is a fascinating mélange of the region's history: Underground Railroad tunnels in **Milton;** the *complete* history of Wisconsin dairying at **Hoard's Dairy Shrine** in Fort Atkinson; burial mounds of some of the state's first (mysterious) residents at **Aztalan State Park** near Lake Mills; and one of the coolest architectural (and historical) sights in the state: Watertown's **Octagon House.**

MILTON

About a half hour southeast of Madison, just off I-90, is flyspeck Milton. At the junction of WI 26 and WI 59 is the **Milton House Museum** (608/868-7772, 10 A.M.–4 P.M. daily Memorial Day weekend–Labor Day, weekends only spring and fall, $6 adults), a 20-room hexagonal erstwhile stagecoach inn once used as part of the Underground Railroad—the stone and earth tunnels still lie beneath it. It was also purportedly the first building made from poured grout "concrete" in the United States. Also on the grounds is an 1837 log cabin (the terminus of the subterranean tunnel) and plenty of 19th-century artifacts.

Milton College, which predated statehood by five decades, shut its doors in 1982, but today the campus supports an antique haven, specialty shops, and the **Main Hall Museum,** detailing the college's and community's history.

FORT ATKINSON

Bisected by the Rock River, which flows sluggishly south and west of town into Lake Koshkonong, Fort Atkinson is a trim slice of Americana. It's been called by *Money* magazine one of the "hottest" small towns in the country in which to live.

The city was born when General Henry Atkinson and his men hastily assembled a rough stockade and crude cabins at the confluence of the Rock and Bark Rivers while pursuing the Sauk Indians in the 1832 Black Hawk War. Dairying truly put the town on the map. William Dempster Hoard, the sort of patron saint of Wisconsin's dairy industry, began *Hoard's Dairyman,* a newsletter-cum-magazine, here in 1873.

◖ Hoard Historical Museum and Dairy Shrine

No visit to America's Dairyland would be complete without a look-see at the Hoard Historical Museum (407 Merchants Ave., 920/563-7769, 9:30 A.M.–4:30 P.M. Tues.–Sat. and 11 A.M.–3 P.M. Sun. June–Labor Day, shorter hours the rest of the year, free), housed in W. D. Hoard's family home, a Gothic revival/mission oak–style mansion. The museum displays a restoration of the Dwight Foster House—the area's first frame house, built in 1841—along with two rooms of exhibits, the anchors of which are an extensive, 15,000-piece Native American artifact collection—so extensive the Smithsonian once eyed it—and a wealth of information on the Black Hawk War. Even Abe Lincoln, who traveled through the county in 1832 with the militia chasing Black Hawk, gets a nod.

The museum is also the site of the **Dairy Shrine,** an assemblage of audiovisual displays, dioramas, and artifacts tracing the history of Wisconsin dairying.

The Fireside

Get your Broadway-style musicals and international revues as well as a copious dinner in a 650-seat in-the-round theater (920/563-9505, www.firesidetheater.com). The gift "shoppes" are as large as some grocery stores. Nine performances, including some matinees, generally run Wednesday–Sunday.

Lake Koshkonong

The second-largest lake in Wisconsin, Lake Koshkonong is fed by the Rock River. The lake's entire circumference is lined with restaurants, inns, resorts, and marinas. For a small village town, Newville's got a lot of action, especially in the way of restaurants and pubs. You'll also find county parks with trails bypassing effigy mounds, covered bridges on bike trails, and canoe rentals.

Accommodations and Food

How about laying your head in a 1928 barn? **La Grange B&B** (1050 East St., 920/563-1421, www.1928barn.com, $75–89) sits in a wooded copse; the French country–themed rooms have shared or private baths.

The town has a couple of nearly-chic eateries that have opened, but you simply must head to the ◖ **Café Carpe** (18 S. Water St., 920/563-9391, www.cafecarpe.com, $4–12), one of the best eateries in the state. The food is a carefree, delicious blend of Midwestern diner and downscale café. But "the Carp" is even more famous as Wisconsin's best venue for folk music. Low-key and friendly, this is one place you'll revisit. Hours vary—but it stays open late!

Information

The **Fort Atkinson Chamber of Commerce** (89 Main St., 920/563-3210 or 888/733-3678, www.fortchamber.com) is open regular business hours.

Side Trip: Jefferson

The next town north of Fort Atkinson (via WI 26) is Jefferson, worth a visit for natural beauty. The **Jefferson Marsh Wildlife and Natural Area,** east of Jefferson via Highway Y, is a 3,129-acre tamarack preserve—the state's largest—and a sanctuary for endangered egrets. It's even got effigy mounds.

◖ AZTALAN STATE PARK

Aztalan State Park, a skip off the interstate, is completely overlooked by 99 percent of passing travelers. Or, for the moment it is. The state has plans to upgrade facilities, reclaim surrounding farmland, add a chic new visitors center, and increase attendance by 700 percent. Visit while it's still an isolated gem.

Surrounded by agrarian stretches, the park

© THOMAS HUHTI

burial mounds near Lake Mills, Aztalan State Park

feels eerily historic; the Rock River rolls by silently, and the only sound audible is the wind shuffling through the leaves of the corn. One of the largest and most carefully researched archaeological sites in Wisconsin, Aztalan covers almost 175 acres and features remnant stockades and hiking trails snaking in and around the large burial mounds. Scientists theorize that this spot was a strategic northern endpoint of a Middle Mississippian culture, whose influence stretched south to New Orleans and into Mexico. If the solitary—if not lonely—park superintendent is around, you may get an impromptu tour.

Lake Mills is an engaging classic small Victorian town nearby. Encircling a central park, it has wide tree-lined avenues, mansions, and droopy willow trees. Visitors can enjoy Lake Mills' free Bartles Beach or, for a fee, Sandy Beach, on the other side of Rock Lake. (An aside: There are those who believe—this is no joke, universities have sent research teams—that there are pyramids beneath the black surface of Rock Lake. Apparently, these structures were produced by copper-mining expeditions from Asia and Europe several thousand years ago. Why they would halt mining and create pyramids hasn't been explained.) The less leisure-minded should head to the junction of WI 89 and Highway A, a node for the **Glacial Drumlin Trail,** a 47-mile multipurpose recreation trail spanning from Waukesha to Cottage Grove east of Madison. The Lake Mills segment may be the most picturesque along the entire trail, with an old depot and trestle at the trailhead not far from Rock Lake. There's also a good wildlife area south of Lake Mills.

Cuisine-wise, the community arguably has the best burgers in the state—butter-filled little heart-attack patties called **sliders** served all summer by the American Legion.

WATERTOWN

Watertown justifies its name: It lies at the bifurcation of the Rock River as it wends through an oxbow bend in the valley. Yankee settlers appeared as early as 1836 and harnessed the

© THOMAS HUHTI

The largest antebellum octagon house in the Midwest is in Watertown.

channel's water power—it drops 20 feet on its course through town for grist and flour mills, some of which still stand.

Historically, besides water power, Watertown was known for geese and Germans. Watertown goose livers were the top of the pâté de foie gras line. The city exported up to 25 tons of the rich organ to eastern markets annually. (Watertown perfected the art of "noodling"—force-feeding the geese with noodles to fatten them up.) The local high school's team nickname is the Goslings—not exactly ferocious, but at least historically relevant.

Until quite recently, the town's name was rendered Wasserstadt on a few business signs, a remnant of the heavy immigration of enlightened freethinkers fleeing political and social persecution in 1848 Germany. Most notable was Carl Schurz, a political reformer who arrived in Watertown in 1855 and eventually left his mark on U.S. politics. His wife put the town on the map, though, in contemporary terms; hers was the first kindergarten in the United States, which continues to be one of the city's primary tourist draws. At a critical transportation point in southern Wisconsin, Watertown was rumored at one time to be on the short list for state capital relocation.

And it warrants mention simply because it is the hometown of a certain travel author . . .

C Octagon House

This house (919 Charles St., 920/261-2796) may be the most impressive in the state. It is certainly the largest pre–Civil War family residence in the Midwest, with more than 8,000 square feet of floor space and 57 rooms (although only one fireplace!). Built during the course of 13 years by John Richards—who owned three mills on the river below the vertiginous hill upon which the house sits—the house sports one of the nation's only cantilevered spiral staircases, a basswood and cherry marvel that pirouettes 40 feet to the upper levels. This baby was so well built that reportedly

not one of the stairs on the staircases creaks! Behind the house on the large grounds is the nation's first kindergarten, and nearby is a restored late-19th-century barn housing an array of agricultural implements. Octagon House hosts activities throughout the year and sits on the best sledding hill (though it's officially not allowed) in the county. The house is open May–October, with docent-led tours 10 A.M.–4 P.M. daily; before Memorial Day and after Labor Day, hours are 11 A.M.–3 P.M. Admission is $7 adults.

Practicalities

Nothing at all to mention lodging-wise (go south eight miles on WI 26 to I-94—tons of chains).

The C **Upper Krust** (1300 Memorial Dr., 920/206-9202, 6 A.M.–9 P.M. Mon.–Sat., 9 A.M.–1:30 P.M. Sun., $3–8) is a creative breakfast/sandwich/hot plate kind of place, but it's absolutely famed for its killer pies. You can't get near this place at lunch; it's so popular that traveling businesspeople will phone a day ahead to reserve pies and then take away a dozen at a time!

The building housing **Elias Inn** (200 N. 2nd St., 920/261-6262, 5–10 P.M. Mon.–Thurs., 4–10:30 P.M. Fri., 5–10 P.M. Sat., from $6) has come a long way from the days when it was a German-style *bierstube*. Farmers coming into town to do their banking on Friday would stop off to quaff a brackish tap in a cloudy glass while suit-and-tie types from the bank munched head cheese or homemade venison sausage. Its present incarnation is a delicious amalgam of straight-up supper club with hints of Midwestern regional cuisine—all in a real-deal rustic interior. Outstanding fish fries.

C **Mullen's** (212 W. Main St., 920/261-4278) is a southeastern Wisconsin landmark. Well into its sixth decade, it's got the best homemade ice cream you'll ever taste and a red-and-white-checked interior reminiscent of bygone times.

The Trollway

Essentially a cobbling together with lots of ancient Indian trails south of the Wisconsin River, the historic Old Military Road, the first overland link east to west in the state, constructed in 1835–1836 by soldier labor, used to stretch as far as Prairie du Chien. Today, you're as likely to see bicyclists along the route as you are cud-chewing bovines on the Fitchburg-Dodgeville Military Ridge State Trail. Our route takes us just as far as "The Trollway," and you'll know why when you see all the Norwegian flags in these parts.

MOUNT HOREB

The "Trollway," as the main drag in predominantly Norwegian Mount Horeb is known, is reminiscent of a northern European mountain village. Predating statehood, Norwegian and Swiss (and a few Irish) farmers staked out the rolling ridges and valleys around these parts, and the whole area boasts a thoroughly northern European brick-and-frame architecture and not a few log structures and octagonal barns.

Mustard mania in Mount Horeb!

© YUKI TAKANO

◖ Mount Horeb Mustard Museum

This town may sport Pippi Longstocking–esque architecture, but it's also fast becoming known as the place where "mustard happens." At the not-nearly-famous-enough **Mount Horeb Mustard Museum** (109 E. Trollway, 608/437-3986, www. mustardmuseum.com, 10 A.M.–5 P.M. daily, free), you're greeted at the door by cheery, delightfully irreverent hosts, their lapels exclaiming, "Just let us know if you need any condiment therapy." And all this because of one of those accursed, classic Boston Red Sox September Swoons—Bill Buckner's infamous boot of that World Series Game 6 groundball, snatching defeat from the jaws of victory for the hapless Bosox. Barry Levenson, a lawyer before that moment, became an apostate to the game. In a scene from a twisted *Field of Dreams,* Barry wandered into a late-night grocery store where the mustard jars were heard to say, "If you collect us, they will come." So he decamped to a small town

in southwestern Wisconsin and opened this eccentric museum featuring the underappreciated spice. What better place to open a mustard museum than a state where bratwurst is king? All kidding aside, this is a serious place, with more than 2,000 mustards on display. It's also the world's largest mustard retailer—400 to buy and 100 to sample. Ladysmith, Wisconsin's own Royal Bohemian Triple Extra Hot Horseradish Mustard is the hottest. The museum has even sponsored National Mustard Day, heretofore known as August 5. One of the most enjoyable stops in southwestern Wisconsin, the Mustard Museum is a must-see.

Note: At the time of this writing, the Mount Horeb Mustard Museum signed a deal to move to the west side of Madison (Middleton Antiques Mall, 1819 Parmenter Street, Middleton), target date October, 2009. Be sure to check the museum's website for its current location.

Other Sights

The **Mount Horeb Area Historical Museum** (Main and 2nd, 608/437-6486, noon–5 P.M. Fri.–Sun., Memorial Day weekend–Labor Day, free) is housed in the old municipal building. This 1918 home features a dozen rooms—more than 4,000 square feet!—that regularly change themes.

Bust-the-wallet-wise, there are more Scandinavian gift huts than trolls in this town.

All you need is at www.trollway.com.

Practicalities

The **Karakahl Inn** (1405 U.S. 18/151, 608/437-5545, www.karakahl.com, $70) is not your average motel. The buildings were designed as a retreat for patients of famed chiropractor Clarence Gonstead. Shaped like a fierce Viking ship, it supposedly follows the dictums of Frank Lloyd Wright.

Actually attached to Clarence Gonstead's original home (read, estate) is the **Gonstead Cottage** (602 S. 2nd St., 608/437-4374, $125 peak rate). It says cottage, but you should think "guest house in prairie school style," and nothing else like it exists for an overnight in the region!

Housed in an old cheese factory, the **Grumpy Troll Brewpub** (608/437-2739, $6–14) is pretty much the perfect spot to unwind after you've just ridden 25 miles on a bike! It sports a dazzling variety of seasonal beers.

Very new to the downtown is what has been described as "upscale tapas" at **Bistro 101** (101 E. Main St., 608/437-9463, 10 A.M.–11 P.M. Thurs.–Sat., till 9 P.M. Wed.–Thurs., till 5 P.M. Sun.–Mon.), with great photos of historic Mount Horeb a nice touch to the global food.

Yet for something special, drive north to Mazomanie (via Hwy. F and U.S. 14), a town that's been gentrifying itself to turn-of-the-century quaintness of late (a few national magazines have featured it as one of the "Quaintest Towns"—or whatever term they use—in the United States. Galleries and shops are springing up and for a town this size, it's got great dining options. At the **C Old Feed Mill** (114 Hwyamer St., 608/795-4909, $11–25), the eclectic heartland fare is luscious, true enough, but the exquisitely well-renovated 1857 mill and period detailing are equally fine—garnering nods from the state's historical society. Lunch and dinner are served Tuesday–Saturday, with a great Sunday brunch added to an evening supper.

BLUE MOUNDS AREA

Three short miles west of Mount Horeb, the town, centered between three highlights on the Old Military Road, began as a tiny mining encampment and an ungodly amount of lead was extracted from its grounds.

Nissedahle

Transliterated, roughly, as "Valley of the Elves" (actually "Nissedahle," but better known as "Little Norway") and tucked into the rain-shadow edge of big Blue Mound next to a bubbly spring, this outdoor living museum (608/437-8211, www.littlenorway.com, 9 A.M.–7 P.M. daily July–Aug., 9 A.M.–5 P.M. May–June and Sept.–Oct., $10 adults) features more than a dozen log buildings from a Norwegian homestead. You can't miss a gorgeous triumvirate of cupolas. The massive Norway Building, a replica of a 12th-century Norway *stavkirke*, or stave church, is replete with Cathay-esque steeples and dragon heads. The interiors of the buildings house what is arguably the most exhaustive display

Norway Building, Nissedahle

of Norwegian-American culture in the United States, including the original manuscript of an Edvard Grieg musical composition and, of course, intricate rosemaling.

Blue Mound State Park

Penning notes of his Wisconsin River explorations in 1776; Jonathan Carver detailed extensively the "mountains" due south of the river. The highest point in southern Wisconsin at 1,719 feet above sea level, the salient upthrust—which can indeed seem a steely blue—doesn't exactly spur migratory peregrinations, but it's rumored to hold Native treasure.

Note the singular Blue Mound park and the plural Blue Mounds town; no historical mistake, there are in fact two mounds—the shorter eastern twin is now Brigham County Park in Dane County. Both are multilayered candy drops of geology.

The Winnebago called it "High Place with Beautiful View" and used it as a landmark on their journeys to today's Lake Mendota in Madison. The U.S. military appropriated the footpath for a section of a military road.

One of the extras at this park is a real swimming pool. For the more ambitious, a number of trails wind throughout the area. Mountain bikers actually have a trail just for themselves, unsurprising as this is in close proximity to the Military Ridge State Trail.

Cave of the Mounds

Cave of the Mounds (608/437-3038) is yet another residual of the eons-old limestone cementation process; another cave, Lost River Cave, exists near Blue Mound State Park.

Oddly, though the area above the subterranean caverns was settled, mined, plowed, and grazed starting as far back as 1828 (making the homestead the oldest in the county), these caves weren't discovered until 1939. It took until the 1980s for geologists of the U.S. Department of the Interior to declare it a National Natural Landmark. It's better known as the "jewel box" of large caverns, neither as large nor as famous as others, but, as the Chicago Academy of Sciences called it, "the significant cave of the upper Midwest."

The farm grounds up top, with a few assorted gardens, also make for great walking and picnicking!

An annual event is the performance of the *Song of Norway,* a romantic musical tracing the life of Norwegian composer Edvard Grieg.

The caverns are open mid-March–mid-November, daily 9 A.M.–6 P.M. summers, less and less toward winter. Admission is $10.

Green County

Green County, south and west of Madison, might as well be called "Little Switzerland." The Swiss culture shows itself most prominently in New Glarus, an amazing alpineesque village. In Monroe, farther south, world-famous swiss cheese comes thanks to a substrata of limestone soil, allowing a certain digestive process by which cows produce creamy gold.

In the '30s, Monroe cheesemaking had grown so prodigious that a postmaster in Iowa grew weary of the waftings of ripe Monroe limburger passing through his tiny post office.

The Depression-era WPA guide captured the moment:

> Cheese was stoutly defended when Monroe's postmaster engaged in a sniffing duel with a postmaster in Iowa to determine whether or not the odor of Limburger in transit was a fragrance or a stench. Well publicized by the press of the Nation, the duel ended when a decision was reached which held that Limburger merely exercised its constitutional right to hold its own against all comers.

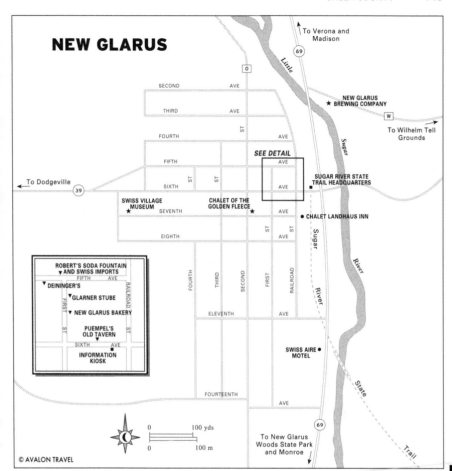

NEW GLARUS

To Verona and Madison

69

0

SECOND AVE

THIRD AVE

ST

FOURTH AVE

SEE DETAIL

FIFTH AVE

To Dodgeville

39

SIXTH AVE

SWISS VILLAGE MUSEUM

SEVENTH

CHALET OF THE GOLDEN FLEECE

EIGHTH AVE

NEW GLARUS BREWING COMPANY

W

To Wilhelm Tell Grounds

Sugar

SUGAR RIVER STATE TRAIL HEADQUARTERS

CHALET LANDHAUS INN

Sugar

River

ROBERT'S SODA FOUNTAIN AND SWISS IMPORTS

FIFTH AVE

RAILROAD

DEININGER'S

FIRST

GLARNER STUBE

NEW GLARUS BAKERY

ST

ST

PUEMPEL'S OLD TAVERN

SIXTH AVE

INFORMATION KIOSK

FOURTH

THIRD

SECOND

FIRST

RAILROAD

River

ELEVENTH AVE

ST

SWISS AIRE MOTEL

State

FOURTEENTH AVE

0   100 yds

0   100 m

69

To New Glarus Woods State Park and Monroe

Trail

© AVALON TRAVEL

NEW GLARUS

In 1845, a group of 190 Swiss left the Canton of Glarus during an economically devastating period. Scouts dispatched earlier had quite literally stumbled into southwestern Wisconsin and marveled at its similarities to Switzerland—nestled in the crook of a short but steep valley. Only 100 made it this far. After toughing out a rough winter, the Swiss farmers attempted to grow wheat, but they were unaccustomed to growing the grain and, returning to dairy, they soon began to pique interest in the east for their trademark cheeses.

Full of white-and-brown architecture, umlauts, and scrolled Swiss-German sayings, gift shops every 10 feet, a Swiss festival that seems biweekly, and Swiss music piped throughout the village—sounds dangerously close to tacky tourist trap. Fear not—it's done with class.

So classy, in fact, that the Swiss ambassador a handful of years ago dropped off a $4 million check for the establishment in New Glarus of a North American Swiss Heritage Center.

Incidentally, from New Glarus, you can either continue south to Monroe the straight shot or, take a detour via **Monticello.**

Sights

One word can fully encapsulate this town: festivals. Celebratory shindigs feting the Swiss heritage are held continually. The big draw is the **Wilhelm Tell Pageant,** held on Labor Day since 1938. Virtually the whole town puts on the lederhosen—half of the town in the grandiloquent play of Swiss independence that nobody in the other half can understand but enjoys nonetheless. The real Independence Day, or **Volksfest,** is celebrated with another festival, this one on the first Sunday in August. Swiss consular officials and other dignitaries often make happy appearances. June features a first-week **Polkafest,** a real hoot; and another popular drama during the **Heidi Festival,** on the last full weekend of the month. And, of course, an obligatory **Oktoberfest** goes down in early October. Most of the festivals feature oddities such as Swiss flag throwing (don't ask), yodeling (of course), *thalerschwingen* (let the locals tell you), or any combination of the above.

Up the hillsides you'll find 13 buildings comprising the **Swiss Village Museum** (612 7th Ave., 608/527-2317, 9 A.M.–4:30 P.M. daily May–Nov., $7 adults), centered around flower gardens and an educational exhibit detailing the Swiss immigrant movement to New Glarus; all have period demonstrations. Local schoolchildren sometimes attend class in the old schoolhouse. A display on the Glarner industries of Sap Sago cheese, slate, and fabrics was donated from Glarus, Switzerland.

The **Chalet of the Golden Fleece** (618 2nd St., 608/527-6838) is a Bernese mountain-style chalet built in 1938 by the founder of the village's Wilhelm Tell tradition. Three creakingly full floors have a huge assortment of immigrant everything-but-the-kitchen-sink—artifacts such as Gregorian chants written on parchment from the 15th century, Etruscan earrings, and a host of folk art. Problem is, it's open only for group tours.

New Glarus has, in this, my humble opinion, the best of the state's small-town breweries, the eponymous **New Glarus Brewing Company** (Hwy. W at WI 69, 608/527-5850, www.newglarusbrewing.com, tours and tastings 10 A.M.–4 P.M.). The *braumeister,* trained in Europe, reaps accolades and ribbons at every World Beer Championship. Do stop by the brewery for its tasting room and views of the brewery process; self-guided tours (free, but $4.50 for the tasting room) leave daily.

Once a dense wood impeding travel to and from Milwaukee, **New Glarus Woods State Park** (608/527-2335) has arguably the best state park campsites (some bike-in!) in this part of Wisconsin. The 11 hiking miles are excellent, through dense woods or deep valleys. This the western endpoint of the **Sugar River State Trail,** a 23-mile path from New Glarus to Brodhead along the Sugar River ravine. (In Monticello it will link up to the Badger State Trail.) The whole shooting match is part of the Ice Age National Scenic Trail. In Brodhead, lots of secondary trails branch off, including one to the popular "Half-Way Tree"—a spot used as a landmark by the Winnebago, who knew this point was equidistant between the Mississippi River and Lake Michigan. Bicycles are available for rent at the refurbished New Glarus depot, the trail headquarters.

Off Highway H on the way to Blanchardville is a gorgeous official state **Rustic Road,** great for a Saturday drive.

Should you wish to get some non-Swiss history, continue to Blanchardville, once a Mormon settlement called Zaramhemba or "City of God." (The Latter-day Saints had fled Illinois after the killing of Joseph Smith.) The only things left are the gravestones in the cemetery at the Highway F and WI 78 junction.

Accommodations

The cheapest lodging in New Glarus is the **Swiss-Aire Motel** (WI 69 S, 608/527-2138 or 800/798-4391, www.swissaire.com, $67), a basic but very good motel with a heated pool and continental breakfast—right on the Sugar River Trail.

The **Chalet Landhaus** (801 WI 69, 608/527-5234 or 800/944-1716, www.chaletlandhaus

.com, $110) is built in rustic, traditional Swiss style. The main room features a bent staircase, Swiss detailing, and a fireplace. Rooms have balconies strewn with geraniums, and there are a few suites available with whirlpools.

You'll find loads of quaint farmhouse B&Bs and cottages in the surrounding countryside; the village's website has 'em all, with pictures.

Food

The eateries listed offer any number of Swiss cuisine items. One unique drink is *rivela,* a malted, milky, alcohol-free, sweet sports drink of sorts popular in Switzerland.

Ruef's Meat Market (538 1st St., 608/527-2554, www.ruefsmeatmarket.com) offers real-deal Swiss. Ruef's smokes its own meats and makes *kalberwurst* and *landjaegers.* The best for cheese variety might be **Prima Kase** (W6117 Hwy C, Monticello, 608/938-4227), a cheesemaker just 10 minutes away in Monticello and the United States' only maker of wheel and sweet swiss cheese.

For delectable Swiss-style baked goods, the (**New Glarus Bakery and Tea Room** (534 1st St., 608/527-2916, 7 A.M.–5 P.M. Tues.–Sat., 9 A.M.–4 P.M. Sun., $2–6) is the only stop necessary. The Swiss-trained bakers turn out the house specialty, "Alpenbread," but you might also find stollen, a dense, *two-pound* bread concoction of raisins, spices, marzipan, and almonds, often served at the end of meals or as the centerpiece at brunches. The tea room is a nice touch.

Along the main drag, **Glarner Stube** (518 1st St., 608/527-2216, lunch and dinner Tues.–Sun., $13–22), on a restaurant site dating from 1901, specializes in fondue (cheese cooked in wine), and *Genschnitzelettes* (tender veal sautéed in white wine sauce). This place is immensely popular and no reservations are taken—so get there early.

(**Deininger's** (119 5th Ave., 608/527-2012, 11 A.M.–2:30 P.M. and 5–7:30 P.M. weekdays, 5–8:30 P.M. weekends, shorter hours in winter, $10–22) was opened by an Alsace-trained chef and his German wife, both groomed in Chicago eateries. An outstanding restaurant

with continental-Swiss-German heavy fare, it's standing-room only on weekends.

For a cool-off after the Sugar River Trail, stop by the **soda fountain** at Roberts' European Imports (608/527-2417, www.shop-swiss.com), which also has some soups and homemade cookies.

The requisite watering hole in New Glarus is a classic 1893 tavern, **Puempel's Old Tavern** (608/527-2045, www.puempels.com). This is the real thing, with the original back bar, dark woods, high ceilings, and the real draw—patriotic folk-art murals painted in 1913 by Andrea Hofer.

Information and Services

The exceedingly tiny New Glarus **information kiosk** is open and run by the New Glarus chamber of commerce (608/527-2095 or 800/527-6838, www.swisstown.com).

MONROE

Swiss settlers in these parts took cheesemaking from a home industry to a little gold mine just before the crack in the state's wheat industry. Fabulous timing: By the 1880s, about 75 area cheese factories were producing swiss, limburger, gruyere, and other of the more odoriferous varieties of cheese.

How serious is cheese in Monroe? Besides "Swiss Cheese Capital of America" everywhere, the biannual Cheese Days draw in more than 100,000 people for equal parts revelry, education, and respect. Monroe has one of the country's only limburger cheese factories, and the only swiss and gruyere cheese factory still using traditional copper vats is in Monroe. Appropriately, the local high school nickname is the "Cheesemakers"—how's a Monroe Cheesemakers sweatshirt for an ineffably kitschy souvenir?

Beyond this, an official from the National Trust for Historic Preservations once said it best: "If you put up a fence around Monroe, you could charge admission to get in."

Note: Listen to the **Swiss Program,** still heard on local radio station WEKZ 1260 AM, around 1 P.M. Monday–Saturday.

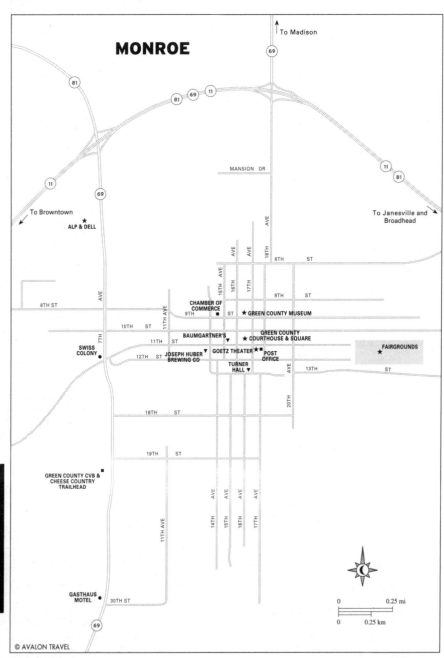

MONROE

To Madison

To Browntown

★ ALP & DELL

To Janesville and Broadhead

MANSION DR

CHAMBER OF COMMERCE
★ GREEN COUNTY MUSEUM

BAUMGARTNER'S
★ GREEN COUNTY COURTHOUSE & SQUARE

SWISS COLONY

GOETZ THEATER ★★ POST OFFICE

JOSEPH HUBER BREWING CO

TURNER HALL ▼

FAIRGROUNDS

GREEN COUNTY CVB & CHEESE COUNTRY TRAILHEAD

GASTHAUS MOTEL

30TH ST

0   0.25 mi

0   0.25 km

© AVALON TRAVEL

Sights

The nucleus of town is the stately, almost baroque **Green County Courthouse,** with a quad-faced clock on the Yankee-style square. The architecture of Monroe displays an intriguing blend of subtle Swiss, common worker bungalow, and gingerbread Victorian, plus the odd octagon house or two. The polished-up 1930s **Goetz Theater** is grand—note the hand-carved reindeer and hammered copper. Free **walking-tour** brochures are available from the Monroe Chamber of Commerce.

The countryside no longer reeks of cheese, but close. No maker receives more attention than **Alp and Dell** (657 2nd St., 608/328-3355 or 800/257-3335). Carpeted walkways with large viewing windows overlook the famed copper vats, this being the only remaining cheese factory still using traditional copper. Open business hours, but it recommends arriving between 9 A.M. and 1 P.M. for optimal cheese-viewing. An aside: Diminutive operation **Franklin Cheese** (7256 Franklin, 608/325-3725, daily except Sun.) is one of the few remaining cooperatives in the United States and still offers tours if you ring 'em up first.

Indescribably pleased was this author upon hearing that tours were finally being offered (damn those insurance companies) at the brewery of the college student's staple beer—eminently rich and tasty yet respectfully undervalued Huber. Its maker, **Minhas Craft Brewery** (1208 14th Ave., 608/325-3191, www.huberbrewery.com), is the oldest continually operating brewery in Wisconsin (and second-longest in the United States). (Actually, the name for more than a century was Joseph Huber Company, and that's still the only way you'll hear it described—just take a look at the website name!) Tours ($10) are offered at 1 P.M. Friday and Saturday, with an additional Saturday tour at 3 P.M., but call ahead.

Starting in Monroe, the **Cheese Country Recreational Trail** rides 47 miles of railroad bed. The multipurpose trail parallels the Pecatonica River and touches the edge of Cadiz Springs State Park and its two lakes. A historic 440-foot skeletal bridge is just west of Browntown; the remainder of the trail, passing through Browntown, South Wayne, Gratiot, Darlington, and Calamine, and finishing in Mineral Point, has an additional 55 or so overpasses. Darlington has refurbished its depot into a historic museum. Gorgeous sections of this trail pass through native grass prairie and magnificent stands of oak. Bikers should be cautioned that sandy spots plague the trail. In Calamine, the trail links up with the **Pecatonica River State Trail,** which itself runs across the Bonner Branch Valley fork of the Pecatonica and leads to an additional 200 miles of trails. A hefty $6 trail fee is assessed.

See rare (today) Old World alpine Swiss cabinetry and folk painting at the studio of **Gottlieb Brandli and Janeen Joy** (508 17th Ave., 608/325-6681, 8 A.M.–6 P.M. weekdays, Sat. by appointment). Gottlieb, a former *Bauernmalerei,* or Swiss-German folk artist immigrant, has lectured on the stylistics of Alpine design at the Smithsonian. Their custom design work can be viewed at the shop, or drive up to New Glarus to see more of it.

West of Monroe, **Argyle** is a lovely little community on the Pecatonica River. Check out the old gristmill on the river and then head for the old Partridge Hall/Star Theatre and gaze at the lovely trim work (it's a restaurant, so perhaps have a bite to eat). Argyle was the boyhood home of Fightin' Bob La Follette, a legendary Badger progressive politico, and local communities are pitching in to preserve and restore his family's home.

Entertainment and Events

Cheese Days, held the third weekend of September *of even-numbered years,* has feted "Cheese Country" since 1914 with celebratory fairs, Swiss musicians, fun runs, a street dance, a carnival, exhibitions, an absolutely enormous cheese-flavored parade, and tons and tons of swiss and limburger (including a 200-pound wheel produced on the square over the weekend).

Accommodations

Cheap and good is the **Gasthaus Motel** (685

WI 69 S, 608/328-8395, www.gasthausmotel .com, $40–50 s or d), a well-spruced little place with a bonus of bike rentals.

But for biking, you can't do better than the  **Earth Rider Cycling Boutique and Hotel** (920 W. Exchange St., 866/245-5276, www .earthridercycling.com, $90–95) in Brodhead, east of Monroe via WI 11. It's a full-service bike shop; better, it's got a handful of comfy Tour de France–themed rooms, as well as house pet Sprocket, the cutest little mischievous pooch in the region!

West of town, **Inn Serendipity** (7843 Hwy. P, 608/329-7056, www.innserendipity .com, $105–125) is in a heavenly, bucolic location, but it's so much more. The innkeepers—corporate refugees from Chicago—show us all what could be done. It's an admirable exercise in purely sustainable living—100 percent powered by renewable sources, organic gardens (their greenhouse even has papayas year-round!), and on and on (it's won virtually every accolade available for their efforts). It's simply a pure escape.

The nearest last-chance public campground would be **New Glarus Woods State Park** back up in New Glarus, or Yellowstone Lake to the northwest.

Food

A prerequisite while in Monroe is the local delicacy, the swiss cheese sandwich, at **Baumgartner's** (608/325-6157), a southwestern Wisconsin institution since 1931. It's a cheese shop and locally favorite tavern, though you'd hardly know the supersized cheese operation when waltzing in the front door. Through the swinging saloon doors you'll enter a six-decade-old Shangri-La of small-town life—a long polished bar, wooden-flat ceiling, horn racks, and mural-maps of Wisconsin. Be daring and go native—try limburger and braunschweiger, just like the locals. From just over a buck. For just a shot-and-a-beer, head for the friendly **Ludlow's Tavern** (407 6th St.), with the best jukebox in Monroe.

Local flavor equally precious is at the

Baumgartner's is a classic southwest Wisconsin tavern.

wonderful 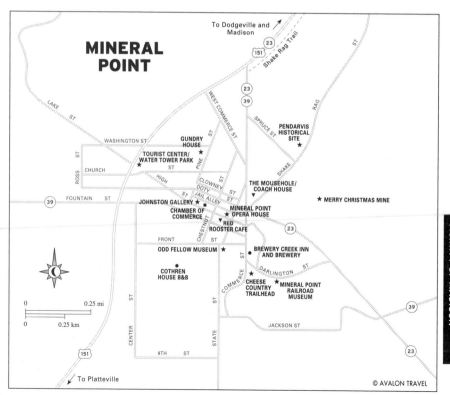 **Turner Hall** (1217 17th Ave., 608/325-3461, $3–7), which serves lunch from noon daily and offers a Friday night fish fry. Great basic Midwestern fare along with some creative Swiss-style food. There's even a great Swiss *Rathskeller* and bowling alley. Show up for polka dances Sunday.

Information and Services

The Monroe Depot (2108 7th Ave., 608/325-7648 or 888/222-9111, www.greencounty .org) is a county tourist information center as well as the trail headquarters of the Cheese Country Recreational Trail and a museum and heritage center to cheesemaking. You could also try the Monroe Chamber of Commerce (www.monroechamber.org)

MINERAL POINT

Mineral Point lies a bit out of the way from New Glarus and Monroe, yet take the time. Seriously.

Only 2,500 friendly souls, yet what a huge place Mineral Point really is, in many ways the heart and soul of the state's heritage. So important was—and still is—it that in 2007 the National Trust for Historic Preservation called it one of America's Dozen Distinctive Destinations.

The name was no fluke—ore fever coursed through the region when a prospector discovered huge deposits under Mineral Point Hill. Hordes of Cornish immigrants took right to the hills. Tirelessly scratching into the hillsides, they even scraped gouges into the bluff

MINERAL POINT

To Dodgeville and Madison

Shake Rag Trail

PENDARVIS HISTORICAL SITE

GUNDRY HOUSE

TOURIST CENTER/ WATER TOWER PARK

THE MOUSEHOLE/ COACH HOUSE

MERRY CHRISTMAS MINE

JOHNSTON GALLERY

CHAMBER OF COMMERCE

MINERAL POINT OPERA HOUSE

RED ROOSTER CAFE

ODD FELLOW MUSEUM

COTHREN HOUSE B&B

BREWERY CREEK INN AND BREWERY

CHEESE COUNTRY TRAILHEAD

MINERAL POINT RAILROAD MUSEUM

JACKSON ST

To Platteville

© AVALON TRAVEL

sides where they could rest and escape the elements. Many thus believe Mineral Point to be the origin of the nickname "badger," as these ubiquitous holes and the miners in them were dubbed.

Soon the heart of the region, it was in Mineral Point that the Territory of Wisconsin was established on July 4, 1836. Elected governor Henry Dodge maintained the political and economic spheres of the territory from temporary offices while Madison was being built. The railroads rolled through, and Mineral Point soon had the largest zinc operation in the United States; it persisted (more or less) through 1979, when the last mine closed down after 150 years.

More than 500 structures in this small town still stand on 1837 plattings. Most buildings contain locally quarried limestone and feature Cornish designs, and all date from the century after 1830. The town's gemlike status has impelled artisans to move to Mineral Point and set up studios, shops, and galleries. "Art" or "gallery" or "antiques" is affixed to absolutely everything; don't be surprised to see "bar-antiques."

And the pervasiveness of "shake rag" this and "shake rag" that stems from a Cornish tradition. At noontime, wives summoned their husbands home from the mines by waving dishcloths. The name stuck.

Sights

Pendarvis and the Merry Christmas Mine

(114 Shake Rag St., 608/987-2122, www.wisconsinhistory.org) is judged by many as the most thorough and best preserved view of the region's mining heritage. While the rest of this historic district was being demolished in the 1930s for scavenged building blocks, a foresighted local bought rundown Cornish cottages and set to renovating. For a while, it was a Cornish restaurant before the state historical society took over. Quite small actually, the complex has a long three-unit rowhouse, the oft-photographed Polperro House, and stone-and-log cottages (six structures in all), linked together by narrow stone paths through gardens.

Even better might be the stroll up, over, and through Mineral Point Hill and the Merry Christmas Mine on a set of trails snaking up from the back of the parking lot. Miners took 80 years to get around to this side of the hill, firing up the lanterns about 1906 and mining for seven years in the largest zinc operation in the area. Assorted hulks of rusting equipment and more than 100 abandoned crevice shafts dot the 43 acres. Native prairie restoration is ongoing, and big bluestem is already blooming again.

The complex is open May–November. Guided tours led by garbed docents depart regularly (schedule varies) daily 10 A.M.–5 P.M., last tickets sales at 4 P.M. Admission is $8 adults.

Up Shake Rag Street from Pendarvis you can espy other stone and stone-and-log dwellings originally put up in the 1830s by Cornish potters, weavers, and other artisans (even Wisconsin's first pottery). This is yer **Shake Rag Alley** (www.shakeragalley.com). Nine historic structures, including one of the oldest log cabins in the state, are surrounded by tailored gardens. Find artisan galleries/workhops, a B&B, a café, and other things; in summer the street even offers theatrical shows under the stars. Just gandering at the classic structures is worth a few minutes.

North of the chamber of commerce is the **Gundry House** (234 Madison St., 608/987-3670, 1–5 P.M. Fri.–Sat., 11 A.M.–2 P.M. Sun., June–late Sept., free), a cut sandstone and limestone Victorian built in 1867 by a prominent local merchant, Joseph Gundry, notable because his business featured the local-legend *Pointer Dog* statue. Otherwise, it's an impressive home with period furnishings, offering tours.

Not many get around to the 1838 **Wisconsin Odd Fellow Museum** (Front St. and State St., 608/987-3093, 9 A.M.–3 P.M. daily June–Sept., free), the first Odd Fellow Hall west of the Allegheny Mountains. Built and dedicated by Thomas Wildey, founder of the order, it's the only hall dedicated by him and still standing.

Mineral Point's classic railroad depot—once called one of the 10 most endangered historic rail structures in the country (it is the oldest in Wisconsin)—has been restored into the **Mineral Point Railroad Museum** (10 A.M.–4 P.M. Thurs.–Sat., noon–4 P.M. Sun., $3 adults) and has collections of southwest Wisconsin rail artifacts. The Wisconsin Trust for Historic Preservation called it the best interpretive site in Wisconsin.

If you're up for a road trip, 13 miles east of town is Hollandale, a mile west of which along WI 39 is **Grandview,** the erstwhile home of folk artist Nick Engelbert. Engelbert, an immigrant dairy farmer turned self-taught artist, in the 1930s began to transform his artistic visions into concrete, glass, and stone and scattered them throughout the gardens around his farm. It's a great minitrip and a splendid look at rural folk art.

Nobody's ever really come here to actually exercise before, but the locals are trying to change that. They've recently completed a dandy **hike/bike trail** to Dodgeville, linking with the Military Ridge State Trail.

The **Mineral Point Chamber of Commerce** (237 High St., 608/987-3201, www.mineralpoint.com) has detailed maps ($3) of **historic walking/driving tours.**

Entertainment

The **Mineral Point Opera House** (139 High St., 608/987-2642) has been undergoing a long, painstaking but loving renovation into its erstwhile grandeur. It features a slate of live performances, mostly folk, during its May–October season. Once a major stop on the Midwest theater tour, it now also shows movies—daily in summer!—as well as occasional theatrical presentations by the local Shake Rag Players and some traveling shows.

Shopping

Get ready to unshackle the calf hide. Ever since some pioneering artisans discovered the tasteful architecture and low-key small-town tranquility in the '40s, Mineral Point has been a hotbed for Wisconsin artisans. More than 40 galleries and studios populate the town, and more seem to spring open

annually. One weekend each October southern Wisconsin artisans open their studio doors for back-room views of the artistic process; Spring Green and Baraboo participate, but Mineral Point is the place to start any tour. The three-day festival is a great combination of art and halcyon autumn. They also do this the first Saturday of April, June, August, and December.

Johnston Gallery (245 High St., 608/987-3787) showcases the works of more than 150 artists. Open daily 10 A.M.–5 P.M. all year.

Accommodations

This is the town that time forgot, so take your pick from lodging in a baker's dozen—or more—absolutely authentic historic structures.

Laying your head on Mineral Point's Shake Rag Street, just a skip from Pendarvis, would be the way to go. Choose between **The Mousehole,** an 1839 cottage, and rooms/suites in the **Coach House,** an 1840s structure. Doesn't get much more historic than these—and for rates starting at $89, for not much moolah. For information, call 608/987-3292, or log on to www.shakeragalley.com.

Stay at the ◖ **Cothren House** (320 Tower St., 608/987-1522, www.cothrenhouse.com, $109–129) and you'd swear you were back in the old country, such is the architecture and landscaping—in fact, it was modeled on Redruth, Cornwall. Choose from a stone cottage or rustic log cabin (both with two bedrooms) and relax in the secluded gardens. The cabin, a pioneer dwelling from 1835, might be the most perfect historic lodging experience in southwestern Wisconsin.

A caveat is perhaps in order. Mineral Point's historic dwellings are legendary for having, er, let's say paranormal guests. Just so you know. . . .

The closest public **campground** is at Governor Dodge State Park in Dodgeville. East and south along Highways D and F is **Yellowstone Lake State Park,** a modest state park with 128 campsites, showers, a good fishing lake, and eight miles of hiking trails.

A wildlife reserve is also part of this 2,600-acre park.

Food

Better get used to hearing *figgyhobbin* (or *figgihobbin*), because you'll see the word incessantly. Yes, it is of course a Cornish dish, and no, it isn't the roast beast the name connotes. It's actually a pastry of raisins and walnuts, and it's quite rich. Other Cornish food might include saffron cakes, Mawgan meatballs, and pasty.

Once a county bank, the (**Red Rooster Café** (158 High St., 608/987-9936, 5 A.M.–5 P.M. daily, $2–7) is a one-of-a-kind road-food-quality eatery where diners sit at a horseshoe-shaped counter on old red vinyl and chrome swivel chairs underneath a coffered ceiling. Pasty and figgyhobbin in a diner atmosphere—classic.

For now, great old mashed with new ambience, courtesy century-old limestone walls of its previous incarnation as a brewery storehouse, comes at **Brewery Creek** (23 Commerce St., 608/987-4747, 11:30 A.M.–8 P.M. daily, $7–15). Today it's a B&B and restaurant. The fare is upper-end pub grub and homebrewed beer, and while you wait, notice the meticulous woodworking and imported tables. The B&B also has historic (from the 1830s!) cottages for rent.

Information and Services

Friendly are those at Mineral Point Chamber of Commerce (237 High St., 608/987-3201, www.mineralpoint.com).

Along the Wisconsin River

(THE LOWER WISCONSIN STATE RIVERWAY

In 1989, the Wisconsin Legislature gave final approval—after seven hard-fought years—to a proposal establishing the 92.5-mile Lower Wisconsin State Riverway. From Sauk Prairie, in south-central Wisconsin just north of Madison, to its confluence with the Mississippi River, it's definitely an "Old Man River," shuffling instead of rushing, lolling instead of cascading. It's also the longest remaining never-dammed stretch of river in Wisconsin.

A grand achievement of civic middle-ground cooperation, these miles couldn't have been better chosen: Precious little development had ever taken place. Ultimately the state hopes to own up to 80,000 acres of riverfront property; slightly more than half that is now under state control.

The riverway subsumes 19 official Natural Areas as diverse as Bakken's Pond near Spring Green, to the haunting battlefield park of the Battle of Wisconsin Heights. It has been called one of the most amazing conglomerations of natural history, ecology, state and Native American history, recreation, flora and fauna, and topography in the Midwest. Shoreline incursion is barred, keeping the bluffs and greenery intact, and any off-bank timber extraction has to first pass muster with a tough advisory-board review. About 350 species of flora and fauna are found inside the riverway's parameters. Sixty or more threatened or endangered species live within its boundaries, as do 35 flora species specific to the unglaciated Driftless Region.

The riverway is also very much a work in progress. Development of new campgrounds, rustic or otherwise, will be taking place, as will a scattering of new boat landings. Most are to be concentrated on the Sauk City–Spring Green upper third and gradually diminish as the river rolls southwest toward Wyalusing State Park. The stretch south and west of Boscobel is earmarked for primitive status.

(Note that many of the highlights here are detailed more in following pages.)

Highlights

Four miles south of Sauk City is the ever-

canoeing on the Wisconsin River

60, you can hop into legendary **Eagle Cave** for a small fee; look for Eagle Cave Road.)

Canoeing

Spring Green marks the southern end of the most populated canoe segment of the 92-mile riverway; Sauk Prairie, 25 miles away, is the northern terminus. Two-thirds of the river's users are active between these points.

The whole of the thing can be canoed, as there is nary a dam, cascade, rapids, or portage—among the longest unimpeded stretches of river in the Midwest. Currents range from five mph on the upper reaches to an absolutely slothful one to two mph near Muscoda. Spring Green to Boscobel is active enough, but beyond Boscobel you'll be alone. Many Spring Green–area travelers pitch a tent at Tower Hill State Park and then reach the river via the park. Other popular access points include Peck's Landing, beneath the WI 23 bridge, and the Lone Rock Landing, just east of the WI 130 bridge.

Hiking

Hiking is grand, with trail networks along the Black Hawk Unit between Mazomanie and Sauk City, and more between Muscoda and Blue River. Better—these 40 grand acres have the wonderful challenge of no established trails. *But: Know where you are, as private land does exist.*

Swimming

No matter what you see the locals doing, respect this river. Monthly drownings are not uncommon. The sandbars make for enticing beach-the-canoe-and-frolic spots, but the current is misleadingly slow; the layered currents can drag you under. Worse, river fluctuations create deep sinkholes, which can be neither seen nor predicted by observing the current—step in one and say bye-bye.

Fishing

Game fish are present in the Wisconsin River's main channel, but pan fish predominate on poles and are especially pervasive in the sloughs

inspiring **Ferry Bluff,** just off WI 60. From the bluff, the Baraboo Range is visible to the east, as is Blue Mound to the south. Many disembark in Spring Green for an extended stay. Near the Lone Rock Boat landing is a protruding cliff called **Devil's Elbow** for its hazardous navigation and numerous wrecks. The **Avoca Prairie,** seven miles west of the WI 133 Lone Rock bridge, is almost 1,000 acres of wet-mezic prairie, the largest tallgrass-prairie remnant east of the Mississippi River. (Turn north off WI 133 onto Hay Lane Road, past Marsh Creek to the parking area; be very aware of wet conditions or you will get stuck.) You'll pass two of the last extant hand-operated drawspan bridges built by the railroads before reaching Bear Creek. After passing Richland City, **Bogus Bluff** comes into view, rich with apocryphal tales of subterranean riches, as well as splendid views. **Muscoda** is the only town of any size before Boscobel, and to the west is the **Blue River Sand Barrens,** a genuine desert—cacti, snakes, and a species of lizard all live here. (On the other side of the river, along WI

© WISCONSIN DEPARTMENT OF TOURISM

VICINITY OF MADISON

and bayous off the river channel. Check locally for regulations and take limits. For serious anglers, it might be worth a 17-mile drive east along U.S. 14 to Black Earth Creek, one of the top 100 trout streams in the country, with more than 1,500 brownies per mile.

Camping

Free dispersed camping is allowed on all state-owned lands, whether inner-stream islands or banks. Trouble is, it isn't always easy to know what land is in state hands—*check locally before setting up camp.* In certain areas, only sandbars are not privately owned, and thus, those are what you've got. They're grand, Huck Finnish ways to experience the river, but then again, this is a river and water levels fluctuate and sandbars disappear, so keep aware. *No glass containers whatsoever are allowed.*

Information

Local chambers of commerce and DNR offices/websites have excellent information—enough to cobble together the entire route. The first place anyone should start is with the Lower Wisconsin State Riverway Commission (800/221-3792, www.lwr.state.wi.us).

SAUK PRAIRIE

Sauk Prairie is actually both Sauk City and Prairie du Sac. In the 1840s, Upper and Lower Sauk were founded by Hungarian immigrant and dandy Agoston Haraszthy, before he lit out for California to become the "Father of the California Wine Industry." Sauk City managed to one-up Prairie du Sac by incorporating first (becoming Wisconsin's oldest incorporated village). It also gained fame throughout Europe as one of the country's last bastions of Freethinkers.

The cities were inspiration for native son August Derleth, the verbose wordsmith who championed the common Wisconsinite (his "Sac Prairie" stories were modeled on the area).

The ice-free and calm, free-flowing waters of the lower Wisconsin River (thanks, oddly, to power plants) and notched sandstone bluffs for roosts have also given rise to a phoenixlike

reappearance of endangered bald eagles. Of the state's nearly 1,150 nesting pairs of eagles, up to 10 percent are concentrated in the Sauk Prairie stretch of river.

Sights and Recreation

Wollersheim Winery (WI 188, 608/643-6515, www.wollersheim.com) has been producing wines since before the Civil War and now accounts for over half of the wine produced in Wisconsin. The antebellum buildings, limestone aging caverns, and vineyards are an official National Historic Site. Popular and fun volunteer grape harvesting and stomping weekends are held in autumn. The winery offers tours ($3.50 adults) hourly 10:15 A.M.–4:15 P.M.

Northwest of Sauk Prairie approximately 10 miles is a day-use and seasonal state park focused on the only natural bridge in Wisconsin, **Natural Bridge State Park.** Crags and battlement outcroppings such as this are found throughout the state's Driftless Area. This wind-eroded hole in a sandstone

Natural Bridge State Park

© THOMAS HUHTI

promontory measures 25 by 35 feet and is one of the oldest sandstone natural features on the planet. Stratigraphic dating has also revealed Paleo-Indian encampments as far back as 12,000 years—among the oldest sites in the Upper Midwest. A couple of trails lead to a natural area. North of the park you'll find **Orchard Drive** (and parts of Schara and Ruff Roads), one of Wisconsin's official Rustic Roads. This six-miler serpentines through grand glacial topography and plenty of wildflowers. This is as off-the-beaten path as it gets.

Approximately eight miles northwest of town via U.S. 12 and Highway C is the amazing **Baxter's Hollow,** a 4,950-acre parcel of the extraordinary Baraboo Hills, itself a vast tract of 144,000 acres and one of the last vestiges of contiguous upland hardwood forest in the United States. So rich with flora and fauna are these regions that it has been listed by The Nature Conservancy as one of the 75 Last Great Places in the Western Hemisphere. Better—in 2005, it was cited as the state's second official Important Birding Area.

The most humbling site in central Wisconsin is the **Black Hawk Unit** of the Lower Wisconsin State Riverway. The unit is of archaeological note for the rare and somewhat mysterious linear-type effigy mounds from the Late Woodland period (A.D. 600–1300), found only in the quad states region including southwestern Wisconsin. Unfortunately, that splendid and cryptic history is overshadowed by the massacre that occurred along the park's northern perimeter—the **Battle of Wisconsin Heights**—between Fox-Sauk warriors and a militia that had pursued them across the state. The park has more than 15 miles of eerily quiet trails taking in the effigy mounds, the battle site, and even late-19th-century log buildings put up when the land was part of a working farm and recreational resort. To get there, take U.S. 12 south to Highway Y and west to WI 78 and then go south.

Sauk Prairie is among the most popular spots to indulge in a favorite pastime on

EAGLE-WATCHING

The bald eagle, on the federal government's endangered species list since 1972, is making a dramatic reappearance in many places. One of the primary eagle habitats is the Lower Wisconsin State Riverway, starting in Sauk City in south-central Wisconsin and stretching to the confluence of the Mississippi River. South of here to the state line, the Upper Mississippi Wildlife Refuge is another, and the Cassville area is one of the best areas to view eagles within that region. Having rebounded from perilously low levels, Wisconsin now has more than 1,000 eagle nesting sites, an eightfold increase in three decades. Though eagles are still getting pushed out by development, poached by knuckleheads, electrocuted by power lines, and poisoned by toxic fish, the future isn't quite so grim. (In fact, the Wisconsin DNR even transplanted four eagle chicks into New York City parks.)

Bald eagles really aren't bald; that false-cognate word came from the Middle English *ball(e)d* – "white spot." The much more impressive scientific name, *Haliaetus leucocephalus*, roughly translates as "white-headed sea bird." (The white head doesn't fully appear until the bird is 4-5 years old.)

Some incidental data: Eagles travel 30-40 mph in flight but in dives can eclipse *100* mph and their vision is six times more acute than a human's!

Eagles generally live 30-50 years, though in the wild that number has slowly dropped. Generally, nesting pairs mate for life; females lay 1-3 eggs in March, and both birds incubate the eggs. One nest weighed in at two tons.

In Sauk Prairie, January eagle-peering comes best in Prairie du Sac, which has an information kiosk and viewing scopes; Veterans Park, which has in-car-only viewing; a mile north of Prairie du Sac and then onto Dam Road to the hydroelectric plant; and, if you're feeling ambitious, head out Highway PF, where you might get a gander at eagles feeding on farmland flotsam.

the lower Wisconsin—**canoeing.** The float from around WI 60 and back to town is easiest; you could theoretically go all the way to Spring Green. Figure $35–40 for a canoe rental and shuttle service on a 2.5-hour trip; multinight trips are also possible. Among the half-dozen outfitters is **Sauk Prairie Canoe Rental** (608/643-6589, www.spcanoerentals.com).

Sauk Prairie is also the proud parent of the annual **Wisconsin State Cow Chip Throw,** held Labor Day weekend. At the **Riverview Ballroom,** built in 1942 and overlooking the Wisconsin River, you can dance to country music Friday nights on the largest dance floor in southern Wisconsin.

Practicalities

The **Skyview Inn** (U.S. 12 and Hwy. PF, 608/643-4344 or 888/643-4344, $50 s or d) offers a spacious, grassy setting (with a view of the De Bluffs over yonder) and one suite with a whirlpool bath.

The dense German food at the 〖 **Dorf Haus** (Hwy. Y in diminutive Roxbury, 608/643-3980, 5–9 P.M. Wed.–Sat., 11:30 A.M.–8:30 P.M. Sun., $8–22) includes real-deal Teutonic specialties—even *leberkaese* (pork and beef loaf)—one of the few spots in the state you'll see it. Special Bavarian smorgasbords are offered the first Monday of every month year-round and the first and third Mondays in summer. And polka predominates!

Frank Lloyd Wright Country

〖 SPRING GREEN

As you trace the final relaxing course of the Wisconsin River westward, the first community, little Spring Green, is nestled and locked into the crook on the north side of a river bight, surrounded by the lushest green imaginable.

Famed Wisconsin curmudgeon Frank Lloyd Wright found the area's beauty to fit his architectural visions so well he founded a groundbreaking design school here and lived here for five decades.

That prime, luck-of-the-draw geographical plunk-down on the edge of the Wyoming Valley has given Spring Green the edge on any tourist town around. From an afterthought hog and cattle shipping point, Spring Green has become a serious tourist town. Mingling are river rats, artisans, and a lot of Wright devotees trooping around to view The Master's works. Yet there's still a large sense of pastoral simplicity. Farmers still roll tractors down the roads and through town. Expansion of village roadwork coincided with equal-size projects to build ponds, wetlands, and a wildlife area, a green tension line of sorts. In fact, Spring Green didn't get a stoplight along busy U.S. 14 until 1995!

Sights

Throw a dart blindfolded in the Spring Green area and it'll hit the word "Wright." In 1911, three miles south of Spring Green's village center in the Jones Valley, Frank Lloyd Wright began work on **Taliesin** (Welsh for "Shining Brow") on the homestead of his Welsh ancestors. He had already made quite a name and reputation for himself in Wisconsin and in architectural circles, both good and bad. An unabashed, monumental egoist, Wright in his lifetime had a profound artistic and architectural influence upon the Badger State. He also enraged proper society with his audacity and uncanny ability to *épater les bourgeois,* that is, to stroke his own famed who-gives-a-damn-what-they-think predilections. When he wasn't dashing off preternaturally radical designs, he was alternately a deadbeat dad, a browbeater, and—one dare say—a megalomaniac. And one who cut a figure with his ever-present cape and porkpie hat. As he said, "I had to choose between hypocritical humility and hated arrogance." His most famous exchange occurred over a client's phoning Wright to inform him that rainwater was dripping on his table in his new Wright home.

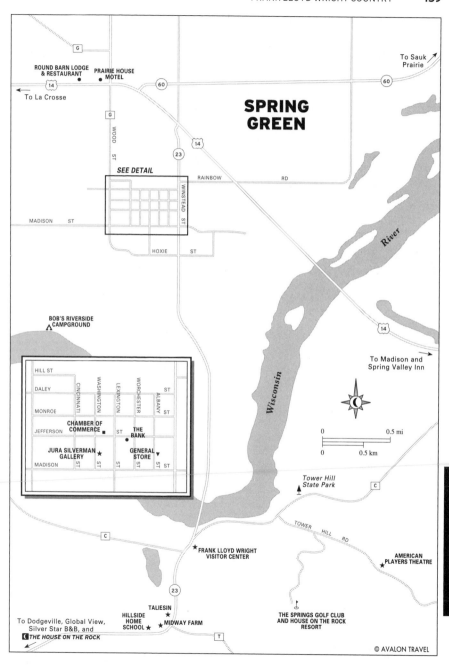

© AVALON TRAVEL

© WISCONSIN DEPARTMENT OF TOURISM

Frank Lloyd Wright's Taliesin

To which the master purportedly replied, "Move your table."

Wright stressed the "organic" in everything, and his devotion to the natural world predated environmental consciousness by generations (though the Japanese had it figured out millennia before Wright visited Tokyo and apparently had an epiphany). Taliesin is a perfect example—gradually pulling itself along the crown of a hill, not dominating the peak.

As it's the preeminent architectural design school, today thousands of acolytes (not really an exaggeration) study under the Taliesin Fellowship. The 600-acre grounds consist of his residence, Taliesin; Hillside Home School, a boardinghouse for a school run by an aunt; a home built for his sister (Yan-Y-Deri, Welsh for "under the oaks"); a windmill (his first commissioned project); and Midway Farm, all built between 1902 and 1930 while Wright and his associates operated his studio and workshop from the main building. Locally quarried sandstone is the predominant rock, and everywhere, those unmistakable Frank Lloyd Wright roofs. Wright would shudder to see how time

has begun to ravage his estate—Herculean efforts are under way to restore aging and nature-damaged structures.

The visitors center (877/588-7900, www.taliesinpreservation.org or www.wrightinwisconsin.org), more like a huge gift shop, is open 9 A.M.–5 P.M. daily May 1–October 31, shorter hours April and November–mid-December.

Myriad tours are available May 1–October 31. The basic Hillside Tour ($17 adults) is an hour long; the biggie is the Estate Tour ($80), a four-hour sweaty traipse around the entire grounds. There are lots of options between these.

Then the wonderful alternative to everything-must-be-Wright: **American Players Theatre** (608/588-2361, www.playinthewoods.org). APT has created a cult following of sorts for its broad palette of offerings and for its accessible direction. Carved into a hillside, it's a personal fave: a steamy evening with nighthawks swooping and actors literally crashing through the underbrush. The theater offers first-rate catered dinners, picnic grounds, and more. Performances generally rotate

Tuesday–Sunday, with matinees Saturday. The season runs mid-June–early October. Prime tickets range $41–55.

In the mid-1800s, what is today **Tower Hill State Park** was the site of a major lead-shot-production operation as cannonballs started to fly across the Mason-Dixon line, but it went belly up in competition with farther-flung and cheaper facilities, all made possible by the railroad. The old shot tower and smelter have been refurbished, and it's a cool (literally and figuratively) traipse down into the cooling tank, where the lead pellets fell 180 feet to the bottom, rounding and cooling as they went.

Events

The last full weekend of June, Spring Green hosts the **Spring Green Arts and Crafts Fair,** with 250 Midwest artisans and craftspeople setting up temporary booths throughout the village.

Shopping

The Wisconsin Artists Showcase at the **Jura Silverman Gallery** (143 S. Washington St., 608/588-7049, 11 A.M.–5 P.M. Wed.–Sun. June–Dec., less often otherwise) has art furniture, slumped glass, handmade-paper art, photography, prints, paintings, and a whole lot more by Wisconsin artists, showcased in a 1900 cheese warehouse.

From the other side of the planet, the wares at **Global View** (608/583-5311), off Highway C along Clyde Road in a reconverted barn, are not your usual import-export, they-don't-know-any-better, Asian "crafts." Global View maintains a reference library and location photographs of the source of each item, if not of the artists themselves, and tours to meet the artists are also organized here.

The whole of the Wisconsin River Valley can be thought of as one big farmers market. Summertime vegetable stands crop up every half mile, or turn up in autumn for pumpkins as big as a kid.

Accommodations

Don't bet on finding too much budget lodging

in Spring Green, at least not between Memorial Day and Labor Day.

Not designed by Wright, but by an "associate," **Prairie House Motel** (U.S. 14, 608/588-2088 or 800/588-2088, $60 s or d) provides a countryside setting, comfortable rooms, a cozy atrium with a gently sloping wood-wainscoted ceiling, a whirlpool, sauna, and exercise room.

Appealing for Wright aficionados is the **Spring Valley Inn** (U.S. 14 and Hwy. C, 608/588-7828, www.springvalleyinn.com, $75–110), designed by Taliesin Associates. You can't miss its steepled upthrust, and its location is secluded but still prime. Large rooms, with an indoor pool, whirlpool, sauna, rec room, and 28 km of cross-country ski trails for guests. The restaurant features alfresco dining by a huge stone fireplace.

The most all-encompassing resort around is indisputably **The Springs Golf Club and House on the Rock Resort** (400 Springs Dr., 608/588-7000 or 800/822-7774, www.house-ontherock.com, $85–205), a luxury spread with a Robert Trent Jones Jr. championship course out your window as well as hiking/biking and tennis. A new inn has more family-style rooms, and lots of package deals are offered.

Cozy B&Bs and historic inns are ubiquitous. You'll find an artistic air at the oversize log building ◖ **Silver Star** (3852 Limmex Hill Rd., 608/935-7297, www.silverstarcountry-inn.com, $95–135), displaying professional regional photographers' works within its chic café/coffeehouse and in all the rooms—minor museums of historical photographic figures. It's all spread out over 300 aces of farmland; sticklers for tradition are happy to find a cozy main room with large fieldstone fireplace.

For the best **camping** head to Tower Hill State Park. For tenters in Spring Green is **Bob's Riverside Resort** (S13220 Shifflet Rd., 608/588-2826), offering canoe rentals.

Food

Classic road-food-quality eats, greasy eggs diners, hard-core Midwest supper clubs, and wannabe chichi restaurants: Check!

A real "I went there" lunch is at the ◖ **Frank Lloyd Wright Visitors Center Riverview Terrace** (lunch only May–Oct., $4–11). Heretofore the planet's only Frank Lloyd Wright–designed restaurant, it was constructed out of a popular 1940s local diner and a WWII aircraft carrier! Grand river views.

A friendly-family-run natural foods café and grocery in an old cheese warehouse, the inimitable ◖ **General Store** (137 S. Albany St., 608/588-7070, 9 A.M.–6 P.M., 8 A.M.–6 P.M. Sat., 8 A.M.–4 P.M. Sun., $4–9) serves healthful yet creative lighter fare—absolutely everything from scratch—keeping vegetarians squarely in mind. Best espresso too. Always on my itinerary.

Originally constructed in 1914 as a dairy barn, the distinctive circular construction of the **Round Barn** (U.S. 14, 608/588-2568, lunch and dinner daily, $6–18) is a good orientation device. Built to save on expensive construction materials and to redirect strong winds, they also, the rumor goes, prevent the devil from finding a corner to hide in! Hearty Midwestern fare is served three times a day (vegetarians/creative cuisine fans are not left out); the Friday night seafood buffet is popular.

At **The Bank** (134 E. Jefferson St., 608/588-7600, www.thebankrestaurantandwinebar.com, $12–25)) the menu changes weekly (they'll cook what locals produce/grow/raise), all in the cozy confines of the erstwhile local neoclassical-style bank and a wondrous new addition (2007) to town. The wine list is astounding.

Information and Services

Contact the **Spring Green Chamber of Commerce** (608/588-2042 or 800/588-2042, www.springgreen.com) for all your needs.

◖ THE HOUSE ON THE ROCK

The House on the Rock (south of Spring Green along WI 23, 608/935-3639, www.thehouseontherock.com) absolutely defies lexical trickery in nailing it down. Novella-length magazine articles have gushed about the, well, left-handed grandeur and spectacle of its true-blue Americana, anything-can-happen overkill. Cynical scribes come and near-religious epiphanies ensue over this Shangri-La—contrived solely to club tourists over the head aesthetically. This is the grandest shakedown of them all in Dairyland, mere miles from the amokdom of the Wisconsin Dells. Best of all, it all goes down less than 10 miles from that enclave to natural architecture—that altar to an ego, that House that Wright Built—Taliesin, in Spring Green.

Come to Wisconsin and you absolutely cannot miss this eighth-dimension tourist trap's ad barrage—Wisconsin's version of a two-drink minimum. Way back in the 1940s, otherwise-sane Alex Jordan literally stumbled over a 60-foot candlelike outcropping in the Wyoming Valley. Intending to construct a weekend retreat and artists' haven, Jordan somehow or other wrestled the original structure into completion atop the chimney. Bit by bit, this architectural gem began to transmogrify into what it is today—the original house atop the rock, plus several other mind-blowing rooms and add-ons, all stuffed with the detritus that Jordan accumulated through a lifetime, much of it museum-worthy in quality or scope.

The catalog: Mill House, Streets of Yesterday, Heritage of the Sea, Pizza Atrium, Transportation Building, Music of Yesterday, World's Largest Carousel (20,000 lights and 275 handcrafted wooden animals, not one of which is a horse), Organ Room (three of the world's greatest right here), and so on ad nauseam.

The best? Try the loopy Infinity Room, a glassed-in room that spikes 218 feet over the valley floor. All told, there are over two *miles* of walking to take in the whole shebang!

But a list doesn't do it justice—it isn't just a selection of junk; it's a wild, shotgun-spattered Attic of the Damned. Is it art? Is it a giant Rorschach test of the mental wilds of an inspired eccentric? Well, equal parts all, perhaps, but an indescribable feeling of visionary honesty pervades the place—never a feeling that it's all a sham or simple stupid overindulgence. The method to the madness is there.

Many visitors overlook what a remarkable artistic and design achievement it was. Jordan never failed to think of how the visitor would see it all, from the 30-mile-panorama observation decks to the floral displays—the gardens based on Asian designs are actually wonderful. Those devoted to tackiness have found their Mecca; best of all, even jaded tourist hacks have to shake their heads and grin. It was undergoing a renovation—renovated House on the Rock, an oxymoron if ever there was one—at the time of writing, so who knows what will be in store for you when you find it?

You can experience all of this March 15 through the last weekend in October. High season hours are 9 A.M.–dusk June–September, shorter hours for the rest of season. There are also special holiday seasons. Three tours are offered: You can fork over $11.50 each or take a package of $27 for the whole slew.

Madison to the Windy City

JANESVILLE

Often overlooked in Madison's glare to the north, this is a hardworking town founded in 1836 by Henry Janes, an ex-military officer who'd heard stories of lush valleys along the Rock River during his military campaigns of the Black Hawk War.

Light manufacturing turned into heavy manufacturing when GM bought out a local factory in 1919 and began Janesville's first assembly line. Within a decade, more than half of the city owed its economic fortunes to GM. Sadly, in 2008 GM closed the plant, despite Herculean efforts by the city and state to save it. No one knows what will become of the massive factory complex (or the thousands of workers).

SIGHTS

Approximately one-fifth of all of Wisconsin's buildings on the National Register of Historic Places can be found in Janesville. The visitors center has the best maps.

One slice of the city's 2,100 acres of park, **Rotary Gardens** (1455 Palmer Dr., 608/752-3885, www.rotarygardens.org) spread over a dozen acres and encompass several landscaping techniques—Japanese rock, English cottage, French, Italian, sunken, and perennial, all united by a theme of Dialogue: World Peace Through Freedom. Across the street you'll find a segment of the Ice Age Trail. The gardens are open year-round during daylight hours.

MIRACLE: THE WHITE BUFFALO

In 1994, an extraordinarily rare white buffalo – Miracle – was born on the Heider Farm near Janesville, the first in the United States since 1933. Spiritually significant to Native Americans, it became a pilgrimage point. Amazingly and admirably, the family refused to profit off it and instead opened its farm to all comers just to share in such a blessing. Miracle died in 2004 but even more amazingly, another white calf was born in 2006, though it lived only a few months.

The Heider Farm family continues to greet visitors (2739 River Rd. S, 608/741-9632, www.whitebuffalomiracle.homestead.com) daily but call first to confirm.

Not far from Rotary Gardens is **Palmer Park,** a large green space with a wading pool, tennis courts, and the CAMDEN Playground, the largest fully accessible playground in the United States.

The **Lincoln-Tallman House** (440 N. Jackson St., 608/752-459), the 1855 home of a prominent abolitionist, is the only private residence in Wisconsin in which Abe Lincoln hung his hat. Architecture mavens have called it one of the finest of its kind in America. Also

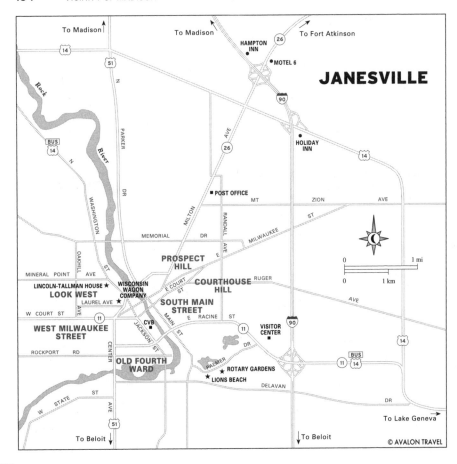

on-site are the original horse barn and a Greek revival stone house used by servants.

A million-dollar-plus renovation added heating and air-conditioning to preserve the original decorations and interiors, including the bed in which Honest Abe slept. Virtually next door is the county historical museum with interactive activities for kids; buy tickets for the Lincoln-Tallman house here. The house is open 9 A.M.–4 P.M. daily June–September, weekends year-round, and for lots of special holiday tours. Admission is $8 adults.

The **Wisconsin Wagon Company** (507 Laurel Ave., 608/754-0026) makes replicas of wooden American Classic coaster wagons—an outstanding bit of Americana brought to life, since the original factory went out of production in 1934 and the Sears-Roebuck catalog was never the same. Tours are available by appointment and cost $3.

Practicalities

Cheapest dependable digs are without question at the local **Motel 6** (3907 Milton Ave., 608/756-1742, $40). A number of other chain motels are nearby.

Looking Glass (18 N. Main, 608/755-9828, 11 A.M.–9 P.M. Mon.–Fri., 11 A.M.–6 P.M. Sat., noon–4 P.M.Sun, $3–7) has pub grub—the interior is a rustic blend of original high, pressed-tin ceilings and polished brass and dark wood bar.

Information

The Janesville Area Visitors and Convention Center (51 S. Jackson St., 608/757-3171 or 800/487-2757, www.janesvillecvb.com) is helpful.

Transportation

Van Galder buses (608/752-5407) stop in Janesville en route to Madison and Chicago up to 10 times a day. The bus stops at the terminal at 3120 North Pontiac.

BELOIT

Beloit lies along a wide expanse of the Rock River at its confluence at Turtle Creek. It is a lovely spot, explaining in part the migration of virtually the entire village of Colebrook, New Hampshire, to this town in 1837.

The city's founders erected a college (respected Beloit College, patterned after eastern religious seminaries) and a church before much of anything else and landscaped the town around designs of a New England village with a square. It must have had a positive effect. In the rough-and-tumble 1840s, a traveler wrote of it as "an unusual community, amid shifting pioneer conditions already evincing character and solidity."

Today, the college still leaves its imprint on the community, though light industry, especially food processing (the world's largest chili can sits in front of the Hormel factory), is the economic linchpin. Anthropologist Margaret Mead once called busy and vibrant Beloit "a microcosm of America." The city's riverfront revitalization stretching from Grand Avenue on the south to Pageant Park on the north transformed coal and rail eyesores into a river tourist hot spot.

The summer brings July's **Riverfest,** a four-day musicfest that's one of the largest of its kind in the country, with more than 50 national acts

© THOMAS HUHTI

Tiffany Bridge, outside Beloit

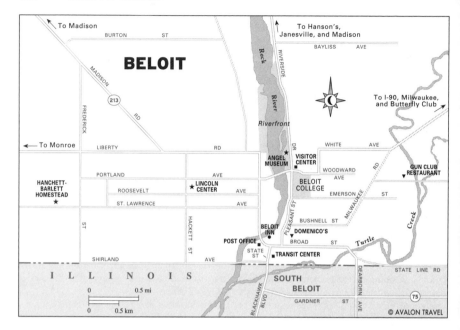

performing. It ranks second in Wisconsin; only Milwaukee's Summerfest is larger.

Turtles in the Park in August is just precious—all turtles, everywhere. Check it out!

Sights

The following is but a small sketch—this city has an inordinate amount of great historic attractions!

The world's largest privately held collection of angel artifacts is on display at Beloit's **Angel Museum** (656 Pleasant St., 608/362-9099, www.angelmuseum.com, $6 adults), housed in a restored church right on the Rock River. Angels of all sorts are on display—more than 12,000 and counting—but the highlight is no doubt the nearly 600 African American angels donated by Oprah Winfrey. Hours are 10 A.M.–4 P.M. Tuesday–Saturday February–December, 1–5 P.M. summer, fewer hours otherwise (closed January).

Founded on the Rock River's east bank as Beloit Seminary, Beloit College (www.beloit .edu) is the oldest college in Wisconsin. Its

founding philosophy was to preserve eastern mores and culture in the heathen "West"—though it could pay its two professors only $600 a year "if they can raise it." The eye-catching buildings include the Middle College building, dating from 1847, the oldest college building north of Chicago. Beloit College's Victorian Gothic **Logan Museum of Anthropology** (College and Bushnell Sts., 608/363-2677, 11 A.M.–4 P.M. Tues.–Sun., free admission) was just a collection of Civil War memorabilia upon inception in 1893, but it's now one of the best museums in the state, with almost a quarter of a million artifacts from around the globe, including the most extensive Stone Age and Paleolithic collections outside of Europe. It's also got a respected Native American collection. Pieces have been collected from six continents on school expeditions, ongoing since the turn of the 20th century. There are those who believe, incidentally, that a certain Beloit College professor was the inspiration for Indiana Jones. Hmm.

The **Wright Museum of Art** (Bushnell St. and Campus Dr., 608/363-2677, 11 A.M.–4 P.M. Tues.–Sun., closed during campus holidays, free admission) displays faculty and student art and hosts art events. Its permanent holdings include American and European paintings and sculpture, Asian decorative arts, and graphics.

The **Thompson Observatory** is at the corner of Emerson and Pleasant Streets and offers tours as well as free open house nights on some—but not all—Wednesdays at 7 P.M. in midfall and midspring. Also, more than two dozen Indian burial mounds dot the campus. Young visitors will want to head straight for the **C House** (or Coughy Haus, or CHAUS) on the Beloit College campus. A dark hall, it feels like the inside of somebody's home, with a loft apartment upstairs. Best of all, there are bands at times, from grunge to jazz-fusion.

The **Near East Side** has more than two dozen structures east of Beloit College; the **Bluff Street** area is also good. Houses in the Near East Side include the unique cobblestone Rasey House, Beloit College's original president's home, and a mélange of mid- to late-19th-century styles. The Bluff Street area across the river also features some houses with delightful cobblestone construction. Maps are available at the visitors center.

Outside of town a bit is the **Hanchett-Bartlett Homestead.** This limestone Greek revival and Italianate mansion, built from locally quarried stone, sits on 15 acres and has been restored to period detail, with special attention to the original color schemes. A great limestone barn filled with farm implements sits on the property, along with a smokehouse nearby. A rural school has been relocated here, and the gray shed-planked Beckman-Howe mill (608/368-1435), on the National Register of Historic Places and dating to the post–Civil War period, is not far away on Highway H. The mill (2149 St. Lawrence Ave., 608/365-7835, 1 P.M.–4 P.M. weekends, June–Sept., $3 adults suggested) has been selected as one of the 10 most endangered historic sites in Wisconsin.

Also outside of town, tough-to-find little **Tiffany** lies northeast of Beloit on Highway S, but it's worth a search; it's got one of the most unusual bridges anywhere, a remnant five-arch iron-truss span based on Roman architecture. Built by the Chicago and Northwestern Railroad in 1869, the structure was modeled after a bridge in Compiegne, France. Each arch spans 50 feet with a 26-foot radius. To reach Tiffany, head east on Highway S from Shopiere and turn left onto Smith Road. You can really view the bridge from the Smith Road iron truss bridge, built in 1890. Tiffany is a personal favorite, an anachronistic relic in the dewy midst of nowhere. The **Tiffany Country Store** (or, Breakfast at Tiffany's) is a wonderful place for breakfast, and even better is the **Tiffany Banquet Inn** for dinner—the fish fry is amazing, and they polka down Friday and Saturday.

Back in Shopiere, check out the village's antique weight-driven timepiece adorned with four lion heads.

Accommodations

Given the proud architecture of Beloit, it's a tad surprising that the city lacks a historic inn or B&B. Good options still exist, most near the I-90 and I-43 interchange, near where you'll find the **Holiday Inn Express** (2790 Milwaukee Rd., 608/365-6000, $79 s, $119 d). The Van Galder bus stops here on the way to Chicago. The Express has some rooms with whirlpools and coffeemakers.

Contemporary cool meets with historic touches at the newish **Beloit Inn** (500 Pleasant St., 608/362-5500, www.beloitinn.com, $99) right downtown. This attractive place has studio and one-bedroom suites with lots of extras.

FOOD

Enjoy *huge* burgers at **Hanson's** (615 E. Cranston, 11 A.M.–variable hours daily, $2–8) on the river along U.S. 51. This is the place for a fish fry as well. It's also the place to experience local flavor, hands down.

The **Circus Drive-In** (3525 Riverside Dr., 608/362-9375, 11 A.M.–8 P.M. daily, from 4 P.M. Mon., $2–5) is a classic, complete with trays hooked on half-open windows.

Domenico's (547 E. Grand Ave., 608/365-9489, 11 A.M.–11 P.M. daily, $6–9) is the pizza joint of choice, with a good veggie pie. Also featured are Italian goodies such as chicken primavera, veal *a'domenico,* and lots of shrimp and seafood.

Locals will likely point you to the **Gun Club** (Colley Rd., 608/362-9900, dinner nightly, $13–23), serving prime rib nightly, along with steaks, seafood, exquisite duck, ribs, and homemade seasonal desserts. Antiques dominate the interiors; live entertainment Friday and Saturday is a nice touch.

Equally traditional, casually ritzy, and open for over seven decades is **❲ The Butterfly Club** (Hwy. K east of town, 608/362-8577, 5–9:30 P.M. daily, noon–8 P.M. Sun., $9–23). Enjoy supper club dining on a patio and likely the best fish fry around (available Wednesday nights as well atourism
s Friday); gotta love fresh-baked cinnamon rolls with your meal. Live entertainment is featured on Friday. The outside is covered with beautiful tulips in season.

INFORMATION

The Beloit Visitor Center (1003 Pleasant St., 608/365-4838 or 800/423-5648, www.visitbeloit.com) is housed in the city's refurbished pump house, built in 1880. You can still wander around and see the workings.

A big hello to the Land of Lincoln is at the Wisconsin Travel Information Center (608/364-4823) south of Beloit at Rest Area 22 on I-90.

TRANSPORTATION

Van Galder buses (608/752-5407) stop in Beloit on their forays to and from Madison and Chicago (O'Hare airport and downtown). The 10 daily buses (each way) stop at the Holiday Inn Express in South Beloit, at the junction of IL 75 and U.S. 51.

The local **Greyhound** (454 St. Paul Ave., 608/365-7808) has daily departures to Madison and Chicago.

BACKGROUND

The Land

Topographically, the region of Wisconsin comprising Milwaukee and Madison may lack the jaw-dropping majesty of other states' vaulting crags or shimmering desert palettes. But it possesses an equable slice of physicality, with fascinating geographical and geological highlights—many of them found nowhere in the country—or world—outside of Wisconsin. You can't help but notice Milwaukee and Madison's tie to water—excellent *feng shui*—one abutting a majestic Great Lake, the other ensconced snugly within four of the state's 16,000-plus glacial lakes. And while you'll of course see moo-cow bucolic, as you'd expect, you'd also be amazed by how a trip westward from Milwaukee to Madison and beyond is a timeline of glacial history. From the eskers and kames (and other glacial era errata) near Milwaukee to flat-earth scoured farmland to the gently rolling, gumdrop fields west of Madison, where the glaciers could not gouge their way through (the only place in North America like it).

Yet never with any drama. This author holds that the Midwestern aw-shucks, taciturn stereotype—not always untrue—stems from an innate sense of the land itself. It takes effort—eminently worthy—to appreciate the understatement.

© THOMAS HUHTI

Where in the World . . . ?

Where is the state? Sticklers say "eastern north-central United States." In a guidebook (*another* guidebook), one outlander classified it simply as "north," which makes sense only if you look at a map. Wisconsinites themselves most often consider their state as part of the Midwest—more specifically, the Upper Midwest. And some even prefer you call it a Great Lakes State.

The Basics

Extend your left hand, palm outward. There—pretty much—is Wisconsin (albeit with a large pinky knuckle and superfluous index finger). Just below the "knuckle" of the thumb lies Milwaukee; trace a line straight west from here to the middle of the back of your hand and you'll hit Madison. Surrounding your thumb is Lake Michigan, precluding easy transportation eastward, one reason why this section of the state was, though not the first port of entry for European explorers and settlers, later the most crucial gateway to the state.

One-third of the U.S. population lives within a day's drive of the state. Its surface area of 56,514 square miles ranks it 26th largest in the nation.

Wisconsin is by no means high, yet this is a state of rolling topography, chock-full of hills and glacial undulation. The highest point is Timm's Hill in north-central Wisconsin; at 1,953 feet it's nothing to sneeze at for the Midwest. (You'll find nothing near this height in southeastern Wisconsin—we get weary biking up a 200-foot glacial hill to the State Capitol.)

Hydrophiles love it here. Even excluding all the access to the Great Lakes, approximately 4 percent of the state's surface is water—including more than 16,000 ancient glacial lakes (40 percent of which have yet to be named).

GEOGRAPHY

Wisconsin was once at the earth's equatorial belt buckle. Plate shifting created the Canadian Shield, which includes about two-thirds of eastern Canada along with Wisconsin, Minnesota, Michigan, and New York. A half billion years ago, a glacial lake flooded the Wisconsin range—the northern section of present-day Wisconsin. Mountains were rounded off in the north and completely covered with sediment in the south. Still later, the northern part of the state rose (up to eight feet per mile) while the southern half was covered with sedimentary debris. Thank intermittent stream erosion, which uplifts more in the north, for all the splendid cataracts.

Glaciation during the two million years of the four glacial periods—geologically, a blink of an eye—is responsible for Wisconsin's one-of-a-kind topography. (The final advance, occurring 70,000–10,000 years ago, was even

WISCONSIN GLACIATION

EXTENT OF GLACIATED AREA

Continental Ice Sheet

Superior Lobe
Chippewa Lobe
Wisconsin Valley Lobe
Terminal Moraine
Chippewa Moraine
Green Bay Lobe
Two Creeks Forest
Northern Kettle Moraine
Campbellsport Drumlins
Horicon Marsh
Terminal Moraine
Lake Michigan Lobe

0   40 mi
0   40 km

© AVALON TRAVEL

named the Wisconsin period.) Wisconsin endured five glacial "lobes" penetrating the state, reducing the state's previous ambitious heights to knobs and slate-flat lands and establishing riverways and streambeds. Only the southwestern lower third of the state escaped the glaciers' penetration, resulting in the world's largest area surrounded completely by glacial drift.

This book emphasizes the southeastern quadrant of the state but does briefly strike out into areas of the northeast, central, and southwestern regions. Knowledge of these zones is crucial, for you won't see any distinct lines of demarcation. (For those zones not touched on within these pages, either use them as rainy-day reading or keep them in mind for your next trip!)

Eastern Ridges and Lowlands

If you look at a map of Wisconsin, this region starts at the base of Door County (near the famous Green Bay) and stretches roughly evenly straight southwest to the Iowa border, subsuming both Milwaukee and Madison (though not always smoothly). Bordered by Lake Michigan on the east and north, this 14,000-square-mile region was much richer in glacial deposits, and the fecund soils attracted the first immigrant farmers. The impeded waterways were ideal conduits for floating timber to mills. It has a smooth, low relief but three prominent cuestas: the Niagara, which forms the eastern side of Lake Winnebago and stretches east all the way to Niagara Falls; another near Ripon in Fond du Lac County; and the last in northeastern Wisconsin in Marinette County.

The Kettle Moraine region southeast of Lake Winnebago as well as the entire Ice Age National Scenic Trail are physical textbooks of glacial geology.

Central (Sand) Plain

Bisected by the mighty Wisconsin River, the crescent-shaped Central Plain region spreads for 13,000 square miles. Once the bottom of enormous glacial Lake Wisconsin, the region is most noted for its oddball topography of sand dune-esque stretches mingled with peat bog, cranberry marsh, and jack pine and scrub oak—all made famous by Aldo Leopold's *A Sand County Almanac.* The central section of this region is relatively flat, but the lower third contains buttes and outliers (younger rock formations)—large sandstone hoodoo-shaped rises visible from many highways. Most impressive are the multihued postglacial sandstone canyons of the Wisconsin Dells region, which any visitor to Madison would be sorely mistaken to miss.

Western Uplands

The Western Uplands region subsumes the radical Driftless Area of the southwestern part of the state (you'll hit it if you drive west of Madison). Geologically the roughest and wildest sector of Wisconsin, it contains rises up to 400 feet higher than the contiguous Central Plain. The unglaciated plateau experienced much stream erosion, and the result is an amazing chocolate-drop topography of rolling hillock and valley—with the odd plateau and ridges not unlike West Virginia—capped by hard rock and sluiced by the lower Wisconsin and Mississippi Rivers.

Northern Highland

Covering 15,000 square miles, the Canadian Shield is the most salient physiogeographical feature of northern Wisconsin. Underlain by crystalline rock on a peneplain, the bedrock and glacial soils are particularly suited to growing timber.

More: Its high concentration of lakes is what separates the region from the rest of the Midwest—and, in fact, distinguishes it in the world, since only the remotest parts of Quebec and Finland have more lakes per square mile.

Other highlights include the Gogebic Iron Range, which stretches from Iron County (natch) into Michigan's Upper Peninsula; Rib Mountain and Timm's Hill; and the underappreciated Blue Hills near Rib Lake.

Lake Superior Lowlands

Wisconsin's northern cap along Lake Superior displays a geological oddity, unique in the

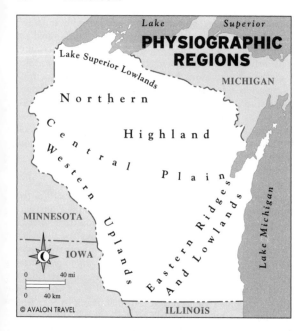

PHYSIOGRAPHIC REGIONS

Lake Superior

Lake Superior Lowlands

MICHIGAN

N o r t h e r n

H i g h l a n d

C e n t r a l

W e s t e r n

P l a i n

MINNESOTA

U p l a n d s

E a s t e r n   R i d g e s   A n d   L o w l a n d s

IOWA

Lake Michigan

0   40 mi
0   40 km

© AVALON TRAVEL

ILLINOIS

near Lake Geneva to be plowing while ice fishers near the Apostle Islands are still drilling holes in the ice.

Temperatures and Precipitation

The state's mean temperature is 43°F, though this is not a terribly useful statistic. You'll find 100°F in the shade come August, 40°F or more below with wind chill in winter, and everything in between.

The annual mean temperature ranges from 41°F in the "Snow Belt," which stretches from Douglas County (Superior) in the west through northern Vilas County, to 48°F in southeastern Kenosha County. This breaks down to a high of 54°F and low of 36°F March–May, 81°F and 57°F June–August, 59°F and 36°F September–November, and 32°F and 12°F December–February.

The average precipitation amount is 38.6 inches annually. Northern counties experience more snowfall than southern ones, and anyplace near the Great Lakes can see some sort of precipitation when the rest of the state is dry. Snow cover ranges from 140 days per annum in the north to 85 days in the south. Snowfall ranges from 30 inches in the extreme south to 120 inches or more in Bayfield County and the Lake Superior cap.

Great Lakes—a fallen trench of Lake Superior, flanked by palisades. Before the glaciers arrived to finish carving, shifting lowered this 10- to 20-mile-wide belt (now a half mile lower than the surrounding land). This wedge-shaped red-clay plain consists mainly of copper-hued outcroppings and numerous streams and rivers. Most of the state's waterfalls cascade off a 400-foot escarpment abutting the southern ridge.

CLIMATE

Contrary to what you may have heard, Wisconsin weather ain't all that bad. Sure, temperatures varying from 110°F to -50°F degrees spice things up a bit and, come late February, most people are psychotically ready for the snow to go, but overall it isn't terrible.

Wisconsin is near the path of the jet stream, and it lacks any declivity large enough to impede precipitation or climatic patterns. Its northerly latitude produces seasonal shifts in the zenith angle, which result in drastic temperature fluctuations. It's not unusual for farmers

"But Cooler Near the Lake"

Wisconsin has two contiguous sea-size bodies of water, which give rise to their own littoral microclimates. In Milwaukee, and anywhere near Lake Michigan, get used to hearing "cooler near the lake" in summer and "warmer near the lake" in winter. This moderating influence is particularly helpful for the orchards and gardens in Door County north of Milwaukee.

THE INLAND SEAS

In their interflowing aggregate, these grand fresh-water seas of ours, —Erie, Ontario, and Huron, and Superior, and Michigan, —possess an oceanlike expansiveness, with many of the ocean's noblest traits.

Herman Melville

Together the Great Lakes account for 20 percent of the planet's fresh water. Fifty million people drink from its basins. Lake Michigan, the only Great Lake wholly within the U.S. boundaries, is so large that it has its own tide (albeit a minute one). Lake Superior is the second-largest lake in the world – Lake Baikal in Russia is more voluminous, but Superior has twice its surface area, larger than South Carolina. It would take 111 years to drain its three billion gallons of water (that's one-eighth the world's supply).

In geological terms, the Great Lakes are young – about 2,000 to 3,500 years old – but initial geological machinations started half a billion years ago, with successive volcanic action and earth shifting during the pre-Cambrian period. The basic formations resulted from movement of the Canadian Shield and rising and falling geosynclines regions during the Paleozoic period. Ancient seas later flooded the entire region, and glaciers bulldozed the existing trenches. Most of what makes up today's Great Lakes was formed in the glacial epoch, streams and waterways gouging and forming channels. Both Lakes Michigan and Superior were once conjoined as part of vast, ancient Lake Nipissing, which also included Lake Huron.

At 820 miles, Wisconsin is second only to Michigan in possessing Great Lake frontage property, with shorelines along hydro-behemoths Michigan and Superior. The Great Lakes were largely responsible for perpetuating Wisconsin as a state, and in many ways they still do today. Early shipbuilding and commercial fishing industries have been joined by sportfishing, at one time over a $75- to $85-million-a-year industry. This approached hard times, however, due to fish stocks plummeting for a variety of reasons (covered under "Environmental Issues").

Tornadoes

Generally, not much here in Wisconsin can kill you—no hurricanes, freeway snipers, or grizzlies. But the state does endure the eye-popping experience of tornadoes, generally averaging six serious twisters and many more near-misses or unsubstantiated touchdowns each year.

And sorry, but Dane County (that is, Madison and environs) historically has the most tornadoes in Wisconsin, though the southwestern (yup, the areas south and west of Madison) and southeastern sectors—especially Waukesha County (west of Milwaukee), Dodge County (smack between the cities), and the area around Eau Claire—also see quite a few. (Don't assume that the north and east are safe!)

Tornado season begins in March and peaks during late May, June—especially—and July. A secondary spike occurs during September and extends occasionally into mid-October. Many of the midsummer tornadoes are smaller and less intense than the ones in April to June or in September.

A **tornado watch** means conditions are favorable for the development of a tornado. A **tornado warning** means one has been sighted in the vicinity. In either case, emergency sirens are active almost everywhere in Wisconsin. Tornadoes appear most often between 3 P.M. and 7 P.M. but can occur at any time.

Seek shelter in a basement and get in the southwest corner (they often, but not always, move from the southwest), under a table if possible. Avoid windows at all costs. If there is no basement, find an interior room, such as a bathroom, with no windows. Avoid rooms with outside walls on the south or west side of a building. If you are driving, position yourself at right angles to the tornado's apparent path. If that's not possible, get out of your car, find a low depression in the ground and lie flat in it, covering your head with your hands.

Thunderstorms and Lightning

Lightning still kills about 200–300 people per year nationwide, *more than tornadoes and hurricanes combined.* Wisconsin averages two serious thunderstorms per year, with a midsummer average of two relatively modest ones each week. Don't let this lull you into complacency in autumn, however; this author scribbled a Wisconsin guidebook during ferocious thunderstorms on Halloween, replete with marble-size hail, flash floods, and tornado activity.

Thunderstorms are often deadlier than tornadoes, particularly when you're driving or when isolated in open areas. Lightning is serious stuff—remember, if you're close enough to hear thunder, you're close enough to get fried. The cardinal rule when lightning is present: Do the opposite of what gut instincts tell you. Avoid anything outside—especially trees. If you cannot get indoors, squat on the balls of your feet, hugging your knees in a balled position, reducing your contact with the ground and your apparent size. If indoors, stay away from anything that has a channel to the outside: telephones, TVs, radios, even plumbing.

Snowstorms

Technically, four inches of snow per 24-hour period qualifies as heavy snowfall (but to that paltry amount a Wisconsinite would just sniff in derision).

Six inches in 8–12 hours will cause serious transportation disruptions and definitely close airports for a while. Snow generally begins to stick in mid- to late October in northern Wisconsin, and early December in southern Wisconsin, though snow has fallen as early as September and as late as May on rare occasions.

Odds are, if you're in Wisconsin in the winter you're going to be driving in the stuff. Still, even the hardiest winter drivers need to practice prudence. If you're a novice at winter driving, don't learn it on the road, especially on a crowded highway at dawn or dusk. Always drive safely—it's important to *slow down.* Be cautious on bridges, even when the rest of the pavement is OK; bridges are always slippery.

© THOMAS HUHTI

a winter scene in one of Madison's lakefront parks

AVERAGE TEMPERATURES

All temperatures are listed in degrees Fahrenheit.

LOCATION	JULY high/low	JANUARY high/low
Superior	78/52	20/0
Ashland	79/54	22/0
St. Croix Falls	82/58	20/-1
Eau Claire	81/58	20/0
Eagle River	78/52	19/1
Wausau	80/57	20/1
Stevens Point	81/58	23/4
Green Bay	80/58	23/6
Sturgeon Bay	76/56	26/11
La Crosse	83/62	23/5
Wisconsin Dells	82/59	25/6
Prairie du Chien	85/62	27/8
Madison	81/57	27/9
Milwaukee	81/59	28/12
Kenosha	81/60	29/13

your owner's manual for the advisability of "rocking" the car; be sure to keep the front wheels cleared *and pointed straight ahead.* Do not race the engine; you'll just spin your wheels into icy ruts. Winterize your vehicle. Most important, carry an emergency kit including anything you may need to spend the night in a snowbank.

And please, if you see someone hung up in a snowbank, stop and help push him or her out.

The Department of Transportation's website (www.511wi.gov) updates winter driving conditions from November to late March four times daily. The website is very useful. You can also call the state's toll-free winter driving conditions hotline (dial 511).

Wind Chill and Frostbite

The most dangerous part of winter in Wisconsin is the wind-chill factor—the biting effect of wind, which makes cold colder and more lethal. For example, when the temperature is 30°F, with a wind of 40 mph the temperature is actually -6°F; if the temperature were 0°F, 40 mph winds would make it -54°F—the point at which it's no longer a joke how cold a Wisconsin winter is.

When the wind chill takes temperatures low enough, exposed skin is in immediate danger. **Frostbite** is the result of skin's prolonged exposure to cold. Like burns, frostbite can range in severity: In minor cases it hurts to take off your boots and mittens, and even lukewarm water is excruciating, but the pain will go away. Lots of Badgers still remember one serious case that they swear they can still feel today when the weather changes. The most serious cases of frostbite—you've seen photos of mountain climbers with black ears and digits—can require amputation.

Worse, without proper clothing, you're at risk for **hypothermia,** a lethal condition in which the body loses the ability to warm itself. Warning signs of hypothermia include unvanquishable chills, slurred speech, and disorientation, among other symptoms.

In controlled skids on ice and snow, take your foot off the accelerator and steer *into* the direction of the skid. Follow all owner's manual advice if your car is equipped with an Anti-Lock Braking System (ABS). Most cars come equipped with all-season radials, so snow tires aren't usually necessary. *Tire chains are illegal in Wisconsin.*

During nighttime snowstorms, keep your lights on low beam. If you get stuck, check

ENVIRONMENTAL ISSUES

A state that produced both John Muir and Aldo Leopold must have a fairly good track record of being "green." If you discount the first century of statehood, during which the state—like most states at the time—pillaged the natural world full-bore, Wisconsin has in fact been ahead of its time environmentally. The state government initiated exceptionally far-sighted environmental laws beginning in the 1950s, when tourism loomed as a major industry. The state was the first to meet the

SAND COUNTY SAGE

There are some who can live without wild things, and some who cannot?.... Like winds and sunsets, wild things were taken for granted until progress began to do away with them.

Aldo Leopold, from the foreword to *A Sand County Almanac and Sketches Here and There*

Leading experts on environmentalism were once asked to name the most influential work in raising ecological consciousness. The hands-down winner was Aldo Leopold's *A Sand County Almanac*.

Aldo Leopold was a seminal naturalist, a pioneering figure in ecology and especially conservation. He introduced the idea of setting aside protected forest land and later devised the concept of wildlife management. Not a native Badger, Leopold nonetheless lived the better part of his life not far from where John Muir grew up. Above all, he was a polished writer, with a lucid, engaging, eloquent style celebrating life and its connection to the land.

EARLY YEARS

After attending Yale – its graduate forestry program was ultraprogressive, controversial, and the first of its kind – in 1909 Leopold went to work for the United States Forest Service (USFS). His seminal moment came in Arizona when he looked into the dying eyes of a wolf that had been shot – eradication was then the norm. His passion for educating people on the need to coexist with forests instead of obliterating them and all life in them in the name of progress may have germinated right there.

He accepted a fortuitous transfer to a new USFS lab in Madison in 1924 and within a few years had revolutionized how we view the natural world. His belief in a cause-and-effect relationship with the land led him to a two-year survey of game in North America and his founding of game-management theory.

By 1933, he was named the chair of UW's new game-management department. Part of his job was to examine and basically repair central Wisconsin, which had been laid waste during previous generations of misinformed agricultural exploitation. Leopold's tenure oversaw reforestation, wetland restoration, establishment of state and county forests, game preserves, parks, and more.

A SAND COUNTY ALMANAC

While covering Wisconsin's central region for his work, Leopold found the perfect retreat. He spent most of the rest of his life in examination of this land. The result is his evenhanded and scientifically pragmatic masterpiece for which he is justly famous, setting down what is now referred to as land ethic, the origin of modern-day land-use management.

A Sand County Almanac was in essence a florid, cheerful way of describing the symbiotic nature of humans and the land. What we today couch in multisyllabic jargon (biodiversity or ecoawareness), Leopold recognized intuitively.

One fantastic way to get a glimpse of the lands he so adored is to travel **Rustic Road 49,** Levee Road – 10 miles stretching along the Wisconsin River between WI 33 and Highway T and passing through the Aldo Leopold Reserve. You can also take self-guided or guided tours of the original **shack** and the wondrous (opened in 2007) **Aldo Leopold Legacy Center** a mile away via a trail. Hours vary; contact the Aldo Leopold Foundation (www.aldoleopold.org).

1972 Clean Water Act; it had put similar legislation on its own books a half decade earlier. Former Wisconsin governor and U.S. senator Gaylord Nelson founded Earth Day in 1970. More than 200 environmental periodicals are published here.

But still, let's be honest here. Milwaukee? Well, besides the fouled beaches due to algae and weeds (see the next section) American Rivers has named Milwaukee's Kinnickinnic River (the KK) as one of the country's ten most endangered rivers due to pollution and runoff. (Just ask any Milwaukeean about the local sewer district and Lake Michigan dumping during storms.) And Madison? Lovely Madison? Its four lakes absolutely reek some summers, with a thick green carpet of algae and weeds (some of which algae can be deadly) floating around and then up on shore, and everyone near the lake shutting their windows and turning on the air conditioning because it's so unbearable. You couldn't pay me to swim in Lake Monona, and I won't let my dog, protest as much as he doth.

Great Lakes No More?

Of all Wisconsin's 16,000-plus lakes (and countless thousand rivers and streams), perhaps the two Great Lakes—Michigan and Superior—are the most important bellwether indicators—if you screw up giants like these, what hope is there for other lakes?

The first thing you'll notice on the Lake Michigan shoreline (from Racine all the way to the Door Peninsula) is the stench. Yes, it is quite powerful at time. Most of this is the residual effect of algae blooms and weeds that ultimately are blown close to and on shore. The main villain? A pesky algae called **Cladophora,** and Wisconsinites now know it well. At times the mess can be so thick it needs to be raked, and at times there's just too much to do it. (And if that's not bad enough, some of it can be harmful, so don't let your dog romp in it.) And even if the algae problem isn't too bad at a spot, the beach may be closed anyway due to bacterial contamination (due to animal or human runoff)—in 2007, just under

20 percent of Wisconsin Great Lakes beaches showed elevated levels of E.coli.

Swimmers are not the only ones seeing major issues with Lake Michigan; sport fishers—a huge economic linchpin in some communities—are being shocked to discover fish stocks plummeting. (And sizes: A 30-pound salmon was no biggie in the 1980s; today, you're lucky to get a 20-pounder.) Lake Huron's salmon stock collapsed after the turn of the millennium. Lake Michigan perhaps isn't so dire, but in some spots the number of prey fish they need have dropped by 90 percent. (On the positive side, the famed yellow perch in the lake have finally begun to rebound.)

A main culprit for the decline in Lake Michigan's overall health is the pesky little mollusk **zebra mussel,** the species best representing what can happen when a nonnative species is introduced into an environment. Transplanted most likely from a visiting freighter from the Caspian Sea in the mid-1980s, the zebra mollusk is a ferocious, tough little Eurasian mollusk that found it loved the warmer waters and phytoplankton of the Great Lakes. Problem is, it loves to breed near warm areas—such as at discharge pipes around power plants. They breed so rapidly they create unbelievably dense barnaclelike crusts that do serious damage. Worse, they're being blamed for the decline if not decimation of native species as they literally suck all the nutrients out of an area. Great Lakes states are frantically fighting a $5 billion-per-year war to keep them from spreading into inland lakes and streams.

But within the past decade, the zebra mussel has become friends with a host of other alien invaders, one of 180 that now populate the Great Lakes. A new one is discovered every six months.

Newest invaders? Scarier even than zebra mussels are **quagga mussels,** new but far worse than zebras since they filter nutrients out of the water year-round (zebras go dormant in winter).

Asian carp, for one. This tough-nut alien species is poised to, quite literally, invade Lake Michigan via Illinois, which is doing everything save for poisoning rivers to keep it out. If it gets into Lake Michigan, it could mean doom for species present there.

Another? It's called VHS for short, but it ain't entertaining. It's **Viral Hemorrhagic Septicemia,** and it is as bad as it sounds—it was responsible for fish kills in 2005 and 2006.

Now for some good news. Quite literally the day this was being written in September 2008, the eight states and Canadian provinces bordering the Great Lakes got some good news when the U.S. Congress passed the sweeping Great Lakes Compact, a multi-billion-dollar plan to protect the Great Lakes (and, importantly, streamline regulations), something President George Bush planned to sign. Even pessimists were surprised and heartened a bit that something was being done.

Superfund Sites and Dirty Water

Things could be better. Wisconsin retains more than three dozen EPA Superfund sites (areas so contaminated that the EPA allots large amounts of money to clean them up). The Wisconsin Department of Natural Resources has found that about 900 miles of rivers in the state flunked environmental standards since the mid-1990s, and another 50 or so lakes were "questionable" or worse. Twenty-two percent of rivers and streams fail, one way or another, to meet the state's clean-water goals. Fish-consumption advisories have been in effect since 2000 for well over 300 lakes and rivers. Though the figures may constitute less than 5 percent of riverways and an even lower percentage of lakes, it portends worse things to come.

Though the state has some of the strictest groundwater laws and is pointed to by the EPA as one of three exemplary states, not enough local water sources pass muster. Land use, particularly agriculture, forestry, and construction, often creates eroded soils and runoff polluted with fertilizers and toxins. But agriculture cannot hold all the blame; urban runoff potentially causes up to 50 times as much soil erosion. Non-point-source pollution (so called

because it isn't traceable to a single source) is no higher than point-source pollution such as factory or industrial discharge. Non-point-source water picks up contaminants from whatever it comes in contact with—soil, pesticides, manure, oils, grass clippings, heavy metals—and winds up in surface water, sediment, or groundwater. Wisconsin's animal-waste runoff problem is among the nation's worst. In 2007 southeastern Wisconsin had its worst winter ever in terms of snowfall—one cannot even begin to imagine how much salt (used as a road de-icer) wound up in streams and rivers (literal saline dead zones were found).

Contaminated sedimentation from decades of abuse remains a secondary problem. In 1970, pulp and paper mills discharged almost 300 million gallons of wastewater, most of it untreated, into surface water, leaving a toxic legacy. The EPA was asked to declare 39 miles of the Fox River—the heart of papermaking—a Superfund site because *40 tons* (of an original 125 tons) of toxic PCBs (polychlorinated biphenyl) remained from factory waste discharge. (One baffling government proposal: Build a sludge pipe *right next to the brand-new Fox River State Trail!* The whole issue is pending.)

As a result of other pollution, the Wisconsin DNR issues almost 200 "boil water" notices annually (one Wisconsin county found half of its 376 wells to be seriously contaminated by pollutants such as atrazine and nitrates). More than 90 percent of state lakes have been affected one way or another, including sedimentation, contamination, and (the most common and difficult to handle) eutrophication—when increased nutrients in the water lead to algae blooms and nuisance weeds, which eventually kill off aquatic life (visit Madison, the city on four lakes, in July and you'll know what I mean). The DNR is in the process of publishing consumption advisories for fish in certain state lakes and the Great Lakes.

In 2000 the state took aim at non-point-source pollution with a set of proposed guidelines over decades that caused immediate debate when Wisconsinites got the bill: $2 billion. The act covers everything from manure spreading to pet droppings.

Mercury and Other Toxins

Some say toxic environmental pollutants are among the most pernicious, silent crises in the health of the North Woods today. No big deal? Environmentalists in 2000 were chagrined at the state's killing of its mercury reduction program, wondering how this could happen when even government statistics estimate that annually 1,200 Wisconsin children are exposed to elevated levels of mercury. The CDC in Atlanta says one woman in 10 in the United States already has dangerous levels of mercury in her blood.

Now, mercury isn't a problem in Lakes Superior and Michigan; however, fish consumption advisories exist there as well because of a cousin toxin—PCBs, different but equally awful. (It can cause cancer.) Mercury warnings for U.S. waters increased more than 100 percent since 1993. In 2004, scientists announced a somewhat shocking discovery—that dioxins were the likely culprit of swooning lake trout stocks, not invasive species or overfishing.

Also in 2004, the U.S. Food and Drug Administration was debating whether to start maintaining statistics on mercury levels in fish; state and local officials have been arguing for years whether it's necessary. No long-term studies have ever been done on humans.

Whether you agree or not on the dangers, here are official government statistics. In bottom feeders such as carp and Mississippi River channel catfish, the ppm contamination levels are at 0.11 and 0.09, respectively. Contrast this with predators such as bass and walleye, both with much higher levels, with the latter at a somewhat whopping 0.52 ppm. Northwestern Wisconsin, oddly enough, despite all those lush tracts of trees, has a rather high level of mercury contamination when compared to the rest of the state, mostly because of airborne contaminants.

This is in part why recommended daily intake of fish for women of childbearing years, nursing mothers, and children under 15 is one meal per week of bluegill, sunfish, yellow perch, and bullheads (among panfish), and one meal per month of walleye, northern pike, bass, channel catfish, and flathead catfish (among predators and bottom feeders). Note: Do not eat walleye longer than 20 inches, northern pike longer than 30 inches, or muskellenge.

For men and women beyond childbearing years, the former isn't limited, the latter is recommended at one meal per week. If you eat fish only during vacation or sporadically otherwise, you can double these amounts. To increase your chances of eating a healthy fish, eat smaller fish, eat panfish (sunfish, crappies, etc.) rather than predators (walleye, northern pike, etc.), and trim skin and fat.

Sprawl Mall Hell

With 90.1 people per square mile, Wisconsin ranks in the middle of American states for population density. However, two-thirds of the people dwell in the dozen southeastern counties, creating a serious land-use and urban-sprawl issue. In southeastern Wisconsin, agricultural land is being converted to urban use at a rate of 10 square miles per year. All of southern Wisconsin may be in danger—Scenic America has declared three sites (Vernon County's Kickapoo River Valley, Washington County around Erin, and Mississippi River bluffs) as some of the worst examples of rural landscape degradation; then again, we're not as bad as Colorado (the entire state made the list).

Northern forests are being encroached upon as flight from burgeoning urban areas continues. This sprawl results in diminished air quality (from excess use of commuters' automobiles), loss of farmland and wildlife habitat, more toxic runoff, and continued erosion.

Air Quality

At one point in the 1970s, fully half of Wisconsin counties failed standards for ozone, total suspended particulates, and sulfur dioxide. All have gotten better, save for ground-level ozone—the main ingredient of smog—still found in 11 southeastern counties. The problem is so severe that southeast Wisconsin was forced by federal law to begin using expensive reformulated gas in the mid-1990s. (Wisconsinites naturally blamed Chicago for the pollution!)

Once a grave crisis for northern lakes and forests, acid deposition, known as acid rain when it falls from the sky, has been slowed, largely through strict national legislation enacted in the mid-'80s. It's still a problem, however; 90 percent of the pollutants in Lake Superior come from the air.

Give 'Em Hell

Pick an issue and Wisconsinites will passionately—but politely—be involved, pro or con. The longstanding tradition of grassroots activism in the state is alive and well, especially in environmental issues. But here's the good part: It often ain't your stereotype granolas versus timber cutters. In fact, in many environmental issues, hunters, fishers, and snowmobilers work for common ground with heretofore "enemies"—the tree-huggers of Madison. No coincidence that the Progressive Party of Fightin' Bob La Follette was founded here. This fight represents what is really going on in the forests.

Visually Busy

In this author's opinion, another piece of the pollution puzzle—not lethal but certainly important—needs scrutiny: Wisconsin's lovely countryside is absolutely scarred by the visual pollution of "litter on a stick," or billboard advertising. States and communities across the nation have awakened to the fact that not only is it disgustingly ugly, but it can also distract drivers. The state has nearly 15,000 ugly popsicles gracelessly attesting to our state's, well, if not greed then certainly bad taste; only three states have more billboard advertising than Wisconsin.

FLORA AND FAUNA
Flora

The Eastern Transition and Great Lakes Forest Zones cover most of Wisconsin. Both are

cherry blossoms

primarily mixed meadow and woodland, a far cry from presettlement periods when 85 percent of the state was covered by forest and the rest by tall grass. By settlement periods, in the mid-19th century, those numbers had dipped to 63 percent forest, 28 percent savanna, and 9 percent grassland. Today, the state's forest cover is 37 percent, and precious little of that is original. Of the two million acres of prairie that once covered the state, only 2,000 scattered acres survive. In all, Wisconsin has more than 2,100 species of plants, approximately a tenth of which are classified as rare, and some of them are threatened.

Four major vegetation types cover Wisconsin. **Boreal forest,** a subarctic coniferous spread across northern North America, is found near Lake Superior in the north. Stretching across the central lowlands of the United States, **deciduous forest** makes up the second-largest swath of Wisconsin woodlands. **Mixed forest,** consisting of species of both, is found throughout the state. **Nonforest/grasslands** are found throughout the southern third of the

© WISCONSIN DEPARTMENT OF TOURISM

state and up into west-central Wisconsin along the Mississippi River.

Pines of all kinds are the most common tree type in Wisconsin. Commercially valuable, they grow quickly (key to recouping harvested lands) and hold well in the sandy, humus-poor soil of Wisconsin's central regions. Virtually all of northern Wisconsin's verdance is pine trees intermingled with northern hardwoods such as maple, birch, and aspen. In the extreme north, along Lake Superior, swamp conifers such as spruce and fir are common, along with tamarack and balsam. In the midsection of the state and to the south, you'll see oak, hickory, beech, and hemlock trees. To the east, lowland hardwoods such as elm, ash, and some cottonwood still grow.

In settlement periods, Wisconsin had a huge expanse of wetlands, including more than 10,000 acres along Green Bay alone. Today, that amount has dwindled by more than half but still constitutes the largest amount remaining on the Great Lakes—a pathetic indication of rapacious development and overuse.

Fauna

Wisconsin lies within three well-defined "life zones" conducive to species diversity: the Canadian, the transition, and the upper austral (or Carolinian). The Canadian, not surprisingly the coldest, features small mammals such as the snowshoe hare but also the state's primary large mammals, the deer and the black bear. The warmest zone, the Carolinian, falls in the southern tier of the state and lacks big game mammals. In total, Wisconsin has 73 species of mammals, 339 native bird species, and more than 200 species of amphibians, reptiles, frogs, bats, butterflies, and insects.

Of Wisconsin's two large mammals, the ubiquitous **white-tailed deer** is so great in number that for the last decade the state Department of Natural Resources (DNR) instituted unheard-of special deer hunts, including a special hunt specifically designed to thin out the doe and fawn population. The other resident big mammal, the **black bear,** is still relatively common in the North Woods and has also been seen in central counties.

Wisconsin lies smack in the middle of several migratory waterfowl flyways, so birding is a big activity in the state. **Tundra swans, sandhill cranes,** and **Canada geese** are three of the most conspicuous species. The latter are so predominant at the Horicon Marsh National Wildlife Refuge that ornithologists make pilgrimages there each spring and especially fall.

Threatened, Endangered, Exterminated

The last plains buffalo was shot five years before the state became a territory. The next to become extinct within the state of Wisconsin were the Richardson's caribou, the American elk, the cougar, the Carolina paroquet, the passenger pigeon (the world's last was shot in Wisconsin), the peregrine falcon, the pine marten, the trumpeter swan, the whooping crane, the wild turkey, the moose, the fisher, and, in 1922, the common wolverine.

Jump forward to today. First, the bad news: Wisconsin has more than 200 species of flora or fauna listed as either endangered or threatened by state or federal agencies. The state ranks in the middle for species diversity and at-risk status—0 percent of mammals are at risk, but 6.2 percent of fish are at serious risk (the rest are in the middle).

Yet all is not lost. Wisconsin instituted preservation measures long before the federal government did and is consistently recognized by environmental groups for at least trying (one reason so many green groups are here). The fisher, falcon, pine marten, trumpeter swan, and wild turkey have been reintroduced to varying degrees of success.

Perhaps befitting a state in which the International Crane Foundation is headquartered, cranes are making a comeback. The regal, French horn–sounding trumpeter swans, once nearly extinct, are well on the way to the target of 51 breeding pairs by 2020 (they now total about 300 birds in 14 counties). A great big by-the-way: **The International Crane Foundation** (www.savingcranes.org) has information on wonderful volunteer opportunities to tramp through central Wisconsin counting the birds—great fun!

In 2000 the state also established nesting sites for whooping cranes over 100,000 acres in central Wisconsin. In 2002, before national media, the first eight whooping cranes made their migration to Florida behind an ultralight plane (most returned). By 2020 hopes are to have 125 of the majestic birds in the state. Most amazing was the return of a nesting pair of **piping plovers** to the shores of the Apostle Islands National Lakeshore in 1999. In the entire Great Lakes only 30 nesting pairs exist, all in Michigan. As a result, the U.S. Fish and Wildlife Service has proposed setting aside nearly 200 miles of shoreline—20 in Wisconsin—for critical habitats, and possibly to establish a colony.

One of the most visually amazing birds—the white pelican—has also made a recent comeback. Thank the universe if you spot one in the Horicon Marsh National Wildlife Refuge.

Though never extinct, the bald eagle, once perilously close to vanishing, may have had the most successful recovery of all. The state now harbors about 850 pairs of breeding eagles, and the birds are so prevalent along the Wisconsin and Mississippi Rivers that certain communities make much of their tourist income because of them. The state is also gobbling up riverine land near Prairie du Sac to continue the comeback.

Wisconsin does take forceful steps to preserve wildlife through its Department of Natural Resources. It was the first state in the United States to designate Natural Areas throughout the state. These vigilantly protected areas harbor fragile geology, archaeology, or plant and animal life; some are even being nudged toward a return to their presettlement ecology.

Absolutely the most intriguing question now is if **cougars** are preying the woods. Since 1994, more than 300 sightings (by quite insistent people) have been reported (the last one supposedly perished in 1908); they're most likely migrating from the Black Hills of South Dakota.

If there is one endangered fish all Badgers worry about, it's the **perch,** especially the yellow perch. In a state that treats fish fries as quasi-religious experiences (there is no better fish than perch for a fish fry), plummeting lake perch populations in the early 1990s absolutely freaked out the fish-loving population. But since the turn of the new millennium, sufficient numbers were being seen for the DNR to be "cautiously optimistic." As of 2007, those numbers were actually pretty good. Trout lovers rejoice—blue-ribbon status streams have increased 1,000 percent in 20 years!

Still, the picture could be much better. Even as many species are rebounding, annually other native species are added to the threatened and endangered lists. Just under 3 percent of native plants are now threatened or endangered. And one-quarter of the state's species are non-native, or invasive.

Birder Heaven

Avian species have always found the state's flyways crucial to survival. With the reintroduction of so many—along with wetlands restoration and protection—the state has fantastic birding opportunities. The statewide **Oak Leaf Birding Trail** (www.dnr .state.wi.us) has 35 prime birding spots; the terminus is Whitnall Park in Milwaukee. Even better is the newer **Great Wisconsin Birding and Nature Trail,** which covers the whole state; check www.wisconsinbirds.org for more information.

One place few people visit is the outstanding **Baraboo Hills** region (in Central Wisconsin), a major node on a transcontinental birding flyway.

History

To understand Madison and Milwaukee, you must understand Wisconsin. And there is a lot there to peruse!

EARLY ARRIVALS

The Siberia-to-Alaska Beringia theory, which posits that the progenitors of North America's Native Americans arrived over a land bridge that rose and submerged in the Bering Strait beginning as many as 20,000 years ago, was dealt serious blows in the late 1990s. Provocative new anthropological discoveries in North and Latin America have forced a radical reconsideration of this theory (a Wisconsin archaeologist was one of the first to bring up the topic—Kenosha County in southeastern Wisconsin has revealed key new finds). The last of the glacial interludes of the Pleistocene era, the Two Rivers, probably saw the first movement into the state of early Paleo-Indians about 11,500 years ago. The time is based on examinations of fluted points as well as a rare mastodon kill site, the Boaz Mastodon, which established Paleo-Indian hunting techniques of the Plains Indians in Wisconsin.

Glacial retreat helps explain why the Paleo-Indian groups entered the state from the south and southwest rather than the more logical north. Nomadic clans followed the mastodon and other large mammals northward as the glaciers shrank. Thus divergent Indian cultures formed in northern and southern Wisconsin, each in a distinct biotic zone created by retreating glaciers, the incipient woodland and prairie, and even nascent littoral environments.

Later Stages

Solid archaeological evidence establishes definite stages in Wisconsin's earliest settlers. The **Archaic** period lasted, approximately, from 8000 b.c. to 750 b.c. The region's deciduous forests and moderate climate required little lifestyle modification. The tribes were still transient, pursuing smaller game and the fish in the newly formed lakes. Around 2000 b.c., these Indians became the first in the New World to fashion copper.

The later **Woodland** Indians, with semipermanent abodes, are generally regarded as the first Natives in Wisconsin to make use of ceramics, elaborate mound burials and, to a lesser extent, domesticated plants such as squash, corn, pumpkins, beans, and tobacco. Lasting from around 750 b.c. until European exploration, the Woodland period was a minor golden age of dramatic change for the Native cultures. Around 100 b.c., the Middle Woodland experienced cultural and technological proliferations, simultaneous with the period of Ohio's and Illinois's Hopewell societies, when villages formed and expanded greatly along waterways. The Late Woodland culture is best represented by the residual ground formations of the effigy mound cultures in the southern third of the state.

The people living during the tail end of the Woodland period have been classified into two additional groups: the **Mississippian** and the **Oneota.** The former's impressive sites can be found from New Orleans all the way north into Wisconsin and parts of Minnesota. Mississippian culture showed high levels of civic planning and complex social hierarchies, and it lasted at least until the Spanish arrived (Spanish records reported contact). Trade was enormous during this period but declined during the Oneota, as did the flowering of culture.

EUROPEAN CONTACT

The Spanish (and Portuguese) in the latter part of the 15th century—the watershed of Europe's first great westward expansion—blazed the trail west looking for the East. The main directive was to circumvent the Arabs, reach the courts of the Great Khan, and establish channels to appropriate the riches of new lands. Along the way, the natives, if any, were to be "pacified" under papal hegemony. After England came to naval power under the

Tudor monarchies and began taking swipes at the French, the New World became the proving ground for the European powers.

New France: Black Robes and the Fur Trade

The French, relative latecomers to maritime and thus expansionist endeavors, were, thanks to the Reformation, conveniently freed of papal dicta for divvying up the new continent and its inherent wealth. Nevertheless, Spanish strength closed them out of much of the Caribbean and Gulf Coast. The up-and-coming English established a foothold in what would become the mid-Atlantic colonies. Hence, France was effectively forced to attempt to penetrate the new land via the northern frontier.

Jacques Cartier first opened the door to the Great Lakes region with his "discovery" of the Gulf of the St. Lawrence River, in 1534. The insular French monarchy, though, were obsessed with keeping up with the Spanish. As a result, the French, content to fish the shoals of Newfoundland, left the scattered outposts to simmer for another 40 years—except for several fur traders, who, it turns out, were on to something.

When, with an eye to establishing a permanent "New France," the French did establish sparse settlements in the early 16th century, they were dismayed by the lack of ready riches, the roughness of the land, and the bitter weather. However, the original traders possessed one superlative talent: forging relationships with the Natives, who became enamored of French metal implements—firearms in particular. Eventually, the French found their coveted mother lode: beavers.

Paris hatmakers discovered that beaver pelts—especially those softened for a year around the waists of Indians—made a superior grade of felt for hats, and these soon became the rage in Paris and other parts of Europe. As beaver was readily available and easily transportable to France from the wilds, it became the lifeblood of the colonies, sustaining the region through the mismanagement and general vagaries of both British and French rule.

Facilitating both the fur trade and French control over the colonies were the missionaries of the Society of Jesus—the Jesuits. These "Black Robes" (so-called by the Huron and Ottawa because of their long dark frocks) first arrived during a time of atavistic religious fervor in France. The Franciscans had originally set down here but found the task of conversion too daunting for their small order. The Jesuits became the very foundation upon which New France operated, serving crucial secular needs as well as religious ones. The traders needed them to foster harmony with Native American traders. More important, the often complicated French systems of operation required that all day-to-day affairs be carried out at the local level. By 1632, all missionary work in French Canada was under the auspices of the Jesuits.

The Jesuits also accompanied voyageurs (explorers) as New France attempted to widen its sphere of influence westward. Eventually, the Black Robes themselves, along with renegade fur traders, were responsible for the initial exploration and settlement of present-day Wisconsin.

THE FRENCH IN WISCONSIN

Samuel de Champlain, who first arrived in Quebec in 1603, was the province's most famous French governor and, in many ways, its most effective, despite ignoring mundane management duties to obsess on the legendary route to the "People of the Seas" and the Great Khan. After arriving and hearing of the "People of the Stinking Waters" (the Winnebago), which he surmised to mean an ocean-dwelling people, he dispatched the first Europeans from Acadia to explore the wild western frontier.

Though there is speculative evidence that Étienne Brulé, Champlain's first explorer, may have poked around Wisconsin as early as 1620—the same year many assume the pilgrims founded the new colonies—most historians credit Jean Nicolet with being the first European to turn up in Green Bay, landing at Red Banks in 1634. Garbed in Chinese damask and using thunderstick histrionics to impress the natives (the Potawatomi he met immediately dubbed him Thunder Beaver), Nicolet efficiently and diplomatically forged immediate ties with the Indians, who guided him throughout the region to meet other tribes, many of whom had never seen a European.

As before, Nicolet couldn't rouse the wilted interest of the French royalty—all it wanted to see was bags of Chinese silk—and the country once again let the matter drop. Legitimate French fur traders were scooped by Pierre Esprit Radisson and Médard Chouart des Groseilliers, two pesky *coureurs-de-bois* (renegade trappers) who couldn't be bothered to get licensed by the crown. They delved farther into Wisconsin than any had before but had nowhere to trade their furs after being blacklisted by the ruling powers in New France. This led them to England, which gave them a charter to establish the Hudson's Bay Company north of New France—one reason for the later conflict between France and Britain. In 1666, these two were followed by Nicholas Perrot, who extended Nicolet's explorations and consequently opened the French fur trade with natives in Wisconsin.

In 1661, the first Black Robe, Father René Ménard, arrived to help the displaced Huron in Chequamegon Bay. Lost in the wilderness, he was replaced by the more seasoned Father Claude Allouez, who founded the first mission at La Pointe in the Apostle Islands. After Perrot opened official commerce with the Indians, Allouez founded St. Francois Xavier, Wisconsin's first permanent European settlement, at De Pere, south of Green Bay. Much of the knowledge of Native American cultures at the time comes from the journals of these Jesuit settlers.

The most famous Jesuit explorer was Father Jacques Marquette, who, along with Louis Jolliet, was sent by La Salle in 1673 to discern whether the Mississippi emptied into the Gulf of Mexico. The first Europeans to cross Wisconsin, they made it to the Mississippi on June 17, 1673, and went as far south as Arkansas, where they saw Indians with European goods, confirming both a route to the Gulf and the presence of the Spanish.

The French hesitated in buttressing their western frontier—and it wound up costing them dearly.

Conflict with the British and British Rule

The fate of New France and, thus, Wisconsin was determined not in the New World but on the European continent, as Louis XIV, who had reigned during a zenith of French power, frittered away French influence bit by bit in frivolous, distracting battles.

The French never fully used the western edges of the Great Lakes. With few royal overseers and inept central planning, the exploration was left to a hodgepodge of fur traders and Jesuits; it proved arbitrary and minimal. James II's rise to the throne in England marked the end of France's never-exactly-halcyon days in the Great Lakes. James forced Louis into wild strategies to protect French interests in the New World—strategies that did lead to further exploration of the hinterlands but also drove France to overextend itself and, eventually, collapse as a power in the region.

At the behest of the Jesuits, who hoped to corral the recalcitrant Indian tribes (who hadn't yet displayed either loyalty to the crown or subservience to God), Louis closed trade completely in the Great Lakes interiors, thus cutting off possible ties between the Indians and the English or the Spanish. Louis correctly reckoned that whoever the Indians sided with would end up controlling the new lands. After realizing this plan was overly rash—and likely was draining royal coffers—he changed tactics and decided instead to keep the Indians, the English, and the Spanish in check by exploring as far inland as possible and trying to establish a line of garrisons from Montreal all the way to New Orleans.

Louis succeeded in this second plan but in the process alienated the uneasy Indians who *had* sworn loyalty to France and, worse, aroused the ire of France's bitterest enemies—the Iroquois and the Fox Indians. Wars with the Fox, which raged 1701–1738, sapped the determination of the French temporarily, but they had enough pluck—and military might—to string forts along the Mississippi to look for inroads into territories already held by the British in the Ohio River Valley. By 1750, British colonists in the western Great Lakes outnumbered French 20 to 1, and many Indians, discovering that the English made higher-quality goods more cheaply, switched to the British side.

Franco-Anglo hostilities ignited for real in 1689, when William of Orange came to power, and the two nations fought four wars over a span of 75 years. The last one—the French and Indian War (1755–1763)—was a thorough thrashing of the French by the British and greatly determined European spheres of influence in North America. The first Treaty of Paris, signed in 1763 as a result of the war, dictated France's ouster from Canada and the Northwest Territory except for minute fisheries on Newfoundland. Spain got New Orleans and Louisiana west of the Mississippi, and Britain got the rest.

Under the British, little changed in daily life. (The English never even had an official presence in present-day Wisconsin.) One Englishman of note, however, was Jonathan Carver, a roguish explorer who roamed the state 1766–1768 and returned to England to publish fanciful, lively, and mostly untrue accounts of the new lands west of the inland seas.

The British crown's ruling philosophy was, for the most part, hands off, except in crucial areas of diplomacy. The French had been content simply to trade and had never made overtures for the land itself. But the British who did come—many barely able to conceal their scorn for the less-than-noble savages—began parceling up property and immediately incited unrest. Pontiac, an Ottawa chieftain, led a revolt against the British at Muscoda.

Additionally, the British monarchy's finances were in disarray from the lengthy conflicts with the French in North America and with other enemies in European theaters. The American colonists had paid very little for the military protection they enjoyed, but the monarchy now decreed that the colonies could foot their own bill for the new lands and instituted the Stamp Act.

THE AMERICAN REVOLUTION

British settlers in Wisconsin who remained after the area was made part of British Quebec Province under the Quebec Act of 1774 stood resolutely loyal to the British crown but never got a real chance to test their mettle. Settlers in Wisconsin remained out of the American Revolution other than scattered attempts by both sides to enlist the Indians.

The 1781 surrender of Cornwallis at Yorktown sealed the fate of the British in the New World. And though they ceded a great part of their holdings, including the Northwest Territory, which included Wisconsin, practical British influence remained in the state until after the War of 1812.

British commercial interests had little desire to abandon the still-lucrative beaver trade, and the Indians had grown, if not loyal to, then at least tolerant of, the British. When hostilities broke out in 1812, the British, aiming to create a buffer zone of Indian alliances in Indiana and Illinois, quickly befriended the Indians—an easy venture, as the Natives were already inflamed over the first of many U.S. government snake-oil land treaties.

The Northwest, including Wisconsin, played a much larger role in this new bellicosity than it had in the Revolution; British loyalists and American frontiersman fought for control of the Natives as well as of the water-route forts of the French and British. British forts, now occupied (and undermanned) by U.S. troops, were easily overwhelmed by English and Indian confederates. However, Commodore Perry's victory on Lake Erie in 1813 swung the momentum to the American side. Treaties signed upon reaching a stalemate in 1814 allowed the United States to regain preexisting national boundaries and, once and for all, sweep the British from the Great Lakes and the Mississippi River. Almost immediately, John Jacob Astor's American Fur Company set up operations in Wisconsin, but by this time the golden age of beaver trade in the area was over.

Though not yet even a territory and despite both the intractability of the Indians and the large populations of British and French, Wisconsin was fully part of the United States by 1815. In 1822, the first wave of immigration began, with thousands of Cornish and other miners burrowing into the hillsides of southwestern Wisconsin to search for lead (the origin of the Badger State moniker). As miners poured into Wisconsin to scavenge lead, speculators multiplied, land offices sprang up, and the first banks opened; everyone was eager to make money off the new immigrants. Before the area achieved territorial status, in 1836, more than 10,000 settlers had inundated the southern part of the state.

NATIVE AMERICAN RELATIONS

Unfortunately, none of the foreign settlers consulted the indigenous residents before carving up the land. The United States practiced a heavy-handed patriarchal policy toward the Native Americans, insisting that they be relocated west—away from white settlers on the eastern seaboard—for the betterment of both sides. Simultaneously, the new government instituted a loony system designed to reprogram the Natives to become happy Christian farmers. American leaders assumed that weaning Native Americans from nomadic hunting tracts would minimize conflict with settlers. Land cessions, begun around the turn of the 19th century, continued regularly until the first general concourse of most western Indian tribes took place, in 1825, at Prairie du Chien, Wisconsin, at which time the first of the more draconian treaties was drawn up. The first New York Indians—the Oneida, Stockbridge, Munsee, and Brothertown—were moved to Wisconsin beginning in 1823. The cocktail of misguided U.S. patronization and helplessly naive Native negotiations turned lethal when many tribes came to realize what had been done to them. The United States began enforcing treaty eviction small print bit by bit, and the forlorn Native Americans, deserted earlier by both the French and the British, were encroached on more and more by a hostile new White Father. Inevitable retaliation followed.

The first skirmish, the so-called Winnebago War of 1827, was nothing more than a frustrated attempt at vengeance by a Winnebago chieftain, Red Bird, who killed two settlers before being convinced to surrender to avert war. The second was more serious—and more legendary.

The Black Hawk War

In 1804, William Henry Harrison, a ruthless longtime foe of Indians in the west, rammed through a treaty with Native Americans in St. Louis that effectively extinguished the tribes' title to most of their land. Part of this land was in southwestern Wisconsin, newly dubbed the "lead region."

Mining operations—wildcatters, mostly—proliferated but ebbed when the miners began to fear the Natives more and more. The ire and paranoia of the federal government, which had assumed carte blanche in the region, was piqued in 1832, when a militant band of Fox-Sauk Indians refused to recognize treaties, including the one that had forcibly moved them out of the southern part of Wisconsin.

Their leader was Black Sparrow Hawk, better known as Black Hawk, a warrior not so much pro-British as fiercely anti-American. With blind faith in the British, obdurate pride, and urging from other Indian tribes (who would later double-cross him), Black Hawk initiated a quixotic stand against the United States, which culminated in tragic battles staged in Wisconsin.

Black Hawk and his group of about 1,000 recalcitrant natives, dubbed "the British Band," balked at U.S. demands that the tribe relocate across the Mississippi. Insisting that they were exempt because Black Hawk had been blacklisted from treaty negotiations, in April 1832 the band began moving up the Rock River to what they deemed their rightful lands. Other tribes had promised support along the way, in both provisions and firepower. Instead, Black Hawk found his erstwhile exhorters—the Potawatomi, Sioux, and Winnebago—turning on him. Worse, news of Black Hawk's actions was sweeping the region with grotesque frontier embellishment, and the U.S. military, private militias, and frontiersmen under their control were all itching for a fight.

His people lacking provisions (one reason for the band's initial decampment was a lack of corn in the area after the settlers squeezed in) and soon tiring, Black Hawk wisely realized his folly and in May sent a truce contingent. Jumpy soldiers under Major Isaiah Stillman instead overreacted and attacked. Black Hawk naturally counterattacked and, although seriously outnumbered, his warriors chased the whites away—an event that became known as Stillman's Run. Nevertheless, the fuse was lit.

The band then crossed into Wisconsin near Lake Koshkonong and began a slow, difficult journey west, back toward the Mississippi River. Two commanders led their forces in pursuit of the hapless Indians, engaging in a war of attrition along the way. They cornered Black Hawk and fought the quick but furious Battle of Wisconsin Heights along the Wisconsin River. The tribe escaped in the darkness, with the soldiers pursuing hungrily. One large group of mostly women, children, and old men tried to float down the Wisconsin toward the Mississippi but was intercepted by soldiers and Indians; most were drowned or killed.

What followed is perhaps the most tragic chapter in Wisconsin history, the Battle of Bad Axe, an episode that garnered shocked national attention and made Black Hawk as well known as the president. On August 1, 1832, Black Hawk made it to the Mississippi River. Hastily throwing together rafts, the band tried to cross but was intercepted by a U.S. gunboat. The U.S. forces opened fire mercilessly for two hours, despite a white flag from the Indians. Black Hawk and a group of 50 escaped, assuming the other group—300 women, children, and elderly—would be left alone. Instead, this group was butchered by General Henry Atkinson's men and their Sioux cohorts when they reached the opposite shore.

Black Hawk and the 50 warriors were pursued by legions of soldiers and Indian accomplices.

Black Hawk was eventually brought in alive to St. Louis (guarded by Jefferson Davis) and later imprisoned on the East Coast, where he found himself in the media spotlight. He later wrote a compelling autobiography, one of the first documents offering a glimpse of the baffled, frustrated Native American point of view. Black Hawk was eventually sent back to Wisconsin.

In truth, Black Hawk was likely never half as belligerent as he's been characterized. By the 1830s he was well into his 60s and weary of protracted and unbalanced negotiations and battles with the whites. The Black Hawk War marked a watershed of Native presence in Wisconsin: By 1833, the few cessions the United States had gained to Native lands below the Fox-Wisconsin Rivers had been extracted. However, in 1837 the northern Wisconsin tribes signed away for a pittance more than half of the land area north of the Fox River, giving free reign to the rapacious lumbermen. Perhaps directly because of Black Hawk's sad grasp for legitimacy, the U.S. government began playing hardball with the Native Americans.

THE WISCONSIN TERRITORY

The Northwest Ordinance of 1787 established many of the borders of present-day Wisconsin; Thomas Jefferson had initially envisioned dividing the region into 10 states. Later, before the War of 1812, Wisconsin became part of first the Indiana Territory and then the Illinois as the Northwest was chiseled down. In 1818, the Illinois Territory was further hacked to create the Michigan Territory. Finally, in 1836, the Wisconsin Territory was established, taking in all of modern Wisconsin, the Upper Peninsula of Michigan, Iowa, Minnesota, and parts of North and South Dakota.

Despite the loss, the Black Hawk fiasco had another effect contrary to the Sauk leader's intentions: The well-publicized battles put Wisconsin on the map. This, combined with the wild mining operations in the southwestern part of the state, burgeoning lumber operations along the Great Lake coast, and discovery of the fecund soils outside of Milwaukee, ensured

Wisconsin's status as the Next Big Thing. The new Erie Canal provided immigrants a direct route to this new land. By 1835, 60,000 eager settlers were pushing through the Erie Canal each year, and most were aiming for what the following year became the Wisconsin Territory. Two years later, in 1838, when the chunk of Wisconsin Territory west of the Mississippi was lopped off, more than half of the 225,000 settlers were in Wisconsin proper. With the enforcement of Indian land cessions after Black Hawk's defeat, up to three *billion* acres became available for government surveyors; the first land title sales started in 1834. Wisconsin had fully arrived—and it still wasn't even a state.

STATEHOOD: GROWING PAINS

Wisconsin's entrance into the Union as the flag's 30th star was a bit anticlimactic; there wasn't even a skirmish with Canada over it. In fact, the populace voted on the issue of statehood in 1841, and every year for nearly the entire decade, but distinctly disinterested voters rejected the idea until 1848, when stratospheric levels of immigration impelled the legislature to more animated attempts, and the first measures passed.

Incessant immigration continued after statehood. Most newcomers arrived from New England or Europe—Ireland, England, Germany, and Scandinavia. The influx of Poles was still decades away. Milwaukee, a diminutive village of 1,500 at the time of territorial status, burgeoned into a rollicking town of 46,000 by the start of the Civil War, by which time the population of the state as a whole was up to 706,000 people.

During the period leading up to the Civil War, Wisconsin was dominated by political (and some social) wrangling over what, exactly, the state was to be. With the influence of Yankee immigrants and the Erie Canal access, much of Wisconsin's cultural, political, and social makeup finally resembled New England. In fact, New York legislation was the model for many early Wisconsin laws. The first university was incorporated almost immediately after statehood, and school codes for primary and secondary education soon followed—a bit ahead of the Union as a whole.

Abolition was a hot issue in Wisconsin's early years. It reached top-level status after the annexation of Texas and the Mexican-American War; as a result of this and many other contentious issues, Ripon, Wisconsin, became the founding spot of the Republican Party, which soon took hold of the legislature and held fast until the Civil War.

During the Civil War, despite being among the first states to near enlistment quotas, Wisconsin suffered some of the fiercest draft rioting in the nation. Many new immigrants had decamped from their European homelands for precisely the reasons for which the government was now pursuing them. Eventually, 96,000 Wisconsinites would serve.

Post-Civil War: Immigrants, Dairy, and Industry

After the Civil War and through the turn of the 20th century, Wisconsin began getting its economic bearings while politicians wrestled over issues as disparate as temperance, railroads, and immigrants' rights. The latter hot potato galvanized enormous enclaves of German Americans into action; they mobilized against anti-immigration laws sweeping through the legislature. Despite the mandates (banning the German language in schools, for one), successive waves of immigrants poured into the state.

The first sawmills had gone up in Wisconsin at the turn of the 19th century. Yankee and British settlers put them up to use the timber they were felling in clearing farmland. Commercial timber exploitation hadn't begun in earnest until the 1830s, initially along the Lake Michigan coast and Fox/Wisconsin Riverway and then creeping northward as the perimeter of forest was hacked away. By 1870, more than one billion board feet of lumber was being churned out through the state's 1,000-plus mills each year, easily making Wisconsin the country's largest timber producer. In time, more than 20 billion board feet were taken from the shores of Green Bay alone; one year, 425 million board feet were shipped through Superior. Wisconsin wood was used in other parts of the expanding country to make homes, wagons, fences, barns, and plank roads. As a result, by the turn of the 20th century, more than 50 million acres of Wisconsin (and Minnesota) forest had been ravaged—most of it unrecoverable. By 1920, most of the state was a cutover wasteland and the timber industry declined to more rational levels, although papermaking continued in overdrive, as it still does.

A handful of years after the Civil War, the state kicked its wheat habit (by 1860, Wisconsin was producing more wheat than any other state in the United States) and began looking for economic diversity. Wheat was sapping the soil fertility in southern Wisconsin, forcing many early settlers to pick up stakes once again and shift to the enormous golden tracts of the western plains states. Later, when railroads and their seemingly arbitrary pricing systems began affecting potential income from wheat, farmers in Wisconsin began seriously reviewing their options. Farmers diversified into corn, cranberries, sorghum, and hops, among others. Sheep and some hogs constituted the spectrum of livestock, but within two decades, the milk cow would surpass everything else on four hooves.

Myriad factors influenced the early trend toward dairy. Most of the European immigrant farmers, many of them dairy farmers in the old country, found the topography and climate in Wisconsin similar to those of their homelands. Transplanted Yankees had seen it before in New York and Vermont and knew a dairy revolution was coming. Led by foresighted dairying advocate William Hoard and his germinal journal, *Hoard's Dairyman,* and by the new Wisconsin Dairymen's Association, farmers began adding dairy cattle to their other crops and livestock until, by 1899, 90 percent of Wisconsin's farmers were keeping cows predominantly.

Butter production initially led the new industry, since it was easier to keep than milk. But technology and industrialization, thanks in large part to the University of Wisconsin Scientific Agriculture Institute, propelled Wisconsin into milk, cheese, and other dairy-product prominence. The institute was responsible for extending the dairy season, introducing several highly productive new methods, and the groundbreaking 1890 Babcock butterfat test, a simple test of chemically separating and centrifuging milk samples to determine its quality, thereby ensuring farmers were paid based on the quality and not just the weight of the milk.

By 1880, despite less-fecund land and a shorter growing season than other agricultural states, Wisconsin ranked fourth in dairy production, thanks to university efficiency, progressive quality control, Herculean effort in the fields, and the later organization of powerful trade exchanges. The southern half of the state, with its minerals in the southwest and rich loamy soils in the southeast, attracted European agrarian and dairy farming immigrants and speculators. "America's Dairyland" made it onto state license plates in the 1930s.

Wisconsin's grand network of northern and central forests and connected waterways, which had supplied humans the means of existence for 10 millennia, was not overshadowed by the southern dairy boom. Ever since the mid-1830s, immigrant tie hacks had moved north along the Lake Michigan coast in search of lumber. The timber industry surpassed dairy until well into the 20th century.

Boom-bust logging ravaged Wisconsin's virgin tracts. One area of the Chippewa River possessed one-sixth of all the pine west of the Adirondacks—and Wisconsin pine was larger and harder than that in surrounding states. Easily floated down streams and rivers, pine became an enormous commodity on the expanding plains. In Wisconsin, even the roads were fashioned from pine and hardwood planks. Though declining in sheer volume after a zenith in the 1870s, lumber led all manufacturing 1890–1910; in 1893, the timber industry provided one-fourth of all wages in the state.

The inevitable downside was the effects of raping the environment. Land eroded, tracts of forest disappeared and weren't replaced, and riparian areas were destroyed to dam for "float flooding." Worst, the average pine tree size was shrinking rapidly, and the lumber barons expressed little interest in preparing for the ultimate eradication of the forests. The small settlement of Peshtigo and more than 1,000 of its people perished in a furious conflagration made worse by logging cutover in 1871, and in the 1890s vast fires swept other central and northern counties.

THE PROGRESSIVE ERA

Wisconsinites have a rather fickle political history. Democrats held sway in the territorial days; then, in 1854, the newly formed Republican Party took the reins. The two monoliths—challenged only occasionally by upstarts such as the Grangers, the Socialists (Milwaukee consistently voted for Socialist representatives), Populists, and the Temperance movement—jockeyed for power until the end of the century.

The Progressive Party movement, formed of equal parts reformed Democrats and Republicans, was the original third-party ticket, molted from the frustrated moderates of the Wisconsin Republican Party keen on challenging the status quo. As progressivism gained steam and was led on by native sons, the citizenry of Wisconsin—tireless and shrewd salt-of-the-earth workers—eventually embraced the movement with open arms, even if the rest of the country didn't always. The Progressive movement was the first serious challenge to the United States' political machine.

Fightin' Bob: Legacy of Progressivism

If there is one piece to the Wisconsin political mosaic that warrants kudos, it's the inveterate inability to follow categorization. Whether politically prescient or simply lacking patience, the state has always ridden the cutting edge. These qualities are best represented physically by the original Progressive: Robert La Follette, a.k.a. "Menace to the Machine." One political writer in the early 20th century said of La Follette: "The story of Wisconsin is the story of Gov. La Follette. He's the head of the state. Not many Governors are that." The seminal force in Wisconsin, La Follette eschewed the pork-barrel status quo to form the Progressive Party. In Wisconsin, the La Follette family dominated the state scene for two generations, fighting for social rights most people had never heard of.

Robert M. La Follette was born on a Dane County farm in 1855, where the typically hard-scrabble life prepared him for the rigors of the University of Wisconsin, which he entered in 1875. He discovered a passion and talent for oratory but, too short for theater, gravitated to politics—a subject befitting the ambitious young man. He was elected Dane County district attorney in 1880. Well liked by the hoi polloi, he gave them resonance with his hand-pumping and his off-the-cuff speeches on hard work and personal responsibility in government. An entrenched Republican, he was more or less ignored by the party brass, so in 1884 he brashly ran for U.S. Congress on his own—and won. He was the youngest state representative in U.S. history.

Initially, La Follette toed the party line fairly well, though he did use his position to crow elegantly against the well-oiled political infrastructure. After the Republicans were voted out en masse in 1890, La Follette returned to Wisconsin and formed the Progressive Party. He ran for governor and, after two tries, landed the nomination. A tireless circuit and chautauqua lecturer, he relied on a salt-of-the-earth theme and left audiences mesmerized. This marked the birth of the "Fightin' Bob" image, which persists to this day. He was elected governor three times, returned to the Senate for a tempestuous career, and made serious runs at the presidency.

La Follette's critics found him as self-righteous and passionately tactless as he was brilliant, forthcoming, gregarious, and every other superlative by which he remains known today. This driven man of the people was no more enigmatically contradictory than many other public figures, but historians have noted that even his most vehement opponents respected his ethics. Under him, Wisconsin instituted the nation's first direct primary and watershed civil-service systems, passed anticorruption legislation and railroad monopoly reforms, and, most important, formed the Wisconsin Idea.

Progressivism and the Wisconsin Idea

Progressivism represented a careful balance of honest-to-goodness idealism and what may today be termed Libertarian tenets. La Follette saw it as an attempt to overcome, on a grassroots level, the dehumanizing aspect of corporate greed and political corruption. *The Progressive,* the Madison-based periodical he founded, remains the country's leading medium for social justice.

Fightin' Bob's most radical creation was the Wisconsin Idea. Officially a system whereby the state used careful research and empirical evidence in governing, in reality it meant that La Follette kept a close-knit core of advisers as de facto aides. His was the first government—state or federal—to maintain expert panels and commissions, a controversial plan at the time. Some criticized it as elitist, but he argued that it was necessary to combat well-funded industry cronyism.

EARLY 20TH CENTURY

Robert La Follette's most (in)famous personal crusade was his strident opposition to U.S. participation in World War I. It was engendered in no small part in Wisconsin's heavy German population but also in La Follette's vehement pacifism. He suffered tremendous regional and national scorn and was booted to the lower echelons of politics. Interestingly, when the United States officially entered the war, Wisconsin was the first state to meet enlistment requirements. Eventually, La Follette enjoyed something of a vindication with a triumphant return to the Senate in 1924, followed by a final real presidential run.

Also a political activist, Bob's wife, Belle La Follette, mounted a long-standing crusade for women's suffrage that helped the 19th Amendment get ratified; Wisconsin was the first state to ratify it. In other political trends starting around the turn of the 20th century, Milwaukee began electing Socialist administrations. Buoyed by nascent labor organizations in the huge factory towns along Lake Michigan, the movement was infused with an immigrant European populace not averse to social radicalism. Milwaukee was the country's most heavily unionized city, and it voted Socialist—at least in part—right through the 1960s. The Progressive banner was picked up by La Follette's sons, Phil and Robert Jr., and the Wisconsin Progressive Party was formed in 1934. Robert Jr. took over for his father in the U.S. Senate, and Phil dominated Wisconsin politics during the '30s. Despite these efforts, the movement waned. Anemic and ineffective from internal splits and World War II, it melded with the Republican Party in 1946.

Dairying became Wisconsin's economic leader by 1920 and gained national prominence as well. The industry brought in nearly $210 million to the state, wholly eclipsing timber and lumber. This turned out to be a savior for the state's fortunes during the Depression; dairy products were less threatened by economic collapse than either forest appropriation or manufacturing, though farmers' management and methodology costs skyrocketed. Papermaking, in which Wisconsin is still a world leader, ameliorated the blow in the jobless cutover north- and east-central parts of the state. Concentrated fully in southeastern Wisconsin, heavy industry—leather, meatpacking, foundries, fabrication, and machine shops—suffered more acutely during the Depression. Sales receipts plummeted by two-thirds and the number of jobs fell by nearly half in five years. Brewing was as yet nonexistent, save for root beer and some backroom swill.

POST-WORLD WAR II TO THE PRESENT

Wisconsin's heavy manufacturing cities drew waves of economic migrants to its factories after World War II, and agribusiness rose in income despite a steady reduction in the number of farms. The state's economic fortunes were generally positive right through the mid-1980s, when the state endured its greatest recession since the catastrophic days of the Depression. Wisconsin companies lost control to or were bought out by competitors in other states. In the early '90s, agribusiness, still one of the top three Wisconsin industries, became vulnerable for the first time when California challenged the state in production of whole milk.

The one industry that blossomed like no other after the war was tourism. Forethinking Wisconsin politicians enacted the first sweeping environmental legislation, and North Woods resort owners instituted effective public relations campaigns. By the late 1950s, Wisconsin had become a full-fledged, four-season vacation destination, and by the early 1990s tourism had become a $6 billion industry in Wisconsin, which established a cabinet-level Department of Tourism and opened regional travel centers in other states.

Government and Economy

GOVERNMENT

Wisconsin entered the Union as the 30th state by Congressional vote in 1846, after two contentious Constitutional Conventions. The final signing, by President James K. Polk, came on May 29, 1848.

Wisconsin has a bicameral legislative system, with a 99-member Assembly elected every two years and a 33-member Senate elected every four years. Both share lawmaking duties with a governor, who is elected every four years. The governor wields veto power and also has a powerful weapon: the line-item veto. Wisconsin has been fighting proposals to shift districts at the national level, which would reduce

© THOMAS HUHTI

The Republican Party started in a blue state!

THE OTHER LA FOLLETTE

While Robert La Follette Sr. dominated Wisconsin politics for most of three decades and left a political footprint still discernible today, he by no means did it alone. He and his wife, Belle, were an inseparable team, both passionate crusaders for social justice — and both well ahead of their time.

Belle La Follette (1859–1931) was behind Bob in every way and in many cases, it could be said, *was* Bob. Her grandmother inculcated in her a fierce determination to obtain the education she herself had been denied. It was at the University of Wisconsin that this very independent woman caught the eye of her soulmate, Bob La Follette. The two rewrote many of society's constricting traditions. They were the first couple in Wisconsin to delete "obey" from their marriage vows. Belle later became the first woman to graduate from the University of Wisconsin law school — this after having their first child.

Her postcollegiate life was an amazing blend of supporting Bob and maintaining her own crusading career as a journalist, editor, and suffrage leader. She marched in the state's first major suffrage parade and became a leading researcher and writer on practices of segregation, welfare, and other social issues. In addition to all that, she lectured, acted as her husband's attorney, and raised the La Follette brood.

She knew Bob would need an enlightened insider, so she chose to study law. She immersed herself in the issues and became his most trusted adviser. When Bob La Follette died, she refused public life; instead, she devoted herself to the *Progressive* magazine, which Bob had founded. Her own activism may be best remembered in her moving, eloquent 1913 speech to a transfixed U.S. Senate Committee on Woman's Suffrage, during which she quoted Abraham Lincoln in asking, "Are women not people?"

the state's representation in the House of Representatives by one member.

Wisconsin has always relished its penchant for progressive, and occasionally even radical, politics. In 1854, Wisconsin made a grand entrance into the national spotlight when dissenters within the Whig Party formed the Republican Party. Wisconsin's real political zenith came with the birth of the Progressive movement, led by Fightin' Bob La Follette. Still, the Republicans retained power whenever the Progressives couldn't cobble together enough votes to sweep them out. By the late 1950s, Wisconsin was showing its Democratic colors. The Democrats constituted the majority in both houses of the state legislature—and held the governor's office—through the early 1990s, when a swing landed a Republican in office for four terms (it's now back to the Democrats). Presidentially, the state virtually always votes Democratic, though it's occasionally by a nose-hair.

ECONOMY

Wisconsin may be "America's Dairyland," but it isn't *only* America's Dairyland. The economic triumvirate of the state is agriculture, manufacturing, and tourism. Wisconsin is an international exporter, tallying $6 billion in receipts in 15–20 foreign markets. Leading exports include computers, industrial machinery, and transportation equipment (crops come fifth).

Since 1990, the state has had one of the country's fastest-growing per capita income levels, topping $18,000. It's been one of the top 10 nationally for fastest-growing economies. This is tempered somewhat by the state's high income tax.

Wisconsin generally shows an above-average economic growth rate (up to 3 percent per annum) and also has defied logic by maintaining an unemployment rate of near *zero* in some communities. Multinational mergers and reorganization of paper companies in the Fox and Wisconsin River Valleys and manufacturing closings in southeastern and northeastern Wisconsin are certainly changing this.

Manufacturing accounts for up to 30 percent of Wisconsin's income—$37.1 billion. Wisconsin leads the nation in the fabrication of small engines, metals, paper products, printing, food processing, mineral extraction equipment, electrical machinery, and transportation equipment. The paper product industry is particularly strong, number one in the nation since 1953. Its 30-plus facilities account for 5.3 million tons of paper, or more than 12 percent of the national total, to the tune of $12.4 billion. One of every 11 jobs in the state is tied to paper.

The new kid on the block, economically speaking, is tourism, which really got its start after World War II. The state now rakes in more than $12 billion annually.

Agriculture is the linchpin: 41 percent of the state remains devoted to agricultural products. The industry is worth more than $80 billion, with 25 percent of that from dairying. Wisconsin ranks first to third in the United States for dairy and a lengthy list of vegetables. Interestingly, it's the fastest-growing state in organic farming (a 92 percent increase 1997–2007): first in organic dairy farms and second in organic farms.

The People

Wisconsin in 1999 reached the six million mark. With 90.1 people per square mile, the state ranks 24th nationally in population density. (It rarely feels that crowded.) General population growth in the state is 3.9 percent annually, unusual because the upper Great Lakes area as a whole shows steadily declining numbers, though this decline is slowing. Wisconsin traces most of its ethnicity (single or multiple ancestries) to Europe, specifically Germany. At the turn of the 20th century, it was the most ethnically diverse state in the Union.

And while still predominantly European-American, the state has a fast-growing nonwhite population—nearly 12 percent and growing fast.

Native Americans

Wisconsin has one of the most diverse Native American populations of any state, taking into account the number of cultures, settlement history, linguistic stock, and affiliations. The state is home to six sovereign Native American nations on 11 reservations, not all of which are demarcated by boundaries. In addition to the six nations, Wisconsin historically has been the home of the Illinois, Fox, Sauk, Miami, Kickapoo, Satee, Ottaway, and Mascouten Indians. The total Native American population is around 40,000, or 1 percent of the population. Native Americans lived in relative harmony with European explorers and trappers and early settlers until federal expansionist efforts began in earnest.

The largest native group is the **Ojibwa.** (Formerly rendered as "Chippewa," the Eurotransliteration of what trappers thought they heard, it has returned to the more appropriate approximations of Ojibway, Ojibwe, and Ojibwa. Ethnologists, historians, linguists, and even tribal members disagree on the spelling. *Ojib* means "to pucker up" and *ub-way* "to roast," and the words together denote the tribe's unique moccasin stitching. In any event, all are really Anish'nabe anyway.) Wisconsin has five Ojibwa tribes. The Ojibwa inhabited the northern woodlands of the upper Great Lakes, especially along Lakes Huron and Superior. They were allied with the Ottawa and Potawatomi but branched off in the 16th century and moved to Michigan's Mackinac Island. The

Ojibwa said that their migration westward was to fulfill the prophecy to find "food that grows on water"—wild rice. The **Bad River** group today lives on a 123,000-acre reservation along Lake Superior in Ashland County. It's the largest reservation in the state and is famed for its wild rice beds on the Kakogan Sloughs. The **Red Cliff** band, the nucleus of the Ojibwa nation, has been organized along the Bayfield Peninsula's shore since 1854. The **St. Croix** band—"homeless" tribes scattered over four counties with no boundaries—lives in northwest Wisconsin. The **Lac du Flambeau** band is the most visited and recognizable because of its proximity to Minocqua and state and federal forests and for exercising its tribal spearfishing rights. **Lac Courte Oreilles** is originally of the *Betonukeengainubejib* Ojibwa division. The **Sokaogan** (Mole Lake) band of Lake Superior Ojibwa is known as the "Lost Tribe" because its original legal treaty title was lost in an 1854 shipwreck. Originally from Canada, the band moved along to Madeline Island before defeating the Sioux near Mole Lake in 1806.

The Algonquian **Menominee** have been in Wisconsin longer than any other tribe. The Menominee once held sway south to Illinois, north into Michigan, and west to the Mississippi River, with a total of 10 million acres. Known as the "Wild Rice People"—the early French explorers called them "Lords of Trade"—the Menominee were divided into sky and earth groups and then subdivided into clans. Though the hegemony of the Menominee lasted up to 10,000 years in Wisconsin, they were almost exterminated by eastern Canadian Indians fleeing Iroquois persecution and by pestilence imported by the Europeans. Today the population has rebounded to around 3,500, and the Menominee reservation constitutes an entire Wisconsin county. The Menominee have been recognized for their forestry conservation methodology.

The Forest County **Potawatomi,** also Algonquian, are the legacy of the tribe that made the most successful move into Wisconsin, beginning in the 1640s. Originally inhabitants of the shores of Lake Huron, the Potawatomi later moved to Michigan, Indiana, and places along the St. Joseph's River. The name means "People of the Fire" or, better, "Keeper of the Fire," after their confederacy with the Ojibwa and Ottawa. The Potawatomi tribe stretched from Chicago to Wisconsin's Door County

a Native American ceremony

© WISCONSIN DEPARTMENT OF TOURISM

and was one of the tribes to greet Jean Nicolet when he arrived in 1634. Wisconsin's band of Potawatomi was one of the few to withstand relocation to Oklahoma in 1838.

Wisconsin's only Mohicans, the **Stockbridge-Munsee,** live on a reservation bordering the Menominee. The Stockbridge (also called Mahican "Wolf") originally occupied the Hudson River and Massachusetts all the way to Lake Champlain. The Munsee are a branch of the Delaware and lived near the headwaters of the Delaware River in New York, New Jersey, and Pennsylvania.

The **Oneida** belonged to the Iroquois Five Nations Confederacy consisting of the Mohawk, Oneida, Onondaga, Cayuga, and Seneca. The Oneida, originally from New York, supported the colonists in the American Revolution but were forced out by Mohawks and land-grabbing settlers along the Erie Canal after the war. Beginning in the 1820s, the Iroquois-speaking Oneida merged with the Mahican, Mohegan, Pequot, Narragansett, Montauk, and other tribes in Wisconsin.

The erstwhile **Winnebago Nation** has reverted to its original name, **Ho Chunk,** or, more appropriately, **Ho Cak** ("Big Voice" or "Mother Voice"), in an attempt to restore the rightful cultural and linguistic heritage to the nation. Also known as Otchangara, the group is related to the Chiwere-Siouxan Iowa, Oto, and Missouri Indians, though their precise origin is unknown. Extremely powerful militarily, they were nonetheless relatively peaceful with the Menominee and Potawatomi, with whom they witnessed Jean Nicolet's 1634 arrival. French scourges and encroaching tribes fleeing Iroquois hostilities in New York devastated Ho Chunk numbers; later, forced relocation nearly killed off the rest. The tribe pulled up stakes in Oklahoma and walked back to Wisconsin, following its chief, Yellow Thunder, who bought the tribe a tract of land, deftly circumventing relocation and leaving the federal government no way to force it out of Wisconsin.

An excellent resource is the website of the Great Lakes Intertribal Council (www.glitc.org).

European Americans

At statehood, only 10 nationalities were represented in Wisconsin. The state organized an immigration council in New York City and on Ellis Island to tout Wisconsin's myriad opportunities to arriving immigrants. By 1900, 25 nationalities populated the state; by 1950, more than 50 could be counted. The vast majority of these were European, and Wisconsin is still 88 percent Caucasian.

A decidedly **German** state, Wisconsin boasts more residents claiming Teutonic roots (54 percent) than anywhere else in the country. So thick is the German milieu of Milwaukee (34 percent) that German chancellors visit the city when they're in the United States for presidential summits. The 2000 census showed that Wisconsin has more than 50,000 native speakers of German—quite remarkable for a century-old ethnic group. Germans came in three waves. The first arrived 1820–1835 from both Pennsylvania and southwestern Germany. German farmers were lured by the chance to buy their own lands—at the time for $1.75 an acre. The second wave, 1840–1860, came mostly from northwest Germany and included the legendary '48ers'—enlightened intellectuals fleeing political persecution. A fairly large number of Catholics and Hussites also came at this time. During this wave, as many as 215,000 Germans moved to Wisconsin each year; by 1855, fully one-third of Wisconsin's Germans had arrived. The third wave occurred after 1880 and drew emigrants mainly from Germany's northeastern region to southeastern Wisconsin, where they worked in the burgeoning factories. Today, the southeast and south-central regions' toponymy reflects its heavily German heritage.

The state's **French** roots can be traced back to the voyageurs, trappers, and Jesuit priests. They started the first settlements, along the Fox and Wisconsin River Valleys. Though Wisconsin shows no strong French presence in anything other than place-names, the Two Rivers area still manifests an Acadian influence.

WISCONSIN LINGUISTIC PRIMER

As with any state, great fun – and occasional consternation – can be had with the anti-English rhythms of Wisconsin place names. The source of the majority of Wisconsin's names is illiterate (and occasionally innumerate) trappers and traders struggling to filter non-Indo European words and speech through Romance and Germanic language sensibilities. Toponymy generally falls into several categories – bastardized Native American lexical items (the peskiest to suss out), practical monikers pertaining to local landforms or natural wonders, and memorials to European American "founding" fathers.

Even "Wisconsin" is etymologically slippery; a historical linguist has called Wisconsin's name the most cryptic of all 27 states with Native American names. As early as 1673, Father Marquette named the river from which some say the state's name derived Meskousing ("red stones"), perhaps because of a red tinge of the banks. "Ouisconsin" appeared on a Jesuit map in 1688. But most widely accepted is the Ojibwa word for the state, *Wees-kon-san* or "gathering place of waters."

WISCONSINISMS

Perhaps the most famous example of a Wisconsinism is "bubbler," for drinking fountain, as in the Cheesehead who travels to another state and asks, "Excuse me, I'm thirsty. Where's the bubbler?" The *Dictionary of American Regional English* (out of UW-Madison) says that the other truly Wisconsin word is "golden birthday," the birthday year that matches the date of the month (for example, if you were born on January 13, your 13th birthday is your golden birthday). Those in common Midwestern (or national) usage, but started in Wisconsin, include "flowage" (water backed up behind a dam), "hot dish" (casserole), and this author's favorite, "ishy" ("icky").

One important one to know is "yooper," for a denizen of Michigan's Upper Peninsula. Another is the regionalism "Tyme machine," which you know as an "ATM."

Milwaukee colloquialisms – though some vociferously deny it – include "bumbershoot," for umbrella, and "ainah hey?" for "isn't that so?" (In Wisconsin outside of Milwaukee, folks – especially this author's mom and aunt! – say, "inso?") You'll also hear "down by" – everything is "down by" something. Or, even "Grease yourself a piece of bread and I'll put you on a hamburger" – a Milwaukeeism if ever there was one. Wisconsinites also seem somewhat averse to liquid sounds; it's "M'waukee" as often as not.

HOWZAT AGAIN?

The phonology of Wisconsin English contains only one dramatic sound: the "ah," seriously emphasized and strongly run though the nasal cavity, as in wis-KHAN-sin. (And please, never, ever, is it WES-khan-sin.)

Algoma – al-GO-muh
Chequamegon National Forest – shuh-WAHM-uh-gun
Fond du Lac – FAHN-duh-lack
Green Bay – green-BAY, *not* GREEN-bay
Kenosha – kuh-NO-shuh
Lac Court Oreilles – la COO-der-ray
Manitowoc – MAN-ih/uh-tuh-wock
Menominee/Menomonie – muh-NAH-muh-nee
Minocqua – min-AHK-wah
Muscoda – MUSS-kuh-day
New Berlin/Berlin – new BER-lin
Nicolet National Forest – nick-oh-LAY (but don't be too surprised to hear "nick-ul-ETT")
Oshkosh – AHSH-kahsh
Prairie du Chien – prairie du SHEEN
Racine – ruh-SEEN
Ripon – RIP-pin
Shawano – SHAW-no (though SHAH-no is possible)
Sheboygan – shuh-BOY-gun
Trempealeau – TREM-puh-low
Waupun – wau-PAHN
Oconomowoc – good luck!

As the **British** and the French haggled and warred over all of the Wisconsin territory, many crown-friendly British Yankees did move here, populating virtually every community. The **Irish** began arriving in the late 19th century in numbers second only to the Germans. Irish influence is found in every community, especially Milwaukee's Bay View, Erin in Washington County, Ozaukee County, Adell and Parnell in Sheboygan County, and Manitowoc County.

Pockets of **Welsh** and **Cornish** are found throughout the state, the latter especially in the southwestern lead-mining region of the state. A distinct **Belgian** influence exists in Kewaunee County, where Walloon can still be heard in local taverns.

Poles represent the primary Eastern European ethnic group. The largest contingent is in Milwaukee, where kielbasa is as common a dietary mainstay as bratwurst. Most Poles arrived 1870–1910. At that time, Poland was not recognized as a country, so Ellis Island officials erroneously categorized many of the immigrants as Prussian, Austrian, or Russian. While 90 percent of Wisconsin's Polish immigrants moved into the cities, about three-tenths of those who arrived farmed, mostly in Portage and Trempealeau Counties; the latter is the oldest Polish settlement in the United States. By 1920, 90,000 Poles inhabited Milwaukee. **Czechs,** another large Eastern European group, live mostly in north and east-central Wisconsin, especially Kewaunee and Manitowoc Counties.

Many **Norwegians** also emigrated to the Upper Midwest, primarily Minnesota and Wisconsin. Most were economic emigrants trying to escape Norway's chronic overpopulation (85 percent of its people were forced onto 3 percent of the arable land). Most Norwegians in Wisconsin wound up in Dane and Rock Counties between 1835 and 1850. **Finnish** immigrants to the United States totaled 300,000 between 1864 and 1920, and many of these settled in the Upper Peninsula of Michigan and northern Wisconsin. **Swedes** made up the smallest Scandinavian contingent, the original settlement made up of a dozen families near Waukesha.

By the turn of the 20th century, Wisconsin was home to almost 10 percent of all the **Danes** in the United States—the second-largest national contingent. Most originally settled in the northeast (the city of Denmark lies just southeast of Green Bay), but later immigrants wound up farther south. To this day, Racine is nicknamed "Kringleville," for its flaky Danish pastry.

The **Dutch** settled primarily in Milwaukee and Florence Counties beginning in the 1840s, when potato crops failed and protests flared over the Reformed Church. These southeastern counties today sport towns such as Oostburg, New Amsterdam, and Holland.

In 1846, a large contingent of **Swiss** from the Glarus canton sent emissaries to the New World to search out a suitable immigration site. Eventually, the two scouts stumbled upon the gorgeous, lush valleys of southwestern Wisconsin. After much travail, hundreds of Swiss forded their way across the country and endured a tough winter to establish themselves here. A great deal of Swiss heritage remains in Green County.

Italians began arriving in the 1830s—many Genoese migrated north from Illinois lead camps to fish and scavenge lead along the Mississippi River—but didn't arrive in substantial numbers until the early 1900s. Most settled in the southeast, specifically Milwaukee, Racine, and especially Kenosha.

Perhaps unique to Wisconsin is the large population of **Icelandic** immigrants, who settled on far-flung Washington Island, northeast of Door Peninsula. It was the largest single Icelandic settlement in the United States when they arrived in 1870 to work as fishers.

African Americans

Some theories hold African Americans first arrived in Wisconsin in 1835, in the entourage of Solomon Juneau, the founder of Milwaukee. But records from the early part of the 18th century detail black trappers, guides, and explorers. In 1791 and 1792, in fact, black fur traders established an encampment estimated to be near present-day Marinette. Though the Michigan Territory, which would become the Wisconsin Territory, was ostensibly free, slavery was not uncommon. Henry Dodge, Wisconsin's first territorial governor, had slaves but freed them two years after leaving office. Other slave owners were transplanted Southerners living in the new lead-mining district of the southwest. Other early African Americans were demi-French African immigrants, who settled near Prairie du Chien in the early 19th century. Wisconsin's first African American settlement was Pleasant Spring, outside Lancaster in southwest Wisconsin; the State Historical Society's Old World Wisconsin in Eagle has a brand-new exhibit on it.

After passage of the Fugitive Slave Act, which allowed slave catchers to cross state lines in pursuit, many freed and escaped slaves flocked to the outer fringes of the country. Wisconsin's opposition to the act was strident. One celebrated case involved Joshua Glover, an escaped slave who had been living free and working in Racine for years. He was caught and imprisoned by his erstwhile master but later broken out by mobs from Ripon, Milwaukee, and southeastern Wisconsin. The state Supreme Court ruled the act unconstitutional.

After the Civil War, the African American population increased, and most chose to live in rural, agricultural settings. Large-scale African American migration to Milwaukee, Racine, and Kenosha took place after World War II, as northern factories revved up for the Korean War and, later, the Cold War. Today, the vast majority of Wisconsin's nearly 300,000, or 80 percent of, African Americans (around 6 percent of the state total) live in these urbanized southeastern counties. The black population is one of the fastest growing—increasing by 25 percent per decade.

Hispanics

Wisconsin's Hispanic population stands at around 140,000 and is growing fast; it more than doubled from 1990 to 2000 and is expected to do so again in the 2010 census. **Puerto Ricans** began arriving in Milwaukee after World War II as blue-collar laborers. In the 1950s, estimates put the Puerto Rican population at perhaps 500; today, the number is near 20,000. **Mexicans** represent one of the more recent immigration waves, many of them having arrived in the mid-1960s, though Mexican immigrants have been in the state since as far back as 1850. Mexicans today live mostly in southeastern Wisconsin—Milwaukee, Madison, and, especially, Racine.

Asians

Wisconsin has upward of 77,000 residents of Asian descent, about 2 percent of the population. One of the fastest-growing elements, **Laotian Hmong,** began arriving during the Vietnam War and settled mostly in Appleton, Green Bay, the Fox River Valley, Manitowoc, Eau Claire, La Crosse, and pockets in southeastern Wisconsin. The state also has substantial **Chinese** and **Korean** populations.

Culture

ART MUSEUMS AND GALLERIES

The smashing addition to the **Milwaukee Art Museum** by Santiago Calatrava has drawn media from around the world, yet don't overlook its phenomenal holdings. Milwaukee otherwise is rated in the top 5 percent for cultural attractions per population in the United States!

Madison has so many museums that one nickname for downtown is "Museum Mile," of which the **Madison Museum of Contemporary Art** and UW's **Chazen Art Museum** will be superb art aficionado bookends.

One would be amazed by how much art is outside the two population centers. Essential art attractions include the **Racine Art Museum** and history at the **Hoard Dairy Museum** in Fort Atkinson. Ditto on the galleries for the diminutive communities of Mineral Point and Spring Green southwest of Madison.

HANDICRAFTS

There are dozens of types of handicrafts in Wisconsin. Every community has artisans specializing in various ethnic styles: Norwegian rosemaling, for example, is a flowery, colorful, painted trim artwork. Unique are the creations of the Amish and the Hmong. A large contingent of Amish families, famed for their quilting, crafts, bent-hickory furniture, and outstanding bakeries, live in the southwestern and west-central sections of Wisconsin.

Hmong crafts include storycloths, which recount narratives visually, and exquisite decorative *paj ntaub,* a 2,000-year-old hybrid of needlework and appliqué, usually featuring geometric designs and, often, animals. These quilts and wall hangings require more than 100 hours of work. Some Amish and Hmong young women are synthesizing their quilt styles into wonderful bicultural mélanges. Hmong artisans are often found at craft fairs and farmers

Norwegian rosemaling

MAJOR EVENTS AND FESTIVALS

One apt nickname for Milwaukee is the "City of Festivals." Milwaukee's **Polish Fest** is one of the larger ethnic festivals in the country, but the city really gets into high gear the last week of June when it hosts the mammoth **Summerfest,** billed as the largest music festival in the United States. In the 11-day extravaganza, more than 2,500 national acts perform everything from big band to heavy metal. It's also a great place to sample Wisconsin food.

In August, Milwaukee also hosts the **Wisconsin State Fair,** the state's largest annual event, with more than a million visitors over 11 days. In late August, Milwaukee features **Irish Fest,** the world's largest Irish cultural event outside of the Emerald Isle. Wisconsin's largest Native American cultural celebration is Milwaukee's **Indian Summer,** in mid-September. Featured are a full competition powwow as well as Native American entertainment and artwork. In mid-November, more than 50 ethnic groups participate in the Milwaukee **Holiday Folk Fair.** The largest annual multiethnic festival in the country, it's a great place to shop for folk art, and the ethnic dancing is quite popular.

These are but a few of the city's more than two dozen *major* festivals – Lord knows how many they really have.

Madison cannot possibly hope to compete with that, but the city does have a couple of great ones. First off, on the weekend nearest July 4, the city hosts **Rhythms & Booms,** the Midwest's largest fireworks show. It's incredible and incredibly popular, so be prepared to get there a day early to find a place to park/sit.

Being America's Dairyland, it seems appropriate for Wisconsin to hold the world's largest dairying trade show, the **World Dairy Expo.** More than 50 countries participate in the event, held yearly in Madison in September.

In the vicinity of the two cities, other major celebrations include the **Heidi Festival** in New Glarus in late April; the **Horicon Marsh Bird Festival** and Burlington's **Chocolate Fest** in May; the world's largest fish fry at Port Washington's **Fish Day** in early July; this author's favorite – **National Mustard Day Festival** in Mount Horeb in August; and New Glarus' **Wilhelm Tell Festival** at the end of August. Personally, however, this author firmly believes that you haven't experienced Wisconsin until you've been to September's **Wisconsin State Cow Chip Throwing Festival** in Sauk Prairie, north of Madison. Yes, it is exactly what you think it is: You throw dried cow dung. Seriously – it's tons of fun!

But here's a personal idea for a celebration: nature. Nature's autumn majesty – -figure mid-to late-September-late-October, north to south in the state – is a big deal in Wisconsin, drawing thousands of tourists annually. Local news reports even feature nightly **leaf color watches.** The state Department of Tourism maintains 24/7 color updates via phone and website. Isn't that indeed the best kind of festival?

---

markets. Amish wares are found both in home shops throughout southwestern Wisconsin and in a few stores.

FOOD

Midwestern cuisine. An oxymoron? Hardly. Banish those visions of tuna casserole dancing in your head. Midwestern cuisine—real, original fare handed down generationally—is more eclectic and more representative of "American" heritage than better-known, better-marketed cooking styles.

If you search out the latent Americana in Wisconsin cooking, you'll be amazed. Wisconsin's best cooking is a thoughtful mélange of ethnicities, stemming from the diverse populace and prairie-cooking fare that reflects a heritage of living off the land. Midwest regional cuisine is a blend of originally wild food such as cranberries, wild rice, pumpkins, blueberries, whitefish livers, catfish cheeks, and morel mushrooms incorporated into standard old country recipes. Added to the mix are game animals, such as deer, pheasant, and goose. Many Midwesterners simply shoot their own, rather than raising them or buying them from a grocery wholesaler. It's a home-based culinary style, perfected from house to house through generations of adaptation.

And while the state features a panorama of European fare, the rest of the culinary spectrum is also represented. Milwaukee's got real-deal soul food and a fantastic array of Puerto Rican and Mexican restaurants, and in Madison you'll find Asian eateries rivaling any city's. In short, despite the preponderance of hot beef and meat loaf, it's quite possible to find good imaginative food in Wisconsin.

Wisconsin is well represented food-wise on the Web. Surprised? The site **www .SavorWisconsin.com** is a wonderful compendium (run by the state government) of information on local agricultural producers, food events, and more. Others of note: www .WisconsinCooks.org, www.chew.wisconsin-cooks.org, www.WisconsinMade.com, and even www.SlowFoodWisconsin.org.

Cheese

Wisconsin produces more than a third of the nation's cheese (leading in cheddar, colby, brick, muenster, limburger, and many Italian varieties). More than 500 varieties of cheese come out of Wisconsin. And, yes, we really do eat a great deal of it. The loyal dairy consumption shouldn't come as a surprise—laws prohibiting the use of margarine remained on the books until 1967.

The most common cheese in Wisconsin is the ever-versatile **cheddar.** It varies in color from nearly white to orange, and its flavor can be almost bland to bitingly sharp (aged versions). For something different, eat it with fruit (apples are best) or melt it on hot apple pie.

Colby cheese was invented in the northern Wisconsin town of the same name. The cheese has a very mild, mellow flavor and a firm, open texture. It's most often eaten breaded and deep fried, but try cubing it in fruit or vegetable salads. Firmer, with a smooth body, **colby jack** cheese is marbled white and yellow—a mixture of the mellow colby cheese along with the

distinctive broad taste of **monterey jack,** a semisoft, creamy white cheese used mostly in Mexican restaurants as a substitute for cheese from the Mexican state of Chihuahua.

Wisconsin effectively brought **swiss** cheese to prominence in the United States more than a century ago. Firm and smooth with large shiny eyes (holes), swiss has an unmistakable nutty flavor. Swiss cheese fans should head immediately for the town of Monroe in southwestern Wisconsin; there you'll find the greatest swiss you've ever tasted, as well as a milder **baby swiss.** While there, slip into a tavern or sandwich shop and really experience

THE BUTTER BATTLE

You doubt Wisconsin's a dairy state? Consider the Butter Battle, or Oleo Wars. Oleomargarine was developed in 1895. It would take until 1967 – that's right – that selling or buying the creamy concoction wasn't a *crime*.

Farmers initially feared that the golden-colored spread would ruin them and demanded the ban; later they would march and protest for a ban on anything resembling butter or anything used like butter. Of course, margarine smuggling started up (kinda lacks the romanticism of moonshine running, doesn't it?), and those consumers watching their diets would cross the Illinois line to the "margarine villages" that sprouted alongside border service stations. Butter's most partisan supporter was Gordon Roseleip, a Republican senator from Darlington, whose rantings against oleo could occasionally overshadow Joseph McCarthy's anti-Communist spewings. But the good senator doomed the butter industry in 1965 when he agreed to take a blind taste test between butter and oleo. And lost. His family later admitted that he had been unknowingly consuming oleo for years; he weighed 275 pounds and his family had switched, hoping to control his weight.

THE POLKA

Wisconsinites possess a genetic predisposition to polka, established by a 1994 statute as the state's official dance. Given the state's heady 19th-century influx of Eastern and Central European immigrants – the highest concentration in America at the time – it's only natural that the peasant dance would take root here. Some cultural historians claim Wisconsin harbors more species of polka than anyplace else in the world. Polka music emanates from across the AM dial. At weddings, one polka per hour is virtually an unwritten house minimum. Polka at Brewers games, polka in the Capitol building, even polka Masses in churches! In Wisconsin, polka is king. (In Milwaukee, head for **Kochanski's Concertina Beer Hall;** in Madison, it's the **Essenhaus.**

Each culture in Europe stylized the polka with its own distinctions. The Swiss did the polka step on the first beat of a bar, while the Austrians did it on the last half beat, made it more prominent, and included some zigzags. The Dutch used a backward swing and omitted the hop, replacing it with only a slight rise or roll of the body to mark the last whole or half beat of a bar. The Poles' polka stepped in measures of four, with the polka lead foot every second step. Czechs did it without a hop. Finns used a 4/4 rhythm and an abrupt heel step and added bits from their own baleful tango. Generally, polka couples turn right continuously without reversing and always move to the right.

Wafting across the Atlantic to the United States, it caught on like wildfire, unlike in Europe (the snobbish elite there considered it a madness of the lowest base order).

Polka has had an unmistakable influence on the Americas. Eastern and Central Europeans also gravitated to the south, where predominantly African American steps were incorporated. A large population of Europeans took their music to Texas and melded border flavors into the music called *conjunto*. Today, some country-western two-steps are being traded back and forth between country and polka camps.

And in Wisconsin, all forms have melded into one eclectic, happy dance. Wisconsin polka is mainly the Polish mazurka and the Dutch, Swiss, and Czech polkas. The best way to experience it is at one of the state's many polka festivals, including the annual Wisconsin Polkafest in mid-May in diminutive Concord. Check out www.wisconsinpolkamusic.com for a great introduction.

Wisconsin culture by sampling a **limburger** sandwich—the pungent, oft-misunderstood swiss on pumpernickel, with onions and radishes. Wisconsin may be the last place on earth where it's couth to munch limburger in polite company; it *is* the last place in the world making the cheese.

Another Wisconsin original is **brick cheese,** a semisoft cheese with a waxy, open texture. Creamy white, young brick has a mild flavor; when aged, it becomes sharp. It's perfect for grilled cheese sandwiches or with mustard on pumpernickel bread.

Two transplants the state produces to near perfection are **gouda** and **edam** cheeses, imported by Western Europeans. They're semisoft to firm and creamy in texture, with small holes and a mild, slightly nutty flavor.

Finally, for the most authentic cheese-eating cultural experience, go to a bar and order **cheese curds,** commonly breaded and deep fried. When bought at a dairy or a farmers market, cheese curds leave a distinctive squeaky feeling on the teeth and are a perfect snack food. Another unique cheese dish, especially in Green Bay, is beer cheese soup.

The Wisconsin Milk Marketing Board (www.wisdairy.com) is a wonderful place to peruse the "Joy of Cheese" and to request a copy of the fantastic *Taster's Guide to Wisconsin,* a scenic agricultural tour of the Dairy State, highlighting each cheese factory (and dairy, winery, brewery, etc.) that offers tours.

FROZEN CUSTARD: A GIFT FROM HEAVEN

What's for dessert? Or a snack? Or for no reason? The answer in Wisconsin is definitively frozen custard. In fact, just mention it to a Wisconsinite – especially a Madisonian or Milwaukeean – and watch them lick their lips, imagining this silky stress-reducer.

What's the deal with frozen custard? Well, start with a minimum of 10 percent butterfat (sounds sublime already, doesn't it?) and 1.4 percent egg yolk. Then, it's churned with far less air in it. For this author, it lacks that palpable sense of, well, ice to it. Trust me – you ain't never gonna be satisfied with anything else after a visit to Wisconsin for its frozen custard.

Supper Clubs

What, exactly, is a supper club? What the *zócalo* is to Latin Americans, the sidewalk café to Parisians, the *biergarten* to Bavarians, so is the supper club to Wisconsinites. It sometimes seems as if the state charter requires every Badger State community to have one. It's the social and culinary underpinning of Wisconsin. Indeed, though supper clubs exist in many Midwestern states, Wisconsin's density is difficult to fathom.

Equal parts homey, casual meat-and-potatoes restaurant and local kaffeeklatsch (better make that "brandyklatsch"), supper clubs traditionally have a triumvirate of obligatory specialties: prime rib, always on Saturday, although some serve it every day; homestyle chicken; and invariably a Friday-night fish fry. No fish fry, no business. Most menus feature steaks in one column, seafood in the other. Regional variations buttress these basics with anything from Teutonic carnivore fare to Turkish food. This being Wisconsin, venison occasionally makes an appearance. One side dish will always be a choice of potato. If it's a true supper club, a relish tray comes out with the dinner rolls. On it, you'll find everything from sliced vegetable sticks to pickles to coleslaw—and sometimes an indescribably weird "salad" concoction such as green Jell-O with shaved carrots inside.

No two supper clubs look alike (the only prerequisites are an attached bar and faux wood paneling), but all can be partially covered by clichés such as "rustic," "cozy," and "like someone's dining room." Nicer supper clubs will have crackling fireplaces; low-end joints feel more like run-down family restaurants, in both decor and menu. The coolest ones have animal heads dangling above the diners; the tackiest ones feature overdone nautical decor. Dress is completely up to you. Wear a suit and you'll be conspicuous. Jeans are perfectly acceptable. In many places—especially Madison—Badger red is de rigueur on football Saturdays. Beware impostors: In recent years, the words "supper club" have been adopted by fancy restaurants on both coasts, but a co-opted supper club is not the real thing. If you ever see a dress code posted, you're not at a real supper club.

A DRINKING LIFE

Yes, Badgers drink a lot. We rank fourth nationally in per capita consumption; 69 percent of drinking-age population report participation in legal imbibing. Madison and surrounding Dane County have one of the highest percentages of binge drinkers in the United States. (Milwaukee was once rated the "Drunkest City in America.") Alcohol is the social lubricant of the state, and many out-of-staters are a bit wide-eyed when they move here. At last count, the state had more than 13,000 taverns, by far the most per capita in the country.

Beer

To disabuse: Wisconsinites do not drink more beer (per capita, anyway) than residents of any other state in the country—Nevada does (though that number is admittedly tourist-heavy). Alas, the days of quaffing a brew with breakfast and finding a *biergarten* on every street corner are long gone.

Wisconsin beer drinking began with the

BRATWURST: THE WISCONSIN DISH

Bratwurst, a Germanic legacy of Wisconsin, is the unofficial state dish. The brat (pronounced to rhyme with "plot," not "splat!") is pervasive here. Supermarkets devote entire lengths of freezers to accommodate sausage-makers. Many towns still have old butcher shops that string up homemade flavors. Watertown, Wisconsin, is being considered for a national Bratwurst Hall of Flame (that's right, Flame).

THE IMMIGRANT EPICURE

Strictly speaking, the bratwurst is but one of hundreds of varieties of sausage, according to official (and draconian) German food law. Actually, sausage-making was here with the Native Americans, who had long stuffed deer intestines and hides with wild rice, grains, meats, offal, and herbs to produce pemmican, which is, technically, a sausage.

From the earliest settlement of the state, immigrants did make their own sausage. Wisconsin's bratwurst, unlike some variet-ies, is almost strictly made from pork. All im-migrant groups traditionally used intestines for bratwurst casings. The internal mixtures would consist of meat, fat, and seasonings, along with occasional starches such as rice and bread. Concoctions were and are highly secret – similar to the recipe for Coca-Cola.

INFINITE VARIETIES

The main categories of Wisconsin sausage are outlined below. In addition, the Czech method includes a rice sausage and head cheese; the Norwegians make *sylte*, which is spiced and salted in brine.

German: There are a zillion kinds of German sausage. Bratwurst are most often seasoned with marjoram, pepper, salt, caraway, and nut-meg, though there are no hard and fast rules.

Italian: Italian sausage is sweeter and hot-ter. Fennel gives it its trademark flavor.

Polish: Think garlic-heavy ring of two-inch-thick, dark pink bologna-esque sausage tradi-tionally steam-fried for dinner (and then cut into sandwiches for leftovers and lunchboxes). Polish recipes often call for red cabbage and mustard sauces.

PREPARATION

Microwave a brat and you'll incur the wrath of any Wisconsinite. Frying one is OK, but tra-ditionally a brat must be grilled. Brats work best if you parboil them in beer and onions for 10-15 minutes before putting them on the grill. Sheboyganites absolutely cringe at parboiling, so don't tell them I told you. Another no-no is any sort of roughage crammed in the bun – lettuce, tomatoes, and so on; even sauerkraut, loved by Milwaukeeans, is barely tolerated by Sheboyganites.

Another option: Parboil brats briefly. Sear in butter in a frying pan. Set aside. Pour two cups dark beer into fry pan and scrape resi-due. Combine a finely chopped onion, some beef stock, juice from one lemon, and maybe one chopped green pepper. Put brats back in and boil 12-15 minutes. Remove brats and place on hot grill. Sauce can be thickened with flour or cornstarch and poured over the top. A cheesehead will stick the sauce in a bun along-side the brat with mustard.

Bratwurst is best when grilled.

hordes of European immigrants. The earliest brewery has been traced back to an 1835 operation in Mineral Point, but there may have been one a few years before that, though what most early southwestern Wisconsin brewers were making was actually top-fermented malt liquor (which to some aficionados is akin to cutting a porter with antifreeze). Surprisingly, Germans did not initiate Milwaukee's legendary beer-making industry; it was instead a couple of upstarts from the British Isles. But massive German settlement did set the state's beer standard, which no other state could hope to match. By 1850, Milwaukee alone had almost 200 breweries, elevating beer-making to the city's number one industry. Throughout the state, every town, once it had been platted and while waiting for incorporation, would build three things—a church, a town hall, and a brewery, not necessarily in that order.

The exact number of breweries in the state in the 19th century isn't known, but it is easily in the thousands; up to 50 years ago, local brew was still common. At that time, beer-making went through a decline; industry giants effectively killed off the regional breweries. But by the 1970s, a backlash against the swill water the big brewers passed off as beer sent profits plummeting. Into the void left by unsatisfied beef aficionados stepped microbreweries and brewpubs, which, with their methodology—nay, artistry—reaching back across generations to the time-honored traditions of *crafting* beer, started a national renaissance of beer crafting, and Wisconsin is no different; Madison and Milwaukee have numerous brewpubs and a few microbreweries. In other parts of the state, anachronistic old breweries are coming back to the fore, usually with the addition of a restaurant and lots of young professional patrons. Time will tell if this trend marks a permanent national shift toward traditional brews (made according to four-century-old purity laws), or if it's simply a fad.

Some local standards still exist. **Leinenkugel's** (or Leinie's) is the preferred choice of North Woods denizens, closely rivaled by Point, which is brewed in Stevens Point. In the southern part of the state, Monroe's Joseph Huber Brewing Company (now named Minhas though the website still uses the old name!) puts out the college-student-standard (cheap but tasty) **Huber**—the Bock is worth the wait. In Middleton, west of Madison, the **Capital Brewery** has been restored to its early-century standards.

Brandy

What traditionally has made a Badger a Badger, drinkwise? Brandy, of any kind. (The author's father still gets stares from *auslander* wait staff with the very Wisconsin drink request of "brandy old-fashioned with mushrooms, not fruit"—they're surprised by the brandy, not the mushrooms, and they usually get it wrong.) When the Wisconsin Badgers play a football game on the road, the 30,000-plus cheeseheads who follow generally get newspaper articles written about their bratwurst, postgame polka dancing, and prodigious brandy drinking. In 1993, when the rowdy Badger faithful descended on the Rose Bowl in a friendly invasion, Los Angeles hotels essentially ran dry of brandy; by the time the Badgers returned in 1999 (and again in 2000), local hoteliers had figured it out!

Truth be told, the state has—egads!—slipped to second place behind Washington, DC (of all places), in per capita consumption, but Korbel still sells just under half its brandy in the state!

Wisconsinites are decidedly *not* connoisseurs of brandy; you'll never hear discussions of "smoky" versus "plump" varieties, or vintages. Try to chat somebody up about cognac versus brandy in a bar and you'll probably just be met with an empty stare. (For the record, cognac is a spirit distilled from the white wine grapes of Cognac in France; brandy is a more general term for a spirit distilled from wine.)

Here's how to make Wisconsin's fave drink: Put ice cubes in a glass. Add two ounces of brandy (any kind you wish), one lump of sugar, and one dash of cocktail bitters. Fill remaining glass with water or white soda. Top off with fruit or mushrooms.

ESSENTIALS

Getting There

BY AIR

The major U.S. airlines have some direct domestic flights into Wisconsin, but you almost always have to stop first in Chicago, Minneapolis, St. Louis, or another major hub. Ticket prices vary wildly depending on when you travel and, more important, when you buy the ticket. Prices are predictably higher around the major holidays (July Fourth, Thanksgiving, Christmas) and to southern destinations in winter, while other times you can fly for as low as $350 from the west coast, slightly less from the east coast; sometimes you can get tickets for half that! The best way to find out about deals is through a travel agent or, yes, mucking about on the Internet.

Milwaukee's **Mitchell International Airport** (www.mitchellairport.com) is the only international airport in the state and the airport offering the most direct flights across the country (Madison has a dozen or so as well). The wonderful **Midwest Airlines** (800/452-2022, www.midwestairlines.com) is a Milwaukee-based service with direct flights and undoubtedly the best service in the country. Imagine two-person-wide leather seats throughout the cabin, exquisite meals (cookies baked on board!), and genuinely solicitous service. The prices are competitive, too, on nonstop flights

to all over the United States. The airline offers excellent package deals including tickets, rental car, and accommodations from a dozen major U.S. cities.

Madison is served by interstate and intrastate flights, often branches of the major carriers.

BY BUS

Greyhound (800/231-2222, www.greyhound.com) operates in both cities (and major Wisconsin cities), but only along major interstate routes.

Van Galder (800/747-0994, www.vangalderbus.com) operates between Chicago (O'Hare airport and downtown) and Madison, making stops at Wisconsin communities along the way. In Milwaukee, besides Greyhound you can also hop aboard Wisconsin Coach Lines' **Airport Express,** which goes from Milwaukee to Chicago via Racine and Kenosha.

Megabus (www.megabus.com) offers rides to Chicago and Minneapolis from both Madison and Milwaukee. This formerly el cheapo option is no longer that; furthermore, there is no terminal, so you have to be aware of where their pick-up point is.

BY TRAIN

Amtrak (800/872-7245) operates trains through Wisconsin. The long-distance **Empire Builder** originates in Chicago and runs through Milwaukee, Columbus, Portage, Wisconsin Dells, Sturtevant, Tomah, and La Crosse on its way to Seattle/Portland.

Metra (312/322-6777, www.metrarail.com) offers train service between Kenosha and Chicago's Madison Street Station.

Many Midwestern states are beginning discussions about creating a Midwest rail network, with Chicago as the hub and Milwaukee as one of many branches. Express light rail between Madison and Milwaukee will probably be debated until the end of time.

BY WATER

The **SS** *Badger* (www.ssbadger.com), the only active passenger/car steamship left on the Great Lakes, is a fantastic way to experience Lake Michigan. It runs daily in season between Manitowoc, Wisconsin, and Ludington, Michigan.

Milwaukee has the high-speed **Lake Express** ferry (866/914-1010, www.lake-express.com) to Muskegon, Michigan, a blessing for those not wanting to suffer the white-knuckle tour of outer Chicago's interstate arteries.

Two more ferries have been discussed within the past five years: One would run from Algoma in East-Central Wisconsin to Michigan, the other a passenger-only ferry from Sturgeon Bay in Door County to Michigan's Upper Peninsula.

On a much smaller scale, one of the few remaining interstate ferries left in America, the **Cassville Car Ferry,** operates seasonally in southwestern Wisconsin. It shuttles passengers across the Mississippi River between Wisconsin and Iowa.

With 1,000 miles of Mississippi River and Great Lakes shoreline, Wisconsin is entered easily in your own craft. Racine has the Great Lakes' largest marina, and every community along both Lake Michigan and Lake Superior offers slips and rentals.

Getting Around

HIGHWAYS

In *Midwest Living* magazine reader surveys, Wisconsin's roadways rank the best in most categories—best roads overall, best maintained, and others. Despite a few problem areas, the state's 110,300 miles of roads are all in pretty good shape. Best of all—no toll roads yet!

Then again, the stretch of I-94 running through Milwaukee is one of the nation's 10 most congested highways, and the resultant transit problems remain unaddressed. The next-worst roads you'll experience are Madison's Beltline Highway and I-90 interchange, both of which, along with Milwaukee's interstates, are inhospitable during rush hours. The state Department of Transportation is now operating under a 20-year plan to improve existing multilane highways and expand certain two-lane highways, including roads linking key tourist centers. These two-lane roads are crucial, as they constitute only 4 percent of the state's highways but carry 42 percent of the traffic.

County roads are designated by letters. You can determine in advance the general condition of the road by the letters designating it. The road deteriorates in direct proportion to the number of letters. Thus, Highway RR will be narrower than Highway R—and possibly decaying. County roads are generally paved, but don't be surprised if they're not. State highway numbers are preceded by the abbreviation WI, federal highways by U.S., and interstates with I.

Regulations and Etiquette

Wisconsin permits radar detectors in cars. There is a mandatory motorcycle helmet law for people under 18 years old. All vehicle passengers are required by law to wear seatbelts. Child restraints are mandatory for children under four.

The speed limit on Wisconsin interstates is 65 mph, reduced to 55 mph in metropolitan areas. Milwaukee's fringes are well monitored, so be forewarned. You can travel 65 mph on some four-lane highways in the northern part of the state, to the relief of many travelers.

Drivers in the state are very courteous. In fact, many acquaintances of this author have grumbled about the, er, *methodical* pace of Wisconsin traffic. The interstate arteries surrounding larger cities, especially Milwaukee, are the only places conducive to speeding.

ROADKILL

Driving in Wisconsin you *will* experience the insanely high numbers of deer (and carcasses roadside). In one traverse of the state you'll likely slam on the brakes at least once, trying to avoid thumping a deer. The modern rite of passage for "my first deer" no longer necessarily implies one downed with a weapon.

DEER DISPLACEMENT

The fecund croplands and suburban gardens that replaced the state's original meadows and forests have also lured back huge numbers of deer, to the point that some suburban areas ringed with rural lands have higher deer concentrations than public parklands. Some wildlife biologists now worry that the social carrying capacity of the land, or the number of deer that humans can tolerate, has been maxed out in the south, while in the sparsely populated north, the reverse is true – the biological carrying capacity is bulging at the seams. The primary cause is once again a lethal modern combination of an abundance of crops available for the deer to eat and refusal to allow hunting on private land, which results in no thinning of the herd. And it's not the same old divisions in this debate – some environmentalists are pro-deer hunting, as enormous deer populations destroy fragile and rare flora in winter feeding.

THE NUMBERS

The Department of Natural Resources estimates the deer herd at anywhere between 1.4 and 1.9 million (estimates vary wildly). It was as high as 1.75 million in 2008. Things have been so bad that the DNR has instituted an unheard-of early-October gun season for does and fawns and earn-a-buck programs, wherein to shoot a trophy buck, you have to kill a doe first. Designed to thin herds to manageable levels, this has continued annually, along with extending periods in November, all to little avail. Annually, more than 20,500 car-deer crashes are reported (causing around 10 deaths and 700 injuries); since these are only the investigated ones, you can probably safely double that number. Statewide, deer account

a typical sight when driving through Wisconsin

© THOMAS HUHTI

for 16 to 17 percent of crashes as of 2007 (up from 5.1 percent in 1978). A conservative estimate puts the damage total, including cars and agricultural losses, at around $100 million per year. Thankfully, less than 2 percent of car-deer crashes result in human fatality.

PREVENTIVE MAINTENANCE

If you're driving in Wisconsin, face the fact that at some point you're going to meet a deer on a highway. October and November are the worst months statistically, but May and June are pretty bad, too. April-August, crashes happen mostly after 8 P.M.; the rest of the year, they typically occur 5-7 P.M. Deer, like any wildlife, are most active around dawn and dusk, but they are active day and night. Most crashes occur on dry roads on mostly clear days. And the old adage about their freezing in the headlights is absolutely true. The best thing you can do is pay close attention, don't speed, and keep an intelligent stopping distance between you and the next car. Use your peripheral vision, and if you see one deer, expect more. If one appears, *do not swerve or slam on the brakes,* even if this, sadly, means running through the deer. All experts agree this only causes much more danger to you and other motorists.

Road Conditions

The state Department of Transportation maintains a **road condition hotline** (800/762-3947, www.dot.wisconsin.gov/travel) detailing the conditions of all major roads across the state; it also lists construction delays.

It's important to winterize your vehicle while driving in Wisconsin. Always keep your antifreeze level prepared for temperatures of -35°F (half water, half fluid usually suffices). Most important: Keep a full tank of gas—it helps prevent freeze-ups in the line and lets you run your car if you're stuck in a ditch.

BY BUS

You can always hop aboard **Greyhound,** but only as long as you're traveling to communities along very main highways. **Lamers** is a bus service traveling to and from central Wisconsin to Milwaukee through the Fox River Valley.

The communities of Janesville, Beloit, Racine, Kenosha, Milwaukee, and Bayfield Peninsula have bus systems linking nearby communities. Madison and Milwaukee are linked by the oft-running **Badger Bus** (608/255-6771, www.badgerbus.com).

Outdoor Recreation

"Work hard, play hard" is the ethic in Wisconsin. There's always a trail, a lake, or an activity within shouting distance. Wisconsin contains a fairly remarkable 95 state parks, forests, and trails, varying in size from Green Bay's 50-acre living museum **Heritage Hill** to the 225,000-acre **Northern Highlands-American Legion State Forest** near Woodruff and Minocqua. A state park lies within an hour of every Wisconsin resident, a deliberate feature of the state park system. The parks offer an admirable mix of history, archaeology, anthropology, recreation, and state preservation; they've been dubbed the most diverse in the Midwest. A few of them— **Devil's Lake State Park, Peninsula State Park,** and the **Kettle Moraine State Forest,** for example—rival other major state parks in the nation. (And at times outdraw even places like Yellowstone National Park!) Since 2000, Wisconsin's state park system has been a finalist in the national Gold Medal Parks award for the best in the country.

For purposes of this book, you'll absolutely not want to bypass the *two* sections of the **Kettle Moraine State Forest** southwest and northwest of Milwaukee and the crown jewel of the state park system, **Devil's Lake State Park** north of Madison one hour.

Wisconsin alone has the **Ice Age National Scientific Reserve,** highlighting crucial zones of the state's 1,200-mile-long Ice Age National Scenic Trail—several of which are outlined within this book.

State parks and forests require a park sticker, which you can buy daily ($7 resident, $10 non-resident) or annually ($25 and $35). Camping fees in state parks are also $10–15 (electricity and prime sites cost more), depending on location and campsite (some primitive camping is free)—nonresidents pay $2 more. Reservations in state parks are a good idea—a must for holiday weekends in summer—and be prepared to reserve 11 months ahead of time for the most popular parks. The Wisconsin Department of Natural Resources (DNR, 608/266-2181, www.wiparks.net) is an invaluable source of information on state lands and environmental issues. A separate entity, ReserveAmerica (888/947-2757, www.reservamerica.com) handles reservations for a $10 fee (fees for canceling or changing).

Wisconsin's mammoth multiuse trail system is also under the Department of Natural Resources, and a trail pass (residents $4 daily, $15 annually) is needed; note that some trails are not *state* trails but county trails and you'll need a different pass—them's the rules! Also note that hikers do *not* need to pay; only those using bikes, horses, skis, or ATVs do.

© WISCONSIN DEPARTMENT OF TOURISM

touring one of Wisconsin's lovely Rustic Roads

National forests now charge a $3–4 daily user fee for things such as picnic areas and beaches, and camping runs $8–18 (though things vary). Reservations (877/444-6777, www.reserveusa.com) are available at some campgrounds.

BIKING

Bicycling magazine rates Wisconsin one of the top three states for cyclists. Madison is second only to Seattle in the list of the nation's most bike-friendly cities; it was, in fact, named number-one in 2006 by both *Bicycling* and *Outside* magazines. The Elroy-Sparta State Recreational Trail was the country's first rail-to-trail system and is regarded as the granddaddy of all multipurpose state recreational trails (many of which are highlighted within this book's pages), and the Chequamegon Area Mountain Bike Trail (CAMBA) system is among the most respected outside Colorado and Utah. All this, combined with the immense concatenate labyrinth of rural Rustic Roads, makes it obvious why Wisconsinites leave bike racks on their cars year-round. In total, the state maintains more than 10,000 miles of established, mapped, and recommended bike routes.

Since the completion of the Elroy-Sparta State Recreational Trail, the state has added 41 other rail beds, logging roads, and state park trails to its State Trail System for a total of nearly 1,700 miles. It's impossible to keep up with how many more miles are added annually since cities and counties are establishing their own networks to link with state trails.

The state of Wisconsin tourist information centers dispense excellent free cycling maps and booklets. Two good organizations are the **Bicycling Federation of Wisconsin** (www.bfw.org) and the **Wisconsin Off-Road Bicycling Association** (www.worba.org).

Trail passes ($4 daily, $15 annually) are *not* required for hikers, but are necessary for all others 16 and over.

HIKING

With more than two million acres of state and federal land open for public consumption, along with 34 state recreation trails, hiking opportunities are endless. Two trails of interest to serious backpackers are the **Ice Age National Scenic Trail** and the **North Country National Scenic Trail.** The ultimate goal is to link Wisconsin's 42 rails-to-trails trails via

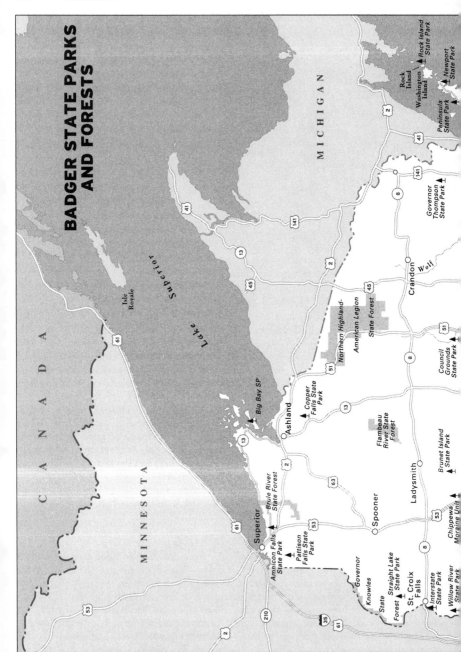

BADGER STATE PARKS AND FORESTS

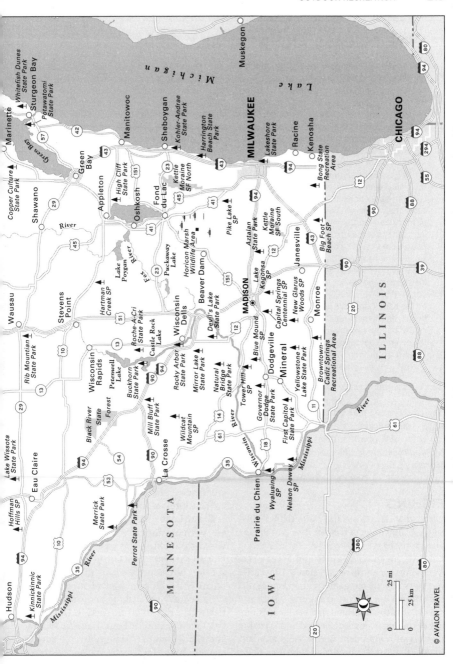

© AVALON TRAVEL

LYME DISEASE AND WEST NILE VIRUS

Since the first diagnosed case of the bacterial plague Lyme disease was isolated in Lyme, Connecticut, in 1975, it has spread across the United States and is now found on the Pacific coast; it is the fastest growing insect-borne infectious disease in the country. In 2007, 1,819 cases were reported in Wisconsin – 20 percent more than 2006.

The cause of Lyme disease is *Borrelia burgdorferi,* carried and transmitted to humans via the *Ixodes dammini,* or deer tick. The deer tick is *not* the only tick (or, some think, insect) to carry the bacterium, but in Wisconsin it is the primary carrier. Distinguishing the maddeningly small deer tick from the more ubiquitous dog tick is easy. The deer tick is exceedingly small – the head and body, 2-4 mm, are only slightly larger than a sesame seed – and reddish brown and black. Dog ticks are twice the size and brown, usually with white markings on the back. Deer ticks are concentrated most heavily in the northwestern quadrant of Wisconsin but have been reported as far south as the counties bordering Illinois and Iowa and as far east as the Wolf River watershed.

West Nile virus has appeared from literally out of nowhere, with more than 4,000 cases and 240 deaths per annum within a half decade. Wisconsin hasn't been hit too hard – a "mere" 13 cases in 2007. These seemingly low numbers may be false hope; Colorado went from none to the country's hot spot in one year. Spread by mosquitoes who feed on infected birds, the virus generally affects those with weakened immune systems and affects the spinal cord and brain membranes, causing encephalitic symptoms. The virus is not transmitted by person-to-person contact. No vaccine exists – all you can do is not get bitten.

PREVENTION

Lyme disease is highly preventable, if you use common sense. Deer ticks are active year-round, so you've always got to be aware. Deer ticks cannot fly or jump. They cling to vegetation and attach themselves to objects pushing through. Always wear light-colored clothing, long sleeves, and long pants, and tuck the cuffs into your boots. A hat is always a good idea. Walk in the center of trails and avoid branches and grasses whenever possible. Check yourself and others *thoroughly,* paying particular

---

city-county-state plans. This would double the state's trail mileage.

Can't miss opportunities for hiking near Milwaukee include the sections of the **Kettle Moraine State Forest** and, near Madison, the sublime trails of **Devil's Lake State Park.**

FISHING

Given that Wisconsin has more than 16,000 lakes, 27,000 miles of fishable river and stream, and more than 1,000 miles of Lake Superior, Lake Michigan, and Mississippi River coastline, and that most of the state's 135 native species of fish are fair game, it's no surprise that the number one activity is angling. Wisconsin ranks in the top five states nationwide for number of fishing licenses dispensed and is first in number of nonresident licenses sold annually (if you're talking freshwater, though even if you

factor in ocean sportfishing, the state still trails only Florida). Though the **muskellunge** is revered as king of the waters, in sheer numbers the most popular sportfish is the **walleye.**

Wisconsin's only native stream trout is the **brook trout,** closely related to the lake trout. Good news—hundreds of blue-ribbon streams are chock-full of these suckers.

Great Lakes fishing has grown to become an enormous industry, with entire fleets devoted to working the well-stocked waters. Not all the fish in the Great Lakes are native species, but nobody seems to mind. Much of the restocking took place in response to early-century overfishing and the decline of fish stocks due to exotic species. In terms of fish taken per angler hour, Kenosha, Racine, and the Kewaunee/Algoma stretch rate extremely high. In all, the state Department attention to the hair. Children are always candidates for tick attachment. Check everybody every 24 hours, even if you haven't been in the deep woods. Studies have indicated that the deer tick must be attached to your skin 24-72 hours before the bacterium is spread. Pet owners beware: Domestic animals can develop Lyme disease, and this is not limited to hunting dogs, so check them as well.

West Nile virus is spread by common mosquitoes, so it's imperative you don't walk around at night in shorts and flip-flops without insect repellent.

People swear by insect repellents using DEET. But remember that DEET's cocktail of toxicology has caused death in children, and unsubstantiated reports have shown that high concentrations of it for long exposures can do very bad things to your nervous system. If you use DEET, buy it in concentrations of no higher than 20 percent for kids, 30 percent for adults. So-called "natural" repellents aren't, this author feels, worth a tinker's darn for ticks, black flies, or mosquitoes.

In 1998 SmithKline Beecham announced it had developed LYMErix, a Lyme disease vaccine. The FDA's governing panel grudgingly OK'd it, despite having serious reservations because of a lack of testing. The efficacy rate tops out at only 79 percent after three expensive doses, and claims of the vaccine's actually causing degenerative arthritis have surfaced. (The company is phasing out the vaccine for humans because of low demand, but it's still in canine form for pets.) In short: It's probably better to skip the vaccine and use preventive measures.

Paramount: Do not panic every time you pull a tick out. The chances are good it's a dog tick, and even if it is a deer tick, it doesn't automatically guarantee Lyme disease. The best way to remove it if you do find one is to grasp it with tweezers as close to the skin as possible and tug it out gently. (Do not jerk or twist, because the head will come off and cause infection. Also, avoid the old method of using a match to "burn" them out; all this does is crisp it and leave the head in.) Disinfect the area thoroughly. You may want to save the tick's body in a plastic bag with a cotton ball soaked in alcohol. Wash your hands after removing the tick.

---

of Natural Resources stocks more than 2.1 million coho and chinook salmon, a million lake trout, and two million brook, brown, and steelhead trout.

Driving the truck out on a frozen lake to a village of shanties erected over drilled holes, sitting on an overturned five-gallon pail, stamping your feet quite a bit, and drinking a lot of schnapps is a time-honored tradition in the Great White North. **Ice fishing** is serious business in Wisconsin: Up to two million angler-days are spent on the ice each year, and ice fishing accounts for up to one-fifth of the state's annual catch.

Lots of minor regulations exist—and regulations vary on boundary waters with Minnesota, Iowa, and Michigan—so be sure to get the rundown from a local bait shop before drilling your hole.

For all information, it's imperative to contact the Wisconsin Department of Natural Resources (877/945-4236, www.dnr.state.wi.us).

HUNTING

Hunting, like fishing, is a well-established business in Wisconsin, though far less so on a tourist level. The nine-day gun deer season alone generates $250 million for the state. Fortunately, hunters are often more conservation-oriented than their civilian brethren. Many animal species owe their continued existence to hunting and conservation groups.

Deer hunting is essentially a rite of passage in Wisconsin's North Woods even today. Entire school districts in the area shut down for the November white-tailed deer season. Other popular hunts include **goose, duck, pheasant,** and especially **ruffed grouse.**

SKIING

Wisconsin mountains will never be mistaken for the Rockies or the Grand Tetons, but the state's heights gives it a fairly decent concentration of downhill ski facilities. Cross-country ski buffs can indulge themselves in an orgy of skiing statewide. It's such a big deal in Wisconsin that the nation's largest cross-country ski race, the Birkebeiner, is held here every year in February, in Hayward.

Including private recreation centers as well as county, state, and federal lands, Wisconsin has more than three dozen downhill facilities and 350 established cross-country ski areas. The tourism department's free book, **Wisconsin Winter Recreation,** details all the sites.

SNOWMOBILING

Snowmobiling is a big deal here. In some communities, snowmobiling accounts for more business than even fishing. In fact, with more than 175,000 registered riders spending $40 million, it accounts for more money in some parts of the state than angling, hunting, and skiing combined. In *Snowgoer* magazine, reader polls have ranked northeastern Wisconsin and Minocqua best overall, eclipsing better-known, better-financed Rocky Mountain operators. Antigo passed ordinances giving snowmobiles rights similar to those of cars on city streets. Restaurants and nightspots often list their addresses according to the snowmobile route you'll find them on.

In total, the state maintains 25,000 miles of interconnected trails, so well linked that you can travel on them continuously from Kenosha in southeastern Wisconsin all the way to Lake Superior in the northwest. Nearly half of the 42 state recreation trails permit snowmobiling, as do 15 state parks and forests; the national forests are wide open.

CANOEING AND KAYAKING

Wisconsin features unbeatable canoeing and kayaking. Nationally regarded or federally designated Wild Rivers include the **Wolf River,** a federal Outstanding Water Resource coursing through the Menominee

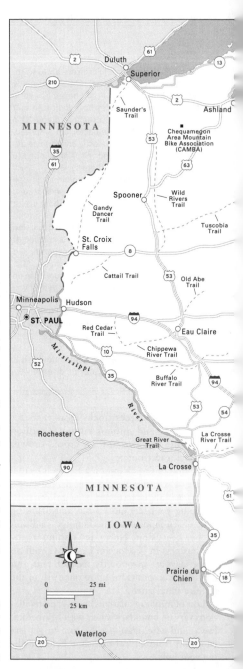

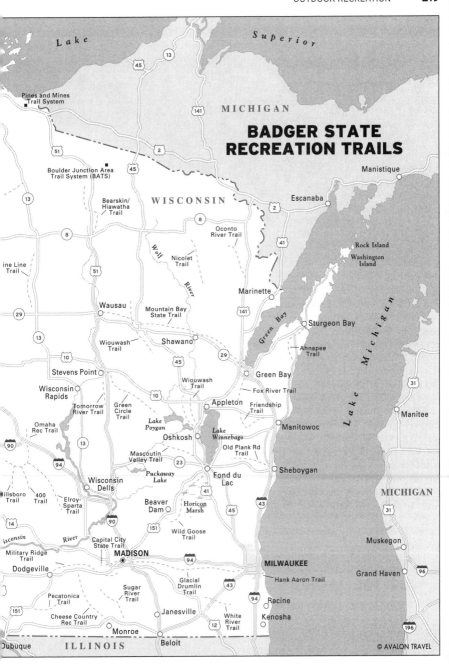

BADGER STATE RECREATION TRAILS

Set down your paddles at a canoe campsite on one of Wisconsin's 16,000 lakes.

Indian Reservation; the **Flambeau River** system, one of the wildest in the Midwest; the **Bois Brule River,** famed for its trout; the **Montreal River,** home of the Junior World Kayak Championships; the unknown but exquisite **Turtle River,** leading into Wisconsin's Turtle-Flambeau Flowage in the most unspoiled section of the state; the **Pine** and **Popple Rivers** in the Nicolet National Forest; the wild **Peshtigo River;** the lazy, classic **Lower Wisconsin State Riverway;** the **La Crosse River;** the **Kickapoo River** (the "crookedest in the world"); the **Yahara River,** one reason *Canoeist* magazine calls Madison a canoeing mecca; and perhaps the most popular, the **Manitowish River,** in the Northern Highlands/American Legion State Forest in one of the planet's densest concentrations of lakes.

The **Namekagon-St. Croix National Scenic Riverway** stretches west from northeast of Cable, joins the St. Croix River and its smashing geology, and eventually flows to the confluence with the Mississippi River.

Kayakers enjoy the superb **Apostle Islands National Lakeshore** along Lake Superior—an experience impossible to overstate—and, to a lesser extent, the magnificence of Door County on the Lake Michigan side. Rentals are plentiful at all locations; kayaks are always much more expensive to rent than canoes but offer a wider range of use, since they can handle rougher waters.

GOLF

Believe it or not, forlorn, wintry Wisconsin has one of the nation's highest concentrations of golf courses per capita. Go figure. Nearly 430 courses are listed in the state's *Wisconsin Golf Guide.* Among the courses most often pursued are **Blackwolf Run** in Kohler, **Lawsonia** in Green Lake, **Sentryworld** in Stevens Point, **University Ridge** in Madison, and **Brown Deer Golf Course** near Milwaukee.

SNOWMOBILE CENTRAL

Wisconsinites had been toying with varieties of homemade "snow machines" for some time before something inspired Carl Eliason to strap a small gas-powered boat engine onto a toboggan, pound on some turnable skis, and let himself loose across the ice near Sayner, Wisconsin, in 1924. Voilà! – the first modern snowmobile, patented in 1927.

Wisconsin has one of the most active populations of snowmobilers of any state. More than 25,000 miles of well-tracked trails are maintained by dozens and dozens of snow clubs throughout the north – the nation's most extensive network. And these are just maintained trails; Wisconsin Trail number 15 bisects the state southeast to northwest – a seeming million frozen miles aboard a sled. One quarter of the nation's 2.7 million sleds are in Wisconsin, and tourism for ´biling equals that generated by certain western states' ski industries (some northern resorts make 85 percent of their income from snowmobilers). *Snowgoer* magazine readers consistently rate northeast Wisconsin tops in the country.

Buzzing machines scrape to a halt next to you at the gas station. Businesses post advertisements along snowmobile trails. Any lodging either caters to snowmobilers exclusively – with rentals, linked trails on-site (they can park at the door) or nearby, guided tours – or at least offers special snowmobile rates.

Some regard ´biling aficionados as single-browed Cro-Magnons who despoil the bucolic landscape. ´Bilers of the true kind cringe at the antics of the few yahoos, the ones fueled as much on Leinenkugel's lager as by the feeling of frigid air. Snowmobile clubs are on the whole a respectable bunch who do as much charity work as they do trail maintenance. However, in a time-honored tradition, making "pit stops" generally translates as bar hopping. And there are many morons zipping home after the bars close or after a festival aboard a 400-pound missile. About 25-40 snowmobilers die every year on the trails and lakes.

Yet keep in mind that snowmobile clubs are actually the ones who best bring together local officials and landowners and even work with environmental groups to share access. It is they who do the maintenance and educate the public – so much so that Wisconsin's club trail network is an officially recognized highway system. And while true that an engine is an engine – thus pumping hydrocarbons into the air – technology is reducing emissions annually. And the number of snowmobiles is still far lower than those pollution machines of other folks' SUVs, lawnmowers, leaf blowers, powerboats, and so on.

© WISCONSIN DEPARTMENT OF TOURISM

a snowmobiling bridge

Tips for Travelers

For information on anything and everything in the state, contact the **Wisconsin Department of Tourism** (800/432-8747, www.travelwisconsin.com), which has a decent website. It does have fantastic printed guides you can request—free, they're dense and very well-designed, covering everything from scenic drives to recreation.

The state operates information centers along major highways entering Wisconsin from neighboring Iowa, Minnesota, Illinois, and Michigan—and also one in Madison.

Regarding the Internet, precious few sites are really all that worthy. First stop for culture, arts, and history should be www.portalwisconsin.org, a superb site; cheekier but filled with tidbits is www.classicwisconsin.com, good for information on fish fries. An idiosyncratic site—is it travel or geography or what?—is www.wisconline.com. You can thereafter peruse all you want, but this author has never found an otherwise worthy website on pan-Wisconsin travel.

GAY AND LESBIAN TRAVELERS

Madison has been ranked third-best (after San Francisco and Bloomington, Indiana) by LGBT media for quality of life, and the gay community is organized and active there. In fact, Madison is actually the place to go for LGBT information. One great website covering everything (clubs to health to accommodations) everywhere is www.madisongaypride.com. Milwaukee's LGBT Community Center (www.mkelgbt.com) can also help.

TRAVEL GREEN WISCONSIN

In 2007, in a U.S. first, Wisconsin launched its *Travel Green* program, designed to highlight businesses, lodging, attractions, and so on for their efforts to reduce the environmental impact of tourism. (And, naturally, to highlight the existence of the fact that this can, in fact, be done.) Kind of a no-brainer, eh? Madison, Bayfield, Rhinelander, and Door County led the 2006 pilot program, and it was a resounding success with travelers. (Another no-brainer, Madison leading the way; it's won about a dozen "Green" Awards – yes, yes, whatever that means – in the last five years, including being named "America's Greenest City" by the Environmental News Network in 2007.) Wanna rent a hybrid car? Wanna eat in a restaurant that follows a protocol of sustainability? Then check out www.travelgreenwisconsin.com and find out what it's all about!

Information and Services

MONEY

Wisconsinites are taxed to high heaven, but in general travelers don't have to share the burden; the state doesn't even have toll roads. Prices in general are lower in Wisconsin than in the rest of the country, and gasoline is usually cheaper than anywhere else in the Midwest except maybe Iowa. Once you get out into the rural areas, prices for goods and services are absolutely dirt cheap. Wisconsin's sales tax is 5 percent. Some counties or cities tack on an additional half percent. There may also be additional room taxes.

Travelers checks are accepted in most hotels and motels; those that don't take them are few and far between, usually the low-end places. Some restaurants will accept them, others won't—inquire ahead of time. Credit cards are widely accepted—though not universally.

Exchanging foreign currency can be a bit more problematic. If you arrive with foreign currency, it may be difficult to exchange it for U.S. dollars. Banks in Madison and Milwaukee will often have just one branch that deals with money-changing. In smaller cities, such as Green Bay, La Crosse, and Appleton, it isn't advisable to arrive with foreign currency.

COMMUNICATIONS
Telephone

Wisconsin has five area codes. Milwaukee, along with most of southeastern Wisconsin, is in the 414 area code; areas immediately outside of Milwaukee are 262 area code; Madison and the southwestern and south-central regions fall in the 608 area code; and the rest—most of the northwest—lies in the 715 area code. All else is area code 920.

Internet

If you need to log on and don't have your laptop, you generally have to go to the public library. Sure, coffee shops exist in spades in Madison and Milwaukee, but they come and go a lot—and are mostly wireless equipped, so if you're sans laptop, you're out of luck. Otherwise, the most popular destinations in this book have wireless-equipped coffee shops and accommodations, but don't absolutely count on it.

MEDIA

The only publication that covers Wisconsin on a macro scale is the monthly magazine *Wisconsin Trails* (www.wistrails.com). It's a slick periodical with a nice balance of road warrior personality and nostalgia. It dispenses with the political and social and just focuses on where and when to go, providing lots of good cultural bits and stunning photography. *Midwest Living* magazine, another monthly, features Wisconsin regularly. More for the conservation-minded, *Wisconsin Natural Resources* (www.wnrmag .com) is published by the state Department of Natural Resources. The well-put-together periodical features detailed natural history and is so well written and photographed that it might let you truly understand and appreciate science for the first time.

Newspapers

The *Journal Sentinel,* the largest and best of Wisconsin's newspapers, is a daily morning paper out of Milwaukee. In Madison, it's down to just the *Wisconsin State Journal,* though the former liberal afternoon *Capital Times* still exists as a free twice-weekly option. (But check out free local weeklies: *Isthmus* in Madison and *Shepherd Express* in Milwaukee.

MAPS

You can get a decent Department of Transportation state road map free by calling the state Department of Tourism hotline (800/432-8747). The *best* maps for snooping around the state are those contained in the *Wisconsin Atlas and Gazetteer,* available from any outdoors store or direct from the DeLorme Publishing Company (207/865-4171, www .delorme.com). On a somewhat smaller scale than topo maps, the maps in this 100-page, large-format book are absolutely indispensable for exploring the back roads.

Topographic, planimetric, and 7.5-minute quadrangle maps can be obtained from the Wisconsin Geological and Natural History Survey (3817 Mineral Point Rd., Madison, WI 53705, 608/263-7389). The 7.5- or 15-minute maps cost $3.50 each. County topographical maps (1:1,000,000 scale) are available for $4 each.

WEIGHTS AND MEASURES
Voltage
Electrical outlets in the United States run on a 110V or 120V AC. Most plugs are either two flat prongs or two flat and one round. Transformers and adapters for 220V appliances are available in hardware or electronics stores.

The Metric System
Let's just say it doesn't come up a whole lot in Wisconsin. Foreign visitors can reference the U.S.-Metric Conversion Table in the back of this book for help with distance and temperature conversions.

Time Zones
All of Wisconsin falls on central standard time (CST), which is six hours earlier than Greenwich mean time. However, if you plan a trip north of the border into Michigan's Upper Peninsula, you'll enter eastern standard time (EST), which is one hour ahead of CST.

RESOURCES

Suggested Reading

If you're in Madison and are serious about reading Wisconsin-oriented books, eschew bookstores and head directly to the State Historical Society Museum, across from the State Capitol. The gift shop is even better in scope than the library.

DESCRIPTION AND TRAVEL

Lyons, John J., ed. *Wisconsin. A Guide to the Badger State.* American Guide Series, Works Projects Administration, 1941. From the mother of all guidebook series, the Wisconsin edition, nearly seven decades old, is still the standard for anyone interested in the history, natural history, and culture of the state. Check the library or used bookstores.

Ostergren, Robert C., and Vale, Thomas R., ed. *Wisconsin Land and Life.* Madison: University of Wisconsin Press, 1997. This amazing book came out in 1997 and was instantly regarded as the most perfect synthesis of natural history and cultural geography that has ever examined the Badger state. Written by two prominent UW-Madison geography professors, this heavy but eminently readable book covers climate, geology, flora and fauna, settlement patterns, cultural geography, regional economies, and changing landscapes, both cultural and ecological.

OUTDOORS AND ENVIRONMENT

Leopold, Aldo. *A Sand County Almanac.* New York: Oxford University Press, 1949. An ab-solute must-read for anyone who considers himself or herself to be at all attuned to the land. Also an education for those superficial enough to think central Wisconsin is a vast nothingland.

Logan, Ben. *The Land Awakens.* Itchy Cat Press: original publication 1975. Could be culture, could be literature, could be history—a wondrous account of growing up on a rural Wisconsin farm in the 1920s and 1930s, you can practically feel the man's love for the land.

Olson, Sigurd. *Collected Works of Sigurd Olson.* Stillwater, MN: 1990. Wisconsin's seminal ecologist besides Aldo Leopold, Olson had as much influence as his more famous contemporary. This is an excellent overview of his life's work, writings that show an incredible depth of ecological awareness but are very approachable for a layperson.

HISTORY
Wisconsin History

The History of Wisconsin. Madison: State Historical Society of Wisconsin, 1973–1988. A massive, multivolume, encyclopedic examination of the state's history.

McAnn, D. *The Wisconsin Story: 150 Years, 150 Stories.* Milwaukee: *Milwaukee Journal Sentinel,* 1998. In contrast to the other two scholarly, somewhat dry reads is this great book, excellent because most articles are about historical minutiae most folks have never heard about but are fascinating highlights to the general history books. Well written and engaging, it's probably your best bet for an easy vacation read.

Nesbit, Robert. *Wisconsin: A History.* Madison: University of Wisconsin Press, 1989. For those with too little time, money, or inclination for the state historical society's version, this is standard reading.

Milwaukee History

Ackerman, Sandra. *Milwaukee Then and Now.* Thunder Bay Press, 2004. The best picture book to me: it compares archival photos with their modern equivalents.

Gurda, John. Just head for a bookshop, the library, or go online and find anything from this man. He is *the* scribe of Milwaukee. My favorite is *Cream City Chronicles* (Wisconsin Historical Society, 2000), though others say you must read *The Making of Milwaukee* (Milwaukee County Historical Society, 1999). Either way you'll be happy.

Knauss Paradis, Trudy. *German Milwaukee: Its History—Its Recipes.* G. Bradley Publishing, 2006. Milwaukee is German to the core, and this book is the best at capturing the entire ethos of this immigrant group.

Zimmerman, H. Russell. *The Heritage Guidebook.* Schwartz Bookshop. Covers more than Milwaukee, but its Milwaukee section is fascinating, a virtual street guide to the former city.

Madison History

Amazingly, not much read-worthy exists out there for Madison (I know I'll hear about this.)

Mollenhoff, David V. *Madison: A History of the Formative Years.* University of Wisconsin Press, 2003. Just a fascinating book.

FOLKLORE

Leary, J. *Wisconsin Folklore.* Madison: University of Wisconsin Press, 1998. This wonderful book runs the gamut of Wisconsin culture: linguistics, storytelling, music, song, dance, folk crafts, and material traditions. The chapter on Milwaukeeisms is worth the price of the book. Even the Smithsonian has recognized the uniqueness of the book.

NATURAL HISTORY

Finley, Robert W. *Geography of Wisconsin: A Content Outline.* Madison: College Printing and Press, 1965. Written by a University of Wisconsin geography professor, this softbound text, found only in libraries, is the best resource for nonscientists. Full of clear maps, it also includes data on climate, agriculture, and topography.

Green, William, et al., eds. "Introduction to Wisconsin Archaeology." *The Wisconsin Archaeologist* (Sept.–Dec. 1986, Vol. 67, no. 3–4). Clearly written.

Martin, Lawrence. *The Physical Geography of Wisconsin.* Madison: University of Wisconsin Press, 1965. This is the granddaddy of all Wisconsin geography books, first published in 1916 and updated in subsequent editions.

Paull, R. and R. *Wisconsin and Upper Michigan Geology.* Dubuque, IA: Kendall/Hunt Publishing, 1980. One in a highly popular series of road guides to geology. These guides have less jargon than a textbook but still adequately cover the complexities of the topic.

Reuss, Henry S. *On the Trail of the Ice Age.* Sheboygan, WI: Ice Age Park and Trail Foundation, 1990. A good compendium of the oddball geology of the state and the effort to establish the Ice Age National Scenic Trail. Plus, buying it supports a good cause.

Schultz, Gwen. *Wisconsin's Foundations.* Dubuque, IA: Kendall/Hunt Publishing,

1986. An excellent primer on the geology of Wisconsin and, more importantly, its effects on Wisconsin's geography and geocultural history.

PEOPLE

The state historical society has produced brief booklets profiling every immigrant group in Wisconsin. They're available from the State Historical Society Museum in Madison.

Bieder, Robert E. *Native American Communities in Wisconsin, 1600–1960*. Madison: University of Wisconsin Press, 1995. The first and, really, only comprehensive, in-depth look at Native Americans in the state.

Freeman, L. *Belle: The Biography of Belle Case La Follette*. Beaufort, SC: Beaufort Books, 1986. An excellent compendium of information on Belle La Follette, suffragist and wife and trusted legal adviser to Progressive governor Robert La Follette.

Maxwell, R. S. *La Follette and the Rise of the Progressives in Wisconsin*. Madison: State Historical Society, 1956. A fine account of Robert La Follette, the much-beloved Progressive Party politician of the late 1800s and early 1900s.

McBride, G. *On Wisconsin Women*. Madison: University of Wisconsin Press, 1993. An excellent newer book, this is one of few sources of information about many of the important women in the state's history.

Meine, C. *Aldo Leopold: His Life and Work*. Madison: University of Wisconsin Press, 1988. The best book on ecologist Aldo Leopold.

Ritzenthaler, Robert E. *Prehistoric Indians of Wisconsin*. Milwaukee Public Museum Popular Science Handbook Series no. 4, 1979. This nifty little booklet, written in layperson's prose, is a condensed introduction to the earliest of Wisconsin's natives.

Tanner, T., ed. *Aldo Leopold: The Man and His Legacy* Ames, IA: Iowa State University Press, 1988. Another good choice, containing multidisciplinary examinations of his life, studies, and effects.

Zaniewski, R. *Atlas of Ethnic Diversity in Wisconsin*. Madison: University of Wisconsin Press, 1998. This outstanding (and huge) tome is the best ever produced covering the peoples of Wisconsin. It's coffee-table-size, it's got excellent color graphics, and it's terribly expensive. Check the library.

LITERATURE

Boudreau, Richard, ed. *The Literary Heritage of Wisconsin: An Anthology of Wisconsin Literature from Beginnings to 1925*. La Crosse, WI: Juniper Press, 1986. A condensed version of the state's literary canon.

Perry, Michael. *Population: 485* (Harper Perennial, 2002) and *Truck: A Love Story* (Harper Perennial, 2006). Wisconsin has had a few luminaries of literature (Jane Hamilton, Kelly Cherry, Lorrie Moore, et al.) but I think he's the oughta-be-read author scribbling in the state. If you want to experience small-town Wisconsin in a wonderfully low-key, hilarious way, read these books. Absolutely the best thing to describe us.

Stephens, Jim, ed. *The Journey Home: The Literature of Wisconsin Through Four Centuries*. Madison: North Country Press, 1989. A remarkable multivolume set of Wisconsin literature, tracing back as far as the trickster cycles of Native Americans. Rich with obscure minutiae, this tome is not readily obtainable for those of modest means but is of paramount importance to anyone hoping to get a complete overview of Wisconsin letters, history, and culture.

Wilder, Laura Ingalls. *Little House in the Big Woods*. New York: Harper Collins Children's Books, 1953. While no one would think it, the series was actually inspired by Wisconsin; Laura Ingalls Wilder was born in a small cabin near the Mississippi River town of Pepin, the source material for many of the books' events.

CUISINE

More and more cookbooks detail Midwestern cuisine. Any bookstore worth its salt will have great selections on regional cooking.

Allen, T. *Wisconsin Food Fests*. Amherst, WI: Amherst Press, 1995. Terese Allen is one of Wisconsin's most noted food writers, so look for her name in bookstores. This book is best for travelers; you can always find a fest somewhere close to you—a good way to sample a sesquicentennial of ethnic cooking.

Apps, Jerry. *Breweries of Wisconsin*. Madison: University of Wisconsin Press, 1992. This amazing book came out and surprised everyone—a thorough examination of the culture of beer in Wisconsin as had never been done

before. Part history of beer, part cultural synopsis, with detailed examinations of major Wisconsin brewers past and present.

Boyer, D. *Great Wisconsin Taverns*. Black Earth, WI: Trails Book Guides, 1999. The name pretty much says it all. It sounds hokey, but the author, a professional folklorist and storyteller, made his peregrinations around the state—not to mention a predilection for imbibing—into a wonderful, offbeat guidebook.

Hachten, Harva. *The Flavor of Wisconsin*. Madison: State Historical Society of Wisconsin, 1981. A dense volume cataloging all—and this means all—the ethnic groups of the state and their contributions to the cuisine.

Revolinski, Kevin. *Wisconsin Beer Guide*. Tynan's Independent Media, 2006. Informative but also fun, from the kind of guy you'd like to have in the shotgun seat on a long trip.

Internet Resources

Sconnie Nation
www.sconnie.com

Wisconsinites will likely appreciate Sconnie Nation. Started by a couple of genius UW undergrads, the online company sells all sorts of apparel with "Sconnie" written on it (I can't stop wearing my camo hat). But they have a hilarious section on what it means to be "Sconnie." You'll spend hours just perusing the videos submitted by proud Badgers (gotta love the tractor square dance…).

TRAVEL

Travel Wisconsin
www.travelwisconsin.com

From the state's Department of Tourism, it's

loads more useful than some other states' websites. Seriously, give it a look. From here you can also link to Madison, Milwaukee, and any other town or city herein as well as many of the sites listed below.

Wisconsin Online
www.wisconline.com

It doesn't have everything in the state, but it has lots!

Wisconsin Association of Convention and Visitors Bureaus (WACVB)
www.escapetowisconsin.com

Run by the association of chambers of commerce, it's a good starting point to local sights around the state.

STATE PARKS

Wisconsin Department of Natural Resources
www.wiparks.net

Good resource from the Department of Natural Resources. It also covers state trails. This site is great for hunting, fishing, and many other outdoors excursions as well.

RECREATION

Wisconsin Bicycling Federation
www.bfw.org

They're an educational and advocacy group working strenuously for bikers' rights (and more trails and bike lanes in cities). What you'll find here are the best bike maps ($3) of southeastern Wisconsin—on or off-road. (And they can answer any questions you might have.)

Wisconsin Off-Road Bicycling Association
www.worba.org

An excellent source for off-pavement riders, check it out for its expanding list of downloadable trail maps.

ARTS AND CULTURE

Portal Wisconsin
www.portalwisconsin.org

A fantastic resource for all visual and performance arts in the state.

Wisconsin Arts Board
www.arts.state.wi.us

The website of the Wisconsin Arts Board has great sections on art fairs, galleries, and art museums.

HISTORY

State Historical Society of Wisconsin
www.wisconsinhistory.org

The best starting place for state history, from the State Historical Society of Wisconsin.

ACCOMMODATIONS

Wisconsin Association of Campground Owners
www.wisconsincampgrounds.com

This site has information on all private campgrounds in the state.

Wisconsin Bed & Breakfast Association
www.wbba.org

From the Wisconsin Bed & Breakfast Association.

Wisconsin Lodging
www.lodging-wi.com

Visit this site to view photos and information of lodging options around the state.

FOOD

Classic Wisonsin
www.classicwisconsin.com

Similar to Wisconsin Made, I like it for its rundown of fish fries statewide!

Culinary History Enthusiasts of Wisconsin
www.chew.wisconsincooks.org

Fabulous site for anything food-worthy in the state.

Wisconsin Agricultural Marketing Board
www.wisdairy.com

From the state's Agricultural Marketing Board, it's a great place to find resources on seeing/tasting/buying cheese or dairy products.

Wisconsin Cooks
www.wisconsincooks.org

A fun guide run by Wisconsin foodies, it has a good list of food-centric events; better is its outstanding database of anything related to Wisconsin: eating, books, articles, recipes, etc.

Wisconsin Department of Agriculture
www.savorwisconsin.com

From the Department of Agriculture, it's got a mammoth list of where to find stuff grown/made here.

Wisconsin Made
www.wisconsinmade.com

Similar to the above but it has a heck of a lot more than just agricultural products—T-shirts and foam cheese hats are also here!

TRANSPORTATION AND ROAD TRIPS

Wisconsin Department of Transportation
www.dot.wisconsin.gov

The state's Department of Transportation website has all necessary information on construction, road conditions, etc. Do check out its "Rustic Roads" section for fantastic country drives.

Index

List of Maps

www.moon.com

MOON.COM is all new, and ready to help plan your next trip! Filled with fresh trip ideas and strategies, author interviews, informative blogs, a detailed map library, and descriptions of all the Moon guidebooks, Moon.com is all you need to get out and explore the world—or even places in your own backyard. As always, when you travel with Moon, expect an experience that is uncommon and truly unique.

MAP SYMBOLS

▦ Expressway	**◖**	Highlight	✗	Airfield	⚓	Golf Course
▦ Primary Road	○	City/Town	✈	Airport	**P**	Parking Area
▦ Secondary Road	◉	State Capital	▲	Mountain	▱	Archaeological Site
▦ Unpaved Road	⊛	National Capital	✦	Unique Natural Feature	▮	Church
▦ Trail	★	Point of Interest			▯	Gas Station
▦ Ferry	●	Accommodation	🀆	Waterfall		Glacier
▦ Railroad	▾	Restaurant/Bar	▲	Park		Mangrove
▦ Pedestrian Walkway	■	Other Location	▯	Trailhead		Reef
▦ Stairs	Λ	Campground	✘	Skiing Area		Swamp

CONVERSION TABLES

°C = (°F - 32) / 1.8
°F = (°C x 1.8) + 32
1 inch = 2.54 centimeters (cm)
1 foot = 0.304 meters (m)
1 yard = 0.914 meters
1 mile = 1.6093 kilometers (km)
1 km = 0.6214 miles
1 fathom = 1.8288 m
1 chain = 20.1168 m
1 furlong = 201.168 m
1 acre = 0.4047 hectares
1 sq km = 100 hectares
1 sq mile = 2.59 square km
1 ounce = 28.35 grams
1 pound = 0.4536 kilograms
1 short ton = 0.90718 metric ton
1 short ton = 2,000 pounds
1 long ton = 1.016 metric tons
1 long ton = 2,240 pounds
1 metric ton = 1,000 kilograms
1 quart = 0.94635 liters
1 US gallon = 3.7854 liters
1 Imperial gallon = 4.5459 liters
1 nautical mile = 1.852 km

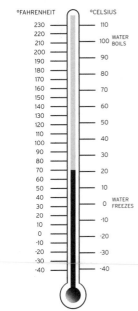

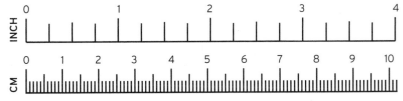

MOON MILWAUKEE & MADISON

Avalon Travel
a member of the Perseus Books Group
1700 Fourth Street
Berkeley, CA 94710, USA
www.moon.com

Editor: Michelle Cadden
Series Manager: Kathryn Ettinger
Copy Editor: Michelle Peters
Graphics and Production Coordinator: Lucie Ericksen
Cover Designer: Stefano Boni
Map Editor: Albert Angulo
Cartography Director: Mike Morgenfeld
Cartographers: Jon Niemczyk, Jon Twena,
  Kat Bennett, Chris Markiewicz
Indexer: Rachel Kuhn

ISBN: 978-1-59880-200-9
ISSN: 1947-4113

Printing History
1st Edition — June 2009
5 4 3 2 1

Front cover photo: Museum of Art, Milwauke
  © Kenneth Ilio/TrekEarth
Title page photo: Family Kite Festival, Milwaukee
  © Donald S. Abrams/Courtesy of Wisconsin
  Department of Tourism
Interior photos pg. 4-7, 10, 13-right © Wisconsin
  Department of Tourism; pg. 9, 11, 12, 13-left, 14,
  15, 17, 18, 20 © Thomas Huhti; pg. 8 © Henryk
  Sadura/123RF; pg. 16 © Yuki Takano; pg. 19-top
  © Nicole LaFevre; 19-bottom © Focus Photography

Printed in the United States by RR Donnelley

KEEPING CURRENT

If you have a favorite gem you'd like to see included in the next edition, or see anything that needs updating, clarification, or correction, please drop us a line. Send your comments via email to feedback@moon.com, or use the address above.